C# 4.0

IN A NUTSHELL

C# 4.0

IN A NUTSHELL

Fourth Edition

Joseph Albahari and Ben Albahari

O'REILLY®

Beijing · Cambridge · Farnham · Köln · Sebastopol · Tokyo

C# 4.0 in a Nutshell, Fourth Edition

by Joseph Albahari and Ben Albahari

Published by O'Reilly Media, Inc., 1005 Gravenstein Highway North, Sebastopol, CA 95472.

O'Reilly books may be purchased for educational, business, or sales promotional use. Online editions are also available for most titles (*http://my.safaribooksonline.com*). For more information, contact our corporate/institutional sales department: (800) 998-9938 or *corporate@oreilly.com*.

Editor: Laurel R.T. Ruma
Production Editor: Loranah Dimant
Copyeditor: Audrey Doyle
Proofreader: Colleen Toporek

Indexer: John Bickelhaupt
Cover Designer: Karen Montgomery
Interior Designer: David Futato
Illustrator: Robert Romano

Printing History:

March 2002:	First Edition.
August 2003:	Second Edition.
September 2007:	Third Edition.
January 2010:	Fourth Edition.

ISBN: 978-0-596-80095-6

[M]   [10/10]

1285900096

Table of Contents

Preface

C# 4.0 further enhances Microsoft's flagship programming language with much-requested features—including support for dynamic programming, type parameter variance, and optional and named parameters. At the same time, the CLR and .NET Framework have grown to include a rich set of features for parallel programming, code contracts, and a new code security model.

The price of this growth is that there's more than ever to learn. Although tools such as Microsoft's IntelliSense—and online references—are excellent in helping you on the job, they presume an existing map of conceptual knowledge. This book provides exactly that map of knowledge in a concise and unified style—free of clutter and long introductions.

Like the previous edition, *C# 4.0 in a Nutshell* is organized entirely around concepts and use cases, making it friendly both to sequential reading and to random browsing. It also plumbs significant depths while assuming only basic background knowledge—making it accessible to intermediate as well as advanced readers.

This book covers C#, the CLR, and the core Framework assemblies. We've chosen this focus to allow space for difficult topics such as concurrency, security, and application domains—without compromising depth or readability. Features new to C# 4.0 and the associated Framework are flagged so that you can also use this book as a C# 3.0 reference.

Intended Audience

This book targets intermediate to advanced audiences. No prior knowledge of C# is required, but some general programming experience is necessary. For the beginner, this book complements, rather than replaces, a tutorial-style introduction to programming.

If you're already familiar with C# 3.0, you'll find more than 100 pages dedicated to the new features of C# 4.0 and Framework 4.0. In addition, many chapters have been enhanced from the previous edition, most notably the chapters on the C# language, .NET Framework fundamentals, memory management, threading, and COM interoperability. We've also updated the LINQ chapters to make the examples friendly to both LINQ to SQL and Entity Framework programmers.

This book is an ideal companion to any of the vast array of books that focus on an applied technology such as WPF, ASP.NET, or WCF. The areas of the language and .NET Framework that such books omit, *C# 4.0 in a Nutshell* covers in detail— and vice versa.

If you're looking for a book that skims every .NET Framework technology, this is not for you. This book is also unsuitable if you want a replacement for IntelliSense (i.e., the alphabetical listings of types and type members that appeared in the C# 1.1 edition of this book).

How This Book Is Organized

The first three chapters after the introduction concentrate purely on C#, starting with the basics of syntax, types, and variables, and finishing with advanced topics such as unsafe code and preprocessor directives. If you're new to the language, you should read these chapters sequentially.

The remaining chapters cover the core .NET Framework, including such topics as LINQ, XML, collections, I/O and networking, memory management, reflection, dynamic programming, attributes, security, concurrency, application domains, and native interoperability. You can read most of these chapters randomly, except for Chapters 6 and 7, which lay a foundation for subsequent topics. The three chapters on LINQ are also best read in sequence.

What You Need to Use This Book

The examples in this book require a C# 4.0 compiler and Microsoft .NET Framework 4.0. You will also find Microsoft's .NET documentation useful to look up individual types and members. The easiest way to get all three—along with an integrated development environment—is to install Microsoft Visual Studio 2010. Any edition is suitable for what's taught in this book, including Visual Studio Express (a free download). Visual Studio also includes an express edition of SQL Server, required to run the LINQ to SQL and Entity Framework examples, and IntelliSense, which pops up type member listings as you type.

For Chapters 2 through 4, Chapter 6, Chapters 8 through 10, and Chapter 24, the code samples are available in the free code-snippet IDE, LINQPad. The samples include everything in those chapters from simple expressions to complete programs and are fully editable, allowing you to learn interactively. You can download LINQ-Pad from *http://www.linqpad.net*; to obtain the additional samples, click "Download more samples" in the Samples tab at the bottom left. You can then advance through each sample with a single click.

Conventions Used in This Book

The book uses basic UML notation to illustrate relationships between types, as shown in Figure P-1. A slanted rectangle means an abstract class; a circle means an interface. A line with a hollow triangle denotes inheritance, with the triangle pointing to the base type. A line with an arrow denotes a one-way association; a line without an arrow denotes a two-way association.

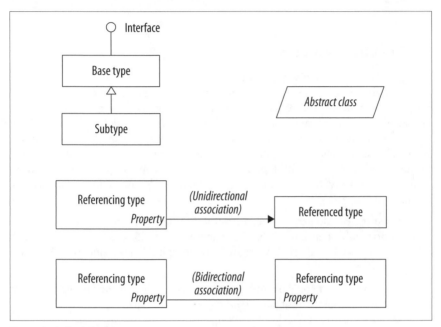

Figure P-1. Sample diagram

The following typographical conventions are used in this book:

Italic
    Indicates new terms, URIs, filenames, and directories

`Constant width`
    Indicates C# code, keywords and identifiers, and program output

`Constant width bold`
    Shows a highlighted section of code

`Constant width italic`
    Shows text that should be replaced with user-supplied values

This icon signifies a tip, suggestion, or general note.

This icon indicates a warning or caution.

Using Code Examples

This book is here to help you get your job done. In general, you may use the code in this book in your programs and documentation. You do not need to contact us for permission unless you're reproducing a significant portion of the code. For example, writing a program that uses several chunks of code from this book does not require permission. Selling or distributing a CD-ROM of examples from O'Reilly books *does* require permission. Answering a question by citing this book and quoting example code does not require permission. Incorporating a significant amount of example code from this book into your product's documentation *does* require permission.

We appreciate, but do not require, attribution. An attribution usually includes the title, author, publisher, and ISBN. For example: "*C# 4.0 in a Nutshell* by Joseph Albahari and Ben Albahari. Copyright 2010 Joseph Albahari and Ben Albahari, 978-0-596-80095-6."

If you feel your use of code examples falls outside fair use or the permission given here, feel free to contact us at *permissions@oreilly.com*.

We'd Like to Hear from You

Please address comments and questions concerning this book to the publisher:

O'Reilly Media, Inc.
1005 Gravenstein Highway North
Sebastopol, CA 95472
800-998-9938 (in the United States or Canada)
707-829-0515 (international or local)
707-829-0104 (fax)

We have a web page for this book, where we list errata, examples, and any additional information. You can access this page at:

http://www.oreilly.com/catalog/9780596800956

Code listings and additional resources are provided at:

http://www.albahari.com/nutshell/

To comment or ask technical questions about this book, send email to the following, quoting the book's ISBN (9780596800956):

> *bookquestions@oreilly.com*

For more information about our books, conferences, Resource Centers, and the O'Reilly Network, see our website at:

> *http://www.oreilly.com*

Safari® Books Online

 Safari Books Online is an on-demand digital library that lets you easily search over 7,500 technology and creative reference books and videos to find the answers you need quickly.

With a subscription, you can read any page and watch any video from our library online. Read books on your cell phone and mobile devices. Access new titles before they are available for print, and get exclusive access to manuscripts in development and post feedback for the authors. Copy and paste code samples, organize your favorites, download chapters, bookmark key sections, create notes, print out pages, and benefit from tons of other time-saving features.

O'Reilly Media has uploaded this book to the Safari Books Online service. To have full digital access to this book and others on similar topics from O'Reilly and other publishers, sign up for free at *http://my.safaribooksonline.com*.

Acknowledgments

Joseph Albahari

First, I want to thank my brother and coauthor, Ben Albahari, for initially persuading me to take on what has become a highly successful project. I particularly enjoy working with Ben in probing difficult topics: he shares my willingness to question conventional wisdom, and the tenacity to pull things apart until it becomes clear how they *really* work.

I am most indebted to the superb technical reviewers. Starting with the reviewers at Microsoft, the extensive input from Stephen Toub (Parallel Programming team) and Chris Burrows (C# Compiler team) significantly enhanced the chapters on concurrency, dynamic programming, and the C# language. From the CLR team, I received invaluable input on security and memory management from Shawn Farkas, Brian Grunkemeyer, Maoni Stephens, and David DeWinter. And on Code Contracts, the feedback from Brian Grunkemeyer, Mike Barnett, and Melitta Andersen raised this chapter to the next quality bar. Thank you, people—both for your prompt feedback and for answering all my questions. I really appreciate it!

I have the highest praise for Jon Skeet (author of *C# in Depth* and Stack Overflow extraordinaire), whose perceptive suggestions enhanced numerous chapters (you work for Google, but we'll forgive you!). I'm similarly grateful for the keen eye of C# MVP Nicholas Paldino, who spotted errors and omissions that others missed. I'd also like to thank C# MVPs Mitch Wheat and Brian Peek, and reviewers of the 3.0 edition upon which this book was based. This includes the aforementioned Nicholas Paldino, who applied his thoroughness and breadth of knowledge to most chapters of the book, and Krzysztof Cwalina, Matt Warren, Joel Pobar, Glyn Griffiths, Ion Vasilian, Brad Abrams, Sam Gentile, and Adam Nathan.

Finally, I want to thank the O'Reilly team, including my prompt and efficient editor, Laurel Ruma, my publicist, Kathryn Barrett, my copyeditor, Audrey Doyle, and members of my family, Miri and Sonia.

Ben Albahari

Because my brother wrote his acknowledgments first, you can infer most of what I want to say :) We've actually both been programming since we were kids (we shared an Apple IIe; he was writing his own operating system while I was writing Hangman), so it's cool that we're now writing books together. I hope the enriching experience we had writing the book will translate into an enriching experience for you reading the book.

I'd also like to thank my former colleagues at Microsoft. Many smart people work there, not just in terms of intellect but also in a broader emotional sense, and I miss working with them. In particular, I learned a lot from Brian Beckman, to whom I am indebted.

1

Introducing C# and the .NET
Framework

C# is a general-purpose, type-safe, object-oriented programming language. The goal of the language is programmer productivity. To this end, the language balances simplicity, expressiveness, and performance. The chief architect of the language since its first version is Anders Hejlsberg (creator of Turbo Pascal and architect of Delphi). The C# language is platform-neutral, but it was written to work well with the Microsoft .NET Framework.

Object Orientation

C# is a rich implementation of the object-orientation paradigm, which includes *encapsulation*, *inheritance*, and *polymorphism*. Encapsulation means creating a boundary around an *object*, to separate its external (public) behavior from its internal (private) implementation details. The distinctive features of C# from an object-oriented perspective are:

Unified type system
   The fundamental building block in C# is an encapsulated unit of data and functions called a *type*. C# has a *unified type system*, where all types ultimately share a common base type. This means that all types, whether they represent business objects or are primitive types such as numbers, share the same basic set of functionality. For example, any type can be converted to a string by calling its `ToString` method.

Classes and interfaces
   In the pure object-oriented paradigm, the only kind of type is a class. In C#, there are several other kinds of types, one of which is an *interface* (similar to Java interfaces). An interface is like a class except it is only a definition for a type, not an implementation. It's particularly useful in scenarios where multiple inheritance is required (unlike languages such as C++ and Eiffel, C# does not support multiple inheritance of classes).

Properties, methods, and events

In the pure object-oriented paradigm, all functions are *methods* (this is the case in Smalltalk). In C#, methods are only one kind of *function member*, which also includes *properties* and *events* (there are others, too). Properties are function members that encapsulate a piece of an object's state, such as a button's color or a label's text. Events are function members that simplify acting on object state changes.

Type Safety

C# is primarily a *type-safe* language, meaning that types can interact only through protocols they define, thereby ensuring each type's internal consistency. For instance, C# prevents you from interacting with a *string* type as though it were an *integer* type.

More specifically, C# supports *static typing*, meaning that the language enforces type safety at *compile time*. This is in addition to *dynamic* type safety, which the .NET CLR enforces at *runtime*.

Static typing eliminates a large class of errors before a program is even run. It shifts the burden away from runtime unit tests onto the compiler to verify that all the types in a program fit together correctly. This makes large programs much easier to manage, more predictable, and more robust. Furthermore, static typing allows tools such as IntelliSense in Visual Studio to help you write a program, since it knows for a given variable what type it is, and hence what methods you can call on that variable.

 C# 4.0 allows parts of your code to be dynamically typed via the new `dynamic` keyword. However, C# remains a predominately statically typed language.

C# is called a *strongly typed language* because its type rules (whether enforced statically or dynamically) are very strict. For instance, you cannot call a function that's designed to accept an integer with a floating-point number, unless you first *explicitly* convert the floating-point number to an integer. This helps prevent mistakes.

Strong typing also plays a role in enabling C# code to run in a sandbox—an environment where every aspect of security is controlled by the host. In a sandbox, it is important that you cannot arbitrarily corrupt the state of an object by bypassing its type rules.

Memory Management

C# relies on the runtime to perform automatic memory management. The CLR has a garbage collector that executes as part of your program, reclaiming memory for objects that are no longer referenced. This frees programmers from explicitly deallocating the memory for an object, eliminating the problem of incorrect pointers encountered in languages such as C++.

C# does not eliminate pointers: it merely makes them unnecessary for most programming tasks. For performance-critical hotspots and interoperability, pointers may be used, but they are permitted only in blocks that are explicitly marked unsafe.

Platform Support

C# is typically used for writing code that runs on Windows platforms. Although Microsoft standardized the C# language and the CLR through ECMA, the total amount of resources (both inside and outside of Microsoft) dedicated to supporting C# on non-Windows platforms is relatively small. This means that languages such as Java are sensible choices when multiplatform support is of primary concern. Having said this, C# can be used to write cross-platform code in the following scenarios:

- C# code may run on the server and dish up DHTML that can run on any platform. This is precisely the case for ASP.NET.

- C# code may run on a runtime other than the Microsoft Common Language Runtime. The most notable example is the Mono project, which has its own C# compiler and runtime, running on Linux, Solaris, Mac OS X, and Windows.

- C# code may run on a host that supports Microsoft Silverlight (supported for Windows and Mac OS X). This is a new technology that is analogous to Adobe's Flash Player.

C#'s Relationship with the CLR

C# depends on a runtime equipped with a host of features such as automatic memory management and exception handling. The design of C# closely maps to the design of the CLR, which provides these runtime features (although C# is technically independent of the CLR). Furthermore, the C# type system maps closely to the CLR type system (e.g., both share the same definitions for primitive types).

The CLR and .NET Framework

The .NET Framework consists of a runtime called the *Common Language Runtime* (CLR) and a vast set of libraries. The libraries consist of core libraries (which this book is concerned with) and applied libraries, which depend on the core libraries. Figure 1-1 is a visual overview of those libraries (and also serves as a navigational aid to the book).

The CLR is the runtime for executing *managed code*. C# is one of several *managed languages* that get compiled into managed code. Managed code is packaged into an *assembly*, in the form of either an executable file (an *.exe*) or a library (a *.dll*), along with type information, or *metadata*.

Managed code is represented in *Intermediate Language* or *IL*. When the CLR loads an assembly, it converts the IL into the native code of the machine, such as x86. This conversion is done by the CLR's JIT (Just-In-Time) compiler. An assembly retains

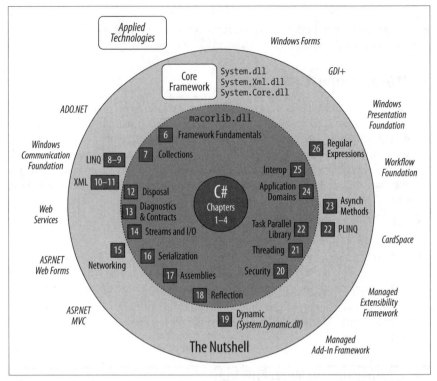

Figure 1-1. This depicts the topics covered in this book and the chapters in which they are found. The names of specialized frameworks and class libraries beyond the scope of this book are grayed out and displayed outside the boundaries of The Nutshell.

almost all of the original source language constructs, which makes it easy to inspect and even generate code dynamically.

> Red Gate's .NET Reflector application is an invaluable tool for examining the contents of an assembly (you can also use it as a decompiler).

The CLR performs as a host for numerous runtime services. Examples of these services include memory management, the loading of libraries, and security services.

The CLR is language-neutral, allowing developers to build applications in multiple languages (e.g., C#, Visual Basic .NET, Managed C++, Delphi.NET, Chrome .NET, and J#).

The .NET Framework consists of libraries for writing just about any Windows- or web-based application. Chapter 5 gives an overview of the .NET Framework libraries.

What's New in C# 4.0

The new features in C# 4.0 are:

- Dynamic binding
- Type variance with generic interfaces and delegates
- Optional parameters
- Named arguments
- COM interoperability improvements

Dynamic binding (Chapters 4 and 19) is C# 4.0's biggest innovation. This feature was inspired by dynamic languages such as Python, Ruby, JavaScript, and Smalltalk. Dynamic binding defers *binding*—the process of resolving types and members— from compile time to runtime. Although C# remains a predominantly statically typed language, a variable of type `dynamic` is resolved in a late-bound manner. For example:

```
dynamic d = "hello";
Console.WriteLine (d.ToUpper());    // HELLO
Console.WriteLine (d.Foo());        // Compiles OK but gives runtime error
```

Calling an object dynamically is useful in scenarios that would otherwise require complicated reflection code. Dynamic binding is also useful when interoperating with dynamic languages and COM components.

Optional parameters (Chapter 2) allow functions to specify default parameter values so that callers can omit arguments. An optional parameter declaration such as:

```
void Foo (int x = 23) { Console.WriteLine (x); }
```

can be called as follows:

```
Foo(); // 23
```

Named arguments (Chapter 2) allow a function caller to identify an argument by name rather than position. For example, the preceding method can now be called as follows:

```
Foo (x:5);
```

Type variance (Chapters 3 and 4) allows generic interfaces and generic delegates to mark their type parameters as covariant or contravariant. This enables code such as the following to work:

```
IEnumerable<string> x = ...;
IEnumerable<object> y = x;
```

COM interoperability (Chapter 25) has been enhanced in C# 4.0 in three ways. First, arguments can be passed by reference without the `ref` keyword. This feature is particularly useful in conjunction with optional parameters. It means that the following C# 3.0 code to open a Word document:

```
object o1 = "foo.doc";
object o2 = Missing.Value;
object o3 = Missing.Value;
...
word.Open (ref o1, ref o2, ref o3...);
```

can now be simplified to:

```
word.Open ("Foo.doc");
```

Second, assemblies that contain COM interop types can now be *linked* rather than *referenced*. Linked interop types support type equivalence, avoiding the need for *Primary Interop Assemblies* and putting an end to versioning and deployment headaches.

Third, functions that return *variant* types from linked interop types are mapped to dynamic rather than object, eliminating the need for casting.

C# Language Basics

In this chapter, we introduce the basics of the C# language.

All programs and code snippets in this and the following two chapters are available as interactive samples in LINQPad. Working through these samples in conjunction with the book accelerates learning in that you can edit the samples and instantly see the results without needing to set up projects and solutions in Visual Studio.

To download the samples, click the Samples tab in LINQPad and then click "Download more samples." LINQPad is free—go to *http://www.linqpad.net*.

A First C# Program

Here is a program that multiplies 12 by 30 and prints the result, 360, to the screen. The double forward slash indicates that the remainder of a line is a *comment*:

```
using System;                   // Importing namespace

class Test                      // Class declaration
{
  static void Main()            //   Method declaration
  {
    int x = 12 * 30;            //     Statement 1
    Console.WriteLine (x);      //     Statement 2
  }                             //   End of method
}                               // End of class
```

At the heart of this program lie two *statements*. Statements in C# execute sequentially. Each statement is terminated by a semicolon:

```
int x = 12 * 30;
Console.WriteLine (x);
```

The first statement computes the *expression* 12 * 30 and stores the result in a *local variable*, named x, which is an integer type. The second statement calls the Console class's WriteLine *method*, to print the variable x to a text window on the screen.

A *method* performs an action in a series of statements, called a *statement block*—a pair of braces containing zero or more statements. We defined a single method named Main:

```
static void Main()
{
  ...
}
```

Writing higher-level functions that call upon lower-level functions simplifies a program. We can *refactor* our program with a reusable method that multiplies an integer by 12 as follows:

```
using System;

class Test
{
  static void Main()
  {
    Console.WriteLine (FeetToInches (30));     // 360
    Console.WriteLine (FeetToInches (100));    // 1200
  }

  static int FeetToInches (int feet)
  {
    int inches = feet * 12;
    return inches;
  }
}
```

A method can receive *input* data from the caller by specifying *parameters* and *output* data back to the caller by specifying a *return type*. We defined a method called FeetToInches that has a parameter for inputting feet, and a return type for outputting inches:

```
static int FeetToInches (int feet) {...}
```

The *literals* 30 and 100 are the *arguments* passed to the FeetToInches method. The Main method in our example has empty parentheses because it has no parameters, and is void because it doesn't return any value to its caller:

```
static void Main()
```

C# recognizes a method called Main as signaling the default entry point of execution. The Main method may optionally return an integer (rather than void) in order to return a value to the execution environment. The Main method can also optionally accept an array of strings as a parameter (that will be populated with any arguments passed to the executable). For example:

```
static int Main (string[] args) {...}
```

An array (such as string[]) represents a fixed number of elements of a particular type. Arrays are specified by placing square brackets after the element type and are described in "Arrays" on page 32.

Methods are one of several kinds of functions in C#. Another kind of function we used was the * *operator*, used to perform multiplication. There are also *constructors*, *properties*, *events*, *indexers*, and *finalizers*.

In our example, the two methods are grouped into a class. A *class* groups function members and data members to form an object-oriented building block. The Console class groups members that handle command-line input/output functionality, such as the WriteLine method. Our Test class groups two methods—the Main method and the FeetToInches method. A class is a kind of *type*, which we will examine in "Type Basics" on page 12.

At the outermost level of a program, types are organized into *namespaces*. The using directive was used to make the System namespace available to our application, to use the Console class. We could define all our classes within the TestPrograms namespace, as follows:

```
using System;

namespace TestPrograms
{
  class Test  {...}
  class Test2 {...}
}
```

The .NET Framework is organized into nested namespaces. For example, this is the namespace that contains types for handling text:

```
using System.Text;
```

The using directive is there for convenience; you can also refer to a type by its fully qualified name, which is the type name prefixed with its namespace, such as System.Text.StringBuilder.

Compilation

The C# compiler compiles source code, specified as a set of files with the *.cs* extension, into an *assembly*. An assembly is the unit of packaging and deployment in .NET. An assembly can be either an *application* or a *library*. A normal console or Windows *application* has a Main method and is an *.exe* file. A library is a *.dll* and is equivalent to an *.exe* without an entry point. Its purpose is to be called upon (*referenced*) by an application or by other libraries. The .NET Framework is a set of libraries.

The name of the C# compiler is *csc.exe*. You can either use an IDE such as Visual Studio to compile, or call `csc` manually from the command line. To compile manually, first save a program to a file such as *MyFirstProgram.cs*, and then go to the command line and invoke `csc` (located under *%SystemRoot%\Microsoft.NET \Framework\<framework-version>* where *%SystemRoot%* is your Windows directory) as follows:

```
csc MyFirstProgram.cs
```

This produces an application named *MyFirstProgram.exe*.

To produce a library (*.dll*), do the following:

```
csc /target:library MyFirstProgram.cs
```

 We explain assemblies in detail in Chapter 16.

Syntax

C# syntax is based on C and C++ syntax. In this section, we will describe C#'s elements of syntax, using the following program:

```
using System;

class Test
{
  static void Main()
  {
    int x = 12 * 30;
    Console.WriteLine (x);
  }
}
```

Identifiers and Keywords

Identifiers are names that programmers choose for their classes, methods, variables, and so on. These are the identifiers in our example program, in the order they appear:

```
System    Test    Main    x    Console    WriteLine
```

An identifier must be a whole word, essentially made up of Unicode characters starting with a letter or underscore. C# identifiers are case-sensitive. By convention, parameters, local variables, and private fields should be in camel case (e.g., `myVariable`), and all other identifiers should be in Pascal case (e.g., `MyMethod`).

Keywords are names reserved by the compiler that you can't use as identifiers. These are the keywords in our example program:

```
using    class    static    void    int
```

Here is the full list of C# keywords:

abstract	as	base	bool	break
byte	case	catch	char	checked
class	const	continue	decimal	default
delegate	do	double	else	enum
event	explicit	extern	false	finally
fixed	float	for	foreach	goto
if	implicit	in	int	interface
internal	is	lock	long	namespace
new	null	object	operator	out
override	params	private	protected	public
readonly	ref	return	sbyte	sealed
short	sizeof	stackalloc	static	string
struct	switch	this	throw	true
try	typeof	uint	ulong	unchecked
unsafe	ushort	using	virtual	volatile
void	while			

Avoiding conflicts

If you really want to use an identifier that clashes with a keyword, you can do so by qualifying it with the @ prefix. For instance:

```
class class  {...}     // Illegal
class @class {...}     // Legal
```

The @ symbol doesn't form part of the identifier itself. So @myVariable is the same as myVariable.

> The @ prefix can be useful when consuming libraries written in other .NET languages that have different keywords.

Contextual keywords

Some keywords are *contextual*, meaning that they can also be used as identifiers—without an @ symbol. These are:

add	ascending	by	descending	dynamic	equals
from	get	global	group	in	into
join	let	on	orderby	partial	remove
select	set	value	var	where	yield

With contextual keywords, ambiguity cannot arise within the context in which they are used.

Literals, Punctuators, and Operators

Literals are primitive pieces of data statically embedded into the program. The literals we used in our example program are 12 and 30.

Punctuators help demarcate the structure of the program. These are the punctuators we used in our example program:

```
;  {  }
```

The semicolon is used to terminate a statement. This means that statements can wrap multiple lines:

```
Console.WriteLine
  (1 + 2 + 3 + 4 + 5 + 6 + 7 + 8 + 9 + 10);
```

The braces are used to group multiple statements into a statement block.

An *operator* transforms and combines expressions. Most operators in C# are denoted with a symbol, such as the multiplication operator, *. We will discuss operators in more detail later in the chapter. These are the operators we used in our example program:

```
.  ()  *  =
```

The period denotes a member of something (or a decimal point with numeric literals). The parentheses are used when declaring or calling a method; empty parentheses are used when the method accepts no arguments. The equals sign is used for *assignment* (the double equals sign, ==, is used for equality comparison, as we'll see later).

Comments

C# offers two different styles of source-code documentation: *single-line comments* and *multiline comments*. A single-line comment begins with a double forward slash and continues until the end of the line. For example:

```
int x = 3;   // Comment about assigning 3 to x
```

A multiline comment begins with /* and ends with */. For example:

```
int x = 3;   /* This is a comment that
                spans two lines */
```

Comments may embed XML documentation tags, explained in "XML Documentation" on page 176 in Chapter 4.

Type Basics

A *type* defines the blueprint for a value. A *value* is a storage location denoted by a *variable* or a *constant*. A variable represents a value that can change, whereas a constant represents an invariant (we will visit constants later in the chapter). We created a local variable named x in our first program:

```
static void Main()
{
  int x = 12 * 30;
  Console.WriteLine (x);
}
```

All values in C# are an *instance* of a specific type. The meaning of a value, and the set of possible values a variable can have, is determined by its type. The type of x is int.

Predefined Type Examples

Predefined types are types that are specially supported by the compiler. The int type is a predefined type for representing the set of integers that fit into 32 bits of memory, from -2^{31} to $2^{31}-1$. We can perform functions such as arithmetic with instances of the int type as follows:

```
int x = 12 * 30;
```

Another predefined C# type is string. The string type represents a sequence of characters, such as ".NET" or "*http://oreilly.com*". We can work with strings by calling functions on them as follows:

```
string message = "Hello world";
string upperMessage = message.ToUpper();
Console.WriteLine (upperMessage);          // HELLO WORLD

int x = 2010;
message = message + x.ToString();
Console.WriteLine (message);               // Hello world2010
```

The predefined bool type has exactly two possible values: true and false. The bool type is commonly used to conditionally branch execution flow based with an if statement. For example:

```
bool simpleVar = false;
if (simpleVar)
  Console.WriteLine ("This will not print");

int x = 5000;
bool lessThanAMile = x < 5280;
if (lessThanAMile)
  Console.WriteLine ("This will print");
```

In C#, predefined types (also referred to as built-in types) are recognized with a C# keyword. The System namespace in the .NET Framework contains many important types that are not predefined by C# (e.g., DateTime).

Custom Type Examples

Just as we can build complex functions from simple functions, we can build complex types from primitive types. In this example, we will define a custom type named UnitConverter—a class that serves as a blueprint for unit conversions:

```
using System;

public class UnitConverter
{
  int ratio;                                              // Field
  public UnitConverter (int unitRatio) {ratio = unitRatio; } // Constructor
  public int Convert   (int unit)     {return unit * ratio; } // Method
}

class Test
{
  static void Main()
  {
    UnitConverter feetToInchesConverter = new UnitConverter (12);
    UnitConverter milesToFeetConverter  = new UnitConverter (5280);

    Console.WriteLine (feetToInchesConverter.Convert(30));    // 360
    Console.WriteLine (feetToInchesConverter.Convert(100));   // 1200
    Console.WriteLine (feetToInchesConverter.Convert(
                       milesToFeetConverter.Convert(1)));    // 63360
  }
}
```

Members of a type

A type contains *data members* and *function members*. The data member of UnitConverter is the *field* called ratio. The function members of UnitConverter are the Convert method and the UnitConverter's *constructor*.

Symmetry of predefined types and custom types

A beautiful aspect of C# is that predefined types and custom types have few differences. The predefined int type serves as a blueprint for integers. It holds data—32 bits—and provides function members that use that data, such as ToString. Similarly, our custom UnitConverter type acts as a blueprint for unit conversions. It holds data—the ratio—and provides function members to use that data.

Constructors and instantiation

Data is created by *instantiating* a type. Predefined types can be instantiated simply by using a literal. For example, the following line instantiates two integers (12 and 30), which are used to compute a third instance, x:

```
int x = 12 * 30;
```

The new operator is needed to create a new instance of a custom type. We created and declared an instance of the UnitConverter type with this statement:

```
UnitConverter feetToInchesConverter = new UnitConverter (12);
```

Immediately after the new operator instantiates an object, the object's *constructor* is called to perform initialization. A constructor is defined like a method, except that the method name and return type are reduced to the name of the enclosing type:

```
public class UnitConverter
{
  ...
  public UnitConverter (int unitRatio) { ratio = unitRatio; }
  ...
}
```

Instance versus static members

The data members and function members that operate on the *instance* of the type are called instance members. The UnitConverter's Convert method and the int's ToString method are examples of instance members. By default, members are instance members.

Data members and function members that don't operate on the instance of the type, but rather on the type itself, must be marked as static. The Test.Main and Console.WriteLine methods are static methods. The Console class is actually a *static class*, which means *all* its members are static. You never actually create instances of a Console—one console is shared across the whole application.

To contrast instance from static members, in the following code the instance field Name pertains to an instance of a particular Panda, whereas Population pertains to the set of all Panda instances:

```
public class Panda
{
  public string Name;              // Instance field
  public static int Population;     // Static field

  public Panda (string n)          // Constructor
  {
    Name = n;                      // Assign the instance field
    Population = Population + 1;    // Increment the static Population field
  }
}
```

The following code creates two instances of the Panda, prints their names, and then prints the total population:

```
using System;

class Program
{
  static void Main()
  {
    Panda p1 = new Panda ("Pan Dee");
    Panda p2 = new Panda ("Pan Dah");

    Console.WriteLine (p1.Name);    // Pan Dee
    Console.WriteLine (p2.Name);    // Pan Dah

    Console.WriteLine (Panda.Population);  // 2
```

```
      }
    }
```

The public keyword

The public keyword exposes members to other classes. In this example, if the Name
field in Panda was not public, the Test class could not access it. Marking a member
public is how a type communicates: "Here is what I want other types to see—
everything else is my own private implementation details." In object-oriented terms,
we say that the public members *encapsulate* the private members of the class.

Conversions

C# can convert between instances of compatible types. A conversion always creates
a new value from an existing one. Conversions can be either *implicit* or *explicit*:
implicit conversions happen automatically, and explicit conversions require a *cast*.
In the following example, we *implicitly* cast an int to a long type (which has twice
the bitwise capacity of an int) and *explicitly* cast an int to a short type (which has
half the capacity of an int):

```
int x = 12345;        // int is a 32-bit integer
long y = x;           // Implicit conversion to 64-bit integer
short z = (short)x;   // Explicit conversion to 16-bit integer
```

Implicit conversions are allowed when both of the following are true:

- The compiler can guarantee they will always succeed.
- No information is lost in conversion.*

Conversely, *explicit* conversions are required when one of the following is true:

- The compiler cannot guarantee they will always succeed.
- Information may be lost during conversion.

> The *numeric conversions* that we just saw are built into the
> language. C# also supports *reference conversions* and *boxing
> conversions* (see Chapter 3) as well as *custom conversions* (see
> "Operator Overloading" on page 153 in Chapter 4). The com-
> piler doesn't enforce the aforementioned rules with custom
> conversions, so it's possible for badly designed types to behave
> otherwise.

Value Types Versus Reference Types

All C# types fall into the following categories:

- Value types
- Reference types

---

* A minor caveat is that very large long values lose some precision when converted to double.

- Generic type parameters
- Pointer types

 In this section, we'll describe value types and reference types. In "Generics" on page 101 in Chapter 3, we'll cover generic type parameters, and in "Unsafe Code and Pointers" on page 170 in Chapter 4, we'll cover pointer types.

Value types comprise most built-in types (specifically, all numeric types, the `char` type, and the `bool` type) as well as custom `struct` and `enum` types.

Reference types comprise all class, array, delegate, and interface types.

The fundamental difference between value types and reference types is how they are handled in memory.

Value types

The content of a *value type* variable or constant is simply a value. For example, the content of the built-in value type, `int`, is 32 bits of data.

You can define a custom value type with the `struct` keyword (see Figure 2-1):

```
public struct Point { public int X, Y; }
```

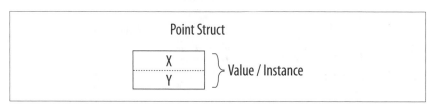

Figure 2-1. A value type instance in memory

The assignment of a value type instance always *copies* the instance. For example:

```
static void Main()
{
  Point p1 = new Point();
  p1.X = 7;

  Point p2 = p1;             // Assignment causes copy

  Console.WriteLine (p1.X);  // 7
  Console.WriteLine (p2.X);  // 7

  p1.X = 9;                  // Change p1.X

  Console.WriteLine (p1.X);  // 9
  Console.WriteLine (p2.X);  // 7
}
```

Figure 2-2 shows that **p1** and **p2** have independent storage.

Figure 2-2. Assignment copies a value-type instance

Reference types

A reference type is more complex than a value type, having two parts: an *object* and the *reference* to that object. The content of a reference-type variable or constant is a reference to an object that contains the value. Here is the `Point` type from our previous example rewritten as a class, rather than a `struct` (shown in Figure 2-3):

```
public class Point { public int X, Y; }
```

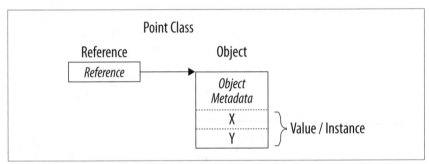

Figure 2-3. A reference-type instance in memory

Assigning a reference-type variable copies the reference, not the object instance. This allows multiple variables to refer to the same object—something not ordinarily possible with value types. If we repeat the previous example, but with `Point` now a class, an operation to X affects Y:

```
static void Main()
{
  Point p1 = new Point();
  p1.X = 7;

  Point p2 = p1;            // Copies p1 reference

  Console.WriteLine (p1.X); // 7
  Console.WriteLine (p2.X); // 7

  p1.X = 9;                 // Change p1.X

  Console.WriteLine (p1.X); // 9
  Console.WriteLine (p2.X); // 9
}
```

Figure 2-4 shows that `p1` and `p2` are two references that point to the same object.

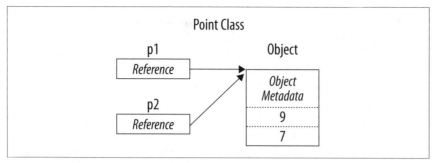

Figure 2-4. Assignment copies a reference

Null

A reference can be assigned the literal null, indicating that the reference points to no object:

```
class Point {...}
...

Point p = null;
Console.WriteLine (p == null);   // True

// The following line generates a runtime error
// (a NullReferenceException is thrown):
Console.WriteLine (p.X);
```

In contrast, a value type cannot ordinarily have a null value:

```
struct Point {...}
...

Point p = null;  // Compile-time error
int x = null;    // Compile-time error
```

 C# also has a construct called *nullable types* for representing value-type nulls (see "Nullable Types" on page 148 in Chapter 4).

Storage overhead

Value-type instances occupy precisely the memory required to store their fields. In this example, Point takes eight bytes of memory:

```
struct Point
{
  int x;  // 4 bytes
  int y;  // 4 bytes
}
```

Technically, the CLR positions fields within the type at an address that's a multiple of the fields' size (up to a maximum of 8 bytes). Thus, the following actually consumes 16 bytes of memory (with the 7 bytes following the first field "wasted"):

```
struct A { byte b; long l; }
```

Reference types require separate allocations of memory for the reference and object. The object consumes as many bytes as its fields, plus additional administrative overhead. The precise overhead is intrinsically private to the implementation of the .NET runtime, but at minimum the overhead is eight bytes, used to store a key to the object's type, as well as temporary information such as its lock state for multithreading and a flag to indicate whether it has been fixed from movement by the garbage collector. Each reference to an object requires an extra 4 or 8 bytes, depending on whether the .NET runtime is running on a 32- or 64-bit platform.

Predefined Type Taxonomy

The predefined types in C# are:

Value types

- Numeric
  — Signed integer (`sbyte`, `short`, `int`, `long`)
  — Unsigned integer (`byte`, `ushort`, `uint`, `ulong`)
  — Real number (`float`, `double`, `decimal`)
- Logical (`bool`)
- Character (`char`)

Reference types

- String (`string`)
- Object (`object`)

Predefined types in C# alias Framework types in the `System` namespace. There is only a syntactic difference between these two statements:

```
int i = 5;
System.Int32 i = 5;
```

The set of predefined *value* types excluding `decimal` are known as *primitive types* in the CLR. Primitive types are so called because they are supported directly via instructions in compiled code, and this usually translates to direct support on the underlying processor. For example:

```
                        // Underlying hexadecimal representation
int i = 7;              // 0x7
bool b = true;          // 0x1
char c = 'A';           // 0x41
float f = 0.5f;         // uses IEEE floating-point encoding
```

The `System.IntPtr` and `System.UIntPtr` types are also primitive (see Chapter 25).

Numeric Types

C# has the predefined numeric types shown in Table 2-1.

Table 2-1. Predefined numeric types in C#

C# type	System type	Suffix	Size	Range
Integral—signed				
sbyte	SByte		8 bits	-2^7 to 2^7-1
short	Int16		16 bits	-2^{15} to $2^{15}-1$
int	Int32		32 bits	-2^{31} to $2^{31}-1$
long	Int64	L	64 bits	-2^{63} to $2^{63}-1$
Integral—unsigned				
byte	Byte		8 bits	0 to 2^8-1
ushort	UInt16		16 bits	0 to $2^{16}-1$
uint	UInt32	U	32 bits	0 to $2^{32}-1$
ulong	UInt64	UL	64 bits	0 to $2^{64}-1$
Real				
float	Single	F	32 bits	$\pm(\sim\!10^{-45}$ to $10^{38})$
double	Double	D	64 bits	$\pm(\sim\!10^{-324}$ to $10^{308})$
decimal	Decimal	M	128 bits	$\pm(\sim\!10^{-28}$ to $10^{28})$

Of the *integral* types, int and long are first-class citizens and are favored by both C# and the runtime. The other integral types are typically used for interoperability or when space efficiency is paramount.

Of the *real* number types, float and double are called *floating-point types*[†] and are typically used for scientific calculations. The decimal type is typically used for financial calculations, where base-10-accurate arithmetic and high precision are required.

Numeric Literals

Integral literals can use decimal or hexadecimal notation; hexadecimal is denoted with the 0x prefix. For example:

```
int x = 127;
long y = 0x7F;
```

Real literals can use decimal and/or exponential notation. For example:

```
double d = 1.5;
double million = 1E06;
```

[†] Technically, decimal is a floating-point type too, although it's not referred to as such in the C# language specification.

Numeric literal type inference

By default, the compiler *infers* a numeric literal to be either `double` or an integral type:

- If the literal contains a decimal point or the exponential symbol (`E`), it is a `double`.
- Otherwise, the literal's type is the first type in this list that can fit the literal's value: `int`, `uint`, `long`, and `ulong`.

For example:

```
Console.WriteLine (        1.0.GetType());  // Double  (double)
Console.WriteLine (      1E06.GetType());  // Double  (double)
Console.WriteLine (         1.GetType());  // Int32   (int)
Console.WriteLine ( 0xF0000000.GetType());  // UInt32  (uint)
```

Numeric suffixes

Numeric suffixes explicitly define the type of a literal. Suffixes can be either lower- or uppercase, and are as follows:

Category	C# type	Notes	Example
F	float		float f = 1.0F;
D	double		double d = 1D;
M	decimal		decimal d = 1.0M;
U	uint or ulong	Combinable with L	uint i = 1U;
L	long or ulong	Combinable with U	ulong i = 1UL;

The suffixes `U` and `L` are rarely necessary, because the `uint`, `long`, and `ulong` types can nearly always be either *inferred* or *implicitly converted* from `int`:

```
long i = 5;     // Implicit lossless conversion from int literal to long
```

The `D` suffix is technically redundant, in that all literals with a decimal point are inferred to be `double`. And you can always add a decimal point to a numeric literal:

```
double x = 4.0;
```

The `F` and `M` suffixes are the most useful and should always be applied when specifying `float` or `decimal` literals. Without the `F` suffix, the following line would not compile, because 4.5 would be inferred to be of type `double`, which has no implicit conversion to `float`:

```
float f = 4.5F;
```

The same principle is true for a decimal literal:

```
decimal d = -1.23M;     // Will not compile without the M suffix.
```

We describe the semantics of numeric conversions in detail in the following section.

Numeric Conversions

Integral to integral conversions

Integral conversions are *implicit* when the destination type can represent every possible value of the source type. Otherwise, an *explicit* conversion is required. For example:

```
int x = 12345;      // int is a 32-bit integral
long y = x;         // Implicit conversion to 64-bit integral
short z = (short)x; // Explicit conversion to 16-bit integral
```

Floating-point to floating-point conversions

A `float` can be implicitly converted to a `double`, since a `double` can represent every possible value of a `float`. The reverse conversion must be explicit.

Floating-point to integral conversions

All integral types may be implicitly converted to all floating-point numbers:

```
int i = 1;
float f = i;
```

The reverse conversion must be explicit:

```
int i2 = (int)f;
```

 When you cast from a floating-point number to an integral, any fractional portion is truncated; no rounding is performed. The static class `System.Convert` provides methods that round while converting between various numeric types (see Chapter 6).

Implicitly converting a large integral type to a floating-point type preserves *magnitude* but may occasionally lose *precision*. This is because floating-point types always have more magnitude than integral types, but may have less precision. Rewriting our example with a larger number demonstrates this:

```
int i1 = 100000001;
float f = i1;       // Magnitude preserved, precision lost
int i2 = (int)f;    // 100000000
```

Decimal conversions

All integral types can be implicitly converted to the decimal type, since a decimal can represent every possible C# integral value. All other numeric conversions to and from a decimal type must be explicit.

Arithmetic Operators

The arithmetic operators (+, -, *, /, %) are defined for all numeric types except the 8- and 16-bit integral types:

```
+    Addition
-    Subtraction
*    Multiplication
/    Division
%    Remainder after division
```

Increment and Decrement Operators

The increment and decrement operators (++, --) increment and decrement numeric types by 1. The operator can either precede or follow the variable, depending on whether you want the variable to be updated *before* or *after* the expression is evaluated. For example:

```
int x = 0;
Console.WriteLine (x++);   // Outputs 0; x is now 1
Console.WriteLine (++x);   // Outputs 2; x is now 2
Console.WriteLine (--x);   // Outputs 1; x is now 1
```

Specialized Integral Operations

Integral division

Division operations on integral types always truncate remainders. Dividing by a variable whose value is zero generates a runtime error (a `DivideByZeroException`):

```
int a = 2 / 3;     // 0

int b = 0;
int c = 5 / b;     // throws DivisionByZeroException
```

Dividing by the *literal* 0 generates a compile-time error.

Integral overflow

At runtime, arithmetic operations on integral types can overflow. By default, this happens silently—no exception is thrown. Although the C# specification is agnostic as to the result of an overflow, the CLR always causes wraparound behavior. For example, decrementing the minimum possible `int` value results in the maximum possible `int` value:

```
int a = int.MinValue;
a--;
Console.WriteLine (a == int.MaxValue); // True
```

Integral arithmetic overflow check operators

The `checked` operator tells the runtime to generate an `OverflowException` rather than failing silently when an integral expression or statement exceeds the arithmetic limits of that type. The `checked` operator affects expressions with the ++, --, +, - (binary and unary), *, /, and explicit conversion operators between integral types.

`checked` can be used around either an expression or a statement block. For example:

```
int a = 1000000;
int b = 1000000;
```

```
int c = checked (a * b);        // Checks just the expression.

checked                         // Checks all expressions
{                               // in statement block.
    ...
    c = a * b;
    ...
}
```

You can make arithmetic overflow checking the default for all expressions in a program by compiling with the /checked+ command-line switch (in Visual Studio, go to Advanced Build Settings). If you then need to disable overflow checking just for specific expressions or statements, you can do so with the unchecked operator. For example, the following code will not throw exceptions—even if compiled with /checked+:

```
int x = int.MaxValue;
int y = unchecked (x + 1);
unchecked { int z = x + 1; }
```

Overflow checking for constant expressions

Regardless of the /checked compiler switch, expressions evaluated at compile time are always overflow-checked—unless you apply the unchecked operator:

```
int x = int.MaxValue + 1;            // Compile-time error
int y = unchecked (int.MaxValue + 1); // No errors
```

Bitwise operators

C# supports the following bitwise operators:

Operator	Meaning	Sample expression	Result
~	Complement	~0xfU	0xfffffff0U
&	And	0xf0 & 0x33	0x30
|	Or	0xf0 | 0x33	0xf3
^	Exclusive Or	0xff00 ^ 0x0ff0	0xf0f0
<<	Shift left	0x20 << 2	0x80
>>	Shift right	0x20 >> 1	0x10

8- and 16-Bit Integrals

The 8- and 16-bit integral types are byte, sbyte, short, and ushort. These types lack their own arithmetic operators, so C# implicitly converts them to larger types as required. This can cause a compile-time error when trying to assign the result back to a small integral type:

```
short x = 1, y = 1;
short z = x + y;        // Compile-time error
```

In this case, x and y are implicitly converted to int so that the addition can be performed. This means the result is also an int, which cannot be implicitly cast back to a short (because it could cause loss of data). To make this compile, we must add an explicit cast:

```
short z = (short) (x + y);   // OK
```

Special Float and Double Values

Unlike integral types, floating-point types have values that certain operations treat specially. These special values are NaN (Not a Number), +∞, -∞, and -0. The float and double classes have constants for NaN, +∞, and -∞, as well as other values (MaxValue, MinValue, and Epsilon). For example:

```
Console.WriteLine (double.NegativeInfinity);   // -Infinity
```

The constants that represent special values for double and float are as follows:

Special value	Double constant	Float constant
NaN	double.NaN	float.NaN
+∞	double.PositiveInfinity	float.PositiveInfinity
-∞	double.NegativeInfinity	float.NegativeInfinity
-0	-0.0	-0.0f

Dividing a nonzero number by zero results in an infinite value. For example:

```
Console.WriteLine ( 1.0 /  0.0);   //  Infinity
Console.WriteLine (-1.0 /  0.0);   // -Infinity
Console.WriteLine ( 1.0 / -0.0);   // -Infinity
Console.WriteLine (-1.0 / -0.0);   //  Infinity
```

Dividing zero by zero, or subtracting infinity from infinity, results in a NaN. For example:

```
Console.WriteLine ( 0.0 /  0.0);             //  NaN
Console.WriteLine ((1.0 /  0.0) - (1.0 / 0.0));   //  NaN
```

When using ==, a NaN value is never equal to another value, even another NaN value:

```
Console.WriteLine (0.0 / 0.0 == double.NaN);   // False
```

To test whether a value is NaN, you must use the float.IsNaN or double.IsNaN method:

```
Console.WriteLine (double.IsNaN (0.0 / 0.0));   // True
```

When using object.Equals, however, two NaN values are equal:

```
Console.WriteLine (object.Equals (0.0 / 0.0, double.NaN));   // True
```

NaNs are sometimes useful in representing special values. In WPF, double.NaN represents a measurement whose value is "Automatic." Another way to represent such a value is with a nullable type (Chapter 4); another is with a custom struct that wraps a numeric type and adds an additional field (Chapter 3).

float and double follow the specification of the IEEE 754 format types, supported natively by almost all processors. You can find detailed information on the behavior of these types at *http://www.ieee.org*.

double Versus decimal

double is useful for scientific computations (such as computing spatial coordinates). decimal is useful for financial computations and values that are "man-made" rather than the result of real-world measurements. Here's a summary of the differences:

Category	double	decimal
Internal representation	Base 2	Base 10
Precision	15–16 significant figures	28–29 significant figures
Range	$\pm(\sim10^{-324}$ to $\sim10^{308})$	$\pm(\sim10^{-28}$ to $\sim10^{28})$
Special values	$+0, -0, +\infty, -\infty$, and NaN	None
Speed	Native to processor	Non-native to processor (about 10 times slower than double)

Real Number Rounding Errors

float and double 1internally represent numbers in base 2. For this reason, only numbers expressible in base 2 are represented precisely. Practically, this means most literals with a fractional component (which are in base 10) will not be represented precisely. For example:

```
float tenth = 0.1f;          // Not quite 0.1
float one   = 1f;
Console.WriteLine (one - tenth * 10f);    // -1.490116E-08
```

This is why float and double are bad for financial calculations. In contrast, decimal works in base 10 and so can precisely represent numbers expressible in base 10 (as well as its factors, base 2 and base 5). Since real literals are in base 10, decimal can precisely represent numbers such as 0.1. However, neither double nor decimal can precisely represent a fractional number whose base 10 representation is recurring:

```
decimal m = 1M / 6M;         // 0.1666666666666666666666666667M
double  d = 1.0 / 6.0;       // 0.16666666666666666
```

This leads to accumulated rounding errors:

```
decimal notQuiteWholeM = m+m+m+m+m+m;   // 1.0000000000000000000000000002M
double  notQuiteWholeD = d+d+d+d+d+d;   // 0.99999999999999989
```

which breaks equality and comparison operations:

```
Console.WriteLine (notQuiteWholeM == 1M);   // False
Console.WriteLine (notQuiteWholeD < 1.0);   // True
```

Boolean Type and Operators

C#'s `bool` type (aliasing the `System.Boolean` type) is a logical value that can be assigned the literal `true` or `false`.

Although a Boolean value requires only one bit of storage, the runtime will use one byte of memory, since this is the minimum chunk that the runtime and processor can efficiently work with. To avoid space inefficiency in the case of arrays, the Framework provides a `BitArray` class in the `System.Collections` namespace that is designed to use just one bit per Boolean value.

Bool Conversions

No conversions can be made from the `bool` type to numeric types or vice versa.

Equality and Comparison Operators

`==` and `!=` test for equality and inequality of any type, but always return a `bool` value.‡ Value types typically have a very simple notion of equality:

```
int x = 1;
int y = 2;
int z = 1;
Console.WriteLine (x == y);   // False
Console.WriteLine (x == z);   // True
```

For reference types, equality, by default, is based on *reference*, as opposed to the actual *value* of the underlying object (more on this in Chapter 6):

```
public class Dude
{
  public string Name;
  public Dude (string n) { Name = n; }
}
...
Dude d1 = new Dude ("John");
Dude d2 = new Dude ("John");
Console.WriteLine (d1 == d2);   // False
Dude d3 = d1;
Console.WriteLine (d1 == d3);   // True
```

The equality and comparison operators, `==`, `!=`, `<`, `>`, `>=`, and `<=`, work for all numeric types, but should be used with caution with real numbers (as we saw in "Real Number Rounding Errors" on page 27). The comparison operators also work on `enum`

---

‡ It's possible to *overload* these operators (Chapter 4) such that they return a non-`bool` type, but this is almost never done in practice.

type members, by comparing their underlying integral values. We describe this in "Enums" on page 97 in Chapter 3.

We explain the equality and comparison operators in greater detail in Chapter 4 in the sections "Operator Overloading" on page 153 and "Equality Comparison" on page 245 and in the section "Order Comparison" on page 255 in Chapter 6.

Conditional Operators

The && and || operators test for *and* and *or* conditions. They are frequently used in conjunction with the ! operator, which expresses *not*. In this example, the UseUmbrella method returns true if it's rainy or sunny (to protect us from the rain or the sun), as long as it's not also windy (since umbrellas are useless in the wind):

```
static bool UseUmbrella (bool rainy, bool sunny, bool windy)
{
  return !windy && (rainy || sunny);
}
```

The && and || operators *short-circuit* evaluation when possible. In the preceding example, if it is windy, the expression (rainy || sunny) is not even evaluated. Short-circuiting is essential in allowing expressions such as the following to run without throwing a NullReferenceException:

```
if (sb != null && sb.Length > 0) ...
```

The & and | operators also test for *and* and *or* conditions:

```
return !windy & (rainy | sunny);
```

The difference is that they *do not short-circuit*. For this reason, they are rarely used in place of conditional operators.

 Unlike in C and C++, the & and | operators perform (non-short-circuiting) *boolean* comparisons when applied to bool expressions. The & and | operators perform *bitwise* operations only when applied to numbers.

The ternary conditional operator (simply called the *conditional operator*) has the form q ? a : b, where if condition q is true, a is evaluated, else b is evaluated. For example:

```
static int Max (int a, int b)
{
  return (a > b) ? a : b;
}
```

The conditional operator is particularly useful in LINQ queries (Chapter 8).

Strings and Characters

C#'s char type (aliasing the System.Char type) represents a Unicode character and occupies two bytes. A char literal is specified inside single quotes:

```
char c = 'A';        // Simple character
```

Escape sequences express characters that cannot be expressed or interpreted literally. An escape sequence is a backslash followed by a character with a special meaning. For example:

```
char newLine = '\n';
char backSlash = '\\';
```

The escape sequence characters are shown in Table 2-2.

Table 2-2. Escape sequence characters

Char	Meaning	Value
\'	Single quote	0x0027
\"	Double quote	0x0022
\\	Backslash	0x005C
\0	Null	0x0000
\a	Alert	0x0007
\b	Backspace	0x0008
\f	Form feed	0x000C
\n	New line	0x000A
\r	Carriage return	0x000D
\t	Horizontal tab	0x0009
\v	Vertical tab	0x000B

The \u (or \x) escape sequence lets you specify any Unicode character via its four-digit hexadecimal code:

```
char copyrightSymbol = '\u00A9';
char omegaSymbol     = '\u03A9';
char newLine         = '\u000A';
```

Char Conversions

An implicit conversion from a char to a numeric type works for the numeric types that can accommodate an unsigned short. For other numeric types, an explicit conversion is required.

String Type

C#'s string type (aliasing the System.String type, covered in depth in Chapter 6) represents an immutable sequence of Unicode characters. A string literal is specified inside double quotes:

```
string a = "Heat";
```

 string is a reference type, rather than a value type. Its equality operators, however, follow value-type semantics:

```
string a = "test";
string b = "test";
Console.Write (a == b);  // True
```

The escape sequences that are valid for char literals also work inside strings:

```
string a = "Here's a tab:\t";
```

The cost of this is that whenever you need a literal backslash, you must write it twice:

```
string a1 = "\\\\server\\fileshare\\helloworld.cs";
```

To avoid this problem, C# allows *verbatim* string literals. A verbatim string literal is prefixed with @ and does not support escape sequences. The following verbatim string is identical to the preceding one:

```
string a2 = @ "\\server\fileshare\helloworld.cs";
```

A verbatim string literal can also span multiple lines:

```
string escaped  = "First Line\r\nSecond Line";
string verbatim = @"First Line
Second Line";

// Assuming your IDE uses CR-LF line separators:
Console.WriteLine (escaped == verbatim);  // True
```

You can include the double-quote character in a verbatim literal by writing it twice:

```
string xml = @"<customer id=""123""></customer>";
```

String concatenation

The + operator concatenates two strings:

```
string s = "a" + "b";
```

The righthand operand may be a nonstring value, in which case ToString is called on that value. For example:

```
string s = "a" + 5;  // a5
```

Since string is immutable, using the + operator repeatedly to build up a string is inefficient: a better solution is to use the System.Text.StringBuilder type (described in Chapter 6).

String comparisons

string does not support < and > operators for comparisons. You must use the string's CompareTo method, described in Chapter 6.

Arrays

An array represents a fixed number of elements of a particular type. The elements in an array are always stored in a contiguous block of memory, providing highly efficient access.

An array is denoted with square brackets after the element type. For example:

```
char[] vowels = new char[5];    // Declare an array of 5 characters
```

Square brackets also *index* the array, accessing a particular element by position:

```
vowels [0] = 'a';
vowels [1] = 'e';
vowels [2] = 'i';
vowels [3] = 'o';
vowels [4] = 'u';
Console.WriteLine (vowels [1]);      // e
```

This prints "e" because array indexes start at 0. We can use a for loop statement to iterate through each element in the array. The for loop in this example cycles the integer i from 0 to 4:

```
for (int i = 0; i < vowels.Length; i++)
    Console.Write (vowels [i]);          // aeiou
```

The Length property of an array returns the number of elements in the array. Once an array has been created, its length cannot be changed. The System.Collection namespace and subnamespaces provide higher-level data structures, such as dynamically sized arrays and dictionaries.

An *array initialization expression* specifies each element of an array. For example:

```
char[] vowels = new char[] {'a','e','i','o','u'};
```

or simply:

```
char[] vowels = {'a','e','i','o','u'};
```

All arrays inherit from the System.Array class, providing common services for all arrays. These members include methods to get and set elements regardless of the array type, and are described in "The Array Class" on page 273 in Chapter 7.

Default Element Initialization

Creating an array always preinitializes the elements with default values. The default value for a type is the result of a bitwise zeroing of memory. For example, consider creating an array of integers. Since int is a value type, this allocates 1,000 integers in one contiguous block of memory. The default value for each element will be 0:

```
int[] a = new int[1000];
Console.Write (a[123]);          // 0
```

Value types versus reference types

Whether an array element type is a value type or a reference type has important performance implications. When the element type is a value type, each element value is allocated as part of the array. For example:

```
public struct Point { public int X, Y; }
...

Point[] a = new Point[1000];
int x = a[500].X;                    // 0
```

Had `Point` been a class, creating the array would have merely allocated 1,000 null references:

```
public class Point { public int X, Y; }


...
Point[] a = new Point[1000];
int x = a[500].X;                    // Runtime error, NullReferenceException
```

To avoid this error, we must explicitly instantiate 1,000 `Point`s after instantiating the array:

```
Point[] a = new Point[1000];
for (int i = 0; i < a.Length; i++) // Iterate i from 0 to 999
    a[i] = new Point();             // Set array element i with new point
```

An array *itself* is always a reference type object, regardless of the element type. For instance, the following is legal:

```
int[] a = null;
```

Multidimensional Arrays

Multidimensional arrays come in two varieties: *rectangular* and *jagged*. Rectangular arrays represent an *n*-dimensional block of memory, and jagged arrays are arrays of arrays.

Rectangular arrays

Rectangular arrays are declared using commas to separate each dimension. The following declares a rectangular two-dimensional array, where the dimensions are 3 by 3:

```
int [,] matrix = new int [3, 3];
```

The `GetLength` method of an array returns the length for a given dimension (starting at 0):

```
for (int i = 0; i < matrix.GetLength(0); i++)
    for (int j = 0; j < matrix.GetLength(1); j++)
        matrix [i, j] = i * 3 + j;
```

A rectangular array can be initialized as follows (each element in this example is initialized to be identical to the previous example):

```
int[,] matrix = new int[,]
{
  {0,1,2},
  {3,4,5},
  {6,7,8}
};
```

Jagged arrays

Jagged arrays are declared using successive square brackets to represent each dimension. Here is an example of declaring a jagged two-dimensional array, where the outermost dimension is 3:

```
int [][] matrix = new int [3][];
```

The inner dimensions aren't specified in the declaration. Unlike a rectangular array, each inner array can be an arbitrary length. Each inner array is implicitly initialized to null rather than an empty array. Each inner array must be created manually:

```
for (int i = 0; i < matrix.Length; i++)
{
  matrix[i] = new int [3];                 // Create inner array
  for (int j = 0; j < matrix[i].Length; j++)
    matrix[i][j] = i * 3 + j;
}
```

A jagged array can be initialized as follows (each element in this example is initialized to be identical to the previous example):

```
int[][] matrix = new int[][]
{
  new int[] {0,1,2},
  new int[] {3,4,5},
  new int[] {6,7,8}
};
```

Simplified Array Initialization Expressions

There are two ways to shorten array initialization expressions. The first is to omit the new operator and type qualifications:

```
char[] vowels = {'a','e','i','o','u'};

int[,] rectangularMatrix =
{
  {0,1,2},
  {3,4,5},
  {6,7,8}
};

int[][] jaggedMatrix =
{
  new int[] {0,1,2},
  new int[] {3,4,5},
  new int[] {6,7,8}
};
```

The second approach is to use the **var** keyword, which tells the compiler to implicitly type a local variable:

```
var i = 3;            // i is implicitly of type int
var s = "sausage";    // s is implicitly of type string

// Therefore:

var rectMatrix = new int[,]    // rectMatrix is implicitly of type int[,]
{
  {0,1,2},
  {3,4,5},
  {6,7,8}
};

var jaggedMat = new int[][]    // jaggedMat is implicitly of type int[][]
{
  new int[] {0,1,2},
  new int[] {3,4,5},
  new int[] {6,7,8}
};
```

Implicit typing can be taken one stage further with single-dimensional arrays. You can omit the type qualifier after the **new** keyword and have the compiler *infer* the array type:

```
var vowels = new[] {'a','e','i','o','u'};    // Compiler infers char[]
```

The elements must all be implicitly convertible to a single type in order for implicit array typing to work. For example:

```
var x = new[] {1,10000000000};    // all convertible to long
```

Bounds Checking

All array indexing is bounds-checked by the runtime. If you use an invalid index, an `IndexOutOfRangeException` is thrown:

```
int[] arr = new int[3];
arr[3] = 1;                 // IndexOutOfRangeException thrown
```

As with Java, array bounds checking is necessary for type safety and simplifies debugging.

> Generally, the performance hit from bounds checking is minor, and the JIT (Just-in-Time) compiler can perform optimizations, such as determining in advance whether all indexes will be safe before entering a loop, thus avoiding a check on each iteration. In addition, C# provides "unsafe" code that can explicitly bypass bounds checking (see the section "Unsafe Code and Pointers" on page 170 in Chapter 4).

Variables and Parameters

A variable represents a storage location that has a modifiable value. A variable can be a *local variable, parameter* (*value, ref,* or *out*), *field* (*instance* or *static*), or *array element.*

The Stack and the Heap

The stack and the heap are the places where variables and constants reside. Each has very different lifetime semantics.

Stack

The stack is a block of memory for storing local variables and parameters. The stack logically grows and shrinks as a function is entered and exited. Consider the following method (to avoid distraction, input argument checking is ignored):

```
static int Factorial (int x)
{
  if (x == 0) return 1;
  return x * Factorial (x-1);
}
```

This method is recursive, meaning that it calls itself. Each time the method is entered, a new `int` is allocated on the stack, and each time the method exits, the `int` is deallocated.

Heap

The heap is a block of memory in which *objects* (i.e., reference-type instances) reside. Whenever a new object is created, it is allocated on the heap, and a reference to that object is returned. During a program's execution, the heap starts filling up as new objects are created. The runtime has a garbage collector that periodically deallocates objects from the heap, so your computer does not run out of memory. An object is eligible for deallocation as soon as nothing references it.

In the following example, we start by creating a `StringBuilder` object referenced by the variable `ref1`, and then write out its content. That `StringBuilder` object is then immediately eligible for garbage collection, because nothing subsequently uses it.

Then, we create another `StringBuilder` referenced by variable `ref2`, and copy that reference to `ref3`. Even though `ref2` is not used after that point, `ref3` keeps the same `StringBuilder` object alive—ensuring that it doesn't become eligible for collection until we've finished using `ref3`.

```
using System;
using System.Text;

class Test
{
  static void Main()
  {
    StringBuilder ref1 = new StringBuilder ("object1");
```

```
    Console.WriteLine (ref1);
    // The StringBuilder referenced by ref1 is now eligible for GC.

    StringBuilder ref2 = new StringBuilder ("object2");
    StringBuilder ref3 = ref2;
    // The StringBuilder referenced by ref2 is NOT yet eligible for GC.

    Console.WriteLine (ref3);                    // object2
  }
}
```

Value-type instances (and object references) live wherever the variable was declared. If the instance was declared as a field within an object, or as an array element, that instance lives on the heap.

 You can't explicitly delete objects in C#, as you can in C++. An unreferenced object is eventually collected by the garbage collector.

The heap also stores static fields and constants. Unlike objects allocated on the heap (which can get garbage-collected), these live until the application domain is torn down.

Definite Assignment

C# enforces a definite assignment policy. In practice, this means that outside of an unsafe context, it's impossible to access uninitialized memory. Definite assignment has three implications:

- Local variables must be assigned a value before they can be read.
- Function arguments must be supplied when a method is called.
- All other variables (such as fields and array elements) are automatically initialized by the runtime.

For example, the following code results in a compile-time error:

```
static void Main()
{
  int x;
  Console.WriteLine (x);       // Compile-time error
}
```

Fields and array elements are automatically initialized with the default values for their type. The following code outputs 0, because array elements are implicitly assigned to their default values:

```
static void Main()
{
  int[] ints = new int[2];
  Console.WriteLine (ints[0]);    // 0
}
```

The following code outputs 0, because fields are implicitly assigned to a default value:

```
class Test
{
  static int x;
  static void Main() { Console.WriteLine (x); }   // 0
}
```

Default Values

All type instances have a default value. The default value for the predefined types is the result of a bitwise zeroing of memory:

Type	Default value
All reference types	null
All numeric and enum types	0
char type	'\0'
bool type	false

You can obtain the default value for any type using the default keyword (in practice, this is useful with generics, which we'll cover in Chapter 3):

```
decimal d = default (decimal);
```

The default value in a custom value type (i.e., struct) is the same as the default value for each field defined by the custom type.

Parameters

A method has a sequence of parameters. Parameters define the set of arguments that must be provided for that method. In this example, the method Foo has a single parameter named p, of type int:

```
static void Foo (int p)
{
  p = p + 1;                // Increment p by 1
  Console.WriteLine(p);     // Write p to screen
}
static void Main() { Foo (8); }
```

You can control how parameters are passed with the ref and out modifiers:

Parameter modifier	Passed by	Variable must be definitely assigned
None	Value	Going *in*
ref	Reference	Going *in*
out	Reference	Going *out*

Passing arguments by value

By default, arguments in C# are *passed by value*, which is by far the most common case. This means a copy of the value is created when passed to the method:

```
class Test
{
  static void Foo (int p)
  {
    p = p + 1;              // Increment p by 1
    Console.WriteLine (p);  // Write p to screen
  }

  static void Main()
  {
    int x = 8;
    Foo (x);                // Make a copy of x
    Console.WriteLine (x);  // x will still be 8
  }
}
```

Assigning p a new value does not change the contents of x, since p and x reside in different memory locations.

Passing a reference-type argument by value copies the *reference*, but not the object. In the following example, Foo sees the same StringBuilder object that Main instantiated, but has an independent *reference* to it. In other words, sb and fooSB are separate variables that reference the same StringBuilder object:

```
class Test
{
  static void Foo (StringBuilder fooSB)
  {
    fooSB.Append ("test");
    fooSB = null;
  }

  static void Main()
  {
    StringBuilder sb = new StringBuilder();
    Foo (sb);
    Console.WriteLine (sb.ToString());   // test
  }
}
```

Because fooSB is a *copy* of a reference, setting it to null doesn't make sb null. (If, however, fooSB was declared and called with the ref modifier, sb *would* become null.)

The ref modifier

To *pass by reference*, C# provides the ref parameter modifier. In the following example, p and x refer to the same memory locations:

```
class Test
{
```

```
static void Foo (ref int p)
{
  p = p + 1;              // Increment p by 1
  Console.WriteLine (p);  // Write p to screen
}

static void Main()
{
  int x = 8;
  Foo (ref x);            // Ask Foo to deal directly with x
  Console.WriteLine (x);  // x is now 9
}
}
```

Now assigning p a new value changes the contents of x. Notice how the ref modifier is required both when writing and when calling the method.§ This makes it very clear what's going on.

The ref modifier is essential in implementing a swap method (later, in "Generics" on page 101 in Chapter 3, we will show how to write a swap method that works with any type):

```
class Test
{
  static void Swap (ref string a, ref string b)
  {
    string temp = a;
    a = b;
    b = temp;
  }

  static void Main()
  {
    string x = "Penn";
    string y = "Teller";
    Swap (ref x, ref y);
    Console.WriteLine (x);   // Teller
    Console.WriteLine (y);   // Penn
  }
}
```

 A parameter can be passed by reference or by value, regardless of whether the parameter type is a reference type or a value type.

The out modifier

An out argument is like a ref argument, except it:

- Need not be assigned before going into the function

---

§ An exception to this rule is when calling COM methods. We discuss this in Chapter 25.

- Must be assigned before it comes *out* of the function

The out modifier is most commonly used to get multiple return values back from a method. For example:

```
class Test
{
  static void Split (string name, out string firstNames,
                     out string lastName)
  {
    int i = name.LastIndexOf (' ');
    firstNames = name.Substring (0, i);
    lastName   = name.Substring (i + 1);
  }

  static void Main()
  {
    string a, b;
    Split ("Stevie Ray Vaughn", out a, out b);
    Console.WriteLine (a);          // Stevie Ray
    Console.WriteLine (b);          // Vaughn
  }
}
```

Like a ref parameter, an out parameter is passed by reference.

Implications of passing by reference

When you pass an argument by reference, you alias the storage location of an existing variable rather than create a new storage location. In the following example, the variables x and y represent the same instance:

```
class Test
{
  static int x;

  static void Main() { Foo (out x); }

  static void Foo (out int y)
  {
    Console.WriteLine (x);          // x is 0
    y = 1;                          // Mutate y
    Console.WriteLine (x);          // x is 1
  }
}
```

The params modifier

The params parameter modifier may be specified on the last parameter of a method so that the method accepts any number of parameters of a particular type. The parameter type must be declared as an array. For example:

```
class Test
{
  static int Sum (params int[] ints)
  {
    int sum = 0;
```

```
    for (int i = 0; i < ints.Length; i++)
        sum += ints[i];                          // Increase sum by ints[i]
      return sum;
    }

    static void Main()
    {
      int total = Sum (1, 2, 3, 4);
      Console.WriteLine (total);                 // 10
    }
  }
```

You can also supply a params argument as an ordinary array. The first line in Main is semantically equivalent to this:

```
int total = Sum (new int[] { 1, 2, 3, 4 } );
```

Optional parameters (C# 4.0)

From C# 4.0, methods, constructors, and indexers (Chapter 3) can declare *optional parameters*. A parameter is optional if it specifies a *default value* in its declaration:

```
void Foo (int x = 23) { Console.WriteLine (x); }
```

Optional parameters may be omitted when calling the method:

```
Foo();     // 23
```

The *default argument* of 23 is actually *passed* to the optional parameter x—the compiler bakes the value 23 into the compiled code at the *calling* side. The preceding call to Foo is semantically identical to:

```
Foo (23);
```

because the compiler simply substitutes the default value of an optional parameter wherever it is used.

> Adding an optional parameter to a public method that's called from another assembly requires recompilation of both assemblies—just as though the parameter were mandatory.

The default value of an optional parameter must be specified by a constant expression, or a parameterless constructor of a value type. Optional parameters cannot be marked with ref or out.

Mandatory parameters must occur *before* optional parameters in both the method declaration and the method call (the exception is with params arguments, which still always come last). In the following example, the explicit value of 1 is passed to x, and the default value of 0 is passed to y:

```
void Foo (int x = 0, int y = 0) { Console.WriteLine (x + ", " + y); }

void Test()
{
  Foo(1);     // 1, 0
}
```

To do the converse (pass a default value to x and an explicit value to y), you must combine optional parameters with *named arguments*.

Named arguments (C# 4.0)

Rather than identifying an argument by position, you can identify an argument by name. For example:

```
void Foo (int x, int y) { Console.WriteLine (x + ", " + y); }

void Test()
{
  Foo (x:1, y:2);  // 1, 2
}
```

Named arguments can occur in any order. The following calls to Foo are semantically identical:

```
Foo (x:1, y:2);
Foo (y:2, x:1);
```

A subtle difference is that argument expressions are evaluated in the order in which they appear at the *calling* site. In general, this makes a difference only with interdependent side-effecting expressions such as the following, which writes 0, 1:

```
int a = 0;
Foo (y: ++a, x: --a);  // ++a is evaluated first
```

Of course, you would almost certainly avoid writing such code in practice!

You can mix named and positional parameters:

```
Foo (1, y:2);
```

However, there is a restriction: positional parameters must come before named arguments. So we couldn't call Foo like this:

```
Foo (x:1, 2);          // Compile-time error
```

Named arguments are particularly useful in conjunction with optional parameters. For instance, consider the following method:

```
void Bar (int a = 0, int b = 0, int c = 0, int d = 0) { ... }
```

We can call this supplying only a value for d as follows:

```
Bar (d:3);
```

This is particularly useful when calling COM APIs, and is discussed in detail in Chapter 25.

var—Implicitly Typed Local Variables

It is often the case that you declare and initialize a variable in one step. If the compiler is able to infer the type from the initialization expression, you can use the keyword var (introduced in C# 3.0) in place of the type declaration. For example:

```
var x = "hello";
var y = new System.Text.StringBuilder();
var z = (float)Math.PI;
```

This is precisely equivalent to:

```
string x = "hello";
System.Text.StringBuilder y = new System.Text.StringBuilder();
float z = (float)Math.PI;
```

Because of this direct equivalence, implicitly typed variables are statically typed. For example, the following generates a compile-time error:

```
var x = 5;
x = "hello";    // Compile-time error; x is of type int
```

 var can decrease code readability in the case when *you can't deduce the type purely by looking at the variable declaration*. For example:

```
Random r = new Random();
var x = r.Next();
```

What type is x?

In "Anonymous Methods" on page 134 in Chapter 4, we will describe a scenario where the use of var is mandatory.

Expressions and Operators

An *expression* essentially denotes a value. The simplest kinds of expressions are constants and variables. Expressions can be transformed and combined using operators. An *operator* takes one or more input *operands* to output a new expression.

Here is an example of a *constant expression*:

```
12
```

We can use the * operator to combine two operands (the literal expressions 12 and 30), as follows:

```
12 * 30
```

Complex expressions can be built because an operand may itself be an expression, such as the operand (12 * 30) in the following example:

```
1 + (12 * 30)
```

Operators in C# are classed as *unary*, *binary*, or *ternary*—depending on the number of operands they work on (one, two, or three). The binary operators always use *infix* notation, where the operator is placed *between* the two operands.

Primary Expressions

Primary expressions include expressions composed of operators that are intrinsic to the basic plumbing of the language. Here is an example:

```
Math.Log (1)
```

This expression is composed of two primary expressions. The first expression performs a member-lookup (with the . operator), and the second expression performs a method call (with the () operator).

Void Expressions

A void expression is an expression that has no value. For example:

```
Console.WriteLine (1)
```

A void expression, since it has no value, cannot be used as an operand to build more complex expressions:

```
1 + Console.WriteLine (1)     // Compile-time error
```

Assignment Expressions

An assignment expression uses the = operator to assign the result of another expression to a variable. For example:

```
x = x * 5
```

An assignment expression is not a void expression. It actually carries the assignment value, and so can be incorporated into another expression. In the following example, the expression assigns 2 to x and 10 to y:

```
y = 5 * (x = 2)
```

This style of expression can be used to initialize multiple values:

```
a = b = c = d = 0
```

The *compound assignment operators* are syntactic shortcuts that combine assignment with another operator. For example:

```
x *= 2    // equivalent to x = x * 2
x <<= 1   // equivalent to x = x << 1
```

(A subtle exception to this rule is with *events*, which we describe in Chapter 4: the += and -= operators here are treated specially and map to the event's add and remove accessors.)

Operator Precedence and Associativity

When an expression contains multiple operators, *precedence* and *associativity* determine the order of evaluation. Operators with higher precedence execute before operators of lower precedence. If the operators have the same precedence, the operator's associativity determines the order of evaluation.

Precedence

The following expression:

```
1 + 2 * 3
```

is evaluated as follows because * has a higher precedence than +:

```
1 + (2 * 3)
```

Left-associative operators

Binary operators (except for assignment, lambda, and null coalescing operators) are *left-associative*; in other words, they are evaluated from left to right. For example, the following expression:

```
8 / 4 / 2
```

is evaluated as follows due to left associativity:

```
( 8 / 4 ) / 2    // 1
```

You can insert parentheses to change the actual order of evaluation:

```
8 / ( 4 / 2 )    // 4
```

Right-associative operators

The *assignment operators*, lambda, null coalescing, and conditional operator are *right-associative*; in other words, they are evaluated from right to left. Right associativity allows multiple assignments such as the following to compile:

```
x = y = 3;
```

This first assigns 3 to y, and then assigns the result of that expression (3) to x.

Operator Table

Table 2-3 lists C#'s operators in order of precedence. Operators in the same category have the same precedence. We explain user-overloadable operators in "Operator Overloading" on page 153 in Chapter 4.

Table 2-3. C# operators (categories in order of precedence)

Category	Operator symbol	Operator name	Example	User-overloadable
Primary	()	Grouping	while(x)	No
	.	Member access	x.y	No

Category	Operator symbol	Operator name	Example	User-overloadable
	->	Pointer to struct (unsafe)	x->y	No
	()	Function call	x()	No
	[]	Array/index	a[x]	Via indexer
	++	Post-increment	x++	Yes
	--	Post-decrement	x--	Yes
	new	Create instance	new Foo()	No
	stackalloc	Unsafe stack allocation	stackalloc(10)	No
	typeof	Get type from identifier	typeof(int)	No
	checked	Integral overflow check on	checked(x)	No
	unchecked	Integral overflow check off	unchecked(x)	No
Unary	sizeof	Get size of struct	sizeof(int)	No
	+	Positive value of	+x	Yes
	-	Negative value of	-x	Yes
	!	Not	!x	Yes
	~	Bitwise complement	~x	Yes
	++	Pre-increment	++x	Yes
	--	Pre-decrement	--x	Yes
	()	Cast	(int)x	No
	*	Value at address (unsafe)	*x	No
	&	Address of value (unsafe)	&x	No
Multiplicative	*	Multiply	x * y	Yes
	/	Divide	x / y	Yes
	%	Remainder	x % y	Yes
Additive	+	Add	x + y	Yes
	-	Subtract	x - y	Yes
Shift	<<	Shift left	x >> 1	Yes
	>>	Shift right	x << 1	Yes
Relational	<	Less than	x < y	Yes
	>	Greater than	x > y	Yes
	<=	Less than or equal to	x <= y	Yes

Category	Operator symbol	Operator name	Example	User-overloadable
	>=	Greater than or equal to	x >= y	Yes
	is	Type is or is subclass of	x is y	No
	as	Type conversion	x as y	No
Equality	==	Equals	x == y	Yes
	!=	Not equals	x != y	Yes
Logical And	&	And	x & y	Yes
Logical Xor	^	Exclusive Or	x ^ y	Yes
Logical Or	|	Or	x | y	Yes
Conditional And	&&	Conditional And	x && y	Via &
Conditional Or	||	Conditional Or	x || y	Via |
Null coalescing	??	Null coalescing	x ?? y	No
Conditional	?:	Conditional	isTrue ? thenThis Value : elseThis Value	No
Assignment	=	Assign	x = y	No
	*=	Multiply self by	x *= 2	Via *
	/=	Divide self by	x /= 2	Via /
	+=	Add to self	x += 2	Via +
	-=	Subtract from self	x -= 2	Via -
	<<=	Shift self left by	x <<= 2	Via <<
	>>=	Shift self right by	x >>= 2	Via >>
	&=	And self by	x &= 2	Via &
	^=	Exclusive-Or self by	x ^= 2	Via ^
	|=	Or self by	x |= 2	Via |
Lambda	=>	Lambda	x => x + 1	No

Statements

Functions comprise statements that execute sequentially in the textual order in which they appear. A *statement block* is a series of statements appearing between braces (the {} tokens).

Declaration Statements

A declaration statement declares a new variable, optionally initializing the variable with an expression. A declaration statement ends in a semicolon. You may declare multiple variables of the same type in a comma-separated list. For example:

```
string someWord = "rosebud";
int someNumber = 42;
bool rich = true, famous = false;
```

A constant declaration is like a variable declaration, except that the variable cannot be changed after it has been declared, and the initialization must occur with the declaration:

```
const double c = 2.99792458E08;
c += 10;                         // Compile-time Error
```

Local variables

The scope of a local or constant variable extends throughout the current block. You cannot declare another local variable with the same name in the current block or in any nested blocks. For example:

```
static void Main()
{
  int x;
  {
    int y;
    int x;          // Error - x already defined
  }
  {
    int y;          // OK - y not in scope
  }
  Console.Write (y);  // Error - y is out of scope
}
```

 A variable's scope extends in *both directions* throughout its code block. This means that if we moved the initial declaration of x in this example to the bottom of the method, we'd get the same error.

Expression Statements

Expression statements are expressions that are also valid statements. An expression statement must either change state or call something that might change state. Changing state essentially means changing a variable. The possible expression statements are:

- Assignment expressions (including increment and decrement expressions)
- Method call expressions (both void and nonvoid)
- Object instantiation expressions

Here are some examples:

```
// Declare variables with declaration statements:
string s;
int x, y;
System.Text.StringBuilder sb;
```

```
// Expression statements
x = 1 + 2;                    // Assignment expression
x++;                          // Increment expression
y = Math.Max (x, 5);          // Assignment expression
Console.WriteLine (y);        // Method call expression
sb = new StringBuilder();     // Assignment expression
new StringBuilder();          // Object instantiation expression
```

When you call a constructor or a method that returns a value, you're not obliged to use the result. However, unless the constructor or method changes state, the statement is completely useless:

```
new StringBuilder();      // Legal, but useless
new string ('c', 3);      // Legal, but useless
x.Equals (y);             // Legal, but useless
```

Selection Statements

C# has the following mechanisms to conditionally control the flow of program execution:

- Selection statements (if, switch)
- Conditional operator (?:)
- Loop statements (while, do..while, for, foreach)

This section covers the simplest two constructs: the if-else statement and the switch statement.

The if statement

An if statement executes a body of code depending on whether a bool expression is true. For example:

```
if (5 < 2 * 3)
{
  Console.WriteLine ("true");      // True
}
```

If the body of code is a single statement, you can optionally omit the braces:

```
if (5 < 2 * 3)
  Console.WriteLine ("true");      // True
```

The else clause

An if statement is optionally followed by an else clause:

```
if (2 + 2 == 5)
  Console.WriteLine ("Does not compute");
else
  Console.WriteLine ("False");        // False
```

Within an else clause, you can nest another if statement:

```
if (2 + 2 == 5)
  Console.WriteLine ("Does not compute");
else
```

```
if (2 + 2 == 4)
    Console.WriteLine ("Computes");    // Computes
```

Changing the flow of execution with braces

An `else` clause always applies to the immediately preceding `if` statement in the statement block. For example:

```
if (true)
    if (false)
        Console.WriteLine();
    else
        Console.WriteLine ("executes");
```

This is semantically identical to:

```
if (true)
{
    if (false)
        Console.WriteLine();
    else
        Console.WriteLine ("executes");
}
```

We can change the execution flow by moving the braces:

```
if (true)
{
    if (false)
        Console.WriteLine();
}
else
    Console.WriteLine ("does not execute");
```

With braces, you explicitly state your intention. This can improve the readability of nested `if` statements—even when not required by the compiler. A notable exception is with the following pattern:

```
static void TellMeWhatICanDo (int age)
{
    if (age >= 35)
        Console.WriteLine ("You can be president!");
    else if (age >= 21)
        Console.WriteLine ("You can drink!");
    else if (age >= 18)
        Console.WriteLine ("You can vote!");
    else
        Console.WriteLine ("You can wait!");
}
```

Here, we've arranged the `if` and `else` statements to mimic the "elsif" construct of other languages (and C#'s `#elif` preprocessor directive). Visual Studio's auto-formatting recognizes this pattern and preserves the indentation. Semantically, though, each `if` statement following an `else` statement is functionally nested within the `else` statement.

The switch statement

switch statements let you branch program execution based on a selection of possible values that a variable may have. switch statements may result in cleaner code than multiple if statements, since switch statements require an expression to be evaluated only once. For instance:

```csharp
static void ShowCard(int cardNumber)
{
  switch (cardNumber)
  {
    case 13:
      Console.WriteLine ("King");
      break;
    case 12:
      Console.WriteLine ("Queen");
      break;
    case 11:
      Console.WriteLine ("Jack");
      break;
    case -1:                          // Joker is -1
      goto case 12;                   // In this game joker counts as queen
    default:                          // Executes for any other cardNumber
      Console.WriteLine (cardNumber);
      break;
  }
}
```

You can only switch on an expression of a type that can be statically evaluated, which restricts it to the built-in integral types, string type, and enum types.

At the end of each case clause, you must say explicitly where execution is to go next, with some kind of jump statement. Here are the options:

- break (jumps to the end of the switch statement)
- goto case x (jumps to another case clause)
- goto default (jumps to the default clause)
- Any other jump statement—namely, return, throw, continue, or goto label

When more than one value should execute the same code, you can list the common cases sequentially:

```csharp
switch (cardNumber)
{
  case 13:
  case 12:
  case 11:
    Console.WriteLine ("Face card");
    break;
  default:
    Console.WriteLine ("Plain card");
    break;
}
```

This feature of a `switch` statement can be pivotal in terms of producing cleaner code than multiple `if-else` statements.

Iteration Statements

C# enables a sequence of statements to execute repeatedly with the `while`, `do-while`, `for`, and `foreach` statements.

while and do-while loops

`while` loops repeatedly execute a body of code while a `bool` expression is true. The expression is tested *before* the body of the loop is executed. For example:

```
int i = 0;
while (i < 3)
{
  Console.WriteLine (i);
  i++;
}

OUTPUT:
0
1
2
```

`do-while` loops differ in functionality from `while` loops only in that they test the expression *after* the statement block has executed (ensuring that the block is always executed at least once). Here's the preceding example rewritten with a `do-while` loop:

```
int i = 0;
do
{
  Console.WriteLine (i);
  i++;
}
while (i < 3);
```

for loops

`for` loops are like `while` loops with special clauses for *initialization* and *iteration* of a loop variable. A `for` loop contains three clauses as follows:

```
for (initialization-clause; condition-clause; iteration-clause)
  statement-or-statement-block
```

Initialization clause
> Executed before the loop begins; used to initialize one or more *iteration* variables

Condition clause
> The `bool` expression that, while true, will execute the body

Iteration clause
> Executed *after* each iteration of the statement block; used typically to update the iteration variable

For example, the following prints the numbers 0 through 2:

```
for (int i = 0; i < 3; i++)
  Console.WriteLine (i);
```

The following prints the first 10 Fibonacci numbers (where each number is the sum of the previous two):

```
for (int i = 0, prevFib = 1, curFib = 1; i < 10; i++)
{
  Console.WriteLine (prevFib);
  int newFib = prevFib + curFib;
  prevFib = curFib; curFib = newFib;
}
```

Any of the three parts of the for statement may be omitted. One can implement an infinite loop such as the following (though while(true) may be used instead):

```
for (;;)
  Console.WriteLine ("interrupt me");
```

foreach loops

The foreach statement iterates over each element in an enumerable object. Most of the types in C# and the .NET Framework that represent a set or list of elements are enumerable. For example, both an array and a string are enumerable. Here is an example of enumerating over the characters in a string, from the first character through to the last:

```
foreach (char c in "beer")   // c is the iteration variable
  Console.WriteLine (c);

OUTPUT:
b
e
e
r
```

We define enumerable objects in "Enumeration and Iterators" on page 143 in Chapter 4.

Jump Statements

The C# jump statements are break, continue, goto, return, and throw.

> Jump statements obey the reliability rules of try statements (see "try Statements and Exceptions" on page 134 in Chapter 4). This means that:
>
> - A jump out of a try block always executes the try's finally block before reaching the target of the jump.
> - A jump cannot be made from the inside to the outside of a finally block.

The break statement

The break statement ends the execution of the body of an iteration or switch statement:

```
int x = 0;
while (true)
{
  if (x++ > 5)
    break ;        // break from the loop
}
// execution continues here after break
...
```

The continue statement

The continue statement forgoes the remaining statements in a loop and makes an early start on the next iteration. The following loop skips even numbers:

```
for (int i = 0; i < 10; i++)
{
  if ((i % 2) == 0)        // If i is even,
    continue;              // continue with next iteration

  Console.Write (i + " ");
}
```

```
OUTPUT: 1 3 5 7 9
```

The goto statement

The goto statement transfers execution to another label within the statement block. The form is as follows:

```
goto statement-label;
```

Or, when used within a switch statement:

```
goto case case-constant;
```

A label statement is just a placeholder in a code block, denoted with a colon suffix. The following iterates the numbers 1 through 5, mimicking a for loop:

```
int i = 1;
startLoop:
if (i <= 5)
{
  Console.Write (i + " ");
  i++;
  goto startLoop;
}
```

```
OUTPUT: 1 2 3 4 5
```

The goto case-constant transfers execution to another case in a switch block (see "The switch statement" on page 52).

The return statement

The `return` statement exits the method and must return an expression of the method's return type if the method is nonvoid:

```
static decimal AsPercentage (decimal d)
{
  decimal p = d * 100m;
  return p;              // Return to the calling method with value
}
```

A `return` statement can appear anywhere in a method.

The throw statement

The `throw` statement throws an exception to indicate an error has occurred (see "try Statements and Exceptions" on page 134 in Chapter 4):

```
if (w == null)
    throw new ArgumentNullException (...);
```

Miscellaneous Statements

The `lock` statement is a syntactic shortcut for calling the `Enter` and `Exit` methods of the `Monitor` class (see Chapter 19).

The `using` statement provides an elegant syntax for calling `Dispose` on objects that implement `IDisposable`, within a `finally` block (see "try Statements and Exceptions" on page 134 in Chapter 4 and "IDisposable, Dispose, and Close" on page 475 in Chapter 12).

> C# overloads the `using` keyword to have independent meanings in different contexts. Specifically, the `using` *directive* is different from the `using` *statement*.

Namespaces

A namespace is a domain within which type names must be unique. Types are typically organized into hierarchical namespaces—both to avoid naming conflicts and to make type names easier to find. For example, the `RSA` type that handles public key encryption is defined within the following namespace:

```
System.Security.Cryptography
```

A namespace forms an integral part of a type's name. The following code calls `RSA`'s `Create` method:

```
System.Security.Cryptography.RSA rsa =
    System.Security.Cryptography.RSA.Create();
```

Namespaces are independent of assemblies, which are units of deployment such as an *.exe* or *.dll* (described in Chapter 16).

Namespaces also have no impact on member visibility—public, internal, private, and so on.

The namepace keyword defines a namespace for types within that block. For example:

```
namespace Outer.Middle.Inner
{
  class Class1 {}
  class Class2 {}
}
```

The dots in the namespace indicate a hierarchy of nested namespaces. The code that follows is semantically identical to the preceding example:

```
namespace Outer
{
  namespace Middle
  {
    namespace Inner
    {
      class Class1 {}
      class Class2 {}
    }
  }
}
```

You can refer to a type with its *fully qualified name*, which includes all namespaces from the outermost to the innermost. For example, we could refer to Class1 in the preceding example as Outer.Middle.Inner.Class1.

Types not defined in any namespace are said to reside in the *global namespace*. The global namespace also includes top-level namespaces, such as Outer in our example.

The using Directive

The using directive *imports* a namespace. This is a convenient way to refer to types without their fully qualified names. This example is semantically identical to our previous example:

```
using Outer.Middle.Inner;

class Test
{
  static void Main()
  {
    Class1 c;
  }
}
```

Rules Within a Namespace

Name scoping

Names declared in outer namespaces can be used unqualified within inner namespaces. Here, the names `Middle` and `Class1` are implicitly imported into `Inner`:

```
namespace Outer
{
  namespace Middle
  {
    class Class1 {}

    namespace Inner
    {
      class Class2 : Class1  {}
    }
  }
}
```

If you want to refer to a type in a different branch of your namespace hierarchy, you can use a partially qualified name. In the following example, we base `SalesReport` on `Common.ReportBase`:

```
namespace MyTradingCompany
{
  namespace Common
  {
    class ReportBase {}
  }
  namespace ManagementReporting
  {
    class SalesReport : Common.ReportBase  {}
  }
}
```

Name hiding

If the same type name appears in both an inner and an outer namespace, the inner name wins. To refer to the type in the outer namespace, you must qualify its name:

```
namespace Outer
{
  class Foo { }

  namespace Inner
  {
    class Foo { }

    class Test
    {
      Foo f1;          // = Outer.Inner.Foo
      Outer.Foo f2;    // = Outer.Foo
    }
  }
}
```

All type names are converted to fully qualified names at compile time. Intermediate Language (IL) code contains no unqualified or partially qualified names.

Repeated namespaces

You can repeat a namespace declaration, as long as the type names within the namespaces don't conflict:

```
namespace Outer.Middle.Inner
{
  class Class1 {}
}

namespace Outer.Middle.Inner
{
  class Class2 {}
}
```

We can even break the example into two source files such that we could compile each class into a different assembly.

Source file 1:

```
namespace Outer.Middle.Inner
{
  class Class1 {}
}
```

Source file 2:

```
namespace Outer.Middle.Inner
{
  class Class2 {}
}
```

Nested using directive

You can nest a `using` directive within a namespace. This allows you to scope the `using` directive within a namespace declaration. In the following example, `Class1` is visible in one scope, but not in another:

```
namespace N1
{
  class Class1 {}
}

namespace N2
{
  using N1;

  class Class2 : Class1 {}
}
```

```
namespace N2
{
  class Class3 : Class1 {}    // Compile-time error
}
```

Aliasing Types and Namespaces

Importing a namespace can result in type-name collision. Rather than importing the whole namespace, you can import just the specific types you need, giving each type an alias. For example:

```
using PropertyInfo2 = System.Reflection.PropertyInfo;
class Program { PropertyInfo2 p; }
```

An entire namespace can be aliased, as follows:

```
using R = System.Reflection;
class Program { R.PropertyInfo p; }
```

Advanced Namespace Features

Extern

Extern aliases allow your program to reference two types with the same fully qualified name (i.e., the namespace and type name are identical). This is an unusual scenario and can occur only when the two types come from different assemblies. Consider the following example:

Library 1:

```
// csc target:library /out:Widgets1.dll widgetsv1.cs

namespace Widgets
{
  public class Widget {}
}
```

Library 2:

```
// csc target:library /out:Widgets2.dll widgetsv2.cs

namespace Widgets
{
  public class Widget {}
}
```

Application:

```
// csc /r:Widgets1.dll /r:Widgets2.dll application.cs

using Widgets;

class Test
{
  static void Main()
```

```
    {
        Widget w = new Widget();
    }
}
```

The application cannot compile, because `Widget` is ambiguous. Extern aliases can resolve the ambiguity in our application:

```
// csc /r:W1=Widgets1.dll /r:W2=Widgets2.dll application.cs

extern alias W1;
extern alias W2;

class Test
{
    static void Main()
    {
        W1.Widgets.Widget w1 = new W1.Widgets.Widget();
        W2.Widgets.Widget w2 = new W2.Widgets.Widget();
    }
}
```

Namespace alias qualifiers

As we mentioned earlier, names in inner namespaces hide names in outer namespaces. However, sometimes even the use of a fully qualified type name does not resolve the conflict. Consider the following example:

```
namespace N
{
    class A
    {
        public class B {}                    // Nested type
        static void Main() { new A.B(); }     // Instantiate class B
    }
}

namespace A
{
    class B {}
}
```

The `Main` method could be instantiating either the nested class `B`, or the class `B` within the namespace `A`. The compiler always gives higher precedence to identifiers in the current namespace; in this case, the nested `B` class.

To resolve such conflicts, a namespace name can be qualified, relative to one of the following:

- The global namespace—the root of all namespaces (identified with the contextual keyword `global`)
- The set of extern aliases

The :: token is used for namespace alias qualification. In this example, we qualify using the global namespace (this is most commonly seen in auto-generated code to avoid name conflicts):

```
namespace N
{
  class A
  {
    static void Main()
    {
      System.Console.WriteLine (new A.B());
      System.Console.WriteLine (new global::A.B());
    }

    public class B {}
  }
}

namespace A
{
  class B {}
}
```

Here is an example of qualifying with an alias (adapted from the example in "Extern" on page 60):

```
extern alias W1;
extern alias W2;

class Test
{
  static void Main()
  {
    W1::Widgets.Widget w1 = new W1::Widgets.Widget();
    W2::Widgets.Widget w2 = new W2::Widgets.Widget();
  }
}
```

3

Creating Types in C#

In this chapter, we will delve into types and type members.

Classes

A class is the most common kind of reference type. The simplest possible class declaration is as follows:

```
class YourClassName
{
}
```

A more complex class optionally has the following:

Preceding the keyword `class`	Attributes and class modifiers. The non-nested class modifiers are `public`, `internal`, `abstract`, `sealed`, `static`, `unsafe`, and `partial`
Following `YourClassName`	Generic type parameters, a base class, and interfaces
Within the braces	Class members (these are methods, properties, indexers, events, fields, constructors, operator functions, nested types, and a finalizer)

This chapter covers all of these constructs except attributes, operator functions, and the `unsafe` keyword, which are covered in Chapter 4. The following sections will enumerate each of the class members.

Fields

A *field* is a variable that is a member of a class or struct. For example:

```
class Octopus
{
  string name;
  public int Age = 10;
}
```

Fields allow the following modifiers:

Static modifier	`static`
Access modifiers	`public internal private protected`
Inheritance modifier	`new`
Unsafe code modifier	`unsafe`
Read-only modifier	`readonly`
Threading modifier	`volatile`

The readonly modifier

The `readonly` modifier prevents a field from being modified after construction. A read-only field can be assigned only in its declaration or within the enclosing type's constructor.

Field initialization

Field initialization is optional. An uninitialized field has a default value (`0`, `\0`, `null`, `false`). Field initializers run before constructors:

```
public int Age = 10;
```

Declaring multiple fields together

For convenience, you may declare multiple fields of the same type in a comma-separated list. This is a convenient way for all the fields to share the same attributes and field modifiers. For example:

```
static readonly int legs = 8,
                    eyes = 1;
```

Methods

A method performs an action in a series of statements. A method can receive *input* data from the caller by specifying *parameters* and *output* data back to the caller by specifying a *return type*. A method can specify a `void` return type, indicating that it doesn't return any value to its caller. A method can also output data back to the caller via `ref`/`out` parameters.

A method's *signature* must be unique within the type. A method's signature comprises its name and parameter types (but not the parameter *names*, nor the return type).

Methods allow the following modifiers:

Static modifier	`static`
Access modifiers	`public internal private protected`
Inheritance modifiers	`new virtual abstract override sealed`
Unmanaged code modifiers	`unsafe extern`

Overloading methods

A type may overload methods (have multiple methods with the same name), as long as the signatures are different. For example, the following methods can all coexist in the same type:

```
void Foo (int x);
void Foo (double x);
void Foo (int x, float y);
void Foo (float x, int y);
```

However, the following pairs of methods cannot coexist in the same type, since the return type and the params modifier are not part of a method's signature:

```
void  Foo (int x);
float Foo (int x);           // Compile-time error

void  Goo (int[] x);
void  Goo (params int[] x);  // Compile-time error
```

Pass-by-value versus pass-by-reference

Whether a parameter is pass-by-value or pass-by-reference is also part of the signature. For example, Foo(int) can coexist with either Foo(ref int) or Foo(out int). However, Foo(ref int) and Foo(out int) cannot coexist:

```
void Foo (int x);
void Foo (ref int x);        // OK so far
void Foo (out int x);        // Compile-time error
```

Instance Constructors

Constructors run initialization code on a class or struct. A constructor is defined like a method, except that the method name and return type are reduced to the name of the enclosing type:

```
public class Panda
{
  string name;                // Define field
  public Panda (string n)     // Define constructor
  {
    name = n;                 // Initialization code (set up field)
  }
}
...

  Panda p = new Panda ("Petey");   // Call constructor
```

Constructors allow the following modifiers:

Access modifiers	public internal private protected
Unmanaged code modifiers	unsafe extern

Overloading constructors

A class or struct may overload constructors. To avoid code duplication, one constructor may call another, using the **this** keyword:

```
using System;

public class Wine
{
  public decimal Price;
  public int Year;
  public Wine (decimal price) { Price = price; }
  public Wine (decimal price, int year) : this (price) { Year = year; }
}
```

When one constructor calls another, the *called constructor* executes first.

You can pass an *expression* into another constructor as follows:

```
public Wine (decimal price, DateTime year) : this (price, year.Year) { }
```

The expression itself cannot make use of the **this** reference, for example, to call an instance method. It can, however, call static methods.

Implicit parameterless constructors

For classes, the C# compiler automatically generates a parameterless constructor if and only if you do not define any constructors. However, as soon as you define at least one constructor, the parameterless constructor is no longer automatically generated.

For structs, a parameterless constructor is intrinsic to the struct; therefore, you cannot define your own. The role of a struct's implicit parameterless constructor is to initialize each field with default values.

Constructor and field initialization order

Previously, we saw that fields can be initialized with default values in their declaration:

```
class Player
{
  int shields = 50;    // Initialized first
  int health = 100;    // Initialized second
}
```

Field initializations occur *before* the constructor is executed, and in the declaration order of the fields.

Nonpublic constructors

Constructors do not need to be public. A common reason to have a nonpublic constructor is to control instance creation via a static method call. The static method could be used to return an object from a pool rather than necessarily creating a new object, or return various subclasses based on input arguments. The template for that pattern is shown next:

```
public class Class1
{
    Class1() {}                              // Private constructor
    public static Class1 Create (...)
    {
        // Perform custom logic here to return an instance of Class1
        ...
    }
}
```

Object Initializers

To simplify object initialization, the accessible fields or properties of an object can be initialized in a single statement directly after construction. For example, consider the following class:

```
public class Bunny
{
    public string Name;
    public bool LikesCarrots;
    public bool LikesHumans;

    public Bunny () {}
    public Bunny (string n) { Name = n; }
}
```

Using object initializers, you can instantiate Bunny objects as follows:

```
// Note parameterless constructors can omit empty parentheses
Bunny b1 = new Bunny { Name="Bo", LikesCarrots=true, LikesHumans=false };
Bunny b2 = new Bunny ("Bo")      { LikesCarrots=true, LikesHumans=false };
```

The code to construct b1 and b2 is precisely equivalent to:

```
Bunny temp1 = new Bunny();      // temp1 is a compiler-generated name
temp1.Name = "Bo";
temp1.LikesCarrots = true;
temp1.LikesHumans = false;
Bunny b1 = temp1;

Bunny temp2 = new Bunny ("Bo");
temp2.LikesCarrots = true;
temp2.LikesHumans = false;
Bunny b2 = temp2;
```

The temporary variables are to ensure that if an exception is thrown during initialization, you can't end up with a half-initialized object.

Object initializers were introduced in C# 3.0.

Object Initializers Versus Optional Parameters

Instead of using object initializers, we could make Bunny's constructor accept optional parameters:

```
public Bunny (string name,
              bool likesCarrots = false,
              bool likesHumans = false)
{
  Name = name;
  LikesCarrots = likesCarrots;
  LikesHumans = likesHumans;
}
```

This would allow us to construct a Bunny as follows:

```
Bunny b1 = new Bunny (name: "Bo",
                      likesCarrots: true);
```

An advantage of this approach is that we could make Bunny's fields (or *properties*, as we'll explain shortly) read-only if we choose. Making fields or properties read-only is good practice when there's no valid reason for them to change throughout the life of the object.

The disadvantage in this approach is that each optional parameter value is baked into the *calling site*. In other words, C# translates our constructor call into this:

```
Bunny b1 = new Bunny ("Bo", true, false);
```

This can be problematic if we instantiate the Bunny class from another assembly, and later modify Bunny by adding another optional parameter—such as likes Cats. Unless the referencing assembly is also recompiled, it will continue to call the (now nonexistent) constructor with three parameters and fail at runtime. (A subtler problem is that if we changed the value of one of the optional parameters, callers in other assemblies would continue to use the old optional value until they were recompiled.)

Hence, optional parameters are best avoided in public functions if you want to offer binary compatibility between assembly versions.

The this Reference

The this reference refers to the instance itself. In the following example, the Marry method uses this to set the partner's mate field:

```
public class Panda
{
  public Panda Mate;

  public void Marry (Panda partner)
  {
    Mate = partner;
    partner.Mate = this;
  }
}
```

The this reference also disambiguates a local variable or parameter from a field. For example:

```
public class Test
{
  string name;
  public Test (string name) { this.name = name; }
}
```

The this reference is valid only within nonstatic members of a class or struct.

Properties

Properties look like fields from the outside, but internally they contain logic, like methods do. For example, you can't tell by looking at the following code whether CurrentPrice is a field or a property:

```
Stock msft = new Stock();
msft.CurrentPrice = 30;
msft.CurrentPrice -= 3;
Console.WriteLine (msft.CurrentPrice);
```

A property is declared like a field, but with a get/set block added. Here's how to implement CurrentPrice as a property:

```
public class Stock
{
  decimal currentPrice;          // The private "backing" field

  public decimal CurrentPrice    // The public property
  {
    get { return currentPrice; } set { currentPrice = value; }
  }
}
```

get and set denote property *accessors*. The get accessor runs when the property is read. It must return a value of the property's type. The set accessor is run when the property is assigned. It has an implicit parameter named value of the property's type that you typically assign to a private field (in this case, currentPrice).

Although properties are accessed in the same way as fields, they differ in that they give the implementer complete control over getting and setting its value. This control enables the implementer to choose whatever internal representation is needed, without exposing the internal details to the user of the property. In this example, the set method could throw an exception if value was outside a valid range of values.

Throughout this book, we use public fields extensively to keep the examples free of distraction. In a real application, you would typically favor public properties over public fields, in order to promote encapsulation.

Properties allow the following modifiers:

Static modifier	`static`
Access modifiers	`public internal private protected`
Inheritance modifiers	`new virtual abstract override sealed`
Unmanaged code modifiers	`unsafe extern`

Read-only and calculated properties

A property is read-only if it specifies only a `get` accessor, and it is write-only if it specifies only a `set` accessor. Write-only properties are rarely used.

A property typically has a dedicated backing field to store the underlying data. However, a property can also be computed from other data. For example:

```
decimal currentPrice, sharesOwned;

public decimal Worth
{
  get { return currentPrice * sharesOwned; }
}
```

Automatic properties

The most common implementation for a property is a getter and/or setter that simply reads and writes to a private field of the same type as the property. An *automatic property* declaration instructs the compiler to provide this implementation. We can redeclare the first example in this section as follows:

```
public class Stock
{
  ...
  public decimal CurrentPrice { get; set; }
}
```

The compiler automatically generates a private backing field of a compiler-generated name that cannot be referred to. The `set` accessor can be marked **private** if you want to expose the property as read-only to other types. Automatic properties were introduced in C# 3.0.

get and set accessibility

The `get` and `set` accessors can have different access levels. The typical use case for this is to have a **public** property with an **internal** or **private** access modifier on the setter:

```
public class Foo
{
  private decimal x;
  public decimal X
  {
    get         { return x;  }
    private set { x = Math.Round (value, 2); }
```

```
  }
}
```

Notice that you declare the property itself with the more permissive access level (`public`, in this case), and then add the modifier to the accessor that you want to be *less* accessible.

CLR property implementation

C# property accessors internally compile to methods called **get_*XXX*** and **set_*XXX*:**

```
public int  get_CurrentPrice {...}
public void set_CurrentPrice (decimal value) {...}
```

Simple nonvirtual property accessors are *inlined* by the JIT (Just-In-Time) compiler, eliminating any performance difference between accessing a property and a field. Inlining is an optimization in which a method call is replaced with the body of that method.

Indexers

Indexers provide a natural syntax for accessing elements in a class or struct that encapsulate a list or dictionary of values. Indexers are similar to properties, but are accessed via an index argument rather than a property name. The **string** class has an indexer that lets you access each of its **char** values via an **int** index:

```
string s = "hello";
Console.WriteLine (s[0]); // 'h'
Console.WriteLine (s[3]); // 'l'
```

The syntax for using indexers is like that for using arrays when the index is an integer type.

 Indexers have the same modifiers as properties (see "Properties" on page 69).

Implementing an indexer

To write an indexer, define a property called **this**, specifying the arguments in square brackets. For instance:

```
class Sentence
{
  string[] words = "The quick brown fox".Split();

  public string this [int wordNum]      // indexer
  {
    get { return words [wordNum];  }
    set { words [wordNum] = value; }
  }
}
```

Here's how we could use this indexer:

```
Sentence s = new Sentence();
Console.WriteLine (s[3]);        // fox
s[3] = "kangaroo";
Console.WriteLine (s[3]);        // kangaroo
```

A type may declare multiple indexers, each with parameters of different types. An indexer can also take more than one parameter:

```
public string this [int arg1, string arg2]
{
  get { ... }  set { ... }
}
```

If you omit the set accessor, an indexer becomes read-only.

CLR indexer implementation

Indexers internally compile to methods called get_Item and set_Item, as follows:

```
public string get_Item (int wordNum) {...}
public void set_Item (int wordNum, string value) {...}
```

The compiler chooses the name "Item" by default—you can actually change this by decorating your indexer with the following attribute:

```
[System.Runtime.CompilerServices.IndexerName ("Blah")]
```

Constants

A *constant* is a field whose value can never change. A constant is evaluated statically at compile time and the compiler literally substitutes its value whenever used, rather like a macro in C++. A constant can be any of the built-in numeric types, bool, char, string, or an enum type.

A constant is declared with the const keyword and must be initialized with a value. For example:

```
public class Test
{
  public const string Message = "Hello World";
}
```

A constant is much more restrictive than a static readonly field—both in the types you can use and in field initialization semantics. A constant also differs from a static readonly field in that the evaluation of the constant occurs at compile time. For example:

```
public static double Circumference (double radius)
{
  return 2 * System.Math.PI * radius;
}
```

is compiled to:

```
public static double Circumference (double radius)
{
  return 6.2831853071795862 * radius;
}
```

It makes sense for PI to be a constant, since it can never change. In contrast, a static readonly field can have a different value per application.

 A static readonly field is also advantageous when exposing to other assemblies a value that might change in a later version. For instance, suppose assembly X exposes a constant as follows:

```
public const int MaximumThreads = 20;
```

If assembly Y references X and uses this constant, the value 20 will be baked into assembly Y when compiled. This means that if X is later recompiled with the constant set to 50, Y will still use the old value of 20 *until* Y *is recompiled*. A static readonly field avoids this problem.

Constants can also be declared local to a method. For example:

```
static void Main()
{
  const double twoPI  = 2 * System.Math.PI;
  ...
}
```

Constants allow the following modifiers:

Access modifiers	public internal private protected
Inheritance modifier	new

Static Constructors

A static constructor executes once per *type*, rather than once per *instance*. A type can define only one static constructor, and it must be parameterless and have the same name as the type:

```
class Test
{
  static Test() { Console.WriteLine ("Type Initialized"); }
}
```

The runtime automatically invokes a static constructor just prior to the type being used. Two things trigger this:

- Instantiating the type
- Accessing a static member in the type

The only modifiers allowed by static constructors are unsafe and extern.

If a static constructor throws an unhandled exception (Chapter 4), that type becomes *unusable* for the life of the application.

Static constructors and field initialization order

Static field initializers run just *before* the static constructor is called. If a type has no static constructor, field initializers will execute just prior to the type being used—or *anytime earlier* at the whim of the runtime. (This means that the presence of a static constructor may cause field initializers to execute later in the program than they would otherwise.)

Static field initializers run in the order in which the fields are declared. The following example illustrates this: X is initialized to 0 and Y is initialized to 3.

```
class Foo
{
  public static int X = Y;    // 0
  public static int Y = 3;    // 3
}
```

If we swap the two field initializers around, both fields are initialized to 3. The next example prints 0 followed by 3 because the field initializer that instantiates a Foo executes before X is initialized to 3:

```
class Program
{
  static void Main() { Console.WriteLine (Foo.X); }    // 3
}

class Foo
{
  public static Foo Instance = new Foo();
  public static int X = 3;

  Foo() { Console.WriteLine (X); }    // 0
}
```

If we swap the two lines in boldface, the example prints 3 followed by 3.

Static Classes

A class can be marked `static`, indicating that it must be composed solely of static members and cannot be subclassed. The `System.Console` and `System.Math` classes are good examples of static classes.

Finalizers

Finalizers are class-only methods that execute before the garbage collector reclaims the memory for an unreferenced object. The syntax for a finalizer is the name of the class prefixed with the ˜ symbol:

```
class Class1
{
  ~Class1()
  {
    ...
  }
}
```

This is actually C# syntax for overriding Object's Finalize method, and the compiler expands it into the following method declaration:

```
protected override void Finalize()
{
  ...
  base.Finalize();
}
```

We discuss garbage collection and finalizers fully in Chapter 12.

Finalizers allow the following modifier:

Unmanaged code modifier   unsafe

Partial Types and Methods

Partial types allow a type definition to be split—typically across multiple files. A common scenario is for a partial class to be auto-generated from some other source (e.g., an XSD), and for that class to be augmented with additional hand-authored methods. For example:

```
// PaymentFormGen.cs - auto-generated
partial class PaymentForm { ... }

// PaymentForm.cs - hand-authored
partial class PaymentForm { ... }
```

Each participant must have the partial declaration; the following is illegal:

```
partial class PaymentForm {}
class PaymentForm {}
```

Participants cannot have conflicting members. A constructor with the same parameters, for instance, cannot be repeated. Partial types are resolved entirely by the compiler, which means that each participant must be available at compile time and must reside in the same assembly.

There are two ways to specify a base class with partial classes:

- Specify the (same) base class on each participant. For example:

  ```
  partial class PaymentForm : ModalForm {}
  partial class PaymentForm : ModalForm {}
  ```

- Specify the base class on just one participant. For example:

  ```
  partial class PaymentForm : ModalForm {}
  partial class PaymentForm {}
  ```

In addition, each participant can independently specify interfaces to implement. We cover base classes and interfaces in "Inheritance" on page 76 and "Interfaces" on page 92.

Partial methods

A partial type may contain *partial methods*. These let an auto-generated partial type provide customizable hooks for manual authoring. For example:

```
partial class PaymentForm    // In auto-generated file
{
  ...
  partial void ValidatePayment (decimal amount);
}

partial class PaymentForm    // In hand-authored file
{
  ...
  partial void ValidatePayment (decimal amount)
  {
    if (amount > 100)
      ...
  }
}
```

A partial method consists of two parts: a *definition* and an *implementation*. The definition is typically written by a code generator, and the implementation is typically manually authored. If an implementation is not provided, the definition of the partial method is compiled away. This allows auto-generated code to be liberal in providing hooks, without having to worry about code bloat. Partial methods must be void and are implicitly private.

Partial methods were introduced in C# 3.0.

Inheritance

A class can *inherit* from another class to extend or customize the original class. Inheriting from a class lets you reuse the functionality in that class instead of building it from scratch. A class can inherit from only a single class, but can itself be inherited by many classes, thus forming a class hierarchy. In this example, we start by defining a class called Asset:

```
public class Asset
{
  public string Name;
}
```

Next, we define classes called Stock and House, which will inherit from Asset. They get everything an Asset has, plus any additional members that they define:

```
public class Stock : Asset   // inherits from Asset
{
  public long SharesOwned;
}
```

```
public class House : Asset    // inherits from Asset
{
  public decimal Mortgage;
}
```

Here's how we can use these classes:

```
Stock msft = new Stock { Name="MSFT",
                         SharesOwned=1000 };

Console.WriteLine (msft.Name);          // MSFT
Console.WriteLine (msft.SharesOwned);   // 1000

House mansion = new House { Name="Mansion",
                            Mortgage=250000 };

Console.WriteLine (mansion.Name);       // Mansion
Console.WriteLine (mansion.Mortgage);   // 250000
```

The *subclasses*, Stock and House, inherit the Name property from the *base class*, Asset.

A subclass is also called a *derived class*.

A base class is also called a *superclass*.

Polymorphism

References are polymorphic. This means a variable of type *x* can refer to an object that subclasses *x*. For instance, consider the following method:

```
public static void Display (Asset asset)
{
  System.Console.WriteLine (asset.Name);
}
```

This method can display both a Stock and a House, since they are both Assets:

```
Stock msft     = new Stock ... ;
House mansion = new House ... ;

Display (msft);
Display (mansion);
```

Polymorphism works on the basis that subclasses (Stock and House) have all the features of their base class (Asset). The converse, however, is not true. If Display was modified to accept a House, you could not pass in an Asset:

```
static void Main() { Display (new Asset()); }    // Compile-time error

public static void Display (House house)          // Will not accept Asset
{
  System.Console.WriteLine (house.Mortgage);
}
```

Casting and Reference Conversions

An object reference can be:

- Implicitly *upcast* to a base class reference
- Explicitly *downcast* to a subclass reference

Upcasting and downcasting between compatible reference types performs *reference conversions*: a new reference is created that points to the *same* object. An upcast always succeeds; a downcast succeeds only if the object is suitably typed.

Upcasting

An upcast operation creates a base class reference from a subclass reference. For example:

```
Stock msft = new Stock();
Asset a = msft;             // Upcast
```

After the upcast, variable a still references the same Stock object as variable msft. The object being referenced is not itself altered or converted:

```
Console.WriteLine (a == msft);      // True
```

Although a and msft refer to the identical object, a has a more restrictive view on that object:

```
Console.WriteLine (a.Name);         // OK
Console.WriteLine (a.SharesOwned);  // Error: SharesOwned undefined
```

The last line generates a compile-time error because the variable a is of type Asset, even though it refers to an object of type Stock. To get to its SharedOwned field, you must *downcast* the Asset to a Stock.

Downcasting

A downcast operation creates a subclass reference from a base class reference. For example:

```
Stock msft = new Stock();
Asset a = msft;                      // Upcast
Stock s = (Stock)a;                  // Downcast
Console.WriteLine (s.SharesOwned);   // <No error>
Console.WriteLine (s == a);          // True
Console.WriteLine (s == msft);       // True
```

As with an upcast, only references are affected—not the underlying object. A downcast requires an explicit cast because it can potentially fail at runtime:

```
House h = new House();
Asset a = h;                // Upcast always succeeds
Stock s = (Stock)a;         // Downcast fails: a is not a Stock
```

If a downcast fails, an InvalidCastException is thrown. This is an example of *runtime type checking* (we will elaborate on this concept in "Static and Runtime Type Checking" on page 87).

The as operator

The as operator performs a downcast that evaluates to null (rather than throwing an exception) if the downcast fails:

```
Asset a = new Asset();
Stock s = a as Stock;      // s is null; no exception thrown
```

This is useful when you're going to subsequently test whether the result is null:

```
if (s != null) Console.WriteLine (s.SharesOwned);
```

Without such a test, a cast is advantageous, because if it fails, a more descriptive exception is thrown. We can illustrate by comparing the following two lines of code:

```
int shares = ((Stock)a).SharesOwned;      // Approach #1
int shares = (a as Stock).SharesOwned;     // Approach #2
```

If a is not a Stock, the first line throws an InvalidCastException, which is an accurate description of what went wrong. The second line throws a NullReferenceException, which is ambiguous. Was a not a Stock or was a null?

The as operator cannot perform *custom conversions* (see "Operator Overloading" on page 153 in Chapter 4) and it cannot do numeric conversions:

```
long x = 3 as long;      // Compile-time error
```

The as and cast operators will also perform upcasts, although this is not terribly useful because an implicit conversion will do the job.

The is operator

The is operator tests whether a reference conversion would succeed; in other words, whether an object derives from a specified class (or implements an interface). It is often used to test before downcasting.

```
if (a is Stock)
    Console.WriteLine (((Stock)a).SharesOwned);
```

The is operator does not consider custom or numeric conversions, but it does consider *unboxing conversions* (see "The object Type" on page 85).

Virtual Function Members

A function marked as virtual can be *overridden* by subclasses wanting to provide a specialized implementation. Methods, properties, indexers, and events can all be declared virtual:

```
public class Asset
{
  public string Name;
  public virtual decimal Liability { get { return 0; } }
}
```

A subclass overrides a virtual method by applying the **override** modifier:

```
public class Stock : Asset
{
  public long SharesOwned;
}

public class House : Asset
{
  public decimal Mortgage;
  public override decimal Liability { get { return Mortgage; } }
}
```

By default, the `Liability` of an `Asset` is 0. A `Stock` does not need to specialize this behavior. However, the `House` specializes the `Liability` property to return the value of the `Mortgage`:

```
House mansion = new House { Name="McMansion", Mortgage=250000 };
Console.WriteLine (mansion.Liability);      // 250000
```

The signatures, return types, and accessibility of the virtual and overridden methods must be identical. An overridden method can call its base class implementation via the **base** keyword (we will cover this in "The base Keyword" on page 82).

Abstract Classes and Abstract Members

A class declared as *abstract* can never be instantiated. Instead, only its concrete *subclasses* can be instantiated.

Abstract classes are able to define *abstract members*. Abstract members are like virtual members, except they don't provide a default implementation. That implementation must be provided by the subclass, unless that subclass is also declared abstract:

```
public abstract class Asset
{
  // Note empty implementation
  public abstract decimal NetValue { get; }
}

public class Stock : Asset
{
  public long SharesOwned;
  public decimal CurrentPrice;

  // Override like a virtual method.
  public override decimal NetValue
  {
    get { return CurrentPrice * SharesOwned; }
```

```
    }
  }
```

Hiding Inherited Members

A base class and a subclass may define identical members. For example:

```
public class A     { public int Counter = 1; }
public class B : A { public int Counter = 2; }
```

The `Counter` field in class `B` is said to *hide* the `Counter` field in class `A`. Usually, this happens by accident, when a member is added to the base type *after* an identical member was added to the subtype. For this reason, the compiler generates a warning, and then resolves the ambiguity as follows:

- References to `A` (at compile time) bind to `A.Counter`.
- References to `B` (at compile time) bind to `B.Counter`.

Occasionally, you want to hide a member deliberately, in which case you can apply the `new` modifier to the member in the subclass. The `new` modifier *does nothing more than suppress the compiler warning that would otherwise result*:

```
public class A     { public     int Counter = 1; }
public class B : A { public new int Counter = 2; }
```

The `new` modifier communicates your intent to the compiler—and other programmers—that the duplicate member is not an accident.

 C# overloads the `new` keyword to have independent meanings in different contexts. Specifically, the `new` *operator* is different from the `new` *member* modifier.

new versus virtual

Consider the following class hierarchy:

```
public class BaseClass
{
  public virtual void Foo()  { Console.WriteLine ("BaseClass.Foo"); }
}

public class Overrider : BaseClass
{
  public override void Foo() { Console.WriteLine ("Overrider.Foo"); }
}

public class Hider : BaseClass
{
  public new void Foo()      { Console.WriteLine ("Hider.Foo"); }
}
```

The differences in behavior between `Overrider` and `Hider` are demonstrated in the following code:

```
Overrider over = new Overrider();
BaseClass b1 = over;
over.Foo();                        // Overrider.Foo
b1.Foo();                          // Overrider.Foo

Hider h = new Hider();
BaseClass b2 = h;
h.Foo();                           // Hider.Foo
b2.Foo();                          // BaseClass.Foo
```

Sealing Functions and Classes

An overridden function member may *seal* its implementation with the `sealed` keyword to prevent it from being overridden by further subclasses. In our earlier virtual function member example, we could have sealed `House`'s implementation of `Liability`, preventing a class that derives from `House` from overriding `Liability`, as follows:

```
public sealed override decimal Liability { get { return Mortgage; } }
```

You can also seal the class itself, implicitly sealing all the virtual functions, by applying the `sealed` modifier to the class itself. Sealing a class is more common than sealing a function member.

The base Keyword

The `base` keyword is similar to the `this` keyword. It serves two essential purposes:

- Accessing an overridden function member from the subclass
- Calling a base class constructor (see the next section)

In this example, `House` uses the `base` keyword to access `Asset`'s implementation of `Liability`:

```
public class House : Asset
{
  ...
  public override decimal Liability
  {
    get { return base.Liability + Mortgage; }
  }
}
```

With the `base` keyword, we access `Asset`'s `Liability` property *nonvirtually*. This means we will always access `Asset`'s version of this property—regardless of the instance's actual runtime type.

The same approach works if `Liability` is *hidden* rather than *overridden*. (You can also access hidden members by casting to the base class before invoking the function.)

Constructors and Inheritance

A subclass must declare its own constructors. For example, if we define `Subclass` as follows:

```
public class Baseclass
{
  public int X;
  public Baseclass () { }
  public Baseclass (int x) { this.X = x; }
}

public class Subclass : Baseclass { }
```

the following is illegal:

```
Subclass s = new Subclass (123);
```

`Subclass` must hence "redefine" any constructors it wants to expose. In doing so, however, it can call any of the base class's constructors with the `base` keyword:

```
public class Subclass : Baseclass
{
  public Subclass (int x) : base (x) { }
}
```

The `base` keyword works rather like the `this` keyword, except that it calls a constructor in the base class.

Base class constructors always execute first; this ensures that *base* initialization occurs before *specialized* initialization.

Implicit calling of the parameterless base class constructor

If a constructor in a subclass omits the `base` keyword, the base type's *parameterless* constructor is implicitly called:

```
public class BaseClass
{
  public int X;
  public BaseClass() { X = 1; }
}

public class Subclass : BaseClass
{
  public Subclass() { Console.WriteLine (X); }  // 1
}
```

If the base class has no parameterless constructor, subclasses are forced to use the `base` keyword in their constructors.

Constructor and field initialization order

When an object is instantiated, initialization takes place in the following order:

1. From subclass to base class:

    a. Fields are initialized.

    b. Arguments to base-class constructor calls are evaluated.

2. From base class to subclass:

    a. Constructor bodies execute.

The following code demonstrates:

```
public class B
{
  int x = 0;          // Executes 3rd
  public B (int x)
  {
    ...               // Executes 4th
  }
}
public class D : B
{
  int y = 0;          // Executes 1st
  public D (int x)
    : base (x + 1)    // Executes 2nd
  {
    ...               // Executes 5th
  }
}
```

Overloading and Resolution

Inheritance has an interesting impact on method overloading. Consider the following two overloads:

```
static void Foo (Asset a) { }
static void Foo (House h) { }
```

When an overload is called, the most specific type has precedence:

```
House h = new House (...);
Foo(h);                         // Calls Foo(House)
```

The particular overload to call is determined statically (at compile time) rather than at runtime. The following code calls `Foo(Asset)`, even though the runtime type of a is `House`:

```
Asset a = new House (...);
Foo(a);                         // Calls Foo(Asset)
```

If you cast Asset to dynamic (Chapter 4), the decision as to which overload to call is deferred until runtime, and is then based on the object's actual type:

```
Asset a = new House (...);
Foo ((dynamic)a);   // Calls Foo(House)
```

The object Type

object (System.Object) is the ultimate base class for all types. Any type can be upcast to object.

To illustrate how this is useful, consider a general-purpose *stack*. A stack is a data structure based on the principle of LIFO—"Last-In First-Out." A stack has two operations: *push* an object on the stack, and *pop* an object off the stack. Here is a simple implementation that can hold up to 10 objects:

```
public class Stack
{
  int position;
  object[] data = new object[10];
  public void Push (object obj)    { data[position++] = obj;  }
  public object Pop()              { return data[--position]; }
}
```

Because Stack works with the object type, we can Push and Pop instances of *any type* to and from the Stack:

```
Stack stack = new Stack();
stack.Push ("sausage");
string s = (string) stack.Pop();   // Downcast, so explicit cast is needed

Console.WriteLine (s);             // sausage
```

object is a reference type, by virtue of being a class. Despite this, value types, such as int, can also be cast to and from object, and so be added to our stack. This feature of C# is called *type unification* and is demonstrated here:

```
stack.Push (3);
int three = (int) stack.Pop();
```

When you cast between a value type and object, the CLR must perform some special work to bridge the difference in semantics between value and reference types. This process is called *boxing* and *unboxing*.

In "Generics" on page 101, we'll describe how to improve our Stack class to better handle stacks with same-typed elements.

Boxing and Unboxing

Boxing is the act of casting a value-type instance to a reference-type instance. The reference type may be either the `object` class or an interface (which we will visit later in the chapter).[*] In this example, we box an `int` into an object:

```
int x = 9;
object obj = x;          // Box the int
```

Unboxing reverses the operation, by casting the object back to the original value type:

```
int y = (int)obj;        // Unbox the int
```

Unboxing requires an explicit cast. The runtime checks that the stated value type matches the actual object type, and throws an `InvalidCastException` if the check fails. For instance, the following throws an exception, because `long` does not exactly match `int`:

```
object obj = 9;          // 9 is inferred to be of type int
long x = (long) obj;     // InvalidCastException
```

The following succeeds, however:

```
object obj = 9;
long x = (int) obj;
```

As does this:

```
object obj = 3.5;          // 3.5 is inferred to be of type double
int x = (int) (double) obj;   // x is now 3
```

In the last example, `(double)` performs an *unboxing* and then `(int)` performs a *numeric conversion*.

> Boxing conversions are crucial in providing a unified type system. The system is not perfect, however: we'll see in "Generics" on page 101 that variance with arrays and generics supports only *reference conversions* and not *boxing conversions*:
>
> ```
> object[] a1 = new string[3];   // Legal
> object[] a2 = new int[3];      // Error
> ```

Copying semantics of boxing and unboxing

Boxing *copies* the value-type instance into the new object, and unboxing *copies* the contents of the object back into a value-type instance. In the following example, changing the value of `i` doesn't change its previously boxed copy:

```
int i = 3;
object boxed = i;
i = 5;
Console.WriteLine (boxed);     // 3
```

---

[*] The reference type may also be `System.ValueType` or `System.Enum` (Chapter 6).

Static and Runtime Type Checking

C# checks types both statically (at compile time) and at runtime.

Static type checking enables the compiler to verify the correctness of your program without running it. The following code will fail because the compiler enforces static typing:

```
int x = "5";
```

Runtime type checking is performed by the CLR when you downcast via a reference conversion or unboxing. For example:

```
object y = "5";
int z = (int) y;        // Runtime error, downcast failed
```

Runtime type checking is possible because each object on the heap internally stores a little type token. This token can be retrieved by calling the GetType method of object.

The GetType Method and typeof Operator

All types in C# are represented at runtime with an instance of System.Type. There are two basic ways to get a System.Type object:

- Call GetType on the instance.
- Use the typeof operator on a type name.

GetType is evaluated at runtime; typeof is evaluated statically at compile time.

System.Type has properties for such things as the type's name, assembly, base type, and so on. For example:

```
using System;

public class Point { public int X, Y; }

class Test
{
  static void Main()
  {
    Point p = new Point();
    Console.WriteLine (p.GetType().Name);             // Point
    Console.WriteLine (typeof (Point).Name);          // Point
    Console.WriteLine (p.GetType() == typeof(Point)); // True
    Console.WriteLine (p.X.GetType().Name);           // Int32
    Console.WriteLine (p.Y.GetType().FullName);       // System.Int32
  }
}
```

System.Type also has methods that act as a gateway to the runtime's reflection model, described in Chapter 17.

The ToString Method

The `ToString` method returns the default textual representation of a type instance. This method is overridden by all built-in types. Here is an example of using the `int` type's `ToString` method:

```
int x = 1;
string s = x.ToString();     // s is "1"
```

You can override the `ToString` method on custom types as follows:

```
public class Panda
{
  public string Name;
  public override string ToString() { return Name; }
}
...

Panda p = new Panda { Name = "Petey" };
Console.WriteLine (p);   // Petey
```

 When you call an *overridden* `object` member such as `ToString` directly on a value type, boxing doesn't occur. Boxing then occurs only if you cast:

```
int x = 1;
string s1 = x.ToString();     // Calling on nonboxed value
object box = x;
string s2 = box.ToString();   // Calling on boxed value
```

Object Member Listing

Here are all the members of `object`:

```
public class Object
{
  public Object();

  public extern Type GetType();

  public virtual bool Equals (object obj);
  public static bool Equals  (object objA, object objB);
  public static bool ReferenceEquals (object objA, object objB);

  public virtual int GetHashCode();

  public virtual string ToString();

  protected override void Finalize();
  protected extern object MemberwiseClone();
}
```

We describe the `Equals`, `ReferenceEquals`, and `GetHashCode` methods in "Equality Comparison" on page 245 in Chapter 6.

Structs

A *struct* is similar to a class, with the following key differences:

- A struct is a value type, whereas a class is a reference type.
- A struct does not support inheritance (other than implicitly deriving from object, or more precisely, System.ValueType).

A struct can have all the members a class can, except the following:

- A parameterless constructor
- A finalizer
- Virtual members

A struct is used instead of a class when value-type semantics are desirable. Good examples of structs are numeric types, where it is more natural for assignment to copy a value rather than a reference. Because a struct is a value type, each instance does not require instantiation of an object on the heap; this incurs a useful savings when creating many instances of a type. For instance, creating an array of value type requires only a single heap allocation.

Struct Construction Semantics

The construction semantics of a struct are as follows:

- A parameterless constructor that you can't override implicitly exists. This performs a bitwise-zeroing of its fields.
- When you define a struct constructor, you must explicitly assign every field.
- You can't have field initializers in a struct.

Here is an example of declaring and calling struct constructors:

```
public struct Point
{
  int x, y;
  public Point (int x, int y) { this.x = x; this.y = y; }
}

...
Point p1 = new Point ();      // p1.x and p1.y will be 0
Point p2 = new Point (1, 1);  // p1.x and p1.y will be 1
```

The next example generates three compile-time errors:

```
public struct Point
{
  int x = 1;                  // Illegal: cannot initialize field
  int y;
  public Point() {}           // Illegal: cannot have
                              // parameterless constructor

  public Point (int x) {this.x = x;}  // Illegal: must assign field y
}
```

Changing struct to class makes this example legal.

Access Modifiers

To promote encapsulation, a type or type member may limit its *accessibility* to other types and other assemblies by adding one of five *access modifiers* to the declaration:

public

Fully accessible; the implicit accessibility for members of an enum or interface

internal

Accessible only within containing assembly or friend assemblies; the default accessibility for non-nested types

private

Visible only within containing type; the default accessibility members of a class or struct

protected

Visible only within containing type or subclasses

protected internal

The *union* of protected and internal accessibility (this is *less* restrictive than protected or internal alone)

 The CLR has the concept of the *intersection* of protected and internal accessibility, but C# does not support this.

Examples

Class2 is accessible from outside its assembly; Class1 is not:

```
class Class1 {}                    // Class1 is internal (default)
public class Class2 {}
```

ClassB exposes field x to other types in the same assembly; ClassA does not:

```
class ClassA { int x;          } // x is private (default)
class ClassB { internal int x; }
```

Functions within Subclass can call Bar but not Foo:

```
class BaseClass
{
  void Foo()           {}     // Foo is private (default)
  protected void Bar() {}
}

class Subclass : BaseClass
{
    void Test1() { Foo(); }    // Error - cannot access Foo
    void Test2() { Bar(); }    // OK
}
```

Friend Assemblies

In advanced scenarios, you can expose internal members to other *friend* assemblies by adding the System.Runtime.CompilerServices.InternalsVisibleTo assembly attribute, specifying the name of the friend assembly as follows:

```
[assembly: InternalsVisibleTo ("Friend")]
```

If the friend assembly has a strong name (see Chapter 17), you must specify its *full* 160-byte public key:

```
[assembly: InternalsVisibleTo ("StrongFriend, PublicKey=0024f000048c...")]
```

You can extract the full public key from a strongly named assembly with a LINQ query (we explain LINQ in detail in Chapter 8):

```
string key = string.Join ("",
    Assembly.GetExecutingAssembly().GetName().GetPublicKey()
    .Select (b => b.ToString ("x2"))
    .ToArray());
```

 The companion sample in LINQPad invites you to browse to an assembly and then copies the assembly's full public key to the clipboard.

Accessibility Capping

A type caps the accessibility of its declared members. The most common example of capping is when you have an internal type with public members. For example:

```
class C { public void Foo() {} }
```

C's (default) internal accessibility caps Foo's accessibility, effectively making Foo internal. A common reason Foo would be marked public is to make for easier refactoring, should C later be changed to public.

Restrictions on Access Modifiers

When overriding a base class function, accessibility must be identical on the overridden function. For example:

```
class BaseClass            { protected virtual  void Foo() {} }
class Subclass1 : BaseClass { protected override void Foo() {} }  // OK
class Subclass2 : BaseClass { public    override void Foo() {} }  // Error
```

The compiler prevents any inconsistent use of access modifiers. For example, a subclass itself can be less accessible than a base class, but not more:

```
internal class A {}
public class B : A {}       // Error
```

Interfaces

An interface is similar to a class, but it provides a specification rather than an implementation for its members. An interface is special in the following ways:

- A class can implement *multiple* interfaces. In contrast, a class can inherit from only a *single* class.

- Interface members are *all implicitly abstract*. In contrast, a class can provide both abstract members and concrete members with implementations.

- *Structs* can implement interfaces. In contrast, a struct cannot inherit from a class.

An interface declaration is like a class declaration, but it provides no implementation for its members, since all its members are implicitly abstract. These members will be implemented by the classes and structs that implement the interface. An interface can contain only methods, properties, events, and indexers, which noncoincidentally are precisely the members of a class that can be abstract.

Here is the definition of the IEnumerator interface, defined in System.Collections:

```
public interface IEnumerator
{
  bool MoveNext();
  object Current { get; }
  void Reset();
}
```

Interface members are always implicitly public and cannot declare an access modifier. Implementing an interface means providing a public implementation for all its members:

```
internal class Countdown : IEnumerator
{
  int count = 11;
  public bool MoveNext () { return count-- > 0 ;              }
  public object Current   { get { return count; }             }
  public void Reset()     { throw new NotSupportedException(); }
}
```

You can implicitly cast an object to any interface that it implements. For example:

```
IEnumerator e = new Countdown();
while (e.MoveNext())
  Console.Write (e.Current);     // 109876543210
```

> Even though Countdown is an internal class, its members that implement IEnumerator can be called publicly by casting an instance of Countdown to IEnumerator. For instance, if a public type in the same assembly defined a method as follows:
>
> ```
> public static class Util
> {
>   public static object GetCountDown()
>   {
> ```

```
                return new CountDown();
        }
    }
```

a caller from another assembly could do this:

```
IEnumerator e = (IEnumerator) Util.GetCountDown();
e.MoveNext();
```

If `IEnumerator` was itself defined as `internal`, this wouldn't be possible.

Extending an Interface

Interfaces may derive from other interfaces. For instance:

```
public interface IUndoable          { void Undo(); }
public interface IRedoable : IUndoable { void Redo(); }
```

`IRedoable` inherits all the members of `IUndoable`.

Explicit Interface Implementation

Implementing multiple interfaces can sometimes result in a collision between member signatures. You can resolve such collisions by *explicitly implementing* an interface member. Consider the following example:

```
interface I1 { void Foo(); }
interface I2 { int Foo(); }

public class Widget : I1, I2
{
    public void Foo ()
    {
        Console.WriteLine ("Widget's implementation of I1.Foo");
    }

    int I2.Foo()
    {
        Console.WriteLine ("Widget's implementation of I2.Foo");
        return 42;
    }
}
```

Because both `I1` and `I2` have conflicting `Foo` signatures, `Widget` explicitly implements `I2`'s `Foo` method. This lets the two methods coexist in one class. The only way to call an explicitly implemented member is to cast to its interface:

```
Widget w = new Widget();
w.Foo();            // Widget's implementation of I1.Foo
((I1)w).Foo();      // Widget's implementation of I1.Foo
((I2)w).Foo();      // Widget's implementation of I2.Foo
```

Another reason to explicitly implement interface members is to hide members that are highly specialized and distracting to a type's normal use case. For example, a type that implements ISerializable would typically want to avoid flaunting its ISerializable members unless explicitly cast to that interface.

Implementing Interface Members Virtually

An implicitly implemented interface member is, by default, sealed. It must be marked **virtual** or **abstract** in the base class in order to be overridden. For example:

```
public interface IUndoable { void Undo(); }

public class TextBox : IUndoable
{
  public virtual void Undo()
  {
    Console.WriteLine ("TextBox.Undo");
  }
}

public class RichTextBox : TextBox
{
  public override void Undo()
  {
    Console.WriteLine ("RichTextBox.Undo");
  }
}
```

Calling the interface member through either the base class or the interface calls the subclass's implementation:

```
RichTextBox r = new RichTextBox();
r.Undo();                           // RichTextBox.Undo
((IUndoable)r).Undo();              // RichTextBox.Undo
((TextBox)r).Undo();                // RichTextBox.Undo
```

An explicitly implemented interface member cannot be marked **virtual**, nor can it be overridden in the usual manner. It can, however, be *reimplemented*.

Reimplementing an Interface in a Subclass

A subclass can reimplement any interface member already implemented by a base class. Reimplementation hijacks a member implementation (when called through the interface) and works whether or not the member is **virtual** in the base class. It also works whether a member is implemented implicitly or explicitly—although it works best in the latter case, as we will demonstrate.

In the following example, TextBox implements IUndoable.Undo explicitly, and so it cannot be marked as **virtual**. In order to "override" it, RichTextBox must reimplement IUndoable's Undo method:

```
public interface IUndoable { void Undo(); }

public class TextBox : IUndoable
{
  void IUndoable.Undo() { Console.WriteLine ("TextBox.Undo"); }
}
```

```
public class RichTextBox : TextBox, IUndoable
{
  public new void Undo() { Console.WriteLine ("RichTextBox.Undo"); }
}
```

Calling the reimplemented member through the interface calls the subclass's implementation:

```
RichTextBox r = new RichTextBox();
r.Undo();                    // RichTextBox.Undo    Case 1
((IUndoable)r).Undo();       // RichTextBox.Undo    Case 2
```

Assuming the same RichTextBox definition, suppose that TextBox implemented Undo *implicitly*:

```
public class TextBox : IUndoable
{
  public void Undo() { Console.WriteLine ("TextBox.Undo"); }
}
```

This would give us another way to call Undo, which would "break" the system, as shown in Case 3:

```
RichTextBox r = new RichTextBox();
r.Undo();                    // RichTextBox.Undo    Case 1
((IUndoable)r).Undo();       // RichTextBox.Undo    Case 2
((TextBox)r).Undo();         // TextBox.Undo        Case 3
```

Case 3 shows that reimplementation hijacking is effective only when a member is called through the interface and not through the base class. This is usually undesirable, as it can mean inconsistent semantics. Reimplementation is most appropriate as a strategy for overriding *explicitly* implemented interface members.

Alternatives to interface reimplementation

Even with explicit member implementation, interface reimplementation is problematic for a couple of reasons:

- The subclass has no way to call the base class method.
- The base class author may not anticipate that a method be reimplemented and may not allow for the potential consequences.

Reimplementation can be a good last resort when subclassing hasn't been anticipated. A better option, however, is to design a base class such that reimplementation will never be required. There are two ways to achieve this:

- When implicitly implementing a member, mark it virtual if appropriate.
- When explicitly implementing a member, use the following pattern if you anticipate that subclasses might need to override any logic:

```
public class TextBox : IUndoable
{
  void IUndoable.Undo()        { Undo(); }    // Calls method below
  protected virtual void Undo() { Console.WriteLine ("TextBox.Undo"); }
}
```

```
public class RichTextBox : TextBox
{
    protected override void Undo() { Console.WriteLine("RichTextBox.Undo"); }
}
```

If you don't anticipate any subclassing, you can mark the class as sealed to preempt interface reimplementation.

Interfaces and Boxing

Casting a struct to an interface causes boxing. Calling an implicitly implemented member on a struct does not cause boxing:

```
interface  I { void Foo();           }
struct S : I { public void Foo() {} }

...
S s = new S();
s.Foo();           // No boxing.

I i = s;           // Box occurs when casting to interface.
i.Foo();
```

Writing a Class Versus an Interface

As a guideline:

- Use classes and subclasses for types that naturally share an implementation.
- Use interfaces for types that have independent implementations.

Consider the following classes:

```
abstract class Animal {}
abstract class Bird          : Animal {}
abstract class Insect         : Animal {}
abstract class FlyingCreature : Animal {}
abstract class Carnivore      : Animal {}

// Concrete classes:

class Ostrich : Bird {}
class Eagle   : Bird, FlyingCreature, Carnivore {}   // Illegal
class Bee     : Insect, FlyingCreature {}            // Illegal
class Flea    : Insect, Carnivore {}                 // Illegal
```

The Eagle, Bee, and Flea classes do not compile because inheriting from multiple classes is prohibited. To resolve this, we must convert some of the types to interfaces. The question then arises, which types? Following our general rule, we could say that insects share an implementation, and birds share an implementation, so they remain classes. In contrast, flying creatures have independent mechanisms for flying, and carnivores have independent strategies for eating animals, so we would convert FlyingCreature and Carnivore to interfaces:

```
interface IFlyingCreature {}
interface ICarnivore      {}
```

> In a typical scenario, `Bird` and `Insect` might correspond to a Windows control and a web control; `FlyingCreature` and `Carnivore` might correspond to `IPrintable` and `IUndoable`.

Enums

An enum is a special value type that lets you specify a group of named numeric constants. For example:

```
public enum BorderSide { Left, Right, Top, Bottom }
```

We can use this enum type as follows:

```
BorderSide topSide = BorderSide.Top;
bool isTop = (topSide == BorderSide.Top);    // true
```

Each enum member has an underlying integral value. By default:

- Underlying values are of type `int`.
- The constants 0, 1, 2... are automatically assigned, in the declaration order of the enum members.

You may specify an alternative integral type, as follows:

```
public enum BorderSide : byte { Left, Right, Top, Bottom }
```

You may also specify an explicit underlying value for each enum member:

```
public enum BorderSide : byte { Left=1, Right=2, Top=10, Bottom=11 }
```

> The compiler also lets you explicitly assign *some* of the enum members. The unassigned enum members keep incrementing from the last explicit value. The preceding example is equivalent to the following:
>
> ```
> public enum BorderSide : byte
>     { Left=1, Right, Top=10, Bottom }
> ```

Enum Conversions

You can convert an enum instance to and from its underlying integral value with an explicit cast:

```
int i = (int) BorderSide.Left;
BorderSide side = (BorderSide) i;
bool leftOrRight = (int) side <= 2;
```

You can also explicitly cast one enum type to another. Suppose `HorizontalAlignment` is defined as follows:

```
public enum HorizontalAlignment
{
  Left = BorderSide.Left,
  Right = BorderSide.Right,
```

```
     Center
}
```

A translation between the enum types uses the underlying integral values:

```
HorizontalAlignment h = (HorizontalAlignment) BorderSide.Right;
// same as:
HorizontalAlignment h = (HorizontalAlignment) (int) BorderSide.Right;
```

The numeric literal 0 is treated specially by the compiler in an enum expression and does not require an explicit cast:

```
BorderSide b = 0;      // No cast required
if (b == 0) ...
```

There are two reasons for the special treatment of 0:

- The first member of an enum is often used as the "default" value.
- For *combined enum* types, 0 means "no flags."

Flags Enums

You can combine enum members. To prevent ambiguities, members of a combinable enum require explicitly assigned values, typically in powers of two. For example:

```
[Flags]
public enum BorderSides { Left=1, Right=2, Top=4, Bottom=8 }
```

To work with combined enum values, you use bitwise operators, such as | and &. These operate on the underlying integral values:

```
BorderSides leftRight = BorderSides.Left | BorderSides.Right;

if ((leftRight & BorderSides.Left) != 0)
    Console.WriteLine ("Includes Left");      // Includes Left

string formatted = leftRight.ToString();    // "Left, Right"

BorderSides s = BorderSides.Left;
s |= BorderSides.Right;
Console.WriteLine (s == leftRight);   // True

s ^= BorderSides.Right;               // Toggles BorderSides.Right
Console.WriteLine (s);                // Left
```

By convention, the Flags attribute should always be applied to an enum type when its members are combinable. If you declare such an enum without the Flags attribute, you can still combine members, but calling ToString on an enum instance will emit a number rather than a series of names.

By convention, a combinable enum type is given a plural rather than singular name.

For convenience, you can include combination members within an enum declaration itself:

```
[Flags]
public enum BorderSides
{
  Left=1, Right=2, Top=4, Bottom=8,
  LeftRight = Left | Right,
  TopBottom = Top  | Bottom,
  All       = LeftRight | TopBottom
}
```

Enum Operators

The operators that work with enums are:

```
=   ==   !=   <   >   <=   >=   +   -   ^   &   |   ~
+=   -=   ++   -   sizeof
```

The bitwise, arithmetic, and comparison operators return the result of processing the underlying integral values. Addition is permitted between an enum and an integral type, but not between two enums.

Type-Safety Issues

Consider the following enum:

```
public enum BorderSide { Left, Right, Top, Bottom }
```

Since an enum can be cast to and from its underlying integral type, the actual value it may have may fall outside the bounds of a legal enum member. For example:

```
BorderSide b = (BorderSide) 12345;
Console.WriteLine (b);          // 12345
```

The bitwise and arithmetic operators can produce similarly invalid values:

```
BorderSide b = BorderSide.Bottom;
b++;                            // No errors
```

An invalid BorderSide would break the following code:

```
void Draw (BorderSide side)
{
  if      (side == BorderSide.Left)  {...}
  else if (side == BorderSide.Right) {...}
  else if (side == BorderSide.Top)   {...}
  else                               {...} // Assume BorderSide.Bottom
}
```

One solution is to add another else clause:

```
...
else if (side == BorderSide.Bottom) ...
else throw new ArgumentException ("Invalid BorderSide: " + side, "side");
```

Another workaround is to explicitly check an enum value for validity. The static Enum.IsDefined method does this job:

```
BorderSide side = (BorderSide) 12345;
Console.WriteLine (Enum.IsDefined (typeof (BorderSide), side));  // False
```

Unfortunately, `Enum.IsDefined` does not work for flagged enums. However, the following helper method (a trick dependent on the behavior of `Enum.ToString()`) returns `true` if a given flagged enum is valid:

```
static bool IsFlagDefined (Enum e)
{
  decimal d;
  return !decimal.TryParse(e.ToString(), out d);
}

[Flags]
public enum BorderSides { Left=1, Right=2, Top=4, Bottom=8 }

static void Main()
{
  for (int i = 0; i <= 16; i++)
  {
    BorderSides side = (BorderSides)i;
    Console.WriteLine (IsFlagDefined (side) + " " + side);
  }
}
```

Nested Types

A *nested type* is declared within the scope of another type. For example:

```
public class TopLevel
{
  public class Nested { }                // Nested class
  public enum Color { Red, Blue, Tan }   // Nested enum
}
```

A nested type has the following features:

- It can access the enclosing type's private members and everything else the enclosing type can access.
- It can be declared with the full range of access modifiers, rather than just `public` and `internal`.
- The default visibility for a nested type is `private` rather than `internal`.
- Accessing a nested type from outside the enclosing type requires qualification with the enclosing type's name (like when accessing static members).

For example, to access `Color.Red` from outside our `TopLevel` class, we'd have to do this:

```
TopLevel.Color color = TopLevel.Color.Red;
```

All types can be nested; however, only classes and structs can *nest*.

Here is an example of accessing a private member of a type from a nested type:

```
public class TopLevel
{
  static int x;
  class Nested
  {
    static void Foo() { Console.WriteLine (TopLevel.x); }
  }
}
```

Here is an example of applying the **protected** access modifier to a nested type:

```
public class TopLevel
{
  protected class Nested { }
}

public class SubTopLevel : TopLevel
{
  static void Foo() { new TopLevel.Nested(); }
}
```

Here is an example of referring to a nested type from outside the enclosing type:

```
public class TopLevel
{
  public class Nested { }
}

class Test
{
  TopLevel.Nested n;
}
```

Nested types are used heavily by the compiler itself when it generates private classes that capture state for constructs such as iterators and anonymous methods.

 If the sole reason for using a nested type is to avoid cluttering a namespace with too many types, consider using a nested namespace instead. A nested type should be used because of its stronger access control restrictions, or when the nested class must access private members of the containing class.

Generics

C# has two separate mechanisms for writing code that is reusable across different types: *inheritance* and *generics*. Whereas inheritance expresses reusability with a base type, generics express reusability with a "template" that contains "placeholder" types. Generics, when compared to inheritance, can *increase type safety* and *reduce casting and boxing*.

C# generics and C++ templates are similar concepts, but they work differently. We explain this difference in "C# Generics Versus C++ Templates" on page 113.

Generic Types

A generic type declares *type parameters*—placeholder types to be filled in by the consumer of the generic type, which supplies the *type arguments*. Here is a generic type Stack<T>, designed to stack instances of type T. Stack<T> declares a single type parameter T:

```
public class Stack<T>
{
  int position;
  T[] data = new T[100];
  public void Push (T obj)   { data[position++] = obj;  }
  public T Pop()             { return data[--position]; }
}
```

We can use Stack<T> as follows:

```
Stack<int> stack = new Stack<int>();
stack.Push(5);
stack.Push(10);
int x = stack.Pop();       // x is 10
int y = stack.Pop();       // y is 5
```

Stack<int> fills in the type parameter T with the type argument int, implicitly creating a type on the fly (the synthesis occurs at runtime). Stack<int> effectively has the following definition (substitutions appear in bold, with the class name hashed out to avoid confusion):

```
public class ###
{
  int position;
  int[] data;
  public void Push (int obj)   { data[position++] = obj;  }
  public int Pop()             { return data[--position]; }
}
```

Technically, we say that Stack<T> is an *open type*, whereas Stack<int> is a *closed type*. At runtime, all generic type instances are closed—with the placeholder types filled in. This means that the following statement is illegal:

```
var stack = new Stack<T>();   // Illegal: What is T?
```

unless inside a class or method which itself defines T as a type parameter:

```
public class Stack<T>
{
  ...
  public Stack<T> Clone()
  {
    Stack<T> clone = new Stack<T>();   // Legal
    ...
```

```
        }
    }
```

Why Generics Exist

Generics exist to write code that is reusable across different types. Suppose we needed a stack of integers, but we didn't have generic types. One solution would be to
hardcode a separate version of the class for every required element type (e.g.,
IntStack, StringStack, etc.). Clearly, this would cause considerable code
duplication. Another solution would be to write a stack that is generalized by using
object as the element type:

```
public class ObjectStack
{
  int position;
  object[] data = new object[10];
  public void Push (object obj) { data[position++] = obj;  }
  public object Pop()           { return data[--position]; }
}
```

An ObjectStack, however, wouldn't work as well as a hardcoded IntStack for specifically stacking integers. Specifically, an ObjectStack would require boxing and
downcasting that could not be checked at compile time:

```
// Suppose we just want to store integers here:
ObjectStack stack = new ObjectStack();

stack.Push ("s");          // Wrong type, but no error!
int i = (int)stack.Pop();  // Downcast - runtime error
```

What we need is both a general implementation of a stack that works for all element
types, and a way to easily specialize that stack to a specific element type for increased
type safety and reduced casting and boxing. Generics give us precisely this, by allowing us to parameterize the element type. Stack<T> has the benefits of both
ObjectStack and IntStack. Like ObjectStack, Stack<T> is written once to work *generally* across all types. Like IntStack, Stack<T> is *specialized* for a particular type—
the beauty is that this type is T, which we substitute on the fly.

  ObjectStack is functionally equivalent to Stack<object>.

Generic Methods

A generic method declares type parameters within the signature of a method.

With generic methods, many fundamental algorithms can be implemented in a
general-purpose way only. Here is a generic method that swaps two values of any
type:

```
static void Swap<T> (ref T a, ref T b)
{
  T temp = a;
  a = b;
  b = temp;
}
```

Swap<T> can be used as follows:

```
int x = 5;
int y = 10;
Swap (ref x, ref y);
```

Generally, there is no need to supply type arguments to a generic method, because the compiler can implicitly infer the type. If there is ambiguity, generic methods can be called with the type arguments as follows:

```
Swap<int> (ref x, ref y);
```

Within a generic *type*, a method is not classed as generic unless it *introduces* type parameters (with the angle bracket syntax). The Pop method in our generic stack merely uses the type's existing type parameter, T, and is not classed as a generic method.

Methods and types are the only constructs that can introduce type parameters. Properties, indexers, events, fields, constructors, operators, and so on cannot declare type parameters, although they can partake in any type parameters already declared by their enclosing type. In our generic stack example, for instance, we could write an indexer that returns a generic item:

```
public T this [int index] { get { return data [index]; } }
```

Similarly, constructors can partake in existing type parameters, but not *introduce* them:

```
public Stack<T>() { }   // Illegal
```

Declaring Type Parameters

Type parameters can be introduced in the declaration of classes, structs, interfaces, delegates (covered in Chapter 4), and methods. Other constructs, such as properties, cannot *introduce* a type parameter, but can *use* one. For example, the property Value uses T:

```
public struct Nullable<T>
{
  public T Value { get; set; }
}
```

A generic type or method can have multiple parameters. For example:

```
class Dictionary<TKey, TValue> {...}
```

To instantiate:

```
Dictionary<int,string> myDic = new Dictionary<int,string>();
```

Or:

```
var myDic = new Dictionary<int,string>();
```

Generic type names and method names can be overloaded as long as the number of type parameters is different. For example, the following two type names do not conflict:

```
class A<T> {}
class A<T1,T2> {}
```

 By convention, generic types and methods with a *single* type parameter typically name their parameter T, as long as the intent of the parameter is clear. When using *multiple* type parameters, each parameter is prefixed with T, but has a more descriptive name.

typeof and Unbound Generic Types

Open generic types do not exist at runtime: open generic types are closed as part of compilation. However, it is possible for an *unbound* generic type to exist at runtime—purely as a Type object. The only way to specify an unbound generic type in C# is with the typeof operator:

```
class A<T> {}
class A<T1,T2> {}
...

Type a1 = typeof (A<>);    // Unbound type (notice no type arguments).
Type a2 = typeof (A<,>);   // Use commas to indicate multiple type args.
```

You can also use the typeof operator to specify a closed type:

```
Type a3 = typeof (A<int,int>);
```

or an open type (which is closed at runtime):

```
class B<T> { void X() { Type t = typeof (T); } }
```

The default Generic Value

The default keyword can be used to get the default value given a generic type parameter. The default value for a reference type is null, and the default value for a value type is the result of bitwise-zeroing the value type's fields:

```
static void Zap<T> (T[] array)
{
  for (int i = 0; i < array.Length; i++)
    array[i] = default(T);
}
```

Generic Constraints

By default, a type parameter can be substituted with any type whatsoever. *Constraints* can be applied to a type parameter to require more specific type arguments. These are the possible constraints:

```
where T : base-class    // Base class constraint
where T : interface     // Interface constraint
where T : class         // Reference-type constraint
where T : struct        // Value-type constraint (excludes Nullable types)
where T : new()         // Parameterless constructor constraint
where U : T             // Naked type constraint
```

In the following example, GenericClass<T,U> requires T to derive from SomeClass and implement Interface1, and requires U to provide a parameterless constructor:

```
class     SomeClass {}
interface Interface1 {}

class GenericClass<T> where T : SomeClass, Interface1
                      where U : new()
{...}
```

Constraints can be applied wherever type parameters are defined, in both methods and type definitions.

A *base class constraint* or *interface constraint* specifies that the type parameter must subclass or implement a particular class or interface. This allows instances of that type to be implicitly cast to that class or interface. For example, suppose we want to write a generic Max method, which returns the maximum of two values. We can take advantage of the generic interface defined in the framework called IComparable<T>:

```
public interface IComparable<T>   // Simplified version of interface
{
  int CompareTo (T other);
}
```

CompareTo returns a positive number if other is greater than this. Using this interface as a constraint, we can write a Max method as follows (to avoid distraction, null checking is omitted):

```
static T Max <T> (T a, T b) where T : IComparable<T>
{
  return a.CompareTo (b) > 0 ? a : b;
}
```

The Max method can accept arguments of any type implementing IComparable<T> (which includes most built-in types such as int and string):

```
int z = Max (5, 10);            // 10
string last = Max ("ant", "zoo"); // zoo
```

The *class constraint* and *struct constraint* specify that T must be a reference type or (non-nullable) value type. A great example of the struct constraint is the `System.Nul lable<T>` struct (we will discuss this class in depth in the section "Nullable Types" on page 148 in Chapter 4):

```
struct Nullable<T> where T : struct {...}
```

The *parameterless constructor constraint* requires T to have a public parameterless constructor. If this constraint is defined, you can call `new()` on T:

```
static void Initialize<T> (T[] array) where T : new()
{
  for (int i = 0; i < array.Length; i++)
    array[i] = new T();
}
```

The *naked type constraint* requires one type parameter to derive from *another type parameter*. In this example, the method `FilteredStack` returns another `Stack`, containing only the subset of elements where the type parameter T is of the type parameter U:

```
class Stack<T>
{
  Stack<U> FilteredStack<U>() where U : T {...}
}
```

Subclassing Generic Types

A generic class can be subclassed just like a nongeneric class. The subclass can leave the base class's type parameters open, as in the following example:

```
class Stack<T>                    {...}
class SpecialStack<T> : Stack<T> {...}
```

Or the subclass can close the generic type parameters with a concrete type:

```
class IntStack : Stack<int>  {...}
```

A subtype can also introduce fresh type arguments:

```
class List<T>                      {...}
class KeyedList<T,TKey> : List<T> {...}
```

> Technically, *all* type arguments on a subtype are fresh: you could say that a subtype closes and then reopens the base type arguments. This means that a subclass can give new (and potentially more meaningful) names to the type arguments it reopens:
>
> ```
> class List<T> {...}
> class KeyedList<TElement,TKey> : List<TElement> {...}
> ```

Self-Referencing Generic Declarations

A type can name *itself* as the concrete type when closing a type argument:

```
public interface IEquatable<T> { bool Equals (T obj); }

public class Balloon : IEquatable<Balloon>
{
  public string Color { get; set; }
  public int CC { get; set; }

  public bool Equals (Balloon b)
  {
    if (b == null) return false;
    return b.Color == Color && b.CC == CC;
  }
}
```

The following are also legal:

```
class Foo<T> where T : IComparable<T> { ... }
class Bar<T> where T : Bar<T> { ... }
```

Static Data

Static data is unique for each closed type:

```
class Bob<T> { public static int Count; }

class Test
{
  static void Main()
  {
    Console.WriteLine (++Bob<int>.Count);     // 1
    Console.WriteLine (++Bob<int>.Count);     // 2
    Console.WriteLine (++Bob<string>.Count);  // 1
    Console.WriteLine (++Bob<object>.Count);  // 1
  }
}
```

Type Parameters and Conversions

C#'s cast operator can perform several kinds of conversion, including:

- Numeric conversion
- Reference conversion
- Boxing/unboxing conversion
- Custom conversion (via operator overloading; see Chapter 4)

The decision as to which kind of conversion will take place happens at *compile time*, based on the known types of the operands. This creates an interesting scenario with generic type parameters, because the precise operand types are unknown at compile time. If this leads to ambiguity, the compiler generates an error.

The most common scenario is when you want to perform a reference conversion:

```
StringBuilder Foo<T> (T arg)
{
  if (arg is StringBuilder)
    return (StringBuilder) arg;    // Will not compile
  ...
}
```

Without knowledge of T's actual type, the compiler is concerned that you might have intended this to be a *custom conversion*. The simplest solution is to instead use the **as** operator, which is unambiguous because it cannot perform custom conversions:

```
StringBuilder Foo<T> (T arg)
{
  StringBuilder sb = arg as StringBuilder;
  if (sb != null) return sb;
  ...
}
```

A more general solution is to first cast to object. This works because conversions to/from object are assumed not to be custom conversions, but reference or boxing/unboxing conversions. In this case, StringBuilder is a reference type, so it has to be a reference conversion:

```
    return (StringBuilder) (object) arg;
```

Unboxing conversions can also introduce ambiguities. The following could be an unboxing, numeric, or custom conversion:

```
    int Foo<T> (T x) {   return (int) x; }    // Compile-time error
```

The solution, again, is to first cast to object and then to int (which then unambiguously signals an unboxing conversion in this case):

```
    int Foo<T> (T x) {   return (int) (object) x; }
```

Covariance

Assuming S subclasses B, type X is *covariant* if X<S> allows a reference conversion to X<B>.

In other words, type IFoo<T> is covariant if the following is legal:

```
    IFoo<string> b = ...;
    IFoo<object> s = b;
```

As of C# 4.0, generic interfaces permit covariance (as do generic delegates—see Chapter 4), but generic classes do not. Arrays also support covariance (S[] can be cast to B[] if S subclasses B), and are discussed here for comparison.

Covariance and contravariance (or simply "variance") are advanced concepts. The motivation behind introducing and enhancing variance in C# was to allow generic interface and generic types (in particular, those defined in the Framework, such as IEnumerable<T>) to work *more as you'd expect*. You can benefit from this without understanding the details behind covariance and contravariance.

Classes

Generic classes are not covariant, to ensure static type safety. Consider the following:

```
class Animal {}
class Bear : Animal {}
class Camel : Animal {}

public class Stack<T>    // A simple Stack implementation
{
  int position;
  T[] data = new T[100];
  public void Push (T obj)    { data[position++] = obj;  }
  public T Pop()              { return data[--position]; }
}
```

The following fails to compile:

```
Stack<Bear> bears = new Stack<Bear>();
Stack<Animal> animals = bears;            // Compile-time error
```

That restriction prevents the possibility of runtime failure with the following code:

```
animals.Push (new Camel());      // Trying to add Camel to bears
```

Lack of covariance, however, can hinder reusability. Suppose, for instance, we wanted to write a method to Wash a stack of animals:

```
public class ZooCleaner
{
  public static void Wash (Stack<Animal> animals) {...}
}
```

Calling Wash with a stack of bears would generate a compile-time error. One workaround is to redefine the Wash method with a constraint:

```
class ZooCleaner
{
  public static void Wash<T> (Stack<T> animals) where T : Animal { ... }
}
```

We can now call Wash as follows:

```
Stack<Bear> bears = new Stack<Bear>();
ZooCleaner.Wash (bears);
```

Another solution is to have Stack<T> implement a covariant generic interface, as we'll see shortly.

Arrays

For historical reasons, array types are covariant. This means that `B[]` can be cast to `A[]` if B subclasses A (and both are reference types). For example:

```
Bear[] bears = new Bear[3];
Animal[] animals = bears;    // OK
```

The downside of this reusability is that element assignments can fail at runtime:

```
animals[0] = new Camel();    // Runtime error
```

Interfaces

As of C# 4.0, generic interfaces support covariance for type parameters marked with the out modifier. This modifier ensures that, unlike with arrays, covariance with interfaces is fully type-safe. To illustrate, suppose that our Stack class implements the following interface:

```
public interface IPoppable<out T> { T Pop(); }
```

The out modifier on T is new to C# 4.0 and indicates that T is used only in *output positions* (e.g., return types for methods). The out modifier flags the interface as *covariant* and allows us to do this:

```
var bears = new Stack<Bear>();
bears.Push (new Bear());
// Bears implements IPoppable<Bear>. We can convert to IPoppable<Animal>:
IPoppable<Animal> animals = bears;    // Legal
Animal a = animals.Pop();
```

The cast from bears to animals is permitted by the compiler—by virtue of the interface being covariant. This is type-safe because the case the compiler is trying to avoid—pushing a Camel onto the stack—can't occur as there's no way to feed a Camel *in*to an interface where T can appear only in *out*put positions.

Covariance (and contravariance) in interfaces is something that you typically *consume*: it's less common that you need to *write* variant interfaces.

Curiously, method parameters marked as out are not eligible for covariance, due to a limitation in the CLR.

We can leverage the ability to cast covariantly to solve the reusability problem described earlier:

```
public class ZooCleaner
{
  public static void Wash (IPoppable<Animal> animals) { ... }
}
```

The `IEnumerator<T>` and `IEnumerable<T>` interfaces described in Chapter 7 are marked as covariant from Framework 4.0. This allows you to cast `IEnumerable<string>` to `IEnumerable<object>`, for instance.

The compiler will generate an error if you use a covariant type parameter in an *input* position (e.g., a parameter to a method or a writable property).

With both generic types and arrays, covariance (and contravariance) is valid only for elements with *reference conversions*—not *boxing conversions*. So, if you wrote a method that accepted a parameter of type `IPoppable<object>`, you could call it with `IPoppable<string>`, but not `IPoppable<int>`.

Contravariance

We previously saw that a type X is covariant if X<S> allows a reference conversion to X<B> where S subclasses B. A type is *contravariant* when you can convert in the reverse direction—from X<B> to X<S>. This is supported in C# 4.0 with generic interfaces—when the generic type parameter only appears in *input* positions, designated with the `in` modifier. Extending our previous example, if the `Stack<T>` class implements the following interface:

```
public interface IPushable<in T> { void Push (T obj); }
```

we can legally do this:

```
IPushable<Animal> animals = new Stack<Animal>();
IPushable<Bear> bears = animals;    // Legal
bears.Push (new Bear());
```

No member in `IPushable` *outputs* a T, so we can't get into trouble by casting `animals` to `bears` (there's no way to `Pop`, for instance, through that interface).

Our `Stack<T>` class can implement both `IPushable<T>` and `IPoppable<T>`—despite T having opposing variance annotations in the two interfaces! This works because you can exercise variance only through an interface; therefore, you must commit to the lens of either `IPoppable` or `IPushable` before performing a variant conversion. This lens then restricts you to the operations that are legal under the appropriate variance rules.

This also illustrates why it would make no sense for *classes* (such as `Stack<T>`) to be variant.

To give another example, consider the following interface, defined as part of the .NET Framework:

```
public interface IComparer<in T>
{
  // Returns a value indicating the relative ordering of a and b
  int Compare (T a, T b);
}
```

Because the interface is contravariant, we can use an IComparer<**object**> to compare two *strings*:

```
var objectComparer = Comparer<object>.Default;
// objectComparer implements IComparer<object>
IComparer<string> stringComparer = objectComparer;
int result = stringComparer.Compare ("Brett", "Jemaine");
```

Mirroring covariance, the compiler will report an error if you try to use a contravariant parameter in an output position (e.g., as a return value, or in a readable property).

C# Generics Versus C++ Templates

C# generics are similar in application to C++ templates, but they work very differently. In both cases, a synthesis between the producer and consumer must take place, where the placeholder types of the producer are filled in by the consumer. However, with C# generics, producer types (i.e., open types such as List<T>) can be compiled into a library (such as *mscorlib.dll*). This works because the synthesis between the producer and the consumer that produces closed types doesn't actually happen until runtime. With C++ templates, this synthesis is performed at compile time. This means that in C++ you don't deploy template libraries as *.dlls*—they exist only as source code. It also makes it difficult to dynamically inspect, let alone create, parameterized types on the fly.

To dig deeper into why this is the case, consider the Max method in C#, once more:

```
static T Max <T> (T a, T b) where T : IComparable<T>
{
  return a.CompareTo (b) > 0 ? a : b;
}
```

Why couldn't we have implemented it like this?

```
static T Max <T> (T a, T b)
{
  return a > b ? a : b;         // Compile error
}
```

Creating Types

The reason is that Max needs to be compiled once and work for all possible values of T. Compilation cannot succeed, because there is no single meaning for > across all values of T—in fact, not every T even has a > operator. In contrast, the following code shows the same Max method written with C++ templates. This code will be compiled separately for each value of T, taking on whatever semantics > has for a particular T, failing to compile if a particular T does not support the > operator:

```
template <class T> T Max (T a, T b)
{
  return a > b ? a : b;
}
```

4

Advanced C#

In this chapter, we cover advanced C# topics that build on concepts explored in previous chapters. You should read the first four sections sequentially; you can read the remaining sections in any order.

Delegates

A delegate dynamically wires up a method caller to its target method. There are two aspects to a delegate: *type* and *instance*. A *delegate type* defines a *protocol* to which the caller and target will conform, comprising a list of parameter types and a return type. A *delegate instance* is an object that refers to one (or more) target methods conforming to that protocol.

A delegate instance literally acts as a delegate for the caller: the caller invokes the delegate, and then the delegate calls the target method. This indirection decouples the caller from the target method.

A delegate type declaration is preceded by the keyword `delegate`, but otherwise it resembles an (abstract) method declaration. For example:

```
delegate int Transformer (int x);
```

To create a delegate instance, you can assign a method to a delegate variable:

```
class Test
{
  static void Main()
  {
    Transformer t = Square;          // Create delegate instance
    int result = t(3);               // Invoke delegate
    Console.WriteLine (result);      // 9
  }
  static int Square (int x) { return x * x; }
}
```

Technically, we are specifying a *method group* when we refer to
Square without brackets or arguments. If the method is overloaded, C# will pick the correct overload based on the signature
of the delegate to which it's being assigned.

Invoking a delegate is just like invoking a method (since the delegate's purpose is
merely to provide a level of indirection):

```
t(3);
```

The statement:

```
Transformer t = Square;
```

is shorthand for:

```
Transformer t = new Transformer (Square);
```

and:

```
t(3)
```

is shorthand for:

```
t.Invoke (3);
```

A delegate is similar to a *callback*, a general term that captures
constructs such as C function pointers.

Writing Plug-in Methods with Delegates

A delegatevariable is assigned a method *dynamically*. This is useful for writing plug-
in methods. In this example, we have a utility method named Transform that applies
a transform to each element in an integer array. The Transform method has a delegate
parameter, for specifying a plug-in transform.

```
public delegate int Transformer (int x);

class Util
{
  public static void Transform (int[] values, Transformer t)
  {
    for (int i = 0; i < values.Length; i++)
      values[i] = t (values[i]);
  }
}

class Test
{
  static void Main()
  {
    int[] values = { 1, 2, 3 };
    Util.Transform (values, Square);      // Dynamically hook in Square
```

```
    foreach (int i in values)
        Console.Write (i + "  ");              // 1    4    9
    }

    static int Square (int x) { return x * x; }
}
```

Multicast Delegates

All delegate instances have *multicast* capability. This means that a delegate instance can reference not just a single target method, but also a list of target methods. The + and += operators combine delegate instances. For example:

```
SomeDelegate d = SomeMethod1;
d += SomeMethod2;
```

The last line is functionally the same as:

```
d = d + SomeMethod2;
```

Invoking d will now call both SomeMethod1 and SomeMethod2. Delegates are invoked in the order they are added.

The - and -= operators remove the right delegate operand from the left delegate operand. For example:

```
d -= SomeMethod1;
```

Invoking d will now cause only SomeMethod2 to be invoked.

Calling + or += on a delegate variable with a null value works, and it is equivalent to assigning the variable to a new value:

```
SomeDelegate d = null;
d += SomeMethod1;       // Equivalent (when d is null) to d = SomeMethod1;
```

Similarly, calling -= on a delegate variable with a single target is equivalent to assigning null to that variable.

 Delegates are *immutable*, so when you call += or -=, you're in fact creating a *new* delegate instance and assigning it to the existing variable.

If a multicast delegate has a nonvoid return type, the caller receives the return value from the last method to be invoked. The preceding methods are still called, but their return values are discarded. In most scenarios in which multicast delegates are used, they have void return types, so this subtlety does not arise.

 All delegate types implicitly derive from System.MulticastDelegate, which inherits from System.Delegate. C# compiles +, -, +=, and -= operations made on a delegate to the static Combine and Remove methods of the System.Delegate class.

Multicast delegate example

Suppose you wrote a routine that took a long time to execute. That routine could regularly report progress to its caller by invoking a delegate. In this example, the HardWork routine has a ProgressReporter delegate parameter, which it invokes to indicate progress:

```
public delegate void ProgressReporter (int percentComplete);

public class Util
{
  public static void HardWork (ProgressReporter p)
  {
    for (int i = 0; i < 10; i++)
    {
      p (i * 10);                              // Invoke delegate
      System.Threading.Thread.Sleep (100);  // Simulate hard work
    }
  }
}
```

To monitor progress, the Main method creates a multicast delegate instance p, such that progress is monitored by two independent methods:

```
class Test
{
  static void Main()
  {
    ProgressReporter p = WriteProgressToConsole;
    p += WriteProgressToFile;
    Util.HardWork (p);
  }

  static void WriteProgressToConsole (int percentComplete)
  {
    Console.WriteLine (percentComplete);
  }

  static void WriteProgressToFile (int percentComplete)
  {
    System.IO.File.WriteAllText ("progress.txt",
                                  percentComplete.ToString());
  }
}
```

Instance Versus Static Method Targets

When a delegate object is assigned to an *instance* method, the delegate object must maintain a reference not only to the method, but also to the *instance* to which the method belongs. The System.Delegate class's Target property represents this instance (and will be null for a delegate referencing a static method). For example:

```
public delegate void ProgressReporter (int percentComplete);

class Test
{
  static void Main()
  {
    X x = new X();
    ProgressReporter p = x.InstanceProgress;
    p(99);                               // 99
    Console.WriteLine (p.Target == x);   // True
    Console.WriteLine (p.Method);        // Void InstanceProgress(Int32)
  }
}

class X
{
  public void InstanceProgress (int percentComplete)
  {
    Console.WriteLine (percentComplete);
  }
}
```

Generic Delegate Types

A delegate type may contain generic type parameters. For example:

```
public delegate T Transformer<T> (T arg);
```

With this definition, we can write a generalized Transform utility method that works on any type:

```
public class Util
{
  public static void Transform<T> (T[] values, Transformer<T> t)
  {
    for (int i = 0; i < values.Length; i++)
      values[i] = t (values[i]);
  }
}

class Test
{
  static void Main()
  {
    int[] values = { 1, 2, 3 };
    Util.Transform (values, Square);     // Dynamically hook in Square
    foreach (int i in values)
      Console.Write (i + "  ");          // 1    4    9
  }

  static int Square (int x) { return x * x; }
}
```

The Func and Action Delegates

With generic delegates, it becomes possible to write a small set of delegate types that are so general they can work for methods of any return type and any (reasonable) number of arguments. These delegates are the Func and Action delegates, defined in the System namespace (the in and out annotations indicate *variance*, which we will cover shortly):

```
delegate TResult Func <out TResult>            ();
delegate TResult Func <in T, out TResult>      (T arg);
delegate TResult Func <in T1, in T2, out TResult>  (T1 arg1, T2 arg2);
... and so on, up to T16

delegate void Action                    ();
delegate void Action <in T>             (T arg);
delegate void Action <in T1, in T2>     (T1 arg1, T2 arg2);
... and so on, up to T16
```

These delegates are extremely general. The Transformer delegate in our previous example can be replaced with a Func delegate that takes a single argument of type T and returns a same-typed value:

```
public static void Transform<T> (T[] values, Func<T,T> transformer)
{
  for (int i = 0; i < values.Length; i++)
    values[i] = transformer (values[i]);
}
```

The only practical scenarios not covered by these delegates are ref/out and pointer parameters.

Delegates Versus Interfaces

A problem that can be solved with a delegate can also be solved with an interface. For instance, the following explains how to solve our filter problem using an ITransformer interface:

```
public interface ITransformer
{
  int Transform (int x);
}

public class Util
{
 public static void TransformAll (int[] values, ITransformer t)
 {
   for (int i = 0; i < values.Length; i++)
     values[i] = t.Transform (values[i]);
 }
}

class Squarer : ITransformer
{
  public int Transform (int x) { return x * x; }
}
```

```
...
static void Main()
{
  int[] values = { 1, 2, 3 };
  Util.TransformAll (values, new Squarer());
  foreach (int i in values)
    Console.WriteLine (i);
}
```

A delegate design may be a better choice than an interface design if one or more of these conditions are true:

- The interface defines only a single method.
- Multicast capability is needed.
- The subscriber needs to implement the interface multiple times.

In the ITransformer example, we don't need to multicast. However, the interface defines only a single method. Furthermore, our subscriber may need to implement ITransformer multiple times, to support different transforms, such as square or cube. With interfaces, we're forced into writing a separate type per transform, since Test can implement ITransformer only once. This is quite cumbersome:

```
class Squarer : ITransformer
{
  public int Transform (int x) { return x * x; }
}

class Cuber : ITransformer
{
  public int Transform (int x) {return x * x * x; }
}
...

static void Main()
{
  int[] values = { 1, 2, 3 };
  Util.TransformAll (values, new Cuber());
  foreach (int i in values)
    Console.WriteLine (i);
}
```

Delegate Compatibility

Type compatibility

Delegate types are all incompatible with each other, even if their signatures are the same:

```
delegate void D1();
delegate void D2();
...

D1 d1 = Method1;
D2 d2 = d1;                    // Compile-time error
```

The following, however, is permitted:

```
D2 d2 = new D2 (d1);
```

Delegate instances are considered equal if they have the same method targets:

```
delegate void D();
...

D d1 = Method1;
D d2 = Method1;
Console.WriteLine (d1 == d2);        // True
```

Multicast delegates are considered equal if they reference the same methods *in the same order*.

Parameter compatibility

When you call a method, you can supply arguments that have more specific types than the parameters of that method. This is ordinary polymorphic behavior. For exactly the same reason, a delegate can have more specific parameter types than its method target. This is called *contravariance*.

Here's an example:

```
delegate void StringAction (string s);

class Test
{
  static void Main()
  {
    StringAction sa = new StringAction (ActOnObject);
    sa ("hello");
  }

  static void ActOnObject (object o)
  {
    Console.WriteLine (o);   // hello
  }
}
```

A delegate merely calls a method on someone else's behalf. In this case, the StringAction is invoked with an argument of type string. When the argument is then relayed to the target method, the argument gets implicitly upcast to an object.

The standard event pattern is designed to help you leverage contravariance through its use of the common EventArgs base class. For example, you can have a single method invoked by two different delegates, one passing a MouseEventArgs and the other passing a KeyEventArgs.

Return type compatibility

If you call a method, you may get back a type that is more specific than what you asked for. This is ordinary polymorphic behavior. For exactly the same reason, the return type of a delegate can be less specific than the return type of its target method. This is called *covariance*. For example:

```
delegate object ObjectRetriever();

class Test
{
  static void Main()
  {
    ObjectRetriever o = new ObjectRetriever (RetriveString);
    object result = o();
    Console.WriteLine (result);      // hello
  }
  static string RetriveString() { return "hello"; }
}
```

The ObjectRetriever expects to get back an object, but an object subclass will also do: delegate return types are *covariant*.

Generic delegate type parameter variance (C# 4.0)

In Chapter 3 we saw how generic interfaces support covariant and contravariant type parameters. The same capability exists for delegates, too.

If you're defining a generic delegate type, it's good practice to:

- Mark a type parameter used only on the return value as covariant (out).
- Mark any type parameters used only on parameters as contravariant (in).

Doing so allows conversions to work naturally by respecting inheritance relationships between types.

The following delegate (defined in the System namespace) supports covariance:

```
delegate TResult Func<out TResult>();
```

allowing:

```
Func<string> x = ...;
Func<object> y = x;
```

The following delegate (defined in the System namespace) supports contravariance:

```
delegate void Action<in T> (T arg);
```

allowing:

```
Action<object> x = ...;
Action<string> y = x;
```

Events

When using delegates, two emergent roles commonly appear: *broadcaster* and *subscriber*.

The *broadcaster* is a type that contains a delegate field. The broadcaster decides when to broadcast, by invoking the delegate.

The *subscribers* are the method target recipients. A subscriber decides when to start and stop listening, by calling += and -= on the broadcaster's delegate. A subscriber does not know about, or interfere with, other subscribers.

Events are a language feature that formalizes this pattern. An **event** is a construct that exposes just the subset of delegate features required for the broadcaster/ subscriber model. The main purpose of events is to *prevent subscribers from interfering with each other*.

The easiest way to declare an event is to put the **event** keyword in front of a delegate member:

```
public class Broadcaster
{
  public event ProgressReporter Progress;
}
```

Code within the `Broadcaster` type has full access to `Progress` and can treat it as a delegate. Code outside of `Broadcaster` can only perform += and -= operations on the `Progress` event.

How Do Events Work on the Inside?

Three things happen under the covers when you declare an event as follows:

```
public class Broadcaster
{
  public event EventHandler Progress;
}
```

First, the compiler translates the event declaration into something close to the following:

```
EventHandler _priceChanged;   // private delegate
public event EventHandler PriceChanged
{
  add    { _priceChanged += value; }
  remove { _priceChanged -= value; }
}
```

The **add** and **remove** keywords denote explicit *event accessors*—which act rather like property accessors. We'll describe how to write these later.

Second, the compiler looks *within* the `Broadcaster` class for references to `PriceChanged` that perform operations other than += or -=, and redirects them to the underlying `_priceChanged` delegate field.

Third, the compiler translates += and -= operations on the event to calls to the event's **add** and **remove** accessors. Interestingly, this makes the behavior of += and -= unique when applied to events: unlike in other scenarios, it's not simply a shortcut for + and - followed by an assignment.

Consider the following example. The Stock class fires its PriceChanged event every time the Price of the Stock changes:

```
public delegate void PriceChangedHandler (decimal oldPrice,
                                           decimal newPrice);

public class Stock
{
  string symbol;
  decimal price;

  public Stock (string symbol) { this.symbol = symbol; }

  public event PriceChangedHandler PriceChanged;

  public decimal Price
  {
    get { return price; }
    set
    {
      if (price == value) return;     // Exit if nothing has changed
      if (PriceChanged != null)       // If invocation list not empty,
        PriceChanged (price, value);  // fire event.
      price = value;
    }
  }
}
```

If we remove the **event** keyword from our example so that PriceChanged becomes an ordinary delegate field, our example would give the same results. However, Stock would be less robust, in that subscribers could do the following things to interfere with each other:

- Replace other subscribers by reassigning PriceChanged (instead of using the += operator).
- Clear all subscribers (by setting PriceChanged to null).
- Broadcast to other subscribers by invoking the delegate.

Standard Event Pattern

The .NET Framework defines a standard pattern for writing events. Its purpose is to provide consistency across both Framework and user code. At the core of the standard event pattern is System.EventArgs: a predefined Framework class with no members (other than the static Empty property). EventArgs is a base class for conveying information for an event. In our Stock example, we would subclass EventArgs to convey the old and new prices when a PriceChanged event is fired:

```
public class PriceChangedEventArgs : System.EventArgs
{
  public readonly decimal LastPrice;
  public readonly decimal NewPrice;


  public PriceChangedEventArgs (decimal lastPrice, decimal newPrice)
  {
    LastPrice = lastPrice;
    NewPrice = newPrice;
  }
}
```

For reusability, the `EventArgs` subclass is named according to the information it contains (rather than the event for which it will be used). It typically exposes data as properties or as read-only fields.

With an `EventArgs` subclass in place, the next step is to choose or define a delegate for the event. There are three rules:

- It must have a **void** return type.
- It must accept two arguments: the first of type `object`, and the second a subclass of `EventArgs`. The first argument indicates the event broadcaster, and the second argument contains the extra information to convey.
- Its name must end with *EventHandler*.

The Framework defines a generic delegate called `System.EventHandler<>` that satisfies these rules:

```
public delegate void EventHandler<TEventArgs>
  (object source, TEventArgs e) where TEventArgs : EventArgs;
```

Before generics existed in the language (prior to C# 2.0), we would have had to instead write a custom delegate as follows:

```
public delegate void PriceChangedHandler
  (object sender, PriceChangedEventArgs e);
```

For historical reasons, most events within the Framework use delegates defined in this way.

The next step is to define an event of the chosen delegate type. Here, we use the generic `EventHandler` delegate:

```
public class Stock
{
  ...
  public event EventHandler<PriceChangedEventArgs> PriceChanged;
}
```

Finally, the pattern requires that you write a protected virtual method that fires the event. The name must match the name of the event, prefixed with the word *On*, and then accept a single `EventArgs` argument:

```
public class Stock
{
  ...

  public event EventHandler<PriceChangedEventArgs> PriceChanged;

  protected virtual void OnPriceChanged (PriceChangedEventArgs e)
  {
    if (PriceChanged != null) PriceChanged (this, e);
  }
}
```

 In multithreaded scenarios (Chapter 21), you need to assign the delegate to a temporary variable before testing and invoking it in order to be thread-safe:

```
var temp = PriceChanged;
if (temp != null) temp (this, e);
```

This provides a central point from which subclasses can invoke or override the event (assuming the class is not sealed). Here's the complete example:

```
using System;

public class PriceChangedEventArgs : EventArgs
{
  public readonly decimal LastPrice;
  public readonly decimal NewPrice;

  public PriceChangedEventArgs (decimal lastPrice, decimal newPrice)
  {
    LastPrice = lastPrice; NewPrice = newPrice;
  }
}

public class Stock
{
  string symbol;
  decimal price;

  public Stock (string symbol) {this.symbol = symbol;}

  public event EventHandler<PriceChangedEventArgs> PriceChanged;

  protected virtual void OnPriceChanged (PriceChangedEventArgs e)
  {
    if (PriceChanged != null) PriceChanged (this, e);
  }

  public decimal Price
  {
    get { return price; }
    set
    {
```

```
      if (price == value) return;
      OnPriceChanged (new PriceChangedEventArgs (price, value));
      price = value;
    }
  }
}

class Test
{
  static void Main()
  {
    Stock stock = new Stock ("THPW");
    stock.Price = 27.10M;
    // Register with the PriceChanged event
    stock.PriceChanged += stock_PriceChanged;
    stock.Price = 31.59M;
  }

  static void stock_PriceChanged (object sender, PriceChangedEventArgs e)
  {
    if ((e.NewPrice - e.LastPrice) / e.LastPrice > 0.1M)
      Console.WriteLine ("Alert, 10% stock price increase!");
  }
}
```

The predefined nongeneric EventHandler delegate can be used when an event doesn't carry extra information. In this example, we rewrite Stock such that the Price Changed event is fired after the price changes, and no information about the event is necessary, other than it happened. We also make use of the EventArgs.Empty property, in order to avoid unnecessarily instantiating an instance of EventArgs.

```
public class Stock
{
  string symbol;
  decimal price;

  public Stock (string symbol) { this.symbol = symbol; }

  public event EventHandler PriceChanged;

  protected virtual void OnPriceChanged (EventArgs e)
  {
    if (PriceChanged != null) PriceChanged (this, e);
  }

  public decimal Price
  {
    get { return price; }
    set
    {
      if (price == value) return;
      price = value;
      OnPriceChanged (EventArgs.Empty);
    }
  }
}
```

Event Accessors

An event's *accessors* are the implementations of its += and -= functions. By default, accessors are implemented implicitly by the compiler. Consider this event declaration:

```
public event EventHandler PriceChanged;
```

The compiler converts this to the following:

- A private delegate field
- A public pair of event accessor functions, whose implementations forward the += and -= operations to the private delegate field

You can take over this process by defining *explicit* event accessors. Here's a manual implementation of the PriceChanged event from our previous example:

```
private EventHandler _priceChanged;        // Declare a private delegate

public event EventHandler PriceChanged
{
  add    { _priceChanged += value; }
  remove { _priceChanged -= value; }
}
```

This example is functionally identical to C#'s default accessor implementation (except that C# also ensures thread safety around updating the delegate—see Chapter 21). By defining event accessors ourselves, we instruct C# not to generate default field and accessor logic.

> Before C# 4.0, the compiler ensured thread safety by locking the containing type or instance around updating the delegate. This is a crude mechanism (as we'll see in "Thread Safety" on page 543 in Chapter 21), and it resulted in some people using explicit event accessors purely to work around this. The good news is that from C# 4.0, the compiler implements thread safety through a superior lock-free compare-and-swap algorithm.

With explicit event accessors, you can apply more complex strategies to the storage and access of the underlying delegate. There are three scenarios where this is useful:

- When the event accessors are merely relays for another class that is broadcasting the event.
- When the class exposes a large number of events, where most of the time very few subscribers exist, such as a Windows control. In such cases, it is better to store the subscriber's delegate instances in a dictionary, since a dictionary will contain less storage overhead than dozens of null delegate field references.
- When explicitly implementing an interface that declares an event.

Here is an example that illustrates the last point:

```
public interface IFoo { event EventHandler Ev; }

class Foo : IFoo
{
  private EventHandler ev;

  event EventHandler IFoo.Ev
  {
    add    { ev += value; }
    remove { ev -= value; }
  }
}
```

 The add and remove parts of an event are compiled to add_*XXX* and remove_*XXX* methods.

The += and -= operations on an event are compiled to calls to the add_*XXX* and remove_*XXX* methods.

Event Modifiers

Like methods, events can be virtual, overridden, abstract, or sealed. Events can also be static:

```
public class Foo
{
  public static event EventHandler<EventArgs> StaticEvent;
  public virtual event EventHandler<EventArgs> VirtualEvent;
}
```

Lambda Expressions

A lambda expression is an unnamed method written in place of a delegate instance. The compiler immediately converts the lambda expression to either:

- A delegate instance.
- An *expression tree*, of type Expression<TDelegate>, representing the code inside the lambda expression in a traversable object model. This allows the lambda expression to be interpreted later at runtime (see "Building Query Expressions" on page 361 in Chapter 8).

Given the following delegate type:

```
delegate int Transformer (int i);
```

we could assign and invoke the lambda expression x => x * x as follows:

```
Transformer sqr = x => x * x;
Console.WriteLine (sqr(3));    // 9
```

Internally, the compiler resolves lambda expressions of this type by writing a private method, and moving the expression's code into that method.

A lambda expression has the following form:

```
(parameters) => expression-or-statement-block
```

For convenience, you can omit the parentheses if and only if there is exactly one parameter of an inferable type.

In our example, there is a single parameter, x, and the expression is x * x:

```
x => x * x;
```

Each parameter of the lambda expression corresponds to a delegate parameter, and the type of the expression (which may be **void**) corresponds to the return type of the delegate.

In our example, x corresponds to parameter i, and the expression x * x corresponds to the return type **int**, therefore being compatible with the Transformer delegate:

```
delegate int Transformer (int i);
```

A lambda expression's code can be a *statement block* instead of an expression. We can rewrite our example as follows:

```
x => { return x * x; };
```

Lambda expressions are used most commonly with the Func and Action delegates, so you will most often see our earlier expression written as follows:

```
Func<int,int> sqr = x => x * x;
```

Here's an example of an expression that accepts two parameters:

```
Func<string,string,int> totalLength = (s1, s2) => s1.Length + s2.Length;
int total = totalLength ("hello", "world");   // total is 10;
```

Lambda expressions were introduced in C# 3.0.

Explicitly Specifying Lambda Parameter Types

The compiler can usually *infer* the type of lambda parameters contextually. When this is not the case, you must specify the type of each parameter explicitly. Consider the following expression:

```
Func<int,int> sqr = x => x * x;
```

The compiler uses *type inference* to infer that x is an **int**.

We could explicitly specify x's type as follows:

```
Func<int,int> sqr = (int x) => x * x;
```

Capturing Outer Variables

A lambda expression can reference the local variables and parameters of the method in which it's defined (*outer variables*). For example:

```
static void Main()
{
  int factor = 2;
  Func<int, int> multiplier = n => n * factor;
  Console.WriteLine (multiplier (3));        // 6
}
```

Outer variables referenced by a lambda expression are called *captured variables*. A lambda expression that captures variables is called a *closure*.

Captured variables are evaluated when the delegate is actually *invoked*, not when the variables were *captured*:

```
int factor = 2;
Func<int, int> multiplier = n => n * factor;
factor = 10;
Console.WriteLine (multiplier (3));        // 30
```

Lambda expressions can themselves update captured variables:

```
int seed = 0;
Func<int> natural = () => seed++;
Console.WriteLine (natural());        // 0
Console.WriteLine (natural());        // 1
Console.WriteLine (seed);             // 2
```

Captured variables have their lifetimes extended to that of the delegate. In the following example, the local variable seed would ordinarily disappear from scope when Natural finished executing. But because seed has been *captured*, its lifetime is extended to that of the capturing delegate, natural:

```
static Func<int> Natural()
{
  int seed = 0;
  return () => seed++;        // Returns a closure
}

static void Main()
{
  Func<int> natural = Natural();
  Console.WriteLine (natural());        // 0
  Console.WriteLine (natural());        // 1
}
```

A local variable *instantiated* within a lambda expression is unique per invocation of the delegate instance. If we refactor our previous example to instantiate seed *within* the lambda expression, we get a different (in this case, undesirable) result:

```
static Func<int> Natural()
{
  return() => { int seed = 0; return seed++; };
}
```

```
static void Main()
{
  Func<int> natural = Natural();
  Console.WriteLine (natural());        // 0
  Console.WriteLine (natural());        // 0
}
```

 Capturing is internally implemented by "hoisting" the captured variables into fields of a private class. When the method is called, the class is instantiated and lifetime-bound to the delegate instance.

Capturing iteration variables

When you capture iteration variables in for and foreach statements, C# treats those iteration variables as though they were declared *outside* the loop. This means that the *same* variable is captured in each iteration. The following program writes 333 instead of writing 012:

```
Action[] actions = new Action[3];

for (int i = 0; i < 3; i++)
  actions [i] = () => Console.Write (i);

foreach (Action a in actions) a();       // 333
```

Each closure (shown in boldface) captures the same variable, i. When the delegates are later invoked, each delegate sees i's value at the time of *invocation*—which is 3. We can illustrate this better by expanding the for loop as follows:

```
Action[] actions = new Action[3];
int i = 0;
actions[0] = () => Console.Write (i);
i = 1;
actions[1] = () => Console.Write (i);
i = 2;
actions[2] = () => Console.Write (i);
i = 3;
foreach (Action a in actions) a();       // 333
```

The solution, if we want to write 012, is to assign the iteration variable to a local variable that's scoped *inside* the loop:

```
Action[] actions = new Action[3];
for (int i = 0; i < 3; i++)
{
  int loopScopedi = i;
  actions [i] = () => Console.Write (loopScopedi);
}
foreach (Action a in actions) a();       // 012
```

This then causes the closure to capture a *different* variable on each iteration.

Anonymous Methods

Anonymous methods are a C# 2.0 feature that has been subsumed largely by C# 3.0 lambda expressions. An anonymous method is like a lambda expression, but it lacks the following features:

- Implicitly typed parameters
- Expression syntax (an anonymous method must always be a statement block)
- The ability to compile to an expression tree, by assigning to `Expression<T>`

To write an anonymous method, you include the `delegate` keyword followed (optionally) by a parameter declaration and then a method body. For example, given this delegate:

```
delegate int Transformer (int i);
```

we could write and call an anonymous method as follows:

```
Transformer sqr = delegate (int x) {return x * x;};
Console.WriteLine (sqr(3));                              // 9
```

The first line is semantically equivalent to the following lambda expression:

```
Transformer sqr =      (int x) => {return x * x;};
```

Or simply:

```
Transformer sqr =        x => x * x;
```

A unique feature of anonymous methods is that you can omit the parameter declaration entirely—even if the delegate expects them. This can be useful in declaring events with a default empty handler:

```
public event EventHandler Clicked = delegate { };
```

This avoids the need for a null check before firing the event. The following is also legal:

```
Clicked += delegate { Console.WriteLine ("clicked"); };  // No parameters
```

Anonymous methods capture outer variables in the same way lambda expressions do.

try Statements and Exceptions

A `try` statement specifies a code block subject to error-handling or cleanup code. The `try` *block* must be followed by a `catch` *block*, a `finally` *block*, or both. The `catch` block executes when an error occurs in the `try` block. The `finally` block executes after execution leaves the `try` block (or if present, the `catch` block), to perform cleanup code, whether or not an error occurred.

A `catch` block has access to an `Exception` object that contains information about the error. You use a `catch` block to either compensate for the error or *rethrow* the exception. You rethrow an exception if you merely want to log the problem, or if you want to rethrow a new, higher-level exception type.

A `finally` block adds determinism to your program, by always executing no matter what. It's useful for cleanup tasks such as closing network connections.

A `try` statement looks like this:

```
try
{
  ... // exception may get thrown within execution of this block
}
catch (ExceptionA ex)
{
  ... // handle exception of type ExceptionA
}
catch (ExceptionB ex)
{
  ... // handle exception of type ExceptionB
}
finally
{
  ... // cleanup code
}
```

Consider the following program:

```
class Test
{
  static int Calc (int x) { return 10 / x; }

  static void Main()
  {
    int y = Calc (0);
    Console.WriteLine (y);
  }
}
```

Because `x` is zero, the runtime throws a `DivideByZeroException`, and our program terminates. We can prevent this by catching the exception as follows:

```
class Test
{
  static int Calc (int x) { return 10 / x; }

  static void Main()
  {
    try
    {
      int y = Calc (0);
      Console.WriteLine (y);
    }
    catch (DivideByZeroException ex)
    {
      Console.WriteLine ("x cannot be zero");
    }
    Console.WriteLine ("program completed");
  }
}
```

```
OUTPUT:
x cannot be zero
program completed
```

 This is a simple example to illustrate exception handling. We could deal with this particular scenario better in practice by checking explicitly for the divisor being zero before calling Calc.

Exceptions are relatively expensive to handle, taking hundreds of clock cycles.

When an exception is thrown, the CLR performs a test:

Is execution currently within a try *statement that can catch the exception?*

- If so, execution is passed to the compatible catch block. If the catch block successfully finishes executing, execution moves to the next statement after the try statement (if present, executing the finally block first).
- If not, execution jumps back to the caller of the function, and the test is repeated (after executing any finally blocks that wrap the statement).

If no function takes responsibility for the exception, an error dialog is displayed to the user, and the program terminates.

The catch Clause

A catch clause specifies what type of exception to catch. This must either be System.Exception or a subclass of System.Exception.

Catching System.Exception catches all possible errors. This is useful when:

- Your program can potentially recover regardless of the specific exception type.
- You plan to rethrow the exception (perhaps after logging it).
- Your error handler is the last resort, prior to termination of the program.

More typically, though, you catch *specific exception types*, in order to avoid having to deal with circumstances for which your handler wasn't designed (e.g., an OutOfMemoryException).

You can handle multiple exception types with multiple catch clauses (again, this example could be written with explicit argument checking rather than exception handling):

```
class Test
{
  static void Main (string[] args)
  {
    try
    {
      byte b = byte.Parse (args[0]);
      Console.WriteLine (b);
    }
```

```
      catch (IndexOutOfRangeException ex)
      {
        Console.WriteLine ("Please provide at least one argument");
      }
      catch (FormatException ex)
      {
        Console.WriteLine ("That's not a number!");
      }
      catch (OverflowException ex)
      {
        Console.WriteLine ("You've given me more than a byte!");
      }
    }
  }
```

Only one catch clause executes for a given exception. If you want to include a safety net to catch more general exceptions (such as System.Exception), you must put the more specific handlers *first*.

An exception can be caught without specifying a variable if you don't need to access its properties:

```
    catch (StackOverflowException)   // no variable
    {
      ...
    }
```

Furthermore, you can omit both the variable and the type (meaning that all exceptions will be caught):

```
    catch { ... }
```

 In languages other than C#, it is possible (though not recommended) to throw an object that does not derive from Exception. The CLR automatically wraps that object in a RuntimeWrappedException class (which does derive from Exception).

The finally Block

A finally block always executes—whether or not an exception is thrown and whether or not the try block runs to completion. finally blocks are typically used for cleanup code.

A finally block executes either:

- After a catch block finishes
- After control leaves the try block because of a jump statement (e.g., return or goto)
- After the try block ends

A finally block helps add determinism to a program. In the following example, the file that we open *always* gets closed, regardless of whether:

- The try block finishes normally.
- Execution returns early because the file is empty (EndOfStream).
- An IOException is thrown while reading the file.

```
static void ReadFile()
{
  StreamReader reader = null;    // In System.IO namespace
  try
  {
    reader = File.OpenText ("file.txt");
    if (reader.EndOfStream) return;
    Console.WriteLine (reader.ReadToEnd());
  }
  finally
  {
    if (reader != null) reader.Dispose();
  }
}
```

In this example, we closed the file by calling Dispose on the StreamReader. Calling Dispose on an object, within a finally block, is a standard convention throughout the .NET Framework and is supported explicitly in C# through the using statement.

The using statement

Many classes encapsulate unmanaged resources, such as file handles, graphics handles, or database connections. These classes implement System.IDisposable, which defines a single parameterless method named Dispose to clean up these resources. The using statement provides an elegant syntax for calling Dispose on an IDisposable object within a finally block.

The following:

```
using (StreamReader reader = File.OpenText ("file.txt"))
{
  ...
}
```

is precisely equivalent to:

```
StreamReader reader = File.OpenText ("file.txt");
try
{
  ...
}
finally
{
  if (reader != null)
    ((IDisposable)reader).Dispose();
}
```

We cover the disposal pattern in more detail in Chapter 12.

Throwing Exceptions

Exceptions can be thrown either by the runtime or in user code. In this example, Display throws a System.ArgumentNullException:

```
class Test
{
  static void Display (string name)
  {
    if (name == null)
      throw new ArgumentNullException ("name");

    Console.WriteLine (name);
  }

  static void Main()
  {
    try { Display (null); }
    catch (ArgumentNullException ex)
    {
      Console.WriteLine ("Caught the exception");
    }
  }
}
```

Rethrowing an exception

You can capture and rethrow an exception as follows:

```
try { ... }
catch (Exception ex)
{
  // Log error
  ...
  throw;          // Rethrow same exception
}
```

Rethrowing in this manner lets you log an error without *swallowing* it. It also lets you back out of handling an exception should circumstances turn out to be outside what you expected:

```
using System.Net;        // (See Chapter 14)
...

string s = null;
using (WebClient wc = new WebClient())
  try { s = wc.DownloadString ("http://www.albahari.com/nutshell/"); }
  catch (WebException ex)
  {
    if (ex.Status == WebExceptionStatus.NameResolutionFailure)
      Console.WriteLine ("Bad domain name");
    else
      throw;        // Can't handle other sorts of WebException, so rethrow
  }
```

The other common scenario is to rethrow a more specific exception type. For example:

```
try
{
    ... // Parse a DateTime from XML element data
}
catch (FormatException ex)
{
    throw new XmlException ("Invalid DateTime", ex);
}
```

Rethrowing an exception does not affect the `StackTrace` property of the exception (see the next section). When rethrowing a different exception, you can set the `InnerException` property with the original exception if doing so could aid debugging. Nearly all types of exceptions provide a constructor for this purpose.

Key Properties of System.Exception

The most important properties of `System.Exception` are the following:

`StackTrace`
A string representing all the methods that are called from the origin of the exception to the `catch` block.

`Message`
A string with a description of the error.

`InnerException`
The inner exception (if any) that caused the outer exception. This, itself, may have another `InnerException`.

All exceptions in C# are runtime exceptions—there is no equivalent to Java's compile-time checked exceptions.

Common Exception Types

The following exception types are used widely throughout the CLR and .NET Framework. You can throw these yourself or use them as base classes for deriving custom exception types:

`System.ArgumentException`
Thrown when a function is called with a bogus argument. This generally indicates a program bug.

`System.ArgumentNullException`
Subclass of `ArgumentException` that's thrown when a function argument is (unexpectedly) null.

`System.ArgumentOutOfRangeException`
Subclass of `ArgumentException` that's thrown when a (usually numeric) argument is too big or too small. For example, this is thrown when passing a negative number into a function that accepts only positive values.

`System.InvalidOperationException`
Thrown when the state of an object is unsuitable for a method to successfully execute, regardless of any particular argument values. Examples include reading an unopened file or getting the next element from an enumerator where the underlying list has been modified partway through the iteration.

`System.NotSupportedException`
Thrown to indicate that a particular functionality is not supported. A good example is calling the `Add` method on a collection for which `IsReadOnly` returns true.

`System.NotImplementedException`
Thrown to indicate that a function has not yet been implemented.

`System.ObjectDisposedException`
Thrown when the object upon which the function is called has been disposed.

Common Patterns

The TryXXX method pattern

When writing a method, you have a choice, when something goes wrong, to return some kind of failure code or throw an exception. In general, you throw an exception when the error is outside the normal workflow—or if you expect that the immediate caller won't be able to cope with it. Occasionally, though, it can be best to offer both choices to the consumer. An example of this is the `int` type, which defines two versions of its `Parse` method:

```
public int Parse    (string input);
public bool TryParse (string input, out int returnValue);
```

If parsing fails, `Parse` throws an exception; `TryParse` returns `false`.

You can implement this pattern by having the *XXX* method call the Try*XXX* method as follows:

```
public return-type XXX (input-type input)
{
  return-type returnValue;
  if (!TryXXX (input, out returnValue))
    throw new YYYException (...)
  return returnValue;
}
```

The atomicity pattern

It can be desirable for an operation to be *atomic*, where it either successfully completes or fails without affecting state. An object becomes unusable when it enters an indeterminate state that is the result of a half-finished operation. `finally` blocks facilitate writing atomic operations.

In the following example, we use an `Accumulator` class that has an `Add` method that adds an array of integers to its field `Total`. The `Add` method will cause an `OverflowException` if `Total` exceeds the maximum value for an `int`. The `Add` method is atomic, either successfully updating `Total` or failing, which leaves `Total` with its former value:

```
class Test
{
  static void Main()
  {
    Accumulator a = new Accumulator();
    try
    {
      a.Add (4, 5);            // a.Total is now 9
      a.Add (1, int.MaxValue);  // Will cause OverflowException
    }
    catch (OverflowException)
    {
      Console.WriteLine (a.Total);  // a.Total is still 9
    }
  }
}
```

In the implementation of `Accumulator`, the `Add` method affects the `Total` field as it executes. However, if *anything goes wrong* during the method (e.g., a numeric overflow, a stack overflow, etc.), `Total` is restored to its initial value at the start of the method.

```
public class Accumulator
{
  public int Total { get; private set; }

  public void Add (params int[] ints)
  {
    bool success = false;
    int totalSnapshot = Total;
    try
    {
      foreach (int i in ints)
      {
        checked { Total += i; }
      }
      success = true;
    }
    finally
    {
      if (! success)
        Total = totalSnapshot;
    }
  }
}
```

Alternatives to exceptions

As with `int.TryParse`, a function can communicate failure by sending an error code back to the calling function via a return type or parameter. Although this can work with simple and predictable failures, it becomes clumsy when extended to all errors, polluting method signatures and creating unnecessary complexity and clutter. It also cannot generalize to functions that are not methods, such as operators (e.g., the division operator) or properties. An alternative is to place the error in a common place where all functions in the call stack can see it (e.g., a static method that stores the current error per thread). This, though, requires each function to participate in an error-propagation pattern that is cumbersome and, ironically, itself error-prone.

Enumeration and Iterators

Enumeration

An *enumerator* is a read-only, forward-only cursor over a *sequence of values*. An enumerator is an object that implements either of the following interfaces:

- `System.Collections.IEnumerator`
- `System.Collections.Generic.IEnumerator<T>`

> Technically, any object that has a method named `MoveNext` and a property called `Current` is treated as an enumerator; this relaxation exists to allow enumeration of value type elements in C# 1.0 without a boxing/unboxing overhead. This optimization is now obsolete with generics, and is, in fact, unsupported with C# 4.0's `dynamic` binding.

The `foreach` statement iterates over an *enumerable* object. An enumerable object is the logical representation of a sequence. It is not itself a cursor, but an object that produces cursors over itself. An enumerable object either:

- Implements `IEnumerable` or `IEnumerable<T>`
- Has a method named `GetEnumerator` that returns an *enumerator*

> `IEnumerator` and `IEnumerable` are defined in `System.Collec`tions. `IEnumerator<T>` and `IEnumerable<T>` are defined in `System.Collections.Generic`.

The enumeration pattern is as follows:

```
class Enumerator   // Typically implements IEnumerator or IEnumerator<T>
{
  public IteratorVariableType Current { get {...} }
  public bool MoveNext() {...}
}
```

```
class Enumerable      // Typically implements IEnumerable or IEnumerable<T>
{
    public Enumerator GetEnumerator() {...}
}
```

Here is the high-level way of iterating through the characters in the word *beer* using a foreach statement:

```
foreach (char c in "beer")
    Console.WriteLine (c);
```

Here is the low-level way of iterating through the characters in *beer* without using a foreach statement:

```
using (var enumerator = "beer".GetEnumerator())
    while (enumerator.MoveNext())
    {
        var element = enumerator.Current;
        Console.WriteLine (element);
    }
```

If the enumerator implements IDisposable, the foreach statement also acts as a using statement, implicitly disposing the enumerator object as in the earlier example.

 Chapter 7 explains the enumeration interfaces in further detail.

Collection Initializers

You can instantiate and populate an enumerable object in a single step. For example:

```
using System.Collections.Generic;
...

List<int> list = new List<int> {1, 2, 3};
```

The compiler translates this to the following:

```
using System.Collections.Generic;
...

List<int> list = new List<int>();
list.Add (1);
list.Add (2);
list.Add (3);
```

This requires that the enumerable object implements the System.Collections.IEnumerable interface, and that it has an Add method that has the appropriate number of parameters for the call.

Iterators

Whereas a foreach statement is a *consumer* of an enumerator, an iterator is a *producer* of an enumerator. In this example, we use an iterator to return a sequence of Fibonacci numbers (where each number is the sum of the previous two):

```
using System;
using System.Collections.Generic;

class Test
{
  static void Main()
  {
    foreach (int fib in Fibs(6))
      Console.Write (fib + "  ");
  }

  static IEnumerable<int> Fibs (int fibCount)
  {
    for (int i = 0, prevFib = 1, curFib = 1; i < fibCount; i++)
    {
      yield return prevFib;
      int newFib = prevFib+curFib;
      prevFib = curFib;
      curFib = newFib;
    }
  }
}
```

OUTPUT: 1 1 2 3 5 8

Whereas a return statement expresses "Here's the value you asked me to return from this method," a yield return statement expresses "Here's the next element you asked me to yield from this enumerator." On each yield statement, control is returned to the caller, but the callee's state is maintained so that the method can continue executing as soon as the caller enumerates the next element. The lifetime of this state is bound to the enumerator, such that the state can be released when the caller has finished enumerating.

> The compiler converts iterator methods into private classes that implement IEnumerable<T> and/or IEnumerator<T>. The logic within the iterator block is "inverted" and spliced into the MoveNext method and Current property on the compiler-written enumerator class. This means that when you call an iterator method, all you're doing is instantiating the compiler-written class; none of your code actually runs! Your code runs only when you start enumerating over the resultant sequence, typically with a foreach statement.

Iterator Semantics

An iterator is a method, property, or indexer that contains one or more `yield` statements. An iterator must return one of the following four interfaces (otherwise, the compiler will generate an error):

```
// Enumerable interfaces
System.Collections.IEnumerable
System.Collections.Generic.IEnumerable<T>

// Enumerator interfaces
System.Collections.IEnumerator
System.Collections.Generic.IEnumerator<T>
```

An iterator has different semantics, depending on whether it returns an *enumerable* interface or an *enumerator* interface. We describe this in Chapter 7.

Multiple yield statements are permitted. For example:

```
class Test
{
  static void Main()
  {
    foreach (string s in Foo())
      Console.WriteLine(s);          // Prints "One","Two","Three"
  }

  static IEnumerable<string> Foo()
  {
    yield return "One";
    yield return "Two";
    yield return "Three";
  }
}
```

yield break

The `yield break` statement indicates that the iterator block should exit early, without returning more elements. We can modify `Foo` as follows to demonstrate:

```
static IEnumerable<string> Foo (bool breakEarly)
{
  yield return "One";
  yield return "Two";

  if (breakEarly)
    yield break;

  yield return "Three";
}
```

 A return statement is illegal in an iterator block—you must use a `yield break` instead.

Iterators and try/catch/finally blocks

A `yield return` statement cannot appear in a `try` block that has a `catch` clause:

```
IEnumerable<string> Foo()
{
  try { yield return "One"; }    // Illegal
  catch { ... }
}
```

Nor can `yield return` appear in a `catch` or `finally` block. These restrictions are due to the fact that the compiler must translate iterators into ordinary classes with `MoveNext`, `Current`, and `Dispose` members, and translating exception handling blocks would create excessive complexity.

You can, however, yield within a `try` block that has (only) a `finally` block:

```
IEnumerable<string> Foo()
{
  try { yield return "One"; }    // OK
  finally { ... }
}
```

The code in the `finally` block executes when the consuming enumerator reaches the end of the sequence or is disposed. A `foreach` statement implicitly disposes the enumerator if you break early, making this a safe way to consume enumerators. When working with enumerators explicitly, a trap is to abandon enumeration early without disposing it, circumventing the `finally` block. You can avoid this risk by wrapping explicit use of enumerators in a `using` statement:

```
string firstElement = null;
var sequence = Foo();
using (var enumerator = sequence.GetEnumerator())
  if (enumerator.MoveNext())
    firstElement = enumerator.Current;
```

Composing Sequences

Iterators are highly composable. We can extend our example, this time to output even Fibonacci numbers only:

```
using System;
using System.Collections.Generic;

class Test
{
  static void Main()
  {
    foreach (int fib in EvenNumbersOnly (Fibs(6)))
      Console.WriteLine (fib);
  }

  static IEnumerable<int> Fibs (int fibCount)
  {
    for (int i = 0, prevFib = 1, curFib = 1; i < fibCount; i++)
    {
```

```
    yield return prevFib;
    int newFib = prevFib+curFib;
    prevFib = curFib;
    curFib = newFib;
  }
}

static IEnumerable<int> EvenNumbersOnly (IEnumerable<int> sequence)
{
  foreach (int x in sequence)
    if ((x % 2) == 0)
      yield return x;
}
}
```

Each element is not calculated until the last moment—when requested by a
MoveNext() operation. Figure 4-1 shows the data requests and data output over time.

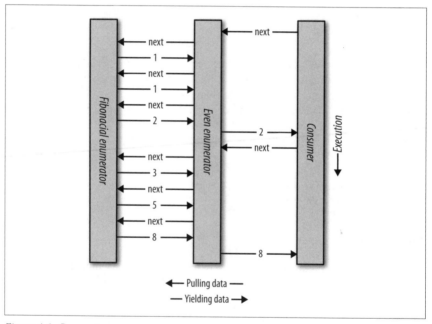

Figure 4-1. Composing sequences

The composability of the iterator pattern is extremely useful in LINQ; we will discuss
the subject again in Chapter 8.

Nullable Types

Reference types can represent a nonexistent value with a null reference. Value types,
however, cannot ordinarily represent null values. For example:

```
string s = null;      // OK, Reference Type
int i = null;         // Compile Error, Value Type cannot be null
```

To represent null in a value type, you must use a special construct called a *nullable type*. A nullable type is denoted with a value type followed by the ? symbol:

```
int? i = null;                      // OK, Nullable Type
Console.WriteLine (i == null);      // True
```

Nullable<T> Struct

T? translates into System.Nullable<T>. Nullable<T> is a lightweight immutable structure, having only two fields, to represent Value and HasValue. The essence of System.Nullable<T> is very simple:

```
public struct Nullable<T> where T : struct
{
  public T Value {get;}
  public bool HasValue {get;}
  public T GetValueOrDefault();
  public T GetValueOrDefault (T defaultValue);
  ...
}
```

The code:

```
int? i = null;
Console.WriteLine (i == null);               // True
```

translates to:

```
Nullable<int> i = new Nullable<int>();
Console.WriteLine (! i.HasValue);            // True
```

Attempting to retrieve Value when HasValue is false throws an InvalidOperationException. GetValueOrDefault() returns Value if HasValue is true; otherwise, it returns new T() or a specified custom default value.

The default value of T? is null.

Implicit and Explicit Nullable Conversions

The conversion from T to T? is implicit, and from T? to T is explicit. For example:

```
int? x = 5;         // implicit
int y = (int)x;     // explicit
```

The explicit cast is directly equivalent to calling the nullable object's Value property. Hence, an InvalidOperationException is thrown if HasValue is false.

Boxing and Unboxing Nullable Values

When T? is boxed, the boxed value on the heap contains T, not T?. This optimization is possible because a boxed value is a reference type that can already express null.

C# also permits the unboxing of nullable types with the as operator. The result will be null if the cast fails:

```
object o = "string";
int? x = o as int?;
Console.WriteLine (x.HasValue);    // False
```

Operator Lifting

The `Nullable<T>` struct does not define operators such as `<`, `>`, or even `==`. Despite this, the following code compiles and executes correctly:

```
int? x = 5;
int? y = 10;
bool b = x < y;        // true
```

This works because the compiler steals or "lifts" the less-than operator from the underlying value type. Semantically, it translates the preceding comparison expression into this:

```
bool b = (x.HasValue && y.HasValue) ? (x.Value < y.Value) : false;
```

In other words, if both x and y have values, it compares via int's less-than operator; otherwise, it returns `false`.

Operator lifting means you can implicitly use T's operators on T?. You can define operators for T? in order to provide special-purpose null behavior, but in the vast majority of cases, it's best to rely on the compiler automatically applying systematic nullable logic for you. Here are some examples:

```
int? x = 5;
int? y = null;

// Equality operator examples
Console.WriteLine (x == y);    // False
Console.WriteLine (x == null); // False
Console.WriteLine (x == 5);    // True
Console.WriteLine (y == null); // True
Console.WriteLine (y == 5);    // False
Console.WriteLine (y != 5);    // True

// Relational operator examples
Console.WriteLine (x < 6);     // True
Console.WriteLine (y < 6);     // False
Console.WriteLine (y > 6);     // False

// All other operator examples
Console.WriteLine (x + 5);     // 10
Console.WriteLine (x + y);     // null (prints empty line)
```

The compiler performs null logic differently depending on the category of operator. The following sections explain these different rules.

Equality operators (== !=)

Lifted equality operators handle nulls just like reference types do. This means two null values are equal:

```
Console.WriteLine (      null ==        null);  // True
Console.WriteLine ((bool?)null == (bool?)null); // True
```

Further:

- If exactly one operand is null, the operands are unequal.
- If both operands are non-null, their Values are compared.

Relational operators (< <= >= >)

The relational operators work on the principle that it is meaningless to compare null operands. This means comparing a null value to either a null or a non-null value returns false.

```
bool b = x < y;    // Translation:
bool b = (x == null || y == null) ? false : (x.Value < y.Value);

// b is false (assuming x is 5 and y is null)
```

All other operators (+ − * / % & | ^ << >> + ++ -- ! ~)

These operators return null when any of the operands are null. This pattern should be familiar to SQL users.

```
int? c = x + y;    // Translation:

int? c = (x == null || y == null)
            ? null
            : (int?) (x.Value + y.Value);

// c is null (assuming x is 5 and y is null)
```

An exception is when the & and | operators are applied to bool?, which we will discuss shortly.

Mixing nullable and non-nullable operators

You can mix and match nullable and non-nullable types (this works because there is an implicit conversion from T to T?):

```
int? a = null;
int b = 2;
int? c = a + b;    // c is null - equivalent to a + (int?)b
```

bool? with & and | Operators

When supplied operands of type bool?, the & and | operators treat null as an *unknown value*. So, null | true is true, because:

- If the unknown value is false, the result would be true.
- If the unknown value is true, the result would be true.

Similarly, null & false is false. This behavior would be familiar to SQL users. The following example enumerates other combinations:

```
bool? n = null;
bool? f = false;
bool? t = true;
Console.WriteLine (n | n);    // (null)
```

```
Console.WriteLine (n | f);   // (null)
Console.WriteLine (n | t);   // True
Console.WriteLine (n & n);   // (null)
Console.WriteLine (n & f);   // False
Console.WriteLine (n & t);   // (null)
```

Null Coalescing Operator

The ?? operator is the null coalescing operator, and it can be used with both nullable
types and reference types. It says, "If the operand is non-null, give it to me; otherwise,
give me a default value." For example:

```
int? x = null;
int y = x ?? 5;        // y is 5

int? a = null, b = 1, c = 2;
Console.WriteLine (a ?? b ?? c);  // 1 (first non-null value)
```

The ?? operator is equivalent to calling GetValueOrDefault with an explicit default
value, except that the expression passed to GetValueOrDefault is never evaluated if
the variable is not null.

Scenarios for Nullable Types

One of the most common scenarios for nullable types is to represent unknown values. This frequently occurs in database programming, where a class is mapped to a
table with nullable columns. If these columns are strings (e.g., an EmailAddress
column on a Customer table), there is no problem, as string is a reference type in
the CLR, which can be null. However, most other SQL column types map to CLR
struct types, making nullable types very useful when mapping SQL to the CLR. For
example:

```
// Maps to a Customer table in a database
public class Customer
{
  ...
  public decimal? AccountBalance;
}
```

A nullable type can also be used to represent the backing field of what's sometimes
called an *ambient property*. An ambient property, if null, returns the value of its
parent. For example:

```
public class Row
{
  ...
  Grid parent;
  Color? color;

  public Color Color
  {
    get { return color ?? parent.Color; }
    set { color = Color == parent.Color ? (Color?)null : value; }
  }
}
```

Alternatives to Nullable Types

Before nullable types were part of the C# language (i.e., before C# 2.0), there were many strategies to deal with nullable value types, examples of which still appear in the .NET Framework for historical reasons. One of these strategies is to designate a particular non-null value as the "null value"; an example is in the string and array classes. `String.IndexOf` returns the magic value of -1 when the character is not found:

```
int i = "Pink".IndexOf ('b');
Console.WriteLine (s);        // -1
```

However, `Array.IndexOf` returns -1 only if the index is 0-bounded. The more general formula is that `IndexOf` returns 1 less than the lower bound of the array. In the next example, `IndexOf` returns 0 when an element is not found:

```
// Create an array whose lower bound is 1 instead of 0:

Array a = Array.CreateInstance (typeof (string),
                        new int[] {2}, new int[] {1});
a.SetValue ("a", 1);
a.SetValue ("b", 2);
Console.WriteLine (Array.IndexOf (a, "c"));  // 0
```

Nominating a "magic value" is problematic for several reasons:

- It means that each value type has a different representation of null. In contrast, nullable types provide one common pattern that works for all value types.

- There may be no reasonable designated value. In the previous example, -1 could not always be used. The same is true for our earlier examples representing an unknown account balance and an unknown temperature.

- Forgetting to test for the magic value results in an incorrect value that may go unnoticed until later in execution—when it pulls an unintended magic trick. Forgetting to test `HasValue` on a null value, however, throws an `InvalidOpera` `tionException` on the spot.

- The ability for a value to be null is not captured in the *type*. Types communicate the intention of a program, allow the compiler to check for correctness, and enable a consistent set of rules enforced by the compiler.

Operator Overloading

Operators can be overloaded to provide more natural syntax for custom types. Operator overloading is most appropriately used for implementing custom structs that represent fairly primitive data types. For example, a custom numeric type is an excellent candidate for operator overloading.

The following symbolic operators can be overloaded:

+ (unary)	– (unary)	!	~	++
--	+	-	*	/
%	&	|	^	<<

```
>>        ==       !=   >   <
>=        <=
```

The following operators are also overloadable:

- Implicit and explicit conversions (with the `implicit` and `explicit` keywords)
- The literals `true` and `false`

The following operators are indirectly overloaded:

- The compound assignment operators (e.g., `+=`, `/=`) are implicitly overridden by overriding the noncompound operators (e.g., `+`, `/`).
- The conditional operators `&&` and `||` are implicitly overridden by overriding the bitwise operators `&` and `|`.

Operator Functions

An operator is overloaded by declaring an *operator function*. An operator function has the following rules:

- The name of the function is specified with the `operator` keyword followed by an operator symbol.
- The operator function must be marked `static`.
- The parameters of the operator function represent the operands.
- The return type of an operator function represents the result of an expression.
- At least one of the operands must be the type in which the operator function is declared.

In the following example, we define a struct called `Note` representing a musical note, and then overload the + operator:

```
public struct Note
{
  int value;
  public Note (int semitonesFromA) { value = semitonesFromA; }
  public static Note operator + (Note x, int semitones)
  {
    return new Note (x.value + semitones);
  }
}
```

This overload allows us to add an `int` to a `Note`:

```
Note B = new Note (2);
Note CSharp = B + 2;
```

Overloading an assignment operator automatically supports the corresponding compound assignment operator. In our example, since we overrode +, we can use += too:

```
CSharp += 2;
```

Overloading Equality and Comparison Operators

Equality and comparison operators are sometimes overridden when writing structs, and in rare cases when writing classes. Special rules and obligations come with overloading the equality and comparison operators, which we explain in Chapter 6. A summary of these rules is as follows:

Pairing
The C# compiler enforces operators that are logical pairs to both be defined. These operators are (== !=), (< >), and (<= >=).

Equals *and* GetHashCode
In most cases, if you overload (==) and (!=), you will usually need to override the Equals and GetHashCode methods defined on object in order to get meaningful behavior. The C# compiler will give a warning if you do not do this. (See "Equality Comparison" on page 245 in Chapter 6 for more details.)

IComparable *and* IComparable<T>
If you overload (< >) and (<= >=), you should implement IComparable and IComparable<T>.

Custom Implicit and Explicit Conversions

Implicit and explicit conversions are overloadable operators. These conversions are typically overloaded to make converting between strongly related types (such as numeric types) concise and natural.

To convert between weakly related types, the following strategies are more suitable:

- Write a constructor that has a parameter of the type to convert from.
- Write To*XXX* and (static) From*XXX* methods to convert between types.

As explained in the discussion on types, the rationale behind implicit conversions is that they are guaranteed to succeed and do not lose information during the conversion. Conversely, an explicit conversion should be required either when runtime circumstances will determine whether the conversion will succeed or if information may be lost during the conversion.

In this example, we define conversions between our musical Note type and a double (which represents the frequency in hertz of that note):

```
...
// Convert to hertz
public static implicit operator double (Note x)
{
  return 440 * Math.Pow (2, (double) x.value / 12 );
}

// Convert from hertz (accurate to the nearest semitone)
public static explicit operator Note (double x)
{
  return new Note ((int) (0.5 + 12 * (Math.Log (x/440) / Math.Log(2) ) ));
}
...
```

```
Note n = (Note)554.37;   // explicit conversion
double x = n;            // implicit conversion
```

Following our own guidelines, this example might be better implemented with a ToFrequency method (and a static FromFrequency method) instead of implicit and explicit operators.

Custom conversions are ignored by the as and is operators:

```
Console.WriteLine (554.37 is Note);   // False
Note n = 554.37 as Note;              // Error
```

Overloading true and false

The true and false operators are overloaded in the extremely rare case of types that are boolean "in spirit," but do not have a conversion to bool. An example is a type that implements three-state logic: by overloading true and false, such a type can work seamlessly with conditional statements and operators—namely, if, do, while, for, &&, ||, and ?:. The System.Data.SqlTypes.SqlBoolean struct provides this functionality. For example:

```
SqlBoolean a = SqlBoolean.Null;
if (a)
  Console.WriteLine ("True");
else if (!a)
  Console.WriteLine ("False");
else
  Console.WriteLine ("Null");

OUTPUT:
Null
```

The following code is a reimplementation of the parts of SqlBoolean necessary to demonstrate the true and false operators:

```
public struct SqlBoolean
{
  public static bool operator true (SqlBoolean x)
  {
    return x.m_value == True.m_value;
  }

  public static bool operator false (SqlBoolean x)
  {
    return x.m_value == False.m_value;
  }


  public static SqlBoolean operator ! (SqlBoolean x)
  {
    if (x.m_value == Null.m_value)  return Null;
```

```
    if (x.m_value == False.m_value) return True;
    return False;
}

public static readonly SqlBoolean Null  = new SqlBoolean(0);
public static readonly SqlBoolean False = new SqlBoolean(1);
public static readonly SqlBoolean True  = new SqlBoolean(2);

private SqlBoolean (byte value) { m_value = value; }
private byte m_value;
}
```

Extension Methods

Extension methods allow an existing type to be extended with new methods without altering the definition of the original type. An extension method is a static method of a static class, where the this modifier is applied to the first parameter. The type of the first parameter will be the type that is extended. For example:

```
public static class StringHelper
{
  public static bool IsCapitalized (this string s)
  {
    if (string.IsNullOrEmpty(s)) return false;
    return char.IsUpper (s[0]);
  }
}
```

The IsCapitalized extension method can be called as though it were an instance method on a string, as follows:

```
Console.WriteLine ("Perth".IsCapitalized());
```

An extension method call, when compiled, is translated back into an ordinary static method call:

```
Console.WriteLine (StringHelper.IsCapitalized ("Perth"));
```

The translation works as follows:

```
arg0.Method (arg1, arg2, ...);            // Extension method call
StaticClass.Method (arg0, arg1, arg2, ...); // Static method call
```

Interfaces can be extended too:

```
public static T First<T> (this IEnumerable<T> sequence)
{
  foreach (T element in sequence)
    return element;

  throw new InvalidOperationException ("No elements!");
}
...
Console.WriteLine ("Seattle".First());   // S
```

Extension methods were added in C# 3.0.

Extension Method Chaining

Extension methods, like instance methods, provide a tidy way to chain functions. Consider the following two functions:

```
public static class StringHelper
{
  public static string Pluralize (this string s) {...}
  public static string Capitalize (this string s) {...}
}
```

x and y are equivalent and both evaluate to "Sausages", but x uses extension methods, whereas y uses static methods:

```
string x = "sausage".Pluralize().Capitalize();
string y = StringHelper.Capitalize (StringHelper.Pluralize ("sausage"));
```

Ambiguity and Resolution

Namespaces

An extension method cannot be accessed unless the namespace is in scope. Consider the extension method IsCapitalized in the following example:

```
using System;

namespace Utils
{
  public static class StringHelper
  {
    public static bool IsCapitalized (this string s)
    {
      if (string.IsNullOrEmpty(s)) return false;
      return char.IsUpper (s[0]);
    }
  }
}
```

To use IsCapitalized, the following application must import Utils, in order to avoid a compile-time error:

```
namespace MyApp
{
  using Utils;

  class Test
  {
    static void Main()
    {
      Console.WriteLine ("Perth".IsCapitalized());
    }
  }
}
```

Extension methods versus instance methods

Any compatible instance method will always take precedence over an extension method. In the following example, Test's Foo method will always take precedence— even when called with an argument x of type int:

```
class Test
{
  public void Foo (object x) { }    // This method always wins
}

static class Extensions
{
  public static void Foo (this Test t, int x) { }
}
```

The only way to call the extension method in this case is via normal static syntax; in other words, Extensions.Foo(...).

Extension methods versus extension methods

If two extension methods have the same signature, the extension method must be called as an ordinary static method to disambiguate the method to call. If one extension method has more specific arguments, however, the more specific method takes precedence.

To illustrate, consider the following two classes:

```
static class StringHelper
{
  public static bool IsCapitalized (this string s) {...}
}
static class ObjectHelper
{
  public static bool IsCapitalized (this object s) {...}
}
```

The following code calls StringHelper's IsCapitalized method:

```
bool test1 = "Perth".IsCapitalized();
```

To call ObjectHelper's IsCapitalized method, we must specify it explicitly:

```
bool test2 = (ObjectHelper.IsCapitalized ("Perth"));
```

Concrete types are considered more specific than interfaces.

Extension Methods on Interfaces

Extension methods can apply to interfaces:

```
using System;
using System.Collections.Generic;

static class Test
{
```

```
static void Main()
{
  string[] strings = { "a", "b", null, "c"};
  foreach (string s in strings.StripNulls())
    Console.WriteLine (s);
}

static IEnumerable<T> StripNulls<T> (this IEnumerable<T> seq)
{
  foreach (T t in seq)
    if (t != null)
      yield return t;
}
}
```

Anonymous Types

An anonymous type is a simple class created by the compiler on the fly to store a set of values. To create an anonymous type, use the new keyword followed by an object initializer, specifying the properties and values the type will contain. For example:

```
var dude = new { Name = "Bob", Age = 1 };
```

The compiler translates this to (approximately) the following:

```
internal class AnonymousGeneratedTypeName
{
  private string name;  // Actual field name is irrelevant
  private int    age;   // Actual field name is irrelevant

  public AnonymousGeneratedTypeName (string name, int age)
  {
    this.name = name; this.age = age;
  }

  public string  Name { get { return name; } }
  public int     Age  { get { return age;  } }

  // The Equals and GetHashCode methods are overridden (see Chapter 6).
  // The ToString method is also overridden.
}
...

  var dude = new AnonymousGeneratedTypeName ("Bob", 1);
```

You must use the var keyword to reference an anonymous type, because the name of the type is compiler-generated.

The property name of an anonymous type can be inferred from an expression that is itself an identifier (or ends with one). For example:

```
int Age = 23;
var dude = new { Name = "Bob", Age, Age.ToString().Length };
```

is equivalent to:

```
var dude = new { Name = "Bob", Age = Age, Length = Age.ToString().Length };
```

Two anonymous type instances will have the same underlying type if their elements are same-typed and they're declared within the same assembly:

```
var a1 = new { X = 2, Y = 4 };
var a2 = new { X = 2, Y = 4 };
Console.WriteLine (a1.GetType() == a2.GetType());   // True
```

Additionally, the `Equals` method is overridden to perform equality comparisons:

```
Console.WriteLine (a1 == a2);        // False
Console.WriteLine (a1.Equals (a2));  // True
```

Anonymous types are used primarily when writing LINQ queries (see Chapter 8), and were added in C# 3.0.

Dynamic Binding

Dynamic binding defers *binding*—the process of resolving types, members, and operations—from compile time to runtime. Dynamic binding is useful when at compile time *you* know that a certain function, member, or operation exists, but the *compiler* does not. This commonly occurs when you are interoperating with dynamic languages (such as IronPython) and COM and in scenarios when you might otherwise use reflection.

A dynamic type is declared with the contextual keyword `dynamic`:

```
dynamic d = GetSomeObject();
d.Quack();
```

A dynamic type tells the compiler to relax. We expect the runtime type of `d` to have a `Quack` method. We just can't prove it statically. Since `d` is dynamic, the compiler defers binding `Quack` to `d` until runtime. To understand what this means requires distinguishing between *static binding* and *dynamic binding*.

Static Binding Versus Dynamic Binding

The canonical binding example is mapping a name to a specific function when compiling an expression. To compile the following expression, the compiler needs to find the implementation of the method named `Quack`:

```
d.Quack();
```

Let's suppose the static type of `d` is `Duck`:

```
Duck d = ...
d.Quack();
```

In the simplest case, the compiler does the binding by looking for a parameterless method named `Quack` on `Duck`. Failing that, the compiler extends its search to methods taking optional parameters, methods on base classes of `Duck`, and extension methods that take `Duck` as its first parameter. If no match is found, you'll get a compilation error. Regardless of what method gets bound, the bottom line is that the binding is done by the compiler, and the binding utterly depends on statically knowing the types of the operands (in this case, `d`). This makes it *static binding*.

Now let's change the static type of d to `object`:

```
object d = ...
d.Quack();
```

Calling `Quack` gives us a compilation error, because although the value stored in d can contain a method called `Quack`, the compiler cannot know it since the only information it has is the type of the variable, which in this case is `object`. But let's now change the static type of d to `dynamic`:

```
dynamic d = ...
d.Quack();
```

A `dynamic` type is like `object`—it's equally nondescriptive about a type. The difference is that it lets you use it in ways that aren't known at compile time. A dynamic object binds at runtime based on its runtime type, not its compile-time type. When the compiler sees a dynamically bound expression (which in general is an expression that contains any value of type `dynamic`), it merely packages up the expression such that the binding can be done later at runtime.

At runtime, if a dynamic object implements `IDynamicMetaObjectProvider`, that interface is used to perform the binding. If not, binding occurs in almost the same way as it would have had the compiler known the dynamic object's runtime type. These two alternatives are called *custom binding* and *language binding*.

 COM interop can be considered to use a third kind of binding (see Chapter 25).

Custom Binding

Custom binding occurs when a dynamic object implements `IDynamicMetaObjectProvider` (IDMOP). Although you can implement IDMOP on types that you write in C#, and that is useful to do, the more common case is that you have acquired an IDMOP object from a dynamic language that is implemented in .NET on the DLR, such as IronPython or IronRuby. Objects from those languages implicitly implement IDMOP as a means by which to directly control the meanings of operations performed on them.

We will discuss custom binders in greater detail in Chapter 19, but we will write a simple one now to demonstrate the feature:

```
using System;
using System.Dynamic;

public class Test
{
  static void Main()
  {
    dynamic d = new Duck();
    d.Quack();              // Quack method was called
    d.Waddle();             // Waddle method was called
```

```
   }
}

public class Duck : DynamicObject
{
  public override bool TryInvokeMember (
    InvokeMemberBinder binder, object[] args, out object result)
  {
    Console.WriteLine (binder.Name + " method was called");
    result = null;
    return true;
  }
}
```

The Duck class doesn't actually have a Quack method. Instead, it uses custom binding to intercept and interpret all method calls.

Language Binding

Language binding occurs when a dynamic object does not implement IDynamicMetaObjectProvider. Language binding is useful when working around imperfectly designed types or inherent limitations in the .NET type system (we'll explore more scenarios in Chapter 19). A typical problem when using numeric types is that they have no common interface. We have seen that methods can be bound dynamically; the same is true for operators:

Advanced C#

```
static dynamic Mean (dynamic x, dynamic y)
{
  return (x + y) / 2;
}

static void Main()
{
  int x = 3, y = 4;
  Console.WriteLine (Mean (x, y));
}
```

The benefit is obvious—you don't have to duplicate code for each numeric type. However, you lose static type safety, risking runtime exceptions rather than compile-time errors.

> Dynamic binding circumvents static type safety, but not runtime type safety. Unlike with reflection (Chapter 18), you can't circumvent member accessibility rules with dynamic binding.

By design, language runtime binding behaves as similarly as possible to static binding, had the runtime types of the dynamic objects been known at compile time. In our previous example, the behavior of our program would be identical if we hardcoded Mean to work with the int type. The most notable exception in parity between static and dynamic binding is for extension methods, which we discuss in "Uncallable Functions" on page 168.

Dynamic binding also incurs a performance hit. Because of the DLR's caching mechanisms, however, repeated calls to the same dynamic expression are optimized—allowing you to efficiently call dynamic expressions in a loop. This optimization brings the typical overhead for a simple dynamic expression on today's hardware down to less than 100 ns.

RuntimeBinderException

If a member fails to bind, a `RuntimeBinderException` is thrown. You can think of this like a compile-time error at runtime:

```
dynamic d = 5;
d.Hello();                  // throws RuntimeBinderException
```

The exception is thrown because the `int` type has no `Hello` method.

Runtime Representation of Dynamic

There is a deep equivalence between the `dynamic` and `object` types. The runtime treats the following expression as `true`:

```
typeof (dynamic) == typeof (object)
```

This principle extends to constructed types and array types:

```
typeof (List<dynamic>) == typeof (List<object>)
typeof (dynamic[]) == typeof (object[])
```

Like an object reference, a dynamic reference can point to an object of any type (except pointer types):

```
dynamic x = "hello";
Console.WriteLine (x.GetType().Name);  // String

x = 123;  // No error (despite same variable)
Console.WriteLine (x.GetType().Name);  // Int32
```

Structurally, there is no difference between an object reference and a dynamic reference. A dynamic reference simply enables dynamic operations on the object it points to. You can convert from `object` to `dynamic` to perform any dynamic operation you want on an `object`:

```
object o = new System.Text.StringBuilder();
dynamic d = o;
d.Append ("hello");
Console.WriteLine (o);   // hello
```

Reflecting on a type exposing (public) dynamic members reveals that those members are represented as annotated objects. For example:

```
public class Test
{
    public dynamic Foo;
}
```

is equivalent to:

```
public class Test
{
    [System.Runtime.CompilerServices.DynamicAttribute]
    public object Foo;
}
```

This allows consumers of that type to know that Foo should be treated as dynamic, while allowing languages that don't support dynamic binding to fall back to object.

Dynamic Conversions

The dynamic type has implicit conversions to and from all other types:[*]

```
int i = 7;
dynamic d = i;
int j = d;          // No cast required (implicit conversion)
```

For the conversion to succeed, the runtime type of the dynamic object must be implicitly convertible to the target static type. The preceding example worked because an int is implicitly convertible to a long.

The following example throws a RuntimeBinderException because an int is not implicitly convertible to a short:

```
int i = 7;
dynamic d = i;
short j = d;        // throws RuntimeBinderException
```

var Versus dynamic

The var and dynamic types bear a superficial resemblance, but the difference is deep:

- var says, "Let the *compiler* figure out the type."
- dynamic says, "Let the *runtime* figure out the type."

```
dynamic x = "hello";  // Static type is dynamic, runtime type is string
var y = "hello";      // Static type is string, runtime type is string
int i = x;            // Runtime error
int j = y;            // Compile-time error
```

---

[*] Technically, the conversion from dynamic to other types is not an *implicit conversion*, but an *assignment conversion*. An assignment conversion is more restrictive in situations that might otherwise create ambiguities, such as overload resolution.

The static type of a variable declared with `var` can be `dynamic`:

```
dynamic x = "hello";
var y = x;            // Static type of y is dynamic
int z = y;            // Runtime error
```

Dynamic Expressions

Fields, properties, methods, events, constructors, indexers, operators, and conversions can all be called dynamically.

Trying to consume the result of a dynamic expression with a `void` return type is prohibited—just as with a statically typed expression. The difference is that the error occurs at runtime:

```
dynamic list = new List<int>();
var result = list.Add (5);      // RuntimeBinderException thrown
```

Expressions involving dynamic operands are typically themselves dynamic, since the effect of absent type information is cascading:

```
dynamic x = 2;
var y = x * 3;      // Static type of y is dynamic
```

There are a couple of obvious exceptions to this rule. First, casting a dynamic expression to a static type yields a static expression:

```
dynamic x = 2;
var y = (int)2;      // Static type of y is int
```

Second, constructor invocations always yield static expressions—even when called with dynamic arguments. In this example, x is statically typed to a `StringBuilder`:

```
dynamic capacity = 10;
var x = new System.Text.StringBuilder (capacity);
```

In addition, there are a few edge cases where an expression containing a dynamic argument is static, including passing an index to an array and delegate creation expressions.

Dynamic Calls Without Dynamic Receivers

The canonical use case for `dynamic` involves a dynamic *receiver*. This means that a dynamic object is the receiver of a dynamic function call:

```
dynamic x = ...;
x.Foo();      // x is the receiver
```

However, you can also call statically known functions with dynamic arguments. Such calls are subject to dynamic overload resolution, and can include:

- Static methods
- Instance constructors
- Instance methods on receivers with a statically known type

In the following example, the particular Foo that gets dynamically bound is dependent on the runtime type of the dynamic argument:

```
class Program
{
  static void Foo (int x)    { Console.WriteLine ("1"); }
  static void Foo (string x) { Console.WriteLine ("2"); }

  static void Main()
  {
    dynamic x = 5;
    dynamic y = "watermelon";

    Foo (x);                 // 1
    Foo (y);                 // 2
  }
}
```

Because a dynamic receiver is not involved, the compiler can statically perform a basic check to see whether the dynamic call will succeed. It checks that a function with the right name and number of parameters exists. If no candidate is found, you get a compile-time error. For example:

```
class Program
{
  static void Foo (int x)    { Console.WriteLine ("1"); }
  static void Foo (string x) { Console.WriteLine ("2"); }

  static void Main()
  {
    dynamic x = 5;
    Foo (x, x);       // Compiler error - wrong number of parameters
    Fook (x);         // Compiler error - no such method name
  }
}
```

Static Types in Dynamic Expressions

It's obvious that dynamic types are used in dynamic binding. It's not so obvious that static types are also used—wherever possible—in dynamic binding. Consider the following:

```
class Program
{
  static void Foo (object x, object y) { Console.WriteLine ("oo"); }
  static void Foo (object x, string y) { Console.WriteLine ("os"); }
  static void Foo (string x, object y) { Console.WriteLine ("so"); }
  static void Foo (string x, string y) { Console.WriteLine ("ss"); }

  static void Main()
  {
    object o = "hello";
    dynamic d = "goodbye";
    Foo (o, d);               // os
  }
}
```

The call to Foo(o,d) is dynamically bound because one of its arguments, d, is dynamic. But since o is statically known, the binding—even though it occurs dynamically—will make use of that. In this case, overload resolution will pick the second implementation of Foo due to the static type of o and the runtime type of d. In other words, the compiler is "as static as it can possibly be."

Uncallable Functions

Some functions cannot be called dynamically. You cannot call:

- Extension methods (via extension method syntax)
- Any member of an interface
- Base members hidden by a subclass

Understanding why this is so is useful in understanding dynamic binding.

Dynamic binding requires two pieces of information: the name of the function to call, and the object upon which to call the function. However, in each of the three uncallable scenarios, an *additional type* is involved, which is known only at compile time. As of C# 4.0, there's no way to specify these additional types dynamically.

When calling extension methods, that additional type is implicit. It's the static class on which the extension method is defined. The compiler searches for it given the using directives in your source code. This makes extension methods compile-time-only concepts, since using directives melt away upon compilation (after they've done their job in the binding process in mapping simple names to namespace-qualified names).

When calling members via an interface, you specify that additional type via an implicit or explicit cast. There are two scenarios where you might want to do this: when calling explicitly implemented interface members, and when calling interface members implemented in a type internal to another assembly. We can illustrate the former with the following two types:

```
interface IFoo    { void Test();        }
class Foo : IFoo { void IFoo.Test() {} }
```

To call the Test method, we must cast to the IFoo interface. This is easy with static typing:

```
IFoo f = new Foo();    // Implicit cast to interface
f.Test();
```

Now consider the situation with dynamic typing:

```
IFoo f = new Foo();
dynamic d = f;
d.Test();               // Exception thrown
```

The implicit cast shown in bold tells the *compiler* to bind subsequent member calls on f to IFoo rather than Foo—in other words, to view that object through the lens of the IFoo interface. However, that lens is lost at runtime, so the DLR cannot complete the binding. The loss is illustrated as follows:

```
Console.WriteLine (f.GetType().Name);    // Foo
```

A similar situation arises when calling a hidden base member: you must specify an additional type via either a cast or the base keyword—and that additional type is lost at runtime.

Attributes

You're already familiar with the notion of attributing code elements of a program with modifiers, such as virtual or ref. These constructs are built into the language. *Attributes* are an extensible mechanism for adding custom information to code elements (assemblies, types, members, return values, and parameters). This extensibility is useful for services that integrate deeply into the type system, without requiring special keywords or constructs in the C# language.

A good scenario for attributes is serialization—the process of converting arbitrary objects to and from a particular format. In this scenario, an attribute on a field can specify the translation between C#'s representation of the field and the format's representation of the field.

Attribute Classes

An attribute is defined by a class that inherits (directly or indirectly) from the abstract class System.Attribute. To attach an attribute to a code element, specify the attribute's type name in square brackets, before the code element. For example, the following attaches the ObsoleteAttribute to the Foo class:

```
[ObsoleteAttribute]
public class Foo {...}
```

This attribute is recognized by the compiler and will cause compiler warnings if a type or member marked obsolete is referenced. By convention, all attribute types end in the word *Attribute*. C# recognizes this and allows you to omit the suffix when attaching an attribute:

```
[Obsolete]
public class Foo {...}
```

ObsoleteAttribute is a type declared in the System namespace as follows (simplified for brevity):

```
public sealed class ObsoleteAttribute : Attribute {...}
```

The C# language and the .NET Framework include a number of predefined attributes. We describe how to write your own attributes in Chapter 17.

Named and Positional Attribute Parameters

Attributes may have parameters. In the following example, we apply XmlElementAttribute to a class. This attribute tells XML serializer (in System.Xml.Serialization) how an object is represented in XML and accepts several *attribute parameters*. The following attribute maps the `CustomerEntity` class to an XML element named `Customer`, belonging to the *http://oreilly.com* namespace:

```
[XmlElement ("Customer", Namespace="http://oreilly.com")]
public class CustomerEntity { ... }
```

Attribute parameters fall into one of two categories: positional or named. In the preceding example, the first argument is a *positional parameter*; the second is a *named parameter*. Positional parameters correspond to parameters of the attribute type's public constructors. Named parameters correspond to public fields or public properties on the attribute type.

When specifying an attribute, you must include positional parameters that correspond to one of the attribute's constructors. Named parameters are optional.

In Chapter 18, we describe the valid parameter types and rules for their evaluation.

Attribute Targets

Implicitly, the target of an attribute is the code element it immediately precedes, which is typically a type or type member. However, you can also attach attributes to an assembly. This requires that you explicitly specify the attribute's target.

Here is an example of using the `CLSCompliant` attribute to specify CLS compliance for an entire assembly:

```
[assembly:CLSCompliant(true)]
```

Specifying Multiple Attributes

Multiple attributes can be specified for a single code element. Each attribute can be listed either within the same pair of square brackets (separated by a comma) or in separate pairs of square brackets (or a combination of the two). The following three examples are semantically identical:

```
[Serializable, Obsolete, CLSCompliant(false)]
public class Bar {...}

[Serializable] [Obsolete] [CLSCompliant(false)]
public class Bar {...}

[Serializable, Obsolete]
[CLSCompliant(false)]
public class Bar {...}
```

Unsafe Code and Pointers

C# supports direct memory manipulation via pointers within blocks of code marked unsafe and compiled with the `/unsafe` compiler option. Pointer types are primarily useful for interoperability with C APIs, but may also be used for accessing memory outside the managed heap or for performance-critical hotspots.

Pointer Basics

For every value type or pointer type *V*, there is a corresponding pointer type *V**. A pointer instance holds the address of a value. This is considered to be of type *V*, but pointer types can be (unsafely) cast to any other pointer type. The main pointer operators are:

Operator	Meaning
&	The *address-of* operator returns a pointer to the address of a value
*	The *dereference* operator returns the value at the address of a pointer
->	The *pointer-to-member* operator is a syntactic shortcut, in which x->y is equivalent to (*x).y

Unsafe Code

By marking a type, type member, or statement block with the unsafe keyword, you're permitted to use pointer types and perform C++ style pointer operations on memory within that scope. Here is an example of using pointers to quickly process a bitmap:

```
unsafe void BlueFilter (int[,] bitmap)
{
  int length = bitmap.Length;
  fixed (int* b = bitmap)
  {
    int* p = b;
    for (int i = 0; i < length; i++)
      *p++ &= 0xFF;
  }
}
```

Unsafe code can run faster than a corresponding safe implementation. In this case, the code would have required a nested loop with array indexing and bounds checking. An unsafe C# method may also be faster than calling an external C function, since there is no overhead associated with leaving the managed execution environment.

The fixed Statement

The fixed statement is required to pin a managed object, such as the bitmap in the previous example. During the execution of a program, many objects are allocated and deallocated from the heap. In order to avoid unnecessary waste or fragmentation of memory, the garbage collector moves objects around. Pointing to an object is futile if its address could change while referencing it, so the fixed statement tells the garbage collector to "pin" the object and not move it around. This may have an impact on the efficiency of the runtime, so fixed blocks should be used only briefly, and heap allocation should be avoided within the fixed block.

Within a fixed statement, you can get a pointer to any value type, an array of value types, or a string. In the case of arrays and strings, the pointer will actually point to the first element, which is a value type.

Value types declared inline within reference types require the reference type to be pinned, as follows:

```
class Test
{
  int x;
  static void Main()
  {
    Test test = new Test();
    unsafe
    {
      fixed (int* p = &test.x)    // Pins test
      {
        *p = 9;
      }
      System.Console.WriteLine (test.x);
    }
  }
}
```

We describe the fixed statement further in "Mapping a Struct to Unmanaged Memory" on page 965 in Chapter 25.

The Pointer-to-Member Operator

In addition to the & and * operators, C# also provides the C++ style -> operator, which can be used on structs:

```
struct Test
{
  int x;
  unsafe static void Main()
  {
    Test test = new Test();
    Test* p = &test;
    p->x = 9;
    System.Console.WriteLine (test.x);
  }
}
```

Arrays

The stackalloc keyword

Memory can be allocated in a block on the stack explicitly using the stackalloc keyword. Since it is allocated on the stack, its lifetime is limited to the execution of the method, just as with any other local variable. The block may use the [ ] operator to index into memory:

```
int* a = stackalloc int [10];
for (int i = 0; i < 10; ++i)
  Console.WriteLine (a[i]);    // Print raw memory
```

Fixed-size buffers

Memory can be allocated in a block within a struct using the `fixed` keyword:

```
unsafe struct UnsafeUnicodeString
{
  public short Length;
  public fixed byte Buffer[30];
}

unsafe class UnsafeClass
{
  UnsafeUnicodeString uus;

  public UnsafeClass (string s)
  {
    uus.Length = (short)s.Length;
    fixed (byte* p = uus.Buffer)
      for (int i = 0; i < s.Length; i++)
        p[i] = (byte) s[i];
  }
}
class Test
{
  static void Main() { new UnsafeClass ("Christian Troy"); }
}
```

The `fixed` keyword is also used in this example to pin the object on the heap that contains the buffer (which will be the instance of `UnsafeClass`).

void*

A *void pointer* (`void*`) makes no assumptions about the type of the underlying data and is useful for functions that deal with raw memory. An implicit conversion exists from any pointer type to `void*`. A `void*` cannot be dereferenced, and arithmetic operations cannot be performed on void pointers. For example:

```
class Test
{
  unsafe static void Main()
  {
    short[ ] a = {1,1,2,3,5,8,13,21,34,55};
    fixed (short* p = a)
    {
      //sizeof returns size of value-type in bytes
      Zap (p, a.Length * sizeof (short));
    }
    foreach (short x in a)
      System.Console.WriteLine (x);   // Prints all zeros
  }

  unsafe static void Zap (void* memory, int byteCount)
  {
    byte* b = (byte*) memory;
      for (int i = 0; i < byteCount; i++)
        *b++ = 0;
```

```
      }
    }
```

Pointers to Unmanaged Code

Pointers are also useful for accessing data outside the managed heap (such as when interacting with C DLLs or COM), or when dealing with data not in the main memory (such as graphics memory or a storage medium on an embedded device).

Preprocessor Directives

Preprocessor directives supply the compiler with additional information about regions of code. The most common preprocessor directives are the conditional directives, which provide a way to include or exclude regions of code from compilation. For example:

```
#define DEBUG
class MyClass
{
  int x;
  void Foo()
  {
    # if DEBUG
    Console.WriteLine ("Testing: x = {0}", x);
    # endif
  }
  ...
}
```

In this class, the statement in Foo is compiled as conditionally dependent upon the presence of the DEBUG symbol. If we remove the DEBUG symbol, the statement is not compiled. Preprocessor symbols can be defined within a source file (as we have done), and they can be passed to the compiler with the /define:symbol command-line option.

With the #if and #elif directives, you can use the ||, &&, and ! operators to perform *or*, *and*, and *not* operations on multiple symbols. The following directive instructs the compiler to include the code that follows if the TESTMODE symbol is defined and the DEBUG symbol is not defined:

```
#if TESTMODE && !DEBUG
...
```

Bear in mind, however, that you're not building an ordinary C# expression, and the symbols upon which you operate have absolutely no connection to *variables*—static or otherwise.

The #error and #warning symbols prevent accidental misuse of conditional directives by making the compiler generate a warning or error given an undesirable set of compilation symbols. Table 4-1 lists the preprocessor directives.

Table 4-1. Preprocessor directives

Preprocessor directive	Action
#define *symbol*	Defines *symbol*
#undef *symbol*	Undefines *symbol*
#if *symbol* [*operator symbol2*]...	*symbol* to test; *operators* are ==, !=, &&, and || followed by #else, #elif, and #endif
#else	Executes code to subsequent #endif
#elif *symbol* [*operator symbol2*]	Combines #else branch and #if test
#endif	Ends conditional directives
#warning *text*	*text* of the warning to appear in compiler output
#error *text*	*text* of the error to appear in compiler output
#line [*number* [*"file"*] | hidden]	*number* specifies the line in source code; *file* is the filename to appear in computer output; hidden instructs debuggers to skip over code from this point until the next #line directive
#region *name*	Marks the beginning of an outline
#end *region*	Ends an outline region

Conditional Attributes

An attribute decorated with the Conditional attribute will be compiled only if a given preprocessor symbol is present. For example:

```
// file1.cs
#define DEBUG
using System;
using System.Diagnostics;
[Conditional("DEBUG")]
public class TestAttribute : Attribute {}

// file2.cs
#define DEBUG
[Test]
class Foo
{
  [Test]
  string s;
}
```

The compiler will not incorporate the [Test] attributes if the DEBUG symbol is in scope for *file2.cs*.

Pragma Warning

The compiler generates a warning when it spots something in your code that seems unintentional. Unlike errors, warnings don't ordinarily prevent your application from compiling.

Compiler warnings can be extremely valuable in spotting bugs. Their usefulness, however, is undermined when you get *false* warnings. In a large application, maintaining a good signal-to-noise ratio is essential if the "real" warnings are to get noticed.

To this effect, the compiler allows you to selectively suppress warnings with the `#pragma warning` directive. In this example, we instruct the compiler not to warn us about the field `Message` not being used:

```
public class Foo
{
  static void Main() { }

  #pragma warning disable 414
  static string Message = "Hello";
  #pragma warning restore 414
}
```

Omitting the number in the `#pragma warning` directive disables or restores all warning codes.

If you are thorough in applying this directive, you can compile with the `/warnaserror` switch—this tells the compiler to treat any residual warnings as errors.

XML Documentation

A *documentation comment* is a piece of embedded XML that documents a type or member. A documentation comment comes immediately before a type or member declaration, and starts with three slashes:

```
/// <summary>Cancels a running query.</summary>
public void Cancel() { ... }
```

Multiline comments can be done either like this:

```
/// <summary>
/// Cancels a running query
/// </summary>
public void Cancel() { ... }
```

or like this (notice the extra star at the start):

```
/**
    <summary> Cancels a running query. </summary>
*/
public void Cancel() { ... }
```

If you compile with the `/doc` directive, the compiler extracts and collates documentation comments into a single XML file. This has two main uses:

- If placed in the same folder as the compiled assembly, Visual Studio automatically reads the XML file and uses the information to provide IntelliSense member listings to consumers of the assembly of the same name.

- Third-party tools (such as Sandcastle and NDoc) can transform XML file into an HTML help file.

Standard XML Documentation Tags

Here are the standard XML tags that Visual Studio and documentation generators recognize:

`<summary>`

```
<summary>...</summary>
```

Indicates the tool tip that IntelliSense should display for the type or member; typically a single phrase or sentence.

`<remarks>`

```
<remarks>...</remarks>
```

Additional text that describes the type or member. Documentation generators pick this up and merge it into the bulk of a type or member's description.

`<param>`

```
<param name="name">...</param>
```

Explains a parameter on a method.

`<returns>`

```
<returns>...</returns>
```

Explains the return value for a method.

`<exception>`

```
<exception [cref="type"]>...</exception>
```

Lists an exception that a method may throw (`cref` refers to the exception type).

`<permission>`

```
<permission [cref="type"]>...</permission>
```

Indicates an `IPermission` type required by the documented type or member.

`<example>`

```
<example>...</example>
```

Denotes an example (used by documentation generators). This usually contains both description text and source code (source code is typically within a `<c>` or `<code>` tag).

`<c>`

```
<c>...</c>
```

Indicates an inline code snippet. This tag is usually used inside an `<example>` block.

`<code>`

```
<code>...</code>
```

Indicates a multiline code sample. This tag is usually used inside an `<example>` block.

`<see>`

```
<see cref="member">...</see>
```

Inserts an inline cross-reference to another type or member. HTML documentation generators typically convert this to a hyperlink. The compiler emits a warning if the type or member name is invalid. To refer to generic types, use curly braces; for example, `cref="Foo{T,U}"`.

`<seealso>`

```
<seealso cref="member">...</seealso>
```

Cross-references another type or member. Documentation generators typically write this into a separate "See Also" section at the bottom of the page.

`<paramref>`

```
<paramref name="name"/>
```

References a parameter from within a `<summary>` or `<remarks>` tag.

`<list>`

```
<list type=[ bullet | number | table ]>
  <listheader>
    <term>...</term>
    <description>...</description>
  </listheader>
  <item>
    <term>...</term>
    <description>...</description>
  </item>
</list>
```

Instructs documentation generators to emit a bulleted, numbered, or table-style list.

`<para>`

```
<para>...</para>
```

Instructs documentation generators to format the contents into a separate paragraph.

`<include>`

Merges an external XML file that contains documentation. The path attribute denotes an XPath query to a specific element in that file.

User-Defined Tags

Little is special about the predefined XML tags recognized by the C# compiler, and you are free to define your own. The only special processing done by the compiler is on the `<param>` tag (in which it verifies the parameter name and that all the parameters on the method are documented) and the `cref` attribute (in which it verifies that the attribute refers to a real type or member and expands it to a fully qualified type or member ID). The `cref` attribute can also be used in your own tags and is verified and expanded just as it is in the predefined `<exception>`, `<permission>`, `<see>`, and `<seealso>` tags.

Type or Member Cross-References

Type names and type or member cross-references are translated into IDs that uniquely define the type or member. These names are composed of a prefix that defines what the ID represents and a signature of the type or member. The member prefixes are:

XML type prefix	ID prefixes applied to...
N	Namespace
T	Type (class, struct, enum, interface, delegate)
F	Field
P	Property (includes indexers)
M	Method (includes special methods)
E	Event
!	Error

The rules describing how the signatures are generated are well documented, although fairly complex.

Here is an example of a type and the IDs that are generated:

```
// Namespaces do not have independent signatures
namespace NS
{
  /// T:NS.MyClass
  class MyClass
  {
    /// F:NS.MyClass.aField
    string aField;

    /// P:NS.MyClass.aProperty
    short aProperty {get {...} set {...}}

    /// T:NS.MyClass.NestedType
    class NestedType {...};

    /// M:NS.MyClass.X()
    void X() {...}


    /// M:NS.MyClass.Y(System.Int32,System.Double@,System.Decimal@)
    void Y(int p1, ref double p2, out decimal p3) {...}
```

```
/// M:NS.MyClass.Z(System.Char[ ],System.Single[0:,0:])
void Z(char[ ] 1, float[,] p2) {...}

/// M:NS.MyClass.op_Addition(NS.MyClass,NS.MyClass)
public static MyClass operator+(MyClass c1, MyClass c2) {...}

/// M:NS.MyClass.op_Implicit(NS.MyClass)~System.Int32
public static implicit operator int(MyClass c) {...}

/// M:NS.MyClass.#ctor
MyClass() {...}

/// M:NS.MyClass.Finalize
~MyClass() {...}

/// M:NS.MyClass.#cctor
static MyClass() {...}
    }
}
```

5

Framework Overview

Almost all the capabilities of the .NET Framework are exposed via a vast set of managed types. These types are organized into hierarchical namespaces and packaged into a set of assemblies, which, together with the CLR, comprise the .NET platform.

Some of the .NET types are used directly by the CLR and are essential for the managed hosting environment. These types reside in an assembly called *mscorlib.dll* and include C#'s built-in types, as well as the basic collection classes, types for stream processing, serialization, reflection, threading, and native interoperability.

At a level above this are additional types that "flesh out" the CLR-level functionality, providing features such as XML, networking, and LINQ. These reside in *System.dll*, *System.Xml.dll*, and *System.Core.dll*, and together with *mscorlib* they provide a rich programming environment upon which the rest of the Framework is built. This "core framework" largely defines the scope of the rest of this book.

The remainder of the .NET Framework consists of applied APIs, most of which cover three areas of functionality:

- User interface technologies
- Backend technologies
- Distributed system technologies

Table 5-1 shows the history of compatibility between each version of C#, the CLR, and the .NET Framework. Interestingly, C# 3.0 targeted a new Framework version while using the same CLR version as its predecessor. With C# 4.0, the numbers align cleanly again.

Table 5-1. C#, CLR, and .NET Framework versions

C# version	CLR version	Framework versions
1.0	1.0	1.0
1.2	1.1	1.1
2.0	2.0	2.0, 3.0
3.0	2.0 (SP1)	3.5
4.0	4.0	4.0

This chapter skims all key areas of the .NET Framework—starting with the core types covered in this book and finishing with an overview of the applied technologies.

 Assemblies and namespaces in the .NET Framework *cross-cut.* The most extreme examples are *System.Core.dll* and *mscorlib.dll*, both defining types in dozens of namespaces, none of which is prefixed with *mscorlib* or *System.Core.* The less obvious cases are the more confusing ones, however, such as the types in `System.Security.Cryptography`. Most types in this namespace reside in *System.dll*, except for a handful, which reside in *System.Security.dll.* This book's companion website (*www.albahari.com/nutshell/NamespaceReference.aspx*) has a complete mapping of Framework namespaces to assemblies.

What's New in .NET Framework 4.0

Framework 4.0 adds the following new features:

- New core types: `BigInteger` (for arbitrarily large numbers), `Complex` (complex numbers), and tuples (Chapter 6)
- A new `SortedSet` collection (Chapter 7)
- *Code contracts*, for enabling methods to interact more reliably through mutual obligations and responsibilities (Chapter 13)
- Direct support for memory-mapped files (Chapter 14)
- Lazy file- and directory-I/O methods that return `IEnumerable<T>` instead of arrays (Chapter 14)
- The *Dynamic Language Runtime* (DLR), which is now part of the .NET Framework (Chapter 19)
- *Security transparency*, which makes it easier to secure libraries in partially trusted environments (Chapter 20)
- New threading constructs, including a more robust `Monitor.Enter` overload, `Thread.Yield`, new signaling classes (`Barrier` and `CountdownEvent`), and lazy initialization primitives (Chapter 21)
- *Parallel programming* APIs for leveraging multicore processors, including Parallel LINQ (PLINQ), imperative data and task parallelism constructs,

concurrent collections, and low-latency synchronization and spinning primitives (Chapter 22)

- Methods for application domain resource monitoring (Chapter 24)

Framework 4.0 also includes enhancements to ASP.NET, including the MVC framework and Dynamic Data, and enhancements to Entity Framework, WPF, WCF, and Workflow. In addition, it includes the new *Managed Extensibility Framework* library, to assist with runtime composition, discovery, and dependency injection.

Many of the core types are defined in the following assemblies: *mscorlib.dll*, *System.dll*, and *System.Core.dll*. The first of these, *mscorlib.dll*, comprises the types required by the runtime environment itself; *System.dll* and *System.Core.dll* contain additional core types required by you as a programmer. The reason the latter two are separate is historical: when the Microsoft team introduced Framework 3.5, they made it *additive* insofar as it ran over the existing CLR 2.0. Therefore, almost all new core types (such as the classes supporting LINQ) went into a new assembly which Microsoft called *System.Core.dll*. With Framework 4.0, separation was maintained to avoid breaking existing applications.

A notable exception is the following types, which in Framework 4.0 have moved from *System.Core.dll* to *mscorlib.dll*:

- The `Action` and `Func` delegates
- `TimeZoneInfo` and associated types
- `System.Threading.LockRecursionException`

Redirections have been set up on these types, so if you ask the reflection API for the "TimeZoneInfo" type in *System.Core.dll*, you'll be given the type in *mscorlib.dll* instead.

The CLR and Core Framework

System Types

The most fundamental types live directly in the `System` namespace. These include C#'s built-in types, the `Exception` base class, the `Enum`, `Array`, and `Delegate` base classes, and `Nullable`, `Type`, `DateTime`, `TimeSpan`, and `Guid`. The `System` namespace also includes types for performing mathematical functions (`Math`), generating random numbers (`Random`), and converting between various types (`Convert` and `BitConverter`).

Chapter 6 describes these types—as well as the interfaces that define standard protocols used across the .NET Framework for such tasks as formatting (`IFormattable`) and order comparison (`IComparable`).

The `System` namespace also defines the `IDisposable` interface and the `GC` class for interacting with the garbage collector. These topics are saved for Chapter 12.

Text Processing

The `System.Text` namespace contains the `StringBuilder` class (the editable or *mutable* cousin of `string`), and the types for working with text encodings, such as UTF-8 (`Encoding` and its subtypes). We cover this in Chapter 6.

The `System.Text.RegularExpressions` namespace contains types that perform advanced pattern-based search and replace operations; these are described in Chapter 26.

Collections

The .NET Framework offers a variety of classes for managing collections of items. These include both list- and dictionary-based structures, and work in conjunction with a set of standard interfaces that unify their common characteristics. All collection types are defined in the following namespaces, covered in Chapter 7:

```
System.Collections              // Nongeneric collections
System.Collections.Generic      // Generic collections
System.Collections.Specialized  // Strongly typed collections
System.Collections.ObjectModel  // Bases for your own collections
System.Collections.Concurrent   // Thread-safe collection (Chapter 20)
```

Queries

Language Integrated Query (LINQ) was added in Framework 3.5. LINQ allows you to perform type-safe queries over local and remote collections (e.g., SQL Server tables) and is described in Chapters 8 through 10. A big advantage of LINQ is that it presents a consistent querying API across a variety of domains. The types for resolving LINQ queries reside in these namespaces:

```
System.Linq              // LINQ to Objects and PLINQ
System.Xml.Linq          // LINQ to XML
System.Data.Linq         // LINQ to SQL
System.Data.Entity       // LINQ to Entities (Entity Framework)
System.Linq.Expressions  // For building expressions manually
```

The LINQ to SQL and Entity Framework APIs leverage lower-level ADO.NET types in the `System.Data` namespace.

XML

XML is used widely within the .NET Framework, and so is supported extensively. Chapter 10 focuses entirely on LINQ to XML—a lightweight XML document object model that can be constructed and queried through LINQ. Chapter 11 describes the older W3C DOM, as well as the performant low-level reader/writer classes and the Framework's support for XML schemas, stylesheets, and XPath. The XML namespaces are:

```
System.Xml          // XmlReader, XmlWriter + the old W3C DOM
System.Xml.Linq     // The LINQ to XML DOM
System.Xml.Schema   // Support for XSD
System.Xml.XPath    // XPath query language
```

```
System.Xml.Xsl              // Stylesheet support
System.Xml.Serialization    // Declarative XML serialization for .NET types
```

Diagnostics and Code Contracts

In Chapter 13, we cover .NET's logging and assertion facilities and the new code contracts system in Framework 4.0. We also describe how to interact with other processes, write to the Windows event log, and use performance counters for monitoring. The types for this are defined in and under `System.Diagnostics`.

Streams and I/O

The Framework provides a stream-based model for low-level input/output. Streams are typically used to read and write directly to files and network connections, and can be chained or wrapped in decorator streams to add compression or encryption functionality. Chapter 14 describes .NET's stream architecture, as well as the specific support for working with files and directories, compression, isolated storage, pipes, and memory-mapped files. The `Stream` and I/O types are defined in and under the `System.IO` namespace.

Networking

You can directly access standard network protocols such as HTTP, FTP, TCP/IP, and SMTP via the types in `System.Net`. In Chapter 15, we demonstrate how to communicate using each of these protocols, starting with simple tasks such as downloading from a web page, and finishing with using TCP/IP directly to retrieve POP3 email. Here are the namespaces we cover:

```
System.Net
System.Net.Mail      // For sending mail via SMTP
System.Net.Sockets   // TCP, UDP, and IP
```

Serialization

The Framework provides several systems for saving and restoring objects to a binary or text representation. Such systems are required for distributed application technologies, such as WCF, Web Services, and Remoting, and also to save and restore objects to a file. In Chapter 16, we cover all three serialization engines: the data contract serializer, the binary serializer, and the XML serializer. The types for serialization reside in the following namespaces:

```
System.Runtime.Serialization
System.Runtime.Serialization.Formatters.Binary
System.Runtime.Serialization.Formatters.SOAP
System.Xml.Serialization
```

Assemblies, Reflection, and Attributes

The assemblies into which C# programs compile comprise executable instructions (stored as intermediate language or IL) and metadata, which describes the program's types, members, and attributes. Through reflection, you can inspect this metadata at runtime, and do such things as dynamically invoke methods. With `Reflection.Emit`, you can construct new code on the fly.

In Chapter 17, we describe the makeup of assemblies and how to sign them, use the global assembly cache and resources, and resolve file references. In Chapter 18, we cover reflection and attributes—describing how to inspect metadata, dynamically invoke functions, write custom attributes, emit new types, and parse raw IL. The types for using reflection and working with assemblies reside in the following namespaces:

```
System
System.Reflection
System.Reflection.Emit
```

Dynamic Programming

In Chapter 19, we look at some of the patterns for dynamic programming and leveraging the Dynamic Language Runtime, which is now part of the CLR. We describe how to implement the Visitor pattern, write custom dynamic objects, and interoperate with IronPython. The types for dynamic programming are in `System.Dynamic`.

Security

The .NET Framework provides its own security layer, allowing you to both sandbox other assemblies and be sandboxed yourself. In Chapter 20, we cover code access, role, and identity security, and the new transparency model in CLR 4.0. We then describe cryptography in the Framework, covering encryption, hashing, and data protection. The types for this are defined in:

```
System.Security
System.Security.Permissions
System.Security.Policy
System.Security.Cryptography
```

Threading and Parallel Programming

Multithreading allows you to execute code in parallel. Chapter 21 explores this subject in detail, describing both the Framework's support for multithreading and the strategies for writing multithreaded applications. In Chapter 22, we cover Framework 4.0's new constructs for leveraging multicore processors, and in Chapter 23, we describe how to use asynchronous methods to write highly concurrent server applications.

All types for threading are in and under the `System.Threading` namespace.

Application Domains

The CLR provides an additional level of isolation within a process, called an *application domain*. In Chapter 24, we examine the properties of an application domain with which you can interact, and demonstrate how to create and use additional application domains within the same process for such purposes as unit testing. We also describe how to use Remoting to communicate with these application domains. The `AppDomain` type is defined in the `System` namespace.

Native and COM Interoperability

You can interoperate with both native and COM code. Native interoperability allows you to call functions in unmanaged DLLs, register callbacks, map data structures, and interoperate with native data types. COM interoperability allows you to call COM types and expose .NET types to COM. The types that support these functions are in `System.Runtime.InteropServices`, and we cover them in Chapter 25.

Applied Technologies

User Interface Technologies

The .NET Framework provides four APIs for user-interface-based applications:

ASP.NET (`System.Web.UI`)
    For writing thin client applications that run over a standard web browser

Silverlight
    For providing a rich user interface inside a web browser

Windows Presentation Foundation (`System.Windows`)
    For writing rich client applications

Windows Forms (`System.Windows.Forms`)
    For maintaining legacy rich client applications

In general, a thin client application amounts to a website; a rich client application is a program the end user must download or install on the client computer.

ASP.NET

Applications written using ASP.NET host under Windows IIS and can be accessed from almost any web browser. Here are the advantages of ASP.NET over rich client technologies:

- There is zero deployment at the client end.
- Clients can run a non-Windows platform.
- Updates are easily deployed.

Further, because most of what you write in an ASP.NET application runs on the server, you design your data access layer to run in the same application domain—without limiting security or scalability. In contrast, a rich client that does the same is not generally as secure or scalable. (The solution, with the rich client, is to insert a *middle tier* between the client and database. The middle tier runs on a remote application server [often alongside the database server] and communicates with the rich clients via WCF, Web Services, or Remoting.)

In writing your web pages, you can choose between the traditional Web Forms and the new MVC (Model-View-Controller) API. Both build on the ASP.NET infrastructure. Web Forms has been part of the Framework since its inception; MVC was written much later in response to the success of Ruby on Rails and MonoRail. Although debuting in Framework 4.0, the MVC framework has benefited from having matured for some time as a public beta. It provides, in general, a better programming abstraction than Web Forms; it also allows more control over the generated HTML. What you lose over Web Forms is a designer. This makes Web Forms still a good choice for web pages with predominately static content.

The limitations of ASP.NET are largely a reflection of the limitations of thin client systems in general:

- A web browser interface significantly restricts what you can do.
- Maintaining state on the client—or on behalf of the client—is cumbersome.

You can improve the interactivity and responsiveness, however, through client-side scripting or technologies such as AJAX: a good resource for this is *http://ajax.asp .net*. Use of AJAX is simplified through the use of libraries such as jQuery.

The types for writing ASP.NET applications are in the `System.Web.UI` namespace and its subnamespaces, and are packed in the *System.Web.dll* assembly.

Silverlight

Silverlight is not technically part of the main .NET Framework: it's a separate Framework that includes a subset of the Framework's core features—plus the ability to run as a web browser plug-in. Its graphics model is essentially a subset of WPF and this allows you to leverage existing knowledge in developing Silverlight applications. Silverlight is available as a small cross-platform download for web browsers—much like Macromedia's Flash.

Flash has a far bigger installation base and so dominates in this area. For this reason, Silverlight tends to be used in fringe scenarios—corporate intranets, for example.

Windows Presentation Foundation (WPF)

WPF was introduced in Framework 3.0 for writing rich client applications. The benefits of WPF over its predecessor, Windows Forms, are as follows:

- It supports sophisticated graphics, such as arbitrary transformations, 3D rendering, and true transparency.
- Its primary measurement unit is not pixel-based, so applications display correctly at any DPI (dots per inch) setting.
- It has extensive dynamic layout support, which means you can localize an application without danger of elements overlapping.
- Rendering uses DirectX and is fast, taking good advantage of graphics hardware acceleration.
- User interfaces can be described declaratively in XAML files that can be maintained independently of the "code-behind" files—this helps to separate appearance from functionality.

WPF's size and complexity, however, make for a steep learning curve.

The types for writing WPF applications are in the System.Windows namespace and all subnamespaces except for System.Windows.Forms.

Windows Forms

Windows Forms is a rich client API that's as old as the .NET Framework. Compared to WPF, Windows Forms is a relatively simple technology that provides most of the features you need in writing a typical Windows application. It also has significant relevancy in maintaining legacy applications. It has a number of drawbacks, though, compared to WPF:

- Controls are positioned and sized in pixels, making it easy to write applications that break on clients whose DPI settings differ from the developer's.
- The API for drawing nonstandard controls is GDI+, which, although reasonably flexible, is slow in rendering large areas (and without double buffering, flickers horribly).
- Controls lack true transparency.
- Dynamic layout is difficult to get right reliably.

The last point is an excellent reason to favor WPF over Windows Forms—even if you're writing a business application that needs just a user interface and not a "user experience." The layout elements in WPF, such as Grid, make it easy to assemble labels and text boxes such that they always align—even after language changing localization—without messy logic and without any flickering. Further, you don't have to bow to the lowest common denominator in screen resolution—WPF layout elements have been designed from the outset to adapt properly to resizing.

On the subject of speed, it was originally thought that graphics card manufacturers would incorporate GDI+ hardware accelerators. This never happened; their focus was instead on DirectX. Consequently, GDI+ is considerably slower than even its predecessor, GDI, let alone WPF.

On the positive side, Windows Forms is relatively simple to learn and has a wealth of support in third-party controls.

The Windows Forms types are in the namespaces System.Windows.Forms (in *System.Windows.Forms.dll*) and System.Drawing (in *System.Drawing.dll*). The latter also contains the GDI+ types for drawing custom controls.

Backend Technologies

ADO.NET

ADO.NET is the managed data access API. Although the name is derived from the 1990s-era ADO (ActiveX Data Objects), the technology is completely different. ADO.NET contains two major low-level components:

Provider layer

The provider model defines common classes and interfaces for low-level access to database providers. These interfaces comprise connections, commands, adapters, and readers (forward-only, read-only cursors over a database). The Framework ships with native support for Microsoft SQL Server and Oracle and has OLE-DB and ODBC providers.

DataSet model

A DataSet is a structured cache of data. It resembles a primitive in-memory database, which defines SQL constructs such as tables, rows, columns, relationships, constraints, and views. By programming against a cache of data, you can reduce the number of trips to the server, increasing server scalability and the responsiveness of a rich-client user interface. DataSets are serializable and are designed to be sent across the wire between client and server applications.

Sitting above the provider layer are two APIs that offer the ability to query databases via LINQ:

- LINQ to SQL (introduced in Framework 3.5)
- Entity Framework (introduced in Framework 3.5 SP1)

Both technologies include *object/relational mappers* (ORMs), meaning they automatically map objects (based on classes that you define) to rows in the database. This allows you to query those objects via LINQ (instead of writing SQL select statements)—and update them without manually writing SQL insert/delete/update statements. This cuts the volume of code in an application's data access layer (particularly the "plumbing" code) and provides strong static type safety. These technologies also avoid the need for DataSets as receptacles of data—although DataSets still provide the unique ability to store and serialize state changes (something particularly useful in multitier applications). You can use LINQ to SQL or Entity Framework in conjunction with DataSets, although the process is somewhat clumsy and DataSets are inherently ungainly. In other words, there's no straightforward out-of-the-box solution for writing *n*-tier applications with Microsoft's ORMs as yet.

LINQ to SQL is simpler and faster than Entity Framework, and tends to produce better SQL. Entity Framework is more flexible in that you can create elaborate mappings between the database and the classes that you query. Entity Framework also has third-party support for databases other than SQL Server.

Windows Workflow

Windows Workflow is a framework for modeling and managing potentially long-running business processes. Workflow targets a standard runtime library, providing consistency and interoperability. Workflow also helps reduce coding for dynamically controlled decision-making trees.

Windows Workflow is not strictly a backend technology—you can use it anywhere (an example is page flow, in the UI).

Workflow came originally with .NET Framework 3.0, with its types defined in the `System.WorkFlow` namespace. Workflow has been substantially revised in Framework 4.0; the new types live in and under the `System.Activities` namespace.

COM+ and MSMQ

The Framework allows you to interoperate with COM+ for services such as distributed transactions, via types in the `System.EnterpriseServices` namespace. It also supports MSMQ (Microsoft Message Queuing) for asynchronous, one-way messaging through types in `System.Messaging`.

Distributed System Technologies

Windows Communication Foundation (WCF)

WCF is a sophisticated communications infrastructure introduced in Framework 3.0. WCF is flexible and configurable enough to make both of its predecessors— Remoting and (.ASMX) Web Services—*mostly* redundant.

WCF, Remoting, and Web Services are all alike in that they implement the following basic model in allowing a client and server application to communicate:

- On the server, you indicate what methods you'd like remote client applications to be able to call.
- On the client, you specify or infer the *signatures* of the server methods you'd like to call.
- On both the server and the client, you choose a transport and communication protocol (in WCF, this is done through a *binding*).
- The client establishes a connection to the server.
- The client calls a remote method, which executes transparently on the server.

WCF further decouples the client and server through service contracts and data contracts. Conceptually, the client sends an (XML or binary) message to an endpoint on a remote *service*, rather than directly invoking a remote *method*. One of the benefits of this decoupling is that clients have no dependency on the .NET platform or on any proprietary communication protocols.

WCF is highly configurable and provides the most extensive support for standardized messaging protocols, including WS-*. This lets you communicate with parties running different software—possibly on different platforms—while still supporting advanced features such as encryption. Another benefit of WCF is that you can change protocols without needing to change other aspects of your client or server applications.

The types for communicating with WCF are in, and are below, the `System.Service Model` namespace.

Remoting and Web Services

Remoting and .ASMX Web Services are WCF's predecessors and are almost redundant in WCF's wake—although Remoting still has a niche in communicating between application domains within the same process (see Chapter 24).

Remoting's functionality is geared toward tightly coupled applications. A typical example is when the client and server are both .NET applications written by the same company (or companies sharing common assemblies). Communication typically involves exchanging potentially complex custom .NET objects that the Remoting infrastructure serializes and deserializes without needing intervention.

The functionality of Web Services is geared toward loosely coupled or SOA-style applications. A typical example is a server designed to accept simple SOAP-based messages that originate from clients running a variety of software—on a variety of platforms. Web Services can only use HTTP and SOAP as transport and formatting protocols, and applications are normally hosted under IIS. The benefits of interoperability come at a performance cost—a Web Services application is typically slower, in both execution and development time, than a well-designed Remoting application.

The types for Remoting are in or under `System.Runtime.Remoting`; the types for Web Services are under `System.Web.Services`.

CardSpace

CardSpace is a token-based authentication and identity management protocol designed to simplify password management for end users. The technology has received little attention because of the difficulty in porting tokens across machines (*OpenID* is a popular alternative that avoids this problem).

CardSpace builds on open XML standards, and parties can participate independently of Microsoft. A user can hold multiple identities, which are maintained by a third party (the *identity provider*). When a user wants to access a resource at site X, the user authenticates to the identity provider, which then issues a token to site X. This avoids having to provide a password directly to site X and reduces the number of identities that the user needs to maintain.

WCF allows you to specify a CardSpace identity when connecting through a secure HTTP channel, through types in the `System.IdentityModel.Claims` and `System.IdentityModel.Policy` namespaces.

6

Framework Fundamentals

Many of the core facilities that you need when programming are provided not by the C# language, but by types in the .NET Framework. In this chapter, we cover the Framework's role in fundamental programming tasks, such as virtual equality comparison, order comparison, and type conversion. We also cover the basic Framework types, such as String, DateTime, and Enum.

The types in this section reside in the System namespace, with the following exceptions:

- StringBuilder is defined in System.Text, as are the types for *text encodings*.
- CultureInfo and associated types are defined in System.Globalization.
- XmlConvert is defined in System.Xml.

String and Text Handling

Char

A C# char represents a single Unicode character and aliases the System.Char struct. In Chapter 2, we described how to express char literals. For example:

```
char c = 'A';
char newLine = '\n';
```

System.Char defines a range of static methods for working with characters, such as ToUpper, ToLower, and IsWhiteSpace. You can call these through either the System.Char type or its char alias:

```
Console.WriteLine (System.Char.ToUpper ('c'));   // C
Console.WriteLine (char.IsWhiteSpace ('\t'));     // True
```

ToUpper and ToLower honor the end user's locale, which can lead to subtle bugs. The following expression evaluates to false in Turkey:

```
char.ToUpper ('i') == 'I'
```

because in Turkey, char.ToUpper ('i') is 'İ' (notice the dot on top!). To avoid this problem, System.Char (and System.String) also provides culture-invariant versions of ToUpper and ToLower ending with the word *Invariant*. These always apply English culture rules:

```
Console.WriteLine (char.ToUpperInvariant ('i'));    // I
```

This is a shortcut for:

```
Console.WriteLine (char.ToUpper ('i', CultureInfo.InvariantCulture))
```

For more on locales and culture, see "Formatting and parsing" on page 212.

Most of char's remaining static methods are related to categorizing characters and are listed in Table 6-1.

Table 6-1. Static methods for categorizing characters

Static method	Characters included	Unicode categories included
IsLetter	A–Z, a–z, and letters of other alphabets	UpperCaseLetter
		LowerCaseLetter
		TitleCaseLetter
		ModifierLetter
		OtherLetter
IsUpper	Uppercase letters	UpperCaseLetter
IsLower	Lowercase letters	LowerCaseLetter
IsDigit	0–9 plus digits of other alphabets	DecimalDigitNumber
IsLetterOrDigit	Letters plus digits	Sum of IsLetter and IsDigit
IsNumber	All digits plus Unicode fractions and Roman numeral symbols	DecimalDigitNumber
		LetterNumber
		OtherNumber
IsSeparator	Space plus all Unicode separator characters	LineSeparator
		ParagraphSeparator
IsWhiteSpace	All separators plus \n, \r, \t, \f, and \v	LineSeparator
		ParagraphSeparator
IsPunctuation	Symbols used for punctuation in Western and other alphabets	DashPunctuation
		ConnectorPunctuation
		InitialQuotePunctuation
		FinalQuotePunctuation
IsSymbol	Most other printable symbols	MathSymbol
		ModifierSymbol
		OtherSymbol

Static method	Characters included	Unicode categories included
IsControl	Nonprintable "control" characters below 0x20, such as \r, \n, \t, \0, and characters between 0x7F and 0x9A	(None)

For more granular categorization, char provides a static method called GetUnicode Category; this returns a UnicodeCategory enumeration whose members are shown in the rightmost column of Table 6-1.

 By explicitly casting from an integer, it's possible to produce a char outside the allocated Unicode set. To test a character's validity, call char.GetUnicodeCategory: if the result is UnicodeCa tegory.OtherNotAssigned, the character is invalid.

A char is 16 bits wide—enough to represent any Unicode character in the *Basic Multilingual Plane*. To go outside this, you must use surrogate pairs: we describe the methods for doing this in "Text Encodings and Unicode" on page 203.

String

A C# string (== System.String) is an immutable (unchangeable) sequence of characters. In Chapter 2, we described how to express string literals, perform equality comparisons, and concatenate two strings. This section covers the remaining functions for working with strings, exposed through the static and instance members of the System.String class.

Constructing strings

The simplest way to construct a string is to assign a literal, as we saw in Chapter 2:

```
string s1 = "Hello";
string s2 = "First Line\r\nSecond Line";
string s3 = @"\\server\fileshare\helloworld.cs";
```

To create a repeating sequence of characters you can use string's constructor:

```
Console.Write (new string ('*', 10));      // **********
```

You can also construct a string from a char array. The ToCharArray method does the reverse:

```
char[] ca = "Hello".ToCharArray();
string s = new string (ca);              // s = "Hello"
```

string's constructor is also overloaded to accept various (unsafe) pointer types, in order to create strings from types such as char*.

Null and empty strings

An empty string has a length of zero. To create an empty string, you can use either a literal or the static string.Empty field; to test for an empty string, you can either perform an equality comparison or test its Length property:

```
string empty = "";
Console.WriteLine (empty == "");              // True
Console.WriteLine (empty == string.Empty);    // True
Console.WriteLine (empty.Length == 0);        // True
```

Because strings are reference types, they can also be null:

```
string nullString = null;
Console.WriteLine (nullString == null);        // True
Console.WriteLine (nullString == "");           // False
Console.WriteLine (nullString.Length == 0);    // NullReferenceException
```

The static `string.IsNullOrEmpty` method is a useful shortcut for testing whether a given string is either null or empty.

Accessing characters within a string

A string's indexer returns a single character at the given index. As with all functions that operate on strings, this is zero-indexed:

```
string str  = "abcde";
char letter = str[1];          // letter == 'b'
```

`string` also implements `IEnumerable<char>`, so you can `foreach` over its characters:

```
foreach (char c in "123") Console.Write (c + ",");     // 1,2,3,
```

Searching within strings

The simplest methods for searching within strings are `Contains`, `StartsWith`, and `EndsWith`. These all return `true` or `false`:

```
Console.WriteLine ("quick brown fox".Contains ("brown"));   // True
Console.WriteLine ("quick brown fox".EndsWith ("fox"));     // True
```

`IndexOf` is more powerful: it returns the first position of a given character or substring (or -1 if the substring isn't found):

```
Console.WriteLine ("abcde".IndexOf ("cd"));    // 2
```

`IndexOf` is overloaded to accept a `startPosition` (an index from which to begin searching) and a `StringComparison` enum. The latter allows you to perform case-insensitive searches:

```
Console.WriteLine ("abcde".IndexOf ("CD",
                   StringComparison.CurrentCultureIgnoreCase));   // 2
```

`LastIndexOf` is like `IndexOf`, but works backward through the string.

`IndexOfAny` returns the first matching position of any one of a set of characters:

```
Console.Write ("ab,cd ef".IndexOfAny (new char[] {' ', ','} ));       // 2
Console.Write ("pas5w0rd".IndexOfAny ("0123456789".ToCharArray() ));  // 3
```

`LastIndexOfAny` does the same in the reverse direction.

Manipulating strings

Because `String` is immutable, all the methods that "manipulate" a string return a new one, leaving the original untouched (the same goes for when you reassign a string variable).

`Substring` extracts a portion of a string:

```
string left3 = "12345".Substring (0, 3);    // left3 = "123";
string mid3  = "12345".Substring (1, 3);    // mid3 = "234";
```

If you omit the length, you get the remainder of the string:

```
string end3  = "12345".Substring (2);       // end3 = "345";
```

`Insert` and `Remove` insert or remove characters at a specified position:

```
string s1 = "helloworld".Insert (5, ", ");  // s1 = "hello, world"
string s2 = s1.Remove (5, 2);               // s2 = "helloworld";
```

`PadLeft` and `PadRight` pad a string to a given length with a specified character (or a space if unspecified):

```
Console.WriteLine ("12345".PadLeft (9, '*'));  // ****12345
Console.WriteLine ("12345".PadLeft (9));       //     12345
```

If the input string is longer than the padding length, the original string is returned unchanged.

`TrimStart` and `TrimEnd` remove specified characters from the beginning or end of a string; `Trim` does both. By default, these functions remove whitespace characters (including spaces, tabs, new lines, and Unicode variations of these):

```
Console.WriteLine ("  abc \t\r\n ".Trim().Length);   // 3
```

`Replace` replaces all occurrences of a particular character or substring:

```
Console.WriteLine ("to be done".Replace (" ", " | ") );  // to | be | done
Console.WriteLine ("to be done".Replace (" ", "")    );  // tobedone
```

`ToUpper` and `ToLower` return upper- and lowercase versions of the input string. By default, they honor the user's current language settings; `ToUpperInvariant` and `ToLowerInvariant` always apply English alphabet rules.

Splitting and joining strings

`Split` takes a sentence and returns an array of words:

```
string[] words = "The quick brown fox".Split();

foreach (string word in words)
  Console.Write (word + "|");   // The|quick|brown|fox|
```

By default, `Split` uses whitespace characters as delimiters; it's also overloaded to accept a `params` array of `char` or `string` delimiters. `Split` also optionally accepts a `StringSplitOptions` enum, which has an option to remove empty entries: this is useful when words are separated by several delimiters in a row.

The static Join method does the reverse of Split. It requires a delimiter and string array:

```
string[] words = "The quick brown fox".Split();
string together = string.Join (" ", words);     // The quick brown fox
```

The static Concat method is similar to Join but accepts only a params string array and applies no separator. Concat is exactly equivalent to the + operator (the compiler, in fact, translates + to Concat):

```
string sentence     = string.Concat ("The", " quick", " brown", " fox");
string sameSentence = "The" + " quick" + " brown" + " fox";
```

String.Format and composite format strings

The static Format method provides a convenient way to build strings that embed variables. The embedded variables can be of any type; the Format simply calls ToString on them.

The master string that includes the embedded variables is called a *composite format string*. When calling String.Format, you provide a composite format string followed by each of the embedded variables. For example:

```
string composite = "It's {0} degrees in {1} on this {2} morning";
string s = string.Format (composite, 35, "Perth", DateTime.Now.DayOfWeek);

// s == "It's 35 degrees in Perth on this Friday morning"
```

(And that's Celsius!)

Each number in curly braces is called a *format item*. The number corresponds to the argument position and is optionally followed by:

- A comma and a *minimum width* to apply
- A colon and a *format string*

The minimum width is useful for aligning columns. If the value is negative, the data is left-aligned; otherwise, it's right-aligned. For example:

```
string composite = "Name={0,-20} Credit Limit={1,15:C}";

Console.WriteLine (string.Format (composite, "Mary", 500));
Console.WriteLine (string.Format (composite, "Elizabeth", 20000));
```

Here's the result:

```
Name=Mary            Credit Limit=      $500.00
Name=Elizabeth       Credit Limit=   $20,000.00
```

The equivalent without using string.Format is this:

```
string s = "Name=" + "Mary".PadRight (20) +
           " Credit Limit=" + 500.ToString ("C").PadLeft (15);
```

The credit limit is formatted as currency by virtue of the "C" format string. We describe format strings in detail in "Formatting and parsing" on page 212.

A disadvantage of composite format strings is that it's easier to make a mistake that goes unnoticed until runtime—such as having greater or fewer format items than values. Such a mistake is harder to make when the format items and values are together.

Comparing Strings

In comparing two values, the .NET Framework differentiates the concepts of *equality comparison* and *order comparison*. Equality comparison tests whether two instances are semantically the same; order comparison tests which of two (if any) instances comes first when arranging them in ascending or descending sequence.

Equality comparison is not a *subset* of order comparison; the two systems have different purposes. It's legal, for instance, to have two unequal values in the same ordering position. We resume this topic in "Equality Comparison" on page 245.

For string equality comparison, you can use the == operator or one of `string`'s `Equals` methods. The latter are more versatile because they allow you to specify options such as case-insensitivity.

Another difference is that == does not work reliably on strings if the variables are cast to the `object` type. We explain why this is so in "Equality Comparison" on page 245.

For string order comparison, you can use either the `CompareTo` instance method or the static `Compare` and `CompareOrdinal` methods: these return a positive or negative number—or zero—depending on whether the first value comes before, after, or alongside the second.

Before going into the details of each, we need to examine .NET's underlying string comparison algorithms.

Ordinal versus culture comparison

There are two basic algorithms for string comparison: *ordinal* and *culture-sensitive*. Ordinal comparisons interpret characters simply as numbers (according to their numeric Unicode value); culture-sensitive comparisons interpret characters with reference to a particular alphabet. There are two special cultures: the "current culture," which is based on settings picked up from the computer's control panel, and the "invariant culture," which is the same on every computer (and closely maps American culture).

For equality comparison, both ordinal and culture-specific algorithms are useful. For ordering, however, culture-specific comparison is nearly always preferable: to order strings alphabetically, you need an alphabet. Ordinal relies on the numeric Unicode point values, which happen to put English characters in alphabetical order—but even then not exactly as you might expect. For example, assuming case-sensitivity, consider the strings "Atom", "atom", and "Zamia". The invariant culture puts them in the following order:

```
"Atom", "atom", "Zamia"
```

Ordinal arranges them instead as follows:

```
"Atom", "Zamia", "atom"
```

This is because the invariant culture encapsulates an alphabet, which considers uppercase characters adjacent to their lowercase counterparts (AaBbCcDd...). The ordinal algorithm, however, puts all the uppercase characters first, and then all lowercase characters (A..Z, a..z). This is essentially a throwback to the ASCII character set invented in the 1960s.

String equality comparison

Despite ordinal's limitations, string's == operator always performs *ordinal case-sensitive* comparison. The same goes for the instance version of string.Equals when called without arguments; this defines the "default" equality comparison behavior for the string type.

> The ordinal algorithm was chosen for string's == and Equals functions because it's both highly efficient and *deterministic*. String equality comparison is considered fundamental and is performed far more frequently than order comparison.
>
> A "strict" notion of equality is also consistent with the general use of the == operator.

The following methods allow culture-aware or case-insensitive comparisons:

```
public bool Equals(string value, StringComparison comparisonType);

public static bool Equals (string a, string b,
                           StringComparison comparisonType);
```

The static version is advantageous in that it still works if one or both of the strings are null. StringComparison is an enum defined as follows:

```
public enum StringComparison
{
  CurrentCulture,              // Case-sensitive
  CurrentCultureIgnoreCase,
  InvariantCulture,           // Case-sensitive
  InvariantCultureIgnoreCase,
  Ordinal,                    // Case-sensitive
  OrdinalIgnoreCase
}
```

For example:

```
Console.WriteLine (string.Equals ("foo", "FOO",
                   StringComparison.OrdinalIgnoreCase));   // True

Console.WriteLine ("ü" == "ü");                            // False

Console.WriteLine (string.Equals ("ü", "ü",
                   StringComparison.CurrentCulture));      // ?
```

(The result of the final comparison is determined by the computer's current language settings.)

String order comparison

String's CompareTo instance method performs *culture-sensitive, case-sensitive* order comparison. Unlike the == operator, CompareTo does not use ordinal comparison: for ordering, a culture-sensitive algorithm is much more useful.

Here's the method's definition:

```
public int CompareTo (string strB);
```

 The CompareTo instance method implements the generic IComparable interface, a standard comparison protocol used across the .NET Framework. This means string's CompareTo defines the default ordering behavior strings, in such applications as sorted collections, for instance. For more information on IComparable, see "Order Comparison" on page 255.

For other kinds of comparison, you can call the static Compare and CompareOrdinal methods:

```
public static int Compare (string strA, string strB,
                           StringComparison comparisonType);

public static int Compare (string strA, string strB, bool ignoreCase,
                           CultureInfo culture);

public static int Compare (string strA, string strB, bool ignoreCase);

public static int CompareOrdinal (string strA, string strB);
```

The last two methods are simply shortcuts for calling the first two methods.

All of the order comparison methods return a positive number, a negative number, or zero, depending on whether the first value comes after, before, or alongside the second value:

```
Console.WriteLine ("Boston".CompareTo ("Austin"));    // 1
Console.WriteLine ("Boston".CompareTo ("Boston"));    // 0
Console.WriteLine ("Boston".CompareTo ("Chicago"));   // -1
Console.WriteLine ("ü".CompareTo ("ü"));              // 0
Console.WriteLine ("foo".CompareTo ("FOO"));          // -1
```

The following performs a case-insensitive comparison using the current culture:

```
Console.WriteLine (string.Compare ("foo", "FOO", true));   // 0
```

By supplying a `CultureInfo` object, you can plug in any alphabet:

```
// CultureInfo is defined in the System.Globalization namespace

CultureInfo german = CultureInfo.GetCultureInfo ("de-DE");
int i = string.Compare ("Müller", "Muller", false, german);
```

StringBuilder

The `StringBuilder` class (`System.Text` namespace) represents a mutable (editable) string. With a `StringBuilder`, you can `Append`, `Insert`, `Remove`, and `Replace` substrings without replacing the whole `StringBuilder`.

`StringBuilder`'s constructor optionally accepts an initial string value, as well as a starting size for its internal capacity (default is 16 characters). If you go above this, `StringBuilder` automatically resizes its internal structures to accommodate (at a slight performance cost) up to its maximum capacity (default is `int.MaxValue`).

A popular use of `StringBuilder` is to build up a long string by repeatedly calling `Append`. This approach is much more efficient than repeatedly concatenating ordinary string types:

```
StringBuilder sb = new StringBuilder();
for (int i = 0; i < 50; i++) sb.Append (i + ",");
```

To get the final result, call `ToString()`:

```
Console.WriteLine (sb.ToString());
```

```
0,1,2,3,4,5,6,7,8,9,10,11,12,13,14,15,16,17,18,19,20,21,22,23,24,25,26,
27,28,29,30,31,32,33,34,35,36,37,38,39,40,41,42,43,44,45,46,47,48,49,
```

In our example, the expression `i + ","` means that we're still repeatedly concatenating strings. However, this incurs only a small performance cost in that the strings in question are small and don't grow with each loop iteration. For maximum performance, however, we could change the loop body to this:

```
{ sb.Append (i.ToString()); sb.Append (","); }
```

`AppendLine` performs an `Append` that adds a new line sequence (`"\r\n"` in Windows). `AppendFormat` accepts a composite format string, just like `String.Format`.

As well as the `Insert`, `Remove`, and `Replace` methods (`Replace` functions such as string's `Replace`), `StringBuilder` defines a `Length` property and a writable indexer for getting/setting individual characters.

To clear the contents of a `StringBuilder`, either instantiate a new one or set its `Length` to zero.

Setting a `StringBuilder`'s `Length` to zero doesn't shrink its *internal* capacity. So, if the `StringBuilder` previously contained 1 million characters, it will continue to occupy around 2 MB of memory after zeroing its `Length`. If you want to release the memory, you must create a new `StringBuilder` and allow the old one to drop out of scope (and be garbage-collected).

Text Encodings and Unicode

A *character set* is an allocation of characters, each with a numeric code or *code point*. There are two character sets in common use: Unicode and ASCII. Unicode has an address space of approximately 1 million characters, of which about 100,000 are currently allocated. Unicode covers most spoken world languages, as well as some historical languages and special symbols. The ASCII set is simply the first 127 characters of the Unicode set, which covers most of what you see on a U.S.-style keyboard. ASCII predates Unicode by 30 years and is still sometimes used for its simplicity and efficiency: each character is represented by one byte.

The .NET type system is designed to work with the Unicode character set. ASCII is implicitly supported, though, by virtue of being a subset of Unicode.

A *text encoding* maps characters from their numeric code point to a binary representation. In .NET, text encodings come into play primarily when dealing with text files or streams. When you read a text file into a string, a *text encoder* translates the file data from binary into the internal Unicode representation that the `char` and `string` types expect. A text encoding can restrict what characters can be represented, as well as impacting storage efficiency.

There are two categories of text encoding in .NET:

- Those that map Unicode characters to another character set
- Those that use standard Unicode encoding schemes

The first category contains legacy encodings such as IBM's EBCDIC and 8-bit character sets with extended characters in the upper-128 region that were popular prior to Unicode (identified by a code page). The ASCII encoding is also in this category: it encodes the first 128 characters and drops everything else. This category contains the *nonlegacy* GB18030 as well, which is the mandatory standard for applications written in China—or sold to China—since 2000.

In the second category are UTF-8, UTF-16, and UTF-32 (and the obsolete UTF-7). Each differs in space efficiency. UTF-8 is the most space-efficient for most kinds of text: it uses *between one and four bytes* to represent each character. The first 128 characters require only a single byte, making it compatible with ASCII. UTF-8 is the most popular encoding for text files and streams (particularly on the Internet), and it is the default for stream I/O in .NET (in fact, it's the default for almost everything that implicitly uses an encoding).

UTF-16 uses one or two 16-bit words to represent each character, and is what .NET uses internally to represent characters and strings. Some programs also write files in UTF-16.

UTF-32 is the least space-efficient: it maps each code point directly to 32 bits, so every character consumes four bytes. UTF-32 is rarely used for this reason. It does, however, make random access very easy because every character takes an equal number of bytes.

Obtaining an Encoding object

The `Encoding` class in `System.Text` is the common base type for classes that encapsulate text encodings. There are several subclasses—their purpose is to encapsulate families of encodings with similar features. The easiest way to instantiate a correctly configured class is to call `Encoding.GetEncoding` with a standard IANA name:

```
Encoding utf8 = Encoding.GetEncoding ("utf-8");
Encoding chinese = Encoding.GetEncoding ("GB18030");
```

The most common encodings can also be obtained through dedicated static properties on `Encoding`:

Encoding name	Static property on Encoding
UTF-8	`Encoding.UTF8`
UTF-16	`Encoding.Unicode` (*not* UTF16)
UTF-32	`Encoding.UTF32`
ASCII	`Encoding.ASCII`

The static `GetEncodings` method returns a list of all supported encodings, with their standard IANA names:

```
foreach (EncodingInfo info in Encoding.GetEncodings())
    Console.WriteLine (info.Name);
```

The other way to obtain an encoding is to directly instantiate an encoding class. Doing so allows you to set various options via constructor arguments, including:

- Whether to throw an exception if an invalid byte sequence is encountered when decoding. The default is false.
- Whether to encode/decode UTF-16/UTF-32 with the most significant bytes first (*big endian*) or the least significant bytes first (*little endian*). The default is *little endian*, the standard on the Windows operating system.
- Whether to emit a byte-order mark (a prefix that indicates *endianness*).

Encoding for file and stream I/O

The most common application for an `Encoding` object is to control how text is read and written to a file or stream. For example, the following writes "Testing..." to a file called *data.txt* in UTF-16 encoding:

```
System.IO.File.WriteAllText ("data.txt", "Testing...", Encoding.Unicode);
```

If you omit the final argument, `WriteAllText` applies the ubiquitous UTF-8 encoding.

UTF-8 is the default text encoding for all file and stream I/O.

We resume this subject in Chapter 14, in "Stream Adapters" on page 552.

Encoding to byte arrays

You can also use an `Encoding` object to go to and from a byte array. The `GetBytes` method converts from `string` to `byte[]` with the given encoding; `GetString` converts from `byte[]` to `string`:

```
byte[] utf8Bytes  = System.Text.Encoding.UTF8.GetBytes    ("0123456789");
byte[] utf16Bytes = System.Text.Encoding.Unicode.GetBytes ("0123456789");
byte[] utf32Bytes = System.Text.Encoding.UTF32.GetBytes   ("0123456789");

Console.WriteLine (utf8Bytes.Length);    // 10
Console.WriteLine (utf16Bytes.Length);   // 20
Console.WriteLine (utf32Bytes.Length);   // 40

string original1 = System.Text.Encoding.UTF8.GetString    (utf8Bytes);
string original2 = System.Text.Encoding.Unicode.GetString (utf16Bytes);
string original3 = System.Text.Encoding.UTF32.GetString   (utf32Bytes);

Console.WriteLine (original1);           // 0123456789
Console.WriteLine (original2);           // 0123456789
Console.WriteLine (original3);           // 0123456789
```

UTF-16 and surrogate pairs

Recall that .NET stores characters and strings in UTF-16. Because UTF-16 requires one or two 16-bit words per character, and a `char` is only 16 bits in length, some Unicode characters require two `char`s to represent. This has a couple of consequences:

- A string's `Length` property may be greater than its real character count.
- A single `char` is not always enough to fully represent a Unicode character.

Most applications ignore this, because nearly all commonly used characters fit into a section of Unicode called the *Basic Multilingual Plane* (BMP), which requires only one 16-bit word in UTF-16. The BMP covers several dozen world languages and includes more than 30,000 Chinese characters. Excluded are characters of some ancient languages, symbols for musical notation, and some less common Chinese characters.

If you need to support two-word characters, the following static methods in `char` convert a 32-bit code point to a string of two `char`s, and back again:

```
string ConvertFromUtf32 (int utf32)
int    ConvertToUtf32   (char highSurrogate, char lowSurrogate)
```

Two-word characters are called *surrogates*. They are easy to spot because each word is in the range 0xD800 to 0xDFFF. You can use the following static methods in char to assist:

```
bool IsSurrogate     (char c)
bool IsHighSurrogate (char c)
bool IsLowSurrogate  (char c)
bool IsSurrogatePair (char highSurrogate, char lowSurrogate)
```

The StringInfo class in the System.Globalization namespace also provides a range of methods and properties for working with two-word characters.

Characters outside the BMP typically require special fonts and have limited operating system support.

Dates and Times

Three immutable structs in the System namespace do the job of representing dates and times: DateTime, DateTimeOffset, and TimeSpan. C# doesn't define any special keywords that map to these types.

TimeSpan

A TimeSpan represents an interval of time—or a time of the day. In the latter role, it's simply the "clock" time (without the date), which is equivalent to the time since midnight, assuming no daylight saving transition. A TimeSpan has a resolution of 100 ns, has a maximum value of about 10 million days, and can be positive or negative.

There are three ways to construct a TimeSpan:

- Through one of the constructors
- By calling one of the static From... methods
- By subtracting one DateTime from another

Here are the constructors:

```
public TimeSpan (int hours, int minutes, int seconds);
public TimeSpan (int days, int hours, int minutes, int seconds);
public TimeSpan (int days, int hours, int minutes, int seconds,
                                              int milliseconds);
public TimeSpan (long ticks);   // Each tick = 100ns
```

The static From... methods are more convenient when you want to specify an interval in just a single unit, such as minutes, hours, and so on:

```
public static TimeSpan FromDays (double value);
public static TimeSpan FromHours (double value);
public static TimeSpan FromMinutes (double value);
public static TimeSpan FromSeconds (double value);
public static TimeSpan FromMilliseconds (double value);
```

For example:

```
Console.WriteLine (new TimeSpan (2, 30, 0));     // 02:30:00
Console.WriteLine (TimeSpan.FromHours (2.5));     // 02:30:00
Console.WriteLine (TimeSpan.FromHours (-2.5));    // -02:30:00
```

TimeSpan overloads the < and > operators, as well as the + and - operators. The following expression evaluates to a TimeSpan of 2.5 hours:

```
TimeSpan.FromHours(2) + TimeSpan.FromMinutes(30);
```

The next expression evaluates to one second short of 10 days:

```
TimeSpan.FromDays(10) - TimeSpan.FromSeconds(1);     // 9.23:59:59
```

Using this expression, we can illustrate the integer properties Days, Hours, Minutes, Seconds, and Milliseconds:

```
TimeSpan nearlyTenDays = TimeSpan.FromDays(10) - TimeSpan.FromSeconds(1);

Console.WriteLine (nearlyTenDays.Days);           // 9
Console.WriteLine (nearlyTenDays.Hours);          // 23
Console.WriteLine (nearlyTenDays.Minutes);        // 59
Console.WriteLine (nearlyTenDays.Seconds);        // 59
Console.WriteLine (nearlyTenDays.Milliseconds);   // 0
```

In contrast, the Total... properties return values of type double describing the entire time span:

```
Console.WriteLine (nearlyTenDays.TotalDays);          // 9.99998842592593
Console.WriteLine (nearlyTenDays.TotalHours);         // 239.999722222222
Console.WriteLine (nearlyTenDays.TotalMinutes);       // 14399.9833333333
Console.WriteLine (nearlyTenDays.TotalSeconds);       // 863999
Console.WriteLine (nearlyTenDays.TotalMilliseconds);  // 863999000
```

The static Parse method does the opposite of ToString, converting a string to a TimeSpan. TryParse does the same, but returns false rather than throwing an exception if the conversion fails. The XmlConvert class also provides TimeSpan/string conversion methods that follow standard XML formatting protocols.

The default value for a TimeSpan is TimeSpan.Zero.

TimeSpan can also be used to represent the time of the day (the elapsed time since midnight). To obtain the current time of day, call DateTime.Now.TimeOfDay.

DateTime and DateTimeOffset

DateTime and DateTimeOffset are immutable structs for representing a date, and optionally, a time. They have a resolution of 100 ns, and a range covering the years 0001 through 9999.

DateTimeOffset was added in Framework 3.5 and is functionally similar to DateTime. Its distinguishing feature is that it also stores a UTC offset; this allows more meaningful results when comparing values across different time zones.

An excellent article on the rationale behind the introduction of DateTimeOffset is available on the MSDN BCL blogs. The title is "A Brief History of DateTime," by Anthony Moore (*http:// blogs.msdn.com/bclteam/archive/2007/06/18/a-brief-history-of -datetime-anthony-moore.aspx*).

Choosing between DateTime and DateTimeOffset

DateTime and DateTimeOffset differ in how they handle time zones. A DateTime incorporates a three-state flag indicating whether the DateTime is relative to:

- The local time on the current computer
- UTC (the modern equivalent of Greenwich Mean Time)
- Unspecified

A DateTimeOffset is more specific—it stores the offset from UTC as a TimeSpan:

```
July 01 2007 03:00:00 -06:00
```

This influences equality comparisons, which is the main factor in choosing between DateTime and DateTimeOffset. Specifically:

- DateTime ignores the three-state flag in comparisons and considers two values equal if they have the same year, month, day, hour, minute, and so on.
- DateTimeOffset considers two values equal if they refer to the *same point in time*.

Daylight saving time can make this distinction important even if your application doesn't need to handle multiple geographic time zones.

So, DateTime considers the following two values different, whereas DateTimeOffset considers them equal:

```
July 01 2007 09:00:00 +00:00 (GMT)
July 01 2007 03:00:00 -06:00 (local time, Central America)
```

In most cases, DateTimeOffset's equality logic is preferable. For example, in calculating which of two international events is more recent, a DateTimeOffset implicitly gives the right answer. Similarly, a hacker plotting a distributed denial of service attack would reach for a DateTimeOffset! To do the same with DateTime requires standardizing on a single time zone (typically UTC) throughout your application. This is problematic for two reasons:

- To be friendly to the end user, UTC DateTimes require explicit conversion to local time prior to formatting.
- It's easy to forget and incorporate a local DateTime.

DateTime is better, though, at specifying a value relative to the local computer at runtime—for example, if you want to schedule an archive at each of your international offices for next Sunday, at 3 A.M. local time (when there's least activity). Here, DateTime would be more suitable because it would respect each site's local time.

 Internally, DateTimeOffset uses a short integer to store the UTC offset in minutes. It doesn't store any regional information, so there's nothing present to indicate whether an offset of +08:00, for instance, refers to Singapore time or Perth time.

We revisit time zones and equality comparison in more depth in "Dates and Time Zones" on page 213.

 SQL Server 2008 introduces direct support for DateTimeOffset through a new data type of the same name.

Constructing a DateTime

DateTime defines constructors that accept integers for the year, month, and day— and optionally, the hour, minute, second, and millisecond:

```
public DateTime (int year, int month, int day);

public DateTime (int year, int month, int day,
                 int hour, int minute, int second, int millisecond);
```

If you specify only a date, the time is implicitly set to midnight (0:00).

The DateTime constructors also allow you to specify a DateTimeKind—an enum with the following values:

```
Unspecified, Local, Utc
```

This corresponds to the three-state flag described in the preceding section. Unspecified is the default and it means that the DateTime is time-zone-agnostic. Local means relative to the local time zone on the current computer. A local Date Time does not include information about *which particular time zone* it refers to, nor, unlike DateTimeOffset, the numeric offset from UTC.

A DateTime's Kind property returns its DateTimeKind.

DateTime's constructors are also overloaded to accept a Calendar object as well— this allows you to specify a date using any of the Calendar subclasses defined in System.Globalization. For example:

```
DateTime d = new DateTime (5767, 1, 1,
                 new System.Globalization.HebrewCalendar());

Console.WriteLine (d);    // 12/12/2006 12:00:00 AM
```

(The formatting of the date in this example depends on your computer's control panel settings.) A DateTime always uses the default Gregorian calendar—this example, a one-time conversion, takes place during construction. To perform computations using another calendar, you must use the methods on the `Calendar` subclass itself.

You can also construct a `DateTime` with a single *ticks* value of type `long`, where *ticks* is the number of 100 ns intervals from midnight 01/01/0001.

For interoperability, `DateTime` provides the static `FromFileTime` and `FromFileTimeUtc` methods for converting from a Windows file time (specified as a `long`) and `FromOADate` for converting from an OLE automation date/time (specified as a `double`).

To construct a `DateTime` from a string, call the static `Parse` or `ParseExact` method. Both methods accept optional flags and format providers; `ParseExact` also accepts a format string. We discuss parsing in greater detail in "Formatting and parsing" on page 212.

Constructing a DateTimeOffset

`DateTimeOffset` has a similar set of constructors. The difference is that you also specify a UTC offset as a `TimeSpan`:

```
public DateTimeOffset (int year, int month, int day,
                       int hour, int minute, int second,
                       TimeSpan offset);

public DateTimeOffset (int year, int month, int day,
                       int hour, int minute, int second, int millisecond,
                       TimeSpan offset);
```

The `TimeSpan` must amount to a whole number of minutes, or an exception is thrown.

`DateTimeOffset` also has constructors that accept a `Calendar` object, a `long` *ticks* value, and static `Parse` and `ParseExact` methods that accept a string.

You can construct a `DateTimeOffset` from an existing `DateTime` either by using these constructors:

```
public DateTimeOffset (DateTime dateTime);
public DateTimeOffset (DateTime dateTime, TimeSpan offset);
```

or with an implicit cast:

```
DateTimeOffset dt = new DateTime (2000, 2, 3);
```

> The implicit cast from `DateTime` to `DateTimeOffset` is handy because most of the .NET Framework supports `DateTime`—not `DateTimeOffset`.

If you don't specify an offset, it's inferred from the `DateTime` value using these rules:

- If the `DateTime` has a `DateTimeKind` of `Utc`, the offset is zero.
- If the `DateTime` has a `DateTimeKind` of `Local` or `Unspecified` (the default), the offset is taken from the current local time zone.

To convert in the other direction, `DateTimeOffset` provides three properties that return values of type `DateTime`:

- The `UtcDateTime` property returns a `DateTime` in UTC time.
- The `LocalDateTime` property returns a `DateTime` in the current local time zone (converting it if necessary).
- The `DateTime` property returns a `DateTime` in whatever zone it was specified, with a `Kind` of `Unspecified` (i.e., it returns the UTC time plus the offset).

The current DateTime/DateTimeOffset

Both `DateTime` and `DateTimeOffset` have a static `Now` property that returns the current date and time:

```
Console.WriteLine (DateTime.Now);          // 11/11/2007 1:23:45 PM
Console.WriteLine (DateTimeOffset.Now);    // 11/11/2007 1:23:45 PM -06:00
```

`DateTime` also provides a `Today` property that returns just the date portion:

```
Console.WriteLine (DateTime.Today);        // 11/11/2007 12:00:00 AM
```

The static `UtcNow` property returns the current date and time in UTC:

```
Console.WriteLine (DateTime.UtcNow);         // 11/11/2007 7:23:45 AM
Console.WriteLine (DateTimeOffset.UtcNow);   // 11/11/2007 7:23:45 AM +00:00
```

The precision of all these methods depends on the operating system and is typically in the 10–20 ms region.

Working with dates and times

`DateTime` and `DateTimeOffset` provide a similar set of instance properties that return various date/time elements:

```
DateTime dt = new DateTime (2000, 2, 3,
                            10, 20, 30);

Console.WriteLine (dt.Year);         // 2000
Console.WriteLine (dt.Month);        // 2
Console.WriteLine (dt.Day);          // 3
Console.WriteLine (dt.DayOfWeek);    // Thursday
Console.WriteLine (dt.DayOfYear);    // 34

Console.WriteLine (dt.Hour);         // 10
Console.WriteLine (dt.Minute);       // 20
Console.WriteLine (dt.Second);       // 30
Console.WriteLine (dt.Millisecond);  // 0
Console.WriteLine (dt.Ticks);        // 630851700300000000
Console.WriteLine (dt.TimeOfDay);    // 10:20:30  (returns a TimeSpan)
```

`DateTimeOffset` also has an `Offset` property of type `TimeSpan`.

Both types provide the following instance methods to perform computations (most accept an argument of type `double` or `int`):

```
AddYears  AddMonths   AddDays
AddHours  AddMinutes  AddSeconds  AddMilliseconds  AddTicks
```

These all return a new `DateTime` or `DateTimeOffset`, and they take into account such things as leap years. You can pass in a negative value to subtract.

The `Add` method adds a `TimeSpan` to a `DateTime` or `DateTimeOffset`. The + operator is overloaded to do the same job:

```
TimeSpan ts = TimeSpan.FromMinutes (90);
Console.WriteLine (dt.Add (ts));        // 3/02/2000 11:50:30 AM
Console.WriteLine (dt + ts);            // 3/02/2000 11:50:30 AM
```

You can also subtract a `TimeSpan` from a `DateTime`/`DateTimeOffset` and subtract one `DateTime`/`DateTimeOffset` from another. The latter gives you a `TimeSpan`:

```
DateTime thisYear = new DateTime (2007, 1, 1);
DateTime nextYear = thisYear.AddYears (1);
TimeSpan oneYear = nextYear - thisYear;
```

Formatting and parsing

Calling `ToString` on a `DateTime` formats the result as a *short date* (all numbers) followed by a *long time* (including seconds). For example:

```
13/02/2000 11:50:30 AM
```

The operating system's control panel, by default, determines such things as whether the day, month, or year comes first, the use of leading zeros, and whether 12- or 24-hour time is used.

Calling `ToString` on a `DateTimeOffset` is the same, except that the offset is returned also:

```
3/02/2000 11:50:30 AM -06:00
```

The `ToShortDateString` and `ToLongDateString` methods return just the date portion. The long date format is also determined by the control panel; an example is "Saturday, 17 February 2007". `ToShortTimeString` and `ToLongTimeString` return just the time portion, such as 17:10:10 (the former excludes seconds).

These four methods just described are actually shortcuts to four different *format strings*. `ToString` is overloaded to accept a format string and provider, allowing you to specify a wide range of options and control how regional settings are applied.

 `DateTime`s and `DateTimeOffset`s can be misparsed if the culture settings differ from those in force when formatting takes place. You can avoid this problem by using `ToString` in conjunction with a format string that ignores culture settings (such as "o"):

```
DateTime dt1 = DateTime.Now;
string cannotBeMisparsed = dt1.ToString ("o");
DateTime dt2 = DateTime.Parse (cannotBeMisparsed);
```

The static `Parse` and `ParseExact` methods do the reverse of `ToString`, converting a string to a `DateTime` or `DateTimeOffset`. The `Parse` method is also overloaded to accept a format provider.

Null DateTime and DateTimeOffset values

Because `DateTime` and `DateTimeOffset` are structs, they are not intrinsically nullable. When you need nullability, there are two ways around this:

- Use a `Nullable` type (i.e., `DateTime?` or `DateTimeOffset?`).
- Use the static field `DateTime.MinValue` or `DateTimeOffset.MinValue` (the *default values* for these types).

A nullable type is usually the best approach because the compiler helps to prevent mistakes. `DateTime.MinValue` is useful for backward compatibility with code written prior to C# 2.0 (when nullable types were introduced).

 Calling `ToUniversalTime` or `ToLocalTime` on a `DateTime.Min Value` can result in it no longer being `DateTime.MinValue` (depending on which side of GMT you are on). If you're right on GMT (England, outside daylight saving), the problem won't arise at all because local and UTC times are the same. This is your compensation for the English winter!

Dates and Time Zones

In this section, we examine in more detail how time zones influence `DateTime` and `DateTimeOffset`. We also look at the `TimeZone` and `TimeZoneInfo` types, which provide information on time zone offsets and daylight saving time.

DateTime and Time Zones

`DateTime` is simplistic in its handling of time zones. Internally, it stores a `DateTime` using two pieces of information:

- A 62-bit number, indicating the number of ticks since 1/1/0001
- A 2-bit enum, indicating the `DateTimeKind` (`Unspecified`, `Local`, or `Utc`)

When you compare two `DateTime` instances, only their *ticks* values are compared; their `DateTimeKind`s are ignored:

```
DateTime dt1 = new DateTime (2000, 1, 1, 10, 20, 30, DateTimeKind.Local);
DateTime dt2 = new DateTime (2000, 1, 1, 10, 20, 30, DateTimeKind.Utc);
Console.WriteLine (dt1 == dt2);        // True
DateTime local = DateTime.Now;
DateTime utc = local.ToUniversalTime();
Console.WriteLine (local == utc);      // False
```

The instance methods `ToUniversalTime`/`ToLocalTime` convert to universal/local time. These apply the computer's current time zone settings and return a new `DateTime` with a `DateTimeKind` of `Utc` or `Local`. No conversion happens if you call `ToUniversal Time` on a `DateTime` that's already `Utc`, or `ToLocalTime` on a `DateTime` that's already `Local`. You will get a conversion, however, if you call `ToUniversalTime` or `ToLocalTime` on a `DateTime` that's `Unspecified`.

You can construct a `DateTime` that differs from another only in `Kind` with the static `DateTime.SpecifyKind` method:

```
DateTime d = new DateTime (2000, 12, 12);  // Unspecified
DateTime utc = DateTime.SpecifyKind (d, DateTimeKind.Utc);
Console.WriteLine (utc);                    // 12/12/2000 12:00:00 AM
```

DateTimeOffset and Time Zones

Internally, `DateTimeOffset` comprises a `DateTime` field whose value is always in UTC, and a 16-bit integer field for the UTC offset in minutes. Comparisons look only at the (UTC) `DateTime`; the `Offset` is used primarily for formatting.

The `ToUniversalTime`/`ToLocalTime` methods return a `DateTimeOffset` representing the same point in time, but with a UTC or local offset. Unlike with `DateTime`, these methods don't affect the underlying date/time value, only the offset:

```
DateTimeOffset local = DateTimeOffset.Now;
DateTimeOffset utc   = local.ToUniversalTime();

Console.WriteLine (local.Offset);   // -06:00:00 (in Central America)
Console.WriteLine (utc.Offset);     // 00:00:00

Console.WriteLine (local == utc);             // True
```

To include the `Offset` in the comparison, you must use the `EqualsExact` method:

```
Console.WriteLine (local.EqualsExact (utc));     // False
```

TimeZone and TimeZoneInfo

The `TimeZone` and `TimeZoneInfo` classes provide information on time zone names, UTC offsets, and daylight saving time rules. `TimeZoneInfo` is the more powerful of the two and was new to Framework 3.5.

The biggest difference between the two types is that `TimeZone` lets you access only the current local time zone, whereas `TimeZoneInfo` provides access to all the world's time zones. Further, `TimeZoneInfo` exposes a richer (although at times, more awkward) rules-based model for describing daylight saving time.

TimeZone

The static `TimeZone.CurrentTimeZone` method returns a `TimeZone` object based on the current local settings. The following demonstrates the result if run in Western Australia:

```
TimeZone zone = TimeZone.CurrentTimeZone;
Console.WriteLine (zone.StandardName);   // W. Australia Standard Time
Console.WriteLine (zone.DaylightName);   // W. Australia Daylight Time
```

The `IsDaylightSavingTime` and `GetUtcOffset` methods work as follows:

```
DateTime dt1 = new DateTime (2008, 1, 1);
DateTime dt2 = new DateTime (2008, 6, 1);
Console.WriteLine (zone.IsDaylightSavingTime (dt1));   // True
Console.WriteLine (zone.IsDaylightSavingTime (dt2));   // False
```

```
Console.WriteLine (zone.GetUtcOffset (dt1));        // 09:00:00
Console.WriteLine (zone.GetUtcOffset (dt2));        // 08:00:00
```

The `GetDaylightChanges` method returns specific daylight saving time information for a given year:

```
DaylightTime day = zone.GetDaylightChanges (2008);
Console.WriteLine (day.Start);   // 26/10/2008 2:00:00 AM  (Note D/M/Y)
Console.WriteLine (day.End);     // 30/03/2008 3:00:00 AM
Console.WriteLine (day.Delta);   // 01:00:00
```

TimeZoneInfo

The `TimeZoneInfo` class works in a similar manner. `TimeZoneInfo.Local` returns the current local time zone:

```
TimeZoneInfo zone = TimeZoneInfo.Local;
Console.WriteLine (zone.StandardName);   // W. Australia Standard Time
Console.WriteLine (zone.DaylightName);   // W. Australia Daylight Time
```

`TimeZoneInfo` also provides `IsDaylightSavingTime` and `GetUtcOffset` methods—the difference is that they accept either a `DateTime` or a `DateTimeOffset`.

You can obtain a `TimeZoneInfo` for any of the world's time zones by calling `FindSystemTimeZoneById` with the zone ID. This feature is unique to `TimeZoneInfo`, as is everything else that we demonstrate from this point on. We'll stick with Western Australia for reasons that will soon become clear:

```
TimeZoneInfo wa = TimeZoneInfo.FindSystemTimeZoneById
  ("W. Australia Standard Time");

Console.WriteLine (wa.Id);               // W. Australia Standard Time
Console.WriteLine (wa.DisplayName);      // (GMT+08:00) Perth
Console.WriteLine (wa.BaseUtcOffset);    // 08:00:00
Console.WriteLine (wa.SupportsDaylightSavingTime);   // True
```

The `Id` property corresponds to the value passed to `FindSystemTimeZoneById`. The static `GetSystemTimeZones` method returns all world time zones; hence, you can list all valid zone ID strings as follows:

```
foreach (TimeZoneInfo z in TimeZoneInfo.GetSystemTimeZones())
  Console.WriteLine (z.Id);
```

You can also create a custom time zone by calling `TimeZoneInfo.CreateCustomTimeZone`. Because `TimeZoneInfo` is immutable, you must pass in all the relevant data as method arguments.

You can serialize a predefined or custom time zone to a (semi) human-readable string by calling `ToSerializedString`—and deserialize it by calling `TimeZoneInfo.FromSerializedString`.

The static `ConvertTime` method converts a `DateTime` or `DateTimeOffset` from one time zone to another. You can include either just a destination `TimeZoneInfo`, or both source and destination `TimeZoneInfo` objects. You can also convert directly from or to UTC with the methods `ConvertTimeFromUtc` and `ConvertTimeToUtc`.

For working with daylight saving time, `TimeZoneInfo` provides the following additional methods:

- `IsInvalidTime` returns `true` if a `DateTime` is within the hour (or delta) that's skipped when the clocks move forward.

- `IsAmbiguousTime` returns `true` if a `DateTime` or `DateTimeOffset` is within the hour (or delta) that's repeated when the clocks move back.

- `GetAmbiguousTimeOffsets` returns an array of `TimeSpans` representing the valid offset choices for an ambiguous `DateTime` or `DateTimeOffset`.

Unlike with `TimeZone`, you can't obtain simple dates from a `DateZoneInfo` indicating the start and end of daylight saving time. Instead, you must call `GetAdjustmentRules`, which returns a declarative summary of all daylight saving rules that apply to all years. Each rule has a `DateStart` and `DateEnd` indicating the date range within which the rule is valid:

```
foreach (TimeZoneInfo.AdjustmentRule rule in wa.GetAdjustmentRules())
    Console.WriteLine ("Rule: applies from " + rule.DateStart +
                       " to " + rule.DateEnd);
```

Western Australia first introduced daylight saving time in 2006, *midseason* (and then rescinded it in 2009). This required a special rule for the first year; hence, there are two rules:

```
Rule: applies from 1/01/2006 12:00:00 AM to 31/12/2006 12:00:00 AM
Rule: applies from 1/01/2007 12:00:00 AM to 31/12/2009 12:00:00 AM
```

Each `AdjustmentRule` has a `DaylightDelta` property of type `TimeSpan` (this is one hour in almost every case) and properties called `DaylightTransitionStart` and `Daylight TransitionEnd`. The latter two are of type `TimeZoneInfo.TransitionTime`, which has the following properties:

```
public bool IsFixedDateRule { get; }
public DayOfWeek DayOfWeek { get; }
public int Week { get; }
public int Day { get; }
public int Month { get; }
public DateTime TimeOfDay { get; }
```

A transition time is somewhat complicated in that it needs to represent both fixed and floating dates. An example of a floating date is "the last Sunday in March." Here are the rules for interpreting a transition time:

1. If, for an end transition, `IsFixedDateRule` is `true`, `Day` is `1`, `Month` is `1`, and `TimeOfDay` is `DateTime.MinValue`, there is no end to daylight saving time in that year (this can happen only in the southern hemisphere, upon the initial introduction of daylight saving time to a region).

2. Otherwise, if `IsFixedDateRule` is `true`, the `Month`, `Day`, and `TimeOfDay` properties determine the start or end of the adjustment rule.

3. Otherwise, if `IsFixedDateRule` is `false`, the `Month`, `DayOfWeek`, `Week`, and `TimeOfDay` properties determine the start or end of the adjustment rule.

In the last case, `Week` refers to the week of the month, with "5" meaning the last week. We can demonstrate this by enumerating the adjustment rules for our `wa` time zone:

```
foreach (TimeZoneInfo.AdjustmentRule rule in wa.GetAdjustmentRules())
{
  Console.WriteLine ("Rule: applies from " + rule.DateStart +
                                " to " + rule.DateEnd);

  Console.WriteLine ("  Delta: " + rule.DaylightDelta);

  Console.WriteLine ("  Start: " + FormatTransitionTime
                            (rule.DaylightTransitionStart, false));

  Console.WriteLine ("  End:   " + FormatTransitionTime
                            (rule.DaylightTransitionEnd, true));
  Console.WriteLine();
}
```

In `FormatTransitionTime`, we honor the rules just described:

```
static string FormatTransitionTime (TimeZoneInfo.TransitionTime tt,
                                    bool endTime)
{
  if (endTime && tt.IsFixedDateRule
            && tt.Day == 1 && tt.Month == 1
            && tt.TimeOfDay == DateTime.MinValue)
    return "-";

  string s;
  if (tt.IsFixedDateRule)
    s = tt.Day.ToString();
  else
    s = "The " +
        "first second third fourth last".Split() [tt.Week - 1] +
        " " + tt.DayOfWeek + " in";

  return s + " " + DateTimeFormatInfo.CurrentInfo.MonthNames [tt.Month-1]
          + " at " + tt.TimeOfDay.TimeOfDay;
}
```

The result with Western Australia is interesting in that it demonstrates both fixed and floating date rules—as well as an absent end date:

```
Rule: applies from 1/01/2006 12:00:00 AM to 31/12/2006 12:00:00 AM
  Delta: 01:00:00
  Start: 3 December at 02:00:00
  End:   -

Rule: applies from 1/01/2007 12:00:00 AM to 31/12/2009 12:00:00 AM
  Delta: 01:00:00
  Start: The last Sunday in October at 02:00:00
  End:   The last Sunday in March at 03:00:00
```

Western Australia is actually unique in this regard. Here's how we found it:

```
from zone in TimeZoneInfo.GetSystemTimeZones()
let rules = zone.GetAdjustmentRules()
where
    rules.Any
    (r => r.DaylightTransitionEnd.IsFixedDateRule) &&
    rules.Any
    (r => !r.DaylightTransitionEnd.IsFixedDateRule)
select zone
```

Daylight Saving Time and DateTime

If you use a `DateTimeOffset` or a UTC `DateTime`, equality comparisons are unimpeded by the effects of daylight saving time. But with local `DateTimes`, daylight saving can be problematic.

The rules can be summarized as follows:

- Daylight saving impacts local time but not UTC time.
- When the clocks turn back, comparisons that rely on time moving forward will break if (and only if) they use local `DateTimes`.
- You can always reliably round-trip between UTC and local times (on the same computer)—even as the clocks turn back.

The `IsDaylightSavingTime` tells you whether a given local `DateTime` is subject to daylight saving time. UTC times always return `false`:

```
Console.Write (DateTime.Now.IsDaylightSavingTime());    // True or False
Console.Write (DateTime.UtcNow.IsDaylightSavingTime()); // Always False
```

Assuming `dto` is a `DateTimeOffset`, the following expression does the same:

```
dto.LocalDateTime.IsDaylightSavingTime
```

The end of daylight saving time presents a particular complication for algorithms that use local time. When the clocks go back, the same hour (or more precisely, `Delta`) repeats itself. We can demonstrate this by instantiating a `DateTime` right in the "twilight zone" on your computer, and then subtracting `Delta` (this example requires that you practice daylight saving time to be interesting!):

```
DaylightTime changes = TimeZone.CurrentTimeZone.GetDaylightChanges (2010);
TimeSpan halfDelta = new TimeSpan (changes.Delta.Ticks / 2);
DateTime utc1 = changes.End.ToUniversalTime() - halfDelta;
DateTime utc2 = utc1 - changes.Delta;
```

Converting these variables to local times demonstrates why you should use UTC and not local time if your code relies on time moving forward:

```
DateTime loc1 = utc1.ToLocalTime();  // (Pacific Standard Time)
DateTime loc2 = utc2.ToLocalTime();
Console.WriteLine (loc1);            // 2/11/2010 1:30:00 AM
Console.WriteLine (loc2);            // 2/11/2010 1:30:00 AM
Console.WriteLine (loc1 == loc2);    // True
```

Despite loc1 and loc2 reporting as equal, they are different inside. DateTime reserves a special bit for indicating on which side of the twilight zone an ambiguous local date lies! This bit is ignored in comparison—as we just saw—but comes into play when you format the DateTime unambiguously:

```
Console.Write (loc1.ToString ("o"));  // 2010-11-02T02:30:00.0000000-08:00
Console.Write (loc2.ToString ("o"));  // 2010-11-02T02:30:00.0000000-07:00
```

This bit also is read when you convert back to UTC, ensuring perfect round-tripping between local and UTC times:

```
Console.WriteLine (loc1.ToUniversalTime() == utc1);  // True
Console.WriteLine (loc2.ToUniversalTime() == utc2);  // True
```

 You can reliably compare any two DateTimes by first calling ToUniversalTime on each. This strategy fails if (and only if) exactly one of them has a DateTimeKind of Unspecified. This potential for failure is another reason for favoring DateTimeOffset.

Formatting and Parsing

Formatting means converting *to* a string; parsing means converting *from* a string. The need to format or parse arises frequently in programming, in a variety of situations. Hence, the .NET Framework provides a variety of mechanisms:

ToString *and* Parse
These methods provide default functionality for many types.

Format providers
These manifest as additional ToString (and Parse) methods that accept a *format string* and/or a *format provider*. Format providers are highly flexible and culture-aware. The .NET Framework includes format providers for the numeric types and DateTime/DateTimeOffset.

XmlConvert
This is a static class with methods that format and parse while honoring XML standards. XmlConvert is also useful for general-purpose conversion when you need culture independence or you want to preempt misparsing. XmlConvert supports the numeric types, bool, DateTime, DateTimeOffset, TimeSpan, and Guid.

Type converters
These target designers and XAML parsers.

In this section, we discuss the first two mechanisms, focusing particularly on format providers. In the section following, we describe XmlConvert and type converters, as well as other conversion mechanisms.

ToString and Parse

The simplest formatting mechanism is the `ToString` method. It gives meaningful output on all simple value types (`bool`, `DateTime`, `DateTimeOffset`, `TimeSpan`, `Guid`, and all the numeric types). For the reverse operation, each of these types defines a static `Parse` method. For example:

```
string s = true.ToString();    // s = "True"
bool b = bool.Parse (s);       // b = true
```

If the parsing fails, a `FormatException` is thrown. Many types also define a `TryParse` method, which returns `false` if the conversion fails, rather than throwing an exception:

```
int i;
bool failure = int.TryParse ("qwerty", out i);
bool success = int.TryParse ("123", out i);
```

If you anticipate an error, calling `TryParse` is faster and more elegant than calling `Parse` in an exception handling block.

The `Parse` and `TryParse` methods on `DateTime(Offset)` and the numeric types respect local culture settings; you can change this by specifying a `CultureInfo` object. Specifying invariant culture is often a good idea. For instance, parsing "1.234" into a double gives us 1234 in Germany:

```
Console.WriteLine (double.Parse ("1.234"));   // 1234  (In Germany)
```

This is because in Germany, the period indicates a thousands separator rather than a decimal point. Specifying *invariant culture* fixes this:

```
double x = double.Parse ("1.234", CultureInfo.InvariantCulture);
```

The same applies when calling `ToString()`:

```
string x = 1.234.ToString (CultureInfo.InvariantCulture);
```

Format Providers

Sometimes you need more control over how formatting and parsing take place. There are dozens of ways to format a `DateTime(Offset)`, for instance. Format providers allow extensive control over formatting and parsing, and are supported for numeric types and date/times. Format providers are also used by user interface controls for formatting and parsing.

The gateway to using a format provider is `IFormattable`. All numeric types—and `DateTime(Offset)`—implement this interface:

```
public interface IFormattable
{
    string ToString (string format, IFormatProvider formatProvider);
}
```

The first argument is the *format string*; the second is the *format provider*. The format string provides instructions; the format provider determines how the instructions are translated. For example:

```
NumberFormatInfo f = new NumberFormatInfo();
f.CurrencySymbol = "$$";
Console.WriteLine (3.ToString ("C", f));          // $$ 3.00
```

Here, "C" is a format string that indicates *currency*, and the NumberFormatInfo object is a format provider that determines how currency—and other numeric representations—are rendered. This mechanism allows for globalization.

 All format strings for numbers and dates are listed in "Standard Format Strings and Parsing Flags" on page 225.

If you specify a null format string or provider, a default is applied. The default format provider is CultureInfo.CurrentCulture, which, unless reassigned, reflects the computer's runtime control panel settings. For example, on this computer:

```
Console.WriteLine (10.3.ToString ("C", null));  // $10.30
```

For convenience, most types overload ToString such that you can omit a null provider:

```
Console.WriteLine (10.3.ToString ("C"));     // $10.30
Console.WriteLine (10.3.ToString ("F4"));    // 10.3000 (Fix to 4 D.P.)
```

Calling ToString on a DateTime(Offset) or a numeric type with no arguments is equivalent to using a default format provider, with an empty format string.

The .NET Framework defines three format providers (all of which implement IFormatProvider):

```
NumberFormatInfo
DateTimeFormatInfo
CultureInfo
```

 All enum types are also formattable, though there's no special IFormatProvider class.

Format providers and CultureInfo

Within the context of format providers, CultureInfo acts as an indirection mechanism for the other two format providers, returning a NumberFormatInfo or DateTime FormatInfo object applicable to the culture's regional settings.

In the following example, we request a specific culture (*en*glish language in *G*reat Britain):

```
CultureInfo uk = CultureInfo.GetCultureInfo ("en-GB");
Console.WriteLine (3.ToString ("C", uk));      // £3.00
```

This executes using the default NumberFormatInfo object applicable to the en-GB culture.

The next example formats a `DateTime` with invariant culture. Invariant culture is always the same, regardless of the computer's settings:

```
DateTime dt = new DateTime (2000, 1, 2);
CultureInfo iv = CultureInfo.InvariantCulture;
Console.WriteLine (dt.ToString (iv));        // 01/02/2000 00:00:00
Console.WriteLine (dt.ToString ("d", iv));   // 01/02/2000
```

 Invariant culture is based on American culture, with the following differences:

- The currency symbol is ✿ instead of $.

- Dates and times are formatted with leading zeros (though still with the month first).

- Time uses the 24-hour format rather than an A.M./P.M. designator.

Using NumberFormatInfo or DateTimeFormatInfo

In the next example, we instantiate a `NumberFormatInfo` and change the group separator from a comma to a space. We then use it to format a number to three decimal places:

```
NumberFormatInfo f = new NumberFormatInfo ();
f.NumberGroupSeparator = " ";
Console.WriteLine (12345.6789.ToString ("N3", f));   // 12 345.679
```

The initial settings for a `NumberFormatInfo` or `DateTimeFormatInfo` are based on the invariant culture. Sometimes, however, it's more useful to choose a different starting point. To do this, you can `Clone` an existing format provider:

```
NumberFormatInfo f = (NumberFormatInfo)
                      CultureInfo.CurrentCulture.NumberFormat.Clone();
```

A cloned format provider is always writable—even if the original was read-only.

Composite formatting

Composite format strings allow you to combine variable substitution with format strings. The static `string.Format` method accepts a composite format string—we illustrated this in "String and Text Handling" on page 193:

```
string composite = "Credit={0:C}";
Console.WriteLine (string.Format (composite, 500));   // Credit=$500.00
```

The `Console` class itself overloads its `Write` and `WriteLine` methods to accept composite format strings, allowing us to shorten this example slightly:

```
Console.WriteLine ("Credit={0:C}", 500);   // Credit=$500.00
```

You can also append a composite format string to a `StringBuilder` (via `AppendFormat`), and to a `TextWriter` for I/O (see Chapter 14).

`string.Format` accepts an optional format provider. A simple application for this is to call `ToString` on an arbitrary object while passing in a format provider. For example:

```
string s = string.Format (CultureInfo.InvariantCulture, "{0}", someObject);
```

This is equivalent to:

```
string s;
if (someObject is IFormattable)
  s = ((IFormattable)someObject).ToString (null,
                              CultureInfo.InvariantCulture);
else if (someObject == null)
  s = "";
else
  s = someObject.ToString();
```

Parsing with format providers

There's no standard interface for parsing through a format provider. Instead, each participating type overloads its static `Parse` (and `TryParse`) method to accept a format provider, and optionally, a `NumberStyles` or `DateTimeStyles` enum.

`NumberStyles` and `DateTimeStyles` control how parsing work: they let you specify such things as whether parentheses or a currency symbol can appear in the input string. (By default, the answer to both of these questions is *no*.) For example:

```
int error = int.Parse ("(2)");   // Exception thrown

int minusTwo = int.Parse ("(2)", NumberStyles.Integer |
                          NumberStyles.AllowParentheses);   // OK

decimal fivePointTwo = decimal.Parse ("£5.20", NumberStyles.Currency,
                        CultureInfo.GetCultureInfo ("en-GB"));
```

The next section lists all `NumberStyles` and `DateTimeStyles` members—as well as the default parsing rules for each type.

IFormatProvider and ICustomFormatter

All format providers implement `IFormatProvider`:

```
public interface IFormatProvider { object GetFormat (Type formatType); }
```

The purpose of this method is to provide indirection—this is what allows `CultureInfo` to defer to an appropriate `NumberFormatInfo` or `DateTimeInfo` object to do the work.

By implementing `IFormatProvider`—along with `ICustomFormatter`—you can also write your own format provider that works in conjunction with existing types. `ICustomFormatter` defines a single method as follows:

```
string Format (string format, object arg, IFormatProvider formatProvider);
```

The following custom format provider writes numbers as words:

```
// Program can be downloaded from http://www.albahari.com/nutshell/

public class WordyFormatProvider : IFormatProvider, ICustomFormatter
{
  static readonly string[] _numberWords =
  "zero one two three four five six seven eight nine minus point".Split();

  IFormatProvider _parent;   // Allows consumers to chain format providers

  public WordyFormatProvider () : this (CultureInfo.CurrentCulture) { }
  public WordyFormatProvider (IFormatProvider parent)
  {
    _parent = parent;
  }

  public object GetFormat (Type formatType)
  {
    if (formatType == typeof (ICustomFormatter)) return this;
    return null;
  }

  public string Format (string format, object arg, IFormatProvider prov)
  {
    // If it's not our format string, defer to the parent provider:
    if (arg == null || format != "W")
      return string.Format (_parent, "{0:" + format + "}", arg);

    StringBuilder result = new StringBuilder();
    string digitList = string.Format (CultureInfo.InvariantCulture,
                                      "{0}", arg);
    foreach (char digit in digitList)
    {
      int i = "0123456789-.".IndexOf (digit);
      if (i == -1) continue;
      if (result.Length > 0) result.Append (' ');
      result.Append (_numberWords[i]);
    }
    return result.ToString();
  }
}
```

Notice that in the Format method we used string.Format to convert the input number
to a string—with InvariantCulture. It would have been much simpler just to call
ToString() on arg, but then CurrentCulture would have been used instead. The
reason for needing the invariant culture is evident a few lines later:

```
int i = "0123456789-.".IndexOf (digit);
```

It's critical here that the number string comprises only the characters 0123456789-.
and not any internationalized versions of these.

Here's an example of using WordyFormatProvider:

```
double n = -123.45;
IFormatProvider fp = new WordyFormatProvider();
```

```
Console.WriteLine (string.Format (fp, "{0:C} in words is {0:W}", n));

// -$123.45 in words is one two three point four five
```

Custom format providers can be used only in composite format strings.

Standard Format Strings and Parsing Flags

The standard format strings control how a numeric type or `DateTime/DateTimeOff` set is converted to a string. There are two kinds of format strings:

Standard format strings
With these, you provide general guidance. A standard format string consists of a single letter, followed, optionally, by a digit (whose meaning depends on the letter). An example is `"C"` or `"F2"`.

Custom format strings
With these, you micromanage every character with a template. An example is `"0:#.000E+00"`.

Custom format strings are unrelated to custom format providers.

Numeric Format Strings

Table 6-2 lists all standard numeric format strings.

Table 6-2. Standard numeric format strings

Letter	Meaning	Sample input	Result	Notes
G or g	"General"	1.2345, "G"	1.2345	Switches to exponential notation for small or large numbers.
		0.00001, "G"	1E-05	
		0.00001, "g"	1e-05	G3 limits precision to three digits in *total* (before + after point).
		1.2345, "G3"	1.23	
		12345, "G3"	1.23E04	
F	Fixed point	2345.678, "F2"	2345.68	F2 rounds to two decimal places.
		2345.6, "F2"	2345.60	
N	Fixed point with group separator ("Numeric")	2345.678, "N2"	2,345.68	As above, with group (1,000s) separator (details from format provider).
		2345.6, "N2"	2,345.60	
D	Pad with leading zeros	123, "D5"	00123	For integral types only.
		123, "D1"	123	D5 pads left to five digits; does not truncate.
E or e	Force exponential notation	56789, "E"	5.678900E+004	Six-digit default precision.
		56789, "e"	5.678900e+004	
		56789, "E2"	5.68E+004	

Letter	Meaning	Sample input	Result	Notes
C	Currency	1.2, "C" 1.2, "C4"	$1.20 $1.2000	C with no digit uses default number of D.P. from format provider.
P	Percent	.503, "P" .503, "P0"	50.30 % 50 %	Uses symbol and layout from format provider. Decimal places can optionally be overridden.
X or x	Hexadecimal	47, "X" 47, "x" 47, "X4"	2F 2f 002F	X for uppercase hex digits; x for lowercase hex digits. Integrals only.
R	Round-trip	1f / 3f, "R"	0.333333343	For the float and double types, R squeezes out all digits to ensure exact round-tripping.

Supplying no numeric format string (or a null or blank string) is equivalent to using the "G" standard format string followed by no digit. This exhibits the following behavior:

- Numbers smaller than 10^{-4} or larger than the type's precision are expressed in exponential (scientific) notation.

- The two decimal places at the limit of float or double's precision are rounded away to mask the inaccuracies inherent in conversion to decimal from their underlying binary form.

> The automatic rounding just described is usually beneficial and goes unnoticed. However, it can cause trouble if you need to round-trip a number; in other words, convert it to a string and back again (maybe repeatedly) while preserving value equality. For this reason, the "R" format string exists to circumvent this implicit rounding.

Table 6-3 lists custom numeric format strings.

Table 6-3. Custom numeric format strings

Specifier	Meaning	Sample input	Result	Notes
#	Digit placeholder	12.345, ".##" 12.345, ".####"	12.35 12.345	Limits digits after D.P.
0	Zero placeholder	12.345, ".00" 12.345, ".0000" 99, "000.00"	12.35 12.3500 099.00	As above, but also pads with zeros before and after D.P.
.	Decimal point			Indicates D.P.

Specifier	Meaning	Sample input	Result	Notes
				Actual symbol comes from NumberFormatInfo.
,	Group separator	1234, "#,###,###"	1,234	Symbol comes from Number FormatInfo.
		1234, "0,000,000"	0,001,234	
, (as above)	Multiplier	1000000, "#,"	1000	If comma is at end or before D.P., it acts as a multiplier— dividing result by 1,000, 1,000,000, etc.
		1000000, "#,,"	1	
	Percent notation	0.6, "00%"	60%	First multiplies by 100 and then substitutes percent symbol obtained from Number FormatInfo.
E0, e0, E +0, e+0 E-0, e-0	Exponent notation	1234, "0E0"	1E0	
		1234, "0E+0"	1E+3	
		1234, "0.00E00"	1.25E03	
		1234, "0.00e00"	1.25e03	
\	Literal character quote	50, @"\#0"	#50	Use in conjunction with an @ prefix on the string—or use \\.
'xx' 'xx'	Literal string quote	50, "0 '...'"	50 ...	
;	Section separator	15, "#;(#);zero"	15	(If positive).
		-5, "#;(#);zero"	-5	(If negative).
		0, "#;(#);zero"	zero	(If zero).
Any other char	Literal	35.2, "$0 . 00c"	$35 . 00c	

NumberStyles

Each numeric type defines a static `Parse` method that accepts a `NumberStyles` argument. `NumberStyles` is a flags enum that lets you determine how the string is read as it's converted to a numeric type. It has the following combinable members:

```
AllowLeadingWhite    AllowTrailingWhite
AllowLeadingSign     AllowTrailingSign
AllowParentheses     AllowDecimalPoint
AllowThousands       AllowExponent
AllowCurrencySymbol  AllowHexSpecifier
```

`NumberStyles` also defines these composite members:

```
None  Integer  Float  Number  HexNumber  Currency  Any
```

Except for `None`, all composite values include `AllowLeadingWhite` and `AllowTrailing White`. Their remaining makeup is shown in Figure 6-1, with the most useful three emphasized.

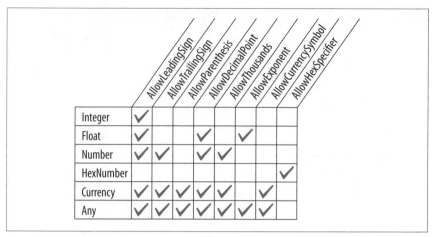

Figure 6-1. Composite NumberStyles

When you call `Parse` without specifying any flags, the defaults in Figure 6-2 are applied.

If you don't want the defaults shown in Figure 6-2, you must explicitly specify `NumberStyles`:

```
int thousand = int.Parse ("3E8", NumberStyles.HexNumber);
int minusTwo = int.Parse ("(2)", NumberStyles.Integer |
                          NumberStyles.AllowParentheses);
double aMillion = double.Parse ("1,000,000", NumberStyles.Any);
decimal threeMillion = decimal.Parse ("3e6", NumberStyles.Any);
decimal fivePointTwo = decimal.Parse ("$5.20", NumberStyles.Currency);
```

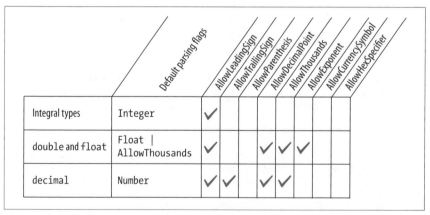

Figure 6-2. Default parsing flags for numeric types

Because we didn't specify a format provider, this example works with your local currency symbol, group separator, decimal point, and so on. The next example is hardcoded to work with the euro sign and a blank group separator for currencies:

```
NumberFormatInfo ni = new NumberFormatInfo();
ni.CurrencySymbol = "€";
ni.CurrencyGroupSeparator = " ";
double million = double.Parse ("€1 000 000", NumberStyles.Currency, ni);
```

Date/Time Format Strings

Format strings for DateTime/DateTimeOffset can be divided into two groups, based on whether they honor culture and format provider settings. Those that do are listed in Table 6-4; those that don't are listed in Table 6-5. The sample output comes from formatting the following DateTime (with *invariant culture*, in the case of Table 6-4):

```
new DateTime (2000, 1, 2, 17, 18, 19);
```

Table 6-4. Culture-sensitive date/time format strings

Format string	Meaning	Sample output
d	Short date	01/02/2000
D	Long date	Sunday, 02 January 2000
t	Short time	17:18
T	Long time	17:18:19
f	Long date + short time	Sunday, 02 January 2000 17:18
F	Long date + long time	Sunday, 02 January 2000 17:18:19
g	Short date + short time	01/02/2000 17:18
G (default)	Short date + long time	01/02/2000 17:18:19
m, M	Month and day	January 02
y, Y	Year and month	2000 January

Table 6-5. Culture-insensitive date/time format strings

Format string	Meaning	Sample output	Notes
o	Round-trippable	2000-01-02T17:18:19.0000000	Will append time zone information unless DateTimeKind is Unspecified
r, R	RFC 1123 standard	Sun, 02 Jan 2000 17:18:19 GMT	You must explicitly convert to UTC with DateTime.ToUniversalTime
s	Sortable; ISO 8601	2000-01-02T17:18:19	Compatible with text-based sorting
u	"Universal" Sortable	2000-01-02 17:18:19Z	Similar to above; must explicitly convert to UTC
U	UTC	Sunday, 02 January 2000 17:18:19	Long date + short time, converted to UTC

The format strings "r", "R", and "u" emit a suffix that implies UTC; yet they don't automatically convert a local to a UTC DateTime (so you must do the conversion yourself). Ironically, "U" automatically converts to UTC, but doesn't write a time zone suffix! In fact, "o" is the only format specifier in the group that can write an unambiguous DateTime without intervention.

DateTimeFormatInfo also supports custom format strings: these are analogous to numeric custom format strings. The list is fairly exhaustive and you can find it in the MSDN. An example of a custom format string is:

```
yyyy-MM-dd HH:mm:ss
```

Parsing and misparsing DateTimes

Strings that put the month or day first are ambiguous and can easily be misparsed—particularly if you or any of your customers live outside the United States and Canada. This is not a problem in user interface controls because the same settings are in force when parsing as when formatting. But when writing to a file, for instance, day/month misparsing can be a real problem. There are two solutions:

- Always state the same explicit culture when formatting and parsing (e.g., invariant culture).
- Format DateTime and DateTimeOffsets in a manner *independent* of culture.

The second approach is more robust—particularly if you choose a format that puts the four-digit year first: such strings are much harder to misparse by another party. Further, strings formatted with a *standards-compliant* year-first format (such as "o") can parse correctly alongside locally formatted strings—rather like a "universal donor." (Dates formatted with "s" or "u" have the further benefit of being sortable.)

To illustrate, suppose we generate a culture-insensitive DateTime string s as follows:

```
string s = DateTime.Now.ToString ("o");
```

 The "o" format string includes milliseconds in the output. The following custom format string gives the same result as "o", but without milliseconds:

```
yyyy-MM-ddTHH:mm:ss K
```

We can reparse this in two ways. ParseExact demands strict compliance with the specified format string:

```
DateTime dt1 = DateTime.ParseExact (s, "o", null);
```

(You can achieve a similar result with XmlConvert's ToString and ToDateTime methods.)

Parse, however, implicitly accepts both the "o" format and the CurrentCulture format:

```
DateTime dt2 = DateTime.Parse (s);
```

This works with both DateTime and DateTimeOffset.

`ParseExact` is usually preferable if you know the format of the string that you're parsing. It means that if the string is incorrectly formatted, an exception will be thrown—which is usually better than risking a misparsed date.

DateTimeStyles

`DateTimeStyles` is a flags enum that provides additional instructions when calling `Parse` on a `DateTime(Offset)`. Here are its members:

```
None,
AllowLeadingWhite, AllowTrailingWhite, AllowInnerWhite,
AssumeLocal, AssumeUniversal, AdjustToUniversal,
NoCurrentDateDefault, RoundTripKind
```

There is also a composite member, `AllowWhiteSpaces`:

```
AllowWhiteSpaces = AllowLeadingWhite | AllowTrailingWhite | AllowInnerWhite
```

The default is `None`. This means that extra whitespace is normally prohibited (whitespace that's part of a standard `DateTime` pattern is exempt).

`AssumeLocal` and `AssumeUniversal` apply if the string doesn't have a time zone suffix (such as `Z` or `+9:00`). `AdjustToUniversal` still honors time zone suffixes, but then converts to UTC using the current regional settings.

If you parse a string comprising a time but no date, today's date is applied by default. If you apply the `NoCurrentDateDefault` flag, however, it instead uses 1st January 0001.

Enum Format Strings

In "Enums" on page 240 in Chapter 3, we describe formatting and parsing enum values. Table 6-6 lists each format string and the result of applying it to the following expression:

```
Console.WriteLine (System.ConsoleColor.Red.ToString (formatString));
```

Table 6-6. Enum format strings

Format string	Meaning	Sample output	Notes
G or g	"General"	Red	Default
F or f	Treat as though `Flags` attribute were present	Red	Works on combined members even if enum has no `Flags` attribute
D or d	Decimal value	12	Retrieves underlying integral value
X or x	Hexadecimal value	0000000C	Retrieves underlying integral value

Other Conversion Mechanisms

In the previous two sections, we covered format providers—.NET's primary mechanism for formatting and parsing. Other important conversion mechanisms are scattered through various types and namespaces. Some convert to and from string, and some do other kinds of conversions. In this section, we discuss the following topics:

- The Convert class and its functions:
  - — Real to integral conversions that round rather than truncate
  - — Parsing numbers in base 2, 8, and 16
  - — Dynamic conversions
  - — Base 64 translations
- XmlConvert and its role in formatting and parsing for XML
- Type converters and their role in formatting and parsing for designers and XAML
- BitConverter, for binary conversions

Convert

The .NET Framework calls the following types *base types*:

- bool, char, string, System.DateTime, and System.DateTimeOffset
- All of the C# numeric types

The static Convert class defines methods for converting every base type to every other base type. Unfortunately, most of these methods are useless: either they throw exceptions or they are redundant alongside implicit casts. Among the clutter, however, are some useful methods, listed in the following sections.

 All base types (explicitly) implement IConvertible, which defines methods for converting to every other base type. In most cases, the implementation of each of these methods simply calls a method in Convert. On rare occasions, it can be useful to write a method that accepts an argument of type IConvertible.

Rounding real to integral conversions

In Chapter 2, we saw how implicit and explicit casts allow you to convert between numeric types. In summary:

- Implicit casts work for nonlossy conversions (e.g., int to double).
- Explicit casts are required for lossy conversions (e.g., double to int).

Casts are optimized for efficiency; hence, they *truncate* data that won't fit. This can be a problem when converting from a real number to an integer, because often you want to *round* rather than truncate. `Convert`'s numerical conversion methods address just this issue; they always *round*:

```
double d = 3.9;
int i = Convert.ToInt32 (d);    // i == 4
```

`Convert` uses banker's rounding, which snaps midpoint values to even integers (this avoids positive or negative bias). If banker's rounding is a problem, first call `Math.Round` on the real number; this accepts an additional argument that allows you to control midpoint rounding.

Parsing numbers in base 2, 8, and 16

Hidden among the To(*integral-type*) methods are overloads that parse numbers in another base:

```
int thirty = Convert.ToInt32  ("1E", 16);   // Parse in hexadecimal
uint five  = Convert.ToUInt32 ("101", 2);   // Parse in binary
```

The second argument specifies the base. It can be any base you like—as long as it's 2, 8, 10, or 16!

Dynamic conversions

Occasionally, you need to convert from one type to another—but you don't know what the types are until runtime. For this, the `Convert` class provides a `ChangeType` method:

```
public static object ChangeType (object value, Type conversionType);
```

The source and target types must be one of the "base" types. `ChangeType` also accepts an optional `IFormatProvider` argument. Here's an example:

```
Type targetType = typeof (int);
object source = "42";

object result = Convert.ChangeType (source, targetType);

Console.WriteLine (result);           // 42
Console.WriteLine (result.GetType()); // System.Int32
```

An example of when this might be useful is in writing a deserializer that can work with multiple types. It can also convert any enum to its integral type (see "Enums" on page 240).

A limitation of `ChangeType` is that you cannot specify a format string or parsing flag.

Base 64 conversions

Sometimes you need to include binary data such as a bitmap within a text document such as an XML file or email message. Base 64 is a ubiquitous means of encoding binary data as readable characters, using 64 characters from the ASCII set.

`Convert`'s `ToBase64String` method converts from a byte array to base 64; `FromBase64String` does the reverse.

XmlConvert

If you're dealing with data that's originated from or destined for an XML file, XmlConvert (the System.Xml namespace) provides the most suitable methods for formatting and parsing. The methods in XmlConvert handle the nuances of XML formatting without needing special format strings. For instance, true in XML is "true" and not "True". The .NET Framework internally uses XmlConvert extensively. XmlConvert is also good for general-purpose culture-independent serialization.

The formatting methods in XmlConvert are all provided as overloaded ToString methods; the parsing methods are called ToBoolean, ToDateTime, and so on. For example:

```
string s = XmlConvert.ToString (true);       // s = "true"
bool isTrue = XmlConvert.ToBoolean (s);
```

The methods that convert to and from DateTime accept an XmlDateTimeSerializationMode argument. This is an enum with the following values:

```
Unspecified, Local, Utc, RoundtripKind
```

Local and Utc cause a conversion to take place when formatting (if the DateTime is not already in that time zone). The time zone is then appended to the string:

```
2010-02-22T14:08:30.9375          // Unspecified
2010-02-22T14:07:30.9375+09:00    // Local
2010-02-22T05:08:30.9375Z         // Utc
```

Unspecified strips away any time zone information embedded in the DateTime (i.e., DateTimeKind) before formatting. RoundtripKind honors the DateTime's DateTimeKind—so when it's reparsed, the resultant DateTime struct will be exactly as it was originally.

Type Converters

Type converters are designed to format and parse in design-time environments. They also parse values in XAML (Extensible Application Markup Language) documents—as used in Windows Presentation Foundation and Workflow Foundation.

In the .NET Framework, there are more than 100 type converters—covering such things as colors, images, and URIs. In contrast, format providers are implemented for only a handful of simple value types.

Type converters typically parse strings in a variety of ways—without needing hints. For instance, in an ASP.NET application in Visual Studio, if you assign a control a BackColor by typing **"Beige"** into the property window, Color's type converter figures out that you're referring to a color name and not an RGB string or system color. This flexibility can sometimes make type converters useful in contexts outside of designers and XAML documents.

All type converters subclass TypeConverter in System.ComponentModel. To obtain a TypeConverter, call TypeDescriptor.GetConverter. The following obtains a

TypeConverter for the `Color` type (in the `System.Drawing` namespace, *System.Drawing.dll*):

```
TypeConverter cc = TypeDescriptor.GetConverter (typeof (Color));
```

Among many other methods, `TypeConverter` defines methods to `ConvertToString` and `ConvertFromString`. We can call these as follows:

```
Color beige  = (Color) cc.ConvertFromString ("Beige");
Color purple = (Color) cc.ConvertFromString ("#800080");
Color window = (Color) cc.ConvertFromString ("Window");
```

By convention, type converters have names ending in *Converter* and are usually in the same namespace as the type they're converting. A type links to its converter via a `TypeConverterAttribute`, allowing designers to pick up converters automatically.

Type converters can also provide design-time services such as generating standard value lists for populating a drop-down list in a designer or assisting with code serialization.

BitConverter

Most base types can be converted to a byte array, by calling `BitConverter.GetBytes`:

```
foreach (byte b in BitConverter.GetBytes (3.5))
  Console.Write (b + " ");                      // 0 0 0 0 0 0 12 64
```

`BitConverter` also provides methods for converting in the other direction, such as `ToDouble`.

The `decimal` and `DateTime(Offset)` types are not supported by `BitConverter`. You can, however, convert a `decimal` to an `int` array by calling `decimal.GetBits`. To go the other way around, `decimal` provides a constructor that accepts an `int` array.

In the case of `DateTime`, you can call `ToBinary` on an instance—this returns a `long` (upon which you can then use `BitConverter`). The static `DateTime.FromBinary` method does the reverse.

Globalization

There are two aspects to *internationalizing* an application: *globalization* and *localization*.

Globalization is concerned with three tasks (in decreasing order of importance):

1. Making sure that your program doesn't *break* when run in another culture
2. Respecting a local culture's formatting rules—for instance, when displaying dates
3. Designing your program so that it picks up culture-specific data and strings from satellite assemblies that you can later write and deploy

Localization means concluding that last task by writing satellite assemblies for specific cultures. This can be done *after* writing your program—we cover the details in "Resources and Satellite Assemblies" on page 663 in Chapter 17.

The .NET Framework helps you with the second task by applying culture-specific rules by default. We've already seen how calling `ToString` on a `DateTime` or number respects local formatting rules. Unfortunately, this makes it easy to fail the first task and have your program break because you're expecting dates or numbers to be formatted according to an assumed culture. The solution, as we've seen, is either to specify a culture (such as the invariant culture) when formatting and parsing, or to use culture-independent methods such as those in `XmlConvert`.

Globalization Checklist

We've already covered the important points in this chapter. Here's a summary of the essential work required:

- Understand Unicode and text encodings (see "Text Encodings and Unicode" on page 203).
- Be mindful that methods such as `ToUpper` and `ToLower` on `char` and `string` are culture-sensitive: use `ToUpperInvariant`/`ToLowerInvariant` unless you want culture-sensitivity.
- Favor culture-independent formatting and parsing mechanisms for `DateTime` and `DateTimeOffset`s such as `ToString("o")` and `XmlConvert`.
- Otherwise, specify a culture when formatting/parsing numbers or date/times (unless you *want* local-culture behavior).

Testing

You can test against different cultures by reassigning `Thread`'s `CurrentCulture` property (in `System.Threading`). The following changes the current culture to Turkey:

```
Thread.CurrentThread.CurrentCulture = CultureInfo.GetCultureInfo ("tr-TR");
```

Turkey is a particularly good test case because:

- `"i".ToUpper()` != `"I"` and `"I".ToLower()` != `"i"`.
- Dates are formatted as day/month/year, and with a period separator.
- The decimal point indicator is a comma instead of a period.

You can also experiment by changing the number and date formatting settings in the Windows Control Panel: these are reflected in the default culture (`CultureInfo.CurrentCulture`).

`CultureInfo.GetCultures()` returns an array of all available cultures.

 `Thread` and `CultureInfo` also support a `CurrentUICulture` property. This is concerned more about localization: we cover this in Chapter 17.

Working with Numbers

Conversions

We covered numeric conversions in previous chapters and sections; Table 6-7 summarizes all the options.

Table 6-7. Summary of numeric conversions

Task	Functions	Examples
Parsing base 10 numbers	Parse	`double d = double.Parse ("3.5");`
	TryParse	`int i;`
		`bool ok = int.TryParse ("3", out i);`
Parsing from base 2, 8, or 16	`Convert.ToIntegral`	`int i = Convert.ToInt32 ("1E", 16);`
Formatting to hexadecimal	`ToString ("X")`	`string hex = 45.ToString ("X");`
Lossless numeric conversion	Implicit cast	`int i = 23;`
		`double d = d;`
Truncating numeric conversion	Explicit cast	`double d = 23.5;`
		`int i = (int) d;`
Rounding numeric conversion (real to integral)	`Convert.ToIntegral`	`double d = 23.5;`
		`int i = Convert.ToInt32 (d);`

Math

Table 6-8 lists the members of the static `Math` class. The trigonometric functions accept arguments of type `double`; other methods such as `Max` are overloaded to operate on all numeric types. The `Math` class also defines the mathematical constants `E` (*e*) and `PI`.

Table 6-8. Methods in the static Math class

Category	Methods
Rounding	`Round, Truncate, Floor, Ceiling`
Maximum/minimum	`Max, Min`
Absolute value and sign	`Abs, Sign`
Square root	`Sqrt`
Raising to a power	`Pow, Exp`
Logarithm	`Log, Log10`
Trigonometric	`Sin, Cos, Tan`
	`Sinh, Cosh, Tanh`
	`Asin, Acos, Atan`

The Round method lets you specify the number of decimal places with which to round, as well as how to handle midpoints (away from zero, or with banker's rounding). Floor and Ceiling round to the nearest integer: Floor always rounds down and Ceiling always rounds up—even with negative numbers.

Max and Min accept only two arguments. If you have an array or sequence of numbers, use the Max and Min extension methods in System.Linq.Enumerable.

BigInteger

The BigInteger struct is a specialized numeric type new to .NET Framework 4.0. It lives in the new System.Numerics namespace in *System.Numerics.dll* and allows you to represent an arbitrarily large integer without any loss of precision.

C# doesn't provide native support for BigInteger, so there's no way to represent BigInteger literals. You can, however, implicitly cast from any other integral type to a BigInteger. For instance:

```
BigInteger twentyFive = 25;     // implicit cast from integer
```

To represent a bigger number, such as one googol (10^{100}), you can use one of BigInteger's static methods, such as Pow (raise to the power):

```
BigInteger googol = BigInteger.Pow (10, 100);
```

Alternatively, you can Parse a string:

```
BigInteger googol = BigInteger.Parse ("1".PadRight (100, '0'));
```

Calling ToString() on this prints every digit:

```
Console.WriteLine (googol.ToString()); // 10000000000000000000000000000000
00000000000000000000000000000000000000000000000000000000000000000000
```

You can implicitly cast a BigInteger to a standard numeric type and explicitly cast in the other direction. For instance:

```
double g1 = 1e100;                  // implicit cast
BigInteger g2 = (BigInteger) g1;    // explicit cast
Console.WriteLine (g2);
```

You lose precision when converting a large BigInteger to another type, such as double. The output of the preceding example demonstrates this:

```
10000000000000000159028911097599180468360808563945281389781327557 74...
```

BigInteger overloads all the arithmetic operators, as well as the comparison, equality, modulus (%), and negation operators.

You can also construct a BigInteger from a byte array. The following code generates a 32-byte random number suitable for cryptography and then assigns it to a BigInteger:

```
// This uses the System.Security.Cryptography namespace:
RandomNumberGenerator rand = RandomNumberGenerator.Create();
byte[] bytes = new byte [32];
rand.GetBytes (bytes);
var bigRandomNumber = new BigInteger (bytes);    // Convert to BigInteger
```

The advantage of storing such a number in a `BigInteger` over a byte array is that you get value-type semantics. Calling `ToByteArray` converts a `BigInteger` back to a byte array.

Complex

The `Complex` struct is another specialized numeric type new to Framework 4.0, and is for representing complex numbers with real and imaginary components of type `double`. `Complex` resides in the *System.Numerics.dll* assembly (along with `BigInteger`).

To use `Complex`, instantiate the struct, specifying the real and imaginary values:

```
var c1 = new Complex (2, 3.5);
var c2 = new Complex (3, 0);
```

There are also implicit conversions from the standard numeric types.

The `Complex` struct exposes properties for the real and imaginary values, as well as the phase and magnitude:

```
Console.WriteLine (c1.Real);       // 2
Console.WriteLine (c1.Imaginary);  // 3.5
Console.WriteLine (c1.Phase);      // 1.05165021254837
Console.WriteLine (c1.Magnitude);  // 4.03112887414927
```

You can also construct a `Complex` number by specifying magnitude and phase:

```
Complex c3 = Complex.FromPolarCoordinates (1.3, 5);
```

The standard arithmetic operators are overloaded to work on `Complex` numbers:

```
Console.WriteLine (c1 + c2);   // (5, 3.5)
Console.WriteLine (c1 * c2);   // (6, 10.5)
```

The `Complex` struct exposes static methods for more advanced functions, including:

- Trigonometric (`Sin`, `Asin`, `Sinh`, `Tan`, etc.)
- Logarithms and exponentiations
- Conjugate

Random

The `Random` class generates a pseudorandom sequence of random `byte`s, `integer`s, or `double`s.

To use `Random`, you first instantiate it, optionally providing a seed to initiate the random number series. Using the same seed guarantees the same series of numbers, which is sometimes useful when you want reproducibility:

```
Random r1 = new Random (1);
Random r2 = new Random (1);
Console.WriteLine (r1.Next (100) + ", " + r1.Next (100));   // 24, 11
Console.WriteLine (r2.Next (100) + ", " + r2.Next (100));   // 24, 11
```

If you don't want reproducibility, you can construct Random with no seed—then it uses the current system time to make one up.

 Because the system clock has limited granularity, two Random instances created close together (typically within 10 ms) will yield the same sequence of values. A common trap is to instantiate a new Random object every time you need a random number, rather than reusing the *same* object.

A good pattern is to declare a single static Random instance. In multithreaded scenarios, however, this can cause trouble because Random objects are not thread-safe. We describe a workaround in "Thread-Local Storage" on page 862 in Chapter 21.

Calling Next(*n*) generates a random integer between 0 and *n*-1. NextDouble generates a random double between 0 and 1. NextBytes fills a byte array with random values.

Random is not considered random enough for high-security applications, such as cryptography. For this, the .NET Framework provides a *cryptographically strong* random number generator, in the System.Security.Cryptography namespace. Here's how it's used:

```
var rand = System.Security.Cryptography.RandomNumberGenerator.Create();
byte[] bytes = new byte [32];
rand.GetBytes (bytes);        // Fill the byte array with random numbers.
```

The downside is that it's less flexible: filling a byte array is the only means of obtaining random numbers. To obtain an integer, you must use BitConverter:

```
byte[] bytes = new byte [4];
rand.GetBytes (bytes);
int i = BitConverter.ToInt32 (bytes, 0);
```

Enums

In Chapter 3, we described C#'s enum type, and showed how to combine members, test equality, use logical operators, and perform conversions. The Framework extends C#'s support for enums through the System.Enum type. This type has two roles: providing type unification for all enum types and defining static utility methods.

Type unification means you can implicitly cast any enum member to a System.Enum instance:

```
enum Nut  { Walnut, Hazelnut, Macadamia }
enum Size { Small, Medium, Large }

static void Main()
{
  Display (Nut.Macadamia);    // Nut.Macadamia
  Display (Size.Large);       // Size.Large
}
```

```
static void Display (Enum value)
{
  Console.WriteLine (value.GetType().Name + "." + value.ToString());
}
```

The static utility methods on System.Enum are primarily related to performing conversions and obtaining lists of members.

Enum Conversions

There are three ways to represent an enum value:

- As an enum member
- As its underlying integral value
- As a string

In this section, we describe how to convert between each.

Enum to integral conversions

Recall that an explicit cast converts between an enum member and its integral value. An explicit cast is the correct approach if you know the enum type at compile time:

```
[Flags] public enum BorderSides { Left=1, Right=2, Top=4, Bottom=8 }
...
int i = (int) BorderSides.Top;          // i == 4
BorderSides side = (BorderSides) i;     // side == BorderSides.Top
```

You can cast a System.Enum instance to its integral type in the same way. The trick is to first cast to an object, and then the integral type:

```
static int GetIntegralValue (Enum anyEnum)
{
  return (int) (object) anyEnum;
}
```

This relies on you knowing the integral type: the method we just wrote would crash if passed an enum whose integral type was long. To write a method that works with an enum of any integral type, you can take one of three approaches. The first is to call Convert.ToDecimal:

```
static decimal GetAnyIntegralValue (Enum anyEnum)
{
  return Convert.ToDecimal (anyEnum);
}
```

This works because every integral type (including ulong) can be converted to decimal without loss of information. The second approach is to call Enum.GetUnderlying Type in order to obtain the enum's integral type, and then call Convert.ChangeType:

```
static object GetBoxedIntegralValue (Enum anyEnum)
{
  Type integralType = Enum.GetUnderlyingType (anyEnum.GetType());
  return Convert.ChangeType (anyEnum, integralType);
}
```

This preserves the original integral type, as the following example shows:

```
object result = GetBoxedIntegralValue (BorderSides.Top);
Console.WriteLine (result);                          // 4
Console.WriteLine (result.GetType());                // System.Int32
```

Our GetBoxedIntegralType method in fact performs no value conversion; rather, it *reboxes* the same value in another type. It translates an integral value in *enum-type* clothing to an integral value in *integral-type* clothing. We describe this further in "How Enums Work" on page 243.

The third approach is to call Format or ToString specifying the "d" or "D" format string. This gives you the enum's integral value as a string, and it is useful when writing custom serialization formatters:

```
static string GetIntegralValueAsString (Enum anyEnum)
{
  return anyEnum.ToString ("D");      // returns something like "4"
}
```

Integral to enum conversions

Enum.ToObject converts an integral value to an enum instance of the given type:

```
object bs = Enum.ToObject (typeof (BorderSides), 3);
Console.WriteLine (bs);                             // Left, Right
```

This is the dynamic equivalent of this:

```
BorderSides bs = (BorderSides) 3;
```

ToObject is overloaded to accept all integral types, as well as object. (The latter works with any boxed integral type.)

String conversions

To convert an enum to a string, you can either call the static Enum.Format method or call ToString on the instance. Each method accepts a format string, which can be "G" for default formatting behavior, "D" to emit the underlying integral value as a string, "X" for the same in hexadecimal, or "F" to format combined members of an enum without the Flags attribute. We listed examples of these in "Standard Format Strings and Parsing Flags" on page 225.

Enum.Parse converts a string to an enum. It accepts the enum type and a string that can include multiple members:

```
BorderSides leftRight = (BorderSides) Enum.Parse (typeof (BorderSides),
                                     "Left, Right");
```

An optional third argument lets you perform case-insensitive parsing. A FormatException is thrown if the member is not found.

Enumerating Enum Values

Enum.GetValues returns an array comprising all members of a particular enum type:

```
foreach (Enum value in Enum.GetValues (typeof (BorderSides)))
  Console.WriteLine (value);
```

Composite members such as LeftRight = Left | Right are included, too.

Enum.GetNames performs the same function, but returns an array of *strings*.

 Internally, the CLR implements GetValues and GetNames by reflecting over the fields in the enum's type. The results are cached for efficiency.

How Enums Work

The semantics of enums are enforced largely by the compiler. In the CLR, there's no runtime difference between an enum instance (when unboxed) and its underlying integral value. Further, an enum definition in the CLR is merely a subtype of System.Enum with static integral-type fields for each member. This makes the ordinary use of an enum highly efficient, with a runtime cost matching that of integral constants.

The downside of this strategy is that enums can provide *static* but not *strong* type safety. We saw an example of this in Chapter 3:

```
public enum BorderSides { Left=1, Right=2, Top=4, Bottom=8 }
...
BorderSides b = BorderSides.Left;
b += 1234;                        // No error!
```

When the compiler is unable to perform validation (as in this example), there's no backup from the runtime to throw an exception.

What we said about there being no runtime difference between an enum instance and its integral value might seem at odds with the following:

```
[Flags] public enum BorderSides { Left=1, Right=2, Top=4, Bottom=8 }
...
Console.WriteLine (BorderSides.Right.ToString());       // Right
Console.WriteLine (BorderSides.Right.GetType().Name);   // BorderSides
```

Given the nature of an enum instance at runtime, you'd expect this to print 2 and Int32! The reason for its behavior is down to some more compile-time trickery. C# explicitly *boxes* an enum instance before calling its virtual methods—such as ToString or GetType. And when an enum instance is boxed, it gains a runtime wrapping that references its enum type.

Tuples

Framework 4.0 provides a new set of generic classes for holding a set of differently typed elements. These are called *tuples*:

```
public class Tuple <T1>
public class Tuple <T1, T2>
public class Tuple <T1, T2, T3>
public class Tuple <T1, T2, T3, T4>
public class Tuple <T1, T2, T3, T4, T5>
public class Tuple <T1, T2, T3, T4, T5, T6>
public class Tuple <T1, T2, T3, T4, T5, T6, T7>
public class Tuple <T1, T2, T3, T4, T5, T6, T7, TRest>
```

Each has read-only properties called Item1, Item2, and so on (one for each type parameter).

You can instantiate a tuple either via its constructor:

```
var t = new Tuple<int,string> (123, "Hello");
```

or via the static helper method Tuple.Create:

```
Tuple<int,string> t = Tuple.Create (123, "Hello");
```

The latter leverages generic type inference. You can combine this with implicit typing:

```
var t = Tuple.Create (123, "Hello");
```

You can then access the properties as follows (notice that each is statically typed):

```
Console.WriteLine (t.Item1 * 2);        // 246
Console.WriteLine (t.Item2.ToUpper());  // HELLO
```

Tuples are convenient in returning more than one value from a method—or creating collections of value *pairs* (we'll cover collections in the following chapter).

An alternative to tuples is to use an object array. However, you then lose static type safety, incur the cost of boxing/unboxing for value types, and require clumsy casts that cannot be validated by the compiler:

```
object[] items = { 123, "Hello" };
Console.WriteLine ( ((int)    items[0]) * 2      );  // 246
Console.WriteLine ( ((string) items[1]).ToUpper() );  // HELLO
```

Comparing Tuples

Tuples are classes (and therefore reference types). In keeping with this, comparing two distinct instances with the equality operator returns false. However, the Equals method is overridden to compare each individual element instead:

```
var t1 = Tuple.Create (123, "Hello");
var t2 = Tuple.Create (123, "Hello");
Console.WriteLine (t1 == t2);         // False
Console.WriteLine (t1.Equals (t2));   // True
```

You can also pass in a custom equality comparer (by virtue of tuples implementing `IStructuralEquatable`). We cover equality and order comparison later in this chapter.

The Guid Struct

The `Guid` struct represents a globally unique identifier: a 16-byte value that, if randomly generated, will almost certainly be unique in the world. `Guid`s are often used for keys of various sorts—in applications and databases. There are 2^{128} or 3.4 × 10^{38} unique `Guid`s.

To create a new random `Guid`, call the static `Guid.NewGuid` method:

```
Guid g = Guid.NewGuid ();
Console.WriteLine (g.ToString()); // 0d57629c-7d6e-4847-97cb-9e2fc25083fe
```

To instantiate an existing value, use one of the constructors. The two most useful constructors are:

```
public Guid (byte[] b);    // Accepts a 16-byte array
public Guid (string g);    // Accepts a formatted string
```

When represented as a string, a `Guid` is formatted as a 32-digit hexadecimal number, with optional hyphens after the 8th, 12th, 16th, and 20th digits. The whole string can also be optionally wrapped in brackets or braces:

```
Guid g1 = new Guid ("{0d57629c-7d6e-4847-97cb-9e2fc25083fe}");
Guid g2 = new Guid ("0d57629c7d6e484797cb9e2fc25083fe");
Console.WriteLine (g1 == g2); // True
```

Being a struct, a `Guid` honors value-type semantics; hence, the equality operator works in the preceding example.

The `ToByteArray` method converts a `Guid` to a byte array.

The static `Guid.Empty` property returns an empty `Guid` (all zeros). This is often used in place of `null`.

Equality Comparison

Until now, we've assumed that the `==` and `!=` operators are all there is to equality comparison. The issue of equality, however, is more complex and subtler, sometimes requiring the use of additional methods and interfaces. This section explores the standard C# and .NET protocols for equality, focusing particularly on two questions:

- When are `==` and `!=` adequate—and inadequate—for equality comparison, and what are the alternatives?
- How and when should you customize a type's equality logic?

But before exploring the details of equality protocols and how to customize them, we must first look at the preliminary concept of value versus referential equality.

Value Versus Referential Equality

There are two kinds of equality:

Value equality
Two values are *equivalent* in some sense.

Referential equality
Two references refer to *exactly the same object.*

By default:

- Value types use *value equality.*
- Reference types use *referential equality.*

Value types, in fact, can *only* use value equality (unless boxed). A simple demonstration of value equality is to compare two numbers:

```
int x = 5, y = 5;
Console.WriteLine (x == y);   // True (by virtue of value equality)
```

A more elaborate demonstration is to compare two DateTimeOffset structs. The following prints True because the two DateTimeOffsets refer to the *same point in time* and so are considered equivalent:

```
var dt1 = new DateTimeOffset (2010, 1, 1, 1, 1, 1, TimeSpan.FromHours(8));
var dt2 = new DateTimeOffset (2010, 1, 1, 2, 1, 1, TimeSpan.FromHours(9));
Console.WriteLine (dt1 == dt2);   // True
```

 DateTimeOffset is a struct whose equality semantics have been tweaked. By default, structs exhibit a special kind of value equality called *structural equality*, where two values are considered equal if all of their members are equal. (You can see this by creating a struct and calling its Equals method; more on this later.)

Reference types exhibit referential equality by default. In the following example, f1 and f2 are not equal—despite their objects having identical content:

```
class Foo { public int X; }
...
Foo f1 = new Foo { X = 5 };
Foo f2 = new Foo { X = 5 };
Console.WriteLine (f1 == f2);   // False
```

In contrast, f3 and f1 are equal because they reference the same object:

```
Foo f3 = f1;
Console.WriteLine (f1 == f3);   // True
```

We'll explain later in this section how reference types can be *customized* to exhibit value equality. An example of this is the Uri class in the System namespace:

```
Uri uri1 = new Uri ("http://www.linqpad.net");
Uri uri2 = new Uri ("http://www.linqpad.net");
Console.WriteLine (uri1 == uri2);            // True
```

Standard Equality Protocols

There are three standard protocols types can implement for equality comparison:

- The == and != operators
- The virtual Equals method in object
- The IEquatable<T> interface

In addition, there are the *pluggable* protocols and the IStructuralEquatable interface which we describe in Chapter 7.

== and !=

We've already seen in many examples how the standard == and != operators perform equality/inequality comparisons. The subtleties with == and != arise because they are *operators*, and so are statically resolved (in fact, they are implemented as static functions). So, when you use == or !=, C# makes a *compile-time* decision as to which type will perform the comparison, and no **virtual** behavior comes into play. This is normally desirable. In the following example, the compiler hard-wires == to the int type because x and y are both int:

```
int x = 5;
int y = 5;
Console.WriteLine (x == y);      // True
```

But in the next example, the compiler wires the == operator to the object type:

```
object x = 5;
object y = 5;
Console.WriteLine (x == y);      // False
```

Because object is a class (and so a reference type), object's == operator uses *referential equality* to compare x and y. The result is false, because x and y each refer to different boxed objects on the heap.

The virtual Object.Equals method

To correctly equate x and y in the preceding example, we can use the virtual Equals method. Equals is defined in System.Object, and so is available to all types:

```
object x = 5;
object y = 5;
Console.WriteLine (x.Equals (y));      // True
```

Equals is resolved at runtime—according to the object's actual type. In this case, it calls Int32's Equals method, which applies *value equality* to the operands, returning true. With reference types, Equals performs referential equality comparison by default; with structs, Equals performs structural comparison by calling Equals on each of its fields.

Why the Complexity?

You might wonder why the designers of C# didn't avoid the problem by making == virtual, and so functionally identical to Equals. There are three reasons for this:

- If the first operand is null, Equals fails with a NullReferenceException; a static operator does not.

- Because the == operator is statically resolved, it executes extremely quickly. This means that you can write computationally intensive code without penalty—and without needing to learn another language such as C++.

- Sometimes it can be useful to have == and Equals apply different definitions of equality. We describe this scenario later in this section.

Hence, Equals is suitable for equating two objects in a type-agnostic fashion. The following method equates two objects of any type:

```
public static bool AreEqual (object obj1, object obj2)
{
  return obj1.Equals (obj2);
}
```

There is one case, however, in which this fails. If the first argument is null, you get a NullReferenceException. Here's the fix:

```
public static bool AreEqual (object obj1, object obj2)
{
  if (obj1 == null) return obj2 == null;
  return obj1.Equals (obj2);
}
```

The static object.Equals method

The object class provides a static helper method that does the work of AreEqual in the preceding example. Its name is Equals—just like the virtual method—but there's no conflict because it accepts *two* arguments:

```
public static bool Equals (object objA, object objB)
```

This provides a null-safe equality comparison algorithm for when the types are unknown at compile time. For example:

```
object x = 3, y = 3;
Console.WriteLine (object.Equals (x, y));   // True
x = null;
Console.WriteLine (object.Equals (x, y));   // False
y = null;
Console.WriteLine (object.Equals (x, y));   // True
```

A useful application is when writing generic types. The following code will not compile if object.Equals is replaced with the == or != operator:

```
class Test <T>
{
  T _value;
  public void SetValue (T newValue)
```

```
    {
      if (!object.Equals (newValue, _value))
      {
        _value = newValue;
        OnValueChanged();
      }
    }
    protected virtual void OnValueChanged() { ... }
}
```

Operators are prohibited here because the compiler cannot bind to the static method of an unknown type.

> A more elaborate way to implement this comparison is with the EqualityComparer<T> class. This has the advantage of avoiding boxing:
>
> ```
> if (!EqualityComparer<T>.Default.Equals (newValue, _value))
> ```
>
> We discuss EqualityComparer<T> in more detail in Chapter 7 (see "Plugging in Equality and Order" on page 304).

The static object.ReferenceEquals method

Occasionally, you need to force referential equality comparison. The static object.ReferenceEquals method does just this:

```
class Widget { ... }

class Test
{
  static void Main()
  {
    Widget w1 = new Widget();
    Widget w2 = new Widget();
    Console.WriteLine (object.ReferenceEquals (w1, w2));     // False
  }
}
```

You might want to do this because it's possible for Widget to override the virtual Equals method, such that w1.Equals(w2) would return true. Further, it's possible for Widget to overload the == operator so that w1==w2 would also return true. In such cases, calling object.ReferenceEquals guarantees normal referential equality semantics.

> Another way to force referential equality comparison is to cast the values to object and then apply the == operator.

The IEquatable<T> interface

A consequence of calling `object.Equals` is that it forces boxing on value types. This is undesirable in highly performance-sensitive scenarios because boxing is relatively expensive compared to the actual comparison. A solution was introduced in C# 2.0, with the `IEquatable<T>` interface:

```
public interface IEquatable<T>
{
  bool Equals (T other);
}
```

The idea is that `IEquatable<T>`, when implemented, gives the same result as calling `object`'s virtual `Equals` method—but more quickly. Most basic .NET types implement `IEquatable<T>`. You can use `IEquatable<T>` as a constraint in a generic type:

```
class Test<T> where T : IEquatable<T>
{
  public bool IsEqual (T a, T b)
  {
    return a.Equals (b);     // No boxing with generic T
  }
}
```

If we remove the generic constraint, the class would still compile, but `a.Equals(b)` would bind to the slower `object.Equals` (slower assuming `T` was a value type).

When Equals and == are not equal

We said earlier that it's sometimes useful for == and `Equals` to apply different definitions of equality. For example:

```
double x = double.NaN;
Console.WriteLine (x == x);          // False
Console.WriteLine (x.Equals (x));    // True
```

The `double` type's == operator enforces that one NaN can never equal anything else—even another NaN. This is most natural from a mathematical perspective, and it reflects the underlying CPU behavior. The `Equals` method, however, is obliged to apply *reflexive* equality; in other words:

> `x.Equals (x)` must *always* return true.

Collections and dictionaries rely on `Equals` behaving this way; otherwise, they could not find an item they previously stored.

Having `Equals` and == apply different definitions of equality is actually quite rare with value types. A more common scenario is with reference types, and happens when the author customizes `Equals` so that it performs value equality while leaving == to perform (default) referential equality. The `StringBuilder` class does exactly this:

```
var sb1 = new StringBuilder ("foo");
var sb2 = new StringBuilder ("foo");
Console.WriteLine (sb1 == sb2);          // False (referential equality)
Console.WriteLine (sb1.Equals (sb2));    // True  (value equality)
```

Let's now look at how to customize equality.

Equality and Custom Types

Recall default equality comparison behavior:

- Value types use *value equality*.
- Reference types use *referential equality*.

Further:

- A struct's `Equals` method applies *structural value equality* by default (i.e., it compares each field in the struct).

Sometimes it makes sense to override this behavior when writing a type. There are two cases for doing so:

- To change the meaning of equality
- To speed up equality comparisons for structs

Changing the meaning of equality

Changing the meaning of equality makes sense when the default behavior of `==` and `Equals` is unnatural for your type and is *not what a consumer would expect*. An example is `DateTimeOffset`, a struct with two private fields: a UTC `DateTime` and a numeric integer offset. If you were writing this type, you'd probably want to ensure that equality comparisons considered only the UTC `DateTime` field and not the offset field. Another example is numeric types that support `NaN` values such as `float` and `double`. If you were implementing such types yourself, you'd want to ensure that `NaN`-comparison logic was supported in equality comparisons.

With classes, it's sometimes more natural to offer *value equality* as the default instead of *referential equality*. This is often the case with small classes that hold a simple piece of data—such as `System.Uri` (or `System.String`).

Speeding up equality comparisons with structs

The default *structural equality* comparison algorithm for structs is relatively slow. Taking over this process by overriding `Equals` can improve performance by a factor of five. Overloading the `==` operator and implementing `IEquatable<T>` allows unboxed equality comparisons, and this can speed things up by a factor of five again.

> Overriding equality semantics for reference types doesn't benefit performance. The default algorithm for referential equality comparison is already very fast because it simply compares two 32- or 64-bit references.

There's actually another, rather peculiar case for customizing equality, and that's to improve a struct's hashing algorithm for better performance in a hashtable. This comes of the fact that equality comparison and hashing are joined at the hip. We'll examine hashing in a moment.

How to override equality semantics

Here is a summary of the steps:

1. Override `GetHashCode()` and `Equals()`.
2. (Optionally) overload `!=` and `==`.
3. (Optionally) implement `IEquatable<T>`.

Overriding GetHashCode

It might seem odd that `System.Object`—with its small footprint of members—defines a method with a specialized and narrow purpose. `GetHashCode` is a virtual method in `Object` that fits this description—it exists primarily for the benefit of just the following two types:

```
System.Collections.Hashtable
System.Collections.Generic.Dictionary<TKey,TValue>
```

These are *hashtables*—collections where each element has a key used for storage and retrieval. A hashtable applies a very specific strategy for efficiently allocating elements based on their key. This requires that each key have an `Int32` number, or *hash code*. The hash code need not be unique for each key, but should be as varied as possible for good hashtable performance. Hashtables are considered important enough that `GetHashCode` is defined in `System.Object`—so that every type can emit a hash code.

 We describe hashtables in detail in "Dictionaries" on page 292 in Chapter 7.

Both reference and value types have default implementations of `GetHashCode`, meaning you don't need to override this method—*unless you override* `Equals`. The converse is also true: override `GetHashCode` and you must also override `Equals`.

Here are the other rules for overriding `object.GetHashCode`:

- It must return the same value on two objects for which `Equals` returns `true` (hence, `GetHashCode` and `Equals` are overridden together).
- It must not throw exceptions.
- It must return the same value if called repeatedly on the same object (unless the object has *changed*).

For maximum performance in hashtables, `GetHashCode` should be written so as to minimize the likelihood of two different values returning the same hash code. This gives rise to the third reason for overriding `Equals` and `GetHashCode` on structs, which is to provide a more efficient hashing algorithm than the default. The default for structs simply performs a bitwise exclusive OR on each of the fields, which typically generates more duplicate codes than if you wrote the algorithm yourself.

In contrast, the default `GetHashCode` implementation for *classes* is based on an internal object token, which is unique for each instance in the CLR's current implementation.

 If an object's hash code changes after it's been added as a key to a dictionary, the object will no longer be accessible in the dictionary. You can preempt this by basing hash code calculations on immutable fields.

A complete example illustrating how to override `GetHashCode` is listed shortly.

Overriding Equals

The axioms for `object.Equals` are as follows:

- An object cannot equal `null` (unless it's a nullable type).
- Equality is *reflexive* (an object equals itself).
- Equality is *commutative* (if `a.Equals(b)`, then `b.Equals(a)`).
- Equality is *transitive* (if `a.Equals(b)` and `b.Equals(c)`, then `a.Equals(c)`).
- Equality operations are repeatable and reliable (they don't throw exceptions).

Overloading == and !=

In addition to overriding `Equals`, you can optionally overload the equality and inequality operators. This is nearly always done with structs, because the consequence of not doing so is that the `==` and `!=` operators will simply not work on your type.

With classes, there are two ways to proceed:

- Leave `==` and `!=` alone—so that they apply referential equality.
- Overload `==` and `!=` in line with `Equals`.

The first approach is most common with custom types—especially *mutable* types. It ensures that your type follows the expectation that `==` and `!=` should exhibit referential equality with reference types and this avoids confusing consumers. We saw an example earlier:

```
var sb1 = new StringBuilder ("foo");
var sb2 = new StringBuilder ("foo");
Console.WriteLine (sb1 == sb2);        // False (referential equality)
Console.WriteLine (sb1.Equals (sb2));  // True  (value equality)
```

The second approach makes sense with types for which a consumer would never want referential equality. These are typically immutable—such as the `string` and `System.Uri` classes—and are sometimes good candidates for `struct`s.

 Although it's possible to overload `!=` such that it means something other than `!(==)`, this is almost never done in practice, except in cases such as comparing `float.NaN`.

Implementing IEquatable<T>

For completeness, it's also good to implement IEquatable<T> when overriding Equals. Its results should always match those of the overridden object's Equals method. Implementing IEquatable<T> comes at no programming cost if you structure your Equals method implementation, as in the following example.

An example: The Area struct

Imagine we need a struct to represent an area whose width and height are interchangeable. In other words, 5 × 10 is equal to 10 × 5. (Such a type would be suitable in an algorithm that arranges rectangular shapes.)

Here's the complete code:

```
public struct Area : IEquatable <Area>
{
  public readonly int Measure1;
  public readonly int Measure2;

  public Area (int m1, int m2)
  {
    Measure1 = Math.Min (m1, m2);
    Measure2 = Math.Max (m1, m2);
  }

  public override bool Equals (object other)
  {
    if (!(other is Area)) return false;
    return Equals ((Area) other);          // Calls method below
  }

  public bool Equals (Area other)          // Implements IEquatable<Area>
  {
    return Measure1 == other.Measure1 && Measure2 == other.Measure2;
  }

  public override int GetHashCode()
  {
    return Measure2 * 31 + Measure1;     // 31 = some prime number
  }

  public static bool operator == (Area a1, Area a2)
  {
    return a1.Equals (a2);
  }

  public static bool operator != (Area a1, Area a2)
  {
    return !a1.Equals (a2);
  }
}
```

Here's another way to implement the Equals method, leveraging nullable types:

```
Area? otherArea = other as Area?;
return otherArea.HasValue && Equals (otherArea.Value);
```

In implementing GetHashCode, we've helped to improve the likelihood of uniqueness by multiplying the larger measure by some prime number (ignoring any overflow) before adding the two together. When there are more than two fields, the following pattern, suggested by Josh Bloch, gives good results while being performant:

```
int hash = 17;   // 17 = some prime number
hash = hash * 31 + field1.GetHashCode();   // 31 = another prime number
hash = hash * 31 + field2.GetHashCode();
hash = hash * 31 + field3.GetHashCode();
...
return hash;
```

Here's a demo of the Area struct:

```
Area a1 = new Area (5, 10);
Area a2 = new Area (10, 5);
Console.WriteLine (a1.Equals (a2));   // True
Console.WriteLine (a1 == a2);   // True
```

Pluggable equality comparers

If you want a type to take on different equality semantics just for a particular scenario, you can use a pluggable IEqualityComparer. This is particularly useful in conjunction with the standard collection classes, and we describe it in the following chapter, in "Plugging in Equality and Order" on page 304.

Order Comparison

As well as defining standard protocols for equality, C# and .NET define standard protocols for determining the order of one object relative to another. The basic protocols are:

- The IComparable interfaces (IComparable and IComparable<T>)
- The > and < operators

The IComparable interfaces are used by general-purpose sorting algorithms. In the following example, the static Array.Sort method works because System.String implements the IComparable interfaces:

```
string[] colors = { "Green", "Red", "Blue" };
Array.Sort (colors);
foreach (string c in colors) Console.Write (c + " ");   // Blue Green Red
```

The < and > operators are more specialized, and they are intended mostly for numeric types. Because they are statically resolved, they can translate to highly efficient byte-code, suitable for computationally intensive algorithms.

The .NET Framework also provides pluggable ordering protocols, via the IComparer interfaces. We describe these in the final section of Chapter 7.

IComparable

The IComparable interfaces are defined as follows:

```
public interface IComparable      { int CompareTo (object other); }
public interface IComparable<in T> { int CompareTo (T other);      }
```

The two interfaces represent the same functionality. With value types, the generic type-safe interface is faster than the nongeneric interface. In both cases, the CompareTo method works as follows:

- If a comes after b, a.CompareTo(b) returns a positive number.
- If a is the same as b, a.CompareTo(b) returns 0.
- If a comes before b, a.CompareTo(b) returns a negative number.

For example:

```
Console.WriteLine ("Beck".CompareTo ("Anne"));     // 1
Console.WriteLine ("Beck".CompareTo ("Beck"));     // 0
Console.WriteLine ("Beck".CompareTo ("Chris"));    // -1
```

Most of the base types implement both IComparable interfaces. These interfaces are also sometimes implemented when writing custom types. An example is given shortly.

IComparable versus Equals

Consider a type that both overrides Equals and implements the IComparable interfaces. You'd expect that when Equals returns true, CompareTo should return 0. And you'd be right. But here's the catch:

When Equals returns false, CompareTo can return what it likes!

In other words, equality can be "fussier" than comparison, but not vice versa (violate this and sorting algorithms will break). So, CompareTo can say "All objects are equal" while Equals says "But some are more equal than others!"

A great example of this is System.String. String's Equals method and == operator use *ordinal* comparison, which compares the Unicode point values of each character. Its CompareTo method, however, uses a less fussy *culture-dependent* comparison. On most computers, for instance, the strings "ü" and "ǔ" are different according to Equals, but the same according to CompareTo.

In Chapter 7, we discuss the pluggable ordering protocol, IComparer, which allows you to specify an alternative ordering algorithm when sorting or instantiating a sorted collection. A custom IComparer can further extend the gap between CompareTo and Equals—a case-insensitive string comparer, for instance, will return 0 when comparing "A" and "a". The reverse rule still applies, however: CompareTo can never be fussier than Equals.

When implementing the `IComparable` interfaces in a custom type, you can avoid running afoul of this rule by writing the first line of `CompareTo` as follows:

```
if (Equals (other)) return 0;
```

After that, it can return what it likes, as long as it's consistent!

< and >

Some types define `<` and `>` operators. For instance:

```
bool after2010 = DateTime.Now > new DateTime (2010, 1, 1);
```

When implemented, the `<` and `>` operators are functionally consistent with the `IComparable` interfaces. This is standard practice across the .NET Framework.

It's also standard practice to implement the `IComparable` interfaces whenever `<` and `>` are overloaded, although the reverse is not true. In fact, most .NET types that implement `IComparable` *do not* overload `<` and `>`. This differs from the situation with equality, where it's normal to overload `==` when overriding `Equals`.

Typically, `>` and `<` are overloaded only when:

* A type has a strong intrinsic concept of "greater than" and "less than" (versus `IComparable`'s broader concepts of "comes before" and "comes after").
* There is only one way *or context* in which to perform the comparison.
* The result is invariant across cultures.

`System.String` doesn't satisfy the last point: the results of string comparisons can vary according to language. Hence, `string` doesn't support the `>` and `<` operators:

```
bool error = "Beck" > "Anne";      // Compile-time error
```

Implementing the IComparable Interfaces

In the following struct, representing a musical note, we implement the `IComparable` interfaces, as well as overloading the `<` and `>` operators. For completeness, we also override `Equals`/`GetHashCode` and overload `==` and `!=`:

```
public struct Note : IComparable<Note>, IEquatable<Note>, IComparable
{
  int _semitonesFromA;
  public int SemitonesFromA { get { return _semitonesFromA; } }

  public Note (int semitonesFromA)
  {
    _semitonesFromA = semitonesFromA;
  }


  public int CompareTo (Note other)          // Generic IComparable<T>
  {
```

```csharp
      if (Equals (other)) return 0;     // Fail-safe check
      return _semitonesFromA.CompareTo (other._semitonesFromA);
    }

    int IComparable.CompareTo (object other)      // Nongeneric IComparable
    {
      if (!(other is Note))
        throw new InvalidOperationException ("CompareTo: Not a note");
      return CompareTo ((Note) other);
    }

    public static bool operator < (Note n1, Note n2)
    {
      return n1.CompareTo (n2) < 0;
    }

    public static bool operator > (Note n1, Note n2)
    {
      return n1.CompareTo (n2) > 0;
    }

    public bool Equals (Note other)      // for IEquatable<Note>
    {
      return _semitonesFromA == other._semitonesFromA;
    }

    public override bool Equals (object other)
    {
      if (!(other is Note)) return false;
      return Equals ((Note) other);
    }

    public override int GetHashCode()
    {
      return _semitonesFromA.GetHashCode();
    }

    public static bool operator == (Note n1, Note n2)
    {
      return n1.Equals (n2);
    }

    public static bool operator != (Note n1, Note n2)
    {
      return !(n1 == n2);
    }
  }
```

Utility Classes

Console

The static Console class handles standard input/output for console-based applications. In a command-line (Console) application, the input comes from the keyboard via Read, ReadKey, and ReadLine, and the output goes to the text window via Write and WriteLine. You can control the window's position and dimensions with the properties WindowLeft, WindowTop, WindowHeight, and WindowWidth. You can also change the BackgroundColor and ForegroundColor properties and manipulate the cursor with the CursorLeft, CursorTop, and CursorSize properties:

```
Console.WindowWidth = Console.LargestWindowWidth;
Console.ForegroundColor = ConsoleColor.Green;
Console.Write ("test... 50%");
Console.CursorLeft -= 3;
Console.Write ("90%");       // test... 90%
```

The Write and WriteLine methods are overloaded to accept a composite format string (see String.Format in "String and Text Handling" on page 193). However, neither method accepts a format provider, so you are stuck with CultureInfo.CurrentCulture. (The workaround, of course, is to explicitly call string.Format.)

The Console.Out property returns a TextWriter. Passing Console.Out to a method that expects a TextWriter is a useful way to get that method to write to the Console for diagnostic purposes.

You can also redirect the Console's input and output streams via the SetIn and SetOut methods:

```
// First save existing output writer:
System.IO.TextWriter oldOut = Console.Out;

// Redirect the console's output to a file:
using (System.IO.TextWriter w = System.IO.File.CreateText
                                 ("e:\\output.txt"))
{
  Console.SetOut (w);
  Console.WriteLine ("Hello world");
}

// Restore standard console output
Console.SetOut (oldOut);

// Open the output.txt file in Notepad:
System.Diagnostics.Process.Start ("e:\\output.txt");
```

In Chapter 14, we describe how streams and text writers work.

 In a Visual Studio Windows application, the Console's output is automatically redirected to Visual Studio's output window (in debug mode). This can make Console.Write useful for diagnostic purposes; although in most cases the Debug and Trace classes in the System.Diagnostics namespace are more appropriate (see Chapter 13).

Environment

The static `System.Environment` class provides a range of useful properties:

Files and folders
    `CurrentDirectory, SystemDirectory, CommandLine`

Computer and operating system
    `MachineName, ProcessorCount, OSVersion`

User logon
    `UserName, UserInteractive, UserDomainName`

Diagnostics
    `TickCount, StackTrace, WorkingSet, Version`

You can obtain additional folders by calling `GetFolderPath`; we describe this in "File and Directory Operations" on page 559 in Chapter 14.

You can access OS environment variables (what you see when you type "set" at the command prompt) with the following three methods: `GetEnvironmentVariable`, `GetEnvironmentVariables`, and `SetEnvironmentVariable`.

The `ExitCode` property lets you set the return code, for when your program is called from a command or batch file, and the `FailFast` method terminates a program immediately, without performing cleanup.

Process

The `Process` class in `System.Diagnostics` allows you to launch a new process.

The static `Process.Start` method has a number of overloads; the simplest accepts a simple filename with optional arguments:

```
Process.Start ("notepad.exe");
Process.Start ("notepad.exe", "e:\\file.txt");
```

You can also specify just a filename, and the registered program for its extension will be launched:

```
Process.Start ("e:\\file.txt");
```

The most flexible overload accepts a `ProcessStartInfo` instance. With this, you can capture and redirect the launched process's input, output, and error output (if you set `UseShellExecute` to `false`). The following captures the output of calling `ipconfig`:

```
ProcessStartInfo psi = new ProcessStartInfo
{
  FileName = "cmd.exe",
  Arguments = "/c ipconfig /all",
  RedirectStandardOutput = true,
  UseShellExecute = false
};
Process p = Process.Start (psi);
string result = p.StandardOutput.ReadToEnd();
Console.WriteLine (result);
```

You can do the same to invoke the csc compiler, if you set Filename to the following:

```
psi.FileName = System.IO.Path.Combine (
    System.Runtime.InteropServices.RuntimeEnvironment.GetRuntimeDirectory(),
    "csc.exe");
```

If you don't redirect output, Process.Start executes the program in parallel to the caller. If you want to wait for the new process to complete, you can call WaitFor Exit on the Process object, with an optional timeout.

The Process class also allows you to query and interact with other processes running on the computer (see Chapter 13).

7

Collections

The .NET Framework provides a standard set of types for storing and managing collections of objects. These include resizable lists, linked lists, and sorted and unsorted dictionaries, as well as arrays. Of these, only arrays form part of the C# language; the remaining collections are just classes you instantiate like any other.

The types in the Framework for collections can be divided into the following categories:

- Interfaces that define standard collection protocols
- Ready-to-use collection classes (lists, dictionaries, etc.)
- Base classes for writing application-specific collections

This chapter covers each of these categories, with an additional section on the types used in determining element equality and order.

The collection namespaces are as follows:

Namespace	Contains
System.Collections	Nongeneric collection classes and interfaces
System.Collections.Specialized	Strongly typed nongeneric collection classes
System.Collections.Generic	Generic collection classes and interfaces
System.Collections.ObjectModel	Proxies and bases for custom collections
System.Collections.Concurrent	Thread-safe collections (see Chapter 22)

Enumeration

In computing, there are many different kinds of collections ranging from simple data structures, such as arrays or linked lists, to more complex ones, such as red/black trees and hashtables. Although the internal implementation and external characteristics of these data structures vary widely, the ability to traverse the contents of the collection is an almost universal need. The Framework supports this need via a pair of interfaces (`IEnumerable`, `IEnumerator`, and their generic counterparts) that allow different data structures to expose a common traversal API. These are part of a larger set of collection interfaces illustrated in Figure 7-1.

Figure 7-1. Collection interfaces

IEnumerable and IEnumerator

The `IEnumerator` interface defines the basic low-level protocol by which elements in a collection are traversed—or enumerated—in a forward-only manner. Its declaration is as follows:

```
public interface IEnumerator
{
  bool MoveNext();
  object Current { get; }
  void Reset();
}
```

`MoveNext` advances the current element or "cursor" to the next position, returning `false` if there are no more elements in the collection. `Current` returns the element at the current position (usually cast from `object` to a more specific type). `MoveNext` must be called before retrieving the first element—this is to allow for an empty collection. The `Reset` method, if implemented, moves back to the start, allowing the collection to be enumerated again. (Calling `Reset` is generally avoided because it's not supported by all enumerators.)

Collections do not *implement* enumerators; instead, they *provide* enumerators, via the interface `IEnumerable`:

```
public interface IEnumerable
{
  IEnumerator GetEnumerator();
}
```

By defining a single method retuning an enumerator, `IEnumerable` provides flexibility in that the iteration logic can be farmed off to another class. Moreover, it means that several consumers can enumerate the collection at once without interfering with each other. `IEnumerable` can be thought of as "IEnumeratorProvider," and it is the most basic interface that collection classes implement.

The following example illustrates low-level use of `IEnumerable` and `IEnumerator`:

```
string s = "Hello";

// Because string implements IEnumerable, we can call GetEnumerator():
IEnumerator rator = s.GetEnumerator();

while (rator.MoveNext())
{
  char c = (char) rator.Current;
  Console.Write (c + ".");
}

// Output:  H.e.l.l.o.
```

However, it's rare to call methods on enumerators directly in this manner, because C# provides a syntactic shortcut: the **foreach** statement. Here's the same example rewritten using **foreach**:

```
string s = "Hello";       // The String class implements IEnumerable

foreach (char c in s)
  Console.Write (c + ".");
```

IEnumerable<T> and IEnumerator<T>

`IEnumerator` and `IEnumerable` are nearly always implemented in conjunction with their extended generic versions:

```
public interface IEnumerator<T> : IEnumerator, IDisposable
{
  T Current { get; }
}

public interface IEnumerable<T> : IEnumerable
{
  IEnumerator<T> GetEnumerator();
}
```

By defining a typed version of `Current` and `GetEnumerator`, these interfaces strengthen static type safety, avoid the overhead of boxing with value-type elements, and are more convenient to the consumer. Arrays automatically implement `IEnumerable<T>` (where T is the member type of the array).

Thanks to the improved static type safety, calling the following method with an array of characters will generate a compile-time error:

```
void Test (IEnumerable<int> numbers) { ... }
```

It's a standard practice for collection classes to publicly expose IEnumerable<T>, while "hiding" the nongeneric IEnumerable through explicit interface implementation. This is so that if you directly call GetEnumerator(), you get back the type-safe generic IEnumerator<T>. There are times, though, when this rule is broken for reasons of backward compatibility (generics did not exist prior to C# 2.0). A good example is arrays—these must return the nongeneric (the nice way of putting it is "classic") IEnumerator to avoid breaking earlier code. In order to get a generic IEnumerator<T>, you must cast to expose the explicit interface:

```
int[] data = { 1, 2, 3 };
var rator = ((IEnumerable <int>)data).GetEnumerator();
```

Fortunately, you rarely need to write this sort of code, thanks to the foreach statement.

IEnumerable<T> and IDisposable

IEnumerable<T> implements IDisposable. This allows enumerators to hold references to resources such as database connections—and ensure that those resources are released when enumeration is complete (or abandoned partway through). The foreach statement recognizes this detail and translates this:

```
foreach (var element in somethingEnumerable) { ... }
```

into this:

```
using (var rator = somethingEnumerable.GetEnumerator())
  while (rator.MoveNext())
  {
    var element = rator.Current;
    ...
  }
```

The using block ensures disposal—more on IDisposable in Chapter 12.

Implementing the Enumeration Interfaces

You might want to implement IEnumerable or IEnumerable<T> for one or more of the following reasons:

- To support the foreach statement
- To interoperate with anything expecting a standard collection
- As part of implementing a more sophisticated collection interface
- To support collection initializers

To implement IEnumerable/IEnumerable<T>, you must provide an enumerator. You can do this in one of three ways:

- If the class is "wrapping" another collection, by returning the wrapped collection's enumerator
- Via an iterator using yield return
- By instantiating your own IEnumerator/IEnumerator<T> implementation

You can also subclass an existing collection: Collection<T> is designed just for this purpose (see "Customizable Collections and Proxies" on page 298). Yet another approach is to use the LINQ query operators that we'll cover in the next chapter.

Returning another collection's enumerator is just a matter of calling GetEnumera tor on the inner collection. However, this is viable only in the simplest scenarios, where the items in the inner collection are exactly what are required. A more flexible approach is to write an iterator, using C#'s yield return statement. An *iterator* is a C# language feature that assists in writing collections, in the same way the foreach statement assists in consuming collections. An iterator automatically handles the implementation of IEnumerable and IEnumerator—or their generic versions. Here's a simple example:

```
public class MyCollection : IEnumerable
{
  int[] data = { 1, 2, 3 };

  public IEnumerator GetEnumerator()
  {
    foreach (int i in data)
      yield return i;
  }
}
```

Notice the "black magic": GetEnumerator doesn't appear to return an enumerator at all! Upon parsing the yield return statement, the compiler writes a hidden nested enumerator class behind the scenes, and then refactors GetEnumerator to instantiate and return that class. Iterators are powerful and simple (and are the basis for LINQ's implementation).

Keeping with this approach, we can also implement the generic interface IEnumerable<T>:

```
public class MyGenCollection : IEnumerable<int>
{
  int[] data = { 1, 2, 3 };

  public IEnumerator<int> GetEnumerator()
  {
    foreach (int i in data)
      yield return i;
  }

  IEnumerator IEnumerable.GetEnumerator()     // Explicit implementation
  {                                            // keeps it hidden.
    return GetEnumerator();
  }
}
```

Because IEnumerable<T> implements IEnumerable, we must implement both the generic and the nongeneric versions of GetEnumerator. In accordance with standard practice, we've implemented the nongeneric version explicitly. It can simply call the generic GetEnumerator because IEnumerator<T> implements IEnumerator.

The class we've just written would be suitable as a basis from which to write a more sophisticated collection. However, if we need nothing above a simple IEnumerable<T> implementation, the yield return statement allows for an easier variation. Rather than writing a class, you can move the iteration logic into a method returning a generic IEnumerable<T> and let the compiler take care of the rest. Here's an example:

```
public class Test
{
  public static IEnumerable <int> GetSomeIntegers()
  {
    yield return 1;
    yield return 2;
    yield return 3;
  }
}
```

Here's our method in use:

```
foreach (int i in Test.GetSomeIntegers())
  Console.WriteLine (i);

// Output
1
2
3
```

The final approach in writing GetEnumerator is to write a class that implements IEnumerator directly. This is exactly what the compiler does behind the scenes, in resolving iterators. (Fortunately, it's rare that you'll need to go this far yourself.) The following example defines a collection that's hardcoded to contain the integers 1, 2, and 3:

```
public class MyIntList : IEnumerable
{
  int[] data = { 1, 2, 3 };

  public IEnumerator GetEnumerator()
  {
    return new Enumerator (this);
  }

  class Enumerator : IEnumerator        // Define an inner class
  {                                     // for the enumerator.
    MyIntList collection;
    int currentIndex = -1;

    internal Enumerator (MyIntList collection)
    {
      this.collection = collection;
    }

    public object Current
```

```
{
  get
  {
    if (currentIndex == -1)
      throw new InvalidOperationException ("Enumeration not started!");
    if (currentIndex == collection.data.Length)
      throw new InvalidOperationException ("Past end of list!");
    return collection.data [currentIndex];
  }
}

public bool MoveNext()
{
  if (currentIndex > collection.data.Length) return false;
  return ++currentIndex < collection.data.Length;
}
public void Reset() { currentIndex = -1; }
}
}
```

Implementing Reset is optional—you can instead throw a NotSupportedException.

Note that the first call to MoveNext should move to the first (and not the second) item in the list.

To get on par with an iterator in functionality, we must also implement IEnumerator<T>. Here's an example with bounds checking omitted for brevity:

```
class MyIntList : IEnumerable<int>
{
  int[] data = { 1, 2, 3 };

  // The generic enumerator is compatible with both IEnumerable and
  // IEnumerable<T>. We implement the nongeneric GetEnumerator method
  // explicitly to avoid a naming conflict.

  public IEnumerator<int> GetEnumerator() { return new Enumerator(this); }
  IEnumerator IEnumerable.GetEnumerator() { return new Enumerator(this); }

  class Enumerator : IEnumerator<int>
  {
    int currentIndex = -1;
    MyIntList collection;

    internal Enumerator (MyIntList collection)
    {
      this.collection = collection;
    }

    public int Current { get { return collection.data [currentIndex]; } }
    object IEnumerator.Current { get { return Current; } }
```

```
public bool MoveNext()
{
  return ++currentIndex < collection.data.Length;
}

public void Reset() { currentIndex = -1; }

// Given we don't need a Dispose method, it's good practice to
// implement it explicitly, so it's hidden from the public interface.

void IDisposable.Dispose() {}
  }
}
```

The example with generics is faster because IEnumerator<int>.Current doesn't require casting from int to object, and so avoids the overhead of boxing.

When to Use the Nongeneric Interfaces

Given the extra type safety of the generic collection interfaces such as IEnumerable<T>, the question arises: do you ever need to use the nongeneric IEnumerable (or ICollection or IList)?

In the case of IEnumerable, you must implement this interface in conjunction with IEnumerable<T>—because the latter derives from the former. However, it's very rare that you actually implement these interfaces from scratch: in nearly all cases, you can take the higher-level approach of using iterator methods, Collection<T>, and LINQ.

So, what about as a consumer? In nearly all cases, you can manage entirely with the generic interfaces. The nongeneric interfaces are still occasionally useful, though, in their ability to provide type unification for collections across all element types. The following method, for instance, counts elements in any collection *recursively*:

```
public static int Count (IEnumerable e)
{
  int count = 0;
  foreach (object element in e)
  {
    var subCollection = element as IEnumerable;
    if (subCollection != null)
      count += Count (subCollection);
    else
      count++;
  }
  return count;
}
```

Because C# 4.0 offers covariance with generic interfaces, it might seem valid to have this method instead accept IEnumerable<object>. This would fail with value-type elements, however. It would also fail with legacy collections that don't implement IEnumerable<T>— an example is ControlCollection in Windows Forms.

The ICollection and IList Interfaces

Although the enumeration interfaces provide a protocol for forward-only iteration over a collection, they don't provide a mechanism to determine the size of the collection, access a member by index, search, or modify the collection. For such functionality, the .NET Framework defines the ICollection, IList, and IDictionary interfaces. Each comes in both generic and nongeneric versions; however, the non-generic versions exist mostly for legacy.

The inheritance hierarchy for these interfaces was shown in Figure 7-1. The easiest way to summarize them is as follows:

IEnumerable<T> *(and* IEnumerable*)*
> Provides minimum functionality (enumeration only)

ICollection<T> *(and* ICollection*)*
> Provides medium functionality (e.g., the Count property)

IList <T>/IDictionary <K,V> *and their nongeneric versions*
> Provide maximum functionality (including "random" access by index/key)

> It's rare that you'll need to *implement* any of these interfaces. In nearly all cases when you need to write a collection class, you can instead subclass Collection<T> (see "Customizable Collections and Proxies" on page 298). LINQ provides yet another option that covers many scenarios.

The generic and nongeneric versions differ in ways over and above what you might expect, particularly in the case of ICollection. The reasons for this are mostly historical: because generics came later, the generic interfaces were developed with the benefit of hindsight. For this reason, ICollection<T> does not extend ICollection, IList<T> does not extend IList, and IDictionary<TKey, TValue> does not extend IDictionary. Of course, a collection class itself is free to implement both versions of an interface if beneficial (which, often, it is).

> Another, subtler reason for IList<T> not extending IList is that casting to IList<T> would then return an interface with both Add(T) and Add(object) members. This would effectively defeat static type safety, because you could call Add with an object of any type.

This section covers ICollection<T>, IList<T>, and their nongeneric versions; "Dictionaries" on page 292 covers the dictionary interfaces.

Collections

There is no *consistent* rationale in the way the words *collection* and *list* are applied throughout the .NET Framework. For instance, since IList<T> is a more functional version of ICollection<T>, you might expect the class List<T> to be correspondingly more functional than the class Collection<T>. This is not the case. It's best to consider the terms *collection* and *list* as broadly synonymous, except when a specific type is involved.

ICollection<T> and ICollection

ICollection<T> is the standard interface for countable collections of objects. It provides the ability to determine the size of a collection (Count), determine whether an item exists in the collection (Contains), copy the collection into an array (ToArray), and determine whether the collection is read-only (IsReadOnly). For writable collections, you can also Add, Remove, and Clear items from the collection. And since it extends IEnumerable<T>, it can also be traversed via the foreach statement:

```
public interface ICollection<T> : IEnumerable<T>, IEnumerable
{
  int Count { get; }

  bool Contains (T item);
  void CopyTo (T[] array, int arrayIndex);
  bool IsReadOnly { get; }

  void Add(T item);
  bool Remove (T item);
  void Clear();
}
```

The nongeneric ICollection is similar in providing a countable collection, but doesn't provide functionality for altering the list or checking for element membership:

```
public interface ICollection : IEnumerable
{
    int Count { get; }
    bool IsSynchronized { get; }
    object SyncRoot { get; }
    void CopyTo (Array array, int index);
}
```

The nongeneric interface also defines properties to assist with synchronization (Chapter 21)—these were dumped in the generic version because thread safety is no longer considered intrinsic to the collection.

Both interfaces are fairly straightforward to implement. If implementing a read-only ICollection<T>, the Add, Remove, and Clear methods should throw a NotSupportedException.

These interfaces are usually implemented in conjunction with either the IList or the IDictionary interface.

IList<T> and IList

IList<T> is the standard interface for collections indexable by position. In addition to the functionality inherited from ICollection<T> and IEnumerable<T>, it provides the ability to read or write an element by position (via an indexer) and insert/remove by position:

```
public interface IList<T> : ICollection<T>, IEnumerable<T>, IEnumerable
{
  T this [int index] { get; set; }
  int IndexOf (T item);
  void Insert (int index, T item);
  void RemoveAt (int index);
}
```

The IndexOf methods perform a linear search on the list, returning -1 if the specified item is not found.

The nongeneric version of IList has more members because it inherits less from ICollection:

```
public interface IList : ICollection, IEnumerable
{
  object this [int index] { get; set }
  bool IsFixedSize { get; }
  bool IsReadOnly  { get; }
  int  Add        (object value);
  void Clear();
  bool Contains (object value);
  int  IndexOf  (object value);
  void Insert   (int index, object value);
  void Remove   (object value);
  void RemoveAt (int index);
}
```

The Add method on the nongeneric IList interface returns an integer—this is the index of the newly added item. In contrast, the Add method on ICollection<T> has a void return type.

The general-purpose List<T> class is the quintessential implementation of both IList<T> and IList. C# arrays also implement both the generic and nongeneric ILists (although the methods that add or remove elements are hidden via explicit interface implementation and throw a NotSupportedException if called).

The Array Class

The Array class is the implicit base class for all single and multidimensional arrays, and it is one of the most fundamental types implementing the standard collection interfaces. The Array class provides type unification, so a common set of methods is available to all arrays, regardless of their declaration or underlying element type.

Since arrays are so fundamental, C# provides explicit syntax for their declaration and initialization, described in Chapters 2 and 3. When an array is declared using C#'s syntax, the CLR implicitly subtypes the Array class—synthesizing a *pseudotype* appropriate to the array's dimensions and element types. This pseudo-type implements the typed generic collection interfaces, such as IList<string>.

The CLR also treats array types specially upon construction, assigning them a contiguous space in memory. This makes indexing into arrays highly efficient, but prevents them from being resized later on.

Array implements the collection interfaces up to IList<T> in both their generic and nongeneric forms. IList<T> itself is implemented explicitly, though, to keep Array's public interface clean of methods such as Add or Remove, which throw an exception on fixed-length collections such as arrays. The Array class does actually offer a static Resize method, although this works by creating a new array and then copying over each element. As well as being inefficient, references to the array elsewhere in the program will still point to the original version. A better solution for resizable collections is to use the List<T> class (described in the following section).

An array can contain value type or reference type elements. Value type elements are stored in place in the array, so an array of three long integers (each 8 bytes) will occupy 24 bytes of contiguous memory. A reference type element, however, occupies only as much space in the array as a reference (4 bytes in a 32-bit environment or 8 bytes in a 64-bit environment). Figure 7-2 illustrates the effect, in memory, of the following program:

```
StringBuilder[] builders = new StringBuilder [5];
builders [0] = new StringBuilder ("builder1");
builders [1] = new StringBuilder ("builder2");
builders [2] = new StringBuilder ("builder3");

long[] numbers = new long [3];
numbers [0] = 12345;
numbers [1] = 54321;
```

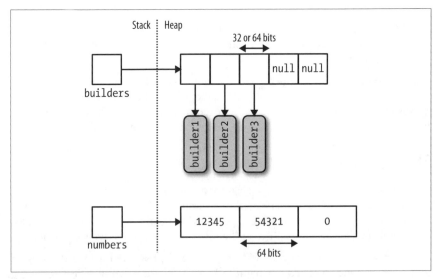

Figure 7-2. Arrays in memory

Because **Array** is a class, arrays are always (themselves) reference types—regardless of the array's element type. This means that the statement **arrayB** = **arrayA** results in two variables that reference the same array. Similarly, two distinct arrays will always fail an equality test—unless you use a custom equality comparer. Framework 4.0 provides one for the purpose of comparing elements in arrays or tuples which you can access via the **StructuralComparisons** type:

```
object[] a1 = { "string", 123, true };
object[] a2 = { "string", 123, true };

Console.WriteLine (a1 == a2);                // False
Console.WriteLine (a1.Equals (a2));          // False

Console.WriteLine (a1.Equals (a2,
  StructuralComparisons.StructuralEqualityComparer));   // True
```

Arrays can be duplicated with the **Clone** method: **arrayB** = **arrayA.Clone()**. However, this results in a shallow clone, meaning that only the memory represented by the array itself is copied. If the array contains value type objects, the values themselves are copied; if the array contains reference type objects, just the references are copied (resulting in two arrays whose members reference the same objects). Figure 7-3 demonstrates the effect of adding the following code to our example:

```
StringBuilder[] builders2 = builders;
StringBuilder[] shallowClone = (StringBuilder[]) builders.Clone();
```

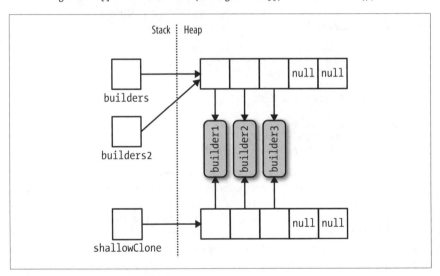

Figure 7-3. Shallow-cloning an array

To create a deep copy—where reference type subobjects are duplicated—you must loop through the array and clone each element manually. The same rules apply to other .NET collection types.

Although **Array** is designed primarily for use with 32-bit indexers, it also has limited support for 64-bit indexers (allowing an array to theoretically address up to 2^{64}

elements) via several methods that accept both Int32 and Int64 parameters. These overloads are useless in practice, because the CLR does not permit any object—including arrays—to exceed 2GB in size (whether running on a 32- or 64-bit environment).

 Many of the methods on the Array class that you expect to be instance methods are in fact static methods. This is an odd design decision, and means you should check for both static and instance methods when looking for a method on Array.

Construction and Indexing

The easiest way to create and index arrays is through C#'s language constructs:

```
int[] myArray = { 1, 2, 3 };
int first = myArray [0];
int last = myArray [myArray.Length - 1];
```

Alternatively, you can instantiate an array dynamically by calling Array.CreateInstance. This allows you to specify element type and rank (number of dimensions) at runtime, as well as allowing nonzero-based arrays through specifying a lower bound. Nonzero-based arrays are not CLS (Common Language Specification)-compliant.

The static GetValue and SetValue methods let you access elements in a dynamically created array (they also work on ordinary arrays):

```
// Create a string array 2 elements in length:
Array a = Array.CreateInstance (typeof(string), 2);
a.SetValue ("hi", 0);                       // → a[0] = "hi";
a.SetValue ("there", 1);                    // → a[1] = "there";
string s = (string) a.GetValue (0);         // → s = a[0];

// We can also cast to a C# array as follows:
string[] cSharpArray = (string[]) a;
string s2 = cSharpArray [0];
```

Zero-indexed arrays created dynamically can be cast to a C# array of a matching or compatible type (compatible by standard array-variance rules). For example, if Apple subclasses Fruit, Apple[] can be cast to Fruit[]. This leads to the issue of why object[] was not used as the unifying array type rather the Array class. The answer is that object[] is incompatible with both multidimensional and value-type arrays (and nonzero-based arrays). An int[] array cannot be cast to object[]. Hence, we require the Array class for full type unification.

GetValue and SetValue also work on compiler-created arrays, and they are useful when writing methods that can deal with an array of any type and rank. For multidimensional arrays, they accept an *array* of indexers:

```
public object GetValue (params int[] indices)
public void    SetValue (object value, params int[] indices)
```

The following method prints the first element of any array, regardless of rank:

```
void WriteFirstValue (Array a)
{
  Console.Write (a.Rank + "-dimensional; ");

  // The indexers array will automatically initialize to all zeros, so
  // passing it into GetValue or SetValue will get/set the zero-based
  // (i.e., first) element in the array.

  int[] indexers = new int[a.Rank];
  Console.WriteLine ("First value is " + a.GetValue (indexers));
}

void Demo()
{
  int[]  oneD = { 1, 2, 3 };
  int[,] twoD = { {5,6}, {8,9} };

  WriteFirstValue (oneD);   // 1-dimensional; first value is 1
  WriteFirstValue (twoD);   // 2-dimensional; first value is 5
}
```

 For working with arrays of unknown type but known rank, generics provide an easier and more efficient solution:

```
void WriteFirstValue<T> (T[] array)
{
  Console.WriteLine (array[0]);
}
```

SetValue throws an exception if the element is of an incompatible type for the array.

When an array is instantiated, whether via language syntax or Array.CreateIn
stance, its elements are automatically initialized. For arrays with reference type elements, this means writing nulls; for arrays with value type elements, this means
calling the value type's default constructor (effectively "zeroing" the members). The
Array class also provides this functionality on demand via the Clear method:

```
public static void Clear (Array array, int index, int length);
```

This method doesn't affect the size of the array. This is in contrast to the usual use
of Clear (such as in ICollection<T>.Clear), where the collection is reduced to zero
elements.

Enumeration

Arrays are easily enumerated with a foreach statement:

```
int[] myArray = { 1, 2, 3};
foreach (int val in myArray)
  Console.WriteLine (val);
```

You can also enumerate using the static Array.ForEach method, defined as follows:

```
public static void ForEach<T> (T[] array, Action<T> action);
```

This uses an `Action` delegate, with this signature:

```
public delegate void Action<T> (T obj);
```

Here's the first example rewritten with `Array.ForEach`:

```
Array.ForEach (new[] { 1, 2, 3 }, Console.WriteLine);
```

Length and Rank

`Array` provides the following methods and properties for querying length and rank:

```
public int  GetLength      (int dimension);
public long GetLongLength  (int dimension);

public int  Length      { get; }
public long LongLength  { get; }

public int GetLowerBound (int dimension);
public int GetUpperBound (int dimension);

public int Rank { get; }    // Returns number of dimensions in array
```

`GetLength` and `GetLongLength` return the length for a given dimension (0 for a single-dimensional array), and `Length` and `LongLength` return the total number of elements in the array—all dimensions included.

`GetLowerBound` and `GetUpperBound` are useful with nonzero indexed arrays. `GetUpperBound` returns the same result as adding `GetLowerBound` to `GetLength` for any given dimension.

Searching

The `Array` class provides a range of methods for finding elements within a one-dimensional array:

```
public static int BinarySearch<T> (T[] array,   object value);
public static int BinarySearch<T> (T[] array,   object value, IComparer<T>
                                                              comparer);
public static int BinarySearch (Array array, object value);
public static int BinarySearch (Array array, object value, IComparer
                                                              comparer);
public static int IndexOf<T>     (T[] array,   T value);
public static int IndexOf        (Array array, object value);
public static int LastIndexOf<T> (T[] array,   T value);
public static int LastIndexOf    (Array array, object value);

// Predicate-based searching:

public static T    Find<T>      (T[] array, Predicate<T> match);
public static T    FindLast<T>  (T[] array, Predicate<T> match);
public static T[]  FindAll<T>   (T[] array, Predicate<T> match);

public static bool Exists<T>    (T[] array, Predicate<T> match);
public static bool TrueForAll<T> (T[] array, Predicate<T> match);
```

```
public static int  FindIndex<T>     (T[] array, Predicate<T> match);
public static int  FindLastIndex<T> (T[] array, Predicate<T> match);
```

The methods shown in bold are also overloaded to accept the following additional arguments:

```
int index   // starting index at which to begin searching
int length  // maximum number of elements to search
```

None of these methods throws an exception if the specified value is not found. Instead, if an item is not found, methods returning an integer return -1 (assuming a zero-indexed array), and methods returning a generic type return the type's default value (e.g., 0 for an integer, or null for a string).

The binary search methods are fast, but they work only on sorted arrays and require that the elements be compared for *order*, rather than simply *equality*. To this effect, the binary search methods can accept an IComparer or IComparer<T> object to arbitrate on ordering decisions (see the section "Plugging in Equality and Order" on page 304, later in this chapter). This must be consistent with any comparer used in originally sorting the array. If no comparer is provided, the type's default ordering algorithm will be applied, based on its implementation of IComparable/ IComparable<T>.

The IndexOf and LastIndexOf methods perform a simple enumeration over the array, returning the position of the first (or last) element that matches the given value.

The predicate-based searching methods allow a method delegate or lambda expression to arbitrate on whether a given element is a "match." A predicate is simply a delegate accepting an object and returning true or false:

```
public delegate bool Predicate<T> (T object);
```

In the following example, we search an array of strings for a name containing the letter "a":

```
static void Main()
{
  string[] names = { "Rodney", "Jack", "Jill" };
  string match = Array.Find (names, ContainsA);
  Console.WriteLine (match);    // Jack
}
static bool ContainsA (string name) { return name.Contains ("a"); }
```

Here's the same code shortened with an anonymous method:

```
string[] names = { "Rodney", "Jack", "Jill" };
string match = Array.Find (names, delegate (string name)
  { return name.Contains ("a"); } );
```

A lambda expression shortens it further:

```
string[] names = { "Rodney", "Jack", "Jill" };
string match = Array.Find (names, n => n.Contains ("a"));    // Jack
```

FindAll returns an array of all items satisfying the predicate. In fact, it's equivalent to Enumerable.Where in the System.Linq namespace, except that FindAll returns an array of matching items rather than an IEnumerable<T> of the same.

Exists returns true if any array member satisfies the given predicate, and is equivalent to Any in System.Linq.Enumerable.

TrueForAll returns true if all items satisfy the predicate, and is equivalent to All in System.Linq.Enumerable.

Sorting

Array has the following built-in sorting methods:

```
// For sorting a single array:

public static void Sort<T> (T[] array);
public static void Sort     (Array array);

// For sorting a pair of arrays:

public static void Sort<TKey,TValue> (TKey[] keys, TValue[] items);
public static void Sort              (Array keys, Array items);
```

Each of these methods is additionally overloaded to also accept:

```
int index                // Starting index at which to begin sorting
int length               // Number of elements to sort
IComparer<T> comparer    // Object making ordering decisions
Comparison<T> comparison // Delegate making ordering decisions
```

The following illustrates the simplest use of Sort:

```
int[] numbers = { 3, 2, 1 };
Array.Sort (numbers);                    // Array is now { 1, 2, 3 }
```

The methods accepting a pair of arrays work by rearranging the items of each array in tandem, basing the ordering decisions on the first array. In the next example, both the numbers and their corresponding words are sorted into numerical order:

```
int[] numbers = { 3, 2, 1 };
string[] words = { "three", "two", "one" };
Array.Sort (numbers, words);

// numbers array is now { 1, 2, 3 }
// words   array is now { "one", "two", "three" }
```

Array.Sort requires that the elements in the array implement IComparable (see the section "Order Comparison" on page 255 in Chapter 6). This means that most primitive C# types (such as integers, as in the preceding example) can be sorted. If the elements are not intrinsically comparable, or you want to override the default ordering, you must provide Sort with a custom comparison provider that reports on the relative position of two elements. There are ways to do this:

- Via a helper object that implements IComparer /IComparer<T> (see the section "Plugging in Equality and Order" on page 304)
- Via a Comparison delegate:

  ```
  public delegate int Comparison<T> (T x, T y);
  ```

The Comparison delegate follows the same semantics as IComparer<T>.CompareTo: if x comes before y, a negative integer is returned; if x comes after y, a positive integer is returned; if x and y have the same sorting position, 0 is returned.

In this example, we sort an array of integers so that the odd numbers come first:

```
int[] numbers = { 1, 2, 3, 4, 5 };
Array.Sort (numbers, (x, y) => x % 2 == y % 2 ? 0 : x % 2 == 1 ? -1 : 1);

// numbers array is now { 3, 5, 1, 2, 4 }
```

> As an alternative to calling Sort, you can use LINQ's OrderBy and ThenBy operators. Unlike Array.Sort, the LINQ operators don't alter the original array, instead emitting the sorted result in a fresh IEnumerable<T> sequence.

Reversing Elements

These Array methods reverse the order of all—or a part of—elements in an array:

```
public static void Reverse (Array array);
public static void Reverse (Array array, int index, int length);
```

Copying, Converting, and Resizing

Array provides shallow copying and cloning methods as follows:

```
// Instance methods:

public object Clone();
public void CopyTo (Array array, int index);

// Static methods:

public static void Copy (Array sourceArray,
                         Array destinationArray,
                         int length);

public static void Copy (Array sourceArray,      int sourceIndex,
                         Array destinationArray, int destinationIndex,
                         int length);

public static void ConstrainedCopy (
                         Array sourceArray,      int sourceIndex,
                         Array destinationArray, int destinationIndex,
                         int length);

public static ReadOnlyCollection<T> AsReadOnly<T> (T[] array)

public static TOutput[] ConvertAll<TInput, TOutput>
  (TInput[] array, Converter<TInput, TOutput> converter)

public static void Resize<T> (ref T[] array, int newSize);
```

The Copy and CopyTo methods are overloaded to accept Int64 index arguments.

The Clone method returns a whole new (shallow-copied) array. The Copy and CopyTo methods copy a contiguous subset of the array. Copying a multidimensional rectangular array requires you to map the multidimensional index to a linear index. For example, the middle square (position[1,1]) in a 3 × 3 array is represented with the index 4, from the calculation: 1*3 + 1. The source and destination ranges can overlap without causing a problem.

ConstrainedCopy performs an *atomic* operation: if all of the requested elements cannot be successfully copied (due to a type error, for instance), the operation is rolled back.

AsReadOnly returns a wrapper that prevents elements from being reassigned. ConvertAll creates and returns a new array of element type TOutput, calling the supplied Converter delegate to copy over the elements. Converter is defined as follows:

```
public delegate TOutput Converter<TInput,TOutput> (TInput input)
```

The following converts an array of floats to an array of integers:

```
float[] reals = { 1.3f, 1.5f, 1.8f };
int[] wholes = Array.ConvertAll (reals, r => Convert.ToInt32 (r));

// wholes array is { 1, 2, 2 }
```

The Resize method works by creating a new array and copying over the elements, returning the new array via the reference parameter. However, any references to the original array in other objects will remain unchanged.

 The System.Linq namespace offers an additional buffet of extension methods suitable for array conversion. These methods return an IEnumerable<T>, which you can convert back to an array via Enumerable's ToArray method.

Lists, Queues, Stacks, and Sets

The Framework provides a comprehensive set of concrete collection classes that implement the interfaces described in this chapter. This section concentrates on the *list-like* collections (versus the *dictionary-like* collections covered in "Dictionaries" on page 292). As with the interfaces we discussed previously, you usually have a choice of generic or nongeneric versions of each type. In terms of flexibility and performance, the generic classes win, making their nongeneric counterparts redundant except for backward compatibility. This differs from the situation with collection interfaces, where the nongeneric versions are still occasionally useful.

Of the classes described in this section, the generic List class is the most commonly used.

List<T> and ArrayList

The generic List and nongeneric ArrayList classes provide a dynamically sized array of objects and are among the most commonly used of the collection classes. Array List implements IList, whereas List<T> implements both IList and IList<T>. Unlike with arrays, all interfaces are implemented publicly, and methods such as Add and Remove are exposed and work as you would expect.

Internally, List<T> and ArrayList work by maintaining an internal array of objects, replaced with a larger array upon reaching capacity. Appending elements is efficient (since there is usually a free slot at the end), but inserting elements can be slow (since all elements after the insertion point have to be shifted to make a free slot). As with arrays, searching is efficient if the BinarySearch method is used on a list that has been sorted, but is otherwise inefficient because each item must be individually checked.

> List<T> is up to several times faster than ArrayList if T is a value type, because List<T> avoids the overhead of boxing and unboxing elements.

List<T> and ArrayList provide constructors that accept an existing collection of elements: these copy each element from the existing collecting into the new List<T> or ArrayList:

```
public class List <T> : IList <T>
{
  public List ();
  public List (IEnumerable<T> collection);
  public List (int capacity);

  // Add+Insert
  public void Add        (T item);
  public void AddRange   (IEnumerable<T> collection);
  public void Insert     (int index, T item);
  public void InsertRange (int index, IEnumerable<T> collection);

  // Remove
  public bool Remove     (T item);
  public void RemoveAt   (int index);
  public void RemoveRange (int index, int count);
  public int  RemoveAll  (Predicate<T> match);

  // Indexing
  public T this [int index] { get; set; }
  public List<T> GetRange (int index, int count);
  public Enumerator<T> GetEnumerator();

  // Exporting, copying and converting:
  public T[] ToArray();
  public void CopyTo (T[] array);
  public void CopyTo (T[] array, int arrayIndex);
  public void CopyTo (int index, T[] array, int arrayIndex, int count);
```

```
public ReadOnlyCollection<T> AsReadOnly();
public List<TOutput> ConvertAll<TOutput> (Converter <T,TOutput>
                                          converter);
// Other:
public void Reverse();              // Reverses order of elements in list.
public int Capacity { get;set; }    // Forces expansion of internal array.
public void TrimExcess();           // Trims internal array back to size.
public void Clear();                // Removes all elements, so Count=0.
}
```

```
public delegate TOutput Converter <TInput, TOutput> (TInput input);
```

In addition to these members, List<T> provides instance versions of all of Array's searching and sorting methods.

The following code demonstrates List's properties and methods. See "The Array Class" on page 273 for examples on searching and sorting:

```
List<string> words = new List<string>();    // New string-typed list

words.Add ("melon");
words.Add ("avocado");
words.AddRange (new[] { "banana", "plum" } );
words.Insert (0, "lemon");                       // Insert at start
words.InsertRange (0, new[] { "peach", "nashi" });  // Insert at start

words.Remove ("melon");
words.RemoveAt (3);                          // Remove the 4th element
words.RemoveRange (0, 2);                     // Remove first 2 elements

// Remove all strings starting in 'n':
words.RemoveAll (s => s.StartsWith ("n"));

Console.WriteLine (words [0]);               // first word
Console.WriteLine (words [words.Count - 1]); // last word
foreach (string s in words) Console.WriteLine (s);  // all words
List<string> subset = words.GetRange (1, 2); // 2nd->3rd words

string[] wordsArray = words.ToArray();    // Creates a new typed array

// Copy first two elements to the end of an existing array:
string[] existing = new string [1000];
words.CopyTo (0, existing, 998, 2);

List<string> upperCastWords = words.ConvertAll (s => s.ToUpper());
List<int> lengths = words.ConvertAll (s => s.Length);
```

The nongeneric ArrayList class is used mainly for backward compatibility with Framework 1.x code and requires clumsy casts—as the following example demonstrates:

```
ArrayList al = new ArrayList();
al.Add ("hello");
string first = (string) al [0];
string[] strArr = (string[]) al.ToArray (typeof (string));
```

Such casts cannot be verified by the compiler; the following compiles successfully but then fails at runtime:

```
int first = (int) al [0];    // Runtime exception
```

 An `ArrayList` is functionally similar to `List<object>`. Both are useful when you need a list of mixed-type elements that share no common base type. A possible advantage of choosing an `ArrayList`, in this case, would be if you need to deal with the list using reflection (Chapter 18). Reflection is easier with a nongeneric `ArrayList` than a `List<object>`.

If you import the `System.Linq` namespace, you can convert an `ArrayList` to a generic `List` by calling `Cast` and then `ToList`:

```
ArrayList al = new ArrayList();
al.AddRange (new[] { 1, 5, 9 } );
List<int> list = al.Cast<int>().ToList();
```

`Cast` and `ToList` are extension methods in the `System.Linq.Enumerable` class, supported from .NET Framework 3.5.

LinkedList<T>

`LinkedList<T>` is a generic doubly linked list (see Figure 7-4). A doubly linked list is a chain of nodes in which each references the node before, the node after, and the actual element. Its main benefit is that an element can always be inserted efficiently anywhere in the list, since it just involves creating a new node and updating a few references. However, finding where to insert the node in the first place can be slow as there's no intrinsic mechanism to index directly into a linked list; each node must be traversed, and binary-chop searches are not possible.

`LinkedList<T>` implements `IEnumerable<T>` and `ICollection<T>` (and their nongeneric versions), but not `IList<T>` since access by index is not supported. List nodes are implemented via the following class:

```
public sealed class LinkedListNode<T>
{
  public LinkedList<T> List { get; }
  public LinkedListNode<T> Next { get; }
  public LinkedListNode<T> Previous { get; }
  public T Value { get; set; }
}
```

When adding a node, you can specify its position either relative to another node or at the start/end of the list. `LinkedList<T>` provides the following methods for this:

```
public void AddFirst(LinkedListNode<T> node);
public LinkedListNode<T> AddFirst (T value);

public void AddLast (LinkedListNode<T> node);
public LinkedListNode<T> AddLast (T value);
```

```
public void AddAfter (LinkedListNode<T> node, LinkedListNode<T> newNode);
public LinkedListNode<T> AddAfter (LinkedListNode<T> node, T value);

public void AddBefore (LinkedListNode<T> node, LinkedListNode<T> newNode);
public LinkedListNode<T> AddBefore (LinkedListNode<T> node, T value);
```

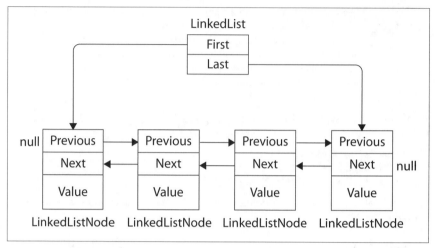

Figure 7-4. LinkedList<T>

Similar methods are provided to remove elements:

```
public void Clear();

public void RemoveFirst();
public void RemoveLast();

public bool Remove (T value);
public void Remove (LinkedListNode<T> node);
```

LinkedList<T> has internal fields to keep track of the number of elements in the list, as well as the head and tail of the list. These are exposed in the following public properties:

```
public int Count { get; }                  // Fast
public LinkedListNode<T> First { get; }     // Fast
public LinkedListNode<T> Last { get; }      // Fast
```

LinkedList<T> also supports the following searching methods (each requiring that the list be internally enumerated):

```
public bool Contains (T value);
public LinkedListNode<T> Find (T value);
public LinkedListNode<T> FindLast (T value);
```

Finally, LinkedList<T> supports copying to an array for indexed processing and obtaining an enumerator to support the foreach statement:

```
public void CopyTo (T[] array, int index);
public Enumerator<T> GetEnumerator();
```

Here's a demonstration on the use of LinkedList<string>:

```
var tune = new LinkedList<string>();
tune.AddFirst ("do");                          // do
tune.AddLast ("so");                           // do - so

tune.AddAfter (tune.First, "re");              // do - re - so
tune.AddAfter (tune.First.Next, "mi");         // do - re - mi - so
tune.AddBefore (tune.Last, "fa");              // do - re - mi - fa - so

tune.RemoveFirst();                            // re - mi - fa - so
tune.RemoveLast();                             // re - mi - fa

LinkedListNode<string> miNode = tune.Find ("mi");
tune.Remove (miNode);                          // re - fa
tune.AddFirst (miNode);                        // mi - re - fa

foreach (string s in tune) Console.WriteLine (s);
```

Queue<T> and Queue

Queue<T> and Queue are first-in first-out (FIFO) data structures, providing methods to Enqueue (add an item to the tail of the queue) and Dequeue (retrieve and remove the item at the head of the queue). A Peek method is also provided to return the element at the head of the queue without removing it, and a Count property (useful in checking that elements are present before dequeuing).

Although queues are enumerable, they do not implement IList<T>/IList, since members cannot be accessed directly by index. A ToArray method is provided, however, for copying the elements to an array where they can be randomly accessed:

```
public class Queue<T> : IEnumerable<T>, ICollection, IEnumerable
{
  public Queue();
  public Queue (IEnumerable<T> collection);   // Copies existing elements
  public Queue (int capacity);                // To lessen auto-resizing
  public void Clear();
  public bool Contains (T item);
  public void CopyTo (T[] array, int arrayIndex);
  public int Count { get; }
  public T Dequeue();
  public void Enqueue (T item);
  public Enumerator<T> GetEnumerator();       // To support foreach
  public T Peek();
  public T[] ToArray();
  public void TrimExcess();
}
```

The following is an example of using Queue<int>:

```
var q = new Queue<int>();
q.Enqueue (10);
q.Enqueue (20);
int[] data = q.ToArray();          // Exports to an array
Console.WriteLine (q.Count);       // "2"
Console.WriteLine (q.Peek());      // "10"
```

```
Console.WriteLine (q.Dequeue());  // "10"
Console.WriteLine (q.Dequeue());  // "20"
Console.WriteLine (q.Dequeue());  // throws an exception (queue empty)
```

Queues are implemented internally using an array that's resized as required—much like the generic List class. The queue maintains indexes that point directly to the head and tail elements; therefore, enqueuing and dequeuing are extremely quick operations (except when an internal resize is required).

Stack<T> and Stack

Stack<T> and Stack are last-in first-out (LIFO) data structures, providing methods to Push (add an item to the top of the stack) and Pop (retrieve and remove an element from the top of the stack). A nondestructive Peek method is also provided, as is a Count property and a ToArray method for exporting the data for random access:

```
public class Stack<T> : IEnumerable<T>, ICollection, IEnumerable
{
  public Stack();
  public Stack (IEnumerable<T> collection);   // Copies existing elements
  public Stack (int capacity);                // Lessens auto-resizing
  public void Clear();
  public bool Contains (T item);
  public void CopyTo (T[] array, int arrayIndex);
  public int Count { get; }
  public Enumerator<T> GetEnumerator();       // To support foreach
  public T Peek();
  public T Pop();
  public void Push (T item);
  public T[] ToArray();
  public void TrimExcess();
}
```

The following example demonstrates Stack<int>:

```
var s = new Stack<int>();
s.Push (1);                     //              Stack = 1
s.Push (2);                     //              Stack = 1,2
s.Push (3);                     //              Stack = 1,2,3
Console.WriteLine (s.Count);    // Prints 3
Console.WriteLine (s.Peek());   // Prints 3,    Stack = 1,2,3
Console.WriteLine (s.Pop());    // Prints 3,    Stack = 1,2
Console.WriteLine (s.Pop());    // Prints 2,    Stack = 1
Console.WriteLine (s.Pop());    // Prints 1,    Stack = <empty>
Console.WriteLine (s.Pop());    // throws exception
```

Stacks are implemented internally with an array that's resized as required, as with Queue<T> and List<T>.

BitArray

A BitArray is a dynamically sized collection of compacted bool values. It is more memory-efficient than both a simple array of bool and a generic List of bool, because it uses only one bit for each value, whereas the bool type otherwise occupies one byte for each value:

```
public sealed class BitArray : ICollection, IEnumerable, ICloneable
{
  // Constructors
  public BitArray (BitArray bits);    // An existing BitArray to copy
  public BitArray (int length);       // Capacity, in bits
  public BitArray (bool[] values);
  public BitArray (byte[] bytes);
  public BitArray (int[] values);
  public BitArray (int length, bool defaultValue);

  // To get/set value
  public bool this [int index] { get; set; }
  public bool Get  (int index);
  public void Set  (int index, bool value);
  public void SetAll (bool value);

  // Bitwise operators
  public BitArray Not();
  public BitArray And (BitArray value);
  public BitArray Or  (BitArray value);
  public BitArray Xor (BitArray value);

  // Copying
  public void CopyTo (Array array, int index);
  public object Clone();

  // Other
  public IEnumerator GetEnumerator();
  public int  Count          { get; }
  public int  Length         { get; set; }
  public bool IsReadOnly     { get; }
  public bool IsSynchronized { get; }
  public object SyncRoot      { get; }
}
```

The following is an example of using the `BitArray` class:

```
var bits = new BitArray(2);
bits[1] = true;
bits.Xor (bits);                    // Bitwise exclusive-OR bits with itself
Console.WriteLine (bits[1]);        // False
```

HashSet<T> and SortedSet<T>

HashSet<T> and SortedSet<T> are generic collections new to Framework 3.5 and 4.0, respectively. Both have the following distinguishing features:

- Their Contains methods execute quickly using a hash-based lookup.
- They do not store duplicate elements and silently ignore requests to add duplicates.
- You cannot access an element by position.

SortedSet<T> keeps elements in order, whereas HashSet<T> does not.

The commonality of these types is captured by the interface ISet<T>.

For historical reasons, HashSet<T> lives in *System.Core.dll* (whereas SortedSet<T> and ISet<T> live in *System.dll*).

HashSet<T> is implemented with a hashtable that stores just keys; SortedSet<T> is implemented with a red/black tree.

Here's the definition for HashSet<T>:

```
public class HashSet<T> : ICollection<T>, IEnumerable<T>, IEnumerable
{
    // Constructors
    public HashSet();
    public HashSet (IEnumerable<T> collection);
    public HashSet (IEqualityComparer<T> comparer);
    public HashSet (IEnumerable<T> collection, IEqualityComparer<T> comparer);

    // Testing for membership
    public bool Contains (T item);

    // Adding / removing
    public bool Add     (T item);
    public bool Remove (T item);
    public int RemoveWhere (Predicate<T> match);
    public void Clear();

    // Set operations - destructive
    public void UnionWith          (IEnumerable<T> other);   // Adds
    public void IntersectWith      (IEnumerable<T> other);   // Removes
    public void ExceptWith         (IEnumerable<T> other);   // Removes
    public void SymmetricExceptWith (IEnumerable<T> other);   // Removes

    // Set operations - bool
    public bool IsSubsetOf         (IEnumerable<T> other);
    public bool IsProperSubsetOf   (IEnumerable<T> other);
    public bool IsSupersetOf       (IEnumerable<T> other);
    public bool IsProperSupersetOf (IEnumerable<T> other);
    public bool Overlaps           (IEnumerable<T> other);
    public bool SetEquals          (IEnumerable<T> other);

    // Other
    public int Count { get; }
    public IEqualityComparer<T> Comparer { get; }
    public void CopyTo (T[] array);
    public void CopyTo (T[] array, int arrayIndex);
    public void CopyTo (T[] array, int arrayIndex, int count);
    public void TrimExcess();
    public static IEqualityComparer<HashSet<T>> CreateSetComparer();
}
```

SortedSet<T> offers the same set of members, plus the following:

```
public virtual SortedSet<T> GetViewBetween (T lowerValue, T upperValue)
public IEnumerable<T> Reverse()

public T Min { get; }
public T Max { get; }
```

SortedSet<T> also accepts an optional IComparer<T> in its constructor (rather than an *equality comparer*).

The following constructs a HashSet<char> from an existing collection, tests for membership, and then enumerates the collection (notice the absence of duplicates):

```
var letters = new HashSet<char> ("the quick brown fox");

Console.WriteLine (letters.Contains ('t'));      // true
Console.WriteLine (letters.Contains ('j'));      // false

foreach (char c in letters) Console.Write (c);   // the quickbrownfx
```

(The reason we can pass a string into HashSet<char>'s constructor is because string implements IEnumerable<char>.)

Here's an example of loading the same letters into a SortedSet<char>:

```
var letters = new SortedSet<char> ("the quick brown fox");
foreach (char c in letters) Console.Write (c);   // bcefhiknoqrtuwx
```

Following on from this, we can obtain the letters between *f* and *j* as follows:

```
foreach (char c in letters.GetViewBetween ('f', 'j'))
  Console.Write (c);                             // fhk
```

The destructive set operators modify the original collection. UnionWith adds all the elements in the second set to the original set (excluding duplicates). Intersects With removes the elements that are not in both sets. We remove all the vowels from our set of characters in the following code:

```
var letters = new HashSet<char> ("the quick brown fox");
letters.IntersectWith ("aeiou");
foreach (char c in letters) Console.Write (c);   // euio
```

ExceptWith removes the specified elements from the source set. Here, we strip all vowels from the set:

```
var letters = new HashSet<char> ("the quick brown fox");
letters.ExceptWith ("aeiou");
foreach (char c in letters) Console.Write (c);   // th qckbrwnfx
```

SymmetricExceptWith removes all but the elements that are unique to one set or the other:

```
var letters = new HashSet<char> ("the quick brown fox");
letters.SymmetricExceptWith ("the lazy brown fox");
foreach (char c in letters) Console.Write (c);   // quicklazy
```

Because HashSet<T> and SortedSet<T> implement IEnumerable<T>, you can use another set as the argument to any of the set operation methods.

Dictionaries

A dictionary is a collection in which each element is a key/value pair. Dictionaries are most commonly used for lookups and sorted lists.

The Framework defines a standard protocol for dictionaries, via the interfaces IDictionary and IDictionary <TKey, TValue>, as well as a set of general-purpose dictionary classes. The classes each differ in the following regard:

- Whether or not items are stored in sorted sequence
- Whether or not items can be accessed by position (index) as well as by key
- Whether generic or nongeneric
- Their performance when large

Table 7-1 summarizes each of the dictionary classes and how they differ in these respects. The performance times are in milliseconds, to perform 50,000 operations on a dictionary with integer keys and values, on a 1.5 GHz PC. (The differences in performance between generic and nongeneric counterparts using the same underlying collection structure are due to boxing, and show up only with value-type elements.)

Table 7-1. Dictionary classes

Type	Internal structure	Retrieve by index?	Memory overhead (avg. bytes per item)	Speed: random insertion	Speed: sequential insertion	Speed: retrieval by key
Unsorted						
Dictionary <K,V>	Hashtable	No	22	30	30	20
Hashtable	Hashtable	No	38	50	50	30
ListDictionary	Linked list	No	36	50,000	50,000	50,000
OrderedDictionary	Hashtable + array	Yes	59	70	70	40
Sorted						
SortedDictionary <K,V>	Red/black tree	No	20	130	100	120
SortedList <K,V>	2xArray	Yes	2	3,300	30	40
SortedList	2xArray	Yes	27	4,500	100	180

In Big-O notation, retrieval time by key is:

- O(1) for Hashtable, Dictionary, and OrderedDictionary
- O(log *n*) for SortedDictionary and SortedList
- O(*n*) for ListDictionary (and nondictionary types such as List<T>)

where *n* is the number of elements in the collection.

IDictionary<TKey,TValue>

IDictionary<TKey,TValue> defines the standard protocol for all key/value-based collections. It extends ICollection<T> by adding methods and properties to access elements based on a key of arbitrary type:

```
public interface IDictionary <TKey, TValue> :
  ICollection <KeyValuePair <TKey, TValue>>, IEnumerable
{
    bool ContainsKey (TKey key);
    bool TryGetValue (TKey key, out TValue value);
    void Add        (TKey key, TValue value);
    bool Remove     (TKey key);

    TValue this [TKey key]      { get; set; } // Main indexer - by key
    ICollection <TKey> Keys     { get; }      // Returns just keys
    ICollection <TValue> Values { get; }      // Returns just values
}
```

To add an item to a dictionary, you either call Add or use the index's set accessor—the latter adds an item to the dictionary if the key is not already present (or updates the item if it is present). Duplicate keys are forbidden in all dictionary implementations, so calling Add twice with the same key throws an exception.

To retrieve an item from a dictionary, use either the indexer or the TryGetValue method. If the key doesn't exist, the indexer throws an exception whereas TryGetValue returns false. You can test for membership explicitly by calling ContainsKey; however, this incurs the cost of two lookups if you then subsequently retrieve the item.

Enumerating directly over an IDictionary<TKey,TValue> returns a sequence of KeyValuePair structs:

```
public struct KeyValuePair <TKey, TValue>
{
    public TKey Key     { get; }
    public TValue Value { get; }
}
```

You can enumerate over just the keys or values via the dictionary's Keys/Values properties.

We demonstrate the use of this interface with the generic Dictionary class in the following section.

IDictionary

The nongeneric IDictionary interface is the same in principle as IDictionary<TKey,TValue>, apart from two important functional differences. It's important to be aware of these differences, because IDictionary appears in legacy code (including the .NET Framework itself in places):

- Retrieving a nonexistent key via the indexer returns null (rather than throwing an exception).

- `Contains` tests for membership rather than `ContainsKey`.

Enumerating over a nongeneric `IDictionary` returns a sequence of `DictionaryEntry` structs:

```
public struct DictionaryEntry
{
  public object Key   { get; set; }
  public object Value { get; set; }
}
```

Dictionary<TKey,TValue> and Hashtable

The generic `Dictionary` class is one of the most commonly used collections (along with the `List<T>` collection). It uses a hashtable data structure to store keys and values, and it is fast and efficient.

> The nongeneric version of `Dictionary<TKey,TValue>` is called `Hashtable`; there is no nongeneric class called `Dictionary`. When we refer simply to `Dictionary`, we mean the generic `Dictionary<TKey,TValue>` class.

`Dictionary` implements both the generic and nongeneric `IDictionary` interfaces, the generic `IDictionary` being exposed publicly. `Dictionary` is, in fact, a "textbook" implementation of the generic `IDictionary`.

Here's how to use it:

```
var d = new Dictionary<string, int>();

d.Add("One", 1);
d["Two"] = 2;      // adds to dictionary because "two" not already present
d["Two"] = 22;     // updates dictionary because "two" is now present
d["Three"] = 3;

Console.WriteLine (d["Two"]);            // Prints "22"
Console.WriteLine (d.ContainsKey ("One"));   // true (fast operation)
Console.WriteLine (d.ContainsValue (3));     // true (slow operation)
int val = 0;
if (!d.TryGetValue ("onE", out val))
  Console.WriteLine ("No val");          // "No val" (case sensitive)

// Three different ways to enumerate the dictionary:

foreach (KeyValuePair<string, int> kv in d)   //   One ; 1
  Console.WriteLine (kv.Key + "; " + kv.Value);   //   Two ; 22
                                                //   Three ; 3

foreach (string s in d.Keys) Console.Write (s);   // OneTwoThree
Console.WriteLine();
foreach (int i in d.Values) Console.Write (i);    // 1223
```

Its underlying hashtable works by converting each element's key into an integer hash code—a pseudounique value—and then applying an algorithm to convert the hash code into a hash key. This hash key is used internally to determine which "bucket" an entry belongs to. If the bucket contains more than one value, a linear search is performed on the bucket. A hashtable typically starts out maintaining a 1:1 ratio of buckets to values (a 1:1 *load factor*), meaning that each bucket contains only one value. However, as more items are added to the hashtable, the load factor dynamically increases, in a manner designed to optimize insertion and retrieval performance as well as memory requirements.

A dictionary can work with keys of any type, providing it's able to determine equality between keys and obtain hash codes. By default, equality is determined via the key's `object.Equals` method, and the pseudounique hash code is obtained via the key's `GetHashCode` method. This behavior can be changed, either by overriding these methods or by providing an `IEqualityComparer` object when constructing the dictionary. A common application of this is to specify a case-insensitive equality comparer when using string keys:

```
var d = new Dictionary<string, int> (StringComparer.OrdinalIgnoreCase);
```

We discuss this further in "Plugging in Equality and Order" on page 304.

As with many other types of collections, the performance of a dictionary can be improved slightly by specifying the collection's expected size in the constructor, avoiding or lessening the need for internal resizing operations.

The nongeneric version is (more aptly) named `Hashtable` and is functionally similar apart from differences stemming from it exposing the nongeneric `IDictionary` interface discussed previously.

The downside to `Dictionary` and `Hashtable` is that the items are not sorted. Furthermore, the original order in which the items were added is not retained. As with all dictionaries, duplicate keys are not allowed.

OrderedDictionary

An `OrderedDictionary` is a nongeneric dictionary that maintains elements in the same order that they were added. With an `OrderedDictionary`, you can access elements both by index and by key.

 An `OrderedDictionary` is not a *sorted* dictionary.

An `OrderedDictionary` is a combination of a `Hashtable` and an `ArrayList`. This means it has all the functionality of a `Hashtable`, plus functions such as `RemoveAt`, as well as an integer indexer. It also exposes `Keys` and `Values` properties that return elements in their original order.

This class was introduced in .NET 2.0, yet peculiarly, there's no generic version.

ListDictionary and HybridDictionary

ListDictionary uses a singly linked list to store the underlying data. It doesn't provide sorting, although it does preserve the original entry order of the items. ListDictionary is extremely slow with large lists. Its only real "claim to fame" is its efficiency with very small lists (fewer than 10 items).

HybridDictionary is a ListDictionary that automatically converts to a Hashtable upon reaching a certain size, to address ListDictionary's problems with performance. The idea is to get a low memory footprint when the dictionary is small, and good performance when the dictionary is large. However, given the overhead in converting from one to the other—and the fact that a Dictionary is not excessively heavy or slow in either scenario—you wouldn't suffer unreasonably by using a Dictionary to begin with.

Both classes come only in nongeneric form.

Sorted Dictionaries

The Framework provides two dictionary classes internally structured such that their content is always sorted by key:

- SortedDictionary<TKey,TValue>
- SortedList<TKey,TValue>*

(In this section, we will abbreviate <TKey,TValue> to <,>.)

SortedDictionary<,> uses a red/black tree: a data structure designed to perform consistently well in any insertion or retrieval scenario.

SortedList<,> is implemented internally with an ordered array pair, providing fast retrieval (via a binary-chop search) but poor insertion performance (because existing values have to be shifted to make room for a new entry).

SortedDictionary<,> is much faster than SortedList<,> at inserting elements in a random sequence (particularly with large lists). SortedList<,>, however, has an extra ability: to access items by index as well as by key. With a sorted list, you can go directly to the *n*th element in the sorting sequence (via the indexer on the Keys/Values properties). To do the same with a SortedDictionary<,>, you must manually enumerate over *n* items. (Alternatively, you could write a class that combines a sorted dictionary with a list class.)

None of the three collections allows duplicate keys (as is the case with all dictionaries).

The following example uses reflection to load all the methods defined in System.Object into a sorted list keyed by name, and then enumerates their keys and values:

```
// MethodInfo is in the System.Reflection namespace
```

---

* There's also a functionally identical nongeneric version of this called SortedList.

```
var sorted = new SortedList <string, MethodInfo>();

foreach (MethodInfo m in typeof (object).GetMethods())
  sorted [m.Name] = m;

foreach (string name in sorted.Keys)
  Console.WriteLine (name);

foreach (MethodInfo m in sorted.Values)
  Console.WriteLine (m.Name + " returns a " + m.ReturnType);
```

Here's the result of the first enumeration:

```
Equals
GetHashCode
GetType
ReferenceEquals
ToString
```

Here's the result of the second enumeration:

```
Equals returns a System.Boolean
GetHashCode returns a System.Int32
GetType returns a System.Type
ReferenceEquals returns a System.Boolean
ToString returns a System.String
```

Notice that we populated the dictionary through its indexer. If we instead used the Add method, it would throw an exception because the object class upon which we're reflecting overloads the Equals method, and you can't add the same key twice to a dictionary. By using the indexer, the later entry overwrites the earlier entry, preventing this error.

 You can store multiple members of the same key by making each value element a list:

```
SortedList <string, List<MethodInfo>>
```

Extending our example, the following retrieves the MethodInfo whose key is "GetHash Code", just as with an ordinary dictionary:

```
Console.WriteLine (sorted ["GetHashCode"]);      // Int32 GetHashCode()
```

So far, everything we've done would also work with a SortedDictionary<,>. The following two lines, however, which retrieve the last key and value, work only with a sorted list:

```
Console.WriteLine (sorted.Keys [sorted.Count - 1]);         // ToString
Console.WriteLine (sorted.Values[sorted.Count - 1].IsVirtual); // True
```

Customizable Collections and Proxies

The collection classes discussed in previous sections are convenient in that they can be directly instantiated, but they don't allow you to control what happens when an item is added to or removed from the collection. With strongly typed collections in an application, you sometimes need this control—for instance:

- To fire an event when an item is added or removed
- To update properties because of the added or removed item
- To detect an "illegal" add/remove operation and throw an exception (for example, if the operation violates a business rule)

The .NET Framework provides collection classes for this exact purpose, in the `System.Collections.ObjectModel` namespace. These are essentially proxies or wrappers that implement `IList<T>` or `IDictionary<,>` by forwarding the methods through to an underlying collection. Each `Add`, `Remove`, or `Clear` operation is routed via a virtual method that acts as a "gateway" when overridden.

Customizable collection classes are commonly used for publicly exposed collections; for instance, a collection of controls exposed publicly on a `System.Windows.Form` class.

Collection<T> and CollectionBase

`Collection<T>` class is a customizable wrapper for `List<T>`.

As well as implementing `IList<T>` and `IList`, it defines four additional virtual methods and a protected property as follows:

```
public class Collection<T> :
  IList<T>, ICollection<T>, IEnumerable<T>, IList, ICollection, IEnumerable
{
  // ...

  protected virtual void ClearItems();
  protected virtual void InsertItem (int index, T item);
  protected virtual void RemoveItem (int index);
  protected virtual void SetItem (int index, T item);

  protected IList<T> Items { get; }
}
```

The virtual methods provide the gateway by which you can "hook in" to change or enhance the list's normal behavior. The protected `Items` property allows the implementer to directly access the "inner list"—this is used to make changes internally without the virtual methods firing.

The virtual methods need not be overridden; they can be left alone until there's a requirement to alter the list's default behavior. The following example demonstrates the typical "skeleton" use of `Collection<T>`:

```
public class Animal
{
  public string Name;
  public int Popularity;

  public Animal (string name, int popularity)
  {
    Name = name; Popularity = popularity;
  }
}

public class AnimalCollection : Collection <Animal>
{
  // AnimalCollection is already a fully functioning list of animals.
  // No extra code is required.
}

public class Zoo    // The class that will expose AnimalCollection.
{                   // This would typically have additional members.

  public readonly AnimalCollection Animals = new AnimalCollection();
}

class Program
{
  static void Main()
  {
    Zoo zoo = new Zoo();
    zoo.Animals.Add (new Animal ("Kangaroo", 10));
    zoo.Animals.Add (new Animal ("Mr Sea Lion", 20));
    foreach (Animal a in zoo.Animals) Console.WriteLine (a.Name);
  }
}
```

As it stands, `AnimalCollection` is no more functional than a simple `List<Animal>`; its role is to provide a base for future extension. To illustrate, we'll now add a `Zoo` property to `Animal`, so it can reference the `Zoo` in which it lives and override each of the virtual methods in `Collection<Animal>` to maintain that property automatically:

```
public class Animal
{
  public string Name;
  public int Popularity;
  public Zoo Zoo { get; internal set; }
  public Animal(string name, int popularity)
  {
    Name = name; Popularity = popularity;
  }
}

public class AnimalCollection : Collection <Animal>
{
  Zoo zoo;
  public AnimalCollection (Zoo zoo) { this.zoo = zoo; }
```

```
protected override void InsertItem (int index, Animal item)
{
  base.InsertItem (index, item);
  item.Zoo = zoo;
}
protected override void SetItem (int index, Animal item)
{
  base.SetItem (index, item);
  item.Zoo = zoo;
}
protected override void RemoveItem (int index)
{
  this [index].Zoo = null;
  base.RemoveItem (index);
}
protected override void ClearItems()
{
  foreach (Animal a in this) a.Zoo = null;
  base.ClearItems();
}
}

public class Zoo
{
  public readonly AnimalCollection Animals;
  public Zoo() { Animals = new AnimalCollection (this); }
}
```

Collection<T> also has a constructor accepting an existing IList<T>. Unlike with other collection classes, the supplied list is *proxied* rather than *copied*, meaning that subsequent changes will be reflected in the wrapping Collection<T> (although *without* Collection<T>'s virtual methods firing). Conversely, changes made via the Collection<T> will change the underlying list.

CollectionBase

CollectionBase is the nongeneric version of Collection<T> introduced in Framework 1.0. This provides most of the same features as Collection<T> but is clumsier to use. Instead of the template methods InsertItem, RemoveItem SetItem, and ClearItem, CollectionBase has "hook" methods that double the number of methods required: OnInsert, OnInsertComplete, OnSet, OnSetComplete, OnRemove, OnRemoveComplete, OnClear, and OnClearComplete. Because CollectionBase is nongeneric, you must also implement typed methods when subclassing it—at a minimum, a typed indexer and Add method.

KeyedCollection<TKey,TItem> and DictionaryBase

KeyedCollection<TKey,TItem> subclasses Collection<TItem>. It both adds and subtracts functionality. What it adds is the ability to access items by key, much like with a dictionary. What it subtracts is the ability to proxy your own inner list.

A keyed collection has some resemblance to an `OrderedDictionary` in that it combines a linear list with a hashtable. However, unlike `OrderedDictionary`, it doesn't implement `IDictionary` and doesn't support the concept of a key/value *pair*. Keys are obtained instead from the items themselves: via the abstract `GetKeyForItem` method. This means enumerating a keyed collection is just like enumerating an ordinary list.

`KeyedCollection<TKey,TItem>` is best thought of as `Collection<TItem>` plus fast lookup by key.

Because it subclasses `Collection<>`, a keyed collection inherits all of `Collection<>`'s functionality, except for the ability to specify an existing list in construction. The additional members it defines are as follows:

```
public abstract class KeyedCollection <TKey, TItem> : Collection <TItem>

// ...

protected abstract TKey GetKeyForItem(TItem item);
protected void ChangeItemKey(TItem item, TKey newKey);

// Fast lookup by key - this is in addition to lookup by index.
public TItem this[TKey key] { get; }

protected IDictionary<TKey, TItem> Dictionary { get; }
}
```

`GetKeyForItem` is what the implementer overrides to obtain an item's key from the underlying object. The `ChangeItemKey` method must be called if the item's key property changes, in order to update the internal dictionary. The `Dictionary` property returns the internal dictionary used to implement the lookup, which is created when the first item is added. This behavior can be changed by specifying a creation threshold in the constructor, delaying the internal dictionary from being created until the threshold is reached (in the interim, a linear search is performed if an item is requested by key). A good reason not to specify a creation threshold is that having a valid dictionary can be useful in obtaining an `ICollection<>` of keys, via the `Dictionary`'s `Keys` property. This collection can then be passed on to a public property.

The most common use for `KeyedCollection<,>` is in providing a collection of items accessible both by index and by name. To demonstrate this, we'll revisit the zoo, this time implementing `AnimalCollection` as a `KeyedCollection<string,Animal>`:

```
public class Animal
{
  string name;
  public string Name
  {
    get { return name; }
    set {
      if (Zoo != null) Zoo.Animals.NotifyNameChange (this, value);
      name = value;
    }
  }
}
```

```csharp
    public int Popularity;
    public Zoo Zoo { get; internal set; }

    public Animal (string name, int popularity)
    {
      Name = name; Popularity = popularity;
    }
  }

  public class AnimalCollection : KeyedCollection <string, Animal>
  {
    Zoo zoo;
    public AnimalCollection (Zoo zoo) { this.zoo = zoo; }

    internal void NotifyNameChange (Animal a, string newName)
    {
      this.ChangeItemKey (a, newName);
    }

    protected override string GetKeyForItem (Animal item)
    {
      return item.Name;
    }

    // The following methods would be implemented as in the previous example
    protected override void InsertItem (int index, Animal item)...
    protected override void SetItem (int index, Animal item)...
    protected override void RemoveItem (int index)...
    protected override void ClearItems()...
  }

  public class Zoo
  {
    public readonly AnimalCollection Animals;
    public Zoo() { Animals = new AnimalCollection (this); }
  }

  class Program
  {
    static void Main()
    {
      Zoo zoo = new Zoo();
      zoo.Animals.Add (new Animal ("Kangaroo", 10));
      zoo.Animals.Add (new Animal ("Mr Sea Lion", 20));
      Console.WriteLine (zoo.Animals [0].Popularity);           // 10
      Console.WriteLine (zoo.Animals ["Mr Sea Lion"].Popularity);  // 20
      zoo.Animals ["Kangaroo"].Name = "Mr Roo";
      Console.WriteLine (zoo.Animals ["Mr Roo"].Popularity);    // 10
    }
  }
```

DictionaryBase

The nongeneric version of KeyedCollection is called DictionaryBase. This legacy class takes very different in its approach: it implements IDictionary and uses clumsy hook methods like `CollectionBase`: `OnInsert`, `OnInsertComplete`, `OnSet`, `OnSetComplete`, `OnRemove`, `OnRemoveComplete`, `OnClear`, and `OnClearComplete` (and additionally, `OnGet`). The primary advantage of implementing `IDictionary` over taking the `KeyedCollection` approach is that you don't need to subclass it in order to obtain keys. But since the very purpose of `DictionaryBase` is to be subclassed, it's no advantage at all. The improved model in `KeyedCollection` is almost certainly due to the fact that it was written some years later, with the benefit of hindsight. `DictionaryBase` is best considered useful for backward compatibility.

ReadOnlyCollection<T>

`ReadOnlyCollection<T>` is a wrapper, or *proxy*, that provides a read-only view of a collection. This is useful in allowing a class to publicly expose read-only access to a collection that the class can still update internally.

A read-only collection accepts the input collection in its constructor, to which it maintains a permanent reference. It doesn't take a static copy of the input collection, so subsequent changes to the input collection are visible through the read-only wrapper.

To illustrate, suppose your class wants to provide read-only public access to a list of strings called `Names`:

```
public class Test
{
  public List<string> Names { get; private set; }
}
```

This only does half the job. Although other types cannot reassign the `Names` property, they can still call `Add`, `Remove`, or `Clear` on the list. The `ReadOnlyCollection<T>` class resolves this:

```
public class Test
{
  List<string> names;
  public ReadOnlyCollection<string> Names { get; private set; }

  public Test()
  {
    names = new List<string>();
    Names = new ReadOnlyCollection<string> (names);
  }

  public void AddInternally() { names.Add ("test"); }
}
```

Now, only members within the `Test` class can alter the list of names:

```
Test t = new Test();

Console.WriteLine (t.Names.Count);      // 0
t.AddInternally();
Console.WriteLine (t.Names.Count);      // 1
```

```
t.Names.Add ("test");                       // Compiler error
((IList<string>) t.Names).Add ("test");     // NotSupportedException
```

Plugging in Equality and Order

In the sections "Equality Comparison" on page 245 and "Order Comparison" on page 255 in Chapter 6, we described the standard .NET protocols that make
a type equatable, hashable, and comparable. A type that implements these protocols
can function correctly in a dictionary or sorted list "out of the box." More
specifically:

- A type for which `Equals` and `GetHashCode` return meaningful results can be used
  as a key in a `Dictionary` or `Hashtable`.

- A type that implements `IComparable` /`IComparable<T>` can be used as a key in
  any of the *sorted* dictionaries or lists.

A type's default equating or comparison implementation typically reflects what is
most "natural" for that type. Sometimes, however, the default behavior is not what
you want. You might need a dictionary whose `string`-type key is treated case-
insensitively. Or you might want a sorted list of customers, sorted by each customer's
postcode. For this reason, the .NET Framework also defines a matching set of "plug-
in" protocols. The plug-in protocols achieve two things:

- They allow you to switch in alternative equating or comparison behavior.

- They allow you to use a dictionary or sorted collection with a key type that's
  not intrinsically equatable or comparable.

The plug-in protocols consist of the following interfaces:

`IEqualityComparer` *and* `IEqualityComparer<T>`
- Performs plug-in *equality comparison and hashing*
- Recognized by `Hashtable` and `Dictionary`

`IComparer` *and* `IComparer<T>`
- Performs plug-in *order comparison*
- Recognized by the sorted dictionaries and collections; also, `Array.Sort`

Each interface comes in generic and nongeneric forms. The `IEqualityComparer` interfaces also have a default implementation in a class called `EqualityComparer`.

In addition, Framework 4.0 adds two new interfaces called `IStructuralEquatable`
and `IStructuralComparable`, which allow the option of structural comparisons on
classes and arrays.

IEqualityComparer and EqualityComparer

An equality comparer switches in nondefault equality and hashing behavior, primarily for the `Dictionary` and `Hashtable` classes.

Recall the requirements of a hashtable-based dictionary. It needs answers to two questions for any given key:

- Is it the same as another?
- What is its integer hash code?

An equality comparer answers these questions by implementing the IEqualityComparer interfaces:

```
public interface IEqualityComparer<T>
{
  bool Equals (T x, T y);
  int GetHashCode (T obj);
}

public interface IEqualityComparer      // Nongeneric version
{
  bool Equals (object x, object y);
  int GetHashCode (object obj);
}
```

To write a custom comparer, you implement one or both of these interfaces (implementing both gives maximum interoperability). As this is somewhat tedious, an alternative is to subclass the abstract EqualityComparer class, defined as follows:

```
public abstract class EqualityComparer<T> : IEqualityComparer,
                                            IEqualityComparer<T>
{
  public abstract bool Equals (T x, T y);
  public abstract int GetHashCode (T obj);

  bool IEqualityComparer.Equals (object x, object y);
  int IEqualityComparer.GetHashCode (object obj);

  public static EqualityComparer<T> Default { get; }
}
```

EqualityComparer implements both interfaces; your job is simply to override the two abstract methods.

The semantics for Equals and GetHashCode follow the same rules for object.Equals and object.GetHashCode, described in Chapter 6. In the following example, we define a Customer class with two fields, and then write an equality comparer that matches both the first and last names:

```
public class Customer
{
  public string LastName;
  public string FirstName;

  public Customer (string last, string first)
  {
    LastName = last;
    FirstName = first;
  }
}
```

```
public class LastFirstEqComparer : EqualityComparer <Customer>
{
  public override bool Equals (Customer x, Customer y)
  {
    return x.LastName == y.LastName && x.FirstName == y.FirstName;
  }

  public override int GetHashCode (Customer obj)
  {
    return (obj.LastName + ";" + obj.FirstName).GetHashCode();
  }
}
```

To illustrate how this works, we'll create two customers:

```
Customer c1 = new Customer ("Bloggs", "Joe");
Customer c2 = new Customer ("Bloggs", "Joe");
```

Because we haven't overridden object.Equals, normal reference type equality semantics apply:

```
Console.WriteLine (c1 == c2);           // False
Console.WriteLine (c1.Equals (c2));     // False
```

.The same default equality semantics apply when using these customers in a Dictionary without specifying an equality comparer:

```
var d = new Dictionary<Customer, string>();
d [c1] = "Joe";
Console.WriteLine (d.ContainsKey (c2));        // False
```

Now with the custom equality comparer:

```
var eqComparer = new LastFirstEqComparer();
var d = new Dictionary<Customer, string> (eqComparer);
d [c1] = "Joe";
Console.WriteLine (d.ContainsKey (c2));        // True
```

In this example, we would have to be careful not to change the customer's FirstName or LastName while it was in use in the dictionary. Otherwise, its hash code would change and the Dictionary would break.

EqualityComparer<T>.Default

Calling EqualityComparer<T>.Default returns a general-purpose equality comparer that can be used as an alternative to the static object.Equals method. The advantage is that first checks if T implements IEquatable<T> and if so, calls that implementation instead, avoiding the boxing overhead. This is particularly useful in generic methods:

```
static bool Foo<T> (T x, T y)
{
  bool same = EqualityComparer<T>.Default.Equals (x, y);
  ...
```

IComparer and Comparer

Comparers are used to switch in custom ordering logic for sorted dictionaries and collections.

Note that a comparer is useless to the unsorted dictionaries such as `Dictionary` and `Hashtable`—these require an `IEqualityComparer` to get hash codes. Similarly, an equality comparer is useless for sorted dictionaries and collections.

Here are the `IComparer` interface definitions:

```
public interface IComparer
{
  int Compare(object x, object y);
}
public interface IComparer <in T>
{
  int Compare(T x, T y);
}
```

As with equality comparers, there's an abstract class you can subtype instead of implementing the interfaces:

```
public abstract class Comparer<T> : IComparer, IComparer<T>
{
  public static Comparer<T> Default { get; }

  public abstract int Compare (T x, T y);      // Implemented by you
  int IComparer.Compare (object x, object y);   // Implemented for you
}
```

The following example illustrates a class that describes a wish, and a comparer that sorts wishes by priority:

```
class Wish
{
  public string Name;
  public int Priority;

  public Wish (string name, int priority)
  {
    Name = name;
    Priority = priority;
  }
}

class PriorityComparer : Comparer <Wish>
{
  public override int Compare (Wish x, Wish y)
  {
    if (object.Equals (x, y)) return 0;        // Fail-safe check
    return x.Priority.CompareTo (y.Priority);
  }
}
```

Collections

The `object.Equals` check ensures that we can never contradict the `Equals` method. Calling the static `object.Equals` method in this case is better than calling `x.Equals` because it still works if x is null!

Here's how our PriorityComparer is used to sort a `List`:

```
var wishList = new List<Wish>();
wishList.Add (new Wish ("Peace", 2));
wishList.Add (new Wish ("Wealth", 3));
wishList.Add (new Wish ("Love", 2));
wishList.Add (new Wish ("3 more wishes", 1));

wishList.Sort (new PriorityComparer());
foreach (Wish w in wishList) Console.Write (w.Name + " | ");

// OUTPUT: 3 more wishes | Love | Peace | Wealth |
```

In the next example, `SurnameComparer` allows you to sort surname strings in an order suitable for a phonebook listing:

```
class SurnameComparer : Comparer <string>
{
  string Normalize (string s)
  {
    s = s.Trim().ToUpper();
    if (s.StartsWith ("MC")) s = "MAC" + s.Substring (2);
    return s;
  }

  public override int Compare (string x, string y)
  {
    return Normalize (x).CompareTo (Normalize (y));
  }
}
```

Here's `SurnameComparer` in use in a sorted dictionary:

```
var dic = new SortedDictionary<string,string> (new SurnameComparer());
dic.Add ("MacPhail", "second!");
dic.Add ("MacWilliam", "third!");
dic.Add ("McDonald", "first!");

foreach (string s in dic.Values)
  Console.Write (s + " ");              // first! second! third!
```

StringComparer

`StringComparer` is a predefined plug-in class for equating and comparing strings, allowing you to specify language and case sensitivity. `StringComparer` implements both `IEqualityComparer` and `IComparer` (and their generic versions), so it can be used with any type of dictionary or sorted collection:

```
// CultureInfo is defined in System.Globalization

public abstract class StringComparer : IComparer, IComparer <string>,
                                       IEqualityComparer,
                                       IEqualityComparer <string>
```

```
{
  public abstract int Compare (string x, string y);
  public abstract bool Equals (string x, string y);
  public abstract int GetHashCode (string obj);

  public static StringComparer Create (CultureInfo culture,
                                       bool ignoreCase);
  public static StringComparer CurrentCulture { get; }
  public static StringComparer CurrentCultureIgnoreCase { get; }
  public static StringComparer InvariantCulture { get; }
  public static StringComparer InvariantCultureIgnoreCase { get; }
  public static StringComparer Ordinal { get; }
  public static StringComparer OrdinalIgnoreCase { get; }
}
```

Because StringComparer is abstract, you obtain instances via its static methods and properties. StringComparer.Ordinal mirrors the default behavior for string equality comparison and StringComparer.CurrentCulture for order comparison.

In the following example, an ordinal case-insensitive dictionary is created, such that dict["Joe"] and dict["JOE"] mean the same thing:

```
var dict = new Dictionary<string, int> (StringComparer.OrdinalIgnoreCase);
```

In the next example, an array of names is sorted, using Australian English:

```
string[] names = { "Tom", "HARRY", "sheila" };
CultureInfo ci = new CultureInfo ("en-AU");
Array.Sort<string> (names, StringComparer.Create (ci, false));
```

The final example is a culture-aware version of the SurnameComparer we wrote in the previous section (to compare names suitable for a phonebook listing):

```
class SurnameComparer : Comparer <string>
{
  StringComparer strCmp;

  public SurnameComparer (CultureInfo ci)
  {
    // Create a case-sensitive, culture-sensitive string comparer
    strCmp = StringComparer.Create (ci, false);
  }

  string Normalize (string s)
  {
    s = s.Trim();
    if (s.ToUpper().StartsWith ("MC")) s = "MAC" + s.Substring (2);
    return s;
  }

  public override int Compare (string x, string y)
  {
    // Directly call Compare on our culture-aware StringComparer
    return strCmp.Compare (Normalize (x), Normalize (y));
  }
}
```

IStructuralEquatable and IStructuralComparable

As we said in the previous chapter, structs implement *structural comparison* by default: two structs are equal if all of their fields are equal. Sometimes, however, structural equality and order comparison are useful as plug-in options on other types as well—such as arrays and tuples. Framework 4.0 introduces two new interfaces to help with this:

```
public interface IStructuralEquatable
{
  bool Equals (object other, IEqualityComparer comparer);
  int GetHashCode (IEqualityComparer comparer);
}

public interface IStructuralComparable
{
  int CompareTo (object other, IComparer comparer);
}
```

The IEqualityComparer/IComparer that you pass in are applied to each individual element in the composite object. We can demonstrate this using arrays and tuples, which implement these interfaces: in the following example, we compare two arrays for equality: first using the default Equals method, and then using IStructuralEquatable's version:

```
int[] a1 = { 1, 2, 3 };
int[] a2 = { 1, 2, 3 };
Console.Write (a1.Equals (a2));                              // False
Console.Write (a1.Equals (a2, EqualityComparer<int>.Default));  // True
```

Here's another example:

```
string[] a1 = "the quick brown fox".Split();
string[] a2 = "THE QUICK BROWN FOX".Split();
bool isTrue = a1.Equals (a2, StringComparer.InvariantCultureIgnoreCase);
```

Tuples work in the same way:

```
var t1 = Tuple.Create (1, "foo");
var t2 = Tuple.Create (1, "FOO");
bool isTrue = t1.Equals (t2, StringComparer.InvariantCultureIgnoreCase);
int zero = t1.CompareTo (t2, StringComparer.InvariantCultureIgnoreCase);
```

The difference with tuples, though, is that their *default* equality and order comparison implementations also apply structural comparisons:

```
var t1 = Tuple.Create (1, "FOO");
var t2 = Tuple.Create (1, "FOO");
Console.WriteLine (t1.Equals (t2));     // True
```

8

LINQ Queries

LINQ, or Language Integrated Query, is a set of language and framework features for writing structured type-safe queries over local object collections and remote data sources. LINQ was introduced in C# 3.0 and Framework 3.5.

LINQ enables you to query any collection implementing IEnumerable<T>, whether an array, list, or XML DOM, as well as remote data sources, such as tables in SQL Server. LINQ offers the benefits of both compile-time type checking and dynamic query composition.

This chapter describes the LINQ architecture and the fundamentals of writing queries. All core types are defined in the System.Linq and System.Linq.Expressions namespaces.

> The examples in this and the following two chapters are preloaded into an interactive querying tool called LINQPad. You can download LINQPad from *www.linqpad.net*.

Getting Started

The basic units of data in LINQ are *sequences* and *elements*. A sequence is any object that implements IEnumerable<T> and an element is each item in the sequence. In the following example, names is a sequence, and Tom, Dick, and Harry are elements:

```
string[] names = { "Tom", "Dick", "Harry" };
```

We call this a *local sequence* because it represents a local collection of objects in memory.

A *query operator* is a method that transforms a sequence. A typical query operator accepts an *input sequence* and emits a transformed *output sequence*. In the Enumerable class in System.Linq, there are around 40 query operators—all implemented as static extension methods. These are called *standard query operators*.

Queries that operate over local sequences are called local queries or *LINQ-to-objects* queries.

LINQ also supports sequences that can be dynamically fed from a remote data source such as a SQL Server. These sequences additionally implement the `IQueryable<T>` interface and are supported through a matching set of standard query operators in the `Queryable` class. We discuss this further in the section "Interpreted Queries" on page 339 later in this chapter.

A query is an expression that transforms sequences with query operators. The simplest query comprises one input sequence and one operator. For instance, we can apply the `Where` operator on a simple array to extract those whose length is at least four characters as follows:

```
string[] names = { "Tom", "Dick", "Harry" };
IEnumerable<string> filteredNames = System.Linq.Enumerable.Where
                                    (names, n => n.Length >= 4);
foreach (string n in filteredNames)
  Console.WriteLine (n);

Dick
Harry
```

Because the standard query operators are implemented as extension methods, we can call `Where` directly on names—as though it were an instance method:

```
IEnumerable<string> filteredNames = names.Where (n => n.Length >= 4);
```

For this to compile, you must import the `System.Linq` namespace. Here's a complete example:

```
using System;
usign System.Collections.Generic;
using System.Linq;

class LinqDemo
{
  static void Main()
  {
    string[] names = { "Tom", "Dick", "Harry" };

    IEnumerable<string> filteredNames = names.Where (n => n.Length >= 4);
    foreach (string name in filteredNames) Console.WriteLine (name);
  }
}

Dick
Harry
```

We could further shorten our code by implicitly typing `filteredNames`:

```
var filteredNames = names.Where (n => n.Length >= 4);
```

This can hinder readability, however, particularly outside of an IDE, where there are no tool tips to help.

In this chapter, we avoid implicitly typing query results except when it's mandatory (as we'll see later, in the section "Projection Strategies" on page 337), or when a query's type is irrelevant to an example.

Most query operators accept a lambda expression as an argument. The lambda expression helps guide and shape the query. In our example, the lambda expression is as follows:

```
n => n.Length >= 4
```

The input argument corresponds to an input element. In this case, the input argument n represents each name in the array and is of type **string**. The **Where** operator requires that the lambda expression return a **bool** value, which if **true**, indicates that the element should be included in the output sequence. Here's its signature:

```
public static IEnumerable<TSource> Where<TSource>
  (this IEnumerable<TSource> source, Func<TSource,bool> predicate)
```

The following query retrieves all names that contain the letter "a":

```
IEnumerable<string> filteredNames = names.Where (n => n.Contains ("a"));

foreach (string name in filteredNames)
  Console.WriteLine (name);          // Harry
```

So far, we've built queries using extension methods and lambda expressions. As we'll see shortly, this strategy is highly composable in that it allows the chaining of query operators. In the book, we refer to this as *fluent syntax*.[*] C# also provides another syntax for writing queries, called *query expression* syntax. Here's our preceding query written as a query expression:

```
IEnumerable<string> filteredNames = from n in names
                                    where n.Contains ("a")
                                    select n;
```

Fluent syntax and query syntax are complementary. In the following two sections, we explore each in more detail.

---

[*] The term is based on Eric Evans and Martin Fowler's work on fluent interfaces.

Fluent Syntax

Fluent syntax is the most flexible and fundamental. In this section, we describe how to chain query operators to form more complex queries—and show why extension methods are important to this process. We also describe how to formulate lambda expressions for a query operator and introduce several new query operators.

Chaining Query Operators

In the preceding section, we showed two simple queries, each comprising a single query operator. To build more complex queries, you append additional query operators to the expression, creating a chain. To illustrate, the following query extracts all strings containing the letter "a", sorts them by length, and then converts the results to uppercase:

```
using System;
using System.Collections.Generic;
using System.Linq;

class LinqDemo
{
  static void Main()
  {
    string[] names = { "Tom", "Dick", "Harry", "Mary", "Jay" };

    IEnumerable<string> query = names
      .Where    (n => n.Contains ("a"))
      .OrderBy  (n => n.Length)
      .Select   (n => n.ToUpper());

    foreach (string name in query) Console.WriteLine (name);
  }
}

JAY
MARY
HARRY
```

 The variable, n, in our example, is privately scoped to each of the lambda expressions. We can reuse n for the same reason we can reuse c in the following method:

```
void Test()
{
  foreach (char c in "string1") Console.Write (c);
  foreach (char c in "string2") Console.Write (c);
  foreach (char c in "string3") Console.Write (c);
}
```

Where, OrderBy, and Select are standard query operators that resolve to extension methods in the Enumerable class (if you import the System.Linq namespace).

We already introduced the Where operator, which emits a filtered version of the input sequence. The OrderBy operator emits a sorted version of its input sequence; the Select method emits a sequence where each input element is transformed or *projected* with a given lambda expression (n.ToUpper(), in this case). Data flows from left to right through the chain of operators, so the data is first filtered, then sorted, then projected.

A query operator never alters the input sequence; instead, it returns a new sequence. This is consistent with the *functional programming* paradigm, from which LINQ was inspired.

Here are the signatures of each of these extension methods (with the OrderBy signature simplified slightly):

```
public static IEnumerable<TSource> Where<TSource>
  (this IEnumerable<TSource> source, Func<TSource,bool> predicate)

public static IEnumerable<TSource> OrderBy<TSource,TKey>
  (this IEnumerable<TSource> source, Func<TSource,TKey> keySelector)

public static IEnumerable<TResult> Select<TSource,TResult>
  (this IEnumerable<TSource> source, Func<TSource,TResult> selector)
```

When query operators are chained as in this example, the output sequence of one operator is the input sequence of the next. The end result resembles a production line of conveyor belts, as illustrated in Figure 8-1.

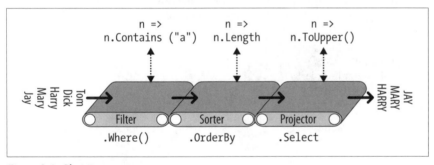

Figure 8-1. Chaining query operators

We can construct the identical query *progressively*, as follows:

```
// You must import the System.Linq namespace for this to compile:

IEnumerable<string> filtered   = names   .Where  (n => n.Contains ("a"));
IEnumerable<string> sorted     = filtered.OrderBy (n => n.Length);
IEnumerable<string> finalQuery = sorted  .Select  (n => n.ToUpper());
```

finalQuery is compositionally identical to the query we had constructed previously. Further, each intermediate step also comprises a valid query that we can execute:

```
foreach (string name in filtered)
  Console.Write (name + "|");        // Harry|Mary|Jay|
```

```
Console.WriteLine();
foreach (string name in sorted)
  Console.Write (name + "|");          // Jay|Mary|Harry|

Console.WriteLine();
foreach (string name in finalQuery)
  Console.Write (name + "|");          // JAY|MARY|HARRY|
```

Why extension methods are important

Instead of using extension method syntax, you can use conventional static method syntax to call the query operators. For example:

```
IEnumerable<string> filtered = Enumerable.Where (names,
                                      n => n.Contains ("a"));
IEnumerable<string> sorted = Enumerable.OrderBy (filtered, n => n.Length);
IEnumerable<string> finalQuery = Enumerable.Select (sorted,
                                      n => n.ToUpper());
```

This is, in fact, how the compiler translates extension method calls. Shunning extension methods comes at a cost, however, if you want to write a query in a single statement as we did earlier. Let's revisit the single-statement query—first in extension method syntax:

```
IEnumerable<string> query = names.Where  (n => n.Contains ("a"))
                                 .OrderBy (n => n.Length)
                                 .Select  (n => n.ToUpper());
```

Its natural linear shape reflects the left-to-right flow of data, as well as keeping lambda expressions alongside their query operators (*infix* notation). Without extension methods, the query loses its *fluency*:

```
IEnumerable<string> query =
  Enumerable.Select (
    Enumerable.OrderBy (
      Enumerable.Where (
        names, n => n.Contains ("a")
      ), n => n.Length
    ), n => n.ToUpper()
  );
```

Composing Lambda Expressions

In previous examples, we fed the following lambda expression to the Where operator:

```
n => n.Contains ("a")      // Input type=string, return type=bool.
```

 An expression returning a bool value is called a *predicate*.

The purpose of the lambda expression depends on the particular query operator. With the Where operator, it indicates whether an element should be included in the output sequence. In the case of the `OrderBy` operator, the lambda expression maps each element in the input sequence to its sorting key. With the `Select` operator, the lambda expression determines how each element in the input sequence is transformed before being fed to the output sequence.

 A lambda expression in a query operator always works on individual elements in the input sequence—not the sequence as a whole.

The query operator evaluates your lambda expression upon demand—typically once per element in the input sequence. Lambda expressions allow you to feed your own logic into the query operators. This makes the query operators versatile—as well as being simple under the hood. Here's a complete implementation of `Enumerable.Where`, exception handling aside:

```
public static IEnumerable<TSource> Where<TSource>
  (this IEnumerable<TSource> source, Func<TSource,bool> predicate)
{
  foreach (TSource element in source)
    if (predicate (element))
      yield return element;
}
```

Lambda expressions and Func signatures

The standard query operators utilize generic `Func` delegates. `Func` is a family of general-purpose generic delegates in `System.Linq`, defined with the following intent:

> The type arguments in `Func` appear in the same order they do in lambda expressions.

Hence, `Func<TSource,bool>` matches a `TSource=>bool` lambda expression: one that accepts a `TSource` argument and returns a `bool` value.

Similarly, `Func<TSource,TResult>` matches a `TSource=>TResult` lambda expression.

The `Func` delegates are listed in the section "Lambda Expressions" on page 130 in Chapter 4.

Lambda expressions and element typing

The standard query operators use the following generic type names:

Generic type letter	Meaning
TSource	Element type for the input sequence
TResult	Element type for the output sequence—if different from TSource
TKey	Element type for the *key* used in sorting, grouping, or joining

`TSource` is determined by the input sequence. `TResult` and `TKey` are *inferred from your lambda expression*.

For example, consider the signature of the Select query operator:

```
public static IEnumerable<TResult> Select<TSource,TResult>
  (this IEnumerable<TSource> source, Func<TSource,TResult> selector)
```

Func<TSource,TResult> matches a TSource=>TResult lambda expression: one that maps an *input element* to an *output element*. TSource and TResult are different types, so the lambda expression can change the type of each element. Further, the lambda expression *determines the output sequence type*. The following query uses Select to transform string type elements to integer type elements:

```
string[] names = { "Tom", "Dick", "Harry", "Mary", "Jay" };
IEnumerable<int> query = names.Select (n => n.Length);

foreach (int length in query)
  Console.Write (length + "|");      // 3|4|5|4|3|
```

The compiler *infers* the type of TResult from the return value of the lambda expression. In this case, TResult is inferred to be of type int.

The Where query operator is simpler and requires no type inference for the output, since input and output elements are of the same type. This makes sense because the operator merely filters elements; it does not *transform* them:

```
public static IEnumerable<TSource> Where<TSource>
  (this IEnumerable<TSource> source, Func<TSource,bool> predicate)
```

Finally, consider the signature of the OrderBy operator:

```
// Slightly simplified:
public static IEnumerable<TSource> OrderBy<TSource,TKey>
  (this IEnumerable<TSource> source, Func<TSource,TKey> keySelector)
```

Func<TSource,TKey> maps an input element to a *sorting key*. TKey is inferred from your lambda expression and is separate from the input and output element types. For instance, we could choose to sort a list of names by length (int key) or alphabetically (string key):

```
string[] names = { "Tom", "Dick", "Harry", "Mary", "Jay" };
IEnumerable<string> sortedByLength, sortedAlphabetically;
sortedByLength        = names.OrderBy (n => n.Length);   // int key
sortedAlphabetically = names.OrderBy (n => n);           // string key
```

You can call the query operators in Enumerable with traditional delegates that refer to methods instead of lambda expressions. This approach is effective in simplifying certain kinds of local queries—particularly with LINQ to XML—and is demonstrated in Chapter 10. It doesn't work with IQueryable<T>-based sequences, however (e.g., when querying a database), because the operators in Queryable require lambda expressions in order to emit expression trees. We discuss this later in the section "Interpreted Queries" on page 339.

Natural Ordering

The original ordering of elements within an input sequence is significant in LINQ. Some query operators rely on this behavior, such as Take, Skip, and Reverse.

The Take operator outputs the first x elements, discarding the rest:

```
int[] numbers = { 10, 9, 8, 7, 6 };
IEnumerable<int> firstThree = numbers.Take (3);    // { 10, 9, 8 }
```

The Skip operator ignores the first x elements and outputs the rest:

```
IEnumerable<int> lastTwo    = numbers.Skip (3);    // { 7, 6 }
```

Reverse does exactly as it says:

```
IEnumerable<int> reversed   = numbers.Reverse();   // { 6, 7, 8, 9, 10 }
```

Operators such as Where and Select preserve the original ordering of the input sequence. LINQ preserves the ordering of elements in the input sequence wherever possible.

Other Operators

Not all query operators return a sequence. The *element* operators extract one element from the input sequence; examples are First, Last, and ElementAt:

```
int[] numbers    = { 10, 9, 8, 7, 6 };
int firstNumber  = numbers.First();                // 10
int lastNumber   = numbers.Last();                 // 6
int secondNumber = numbers.ElementAt(1);           // 9
int lowestNumber = numbers.OrderBy (n => n).First();  // 6
```

The *aggregation* operators return a scalar value; usually of numeric type:

```
int count = numbers.Count();    // 5;
int min = numbers.Min();        // 6;
```

The *quantifiers* return a bool value:

```
bool hasTheNumberNine = numbers.Contains (9);        // true
bool hasMoreThanZeroElements = numbers.Any();        // true
bool hasAnOddElement = numbers.Any (n => n % 2 == 1); // true
```

Because these operators don't return a collection, you can't call further query operators on their result. In other words, they must appear as the last operator in a query.

Some query operators accept two input sequences. Examples are Concat, which appends one sequence to another, and Union, which does the same but with duplicates removed:

```
int[] seq1 = { 1, 2, 3 };
int[] seq2 = { 3, 4, 5 };
IEnumerable<int> concat = seq1.Concat (seq2);   // { 1, 2, 3, 3, 4, 5 }
IEnumerable<int> union  = seq1.Union (seq2);    // { 1, 2, 3, 4, 5 }
```

The joining operators also fall into this category. Chapter 9 covers all the query operators in detail.

Query Expressions

C# provides a syntactic shortcut for writing LINQ queries, called *query expressions*. Contrary to popular belief, query expressions are based not on SQL, but on *list comprehensions* from functional programming languages such as LISP and Haskell.

 In this book we refer to query expression syntax simply as "query syntax."

In the preceding section, we wrote a fluent-syntax query to extract strings containing the letter "a", sorted by length and converted to uppercase. Here's the same thing in query syntax:

```
using System;
using System.Collections.Generic;
using System.Linq;

class LinqDemo
{
  static void Main()
  {
    string[] names = { "Tom", "Dick", "Harry", "Mary", "Jay" };

    IEnumerable<string> query =
      from    n in names
      where   n.Contains ("a")       // Filter elements
      orderby n.Length               // Sort elements
      select  n.ToUpper();           // Translate each element (project)

    foreach (string name in query) Console.WriteLine (name);
  }
}

JAY
MARY
HARRY
```

Query expressions always start with a `from` clause and ends with either a `select` or `group` clause. The `from` clause declares an *range variable* (in this case, n), which you can think of as traversing the input sequence—rather like `foreach`. Figure 8-2 illustrates the complete syntax as a railroad diagram.

 To read this diagram, start at the left and then proceed along the track as if you were a train. For instance, after the mandatory `from` clause, you can optionally include an `orderby`, `where`, `let`, or `join` clause. After that, you can either continue with a `select` or `group` clause, or go back and include another `from`, `orderby`, `where`, `let` or `join` clause.

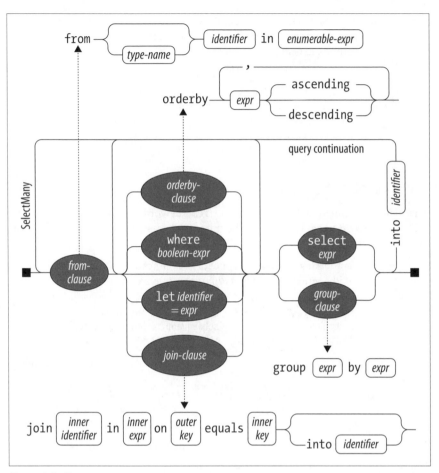

Figure 8-2. Query syntax

The compiler processes a query expression by translating it into fluent syntax. It does this in a fairly mechanical fashion—much like it translates `foreach` statements into calls to `GetEnumerator` and `MoveNext`. This means that anything you can write in query syntax you can also write in fluent syntax. The compiler (initially) translates our example query into the following:

```
IEnumerable<string> query = names.Where   (n => n.Contains ("a"))
                                 .OrderBy (n => n.Length)
                                 .Select  (n => n.ToUpper());
```

The `Where`, `OrderBy`, and `Select` operators then resolve using the same rules that would apply if the query were written in fluent syntax. In this case, they bind to extension methods in the `Enumerable` class, because the `System.Linq` namespace is imported and `names` implements `IEnumerable<string>`. The compiler doesn't specifically favor the `Enumerable` class, however, when translating query expressions. You can think of the compiler as mechanically injecting the words "Where," "OrderBy," and "Select" into the statement, and then compiling it as though you'd typed the method names yourself. This offers flexibility in how they resolve. The operators in the database queries that we'll write in later sections, for instance, will bind instead to extension methods in Queryable.

 If we remove the using System.Linq directive from our program, the query would not compile, because the Where, OrderBy, and Select methods would have nowhere to bind. Query expressions *cannot compile* unless you import a namespace (or write an instance method for every query operator!).

Range Variables

The identifier immediately following the from keyword syntax is called the *range variable*. A range variable refers to the current element in the sequence that the operation is to be performed on.

In our examples, the range variable n appears in every clause in the query. And yet, the variable actually enumerates over a *different* sequence with each clause:

```
from    n in names          // n is our range variable
where   n.Contains ("a")    // n = directly from the array
orderby n.Length            // n = subsequent to being filtered
select  n.ToUpper()         // n = subsequent to being sorted
```

This becomes clear when we examine the compiler's mechanical translation to fluent syntax:

```
names.Where   (n => n.Contains ("a"))    // Privately scoped n
     .OrderBy (n => n.Length)            // Privately scoped n
     .Select  (n => n.ToUpper())         // Privately scoped n
```

As you can see, each instance of n is scoped privately to its own lambda expression.

Query expressions also let you introduce new range variables, via the following clauses:

- let
- into
- An additional from clause

We will cover these later in this chapter in "Composition Strategies" on page 333, and also in Chapter 9, in "Projecting" on page 369 and "Joining" on page 370.

Query Syntax Versus SQL Syntax

Query expressions look superficially like SQL, yet the two are very different. A LINQ query boils down to a C# expression, and so follows standard C# rules. For example, with LINQ, you cannot use a variable before you declare it. In SQL, you reference a table alias in the SELECT clause before defining it in a FROM clause.

A subquery in LINQ is just another C# expression and so requires no special syntax. Subqueries in SQL are subject to special rules.

With LINQ, data logically flows from left to right through the query. With SQL, the order is less well-structured with regard data flow.

A LINQ query comprises a conveyor belt or *pipeline* of operators that accept and emit *ordered sequences*. A SQL query comprises a *network* of clauses that work mostly with *unordered sets*.

Query Syntax Versus Fluent Syntax

Query and fluent syntax each have advantages.

Query syntax is simpler for queries that involve any of the following:

- A `let` clause for introducing a new variable alongside the range variable
- `SelectMany`, `Join`, or `GroupJoin`, followed by an outer range variable reference

(We describe the `let` clause in the later section, "Composition Strategies" on page 333; we describe `SelectMany`, `Join`, and `GroupJoin` in Chapter 9.)

The middle ground is queries that involve the simple use of `Where`, `OrderBy`, and `Select`. Either syntax works well; the choice here is largely personal.

For queries that comprise a single operator, fluent syntax is shorter and less cluttered.

Finally, there are many operators that have no keyword in query syntax. These require that you use fluent syntax—at least in part. This means any operator outside of the following:

```
Where, Select, SelectMany
OrderBy, ThenBy, OrderByDescending, ThenByDescending
GroupBy, Join, GroupJoin
```

Mixed Syntax Queries

If a query operator has no query-syntax support, you can mix query syntax and fluent syntax. The only restriction is that each query-syntax component must be complete (i.e., start with a `from` clause and end with a `select` or `group` clause).

Assuming this array declaration:

```
string[] names = { "Tom", "Dick", "Harry", "Mary", "Jay" };
```

the following example counts the number of names containing the letter "a":

```
int matches = (from n in names where n.Contains ("a") select n).Count();
// 3
```

The next query obtains the first name in alphabetical order:

```
string first = (from n in names orderby n select n).First();   // Dick
```

The mixed syntax approach is sometimes beneficial in more complex queries. With these simple examples, however, we could stick to fluent syntax throughout without penalty:

```
int matches = names.Where (n => n.Contains ("a")).Count();   // 3
string first = names.OrderBy (n => n).First();               // Dick
```

 There are times when mixed syntax queries offer by far the highest "bang for the buck" in terms of function and simplicity. It's important not to unilaterally favor either query or fluent syntax; otherwise, you'll be unable to write mixed syntax queries without feeling a sense of failure!

The remainder of this chapter will show key concepts in both fluent and query syntax, where applicable.

Deferred Execution

An important feature of most query operators is that they execute not when constructed, but when *enumerated* (in other words, when MoveNext is called on its enumerator). Consider the following query:

```
var numbers = new List<int>();
numbers.Add (1);

IEnumerable<int> query = numbers.Select (n => n * 10);   // Build query

numbers.Add (2);                        // Sneak in an extra element

foreach (int n in query)
    Console.Write (n + "|");            // 10|20|
```

The extra number that we sneaked into the list *after* constructing the query is included in the result, because it's not until the foreach statement runs that any filtering or sorting takes place. This is called *deferred* or *lazy* execution. All standard query operators provide deferred execution, with the following exceptions:

- Operators that return a single element or scalar value, such as First or Count
- The following *conversion operators*:

    ToArray, ToList, ToDictionary, ToLookup

These operators cause immediate query execution because their result types have no mechanism for providing deferred execution. The Count method, for instance, returns a simple integer, which then doesn't get enumerated. The following query is executed immediately:

```
int matches = numbers.Where (n => n < 2).Count();   // 1
```

Deferred execution is important because it decouples query *construction* from query *execution*. This allows you to construct a query in several steps, as well as making database queries possible.

Subqueries provide another level of indirection. Everything in a subquery is subject to deferred execution—including aggregation and conversion methods. We describe this in the section "Subqueries" on page 330 later in this chapter.

Reevaluation

Deferred execution has another consequence: a deferred execution query is reevaluated when you re-enumerate:

```
var numbers = new List<int>() { 1, 2 };

IEnumerable<int> query = numbers.Select (n => n * 10);
foreach (int n in query) Console.Write (n + "|");    // 10|20|

numbers.Clear();
foreach (int n in query) Console.Write (n + "|");    // <nothing>
```

There are a couple of reasons why reevaluation is sometimes disadvantageous:

- Sometimes you want to "freeze" or cache the results at a certain point in time.
- Some queries are computationally intensive (or rely on querying a remote database), so you don't want to unnecessarily repeat them.

You can defeat reevaluation by calling a conversion operator, such as ToArray or ToList. ToArray copies the output of a query to an array; ToList copies to a generic List<>:

```
var numbers = new List<int>() { 1, 2 };

List<int> timesTen = numbers
  .Select (n => n * 10)

  .ToList();                 // Executes immediately into a List<int>

numbers.Clear();
Console.WriteLine (timesTen.Count);    // Still 2
```

Captured Variables

Deferred execution also has a sinister effect. If your query's lambda expressions reference local variables, these variables are subject to *captured variable* semantics. This means that if you later change their value, the query changes as well:

```
int[] numbers = { 1, 2 };

int factor = 10;
IEnumerable<int> query = numbers.Select (n => n * factor);
factor = 20;
foreach (int n in query) Console.Write (n + "|");    // 20|40|
```

LINQ Queries

This can be a real trap when building up a query within a **foreach** loop. For example, suppose we wanted to remove all vowels from a string. The following, although inefficient, gives the correct result:

```
IEnumerable<char> query = "Not what you might expect";

query = query.Where (c => c != 'a');
query = query.Where (c => c != 'e');
query = query.Where (c => c != 'i');
query = query.Where (c => c != 'o');
query = query.Where (c => c != 'u');

foreach (char c in query) Console.Write (c);  // Nt wht y mght xpct
```

Now watch what happens when we refactor this with a **foreach** loop:

```
IEnumerable<char> query = "Not what you might expect";

foreach (char vowel in "aeiou")
  query = query.Where (c => c != vowel);

foreach (char c in query) Console.Write (c);   // Not what yo might expect
```

Only the **'u'** is stripped! This is because, as we saw in Chapter 4 (see "Capturing Outer Variables" on page 132 in "Lambda Expressions" on page 130), the compiler scopes the iteration variable in the **foreach** loop as if it was declared *outside* the loop:

```
IEnumerable<char> vowels = "aeiou";
using (IEnumerator<char> rator = vowels.GetEnumerator())
{
  char vowel;
  while (rator.MoveNext())
  {
    vowel = rator.Current;
    query = query.Where (c => c != vowel);
  }
}
```

Because **vowel** is declared outside the loop, the *same* variable is repeatedly updated, so each lambda expression captures the same **vowel**. When we later enumerate the query, all lambda expressions reference that single variable's current value, which is **'u'**. To solve this, you must assign the loop variable to another variable declared *inside* the statement block:

```
foreach (char vowel in "aeiou")
{
  char temp = vowel;
  query = query.Where (c => c != temp);
}
```

This forces a fresh variable to be used on each loop iteration.

How Deferred Execution Works

Query operators provide deferred execution by returning *decorator* sequences.

Unlike a traditional collection class such as an array or linked list, a decorator sequence (in general) has no backing structure of its own to store elements. Instead, it wraps another sequence that you supply at runtime, to which it maintains a permanent dependency. Whenever you request data from a decorator, it in turn must request data from the wrapped input sequence.

 The query operator's transformation constitutes the "decoration." If the output sequence performed no transformation, it would be a *proxy* rather than a decorator.

Calling `Where` merely constructs the decorator wrapper sequence, holding a reference to the input sequence, the lambda expression, and any other arguments supplied. The input sequence is enumerated only when the decorator is enumerated.

Figure 8-3 illustrates the composition of the following query:

```
IEnumerable<int> lessThanTen = new int[] { 5, 12, 3 }.Where (n => n < 10);
```

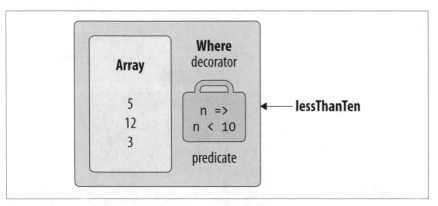

Figure 8-3. Decorator sequence

When you enumerate `lessThanTen`, you're, in effect, querying the array through the `Where` decorator.

The good news—if you ever want to write your own query operator—is that implementing a decorator sequence is easy with a C# iterator. Here's how you can write your own `Select` method:

```
public static IEnumerable<TResult> Select<TSource,TResult>
  (this IEnumerable<TSource> source, Func<TSource,TResult> selector)
{
  foreach (TSource element in source)
    yield return selector (element);
}
```

This method is an iterator by virtue of the `yield return` statement. Functionally, it's a shortcut for the following:

```
public static IEnumerable<TResult> Select<TSource,TResult>
  (this IEnumerable<TSource> source, Func<TSource,TResult> selector)
{
  return new SelectSequence (source, selector);
}
```

where *SelectSequence* is a (compiler-written) class whose enumerator encapsulates the logic in the iterator method.

Hence, when you call an operator such as `Select` or `Where`, you're doing nothing more than instantiating an enumerable class that decorates the input sequence.

Chaining Decorators

Chaining query operators creates a layering of decorators. Consider the following query:

```
IEnumerable<int> query = new int[] { 5, 12, 3 }.Where   (n => n < 10)
                                              .OrderBy (n => n)
                                              .Select  (n => n * 10);
```

Each query operator instantiates a new decorator that wraps the previous sequence (rather like a Russian doll). The object model of this query is illustrated in Figure 8-4. Note that this object model is fully constructed prior to any enumeration.

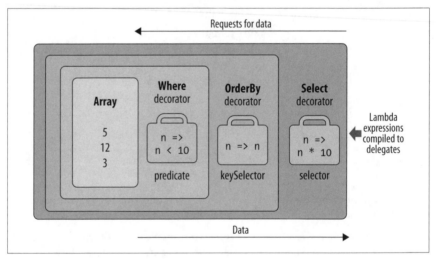

Figure 8-4. Layered decorator sequences

When you enumerate `query`, you're querying the original array, transformed through a layering or chain of decorators.

Adding ToList onto the end of this query would cause the preceding operators to execute right away, collapsing the whole
object model into a single list.

Figure 8-5 shows the same object composition in UML syntax. Select's decorator
references the OrderBy decorator, which references Where's decorator, which references the array. A feature of deferred execution is that you build the identical object
model if you compose the query progressively:

```
IEnumerable<int>
  source   = new int[] { 5, 12, 3 },
  filtered = source   .Where   (n => n < 10),
  sorted   = filtered .OrderBy (n => n),
  query    = sorted   .Select  (n => n * 10);
```

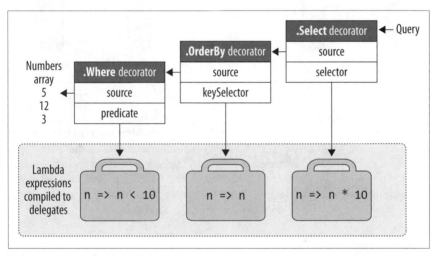

Figure 8-5. UML decorator composition

How Queries Are Executed

Here are the results of enumerating the preceding query:

```
foreach (int n in query) Console.WriteLine (n);
```

```
30
50
```

Behind the scenes, the foreach calls GetEnumerator on Select's decorator (the last or
outermost operator), which kicks everything off. The result is a chain of enumerators
that structurally mirrors the chain of decorator sequences. Figure 8-6 illustrates the
flow of execution as enumeration proceeds.

In the first section of this chapter, we depicted a query as a production line of conveyor belts. Extending this analogy, we can say a LINQ query is a lazy production

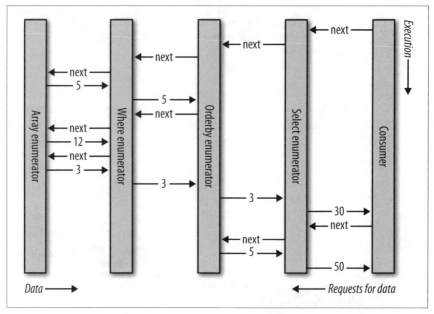

Figure 8-6. Execution of a local query

line, where the conveyor belts roll elements only upon *demand*. Constructing a query constructs a production line—with everything in place—but with nothing rolling. Then when the consumer requests an element (enumerates over the query), the rightmost conveyor belt activates; this in turn triggers the others to roll—as and when input sequence elements are needed. LINQ follows a demand-driven *pull* model, rather than a supply-driven *push* model. This is important—as we'll see later—in allowing LINQ to scale to querying SQL databases.

Subqueries

A subquery is a query contained within another query's lambda expression. The following example uses a subquery to sort musicians by their last name:

```
string[] musos = { "David Gilmour", "Roger Waters", "Rick Wright" };
IEnumerable<string> query = musos.OrderBy (m => m.Split().Last());
```

`m.Split` converts each string into a collection of words, upon which we then call the `Last` query operator. `m.Split().Last` is the subquery; `query` references the *outer query*.

Subqueries are permitted because you can put any valid C# expression on the right-hand side of a lambda. A subquery is simply another C# expression. This means that the rules for subqueries are a consequence of the rules for lambda expressions (and the behavior of query operators in general).

The term *subquery*, in the general sense, has a broader meaning. For the purpose of describing LINQ, we use the term only for a query referenced from within the lambda expression of another query. In a query expression, a subquery amounts to a query referenced from an expression in any clause except the `from` clause.

A subquery is privately scoped to the enclosing expression and is able to reference the outer lambda argument (or range variable in a query expression).

`m.Split().Last` is a very simple subquery. The next query retrieves all strings in an array whose length matches that of the shortest string:

```
string[] names = { "Tom", "Dick", "Harry", "Mary", "Jay" };

IEnumerable<string> outerQuery = names
  .Where (n => n.Length == names.OrderBy (n2 => n2.Length)
                                 .Select (n2 => n2.Length).First());
```

```
Tom, Jay
```

Here's the same thing as a query expression:

```
IEnumerable<string> outerQuery =
  from  n in names
  where n.Length ==
        (from n2 in names orderby n2.Length select n2.Length).First()
  select n;
```

Because the outer range variable (n) is in scope for a subquery, we cannot reuse n as the subquery's range variable.

A subquery is executed whenever the enclosing lambda expression is evaluated. This means a subquery is executed upon demand, at the discretion of the outer query. You could say that execution proceeds from the *outside in*. Local queries follow this model literally; interpreted queries (e.g., database queries) follow this model *conceptually*.

The subquery executes as and when required, to feed the outer query. In our example, the subquery (the top conveyor belt in Figure 8-7) executes once for every outer loop iteration. This is illustrated in Figures 8-7 and 8-8.

We can express our preceding subquery more succinctly as follows:

```
IEnumerable<string> query =
  from  n in names
  where n.Length == names.OrderBy (n2 => n2.Length).First().Length
  select n;
```

With the `Min` aggregation function, we can simplify the query further:

```
IEnumerable<string> query =
  from  n in names
  where n.Length == names.Min (n2 => n2.Length)
  select n;
```

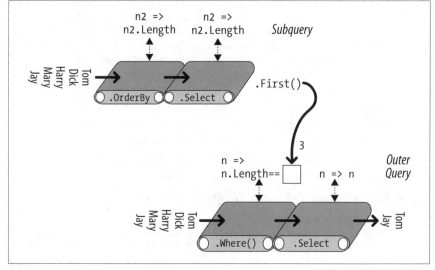

Figure 8-7. Subquery composition

In the later section "Interpreted Queries" on page 339, we'll describe how remote sources such as SQL tables can be queried. Our example makes an ideal database query, because it would be processed as a unit, requiring only one round trip to the database server. This query, however, is inefficient for a local collection because the subquery is recalculated on each outer loop iteration. We can avoid this inefficiency by running the subquery separately (so that it's no longer a subquery):

```
int shortest = names.Min (n => n.Length);

IEnumerable<string> query = from   n in names
                            where  n.Length == shortest
                            select n;
```

Factoring out subqueries in this manner is nearly always desirable when querying local collections. An exception is when the subquery is *correlated*, meaning that it references the outer range variable. We explore correlated subqueries in the following chapter, in the section "Projecting" on page 369.

Subqueries and Deferred Execution

An element or aggregation operator such as `First` or `Count` in a subquery doesn't force the *outer* query into immediate execution—deferred execution still holds for the outer query. This is because subqueries are called *indirectly*—through a delegate in the case of a local query, or through an expression tree in the case of an interpreted query.

An interesting case arises when you include a subquery within a `Select` expression. In the case of a local query, you're actually *projecting a sequence of queries*—each

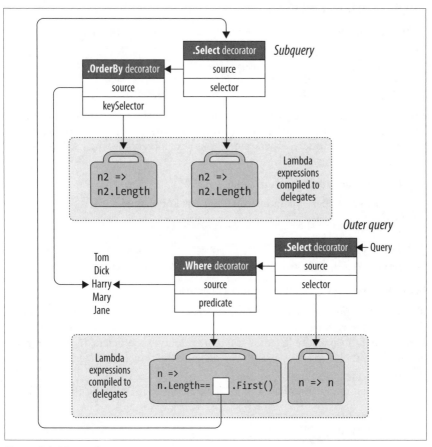

Figure 8-8. UML subquery composition

itself subject to deferred execution. The effect is generally transparent, and it serves to further improve efficiency. We revisit Select subqueries in some detail in Chapter 9.

Composition Strategies

In this section, we describe three strategies for building more complex queries:

- Progressive query construction
- Using the into keyword
- Wrapping queries

All are *chaining* strategies and produce identical runtime queries.

Progressive Query Building

At the start of the chapter, we demonstrated how you could build a fluent query progressively:

```
var filtered  = names    .Where   (n => n.Contains ("a"));
var sorted    = filtered .OrderBy (n => n);
var query     = sorted   .Select  (n => n.ToUpper());
```

Because each of the participating query operators returns a decorator sequence, the resultant query is the same chain or layering of decorators that you would get from a single-expression query. There are a couple of potential benefits, however, to building queries progressively:

- It can make queries easier to write.
- You can add query operators *conditionally*. For example:

```
if (includeFilter) query = query.Where (...)
```

This is more efficient than:

```
query = query.Where (n => !includeFilter || <expression>)
```

because it avoids adding an extra query operator if `includeFilter` is false.

A progressive approach is often useful in query comprehensions. To illustrate, imagine we want to remove all vowels from a list of names, and then present in alphabetical order those whose length is still more than two characters. In fluent syntax, we could write this query as a single expression—by projecting *before* we filter:

```
IEnumerable<string> query = names
  .Select  (n => n.Replace ("a", "").Replace ("e", "").Replace ("i", "")
                  .Replace ("o", "").Replace ("u", ""))
  .Where   (n => n.Length > 2)
  .OrderBy (n => n);

RESULT: { "Dck", "Hrry", "Mry" }
```

 Rather than calling `string`'s `Replace` method five times, we could remove vowels from a string more efficiently with a regular expression:

```
n => Regex.Replace (n, "[aeiou]", "")
```

`string`'s `Replace` method has the advantage, though, of also working in database queries.

Translating this directly into a query expression is troublesome because the `select` clause must come after the `where` and `orderby` clauses. And if we rearrange the query so as to project last, the result would be different:

```
IEnumerable<string> query =
  from  n in names
  where n.Length > 2
  orderby n
```

```
select n.Replace ("a", "").Replace ("e", "").Replace ("i", "")
       .Replace ("o", "").Replace ("u", "");
```

RESULT: { "Dck", "Hrry", "Jy", "Mry", "Tm" }

Fortunately, there are a number of ways to get the original result in query syntax. The first is by querying progressively:

```
IEnumerable<string> query =
  from   n in names
  select n.Replace ("a", "").Replace ("e", "").Replace ("i", "")
         .Replace ("o", "").Replace ("u", "");

query = from n in query where n.Length > 2 orderby n select n;
```

RESULT: { "Dck", "Hrry", "Mry" }

The into Keyword

The into keyword is interpreted in two very different ways by query expressions, depending on context. The meaning we're describing now is for signaling *query continuation* (the other is for signaling a GroupJoin).

The into keyword lets you "continue" a query after a projection and is a shortcut for progressively querying. With into, we can rewrite the preceding query as:

```
IEnumerable<string> query =
  from   n in names
  select n.Replace ("a", "").Replace ("e", "").Replace ("i", "")
         .Replace ("o", "").Replace ("u", "")
  into noVowel
    where noVowel.Length > 2 orderby noVowel select noVowel;
```

The only place you can use into is after a select or group clause. into "restarts" a query, allowing you to introduce fresh where, orderby, and select clauses.

Although it's easiest to think of into as restarting a query from the perspective of a query expression, it's *all one query* when translated to its final fluent form. Hence, there's no intrinsic performance hit with into. Nor do you lose any points for its use!

The equivalent of into in fluent syntax is simply a longer chain of operators.

Scoping rules

All query variables are out of scope following an into keyword. The following will not compile:

LINQ Queries

```
var query =
  from n1 in names
  select n1.ToUpper()
  into n2                           // Only n2 is visible from here on.
    where n1.Contains ("x")         // Illegal: n1 is not in scope.
    select n2;
```

To see why, consider how this maps to fluent syntax:

```
var query = names
  .Select (n1 => n1.ToUpper())
  .Where  (n2 => n1.Contains ("x"));    // Error: n1 no longer in scope
```

The original name (n1) is lost by the time the Where filter runs. Where's input sequence contains only uppercase names, so it cannot filter based on n1.

Wrapping Queries

A query built progressively can be formulated into a single statement by wrapping one query around another. In general terms:

```
var tempQuery = tempQueryExpr
var finalQuery = from ... in tempQuery ...
```

can be reformulated as:

```
var finalQuery = from ... in (tempQueryExpr)
```

Wrapping is semantically identical to progressive query building or using the into keyword (without the intermediate variable). The end result in all cases is a linear chain of query operators. For example, consider the following query:

```
IEnumerable<string> query =
  from   n in names
  select n.Replace ("a", "").Replace ("e", "").Replace ("i", "")
         .Replace ("o", "").Replace ("u", "");

query = from n in query where n.Length > 2 orderby n select n;
```

Reformulated in wrapped form, it's the following:

```
IEnumerable<string> query =
  from n1 in
  (
    from   n2 in names
    select n2.Replace ("a", "").Replace ("e", "").Replace ("i", "")
           .Replace ("o", "").Replace ("u", "")
  )
  where n1.Length > 2 orderby n1 select n1;
```

When converted to fluent syntax, the result is the same linear chain of operators as in previous examples.

```
IEnumerable<string> query = names
  .Select (n => n.Replace ("a", "").Replace ("e", "").Replace ("i", "")
                 .Replace ("o", "").Replace ("u", ""))
  .Where  (n => n.Length > 2)
  .OrderBy (n => n);
```

(The compiler does not emit the final `.Select (n => n)` because it's redundant.)

Wrapped queries can be confusing because they resemble the *subqueries* we wrote earlier. Both have the concept of an inner and outer query. When converted to fluent syntax, however, you can see that wrapping is simply a strategy for sequentially chaining operators. The end result bears no resemblance to a subquery, which embeds an inner query within the *lambda expression* of another.

Returning to a previous analogy: when wrapping, the "inner" query amounts to the *preceding conveyor belts*. In contrast, a subquery rides above a conveyor belt and is activated upon demand through the conveyor belt's lambda worker (as illustrated in Figure 8-7).

Projection Strategies

Object Initializers

So far, all our `select` clauses have projected scalar element types. With C# object initializers, you can project into more complex types. For example, suppose, as a first step in a query, we want to strip vowels from a list of names while still retaining the original versions alongside, for the benefit of subsequent queries. We can write the following class to assist:

```
class TempProjectionItem
{
  public string Original;    // Original name
  public string Vowelless;   // Vowel-stripped name
}
```

and then project into it with object initializers:

```
string[] names = { "Tom", "Dick", "Harry", "Mary", "Jay" };

IEnumerable<TempProjectionItem> temp =
  from n in names
  select new TempProjectionItem
  {
    Original  = n,
    Vowelless = n.Replace ("a", "").Replace ("e", "").Replace ("i", "")
                 .Replace ("o", "").Replace ("u", "")
  };
```

The result is of type `IEnumerable<TempProjectionItem>`, which we can subsequently query:

```
IEnumerable<string> query = from   item in temp
                            where  item.Vowelless.Length > 2
                            select item.Original;
Dick
Harry
Mary
```

Anonymous Types

Anonymous types allow you to structure your intermediate results without writing special classes. We can eliminate the `TempProjectionItem` class in our previous example with anonymous types:

```
var intermediate = from n in names

  select new
  {
    Original = n,
    Vowelless = n.Replace ("a", "").Replace ("e", "").Replace ("i", "")
               .Replace ("o", "").Replace ("u", "")
  };

IEnumerable<string> query = from    item in intermediate
                            where   item.Vowelless.Length > 2
                            select  item.Original;
```

This gives the same result as the previous example, but without needing to write a one-off class. The compiler does the job instead, writing a temporary class with fields that match the structure of our projection. This means, however, that the `intermediate` query has the following type:

```
IEnumerable <random-compiler-produced-name>
```

The only way we can declare a variable of this type is with the `var` keyword. In this case, `var` is more than just a clutter reduction device; it's a necessity.

We can write the whole query more succinctly with the `into` keyword:

```
var query = from n in names
  select new
  {
    Original = n,
    Vowelless = n.Replace ("a", "").Replace ("e", "").Replace ("i", "")
               .Replace ("o", "").Replace ("u", "")
  }
  into temp
  where temp.Vowelless.Length > 2
  select temp.Original;
```

Query expressions provide a shortcut for writing this kind of query: the `let` keyword.

The let Keyword

The `let` keyword introduces a new variable alongside the range variable.

With `let`, we can write a query extracting strings whose length, excluding vowels, exceeds two characters, as follows:

```
string[] names = { "Tom", "Dick", "Harry", "Mary", "Jay" };

IEnumerable<string> query =
  from n in names
  let vowelless = n.Replace ("a", "").Replace ("e", "").Replace ("i", "")
                 .Replace ("o", "").Replace ("u", "")
```

```
where vowelless.Length > 2
orderby vowelless
select n;      // Thanks to let, n is still in scope.
```

The compiler resolves a let clause by projecting into a temporary anonymous type that contains both the range variable and the new expression variable. In other words, the compiler translates this query into the preceding example.

let accomplishes two things:

• It projects new elements alongside existing elements.

• It allows an expression to be used repeatedly in a query without being rewritten.

The let approach is particularly advantageous in this example, because it allows the select clause to project either the original name (n) or its vowel-removed version (v).

You can have any number of let statements, before or after a where statement (see Figure 8-2). A let statement can reference variables introduced in earlier let statements (subject to the boundaries imposed by an into clause). let *reprojects* all existing variables transparently.

A let expression need not evaluate to a scalar type: sometimes it's useful to have it evaluate to a subsequence, for instance.

Interpreted Queries

LINQ provides two parallel architectures: *local* queries for local object collections, and *interpreted* queries for remote data sources. So far, we've examined the architecture of local queries, which operate over collections implementing IEnumerable<>. Local queries resolve to query operators in the Enumerable class, which in turn resolve to chains of decorator sequences. The delegates that they accept—whether expressed in query syntax, fluent syntax, or traditional delegates—are fully local to Intermediate Language (IL) code, just like any other C# method.

By contrast, interpreted queries are *descriptive*. They operate over sequences that implement IQueryable<T>, and they resolve to the query operators in the Queryable class, which emit *expression trees* that are interpreted at runtime.

> The query operators in Enumerable can actually work with IQueryable<T> sequences. The difficulty is that the resultant queries always execute locally on the client—this is why a second set of query operators is provided in the Queryable class.

There are two IQueryable<T> implementations in the .NET Framework:

• LINQ to SQL

• Entity Framework (EF)

These *LINQ-to-db* technologies are very similar in their LINQ support: the LINQ-to-db queries in this book will work with both LINQ to SQL and EF unless otherwise specified.

It's also possible to generate an `IQueryable<T>` wrapper around an ordinary enumerable collection by calling the `AsQueryable` method. We describe `AsQueryable` in the section "Building Query Expressions" on page 361 later in this chapter.

In this section, we'll use LINQ to SQL to illustrate interpreted query architecture because LINQ to SQL lets us query without having to first write an Entity Data Model. The queries that we write, however, work equally well with Entity Framework (and also many third-party products).

 `IQueryable<T>` is an extension of `IEnumerable<>` with additional methods for constructing expression trees. Most of the time you can ignore the details of these methods; they're called indirectly by the Framework. The section "Building Query Expressions" on page 361 covers `IQueryable<T>` in more detail.

Suppose we create a simple customer table in SQL Server and populate it with a few names using the following SQL script:

```
create table Customer
(
  ID int not null primary key,
  Name varchar(30)
)
insert Customer values (1, 'Tom')
insert Customer values (2, 'Dick')
insert Customer values (3, 'Harry')
insert Customer values (4, 'Mary')
insert Customer values (5, 'Jay')
```

With this table in place, we can write an interpreted LINQ query in C# to retrieve customers whose name contains the letter "a" as follows:

```
using System;
using System.Linq;
using System.Data.Linq;          // in System.Data.Linq.dll
using System.Data.Linq.Mapping;

[Table] public class Customer
{
  [Column(IsPrimaryKey=true)] public int ID;
  [Column]                    public string Name;
}

class Test
{
  static void Main()
  {
    DataContext dataContext = new DataContext ("connection string");
    Table<Customer> customers = dataContext.GetTable <Customer>();
```

```
IQueryable<string> query = from c in customers
    where   c.Name.Contains ("a")
    orderby c.Name.Length
    select  c.Name.ToUpper();

foreach (string name in query) Console.WriteLine (name);
}
}
```

LINQ to SQL translates this query into the following SQL:

```
SELECT UPPER([t0].[Name]) AS [value]
FROM [Customer] AS [t0]
WHERE [t0].[Name] LIKE @p0
ORDER BY LEN([t0].[Name])
```

with the following end result:

```
JAY
MARY
HARRY
```

How Interpreted Queries Work

Let's examine how the preceding query is processed.

First, the compiler converts query syntax to fluent syntax. This is done exactly as with local queries:

```
IQueryable<string> query = customers.Where  (n => n.Name.Contains ("a"))
                                    .OrderBy (n => n.Name.Length)
                                    .Select  (n => n.Name.ToUpper());
```

Next, the compiler resolves the query operator methods. Here's where local and interpreted queries differ—interpreted queries resolve to query operators in the Queryable class instead of the Enumerable class.

To see why, we need to look at the customers variable, the source upon which the whole query builds. customers is of type Table<>, which implements IQueryable<T> (a subtype of IEnumerable<>). This means the compiler has a choice in resolving Where: it could call the extension method in Enumerable or the following extension method in Queryable:

```
public static IQueryable<TSource> Where<TSource> (this
    IQueryable<TSource> source, Expression <Func<TSource,bool>> predicate)
```

The compiler chooses Queryable.Where because its signature is a *more specific match*.

Queryable.Where accepts a predicate wrapped in an Expression<TDelegate> type. This instructs the compiler to translate the supplied lambda expression—in other words, n=>n.Name.Contains("a")—to an *expression tree* rather than a compiled delegate. An expression tree is an object model based on the types in System.Linq.Expressions that can be inspected at runtime (so that LINQ to SQL or EF can later translate it to a SQL statement).

LINQ Queries

Because `Queryable.Where` also returns `IQueryable<T>`, the same process follows with the `OrderBy` and `Select` operators. The end result is illustrated in Figure 8-9. In the shaded box, there is an *expression tree* describing the entire query, which can be traversed at runtime.

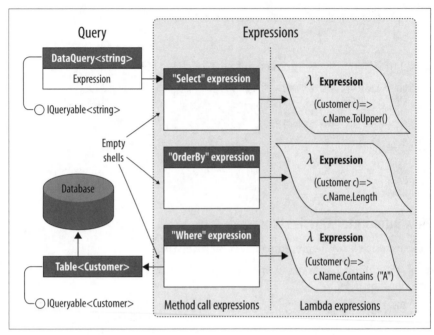

Figure 8-9. Interpreted query composition

Execution

Interpreted queries follow a deferred execution model—just like local queries. This means that the SQL statement is not generated until you start enumerating the query. Further, enumerating the same query twice results in the database being queried twice.

Under the covers, interpreted queries differ from local queries in how they execute. When you enumerate over an interpreted query, the outermost sequence runs a program that traverses the entire expression tree, processing it as a unit. In our example, LINQ to SQL translates the expression tree to a SQL statement, which it then executes, yielding the results as a sequence.

To work, LINQ to SQL needs some clues as to the schema of the database. The Table and Column attributes that we applied to the Customer class serve just this function. The section "LINQ to SQL and Entity Framework" on page 346 describes these attributes in more detail. Entity Framework is similar except that it also requires an Entity Data Model (EDM)—an XML file describing the mapping between database and entities.

We said previously that a LINQ query is like a production line. When you enumerate an IQueryable conveyor belt, though, it doesn't start up the whole production line, like with a local query. Instead, just the IQueryable belt starts up, with a special enumerator that calls upon a production manager. The manager reviews the entire production line—which consists not of compiled code, but of *dummies* (method call expressions) with instructions pasted to their *foreheads* (expression trees). The manager then traverses all the expressions, in this case transcribing them to a single piece of paper (a SQL statement), which it then executes, feeding the results back to the consumer. Only one belt turns; the rest of the production line is a network of empty shells, existing just to describe what has to be done.

This has some practical implications. For instance, with local queries, you can write your own query methods (fairly easily, with iterators) and then use them to supplement the predefined set. With remote queries, this is difficult, and even undesirable. If you wrote a MyWhere extension method accepting IQueryable<T>, it would be like putting your own dummy into the production line. The production manager wouldn't know what to do with your dummy. Even if you intervened at this stage, your solution would be hard-wired to a particular provider, such as LINQ to SQL, and would not work with other IQueryable implementations. Part of the benefit of having a standard set of methods in Queryable is that they define a *standard vocabulary* for querying *any* remote collection. As soon as you try to extend the vocabulary, you're no longer interoperable.

Another consequence of this model is that an IQueryable provider may be unable to cope with some queries—even if you stick to the standard methods. LINQ to SQL and EF are both limited by the capabilities of the database server; some LINQ queries have no SQL translation. If you're familiar with SQL, you'll have a good intuition for what these are, although at times you have to experiment to see what causes a runtime error; it can be surprising what *does* work!

Combining Interpreted and Local Queries

A query can include both interpreted and local operators. A typical pattern is to have the local operators on the *outside* and the interpreted components on the *inside*; in other words, the interpreted queries feed the local queries. This pattern works well with LINQ-to-database queries.

LINQ Queries

For instance, suppose we write a custom extension method to pair up strings in a collection:

```
public static IEnumerable<string> Pair (this IEnumerable<string> source)
{
  string firstHalf = null;
  foreach (string element in source)
    if (firstHalf == null)
      firstHalf = element;
    else
    {
      yield return firstHalf + ", " + element;
      firstHalf = null;
    }
}
```

We can use this extension method in a query that mixes LINQ to SQL and local operators:

```
DataContext dataContext = new DataContext ("connection string");
Table<Customer> customers = dataContext.GetTable <Customer>();

IEnumerable<string> q = customers
  .Select (c => c.Name.ToUpper())
  .OrderBy (n => n)
  .Pair()                         // Local from this point on.
  .Select ((n, i) => "Pair " + i.ToString() + " = " + n);

foreach (string element in q) Console.WriteLine (element);

Pair 0 = HARRY, MARY
Pair 1 = TOM, DICK
```

Because customers is of a type implementing IQueryable<T>, the Select operator resolves to Queryable.Select. This returns an output sequence also of type IQueryable<T>. But the next query operator, Pair, has no overload accepting IQuery able<T>, only the less specific IEnumerable<>. So, it resolves to our local Pair method—wrapping the interpreted query in a local query. Pair also emits IEnumer able, so OrderBy wraps another local operator.

On the LINQ to SQL side, the resulting SQL statement is equivalent to:

```
SELECT UPPER (Name) FROM Customer ORDER BY UPPER (Name)
```

The remaining work is done locally. Figure 8-10 shows the query diagrammatically. In effect, we have a local query (on the outside), whose source is an interpreted query (the inside).

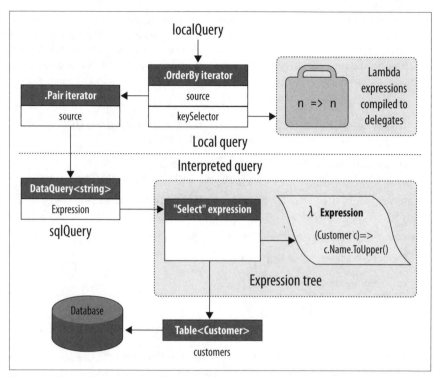

Figure 8-10. Combining local and interpreted queries

AsEnumerable

`Enumerable.AsEnumerable` is the simplest of all query operators. Here's its complete
definition:

```
public static IEnumerable<TSource> AsEnumerable<TSource>
               (this IEnumerable<TSource> source)
{
    return source;
}
```

Its purpose is to cast an `IQueryable<T>` sequence to `IEnumerable<T>`, forcing subsequent query operators to bind to `Enumerable` operators instead of `Queryable` operators. This causes the remainder of the query to execute locally.

To illustrate, suppose we had a `MedicalArticles` table in SQL Server and wanted to
use LINQ to SQL or EF to retrieve all articles on influenza whose abstract contained
less than 100 words. For the latter predicate, we need a regular expression:

```
Regex wordCounter = new Regex (@"\b(\w|[-'])+\b");

var query = dataContext.MedicalArticles
  .Where (article => article.Topic == "influenza" &&
                 wordCounter.Matches (article.Abstract).Count < 100);
```

The problem is that SQL Server doesn't support regular expressions, so the LINQ-to-db providers will throw an exception, complaining that the query cannot be translated to SQL. We can solve this by querying in two steps: first retrieving all articles on influenza through a LINQ to SQL query, and then filtering *locally* for abstracts of less than 100 words:

```
Regex wordCounter = new Regex (@"\b(\w|[-'])+\b");

IEnumerable<MedicalArticle> sqlQuery = dataContext.MedicalArticles
  .Where (article => article.Topic == "influenza");

IEnumerable<MedicalArticle> localQuery = sqlQuery
  .Where (article => wordCounter.Matches (article.Abstract).Count < 100);
```

Because `sqlQuery` is of type `IEnumerable<MedicalArticle>`, the second query binds to the local query operators, forcing that part of the filtering to run on the client.

With `AsEnumerable`, we can do the same in a single query:

```
Regex wordCounter = new Regex (@"\b(\w|[-'])+\b");

var query = dataContext.MedicalArticles
  .Where (article => article.Topic == "influenza")

  .AsEnumerable()
  .Where (article => wordCounter.Matches (article.Abstract).Count < 100);
```

An alternative to calling `AsEnumerable` is to call `ToArray` or `ToList`. The advantage of `AsEnumerable` is that it doesn't force immediate query execution, nor does it create any storage structure.

> Moving query processing from the database server to the client can hurt performance, especially if it means retrieving more rows. A more efficient (though more complex) way to solve our example would be to use SQL CLR integration to expose a function on the database that implemented the regular expression.

We demonstrate combined interpreted and local queries further in Chapter 10.

LINQ to SQL and Entity Framework

Throughout this and the following chapter, we use LINQ to SQL (L2S) and Entity Framework (EF) to demonstrate interpreted queries. We'll now examine the key features of these technologies.

> If you're already familiar with L2S, take an advance look at Table 8-1 (at end of this section) for a summary of the API differences with respect to querying.

LINQ to SQL Versus Entity Framework

Both LINQ to SQL and Entity Framework are LINQ-enabled object-relational mappers. The essential difference is that EF allows for stronger decoupling between the database schema and the classes that you query. Instead of querying classes that closely represent the database schema, you query a higher-level abstraction described by an *Entity Data Model*. This offers extra flexibility, but incurs a cost in both performance and simplicity.

L2S was written by the C# team and was released with Framework 3.5; EF was written by the ADO.NET team and was released later as part of Service Pack 1. L2S has since been taken over by the ADO.NET team. This has resulted in the product receiving only minor improvements in Framework 4.0, with the team concentrating more on EF.

EF has improved considerably in Framework 4.0, although each technology still has unique strengths. L2S's strengths are ease of use, simplicity, performance, and the quality of its SQL translations. EF's strength is its flexibility in creating sophisticated mappings between the database and entity classes. EF also allows for databases other than SQL Server via a *provider model* (L2S also features a provider model, but this was made internal to encourage third parties to focus on EF instead).

A welcome enhancement in EF 4.0 is that it now supports (almost) the same querying functionality as L2S. This means that the LINQ-to-db queries that we demonstrate in this book work with either technology. Further, it makes L2S excellent for learning how to query databases in LINQ—because it keeps the object-relational side of things simple while you learn querying principles that also work with EF.

LINQ to SQL Entity Classes

L2S allows you to use any class to represent data, as long as you decorate it with appropriate attributes. Here's a simple example:

```
[Table]
public class Customer
{
  [Column(IsPrimaryKey=true)]
  public int ID;

  [Column]
  public string Name;
}
```

The [Table] attribute, in the System.Data.Linq.Mapping namespace, tells L2S that an object of this type represents a row in a database table. By default, it assumes the table name matches the class name; if this is not the case, you can specify the table name as follows:

```
[Table (Name="Customers")]
```

A class decorated with the [Table] attribute is called an *entity* in L2S. To be useful, its structure must closely—or exactly—match that of a database table, making it a low-level construct.

The [Column] attribute flags a field or property that maps to a column in a table. If the column name differs from the field or property name, you can specify the column name as follows:

```
[Column (Name="FullName")]
public string Name;
```

The IsPrimaryKey property in the [Column] attribute indicates that the column partakes in the table's primary key and is required for maintaining object identity, as well as allowing updates to be written back to the database.

Instead of defining public fields, you can define public properties in conjunction with private fields. This allows you to write validation logic into the property accessors. If you take this route, you can optionally instruct L2S to bypass your property accessors and write to the field directly when populating from the database:

```
string _name;

[Column (Storage="_name")]
public string Name { get { return _name; } set { _name = value; } }
```

Column(Storage="_name") tells L2S to write directly to the _name field (rather than the Name property) when populating the entity. L2S's use of reflection allows the field to be private—as in this example.

 You can generate entity classes automatically from a database using either Visual Studio (add a new "LINQ to SQL Classes" project item) or with the *SqlMetal* command-line tool.

Entity Framework Entity Classes

As with L2S, EF lets you use any class to represent data (although you have to implement special interfaces if you want functionality such as navigation properties).

The following entity class, for instance, represents a customer that ultimately maps to a *customer* table in the database:

```
// You'll need to reference System.Data.Entity.dll

[EdmEntityType (NamespaceName = "NutshellModel", Name = "Customer")]
public partial class Customer
{
    [EdmScalarPropertyAttribute (EntityKeyProperty = true, IsNullable = false)]
    public int ID { get; set; }

    [EdmScalarProperty (EntityKeyProperty = false, IsNullable = false)]
    public string Name { get; set; }
}
```

Unlike with L2S, however, a class such as this is not enough on its own. Remember that with EF, you're not querying the database directly—you're querying a higher-level model called the *Entity Data Model* (EDM). There needs to be some way to describe the EDM, and this is most commonly done via an XML file with an *.edmx* extension, which contains three parts:

- The *conceptual model*, which describes the EDM in isolation of the database
- The *store model*, which describes the database schema
- The *mapping*, which describes how the conceptual model maps to the store

The easiest way to create an *.edmx* file is to add an "ADO.NET Entity Data Model" project item in Visual Studio and then follow the wizard for generating entities from a database. This creates not only the *.edmx* file, but the entity classes as well.

 The entity classes in EF map to the *conceptual model*. The types that support querying and updating the conceptual model are collectively called *Object Services*.

The designer assumes that you initially want a simple 1:1 mapping between tables and entities. You can enrich this, however, by tweaking the EDM either with the designer or by editing the underlying *.edmx* file that it creates for you. Here are some of the things you can do:

- Map several tables into one entity.
- Map one table into several entities.
- Map inherited types to tables using the three standard kinds of strategies popular in the ORM world.

The three kinds of inheritance strategies are:

Table per hierarchy
A single table maps to a whole class hierarchy. The table contains a discriminator column to indicate which type each row should map to.

Table per type
A single table maps to one type, meaning that an inherited type maps to several tables. EF generates a SQL JOIN when you query an entity, to merge all its base types together.

Table per concrete type
A separate table maps to each concrete type. This means that a base type maps to several tables and EF generates a SQL UNION when you query for entities of a base type.

(In contrast, L2S supports only table per hierarchy.)

The EDM is complex: a thorough discussion can fill hundreds of pages! A good book that describes this in detail is Julia Lerman's *Programming Entity Framework*.

EF also lets you query through the EDM without LINQ—using a textual language called Entity SQL (ESQL). This can be useful for dynamically constructed queries.

DataContext and ObjectContext

Once you've defined entity classes (and an EDM in the case of EF), you can start querying. The first step is to instantiate a `DataContext` (L2S) or `ObjectContext` (EF), specifying a connection string:

```
var l2sContext = new DataContext ("database connection string");
var efContext = new ObjectContext ("entity connection string");
```

Instantiating a `DataContext`/`ObjectContext` directly is a low-level approach and is good for demonstrating how the classes work. More typically, though, you instantiate a *typed context* (a subclassed version of these classes), a process we'll describe shortly.

With L2S, you pass in the database connection string; with EF, you must pass an *entity connection string*, which incorporates the database connection string plus information on how to find the EDM. (If you've created an EDM in Visual Studio, you can find the entity connection string for your EDM in the *app.config* file.)

You can then obtain a queryable object calling `GetTable` (L2S) or `CreateObjectSet` (EF). The following example uses the `Customer` class that we defined earlier:

```
var context = new DataContext ("database connection string");
Table<Customer> customers = context.GetTable <Customer>();

Console.WriteLine (customers.Count());          // # of rows in table.

Customer cust = customers.Single (c => c.ID == 2);  // Retrieves Customer
                                                     // with ID of 2.
```

Here's the same thing with EF:

```
var context = new ObjectContext ("entity connection string");
context.DefaultContainerName = "NutshellEntities";
ObjectSet<Customer> customers = context.CreateObjectSet<Customer>();

Console.WriteLine (customers.Count());          // # of rows in table.

Customer cust = customers.Single (c => c.ID == 2);  // Retrieves Customer
                                                     // with ID of 2.
```

The `Single` operator is ideal for retrieving a row by primary key. Unlike `First`, it throws an exception if more than one element is returned.

A `DataContext`/`ObjectContext` object does two things. First, it acts as a factory for generating objects that you can query. Second, it keeps track of any changes that you make to your entities so that you can write them back. We can continue our previous example to update a customer with L2S as follows:

```
Customer cust = customers.OrderBy (c => c.Name).First();
cust.Name = "Updated Name";
context.SubmitChanges();
```

With EF, the only difference is that you call `SaveChanges` instead:

```
Customer cust = customers.OrderBy (c => c.Name).First();
cust.Name = "Updated Name";
context.SaveChanges();
```

Typed contexts

Having to call `GetTable<Customer>()` or `CreateObjectSet<Customer>()` all the time is awkward. A better approach is to subclass `DataContext`/`ObjectContext` for a particular database, adding properties that do this for each entity. This is called a *typed context*:

```
class NutshellContext : DataContext    // For LINQ to SQL
{
  public Table<Customer> Customers
  {
    get { return GetTable<Customer>(); }
  }
  // ... and so on, for each table in the database
}
```

Here's the same thing for EF:

```
class NutshellContext : ObjectContext    // For Entity Framework
{
  public ObjectSet<Customer> Customers
  {
    get { return CreateObjectSet<Customer>(); }
  }
  // ... and so on, for each entity in the conceptual model
}
```

You can then simply do this:

```
var context = new NutshellContext ("connection string");
Console.WriteLine (context.Customers.Count());
```

If you use Visual Studio to create a "LINQ to SQL Classes" or "ADO.NET Entity Data Model" project item, it builds a typed context for you automatically. The designers can also do additional work such as pluralizing identifiers—in this example, it's `context.Customers` and not `context.Customer`, even though the SQL table and entity class are both called `Customer`.

Disposing DataContext/ObjectContext

Although `DataContext`/`ObjectContext` implement `IDisposable`, you can (in general) get away without disposing instances. Disposing forces the context's connection to dispose—but this is usually unnecessary because L2S and EF close connections automatically whenever you finish retrieving results from a query.

Disposing a context can actually be problematic because of lazy evaluation. Consider the following:

```
IQueryable<Customer> GetCustomers (string prefix)
{
    using (var dc = new NutshellContext ("connection string"))
        return dc.GetTable<Customer>()
                 .Where (c => c.Name.StartsWith (prefix));
}
...
foreach (Customer c in GetCustomers ("a"))
    Console.WriteLine (c.Name);
```

This will fail because the query is evaluated when we enumerate it—which is *after* disposing its `DataContext`.

There are some caveats, though, on not disposing contexts:

- It relies on the connection object releasing all unmanaged resources on the `Close` method. While this holds true with `SqlConnection`, it's theoretically possible for a third-party connection to keep resources open if you call `Close` but not `Dispose` (though this would arguably violate the contract defined by `IDbConnection.Close`).

- If you manually call `GetEnumerator` on a query (instead of using `foreach`) and then fail to either dispose the enumerator or consume the sequence, the connection will remain open. Disposing the `DataContext`/`ObjectContext` provides a backup in such scenarios.

- Some people feel that it's tidier to dispose contexts (and all objects that implement `IDisposable`).

If you want to explicitly dispose contexts, you must pass a `DataContext`/`Object Context` instance into methods such as `GetCustomers` to avoid the problem described.

Object tracking

A `DataContext`/`ObjectContext` instance keeps track of all the entities it instantiates, so it can feed the same ones back to you whenever you request the same rows in a table. In other words, a context in its lifetime will never emit two separate entities that refer to the same row in a table (where a row is identified by primary key).

You can disable this behavior in L2S by setting `ObjectTrackin gEnabled` to `false` on the `DataContext` object. In EF, you can disable change tracking on a per-type basis:

```
context.Customers.MergeOption = MergeOption.NoTracking;
```

Disabling object tracking also prevents you from submitting updates to the data.

To illustrate object tracking, suppose the customer whose name is alphabetically first also has the lowest ID. In the following example, a and b will reference the same object:

```
var context = new NutshellContext ("connection string");

Customer a = context.Customers.OrderBy (c => c.Name).First();
Customer b = context.Customers.OrderBy (c => c.ID).First();
```

This has a couple of interesting consequences. First, consider what happens when L2S or EF encounters the second query. It starts by querying the database—and obtaining a single row. It then reads the primary key of this row and performs a lookup in the context's entity cache. Seeing a match, it returns the existing object *without updating any values*. So, if another user had just updated that customer's Name in the database, the new value would be ignored. This is essential for avoiding unexpected side effects (the `Customer` object could be in use elsewhere) and also for managing concurrency. If you had altered properties on the `Customer` object and not yet called `SubmitChanges`/`SaveChanges`, you wouldn't want your properties automatically overwritten.

To get fresh information from the database, you must either instantiate a new context or call its `Refresh` method, passing in the entity or entities that you want refreshed.

The second consequence is that you cannot explicitly project into an entity type—to select a subset of the row's columns—without causing trouble. For example, if you want to retrieve only a customer's name, any of the following approaches is valid:

```
customers.Select (c => c.Name);
customers.Select (c => new { Name = c.Name } );
customers.Select (c => new MyCustomType { Name = c.Name } );
```

The following, however, is not:

```
customers.Select (c => new Customer { Name = c.Name } );
```

This is because the `Customer` entities will end up partially populated. So, the next time you perform a query that requests *all* customer columns, you get the same cached `Customer` objects with only the `Name` property populated.

LINQ Queries

In a multitier application, you cannot use a single static instance of a `DataContext` or `ObjectContext` in the middle tier to handle all requests, because contexts are not thread-safe. Instead, middle-tier methods must create a fresh context per client request. This is actually beneficial because it shifts the burden in handling simultaneous updates to the database server, which is properly equipped for the job. A database server, for instance, will apply transaction isolation-level semantics.

Associations

The entity generation tools perform another useful job. For each relationship defined in your database, they generate properties on each side that allow you to query that relationship. For example, suppose we define a customer and purchase table in a one-to-many relationship:

```
create table Customer
(
  ID int not null primary key,
  Name varchar(30) not null
)

create table Purchase
(
  ID int not null primary key,
  CustomerID int references Customer (ID),
  Description varchar(30) not null,
  Price decimal not null
)
```

With automatically generated entity classes, we can write queries such as this:

```
var context = new NutshellContext ("connection string");

// Retrieve all purchases made by the first customer (alphabetically):

Customer cust1 = context.Customers.OrderBy (c => c.Name).First();
foreach (Purchase p in cust1.Purchases)
  Console.WriteLine (p.Price);

// Retrieve the customer who made the lowest value purchase:

Purchase cheapest = context.Purchases.OrderBy (p => p.Price).First();
Customer cust2 = cheapest.Customer;
```

Further, if cust1 and cust2 happened to refer to the same customer, c1 and c2 would *refer to the same object*: cust1==cust2 would return true.

Let's examine the signature of the automatically generated Purchases property on the Customer entity. With L2S:

```
[Association (Storage="_Purchases", OtherKey="CustomerID")]
public EntitySet <Purchase> Purchases { get {...} set {...} }
```

With EF:

```
[EdmRelationshipNavigationProperty ("NutshellModel", "FK...", "Purchase")]
public EntityCollection<Purchase> Purchases { get {...} set {...} }
```

An `EntitySet` or `EntityCollection` is like a predefined query, with a built-in `Where` clause that extracts related entities. The `[Association]` attribute gives L2S the information it needs to formulate the SQL query; the `[EdmRelationshipNavigation Property]` attribute tells EF where to look in the EDM for information about that relationship.

As with any other type of query, you get deferred execution. With L2S, an `EntitySet` is populated when you enumerate over it; with EF, an `EntityCollection` is populated when you explicitly call its `Load` method.

Here's the `Purchases.Customer` property, on the other side of the relationship, with L2S:

```
[Association (Storage="_Customer",ThisKey="CustomerID",IsForeignKey=true)]
public Customer Customer { get {...} set {...} }
```

Although the property is of type `Customer`, its underlying field (`_Customer`) is of type `EntityRef`. The `EntityRef` type implements deferred loading, so the related `Customer` is not retrieved from the database until you actually ask for it.

EF works in the same way, except that it doesn't populate the property simply by you accessing it: you must call `Load` on its `EntityReference` object. This means EF contexts must expose properties for both the actual parent object and its `EntityRe ference` wrapper:

```
[EdmRelationshipNavigationProperty ("NutshellModel", "FK...", "Customer")]
public Customer Customer { get {...} set {...} }

public EntityReference<Customer> CustomerReference { get; set; }
```

> You can make EF behave like L2S and have it populate `Entity Collections` and `EntityReferences` simply by virtue of their properties being accessed as follows:
>
> ```
> context.ContextOptions.DeferredLoadingEnabled = true;
> ```

Deferred Execution with L2S and EF

L2S and EF queries are subject to deferred execution, just like local queries. This allows you to build queries progressively. There is one aspect, however, in which L2S/EF have special deferred execution semantics, and that is when a subquery appears inside a `Select` expression:

- With local queries, you get double deferred execution, because from a functional perspective, you're selecting a sequence of *queries*. So, if you enumerate the outer result sequence, but never enumerate the inner sequences, the subquery will never execute.

- With L2S/EF, the subquery is executed at the same time as the main outer query. This avoids excessive round-tripping.

For example, the following query executes in a single round trip upon reaching the first `foreach` statement:

```
var context = new NutshellContext ("connection string");

var query = from c in context.Customers
            select
                from p in c.Purchases
                select new { c.Name, p.Price };

foreach (var customerPurchaseResults in query)
    foreach (var namePrice in customerPurchaseResults)
        Console.WriteLine (namePrice.Name + " spent " + namePrice.Price);
```

Any `EntitySets`/`EntityCollections` that you explicitly project are fully populated in a single round trip:

```
var query = from c in context.Customers
            select new { c.Name, c.Purchases };

foreach (var row in query)
    foreach (Purchase p in row.Purchases)    // No extra round-tripping
        Console.WriteLine (row.Name + " spent " + p.Price);
```

But if we enumerate `EntitySet`/`EntityCollection` properties without first having projected, deferred execution rules apply. In the following example, L2S and EF execute another `Purchases` query on each loop iteration:

```
context.ContextOptions.DeferredLoadingEnabled = true;   // For EF only.

foreach (Customer c in context.Customers)
    foreach (Purchase p in c.Purchases)    // Another SQL round-trip
        Console.WriteLine (c.Name + " spent " + p.Price);
```

This model is advantageous when you want to *selectively* execute the inner loop, based on a test that can be performed only on the client:

```
foreach (Customer c in context.Customers)
    if (myWebService.HasBadCreditHistory (c.ID))
        foreach (Purchase p in c.Purchases)    // Another SQL round trip
            Console.WriteLine (...);
```

(In Chapter 9, we will explore `Select` subqueries in more detail, in "Projecting" on page 369.)

We've seen that you can avoid round-tripping by explicitly projecting associations. L2S and EF offer other mechanisms for this too, which we cover in the following two sections.

DataLoadOptions

The `DataLoadOptions` class is specific to L2S. It has two distinct uses:

- It lets you specify, in advance, a filter for `EntitySet` associations (`AssociateWith`).

- It lets you request that certain `EntitySet`s be eagerly loaded, to lessen round-tripping (`LoadWith`).

Specifying a filter in advance

Let's refactor our previous example as follows:

```
foreach (Customer c in context.Customers)
  if (myWebService.HasBadCreditHistory (c.ID))
    ProcessCustomer (c);
```

We'll define `ProcessCustomer` like this:

```
void ProcessCustomer (Customer c)
{
  Console.WriteLine (c.ID + " " + c.Name);
  foreach (Purchase p in c.Purchases)
    Console.WriteLine ("  - purchased a " + p.Description);
}
```

Now suppose we want to feed `ProcessCustomer` only a *subset* of each customer's purchases; say, the high-value ones. Here's one solution:

```
foreach (Customer c in context.Customers)
  if (myWebService.HasBadCreditHistory (c.ID))
    ProcessCustomer (c.ID,
                     c.Name,
                     c.Purchases.Where (p => p.Price > 1000));
...
void ProcessCustomer (int custID, string custName,
                      IEnumerable<Purchase> purchases)
{
  Console.WriteLine (custID + " " + custName);
  foreach (Purchase p in purchases)
    Console.WriteLine ("  - purchased a " + p.Description);
}
```

This is messy. It would get messier still if `ProcessCustomer` required more `Customer` fields. A better solution is to use `DataLoadOptions`'s `AssociateWith` method:

```
DataLoadOptions options = new DataLoadOptions();
options.AssociateWith <Customer>
 (c => c.Purchases.Where (p => p.Price > 1000));
context.LoadOptions = options;
```

This instructs our `DataContext` instance always to filter a `Customer`'s `Purchases` using the given predicate. We can now use the original version of `ProcessCustomer`.

`AssociateWith` doesn't change deferred execution semantics. When a particular relationship is used, it simply instructs to implicitly add a particular filter to the equation.

Eager loading

The second use for a `DataLoadOptions` is to request that certain `EntitySet`s be eagerly loaded with their parent. For instance, suppose you want to load all customers and their purchases in a single SQL round trip:

```
DataLoadOptions options = new DataLoadOptions();
options.LoadWith <Customer> (c => c.Purchases);
context.LoadOptions = options;

foreach (Customer c in context.Customers)      // One round trip:
  foreach (Purchase p in c.Purchases)
    Console.WriteLine (c.Name + " bought a " + p.Description);
```

This instructs that whenever a Customer is retrieved, its Purchases should also be retrieved at the same time. You can combine LoadWith with AssociateWith. The following instructs that whenever a customer is retrieved, its *high-value* purchases should be retrieved in the same round trip:

```
options.LoadWith <Customer> (c => c.Purchases);
options.AssociateWith <Customer>
  (c => c.Purchases.Where (p => p.Price > 1000));
```

Eager Loading in Entity Framework

You can request in EF that associations be eagerly loaded with the Include method. The following enumerates over each customer's purchases—while generating just one SQL query:

```
foreach (var c in context.Customers.Include ("Purchases"))
  foreach (var p in c.Purchases)
    Console.WriteLine (p.Description);
```

Include can be used with arbitrary breadth and depth. For example, if each Purchase also had PurchaseDetails and SalesPersons navigation properties, the entire nested structure could be eagerly loaded as follows:

```
context.Customers.Include ("Purchases.PurchaseDetails")
                 .Include ("Purchases.SalesPersons")
```

Updates

L2S and EF also keep track of changes that you make to your entities and allow you to write them back to the database by calling SubmitChanges on the DataContext object, or SaveChanges on the ObjectContext object.

L2S's Table<> class provides InsertOnSubmit and DeleteOnSubmit methods for inserting and deleting rows in a table; EF's ObjectSet<> class provides AddObject and DeleteObject methods to do the same thing. Here's how to insert a row:

```
var context = new NutshellContext ("connection string");

Customer cust = new Customer { ID=1000, Name="Bloggs" };
context.Customers.InsertOnSubmit (cust);   // AddObject with EF
context.SubmitChanges();                   // SaveChanges with EF
```

We can later retrieve that row, update it, and then delete it:

```
var context = new NutshellContext ("connection string");

Customer cust = context.Customers.Single (c => c.ID == 1000);
cust.Name = "Bloggs2";
```

```
context.SubmitChanges();                        // Updates the customer

context.Customers.DeleteOnSubmit (cust);  // DeleteObject with EF
context.SubmitChanges();                        // Deletes the customer
```

SubmitChanges/SaveChanges gathers all the changes that were made to its entities since the context's creation (or the last save), and then executes a SQL statement to write them to the database. Any TransactionScope is honored; if none is present, it wraps all statements in a new transaction.

You can also add new or existing rows to an EntitySet/EntityCollection by calling Add. L2S and EF automatically populate the foreign keys when you do this (after calling SubmitChanges or SaveChanges):

```
Purchase p1 = new Purchase { ID=100, Description="Bike",  Price=500 };
Purchase p2 = new Purchase { ID=101, Description="Tools", Price=100 };

Customer cust = context.Customers.Single (c => c.ID == 1);

cust.Purchases.Add (p1);
cust.Purchases.Add (p2);

context.SubmitChanges();  // (or SaveChanges with EF)
```

 If you don't want the burden of allocating unique keys, you can use either an auto-incrementing field (IDENTITY in SQL Server) or a Guid for the primary key.

In this example, L2S/EF automatically writes 1 into the CustomerID column of each of the new purchases (L2S knows to do this because of the association attribute that we defined on the Purchases property; EF knows to do this because of information in the EDM).

```
[Association (Storage="_Purchases", OtherKey="CustomerID")]
public EntitySet <Purchase> Purchases { get {...} set {...} }
```

If the Customer and Purchase entities were generated by the Visual Studio designer or the *SqlMetal* command-line tool, the generated classes would include further code to keep the two sides of each relationship in sync. In other words, assigning the Purchase.Customer property would automatically add the new customer to the Customer.Purchases entity set—and vice versa. We can illustrate this by rewriting the preceding example as follows:

```
var context = new NutshellContext ("connection string");

Customer cust = context.Customers.Single (c => c.ID == 1);
new Purchase { ID=100, Description="Bike",  Price=500, Customer=cust };
new Purchase { ID=101, Description="Tools", Price=100, Customer=cust };

context.SubmitChanges();  // (SaveChanges with EF)
```

When you remove a row from an `EntitySet`/`EntityCollection`, its foreign key field is automatically set to `null`. The following disassociates our two recently added purchases from their customer:

```
var context = new NutshellContext ("connection string");

Customer cust = context.Customers.Single (c => c.ID == 1);

cust.Purchases.Remove (cust.Purchases.Single (p => p.ID == 100));
cust.Purchases.Remove (cust.Purchases.Single (p => p.ID == 101));

context.SubmitChanges();    // Submit SQL to database (SaveChanges in EF)
```

Because this tries to set each purchase's `CustomerID` field to `null`, `Purchase.CustomerID` must be nullable in the database; otherwise, an exception is thrown. (Further, the `CustomerID` field or property in the entity class must be a nullable type.)

To delete child entities entirely, remove them from the `Table<>` or `ObjectSet<>` instead. With L2S:

```
var c = context;
c.Purchases.DeleteOnSubmit (c.Purchases.Single (p => p.ID == 100));
c.Purchases.DeleteOnSubmit (c.Purchases.Single (p => p.ID == 101));
c.SubmitChanges();          // Submit SQL to database
```

With EF:

```
var c = context;
c.Purchases.DeleteObject (c.Purchases.Single (p => p.ID == 100));
c.Purchases.DeleteObject (c.Purchases.Single (p => p.ID == 101));
c.SaveChanges();            // Submit SQL to database
```

API Differences Between L2S and EF

As we've seen, L2S and EF are similar in the aspect of querying with LINQ and performing updates. Table 8-1 summarizes the API differences.

Table 8-1. API differences between L2S and EF

Purpose	LINQ to SQL	Entity Framework
Gatekeeper class for all CRUD operations	DataContext	ObjectContext
Method to (lazily) retrieve all entities of a given type from the store	GetTable	CreateObjectSet
Type returned by the above method	Table<T>	ObjectSet<T>
Method to update the store with any additions, modifications, or deletions to entity objects	SubmitChanges	SaveChanges
Method to add a new entity to the store when the context is updated	InsertOnSubmit	AddObject
Method to delete an entity from the store when the context is updated	DeleteOnSubmit	DeleteObject
Type to represent one side of a relationship property, when that side has a multiplicity of many	EntitySet<T>	EntityCollection<T>

Purpose	LINQ to SQL	Entity Framework
Type to represent one side of a relationship property, when that side has a multiplicity of one	EntityRef<T>	EntityReference<T>
Default strategy for loading relationship properties	Lazy	Explicit
Construct that enables eager loading	DataLoadOptions	.Include()

Building Query Expressions

So far in this chapter, when we've needed to dynamically compose queries, we've done so by conditionally chaining query operators. Although this is adequate in many scenarios, sometimes you need to work at a more granular level and dynamically compose the lambda expressions that feed the operators.

In this section, we'll assume the following Product class:

```
[Table] public partial class Product
{
  [Column(IsPrimaryKey=true)] public int ID;
  [Column]                    public string Description;
  [Column]                    public bool Discontinued;
  [Column]                    public DateTime LastSale;
}
```

Delegates Versus Expression Trees

Recall that:

- Local queries, which use Enumerable operators, take delegates.
- Interpreted queries, which use Queryable operators, take expression trees.

We can see this by comparing the signature of the Where operator in Enumerable and Queryable:

```
public static IEnumerable<TSource> Where<TSource> (this
  IEnumerable<TSource> source, Func<TSource,bool> predicate)

public static IQueryable<TSource> Where<TSource> (this
  IQueryable<TSource> source, Expression<Func<TSource,bool>> predicate)
```

When embedded within a query, a lambda expression looks identical whether it binds to Enumerable's operators or Queryable's operators:

```
IEnumerable<Product> q1 = localProducts.Where (p => !p.Discontinued);
IQueryable<Product>  q2 = sqlProducts.Where   (p => !p.Discontinued);
```

When you assign a lambda expression to an intermediate variable, however, you must be explicit on whether to resolve to a delegate (i.e., Func<>) or an expression tree (i.e., Expression<Func<>>). In the following example, predicate1 and predicate2 are not interchangeable:

```
Func <Product, bool> predicate1 = p => !p.Discontinued;
IEnumerable<Product> q1 = localProducts.Where (predicate1);

Expression <Func <Product, bool>> predicate2 = p => !p.Discontinued;
IQueryable<Product> q2 = sqlProducts.Where (predicate2);
```

Compiling expression trees

You can convert an expression tree to a delegate by calling Compile. This is of particular value when writing methods that return reusable expressions. To illustrate, we'll add a static method to the Product class that returns a predicate evaluating to true if a product is not discontinued and has sold in the past 30 days:

```
public partial class Product
{
  public static Expression<Func<Product, bool>> IsSelling()
  {
    return p => !p.Discontinued && p.LastSale > DateTime.Now.AddDays (-30);
  }
}
```

(We've defined this in a separate partial class to avoid being overwritten by an automatic DataContext generator such as Visual Studio's code generator.)

The method just written can be used both in interpreted and in local queries:

```
void Test()
{
  var dataContext = new NutshellContext ("connection string");
  Product[] localProducts = dataContext.Products.ToArray();

  IQueryable<Product> sqlQuery =
    dataContext.Products.Where (Product.IsSelling());

  IEnumerable<Product> localQuery =
    localProducts.Where (Product.IsSelling.Compile());
}
```

> You cannot convert in the reverse direction, from a delegate to an expression tree. This makes expression trees more versatile.

AsQueryable

The AsQueryable operator lets you write whole *queries* that can run over either local or remote sequences:

```
IQueryable<Product> FilterSortProducts (IQueryable<Product> input)
{
  return from p in input
         where ...
         order by ...
         select p;
}
```

```
void Test()
{
  var dataContext = new NutshellContext ("connection string");
  Product[] localProducts = dataContext.Products.ToArray();

  var sqlQuery   = FilterSortProducts (dataContext.Products);
  var localQuery = FilterSortProducts (localProducts.AsQueryable());
  ...
}
```

AsQueryable wraps IQueryable<T> clothing around a local sequence so that subsequent query operators resolve to expression trees. When you later enumerate over the result, the expression trees are implicitly compiled (at a small performance cost), and the local sequence enumerates as it would ordinarily.

Expression Trees

We said previously, that assigning a lambda expression to a variable of type Expression<TDelegate> causes the C# compiler to emit an expression tree. With some programming effort, you can do the same thing manually at runtime—in other words, dynamically build an expression tree from scratch. The result can be cast to an Expression<TDelegate> and used in LINQ-to-db queries, or compiled into an ordinary delegate by calling Compile.

The Expression DOM

An expression tree is a miniature code DOM. Each node in the tree is represented by a type in the System.Linq.Expressions namespace; these types are illustrated in Figure 8-11.

Figure 8-11. Expression types

From Framework 4.0, this namespace features additional expression types and methods to support language constructs that can appear in code blocks. These are for the benefit of the DLR and not lambda expressions. In other words, code-block-style lambdas still cannot be converted to expression trees:

```
Expression<Func<Customer,bool>> invalid =
    { return true; ]   // Code blocks not permitted
```

The base class for all nodes is the (nongeneric) `Expression` class. The generic `Expression<TDelegate>` class actually means "typed lambda expression" and might have been named `LambdaExpression<TDelegate>` if it wasn't for the clumsiness of this:

```
LambdaExpression<Func<Customer,bool>> f = ...
```

`Expression<>`'s base type is the (nongeneric) `LambdaExpression` class. `LamdbaExpression` provides type unification for lambda expression trees: any typed `Expression<>` can be cast to a `LambdaExpression`.

The thing that distinguishes `LambdaExpression`s from ordinary `Expression`s is that lambda expressions have *parameters*.

To create an expression tree, don't instantiate node types directly; rather, call static methods provided on the `Expression` class. Here are all the methods:

Add	ElementInit	MakeMemberAccess	Or
AddChecked	Equal	MakeUnary	OrElse
And	ExclusiveOr	MemberBind	Parameter
AndAlso	Field	MemberInit	Power
ArrayIndex	GreaterThan	Modulo	Property
ArrayLength	GreaterThanOrEqual	Multiply	PropertyOrField
Bind	Invoke	MultiplyChecked	Quote
Call	Lambda	Negate	RightShift
Coalesce	LeftShift	NegateChecked	Subtract
Condition	LessThan	New	SubtractChecked
Constant	LessThanOrEqual	NewArrayBounds	TypeAs
Convert	ListBind	NewArrayInit	TypeIs
ConvertChecked	ListInit	Not	UnaryPlus
Divide	MakeBinary	NotEqual	

Figure 8-12 shows the expression tree that the following assignment creates:

```
Expression<Func<string, bool>> f = s => s.Length < 5;
```

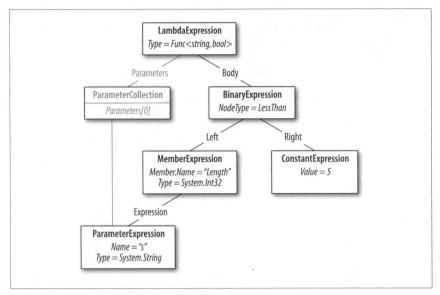

Figure 8-12. Expression tree

We can demonstrate this as follows:

```
Console.WriteLine (f.Body.NodeType);                    // LessThan
Console.WriteLine (((BinaryExpression) f.Body).Right);  // 5
```

Let's now build this expression from scratch. The principle is that you start from the bottom of the tree and work your way up. The bottommost thing in our tree is a `ParameterExpression`, the lambda expression parameter called "s" of type `string`:

```
ParameterExpression p = Expression.Parameter (typeof (string), "s");
```

The next step is to build the `MemberExpression` and `ConstantExpression`. In the former case, we need to access the `Length` *property* of our parameter, "s":

```
MemberExpression stringLength = Expression.Property (p, "Length");
ConstantExpression five = Expression.Constant (5);
```

Next is the `LessThan` comparison:

```
BinaryExpression comparison = Expression.LessThan (stringLength, five);
```

The final step is to construct the lambda expression, which links an expression `Body` to a collection of parameters:

```
Expression<Func<string, bool>> lambda
    = Expression.Lambda<Func<string, bool>> (comparison, p);
```

A convenient way to test our lambda is by compiling it to a delegate:

```
Func<string, bool> runnable = lambda.Compile();

Console.WriteLine (runnable ("kangaroo"));    // False
Console.WriteLine (runnable ("dog"));         // True
```

The easiest way to figure out which expression type to use is to examine an existing lambda expression in the Visual Studio debugger.

We continue this discussion online, at *http://www.albahari.com/expressions/*.

9

LINQ Operators

This chapter describes each of the LINQ query operators. As well as serving as a reference, two of the sections, "Projecting" on page 375 and "Joining" on page 370, cover a number of conceptual areas:

- Projecting object hierarchies
- Joining with Select, SelectMany, Join, and GroupJoin
- Outer range variables in query expressions

All of the examples in this chapter assume that a names array is defined as follows:

```
string[] names = { "Tom", "Dick", "Harry", "Mary", "Jay" };
```

Examples that query a database assume that a typed DataContext variable called dataContext is instantiated as follows:

```
var dataContext = new NutshellContext ("connection string...");

...

public class NutshellContext : DataContext
{
  public NutshellContext (string cxString) : base (cxString) {}

  public Table<Customer> Customers { get { return GetTable<Customer>(); } }
  public Table<Purchase> Purchases { get { return GetTable<Purchase>(); } }
}

[Table] public class Customer
{
  [Column(IsPrimaryKey=true)]  public int ID;
  [Column]                     public string Name;

  [Association (OtherKey="CustomerID")]
  public EntitySet<Purchase> Purchases = new EntitySet<Purchase>();
}
```

```
[Table] public class Purchase
{
    [Column(IsPrimaryKey=true)]   public int ID;
    [Column]                      public int? CustomerID;
    [Column]                      public string Description;
    [Column]                      public decimal Price;
    [Column]                      public DateTime Date;

    EntityRef<Customer> custRef;

    [Association (Storage="custRef",ThisKey="CustomerID",IsForeignKey=true)]
    public Customer Customer
    {
      get { return custRef.Entity; } set { custRef.Entity = value; }
    }
}
```

All the examples in this chapter are preloaded into LINQPad, along with a sample database with a matching schema. You can download LINQPad from *http://www.linqpad.net*.

The entity classes shown are a simplified version of what LINQ to SQL tools typically produce, and do not include code to update the opposing side in a relationship when their entities have been reassigned.

Here are the corresponding SQL table definitions:

```
create table Customer
(
  ID int not null primary key,
  Name varchar(30) not null
)
create table Purchase
(
  ID int not null primary key,
  CustomerID int references Customer (ID),
  Description varchar(30) not null,
  Price decimal not null
)
```

All examples will also work with Entity Framework, except where otherwise indicated. You can build an Entity Framework ObjectContext from these tables by creating a new Entity Data Model in Visual Studio, and then dragging the tables on to the designer surface.

Overview

In this section, we provide an overview of the standard query operators.

The standard query operators fall into three categories:

- Sequence in, sequence out (sequence-to-sequence)
- Sequence in, single element or scalar value out
- Nothing in, sequence out (*generation* methods)

We first present each of the three categories and the query operators they include, and then we take up each individual query operator in detail.

Sequence→Sequence

Most query operators fall into this category—accepting one or more sequences as input and emitting a single output sequence. Figure 9-1 illustrates those operators that restructure the shape of the sequences.

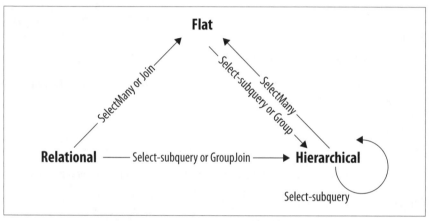

Figure 9-1. Shape-changing operators

Filtering

`IEnumerable<TSource>→IEnumerable<TSource>`

Returns a subset of the original elements.

    Where, Take, TakeWhile, Skip, SkipWhile, Distinct

Projecting

`IEnumerable<TSource>→IEnumerable<TResult>`

Transforms each element with a lambda function. `SelectMany` flattens nested sequences; `Select` and `SelectMany` perform inner joins, left outer joins, cross joins, and non-equi joins with LINQ to SQL and EF.

    Select, SelectMany

Joining

```
IEnumerable<TOuter>, IEnumerable<TInner>→IEnumerable<TResult>
```

Meshes elements of one sequence with another. The joining operators are designed to be efficient with local queries and support inner and left outer joins.

```
Join, GroupJoin
```

Ordering

```
IEnumerable<TSource>→IOrderedEnumerable<TSource>
```

Returns a reordering of a sequence.

```
OrderBy, ThenBy, Reverse
```

Grouping

```
IEnumerable<TSource>→IEnumerable<IGrouping<TSource,TElement>>
```

Groups a sequence into subsequences.

```
GroupBy
```

Set operators

```
IEnumerable<TSource>, IEnumerable<TSource>→IEnumerable<TSource>
```

Takes two same-typed sequences and returns their commonality, sum, or difference.

```
Concat, Union, Intersect, Except
```

Zip operator

```
IEnumerable<TFirst>, IEnumerable<TSecond>→IEnumerable<TResult>
```

Enumerates two sequences in step, applying a function over each element pair.

Conversion methods: Import

```
IEnumerable→IEnumerable<TResult>
```

```
OfType, Cast
```

Conversion methods: Export

```
IEnumerable<TSource>→An array, list, dictionary, lookup, or sequence
```

```
ToArray, ToList, ToDictionary, ToLookup, AsEnumerable, AsQueryable
```

Sequence→Element or Scalar

The following query operators accept an input sequence and emit a single element or scalar value.

Element operators

```
IEnumerable<TSource>→TSource
```

Picks a single element from a sequence.

```
First, FirstOrDefault, Last, LastOrDefault, Single, SingleOrDefault,
ElementAt, ElementAtOrDefault, DefaultIfEmpty
```

Aggregation methods

IEnumerable<TSource>→*scalar*

Performs a computation across a sequence, returning a scalar value (typically a number).

```
Aggregate, Average, Count, LongCount, Sum, Max, Min
```

Quantifiers

IEnumerable<TSource>→*bool*

An aggregation returning true or false.

```
All, Any, Contains, SequenceEqual
```

Void→Sequence

In the third and final category are query operators that produce an output sequence from scratch.

Generation methods

void→IEnumerable<TResult>

Manufactures a simple sequence.

```
Empty, Range, Repeat
```

Filtering

IEnumerable<TSource>→ IEnumerable<TSource>

Method	Description	SQL equivalents
Where	Returns a subset of elements that satisfy a given condition	WHERE
Take	Returns the first count elements and discards the rest	WHERE ROW_NUMBER()... *or* TOP *n* subquery
Skip	Ignores the first count elements and returns the rest	WHERE ROW_NUMBER()... *or* NOT IN (SELECT TOP *n*...)
TakeWhile	Emits elements from the input sequence until the predicate is false	Exception thrown
SkipWhile	Ignores elements from the input sequence until the predicate is false, and then emits the rest	Exception thrown
Distinct	Returns a sequence that excludes duplicates	SELECT DISTINCT...

The "SQL equivalents" column in the reference tables in this chapter do not necessarily correspond to what an IQueryable implementation such as LINQ to SQL will produce. Rather, it indicates what you'd typically use to do the same job if you were writing the SQL query yourself. Where there is no simple translation, the column is left blank. Where there is no translation at all, the column reads "Exception thrown".

Enumerable implementation code, when shown, excludes checking for null arguments and indexing predicates.

With each of the filtering methods, you always end up with either the same number or fewer elements than you started with. You can never get more! The elements are also identical when they come out; they are not transformed in any way.

Where

Argument	Type
Source sequence	IEnumerable<TSource>
Predicate	TSource => bool or (TSource,int) => bool[a]

a Prohibited with LINQ to SQL and Entity Framework.

Query syntax

```
where bool-expression
```

Enumerable.Where implementation

The internal implementation of Enumerable.Where, null checking aside, is functionally equivalent to the following:

```
public static IEnumerable<TSource> Where<TSource>
  (this IEnumerable<TSource> source, Func <TSource, bool> predicate)
{
  foreach (TSource element in source)
    if (predicate (element))
      yield return element;
}
```

Overview

Where returns the elements from the input sequence that satisfy the given predicate.

For instance:

```
string[] names = { "Tom", "Dick", "Harry", "Mary", "Jay" };
IEnumerable<string> query = names.Where (name => name.EndsWith ("y"));

// Result: { "Harry", "Mary", "Jay" }
```

In query syntax:

```
IEnumerable<string> query = from n in names
                            where n.EndsWith ("y")
                            select n;
```

A where clause can appear more than once in a query and be interspersed with let clauses:

```
from n in names
where n.Length > 3
let u = n.ToUpper()
where u.EndsWith ("Y")
select u;                 // Result: { "HARRY", "MARY" }
```

Standard C# scoping rules apply to such queries. In other words, you cannot refer to a variable prior to declaring it with an range variable or a let clause.

Indexed filtering

Where's predicate optionally accepts a second argument, of type int. This is fed with the position of each element within the input sequence, allowing the predicate to use this information in its filtering decision. For example, the following skips every second element:

```
IEnumerable<string> query = names.Where ((n, i) => i % 2 == 0);

// Result: { "Tom", "Harry", "Jay" }
```

An exception is thrown if you use indexed filtering in LINQ to SQL or EF.

SQL LIKE comparisons in LINQ to SQL and EF

The following methods on string translate to SQL's LIKE operator:

```
Contains, StartsWith, EndsWith
```

For instance, c.Name.Contains ("abc") translates to customer.Name LIKE '%abc%' (or more accurately, a parameterized version of this). Contains lets you compare only a against a locally evaluated expression; to compare against another column, you must use the SqlMethods.Like method:

```
... where SqlMethods.Like (c.Description, "%" + c.Name + "%")
```

SqlMethods.Like also lets you perform more complex comparisons (e.g., LIKE 'abc%def%').

< and > string comparisons in LINQ to SQL and EF

You can perform *order* comparison on strings with string's CompareTo method; this maps to SQL's < and > operators:

```
dataContext.Purchases.Where (p => p.Description.CompareTo ("C") < 0)
```

WHERE x IN (..., ..., ...) in LINQ to SQL and EF

With LINQ to SQL and EF, you can apply the `Contains` operator to a local collection within a filter predicate. For instance:

```
string[] chosenOnes = { "Tom", "Jay" };

from c in dataContext.Customers
where chosenOnes.Contains (c.Name)
...
```

This maps to SQL's `IN` operator—in other words:

```
WHERE customer.Name IN ("Tom", "Jay")
```

If the local collection is an array of entities or nonscalar types, LINQ to SQL or EF may instead emit an `EXISTS` clause.

Take and Skip

Argument	Type
Source sequence	IEnumerable<TSource>
Number of elements to take or skip	int

`Take` emits the first *n* elements and discards the rest; `Skip` discards the first *n* elements and emits the rest. The two methods are useful together when implementing a web page allowing a user to navigate through a large set of matching records. For instance, suppose a user searches a book database for the term "mercury," and there are 100 matches. The following returns the first 20:

```
IQueryable<Book> query = dataContext.Books
  .Where  (b => b.Title.Contains ("mercury"))
  .OrderBy (b => b.Title)
  .Take (20);
```

The next query returns books 21 to 40:

```
IQueryable<Book> query = dataContext.Books
  .Where  (b => b.Title.Contains ("mercury"))
  .OrderBy (b => b.Title)
  .Skip (20).Take (20);
```

LINQ to SQL and EF translate `Take` and `Skip` to the `ROW_NUMBER` function in SQL Server 2005, or a `TOP` *n* subquery in earlier versions of SQL Server.

TakeWhile and SkipWhile

Argument	Type
Source sequence	IEnumerable<TSource>
Predicate	TSource => bool or (TSource,int) => bool

TakeWhile enumerates the input sequence, emitting each item, until the given predicate is false. It then ignores the remaining elements:

```
int[] numbers      = { 3, 5, 2, 234, 4, 1 };
var takeWhileSmall = numbers.TakeWhile (n => n < 100);   // { 3, 5, 2 }
```

SkipWhile enumerates the input sequence, ignoring each item until the given predicate is false. It then emits the remaining elements:

```
int[] numbers      = { 3, 5, 2, 234, 4, 1 };
var skipWhileSmall = numbers.SkipWhile (n => n < 100);   // { 234, 4, 1 }
```

TakeWhile and SkipWhile have no translation to SQL and cause a runtime error if used in a LINQ-to-db query.

Distinct

Distinct returns the input sequence, stripped of duplicates. Only the default equality comparer can be used for equality comparison. The following returns distinct letters in a string:

```
char[] distinctLetters = "HelloWorld".Distinct().ToArray();
string s = new string (distinctLetters);                    // HeloWrd
```

We can call LINQ methods directly on a string, because string implements IEnumerable<char>.

Projecting

IEnumerable<TSource>→IEnumerable<TResult>

Method	Description	SQL equivalents
Select	Transforms each input element with the given lambda expression	SELECT
SelectMany	Transforms each input element, and then flattens and concatenates the resultant subsequences	INNER JOIN, LEFT OUTER JOIN, CROSS JOIN

When querying a database, Select and SelectMany are the most versatile joining constructs; for local queries, Join and Group Join are the most *efficient* joining constructs.

Select

Argument	Type
Source sequence	IEnumerable<TSource>
Result selector	TSource => TResult or (TSource,int) => TResult[a]

a Prohibited with LINQ to SQL and Entity Framework.

Query syntax

```
select projection-expression
```

Enumerable implementation

```csharp
public static IEnumerable<TResult> Select<TSource,TResult>
  (this IEnumerable<TSource> source, Func<TSource,TResult> selector)
{
  foreach (TSource element in source)
    yield return selector (element);
}
```

Overview

With Select, you always get the same number of elements that you started with. Each element, however, can be transformed in any manner by the lambda function.

The following selects the names of all fonts installed on the computer (from System.Drawing):

```csharp
IEnumerable<string> query = from f in FontFamily.Families
                            select f.Name;

foreach (string name in query) Console.WriteLine (name);
```

In this example, the select clause converts a FontFamily object to its name. Here's the lambda equivalent:

```csharp
IEnumerable<string> query = FontFamily.Families.Select (f => f.Name);
```

Select statements are often used to project into anonymous types:

```csharp
var query =
  from f in FontFamily.Families
  select new { f.Name, LineSpacing = f.GetLineSpacing (FontStyle.Bold) };
```

A projection with no transformation is sometimes used with query syntax, in order to satisfy the requirement that the query end in a select or group clause. The following selects fonts supporting strikeout:

```csharp
IEnumerable<FontFamily> query =
  from f in FontFamily.Families
  where f.IsStyleAvailable (FontStyle.Strikeout)
  select f;

foreach (FontFamily ff in query) Console.WriteLine (ff.Name);
```

In such cases, the compiler omits the projection when translating to fluent syntax.

Indexed projection

The selector expression can optionally accept an integer argument, which acts as an indexer, providing the expression with the position of each input in the input sequence. This works only with local queries:

```csharp
string[] names = { "Tom", "Dick", "Harry", "Mary", "Jay" };
```

```
IEnumerable<string> query = names
  .Select ((s,i) => i + "=" + s);     //  { "0=Tom", "1=Dick", ... }
```

Select subqueries and object hierarchies

You can nest a subquery in a select clause to build an object hierarchy. The following example returns a collection describing each directory under *D:\source*, with a subcollection of files under each directory:

```
DirectoryInfo[] dirs = new DirectoryInfo (@"d:\source").GetDirectories();

var query =
  from d in dirs
  where (d.Attributes & FileAttributes.System) == 0
  select new
  {
    DirectoryName = d.FullName,
    Created = d.CreationTime,

    Files = from f in d.GetFiles()
            where (f.Attributes & FileAttributes.Hidden) == 0
            select new { FileName = f.Name, f.Length, }
  };

foreach (var dirFiles in query)
{
  Console.WriteLine ("Directory: " + dirFiles.DirectoryName);
  foreach (var file in dirFiles.Files)
    Console.WriteLine ("   " + file.FileName + "Len: " + file.Length);
}
```

The inner portion of this query can be called a *correlated subquery*. A subquery is correlated if it references an object in the outer query—in this case, it references d, the directory being enumerated.

 A subquery inside a Select allows you to map one object hierarchy to another, or map a relational object model to a hierarchical object model.

With local queries, a subquery within a Select causes double-deferred execution. In our example, the files don't get filtered or projected until the inner foreach statement enumerates.

Subqueries and joins in LINQ to SQL and EF

Subquery projections work well in LINQ to SQL and EF and can be used to do the work of SQL-style joins. Here's how we retrieve each customer's name along with their high-value purchases:

```
var query =
  from c in dataContext.Customers
  select new {
              c.Name,
              Purchases = from p in dataContext.Purchases
                          where p.CustomerID == c.ID && p.Price > 1000
                          select new { p.Description, p.Price }
             };

foreach (var namePurchases in query)
{
  Console.WriteLine ("Customer: " + namePurchases.Name);
  foreach (var purchaseDetail in namePurchases.Purchases)
    Console.WriteLine ("  - $$$: " + purchaseDetail.Price);
}
```

 This style of query is ideally suited to interpreted queries. The outer query and subquery are processed as a unit, avoiding unnecessary round-tripping. With local queries, however, it's inefficient because every combination of outer and inner elements must be enumerated to get the few matching combinations. A better choice for local queries is Join or GroupJoin, described in the following sections.

This query matches up objects from two disparate collections, and it can be thought of as a "Join." The difference between this and a conventional database join (or subquery) is that we're not flattening the output into a single two-dimensional result set. We're mapping the relational data to hierarchical data, rather than to flat data.

Here's the same query simplified by using the Purchases association property on the Customer entity:

```
from c in dataContext.Customers
select new
{
  c.Name,
  Purchases = from p in c.Purchases      // Purchases is EntitySet<Purchase>
              where p.Price > 1000
              select new { p.Description, p.Price }
};
```

Both queries are analogous to a left outer join in SQL in the sense that we get all customers in the outer enumeration, regardless of whether they have any purchases. To emulate an inner join—where customers without high-value purchases are excluded—we would need to add a filter condition on the purchases collection:

```
from c in dataContext.Customers
where c.Purchases.Any (p => p.Price > 1000)
select new {
            c.Name,
            Purchases = from p in c.Purchases
                        where p.Price > 1000
                        select new { p.Description, p.Price }
           };
```

This is slightly untidy, however, in that we've written the same predicate (`Price >
1000`) twice. We can avoid this duplication with a `let` clause:

```
from c in dataContext.Customers
let highValueP = from p in c.Purchases
                 where p.Price > 1000
                 select new { p.Description, p.Price }
where highValueP.Any()
select new { c.Name, Purchases = highValueP };
```

This style of query is flexible. By changing `Any` to `Count`, for instance, we can modify
the query to retrieve only customers with at least two high-value purchases:

```
...
where highValueP.Count() >= 2
select new { c.Name, Purchases = highValueP };
```

Projecting into concrete types

Projecting into anonymous types is useful in obtaining intermediate results, but not
so useful if you want to send a result set back to a client, for instance, because
anonymous types can exist only as local variables within a method. An alternative
is to use concrete types for projections, such as DataSets or custom business entity
classes. A custom business entity is simply a class that you write with some properties, similar to a LINQ to SQL [Table] annotated class or an EF Entity, but designed
to hide lower-level (database-related) details. You might exclude foreign key fields
from business entity classes, for instance. Assuming we wrote custom entity classes
called `CustomerEntity` and `PurchaseEntity`, here's how we could project into them:

```
IQueryable<CustomerEntity> query =
  from c in dataContext.Customers
  select new CustomerEntity
  {
    Name = c.Name,
    Purchases =
      (from p in c.Purchases
       where p.Price > 1000
       select new PurchaseEntity {
                                   Description = p.Description,
                                   Value = p.Price
                                 }
      ).ToList()
  };

// Force query execution, converting output to a more convenient List:
List<CustomerEntity> result = query.ToList();
```

Notice that so far, we've not had to use a `Join` or `SelectMany` statement. This is
because we're maintaining the hierarchical shape of the data, as illustrated in Figure 9-2. With LINQ, you can often avoid the traditional SQL approach of flattening
tables into a two-dimensional result set.

Customer	CustomerEntity
Purchase	PurchaseEntity
Purchase	PurchaseEntity

Customer	CustomerEntity
Purchase	PurchaseEntity
Purchase	PurchaseEntity

LINQ to SQL types → **Custom types**

Figure 9-2. Projecting an object hierarchy

SelectMany

Argument	Type
Source sequence	IEnumerable<TSource>
Result selector	TSource => IEnumerable<TResult>
	or (TSource,int) => IEnumerable<TResult>[a]

a Prohibited with LINQ to SQL

Query syntax

```
from identifier1 in enumerable-expression1
from identifier2 in enumerable-expression2
...
```

Enumerable implementation

```
public static IEnumerable<TResult> SelectMany<TSource,TResult>
  (IEnumerable<TSource> source,
   Func <TSource,IEnumerable<TResult>> selector)
{
  foreach (TSource element in source)
    foreach (TResult subElement in selector (element))
      yield return subElement;
}
```

Overview

SelectMany concatenates subsequences into a single flat output sequence.

Recall that for each input element, Select yields exactly one output element. In contrast, SelectMany yields *0..n* output elements. The *0..n* elements come from a subsequence or child sequence that the lambda expression must emit.

SelectMany can be used to expand child sequences, flatten nested collections, and join two collections into a flat output sequence. Using the conveyor belt analogy, SelectMany funnels fresh material onto a conveyor belt. With SelectMany, each input element is the *trigger* for the introduction of fresh material. The fresh material is emitted by the `selector` lambda expression and must be a sequence. In other words, the lambda expression must emit a *child sequence* per input *element*. The final result is a concatenation of the child sequences emitted for each input element.

Starting with a simple example, suppose we have an array of names as follows:

```
string[] fullNames = { "Anne Williams", "John Fred Smith", "Sue Green" };
```

which we wish to convert to a single flat collection of words—in other words:

```
"Anne", "Williams", "John", "Fred", "Smith", "Sue", Green"
```

`SelectMany` is ideal for this task, because we're mapping each input element to a variable number of output elements. All we must do is come up with a `selector` expression that converts each input element to a child sequence. `string.Split` does the job nicely: it takes a string and splits it into words, emitting the result as an array:

```
string testInputElement = "Anne Williams";
string[] childSequence  = testInputElement.Split();

// childSequence is { "Anne", "Williams" };
```

So, here's our `SelectMany` query and the result:

```
IEnumerable<string> query = fullNames.SelectMany (name => name.Split());

foreach (string name in query)
  Console.Write (name + "|"); // Anne|Williams|John|Fred|Smith|Sue|Green|
```

 If you replace `SelectMany` with `Select`, you get the same results in hierarchical form. The following emits a sequence of string *arrays*, requiring nested `foreach` statements to enumerate:

```
IEnumerable<string[]> query =
  fullNames.Select (name => name.Split());

foreach (string[] stringArray in query)
  foreach (string name in stringArray)
    Console.Write (name + "/");
```

The benefit of `SelectMany` is that it yields a single *flat* result sequence.

`SelectMany` is supported in query syntax and is invoked by having an *additional generator*—in other words, an extra `from` clause in the query. The `from` keyword has two meanings in query syntax. At the start of a query, it introduces the original range variable and input sequence. *Anywhere else* in the query, it translates to `SelectMany`. Here's our query in query syntax:

```
IEnumerable<string> query =
  from fullName in fullNames
  from name in fullName.Split()      // Translates to SelectMany
  select name;
```

Note that the additional generator introduces a new query variable—in this case, name. The new query variable becomes the range variable from then on, and the old range variable is demoted to an *outer range variable*.

Outer range variables

In the preceding example, fullName becomes an outer range variable after SelectMany. Outer range variables remain in scope until the query either ends or reaches an into clause. The extended scope of these variables is *the* killer scenario for query syntax over fluent syntax.

To illustrate, we can take the preceding query and include fullName in the final projection:

```
IEnumerable<string> query =
    from fullName in fullNames     // fullName = outer variable
    from name in fullName.Split()  // name = range variable
    select name + " came from " + fullName;

Anne came from Anne Williams
Williams came from Anne Williams
John came from John Fred Smith
...
```

Behind the scenes, the compiler must pull some tricks to resolve outer references. A good way to appreciate this is to try writing the same query in fluent syntax. It's tricky! It gets harder still if you insert a where or orderby clause before projecting:

```
from fullName in fullNames
from name in fullName.Split()
orderby fullName, name
select name + " came from " + fullName;
```

The problem is that SelectMany emits a flat sequence of child elements—in our case, a flat collection of words. The original outer element from which it came (fullName) is lost. The solution is to "carry" the outer element with each child, in a temporary anonymous type:

```
from fullName in fullNames
from x in fullName.Split().Select (name => new { name, fullName } )
orderby x.fullName, x.name
select x.name + " came from " + x.fullName;
```

The only change here is that we're wrapping each child element (name) in an anonymous type that also contains its fullName. This is similar to how a let clause is resolved. Here's the final conversion to fluent syntax:

```
IEnumerable<string> query = fullNames
    .SelectMany (fName => fName.Split()
                                .Select (name => new { name, fName } ))
    .OrderBy (x => x.fName)
    .ThenBy (x => x.name)
    .Select (x => x.name + " came from " + x.fName);
```

Thinking in query syntax

As we just demonstrated, there are good reasons to use query syntax if you need the outer range variable. In such cases, it helps not only to use query syntax, but also to think directly in its terms.

There are two basic patterns when writing additional generators. The first is *expanding and flattening subsequences*. To do this, you call a property or method on an existing query variable in your additional generator. We did this in the previous example:

```
from fullName in fullNames
from name in fullName.Split()
```

Here, we've expanded from enumerating full names to enumerating words. An analogous LINQ-to-db query is when you expand child association properties. The following query lists all customers along with their purchases:

```
IEnumerable<string> query = from c in dataContext.Customers
                            from p in c.Purchases
                            select c.Name + " bought a " + p.Description;

Tom bought a Bike
Tom bought a Holiday
Dick bought a Phone
Harry bought a Car
...
```

Here, we've expanded each customer into a subsequence of purchases.

The second pattern is performing a *cross product* or *cross join*—where every element of one sequence is matched with every element of another. To do this, introduce a generator whose `selector` expression returns a sequence unrelated to a range variable:

```
int[] numbers = { 1, 2, 3 };  string[] letters = { "a", "b" };

IEnumerable<string> query = from n in numbers
                            from l in letters
                            select n.ToString() + l;

RESULT: { "1a", "1b", "2a", "2b", "3a", "3b" }
```

This style of query is the basis of `SelectMany`-style *joins*.

Joining with SelectMany

You can use `SelectMany` to join two sequences, simply by filtering the results of a cross product. For instance, suppose we wanted to match players for a game. We could start as follows:

```
string[] players = { "Tom", "Jay", "Mary" };

IEnumerable<string> query = from name1 in players
                            from name2 in players
                            select name1 + " vs " + name2;
```

```
RESULT: { "Tom vs Tom", "Tom vs Jay", "Tom vs Mary",
          "Jay vs Tom", "Jay vs Jay", "Jay vs Mary",
          "Mary vs Tom", "Mary vs "Jay", "Mary vs Mary" }
```

The query reads: "For every player, reiterate every player, selecting player 1 vs player 2". Although we got what we asked for (a cross join), the results are not useful until we add a filter:

```
IEnumerable<string> query = from name1 in players
                            from name2 in players
                            where name1.CompareTo (name2) < 0
                            orderby name1, name2
                            select name1 + " vs " + name2;

RESULT: { "Jay vs Mary", "Jay vs Tom", "Mary vs Tom" }
```

The filter predicate constitutes the *join condition*. Our query can be called a *non-equi join*, because the join condition doesn't use an equality operator.

We'll demonstrate the remaining types of joins with LINQ to SQL (they'll also work with EF except where we explicitly use a foreign key field).

SelectMany in LINQ to SQL and EF

SelectMany in LINQ to SQL and EF can perform cross joins, non-equi joins, inner joins, and left outer joins. You can use SelectMany with both predefined associations and ad hoc relationships—just as with Select. The difference is that SelectMany returns a flat rather than a hierarchical result set.

A LINQ-to-db cross join is written just as in the preceding section. The following query matches every customer to every purchase (a cross join):

```
var query = from c in dataContext.Customers
            from p in dataContext.Purchases
            select c.Name + " might have bought a " + p.Description;
```

More typically, though, you'd want to match customers to their own purchases only. You achieve this by adding a where clause with a joining predicate. This results in a standard SQL-style equi-join:

```
var query = from c in dataContext.Customers
            from p in dataContext.Purchases
            where c.ID == p.CustomerID
            select c.Name + " bought a " + p.Description;
```

 This translates well to SQL. In the next section, we'll see how it extends to support outer joins. Reformulating such queries with LINQ's Join operator actually makes them *less* extensible—LINQ is opposite to SQL in this sense.

If you have association properties for relationships in your entities, you can express the same query by expanding the subcollection instead of filtering the cross product:

```
from c in dataContext.Customers
from p in c.Purchases
select new { c.Name, p.Description };
```

 Entity Framework doesn't expose foreign keys in the entities, so for recognized relationships you *must* use its association properties rather than joining manually as we did previously.

The advantage is that we've eliminated the joining predicate. We've gone from filtering a cross product to expanding and flattening. Both queries, however, will result in the same SQL.

You can add where clauses to such a query for additional filtering. For instance, if we wanted only customers whose names started with "T", we could filter as follows:

```
from c in dataContext.Customers
where c.Name.StartsWith ("T")
from p in c.Purchases
select new { c.Name, p.Description };
```

This LINQ-to-db query would work equally well if the where clause is moved one line down. If it is a local query, however, moving the where clause down would make it less efficient. With local queries, you should filter *before* joining.

You can introduce new tables into the mix with additional from clauses. For instance, if each purchase had purchase item child rows, you could produce a flat result set of customers with their purchases, each with their purchase detail lines as follows:

```
from c in dataContext.Customers
from p in c.Purchases
from pi in p.PurchaseItems
select new { c.Name, p.Description, pi.DetailLine };
```

Each from clause introduces a new *child* table. To include data from a *parent* table (via an association property), you don't add a from clause—you simply navigate to the property. For example, if each customer has a salesperson whose name you want to query, just do this:

```
from c in dataContext.Customers
select new { Name = c.Name, SalesPerson = c.SalesPerson.Name };
```

You don't use SelectMany in this case because there's no subcollection to flatten. Parent association properties return a single item.

Outer joins with SelectMany

We saw previously that a Select subquery yields a result analogous to a left outer join:

```
from c in dataContext.Customers
select new {
          c.Name,
          Purchases = from p in c.Purchases
                      where p.Price > 1000
```

```
                    select new { p.Description, p.Price }
        };
```

In this example, every outer element (customer) is included, regardless of whether the customer has any purchases. But suppose we rewrite this query with SelectMany, so we can obtain a single flat collection rather than a hierarchical result set:

```
from c in dataContext.Customers
from p in c.Purchases
where p.Price > 1000
select new { c.Name, p.Description, p.Price };
```

In the process of flattening the query, we've switched to an inner join: customers are now included only for whom one or more high-value purchases exist. To get a left outer join with a flat result set, we must apply the DefaultIfEmpty query operator on the inner sequence. This method returns null if its input sequence has no elements. Here's such a query, price predicate aside:

```
from c in dataContext.Customers
from p in c.Purchases.DefaultIfEmpty()
select new { c.Name, p.Description, Price = (decimal?) p.Price };
```

This works perfectly with LINQ to SQL and EF, returning all customers, even if they have no purchases. But if we were to run this as a local query, it would crash, because when p is null, p.Description and p.Price throw a NullReferenceException. We can make our query robust in either scenario as follows:

```
from c in dataContext.Customers
from p in c.Purchases.DefaultIfEmpty()
select new {
            c.Name,
            Descript = p == null ? null : p.Description,
            Price = p == null ? (decimal?) null : p.Price
        };
```

Let's now reintroduce the price filter. We cannot use a where clause as we did before, because it would execute *after* DefaultIfEmpty:

```
from c in dataContext.Customers
from p in c.Purchases.DefaultIfEmpty()
where p.Price > 1000...
```

The correct solution is to splice the Where clause *before* DefaultIfEmpty with a subquery:

```
from c in dataContext.Customers
from p in c.Purchases.Where (p => p.Price > 1000).DefaultIfEmpty()
select new {
            c.Name,
            Descript = p == null ? null : p.Description,
            Price = p == null ? (decimal?) null : p.Price
        };
```

LINQ to SQL and EF translate this to a left outer join. This is an effective pattern for writing such queries.

If you're used to writing outer joins in SQL, you might be tempted to overlook the simpler option of a `Select` subquery for this style of query, in favor of the awkward but familiar SQL-centric flat approach. The hierarchical result set from a `Select` subquery is often better suited to outer join-style queries because there are no additional nulls to deal with.

Joining

`IEnumerable<TOuter>`, `IEnumerable<TInner>→IEnumerable<TResult>`

Method	Description	SQL equivalents
Join	Applies a lookup strategy to match elements from two collections, emitting a flat result set	INNER JOIN
GroupJoin	As above, but emits a *hierarchical* result set	INNER JOIN, LEFT OUTER JOIN

Join and GroupJoin

Join arguments

Argument	Type
Outer sequence	IEnumerable<TOuter>
Inner sequence	IEnumerable<TInner>
Outer key selector	TOuter => TKey
Inner key selector	TInner => TKey
Result selector	(TOuter,TInner) => TResult

GroupJoin arguments

Argument	Type
Outer sequence	IEnumerable<TOuter>
Inner sequence	IEnumerable<TInner>
Outer key selector	TOuter => TKey
Inner key selector	TInner => TKey
Result selector	(TOuter,**IEnumerable<TInner>**) => TResult

Query syntax

```
from outer-var in outer-enumerable
join inner-var in inner-enumerable on outer-key-expr equals inner-key-expr
  [ into identifier ]
```

LINQ Operators

Overview

Join and GroupJoin mesh two input sequences into a single output sequence. Join emits flat output; GroupJoin emits hierarchical output.

Join and GroupJoin provide an alternative strategy to Select and SelectMany. The advantage of Join and GroupJoin is that they execute efficiently over local in-memory collections, since they first load the inner sequence into a keyed lookup, avoiding the need to repeatedly enumerate over every inner element. The disadvantage is that they offer the equivalent of inner and left outer joins only; cross joins and non-equi joins must still be done with Select/SelectMany. With LINQ to SQL and Entity Framework queries, Join and GroupJoin offer no real benefits over Select and SelectMany.

Table 9-1 summarizes the differences between each of the joining strategies.

Table 9-1. Joining strategies

Strategy	Result shape	Local query efficiency	Inner joins	Left outer joins	Cross joins	Non-equi joins
Select + SelectMany	Flat	Bad	Yes	Yes	Yes	Yes
Select + Select	Nested	Bad	Yes	Yes	Yes	Yes
Join	Flat	Good	Yes	-	-	-
GroupJoin	Nested	Good	Yes	Yes	-	-
GroupJoin + SelectMany	Flat	Good	Yes	Yes	-	-

Join

The Join operator performs an inner join, emitting a flat output sequence.

 Entity Framework hides foreign key fields, so you can't manually join across natural relationships (instead, you can query across association properties, as we described in the previous two sections).

The simplest way to demonstrate Join is with LINQ to SQL. The following query lists all customers alongside their purchases, without using an association property:

```
IQueryable<string> query =
    from c in dataContext.Customers
    join p in dataContext.Purchases on c.ID equals p.CustomerID
    select c.Name + " bought a " + p.Description;
```

The results match what we would get from a SelectMany-style query:

```
Tom bought a Bike
Tom bought a Holiday
Dick bought a Phone
Harry bought a Car
```

To see the benefit of `Join` over `SelectMany`, we must convert this to a local query. We can demonstrate this by first copying all customers and purchases to arrays, and then querying the arrays:

```
Customer[] customers = dataContext.Customers.ToArray();
Purchase[] purchases = dataContext.Purchases.ToArray();
var slowQuery = from c in customers
                from p in purchases where c.ID == p.CustomerID
                select c.Name + " bought a " + p.Description;

var fastQuery = from c in customers
                join p in purchases on c.ID equals p.CustomerID
                select c.Name + " bought a " + p.Description;
```

Although both queries yield the same results, the `Join` query is considerably faster because its implementation in `Enumerable` preloads the inner collection (`purchases`) into a keyed lookup.

The query syntax for `join` can be written in general terms as follows:

```
join inner-var in inner-sequence on outer-key-expr equals inner-key-expr
```

Join operators in LINQ differentiate between the *outer sequence* and *inner sequence*. Syntactically:

- The *outer sequence* is the input sequence (in this case, `customers`).

- The *inner sequence* is the new collection you introduce (in this case, `purchases`).

`Join` performs inner joins, meaning customers without purchases are excluded from the output. With inner joins, you can swap the inner and outer sequences in the query and still get the same results:

```
from p in purchases                                  // p is now outer
join c in customers on p.CustomerID equals c.ID      // c is now inner
...
```

You can add further `join` clauses to the same query. If each purchase, for instance, has one or more purchase items, you could join the purchase items as follows:

```
from c in customers
join p in purchases on c.ID equals p.CustomerID      // first join
join pi in purchaseItems on p.ID equals pi.PurchaseID // second join
...
```

`purchases` acts as the *inner* sequence in the first join and as the *outer* sequence in the second join. You could obtain the same results (inefficiently) using nested `foreach` statements as follows:

```
foreach (Customer c in customers)
  foreach (Purchase p in purchases)
    if (c.ID == p.CustomerID)
      foreach (PurchaseItem pi in purchaseItems)
        if (p.ID == pi.PurchaseID)
          Console.WriteLine (c.Name + "," + p.Price + "," + pi.Detail);
```

In query syntax, variables from earlier joins remain in scope—just as outer range variables do with `SelectMany`-style queries. You're also permitted to insert `where` and `let` clauses in between `join` clauses.

Joining on multiple keys

You can join on multiple keys with anonymous types as follows:

```
from x in sequenceX
join y in sequenceY on new { K1 = x.Prop1, K2 = x.Prop2 }
                equals new { K1 = y.Prop3, K2 = y.Prop4 }
...
```

For this to work, the two anonymous types must be structured identically. The compiler then implements each with the same internal type, making the joining keys compatible.

Joining in fluent syntax

The following query syntax join:

```
from c in customers
join p in purchases on c.ID equals p.CustomerID
select new { c.Name, p.Description, p.Price };
```

in fluent syntax is as follows:

```
customers.Join (                    // outer collection
    purchases,                      // inner collection
    c => c.ID,                      // outer key selector
    p => p.CustomerID,              // inner key selector
    (c, p) => new
        { c.Name, p.Description, p.Price }    // result selector
);
```

The result selector expression at the end creates each element in the output sequence. If you have additional clauses prior to projecting, such as `orderby` in this example:

```
from c in customers
join p in purchases on c.ID equals p.CustomerID
orderby p.Price
select c.Name + " bought a " + p.Description;
```

you must manufacture a temporary anonymous type in the result selector in fluent syntax. This keeps both `c` and `p` in scope following the join:

```
customers.Join (                    // outer collection
    purchases,                      // inner collection
    c => c.ID,                      // outer key selector
    p => p.CustomerID,              // inner key selector
    (c, p) => new { c, p } )        // result selector
.OrderBy (x => x.p.Price)
.Select (x => x.c.Name + " bought a " + x.p.Description);
```

Query syntax is usually preferable when joining; it's less fiddly.

GroupJoin

GroupJoin does the same work as Join, but instead of yielding a flat result, it yields a hierarchical result, grouped by each outer element. It also allows left outer joins.

The query syntax for GroupJoin is the same as for Join, but is followed by the into keyword.

Here's the most basic example:

```
IEnumerable<IEnumerable<Purchase>> query =
  from c in customers
  join p in purchases on c.ID equals p.CustomerID
  into custPurchases
  select custPurchases;   // custPurchases is a sequence
```

> An into clause translates to GroupJoin only when it appears directly after a join clause. After a select or group clause, it means *query continuation*. The two uses of the into keyword are quite different, although they have one feature in common: they both introduce a new query variable.

The result is a sequence of sequences, which we could enumerate as follows:

```
foreach (IEnumerable<Purchase> purchaseSequence in query)
  foreach (Purchase p in purchaseSequence)
    Console.WriteLine (p.Description);
```

This isn't very useful, however, because outerSeq has no reference to the outer customer. More commonly, you'd reference the outer range variable in the projection:

```
from c in customers
join p in purchases on c.ID equals p.CustomerID
into custPurchases
select new { CustName = c.Name, custPurchases };
```

This gives the same results as the following (inefficient) Select subquery:

```
from c in customers
select new
{
  CustName = c.Name,
  custPurchases = purchases.Where (p => c.ID == p.CustomerID)
};
```

By default, GroupJoin does the equivalent of a left outer join. To get an inner join—where customers without purchases are excluded—filter on custPurchases:

```
from c in customers join p in purchases on c.ID equals p.CustomerID
into custPurchases
where custPurchases.Any()
select ...
```

Clauses after a group-join into operate on *subsequences* of inner child elements, not *individual* child elements. This means that to filter individual purchases, you'd have to call Where *before* joining:

```
from c in customers
join p in purchases.Where (p2 => p2.Price > 1000)
  on c.ID equals p.CustomerID
into custPurchases ...
```

You can construct lambda queries with GroupJoin as you would with Join.

Flat outer joins

You run into a dilemma if you want both an outer join and a flat result set. Group
Join gives you the outer join; Join gives you the flat result set. The solution is to first
call GroupJoin, and then DefaultIfEmpty on each child sequence, and then finally
SelectMany on the result:

```
from c in customers
join p in purchases on c.ID equals p.CustomerID into custPurchases
from cp in custPurchases.DefaultIfEmpty()
select new
{
  CustName = c.Name,
  Price = cp == null ? (decimal?) null : cp.Price
};
```

DefaultIfEmpty emits a null value if a subsequence of purchases is empty. The second
from clause translates to SelectMany. In this role, it *expands and flattens* all the purchase subsequences, concatenating them into a single sequence of purchase
elements.

Joining with lookups

The Join and GroupJoin methods in Enumerable work in two steps. First, they load
the inner sequence into a *lookup*. Second, they query the outer sequence in combination with the lookup.

A *lookup* is a sequence of groupings that can be accessed directly by key. Another
way to think of it is as a dictionary of sequences—a dictionary that can accept many
elements under each key. Lookups are read-only and defined by the following
interface:

```
public interface ILookup<TKey,TElement> :
  IEnumerable<IGrouping<TKey,TElement>>, IEnumerable
{
  int Count { get; }
  bool Contains (TKey key);
  IEnumerable<TElement> this [TKey key] { get; }
}
```

 The joining operators—like other sequence-emitting
operators—honor deferred or lazy execution semantics. This
means the lookup is not built until you begin enumerating the
output sequence.

You can create and query lookups manually as an alternative strategy to using the joining operators, when dealing with local collections. There are a couple of benefits in doing so:

- You can reuse the same lookup over multiple queries—as well as in ordinary imperative code.
- Querying a lookup is an excellent way of understanding how `Join` and `GroupJoin` work.

The `ToLookup` extension method creates a lookup. The following loads all purchases into a lookup—keyed by their `CustomerID`:

```
ILookup<int?,Purchase> purchLookup =
   purchases.ToLookup (p => p.CustomerID, p => p);
```

The first argument selects the key; the second argument selects the objects that are to be loaded as values into the lookup.

Reading a lookup is rather like reading a dictionary, except that the indexer returns a *sequence* of matching items, rather than a *single* matching item. The following enumerates all purchases made by the customer whose ID is 1:

```
foreach (Purchase p in purchLookup [1])
   Console.WriteLine (p.Description);
```

With a lookup in place, you can write `SelectMany`/`Select` queries that execute as efficiently as `Join`/`GroupJoin` queries. `Join` is equivalent to using `SelectMany` on a lookup:

```
from c in customers
from p in purchLookup [c.ID]
select new { c.Name, p.Description, p.Price };

Tom Bike 500
Tom Holiday 2000
Dick Bike 600
Dick Phone 300
...
```

Adding a call to `DefaultIfEmpty` makes this into an outer join:

```
from c in customers
from p in purchLookup [c.ID].DefaultIfEmpty()
 select new {
            c.Name,
            Descript = p == null ? null : p.Description,
            Price = p == null ? (decimal?) null : p.Price
         };
```

GroupJoin is equivalent to reading the lookup inside a projection:

```
from c in customers
select new {
        CustName = c.Name,
        CustPurchases = purchLookup [c.ID]
     };
```

Enumerable implementations

Here's the simplest valid implementation of `Enumerable.Join`, null checking aside:

```
public static IEnumerable <TResult> Join
                         <TOuter,TInner,TKey,TResult> (
    this IEnumerable <TOuter>       outer,
    IEnumerable <TInner>            inner,
    Func <TOuter,TKey>              outerKeySelector,
    Func <TInner,TKey>              innerKeySelector,
    Func <TOuter,TInner,TResult>    resultSelector)
{
    ILookup <TKey, TInner> lookup = inner.ToLookup (innerKeySelector);
    return
      from outerItem in outer
      from innerItem in lookup [outerKeySelector (outerItem)]
      select resultSelector (outerItem, innerItem);
}
```

GroupJoin's implementation is like that of Join, but simpler:

```
public static IEnumerable <TResult> GroupJoin
                         <TOuter,TInner,TKey,TResult> (
    this IEnumerable <TOuter>       outer,
    IEnumerable <TInner>            inner,
    Func <TOuter,TKey>              outerKeySelector,
    Func <TInner,TKey>              innerKeySelector,
    Func <TOuter,IEnumerable<TInner>,TResult>  resultSelector)
{
    ILookup <TKey, TInner> lookup = inner.ToLookup (innerKeySelector);
    return
      from outerItem in outer
      select resultSelector
        (outerItem, lookup [outerKeySelector (outerItem)]);
}
```

Ordering

IEnumerable<TSource>→IOrderedEnumerable<TSource>

Method	Description	SQL equivalents
OrderBy, ThenBy	Sorts a sequence in ascending order	ORDER BY ...
OrderByDescending, ThenByDescending	Sorts a sequence in descending order	ORDER BY ... DESC
Reverse	Returns a sequence in reverse order	Exception thrown

Ordering operators return the same elements in a different order.

OrderBy, OrderByDescending, ThenBy, and ThenByDescending

OrderBy and OrderByDescending arguments

Argument	Type
Input sequence	IEnumerable<TSource>
Key selector	TSource => TKey

Return type = IOrderedEnumerable<TSource>

ThenBy and ThenByDescending arguments

Argument	Type
Input sequence	IOrderedEnumerable<TSource>
Key selector	TSource => TKey

Query syntax

```
orderby expression1 [descending] [, expression2 [descending] ... ]
```

Overview

OrderBy returns a sorted version of the input sequence, using the keySelector expression to make comparisons. The following query emits a sequence of names in alphabetical order:

```
IEnumerable<string> query = names.OrderBy (s => s);
```

The following sorts names by length:

```
IEnumerable<string> query = names.OrderBy (s => s.Length);

// Result: { "Jay", "Tom", "Mary", "Dick", "Harry" };
```

The relative order of elements with the same sorting key (in this case, Jay/Tom and Mary/Dick) is indeterminate—unless you append a ThenBy operator:

```
IEnumerable<string> query = names.OrderBy (s => s.Length).ThenBy (s => s);

// Result: { "Jay", "Tom", "Dick", "Mary", "Harry" };
```

ThenBy reorders only elements that had the same sorting key in the preceding sort. You can chain any number of ThenBy operators. The following sorts first by length, then by the second character, and finally by the first character:

```
names.OrderBy (s => s.Length).ThenBy (s => s[1]).ThenBy (s => s[0]);
```

The equivalent in query syntax is this:

```
from s in names
orderby s.Length, s[1], s[0]
select s;
```

LINQ also provides `OrderByDescending` and `ThenByDescending` operators, which do the same things, emitting the results in reverse order. The following LINQ-to-db query retrieves purchases in descending order of price, with those of the same price listed alphabetically:

```
dataContext.Purchases.OrderByDescending (p => p.Price)
    .ThenBy (p => p.Description);
```

In query syntax:

```
from p in dataContext.Purchases
orderby p.Price descending, p.Description
select p;
```

Comparers and collations

In a local query, the key selector objects themselves determine the ordering algorithm via their default `IComparable` implementation (see Chapter 7). You can override the sorting algorithm by passing in an `IComparer` object. The following performs a case-insensitive sort:

```
names.OrderBy (n => n, StringComparer.CurrentCultureIgnoreCase);
```

Passing in a comparer is not supported in query syntax, nor in any way by LINQ to SQL or EF. When querying a database, the comparison algorithm is determined by the participating column's collation. If the collation is case-sensitive, you can request a case-insensitive sort by calling `ToUpper` in the key selector:

```
from p in dataContext.Purchases
orderby p.Description.ToUpper()
select p;
```

IOrderedEnumerable and IOrderedQueryable

The ordering operators return special subtypes of `IEnumerable<T>`. Those in `Enumerable` return `IOrderedEnumerable`; those in `Queryable` return `IOrderedQueryable`. These subtypes allow a subsequent `ThenBy` operator to refine rather than replace the existing ordering.

The additional members that these subtypes define are not publicly exposed, so they present like ordinary sequences. The fact that they are different types comes into play when building queries progressively:

```
IOrderedEnumerable<string> query1 = names.OrderBy (s => s.Length);
IOrderedEnumerable<string> query2 = query1.ThenBy (s => s);
```

If we instead declare `query1` of type `IEnumerable<string>`, the second line would not compile—`ThenBy` requires an input of type `IOrderedEnumerable<string>`. You can avoid worrying about this by implicitly typing query variables:

```
var query1 = names.OrderBy (s => s.Length);
var query2 = query1.ThenBy (s => s);
```

Implicit typing can create problems of its own, though. The following will not compile:

```
var query = names.OrderBy (s => s.Length);
query = query.Where (n => n.Length > 3);        // Compile-time error
```

The compiler infers `query` to be of type `IOrderedEnumerable<string>`, based on
`OrderBy`'s output sequence type. However, the `Where` on the next line returns an
ordinary `IEnumerable<string>`, which cannot be assigned back to `query`. You can
work around this either with explicit typing or by calling `AsEnumerable()` after
`OrderBy`:

```
var query = names.OrderBy (s => s.Length).AsEnumerable();
query = query.Where (n => n.Length > 3);                 // OK
```

The equivalent in interpreted queries is to call `AsQueryable`.

Grouping

`IEnumerable<TSource>`→`IEnumerable<IGrouping<TSource,TElement>>`

Method	Description	SQL equivalents
GroupBy	Groups a sequence into subsequences	GROUP BY

GroupBy

Argument	Type
Input sequence	IEnumerable<TSource>
Key selector	TSource => TKey
Element selector (optional)	TSource => TElement
Comparer (optional)	IEqualityComparer<TKey>

Query syntax

```
group element-expression by key-expression
```

Overview

`GroupBy` organizes a flat input sequence into sequences of *groups*. For example, the
following organizes all the files in *c:\temp* by extension:

```
string[] files = Directory.GetFiles ("c:\\temp");

IEnumerable<IGrouping<string,string>> query =
  files.GroupBy (file => Path.GetExtension (file));
```

Or if you're comfortable with implicit typing:

```
var query = files.GroupBy (file => Path.GetExtension (file));
```

Here's how to enumerate the result:

```
```

```
foreach (IGrouping<string,string> grouping in query)
{
  Console.WriteLine ("Extension: " + grouping.Key);
  foreach (string filename in grouping)
    Console.WriteLine ("   - " + filename);
}

Extension: .pdf
  -- chapter03.pdf
  -- chapter04.pdf
Extension: .doc
  -- todo.doc
  -- menu.doc
  -- Copy of menu.doc
...
```

Enumerable.GroupBy works by reading the input elements into a temporary dictionary of lists so that all elements with the same key end up in the same sublist. It then emits a sequence of *groupings*. A grouping is a sequence with a Key property:

```
public interface IGrouping <TKey,TElement> : IEnumerable<TElement>,
                                             IEnumerable
{
  TKey Key { get; }    // Key applies to the subsequence as a whole
}
```

By default, the elements in each grouping are untransformed input elements, unless you specify an elementSelector argument. The following projects each input element to uppercase:

```
files.GroupBy (file => Path.GetExtension (file), file => file.ToUpper());
```

An elementSelector is independent of the keySelector. In our case, this means that the Key on each grouping is still in its original case:

```
Extension: .pdf
  -- CHAPTER03.PDF
  -- CHAPTER04.PDF
Extension: .doc
  -- TODO.DOC
```

Note that the subcollections are not emitted in alphabetical order of key. GroupBy groups only; it does not *sort*; in fact, it preserves the original ordering. To sort, you must add an OrderBy operator:

```
files.GroupBy (file => Path.GetExtension (file), file => file.ToUpper())
     .OrderBy (grouping => grouping.Key);
```

GroupBy has a simple and direct translation in query syntax:

```
group element-expr by key-expr
```

Here's our example in query syntax:

```
from file in files
group file.ToUpper() by Path.GetExtension (file);
```

As with select, group "ends" a query—unless you add a query continuation clause:

```
from file in files
group file.ToUpper() by Path.GetExtension (file) into grouping
orderby grouping.Key
select grouping;
```

Query continuations are often useful in a **group by** query. The next query filters out groups that have fewer than five files in them:

```
from file in files
group file.ToUpper() by Path.GetExtension (file) into grouping
where grouping.Count() < 5
select grouping;
```

 A where after a group by is equivalent to HAVING in SQL. It applies to each subsequence or grouping as a whole, rather than the individual elements.

Sometimes you're interested purely in the result of an aggregation on a grouping and so can abandon the subsequences:

```
string[] votes = { "Bush", "Gore", "Gore", "Bush", "Bush" };

IEnumerable<string> query = from vote in votes
                            group vote by vote into g
                            orderby g.Count() descending
                            select g.Key;

string winner = query.First();    // Bush
```

GroupBy in LINQ to SQL and EF

Grouping works in the same way when querying a database. If you have association properties set up, you'll find, however, that the need to group arises less frequently than with standard SQL. For instance, to select customers with at least two purchases, you don't need to **group**; the following query does the job nicely:

```
from c in dataContext.Customers
where c.Purchases.Count >= 2
select c.Name + " has made " + c.Purchases.Count + " purchases";
```

An example of when you might use grouping is to list total sales by year:

```
from p in dataContext.Purchases
group p.Price by p.Date.Year into salesByYear
select new {
            Year       = salesByYear.Key,
            TotalValue = salesByYear.Sum()
           };
```

LINQ's grouping operators expose a superset of SQL's "GROUP BY" functionality.

Another departure from traditional SQL comes in there being no obligation to project the variables or expressions used in grouping or sorting.

Grouping by multiple keys

You can group by a composite key, using an anonymous type:

```
from n in names
group n by new { FirstLetter = n[0], Length = n.Length };
```

Custom equality comparers

You can pass a custom equality comparer into GroupBy, in a local query, to change the algorithm for key comparison. Rarely is this required, though, because changing the key selector expression is usually sufficient. For instance, the following creates a case-insensitive grouping:

```
group name by name.ToUpper()
```

Set Operators

IEnumerable<TSource>, IEnumerable<TSource>→IEnumerable<TSource>

Method	Description	SQL equivalents
Concat	Returns a concatenation of elements in each of the two sequences	UNION ALL
Union	Returns a concatenation of elements in each of the two sequences, excluding duplicates	UNION
Intersect	Returns elements present in both sequences	WHERE ... IN (...)
Except	Returns elements present in the first, but not the second sequence	EXCEPT
		or
		WHERE ... NOT IN (...)

Concat and Union

Contact returns all the elements of the first sequence, followed by all the elements of the second. Union does the same, but removes any duplicates:

```
int[] seq1 = { 1, 2, 3 }, seq2 = { 3, 4, 5 };

IEnumerable<int>
  concat = seq1.Concat (seq2),    // { 1, 2, 3, 3, 4, 5 }
  union  = seq1.Union  (seq2);    // { 1, 2, 3, 4, 5 }
```

Specifying the type argument explicitly is useful when the sequences are differently typed, but the elements have a common base type. For instance, with the reflection API (Chapter 18), methods and properties are represented with MethodInfo and PropertyInfo classes, which have a common base class called MemberInfo. We can concatenate methods and properties by stating that base class explicitly when calling Concat:

```
MethodInfo[] methods = typeof (string).GetMethods();
PropertyInfo[] props = typeof (string).GetProperties();
IEnumerable<MemberInfo> both = methods.Concat<MemberInfo> (props);
```

In the next example, we filter the methods before concatenating:

```
var methods = typeof (string).GetMethods().Where (m => !m.IsSpecialName);
var props = typeof (string).GetProperties();
var both = methods.Concat<MemberInfo> (props);
```

Interestingly, this example compiles in C# 4.0 but not in C# 3.0 because it relies on interface type parameter variance: methods is of type IEnumerable<MethodInfo>, which requires a covariant conversion to IEnumerable<MemberInfo>. It's a good illustration of how variance makes things work more as you'd expect.

Intersect and Except

Intersect returns the elements that two sequences have in common. Except returns the elements in the first input sequence that are *not* present in the second:

```
int[] seq1 = { 1, 2, 3 }, seq2 = { 3, 4, 5 };

IEnumerable<int>
  commonality = seq1.Intersect (seq2),    // { 3 }
  difference1 = seq1.Except    (seq2),    // { 1, 2 }
  difference2 = seq2.Except    (seq1);    // { 4, 5 }
```

Enumerable.Except works internally by loading all of the elements in the first collection into a dictionary, then removing from the dictionary all elements present in the second sequence. The equivalent in SQL is a NOT EXISTS or NOT IN subquery:

```
SELECT number FROM numbers1Table
WHERE number NOT IN (SELECT number FROM numbers2Table)
```

The Zip Operator

```
IEnumerable<TFirst>, IEnumerable<TSecond>→IEnumerable<TResult>
```

The Zip operator was added in Framework 4.0. It enumerates two sequences in step (like a zipper), returning a sequence based on applying a function over each element pair. For instance, the following:

```
int[] numbers = { 3, 5, 7 };
string[] words = { "three", "five", "seven", "ignored" };
IEnumerable<string> zip = numbers.Zip (words, (n, w) => n + "=" + w);
```

produces a sequence with the following elements:

```
3=three
5=five
7=seven
```

Extraneous elements in either input sequence are ignored. Zip is not supported when querying a database.

Conversion Methods

LINQ deals primarily in sequences—collections of type IEnumerable<T>, in other words. The conversion methods convert to and from other types of collections:

Method	Description
OfType	Converts IEnumerable to IEnumerable<T>, discarding wrongly typed elements
Cast	Converts IEnumerable to IEnumerable<T>, throwing an exception if there are any wrongly typed elements
ToArray	Converts IEnumerable<T> to T[]
ToList	Converts IEnumerable<T> to List<T>
ToDictionary	Converts IEnumerable<T> to Dictionary<TKey,TValue>
ToLookup	Converts IEnumerable<T> to ILookup<TKey,TElement>
AsEnumerable	Downcasts to IEnumerable<T>
AsQueryable	Casts or converts to IQueryable<T>

OfType and Cast

OfType and Cast accept a nongeneric IEnumerable collection and emit a generic IEnumerable<T> sequence that you can subsequently query:

```
ArrayList classicList = new ArrayList();        // in System.Collections
classicList.AddRange ( new int[] { 3, 4, 5 } );
IEnumerable<int> sequence1 = classicList.Cast<int>();
```

Cast and OfType differ in their behavior when encountering an input element that's of an incompatible type. Cast throws an exception; OfType ignores the incompatible element. Continuing the preceding example:

```
DateTime offender = DateTime.Now;
classicList.Add (offender);
IEnumerable<int>
  sequence2 = classicList.OfType<int>(), // OK - ignores offending DateTime
  sequence3 = classicList.Cast<int>();   // Throws exception
```

The rules for element compatibility exactly follow those of C#'s is operator, and therefore consider only reference conversions and unboxing conversions. We can see this by examining the internal implementation of OfType:

```
public static IEnumerable<TSource> OfType <TSource> (IEnumerable source)
{
  foreach (object element in source)
    if (element is TSource)
      yield return (TSource)element;
}
```

Cast has an identical implementation, except that it omits the type compatibility test:

```
public static IEnumerable<TSource> Cast <TSource> (IEnumerable source)
{
  foreach (object element in source)
    yield return (TSource)element;
}
```

A consequence of these implementations is that you cannot use Cast to perform numeric or custom conversions (for these, you must perform a Select operation instead). In other words, Cast is not as flexible as C#'s cast operator:

```
int i = 3;
long l = i;        // Implicit numeric conversion int->long
int i2 = (int) l;  // Explicit numeric conversion long->int
```

We can demonstrate this by attempting to use OfType or Cast to convert a sequence of ints to a sequence of longs:

```
int[] integers = { 1, 2, 3 };

IEnumerable<long> test1 = integers.OfType<long>();
IEnumerable<long> test2 = integers.Cast<long>();
```

When enumerated, test1 emits zero elements and test2 throws an exception. Examining OfType's implementation, it's fairly clear why. After substituting TSource, we get the following expression:

```
(element is long)
```

which returns false for an int element, due to the lack of an inheritance relationship.

 The reason for test2 throwing an exception, when enumerated, is subtler. Notice in Cast's implementation that element is of type object. When TSource is a value type, the CLR assumes this is an *unboxing conversion*, and synthesizes a method that reproduces the scenario described in the section "Boxing and Unboxing" on page 86 in Chapter 3:

```
int value = 123;
object element = value;
long result = (long) element;  // exception
```

Because the element variable is declared of type object, an object-to-long cast is performed (an unboxing) rather than an int-to-long numeric conversion. Unboxing operations require an exact type match, so the object-to-long unbox fails when given an int.

As we suggested previously, the solution is to use an ordinary Select:

```
IEnumerable<long> castLong = integers.Select (s => (long) s);
```

OfType and Cast are also useful in downcasting elements in a generic input sequence. For instance, if you have an input sequence of type IEnumerable<Fruit>, OfType<Apple> would return just the apples. This is particularly useful in LINQ to XML (see Chapter 10).

Cast has query syntax support: simply precede the range variable with a type:

```
from TreeNode node in myTreeView.Nodes
...
```

ToArray, ToList, ToDictionary, and ToLookup

ToArray and ToList emit the results into an array or generic list. These operators force the immediate enumeration of the input sequence (unless indirected via a subquery or expression tree). For examples, refer to the section "Deferred Execution" on page 324 in Chapter 8.

ToDictionary and ToLookup accept the following arguments:

Argument	Type
Input sequence	IEnumerable<TSource>
Key selector	TSource => TKey
Element selector (optional)	TSource => TElement
Comparer (optional)	IEqualityComparer<TKey>

ToDictionary also forces immediate execution of a sequence, writing the results to a generic Dictionary. The keySelector expression you provide must evaluate to a unique value for each element in the input sequence; otherwise, an exception is thrown. In contrast, ToLookup allows many elements of the same key. We describe lookups in the earlier section "Joining with lookups" on page 392.

AsEnumerable and AsQueryable

AsEnumerable upcasts a sequence to IEnumerable<T>, forcing the compiler to bind subsequent query operators to methods in Enumerable, instead of Queryable. For an example, see the section "Combining Interpreted and Local Queries" on page 343 in Chapter 8.

AsQueryable downcasts a sequence to IQueryable<T> if it implements that interface. Otherwise, it instantiates an IQueryable<T> wrapper over the local query.

Element Operators

IEnumerable<TSource>→TSource

Method	Description	SQL equivalents
First, FirstOrDefault	Returns the first element in the sequence, optionally satisfying a predicate	SELECT TOP 1 ... ORDER BY ...
Last, LastOrDefault	Returns the last element in the sequence, optionally satisfying a predicate	SELECT TOP 1 ... ORDER BY ... DESC

Method	Description	SQL equivalents
`Single, SingleOrDefault`	Equivalent to `First`/`FirstOrDefault`, but throws an exception if there is more than one match	
`ElementAt, ElementAtOrDefault`	Returns the element at the specified position	Exception thrown
`DefaultIfEmpty`	Returns null or `default(TSource)` if the sequence has no elements	OUTER JOIN

Methods ending in "OrDefault" return `default(TSource)` rather than throwing an exception if the input sequence is empty or if no elements match the supplied predicate.

`default(TSource)` is null for reference type elements, or "blank" (usually zero) for value type elements.

First, Last, and Single

Argument	Type
Source sequence	`IEnumerable<TSource>`
Predicate (optional)	`TSource => bool`

The following example demonstrates `First` and `Last`:

```
int[] numbers   = { 1, 2, 3, 4, 5 };
int first       = numbers.First();                          // 1
int last        = numbers.Last();                           // 5
int firstEven   = numbers.First  (n => n % 2 == 0);         // 2
int lastEven    = numbers.Last   (n => n % 2 == 0);         // 4
```

The following demonstrates `First` versus `FirstOrDefault`:

```
int firstBigError  = numbers.First          (n => n > 10);  // Exception
int firstBigNumber = numbers.FirstOrDefault (n => n > 10);  // 0
```

To avoid an exception, `Single` requires exactly one matching element; `SingleOrDefault` requires one *or zero* matching elements:

```
int onlyDivBy3 = numbers.Single (n => n % 3 == 0);  // 3
int divBy2Err  = numbers.Single (n => n % 2 == 0);  // Error: 2 & 4 match

int singleError = numbers.Single          (n => n > 10);    // Error
int noMatches   = numbers.SingleOrDefault (n => n > 10);    // 0
int divBy2Error = numbers.SingleOrDefault (n => n % 2 == 0); // Error
```

`Single` is the "fussiest" in this family of element operators. `FirstOrDefault` and `LastOrDefault` are the most tolerant.

LINQ Operators

In LINQ to SQL and EF, `Single` is often used to retrieve a row from a table by primary key:

```
Customer cust = dataContext.Customers.Single (c => c.ID == 3);
```

ElementAt

Argument	Type
Source sequence	IEnumerable<TSource>
Index of element to return	int

`ElementAt` picks the *n*th element from the sequence:

```
int[] numbers    = { 1, 2, 3, 4, 5 };
int third        = numbers.ElementAt (2);          // 3
int tenthError   = numbers.ElementAt (9);          // Exception
int tenth        = numbers.ElementAtOrDefault (9); // 0
```

`Enumerable.ElementAt` is written such that if the input sequence happens to implement `IList<T>`, it calls `IList<T>`'s indexer. Otherwise, it enumerates *n* times, and then returns the next element. `ElementAt` is not supported in LINQ to SQL or EF.

DefaultIfEmpty

`DefaultIfEmpty` converts empty sequences to null/`default()`. This is used in writing flat outer joins: see the earlier sections "Outer joins with SelectMany" on page 385 and "Flat outer joins" on page 392.

Aggregation Methods

IEnumerable<TSource>→ *scalar*

Method	Description	SQL equivalents
Count, LongCount	Returns the number of elements in the input sequence, optionally satisfying a predicate	COUNT (...)
Min, Max	Returns the smallest or largest element in the sequence	MIN (...), MAX (...)
Sum, Average	Calculates a numeric sum or average over elements in the sequence	SUM (...), AVG (...)
Aggregate	Performs a custom aggregation	Exception thrown

Count and LongCount

Argument	Type
Source sequence	IEnumerable<TSource>
Predicate (optional)	TSource => bool

Count simply enumerates over a sequence, returning the number of items:

```
int fullCount = new int[] { 5, 6, 7 }.Count();    // 3
```

The internal implementation of `Enumerable.Count` tests the input sequence to see whether it happens to implement `ICollection<T>`. If it does, it simply calls `ICollection<T>.Count`. Otherwise, it enumerates over every item, incrementing a counter.

You can optionally supply a predicate:

```
int digitCount = "pa55w0rd".Count (c => char.IsDigit (c));    // 3
```

`LongCount` does the same job as `Count`, but returns a 64-bit integer, allowing for sequences of greater than 2 billion elements.

Min and Max

Argument	Type
Source sequence	IEnumerable<TSource>
Result selector (optional)	TSource => TResult

`Min` and `Max` return the smallest or largest element from a sequence:

```
int[] numbers = { 28, 32, 14 };
int smallest = numbers.Min();  // 14;
int largest  = numbers.Max();  // 32;
```

If you include a `selector` expression, each element is first projected:

```
int smallest = numbers.Max (n => n % 10);  // 8;
```

A `selector` expression is mandatory if the items themselves are not intrinsically comparable—in other words, if they do not implement `IComparable<T>`:

```
Purchase runtimeError = dataContext.Purchases.Min ();          // Error
decimal? lowestPrice = dataContext.Purchases.Min (p => p.Price); // OK
```

A `selector` expression determines not only how elements are compared, but also the final result. In the preceding example, the final result is a decimal value, not a purchase object. To get the cheapest purchase, you need a subquery:

```
Purchase cheapest = dataContext.Purchases
  .Where (p => p.Price == dataContext.Purchases.Min (p2 => p2.Price))
  .FirstOrDefault();
```

In this case, you could also formulate the query without an aggregation—using an `OrderBy` followed by `FirstOrDefault`.

Sum and Average

Argument	Type
Source sequence	IEnumerable<TSource>
Result selector (optional)	TSource => TResult

Sum and Average are aggregation operators that are used in a similar manner to Min and Max:

```
decimal[] numbers  = { 3, 4, 8 };
decimal sumTotal   = numbers.Sum();           // 15
decimal average    = numbers.Average();       // 5   (mean value)
```

The following returns the total length of each of the strings in the names array:

```
int combinedLength = names.Sum (s => s.Length);   // 19
```

Sum and Average are fairly restrictive in their typing. Their definitions are hard-wired to each of the numeric types (int, long, float, double, decimal, and their nullable versions). In contrast, Min and Max can operate directly on anything that implements IComparable<T>—such as a string, for instance.

Further, Average always returns either decimal or double, according to the following table:

Selector type	Result type
decimal	decimal
int, long, float, double	double

This means the following does not compile ("cannot convert double to int"):

```
int avg = new int[] { 3, 4 }.Average();
```

But this will compile:

```
double avg = new int[] { 3, 4 }.Average();   // 3.5
```

Average implicitly upscales the input values to avoid loss of precision. In this example, we averaged integers and got 3.5, without needing to resort to an input element cast:

```
double avg = numbers.Average (n => (double) n);
```

When querying a database, Sum and Average translate to the standard SQL aggregations. The following query returns customers whose average purchase was more than $500:

```
from c in dataContext.Customers
where c.Purchases.Average (p => p.Price) > 500
select c.Name;
```

Aggregate

Aggregate allows you to specify a custom accumulation algorithm for implementing unusual aggregations. Aggregate is not supported in LINQ to SQL or Entity Framework, and is somewhat specialized in its use cases. The following demonstrates how Aggregate can do the work of Sum:

```
int[] numbers = { 2, 3, 4 };
int sum = numbers.Aggregate (0, (total, n) => total + n);   // 9
```

The first argument to `Aggregate` is the *seed*, from which accumulation starts. The second argument is an expression to update the accumulated value, given a fresh element. You can optionally supply a third argument to project the final result value from the accumulated value.

 Most problems for which `Aggregate` has been designed can be solved as easily with a `foreach` loop—and with more familiar syntax. The advantage of using `Aggregate` is that with large or complex aggregations, you can automatically parallelize the operation with PLINQ (see Chapter 22).

Unseeded aggregations

You can omit the seed value when calling `Aggregate`, in which case the first element becomes the *implicit* seed, and aggregation proceeds from the second element. Here's the preceding example, *unseeded*:

```
int[] numbers = { 1, 2, 3 };
int sum = numbers.Aggregate ((total, n) => total + n);    // 6
```

This gives the same result as before, but we're actually doing a *different calculation*. Before, we were calculating 0+1+2+3; now we're calculating 1+2+3. We can better illustrate the difference by multiplying instead of adding:

```
int[] numbers = { 1, 2, 3 };
int x = numbers.Aggregate (0, (prod, n) => prod * n);    // 0*1*2*3 = 0
int y = numbers.Aggregate (   (prod, n) => prod * n);    //   1*2*3 = 6
```

As we'll see in Chapter 22, unseeded aggregations have the advantage of being parallelizable without requiring the use of special overloads. However, there are some traps with unseeded aggregations.

Traps with unseeded aggregations

The unseeded aggregation methods are intended for use with delegates that are *commutative* and *associative*. If used otherwise, the result is either *unintuitive* (with ordinary queries) or *nondeterministic* (in the case that you parallelize the query with PLINQ). For example, consider the following function:

```
(total, n) => total + n * n
```

This is neither commutative nor associative. (For example, 1+2*2 != 2+1*1). Let's see what happens when we use it to sum the square of the numbers 2, 3, and 4:

```
int[] numbers = { 2, 3, 4 };
int sum = numbers.Aggregate ((total, n) => total + n * n);    // 27
```

Instead of calculating:

```
2*2 + 3*3 + 4*4    // 29
```

it calculates:

```
2 + 3*3 + 4*4    // 27
```

We can fix this in a number of ways. First, we could include 0 as the first element:

```
int[] numbers = { 0, 2, 3, 4 };
```

Not only is this inelegant, but it will still give incorrect results if parallelized—because PLINQ leverages the function's assumed associativity by selecting *multiple* elements as seeds. To illustrate, if we denote our aggregation function as follows:

```
f(total, n) => total + n * n
```

then LINQ to Objects would calculate this:

```
f(f(f(0, 2),3),4)
```

whereas PLINQ may do this:

```
f(f(0,2),f(3,4))
```

with the following result:

```
First partition:    a = 0 + 2*2   (= 4)
Second partition:   b = 3 + 4*4   (= 19)
Final result:       a + b*b       (= 365!)
OR EVEN:            b + a*a       (= 35!)
```

There are two good solutions. The first is to turn this into a seeded aggregation—with zero as the seed. The only complication is that with PLINQ, we'd need to use a special overload in order for the query not to execute sequentially (see "Optimizing PLINQ" on page 886 in Chapter 22).

The second solution is to restructure the query such that the aggregation function is commutative and associative:

```
int sum = numbers.Select (n => n * n).Aggregate ((total, n) => total + n);
```

> Of course, in such simple scenarios you can (and should) use the Sum operator instead of Aggregate:
>
> ```
> int sum = numbers.Sum (n => n * n);
> ```
>
> You can actually go quite far just with Sum and Average. For instance, you can use Average to calculate a root-mean-square:
>
> ```
> Math.Sqrt (numbers.Average (n => n * n))
> ```
>
> and even standard deviation:
>
> ```
> double mean = numbers.Average();
> double sdev = Math.Sqrt (numbers.Average (n =>
>                 {
>                   double dif = n - mean;
>                   return dif * dif;
>                 }));
> ```
>
> Both are safe, efficient and fully parallelizable. In Chapter 22, we'll give a practical example of a custom aggregation that can't be reduced to Sum or Average.

Quantifiers

IEnumerable<TSource>→*bool*

Method	Description	SQL equivalents
Contains	Returns true if the input sequence contains the given element	WHERE ... IN (...)
Any	Returns true if any elements satisfy the given predicate	WHERE ... IN (...)
All	Returns true if all elements satisfy the given predicate	WHERE (...)
SequenceEqual	Returns true if the second sequence has identical elements to the input sequence	

Contains and Any

The Contains method accepts an argument of type TSource; Any accepts an optional *predicate*.

Contains returns true if the given element is present:

```
bool hasAThree = new int[] { 2, 3, 4 }.Contains (3);      // true;
```

Any returns true if the given expression is true for at least one element. We can rewrite the preceding query with Any as follows:

```
bool hasAThree = new int[] { 2, 3, 4 }.Any (n => n == 3);  // true;
```

Any can do everything that Contains can do, and more:

```
bool hasABigNumber = new int[] { 2, 3, 4 }.Any (n => n > 10);  // false;
```

Calling Any without a predicate returns true if the sequence has one or more elements. Here's another way to write the preceding query:

```
bool hasABigNumber = new int[] { 2, 3, 4 }.Where (n => n > 10).Any();
```

Any is particularly useful in subqueries and is used often when querying databases, for example:

```
from c in dataContext.Customers
where c.Purchases.Any (p => p.Price > 1000)
select c
```

All and SequenceEqual

All returns true if all elements satisfy a predicate. The following returns customers whose purchases are less than $100:

```
dataContext.Customers.Where (c => c.Purchases.All (p => p.Price < 100));
```

SequenceEqual compares two sequences. To return true, each sequence must have identical elements, in the identical order.

LINQ Operators

Generation Methods

void→IEnumerable<TResult>

Method	Description
Empty	Creates an empty sequence
Repeat	Creates a sequence of repeating elements
Range	Creates a sequence of integers

Empty, Repeat, and Range are static (nonextension) methods that manufacture simple local sequences.

Empty

Empty manufactures an empty sequence and requires just a type argument:

```
foreach (string s in Enumerable.Empty<string>())
  Console.Write (s);                            // <nothing>
```

In conjunction with the ?? operator, Empty does the reverse of DefaultIfEmpty. For example, suppose we have a jagged array of integers, and we want to get all the integers into a single flat list. The following SelectMany query fails if any of the inner arrays is null:

```
int[][] numbers =
{
  new int[] { 1, 2, 3 },
  new int[] { 4, 5, 6 },
  null                     // this null makes the query below fail.
};

IEnumerable<int> flat = numbers.SelectMany (innerArray => innerArray);
```

Empty in conjunction with ?? fixes the problem:

```
IEnumerable<int> flat = numbers
  .SelectMany (innerArray => innerArray ?? Enumerable.Empty <int>());

foreach (int i in flat)
  Console.Write (i + " ");   // 1 2 3 4 5 6
```

Range and Repeat

Range and Repeat work only with integers. Range accepts a starting index and count:

```
foreach (int i in Enumerable.Range (5, 5))
  Console.Write (i + " ");              // 5 6 7 8 9
```

Repeat accepts the number to repeat, and the number of iterations:

```
foreach (int i in Enumerable.Repeat (5, 3))
  Console.Write (i + " ");              // 5 5 5
```

10

LINQ to XML

The .NET Framework provides a number of APIs for working with XML data. From Framework 3.5, the primary choice for general-purpose XML document processing is *LINQ to XML*. LINQ to XML comprises a lightweight LINQ-friendly XML document object model, and a set of supplementary query operators. In most scenarios, it can be considered a complete replacement for the preceding W3C-compliant DOM, a.k.a. `XmlDocument`.

In this chapter, we concentrate entirely on LINQ to XML. In the following chapter, we cover the more specialized XML types and APIs, including the forward-only reader/writer, the types for working with schemas, stylesheets and XPaths, and the legacy W3C-compliant DOM.

The LINQ to XML DOM is extremely well designed and highly performant. Even without LINQ, the LINQ to XML DOM is valuable as a lightweight façade over the low-level `XmlReader` and `XmlWriter` classes.

All LINQ to XML types are defined in the `System.Xml.Linq` namespace.

Architectural Overview

This section starts with a very brief introduction to the concept of a DOM, and then explains the rationale behind LINQ to XML's DOM.

What Is a DOM?

Consider the following XML file:

```xml
<?xml version="1.0" encoding="utf-8" standalone="yes"?>
<customer id="123" status="archived">
  <firstname>Joe</firstname>
  <lastname>Bloggs</lastname>
</customer>
```

As with all XML files, we start with a *declaration*, and then a root *element*, whose name is `customer`. It has two *attributes*, each with a name (`id` and `status`) and value (`"123"` and `"archived"`). Within `customer`, there are two child elements, `firstname` and `lastname`, each having simple text content (`"Joe"` and `"Bloggs"`).

Each of these constructs—declaration, element, attribute, value, and text content—can be represented with a class. And if such classes have collection properties for storing child content, we can assemble a *tree* of objects to fully describe a document. This is called a *document object model*, or DOM.

The LINQ to XML DOM

LINQ to XML comprises two things:

- An XML DOM, which we call the *X-DOM*
- A set of about 10 supplementary query operators

As you might expect, the X-DOM consists of types such as `XDocument`, `XElement`, and `XAttribute`. Interestingly, the X-DOM types are not tied to LINQ—you can load, instantiate, update, and save an X-DOM without ever writing a LINQ query.

Conversely, you could use LINQ to query a DOM created of the older W3C-compliant types. However, this would be frustrating and limiting. The distinguishing feature of the X-DOM is that it's *LINQ-friendly*. This means:

- It has methods that emit useful `IEnumerable` sequences, upon which you can query.
- Its constructors are designed such that you can build an X-DOM tree through a LINQ projection.

X-DOM Overview

Figure 10-1 shows the core X-DOM types. The most frequently used of these types is `XElement`. `XObject` is the root of the *inheritance* hierarchy; `XElement` and `XDocument` are roots of the *containership* hierarchy. Figure 10-2 shows the X-DOM tree created from the following code:

```csharp
string xml = @"<customer id='123' status='archived'>
                 <firstname>Joe</firstname>
                 <lastname>Bloggs<!--nice name--></lastname>
               </customer>";

XElement customer = XElement.Parse (xml);
```

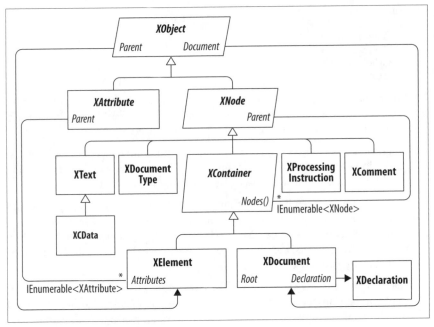

Figure 10-1. Core X-DOM types

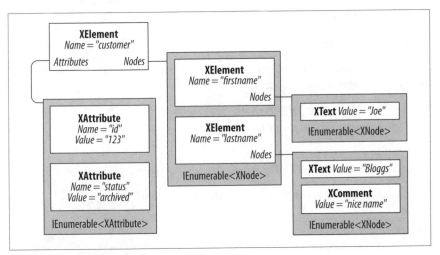

Figure 10-2. A simple X-DOM tree

XObject is the abstract base class for all XML content. It defines a link to the Parent element in the containership tree as well as an optional XDocument.

XNode is the base class for most XML content excluding attributes. The distinguishing feature of XNode is that it can sit in an ordered collection of mixed-type XNodes. For instance, consider the following XML:

```
<data>
  Hello world
  <subelement1/>
  <!--comment-->
  <subelement2/>
</data>
```

Within the parent element `<data>`, there's first an XText node (Hello world), then an XElement node, then an XComment node, and then a second XElement node. In contrast, an XAttribute will tolerate only other XAttributes as peers.

Although an XNode can access its parent XElement, it has no concept of *child* nodes: this is the job of its subclass XContainer. XContainer defines members for dealing with children and is the abstract base class for XElement and XDocument.

XElement introduces members for managing attributes—as well as a Name and Value. In the (fairly common) case of an element having a single XText child node, the Value property on XElement encapsulates this child's content for both get and set operations, cutting unnecessary navigation. Thanks to Value, you can mostly avoid working directly with XText nodes.

XDocument represents the root of an XML tree. More precisely, it *wraps* the root XElement, adding an XDeclaration, processing instructions, and other root-level "fluff." Unlike with the W3C DOM, its use is optional: you can load, manipulate, and save an X-DOM without ever creating an XDocument! The nonreliance on XDocument also means you can efficiently and easily move a node subtree to another X-DOM hierarchy.

Loading and Parsing

Both XElement and XDocument provide static Load and Parse methods to build an X-DOM tree from an existing source:

- Load builds an X-DOM from a file, URI, Stream, TextReader, or XmlReader.
- Parse builds an X-DOM from a string.

For example:

```
XDocument fromWeb = XDocument.Load ("http://albahari.com/sample.xml");

XElement fromFile = XElement.Load (@"e:\media\somefile.xml");

XElement config = XElement.Parse (
@"<configuration>
    <client enabled='true'>
      <timeout>30</timeout>
    </client>
  </configuration>");
```

In later sections, we describe how to traverse and update an X-DOM. As a quick preview, here's how to manipulate the config element we just populated:

```
foreach (XElement child in config.Elements())
  Console.WriteLine (child.Name);                    // client
```

```
XElement client = config.Element ("client");

bool enabled = (bool) client.Attribute ("enabled");   // Read attribute
Console.WriteLine (enabled);                           // True
client.Attribute ("enabled").SetValue (!enabled);      // Update attribute

int timeout = (int) client.Element ("timeout");        // Read element
Console.WriteLine (timeout);                            // 30
client.Element ("timeout").SetValue (timeout * 2);     // Update element

client.Add (new XElement ("retries", 3));              // Add new element

Console.WriteLine (config);        // Implicitly call config.ToString()
```

Here's the result of that last `Console.WriteLine`:

```
<configuration>
  <client enabled="false">
    <timeout>60</timeout>
    <retries>3</retries>
  </client>
</configuration
```

> `XNode` also provides a static `ReadFrom` method that instantiates and populates any type of node from an `XmlReader`. Unlike `Load`, it stops after reading one (complete) node, so you can continue to read manually from the `XmlReader` afterward.
>
> You can also do the reverse and use an `XmlReader` or `XmlWriter` to read or write an `XNode`, via its `CreateReader` and `Create Writer` methods.
>
> We describe XML readers and writers and how to use them with the X-DOM in Chapter 11.

Saving and Serializing

Calling `ToString` on any node converts its content to an XML string—formatted with line breaks and indentation as we just saw. (You can disable the line breaks and indentation by specifying `SaveOptions.DisableFormatting` when calling `ToString`.)

`XElement` and `XDocument` also provide a `Save` method that writes an X-DOM to a file, `Stream`, `TextWriter`, or `XmlWriter`. If you specify a file, an XML declaration is automatically written. There is also a `WriteTo` method defined in the `XNode` class, which accepts just an `XmlWriter`.

We describe the handling of XML declarations when saving in more detail in the section "Documents and Declarations" on page 431 later in this chapter.

Instantiating an X-DOM

Rather than using the Load or Parse methods, you can build an X-DOM tree by manually instantiating objects and adding them to a parent via XContainer's Add method.

To construct an XElement and XAttribute, simply provide a name and value:

```
XElement lastName = new XElement ("lastname", "Bloggs");
lastName.Add (new XComment ("nice name"));

XElement customer = new XElement ("customer");
customer.Add (new XAttribute ("id", 123));
customer.Add (new XElement ("firstname", "Joe"));
customer.Add (lastName);

Console.WriteLine (customer.ToString());
```

The result:

```
<customer id="123">
  <firstname>Joe</firstname>
  <lastname>Bloggs<!--nice name--></lastname>
</customer>
```

A value is optional when constructing an XElement—you can provide just the element name and add content later. Notice that when we did provide a value, a simple string sufficed—we didn't need to explicitly create and add an XText child node. The X-DOM does this work automatically, so you can deal simply with "values."

Functional Construction

In our preceding example, it's hard to glean the XML structure from the code. X-DOM supports another mode of instantiation, called *functional construction* (from functional programming). With functional construction, you build an entire tree in a single expression:

```
XElement customer =
  new XElement ("customer", new XAttribute ("id", 123),
    new XElement ("firstname", "joe"),
    new XElement ("lastname", "bloggs",
      new XComment ("nice name")
    )
  );
```

This has two benefits. First, the code resembles the shape of the XML. Second, it can be incorporated into the select clause of a LINQ query. For example, the following LINQ to SQL query projects directly into an X-DOM:

```
XElement query =
  new XElement ("customers",
    from c in dataContext.Customers
    select
      new XElement ("customer", new XAttribute ("id", c.ID),
        new XElement ("firstname", c.FirstName),
```

```
      new XElement ("lastname", c.LastName,
        new XComment ("nice name")
      )
    )
);
```

More on this later in this chapter, in the section "Projecting into an X-DOM" on page 441.

Specifying Content

Functional construction is possible because the constructors for XElement (and XDocument) are overloaded to accept a params object array:

```
public XElement (XName name, params object[] content)
```

The same holds true for the Add method in XContainer:

```
public void Add (params object[] content)
```

Hence, you can specify any number of child objects of any type when building or appending an X-DOM. This works because *anything* counts as legal content. To see how, we need to examine how each content object is processed internally. Here are the decisions made by XContainer, in order:

1. If the object is null, it's ignored.

2. If the object is based on XNode or XStreamingElement, it's added as is to the Nodes collection.

3. If the object is an XAttribute, it's added to the Attributes collection.

4. If the object is a string, it gets wrapped in an XText node and added to Nodes.*

5. If the object implements IEnumerable, it's enumerated, and the same rules are applied to each element.

6. Otherwise, the object is converted to a string, wrapped in an XText node, and then added to Nodes.†

Everything ends up in one of two buckets: Nodes or Attributes. Furthermore, any object is valid content because it can always ultimately call ToString on it and treat it as an XText node.

---

* The X-DOM actually optimizes this step internally by storing simple text content in a string. The XTEXT node is not actually created until you call Nodes( ) on the XContainer.

† See the previous footnote.

Before calling `ToString` on an arbitrary type, `XContainer` first tests whether it is one of the following types:

```
float, double, decimal, bool,
DateTime, DateTimeOffset, TimeSpan
```

If so, it calls an appropriate typed `ToString` method on the `XmlConvert` helper class instead of calling `ToString` on the object itself. This ensures that the data is round-trippable and compliant with standard XML formatting rules.

Automatic Deep Cloning

When a node or attribute is added to an element (whether via functional construction or an `Add` method), the node or attribute's `Parent` property is set to that element. A node can have only one parent element: if you add an already parented node to a second parent, the node is automatically *deep-cloned*. In the following example, each customer has a separate copy of `address`:

```
var address = new XElement ("address",
                new XElement ("street", "Lawley St"),
                new XElement ("town", "North Beach")
            );
var customer1 = new XElement ("customer1", address);
var customer2 = new XElement ("customer2", address);

customer1.Element ("address").Element ("street").Value = "Another St";
Console.WriteLine (
    customer2.Element ("address").Element ("street").Value);   // Lawley St
```

This automatic duplication keeps X-DOM object instantiation free of side effects—another hallmark of functional programming.

Navigating and Querying

As you might expect, the `XNode` and `XContainer` classes define methods and properties for traversing the X-DOM tree. Unlike a conventional DOM, however, these functions don't return a collection that implements `IList<T>`. Instead, they return either a single value or a *sequence* that implements `IEnumerable<T>`—upon which you are then expected to execute a LINQ query (or enumerate with a `foreach`). This allows for advanced queries as well as simple navigation tasks—using familiar LINQ query syntax.

Element and attribute names are case-sensitive in the X-DOM—just as they are in XML.

Child Node Navigation

Return type	Members	Works on
XNode	FirstNode { get; }	XContainer
	LastNode { get; }	XContainer
IEnumerable<XNode>	Nodes()	XContainer*
	DescendantNodes()	XContainer*
	DescendantNodesAndSelf()	XElement*
XElement	Element (XName)	XContainer
IEnumerable<XElement>	Elements()	XContainer*
	Elements (XName)	XContainer*
	Descendants()	XContainer*
	Descendants (XName)	XContainer*
	DescendantsAndSelf()	XElement*
	DescendantsAndSelf (XName)	XElement*
bool	HasElements { get; }	XElement

Functions marked with an asterisk in the third column of this and other tables also operate on *sequences* of the same type. For instance, you can call Nodes on either an XContainer or a sequence of XContainer objects. This is possible because of extension methods defined in System.Xml.Linq—the supplementary query operators we talked about in the overview.

FirstNode, LastNode, and Nodes

FirstNode and LastNode give you direct access to the first or last child node; Nodes returns all children as a sequence. All three functions consider only direct descendants. For example:

```
var bench = new XElement ("bench",
              new XElement ("toolbox",
                new XElement ("handtool", "Hammer"),
                new XElement ("handtool", "Rasp")
              ),
              new XElement ("toolbox",
                new XElement ("handtool", "Saw"),
                new XElement ("powertool", "Nailgun")
              ),
              new XComment ("Be careful with the nailgun")
            );
foreach (XNode node in bench.Nodes())
  Console.WriteLine (node.ToString (SaveOptions.DisableFormatting) + ".");
```

This is the output:

```
<toolbox><handtool>Hammer</handtool><handtool>Rasp</handtool></toolbox>.
<toolbox><handtool>Saw</handtool><powertool>Nailgun</powertool></toolbox>.
<!--Be careful with the nailgun-->.
```

Retrieving elements

The `Elements` method returns just the child nodes of type `XElement`:

```
foreach (XElement e in bench.Elements())
    Console.WriteLine (e.Name + "=" + e.Value);    // toolbox=HammerRasp
                                                   // toolbox=SawNailgun
```

The following LINQ query finds the toolbox with the nail gun:

```
IEnumerable<string> query =
    from toolbox in bench.Elements()
    where toolbox.Elements().Any (tool => tool.Value == "Nailgun")
    select toolbox.Value;

RESULT: { "SawNailgun" }
```

The next example uses a `SelectMany` query to retrieve the hand tools in all toolboxes:

```
IEnumerable<string> query =
    from toolbox in bench.Elements()
    from tool in toolbox.Elements()
    where tool.Name == "handtool"
    select tool.Value;

RESULT: { "Hammer", "Rasp", "Saw" }
```

 `Elements` itself is equivalent to a LINQ query on `Nodes`. Our preceding query could be started as follows:

```
from toolbox in bench.Nodes().OfType<XElement>()
where ...
```

`Elements` can also return just the elements of a given name. For example:

```
int x = bench.Elements ("toolbox").Count();    // 2
```

This is equivalent to:

```
int x = bench.Elements().Where (e => e.Name == "toolbox").Count();  // 2
```

`Elements` is also defined as an extension method accepting `IEnumerable<XCon tainer>` or, more precisely, it accepts an argument of this type:

```
IEnumerable<T> where T : XContainer
```

This allows it to work with sequences of elements, too. Using this method, we can rewrite the query that finds the hand tools in all toolboxes as follows:

```
from tool in bench.Elements ("toolbox").Elements ("handtool")
select tool.Value.ToUpper();
```

The first call to `Elements` binds to `XContainer`'s instance method; the second call to `Elements` binds to the extension method.

Retrieving a single element

The method `Element` (singular) returns the first matching element of the given name. `Element` is useful for simple navigation, as follows:

```
XElement settings = XElement.Load ("databaseSettings.xml");
string cx = settings.Element ("database").Element ("connectString").Value;
```

`Element` is equivalent to calling `Elements()` and then applying LINQ's `FirstOrDefault` query operator with a name-matching predicate. `Element` returns `null` if the requested element doesn't exist.

 `Element("xyz").Value` will throw a `NullReferenceException` if element `xyz` does not exist. If you'd prefer a `null` rather than an exception, cast the `XElement` to a `string` instead of querying its `Value` property. In other words:

```
string xyz = (string) settings.Element ("xyz");
```

This works because `XElement` defines an explicit `string` conversion—just for this purpose!

Recursive functions

`XContainer` also provides `Descendants` and `DescendantNodes` methods that return child elements or nodes, *recursively*. `Descendants` accepts an optional element name. Returning to our earlier example, we can use `Descendants` to find all the hand tools as follows:

```
Console.WriteLine (bench.Descendants ("handtool").Count()); // 3
```

Both parent and leaf nodes are included, as the following example demonstrates:

```
foreach (XNode node in bench.DescendantNodes())
  Console.WriteLine (node.ToString (SaveOptions.DisableFormatting));
```

```
<toolbox><handtool>Hammer</handtool><handtool>Rasp</handtool></toolbox>
<handtool>Hammer</handtool>
Hammer
<handtool>Rasp</handtool>
Rasp
<toolbox><handtool>Saw</handtool><powertool>Nailgun</powertool></toolbox>
<handtool>Saw</handtool>
Saw
<powertool>Nailgun</powertool>
Nailgun
<!--Be careful with the nailgun-->
```

The next query extracts all comments anywhere within the X-DOM that contain the word "careful":

```
IEnumerable<string> query =
  from c in bench.DescendantNodes().OfType<XComment>()
  where c.Value.Contains ("careful")
  orderby c.Value
  select c.Value;
```

Parent Navigation

All XNodes have a `Parent` property and `AncestorXXX` methods for parent navigation. A parent is always an XElement:

Return type	Members	Works on
XElement	Parent { get; }	XNode*
Enumerable<XElement>	Ancestors()	XNode*
	Ancestors (XName)	XNode*
	AncestorsAndSelf()	XElement*
	AncestorsAndSelf (XName)	XElement*

If x is an XElement, the following always prints true:

```
foreach (XNode child in x.Nodes())
  Console.WriteLine (child.Parent == x);
```

The same is not the case, however, if x is an XDocument. XDocument is peculiar: it can have children, but can never be anyone's parent! To access the XDocument, you instead use the `Document` property—this works on any object in the X-DOM tree.

`Ancestors` returns a sequence whose first element is `Parent`, and whose next element is `Parent.Parent`, and so on, until the root element.

You can navigate to the root element with the LINQ query `AncestorsAndSelf().Last()`.

Another way to achieve the same thing is to call `Document.Root`—although this works only if an XDocument is present.

Peer Node Navigation

Return type	Members	Defined in
bool	IsBefore (XNode node)	XNode
	IsAfter (XNode node)	XNode
XNode	PreviousNode { get; }	XNode
	NextNode { get; }	XNode
IEnumerable<XNode>	NodesBeforeSelf()	XNode
	NodesAfterSelf()	XNode

Return type	Members	Defined in
IEnumerable<XElement>	ElementsBeforeSelf()	XNode
	ElementsBeforeSelf (XName name)	XNode
	ElementsAfterSelf()	XNode
	ElementsAfterSelf (XName name)	XNode

With PreviousNode and NextNode (and FirstNode/LastNode), you can traverse nodes with the feel of a linked list. This is noncoincidental: internally, nodes are stored in a linked list.

XNode internally uses a *singly* linked list, so PreviousNode is not performant.

Attribute Navigation

Return type	Members	Defined in
bool	HasAttributes { get; }	XElement
XAttribute	Attribute (XName name)	XElement
	FirstAttribute { get; }	XElement
	LastAttribute { get; }	XElement
IEnumerable<XAttribute>	Attributes()	XElement
	Attributes (XName name)	XElement

In addition, XAttribute defines PreviousAttribute and NextAttribute properties, as well as Parent.

The Attributes method that accepts a name returns a sequence with either zero or one element; an element cannot have duplicate attribute names in XML.

Updating an X-DOM

You can update elements and attributes in the following ways:

- Call SetValue or reassign the Value property.
- Call SetElementValue or SetAttributeValue.
- Call one of the RemoveXXX methods.
- Call one of the AddXXX or ReplaceXXX methods, specifying fresh content.

You can also reassign the Name property on XElement objects.

Simple Value Updates

Members	Works on
SetValue (object value)	XElement, XAttribute
Value { get; set }	XElement, XAttribute

The `SetValue` method replaces an element or attribute's content with a simple value. Setting the `Value` property does the same, but accepts string data only. We describe both of these functions in detail later in this chapter (see the section "Working with Values" on page 428).

An effect of calling `SetValue` (or reassigning `Value`) is that it replaces all child nodes:

```
XElement settings = new XElement ("settings",
                       new XElement ("timeout", 30)
                    );
settings.SetValue ("blah");
Console.WriteLine (settings.ToString());  // <settings>blah</settings>
```

Updating Child Nodes and Attributes

Category	Members	Works on
Add	Add (params object[] content)	XContainer
	AddFirst (params object[] content)	XContainer
Remove	RemoveNodes()	XContainer
	RemoveAttributes()	XElement
	RemoveAll()	XElement
Update	ReplaceNodes (params object[] content)	XContainer
	ReplaceAttributes (params object[] content)	XElement
	ReplaceAll (params object[] content	XElement
	SetElementValue (XName name, object value)	XElement
	SetAttributeValue (XName name, object value)	XElement

The most convenient methods in this group are the last two: `SetElementValue` and `SetAttributeValue`. They serve as shortcuts for instantiating an `XElement` or `XAttribute` and then Adding it to a parent, replacing any existing element or attribute of that name:

```
XElement settings = new XElement ("settings");
settings.SetElementValue ("timeout", 30);   // Adds child node
settings.SetElementValue ("timeout", 60);   // Update it to 60
```

Add appends a child node to an element or document. `AddFirst` does the same thing, but inserts at the beginning of the collection rather than the end.

You can remove all child nodes or attributes in one hit with `RemoveNodes` or `RemoveAttributes`. `RemoveAll` is equivalent to calling both of these methods.

The ReplaceXXX methods are equivalent to Removing and then Adding. They take a snapshot of the input, so e.ReplaceNodes(e.Nodes()) works as expected.

Updating Through the Parent

Members	Works on
AddBeforeSelf (params object[] content)	XNode
AddAfterSelf (params object[] content)	XNode
Remove()	XNode*, XAttribute*
ReplaceWith (params object[] content)	XNode

The methods AddBeforeSelf, AddAfterSelf, Remove, and ReplaceWith don't operate on the node's children. Instead, they operate on the collection in which the node itself is in. This requires that the node have a parent element—otherwise, an exception is thrown. AddBeforeSelf and AddAfterSelf are useful for inserting a node into an arbitrary position:

```
XElement items = new XElement ("items",
                new XElement ("one"),
                new XElement ("three")
             );
items.FirstNode.AddAfterSelf (new XElement ("two"));
```

Here's the result:

```
<items><one /><two /><three /></items>
```

Inserting into an arbitrary position within a long sequence of elements is actually quite efficient, because nodes are stored internally in a linked list.

The Remove method removes the current node from its parent. ReplaceWith does the same—and then inserts some other content at the same position. For instance:

```
XElement items = XElement.Parse ("<items><one/><two/><three/></items>");
items.FirstNode.ReplaceWith (new XComment ("One was here"));
```

Here's the result:

```
<items><!--one was here--><two /><three /></items>
```

Removing a sequence of nodes or attributes

Thanks to extension methods in System.Xml.Linq, you can also call Remove on a *sequence* of nodes or attributes. Consider this X-DOM:

```
XElement contacts = XElement.Parse (
@"<contacts>
    <customer name='Mary'/>
    <customer name='Chris' archived='true'/>
    <supplier name='Susan'>
       <phone archived='true'>012345678<!--confidential--></phone>
    </supplier>
 </contacts>");
```

The following removes all customers:

```
contacts.Elements ("customer").Remove();
```

The next statement removes all archived contacts (so *Chris* disappears):

```
contacts.Elements().Where (e => (bool?) e.Attribute ("archived") == true)
              .Remove();
```

If we replaced `Elements()` with `Descendants()`, all archived elements throughout the DOM would disappear, with this result:

```
<contacts>
  <customer name="Mary" />
  <supplier name="Susan" />
</contacts>
```

The next example removes all contacts that feature the comment "confidential" anywhere in their tree:

```
contacts.Elements().Where (e => e.DescendantNodes()
                           .OfType<XComment>()
                           .Any (c => c.Value == "confidential")
                        ).Remove();
```

This is the result:

```
<contacts>
  <customer name="Mary" />
  <customer name="Chris" archived="true" />
</contacts>
```

Contrast this with the following simpler query, which strips all comment nodes from the tree:

```
contacts.DescendantNodes().OfType<XComment>().Remove();
```

 Internally, the `Remove` methods first read all matching elements into a temporary list, and then enumerate over the temporary list to perform the deletions. This avoids errors that could otherwise result from deleting and querying at the same time.

Working with Values

`XElement` and `XAttribute` both have a `Value` property of type `string`. If an element has a single `XText` child node, `XElement`'s `Value` property acts as a convenient shortcut to the content of that node. With `XAttribute`, the `Value` property is simply the attribute's value.

Despite the storage differences, the X-DOM provides a consistent set of operations for working with element and attribute values.

Setting Values

There are two ways to assign a value: call `SetValue` or assign the `Value` property. `SetValue` is more flexible because it accepts not just strings, but other simple data types too:

```
var e = new XElement ("date", DateTime.Now);
e.SetValue (DateTime.Now.AddDays(1));
Console.Write (e.Value);          // 2007-03-02T16:39:10.734375+09:00
```

We could have instead just set the element's `Value` property, but this would mean manually converting the `DateTime` to a string. This is more complicated than calling `ToString`—it requires the use of `XmlConvert` for an XML-compliant result.

When you pass a *value* into `XElement` or `XAttribute`'s constructor, the same automatic conversion takes place for nonstring types. This ensures that `DateTimes` are correctly formatted; `true` is written in lowercase, and `double.NegativeInfinity` is written as "-INF".

Getting Values

To go the other way around and parse a `Value` back to a base type, you simply cast the `XElement` or `XAttribute` to the desired type. It sounds like it shouldn't work—but it does! For instance:

```
XElement e = new XElement ("now", DateTime.Now);
DateTime dt = (DateTime) e;

XAttribute a = new XAttribute ("resolution", 1.234);
double res = (double) a;
```

An element or attribute doesn't store `DateTimes` or numbers natively—they're always stored as text, and then parsed as needed. It also doesn't "remember" the original type, so you must cast it correctly to avoid a runtime error. To make your code robust, you can put the cast in a `try/catch` block, catching a `FormatException`.

Explicit casts on `XElement` and `XAttribute` can parse to the following types:

- All standard numeric types
- `string`, `bool`, `DateTime`, `DateTimeOffset`, `TimeSpan`, and `Guid`
- `Nullable<>` versions of the aforementioned value types

Casting to a nullable type is useful in conjunction with the `Element` and `Attribute` methods, because if the requested name doesn't exist, the cast still works. For instance, if x has no `timeout` element, the first line generates a runtime error and the second line does not:

```
int timeout = (int) x.Element ("timeout");       // Error
int? timeout = (int?) x.Element ("timeout");     // OK; timeout is null.
```

You can factor away the nullable type in the final result with the `??` operator. The following evaluates to `1.0` if the `resolution` attribute doesn't exist:

```
double resolution = (double?) x.Attribute ("resolution") ?? 1.0;
```

Casting to a nullable type won't get you out of trouble, though, if the element or attribute *exists* and has an empty (or improperly formatted) value. For this, you must catch a `FormatException`.

You can also use casts in LINQ queries. The following returns "John":

```
var data = XElement.Parse (
  @"<data>
      <customer id='1' name='Mary' credit='100' />
      <customer id='2' name='John' credit='150' />
      <customer id='3' name='Anne' />
    </data>");

IEnumerable<string> query = from cust in data.Elements()
                           where (int?) cust.Attribute ("credit") > 100
                           select cust.Attribute ("name").Value;
```

Casting to a nullable `int` avoids a `NullReferenceException` in the case of Anne, who has no `credit` attribute. Another solution would be to add a predicate to the `where` clause:

```
where cust.Attributes ("credit").Any() && (int) cust.Attribute...
```

The same principles apply in querying element values.

Values and Mixed Content Nodes

Giventhe value of `Value`, you might wonder when you'd ever need to deal directly with `XText` nodes. The answer is when you have mixed content. For example:

```
<summary>An XAttribute is <bold>not</bold> an XNode</summary>
```

A simple `Value` property is not enough to capture `summary`'s content. The `summary` element contains three children: an `XText` node followed by an `XElement`, followed by another `XText` node. Here's how to construct it:

```
XElement summary = new XElement ("summary",
                     new XText ("An XAttribute is "),
                     new XElement ("bold", "not"),
                     new XText (" an XNode")
                   );
```

Interestingly, we can still query `summary`'s `Value`—without getting an exception. Instead, we get a concatenation of each child's value:

```
An XAttribute is not an XNode
```

It's also legal to reassign `summary`'s `Value`, at the cost of replacing all previous children with a single new `XText` node.

Automatic XText Concatenation

When you add simple content to an `XElement`, the X-DOM appends to the existing `XText` child rather than creating a new one. In the following examples, `e1` and `e2` end up with just one child `XText` element whose value is `HelloWorld`:

```
var e1 = new XElement ("test", "Hello"); e1.Add ("World");
var e2 = new XElement ("test", "Hello", "World");
```

If you specifically create XText nodes, however, you end up with multiple children:

```
var e = new XElement ("test", new XText ("Hello"), new XText ("World"));
Console.WriteLine (e.Value);             // HelloWorld
Console.WriteLine (e.Nodes().Count());   // 2
```

XElement doesn't concatenate the two XText nodes, so the nodes' object identities are preserved.

Documents and Declarations

XDocument

As we said previously, an XDocument wraps a root XElement and allows you to add an XDeclaration, processing instructions, a document type, and root-level comments. An XDocument is optional and can be ignored or omitted: unlike with the W3C DOM, it does not serve as glue to keep everything together.

An XDocument provides the same functional constructors as XElement. And because it's based on XContainer, it also supports the AddXXX, RemoveXXX, and ReplaceXXX methods. Unlike XElement, however, an XDocument can accept only limited content:

- A single XElement object (the "root")
- A single XDeclaration object
- A single XDocumentType object (to reference a DTD)
- Any number of XProcessingInstruction objects
- Any number of XComment objects

 Of these, only the root XElement is mandatory in order to have a valid XDocument. The XDeclaration is optional—if omitted, default settings are applied during serialization.

The simplest valid XDocument has just a root element:

```
var doc = new XDocument (
        new XElement ("test", "data")
        );
```

Notice that we didn't include an XDeclaration object. The file generated by calling doc.Save would still contain an XML declaration, however, because one is generated by default.

The next example produces a simple but correct XHTML file, illustrating all the constructs that an XDocument can accept:

```
var styleInstruction = new XProcessingInstruction (
  "xml-stylesheet", "href='styles.css' type='text/css'");

var docType = new XDocumentType ("html",
  "-//W3C//DTD XHTML 1.0 Strict//EN",
  "http://www.w3.org/TR/xhtml1/DTD/xhtml1-strict.dtd", null);

XNamespace ns = "http://www.w3.org/1999/xhtml";
var root =
  new XElement (ns + "html",
    new XElement (ns + "head",
      new XElement (ns + "title", "An XHTML page")),
    new XElement (ns + "body",
      new XElement (ns + "p", "This is the content"))
  );

var doc =
  new XDocument (
    new XDeclaration ("1.0", "utf-8", "no"),
    new XComment ("Reference a stylesheet"),
    styleInstruction,
    docType,
    root);

doc.Save ("test.html");
```

The resultant *test.html* reads as follows:

```
<?xml version="1.0" encoding="utf-8" standalone="no"?>
<!--Reference a stylesheet-->
<?xml-stylesheet href='styles.css' type='text/css'?>
<!DOCTYPE html PUBLIC "-//W3C//DTD XHTML 1.0 Strict//EN"
                      "http://www.w3.org/TR/xhtml1/DTD/xhtml1-strict.dtd">
<html xmlns="http://www.w3.org/1999/xhtml">
  <head>
    <title>An XHTML page</title>
  </head>
  <body>
    <p>This is the content</p>
  </body>
</html>
```

XDocument has a Root property that serves as a shortcut for accessing a document's single XElement. The reverse link is provided by XObject's Document property, which works for all objects in the tree:

```
Console.WriteLine (doc.Root.Name.LocalName);        // html
XElement bodyNode = doc.Root.Element (ns + "body");
Console.WriteLine (bodyNode.Document == doc);        // True
```

Recall that a document's children have no Parent:

```
Console.WriteLine (doc.Root.Parent == null);       // True
foreach (XNode node in doc.Nodes())
    Console.Write (node.Parent == null);           // TrueTrueTrueTrue
```

 An XDeclaration is not an XNode and does not appear in the document's Nodes collection—unlike comments, processing instructions, and the root element. Instead, it gets assigned to a dedicated property called Declaration. This is why "True" is repeated four and not five times in the last example.

XML Declarations

A standard XML file starts with a declaration such as the following:

```
<?xml version="1.0" encoding="utf-8" standalone="yes"?>
```

An XML declaration ensures that the file will be correctly parsed and understood by a reader. XElement and XDocument follow these rules in emitting XML declarations:

- Calling Save with a filename always writes a declaration.
- Calling Save with an XmlWriter writes a declaration unless the XmlWriter is instructed otherwise.
- The ToString method never emits an XML declaration.

 You can instruct an XmlWriter not to produce a declaration by setting the OmitXmlDeclaration and ConformanceLevel properties of an XmlWriterSettings object when constructing the XmlWriter. We describe this in Chapter 11.

The presence or absence of an XDeclaration object has no effect on whether an XML declaration gets written. The purpose of an XDeclaration is instead to *hint the XML serialization*—in two ways:

- What text encoding to use
- What to put in the XML declaration's encoding and standalone attributes (should a declaration be written)

XDeclaration's constructor accepts three arguments, which correspond to the attributes version, encoding, and standalone. In the following example, *test.xml* is encoded in UTF-16:

```
var doc = new XDocument (
        new XDeclaration ("1.0", "utf-16", "yes"),
        new XElement ("test", "data")
        );
doc.Save ("test.xml");
```

Whatever you specify for the XML version is ignored by the XML writer: it always writes "1.0".

The encoding must use an IETF code such as "utf-16"—just as it would appear in the XML declaration.

Writing a declaration to a string

Suppose we want to serialize an XDocument to a string—including the XML declaration. Because ToString doesn't write a declaration, we'd have to use an XmlWriter instead:

```
var doc = new XDocument (
            new XDeclaration ("1.0", "utf-8", "yes"),
            new XElement ("test", "data")
         );
var output = new StringBuilder();
var settings = new XmlWriterSettings { Indent = true };
using (XmlWriter xw = XmlWriter.Create (output, settings))
  doc.Save (xw);
Console.WriteLine (output.ToString());
```

This is the result:

```
<?xml version="1.0" encoding="utf-16" standalone="yes"?>
<test>data</test>
```

Notice that we got UTF-16 in the output—even though we explicitly requested UTF-8 in an XDeclaration! This might look like a bug, but in fact, XmlWriter is being remarkably smart. Because we're writing to a string and not a file or stream, it's impossible to apply any encoding other than UTF-16—the format in which strings are internally stored. Hence, XmlWriter writes "utf-16"—so as not to lie.

This also explains why the ToString method doesn't emit an XML declaration. Imagine that instead of calling Save, you did the following to write an XDocument to a file:

```
File.WriteAllText ("data.xml", doc.ToString());
```

As it stands, *data.xml* would lack an XML declaration, making it incomplete but still parsable (you can infer the text encoding). But if ToString() emitted an XML declaration, *data.xml* would actually contain an *incorrect* declaration (encoding="utf-16"), which might prevent it from being read at all, because WriteAllText encodes using UTF-8.

Names and Namespaces

Just as .NET types can have namespaces, so too can XML elements and attributes.

XML namespaces achieve two things. First, rather like namespaces in C#, they help avoid naming collisions. This can become an issue when you merge data from one

XML file into another. Second, namespaces assign *absolute* meaning to a name. The name "nil," for instance, could mean anything. Within the *http://www.w3.org/2001/ xmlschema-instance* namespace, however, "nil" means something equivalent to null in C# and comes with specific rules on how it can be applied.

Because XML namespaces are a significant source of confusion, we'll cover the topic first in general, and then move on to how they're used in LINQ to XML.

Namespaces in XML

Suppose we want to define a `customer` element in the namespace `OReilly.Nut shell.CSharp`. There are two ways to proceed. The first is to use the `xmlns` attribute as follows:

```
<customer xmlns="OReilly.Nutshell.CSharp"/>
```

`xmlns` is a special reserved attribute. When used in this manner, it performs two functions:

- It specifies a namespace for the element in question.
- It specifies a default namespace for all descendant elements.

This means that in the following example, `address` and `postcode` implicitly live in the `OReilly.Nutshell.CSharp` namespace:

```
<customer xmlns="OReilly.Nutshell.CSharp">
  <address>
    <postcode>02138</postcode>
  </address>
</customer>
```

If we want `address` and `postcode` to have *no* namespace, we'd have to do this:

```
<customer xmlns="OReilly.Nutshell.CSharp"s>
  <address xmlns="">
    <postcode>02138</postcode>      <!-- postcode now inherits empty ns -->
  </address>
</customer>
```

Prefixes

The other way to specify a namespace is with a *prefix*. A prefix is an alias that you assign to a namespace to save typing. There are two steps in using a prefix—*defining* the prefix and *using* it. You can do both together as follows:

```
<nut:customer xmlns:nut="OReilly.Nutshell.CSharp"/>
```

Two distinct things are happening here. On the right, `xmlns:nut="..."` defines a prefix called `nut` and makes it available to this element and all its descendants. On the left, `nut:customer` assigns the newly allocated prefix to the `customer` element.

A prefixed element *does not* define a default namespace for descendants. In the following XML, `firstname` has an empty namespace:

```
<nut:customer nut:xmlns="OReilly.Nutshell.CSharp">
  <firstname>Joe</firstname>
</customer>
```

To give `firstname` the `OReilly.Nutshell.CSharp` prefix, we must do this:

```
<nut:customer xmlns:nut="OReilly.Nutshell.CSharp">
  <nut:firstname>Joe</firstname>
</customer>
```

You can also define a prefix—or prefixes—for the convenience of your descendants, without assigning any of them to the parent element itself. The following defines two prefixes, `i` and `z`, while leaving the `customer` element itself with an empty namespace:

```
<customer xmlns:i="http://www.w3.org/2001/XMLSchema-instance"
          xmlns:z="http://schemas.microsoft.com/2003/10/Serialization/">
  ...
</customer>
```

If this was the root node, the whole document would have `i` and `z` at its fingertips. Prefixes are convenient when elements need to draw from a number of namespaces.

Notice that both namespaces in this example are URIs. Using URIs (that you own) is standard practice: it ensures namespace uniqueness. So, in real life, our `customer` element would more likely be:

```
<customer xmlns="http://oreilly.com/schemas/nutshell/csharp"/>
```

or:

```
<nut:customer xmlns:nut="http://oreilly.com/schemas/nutshell/csharp"/>
```

Attributes

You can assign namespaces to attributes too. The main difference is that it always requires a prefix. For instance:

```
<customer xmlns:nut="OReilly.Nutshell.CSharp" nut:id="123" />
```

Another difference is that an unqualified attribute always has an empty namespace: it never inherits a default namespace from a parent element.

Attributes tend not to need namespaces because their meaning is usually local to the element. An exception is with general-purpose or metadata attributes, such as the `nil` attribute defined by W3C:

```
<customer xmlns:xsi="http://www.w3.org/2001/XMLSchema-instance">
  <firstname>Joe</firstname>
  <lastname xsi:nil="true"/>
</customer>
```

This indicates unambiguously that `lastname` is `nil` (`null` in C#) and not an empty string. Because we've used the standard namespace, a general-purpose parsing utility could know with certainty our intention.

Specifying Namespaces in the X-DOM

So far in this chapter, we've used just simple strings for XElement and XAttribute names. A simple string corresponds to an XML name with an empty namespace—rather like a .NET type defined in the global namespace.

There are a couple of ways to specify an XML namespace. The first is to enclose it in braces, before the local name. For example:

```
var e = new XElement ("{http://domain.com/xmlspace}customer", "Bloggs");
Console.WriteLine (e.ToString());
```

Here's the resulting XML:

```
<customer xmlns="http://domain.com/xmlspace">Bloggs</customer>
```

The second (and more performant) approach is to use the XNamespace and XName types. Here are their definitions:

```
public sealed class XNamespace
{
  public string NamespaceName { get; }
}

public sealed class XName      // A local name with optional namespace
{
  public string LocalName { get; }
  public XNamespace Namespace { get; }   // Optional
}
```

Both types define implicit casts from string, so the following is legal:

```
XNamespace ns    = "http://domain.com/xmlspace";
XName localName  = "customer";
XName fullName   = "{http://domain.com/xmlspace}customer";
```

XName also overloads the + operator, allowing you to combine a namespace and name without using braces:

```
XNamespace ns = "http://domain.com/xmlspace";
XName fullName = ns + "customer";
Console.WriteLine (fullName);    // {http://domain.com/xmlspace}customer
```

All constructors and methods in the X-DOM that accept an element or attribute name actually accept an XName object rather than a string. The reason you can substitute a string—as in all our examples to date—is because of the implicit cast.

Specifying a namespace is the same whether for an element or an attribute:

```
XNamespace ns = "http://domain.com/xmlspace";
var data = new XElement (ns + "data",
            new XAttribute (ns + "id", 123)
          );
```

The X-DOM and Default Namespaces

The X-DOM ignores the concept of default namespaces until it comes time to actually output XML. This means that when you construct a child XElement, you must give it a namespace explicitly if needed: it *will not* inherit from the parent:

```
XNamespace ns = "http://domain.com/xmlspace";
var data = new XElement (ns + "data",
                new XElement (ns + "customer", "Bloggs"),
                new XElement (ns + "purchase", "Bicycle")
            );
```

The X-DOM does, however, apply default namespaces when reading and outputting XML:

```
Console.WriteLine (data.ToString());
```

OUTPUT:
```
<data xmlns="http://domain.com/xmlspace">
  <customer>Bloggs</customer>
  <purchase>Bicycle</purchase>
</data>
```

```
Console.WriteLine (data.Element (ns + "customer").ToString());
```

OUTPUT:
```
<customer xmlns="http://domain.com/xmlspace">Bloggs</customer>
```

If you construct XElement children without specifying namespaces—in other words:

```
XNamespace ns = "http://domain.com/xmlspace";
var data = new XElement (ns + "data",
                new XElement ("customer", "Bloggs"),
                new XElement ("purchase", "Bicycle")
            );
Console.WriteLine (data.ToString());
```

you get this result instead:

```
<data xmlns="http://domain.com/xmlspace">
  <customer xmlns="">Bloggs</customer>
  <purchase xmlns="">Bicycle</purchase>
</data>
```

Another trap is failing to include a namespace when navigating an X-DOM:

```
XNamespace ns = "http://domain.com/xmlspace";
var data = new XElement (ns + "data",
                new XElement (ns + "customer", "Bloggs"),
                new XElement (ns + "purchase", "Bicycle")
            );
XElement x = data.Element (ns + "customer");   // ok
XElement y = data.Element ("customer");        // null
```

If you build an X-DOM tree without specifying namespaces, you can subsequently assign every element to a single namespace as follows:

```
foreach (XElement e in data.DescendantsAndSelf())
  if (e.Name.Namespace == "")
    e.Name = ns + e.Name.LocalName;
```

Prefixes

The X-DOM treats prefixes just as it treats namespaces: purely as a serialization
function. This means you can choose to completely ignore the issue of prefixes—
and get by! The only reason you might want to do otherwise is for efficiency when
outputting to an XML file. For example, consider this:

```
XNamespace ns1 = "http://domain.com/space1";
XNamespace ns2 = "http://domain.com/space2";

var mix = new XElement (ns1 + "data",
            new XElement (ns2 + "element", "value"),
            new XElement (ns2 + "element", "value"),
            new XElement (ns2 + "element", "value")
          );
```

By default, XElement will serialize this as follows:

```
<data xmlns="http://domain.com/space1">
  <element xmlns="http://domain.com/space2">value</element>
  <element xmlns="http://domain.com/space2">value</element>
  <element xmlns="http://domain.com/space2">value</element>
</data>
```

As you can see, there's a bit of unnecessary duplication. The solution is *not* to change
the way you construct the X-DOM, but instead to give the serializer a hint prior to
writing the XML. Do this by adding attributes defining prefixes that you want to see
applied. This is typically done on the root element:

```
mix.SetAttributeValue (XNamespace.Xmlns + "ns1", ns1);
mix.SetAttributeValue (XNamespace.Xmlns + "ns2", ns2);
```

This assigns the prefix "ns1" to our XNamespace variable ns1, and "ns2" to ns2. The
X-DOM automatically picks up these attributes when serializing and uses them to
condense the resulting XML. Here's the result now of calling ToString on mix:

```
<ns1:data xmlns:ns1="http://domain.com/space1"
          xmlns:ns2="http://domain.com/space2">
  <ns2:element>value</ns2:element>
  <ns2:element>value</ns2:element>
  <ns2:element>value</ns2:element>
</ns1:data>
```

Prefixes don't change the way you construct, query, or update the X-DOM—for
these activities, you ignore the presence of prefixes and continue to use full names.
Prefixes come into play only when converting to and from XML files or streams.

Prefixes are also honored in serializing attributes. In the following example, we record a customer's date of birth and credit as "nil", using the W3C-standard attribute. The highlighted line ensures that the prefix is serialized without unnecessary
namespace repetition:

```
```

```
XNamespace xsi = "http://www.w3.org/2001/XMLSchema-instance";
var nil = new XAttribute (xsi + "nil", true);

var cust = new XElement ("customers",
              new XAttribute (XNamespace.Xmlns + "xsi", xsi),
              new XElement ("customer",
                new XElement ("lastname", "Bloggs"),
                new XElement ("dob", nil),
                new XElement ("credit", nil)
              )
            );
```

This is its XML:

```
<customers xmlns:xsi="http://www.w3.org/2001/XMLSchema-instance">
  <customer>
    <lastname>Bloggs</lastname>
    <dob xsi:nil="true" />
    <credit xsi:nil="true" />
  </customer>
</customers>
```

For brevity, we predeclared the nil XAttribute so that we could use it twice in building the DOM. You're allowed to reference the same attribute twice because it's automatically duplicated as required.

Annotations

You can attach custom data to any XObject with an annotation. Annotations are intended for your own private use and are treated as black boxes by X-DOM. If you've ever used the Tag property on a Windows Forms or WPF control, you'll be familiar with the concept—the difference is that you have multiple annotations, and your annotations can be *privately scoped*. You can create an annotation that other types cannot even see—let alone overwrite.

The following methods on XObject add and remove annotations:

```
public void AddAnnotation (object annotation)
public void RemoveAnnotations<T>()     where T : class
```

The following methods retrieve annotations:

```
public T Annotation<T>()               where T : class
public IEnumerable<T> Annotations<T>() where T : class
```

Each annotation is keyed by its *type*, which must be a reference type. The following adds and then retrieves a string annotation:

```
XElement e = new XElement ("test");
e.AddAnnotation ("Hello");
Console.WriteLine (e.Annotation<string>());   // Hello
```

You can add multiple annotations of the same type, and then use the Annotations method to retrieve a *sequence* of matches.

A public type such as **string** doesn't make a great key, however, because code in other types can interfere with your annotations. A better approach is to use an internal or (nested) private class:

```
class X
{
  class CustomData { internal string Message; }   // Private nested type

  static void Test()
  {
    XElement e = new XElement ("test");
    e.AddAnnotation (new CustomData { Message = "Hello" } );
    Console.Write (e.Annotations<CustomData>().First().Message);  // Hello
  }
}
```

To remove annotations, you must also have access to the key's type:

```
e.RemoveAnnotations<CustomData>();
```

Projecting into an X-DOM

So far, we've shown how to use LINQ to get data *out* of an X-DOM. You can also use LINQ queries to project *into* an X-DOM. The source can be anything over which LINQ can query, such as:

- LINQ to SQL or Entity Framework queries
- A local collection
- Another X-DOM

Regardless of the source, the strategy is the same in using LINQ to emit an X-DOM: first write a *functional construction* expression that produces the desired X-DOM shape, and then build a LINQ query around the expression.

For instance, suppose we want to retrieve customers from a database into the following XML:

```
<customers>
  <customer id="1">
    <name>Sue</name>
    <buys>3</buys>
  </customer>
  ...
</customers>
```

We start by writing a functional construction expression for the X-DOM using simple literals:

```
var customers =
  new XElement ("customers",
    new XElement ("customer", new XAttribute ("id", 1),
      new XElement ("name", "Sue"),
      new XElement ("buys", 3)
    )
  );
```

We then turn this into a projection and build a LINQ query around it:

```
var customers =
  new XElement ("customers",
    from c in dataContext.Customers
    select
      new XElement ("customer", new XAttribute ("id", c.ID),
        new XElement ("name", c.Name),
        new XElement ("buys", c.Purchases.Count)
      )
  );
```

 In Entity Framework, you must call .ToList() after retrieving customers, so that the third line reads:

```
from c in objectContext.Customers.ToList()
```

Here's the result:

```
<customers>
  <customer id="1">
    <name>Tom</name>
    <buys>3</buys>
  </customer>
  <customer id="2">
    <name>Harry</name>
    <buys>2</buys>
  </customer>
  ...
</customers>
```

We can see how this works more clearly by constructing the same query in two steps. First:

```
IEnumerable<XElement> sqlQuery =
  from c in dataContext.Customers
  select
    new XElement ("customer", new XAttribute ("id", c.ID),
      new XElement ("name", c.Name),
      new XElement ("buys", c.Purchases.Count)
    );
```

This inner portion is a normal LINQ to SQL query that projects into custom types (from LINQ to SQL's perspective). Here's the second step:

```
var customers = new XElement ("customers", sqlQuery);
```

This constructs the root XElement. The only thing unusual is that the content, sqlQuery, is not a single XElement but an IQueryable<XElement>—which implements IEnumerable<XElement>. Remember that in the processing of XML content, collections are automatically enumerated. So, each XElement gets added as a child node.

This outer query also defines the line at which the query transitions from being a database query to a local LINQ to enumerable query. XElement's constructor doesn't know about `IQueryable<>`, so it forces enumeration of the database query—and execution of the SQL statement.

Eliminating Empty Elements

Suppose in the preceding example that we also wanted to include details of the customer's most recent high-value purchase. We could do this as follows:

```
var customers =
  new XElement ("customers",
    from c in dataContext.Customers
    let lastBigBuy = (from p in c.Purchases
                      where p.Price > 1000
                      orderby p.Date descending
                      select p).FirstOrDefault()
    select
      new XElement ("customer", new XAttribute ("id", c.ID),
        new XElement ("name", c.Name),
        new XElement ("buys", c.Purchases.Count),
        new XElement ("lastBigBuy",
          new XElement ("description",
            lastBigBuy == null ? null : lastBigBuy.Description),
          new XElement ("price",
            lastBigBuy == null ? 0m : lastBigBuy.Price)
        )
      )
  );
```

This emits empty elements, though, for customers with no high-value purchases. (If it was a local query rather than a database query, it would throw a `NullReferenceEx ception`.) In such cases, it would be better to omit the `lastBigBuy` node entirely. We can achieve this by wrapping the constructor for the `lastBigBuy` element in a conditional operator:

```
select
  new XElement ("customer", new XAttribute ("id", c.ID),
    new XElement ("name", c.Name),
    new XElement ("buys", c.Purchases.Count),
    lastBigBuy == null ? null :
      new XElement ("lastBigBuy",
        new XElement ("description", lastBigBuy.Description),
        new XElement ("price", lastBigBuy.Price)
```

For customers with no `lastBigBuy`, a `null` is emitted instead of an empty `XElement`. This is what we want, because `null` content is simply ignored.

Streaming a Projection

If you're projecting into an X-DOM only to `Save` it (or call `ToString` on it), you can improve memory efficiency through an `XStreamingElement`. An `XStreamingElement` is a cut-down version of `XElement` that applies *deferred loading* semantics to its child content. To use it, you simply replace the outer `XElement`s with `XStreamingElement`s:

```
var customers =
  new XStreamingElement ("customers",
    from c in dataContext.Customers
    select
      new XStreamingElement ("customer", new XAttribute ("id", c.ID),
        new XElement ("name", c.Name),
        new XElement ("buys", c.Purchases.Count)
      )
    );
customers.Save ("data.xml");
```

The queries passed into an XStreamingElement's constructor are not enumerated until you call Save, ToString, or WriteTo on the element; this avoids loading the whole X-DOM into memory at once. The flipside is that the queries are reevaluated, should you re-Save. Also, you cannot traverse an XStreamingElement's child content—it does not expose methods such as Elements or Attributes.

XStreamingElement is not based on XObject—or any other class—because it has such a limited set of members. The only members it has, besides Save, ToString, and WriteTo, are an Add method, which accepts content like the constructor and a Name property.

XStreamingElement does not allow you to *read* content in a streamed fashion—for this, you must use an XmlReader in conjunction with the X-DOM. We describe how to do this in the section "Patterns for Using XmlReader/XmlWriter" on page 459 in Chapter 11.

Transforming an X-DOM

You can transform an X-DOM by reprojecting it. For instance, suppose we want to transform an *msbuild* XML file, used by the C# compiler and Visual Studio to describe a project, into a simple format suitable for generating a report. An *msbuild* file looks like this:

```
<Project DefaultTargets="Build" xmlns="http://schemas.microsoft.com/dev...>
  <PropertyGroup>
    <Platform Condition=" '$(Platform)' == '' ">AnyCPU</Platform>
    <ProductVersion>9.0.11209</ProductVersion>
    ...
  </PropertyGroup>
  <ItemGroup>
    <Compile Include="ObjectGraph.cs" />
    <Compile Include="Program.cs" />
    <Compile Include="Properties\AssemblyInfo.cs" />
    <Compile Include="Tests\Aggregation.cs" />
    <Compile Include="Tests\Advanced\RecursiveXml.cs" />
  </ItemGroup>
  <ItemGroup>
    ...
  </ItemGroup>
  ...
</Project>
```

Let's say we want to include only files, as follows:

```
<ProjectReport>
  <File>ObjectGraph.cs</File>
  <File>Program.cs</File>
  <File>Properties\AssemblyInfo.cs</File>
  <File>Tests\Aggregation.cs</File>
  <File>Tests\Advanced\RecursiveXml.cs</File>
</ProjectReport>
```

The following query performs this transformation:

```
XElement project = XElement.Load ("myProjectFile.csproj");
XNamespace ns = project.Name.Namespace;
var query =
  new XElement ("ProjectReport",
    from compileItem in
      project.Elements (ns + "ItemGroup").Elements (ns + "Compile")
    let include = compileItem.Attribute ("Include")
    where include != null
    select new XElement ("File", include.Value)
  );
```

The query first extracts all **ItemGroup** elements, and then uses the **Elements** extension method to obtain a flat sequence of all their **Compile** subelements. Notice that we had to specify an XML namespace—everything in the original file inherits the namespace defined by the **Project** element—so a local element name such as **ItemGroup** won't work on its own. Then, we extracted the **Include** attribute value and projected its value as an element.

Advanced transformations

When querying a local collection such as an X-DOM, you're free to write custom query operators to assist with more complex queries.

Suppose in the preceding example that we instead wanted a hierarchical output, based on folders:

```
<Project>
  <File>ObjectGraph.cs</File>
  <File>Program.cs</File>
  <Folder name="Properties">
    <File>AssemblyInfo.cs</File>
  </Folder>
  <Folder name="Tests">
    <File>Aggregation.cs</File>
    <Folder name="Advanced">
      <File>RecursiveXml.cs</File>
    </Folder>
  </Folder>
</Project>
```

To produce this, we need to process path strings such as *Tests\Advanced\RecursiveXml.cs* recursively. The following method does just this: it accepts a sequence of path strings and emits an X-DOM hierarchy consistent with our desired output:

```
static IEnumerable<XElement> ExpandPaths (IEnumerable<string> paths)
{
  var brokenUp = from path in paths
                 let split = path.Split (new char[] { '\\' }, 2)
                 orderby split[0]
                 select new
                 {
                   name = split[0],
                   remainder = split.ElementAtOrDefault (1)
                 };

  IEnumerable<XElement> files = from b in brokenUp
                                where b.remainder == null
                                select new XElement ("file", b.name);

  IEnumerable<XElement> folders = from b in brokenUp
                                  where b.remainder != null
                                  group b.remainder by b.name into grp
                                  select new XElement ("folder",
                                    new XAttribute ("name", grp.Key),
                                    ExpandPaths (grp)
                                  );
  return files.Concat (folders);
}
```

The first query splits each path string at the first backslash, into a name + remainder:

```
Tests\Advanced\RecursiveXml.cs -> Tests + Advanced\RecursiveXml.cs
```

If remainder is null, we're dealing with a straight filename. The files query extracts these cases.

If remainder is not null, we've got a folder. The folders query handles these cases. Because other files can be in the same folder, it must group by folder name to bring them all together. For each group, it then executes the same function for the sub-elements.

The final result is a concatenation of files and folders. The Concat operator preserves order, so all the files come first, alphabetically, then all the folders, alphabetically.

With this method in place, we can complete the query in two steps. First, we extract a simple sequence of path strings:

```
IEnumerable<string> paths =
  from compileItem in
    project.Elements (ns + "ItemGroup").Elements (ns + "Compile")
  let include = compileItem.Attribute ("Include")
  where include != null
  select include.Value;
```

Then, we feed this into our ExpandPaths method for the final result:

```
var query = new XElement ("Project", ExpandPaths (paths));
```

11

Other XML Technologies

The System.Xml namespace comprises the following namespaces and core classes:

System.Xml.*

XmlReader *and* XmlWriter
High-performance, forward-only cursors for reading or writing an XML stream

XmlDocument
Represents an XML document in a W3C-style DOM

System.Xml.XPath
Infrastructure and API (XPathNavigator) for XPath, a string-based language for querying XML

System.Xml.XmlSchema
Infrastructure and API for (W3C) XSD schemas

System.Xml.Xsl
Infrastructure and API (XslCompiledTransform) for performing (W3C) XSLT transformations of XML

System.Xml.Serialization
Supports the serialization of classes to and from XML (see Chapter 16)

System.Xml.XLinq
Modern, simplified, LINQ-centric version of XmlDocument (see Chapter 10)

W3C is an abbreviation for World Wide Web Consortium, where the XML standards are defined.

XmlConvert, the static class for parsing and formatting XML strings, is covered in Chapter 6.

XmlReader

`XmlReader` is a high-performance class for reading an XML stream in a low-level, forward-only manner.

Consider the following XML file:

```
<?xml version="1.0" encoding="utf-8" standalone="yes"?>
<customer id="123" status="archived">
  <firstname>Jim</firstname>
  <lastname>Bo</lastname>
</customer>
```

To instantiate an `XmlReader`, you call the static `XmlReader.Create` method, passing in a `Stream`, a `TextReader`, or a URI string. For example:

```
using (XmlReader reader = XmlReader.Create ("customer.xml"))
  ...
```

To construct an `XmlReader` that reads from a string:

```
XmlReader reader = XmlReader.Create (
  new System.IO.StringReader (myString));
```

You can also pass in an `XmlReaderSettings` object to control parsing and validation options. The following three properties on `XmlReaderSettings` are particularly useful for skipping over superfluous content:

```
bool IgnoreComments                // Skip over comment nodes?
bool IgnoreProcessingInstructions  // Skip over processing instructions?
bool IgnoreWhitespace              // Skip over whitespace?
```

In the following example, we instruct the reader not to emit whitespace nodes, which are a distraction in typical scenarios:

```
XmlReaderSettings settings = new XmlReaderSettings();
settings.IgnoreWhitespace = true;

using (XmlReader reader = XmlReader.Create ("customer.xml", settings))
  ...
```

Another useful property on `XmlReaderSettings` is `ConformanceLevel`. Its default value of `Document` instructs the reader to assume a valid XML document with a single root node. This is a problem if you want to read just an inner portion of XML, containing multiple nodes:

```
<firstname>Jim</firstname>
<lastname>Bo</lastname>
```

To read this without throwing an exception, you must set `ConformanceLevel` to `Fragment`.

`XmlReaderSettings` also has a property called `CloseInput`, which indicates whether to close the underlying stream when the reader is closed (there's an analogous property on `XmlWriterSettings` called `CloseOutput`). The default value for `CloseInput` and `CloseOutput` is true.

Reading Nodes

The units of an XML stream are *XML nodes*. The reader traverses the stream in textual (depth-first) order. The Depth property of the reader returns the current depth of the cursor.

The most primitive way to read from an XmlReader is to call Read. It advances to the next node in the XML stream, rather like MoveNext in IEnumerator. The first call to Read positions the cursor at the first node. When Read returns false, it means the cursor has advanced *past* the last node, at which point the XmlReader should be closed and abandoned.

In this example, we read every node in the XML stream, outputting each node type as we go:

```
XmlReaderSettings settings = new XmlReaderSettings();
settings.IgnoreWhitespace = true;

using (XmlReader reader = XmlReader.Create ("customer.xml", settings))
  while (reader.Read())
  {
    Console.Write (new string (' ',reader.Depth*2));  // Write indentation
    Console.WriteLine (reader.NodeType);
  }
```

The output is as follows:

```
XmlDeclaration
Element
  Element
    Text
  EndElement
  Element
    Text
  EndElement
EndElement
```

 Attributes are not included in Read-based traversal (see the section "Reading Attributes" on page 454, later in this chapter).

NodeType is of type XmlNodeType, which is an enum with these members:

None	Comment	Document
XmlDeclaration	Entity	DocumentType
Element	EndEntity	DocumentFragment
EndElement	EntityReference	Notation
Text	ProcessingInstruction	Whitespace
Attribute	CDATA	SignificantWhitespace

Two **string** properties on XmlReader provide access to a node's content: Name and
Value. Depending on the node type, either Name or Value (or both) is populated:

```
XmlReaderSettings settings = new XmlReaderSettings();
settings.IgnoreWhitespace = true;
settings.ProhibitDtd = false;      // Must set this to read DTDs

using (XmlReader r = XmlReader.Create ("customer.xml", settings))
  while (r.Read())
  {
    Console.Write (r.NodeType.ToString().PadRight (17, '-'));
    Console.Write ("> ".PadRight (r.Depth * 3));

    switch (r.NodeType)
    {
      case XmlNodeType.Element:
      case XmlNodeType.EndElement:
        Console.WriteLine (r.Name); break;

      case XmlNodeType.Text:
      case XmlNodeType.CDATA:
      case XmlNodeType.Comment:
      case XmlNodeType.XmlDeclaration:
        Console.WriteLine (r.Value); break;

      case XmlNodeType.DocumentType:
        Console.WriteLine (r.Name + " - " + r.Value); break;

      default: break;
    }
  }
```

To demonstrate this, we'll expand our XML file to include a document type, entity,
CDATA, and comment:

```
<?xml version="1.0" encoding="utf-8" ?>
<!DOCTYPE customer [ <!ENTITY tc "Top Customer"> ]>
<customer id="123" status="archived">
  <firstname>Jim</firstname>
  <lastname>Bo</lastname>
  <quote><![CDATA[C#'s operators include: < > &]]></quote>
  <notes>Jim Bo is a &tc;</notes>
  <!-- That wasn't so bad! -->
</customer>
```

An entity is like a macro; a CDATA is like a verbatim string (@"...") in C#. Here's
the result:

```
XmlDeclaration---> version="1.0" encoding="utf-8"
DocumentType-----> customer -  <!ENTITY tc "Top Customer">
Element----------> customer
Element----------> firstname
Text-------------> Jim
EndElement-------> firstname
Element----------> lastname
Text-------------> Bo
EndElement-------> lastname
```

```
Element---------->  quote
CDATA------------>      C#'s operators include: < > &
EndElement------->  quote
Element---------->  notes
Text------------->      Jim Bo is a Top Customer
EndElement------->  notes
Comment---------->      That wasn't so bad!
EndElement------->  customer
```

XmlReader automatically resolves entities, so in our example, the entity reference &tc; expands into Top Customer.

Reading Elements

Often, you already know the structure of the XML document that you're reading. To help with this, XmlReader provides a range of methods that read while *presuming* a particular structure. This simplifies your code, as well as performing some validation at the same time.

 XmlReader throws an XmlException if any validation fails. XmlException has LineNumber and LinePosition properties indicating where the error occurred—logging this information is essential if the XML file is large!

ReadStartElement verifies that the current NodeType is StartElement, and then calls Read. If you specify a name, it verifies that it matches that of the current element.

ReadEndElement verifies that the current NodeType is EndElement, and then calls Read.

For instance, we could read this:

```
<firstname>Jim</firstname>
```

as follows:

```
reader.ReadStartElement ("firstname");
Console.WriteLine (reader.Value);
reader.ReadEndElement();
```

The ReadElementContentAsString method does all of this in one hit. It reads a start element, a text node, and an end element, returning the content as a string:

```
string firstName = reader.ReadElementContentAsString ("firstname", "");
```

The second argument refers to the namespace, which is blank in this example. There are also typed versions of this method, such as ReadElementContentAsInt, which parse the result. Returning to our original XML document:

```
<?xml version="1.0" encoding="utf-8" standalone="yes"?>
<customer id="123" status="archived">
  <firstname>Jim</firstname>
  <lastname>Bo</lastname>
  <creditlimit>500.00</creditlimit>    <!-- OK, we sneaked this in! -->
</customer>
```

We could read it in as follows:

```
XmlReaderSettings settings = new XmlReaderSettings();
settings.IgnoreWhitespace = true;

using (XmlReader r = XmlReader.Create ("customer.xml", settings))
{
  r.MoveToContent();                    // Skip over the XML declaration
  r.ReadStartElement ("customer");
  string firstName    = r.ReadElementContentAsString ("firstname", "");
  string lastName     = r.ReadElementContentAsString ("lastname", "");
  decimal creditLimit = r.ReadElementContentAsDecimal ("creditlimit", "");

  r.MoveToContent();      // Skip over that pesky comment
  r.ReadEndElement();     // Read the closing customer tag
}
```

 The MoveToContent method is really useful. It skips over all the fluff: XML declarations, whitespace, comments, and processing instructions. You can also instruct the reader to do most of this automatically through the properties on XmlReaderSettings.

Optional elements

In the previous example, suppose that `<lastname>` was optional. The solution to this is straightforward:

```
r.ReadStartElement ("customer");
string firstName    = r. ReadElementContentAsString ("firstname", "");
string lastName     = r.Name == "lastname"
                       ? r.ReadElementContentAsString() : null;
decimal creditLimit = r.ReadElementContentAsDecimal ("creditlimit", "");
```

Random element order

The examples in this section rely on elements appearing in the XML file in a set order. If you need to cope with elements appearing in any order, the easiest solution is to read that section of the XML into an X-DOM. We describe how to do this later in the section "Patterns for Using XmlReader/XmlWriter" on page 459.

Empty elements

The way that XmlReader handles empty elements presents a horrible trap. Consider the following element:

```
<customerList></customerList>
```

In XML, this is equivalent to:

```
<customerList/>
```

And yet, XmlReader treats the two differently. In the first case, the following code works as expected:

```
reader.ReadStartElement ("customerList");
reader.ReadEndElement();
```

In the second case, `ReadEndElement` throws an exception, because there is no separate "end element" as far as `XmlReader` is concerned. The workaround is to check for an empty element as follows:

```
bool isEmpty = reader.IsEmptyElement;
reader.ReadStartElement ("customerList");
if (!isEmpty) reader.ReadEndElement();
```

In reality, this is a nuisance only when the element in question may contain child elements (such as a customer list). With elements that wrap simple text (such as `firstname`), you can avoid the whole issue by calling a method such as `ReadElement ContentAsString`. The `ReadElementXXX` methods handle both kinds of empty elements correctly.

Other ReadXXX methods

Table 11-1 summarizes all `ReadXXX` methods in `XmlReader`. Most of these are designed to work with elements. The sample XML fragment shown in bold is the section read by the method described.

Table 11-1. Read methods

Members	Works on NodeType	Sample XML fragment	Input parameters	Data returned
ReadContentAsXXX	Text	`<a>`x`</a>`		x
ReadString	Text	`<a>`x`</a>`		x
ReadElementString	Element	**`<a>x</a>`**		x
ReadElementContentAsXXX	Element	**`<a>x</a>`**		x
ReadInnerXml	Element	**`<a>x</a>`**		x
ReadOuterXml	Element	**`<a>x</a>`**		`<a>`x`</a>`
ReadStartElement	Element	**`<a>`**x`</a>`		
ReadEndElement	Element	`<a>`x**`</a>`**		
ReadSubtree	Element	**`<a>x</a>`**		`<a>`x`</a>`
ReadToDescendent	Element	`<a>`x**`<b></b>`**`</a>`	"b"	
ReadToFollowing	Element	`<a>`x**`<b></b>`**`</a>`	"b"	
ReadToNextSibling	Element	`<a>`x`</a>`**`<b></b>`**	"b"	
ReadAttributeValue	Attribute	See "Reading Attributes" on page 454		

The `ReadContentAsXXX` methods parse a text node into type *XXX*. Internally, the `XmlConvert` class performs the string-to-type conversion. The text node can be within an element or an attribute.

The `ReadElementContentAsXXX` methods are wrappers around corresponding `Read ContentAsXXX` methods. They apply to the *element* node, rather than the *text* node enclosed by the element.

 The typed `ReadXXX` methods also include versions that read base 64 and BinHex formatted data into a byte array.

`ReadInnerXml` is typically applied to an element, and it reads and returns an element and all its descendents. When applied to an attribute, it returns the value of the attribute.

`ReadOuterXml` is the same as `ReadInnerXml`, except it includes rather than excludes the element at the cursor position.

`ReadSubtree` returns a proxy reader that provides a view over just the current element (and its descendents). The proxy reader must be closed before the original reader can be safely read again. At the point the proxy reader is closed, the cursor position of the original reader moves to the end of the subtree.

`ReadToDescendent` moves the cursor to the start of the first descendent node with the specified name/namespace.

`ReadToFollowing` moves the cursor to the start of the first node—regardless of depth—with the specified name/namespace.

`ReadToNextSibling` moves the cursor to the start of the first sibling node with the specified name/namespace.

`ReadString` and `ReadElementString` behave like `ReadContentAsString` and `ReadEle mentContentAsString`, except that they throw an exception if there's more than a *single* text node within the element. In general, these methods should be avoided, as they throw an exception if an element contains a comment.

Reading Attributes

`XmlReader` provides an indexer giving you direct (random) access to an element's attributes—by name or position. Using the indexer is equivalent to calling `GetAttribute`.

Given the following XML fragment:

```
<customer id="123" status="archived"/>
```

we could read its attributes as follows:

```
Console.WriteLine (reader ["id"]);          // 123
Console.WriteLine (reader ["status"]);      // archived
Console.WriteLine (reader ["bogus"] == null);  // True
```

The XmlReader must be positioned *on a start element* in order to read attributes. *After* calling ReadStartElement, the attributes are gone forever!

Although attribute order is semantically irrelevant, you can access attributes by their ordinal position. We could rewrite the preceding example as follows:

```
Console.WriteLine (reader [0]);       // 123
Console.WriteLine (reader [1]);       // archived
```

The indexer also lets you specify the attribute's namespace—if it has one.

AttributeCount returns the number of attributes for the current node.

Attribute nodes

To explicitly traverse attribute nodes, you must make a special diversion from the normal path of just calling Read. A good reason to do so is if you want to parse attribute values into other types, via the ReadContentAs*XXX* methods.

The diversion must begin from a *start element*. To make the job easier, the forward-only rule is relaxed during attribute traversal: you can jump to any attribute (forward or backward) by calling MoveToAttribute.

MoveToElement returns you to the start element from anyplace within the attribute node diversion.

Returning to our previous example:

```
<customer id="123" status="archived"/>
```

we can do this:

```
reader.MoveToAttribute ("status");
string status = ReadContentAsString();

reader.MoveToAttribute ("id");
int id = ReadContentAsInt();
```

MoveToAttribute returns false if the specified attribute doesn't exist.

You can also traverse each attribute in sequence by calling the MoveToFirstAttribute and then the MoveToNextAttribute methods:

```
if (reader.MoveToFirstAttribute())
  do
  {
    Console.WriteLine (reader.Name + "=" + reader.Value);
  }
  while (reader.MoveToNextAttribute());

// OUTPUT:
```

```
id=123
status=archived
```

Namespaces and Prefixes

XmlReader provides two parallel systems for referring to element and attribute names:

- Name
- NamespaceURI and LocalName

Whenever you read an element's Name property or call a method that accepts a single name argument, you're using the first system. This works well if no namespaces or prefixes are present; otherwise, it acts in a crude and literal manner. Namespaces are ignored, and prefixes are included exactly as they were written. For example:

Sample fragment	Name
<customer ...>	customer
<customer xmlns='blah' ...>	customer
<x:customer ...>	x:customer

The following code works with the first two cases:

```
reader.ReadStartElement ("customer");
```

The following is required to handle the third case:

```
reader.ReadStartElement ("x:customer");
```

The second system works through two *namespace-aware* properties: NamespaceURI and LocalName. These properties take into account prefixes and default namespaces defined by parent elements. Prefixes are automatically expanded. This means that NamespaceURI always reflects the semantically correct namespace for the current element, and LocalName is always free of prefixes.

When you pass two name arguments into a method such as ReadStartElement, you're using this same system. For example, consider the following XML:

```
<customer xmlns="DefaultNamespace" xmlns:other="OtherNamespace">
  <address>
    <other:city>
    ...
```

We could read this as follows:

```
reader.ReadStartElement ("customer", "DefaultNamespace");
reader.ReadStartElement ("address",  "DefaultNamespace");
reader.ReadStartElement ("city",     "OtherNamespace");
```

Abstracting away prefixes is usually exactly what you want. If necessary, you can see what prefix was used through the Prefix property and convert it into a namespace by calling LookupNamespace.

XmlWriter

`XmlWriter` is a forward-only writer of an XML stream. The design of `XmlWriter` is symmetrical to `XmlReader`.

As with `XmlTextReader`, you construct an `XmlWriter` by calling `Create` with an optional `settings` object. In the following example, we enable indenting to make the output more human-readable, and then write a simple XML file:

```
XmlWriterSettings settings = new XmlWriterSettings();
settings.Indent = true;

using (XmlWriter writer = XmlWriter.Create ("..\\..\\foo.xml", settings))
{
  writer.WriteStartElement ("customer");
  writer.WriteElementString ("firstname", "Jim");
  writer.WriteElementString ("lastname"," Bo");
  writer.WriteEndElement();
}
```

This produces the following document (the same as the file we read in the first example of `XmlReader`):

```
<?xml version="1.0" encoding="utf-8" ?>
<customer>
  <firstname>Jim</firstname>
  <lastname>Bo</lastname>
</customer>
```

`XmlWriter` automatically writes the declaration at the top unless you indicate otherwise in `XmlWriterSettings`, by setting `OmitXmlDeclaration` to `true` or `ConformanceLevel` to `Fragment`. The latter also permits writing multiple root nodes—something that otherwise throws an exception.

The `WriteValue` method writes a single text node. It accepts both string and nonstring types such as `bool` and `DateTime`, internally calling `XmlConvert` to perform XML-compliant string conversions:

```
writer.WriteStartElement ("birthdate");
writer.WriteValue (DateTime.Now);
writer.WriteEndElement();
```

In contrast, if we call:

```
WriteElementString ("birthdate", DateTime.Now.ToString());
```

the result would be both non-XML-compliant and vulnerable to incorrect parsing.

`WriteString` is equivalent to calling `WriteValue` with a string. `XmlWriter` automatically escapes characters that would otherwise be illegal within an attribute or element, such as `&` `<` `>`, and extended Unicode characters.

Writing Attributes

You can write attributes immediately after writing a start element:

```
writer.WriteStartElement ("customer");
writer.WriteAttributeString ("id", "1");
writer.WriteAttributeString ("status", "archived");
```

To write nonstring values, call WriteStartAttribute, WriteValue, and then WriteEndAttribute.

Writing Other Node Types

XmlWriter also defines the following methods for writing other kinds of nodes:

```
WriteBase64          // for binary data
WriteBinHex          // for binary data
WriteCData
WriteComment
WriteDocType
WriteEntityRef
WriteProcessingInstruction
WriteRaw
WriteWhitespace
```

WriteRaw directly injects a string into the output stream. There is also a WriteNode method that accepts an XmlReader, echoing everything from the given XmlReader.

Namespaces and Prefixes

The overloads for the Write* methods allow you to associate an element or attribute with a namespace. Let's rewrite the contents of the XML file in our previous example. This time we will associate all the elements with the *http://oreilly.com* namespace, declaring the prefix o at the customer element:

```
writer.WriteStartElement ("o", "customer", "http://oreilly.com");
writer.WriteElementString ("o", "firstname", "http://oreilly.com", "Jim");
writer.WriteElementString ("o", "lastname", "http://oreilly.com", "Bo");
writer.WriteEndElement();
```

The output is now as follows:

```
<?xml version="1.0" encoding="utf-8" standalone="yes"?>
<o:customer xmlns:o='http://oreilly.com'>
  <o:firstname>Jim</o:firstname>
  <o:lastname>Bo</o:lastname>
</o:customer>
```

Notice how for brevity XmlWriter omits the child element's namespace declarations when they are already declared by the parent element.

Patterns for Using XmlReader/XmlWriter

Working with Hierarchical Data

Consider the following classes:

```
public class Contacts
{
  public IList<Customer> Customers = new List<Customer>();
  public IList<Supplier> Suppliers = new List<Supplier>();
}

public class Customer { public string FirstName, LastName; }
public class Supplier { public string Name;              }
```

Suppose you want to use `XmlReader` and `XmlWriter` to serialize a `Contacts` object to XML as in the following:

```
<?xml version="1.0" encoding="utf-8" standalone="yes"?>
<contacts>
  <customer id="1">
    <firstname>Jay</firstname>
    <lastname>Dee</lastname>
  </customer>
  <customer>                        <!-- we'll assume id is optional -->
    <firstname>Kay</firstname>
    <lastname>Gee</lastname>
  </customer>
  <supplier>
    <name>X Technologies Ltd</name>
  </supplier>
</contacts>
```

The best approach is not to write one big method, but to encapsulate XML functionality in the `Customer` and `Supplier` types themselves by writing `ReadXml` and `WriteXml` methods on these types. The pattern in doing so is straightforward:

- `ReadXml` and `WriteXml` leave the reader/writer at the same depth when they exit.
- `ReadXml` reads the outer element, whereas `WriteXml` writes only its inner content.

Here's how we would write the `Customer` type:

```
public class Customer
{
  public const string XmlName = "customer";
  public int? ID;
  public string FirstName, LastName;

  public Customer () { }
  public Customer (XmlReader r) { ReadXml (r); }

  public void ReadXml (XmlReader r)
  {
    if (r.MoveToAttribute ("id")) ID = r.ReadContentAsInt();
    r.ReadStartElement();
```

```
      FirstName = r.ReadElementContentAsString ("firstname", "");
      LastName = r.ReadElementContentAsString ("lastname", "");
      r.ReadEndElement();
    }

    public void WriteXml (XmlWriter w)
    {
      if (ID.HasValue) w.WriteAttributeString ("id", "", ID.ToString());
      w.WriteElementString ("firstname", FirstName);
      w.WriteElementString ("lastname", LastName);
    }
  }
}
```

Notice that `ReadXml` reads the outer start and end element nodes. If its caller did this job instead, `Customer` couldn't read its own attributes. The reason for not making `WriteXml` symmetrical in this regard is twofold:

- The caller might need to choose how the outer element is named.
- The caller might need to write extra XML attributes, such as the element's *subtype* (which could then be used to decide which class to instantiate when reading back the element).

Another benefit of following this pattern is that it makes your implementation compatible with `IXmlSerializable` (see Chapter 16).

The `Supplier` class is analogous:

```
public class Supplier
{
  public const string XmlName = "supplier";
  public string Name;

  public Supplier () { }
  public Supplier (XmlReader r) { ReadXml (r); }

  public void ReadXml (XmlReader r)
  {
    r.ReadStartElement();
    Name = r.ReadElementContentAsString ("name", "");
    r.ReadEndElement();
  }

  public void WriteXml (XmlWriter w)
  {
    w.WriteElementString ("name", Name);
  }
}
```

With the `Contacts` class, we must enumerate the `customers` element in `ReadXml`, checking whether each subelement is a customer or a supplier. We also have to code around the empty element trap:

```
public void ReadXml (XmlReader r)
{
  bool isEmpty = r.IsEmptyElement;        // This ensures we don't get
  r.ReadStartElement();                   // snookered by an empty
```

```
    if (isEmpty) return;                    // <contacts/> element!
    while (r.NodeType == XmlNodeType.Element)
    {
      if (r.Name == Customer.XmlName)     Customers.Add (new Customer (r));
      else if (r.Name == Supplier.XmlName) Suppliers.Add (new Supplier (r));
      else
        throw new XmlException ("Unexpected node: " + r.Name);
    }
    r.ReadEndElement();
  }

  public void WriteXml (XmlWriter w)
  {
    foreach (Customer c in Customers)
    {
      w.WriteStartElement (Customer.XmlName);
      c.WriteXml (w);
      w.WriteEndElement();
    }
    foreach (Supplier s in Suppliers)
    {
      w.WriteStartElement (Supplier.XmlName);
      s.WriteXml (w);
      w.WriteEndElement();
    }
  }
}
```

Mixing XmlReader/XmlWriter with an X-DOM

You can fly in an X-DOM at any point in the XML tree where XmlReader or
XmlWriter becomes too cumbersome. Using the X-DOM to handle inner elements
is an excellent way to combine X-DOM's ease of use with the low-memory footprint
of XmlReader and XmlWriter.

Using XmlReader with XElement

To read the current element into an X-DOM, you call XNode.ReadFrom, passing in
the XmlReader. Unlike XElement.Load, this method is not "greedy" in that it doesn't
expect to see a whole document. Instead, it reads just the end of the current subtree.

For instance, suppose we have an XML logfile structured as follows:

```
<log>
  <logentry id="1">
    <date>...</date>
    <source>...</source>
    ...
  </logentry>
  ...
</log>
```

If there were 1 million `logentry` elements, reading the whole thing into an X-DOM would waste memory. A better solution is to traverse each `logentry` with an `XmlReader`, and then use `XElement` to process the elements individually:

```
XmlReaderSettings settings = new XmlReaderSettings();
settings.IgnoreWhitespace = true;

using (XmlReader r = XmlReader.Create ("logfile.xml", settings))
{
  r.ReadStartElement ("log");
  while (r.Name == "logentry")
  {
    XElement logEntry = (XElement) XNode.ReadFrom (r);
    int id = (int) logEntry.Attribute ("id");
    DateTime date = (DateTime) logEntry.Element ("date");
    string source = (string) logEntry.Element ("source");
    ...
  }
  r.ReadEndElement();
}
```

If you follow the pattern described in the previous section, you can slot an `XElement` into a custom type's `ReadXml` or `WriteXml` method without the caller ever knowing you've cheated! For instance, we could rewrite `Customer`'s `ReadXml` method as follows:

```
public void ReadXml (XmlReader r)
{
  XElement x = (XElement) XNode.ReadFrom (r);
  FirstName = (string) x.Element ("firstname");
  LastName = (string) x.Element ("lastname");
}
```

`XElement` collaborates with `XmlReader` to ensure that namespaces are kept intact and prefixes are properly expanded—even if defined at an outer level. So, if our XML file read like this:

```
<log xmlns="http://loggingspace">
  <logentry id="1">
  ...
```

the `XElements` we constructed at the `logentry` level would correctly inherit the outer namespace.

Using XmlWriter with XElement

You can use an `XElement` just to write inner elements to an `XmlWriter`. The following code writes 1 million `logentry` elements to an XML file using `XElement`—without storing the whole thing in memory:

```
using (XmlWriter w = XmlWriter.Create ("log.xml"))
{
  w.WriteStartElement ("log");
  for (int i = 0; i < 1000000; i++)
  {
    XElement e = new XElement ("logentry",
                   new XAttribute ("id", i),
                   new XElement ("date", DateTime.Today.AddDays (-1)),
                   new XElement ("source", "test"));
    e.WriteTo (w);
  }
  w.WriteEndElement ();
}
```

Using an XElement incurs minimal execution overhead. If we amend this example to use XmlWriter throughout, there's no measurable difference in execution time.

XmlDocument

XmlDocument is an in-memory representation of an XML document. Its object model and the methods that its types expose conform to a pattern defined by the W3C. So, if you're familiar with another W3C-compliant XML DOM (e.g., in Java), you'll be at home with XmlDocument. When compared to the X-DOM, however, the W3C model is much "clunkier."

The base type for all objects in an XmlDocument tree is XmlNode. The following types derive from XmlNode:

```
XmlNode
  XmlDocument
  XmlDocumentFragment
  XmlEntity
  XmlNotation
  XmlLinkedNode
```

XmlLinkedNode exposes NextSibling and PreviousSibling properties and is an abstract base for the following subtypes:

```
XmlLinkedNode
  XmlCharacterData
  XmlDeclaration
  XmlDocumentType
  XmlElement
  XmlEntityReference
  XmlProcesingInstruction
```

Loading and Saving an XmlDocument

To load an XmlDocument from an existing source, you instantiate an XmlDocument and then call Load or LoadXml:

- Load accepts a filename, Stream, TextReader, or XmlReader.
- LoadXml accepts a literal XML string.

To save a document, call Save with a filename, Stream, TextWriter, or XmlWriter:

```
XmlDocument doc = new XmlDocument();
doc.Load ("customer1.xml");
doc.Save ("customer2.xml");
```

Traversing an XmlDocument

To illustrate traversing an XmlDocument, we'll use the following XML file:

```
<?xml version="1.0" encoding="utf-8" standalone="yes"?>
<customer id="123" status="archived">
  <firstname>Jim</firstname>
  <lastname>Bo</lastname>
</customer>
```

The ChildNodes property (defined in XNode) allows you to descend into the tree structure. This returns an indexable collection:

```
XmlDocument doc = new XmlDocument();
doc.Load ("customer.xml");

Console.WriteLine (doc.DocumentElement.ChildNodes[0].InnerText);   // Jim
Console.WriteLine (doc.DocumentElement.ChildNodes[1].InnerText);   // Bo
```

With the ParentNode property, you can ascend back up the tree:

```
Console.WriteLine (
    doc.DocumentElement.ChildNodes[1].ParentNode.Name);         // customer
```

The following properties also help traverse the document (all of which return null if the node does not exist):

```
FirstChild
LastChild
NextSibling
PreviousSibling
```

The following two statements both output firstname:

```
Console.WriteLine (doc.DocumentElement.FirstChild.Name);
Console.WriteLine (doc.DocumentElement.LastChild.PreviousSibling.Name);
```

XmlNode exposes an Attributes property for accessing attributes either by name (and namespace) or by ordinal position. For example:

```
Console.WriteLine (doc.DocumentElement.Attributes ["id"].Value);
```

InnerText and InnerXml

The InnerText property represents the concatenation of all child text nodes. The following two lines both output Jim, since our XML document contains only a single text node:

```
Console.WriteLine (doc.DocumentElement.ChildNodes[0].InnerText);
Console.WriteLine (doc.DocumentElement.ChildNodes[0].FirstChild.Value);
```

Setting the `InnerText` property replaces *all* child nodes with a single text node. Be careful when setting `InnerText` to not accidentally wipe over element nodes. For example:

```
doc.DocumentElement.ChildNodes[0].InnerText = "Jo";            // wrong
doc.DocumentElement.ChildNodes[0].FirstChild.InnerText = "Jo"; // right
```

The `InnerXml` property represents the XML fragment *within* the current node. You typically use `InnerXml` on elements:

```
Console.WriteLine (doc.DocumentElement.InnerXml);

// OUTPUT:
<firstname>Jim</firstname><lastname>Bo</lastname>
```

`InnerXml` throws an exception if the node type cannot have children.

Creating and Manipulating Nodes

To create and add new nodes:

1. Call one of the `CreateXXX` methods on the `XmlDocument`, such as `CreateElement`.
2. Add the new node into the tree by calling `AppendChild`, `PrependChild`, `InsertBefore`, or `InsertAfter` on the desired parent node.

> Creating nodes requires that you first have an `XmlDocument`— you cannot simply instantiate an `XmlElement` on its own like with the X-DOM. Nodes rely on a host `XmlDocument` for sustenance.

For example:

```
XmlDocument doc = new XmlDocument();
XmlElement customer = doc.CreateElement ("customer");
doc.AppendChild (customer);
```

The following creates a document matching the XML we started with earlier in this chapter in the section "XmlReader" on page 448:

```
XmlDocument doc = new XmlDocument ();
doc.AppendChild (doc.CreateXmlDeclaration ("1.0", null, "yes"));

XmlAttribute id     = doc.CreateAttribute ("id");
XmlAttribute status = doc.CreateAttribute ("status");
id.Value     = "123";
status.Value = "archived";

XmlElement firstname = doc.CreateElement ("firstname");
XmlElement lastname  = doc.CreateElement ("lastname");
firstname.AppendChild (doc.CreateTextNode ("Jim"));
lastname.AppendChild  (doc.CreateTextNode ("Bo"));

XmlElement customer = doc.CreateElement ("customer");
customer.Attributes.Append (id);
customer.Attributes.Append (status);
```

```
customer.AppendChild (lastname);
customer.AppendChild (firstname);

doc.AppendChild (customer);
```

You can construct the tree in any order. In the previous example, it doesn't matter if you rearrange the order of the lines that append child nodes.

To remove a node, you call `RemoveChild`, `ReplaceChild`, or `RemoveAll`.

Namespaces

 See Chapter 10 for an introduction to XML namespaces and prefixes.

The `CreateElement` and `CreateAttribute` methods are overloaded to let you specify a namespace and prefix:

```
CreateXXX (string name);
CreateXXX (string name, string namespaceURI);
CreateXXX (string prefix, string localName, string namespaceURI);
```

The `name` parameter refers to either a local name (i.e., no prefix) or a name qualified with a prefix. The `namespaceURI` parameter is used if and only if you are *declaring* (rather than merely referring to) a namespace.

Here is an example of *declaring* a namespace with a prefix while creating an element:

```
XmlElement customer = doc.CreateElement ("o", "customer",
                                         "http://oreilly.com");
```

Here is an example of *referring* to a namespace with a prefix while creating an element:

```
XmlElement customer = doc.CreateElement ("o:firstname");
```

In the next section, we will explain how to deal with namespaces when writing XPath queries.

XPath

XPath is the W3C standard for XML querying. In the .NET Framework, XPath can query an `XmlDocument` rather like LINQ queries an X-DOM. XPath has a wider scope, though, in that it's also used by other XML technologies, such as XML schema, XLST, and XAML.

XPath queries are expressed in terms of the XPath 2.0 Data Model. Both the DOM and the XPath Data Model represent an XML document as a tree. The difference is that the XPath Data Model is purely data-centric, abstracting away the formatting aspects of XML text. For example, CDATA sections are not required in the XPath Data Model, since the only reason CDATA sections exist is to enable text to contain markup character sequences. The XPath specification is at *http://www.w3.org/tr/xpath20/*.

The examples in this section all use the following XML file:

```xml
<?xml version="1.0" encoding="utf-8" standalone="yes"?>
<customers>
  <customer id="123" status="archived">
    <firstname>Jim</firstname>
    <lastname>Bo</lastname>
  </customer>
  <customer>
    <firstname>Thomas</firstname>
    <lastname>Jefferson</lastname>
  </customer>
</customers>
```

You can write XPath queries within code in the following ways:

- Call one of the Select*XXX* methods on an XmlDocument or XmlNode.
- Spawn an XPathNavigator from either:
  — An XmlDocument
  — An XPathDocument
- Call an XPath*XXX* extension method on an XNode.

The Select*XXX* methods accept an XPath query string. For example, the following finds the firstname node of an XmlDocument:

```
XmlDocument doc = new XmlDocument();
doc.Load ("customers.xml");
XmlNode n = doc.SelectSingleNode ("customers/customer[firstname='Jim']");
Console.WriteLine (n.InnerText);   // JimBo
```

The Select*XXX* methods delegate their implementation to XPathNavigator, which you can also use directly—over either an XmlDocument or a read-only XPathDocument.

You can also execute XPath queries over an X-DOM, via extension methods defined in System.Xml.XPath:

```
XDocument doc = XDocument.Load (@"Customers.xml");
XElement e = e.XPathSelectElement ("customers/customer[firstname='Jim']");
Console.WriteLine (e.Value);   // JimBo
```

The extension methods for use with XNodes are:

```
CreateNavigator
XPathEvaluate
XPathSelectElement
XPathSelectElements
```

Common XPath Operators

The XPath specification is huge. However, you can get by knowing just a few operators (see Table 11-2), just as you can play a lot of songs knowing just three chords.

Table 11-2. Common XPath operators

Operator	Description
/	Children
//	Recursively children
.	Current node (usually implied)
..	Parent node
*	Wildcard
@	Attribute
[ ]	Filter
:	Namespace separator

To find the customers node:

```
XmlNode node = doc.SelectSingleNode ("customers");
```

The / symbol queries child nodes. To select the customer nodes:

```
XmlNode node = doc.SelectSingleNode ("customers/customer");
```

The // operator includes all child nodes, regardless of nesting level. To select all lastname nodes:

```
XmlNodeList nodes = doc.SelectNodes ("//lastname");
```

The .. operator selects parent nodes. This example is a little silly because we're starting from the root anyway, but it serves to illustrate the functionality:

```
XmlNodeList nodes = doc.SelectNodes ("customers/customer..customers");
```

The * operator selects nodes regardless of name. The following selects the child nodes of customer, regardless of name:

```
XmlNodeList nodes = doc.SelectNodes ("customers/customer/*");
```

The @ operator selects attributes. * can be used as a wildcard. Here is how to select the id attribute:

```
XmlNode node = doc.SelectSingleNode ("customers/customer/@id");
```

The [ ] operator filters a selection, in conjunction with the operators =, !=, <, >, not(), and, and or. In this example, we filter on `firstname`:

```
XmlNode n = doc.SelectSingleNode ("customers/customer[firstname='Jim']");
```

The : operator qualifies a namespace. Had the `customers` element been qualified with the x namespace, we would access it as follows:

```
XmlNode node = doc.SelectSingleNode ("x:customers");
```

XPathNavigator

`XPathNavigator` is a cursor over the XPath Data Model representation of an XML document. It is loaded with primitive methods that move the cursor around the tree (e.g., move to parent, move to first child, etc.). The `XPathNavigator`'s `Select*` methods take an XPath string to express more complex navigations or queries that return multiple nodes.

Spawn instances of `XPathNavigator` from an `XmlDocument`, an `XPathDocument`, or another `XPathNavigator`. Here is an example of spawning an `XPathNavigator` from an `XmlDoument`:

```
XPathNavigator nav = doc.CreateNavigator();
XPathNavigator jim = nav.SelectSingleNode
  (
    "customers/customer[firstname='Jim']"
  );

Console.WriteLine (jim.Value);                    // JimBo
```

In the XPath Data Model, the value of a node is the concatenation of the text elements, equivalent to `XmlDocument`'s `InnerText` property.

The `SelectSingleNode` method returns a single `XPathNavigator`. The `Select` method returns an `XPathNodeIterator`, which simply iterates over multiple `XPathNavigator`s. For example:

```
XPathNavigator nav = doc.CreateNavigator();
string xPath = "customers/customer/firstname/text()";
foreach (XPathNavigator navC in nav.Select (xPath))
  Console.WriteLine (navC.Value);

OUTPUT:
Jim
Thomas
```

To perform faster queries, you can compile an XPath query into an `XPathExpression`. You then pass the compiled expression to a `Select*` method, instead of a string. For example:

```
XPathNavigator nav = doc.CreateNavigator();
XPathExpression expr = nav.Compile ("customers/customer/firstname");
foreach (XPathNavigator a in nav.Select (expr))
  Console.WriteLine (a.Value);
```

```
OUTPUT:
Jim
Thomas
```

Querying with Namespaces

Querying elements and attributes that contain namespaces requires some extra un-intuitive steps. Consider the following XML file:

```
<?xml version="1.0" encoding="utf-8" standalone="yes"?>

<o:customers xmlns:o='http://oreilly.com'>
  <o:customer id="123" status="archived">
    <firstname>Jim</firstname>
    <lastname>Bo</lastname>
  </o:customer>
  <o:customer>
    <firstname>Thomas</firstname>
    <lastname>Jefferson</lastname>
  </o:customer>
</o:customers>
```

The following query will fail, despite qualifying the nodes with the prefix o:

```
XmlDocument doc = new XmlDocument();
doc.Load ("customers.xml");
XmlNode n = doc.SelectSingleNode ("o:customers/o:customer");
Console.WriteLine (n.InnerText);   // JimBo
```

To make this query work, you must first create an `XmlNamespaceManager` instance as follows:

```
XmlNamespaceManager xnm = new XmlNamespaceManager (doc.NameTable);
```

You can treat `NameTable` as a black box (`XmlNamespaceManager` uses it internally to cache and reuse strings). Once we create the namespace manager, we can add prefix/namespace pairs to it as follows:

```
xnm.AddNamespace ("o", "http://oreilly.com");
```

The `Select*` methods on `XmlDocument` and `XPathNavigator` have overloads that accept an `XmlNamespaceManager`. We can successfully rewrite the previous query as follows:

```
XmlNode n = doc.SelectSingleNode ("o:customers/o:customer", xnm);
```

XPathDocument

`XPathDocument` is used for read-only XML documents that conform to the W3C XPath Data Model. An `XPathNavigator` backed by an `XPathDocument` is faster than an `XmlDocument`, but it cannot make changes to the underlying document:

```
XPathDocument doc = new XPathDocument ("customers.xml");
XPathNavigator nav = doc.CreateNavigator();
foreach (XPathNavigator a in nav.Select ("customers/customer/firstname"))
  Console.WriteLine (a.Value);
```

```
OUTPUT:
Jim
Thomas
```

XSD and Schema Validation

The content of a particular XML document is nearly always domain-specific, such
as a Microsoft Word document, an application configuration document, or a web
service. For each domain, the XML file conforms to a particular pattern. There are
several standards for describing the schema of such a pattern, to standardize and
automate the interpretation and validation of XML documents. The most widely
accepted standard is *XSD*, short for *XML Schema Definition*. Its precursors, DTD
and XDR, are also supported by System.Xml.

Consider the following XML document:

```
<?xml version="1.0"?>
<customers>
  <customer id="1" status="active">
    <firstname>Jim</firstname>
    <lastname>Bo</lastname>
  </customer>
  <customer id="1" status="archived">
    <firstname>Thomas</firstname>
    <lastname>Jefferson</lastname>
  </customer>
</customers>
```

We can write an XSD for this document as follows:

```
<?xml version="1.0" encoding="utf-8"?>
<xs:schema attributeFormDefault="unqualified"
           elementFormDefault="qualified"
           xmlns:xs="http://www.w3.org/2001/XMLSchema">
  <xs:element name="customers">
    <xs:complexType>
      <xs:sequence>
        <xs:element maxOccurs="unbounded" name="customer">
          <xs:complexType>
            <xs:sequence>
              <xs:element name="firstname" type="xs:string" />
              <xs:element name="lastname" type="xs:string" />
            </xs:sequence>
            <xs:attribute name="id" type="xs:int" use="required" />
            <xs:attribute name="status" type="xs:string" use="required" />
          </xs:complexType>
        </xs:element>
      </xs:sequence>
    </xs:complexType>
  </xs:element>
</xs:schema>
```

As you can see, XSD documents are themselves written in XML. Furthermore, an
XSD document is describable with XSD—you can find that definition at *http://www
.w3.org/2001/xmlschema.xsd*.

Performing Schema Validation

You can validate an XML file or document against one or more schemas before reading or processing it. There are a number of reasons to do so:

- You can get away with less error checking and exception handling.
- Schema validation picks up errors you might otherwise overlook.
- Error messages are detailed and informative.

To perform validation, plug a schema into an XmlReader, an XmlDocument, or an X-DOM object, and then read or load the XML as you would normally. Schema validation happens automatically as content is read, so the input stream is not read twice.

Validating with an XmlReader

Here's how to plug a schema from the file *customers.xsd* into an XmlReader:

```
XmlReaderSettings settings = new XmlReaderSettings();
settings.ValidationType = ValidationType.Schema;
settings.Schemas.Add (null, "customers.xsd");

using (XmlReader r = XmlReader.Create ("customers.xml", settings))
  ...
```

If the schema is inline, set the following flag instead of adding to Schemas:

```
settings.ValidationFlags |= XmlSchemaValidationFlags.ProcessInlineSchema;
```

You then Read as you would normally. If schema validation fails at any point, an XmlSchemaValidationException is thrown.

 Calling Read on its own validates both elements and attributes: you don't need to navigate to each individual attribute for it to be validated.

If you want *only* to validate the document, you can do this:

```
using (XmlReader r = XmlReader.Create ("customers.xml", settings))
  try { while (r.Read()) ; }
  catch (XmlSchemaValidationException ex)
  {
    ...
  }
```

XmlSchemaValidationException has properties for the error Message, LineNumber, and LinePosition. In this case, it only tells you about the first error in the document. If you want to report on all errors in the document, you instead must handle the ValidationEventHandler event:

```
XmlReaderSettings settings = new XmlReaderSettings();
settings.ValidationType = ValidationType.Schema;
settings.Schemas.Add (null, "customers.xsd");
```

```
settings.ValidationEventHandler += ValidationHandler;
using (XmlReader r = XmlReader.Create ("customers.xml", settings))
  while (r.Read()) ;
```

When you handle this event, schema errors no longer throw exceptions. Instead, they fire your event handler:

```
static void ValidationHandler (object sender, ValidationEventArgs e)
{
  Console.WriteLine ("Error: " + e.Exception.Message);
}
```

The Exception property of ValidationEventArgs contains the XmlSchemaValidatio nException that would have otherwise been thrown.

> The System.Xml namespace also contains a class called XmlVali datingReader. This was used to perform schema validation prior to Framework 2.0, and it is now deprecated.

Validating an X-DOM or XmlDocument

To validate an XML file or stream while reading into an X-DOM or XmlDocument, you create an XmlReader, plug in the schemas, and then use the reader to load the DOM:

```
XmlReaderSettings settings = new XmlReaderSettings();
settings.ValidationType = ValidationType.Schema;
settings.Schemas.Add (null, "customers.xsd");

XDocument doc;
using (XmlReader r = XmlReader.Create ("customers.xml", settings))
  try { doc = XDocument.Load (r); }
  catch (XmlSchemaValidationException ex) { ... }

XmlDocument xmlDoc = new XmlDocument();
using (XmlReader r = XmlReader.Create ("customers.xml", settings))
  try { xmlDoc.Load (r); }
  catch (XmlSchemaValidationException ex) { ... }
```

You can also validate an XDocument or XElement that's already in memory, by calling extension methods in System.Xml.Schema. These methods accept an XmlSchemaSet (a collection of schemas) and a validation event handler:

```
XDocument doc = XDocument.Load (@"customers.xml");
XmlSchemaSet set = new XmlSchemaSet ();
set.Add (null, @"customers.xsd");
StringBuilder errors = new StringBuilder ();
doc.Validate (set, (sender, args) => { errors.AppendLine
                                       (args.Exception.Message); }
             );
Console.WriteLine (errors.ToString());
```

To validate an `XmlDocument` already in memory, add the schema(s) to the `XmlDocument`'s `Schemas` collection and then call the document's `Validate` method, passing in a `ValidationEventHandler` to process the errors.

XSLT

XSLT stands for *Extensible Stylesheet Language Transformations*. It is an XML language that describes how to transform one XML language into another. The quintessential example of such a transformation is transforming an XML document (that typically describes data) into an XHTML document (that describes a formatted document).

Consider the following XML file:

```
<customer>
  <firstname>Jim</firstname>
  <lastname>Bo</lastname>
</customer>
```

The following XSLT file describes such a transformation:

```
<?xml version="1.0" encoding="UTF-8"?>
  <xsl:stylesheet xmlns:xsl="http://www.w3.org/1999/XSL/Transform"
  version="1.0">
  <xsl:template match="/">
    <html>
      <p><xsl:value-of select="//firstname"/></p>
      <p><xsl:value-of select="//lastname"/></p>
    </html>
  </xsl:template>
</xsl:stylesheet>
```

The output is as follows:

```
<html>
  <p>Jim</p>
  <p>Bo</p>
</html>
```

The `System.Xml.Xsl.XslCompiledTransform` transform class efficiently performs XLST transforms. It renders `XmlTransform` obsolete. `XmlTransform` works very simply:

```
XslCompiledTransform transform = new XslCompiledTransform();
transform.Load ("test.xslt");
transform.Transform ("input.xml", "output.xml");
```

Generally, it's more useful to use the overload of `Transform` that accepts an `XmlWriter` rather than an output file, so you can control the formatting.

12

Disposal and Garbage Collection

Some objects require explicit tear-down code to release resources such as open files, locks, operating system handles, and unmanaged objects. In .NET parlance, this is called *disposal*, and it is supported through the IDisposable interface. The managed memory occupied by unused objects must also be reclaimed at some point; this function is known as *garbage collection* and is performed by the CLR.

Disposal differs from garbage collection in that disposal is usually explicitly instigated; garbage collection is totally automatic. In other words, the programmer takes care of such things as releasing file handles, locks, and operating system resources while the CLR takes care of releasing memory.

This chapter discusses both disposal and garbage collection, also describing C# finalizers and the pattern by which they can provide a backup for disposal. Lastly, we discuss the intricacies of the garbage collector and other memory management options.

IDisposable, Dispose, and Close

The .NET Framework defines a special interface for types requiring a tear-down method:

```
public interface IDisposable
{
  void Dispose();
}
```

C#'s using statement provides a syntactic shortcut for calling Dispose on objects that implement IDisposable, using a try/finally block. For example:

```
using (FileStream fs = new FileStream ("myFile.txt", FileMode.Open))
{
  // ... Write to the file ...
}
```

The compiler converts this to:

```
FileStream fs = new FileStream ("myFile.txt", FileMode.Open);
try
{
  // ... Write to the file ...
}
finally
{
  if (fs != null) ((IDisposable)fs).Dispose();
}
```

The `finally` block ensures that the `Dispose` method is called even when an exception is thrown,* or the code exits the block early.

In simple scenarios, writing your own disposable type is just a matter of implementing `IDisposable` and writing the `Dispose` method:

```
sealed class Demo : IDisposable
{
  public void Dispose()
  {
    // Perform cleanup / tear-down.
    ...
  }
}
```

 This pattern works well in simple cases and is appropriate for sealed classes. We'll describe a more elaborate pattern that can provide a backup for consumers that forget to call `Dispose` in "Calling Dispose from a Finalizer" on page 484. With unsealed types, there's a strong case for following this latter pattern from the outset—otherwise, it becomes very messy if the subtype wants to add such functionality itself.

Standard Disposal Semantics

The Framework follows a de facto set of rules in its disposal logic. These rules are not hard-wired to the Framework or C# language in any way; their purpose is to define a consistent protocol to consumers. Here they are:

1. Once disposed, an object is beyond redemption. It cannot be reactivated, and calling its methods or properties throws an `ObjectDisposedException`.
2. Calling an object's `Dispose` method repeatedly causes no error.
3. If disposable object *x* contains or "wraps" or "possesses" disposable object *y*, *x*'s `Dispose` method automatically calls *y*'s `Dispose` method—unless instructed otherwise.

---

* In "Interrupt and Abort" on page 855 in Chapter 21, we describe how aborting a thread can violate the safety of this pattern. This is rarely an issue in practice because aborting threads is widely discouraged for precisely this (and other) reasons.

These rules are also helpful when writing your own types, though not mandatory. Nothing prevents you from writing an "Undispose" method, other than, perhaps, the flak you might cop from colleagues!

According to rule 3, a container object automatically disposes its child objects. A good example is a Windows container control such as a `Form` or `Panel`. The container may host many child controls, yet you don't dispose every one of them explicitly: closing or disposing the parent control or form takes care of the whole lot. Another example is when you wrap a `FileStream` in a `DeflateStream`. Disposing the `DeflateStream` also disposes the `FileStream`—unless you instructed otherwise in the constructor.

Close and Stop

Some types define a method called `Close` in addition to `Dispose`. The Framework is not completely consistent on the semantics of a `Close` method, although in nearly all cases it's either:

- Functionally identical to `Dispose`
- A functional *subset* of `Dispose`

An example of the latter is `IDbConnection`: a `Closed` connection can be re-`Opened`; a `Disposed` connection cannot. Another example is a Windows `Form` activated with `ShowDialog`: `Close` hides it; `Dispose` releases its resources.

Some classes define a `Stop` method (e.g., `Timer` or `HttpListener`), which may release unmanaged resources, like `Dispose`, but unlike `Dispose`, it allows for re-`Start`ing.

When to Dispose

A safe rule to follow (in nearly all cases) is "If in doubt, dispose." A disposable object—if it could talk—would say the following:

> When you've finished with me, let me know. If simply abandoned, I might cause trouble for other object instances, the application domain, the computer, the network, or the database!

Objects wrapping an unmanaged resource handle will nearly always require disposal, in order to free the handle. Examples include Windows Forms controls, file or network streams, network sockets, GDI+ pens, brushes, and bitmaps. Conversely, if a type is disposable, it will often (but not always) reference an unmanaged handle, directly or indirectly. This is because unmanaged handles provide the gateway to the "outside world" of operating system resources, network connections, database locks—the primary means by which objects can create trouble outside of themselves if improperly abandoned.

There are, however, three scenarios for *not* disposing:

- When obtaining a *shared* object via a static field or property
- When an object's `Dispose` method does something that you don't want

- When an object's `Dispose` method is unnecessary *by design*, and disposing that object would add complexity to your program

The first category is rare. The main cases are in the `System.Drawing` namespace: the GDI+ objects obtained through *static fields or properties* (such as `Brushes.Blue`) must never be disposed because the same instance is used throughout the life of the application. Instances that you obtain through constructors, however (such as new `SolidBrush`), *should* be disposed, as should instances obtained through static *methods* (such as `Font.FromHdc`).

The second category is more common. There are some good examples in the `System.IO` and `System.Data` namespaces:

Type	Disposal function	When not to dispose
`MemoryStream`	Prevents further I/O	When you later need to read/write the stream
`StreamReader`, `StreamWriter`	Flushes the reader/writer and closes the underlying stream	When you want to keep the underlying stream open (you must instead call `Flush` on a `StreamWriter` when you're done)
`IDbConnection`	Releases a database connection and clears the connection string	If you need to re-Open it, you should call `Close` instead of `Dispose`
`DataContext` (LINQ to SQL)	Prevents further use	When you might have lazily evaluated queries connected to that context

`MemoryStream`'s `Dispose` method disables only the object; it doesn't perform any critical cleanup because a `MemoryStream` holds no unmanaged handles or other such resources.

The third category includes the following classes: `WebClient`, `StringReader`, `String Writer`, and `BackgroundWorker` (in `System.ComponentModel`). These types are disposable under the duress of their base class rather than through a genuine need to perform essential cleanup. If you happen to instantiate and work with such an object entirely in one method, wrapping it in a `using` block adds little inconvenience. But if the object is longer-lasting, keeping track of when it's no longer used so that you can dispose of it adds unnecessary complexity. In such cases, you can simply ignore object disposal.

Opt-in Disposal

Because `IDisposable` makes a type tractable with C#'s `using` construct, there's a temptation to extend the reach of `IDisposable` to nonessential activities. For instance:

```
public sealed class HouseManager : IDisposable
{
  public void Dispose()
  {
    CheckTheMail();
  }
  ...
}
```

The idea is that a consumer of this class can choose to circumvent the nonessential cleanup—simply by not calling Dispose. This, however, relies on the consumer knowing what's inside Demo's Dispose method. It also breaks if *essential* cleanup activity is later added:

```
public void Dispose()
{
  CheckTheMail();   // Nonessential
  LockTheHouse();   // Essential
}
```

The solution to this problem is the opt-in disposal pattern:

```
public sealed class HouseManager : IDisposable
{
  public readonly bool CheckMailOnDispose;

  public Demo (bool checkMailOnDispose)
  {
    CheckMailOnDispose = checkMailOnDispose;
  }

  public void Dispose()
  {
    if (CheckMailOnDispose) CheckTheMail();
    LockTheHouse();
  }
  ...
}
```

The consumer can then always call Dispose—providing simplicity and avoiding the need for special documentation or reflection. An example of where this pattern is implemented is in the DeflateStream class, in System.IO.Compression. Here's its constructor:

```
public DeflateStream (Stream stream, CompressionMode mode, bool leaveOpen)
```

The nonessential activity is closing the inner stream (the first parameter) upon disposal. There are times when you want to leave the inner stream open and yet still dispose the DeflateStream to perform its *essential* tear-down activity (flushing buffered data).

This pattern might look simple, yet it escaped StreamReader and StreamWriter (the System.IO namespace). The result is messy: StreamWriter must expose another method (Flush) to perform essential cleanup for consumers not calling Dispose. The CryptoStream class in System.Security.Cryptography suffers a similar problem and requires that you call FlushFinalBlock to tear it down while keeping the inner stream open.

You could describe this as an *ownership* issue. The question for a disposable object is: do I really own the underlying resource that I'm using? Or am I just renting it from someone else who manages both the underlying resource lifetime and, by some undocumented contract, my lifetime?

Following the opt-in pattern avoids this problem by making the ownership contract documented and explicit.

Clearing Fields in Disposal

In general, you don't need to clear an object's fields in its `Dispose` method. However, it is good practice to unsubscribe from events that the object has subscribed to internally over its lifetime (see "Managed Memory Leaks" on page 491 for an example). Unsubscribing from such events avoids receiving unwanted event notifications—and avoids unintentionally keeping the object alive in the eyes of the garbage collector (GC).

 A `Dispose` method itself does not cause memory to be released— this can happen only in garbage collection.

It's also worth setting a field to indicate that the object is disposed so that you can throw an `ObjectDisposedException` if a consumer later tries to call members on the object. A good pattern is to use a publicly readable automatic property for this:

```
public bool IsDisposed { get; private set; }
```

Although technically unnecessary, it can also be good to clear an object's own event handlers (by setting them to `null`) in the `Dispose` method. This eliminates the possibility of those events firing during or after disposal.

Occasionally, an object holds high-value secrets, such as encryption keys. In these cases, it can make sense to clear such data from fields during disposal (to avoid discovery by less privileged assemblies or malware). The `SymmetricAlgorithm` class in `System.Security.Cryptography` does exactly this, by calling `Array.Clear` on the byte array holding the encryption key.

Automatic Garbage Collection

Regardless of whether an object requires a `Dispose` method for custom tear-down logic, at some point the memory it occupies on the heap must be freed. The CLR handles this side of it entirely automatically, via an automatic GC. You never deallocate managed memory yourself. For example, consider the following method:

```
public void Test()
{
  byte[] myArray = new byte[1000];
  ...
}
```

Garbage Collection and Memory Consumption

The GC tries to strike a balance between the time it spends doing garbage collection and the application's memory consumption (working set). Consequently, applications can consume more memory than they need, particularly if large temporary arrays are constructed.

The problem can look worse than it is, though, if you judge memory consumption by the "Memory Usage" figure reported by the Task Manager in Windows XP. Unlike with later versions of Windows (which report *private working set*), the XP figure includes memory that a process has internally deallocated and is willing to rescind immediately to the operating system should another process need it. (It doesn't return the memory to the operating system immediately to avoid the overhead of asking for it back, should it be required a short while later. It reasons: "If the computer has plenty of free memory, why not use it to lessen allocation/deallocation overhead?")

You can determine your process's real memory consumption by querying a performance counter (`System.Diagnostics`):

```
string procName = Process.GetCurrentProcess().ProcessName;
using (PerformanceCounter pc = new PerformanceCounter
    ("Process", "Private Bytes", procName))
  Console.WriteLine (pc.NextValue());
```

Reading performance counters requires administrative privileges.

When `Test` executes, an array to hold 1,000 bytes is allocated on the memory heap. The array is referenced by the variable `myArray`, stored on the local variable stack. When the method exits, this local variable `myArray` pops out of scope, meaning that nothing is left to reference the array on the memory heap. The orphaned array then becomes eligible to be reclaimed in garbage collection.

> In debug mode with optimizations disabled, the lifetime of an object referenced by a local variable extends to the end of the code block to ease debugging. Otherwise, it becomes eligible for collection at the earliest point at which it's no longer used.

Garbage collection does not happen immediately after an object is orphaned. Rather like garbage collection on the street, it happens periodically, although (unlike garbage collection on the street) not to a fixed schedule. The CLR bases its decision on when to collect upon a number of factors, such as the available memory, the amount of memory allocation, and the time since the last collection. This means that there's an indeterminate delay between an object being orphaned and being released from memory. Theoretically, it can range from nanoseconds to days.

 The GC doesn't collect all garbage with every collection. Instead, the memory manager divides objects into *generations* and the GC collects new generations (recently allocated objects) more frequently than old generations (long-lived objects). We'll discuss this in more detail in "How the Garbage Collector Works" on page 487.

Roots

A root is something that keeps an object alive. If an object is not directly or indirectly referenced by a root, it will be eligible for garbage collection.

A root is one of the following:

- A local variable or parameter in an executing method (or in any method in its call stack)
- A static variable
- An object on the queue that stores objects ready for finalization (see the next section)

It's impossible for code to execute in a deleted object, so if there's any possibility of an (instance) method executing, its object must somehow be referenced in one of these ways.

Note that a group of objects that reference each other cyclically are considered dead without a root referee (see Figure 12-1). To put it in another way, objects that cannot be accessed by following the arrows (references) from a root object are *unreachable*—and therefore subject to collection.

Finalizers

Prior to an object being released from memory, its *finalizer* runs, if it has one. A finalizer is declared in the same way as a constructor, but it is prefixed by the ˜ symbol:

```
class Test
{
  ˜Test()
  {
    // Finalizer logic...
  }
}
```

Finalizers are possible because garbage collection works in distinct phases. First, the GC identifies the unused objects ripe for deletion. Those without finalizers are

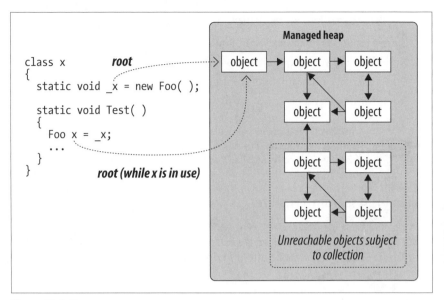

```
class x          root
{
  static void _x = new Foo( );

  static void Test( )
  {
    Foo x = _x;
    ...
  }
}
          root (while x is in use)
```

Managed heap

Unreachable objects subject
to collection

Figure 12-1. Roots

deleted right away. Those with pending (unrun) finalizers are kept alive (for now) and are put onto a special queue.

At that point, garbage collection is complete, and your program continues executing. The *finalizer thread* then kicks in and starts running in parallel to your program, picking objects off that special queue and running their finalization methods. Prior to each object's finalizer running, it's still very much alive—that queue acts as a root object. Once it's been dequeued and the finalizer executed, the object becomes orphaned and will get deleted in the next collection (for that object's *generation*).

Finalizers can be useful, but they come with some provisos:

- Finalizers slow the allocation and collection of memory (the GC needs to keep track of which finalizers have run).
- Finalizers prolong the life of the object and any *referred* objects (they must all await the next garbage truck for actual deletion).
- It's impossible to predict in what order the finalizers for a set of objects will be called.
- You have limited control over when the finalizer for an object will be called.
- If code in a finalizer blocks, other objects cannot get finalized.
- Finalizers may be circumvented altogether if an application fails to unload cleanly.

In summary, finalizers are somewhat like lawyers—although there are cases in which you really need them, in general you don't want to use them unless absolutely necessary. If you do use them, you need to be 100% sure you understand what they are doing for you.

Here are some guidelines for implementing finalizers:

- Ensure that your finalizer executes quickly.
- Never block in your finalizer (Chapter 21).
- Don't reference other finalizable objects.
- Don't throw exceptions.

 An object's finalizer can get called even if an exception is thrown during construction. For this reason, it pays not to assume that fields are correctly initialized when writing a finalizer.

Calling Dispose from a Finalizer

One excellent use for finalizers is to provide a backup for cases when you forget to call Dispose on a disposable object; it's usually better to have an object disposed late than never! There's a standard pattern for implementing this, as follows:

```
class Test : IDisposable
{
  public void Dispose()            // NOT virtual
  {
    Dispose (true);
    GC.SuppressFinalize (this);    // Prevent finalizer from running.
  }

  protected virtual void Dispose (bool disposing)
  {
    if (disposing)
    {
      // Call Dispose() on other objects owned by this instance.
      // You can reference other finalizable objects here.
      // ...
    }

    // Release unmanaged resources owned by (just) this object.
    // ...
  }

  ~Test()
  {
    Dispose (false);
  }
}
```

Dispose is overloaded to accept a bool disposing flag. The parameterless version is *not* declared as virtual and simply calls the enhanced version with true.

The enhanced version contains the actual disposal logic and is protected and virtual; this provides a safe point for subclasses to add their own disposal logic. The disposing flag means it's being called "properly" from the Dispose method rather than in "last-resort mode" from the finalizer. The idea is that when called with disposing set to false, this method should not, in general, reference other objects with finalizers (because such objects may themselves have been finalized and so be in an unpredictable state). This rules out quite a lot! Here are a couple of tasks it can still perform in last-resort mode, when `disposing` is `false`:

- Releasing any *direct references* to operating system resources (obtained, perhaps, via a P/Invoke call to the Win32 API)
- Deleting a temporary file created on construction

To make this robust, any code capable of throwing an exception should be wrapped in a `try`/`catch` block, and the exception, ideally, logged. Any logging should be as simple and robust as possible.

Notice that we call `GC.SuppressFinalize` in the parameterless `Dispose` method—this prevents the finalizer from running when the GC later catches up with it. Technically, this is unnecessary, as `Dispose` methods must tolerate repeated calls. However, doing so improves performance because it allows the object (and its referenced objects) to be garbage-collected in a single cycle.

> This pattern is intended more as a backup than a replacement for calling `Dispose`. A difficulty with relying on it completely is that you couple resource deallocation to memory deallocation—two things with potentially divergent interests. You also increase the burden on the finalization thread.

Resurrection

Suppose a finalizer modifies a living object such that it refers back to the dying object. When the next garbage collection happens (for the object's generation), the CLR will see the previously dying object as no longer orphaned—and so it will evade garbage collection. This is an advanced scenario, and is called *resurrection*.

To illustrate, suppose we want to write a class that manages a temporary file. When an instance of that class is garbage-collected, we'd like the finalizer to delete the temporary file. It sounds easy:

```
public class TempFileRef
{
  public readonly string FilePath;
  public TempFileRef (string filePath) { FilePath = filePath; }

  ~TempFileRef() { File.Delete (FilePath); }
}
```

Unfortunately, this has a bug: `File.Delete` might throw an exception (due to a lack of permissions, perhaps, or the file being in use). Such an exception would take down the whole application (as well as preventing other finalizers from running). We could simply "swallow" the exception with an empty catch block, but then we'd never know that anything went wrong. Calling some elaborate error reporting API would also be undesirable because it would burden the finalizer thread, hindering garbage collection for other objects. We want to restrict finalization actions to those that are simple, reliable, and quick.

A better option is to record the failure to a static collection as follows:

```
public class TempFileRef
{
  static ConcurrentQueue<TempFileRef> _failedDeletions
    = new ConcurrentQueue<TempFileRef>();

  public readonly string FilePath;
  public Exception DeletionError { get; private set; }

  public TempFileRef (string filePath) { FilePath = filePath; }

  ~TempFileRef()
  {
    try { File.Delete (FilePath); }
    catch (Exception ex)
    {
      DeletionError = ex;
      _failedDeletions.Enqueue (this);    // Resurrection
    }
  }
}
```

Enqueuing the object to the static _failedDeletions collection gives the object another referee, ensuring that it remains alive until the object is eventually dequeued.

 ConcurrentQueue<T> is a thread-safe version of Queue<T> and is defined in System.Collections.Concurrent (see Chapter 22). There are a couple of reasons for using a thread-safe collection. First, the CLR reserves the right to execute finalizers on more than one thread in parallel. This means that when accessing shared state such as a static collection, we must consider the possibility of two objects being finalized at once. Second, at some point we're going to want to dequeue items from _failed Deletions so that we can do something about them. This also has to be done in a thread-safe fashion, because it could happen while the finalizer is concurrently enqueuing another object.

GC.ReRegisterForFinalize

A resurrected object's finalizer will not run a second time—unless you call GC.ReRegisterForFinalize.

In the following example, we try to delete a temporary file in a finalizer (as in the last example). But if the deletion fails, we reregister the object so as to try again in the next garbage collection:

```
public class TempFileRef
{
  public readonly string FilePath;
  int _deleteAttempt;

  public TempFileRef (string filePath) { FilePath = filePath; }

  ~TempFileRef()
  {
    try { File.Delete (FilePath); }
    catch
    {
      if (_deleteAttempt++ < 3) GC.ReRegisterForFinalize (this);
    }
  }
}
```

After the third failed attempt, our finalizer will silently give up trying to delete the file. We could enhance this by combining it with the previous example—in other words, adding it to the _failedDeletions queue after the third failure.

> Be careful to call ReRegisterForFinalize just once in the finalizer method. If you call it twice, the object will be reregistered twice and will have to undergo two more finalizations!

How the Garbage Collector Works

The CLR uses a generational mark-and-compact GC that performs automatic memory management for objects stored on the managed heap. The GC is considered to be a *tracing* garbage collector in that it doesn't interfere with every access to an object, but rather wakes up intermittently and traces the graph of objects stored on the managed heap to determine which objects can be considered garbage and therefore collected.

The GC initiates a garbage collection upon performing a memory allocation (via the new keyword) either after a certain threshold of memory has been allocated, or at other times to reduce the application's memory footprint. This process can also be initiated manually by calling System.GC.Collect. During a garbage collection, all threads may by frozen (more on this in the next section).

The GC begins with its root object references, and walks the object graph, marking all the objects it touches as reachable. Once this process is complete, all objects that have not been marked are considered unused, and are subject to garbage collection.

Unused objects without finalizers are immediately discarded; unused objects with finalizers are enqueued for processing on the finalizer thread after the GC is complete. These objects then become eligible for collection in the next GC for the object's generation (unless resurrected).

The remaining "live" objects are then shifted to the start of the heap (compacted), freeing space for more objects. This compaction serves two purposes: it avoids memory fragmentation, and it allows the GC to employ a very simple strategy when allocating new objects, which is to always allocate memory at the end of the heap. This avoids the potentially time-consuming task of maintaining a list of free memory segments.

If there is insufficient space to allocate memory for a new object after garbage collection, and the operating system is unable to grant further memory, an OutOfMemoryException is thrown.

Optimization Techniques

The GC incorporates various optimization techniques to reduce the garbage collection time.

Generational collection

The most important optimization is that the GC is generational. This takes advantage of the fact that although many objects are allocated and discarded rapidly, certain objects are long-lived and thus don't need to be traced during every collection.

Basically, the GC divides the managed heap into three generations. Objects that have just been allocated are in *Gen0* and objects that have survived one collection cycle are in *Gen1*; all other objects are in *Gen2*.

The CLR keeps the Gen0 section relatively small (a maximum of 16 MB on the 32-bit workstation CLR, with a typical size of a few hundred KB to a few MB). When the Gen0 section fills up, the GC instigates a Gen0 collection—which happens relatively often. The GC applies a similar memory threshold to Gen1 (which acts as a buffer to Gen2), and so Gen1 collections are relatively quick and frequent too. Full collections that include Gen2, however, take much longer and so happen infrequently. Figure 12-2 shows the effect of a full collection.

To give some very rough ballpark figures, a Gen0 collection might take less than 1 ms, which is not enough to be noticed in a typical application. A full collection, however, might take as long as 100 ms on a program with large object graphs. These figures depend on numerous factors and so may vary considerably—particularly in the case of Gen2 whose size is *unbounded* (unlike Gen0 and Gen1).

The upshot is that short-lived objects are very efficient in their use of the GC. The StringBuilders created in the following method would almost certainly be collected in a fast Gen0:

```
string Foo()
{
  var sb1 = new StringBuilder ("test");
  sb1.Append ("...");
  var sb2 = new StringBuilder ("test");
  sb2.Append (sb1.ToString());
  return sb2.ToString();
}
```

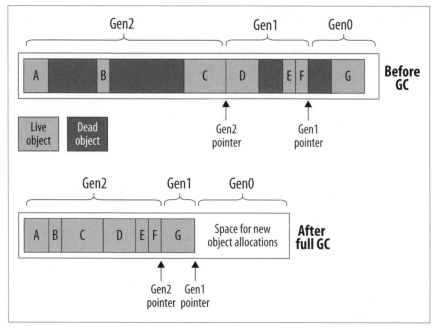

Figure 12-2. Heap generations

The large object heap

The GC uses a separate heap called the Large Object Heap (LOH) for objects larger than a certain threshold (currently 85,000 bytes). This avoids excessive Gen0 collections—without the LOH, allocating a series of 16 MB objects might trigger a Gen0 collection after every allocation.

The LOH is not subject to compaction, because moving large blocks of memory during garbage collection would be prohibitively expensive. This has two consequences:

- Allocations can be slower, because the GC can't always simply allocate objects at the end of the heap—it must also look in the middle for gaps, and this requires maintaining a linked list of free memory blocks.[†]

- The LOH is subject to *fragmentation*. This means that the freeing of an object can create a hole in the LOH that may be hard to fill later. For instance, a hole left by an 86,000-byte object can be filled only by an object of between 85,000 bytes and 86,000 bytes (unless adjoined by another hole).

The large object heap is also nongenerational: all objects are treated as Gen2.

---

† The same thing may occur occasionally in the generational heap due to pinning (see "The fixed Statement" on page 171 in Chapter 4).

Concurrent and background collection

The GC must freeze (block) your execution threads for periods during a collection. This includes the entire period during which a Gen0 or Gen1 collection takes place.

The GC makes a special attempt, though, at allowing threads to run during a Gen2 collection, as it's undesirable to freeze an application for a potentially long period. This optimization applies to the workstation version of the CLR only, which is used on desktop versions of Windows (and on all versions of Windows with standalone applications). The rationale is that the latency from a blocking collection is less likely to be a problem for server applications thats don't have a user interface.

 A mitigating factor is that the server CLR leverages all available cores to perform GCs, so an eight-core server will perform a full GC many times faster. In effect, the server GC is tuned for throughput rather than latency.

The workstation optimization has historically been called *concurrent collection*. From CLR 4.0, it's been revamped and renamed to *background collection*. Background collection removes a limitation whereby a concurrent collection would cease to be concurrent if the Gen0 section filled up while a Gen2 collection was running. This means that from CLR 4.0, applications that continually allocate memory will be more responsive.

GC notifications (server CLR)

From Framework 3.5 SP1, the server version of the CLR can notify you just before a full GC will occur. This is intended for server farm configurations: the idea is that you divert requests to another server just before a collection. You then instigate the collection immediately and wait for it to complete before rerouting requests back to that server.

To start notification, call GC.RegisterForFullGCNotification. Then start up another thread (see Chapter 21) that first calls GC.WaitForFullGCApproach. When this method returns a GCNotificationStatus indicating that a collection is near, you can reroute requests to other servers and force a manual collection (see the following section). You then call GC.WaitForFullGCComplete: when this method returns, GC is complete and you can again accept requests. You then repeat the whole cycle.

Forcing Garbage Collection

You can manually force a GC at any time, by calling GC.Collect. Calling GC.Collect without an argument instigates a full collection. If you pass in an integer value, only generations to that value are collected, so GC.Collect(0) performs only a fast Gen0 collection.

In general, you get the best performance by allowing the GC to decide when to collect: forcing collection can hurt performance by unnecessarily promoting Gen0 objects to Gen1. It can also upset the GC's *self-tuning* ability, whereby the GC dynamically tweaks the thresholds for each generation to maximize performance as the application executes.

There are exceptions, however. The most common case for intervention is when an application goes to sleep for a while: a good example is a Windows Service that performs a daily activity (checking for updates, perhaps). Such an application might use a `System.Timers.Timer` to initiate the activity every 24 hours. After completing the activity, no further code executes for 24 hours, which means that for this period, no memory allocations are made and so the GC has no opportunity to activate. Whatever memory the service consumed in performing its activity, it will continue to consume for the following 24 hours—even with an empty object graph! The solution is to call `GC.Collect` right after the daily activity completes.

To ensure the collection of objects for which collection is delayed by finalizers, you can take the additional step of calling `WaitForPendingFinalizers` and re-collecting:

```
GC.Collect();
GC.WaitForPendingFinalizers();
GC.Collect();
```

Memory Pressure

The runtime decides when to initiate collections based on a number of factors, including the total memory load on the machine. If your program allocates unmanaged memory (Chapter 25), the runtime will get an unrealistically optimistic perception of its memory usage, because the CLR knows only about managed memory. You can mitigate this by telling the CLR to *assume* a specified quantity of unmanaged memory has been allocated, by calling `GC.AddMemoryPressure`. To undo this (when the unmanaged memory is released) call `GC.RemoveMemoryPressure`.

Managed Memory Leaks

In unmanaged languages such as C++, you must remember to manually deallocate memory when an object is no longer required; otherwise, a *memory leak* will result. In the managed world, this kind of error is impossible due to the CLR's automatic garbage collection system.

Nonetheless, large and complex .NET applications can exhibit a milder form of the same syndrome with the same end result: the application consumes more and more memory over its lifetime, until it eventually has to be restarted. The good news is that managed memory leaks are usually easier to diagnose and prevent.

Managed memory leaks are caused by unused objects remaining alive by virtue of unused or forgotten references. A common candidate is event handlers—these hold a reference to the target object (unless the target is a static method). For instance, consider the following classes:

```
class Host
{
  public event EventHandler Click;
}
```

```
class Client
{
  Host _host;
  public Client (Host host)
  {
    _host = host;
    _host.Click += HostClicked;
  }

  void HostClicked (object sender, EventArgs e) { ... }
}
```

The following test class contains a method that instantiates 1,000 clients:

```
class Test
{
  static Host _host = new Host();

  public static void CreateClients()
  {
    Client[] clients = Enumerable.Range (0, 1000)
      .Select (i => new Client (_host))
      .ToArray();

    // Do something with clients ...
  }
}
```

You might expect that after CreateClients finishes executing, the 1,000 Client objects will become eligible for collection. Unfortunately, each client has another referee: the _host object whose Click event now references each Client instance. This may go unnoticed if the Click event doesn't fire—or if the HostClicked method doesn't do anything to attract attention.

One way to solve this is to make Client implement IDisposable, and in the Dispose method, unhook the event handler:

```
public void Dispose() { _host.Click -= HostClicked; }
```

Consumers of Client then dispose of the instances when they're done with them:

```
Array.ForEach (clients, c => c.Dispose());
```

> In "Weak References" on page 494, we'll describe another solution to this problem, which can be useful in environments which tend not to use disposable objects (an example is WPF). In fact, the WPF framework offers a class called WeakEventManager that leverages a pattern employing weak references.
>
> On the topic of WPF, *data binding* is another common cause for memory leaks: the issue is described at *http://support.microsoft.com/kb/938416*.

Timers

Forgotten timers can also cause memory leaks (we discuss timers in Chapter 21). There are two distinct scenarios, depending on the kind of timer. Let's first look at the timer in the System.Timers namespace. In the following example, the Foo class (when instantiated) calls the tmr_Elapsed method once every second:

```
using System.Timers;

class Foo
{
  Timer _timer;

  Foo()
  {
    _timer = new System.Timers.Timer { Interval = 1000 };
    _timer.Elapsed += tmr_Elapsed;
    _timer.Start();
  }

  void tmr_Elapsed (object sender, ElapsedEventArgs e) { ... }
}
```

Unfortunately, instances of Foo can never be garbage-collected! The problem is the .NET Framework itself holds references to active timers so that it can fire their Elapsed events. Hence:

- The .NET Framework will keep _timer alive.
- _timer will keep the Foo instance alive, via the tmr_Elapsed event handler.

The solution is obvious when you realize that Timer implements IDisposable. Disposing of the timer stops it and ensures that the .NET Framework no longer references the object:

```
class Foo : IDisposable
{
  ...
  public void Dispose() { _timer.Dispose(); }
}
```

 A good guideline is to implement IDisposable yourself if any field in your class is assigned an object that implements IDisposable.

The WPF and Windows Forms timers behave in exactly the same way, with respect to what's just been discussed.

The timer in the System.Threading namespace, however, is special. The .NET Framework doesn't hold references to active threading timers; it instead references the callback delegates directly. This means that if you forget to dispose of a threading timer, a finalizer can (and will) fire—and this will automatically stop and dispose the timer. This can create a different problem, however, which we can illustrate as follows:

```
static void Main()
{
  var tmr = new System.Threading.Timer (TimerTick, null, 1000, 1000);
  GC.Collect();
  System.Threading.Thread.Sleep (10000);    // Wait 10 seconds
}

static void TimerTick (object notUsed) { Console.WriteLine ("tick"); }
```

If this example is compiled in "release" mode (debugging disabled and optimizations enabled), the timer will be collected and finalized before it has a chance to fire even once! Again, we can fix this by disposing of the timer when we're done with it:

```
using (var tmr = new System.Threading.Timer (TimerTick, null, 1000, 1000))
{
  GC.Collect();
  System.Threading.Thread.Sleep (10000);    // Wait 10 seconds
}
```

The implicit call to `tmr.Dispose` at the end of the `using` block ensures that the `tmr` variable is "used" and so not considered dead by the GC until the end of the block. Ironically, this call to `Dispose` actually keeps the object alive *longer*!

Diagnosing Memory Leaks

The easiest way to avoid managed memory leaks is to proactively monitor memory consumption as an application is written. You can obtain the current memory consumption of a program's objects as follows (the `true` argument tells the GC to perform a collection first):

```
long memoryUsed = GC.GetTotalMemory (true);
```

If you're practicing test-driven development, one possibility is to use unit tests to assert that memory is reclaimed as expected. If such an assertion fails, you then have to examine only the changes that you've made recently.

If you already have a large application with a managed memory leak, the *windbg.exe* tool can assist in finding it. There are also friendlier graphical tools such as Microsoft's CLR Profiler, SciTech's Memory Profiler, and Red Gate's ANTS Memory Profiler.

The CLR also exposes numerous Windows WMI counters to assist with resource monitoring.

Weak References

Occasionally, it's useful to hold a reference to an object that's "invisible" to the GC in terms of keeping the object alive. This is called a *weak reference*, and is implemented by the `System.WeakReference` class.

To use `WeakReference`, construct it with a target object as follows:

```
var sb = new StringBuilder ("this is a test");
var weak = new WeakReference (sb);
Console.WriteLine (weak.Target);     // This is a test
```

If a target is referenced *only* by one or more weak references, the GC will consider the target eligible for collection. When the target gets collected, the `Target` property of the `WeakReference` will be null:

```
var weak = new WeakReference (new StringBuilder ("weak"));
Console.WriteLine (weak.Target);   // weak
GC.Collect();
Console.WriteLine (weak.Target);   // (nothing)
```

To avoid the target being collected in between testing for it being null and consuming it, assign the target to a local variable:

```
var weak = new WeakReference (new StringBuilder ("weak"));
var sb = (StringBuilder) weak.Target;
if (sb != null) { /* Do something with sb */ }
```

Once a target's been assigned to a local variable, it has a strong root and so cannot be collected while that variable's in use.

The following class uses weak references to keep track of all `Widget` objects that have been instantiated, without preventing those objects from being collected:

```
class Widget
{
  static List<WeakReference> _allWidgets = new List<WeakReference>();

  public readonly string Name;

  public Widget (string name)
  {
    Name = name;
    _allWidgets.Add (new WeakReference (this));
  }

  public static void ListAllWidgets()
  {
    foreach (WeakReference weak in _allWidgets)
    {
      Widget w = (Widget)weak.Target;
      if (w != null) Console.WriteLine (w.Name);
    }
  }
}
```

The only proviso with such a system is that the static list will grow over time, accumulating weak references with null targets. So you need to implement some cleanup strategy.

Weak References and Caching

One use for `WeakReference` is to cache large object graphs. This allows memory-intensive data to be cached briefly without causing excessive memory consumption:

```
_weakCache = new WeakReference (...);    // _weakCache is a field
...
var cache = _weakCache.Target;
if (cache == null) { /* Re-create cache & assign it to _weakCache */ }
```

This strategy may be only mildly effective in practice, because you have little control over when the GC fires and what generation it chooses to collect. In particular, if your cache remains in Gen0, it may be collected within microseconds (and remember that the GC doesn't collect only when memory is low—it collects regularly under normal memory conditions). So at a minimum, you should employ a two-level cache whereby you start out by holding strong references that you convert to weak references over time.

Weak References and Events

We saw earlier how events can cause managed memory leaks. The simplest solution is to either avoid subscribing in such conditions, or implement a Dispose method to unsubscribe. Weak references offer another solution.

Imagine a delegate that holds only weak references to its targets. Such a delegate would not keep its targets alive—unless those targets had independent referees. Of course, this wouldn't prevent a firing delegate from hitting an unreferenced target— in the time between the target being eligible for collection and the GC catching up with it. For such a solution to be effective, your code must be robust in that scenario. Assuming that is the case, a *weak delegate* class can be implemented as follows:

```
class WeakDelegate<TDelegate> where TDelegate : class
{
  List<WeakReference> _targets = new List<WeakReference>();

  public WeakDelegate()
  {
    if (!typeof (TDelegate).IsSubclassOf (typeof (Delegate)))
      throw new InvalidOperationException
        ("TDelegate must be a delegate type");
  }

  public void Combine (TDelegate target)
  {
    if (target == null) return;
    foreach (Delegate d in (target as Delegate).GetInvocationList())
      _targets.Add (new WeakReference (d));
  }

  public void Remove (TDelegate target)
  {
    if (target == null) return;
    foreach (Delegate d in (target as Delegate).GetInvocationList())
    {
      WeakReference weak = _targets.Find (w => d.Equals (w.Target));
      if (weak != null) _targets.Remove (weak);
    }
  }
```

```
public TDelegate Target
{
  get
  {
    var deadRefs = new List<WeakReference>();
    Delegate combinedTarget = null;

    foreach (WeakReference weak in _targets)
    {
      Delegate target = (Delegate)weak.Target;
      if (target != null)
        combinedTarget = Delegate.Combine (combinedTarget, target);
      else
        deadRefs.Add (weak);
    }
    foreach (WeakReference weak in deadRefs)   // Remove dead references
      _targets.Remove (weak);                  // from _targets.

    return combinedTarget as TDelegate;
  }
  set
  {
    _targets.Clear();
    Combine (value);
  }
}
}
```

This code illustrates a number of interesting points in C# and the CLR. First, note that we check that TDelegate is a delegate type in the constructor. This is because of a limitation in C#—the following type constraint is illegal because C# considers System.Delegate a special type for which constraints are not supported:

```
... where TDelegate : Delegate   // Compiler doesn't allow this
```

Instead, we must choose a class constraint, and perform a runtime check in the constructor.

In the Combine and Remove methods, we perform the reference conversion from target to Delegate via the as operator, rather than the more usual cast operator. This is because C# disallows the cast operator with this type parameter—because of a potential ambiguity between a *custom conversion* and a *reference conversion*.

We then call GetInvocationList because these methods might be called with multicast delegates—delegates with more than one method recipient.

In the Target property, we build up a multicast delegate that combines all the delegates referenced by weak references whose targets are alive. We then clear out the remaining (dead) references from the list—to avoid the _targets list endlessly growing. (We could improve our class by doing the same in the Combine method; yet another improvement would be to add locks for thread safety [Chapter 21]).

The following illustrates how to consume this delegate in implementing an event:

```
public class Foo
{
  WeakDelegate<EventHandler> _click = new WeakDelegate<EventHandler>();

  public event EventHandler Click
  {
    add { _click.Combine (value); } remove { _click.Remove (value); }
  }

  protected virtual void OnClick (EventArgs e)
  {
    EventHandler target = _click.Target;
    if (target != null) target (this, e);
  }
}
```

Notice that in firing the event, we assign _click.Target to a temporary variable before checking and invoking it. This avoids the possibility of targets being collected in the interim.

13

Diagnostics and Code Contracts

When things go wrong, it's important that information is available to aid in diagnosing the problem. An IDE or debugger can assist greatly to this effect—but it is usually available only during development. Once an application ships, the application itself must gather and record diagnostic information. To meet this requirement, the .NET Framework provides a set of facilities to log diagnostic information, monitor application behavior, detect runtime errors, and integrate with debugging tools if available.

From Framework 4.0, there are also a new set of types to enforce *code contracts*. These allow methods to interact through a set of mutual obligations, and fail *early* if those obligations are violated.

The types in this chapter are defined primarily in the `System.Diagnostics` and `System.Diagnostics.Contracts` namespaces.

Conditional Compilation

You can conditionally compile any section of code in C# with *preprocessor directives*. Preprocessor directives are special instructions to the compiler that begin with the # symbol (and, unlike other C# constructs, must appear on a line of their own). The preprocessor directives for conditional compilation are #if, #else, #endif, and #elif.

The #if directive instructs the compiler to ignore a section of code unless a specified *symbol* has been defined. You can define a symbol with either the #define directive or a compilation switch. #define applies to a particular *file*; a compilation switch applies to a whole *assembly*:

```
#define TESTMODE        // #define directives must be at top of file
                        // Symbol names are uppercase by convention.
using System;

class Program
{
```

```
    static void Main()
    {
#if TESTMODE
        Console.WriteLine ("in test mode!");     // OUTPUT: in test mode!
#endif
    }
}
```

If we deleted the first line, the program would compile with the `Console.WriteLine` statement completely eliminated from the executable.

The `#else` statement is analogous to C#'s `else` statement, and `#elif` is equivalent to `#else` followed by `#if`. The `||`, `&&`, and `!` operators can be used to perform *or*, *and*, and *not* operations:

```
#if TESTMODE && !PLAYMODE      // if TESTMODE and not PLAYMODE
    ...
```

Bear in mind, however, that you're not building an ordinary C# expression, and the symbols upon which you operate have absolutely no connection to *variables*—static or otherwise.

To define a symbol assembly-wide, specify the `/define` switch when compiling:

```
csc Program.cs /define:TESTMODE,PLAYMODE
```

Visual Studio provides an option to enter conditional compilation symbols under Project Properties.

If you've defined a symbol at the assembly level and then want to "undefine" it for a particular file, you can do so with the `#undef` directive.

Conditional Compilation Versus Static Variable Flags

The preceding example could instead be implemented with a simple static field:

```
static internal bool TestMode = true;

static void Main()
{
    if (TestMode) Console.WriteLine ("in test mode!");
}
```

This has the advantage of allowing runtime configuration. So, why choose conditional compilation? The reason is that conditional compilation can take you places variable flags cannot, such as:

- Conditionally including an attribute
- Changing the declared type of variable
- Switching between different namespaces or type aliases in a `using` directive— for example:

```
using TestType =
#if V2
    MyCompany.Widgets.GadgetV2;
#else
```

```
            MyCompany.Widgets.Gadget;
        #endif
```

You can even perform major refactoring under a conditional compilation directive, so you can instantly switch between old and new versions, and write libraries that can compile against multiple Framework versions, leveraging the latest Framework features where available.

Another advantage of conditional compilation is that debugging code can refer to types in assemblies that are not included in deployment.

The Conditional Attribute

The `Conditional` attribute instructs the compiler to ignore any calls to a particular class or method, if the specified symbol has not been defined.

To see how this is useful, suppose you write a method for logging status information as follows:

```
static void LogStatus (string msg)
{
    string logFilePath = ...
    System.IO.File.AppendAllText (logFilePath, msg + "\r\n");
}
```

Now imagine you wanted this to execute only if the `LOGGINGMODE` symbol is defined. The first solution is to wrap all calls to `LogStatus` around an `#if` directive:

```
#if LOGGINGMODE
LogStatus ("Message Headers: " + GetMsgHeaders());
#endif
```

This gives an ideal result, but it is tedious. The second solution is to put the `#if` directive inside the `LogStatus` method. This, however, is problematic should `LogStatus` be called as follows:

```
LogStatus ("Message Headers: " + GetComplexMessageHeaders());
```

`GetComplexMessageHeaders` would always get called—which might incur a performance hit.

We can combine the functionality of the first solution with the convenience of the second by attaching the `Conditional` attribute (defined in `System.Diagnostics`) to the `LogStatus` method:

```
[Conditional ("LOGGINGMODE")]
static void LogStatus (string msg)
{
    ...
}
```

This instructs the compiler to implicitly wrap any calls to `LogStatus` in an `#if` `LOGGINGMODE` directive. If the symbol is not defined, any calls to `LogStatus` get eliminated entirely in compilation—including their argument evaluation expressions. This works even if `LogStatus` and the caller are in different assemblies.

Another benefit of [Conditional] is that the conditionality check is performed when the *caller* is compiled, rather than when the *called method* is compiled. This is beneficial because it allows you to write a library containing methods such as LogStatus—and build just one version of that library.

The Conditional attribute is ignored at runtime—it's purely an instruction to the compiler.

Alternatives to the Conditional attribute

The Conditional attribute is useless if you need to dynamically enable or disable functionality at runtime: instead, you must use a variable-based approach. This leaves the question of how to elegantly circumvent the evaluation of arguments when calling conditional logging methods. A functional approach solves this:

```
using System;
using System.Linq;

class Program
{
  public static bool EnableLogging;

  static void LogStatus (Func<string> message)
  {
    string logFilePath = ...
    if (EnableLogging)
      System.IO.File.AppendAllText (logFilePath, message() + "\r\n");
  }
}
```

A lambda expression lets you call this method without syntax bloat:

```
LogStatus ( () => "Message Headers: " + GetComplexMessageHeaders() );
```

If EnableLogging is false, GetComplexMessageHeaders is never evaluated.

Debug and Trace Classes

Debug and Trace are static classes that provide basic logging and assertion capabilities. The two classes are very similar; the main differentiator is their intended use. The Debug class is intended for debug builds; the Trace class is intended for both debug and release builds. To this effect:

All methods of the Debug class are defined with [Conditional("DEBUG")].
All methods of the Trace class are defined with [Conditional("TRACE")].

This means that all calls that you make to Debug or Trace are eliminated by the compiler unless you define DEBUG or TRACE symbols. By default, Visual Studio defines both DEBUG and TRACE symbols in a project's *debug* configuration—and just the TRACE symbol in the *release* configuration.

Both the `Debug` and `Trace` classes provide `Write`, `WriteLine`, and `WriteIf` methods. By default, these send messages to the debugger's output window:

```
Debug.Write      ("Data");
Debug.WriteLine  (23 * 34);
int x = 5, y = 3;
Debug.WriteIf    (x > y, "x is greater than y");
```

The `Trace` class also provides the methods `TraceInformation`, `TraceWarning`, and `TraceError`. The difference in behavior between these and the `Write` methods depends on the active `TraceListeners` (we will cover this in the section "TraceListener" on page 504).

Fail and Assert

The `Debug` and `Trace` classes both provide `Fail` and `Assert` methods. `Fail` sends the message to each `TraceListener` in the `Debug` or `Trace` class's `Listeners` collection (see the following section), which by default writes the message to the debug output as well as displaying it in a dialog:

```
Debug.Fail ("File data.txt does not exist!");
```

The dialog that appears asks you whether to ignore, abort, or retry. The latter then lets you attach a debugger, which is useful in instantly diagnosing the problem.

`Assert` simply calls `Fail` if the `bool` argument is `false`—this is called *making an assertion*. Specifying a failure message is optional:

```
Debug.Assert (File.Exists ("data.txt"), "File data.txt does not exist!");
var result = ...
Debug.Assert (result != null);
```

The `Write`, `Fail`, and `Assert` methods are also overloaded to accept a `string` category in addition to the message, which can be useful in processing the output.

An alternative way to make an assertion is to throw an exception if the opposite condition is true. This is a common practice when validating method arguments:

```
public void ShowMessage (string message)
{
  if (message != null) throw new ArgumentNullException ("message");
  ...
}
```

Assertions made in this way are compiled unconditionally and are less flexible in that you can't control the outcome of a failed assertion via `TraceListeners`.

We'll see soon how *code contracts* extend the principles of `Fail` and `Assert`, providing more power and flexibility.

TraceListener

The `Debug` and `Trace` classes each have a `Listeners` property, comprising a static collection of `TraceListener` instances. These are responsible for processing the content emitted by the `Write`, `Fail`, and `Trace` methods.

By default, the `Listeners` collection of each includes a single listener (`DefaultTrace Listener`). The default listener has two key features:

- When connected to a debugger such as Visual Studio, messages are written to the debug output window; otherwise, message content is ignored.
- When the `Fail` method is called (or an assertion fails), a dialog appears asking the user whether to continue, abort, or retry (attach/debug)—regardless of whether a debugger is attached.

You can change this behavior by (optionally) removing the default listener, and then adding one or more of your own. You can write trace listeners from scratch (by subclassing `TraceListener`) or use one of the predefined types:

- `TextWriterTraceListener` writes to a `Stream` or `TextWriter` or appends to a file.
- `EventLogTraceListener` writes to the Windows event log.
- `EventProviderTraceListener` writes to the Event Tracing for Windows (ETW) subsystem in Windows Vista and later.
- `WebPageTraceListener` writes to an ASP.NET web page.

`TextWriterTraceListener` is further subclassed to `ConsoleTraceListener`, `Delimited ListTraceListener`, `XmlWriterTraceListener`, and `EventSchemaTraceListener`.

 None of these listeners display a dialog when `Fail` is called— only `DefaultTraceListener` has this behavior.

The following example clears `Trace`'s default listener, then adds three listeners—one that appends to a file, one that writes to the console, and one that writes to the Windows event log:

```
// Clear the default listener:
Trace.Listeners.Clear();

// Add a writer that appends to the trace.txt file:
Trace.Listeners.Add (new TextWriterTraceListener ("trace.txt"));

// Obtain the Console's output stream, then add that as a listener:
System.IO.TextWriter tw = Console.Out;
Trace.Listeners.Add (new TextWriterTraceListener (tw));

// Set up a Windows Event log source and then create/add listener.
// CreateEventSource requires administrative elevation, so this would
// typically be done in application setup.
if (!EventLog.SourceExists ("DemoApp"))
```

```
EventLog.CreateEventSource ("DemoApp", "Application");

Trace.Listeners.Add (new EventLogTraceListener ("DemoApp"));
```

In the case of the Windows event log, messages that you write with the `Write`, `Fail`, or `Assert` method always display as "Information" messages in the Windows event viewer. Messages that you write via the `TraceWarning` and `TraceError` methods, however, show up as warnings or errors.

`TraceListener` also has a `Filter` of type `TraceFilter` that you can set to control whether a message gets written to that listener. To do this, you either instantiate one of the predefined subclasses (`EventTypeFilter` or `SourceFilter`), or subclass `TraceFilter` and override the `ShouldTrace` method. You could use this to filter by category, for instance.

`TraceListener` also defines `IndentLevel` and `IndentSize` properties for controlling indentation, and the `TraceOutputOptions` property for writing extra data:

```
TextWriterTraceListener tl = new TextWriterTraceListener (Console.Out);
tl.TraceOutputOptions = TraceOptions.DateTime | TraceOptions.Callstack;
```

`TraceOutputOptions` are applied when using the `Trace` methods:

```
Trace.TraceWarning ("Orange alert");
```

```
DiagTest.vshost.exe Warning: 0 : Orange alert
    DateTime=2007-03-08T05:57:13.6250000Z
    Callstack=    at System.Environment.GetStackTrace(Exception e, Boolean
needFileInfo)
    at System.Environment.get_StackTrace()        at ...
```

Flushing and Closing Listeners

Some listeners, such as `TextWriterTraceListener`, ultimately write to a stream that is subject to caching. This has two implications:

- A message may not appear in the output stream or file immediately.
- You must close—or at least flush—the listener before your application ends; otherwise, you lose what's in the cache (up to 4 KB, by default, if you're writing to a file).

The `Trace` and `Debug` classes provide static `Close` and `Flush` methods that call `Close` or `Flush` on all listeners (which in turn calls `Close` or `Flush` on any underlying writers and streams). `Close` implicitly calls `Flush`, closes file handles, and prevents further data from being written.

As a general rule, call `Close` before an application ends and call `Flush` anytime you want to ensure that current message data is written. This applies if you're using stream- or file-based listeners.

`Trace` and `Debug` also provide an `AutoFlush` property, which, if `true`, forces a `Flush` after every message.

It's a good policy to set `AutoFlush` to `true` on `Debug` and `Trace` if you're using any file- or stream-based listeners. Otherwise, if an unhandled exception or critical error occurs, the last 4 KB of diagnostic information may be lost.

Code Contracts Overview

We mentioned previously the concept of an *assertion*, whereby you check that certain conditions are met throughout your program. If a condition fails, it indicates a bug, which should typically be handled by invoking a debugger (in debug builds) or throwing an exception (in release builds).

Assertions follow the principle that if something goes wrong, it's best to fail early and close to the source of the error. This is usually better than trying to continue with invalid data—which can result in incorrect results or an exception later on in the program (which is harder to diagnose).

Historically, there have been two ways to enforce assertions:

- By calling the `Assert` method on `Debug` or `Trace`
- By throwing exceptions (such as `ArgumentNullException`)

Framework 4.0 provides a new feature called *code contracts*, which replaces both of these approaches with a unified system. That system allows you to make not only simple assertions but also more powerful *contract*-based assertions.

Code contracts derive from the principle of "Design by Contract" from the Eiffel programming language, where functions interact with each other through a system of mutual obligations and benefits. Essentially, a function specifies *preconditions* that must be met by the client (caller), and in return guarantees *postconditions* which the client can depend on when the function returns.

The types for code contracts live in the `System.Diagnostics.Contracts` namespace.

Although the types that support code contracts are built into .NET Framework 4.0, the binary rewriter and the static checking tools are available as a separate download at the Microsoft DevLabs site (*http://msdn.microsoft.com/devlabs*). You must install these tools before you can use code contracts in Visual Studio 2010.

Why Use Code Contracts?

To illustrate, we'll write a method that adds an item to a list only if it's not already present—with two *preconditions* and a *postcondition*:

```
public static bool AddIfNotPresent<T> (IList<T> list, T item)
{
    Contract.Requires (list != null);       // Precondition
    Contract.Requires (!list.IsReadOnly);   // Precondition
```

```
Contract.Ensures (list.Contains (item));    // Postcondition
if (list.Contains(item)) return false;
list.Add (item);
return true;
}
```

The preconditions are defined by `Contract.Requires` and are verified when the method starts. The postcondition is defined by `Contract.Ensures` and is verified not where it appears in the code, but *when the method exits*.

Preconditions and postconditions act like assertions and, in this case, detect the following errors:

- Calling the method with a null or read-only list
- A bug in the method whereby we forgot to add the item to the list

 Preconditions and postconditions must appear at the start of the method. This is conducive to good design: if you fail to fulfill the contract in subsequently writing the method, the error will be detected.

Moreover, these conditions form a discoverable *contract* for that method. `AddIfNotPresent` advertises to consumers:

- "You must call me with a non-null writable list."
- "When I return, that list will contain the item you specified."

These facts can be emitted into the assembly's XML documentation file (you can do this in Visual Studio by going to the Code Contracts tab of the Project Properties window, enabling the building of a contracts reference assembly, and checking "Emit Contracts into XML doc file"). Tools such as SandCastle can then incorporate contract details into documentation files.

Contracts also enable your program to be analyzed for correctness by static contract validation tools. If you try to call `AddIfNotPresent` with a `list` whose value might be null, for example, a static validation tool could warn you before you even run the program.

Another benefit of contracts is ease of use. In our example, it's easier to code the postcondition upfront than at both exit points. Contracts also support *object invariants*—which further reduce repetitive coding and make for more reliable enforcement.

Conditions can also be placed on interface members and abstract methods, something that is impossible with standard validation approaches. And conditions on virtual methods cannot be accidentally circumvented by subclasses.

Yet another benefit of code contracts is that contract violation behavior can be customized easily and in more ways than if you rely on calling `Debug.Assert` or throwing exceptions. And it's possible to ensure that contract violations are always recorded—even if contract violation exceptions are swallowed by exception handlers higher in the call stack.

The disadvantage of using code contracts is that the .NET implementation relies on a *binary rewriter*—a tool that mutates the assembly after compilation. This slows the build process, as well as complicating services that rely on calling the C# compiler (whether explicitly or via the `CSharpCodeProvider` class).

The enforcing of code contracts may also incur a runtime performance hit, although this is easily mitigated by scaling back contract checking in release builds.

 Another limitation of code contracts is that you can't use them to enforce security-sensitive checks, because they can be circumvented at runtime (by handling the `ContractFailed` event).

Contract Principles

Code contracts comprise *preconditions*, *postconditions*, *assertions*, and *object invariants*. These are all discoverable assertions. They differ based on when they are verified:

- *Preconditions* are verified when a function starts.
- *Postconditions* are verified before a function exits.
- *Assertions* are verified wherever they appear in the code.
- *Object invariants* are verified after every public function in a class.

Code contracts are defined entirely by calling (static) methods in the `Contract` class. This makes contracts *language-independent*.

Contracts can appear not only in methods, but in other functions as well, such as constructors, properties, indexers, and operators.

Compilation

Almost all methods in the `Contract` class are defined with the `[Conditional("CONTRACTS_FULL")]` attribute. This means that unless you define the `CONTRACTS_FULL` symbol, (most) contract code is stripped out. Visual Studio defines the `CONTRACTS_FULL` symbol automatically if you enable contract checking in the Code Contracts tab of the Project Properties page. (For this tab to appear, you must download and install the Contracts tools from the Microsoft DevLabs site.)

 Removing the `CONTRACTS_FULL` symbol might seem like an easy way to disable all contract checking. However, it doesn't apply to `Requires<TException>` conditions (which we'll describe in detail soon).

The only way to disable contracts in code that uses `Requires<TException>` is to enable the `CONTRACTS_FULL` symbol and then get the binary rewriter to strip out contract code by choosing an enforcement level of "none".

The binary rewriter

After compiling code that contains contracts, you must call the binary rewriter tool, *ccrewrite.exe* (Visual Studio does this automatically if contract checking is enabled). The binary rewriter moves postconditions (and object invariants) into the right place, calls any conditions and object invariants in overridden methods, and replaces calls to `Contract` with calls to a *contracts runtime class*. Here's a (simplified) version of what our earlier example would look like after rewriting:

```
static bool AddIfNotPresent<T> (IList<T> list, T item)
{
  __ContractsRuntime.Requires (list != null);
  __ContractsRuntime.Requires (!list.IsReadOnly);
  bool result;
  if (list.Contains (item))
    result = false;
  else
  {
    list.Add (item);
    result = true;
  }
  __ContractsRuntime.Ensures (list.Contains (item));   // Postcondition
  return result;
}
```

If you fail to call the binary rewriter, `Contract` won't get replaced with `__ContractsRuntime` and the former will end up throwing exceptions.

> The `__ContractsRuntime` type is the default contracts runtime class. In advanced scenarios, you can specify your own contracts runtime class via the `/rw` switch or Visual Studio's Code Contracts tab in Project Properties.
>
> Because `__ContractsRuntime` is shipped with the binary rewriter (which is not a standard part of the .NET Framework), the binary rewriter actually injects the `__ContractsRuntime` class into your compiled assembly. You can examine its code by disassembling any assembly that enables code contracts.

The binary rewriter also offers switches to strip away some or all contract checking: we describe these in "Selectively Enforcing Contracts" on page 521. You typically enable full contract checking in debug build configurations and a subset of contract checking in release configurations.

Asserting versus throwing on failure

The binary rewriter also lets you choose between displaying a dialog and throwing a `ContractException` upon contract failure. The former is typically used for debug builds; the latter for release builds. To enable the latter, specify `/throwonfailure` when calling the binary rewriter, or uncheck the "Assert on contract failure" checkbox in Visual Studio's Code Contracts tab in Project Properties.

See "Dealing with Contract Failure" on page 519 for more detail.

Purity

All functions that you call from arguments passed to contract methods (`Requires`, `Assumes`, `Assert`, etc.) must be *pure*—that is, side-effect-free (they must not alter the values of fields). You must signal to the binary rewriter that any functions you call are pure by applying the [`Pure`] attribute:

```
[Pure]
public static bool IsValidUri (string uri) { ... }
```

This makes the following legal:

```
Contract.Requires (IsValidUri (uri));
```

The contract tools implicitly assume that all property get accessors are pure, as are all C# operators (+, *, %, etc.) and members on selected Framework types, including `string`, `Contract`, `Type`, `System.IO.Path`, and LINQ's query operators. It also assumes that methods invoked via delegates marked with the [`Pure`] attribute are pure (the `Comparison<T>` and `Predicate<T>` attributes are marked with this attribute).

Preconditions

You can define code contract preconditions by calling `Contract.Requires`, `Contract.Requires<TException>`, or `Contract.EndContractBlock`.

Contract.Requires

Calling `Contract.Requires` at the start of a function enforces a precondition:

```
static string ToProperCase (string s)
{
  Contract.Requires (!string.IsNullOrEmpty(s));
  ...
}
```

This is like making an assertion, except that the precondition forms a discoverable fact about your function that can be extracted from the compiled code and consumed by documentation or static checking tools (so that they can warn you should they see some code elsewhere in your program that tries to call `ToProperCase` with a null or empty string).

A further benefit of preconditions is that subclasses that override virtual methods with preconditions cannot prevent the base class method's preconditions from being checked. And preconditions defined on *interface* members will be implicitly woven into the concrete implementations (see "Contracts on Interfaces and Abstract Methods" on page 518).

Preconditions should access only members that are at least as accessible as the function itself—this ensures that callers can make sense of the contract. If you need to read or call less accessible members, it's likely that you're validating *internal state* rather than enforcing the *calling contract*, in which case you should make an assertion instead.

You can call `Contract.Requires` as many times as necessary at the start of the method to enforce different conditions.

What Should You Put in Preconditions?

The guideline from the Code Contracts team is that preconditions should:

- Be possible for the client (caller) to easily validate
- Rely only on data & functions at least as accessible as the method itself
- Always indicate a *bug* if violated

A consequence of the last point is that a client should never specifically "catch" a contract failure (the `ContractException` type, in fact, is internal to help enforce that principle). Instead, the client should call the target properly; if it fails, this indicates a bug that should be handled via your general exception backstop (which may include terminating the application). In other words, if you decide control-flow or do other things based on a precondition failure, it's not really a contract because you can continue executing if it fails.

This leads to the following advice, when choosing between preconditions and throwing ordinary exceptions:

- If failure *always* indicates a bug in the client, favor a precondition.
- If failure indicates an *abnormal condition*, which *may* mean a bug in the client, throw a (catchable) exception instead.

To illustrate, suppose we're writing the `Int32.Parse` function. It's reasonable to assume that a null input string always indicates a bug in the caller, so we'd enforce this with a precondition:

```
public static int Parse (string s)
{
  Contract.Requires (s != null);
}
```

Next, we need to check that the string contains only digits and symbols such as + and - (in the right place). It would place an unreasonable burden on the caller to validate this and so we'd enforce it not as a precondition, but a manual check that throws a (catchable) `FormatException` if violated.

To illustrate the member accessibility issue, consider the following code, which often appears in types implementing the `IDisposable` interface:

```
public void Foo()
{
  if (_isDisposed)  // _isDisposed is a private field
    throw new ObjectDisposedException();
  ...
}
```

This check should not be made into a precondition unless we make _isDisposed accessible to the caller (by refactoring it into a publicly readable property, for instance).

Finally, consider the `File.ReadAllText` method. The following would be *inappropriate* use of a precondition:

```
public static string ReadAllText (string path)
{
    Contract.Requires (File.Exists (path));
    ...
}
```

The caller cannot reliably know that the file exists before calling this method (it could be deleted between making that check and calling the method). So, we'd enforce this in the old-fashioned way—by throwing a catchable `FileNotFoundException` instead.

Contract.Requires<TException>

The introduction of code contracts challenges the following deeply entrenched pattern established in the .NET Framework from version 1.0:

```
static void SetProgress (string message, int percent)  // Classic approach
{
  if (message == null)
    throw new ArgumentNullException ("message");

  if (percent < 0 || percent > 100)
    throw new ArgumentOutOfRangeException ("percent");
  ...
}

static void SetProgress (string message, int percent)  // Modern approach
{
  Contract.Requires (message != null);
  Contract.Requires (percent >= 0 && percent <= 100);
  ...
}
```

If you have a large assembly that enforces classic argument checking, writing new methods with preconditions will create an inconsistent library: some methods will throw argument exceptions whereas others will throw a `ContractException`. One solution is to update all existing methods to use contracts, but this has two problems:

- It's time-consuming.

- Callers may have come to *depend* on an exception type such as `ArgumentNullException` being thrown. (This almost certainly indicates bad design, but may be the reality nonetheless.)

The solution is to call the generic version of `Contract.Requires`. This lets you specify an exception type to throw upon failure:

```
Contract.Requires<ArgumentNullException> (message != null, "message");
Contract.Requires<ArgumentOutOfRangeException>
  (percent >= 0 && percent <= 100, "percent");
```

(The second argument gets passed to the constructor of the exception class).

This results in the same behavior as with old-fashioned argument checking, while delivering the benefits of contracts (conciseness, support for interfaces, implicit documentation, static checking, and runtime customization).

 The specified exception is thrown only if you specify /throwonfailure when rewriting the assembly (or *uncheck* the *Assert on Contract Failure* checkbox in Visual Studio). Otherwise, a dialog appears.

It's also possible to specify a contract-checking level of *ReleaseRequires* in the binary rewriter (see "Selectively Enforcing Contracts" on page 521). Calls to the generic `Contract.Requires<TException>` then remain in place while all other checks are stripped away: this results in an assembly that behaves just as in the past.

Contract.EndContractBlock

The `Contract.EndContractBlock` method lets you get the benefit of code contracts with traditional argument-checking code—avoiding the need to refactor code that you wrote prior to Framework 4.0. All you do is call this method after performing manual argument checks:

```
static void Foo (string name)
{
  if (name == null) throw new ArgumentNullException ("name");
  Contract.EndContractBlock();
  ...
}
```

The binary rewriter then converts this code into something equivalent to:

```
static void Foo (string name)
{
  Contract.Requires<ArgumentNullException> (name != null, "name");
  ...
}
```

The code that precedes `EndContractBlock` must comprise simple statements of the form:

```
if <condition> throw <expression>;
```

You can mix traditional argument checking with code contract calls: simply put the latter after the former:

```
static void Foo (string name)
{
  if (name == null) throw new ArgumentNullException ("name");
  Contract.Requires (name.Length >= 2);
  ...
}
```

Calling any of the contract-enforcing methods implicitly ends the contract block.

The point is to define a region at the beginning of the method where the contract rewriter knows that every `if` statement is part of a contract. Calling any of the contract-enforcing methods implicitly extends the contract block, so you don't need to use `EndContractBlock` if you use another method such as `Contract.Ensures`, etc.

Preconditions and Overridden Methods

An overridden method cannot add preconditions, because doing so would *change the contract* (by making it more restrictive)—breaking the principles of polymorphism.

(Technically, the designers could have allowed overridden methods to *weaken* preconditions; they decided against this because the scenarios weren't sufficiently compelling to justify adding this complexity).

 The binary rewriter ensures that a base method's preconditions are always enforced in subclasses—whether or not the overridden method calls the base method.

Postconditions

Contract.Ensures

`Contract.Ensures` enforces a postcondition: something which must be true when the method exits. We saw an example earlier:

```
static bool AddIfNotPresent<T> (IList<T> list, T item)
{
  Contract.Requires (list != null);          // Precondition
  Contract.Ensures (list.Contains (item));   // Postcondition
  if (list.Contains(item)) return false;
  list.Add (item);
  return true;
}
```

The binary rewriter moves postconditions to the exit points of the method. Post-conditions are checked if you return early from a method (as in this example)—but not if you return early via an unhandled exception.

Unlike preconditions, which detect misuse by the *caller*, postconditions detect an error in the function itself (rather like assertions). Therefore, postconditions may access private state (subject to the caveat stated shortly, in "Postconditions and Overridden Methods" on page 516).

Postconditions and Thread Safety

Multithreaded scenarios (Chapter 21) challenge the usefulness of postconditions. For instance, suppose we wrote a thread-safe wrapper for a List<T> with a method as follows:

```
public class ThreadSafeList<T>
{
  List<T> _list = new List<T>();
  object _locker = new object();

  public bool AddIfNotPresent (T item)
  {
    Contract.Ensures (_list.Contains (item));
    lock (_locker)
    {
      if (_list.Contains(item)) return false;
      _list.Add (item);
      return true;
    }
  }

  public void Remove (T item)
  {
    lock (_locker)
      _list.Remove (item);
  }
}
```

The postcondition in the AddIfNotPresent method is checked *after* the lock is released—at which point the item may no longer exist in the list if another thread called Remove right then. There is currently no workaround for this problem, other than to enforce such conditions as assertions (see next section) rather than postconditions.

Contract.EnsuresOnThrow<TException>

Occasionally, it's useful to ensure that a certain condition holds should a particular type of exception be thrown. The EnsuresOnThrow method does exactly this:

```
Contract.EnsuresOnThrow<WebException> (this.ErrorMessage != null);
```

Contract.Result<T> and Contract.ValueAtReturn<T>

Because postconditions are not evaluated until a function ends, it's reasonable to want to access the return value of a method. The `Contract.Result<T>` method does exactly that:

```
Random _random = new Random();
int GetOddRandomNumber()
{
  Contract.Ensures (Contract.Result<int>() % 2 == 1);
  return _random.Next (100) * 2 + 1;
}
```

The `Contract.ValueAtReturn<T>` method fulfills the same function—but for `ref` and `out` parameters.

Contract.OldValue<T>

`Contract.OldValue<T>` returns the original value of a method parameter. This is useful with postconditions because the latter are checked at the *end* of a function. Therefore, any expressions in postconditions that incorporate parameters will read the *modified* parameter values.

For example, the postcondition in the following method will always fail:

```
static string Middle (string s)
{
  Contract.Requires (s != null && s.Length >= 2);
  Contract.Ensures (Contract.Result<string>().Length < s.Length);
  s = s.Substring (1, s.Length - 2);
  return s.Trim();
}
```

Here's how we can correct it:

```
static string Middle (string s)
{
  Contract.Requires (s != null && s.Length >= 2);
  Contract.Ensures (Contract.Result<string>().Length <
                    Contract.OldValue (s).Length);
  s = s.Substring (1, s.Length - 2);
  return s.Trim();
}
```

Postconditions and Overridden Methods

An overridden method cannot circumvent postconditions defined by its base, but it can add new ones. The binary rewriter ensures that a base method's postconditions are always checked—even if the overridden method doesn't call the base implementation.

For the reason just stated, postconditions on virtual methods should not access private members. Doing so will result in the binary rewriter weaving code into the subclass that will try to access private members in the base class—causing a runtime error.

Assertions and Object Invariants

In addition to preconditions and postconditions, the code contracts API lets you make assertions and define *object invariants*.

Assertions

Contract.Assert

You can make assertions anywhere in a function by calling `Contract.Assert`. You can optionally specify an error message if the assertion fails:

```
...
int x = 3;
...
Contract.Assert (x == 3);                  // Fail unless x is 3
Contract.Assert (x == 3, "x must be 3");
...
```

The binary rewriter doesn't move assertions around. There are two reasons for favoring `Contract.Assert` over `Debug.Assert`:

- You can leverage the more flexible failure-handling mechanisms offered by code contracts

- Static checking tools can attempt to validate `Contract.Assert`s

Contract.Assume

`Contract.Assume` behaves exactly like `Contract.Assert` at runtime, but has slightly different implications for static checking tools. Essentially, static checking tools won't *challenge* an assumption, whereas they may challenge an assertion. This is useful in that there will always be things a static checker is unable to prove, and this may lead to it "crying wolf" over a valid assertion. Changing the assertion to an assumption keeps the static checker quiet.

Object Invariants

For a class, you can specify one or more *object invariant* methods. These methods run automatically after every *public* function in the class, and allow you to assert that the object is in an internally consistent state.

Support for multiple object invariant methods was included to make object invariants work well with partial classes.

To define an object invariant method, write a parameterless void method and annotate it with the `[ContractInvariantMethod]` attribute. In that method, call `Contract.Invariant` to enforce each condition that should hold true if your object is a valid state:

```
class Test
{
  int _x, _y;

  [ContractInvariantMethod]
  void ObjectInvariant()
  {
    Contract.Invariant (_x >= 0);
    Contract.Invariant (_y >= _x);
  }

  public int X { get { return _x; } set { _x = value; } }
  public void Test1() { _x = -3; }
  void Test2()        { _x = -3; }
}
```

The binary rewriter translates the X property, `Test1` method, and `Test2` method to something equivalent to this:

```
public void X { get { return _x; } set { _x = value; ObjectInvariant(); } }
public void Test1() { _x = -3; ObjectInvariant(); }
void Test2()        { _x = -3; }    // No change because it's private
```

Object invariants don't *prevent* an object from entering an invalid state: they merely *detect* when that condition has occurred.

`Contract.Invariant` is rather like `Contract.Assert`, except that it can appear only in a method marked with the `[ContractInvariantMethod]` attribute. And conversely, a contract invariant method can only contain calls to `Contract.Invariant`.

A subclass can introduce its own object invariant method, too, and this will be checked in addition to the base class's invariant method. The caveat, of course, is that the check will take place only after a public method is called.

Contracts on Interfaces and Abstract Methods

A powerful feature of code contracts is that you can attach conditions to interface members and abstract methods. The binary rewriter then automatically weaves these conditions into the members' concrete implementations.

A special mechanism lets specify a separate contract class for interfaces and abstract methods, so that you can write method bodies to house the contract conditions. Here's how it works:

```
[ContractClass (typeof (ContractForITest))]
interface ITest
{
  int Process (string s);
}

[ContractClassFor (typeof (ITest))]
sealed class ContractForITest : ITest
{
  int ITest.Process (string s)     // Must use explicit implementation.
  {
    Contract.Requires (s != null);
    return 0;                       // Dummy value to satisfy compiler.
  }
}
```

Notice that we had to return a value when implementing ITest.Process to satisfy the compiler. The code that returns 0 will not run, however. Instead, the binary rewriter extracts just the conditions from that method, and weaves them into the real implementations of ITest.Process. This means that the contract class is never actually instantiated (and any constructors that you write will not execute).

You can assign a temporary variable within the contract block to make it easier to reference other members of the interface. For instance, if our ITest interface also defined a Message property of type string, we could write the following in ITest.Process:

```
int ITest.Process (string s)
{
  ITest test = this;
  Contract.Requires (s != test.Message);
  ...
}
```

This is easier than:

```
Contract.Requires (s != ((ITest)this).Message);
```

(Simply using this.Message won't work because Message must be explicitly implemented.) The process of defining contract classes for abstract classes is exactly the same, except that the contract class should be marked abstract instead of sealed.

Dealing with Contract Failure

The binary rewriter lets you specify what happens when a contract condition fails, via the /throwonfailure switch (or the *Assert on Contract Failure* checkbox in Visual Studio's *Contracts* tab in *Project Properties*).

If you don't specify /throwonfailure—or check *Assert on Contract Failure*—a dialog appears upon contract failure, allowing you to abort, debug or ignore the error.

There are a couple of nuances to be aware of:

- If the CLR is hosted (i.e., in SQL Server or Exchange), the host's escalation policy is triggered instead of a dialog appearing.
- Otherwise, if the current process can't pop up a dialog box to the user, `Environment.FailFast` is called.

The dialog is useful in debug builds for a couple of reasons:

- It makes it easy to diagnose and debug contract failures on the spot—without having to re-run the program. This works regardless of whether Visual Studio is configured to break on first-chance exceptions. And unlike with exceptions in general, contract failure almost certainly means a bug in your code.
- It lets you know about contract failure—even if a caller higher up in the stack "swallows" exceptions as follows:

```
try
{
    // Call some method whose contract fails
}
catch { }
```

The code above is considered an antipattern in most scenarios because it *masks* failures, including conditions that the author never anticipated.

If you specify the `/throwonfailure` switch—or uncheck *Assert on Contract Failure* in Visual Studio—a `ContractException` is thrown upon failure. This is desirable for:

- Release builds—where you would let the exception bubble up the stack and be treated like any other unexpected exception (perhaps by having a top-level exception handler log the error or invite the user to report it).
- Unit testing environments— where the process of logging errors is automated.

`ContractException` cannot appear in a `catch` block because this type is not public. The rationale is that there's no reason that you'd want to *specifically* catch a `ContractException`—you'd want to catch it only as part of a general exception backstop.

The ContractFailed Event

When a contract fails, the static `Contract.ContractFailed` event fires before any further action is taken. If you handle this event, you can query the event arguments object for details of the error. You can also call `SetHandled` to prevent a `ContractEx ception` from being subsequently thrown (or a dialog appearing).

Handling this event is particularly useful when `/throwonfailure` is specified, because it lets you log *all* contract failures—even if code higher in the call stack swallows exceptions as we described just before. A great example is with automated unit testing:

```
Contract.ContractFailed += (sender, args) =>
{
  string failureMessage = args.FailureKind + ": " + args.Message;
  // Log failureMessage with unit testing framework:
  // ...
  args.SetUnwind();
};
```

This handler logs all contract failures, while allowing the normal `ContractException` (or contract failure dialog) to run its course after the event handler has finished. Notice that we also call `SetUnwind`: this neutralizes the effect of any calls to `SetHandled` from other event subscribers. In other words, it ensures that a `ContractException` (or dialog) will always follow after all event handlers have run.

If you throw an exception from within this handler, any other event handlers will still execute. The exception that you threw then populates the `InnerException` property of the `ContractException` that's eventually thrown.

Exceptions Within Contract Conditions

If an exception is thrown within a contract condition itself, then that exception propagates like any other—regardless of whether `/throwonfailure` is specified. The following method throws a `NullReferenceException` if called with a null string:

```
string Test (string s)
{
  Contract.Requires (s.Length > 0);
  ...
}
```

This precondition is essentially faulty. It should instead be:

```
Contract.Requires (!string.IsNullOrEmpty (s));
```

Selectively Enforcing Contracts

The binary rewriter offers two switches that strip away some or all contract checking: `/publicsurface` and `/level`. You can control these from Visual Studio via the *Code Contracts* tab of *Project Properties*. The `/publicsurface` switch tells the rewriter to check contracts only on public members. The `/level` switch has the following options:

None (Level 0)
    Strips out *all* contract verification

ReleaseRequires (Level 1)
    Enables only calls to the generic version of `Contract.Requires<TException>`

Preconditions (Level 2)
   Enables all preconditions (Level 1 plus normal preconditions)

Pre and Post (Level 3)
   Enables Level2 checking plus postconditions

Full (Level 4)
   Enables Level 3 checking plus object invariants and assertions (i.e., everything)

You typically enable full contract checking in debug build configurations.

Contracts in Release Builds

When it comes to making release builds, there are two general philosophies:

- Favor safety and enable full contract checking
- Favor performance and disable all contract checking

If you're building a library for public consumption, though, the second approach creates a problem. Imagine that you compile and distribute library L in release mode with contract checking disabled. A client then builds project C in *debug* mode that references library L. Assembly C can then call members of L incorrectly without contract violations! In this situation, you actually want to enforce the parts of L's contract that ensure correct usage of L—in other words, the *preconditions* in L's *public* members.

The simplest way to resolve this is to enable `/publicsurface` checking in L with a level of *Preconditions* or *ReleaseRequires*. This ensures that the essential preconditions are enforced for the benefit of consumers, while incurring the performance cost of only those preconditions.

In extreme cases, you might not want to pay even this small performance price—in which case, you can take the more elaborate approach of *call-site checking*.

Call-Site Checking

Call-site checking moves precondition validation from *called* methods into *calling* methods (call sites). This solves the problem just described—by enabling consumers of library L to perform L's precondition validation themselves in debug configurations.

To enable call-site checking, you must first build a separate *contracts reference assembly*—a supplementary assembly that contains just the preconditions for the referenced assembly. To do this, you can either use the *ccrefgen* command-line tool, or proceed in Visual Studio as follows:

1. In the release configuration of the *referenced library* (L), go to the *Code Contracts* tab of *Project Properties* and disable runtime contract checking while ticking "Build a Contract Reference Assembly". This then generates a supplementary contracts reference assembly (with the suffix *.contracts.dll*).

2. In the *release* configuration of the *referencing* assemblies, disable all contract checking.

3. In the *debug* configuration of the *referencing* assemblies, tick "Call-site Requires Checking."

The third step is equivalent to calling *ccrewrite* with the `/callsiterequires` switch. It reads the preconditions from the contracts reference assembly and weaves them into the calling sites in the referencing assembly.

Static Contract Checking

Code contracts permit *static contract checking*, whereby a tool analyzes contract conditions to find potential bugs in your program before it's run. For example, statically checking the following code generates a warning:

```
static void Main()
{
  string message = null;
  WriteLine (message);    // Static checking tool will generate warning
}

static void WriteLine (string s)
{
  Contract.Requires (s != null);
  Console.WriteLine (s);
}
```

You can run Microsoft's static contracts tool either from the command line via *cccheck*, or by enabling static contract checking in Visual Studio's project properties dialog (the commercial version is supported with Visual Studio *Premium and Ultimate editions* only).

For static checking to work, you may need to add preconditions and postconditions to your methods. To give a simple example, the following will generate a warning:

```
static void WriteLine (string s, bool b)
{
  if (b)
    WriteLine (s);    // Warning: requires unproven
}

static void WriteLine (string s)
{
  Contract.Requires (s != null);
  Console.WriteLine (s);
}
```

Because we're calling a method that requires the parameter to be non-null, we must prove that the argument is non-null. To do this, we can add a precondition to the first method as follows:

```
static void WriteLine (string s, bool b)
{
  Contract.Requires (s != null);
  if (b)
    WriteLine (s);    // OK
}
```

The ContractVerification Attribute

Static checking is easiest if instigated from the beginning of a project's lifecycle—otherwise you're likely to get overwhelmed with warnings.

If you do want to apply static contract checking to an existing codebase, it can help by initially applying it just to selective parts of a program—via the `ContractVerification` attribute (in `System.Diagnostics.Contracts`). This attribute can be applied at the assembly, type, and member level. If you apply it at multiple levels, the more granular wins. Therefore, to enable static contract verification just for a particular class, start by disabling verification at the assembly-level as follows:

```
[assembly: ContractVerification (false)]
```

and then enable it just for the desired class:

```
[ContractVerification (true)]
class Foo { ... }
```

Baselines

Another tactic in applying static contract verification to an existing codebase is to run the static checker with the *Baseline* option checked in Visual Studio. All the warnings that are produced are then written to a specified XML file. Next time you run static verification, all the warnings in that that file are ignored—so you see only messages generated as a result of *new* code that you've written.

The SuppressMessage Attribute

You can also tell the static checker to ignore certain types of warnings via the `SuppressMessage` attribute (in `System.Diagnostics.CodeAnalysis`):

```
[SuppressMessage ("Microsoft.Contracts", warningFamily)]
```

where *warningFamily* is one of the following values:

```
Requires Ensures Invariant NonNull DivByZero MinValueNegation
ArrayCreation ArrayLowerBound ArrayUpperBound
```

You can apply this attribute at an assembly or type level.

Debugger Integration

Sometimes it's useful for an application to interact with a debugger if one is available. During development, the debugger is usually your IDE (e.g., Visual Studio); in deployment, the debugger is more likely to be:

- DbgCLR
- One of the lower-level debugging tools, such as WinDbg, Cordbg, or Mdbg

DbgCLR is Visual Studio stripped of everything but the debugger, and it is a free download with the .NET Framework SDK. It's the easiest debugging option when an IDE is not available, although it requires that you download the whole SDK.

Attaching and Breaking

The static `Debugger` class in `System.Diagnostics` provides basic functions for interacting with a debugger—namely `Break`, `Launch`, `Log`, and `IsAttached`.

A debugger must first attach to an application in order to debug it. If you start an application from within an IDE, this happens automatically, unless you request otherwise (by choosing "Start without debugging"). Sometimes, though, it's inconvenient or impossible to start an application in debug mode within the IDE. An example is a Windows Service application or (ironically) a Visual Studio designer. One solution is to start the application normally, and then choose Debug Process in your IDE. This doesn't allow you to set breakpoints early in the program's execution, however.

The workaround is to call `Debugger.Break` from within your application. This method launches a debugger, attaches to it, and suspends execution at that point. (`Launch` does the same, but without suspending execution.) Once attached, you can log messages directly to the debugger's output window with the `Log` method. You can tell whether you're attached to a debugger with the `IsAttached` property.

Debugger Attributes

The `DebuggerStepThrough` and `DebuggerHidden` attributes provide suggestions to the debugger on how to handle single-stepping for a particular method, constructor, or class.

`DebuggerStepThrough` requests that the debugger step through a function without any user interaction. This attribute is useful in automatically generated methods and in proxy methods that forward the real work to a method somewhere else. In the latter case, the debugger will still show the proxy method in the call stack if a breakpoint is set within the "real" method—unless you also add the `DebuggerHidden` attribute. These two attributes can be combined on proxies to help the user focus on debugging the application logic rather than the plumbing:

```
[DebuggerStepThrough, DebuggerHidden]
void DoWorkProxy()
{
  // setup...
  DoWork();
  // teardown...
}

void DoWork() {...}   // Real method...
```

Processes and Process Threads

In the last section of Chapter 6, we described how to launch a new process with `Process.Start`. The `Process` class also allows you to query and interact with other processes running on the same, or another, computer.

Examining Running Processes

The `Process.GetProcessXXX` methods retrieve a specific process by name or process ID, or all processes running on the current or nominated computer. This includes both managed and unmanaged processes. Each `Process` instance has a wealth of properties mapping statistics such as name, ID, priority, memory and processor utilization, window handles, and so on. The following sample enumerates all the running processes on the current computer:

```
foreach (Process p in Process.GetProcesses())
using (p)
{
  Console.WriteLine (p.ProcessName);
  Console.WriteLine ("    PID:    " + p.Id);
  Console.WriteLine ("    Memory: " + p.WorkingSet64);
  Console.WriteLine ("    Threads: " + p.Threads.Count);
}
```

`Process.GetCurrentProcess` returns the current process. If you've created additional application domains, all will share the same process.

You can terminate a process by calling its `Kill` method.

Examining Threads in a Process

You can also enumerate over the threads of other processes, with the `Process.Threads` property. The objects that you get, however, are not `System.Threading.Thread` objects, but rather `ProcessThread` objects, and are intended for administrative rather than synchronization tasks. A `ProcessThread` object provides diagnostic information about the underlying thread and allows you to control some aspects of it such as its priority and processor affinity:

```
public void EnumerateThreads (Process p)
{
  foreach (ProcessThread pt in p.Threads)
  {
    Console.WriteLine (pt.Id);
    Console.WriteLine ("   State:    " + pt.ThreadState);
    Console.WriteLine ("   Priority: " + pt.PriorityLevel);
    Console.WriteLine ("   Started:  " + pt.StartTime);
    Console.WriteLine ("   CPU time: " + pt.TotalProcessorTime);
  }
}
```

StackTrace and StackFrame

The `StackTrace` and `StackFrame` classes provide a read-only view of an execution call stack. You can obtain stack traces for the current thread, another thread in the same process, or an `Exception` object. Such information is useful mostly for diagnostic purposes, though it can also be used in programming (hacks). `StackTrace` represents a complete call stack; `StackFrame` represents a single method call within that stack.

If you instantiate a StackTrace object with no arguments—or with a bool argument—you get a snapshot of the current thread's call stack. The bool argument, if true, instructs StackTrace to read the assembly .pdb (project debug) files if they are present, giving you access to filename, line number, and column offset data.

 Project debug files are generated when you compile with the /debug switch. Visual Studio compiles with this switch unless you request otherwise via *Advanced Build Settings*.

Once you've obtained a StackTrace, you can examine a particular frame by calling GetFrame—or obtain the whole lot with GetFrames:

```
static void Main() { A (); }
static void A()    { B (); }
static void B()    { C (); }
static void C()
{
  StackTrace s = new StackTrace (true);

  Console.WriteLine ("Total frames:   " + s.FrameCount);
  Console.WriteLine ("Current method: " + s.GetFrame(0).GetMethod().Name);
  Console.WriteLine ("Calling method: " + s.GetFrame(1).GetMethod().Name);
  Console.WriteLine ("Entry method:   " + s.GetFrame
                                    (s.FrameCount-1).GetMethod().Name);
  Console.WriteLine ("Call Stack:");
  foreach (StackFrame f in s.GetFrames())
    Console.WriteLine (
      " File: "   + f.GetFileName() +
      " Line: "   + f.GetFileLineNumber() +
      " Col: "    + f.GetFileColumnNumber() +
      " Offset: " + f.GetILOffset() +
      " Method: " + f.GetMethod().Name);
}
```

Here's the output:

```
Total frames:   4
Current method: C
Calling method: B
Entry method: Main
Call stack:
  File: C:\Test\Program.cs  Line: 15  Col: 4   Offset: 7  Method: C
  File: C:\Test\Program.cs  Line: 12  Col: 22  Offset: 6  Method: B
  File: C:\Test\Program.cs  Line: 11  Col: 22  Offset: 6  Method: A
  File: C:\Test\Program.cs  Line: 10  Col: 25  Offset: 6  Method: Main
```

A shortcut to obtaining the essential information for an entire StackTrace is to call ToString on it. Here's what the result looks like:

```
   at DebugTest.Program.C() in C:\Test\Program.cs:line 16
   at DebugTest.Program.B() in C:\Test\Program.cs:line 12
   at DebugTest.Program.A() in C:\Test\Program.cs:line 11
   at DebugTest.Program.Main() in C:\Test\Program.cs:line 10
```

To obtain the stack trace for another thread, pass the other `Thread` into `StackTrace`'s constructor. This can be a useful strategy for profiling a program. The one proviso is that you suspend the thread first, by calling its `Suspend` method (and `Resume` when you're done). This is the one valid use for `Thread`'s deprecated `Suspend` and `Resume` methods!

You can also obtain the stack trace for an `Exception` object (showing what led up to the exception being thrown) by passing the `Exception` into `StackTrace`'s constructor.

> `Exception` already has a `StackTrace` property; however, this property returns a simple string—not a `StackTrace` object. A `StackTrace` object is far more useful in logging exceptions that occur after deployment—where no *.pdb* files are available—because you can log the *IL offset* in lieu of line and column numbers. With an IL offset and *ildasm*, you can pinpoint where within a method an error occurred.

Windows Event Logs

The Win32 platform provides a centralized logging mechanism, in the form of the Windows event logs.

The `Debug` and `Trace` classes we used earlier write to a Windows event log if you register an `EventLogTraceListener`. With the `EventLog` class, however, you can write directly to a Windows event log without using `Trace` or `Debug`. You can also use this class to read and monitor event data.

> Writing to the Windows event log makes sense in a Windows Service application, because if something goes wrong, you can't pop up a user interface directing the user to some special file where diagnostic information has been written. Also, because it's common practice for services to write to the Windows event log, this is the first place an administrator is likely to look if your service falls over.

There are three standard Windows event logs, identified by these names:

- Application
- System
- Security

The *Application* log is where most applications normally write.

Writing to the Event Log

To write to a Windows event log:

1. Choose one of the three event logs (usually *Application*).

---

2. Decide on a *source name* and create it if necessary.

3. Call `EventLog.WriteEntry` with the log name, source name, and message data.

The *source name* is an easily identifiable name for your application. You must register a source name before you use it—the `CreateEventSource` method performs this function. You can then call `WriteEntry`:

```
const string SourceName = "MyCompany.WidgetServer";

// CreateEventSource requires administrative permissions, so this would
// typically be done in application setup.
if (!EventLog.SourceExists (SourceName))
  EventLog.CreateEventSource (SourceName, "Application");

EventLog.WriteEntry (SourceName,
  "Service started; using configuration file=...",
  EventLogEntryType.Information);
```

`EventLogEntryType` can be `Information`, `Warning`, `Error`, `SuccessAudit`, or `FailureAudit`. Each displays with a different icon in the Windows event viewer. You can also optionally specify a category and event ID (each is a number of your own choosing) and provide optional binary data.

`CreateEventSource` also allows you to specify a machine name: this is to write to another computer's event log, if you have sufficient permissions.

Reading the Event Log

To read an event log, instantiate the `EventLog` class with the name of the log you wish to access and optionally the name of another computer on which the log resides. Each log entry can then be read via the `Entries` collection property:

```
EventLog log = new EventLog ("Application");

Console.WriteLine ("Total entries: " + log.Entries.Count);

EventLogEntry last = log.Entries [log.Entries.Count - 1];
Console.WriteLine ("Index:    " + last.Index);
Console.WriteLine ("Source:   " + last.Source);
Console.WriteLine ("Type:     " + last.EntryType);
Console.WriteLine ("Time:     " + last.TimeWritten);
Console.WriteLine ("Message:  " + last.Message);
```

You can enumerate over all logs for the current (or another) computer with the static method `EventLog.GetEventLogs` (this requires administrative privileges):

```
foreach (EventLog log in EventLog.GetEventLogs())
  Console.WriteLine (log.LogDisplayName);
```

This normally prints, at a minimum, *Application*, *Security*, and *System*.

Monitoring the Event Log

You can be alerted whenever an entry is written to a Windows event log, via the `EntryWritten` event. This works for event logs on the local computer, and it fires regardless of what application logged the event.

To enable log monitoring:

1. Instantiate an `EventLog` and set its `EnableRaisingEvents` property to `true`.
2. Handle the `EntryWritten` event.

For example:

```
static void Main()
{
  using (var log = new EventLog ("Application"))
  {
    log.EnableRaisingEvents = true;
    log.EntryWritten += DisplayEntry;
    Console.ReadLine();
  }
}

static void DisplayEntry (object sender, EntryWrittenEventArgs e)
{
  EventLogEntry entry = e.Entry;
  Console.WriteLine (entry.Message);
}
```

Performance Counters

The logging mechanisms we've discussed to date are useful for capturing information for future analysis. However, to gain insight into the current state of an application (or the system as a whole), a more real-time approach is needed. The Win32 solution to this need is the performance-monitoring infrastructure, which consists of a set of performance counters that the system and applications expose, and the Microsoft Management Console (MMC) snap-ins used to monitor these counters in real time.

Performance counters are grouped into categories such as "System," "Processor," ".NET CLR Memory," and so on. These categories are sometimes also referred to as "performance objects" by the GUI tools. Each category groups a related set of performance counters that monitor one aspect of the system or application. Examples of performance counters in the ".NET CLR Memory" category include "% Time in GC," "# Bytes in All Heaps," and "Allocated bytes/sec."

Each category may optionally have one or more instances that can be monitored independently. For example, this is useful in the "% Processor Time" performance counter in the "Processor" category, which allows one to monitor CPU utilization. On a multiprocessor machine, this counter supports an instance for each CPU, allowing one to monitor the utilization of each CPU independently.

The following sections illustrate how to perform commonly needed tasks, such as determining which counters are exposed, monitoring a counter, and creating your own counters to expose application status information.

 Reading performance counters or categories may require administrator privileges on the local or target computer, depending on what is accessed.

Enumerating the Available Counters

The following example enumerates over all of the available performance counters on the computer. For those that have instances, it enumerates the counters for each instance:

```
PerformanceCounterCategory[] cats =
  PerformanceCounterCategory.GetCategories();

foreach (PerformanceCounterCategory cat in cats)
{
  Console.WriteLine ("Category: " + cat.CategoryName);

  string[] instances = cat.GetInstanceNames();
  if (instances.Length == 0)
  {
    foreach (PerformanceCounter ctr in cat.GetCounters())
      Console.WriteLine ("  Counter: " + ctr.CounterName);
  }
  else   // Dump counters with instances
  {
    foreach (string instance in instances)
    {
      Console.WriteLine ("  Instance: " + instance);
      if (cat.InstanceExists (instance))
        foreach (PerformanceCounter ctr in cat.GetCounters (instance))
          Console.WriteLine ("    Counter: " + ctr.CounterName);
    }
  }
}
```

 The result is more than 10,000 lines long! It also takes a while to execute because `PerformanceCounterCategory.InstanceEx ists` has an inefficient implementation. In a real system, you'd want to retrieve the more detailed information only on demand.

The next example uses a LINQ query to retrieve just .NET performance counters, writing the result to an XML file:

```
var x =
  new XElement ("counters",
    from PerformanceCounterCategory cat in
      PerformanceCounterCategory.GetCategories()
    where cat.CategoryName.StartsWith (".NET")
```

```
      let instances = cat.GetInstanceNames()
      select new XElement ("category",
        new XAttribute ("name", cat.CategoryName),
        instances.Length == 0
        ?
          from c in cat.GetCounters()
          select new XElement ("counter",
            new XAttribute ("name", c.CounterName))
        :
          from i in instances
          select new XElement ("instance", new XAttribute ("name", i),
            !cat.InstanceExists (i)
            ?
              null
            :
              from c in cat.GetCounters (i)
              select new XElement ("counter",
                new XAttribute ("name", c.CounterName))
          )
      )
    );
x.Save ("counters.xml");
```

Reading Performance Counter Data

To retrieve the value of a performance counter, instantiate a `PerformanceCounter` object and then call the `NextValue` or `NextSample` method. `NextValue` returns a simple `float` value; `NextSample` returns a `CounterSample` object that exposes a more advanced set of properties, such as `CounterFrequency`, `TimeStamp`, `BaseValue`, and `RawValue`.

`PerformanceCounter`'s constructor takes a category name, counter name, and optional instance. So, to display the current processor utilization for all CPUs, you would do the following:

```
using (PerformanceCounter pc = new PerformanceCounter ("Processor",
                                                       "% Processor Time",
                                                       "_Total"))
  Console.WriteLine (pc.NextValue());
```

Or to display the "real" (i.e., private) memory consumption of the current process:

```
string procName = Process.GetCurrentProcess().ProcessName;
using (PerformanceCounter pc = new PerformanceCounter ("Process",
                                                       "Private Bytes",
                                                       procName))
  Console.WriteLine (pc.NextValue());
```

`PerformanceCounter` doesn't expose a `ValueChanged` event, so if you want to monitor for changes, you must poll. In the next example, we poll every 200 ms—until signaled to quit by an `EventWaitHandle`:

```
// need to import System.Threading as well as System.Diagnostics

static void Monitor (string category, string counter, string instance,
                     EventWaitHandle stopper)
```

```
{
  if (!PerformanceCounterCategory.Exists (category))
    throw new InvalidOperationException ("Category does not exist");

  if (!PerformanceCounterCategory.CounterExists (counter, category))
    throw new InvalidOperationException ("Counter does not exist");

  if (instance == null) instance = "";   // "" == no instance (not null!)
  if (instance != "" &&
      !PerformanceCounterCategory.InstanceExists (instance, category))
    throw new InvalidOperationException ("Instance does not exist");

  float lastValue = 0f;
  using (PerformanceCounter pc = new PerformanceCounter (category,
                                               counter, instance))
    while (!stopper.WaitOne (200, false))
    {
      float value = pc.NextValue();
      if (value != lastValue)        // Only write out the value
      {                              // if it has changed.
        Console.WriteLine (value);
        lastValue = value;
      }
    }
}
```

Here's how we can use this method to simultaneously monitor processor and hard-disk activity:

```
static void Main()
{
  EventWaitHandle stopper = new ManualResetEvent (false);

  new Thread (() =>
    Monitor ("Processor", "% Processor Time", "_Total", stopper)
  ).Start();

  new Thread (() =>
    Monitor ("LogicalDisk", "% Idle Time", "C:", stopper)
  ).Start();

  Console.WriteLine ("Monitoring - press any key to quit");
  Console.ReadKey();
  stopper.Set();
}
```

Creating Counters and Writing Performance Data

Before writing performance counter data, you need to create a performance category and counter. You must create the performance category along with all the counters that belong to it in one step, as follows:

```
string category = "Nutshell Monitoring";

// We'll create two counters in this category:
```

```
string eatenPerMin = "Macadamias eaten so far";
string tooHard = "Macadamias deemed too hard";

if (!PerformanceCounterCategory.Exists (category))
{
  CounterCreationDataCollection cd = new CounterCreationDataCollection();

  cd.Add (new CounterCreationData (eatenPerMin,
          "Number of macadamias consumed, including shelling time",
          PerformanceCounterType.NumberOfItems32));

  cd.Add (new CounterCreationData (tooHard,
          "Number of macadamias that will not crack, despite much effort",
          PerformanceCounterType.NumberOfItems32));

  PerformanceCounterCategory.Create (category, "Test Category",
    PerformanceCounterCategoryType.SingleInstance, cd);
}
```

The new counters then show up in the Windows performance-monitoring tool when you choose Add Counters, as shown in Figure 13-1.

Figure 13-1. Custom performance counter

If you later want to define more counters in the same category, you must first delete the old category by calling `PerformanceCounterCategory.Delete`.

 Creating and deleting performance counters requires administrative privileges. For this reason, it's usually done as part of the application setup.

Once a counter is created, you can update its value by instantiating a `Performance Counter`, setting `ReadOnly` to `false`, and setting `RawValue`. You can also use the `Increment` and `IncrementBy` methods to update the existing value:

```
string category = "Nutshell Monitoring";
string eatenPerMin = "Macadamias eaten so far";

using (PerformanceCounter pc = new PerformanceCounter (category,
                                                eatenPerMin, ""))
{
  pc.ReadOnly = false;
  pc.RawValue = 1000;
  pc.Increment();
  pc.IncrementBy (10);
  Console.WriteLine (pc.NextValue());     // 1011
}
```

The Stopwatch Class

The `Stopwatch` class provides a convenient mechanism for measuring execution times. `Stopwatch` uses the highest-resolution mechanism that the operating system and hardware provide, which is typically less than a microsecond. (In contrast, `DateTime.Now` and `Environment.TickCount` have a resolution of about 15 ms.)

To use `Stopwatch`, call `StartNew`—this instantiates a `Stopwatch` and starts it ticking. (Alternatively, you can instantiate it manually and then call `Start`.) The `Elapsed` property returns the elapsed interval as a `TimeSpan`:

```
Stopwatch s = Stopwatch.StartNew();
System.IO.File.WriteAllText ("test.txt", new string ('*', 30000000));
Console.WriteLine (s.Elapsed);         // 00:00:01.4322661
```

`Stopwatch` also exposes an `ElapsedTicks` property, which returns the number of elapsed "ticks" as a `long`. To convert from ticks to seconds, divide by `StopWatch.Fre quency`. There's also an `ElapsedMilliseconds` property, which is often the most convenient.

Calling `Stop` freezes `Elapsed` and `ElapsedTicks`. There's no background activity incurred by a "running" `Stopwatch`, so calling `Stop` is optional.

14

Streams and I/O

This chapter describes the fundamental types for input and output in .NET, with emphasis on the following topics:

- The .NET stream architecture and how it provides a consistent programming interface for reading and writing across a variety of I/O types
- Manipulating files and directories on disk
- Isolated storage and its role in segregating data by program and user

This chapter concentrates on the types in the System.IO namespace, the home of lower-level I/O functionality. The .NET Framework also provides higher-level I/O functionality in the form of SQL connections and commands, LINQ to SQL and LINQ to XML, Windows Communication Foundation, Web Services, and Remoting.

Stream Architecture

The .NET stream architecture centers on three concepts: backing stores, decorators, and adapters, as shown in Figure 14-1.

A *backing store* is the endpoint that makes input and output useful, such as a file or network connection. Precisely, it is either or both of the following:

- A source from which bytes can be sequentially read
- A destination to which bytes can be sequentially written

A backing store is of no use, though, unless exposed to the programmer. A Stream is the standard .NET class for this purpose; it exposes a standard set of methods for reading, writing, and positioning. Unlike an array, where all the backing data exists in memory at once, a stream deals with data serially—either one byte at a time or in blocks of a manageable size. Hence, a stream can use little memory regardless of the size of its backing store.

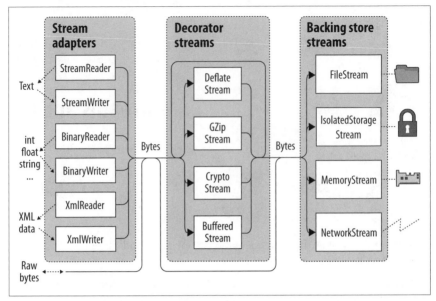

Figure 14-1. Stream architecture

Streams fall into two categories:

Backing store streams

> These are hard-wired to a particular type of backing store, such as `FileStream` or `NetworkStream`

Decorator streams

> These feed off another stream, transforming the data in some way, such as `DeflateStream` or `CryptoStream`

Decorator streams have the following architectural benefits:

- They liberate backing store streams from needing to implement such features as compression and encryption themselves.
- Streams don't suffer a change of interface when decorated.
- You connect decorators at runtime.
- You can chain decorators together (e.g., a compressor followed by an encryptor).

Both backing store and decorator streams deal exclusively in bytes. Although this is flexible and efficient, applications often work at higher levels such as text or XML. *Adapters* bridge this gap by wrapping a stream in a class with specialized methods typed to a particular format. For example, a text reader exposes a `ReadLine` method; an XML writer exposes a `WriteAttributes` method.

An adapter wraps a stream, just like a decorator. Unlike a decorator, however, an adapter is not *itself* a stream; it typically hides the byte-oriented methods completely.

To summarize, backing store streams provide the raw data; decorator streams provide transparent binary transformations such as encryption; adapters offer typed methods for dealing in higher-level types such as strings and XML. Figure 14-1 illustrates their associations. To compose a chain, you simply pass one object into another's constructor.

Using Streams

The abstract `Stream` class is the base for all streams. It defines methods and properties for three fundamental operations, *reading*, *writing*, and *seeking*, as well as for administrative tasks such as closing, flushing, and configuring timeouts (see Table 14-1).

Table 14-1. Stream class members

Category	Members
Reading	`public abstract bool CanRead { get; }`
	`public abstract int Read (byte[] buffer, int offset, int count)`
	`public virtual int ReadByte();`
Writing	`public abstract bool CanWrite { get; }`
	`public abstract void Write (byte[] buffer, int offset, int count);`
	`public virtual void WriteByte (byte value);`
Seeking	`public abstract bool CanSeek { get; }`
	`public abstract long Position { get; set; }`
	`public abstract void SetLength (long value);`
	`public abstract long Length { get; }`
	`public abstract long Seek (long offset, SeekOrigin origin);`
Closing/flushing	`public virtual void Close();`
	`public void Dispose();`
	`public abstract void Flush();`
Timeouts	`public virtual bool CanTimeout { get; }`
	`public virtual int ReadTimeout { get; set; }`
	`public virtual int WriteTimeout { get; set; }`
Other	`public static readonly Stream Null; // "Null" stream`
	`public static Stream Synchronized (Stream stream);`

In the following example, we use a file stream to read, write, and seek:

```
using System;
using System.IO;

class Program
{
  static void Main()
  {
    // Create a file called test.txt in the current directory:
    using (Stream s = new FileStream ("test.txt", FileMode.Create))
    {
      Console.WriteLine (s.CanRead);       // True
      Console.WriteLine (s.CanWrite);      // True
      Console.WriteLine (s.CanSeek);       // True

      s.WriteByte (101);
      s.WriteByte (102);
      byte[] block = { 1, 2, 3, 4, 5 };
      s.Write (block, 0, block.Length);    // Write block of 5 bytes

      Console.WriteLine (s.Length);        // 7
      Console.WriteLine (s.Position);      // 7
      s.Position = 0;                      // Move back to the start

      Console.WriteLine (s.ReadByte());    // 101
      Console.WriteLine (s.ReadByte());    // 102

      // Read from the stream back into the block array:
      Console.WriteLine (s.Read (block, 0, block.Length));   // 5

      // Assuming the last Read returned 5, we'll be at
      // the end of the file, so Read will now return 0:
      Console.WriteLine (s.Read (block, 0, block.Length));   // 0
    }
  }
}
```

Reading and Writing

A stream may support reading, writing, or both. If CanWrite returns false, the stream is read-only; if CanRead returns false, the stream is write-only.

Read receives a block of data from the stream into an array. It returns the number of bytes received, which is always either less than or equal to the count argument. If it's less than count, it means either that the end of the stream has been reached or the stream is giving you the data in smaller chunks (as is often the case with network streams). In either case, the balance of bytes in the array will remain unwritten, their previous values preserved.

With Read, you can be certain you've reached the end of the stream only when the method returns 0. So, if you have a 1,000-byte stream, the following code may fail to read it all into memory:

```
// Assuming s is a stream:
byte[] data = new byte [1000];
s.Read (data, 0, data.Length);
```

The Read method could read anywhere from 1 to 1,000 bytes, leaving the balance of the stream unread.

Here's the correct way to read a 1,000-byte stream:

```
byte[] data = new byte [1000];

// bytesRead will always end up at 1000, unless the stream is
// itself smaller in length:

int bytesRead = 0;
int chunkSize = 1;
while (bytesRead < data.Length && chunkSize > 0)
  bytesRead +=
    chunkSize = s.Read (data, bytesRead, data.Length - bytesRead);
```

Fortunately, the BinaryReader type provides a simpler way to achieve the same result:

```
byte[] data = new BinaryReader (s).ReadBytes (1000);
```

If the stream is less than 1,000 bytes long, the byte array returned reflects the actual stream size. If the stream is seekable, you can read its entire contents by replacing 1000 with (int)s.Length.

We describe the BinaryReader type further in the section "Stream Adapters" on page 552, later in this chapter.

The ReadByte method is simpler: it reads just a single byte, returning –1 to indicate the end of the stream. ReadByte actually returns an int rather than a byte, as the latter cannot return –1.

The Write and WriteByte methods send data to the stream. If they are unable to send the specified bytes, an exception is thrown.

In the Read and Write methods, the offset argument refers to the index in the buffer array at which reading or writing begins, not the position within the stream.

Streams also support asynchronous reading and writing through the methods Begin Read and BeginWrite. Asynchronous methods are intended for high-throughput server applications, and we describe them in Chapter 23.

Seeking

A stream is seekable if `CanSeek` returns `true`. With a seekable stream (such as a file stream), you can query or modify its `Length` (by calling `SetLength`), and at any time change the `Position` at which you're reading or writing. The `Position` property is relative to the beginning of the stream; the `Seek` method, however, allows you to move relative to the current position or the end of the stream.

 Changing the `Position` on a `FileStream` typically takes a few microseconds. If you're doing this millions of times in a loop, Framework 4.0's new `MemoryMappedFile` class may be a better choice than a `FileStream` (for more, see "Memory-Mapped Files" on page 569, later in this chapter).

With a nonseekable stream (such as an encryption stream), the only way to determine its length is to read it right through. Furthermore, if you need to reread a previous section, you must close the stream and start afresh with a new one.

Closing and Flushing

Streams must be disposed after use to release underlying resources such as file and socket handles. A simple way to guarantee this is by instantiating streams within `using` blocks. In general, streams follow standard disposal semantics:

- `Dispose` and `Close` are identical in function.
- Disposing or closing a stream repeatedly causes no error.

Closing a decorator stream closes both the decorator and its backing store stream. With a chain of decorators, closing the outermost decorator (at the head of the chain) closes the whole lot.

Some streams internally buffer data to and from the backing store to lessen round-tripping and so improve performance (file streams are a good example of this). This means data you write to a stream may not hit the backing store immediately; it can be delayed as the buffer fills up. The `Flush` method forces any internally buffered data to be written immediately. `Flush` is called automatically when a stream is closed, so you never need to do the following:

```
s.Flush(); s.Close();
```

Timeouts

A stream supports read and write timeouts if `CanTimeout` returns `true`. Network streams support timeouts; file and memory streams do not. For streams that support timeouts, the `ReadTimeout` and `WriteTimeout` properties determine the desired timeout in milliseconds, where 0 means no timeout. The `Read` and `Write` methods indicate that a timeout has occurred by throwing an exception.

Thread Safety

As a rule, streams are not thread-safe, meaning that two threads cannot concurrently read or write to the same stream without possible error. The Stream class offers a simple workaround via the static Synchronized method. This method accepts a stream of any type and returns a thread-safe wrapper. The wrapper works by obtaining an exclusive lock around each read, write, or seek, ensuring that only one thread can perform such an operation at a time. In practice, this allows multiple threads to simultaneously append data to the same stream—other kinds of activities (such as concurrent reading) require additional locking to ensure that each thread accesses the desired portion of the stream. We discuss thread safety fully in Chapter 21.

Backing Store Streams

Figure 14-2 shows the key backing store streams provided by the .NET Framework. A "null stream" is also available, via the Stream's static Null field.

In the following sections, we describe FileStream and MemoryStream; in the final section in this chapter, we describe IsolatedStorageStream. In Chapter 15, we cover NetworkStream.

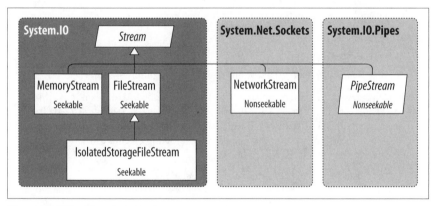

Figure 14-2. Backing store streams

FileStream

Earlier in this section, we demonstrated the basic use of a FileStream to read and write bytes of data. We'll now examine the special features of this class.

Constructing a FileStream

The simplest way to instantiate a FileStream is to use one of the following static façade methods on the File class:

```
FileStream fs1 = File.OpenRead  ("readme.bin");             // Read-only
FileStream fs2 = File.OpenWrite (@"c:\temp\writeme.tmp");   // Write-only
FileStream fs3 = File.Create    (@"c:\temp\writeme.tmp");   // Read/write
```

`OpenWrite` and `Create` differ in behavior if the file already exists. `Create` truncates any existing content; `OpenWrite` leaves existing content intact with the stream positioned at zero. If you write fewer bytes than were previously in the file, `OpenWrite` leaves you with a mixture of old and new content.

You can also instantiate a `FileStream` directly. Its constructors provide access to every feature, allowing you to specify a filename or low-level file handle, file creation and access modes, and options for sharing, buffering, and security. The following opens an existing file for read/write access without overwriting it:

```
var fs = new FileStream ("readwrite.tmp", FileMode.Open);  // Read/write
```

More on `FileMode` shortly.

Shortcut Methods on the File Class

The following static methods read an entire file into memory in one step:

- `File.ReadAllText` (returns a string)
- `File.ReadAllLines` (returns an array of strings)
- `File.ReadAllBytes` (returns a byte array)

The following static methods write an entire file in one step:

- `File.WriteAllText`
- `File.WriteAllLines`
- `File.WriteAllBytes`
- `File.AppendAllText` (great for appending to a log file)

From Framework 4.0 there's also a static method called `File.ReadLines`: this is like `ReadAllLines` except that it returns a lazily-evaluated `IEnumerable<string>`. This is more efficient because it doesn't load the entire file into memory at once. LINQ is ideal for consuming the results: the following calculates the number of lines greater than 80 characters in length:

```
int longLines = File.ReadLines ("filePath")
                    .Count (l => l.Length > 80);
```

Specifying a filename

A filename can be either absolute (e.g., *c:\temp\test.txt*) or relative to the current directory (e.g., *test.txt* or *temp\test.txt*). You can access or change the current directory via the static `Environment.CurrentDirectory` property.

> When a program starts, the current directory may or may not coincide with that of the program's executable. For this reason, you should never rely on the current directory for locating additional runtime files packaged along with your executable.

`AppDomain.CurrentDomain.BaseDirectory` returns the *application base directory*, which in normal cases is the folder containing the program's executable. To specify a filename relative to this directory, you can call `Path.Combine`:

```
string baseFolder = AppDomain.CurrentDomain.BaseDirectory;
string logoPath = Path.Combine (baseFolder, "logo.jpg");
Console.WriteLine (File.Exists (logoPath));
```

You can read and write across a network via a UNC path, such as *\\JoesPC\PicShare \pic.jpg* or *\\10.1.1.2\PicShare\pic.jpg*.

Specifying a FileMode

All of `FileStream`'s constructors that accept a filename also require a `FileMode` enum argument. Figure 14-3 shows how to choose a `FileMode`, and the choices yield results akin to calling a static method on the `File` class.

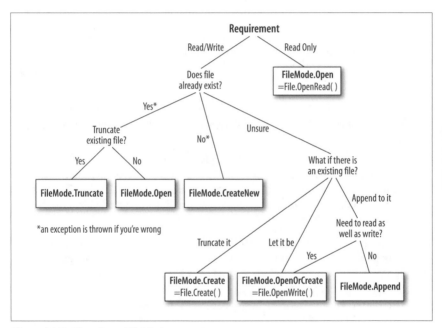

Figure 14-3. Choosing a FileMode

 `File.Create` and `FileMode.Create` will throw an exception if used on hidden files. To overwrite a hidden file, you must delete and re-create it:

```
if (File.Exists ("hidden.txt")) File.Delete ("hidden.txt");
```

Constructing a `FileStream` with just a filename and `FileMode` gives you (with just one exception) a readable writable stream. You can request a downgrade if you also supply a `FileAccess` argument:

```
[Flags]
public enum FileAccess { Read = 1, Write = 2, ReadWrite = 3 }
```

The following returns a read-only stream, equivalent to calling `File.OpenRead`:

```
using (var fs = new FileStream ("x.bin", FileMode.Open, FileAccess.Read))
  ...
```

`FileMode.Append` is the odd one out: with this mode, you get a *write-only* stream. To append with read-write support, you must instead use `FileMode.Open` or `File Mode.OpenOrCreate`, and then seek the end of the stream:

```
using (var fs = new FileStream ("myFile.bin", FileMode.Open))
{
  fs.Seek (0, SeekOrigin.End);
  ...
```

Advanced FileStream features

Here are other optional arguments you can include when constructing a `FileStream`:

- A `FileShare` enum describing how much access to grant other processes wanting to dip into the same file before you've finished (`None`, `Read` [default], `ReadWrite`, or `Write`).
- The size, in bytes, of the internal buffer (default is currently 4 KB).
- A flag indicating whether to defer to the operating system for asynchronous I/O.
- A `FileSecurity` object describing what user and role permissions to assign a new file.
- A `FileOptions` flags enum for requesting operating system encryption (`Encrypted`), automatic deletion upon closure for temporary files (`DeleteOn Close`), and optimization hints (`RandomAccess` and `SequentialScan`). There is also a `WriteThrough` flag that requests that the operating system disable write-behind caching; this is for transactional files or logs.

Opening a file with `FileShare.ReadWrite` allows other processes or users to simultaneously read and write to the same file. To avoid chaos, you can all agree to lock specified portions of the file before reading or writing, using these methods:

```
// Defined on the FileStream class:
public virtual void Lock   (long position, long length);
public virtual void Unlock (long position, long length);
```

`Lock` throws an exception if part or all of the requested file section has already been locked. This is the system used in file-based databases such as Access and FoxPro.

MemoryStream

`MemoryStream` uses an array as a backing store. This partly defeats the purpose of having a stream, because the entire backing store must reside in memory at once. `MemoryStream` still has uses, however; an example is when you need random access to a nonseekable stream. If you know the source stream will be of a manageable size, you can copy it into a `MemoryStream` as follows:

```
static MemoryStream ToMemoryStream (this Stream input, bool closeInput)
{
  try
  {                                      // Read and write in
    byte[] block = new byte [0×1000];    // blocks of 4K.
    MemoryStream ms = new MemoryStream();
    while (true)
    {
      int bytesRead = input.Read (block, 0, block.Length);
      if (bytesRead == 0) return ms;
      ms.Write (block, 0, bytesRead);
    }
  }
  finally { if (closeInput) input.Close (); }
}
```

The reason for the `closeInput` argument is to avoid a situation where the method author and consumer each think the other will close the stream.

You can convert a `MemoryStream` to a byte array by calling `ToArray`. The `GetBuffer` method does the same job more efficiently by returning a direct reference to the underlying storage array; unfortunately, this array is usually longer than the stream's real length.

> Closing and flushing a `MemoryStream` is optional. If you close a `MemoryStream`, you can no longer read or write to it, but you are still permitted to call `ToArray` to obtain the underlying data. `Flush` does absolutely nothing on a memory stream.

You can find further `MemoryStream` examples in the section "Compression" on page 571 later in this chapter, and in the section "Cryptography Overview" on page 776 in Chapter 20.

PipeStream

`PipeStream` was introduced in Framework 3.5. It provides a simple means by which one process can communicate with another through the Windows *pipes* protocol. There are two kinds of pipe:

Anonymous pipe
Allows one-way communication between a parent and child process on the same computer.id

Named pipe
Allows two-way communication between arbitrary processes on the same computer—or different computers across a Windows network.

A pipe is good for interprocess communication (IPC) on a single computer: it doesn't rely on a network transport, which equates to good performance and no issues with firewalls.

Pipes are stream-based, so one process waits to receive a series of bytes while another process sends them. An alternative is for processes to communicate via a block of shared memory—we describe how to do this later, in the section "Memory-Mapped Files" on page 569.

PipeStream is an abstract class with four concrete subtypes. Two are used for anonymous pipes and the other two for named pipes:

Anonymous pipes
AnonymousPipeServerStream and AnonymousPipeClientStream

Named pipes
NamedPipeServerStream and NamedPipeClientStream

Named pipes are simpler to use, so we'll describe them first.

A pipe is a low-level construct that allows just the sending and receiving of bytes (or *messages*, which are groups of bytes). The WCF and Remoting APIs offer higher-level messaging frameworks with the option of using an IPC channel for communication.

Named pipes

With named pipes, the parties communicate through a pipe of the same name. The protocol defines two distinct roles: the client and server. Communication happens between the client and server as follows:

- The server instantiates a NamedPipeServerStream and then calls WaitForConnection.
- The client instantiates a NamedPipeClientStream and then calls Connect (with an optional timeout).

The two parties then read and write the streams to communicate.

The following example demonstrates a server that sends a single byte (100), and then waits to receive a single byte:

```
using (var s = new NamedPipeServerStream ("pipedream"))
{
  s.WaitForConnection();
  s.WriteByte (100);
  Console.WriteLine (s.ReadByte());
}
```

Here's the corresponding client code:

```
using (var s = new NamedPipeClientStream ("pipedream"))
{
  s.Connect();
  Console.WriteLine (s.ReadByte());
```

```
  s.WriteByte (200);                 // Send the value 200 back.
}
```

Named pipe streams are bidirectional by default, so either party can read or write their stream. This means the client and server must agree on some protocol to co-ordinate their actions, so both parties don't end up sending or receiving at once.

There also needs to be agreement on the length of each transmission. Our example was trivial in this regard, because we bounced just a single byte in each direction. To help with messages longer than one byte, pipes provide a *message* transmission mode. If this is enabled, a party calling Read can know when a message is complete by checking the IsMessageComplete property. To demonstrate, we'll start by writing a helper method that reads a whole message from a message-enabled PipeStream— in other words, reads until IsMessageComplete is true:

```
static byte[] ReadMessage (PipeStream s)
{
  MemoryStream ms = new MemoryStream();
  byte[] buffer = new byte [0x1000];      // Read in 4 KB blocks

  do    { ms.Write (buffer, 0, s.Read (buffer, 0, buffer.Length)); }
  while (!s.IsMessageComplete);

  return ms.ToArray();
}
```

 You cannot determine whether a PipeStream has finished read-ing a message simply by waiting for Read to return 0. This is because, unlike most other kinds of stream, pipe streams and network streams have no definite end. Instead, they temporarily "dry up" between message transmissions.

Now we can activate message transmission mode. On the server, this is done by specifying PipeTransmissionMode.Message when constructing the stream:

```
using (var s = new NamedPipeServerStream ("pipedream", PipeDirection.InOut,
                                1, PipeTransmissionMode.Message))
{
  s.WaitForConnection();

  byte[] msg = Encoding.UTF8.GetBytes ("Hello");
  s.Write (msg, 0, msg.Length);

  Console.WriteLine (Encoding.UTF8.GetString (ReadMessage (s)));
}
```

On the client, we activate message transmission mode by setting ReadMode after call-ing Connect:

```
using (var s = new NamedPipeClientStream ("pipedream"))
{
  s.Connect();
  s.ReadMode = PipeTransmissionMode.Message;
```

```
Console.WriteLine (Encoding.UTF8.GetString (ReadMessage (s)));

  byte[] msg = Encoding.UTF8.GetBytes ("Hello right back!");
  s.Write (msg, 0, msg.Length);
}
```

Anonymous pipes

An anonymous pipe provides a one-way communication stream between a parent and child process. Instead of using a system-wide name, anonymous pipes tune in through a private handle.

As with named pipes, there are distinct client and server roles. The system of communication is a little different, however, and proceeds as follows:

1. The server instantiates an `AnonymousPipeServerStream`, committing to a `PipeDirection` of `In` or `Out`.

2. The server calls `GetClientHandleAsString` to obtain an identifier for the pipe, which it then passes to the client (typically as an argument when starting the child process).

3. The child process instantiates an `AnonymousPipeClientStream`, specifying the opposite `PipeDirection`.

4. The server releases the local handle that was generated in step 2, by calling `DisposeLocalCopyOfClientHandle`.

5. The parent and child processes communicate by reading/writing the stream.

Because anonymous pipes are unidirectional, a server must create two pipes for bidirectional communication. The following demonstrates a server that sends a single byte to the child process, and then receives a single byte back from that process:

```
string clientExe = @"d:\PipeDemo\ClientDemo.exe";

HandleInheritability inherit = HandleInheritability.Inheritable;

using (var tx = new AnonymousPipeServerStream (PipeDirection.Out, inherit))
using (var rx = new AnonymousPipeServerStream (PipeDirection.In, inherit))
{
  string txID = tx.GetClientHandleAsString();
  string rxID = rx.GetClientHandleAsString();

  var startInfo = new ProcessStartInfo (clientExe, txID + " " + rxID);
  startInfo.UseShellExecute = false;        // Required for child process
  Process p = Process.Start (startInfo);

  tx.DisposeLocalCopyOfClientHandle();      // Release unmanaged
  rx.DisposeLocalCopyOfClientHandle();      // handle resources.

  tx.WriteByte (100);
  Console.WriteLine ("Server received: " + rx.ReadByte());

  p.WaitForExit();
}
```

Here's the corresponding client code that would be compiled to *d:\PipeDemo\ClientDemo.exe*:

```
string rxID = args[0];    // Note we're reversing the
string txID = args[1];    // receive and transmit roles.

using (var rx = new AnonymousPipeClientStream (PipeDirection.In, rxID))
using (var tx = new AnonymousPipeClientStream (PipeDirection.Out, txID))
{
  Console.WriteLine ("Client received: " + rx.ReadByte());
  tx.WriteByte (200);
}
```

As with named pipes, the client and server must coordinate their sending and receiving and agree on the length of each transmission. Anonymous pipes don't, unfortunately, support message mode, so you must implement your own protocol for message length agreement. One solution is to send, in the first four bytes of each transmission, an integer value defining the length of the message to follow. The `BitConverter` class provides methods for converting between an integer and an array of four bytes.

BufferedStream

`BufferedStream` decorates, or wraps, another stream with buffering capability, and it is one of a number of decorator stream types in the core .NET Framework, all of which are illustrated in Figure 14-4.

Figure 14-4. Decorator streams

Buffering improves performance by reducing round trips to the backing store. Here's how we wrap a `FileStream` in a 20 KB `BufferedStream`:

```
// Write 100K to a file:
File.WriteAllBytes ("myFile.bin", new byte [100000]);

using (FileStream fs = File.OpenRead ("myFile.bin"))
using (BufferedStream bs = new BufferedStream (fs, 20000))  //20K buffer
{
  bs.ReadByte();
}
```

```
    Console.WriteLine (fs.Position);        // 20000
}
```

In this example, the underlying stream advances 20,000 bytes after reading just 1 byte, thanks to the read-ahead buffering. We could call ReadByte another 19,999 times before the FileStream would be hit again.

Coupling a BufferedStream to a FileStream, as in this example, is of limited value because FileStream already has built-in buffering. Its only use might be in enlarging the buffer on an already constructed FileStream.

Closing a BufferedStream automatically closes the underlying backing store stream.

Stream Adapters

A Stream deals only in bytes; to read or write data types such as strings, integers, or XML elements, you must plug in an adapter. Here's what the Framework provides:

Text adapters (for string and character data)
TextReader, TextWriter

StreamReader, StreamWriter

StringReader, StringWriter

Binary adapters (for primitive types such as int, bool, string, *and* float*)*
BinaryReader, BinaryWriter

XML adapters (covered in Chapter 11)
XmlReader, XmlWriter

The relationships between these types are illustrated in Figure 14-5.

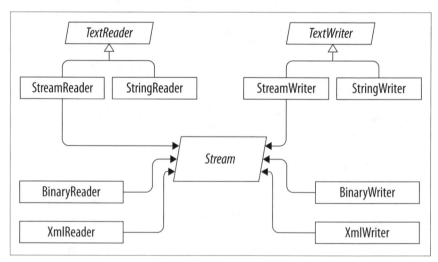

Figure 14-5. Readers and writers

Text Adapters

`TextReader` and `TextWriter` are the abstract base classes for adapters that deal exclusively with characters and strings. Each has two general-purpose implementations in the framework:

`StreamReader/StreamWriter`
 Uses a `Stream` for its raw data store, translating the stream's bytes into characters or strings

`StringReader/StringWriter`
 Implements `TextReader/TextWriter` using in-memory strings

Table 14-2 lists `TextReader`'s members by category. `Peek` returns the next character in the stream without advancing the position. Both `Peek` and the zero-argument version of `Read` return –1 if at the end of the stream; otherwise, they return an integer that can be cast directly to a `char`. The overload of `Read` that accepts a `char[]` buffer is identical in functionality to the `ReadBlock` method. `ReadLine` reads until reaching either a CR (character 13) or LF (character 10), or a CR+LF pair in sequence. It then returns a string, discarding the CR/LF characters.

Table 14-2. TextReader members

Category	Members
Reading one char	`public virtual int Peek(); // Cast the result to a char`
	`public virtual int Read(); // Cast the result to a char`
Reading many chars	`public virtual int Read (char[] buffer, int index, int count);`
	`public virtual int ReadBlock (char[] buffer, int index, int count);`
	`public virtual string ReadLine();`
	`public virtual string ReadToEnd();`
Closing	`public virtual void Close();`
	`public void Dispose(); // Same as Close`
Other	`public static readonly TextReader Null;`
	`public static TextReader Synchronized (TextReader reader);`

> The new line sequence in Windows is loosely modeled on a mechanical typewriter: a carriage return (character 13) followed by a line feed (character 10). The C# string is "\r\n" (think "ReturN"). Reverse the order and you'll get either two new lines or none!

`TextWriter` has analogous methods for writing, as shown in Table 14-3. The `Write` and `WriteLine` methods are additionally overloaded to accept every primitive type, plus the `object` type. These methods simply call the `ToString` method on whatever is passed in (optionally through an `IFormatProvider` specified either when calling the method or when constructing the `TextWriter`).

Table 14-3. TextWriter members

Category	Members
Writing one char	`public virtual void Write (char value);`
Writing many chars	`public virtual void Write (string value);`
	`public virtual void Write (char[] buffer, int index, int count);`
	`public virtual void Write (string format, params object[] arg);`
	`public virtual void WriteLine (string value);`
Closing and flushing	`public virtual void Close();`
	`public void Dispose(); // Same as Close`
	`public virtual void Flush();`
Formatting and encoding	`public virtual IFormatProvider FormatProvider { get; }`
	`public virtual string NewLine { get; set; }`
	`public abstract Encoding Encoding { get; }`
Other	`public static readonly TextWriter Null;`
	`public static TextWriter Synchronized (TextWriter writer);`

`WriteLine` simply appends the given text with CR+LF. You can change this via the `NewLine` property (this can be useful for interoperability with Unix file formats).

StreamReader and StreamWriter

In the following example, a `StreamWriter` writes two lines of text to a file, and then a `StreamReader` reads the file back:

```
using (FileStream fs = File.Create ("test.txt"))
using (TextWriter writer = new StreamWriter (fs))
{
  writer.WriteLine ("Line1");
  writer.WriteLine ("Line2");
}

using (FileStream fs = File.OpenRead ("test.txt"))
using (TextReader reader = new StreamReader (fs))
{
  Console.WriteLine (reader.ReadLine());       // Line1
  Console.WriteLine (reader.ReadLine());       // Line2
}
```

Because text adapters are so often coupled with files, the `File` class provides the static methods `CreateText`, `AppendText`, and `OpenText` to shortcut the process:

```
using (TextWriter writer = File.CreateText ("test.txt"))
{
  writer.WriteLine ("Line1");
```

```
  writer.WriteLine ("Line2");
}

using (TextWriter writer = File.AppendText ("test.txt"))
  writer.WriteLine ("Line3");

using (TextReader reader = File.OpenText ("test.txt"))
  while (reader.Peek() > -1)
    Console.WriteLine (reader.ReadLine());        // Line1
                                                  // Line2
                                                  // Line3
```

This also illustrates how to test for the end of a file (viz. `reader.Peek()`). Another option is to read until `reader.ReadLine` returns null.

You can also read and write other types such as integers, but because `TextWriter` invokes `ToString` on your type, you must parse a string when reading it back:

```
using (TextWriter w = File.CreateText ("data.txt"))
{
  w.WriteLine (123);        // Writes "123"
  w.WriteLine (true);       // Writes the word "true"
}

using (TextReader r = File.OpenText ("data.txt"))
{
  int myInt = int.Parse (r.ReadLine());      // myInt == 123
  bool yes = bool.Parse (r.ReadLine());      // yes == true
}
```

Character encodings

`TextReader` and `TextWriter` are by themselves just abstract classes with no connection to a stream or backing store. The `StreamReader` and `StreamWriter` types, however, are connected to an underlying byte-oriented stream, so they must convert between characters and bytes. They do so through an `Encoding` class from the `System.Text` namespace, which you choose when constructing the `StreamReader` or `Stream Writer`. If you choose none, the default UTF-8 encoding is used.

 A `StreamReader` or `StreamWriter` will throw an exception if it encounters bytes that do not have a valid string translation for their encoding.

The simplest of the encodings is ASCII, because each character is represented by one byte. The ASCII encoding maps the first 127 characters of the Unicode set into its single byte, covering what you see on a U.S.-style keyboard. Most other characters, including specialized symbols and non-English characters, cannot be represented and are converted to the □ character. The default UTF-8 encoding can map all allocated Unicode characters, but it is more complex. The first 127 characters encode to a single byte, for ASCII compatibility; the remaining characters encode to a variable number of bytes (most commonly two or three). Consider this:

```
using (TextWriter w = File.CreateText ("but.txt"))    // Use default UTF-8
  w.WriteLine ("but-");                                // encoding.

using (Stream s = File.OpenRead ("but.txt"))
  for (int b; (b = s.ReadByte()) > -1;)
    Console.WriteLine (b);
```

The word "but" is followed not by a stock-standard hyphen, but by the longer em dash (—) character, U+2014. This is the one that won't get you into trouble with your book editor! Let's examine the output:

```
98      // b
117     // u
116     // t
226     // em dash byte 1      Note that the byte values
128     // em dash byte 2      are >= 128 for each part
148     // em dash byte 3      of the multibyte sequence.
13      // <CR>
10      // <LF>
```

Because the em dash is outside the first 127 characters of the Unicode set, it requires more than a single byte to encode in UTF-8 (in this case, three). UTF-8 is efficient with the Western alphabet, as most popular characters consume just one byte. It also downgrades easily to ASCII simply by ignoring all bytes above 127. Its disadvantage is that seeking within a stream is troublesome, since a character's position does not correspond to its byte position in the stream. An alternative is UTF-16 (labeled just "Unicode" in the Encoding class). Here's how we write the same string with UTF-16:

```
using (Stream s = File.Create ("but.txt"))
using (TextWriter w = new StreamWriter (s, Encoding.Unicode))
  w.WriteLine ("but-");

foreach (byte b in File.ReadAllBytes ("but.txt"))
  Console.WriteLine (b);
```

The output is then:

```
255     // Byte-order mark 1
254     // Byte-order mark 2
98      // 'b' byte 1
0       // 'b' byte 2
117     // 'u' byte 1
0       // 'u' byte 2
116     // 't' byte 1
0       // 't' byte 2
20      // '--' byte 1
32      // '--' byte 2
13      // <CR> byte 1
0       // <CR> byte 2
10      // <LF> byte 1
0       // <LF> byte 2
```

Technically, UTF-16 uses either two or four bytes per character (there are close to a million Unicode characters allocated or reserved, so 2 bytes is not always enough). However, because the C# char type is itself only 16 bits wide, a UTF-16 encoding will always use exactly two bytes per .NET `char`. This makes it easy to jump to a particular character index within a stream.

UTF-16 uses a two-byte prefix to identify whether the byte pairs are written in a "little-endian" or "big-endian" order (the least significant byte first or the most significant byte first). The default little-endian order is standard for Windows-based systems.

StringReader and StringWriter

The `StringReader` and `StringWriter` adapters don't wrap a stream at all; instead, they use a string or `StringBuilder` as the underlying data source. This means no byte translation is required—in fact, the classes do nothing you couldn't easily achieve with a string or `StringBuilder` coupled with an index variable. Their advantage, though, is that they share a base class with `StreamReader`/`StreamWriter`. For instance, suppose we have a string containing XML and want to parse it with an `XmlReader`. The `XmlReader.Create` method accepts one of the following:

- A `URI`
- A `Stream`
- A `TextReader`

So, how do we XML-parse our string? Because `StringReader` is a subclass of `TextReader`, we're in luck. We can instantiate and pass in a `StringReader` as follows:

```
XmlReader r = XmlReader.Create (new StringReader (myString));
```

Binary Adapters

`BinaryReader` and `BinaryWriter` read and write native data types: `bool`, `byte`, `char`, `decimal`, `float`, `double`, `short`, `int`, `long`, `sbyte`, `ushort`, `uint`, and `ulong`, as well as strings and arrays of the primitive data types.

Unlike `StreamReader` and `StreamWriter`, binary adapters store primitive data types efficiently, as they are represented in memory. So, an `int` uses four bytes; a `double` eight bytes. Strings are written through a text encoding (as with `StreamReader` and `StreamWriter`) but are length-prefixed, in order to make it possible to read back a series of strings without needing special delimiters.

Imagine we have a simple type, defined as follows:

```
public class Person
{
  public string Name;
  public int    Age;
  public double Height;
}
```

We can add the following methods to `Person` to save/load its data to/from a stream using binary adapters:

```
public void SaveData (Stream s)
{
  var w = new BinaryWriter (s);
  w.Write (Name);
  w.Write (Age);
  w.Write (Height);
  w.Flush();          // Ensure the BinaryWriter buffer is cleared.
                      // We won't dispose/close it, so more data
}                     // can be written to the stream.

public void LoadData (Stream s)
{
  var r = new BinaryReader (s);
  Name   = r.ReadString();
  Age    = r.ReadInt32();
  Height = r.ReadDouble();
}
```

BinaryReader can also read into byte arrays. The following reads the entire contents of a seekable stream:

```
byte[] data = new BinaryReader (s).ReadBytes ((int) s.Length);
```

This is more convenient than reading directly from a stream, because it doesn't require a loop to ensure that all data has been read.

Closing and Disposing Stream Adapters

You have four choices in tearing down stream adapters:

1. Close the adapter only.
2. Close the adapter, and then close the stream.
3. (For writers) Flush the adapter, and then close the stream.
4. (For readers) Close just the stream.

 Close and Dispose are synonymous with adapters, just as they are with streams.

Options 1 and 2 are semantically identical, because closing an adapter automatically closes the underlying stream. Whenever you nest using statements, you're implicitly taking option 2:

```
using (FileStream fs = File.Create ("test.txt"))
using (TextWriter writer = new StreamWriter (fs))
  writer.WriteLine ("Line");
```

Because the nest disposes from the inside out, the adapter is first closed, and then the stream. Furthermore, if an exception is thrown within the adapter's constructor, the stream still closes. It's hard to go wrong with nested using statements!

Never close a stream before closing or flushing its writer—you'll amputate any data that's buffered in the adapter.

Options 3 and 4 work because adapters are in the unusual category of *optionally disposable objects*. An example of when you might choose not to dispose an adapter is when you've finished with the adapter, but you want to leave the underlying stream open for subsequent use:

```
using (FileStream fs = new FileStream ("test.txt", FileMode.Create))
{
  StreamWriter writer = new StreamWriter (fs);
  writer.WriteLine ("Hello");
  writer.Flush();

  fs.Position = 0;
  Console.WriteLine (fs.ReadByte());
}
```

Here we write to a file, reposition the stream, and then read the first byte before closing the stream. If we disposed the `StreamWriter`, it would also close the underlying `FileStream`, causing the subsequent read to fail. The proviso is that we call `Flush` to ensure that the `StreamWriter`'s buffer is written to the underlying stream.

Stream adapters—with their optional disposal semantics—do not implement the extended disposal pattern where the finalizer calls `Dispose`. This allows an abandoned adapter to evade automatic disposal when the garbage collector catches up with it.

File and Directory Operations

The `System.IO` namespace provides a set of types for performing "utility" file and directory operations, such as copying and moving, creating directories, and setting file attributes and permissions. For most features, you can choose between two classes, one offering static methods and the other instance methods:

Static classes
  `File` and `Directory`

Instance method classes (constructed with a file or directory name)
  `FileInfo` and `DirectoryInfo`

Additionally, there's a static class called `Path`. This does nothing to files or directories; instead, it provides string manipulation methods for filenames and directory paths. `Path` also assists with temporary files.

The File Class

`File` is a static class whose methods all accept a filename. The filename can be either relative to the current directory or fully qualified with a directory. Here are its methods (all `public` and `static`):

```
bool Exists (string path);        // Returns true if the file is present

void Delete  (string path);
void Copy    (string sourceFileName, string destFileName);
void Move    (string sourceFileName, string destFileName);
void Replace (string sourceFileName, string destinationFileName,
                                     string destinationBackupFileName);

FileAttributes GetAttributes (string path);
void SetAttributes            (string path, FileAttributes fileAttributes);

void Decrypt (string path);
void Encrypt (string path);

DateTime GetCreationTime   (string path);    // UTC versions are
DateTime GetLastAccessTime (string path);    // also provided.
DateTime GetLastWriteTime  (string path);

void SetCreationTime   (string path, DateTime creationTime);
void SetLastAccessTime (string path, DateTime lastAccessTime);
void SetLastWriteTime  (string path, DateTime lastWriteTime);

FileSecurity GetAccessControl (string path);
FileSecurity GetAccessControl (string path,
                               AccessControlSections includeSections);
void SetAccessControl (string path, FileSecurity fileSecurity);
```

`Move` throws an exception if the destination file already exists; `Replace` does not. Both methods allow the file to be renamed as well as moved to another directory.

`Delete` throws an `UnauthorizedAccessException` if the file is marked read-only; you can tell this in advance by calling `GetAttributes`. Here are all the members of the `FileAttribute` enum that `GetAttributes` returns:

```
Archive, Compressed, Device, Directory, Encrypted,
Hidden, Normal, NotContentIndexed, Offline, ReadOnly,
ReparsePoint, SparseFile, System, Temporary
```

Members in this enum are combinable. Here's how to toggle a single file attribute without upsetting the rest:

```
string filePath = @"c:\temp\test.txt";

FileAttributes fa = File.GetAttributes (filePath);
if ((fa & FileAttributes.ReadOnly) > 0)
{
    fa ^= FileAttributes.ReadOnly;
    File.SetAttributes (filePath, fa);
}
```

```
// Now we can delete the file, for instance:
File.Delete (filePath);
```

 FileInfo offers an easier way to change a file's read-only flag:

```
new FileInfo (@"c:\temp\test.txt").IsReadOnly = false;
```

Compression and encryption attributes

The `Compressed` and `Encrypted` file attributes correspond to the compression and encryption checkboxes on a file or directory's *properties* dialog in Windows Explorer. This type of compression and encryption is *transparent* in that the operating system does all the work behind the scenes, allowing you to read and write plain data.

You cannot use `SetAttributes` to change a file's `Compressed` or `Encrypted` attributes—it fails silently if you try! The workaround is simple in the latter case: you instead call the `Encrypt()` and `Decrypt()` methods in the `File` class. With compression, it's more complicated; one solution is to use the Windows Management Instrumentation (WMI) API in `System.Management`. The following method compresses a directory, returning 0 if successful (or a WMI error code if not):

```
static uint CompressFolder (string folder, bool recursive)
{
  string path = "Win32_Directory.Name='" + folder + "'";
  using (ManagementObject dir = new ManagementObject (path))
  using (ManagementBaseObject p = dir.GetMethodParameters ("CompressEx"))
  {
    p ["Recursive"] = recursive;
    using (ManagementBaseObject result = dir.InvokeMethod ("CompressEx",
                                                           p, null))
      return (uint) result.Properties ["ReturnValue"].Value;
  }
}
```

To uncompress, replace `CompressEx` with `UncompressEx`.

Transparent encryption relies on a key seeded from the logged-in user's password. The system is robust to password changes performed by the authenticated user, but if a password is reset via an administrator, data in encrypted files is unrecoverable.

 Transparent encryption and compression require special file-system support. NTFS (used most commonly on hard drives) supports these features; CDFS (on CD-ROMs) and FAT (on removable media cards) do not.

You can determine whether a volume supports compression and encryption with Win32 interop:

```
using System;
using System.IO;
using System.Text;
```

```
using System.Runtime.InteropServices;

class SupportsCompressionEncryption
{
  const int SupportsCompression = 0x10;
  const int SupportsEncryption = 0x20000;

  [DllImport ("Kernel32.dll", SetLastError = true)]
  extern static bool GetVolumeInformation (string vol, StringBuilder name,
    int nameSize, out uint serialNum, out uint maxNameLen, out uint flags,
    StringBuilder fileSysName, int fileSysNameSize);

  static void Main()
  {
    uint serialNum, maxNameLen, flags;
    bool ok = GetVolumeInformation (@"C:\", null, 0, out serialNum,
                                    out maxNameLen, out flags, null, 0);
    if (!ok)
      throw new Win32Exception();

    bool canCompress = (flags & SupportsCompression) > 0;
    bool canEncrypt = (flags & SupportsEncryption) > 0;
  }
}
```

File security

The `GetAccessControl` and `SetAccessControl` methods allow you to query
and change the operating system permissions assigned to users and roles via a
`FileSecurity` object (namespace `System.Security.AccessControl`). You can also pass
a `FileSecurity` object to a `FileStream`'s constructor to specify permissions when
creating a new file.

In this example, we list a file's existing permissions, and then assign execution permission to the "Users" group:

```
using System;
using System.IO;
using System.Security.AccessControl;
using System.Security.Principal;

...

FileSecurity sec = File.GetAccessControl (@"c:\temp\test.txt");
AuthorizationRuleCollection rules = sec.GetAccessRules (true, true,
                                          typeof (NTAccount));
foreach (FileSystemAccessRule rule in rules)
{
  Console.WriteLine (rule.AccessControlType);        // Allow or Deny
  Console.WriteLine (rule.FileSystemRights);          // e.g., FullControl
  Console.WriteLine (rule.IdentityReference.Value);   // e.g., MyDomain/Joe
}

FileSystemAccessRule newRule = new FileSystemAccessRule
  ("Users", FileSystemRights.ExecuteFile, AccessControlType.Allow);
```

```
    sec.AddAccessRule (newRule);
    File.SetAccessControl (@"c:\temp\test.txt", sec);
```

The Directory Class

The static `Directory` class provides a set of methods analogous to those in the `File` class—for checking whether a directory exists (`Exists`), moving a directory (`Move`), deleting a directory (`Delete`), getting/setting times of creation or last access, and getting/setting security permissions. Furthermore, `Directory` exposes the following static methods:

```
string GetCurrentDirectory ();
void   SetCurrentDirectory (string path);

DirectoryInfo CreateDirectory  (string path);
DirectoryInfo GetParent        (string path);
string        GetDirectoryRoot (string path);

string[] GetLogicalDrives();

// The following methods all return full paths:

string[] GetFiles            (string path);
string[] GetDirectories      (string path);
string[] GetFileSystemEntries (string path);

IEnumerable<string> EnumerateFiles            (string path);
IEnumerable<string> EnumerateDirectories      (string path);
IEnumerable<string> EnumerateFileSystemEntries (string path);
```

 The last three methods were added in Framework 4.0. They're potentially more efficient than the `Get*` variants, because they're lazily evaluated—fetching data from the filesystem as you enumerate the sequence. They're particularly well-suited to LINQ queries.

The `Enumerate*` and `Get*` methods are overloaded to also accept `searchPattern` (string) and `searchOption` (enum) parameters. If you specify `SearchOption.Search AllSubDirectories`, a recursive subdirectory search is performed. The `*FileSyste mEntries` methods combine the results of `*Files` with `*Directories`.

Here's how to create a directory if it doesn't already exist:

```
if (!Directory.Exists (@"c:\temp"))
    Directory.CreateDirectory (@"c:\temp");
```

FileInfo and DirectoryInfo

The static methods on `File` and `Directory` are convenient for executing a single file or directory operation. If you need to call a series of methods in a row, the `FileInfo` and `DirectoryInfo` classes provide an object model that makes the job easier.

FileInfo offers most of the File's static methods in instance form—with some additional properties such as Extension, Length, IsReadOnly, and Directory—for returning a DirectoryInfo object. For example:

```
FileInfo fi = new FileInfo (@"c:\temp\FileInfo.txt");
Console.WriteLine (fi.Exists);          // false

using (TextWriter w = fi.CreateText())
  w.Write ("Some text");

Console.WriteLine (fi.Exists);          // false (still)
fi.Refresh();
Console.WriteLine (fi.Exists);          // true

Console.WriteLine (fi.Name);            // FileInfo.txt
Console.WriteLine (fi.FullName);        // c:\temp\FileInfo.txt
Console.WriteLine (fi.DirectoryName);   // c:\temp
Console.WriteLine (fi.Directory.Name);  // temp
Console.WriteLine (fi.Extension);       // .txt
Console.WriteLine (fi.Length);          // 9

fi.Encrypt();
fi.Attributes ^= FileAttributes.Hidden;   // (Toggle hidden flag)
fi.IsReadOnly = true;

Console.WriteLine (fi.Attributes);      // ReadOnly,Archive,Hidden,Encrypted
Console.WriteLine (fi.CreationTime);

fi.MoveTo (@"c:\temp\FileInfoX.txt");

DirectoryInfo di = fi.Directory;
Console.WriteLine (di.Name);            // temp
Console.WriteLine (di.FullName);        // c:\temp
Console.WriteLine (di.Parent.FullName); // c:\
di.CreateSubdirectory ("SubFolder");
```

Here's how to use DirectoryInfo to enumerate files and subdirectories:

```
DirectoryInfo di = new DirectoryInfo (@"e:\photos");

foreach (FileInfo fi in di.GetFiles ("*.jpg"))
  Console.WriteLine (fi.Name);

foreach (DirectoryInfo subDir in di.GetDirectories())
  Console.WriteLine (subDir.FullName);
```

Path

The static Path class defines methods and fields for working with paths and filenames. Assuming this setup code:

```
string dir  = @"c:\mydir";
string file = "myfile.txt";
string path = @"c:\mydir\myfile.txt";

Directory.SetCurrentDirectory (@"k:\demo");
```

we can demonstrate Path's methods and fields with the following expressions:

Expression:	Result
Directory.GetCurrentDirectory()	k:\demo\
Path.IsPathRooted (file)	False
Path.IsPathRooted (path)	True
Path.GetPathRoot (path)	c:\
Path.GetDirectoryName (path)	c:\mydir
Path.GetFileName (path)	myfile.txt
Path.GetFullPath (file)	k:\demo\myfile.txt
Path.Combine (dir, file)	c:\mydir\myfile.txt
File extensions:	
Path.HasExtension (file)	True
Path.GetExtension (file)	.txt
Path.GetFileNameWithoutExtension (file)	myfile
Path.ChangeExtension (file, ".log")	myfile.log
Separators and characters:	
Path.AltDirectorySeparatorChar	/
Path.PathSeparator	;
Path.VolumeSeparatorChar	:
Path.GetInvalidPathChars()	chars 0 to 31 and "<>|
Path.GetInvalidFileNameChars()	chars 0 to 31 and "<>|:*?\/
Temporary files:	
Path.GetTempPath()	*<local user folder>*\Temp
Path.GetRandomFileName()	*d2dwuzjf.dnp*
Path.GetTempFileName()	*<local user folder>*\Temp*tmp14B.tmp*

Combine is particularly useful: it allows you to combine a directory and filename—or two directories—without first having to check whether a trailing backslash is present.

GetFullPath converts a path relative to the current directory to an absolute path. It accepts values such as *..\..\file.txt*.

GetRandomFileName returns a genuinely unique 8.3 character filename, without actually creating any file. GetTempFileName generates a temporary filename using an auto-incrementing counter that repeats every 65,000 files. It then creates a zero-byte file of this name in the local temporary directory.

You must delete the file generated by `GetTempFileName` when you're done; otherwise, it will eventually throw an exception (after your 65,000th call to `GetTempFileName`). If this is a problem, you can instead Combine `GetTempPath` with `GetRandomFile Name`. Just be careful not to fill up the user's hard drive!

Special Folders

One thing missing from `Path` and `Directory` is a means to locate folders such as *My Documents*, *Program Files*, *Application Data*, and so on. This is provided instead by the `GetFolderPath` method in the `System.Environment` class:

```
string myDocPath = Environment.GetFolderPath
    (Environment.SpecialFolder.MyDocuments);
```

`Environment.SpecialFolder` is an enum whose values encompass all special directories in Windows:

AdminTools	CommonVideos	Personal
ApplicationData	Cookies	PrinterShortcuts
CDBurning	Desktop	ProgramFiles
CommonAdminTools	DesktopDirectory	ProgramFilesX86
CommonApplicationData	Favorites	Programs
CommonDesktopDirectory	Fonts	Recent
CommonDocuments	History	Resources
CommonMusic	InternetCache	SendTo
CommonOemLinks	LocalApplicationData	StartMenu
CommonPictures	LocalizedResources	Startup
CommonProgramFiles	MyComputer	System
CommonProgramFilesX86	MyDocuments	SystemX86
CommonPrograms	MyMusic	Templates
CommonStartMenu	MyPictures	UserProfile
CommonStartup	MyVideos	Windows
CommonTemplates	NetworkShortcuts	

Of particular value is `ApplicationData`: this is where you can store settings that travel with a user across a network (if roaming profiles are enabled on the network domain). `LocalApplicationData` is for non-roaming data; `CommonApplicationData` is shared by every user of the computer. Writing application data to these folders is considered preferable to using the Windows Registry. A better option still, in most cases, is to use isolated storage (described in the final section of this chapter).

The simplest place to write configuration and log files is to the application's base directory, which you can obtain with AppDomain.CurrentDomain.BaseDirectory. This is not recommended, however, because the operating system is likely to deny your application permissions to write to this folder after initial installation (without administrative elevation).

The following method returns the .NET Framework directory:

```
System.Runtime.InteropServices.RuntimeEnvironment.GetRuntimeDirectory()
```

Querying Volume Information

You can query the drives on a computer with the DriveInfo class:

```
DriveInfo c = new DriveInfo ("C");      // Query the C: drive.

long totalSize = c.TotalSize;           // Size in bytes.
long freeBytes = c.TotalFreeSpace;      // Ignores disk quotas.
long freeToMe  = c.AvailableFreeSpace;  // Takes quotas into account.

foreach (DriveInfo d in DriveInfo.GetDrives())    // All defined drives.
{
  Console.WriteLine (d.Name);            // C:\
  Console.WriteLine (d.DriveType);       // Fixed
  Console.WriteLine (d.RootDirectory);   // C:\

  if (d.IsReady)   // If the drive is not ready, the following two
                   // properties will throw exceptions:
  {
    Console.WriteLine (d.VolumeLabel);   // The Sea Drive
    Console.WriteLine (d.DriveFormat);   // NTFS
  }
}
```

The static GetDrives method returns all mapped drives, including CD-ROMs, media cards, and network connections. DriveType is an enum with the following values:

```
Unknown, NoRootDirectory, Removable, Fixed, Network, CDRom, Ram
```

Catching Filesystem Events

The FileSystemWatcher class lets you monitor a directory (and optionally, subdirectories) for activity. FileSystemWatcher has events that fire when files or subdirectories are created, modified, renamed, and deleted, as well as when their attributes change. These events fire regardless of the user or process performing the change. Here's an example:

```
static void Main() { Watch (@"c:\temp", "*.txt", true); }

static void Watch (string path, string filter, bool includeSubDirs)
{
  using (var watcher = new FileSystemWatcher (path, filter))
  {
```

Streams and I/O

```
    watcher.Created += FileCreatedChangedDeleted;
    watcher.Changed += FileCreatedChangedDeleted;
    watcher.Deleted += FileCreatedChangedDeleted;
    watcher.Renamed += FileRenamed;
    watcher.Error   += FileError;

    watcher.IncludeSubdirectories = includeSubDirs;
    watcher.EnableRaisingEvents = true;

    Console.WriteLine ("Listening for events - press <enter> to end");
    Console.ReadLine();
  }
  // Disposing the FileSystemWatcher stops further events from firing.
}

static void FileCreatedChangedDeleted (object o, FileSystemEventArgs e)
{
  Console.WriteLine ("File {0} has been {1}", e.FullPath, e.ChangeType);
}

static void FileRenamed (object o, RenamedEventArgs e)
{
  Console.WriteLine ("Renamed: {0}->{1}", e.OldFullPath, e.FullPath);
}

static void FileError (object o, ErrorEventArgs e)
{
  Console.WriteLine ("Error: " + e.GetException().Message);
}
```

 Because FileSystemWatcher raises events on a separate thread, you must exception-handle the event handling code to prevent an error from taking down the application. See "Exception Handling" on page 591 for more information on this.

The Error event does not inform you of filesystem errors; instead, it indicates that the FileSystemWatcher's event buffer overflowed because it was overwhelmed by Changed, Created, Deleted, or Renamed events. You can change the buffer size via the InternalBufferSize property.

IncludeSubdirectories applies recursively. So, if you create a FileSystemWatcher on C:\ with IncludeSubdirectories true, its events will fire when a file or directory changes anywhere on the hard drive.

 A trap in using FileSystemWatcher is to open and read newly created or updated files before the file has been fully populated or updated. If you're working in conjunction with some other software that's creating files, you might need to consider a strategy to mitigate this, such as creating files with an unwatched extension and then renaming them once fully written.

Memory-Mapped Files

Memory-mapped files are new to Framework 4.0. They provide two key features:

- Efficient random access to file data
- The ability to share memory between different processes on the same computer

The types for memory-mapped files reside in the `System.IO.MemoryMappedFiles` namespace. Internally, they work by wrapping the Win32 API for memory-mapped files.

Memory-Mapped Files and Random File I/O

Although an ordinary `FileStream` allows random file I/O (by setting the stream's `Position` property), it's optimized for sequential I/O. As a rough rule of thumb:

- `FileStream`s are 10 times faster than memory-mapped files for sequential I/O.
- Memory-mapped files are 10 times faster than `FileStream`s for random I/O.

Changing a `FileStream`'s `Position` can cost several microseconds—which adds up if done within a loop. A `FileStream` is also unsuitable for multithreaded access—because its position changes as it is read or written.

To create a memory-mapped file:

1. Obtain a `FileStream` as you would ordinarily.
2. Instantiate a `MemoryMappedFile`, passing in the file stream.
3. Call `CreateViewAccessor` on the memory-mapped file object.

The last step gives you a `MemoryMappedViewAccessor` object, which provides methods for randomly reading and writing simple types, structures, and arrays (more on this in "Working with View Accessors" on page 570).

The following creates a 1 million-byte file and then uses the memory-mapped file API to read and then write a byte at position 500,000:

```
File.WriteAllBytes ("long.bin", new byte [1000000]);

using (MemoryMappedFile mmf = MemoryMappedFile.CreateFromFile ("long.bin"))
using (MemoryMappedViewAccessor accessor = mmf.CreateViewAccessor())
{
  accessor.Write (500000, (byte) 77);
  Console.WriteLine (accessor.ReadByte (500000));   // 77
}
```

You can also specify a map name and capacity when calling `CreateFromFile`. Specifying a non-null map name allows the memory block to be shared with other processes (see the following section); specifying a capacity automatically enlarges the file to that value. The following creates a 1,000-byte file:

```
using (var mmf = MemoryMappedFile.CreateFromFile
                  ("long.bin", FileMode.Create, null, 1000))
  ...
```

Memory-Mapped Files and Shared Memory

You can also use memory-mapped files as a means of sharing memory between processes on the same computer. One process creates a shared memory block by calling MemoryMappedFile.CreateNew, while other processes subscribe to that same memory block by calling MemoryMappedFile.OpenExisting with the same name. Although it's still referred to as a memory-mapped "file," it lives entirely in memory and has no disk presence.

The following creates a 500-byte shared memory-mapped file, and writes the integer 12345 at position 0:

```
using (MemoryMappedFile mmFile = MemoryMappedFile.CreateNew ("Demo", 500))
using (MemoryMappedViewAccessor accessor = mmFile.CreateViewAccessor())
{
  accessor.Write (0, 12345);
  Console.ReadLine();   // Keep shared memory alive until user hits Enter.
}
```

while the following opens that same memory-mapped file and reads that integer:

```
// This can run in a separate EXE:
using (MemoryMappedFile mmFile = MemoryMappedFile.OpenExisting ("Demo"))
using (MemoryMappedViewAccessor accessor = mmFile.CreateViewAccessor())
  Console.WriteLine (accessor.ReadInt32 (0));   // 12345
```

Working with View Accessors

Calling CreateViewAccessor on a MemoryMappedFile gives you a view accessor that lets you read/write values at random positions.

The Read*/Write* methods accept numeric types, bool, and char, as well as arrays and structs that contain value-type elements or fields. Reference types—and arrays or structs that contain reference types—are prohibited because they cannot map into unmanaged memory. So if you want to write a string, you must encode it into an array of bytes:

```
byte[] data = Encoding.UTF8.GetBytes ("This is a test");
accessor.Write (0, data.Length);
accessor.WriteArray (4, data, 0, data.Length);
```

Notice that we wrote the length first. This means we know how many bytes to read back later:

```
byte[] data = new byte [accessor.ReadInt32 (0)];
accessor.ReadArray (4, data, 0, data.Length);
Console.WriteLine (Encoding.UTF8.GetString (data));   // This is a test
```

Here's an example of reading/writing a struct:

```
struct Data { public int X, Y; }
...
var data = new Data { X = 123, Y = 456 };
accessor.Write (0, ref data);
accessor.Read (0, out data);
Console.WriteLine (data.X + " " + data.Y);   // 123 456
```

You can also directly access the underlying unmanaged memory via a pointer. Following on from the previous example:

```
unsafe
{
  byte* pointer = null;
  accessor.SafeMemoryMappedViewHandle.AcquirePointer (ref pointer);
  int* intPointer = (int*) pointer;
  Console.WriteLine (*intPointer);           // 123
}
```

Pointers can be advantageous when working with large structures: they let you work directly with the raw data rather than using Read/Write to *copy* data between managed and unmanaged memory. We explore this further in Chapter 25.

Compression

Two general-purpose compression streams are provided in the System.IO.Compres sion namespace: DeflateStream and GZipStream. Both use a popular compression algorithm similar to that of the ZIP format. They differ in that GZipStream writes an additional protocol at the start and end—including a CRC to detect for errors. GZipStream also conforms to a standard recognized by other software.

Both streams allow reading and writing, with the following provisos:

- You always *write* to the stream when compressing.
- You always *read* from the stream when decompressing.

DeflateStream and GZipStream are decorators; they compress or decompress data from another stream that you supply in construction. In the following example, we compress and decompress a series of bytes, using a FileStream as the backing store:

```
using (Stream s = File.Create ("compressed.bin"))
using (Stream ds = new DeflateStream (s, CompressionMode.Compress))
  for (byte i = 0; i < 100; i++)
    ds.WriteByte (i);

using (Stream s = File.OpenRead ("compressed.bin"))
using (Stream ds = new DeflateStream (s, CompressionMode.Decompress))
  for (byte i = 0; i < 100; i++)
    Console.WriteLine (ds.ReadByte());    // Writes 0 to 99
```

Even with the smaller of the two algorithms, the compressed file is 241 bytes long: more than double the original! Compression works poorly with "dense," nonrepetitive binary files. It works well with most text files; in the next example, we compress and decompress a text stream composed of 1,000 words chosen randomly from a small sentence. This also demonstrates chaining a backing store stream, a decorator stream, and an adapter, as depicted at the start of the chapter in Figure 14-1:

```
string[] words = "The quick brown fox jumps over the lazy dog".Split();
Random rand = new Random();

using (Stream s = File.Create ("compressed.bin"))
using (Stream ds = new DeflateStream (s, CompressionMode.Compress))
```

```
using (TextWriter w = new StreamWriter (ds))
  for (int i = 0; i < 1000; i++)
    w.Write (words [rand.Next (words.Length)] + " ");

Console.WriteLine (new FileInfo ("compressed.bin").Length);      // 1073

using (Stream s = File.OpenRead ("compressed.bin"))
using (Stream ds = new DeflateStream (s, CompressionMode.Decompress))
using (TextReader r = new StreamReader (ds))
  Console.Write (r.ReadToEnd());                     // Output below:

lazy lazy the fox the quick The brown fox jumps over fox over fox The
brown brown brown over brown quick fox brown dog dog lazy fox dog brown
over fox jumps lazy lazy quick The jumps fox jumps The over jumps dog...
```

In this case, DeflateStream compresses efficiently to 1,073 bytes—slightly more than 1 byte per word.

Compressing in Memory

Sometimes you need to compress entirely in memory. Here's how to use a MemoryStream for this purpose:

```
byte[] data = new byte[1000];           // We can expect a good compression
                                        // ratio from an empty array!
var ms = new MemoryStream();
using (Stream ds = new DeflateStream (ms, CompressionMode.Compress))
  ds.Write (data, 0, data.Length);

byte[] compressed = ms.ToArray();
Console.WriteLine (compressed.Length);        // 113

// Decompress back to the data array:
ms = new MemoryStream (compressed);
using (Stream ds = new DeflateStream (ms, CompressionMode.Decompress))
  for (int i = 0; i < 1000; i += ds.Read (data, i, 1000 - i));
```

The using statement around the DeflateStream closes it in a textbook fashion, flushing any unwritten buffers in the process. This also closes the MemoryStream it wraps—meaning we must then call ToArray to extract its data.

Here's an alternative that avoids closing the MemoryStream:

```
byte[] data = new byte[1000];

MemoryStream ms = new MemoryStream();
using (Stream ds = new DeflateStream (ms, CompressionMode.Compress, true))
  ds.Write (data, 0, data.Length);

Console.WriteLine (ms.Length);              // 113
ms.Position = 0;
using (Stream ds = new DeflateStream (ms, CompressionMode.Decompress))
  for (int i = 0; i < 1000; i += ds.Read (data, i, 1000 - i));
```

The additional flag sent to `DeflateStream`'s constructor tells it not to follow the usual protocol of taking the underlying stream with it in disposal. In other words, the `MemoryStream` is left open, allowing us to position it back to zero and reread it.

Isolated Storage

Each .NET program has access to a special filesystem unique to that program, called *isolated storage*. Isolated storage is useful and important for a number of reasons:

- Your application, if subject to code access security, is more likely to be granted permission to isolated storage than any other form of file I/O (by default, even applications running from an Internet URI or Silverlight sandbox have some access to isolated storage).
- Data that you create is segregated from other applications.
- Isolated storage is UAC-friendly.

In terms of security, isolated storage is a fence designed more to keep you in than to keep other applications out! Data in isolated storage is strongly protected against intrusion from other .NET applications running under the most restricted permission set (i.e., the "Internet" zone). In other cases, there's no hard security preventing another application from accessing your isolated storage *if it really wants to*. The benefit of using isolated storage over `CommonApplicationData` is that applications must go out of their way to interfere with each other—it cannot happen through carelessness or by accident.

Applications running in a sandbox can have their quota of isolated storage limited via permissions. The default, for Internet and Silverlight applications, is 1MB in Framework 4.0.

> From Framework 4.0, a hosted UI-based application (e.g., Silverlight) can ask the user for permission to increase the isolated storage quota by calling the `IncreaseQuotaTo` method on an `IsolatedStorageFile` object. This must be called from a user-initiated event, such as a button click. If the user agrees, the method returns true.
>
> You can query the current allowance via the `Quota` property.

Isolated storage also has disadvantages:

- The API is somewhat awkward to use—particularly when accessing roaming stores.
- You can read/write only with an `IsolatedStorageStream`; you cannot obtain a file or directory path and then use ordinary file I/O.

Isolation Types

Isolated storage can separate by both program and user. This results in three basic types of compartments:

Local user compartments
    One per user, per program, per computer

Roaming user compartments
    One per user, per program

Machine compartments
    One per program, per computer (shared by all users of a program)

The data in a roaming user compartment follows the user across a network—with appropriate operating system and domain support. If this support is unavailable, it behaves like a local user compartment.

So far, we've talked about how isolated storage separates by "program." Isolated storage considers a program to be one of two things, depending on which mode you choose:

- An assembly
- An assembly running within the context of a particular application

The latter is called *domain isolation* and is more commonly used than *assembly isolation*. Domain isolation segregates according to two things: the currently executing assembly and the executable or web application that originally started it. Assembly isolation segregates only according to the currently executing assembly—so different applications calling the same assembly will share the same store.

 Assemblies and applications are identified by their strong name. If no strong name is present, the assembly's full file path or URI is used instead. This means that if you move or rename a weakly named assembly, its isolated storage is reset.

In total, then, there are six kinds of isolated storage compartments. Table 14-4 compares the isolation provided by each.

Table 14-4. Isolated storage containers

Type	Computer?	Application?	Assembly?	User?	Method to obtain store
Domain User (default)	✓	✓	✓	✓	GetUserStoreForDomain
Domain Roaming		✓	✓	✓	
Domain Machine	✓	✓	✓		GetMachineStoreForDomain
Assembly User	✓		✓	✓	GetUserStoreForAssembly

Type	Computer?	Application?	Assembly?	User?	Method to obtain store
Assembly Roaming		✓		✓	
Assembly Machine	✓		✓		`GetMachineStoreForAssembly`

There is no such thing as domain-only isolation. If you want to share an isolated store across all assemblies within an application, there's a simple workaround, however. Just expose a public method in one of the assemblies that instantiates and returns an `IsolatedStorageFileStream` object. Any assembly can access any isolated store if given an `IsolatedStorageFile` object—isolation restrictions are imposed upon construction, not subsequent use.

Similarly, there's no such thing as machine-only isolation. If you want to share an isolated store across a variety of applications, the workaround is to write a common assembly that all applications reference, and then expose a method on the common assembly that creates and returns an assembly-isolated `IsolatedStorageFileStream`. The common assembly must be strongly named for this to work.

Reading and Writing Isolated Storage

Isolated storage uses streams that work much like ordinary file streams. To obtain an isolated storage stream, you first specify the kind of isolation you want by calling one of the static methods on `IsolatedStorageFile`—as shown previously in Table 14-4. You then use it to construct an `IsolatedStorageFileStream`, along with a filename and `FileMode`:

```
// IsolatedStorage classes live in System.IO.IsolatedStorage

using (IsolatedStorageFile f =
      IsolatedStorageFile.GetMachineStoreForDomain())
using (var s = new IsolatedStorageFileStream ("hi.txt",FileMode.Create,f))
using (var writer = new StreamWriter (s))
  writer.WriteLine ("Hello, World");

// Read it back:

using (IsolatedStorageFile f =
      IsolatedStorageFile.GetMachineStoreForDomain())
using (var s = new IsolatedStorageFileStream ("hi.txt", FileMode.Open, f))
using (var reader = new StreamReader (s))
  Console.WriteLine (reader.ReadToEnd());          // Hello, world
```

You can optionally omit the first step, and then the default isolation (Domain User) is used:

```
using (var s = new IsolatedStorageFileStream ("a.txt", FileMode.Create))
using (var writer = new StreamWriter (s))
  ...
```

IsolatedStorageFile is poorly named in that it doesn't represent a file, but rather a *container* for files (basically, a directory).

IsolatedStorageFile doesn't provide methods to directly access the roaming stores: you must instead call GetStore with an IsolatedStorageScope argument. IsolatedStorageScope is a flags enum whose members you must combine in exactly the right way to get a valid store. Figure 14-6 lists all the valid combinations.

	Assembly	Assembly & domain
Local user	Assembly | User	Assembly | Domain | User
Roaming user	Assembly | User | Roaming	Assembly | Domain | User | Roaming
Machine	Assembly | Machine	Assembly | Domain | Machine

Figure 14-6. Valid IsolatedStorageScope combinations

Here's how to write to a store isolated by assembly and roaming user:

```
var flags = IsolatedStorageScope.Assembly
          | IsolatedStorageScope.User
          | IsolatedStorageScope.Roaming;

using (IsolatedStorageFile f = IsolatedStorageFile.GetStore (flags,
                                                             null, null))
using (var s = new IsolatedStorageFileStream ("a.txt", FileMode.Create, f))
using (var writer = new StreamWriter (s))
  writer.WriteLine ("Hello, World");
```

Store Location

Here's where .NET writes isolated storage files:

Scope	Location
Local user	[LocalApplicationData]*IsolatedStorage*
Roaming user	[ApplicationData]*IsolatedStorage*
Machine	[CommonApplicationData]*IsolatedStorage*

You can obtain the locations of each of the folders in square brackets by calling the Environment.GetFolderPath method. Here are the defaults for Windows Vista and above:

Scope	Location
Local user	\Users\<user>\AppData\Local\IsolatedStorage
Roaming user	\Users\<user>\AppData\Roaming\IsolatedStorage
Machine	\ProgramData\IsolatedStorage

For Windows XP:

Scope	Location
Local user	\Documents and Settings\<user>\Local Settings\Application Data\Isolated-Storage
Roaming user	\Documents and Settings\<user>\Application Data\IsolatedStorage
Machine	\Documents and Settings\All Users\Application Data\IsolatedStorage

These are merely the base folders; the data files themselves are buried deep in a labyrinth of subdirectories whose names derive from hashed assembly names. This is both a reason to use—and not to use—isolated storage. On the one hand, it makes isolation possible: a permission-restricted application wanting to interfere with another can be stumped by being denied a directory listing—despite having the same filesystem rights as its peers. On the other hand, it makes administration impractical from outside the application. Sometimes it's handy—or essential—to edit an XML configuration file in Notepad so that an application can start up properly. Isolated storage makes this impractical.

Enumerating Isolated Storage

An IsolatedStorageFile object also provides methods for listing files in the store:

```
using (IsolatedStorageFile f = IsolatedStorageFile.GetUserStoreForDomain())
{
  using (var s = new IsolatedStorageFileStream ("f1.x",FileMode.Create,f))
    s.WriteByte (123);

  using (var s = new IsolatedStorageFileStream ("f2.x",FileMode.Create,f))
    s.WriteByte (123);

  foreach (string s in f.GetFileNames ("*.*"))
    Console.Write (s + " ");                    // f1.x f2.x
}
```

You can also create and remove subdirectories, as well as files:

```
using (IsolatedStorageFile f = IsolatedStorageFile.GetUserStoreForDomain())
{
  f.CreateDirectory ("subfolder");

  foreach (string s in f.GetDirectoryNames ("*.*"))
    Console.WriteLine (s);                       // subfolder

  using (var s = new IsolatedStorageFileStream (@"subfolder\sub1.txt",
```

```
                                          FileMode.Create, f))
    s.WriteByte (100);

  f.DeleteFile (@"subfolder\sub1.txt");
  f.DeleteDirectory ("subfolder");
}
```

With sufficient permissions, you can also enumerate over all isolated stores created by the current user, as well as all machine stores. This function can violate program privacy, but not user privacy. Here's an example:

```
System.Collections.IEnumerator rator =
  IsolatedStorageFile.GetEnumerator (IsolatedStorageScope.User);

while (rator.MoveNext())
{
  var isf = (IsolatedStorageFile) rator.Current;

  Console.WriteLine (isf.AssemblyIdentity);      // Strong name or URI
  Console.WriteLine (isf.CurrentSize);
  Console.WriteLine (isf.Scope);                 // User + ...
}
```

The GetEnumerator method is unusual in accepting an argument (this makes its containing class foreach-unfriendly). GetEnumerator accepts one of three values:

IsolatedStorageScope.User
    Enumerates all local stores belonging to the current user

IsolatedStorageScope.User | IsolatedStorageScope.Roaming
    Enumerates all roaming stores belonging to the current user

IsolatedStorageScope.Machine
    Enumerates all machine stores on the computer

Once you have the IsolatedStorageFile object, you can list its content by calling GetFiles and GetDirectories.

15

Networking

The Framework offers a variety of classes in the System.Net.* namespaces for communicating via standard network protocols, such as HTTP, TCP/IP, and FTP. Here's a summary of the key components:

- A WebClient façade class for simple download/upload operations via HTTP or FTP

- WebRequest and WebResponse classes for more control over client-side HTTP or FTP operations

- HttpListener for writing an HTTP server

- SmtpClient for constructing and sending mail messages via SMTP

- Dns for converting between domain names and addresses

- TcpClient, UdpClient, TcpListener, and Socket classes for direct access to the transport and network layers

The Framework supports primarily Internet-based protocols, although this doesn't limit applicability to the Internet; protocols such as TCP/IP also dominate local area networks.

The types described in this chapter are defined mostly in the System.Net and System.Net.Sockets namespaces; however, many of the examples also use types in System.IO.

Network Architecture

Figure 15-1 illustrates the .NET networking types and the communication layers in which they reside. Most types reside in the *transport layer* or *application layer*. The transport layer defines basic protocols for sending and receiving bytes (TCP and UDP); the application layer defines higher-level protocols designed for specific applications such as retrieving web pages (HTTP), transferring files (FTP), sending mail (SMTP), and converting between domain names and IP addresses (DNS).

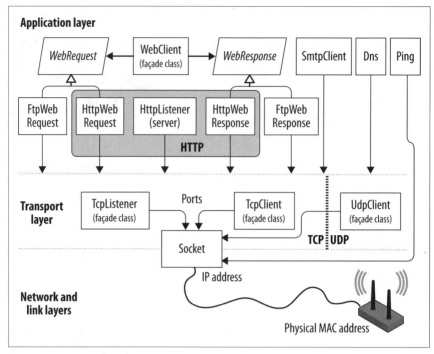

Figure 15-1. Network architecture

It's usually most convenient to program at the application layer; however, there are a couple of reasons you might want to work directly at the transport layer. One is if you need an application protocol not provided in the Framework, such as POP3 for retrieving mail. Another is if you want to invent a custom protocol for a special application, such as a peer-to-peer client.

Of the application protocols, HTTP is special in that its use has extended to general-purpose communication. Its basic mode of operation—"give me the web page with this URL"—adapts nicely to "give me the return value from calling this method with these arguments." HTTP has a rich set of features that are useful in multitier business applications and service-oriented architectures, such as protocols for authentication and encryption, message chunking, extensible headers and cookies, and the ability to have many server applications share a single port and IP address. For these reasons, HTTP is well supported in the Framework—both directly, as described in this chapter, and at a higher level, through such technologies as WCF, Web Services, and ASP.NET.

The Framework provides client-side support for FTP, the popular Internet protocol for sending and receiving files. Server-side support comes in the form of IIS or Unix-based server software.

As the preceding discussion makes clear, networking is a field that is awash in acronyms. Table 15-1 is a handy Network TLA (three-letter and more acronym buster).

Table 15-1. Network TLA (three-letter acronym) buster

Acronym	Expansion	Notes
DNS	Domain Name Service	Converts between domain names (e.g., *ebay.com*) and IP addresses (e.g., 199.54.213.2)
FTP	File Transfer Protocol	Internet-based protocol for sending and receiving files
HTTP	Hypertext Transfer Protocol	Retrieves web pages and runs web services
IIS	Internet Information Services	Microsoft's web server software
IP	Internet Protocol	Network-layer protocol below TCP and UDP
LAN	Local Area Network	Most LANs use Internet-based protocols such as TCP/IP
POP	Post Office Protocol	Retrieves Internet mail
SMTP	Simple Mail Transfer Protocol	Sends Internet mail
TCP	Transmission and Control Protocol	Transport-layer Internet protocol on top of which most higher-layer services are built
UDP	Universal Datagram Protocol	Transport-layer Internet protocol used for low-overhead services such as VoIP
UNC	Universal Naming Convention	*\\computer\sharename\filename*
URI	Uniform Resource Identifier	Ubiquitous resource naming system (e.g., *http://www.amazon.com* or *mailto:joe@bloggs.org*)
URL	Uniform Resource Locator	Technical meaning (fading from use): subset of URI; popular meaning: synonym of URI

Addresses and Ports

For communication to work, a computer or device requires an address. The Internet uses two addressing systems:

IPv4

Currently the dominant addressing system; IPv4 addresses are 32 bits wide. When string-formatted, IPv4 addresses are written as four dot-separated decimals (e.g., 101.102.103.104). An address can be unique in the world—or unique within a particular *subnet* (such as on a corporate network).

IPv6

The newer 128-bit addressing system. Addresses are string-formatted in hexadecimal with a colon separator (e.g., [3EA0:FFFF:198A:E4A3:4FF2:54f-A: 41BC:8D31]). The .NET Framework requires that you add square brackets around the address.

The `IPAddress` class in the `System.Net` namespace represents an address in either protocol. It has a constructor accepting a byte array, and a static `Parse` method accepting a correctly formatted string:

```
IPAddress a1 = new IPAddress (new byte[] { 101, 102, 103, 104 });
IPAddress a2 = IPAddress.Parse ("101.102.103.104");
Console.WriteLine (a1.Equals (a2));          // True
Console.WriteLine (a1.AddressFamily);        // InterNetwork
```

```
IPAddress a3 = IPAddress.Parse
  ("[3EA0:FFFF:198A:E4A3:4FF2:54fA:41BC:8D31]");
Console.WriteLine (a3.AddressFamily);   // InterNetworkV6
```

The TCP and UDP protocols break out each IP address into 65,535 ports, allowing
a computer on a single address to run multiple applications, each on its own port.
Many applications have standard port assignments; for instance, HTTP uses port
80; SMTP uses port 25.

> The TCP and UDP ports from 49152 to 65535 are officially
> unassigned, so they are good for testing and small-scale
> deployments.

An IP address and port combination is represented in the .NET Framework by the
IPEndPoint class:

```
IPAddress a = IPAddress.Parse ("101.102.103.104");
IPEndPoint ep = new IPEndPoint (a, 222);        // Port 222
Console.WriteLine (ep.ToString());              // 101.102.103.104:222
```

> Firewalls block ports. In many corporate environments, only a
> few ports are in fact open—typically, port 80 (for unencrypted
> HTTP) and port 443 (for secure HTTP).

URIs

A URI is a specially formatted string that describes a resource on the Internet or a
LAN, such as a web page, file, or email address. Examples include *http://www.ietf*
.org, *ftp://myisp/doc.txt*, and *mailto:joe@bloggs.com*. The exact formatting is defined
by the Internet Engineering Task Force (*http://www.ietf.org/*).

A URI can be broken up into a series of elements—typically, *scheme*, *authority*, and
path. The Uri class in the System namespace performs just this division, exposing a
property for each element. This is illustrated in Figure 15-2.

> The Uri class is useful when you need to validate the format of
> a URI string or to split a URI into its component parts. Other-
> wise, you can treat a URI simply as a string—most networking
> methods are overloaded to accept either a Uri object or a string.

You can construct a Uri object by passing any of the following strings into its
constructor:

- A URI string, such as *http://www.ebay.com* or *file://janespc/sharedpics/dol-
  phin.jpg*

- An absolute path to a file on your hard disk, such as *c:\myfiles\data.xls*
- A UNC path to a file on the LAN, such as *\\janespc\sharedpics\dolphin.jpg*

Figure 15-2. URI properties

File and UNC paths are automatically converted to URIs: the "file:" protocol is added, and backslashes are converted to forward slashes. The Uri constructors also perform some basic cleanup on your string before creating the Uri, including converting the scheme and hostname to lowercase and removing default and blank port numbers. If you supply a URI string without the scheme, such as "*www.test.com*", a UriFormatException is thrown.

Uri has an IsLoopback property, which indicates whether the Uri references the local host (IP address 127.0.0.1), and an IsFile property, which indicates whether the Uri references a local or UNC (IsUnc) path. If IsFile returns true, the LocalPath property returns a version of AbsolutePath that is friendly to the local operating system (with backslashes), on which you can call File.Open.

Instances of Uri have read-only properties. To modify an existing Uri, instantiate a UriBuilder object—this has writable properties and can be converted back via its Uri property.

Uri also provides methods for comparing and subtracting paths:

```
Uri info = new Uri ("http://www.domain.com:80/info/");
Uri page = new Uri ("http://www.domain.com/info/page.html");

Console.WriteLine (info.Host);        // www.domain.com
Console.WriteLine (info.Port);        // 80
Console.WriteLine (page.Port);        // 80  (Uri knows the default HTTP port)

Console.WriteLine (info.IsBaseOf (page));      // True
Uri relative = info.MakeRelativeUri (page);
Console.WriteLine (relative.IsAbsoluteUri);    // False
Console.WriteLine (relative.ToString());       // page.html
```

A relative Uri, such as *page.html* in this example, will throw an exception if you call almost any property or method other than IsAbsoluteUri and ToString(). You can instantiate a relative Uri directly as follows:

```
Uri u = new Uri ("page.html", UriKind.Relative);
```

 A trailing slash is significant in a URI and makes a difference as to how a server processes a request if a path component is present.

For instance, given the URI *http://www.albahari.com/nutshell/*, you can expect an HTTP web server to look in the *nutshell* subdirectory in the site's web folder and return the default document (usually *index.html*).

Without the trailing slash, the web server will instead look for a file called *nutshell* (without an extension) directly in the site's root folder—which is usually not what you want. If no such file exists, most web servers will assume the user mistyped and will return a 301 *Permanent Redirect* error, suggesting the client retries with the trailing slash. A .NET HTTP client, by default, will respond transparently to a 301 in the same way as a web browser—by retrying with the suggested URI. This means that if you omit a trailing slash when it should have been included, your request will still work—but will suffer an unnecessary extra round trip.

The `Uri` class also provides static helper methods such as `EscapeUriString()`, which converts a string to a valid URL by converting all characters with an ASCII value greater than 127 to hexadecimal representation. The `CheckHostName()` and `CheckSchemeName()` methods accept a string and check whether it is syntactically valid for the given property (although they do not attempt to determine whether a host or URI exists).

Request/Response Architecture

`WebRequest` and `WebResponse` are the common base classes for managing both HTTP and FTP client-side activity, as well as the "file:" protocol. They encapsulate the "request/response" model that these protocols all share: the client makes a request, and then awaits a response from a server.

`WebClient` is simply a façade class that does the work of calling `WebRequest` and `WebResponse`, saving you some coding. `WebClient` gives you a choice of dealing in strings, byte arrays, files, or streams; `WebRequest` and `WebResponse` support just streams. Unfortunately, you cannot rely entirely on `WebClient`; some features (such as cookies) are available only through `WebRequest` and `WebResponse`.

WebClient

Here are the steps in using `WebClient`:

1. Instantiate a `WebClient` object.

2. Assign the `Proxy` property.

3. Assign the `Credentials` property if authentication is required.

4. Call a Download*XXX* or Upload*XXX* method with the desired URI.

Its download methods are as follows:

```
public void   DownloadFile   (string address, string fileName);
public string DownloadString (string address);
public byte[] DownloadData   (string address);
public Stream OpenRead        (string address);
```

Each is overloaded to accept a `Uri` object instead of a string address. The upload methods are similar; their return values contain the response (if any) from the server:

```
public byte[] UploadFile   (string address, string fileName);
public byte[] UploadFile   (string address, string method, string fileName);
public string UploadString(string address, string data);
public string UploadString(string address, string method, string data);
public byte[] UploadData   (string address, byte[] data);
public byte[] UploadData   (string address, string method, byte[] data);
public byte[] UploadValues(string address, NameValueCollection data);
public byte[] UploadValues(string address, string method,
                                            NameValueCollection data);
public Stream OpenWrite     (string address);
public Stream OpenWrite     (string address, string method);
```

The `UploadValues` methods can be used to post values to an HTTP form, with a method argument of "POST". `WebClient` also has a `BaseAddress` property; this allows you to specify a string to be prefixed to all addresses, such as *http://www.mysite.com/data/*.

Here's how to download the code samples page for this book to a file in the current folder, and then display it in the default web browser:

```
WebClient wc = new WebClient();
wc.Proxy = null;
wc.DownloadFile ("http://www.albahari.com/nutshell/code.aspx", "code.htm");
System.Diagnostics.Process.Start ("code.htm");
```

 `WebClient` implements `IDisposable` under *duress*—by virtue of deriving from `Component` (this allows it to be sited in Visual Studio's designer). Its `Dispose` method does nothing useful at run-time, however, so you don't need to dispose `WebClient` instances.

You can use the same `WebClient` object to perform many tasks in sequence. It will crash, however, if you try to make it do two things at once with multithreading. Instead, you must create a separate `WebClient` object for each thread.

WebRequest and WebResponse

`WebRequest` and `WebResponse` are more complex to use than `WebClient`, but also more flexible. Here's how to get started:

1. Call `WebRequest.Create` with a URI to instantiate a web request.

2. Assign the `Proxy` property.

3. Assign the `Credentials` property if authentication is required.

To upload data:

4. Call `GetRequestStream` on the request object, and then write to the stream. Go to step 5 if a response is expected.

To download data:

5. Call `GetResponse` on the request object to instantiate a web response.

6. Call `GetResponseStream` on the response object, and then read the stream (a `StreamReader` can help!).

The following downloads and displays the code samples web page (a rewrite of the preceding example):

```
WebRequest req = WebRequest.Create
                ("http://www.albahari.com/nutshell/code.html");
req.Proxy = null;
using (WebResponse res = req.GetResponse())
using (Stream s = res.GetResponseStream())
using (StreamReader sr = new StreamReader(s))
  File.WriteAllText ("code.html", sr.ReadToEnd());

System.Diagnostics.Process.Start ("code.html");
```

The web response object has a `ContentLength` property, indicating the length of the response stream in bytes, as reported by the server. This value comes from the response headers and may be missing or incorrect. In particular, if an HTTP server chooses the "chunked" mode to break up a large response, the `ContentLength` value is usually –1. The same can apply with dynamically generated pages.

The static `Create` method instantiates a subclass of the `WebRequest` type, such as `HttpWebRequest` or `FtpWebRequest`. Its choice of subclass depends on the URI's prefix, and is shown in Table 15-2.

Table 15-2. URI prefixes and web request types

Prefix	Web request type
http: or https:	HttpWebRequest
ftp:	FtpWebRequest
file:	FileWebRequest

Casting a web request object to its concrete type (`HttpWebRequest` or `FtpWebRequest`) allows you to access its protocol-specific features.

You can also register your own prefixes by calling WebRequest.RegisterPrefix. This requires a prefix along with a factory object with a Create method that instantiates an appropriate web request object.

The "https:" protocol is for secure (encrypted) HTTP, via Secure Sockets Layer or SSL. Both WebClient and WebRequest activate SSL transparently upon seeing this prefix (see "SSL" on page 596 under "HTTP-Specific Support" on page 592, later in this chapter). The "file:" protocol simply forwards requests to a FileStream object. Its purpose is in meeting a consistent protocol for reading a URI, whether it be a web page, FTP site, or file path.

WebRequest has a Timeout property, in milliseconds. If a timeout occurs, a WebException is thrown with a Status property of WebExceptionStatus.Timeout. The default timeout is 100 seconds for HTTP and infinite for FTP.

You cannot recycle a WebRequest object for multiple requests—each instance is good for one job only.

Proxies

A *proxy server* is an intermediary through which HTTP and FTP requests can be routed. Organizations sometimes set up a proxy server as the only means by which employees can access the Internet—primarily because it simplifies security. A proxy has an address of its own and can demand authentication so that only selected users on the local area network can access the Internet.

You can instruct a WebClient or WebRequest object to route requests through a proxy server with a WebProxy object:

```
// Create a WebProxy with the proxy's IP address and port. You can
// optionally set Credentials if the proxy needs a username/password.

WebProxy p = new WebProxy ("192.178.10.49", 808);
p.Credentials = new NetworkCredential ("username", "password");
// or:
p.Credentials = new NetworkCredential ("username", "password", "domain");

WebClient wc = new WebClient();
wc.Proxy = p;
  ...

// Same procedure with a WebRequest object:
WebRequest req = WebRequest.Create ("...");
req.Proxy = p;
```

If you supply a domain when constructing the NetworkCredential, Windows-based authentication protocols are used. To use the currently authenticated Windows user, assign the static CredentialCache.DefaultNetworkCredentials value to the proxy's Credentials property.

If you don't have a proxy, you must set the `Proxy` property to `null` on all `WebClient` and `WebRequest` objects. Otherwise, the Framework may attempt to "auto-detect" your proxy settings, adding up to 30 seconds to your request. If you're wondering why your web requests execute slowly, this is probably it!

As an alternative to setting the `Proxy` on every `WebClient` and `WebRequest` object, you can set the global default as follows:

```
WebRequest.DefaultWebProxy = myWebProxy;
```

or:

```
WebRequest.DefaultWebProxy = null;
```

Whatever you set applies for the life of the application domain (unless some other code changes it!).

Authentication

You can supply a username and password to an HTTP or FTP site by creating a `NetworkCredential` object and assigning it to the `Credentials` property of `WebClient` or `WebRequest`:

```
WebClient wc = new WebClient();
wc.Proxy = null;
wc.BaseAddress = "ftp://ftp.albahari.com";

// Authenticate, then upload and download a file to the FTP server.
// The same approach also works for HTTP and HTTPS.

string username = "nutshell";
string password = "oreilly";
wc.Credentials = new NetworkCredential (username, password);

wc.DownloadFile ("guestbook.txt", "guestbook.txt");

string data = "Hello from " + Environment.UserName + "!\r\n";
File.AppendAllText ("guestbook.txt", data);

wc.UploadFile ("guestbook.txt", "guestbook.txt");
```

This works with dialog-based authentication protocols, such as Basic and Digest, and is extensible through the `AuthenticationManager` class. It also supports Windows NTLM and Kerberos (if you include a domain name when constructing the `NetworkCredential` object). If you want to use the currently authenticated Windows user, you can leave the `Credentials` property `null` and instead set `UseDefaultCreden tials true`.

Assigning `Credentials` is useless for getting through forms-based authentication. We discuss forms-based authentication separately, in "HTTP-Specific Support" on page 592.

The authentication is ultimately handled by a `WebRequest` subtype (in this case, `FtpWebRequest`), which automatically negotiates a compatible protocol. In the case of HTTP, there can be a choice: if you examine the initial response from a Microsoft Exchange server web mail page, for instance, it might contain the following headers:

```
HTTP/1.1 401 Unauthorized
Content-Length: 83
Content-Type: text/html
Server: Microsoft-IIS/6.0
WWW-Authenticate: Negotiate
WWW-Authenticate: NTLM
WWW-Authenticate: Basic realm="exchange.somedomain.com"
X-Powered-By: ASP.NET
Date: Sat, 05 Aug 2006 12:37:23 GMT
```

The 401 code signals that authorization is required; the "WWW-Authenticate" headers indicate what authentication protocols are understood. If you configure a `WebClient` or `WebRequest` object with the correct username and password, however, this message will be hidden from you because the Framework responds automatically by choosing a compatible authentication protocol, and then resubmitting the original request with an extra header. For example:

```
Authorization: Negotiate TlRMTVNTUAAABAAAt5II2gjACDArAAACAwACACgAAAAQ
ATmKAAAADOlVDRdPUksHUq9VUA==
```

This mechanism provides transparency, but generates an extra round trip with each request. You can avoid the extra round trips on subsequent requests to the same URI by setting the `PreAuthenticate` property to `true`. This property is defined on the `WebRequest` class (and works only in the case of `HttpWebRequest`). `WebClient` doesn't support this feature at all.

CredentialCache

You can force a particular authentication protocol with a `CredentialCache` object. A credential cache contains one or more `NetworkCredential` objects, each keyed to a particular protocol and URI prefix. For example, you might want to avoid the Basic protocol when logging into an Exchange Server, as it transmits passwords in plain text:

```
CredentialCache cache = new CredentialCache();
Uri prefix = new Uri ("http://exchange.somedomain.com");
cache.Add (prefix, "Digest",  new NetworkCredential ("joe", "passwd"));
cache.Add (prefix, "Negotiate", new NetworkCredential ("joe", "passwd"));

WebClient wc = new WebClient();
wc.Credentials = cache;
...
```

An authentication protocol is specified as a string. The valid values are as follows:

```
Basic, Digest, NTLM, Kerberos, Negotiate
```

In this particular example, `WebClient` will choose Negotiate, because the server didn't indicate that it supported Digest in its authentication headers. Negotiate is a

Windows protocol that boils down to either Kerberos or NTLM, depending on the capabilities of the server.

The static `CredentialCache.DefaultNetworkCredentials` property allows you to add the currently authenticated Windows user to the credential cache without having to specify a password:

```
cache.Add (prefix, "Negotiate", CredentialCache.DefaultNetworkCredentials);
```

Concurrency

Because communicating across a network can be time-consuming, it makes sense to run `WebClient` or `WebRequest` on a parallel execution path. This allows you to do other things at the same time, and also maintain a responsive user interface. There are a number of ways to achieve parallel execution:

- Create a new thread.
- Use the Task Parallel Library's `Task` class.
- Use asynchronous delegates.
- Use `BackgroundWorker`.

We describe each in Chapter 21. Creating a new thread is simplest, although you must deal with exceptions explicitly on the worker thread:

```
using System;
using System.Net;
using System.Threading;

class ThreadTest
{
  static void Main()
  {
    new Thread (Download).Start();
    Console.WriteLine ("I'm still here while the download's happening!");
    Console.ReadLine();
  }

  static void Download()
  {
    WebClient wc = new WebClient();
    try
    {
      wc.Proxy = null;
      wc.DownloadFile ("http://www.oreilly.com", "oreilly.html");
      Console.WriteLine ("Finished!");
    }
    catch (Exception ex)
    {
      // Process exception...
    }
  }
}
```

You can cancel an active WebClient operation from another thread by calling CancelAsync. (This works whether or not you used an "asynchronous" method to initiate the download or upload.) You can cancel a WebRequest in a similar manner, by calling its Abort method from another thread.

 Another way to achieve parallel execution is to call the asynchronous event methods on WebClient (ending in "Asynch"), such as DownloadFileAsynch. In theory, these methods return instantly, allowing the caller to do other things while they run. Unfortunately, these methods are flawed—they block the caller for a portion of the download or upload.

The asynchronous *methods* on WebRequest and WebResponse (starting in "Begin" and "End") should also be avoided if you're simply after parallel execution—these methods serve a subtly different purpose, described in Chapter 23.

When a WebClient or WebRequest is canceled, a WebException is thrown on its thread. The exception has a Status property of WebExceptionStatus.RequestCanceled. You can catch and deal with this exception just as you would any other, such as an invalid domain name.

Exception Handling

WebRequest, WebResponse, WebClient, and their streams all throw a WebException in the case of a network or protocol error. You can determine the specific error via the WebException's Status property; this returns a WebExceptionStatus enum that has the following members:

CacheEntryNotFound	PipelineFailure	SecureChannelFailure
ConnectFailure	ProtocolError	SendFailure
ConnectionClosed	ProxyNameResolutionFailure	ServerProtocolViolation
KeepAliveFailure	ReceiveFailure	Success
MessageLengthLimitExceeded	RequestCanceled	Timeout
NameResolutionFailure	RequestProhibitedByCachePolicy	TrustFailure
Pending	RequestProhibitedByProxy	UnknownError

An invalid domain name causes a NameResolutionFailure; a dead network causes a ConnectFailure; a request exceeding WebRequest.Timeout milliseconds causes a Timeout.

Errors such as "Page not found," "Moved Permanently," and "Not Logged In" are specific to the HTTP or FTP protocols, and so are all lumped together under the ProtocolError status. To get a more specific code:

1. Cast the WebException's Response property to HttpWebResponse or FtpWebResponse.

Networking

2. Examine the response object's Status property (an HttpStatusCode or FtpStatusCode enum) and/or its StatusDescription property (string).

For example:

```
WebClient wc = new WebClient();
try
{
  wc.Proxy = null;
  string s = wc.DownloadString ("http://www.albahari.com/notthere");
}
catch (WebException ex)
{
  if (ex.Status == WebExceptionStatus.NameResolutionFailure)
    Console.WriteLine ("Bad domain name");
  else if (ex.Status == WebExceptionStatus.ProtocolError)
  {
    HttpWebResponse response = (HttpWebResponse) ex.Response;
    Console.WriteLine (response.StatusDescription);      // "Not Found"
    if (response.StatusCode == HttpStatusCode.NotFound)
      Console.WriteLine ("Not there!");                  // "Not there!"
  }
  else throw;
}
```

If you want the three-digit status code, such as 401 or 404, simply cast the HttpStatusCode or FtpStatusCode enum to an integer.

By default, you'll never get a redirection error because WebClient and WebRequest automatically follow redirection responses. You can switch off this behavior in a WebRequest object by setting AllowAutoRedirect to false.

The redirection errors are 301 (Moved Permanently), 302 (Found/Redirect), and 307 (Temporary Redirect).

If an exception is thrown because you've incorrectly used the WebClient or WebRequest classes, it will more likely be an InvalidOperationException or ProtocolViolationException than a WebException.

HTTP-Specific Support

This section describes HTTP-specific request and response features.

Headers

Both WebClient and WebRequest allow you to add custom HTTP headers, as well as enumerate the headers in a response. A header is simply a key/value pair containing metadata, such as the message content type or server software. Here's how to add a custom header to a request, then list all headers in a response message:

```
WebClient wc = new WebClient();
wc.Proxy = null;
wc.Headers.Add ("CustomHeader", "JustPlaying/1.0");
wc.DownloadString ("http://www.oreilly.com");

foreach (string name in wc.ResponseHeaders.Keys)
  Console.WriteLine (name + "=" + wc.ResponseHeaders [name]);
```

Age=51
X-Cache=HIT from oregano.bp
X-Cache-Lookup=HIT from oregano.bp:3128
Connection=keep-alive
Accept-Ranges=bytes
Content-Length=95433
Content-Type=text/html
...

Query Strings

A query string is simply a string appended to a URI with a question mark, used to send simple data to the server. You can specify multiple key/value pairs in a query string with the following syntax:

```
?key1=value1&key2=value2&key3=value3...
```

WebClient provides an easy way to add query strings through a dictionary-style property. The following searches Google for the word "WebClient", displaying the result page in French:

```
WebClient wc = new WebClient();
wc.Proxy = null;
wc.QueryString.Add ("q", "WebClient");    // Search for "WebClient"
wc.QueryString.Add ("hl", "fr");          // Display page in French
wc.DownloadFile ("http://www.google.com/search", "results.html");
System.Diagnostics.Process.Start ("results.html");
```

To achieve the same result with WebRequest, you must manually append a correctly formatted string to the request URI:

```
string requestURI = "http://www.google.com/search?q=WebClient&hl=fr";
```

Uploading Form Data

WebClient provides UploadValues methods for posting data to an HTML form. Here's how to query the Safari website for books containing the term "WebClient":

```
WebClient wc = new WebClient();
wc.Proxy = null;

var data = new System.Collections.Specialized.NameValueCollection();
data.Add ("searchtextbox", "webclient");
data.Add ("searchmode", "simple");

byte[] result = wc.UploadValues ("http://my.safaribooksonline.com/search",
                                 "POST", data);
```

```
System.IO.File.WriteAllBytes ("SearchResults.html", result);
System.Diagnostics.Process.Start ("SearchResults.html");
```

The keys in the NameValueCollection, such as searchtextbox and searchMode, correspond to the names of input boxes on the HTML form.

Uploading form data is more work via WebRequest. (You'll need to take this route if
you need to use features such as cookies.) Here's the procedure:

1. Set the request's ContentType to "application/x-www-form-urlencoded" and its
   Method to "POST".

2. Build a string containing the data to upload, encoded as follows:

   ```
   name1=value1&name2=value2&name3=value3...
   ```

3. Convert the string to a byte array, with Encoding.UTF8.GetBytes.

4. Set the web request's ContentLength property to the byte array length.

5. Call GetRequestStream on the web request and write the data array.

6. Call GetResponse to read the server's response.

Here's the previous example written with WebRequest:

```
WebRequest req = WebRequest.Create ("http://safari.oreilly.com/search");

req.Proxy = null;
req.Method = "POST";
req.ContentType = "application/x-www-form-urlencoded";

string reqString = "searchtextbox=webclient&searchmode=simple";
byte[] reqData = Encoding.UTF8.GetBytes (reqString);
req.ContentLength = reqData.Length;

using (Stream reqStream = req.GetRequestStream())
  reqStream.Write (reqData, 0, reqData.Length);

using (WebResponse res = req.GetResponse())
using (Stream resSteam = res.GetResponseStream())
using (StreamReader sr = new StreamReader (resSteam))
  File.WriteAllText ("SearchResults.html", sr.ReadToEnd());

System.Diagnostics.Process.Start ("SearchResults.html");
```

Cookies

A cookie is a name/value string pair that an HTTP server sends to a client in a
response header. A web browser client typically remembers cookies, and replays
them to the server in each subsequent request (to the same address) until their expiry.
A cookie allows a server to know whether it's talking to the same client it was a
minute ago—or yesterday—without needing a messy query string in the URI.

By default, HttpWebRequest ignores any cookies received from the server. To accept
cookies, create a CookieContainer object and assign it to the WebRequest. The cookies
received in a response can then be enumerated:

```
var cc = new CookieContainer();

var request = (HttpWebRequest) WebRequest.Create ("http://www.google.com");
request.Proxy = null;
request.CookieContainer = cc;
using (var response = (HttpWebResponse) request.GetResponse())
{
  foreach (Cookie c in response.Cookies)
  {
    Console.WriteLine (" Name:   " + c.Name);
    Console.WriteLine (" Value:  " + c.Value);
    Console.WriteLine (" Path:   " + c.Path);
    Console.WriteLine (" Domain: " + c.Domain);
  }
  // Read response stream...
}

Name:    PREF
Value:   ID=6b10df1da493a9c4:TM=1179025486:LM=1179025486:S=EJCZriOaWEHlk4tt
Path:    /
Domain: .google.com
```

 The WebClient façade class does not provide direct support for cookies.

To replay the received cookies in future requests, simply assign the same CookieCon tainer object to each new WebRequest object. (CookieContainer is serializable, so it can be written to disk—see Chapter 16.) Alternatively, you can start with a fresh CookieContainer, and then add cookies manually as follows:

```
Cookie c = new Cookie ("PREF",
                       "ID=6b10df1da493a9c4:TM=1179...",
                       "/",
                       ".google.com");
freshCookieContainer.Add (c);
```

The third and fourth arguments indicate the path and domain of the originator. A CookieContainer on the client can house cookies from many different places; WebRequest sends only those cookies whose path and domain match those of the server.

Forms Authentication

We saw in the previous section how a NetworkCredentials object can satisfy authentication systems such as Basic or NTLM (that pop up a dialog in a web browser). Most websites requiring authentication, however, use some type of forms-based approach. Enter your username and password into text boxes that are part of an HTML form decorated in appropriate corporate graphics, press a button to post the data, and then receive a cookie upon successful authentication. The cookie allows you greater privileges in browsing pages in the website. With WebRequest, you can do all this with the features discussed in the preceding two sections.

A typical website that implements forms authentication will contain HTML like this:

```
<form action="http://www.somesite.com/login" method="post">
  <input type="text" id="user" name="username">
  <input type="password" id="pass" name="password">
  <button type="submit" id="login-btn">Log In</button>
</form>
```

Here's how to log into such a site:

```
string loginUri = "http://www.somesite.com/login";
string username = "username";
string password = "password";
string reqString = "username=" + username + "&password=" + password;
byte[] requestData = Encoding.UTF8.GetBytes (reqString);

CookieContainer cc = new CookieContainer();
var request = (HttpWebRequest)WebRequest.Create (loginUri);
request.Proxy = null;
request.CookieContainer = cc;
request.Method = "POST";

request.ContentType = "application/x-www-form-urlencoded";
request.ContentLength = requestData.Length;
using (Stream s = request.GetRequestStream())
  s.Write (requestData, 0, requestData.Length);

using (var response = (HttpWebResponse) request.GetResponse())
  foreach (Cookie c in response.Cookies)
    Console.WriteLine (c.Name + " = " + c.Value);

// We're now logged in. As long as we assign cc to subsequent WebRequest
// objects, we'll be treated as an authenticated user.
```

SSL

Both WebClient and WebRequest use SSL automatically when you specify an "https:" prefix. The only complication that can arise relates to bad X.509 certificates. If the server's site certificate is invalid in any way (for instance, if it's a test certificate), an exception is thrown when you attempt to communicate. To work around this, you can attach a custom certificate validator to the static ServicePointManager class:

```
using System.Net;
using System.Net.Security;
using System.Security.Cryptography.X509Certificates;
...
static void ConfigureSSL()
{
  ServicePointManager.ServerCertificateValidationCallback = CertChecker;
}
```

ServerCertificateValidationCallback is a delegate. If it returns true, the certificate is accepted:

```
static bool CertChecker (object sender, X509Certificate certificate,
                         X509Chain chain, SslPolicyErrors errors)
{
  // Return true if you're happy with the certificate
  ...
}
```

Writing an HTTP Server

You can write your own HTTP server with the HttpListener class. The following is
a simple server that listens on port 51111, waits for a single client request, and then
returns a one-line reply.

 HttpListener does not work on operating systems prior to Windows XP.

```
static void Main()
{
  new System.Threading.Thread (Listen).Start();  // Run server in parallel.
  Thread.Sleep (500);                            // Wait half a second.

  WebClient wc = new WebClient();                // Make a client request.
  Console.WriteLine (wc.DownloadString
    ("http://localhost:51111/MyApp/Request.txt"));
}

static void Listen()
{
  HttpListener listener = new HttpListener();
  listener.Prefixes.Add ("http://localhost:51111/MyApp/");  // Listen on
  listener.Start();                                         // port 51111.

  // Wait for a client request:
  HttpListenerContext context = listener.GetContext();

  // Respond to the request:
  string msg = "You asked for: " + context.Request.RawUrl;
  context.Response.ContentLength64 = Encoding.UTF8.GetByteCount (msg);
  context.Response.StatusCode = (int) HttpStatusCode.OK;

  using (Stream s = context.Response.OutputStream)
  using (StreamWriter writer = new StreamWriter (s))
    writer.Write (msg);

  listener.Stop();
}

OUTPUT: You asked for: /MyApp/Request.txt
```

In this example, we sleep for 500 ms to give the server time to start before connecting to it. A better solution would be for the server to signal that it's ready with an `EventWaitHandle` (described in Chapter 21). An example of when you might consider doing this in real life is if writing a unit testing framework for your HTTP server.

`HttpListener` does not internally use .NET `Socket` objects; it instead calls the Windows HTTP Server API. This is supported on Windows XP and above and allows many applications on a computer to listen on the same IP address and port—as long as each registers different address prefixes. In our example, we registered the prefix *http://localhost/myapp*, so another application would be free to listen on the same IP and port on another prefix such as *http://localhost/anotherapp*. This is of value because opening new ports on corporate firewalls can be politically arduous.

`HttpListener` waits for the next client request when you call `GetContext`, returning an object with `Request` and `Response` properties. Each is analogous to a `WebRequest` and `WebResponse` object, but from the server's perspective. You can read and write headers and cookies, for instance, to the request and response objects, much as you would at the client end.

You can choose how fully to support features of the HTTP protocol, based on your anticipated client audience. At a bare minimum, you should set the content length and status code on each request.

Here's a very simple web page server that handles up to 50 concurrent requests:

```csharp
using System;
using System.IO;
using System.Net;
using System.Text;
using System.Threading;

class WebServer
{
  HttpListener _listener;
  string _baseFolder;      // Your web page folder.

  public WebServer (string uriPrefix, string baseFolder)
  {
    System.Threading.ThreadPool.SetMaxThreads (50, 1000);
    System.Threading.ThreadPool.SetMinThreads (50, 50);
    _listener = new HttpListener();
    _listener.Prefixes.Add (uriPrefix);
    _baseFolder = baseFolder;
  }

  public void Start()             // Run this on a separate thread, as
  {                               // we did before.
    _listener.Start();
    while (true)
      try
      {
```

```
      HttpListenerContext request = _listener.GetContext();
      ThreadPool.QueueUserWorkItem (ProcessRequest, request);
    }
    catch (HttpListenerException)    { break; }   // Listener stopped.
    catch (InvalidOperationException) { break; }   // Listener stopped.
  }

  public void Stop() { _listener.Stop(); }

  void ProcessRequest (object listenerContext)
  {
    try
    {
      var context = (HttpListenerContext) listenerContext;
      string filename = Path.GetFileName (context.Request.RawUrl);
      string path = Path.Combine (_baseFolder, filename);
      byte[] msg;
      if (!File.Exists (path))
      {
        context.Response.StatusCode = (int) HttpStatusCode.NotFound;
        msg = Encoding.UTF8.GetBytes ("Sorry, that page does not exist");
      }
      else
      {
        context.Response.StatusCode = (int) HttpStatusCode.OK;
        msg = File.ReadAllBytes (path);
      }
      context.Response.ContentLength64 = msg.Length;
      using (Stream s = context.Response.OutputStream)
        s.Write (msg, 0, msg.Length);
    }
    catch (Exception ex) { Console.WriteLine ("Request error: " + ex); }
  }
}
```

Here's a main method to set things in motion:

```
static void Main()
{
  // Listen on the default port (80), serving files in e:\mydocs\webroot:
  var server = new WebServer ("http://localhost/", @"e:\mydocs\webroot");

  // Start the server on a parallel thread:
  new System.Threading.Thread (server.Start).Start();

  Console.WriteLine ("Server running... press Enter to stop");
  Console.ReadLine();
  server.Stop();
}
```

You can test this at the client end with any web browser; the URI in this case will be *http://localhost/* plus the name of the web page.

Calling SetMinThreads instructs the thread pool not to delay the allocation of threads in an attempt to save memory. This results in a responsive and performant server, up to its limit of 50 requests. If you want to go higher, you can—much higher, and without needing more threads—by following the asynchronous method pattern. This means calling `BeginRead` and `BeginWrite` on the request and response streams, each time exiting with a callback (bringing the investment in programming time almost on par with configuring IIS!). We describe this in detail in Chapter 23.

 `HttpListener` will not start if other software is competing for the same port (unless that software also uses the Windows HTTP Server API). Examples of applications that might listen on port 80 include a web server or a peer-to-peer program such as Skype.

Using FTP

For simple FTP upload and download operations, you can use `WebClient` as we did previously:

```
WebClient wc = new WebClient();
wc.Proxy = null;
wc.Credentials = new NetworkCredential ("nutshell", "oreilly");
wc.BaseAddress = "ftp://ftp.albahari.com";
wc.UploadString ("tempfile.txt", "hello!");
Console.WriteLine (wc.DownloadString ("tempfile.txt"));    // hello!
```

There's more to FTP, however, than just uploading and downloading files. The protocol also lists a set of commands or "methods," defined as string constants in `WebRequestMethods.Ftp`:

AppendFile	ListDirectory	Rename
DeleteFile	ListDirectoryDetails	UploadFile
DownloadFile	MakeDirectory	UploadFileWithUniqueName
GetDateTimestamp	PrintWorkingDirectory	
GetFileSize	RemoveDirectory	

To run one of these commands, you assign its string constant to the web request's `Method` property, and then call `GetResponse()`. Here's how to get a directory listing:

```
var req = (FtpWebRequest) WebRequest.Create ("ftp://ftp.albahari.com");
req.Proxy = null;
req.Credentials = new NetworkCredential ("nutshell", "oreilly");
req.Method = WebRequestMethods.Ftp.ListDirectory;

using (WebResponse resp = req.GetResponse())
using (StreamReader reader = new StreamReader (resp.GetResponseStream()))
  Console.WriteLine (reader.ReadToEnd());

RESULT:
.
..
guestbook.txt
tempfile.txt
test.doc
```

In the case of getting a directory listing, we needed to read the response stream to get the result. Most other commands, however, don't require this step. For instance, to get the result of the `GetFileSize` command, just query the response's `ContentLength` property:

```
var req = (FtpWebRequest) WebRequest.Create (
                          "ftp://ftp.albahari.com/tempfile.txt");
req.Proxy = null;
req.Credentials = new NetworkCredential ("nutshell", "oreilly");

req.Method = WebRequestMethods.Ftp.GetFileSize;

using (WebResponse resp = req.GetResponse())
   Console.WriteLine (resp.ContentLength);           // 6
```

The `GetDateTimestamp` command works in a similar way, except that you query the response's `LastModified` property. This requires that you cast to `FtpWebResponse`:

```
...
req.Method = WebRequestMethods.Ftp.GetDateTimestamp;

using (var resp = (FtpWebResponse) req.GetResponse() )
   Console.WriteLine (resp.LastModified);
```

To use the `Rename` command, you must populate the request's `RenameTo` property with the new filename (without a directory prefix). For example, to rename a file in the *incoming* directory from *tempfile.txt* to *deleteme.txt*:

```
var req = (FtpWebRequest) WebRequest.Create (
                          "ftp://ftp.albahari.com/tempfile.txt");
req.Proxy = null;
req.Credentials = new NetworkCredential ("nutshell", "oreilly");

req.Method = WebRequestMethods.Ftp.Rename;
req.RenameTo = "deleteme.txt";

req.GetResponse().Close();           // Perform the rename
```

Here's how to delete a file:

```
var req = (FtpWebRequest) WebRequest.Create (
                          "ftp://ftp.albahari.com/deleteme.txt");
req.Proxy = null;
req.Credentials = new NetworkCredential ("nutshell", "oreilly");

req.Method = WebRequestMethods.Ftp.DeleteFile;

req.GetResponse().Close();           // Perform the deletion
```

In all these examples, you would typically use an exception handling block to catch network and protocol errors. A typical catch block looks like this:

```
catch (WebException ex)
{
    if (ex.Status == WebExceptionStatus.ProtocolError)
    {
        // Obtain more detail on error:
        var response = (FtpWebResponse) ex.Response;
        FtpStatusCode errorCode = response.StatusCode;
        string errorMessage = response.StatusDescription;
        ...
    }
    ...
}
```

Using DNS

The static `Dns` class encapsulates the Domain Name Service, which converts between a raw IP address, such as 66.135.192.87, and a human-friendly domain name, such as *ebay.com*.

The `GetHostAddresses` method converts from domain name to IP address (or addresses):

```
foreach (IPAddress a in Dns.GetHostAddresses ("albahari.com"))
    Console.WriteLine (a.ToString());      // 208.43.7.176
```

The `GetHostEntry` method goes the other way around, converting from address to domain name:

```
IPHostEntry entry = Dns.GetHostEntry ("208.43.7.176");
Console.WriteLine (entry.HostName);                    // si-eios.com
```

`GetHostEntry` also accepts an `IPAddress` object, so you can specify an IP address as a byte array:

```
IPAddress address = new IPAddress (new byte[] { 208, 43, 7, 176 });
IPHostEntry entry = Dns.GetHostEntry (address);
Console.WriteLine (entry.HostName);                    // si-eios.com
```

Domain names are automatically resolved to IP addresses when you use a class such as `WebRequest` or `TcpClient`. If you plan to make many network requests to the same address over the life of an application, however, you can sometimes improve performance by first using `Dns` to explicitly convert the domain name into an IP address, and then communicating directly with the IP address from that point on. This avoids repeated round-tripping to resolve the same domain name, and it can be of benefit when dealing at the transport layer (via `TcpClient`, `UdpClient`, or `Socket`).

The DNS class also provides asynchronous methods for high-concurrency applications (see Chapter 23).

Sending Mail with SmtpClient

The `SmtpClient` class in the `System.Net.Mail` namespace allows you to send mail messages through the ubiquitous Simple Mail Transfer Protocol. To send a simple text message, instantiate `SmtpClient`, set its `Host` property to your SMTP server address, and then call `Send`:

```
SmtpClient client = new SmtpClient();
client.Host = "mail.myisp.net";
client.Send ("from@adomain.com", "to@adomain.com", "subject", "body");
```

To frustrate spammers, most SMTP servers on the Internet will accept connections only from the ISP's subscribers, so you need the SMTP address appropriate to the current connection for this to work.

Constructing a `MailMessage` object exposes further options, including the ability to add attachments:

```
SmtpClient client = new SmtpClient();
client.Host = "mail.myisp.net";
MailMessage mm = new MailMessage();

mm.Sender = new MailAddress ("kay@domain.com", "Kay");
mm.From   = new MailAddress ("kay@domain.com", "Kay");
mm.To.Add (new MailAddress ("bob@domain.com", "Bob"));
mm.CC.Add (new MailAddress ("dan@domain.com", "Dan"));
mm.Subject = "Hello!";
mm.Body = "Hi there. Here's the photo!";
mm.IsBodyHtml = false;
mm.Priority = MailPriority.High;

Attachment a = new Attachment ("photo.jpg",
                        System.Net.Mime.MediaTypeNames.Image.Jpeg);
mm.Attachments.Add (a);
client.Send (mm);
```

`SmtpClient` allows you to specify `Credentials` for servers requiring authentication, `EnableSsl` if supported, and change the TCP `Port` to a nondefault value. By changing the `DeliveryMethod` property, you can instruct the `SmtpClient` to instead use IIS to send mail messages or simply to write each message to an *.eml* file in a specified directory:

```
SmtpClient client = new SmtpClient();
client.DeliveryMethod = SmtpDeliveryMethod.SpecifiedPickupDirectory;
client.PickupDirectoryLocation = @"c:\mail";
```

Using TCP

TCP and UDP constitute the transport layer protocols on top of which most Internet—and local area network—services are built. HTTP, FTP, and SMTP use TCP; DNS uses UDP. TCP is connection-oriented and includes reliability mechanisms; UDP is connectionless, has a lower overhead, and supports broadcasting. *BitTorrent* uses UDP, as does Voice over IP.

The transport layer offers greater flexibility—and potentially improved performance—over the higher layers, but it requires that you handle such tasks as authentication and encryption yourself.

 The good news with the TCP and UDP classes is that you don't have to worry about setting Proxy to null. The bad news is that if your only access to the Internet is through a web proxy, you can forget about working directly at the TCP or UDP layer!

With TCP, you have a choice of either the easier-to-use `TcpClient` and `TcpListener` façade classes, or the feature-rich `Socket` class. (In fact, you can mix and match, because `TcpClient` exposes the underlying `Socket` object through the `Client` property.) The `Socket` class exposes more configuration options and allows direct access to the network layer (IP) and non-Internet-based protocols such as Novell's SPX/IPX.

As with other protocols, TCP differentiates a client and server: the client initiates a request, while the server waits for a request. Here's the basic structure for a TCP client request:

```
using (TcpClient client = new TcpClient ("address", port))
using (NetworkStream n = client.GetStream())
{
  // Read and write to the network stream...
}
```

`TcpClient` immediately establishes a connection upon construction to a server at the given IP or domain name address and port. The constructor blocks until a connection is established. The `NetworkStream` then provides a means of two-way communication, for both transmitting and receiving bytes of data from a server.

A simple TCP server looks like this:

```
TcpListener listener = new TcpListener (<ip address>, port);
listener.Start();

while (keepProcessingRequests)
  using (TcpClient c = listener.AcceptTcpClient())
  using (NetworkStream n = c.GetStream())
  {
    // Read and write to the network stream...
  }

listener.Stop();
```

`TcpListener` requires the local IP address on which to listen (a computer with two network cards, for instance, may have two addresses). You can use `IPAddress.Any` to tell it to listen on all (or the only) local IP addresses. `AcceptTcpClient` blocks until a client request is received, at which point we call `GetStream`, just as on the client side.

When working at the transport layer, you need to decide on a protocol for who talks when, and for how long—rather like with a walkie-talkie. If both parties talk or listen at the same time, communication breaks down!

Let's invent a protocol where the client speaks first, saying "Hello," and then the server responds by saying "Hello right back!" Here's the code:

```
using System;
using System.IO;
using System.Net;
using System.Net.Sockets;
using System.Threading;

class TcpDemo
{
  static void Main()
  {
    new Thread (Server).Start();    // Run server method concurrently.
    Thread.Sleep (500);             // Give server time to start.
    Client();
  }

  static void Client()
  {
    using (TcpClient client = new TcpClient ("localhost", 51111))
    using (NetworkStream n = client.GetStream())
    {
      BinaryWriter w = new BinaryWriter (n);
      w.Write ("Hello");
      w.Flush();
      Console.WriteLine (new BinaryReader (n).ReadString());
    }
  }

  static void Server()     // Handles a single client request, then exits.
  {
    TcpListener listener = new TcpListener (IPAddress.Any, 51111);
    listener.Start();
    using (TcpClient c = listener.AcceptTcpClient())
    using (NetworkStream n = c.GetStream())
    {
      string msg = new BinaryReader (n).ReadString();
      BinaryWriter w = new BinaryWriter (n);
      w.Write (msg + " right back!");
      w.Flush();                       // Must call Flush because we're not
    }                                  // disposing the writer.
    listener.Stop();
  }
}
```

```
Hello
Hello right back!
```

In this example, we're using the localhost loopback to run the client and server on the same machine. We've arbitrarily chosen a port in the unallocated range (above 49152) and used a BinaryWriter and BinaryReader to encode the text messages. We've avoided closing or disposing the readers and writers in order to keep the underlying NetworkStream open until our conversation completes.

BinaryReader and BinaryWriter might seem like odd choices for reading and writing strings. However, they have a major advantage over StreamReader and Stream Writer: they prefix strings with an integer indicating the length, so a BinaryReader always knows exactly how many bytes to read. If you call StreamReader.ReadToEnd you might block indefinitely—because a NetworkStream doesn't have an end! As long as the connection is open, the network stream can never be sure that the client isn't going to send more data.

> StreamReader is in fact completely out of bounds with NetworkStream, even if you plan only to call ReadLine. This is because StreamReader has a read-ahead buffer, which can result in it reading more bytes than are currently available, blocking indefinitely (or until the socket times out). Other streams such as FileStream don't suffer this incompatibility with StreamReader because they have a definite *end*—at which point Read returns immediately with a value of 0.

Concurrency

You'll often want to do other things at the same time as reading or writing a TCP stream. If you need to manage just a few concurrent activities, any multithreading option described in Chapters 21 and 22 is viable: a new thread, a TPL Task, asynchronous delegates, ThreadPool.QueueUserWorkItem or BackgroundWorker. On a highly concurrent server, however, you need to be choosier. As a simple rule of thumb:

- For less than 50 concurrent connections, think *simplicity* and use the Task Parallel Library or ThreadPool.QueueUserWorkItem.
- For more than 50 concurrent connections, think *efficiency* and go for asynchronous methods.

Chapter 23 describes how to write a TCP server using each of these models.

Receiving POP3 Mail with TCP

The .NET Framework provides no application-layer support for POP3, so you have to write at the TCP layer in order to receive mail from a POP3 server. Fortunately, this is a simple protocol; a POP3 conversation goes like this:

Client	Mail server	Notes
Client connects...	`+OK Hello there.`	Welcome message
`USER joe`	`+OK Password required.`	
`PASS password`	`+OK Logged in.`	
`LIST`	`+OK`	Lists the ID and file size of each message on the server
	`1 1876`	
	`2 5412`	
	`3 845`	
	.	
`RETR 1`	`+OK 1876 octets`	Retrieves the message with the specified ID
	Content of message #1...	
	.	
`DELE 1`	`+OK Deleted.`	Deletes a message from the server
`QUIT`	`+OK Bye-bye.`	

Each command and response is terminated by a new line (CR + LF) except for the multiline LIST and RETR commands, which are terminated by a single dot on a separate line. Because we can't use `StreamReader` with `NetworkStream`, we can start by writing a helper method to read a line of text in a nonbuffered fashion:

```
static string ReadLine (Stream s)
{
  List<byte> lineBuffer = new List<byte>();
  while (true)
  {
    int b = s.ReadByte();
    if (b == 10 || b < 0) break;
    if (b != 13) lineBuffer.Add ((byte)b);
  }
  return Encoding.UTF8.GetString (lineBuffer.ToArray());
}
```

We also need a helper method to send a command. Because we always expect to receive a response starting with "+OK," we can read and validate the response at the same time:

```
static void SendCommand (Stream stream, string line)
{
  byte[] data = Encoding.UTF8.GetBytes (line + "\r\n");
  stream.Write (data, 0, data.Length);
  string response = ReadLine (stream);
  if (!response.StartsWith ("+OK"))
    throw new Exception ("POP Error: " + response);
}
```

With these methods written, the job of retrieving mail is easy. We establish a TCP connection on port 110 (the default POP3 port), and then start talking to the server.

In this example, we write each mail message to a randomly named file with an *.eml* extension, before deleting the message off the server:

```
using (TcpClient client = new TcpClient ("mail.isp.com", 110))
using (NetworkStream n = client.GetStream())
{
  ReadLine (n);                              // Read the welcome message.
  SendCommand (n, "USER username");
  SendCommand (n, "PASS password");
  SendCommand (n, "LIST");                   // Retrieve message IDs
  List<int> messageIDs = new List<int>();
  while (true)
  {
    string line = ReadLine (n);              // e.g., "1 1876"
    if (line == ".") break;
    messageIDs.Add (int.Parse (line.Split (' ')[0] ));   // Message ID
  }

  foreach (int id in messageIDs)             // Retrieve each message.
  {
    SendCommand (n, "RETR " + id);
    string randomFile = Guid.NewGuid().ToString() + ".eml";
    using (StreamWriter writer = File.CreateText (randomFile))
      while (true)
      {
        string line = ReadLine (n);          // Read next line of message.
        if (line == ".") break;              // Single dot = end of message.
        if (line == "..") line = ".";        // "Escape out" double dot.
        writer.WriteLine (line);             // Write to output file.
      }
    SendCommand (n, "DELE " + id);           // Delete message off server.
  }
  SendCommand (n, "QUIT");
}
```

16

Serialization

This chapter introduces serialization and deserialization, the mechanism by which objects can be represented in a flat text or binary form. Unless otherwise stated, the types in this chapter all exist in the following namespaces:

```
System.Runtime.Serialization
System.Xml.Serialization
```

Serialization Concepts

Serialization is the act of taking an in-memory object or *object graph* (set of objects that reference each other) and flattening it into a stream of bytes or XML nodes that can be stored or transmitted. *Deserialization* works in reverse, taking a data stream and reconstituting it into an in-memory object or object graph.

Serialization and deserialization are typically used to:

- Transmit objects across a network or application boundary.
- Store representations of objects within a file or database.

Another, less common use is to deep-clone objects. The data contract and XML serialization engines can also be used as general-purpose tools for loading and saving XML files of a known structure.

The .NET Framework supports serialization and deserialization both from the perspective of clients wanting to serialize and deserialize objects, and from the perspective of types wanting some control over how they are serialized.

Serialization Engines

There are four serialization mechanisms in the .NET Framework:

- The data contract serializer
- The binary serializer
- The (attribute-based) XML serializer (`XmlSerializer`)
- The `IXmlSerializable` interface

Of these, the first three are serialization "engines" that do most or all of the serialization work for you. The last is just a hook for doing the serialization yourself, using `XmlReader` and `XmlWriter`. `IXmlSerializable` can work in conjunction with the data contract serializer or `XmlSerializer`, to handle the more complicated XML serialization tasks.

Table 16-1 compares each of the engines.

Table 16-1. Serialization engine comparison

Feature	Data contract serializer	Binary serializer	XmlSerializer	IXmlSerializable
Level of automation	***	*****	****	*
Type coupling	Choice	Tight	Loose	Loose
Version tolerance	*****	***	*****	*****
Preserves object references	Choice	Yes	No	Choice
Can serialize nonpublic fields	Yes	Yes	No	Yes
Suitability for interoperable messaging	*****	**	****	****
Flexibility in reading/writing XML files	**	-	****	*****
Compact output	**	****	**	**
Performance	***	****	* to ***	***

The scores for `IXmlSerializable` assume you've (hand) coded optimally using `XmlReader` and `XmlWriter`. The XML serialization engine requires that you recycle the same `XmlSerializer` object for good performance.

Why three engines?

The reason for three engines is partly historical. The Framework started out with two distinct goals in serialization:

- Serializing .NET object graphs with type and reference fidelity
- Interoperating with XML and SOAP messaging standards

The first was led by the requirements of Remoting; the second, by Web Services. The job of writing one serialization engine to do both was too daunting, so Microsoft wrote two engines: the binary serializer and the XML serializer.

When Windows Communication Foundation (WCF) was later written, as part of Framework 3.0, part of the goal was to unify Remoting and Web Services. This required a new serialization engine—hence, the *data contract serializer*. The data contract serializer unifies the features of the older two engines *relevant to (interoperable) messaging*. Outside of this context, however, the two older engines are still important.

The data contract serializer

The data contract serializer is the newest and the most versatile of the three serialization engines and is used by WCF. The serializer is particularly strong in two scenarios:

- When exchanging information through standards-compliant messaging protocols
- When you need good version tolerance, plus the option of preserving object references

The data contract serializer supports a *data contract* model that helps you decouple the low-level details of the types you want to serialize from the structure of the serialized data. This provides excellent version tolerance, meaning you can deserialize data that was serialized from an earlier or later version of a type. You can even deserialize types that have been renamed or moved to a different assembly.

The data contract serializer can cope with most object graphs, although it can require more assistance than the binary serializer. It can also be used as a general-purpose tool for reading/writing XML files, if you're flexible on how the XML is structured. (If you need to store data in attributes or cope with XML elements presenting in a random order, you cannot use the data contract serializer.)

The binary serializer

The binary serialization engine is easy to use, highly automatic, and well supported throughout the .NET Framework. Remoting uses binary serialization—including when communicating between two application domains in the same process (see Chapter 24).

The binary serializer is highly automated: quite often, a single attribute is all that's required to make a complex type fully serializable. The binary serializer is also faster than the data contract serializer when full type fidelity is needed. However, it tightly couples a type's internal structure to the format of the serialized data, resulting in poor version tolerance. (Prior to Framework 2.0, even adding a simple field was a version-breaking change.) The binary engine is also not really designed to produce XML, although it offers a formatter for SOAP-based messaging that provides limited interoperability with simple types.

XmlSerializer

The XML serialization engine can *only* produce XML, and it is less powerful than other engines in saving and restoring a complex object graph (it cannot restore shared object references). It's the most flexible of the three, however, in following an arbitrary XML structure. For instance, you can choose whether properties are serialized to elements or attributes and the handling of a collection's outer element. The XML engine also provides excellent version tolerance.

XmlSerializer is used by ASMX Web Services.

IXmlSerializable

Implementing IXmlSerializable means to do the serialization yourself with an XmlReader and XmlWriter. The IXmlSerializable interface is recognized both by XmlSerializer and by the data contract serializer, so it can be used selectively to handle the more complicated types. (It also can be used directly by WCF and ASMX Web Services.) We describe XmlReader and XmlWriter in detail in Chapter 11.

Formatters

The output of the data contract and binary serializers is shaped by a pluggable *formatter*. The role of a formatter is the same with both serialization engines, although they use completely different classes to do the job.

A formatter shapes the final presentation to suit a particular medium or context of serialization. In general, you can choose between XML and binary formatters. An XML formatter is designed to work within the context of an XML reader/writer, text file/stream, or SOAP messaging packet. A binary formatter is designed to work in a context where an arbitrary stream of bytes will do—typically a file/stream or proprietary messaging packet. Binary output is usually smaller than XML—sometimes radically so.

 The term "binary" in the context of a formatter is unrelated to the "binary" serialization engine. Each of the two engines ships with both XML and binary formatters!

In theory, the engines are decoupled from their formatters. In practice, the design of each engine is geared toward one kind of formatter. The data contract serializer is geared toward the interoperability requirements of XML messaging. This is good for the XML formatter but means its binary formatter doesn't always achieve the gains you might hope. In contrast, the binary engine provides a relatively good binary formatter, but its XML formatter is highly limited, offering only crude SOAP interoperability.

Explicit Versus Implicit Serialization

Serialization and deserialization can be initiated in two ways.

The first is *explicitly*, by requesting that a particular object be serialized or deserialized. When you serialize or deserialize explicitly, you choose both the serialization engine and the formatter.

In contrast, *implicit* serialization is initiated by the Framework. This happens when:

- A serializer recurses a child object.
- You use a feature that relies on serialization, such as WCF, Remoting, or Web Services.

WCF always uses the data contract serializer, although it can interoperate with the attributes and interfaces of the other engines.

Remoting always uses the binary serialization engine.

Web Services always uses XmlSerializer.

The Data Contract Serializer

Here are the basic steps in using the data contract serializer:

1. Decide whether to use the DataContractSerializer or the NetDataContract-Serializer.
2. Decorate the types and members you want to serialize with [DataContract] and [DataMember] attributes, respectively.
3. Instantiate the serializer and call WriteObject or ReadObject.

If you chose the DataContractSerializer, you will also need to register "known types" (subtypes that can also be serialized), and decide whether to preserve object references.

You may also need to take special action to ensure that collections are properly serialized.

 Types for the data contract serializer are defined in the System.Runtime.Serialization namespace, in an assembly of the same name.

DataContractSerializer Versus NetDataContractSerializer

There are two data contract serializers:

DataContractSerializer
: Loosely couples .NET types to data contract types

NetDataContractSerializer
: Tightly couples .NET types to data contract types

The DataContractSerializer can produce interoperable standards-compliant XML such as this:

```
<Person xmlns="...">
  ...
</Person>
```

It requires, however, that you explicitly register serializable subtypes in advance so that it can map a data contract name such as "Person" to the correct .NET type. The `NetDataContractSerializer` requires no such assistance, because it writes the full type and assembly names of the types it serializes, rather like the binary serialization engine:

```
<Person z:Type="SerialTest.Person" z:Assembly=
  "SerialTest, Version=1.0.0.0, Culture=neutral, PublicKeyToken=null">
  ...
</Person>
```

Such output, however, is proprietary. It also relies on the presence of a specific .NET type in a specific namespace and assembly in order to deserialize.

If you're saving an object graph to a "black box," you can choose either serializer, depending on what benefits are more important to you. If you're communicating through WCF, or reading/writing an XML file, you'll most likely want the `DataContractSerializer`.

Another difference between the two serializers is that `NetDataContractSerializer` always preserves referential equality; `DataContractSerializer` does so only upon request.

We'll go into each of these topics in more detail in the following sections.

Using the Serializers

After choosing a serializer, the next step is to attach attributes to the types and members you want to serialize. At a minimum:

- Add the [`DataContract`] attribute to each type.
- Add the [`DataMember`] attribute to each member that you want to include.

Here's an example:

```
namespace SerialTest
{
  [DataContract] public class Person
  {
    [DataMember] public string Name;
    [DataMember] public int Age;
  }
}
```

These attributes are enough to make a type *implicitly* serializable through the data contract engine.

You can then *explicitly* serialize or deserialize an object instance by instantiating a `DataContractSerializer` or `NetDataContractSerializer` and calling `WriteObject` or `ReadObject`:

```
Person p = new Person { Name = "Stacey", Age = 30 };

var ds = new DataContractSerializer (typeof (Person));
```

```
using (Stream s = File.Create ("person.xml"))
  ds.WriteObject (s, p);                              // Serialize

Person p2;
using (Stream s = File.OpenRead ("person.xml"))
  p2 = (Person) ds.ReadObject (s);                    // Deserialize

Console.WriteLine (p2.Name + " " + p2.Age);           // Stacey 30
```

`DataContractSerializer`'s constructor requires the *root object* type (the type of the object you're explicitly serializing). In contrast, `NetDataContractSerializer` does not:

```
var ns = new NetDataContractSerializer();

// NetDataContractSerializer is otherwise the same to use
// as DataContractSerializer.
...
```

Both types of serializer use the XML formatter by default. With an `XmlWriter`, you can request that the output be indented for readability:

```
Person p = new Person { Name = "Stacey", Age = 30 };
var ds = new DataContractSerializer (typeof (Person));

XmlWriterSettings settings = new XmlWriterSettings() { Indent = true };
using (XmlWriter w = XmlWriter.Create ("person.xml", settings))
  ds.WriteObject (w, p);

System.Diagnostics.Process.Start ("person.xml");
```

Here's the result:

```
<Person xmlns="http://schemas.datacontract.org/2004/07/SerialTest"
        xmlns:i="http://www.w3.org/2001/XMLSchema-instance">
  <Age>30</Age>
  <Name>Stacey</Name>
</Person>
```

The XML element name `<Person>` reflects the *data contract name*, which, by default, is the .NET type name. You can override this and explicitly state a data contract name as follows:

```
[DataContract (Name="Candidate")]
public class Person { ... }
```

The XML namespace reflects the *data contract namespace*, which, by default, is *http://schemas.datacontract.org/2004/07/*, plus the .NET type namespace. You can override this in a similar fashion:

```
[DataContract (Namespace="http://oreilly.com/nutshell")]
public class Person { ... }
```

Specifying a name and namespace decouples the contract identity from the .NET type name. It ensures that, should you later refactor and change the type's name or namespace, serialization is unaffected.

You can also override names for data members:

```
[DataContract (Name="Candidate", Namespace="http://oreilly.com/nutshell")]
public class Person
{
  [DataMember (Name="FirstName")]  public string Name;
  [DataMember (Name="ClaimedAge")] public int Age;
}
```

Here's the output:

```
<?xml version="1.0" encoding="utf-8"?>
<Candidate xmlns="http://oreilly.com/nutshell"
           xmlns:i="http://www.w3.org/2001/XMLSchema-instance" >
  <ClaimedAge>30</ClaimedAge>
  <FirstName>Stacey</FirstName>
</Candidate>
```

[DataMember] supports both fields and properties—public and private. The field or property's data type can be any of the following:

- Any primitive type
- DateTime, TimeSpan, Guid, Uri, or an Enum value
- Nullable versions of the above
- byte[] (serializes in XML to base 64)
- Any "known" type decorated with DataContract
- Any IEnumerable type (see the section "Serializing Collections" on page 642, later in this chapter)
- Any type with the [Serializable] attribute or implementing ISerializable (see the section "Extending Data Contracts" on page 625 later in this chapter)
- Any type implementing IXmlSerializable

Specifying a binary formatter

You can use a binary formatter with DataContractSerializer or NetDataContract Serializer. The process is the same:

```
Person p = new Person { Name = "Stacey", Age = 30 };
var ds = new DataContractSerializer (typeof (Person));

var s = new MemoryStream();
using (XmlDictionaryWriter w = XmlDictionaryWriter.CreateBinaryWriter (s))
  ds.WriteObject (w, p);

var s2 = new MemoryStream (s.ToArray());
Person p2;
```

```
using (XmlDictionaryReader r = XmlDictionaryReader.CreateBinaryReader (s2,
                                    XmlDictionaryReaderQuotas.Max))
  p2 = (Person) ds.ReadObject (r);
```

The output varies between being slightly smaller than that of the XML formatter, and radically smaller if your types contain large arrays.

Serializing Subclasses

You don't need to do anything special to handle the serializing of subclasses with the NetDataContractSerializer. The only requirement is that subclasses have the DataContract attribute. The serializer will write the fully qualified names of the actual types that it serializes as follows:

```
<Person ... z:Type="SerialTest.Person" z:Assembly=
  "SerialTest, Version=1.0.0.0, Culture=neutral, PublicKeyToken=null">
```

A DataContractSerializer, however, must be informed about all subtypes that it may have to serialize or deserialize. To illustrate, suppose we subclass Person as follows:

```
[DataContract] public class Person
{
  [DataMember] public string Name;
  [DataMember] public int Age;
}
[DataContract] public class Student : Person { }
[DataContract] public class Teacher : Person { }
```

and then write a method to clone a Person:

```
static Person DeepClone (Person p)
{
  var ds = new DataContractSerializer (typeof (Person));
  MemoryStream stream = new MemoryStream();
  ds.WriteObject (stream, p);
  stream.Position = 0;
  return (Person) ds.ReadObject (stream);
}
```

which we call as follows:

```
Person person  = new Person  { Name = "Stacey", Age = 30 };
Student student = new Student { Name = "Stacey", Age = 30 };
Teacher teacher = new Teacher { Name = "Stacey", Age = 30 };

Person p2 =           DeepClone (person);   // OK
Student s2 = (Student) DeepClone (student);  // SerializationException
Teacher t2 = (Teacher) DeepClone (teacher);  // SerializationException
```

DeepClone works if called with a Person but throws an exception with a Student or Teacher, because the deserializer has no way of knowing what .NET type (or assembly) a "Student" or "Teacher" should resolve to. This also helps with security, in that it prevents the deserialization of unexpected types.

The solution is to specify all permitted or "known" subtypes. You can do this either when constructing the DataContractSerializer:

```
var ds = new DataContractSerializer (typeof (Person),
  new Type[] { typeof (Student), typeof (Teacher) } );
```

or in the type itself, with the KnownType attribute:

```
[DataContract, KnownType (typeof (Student)), KnownType (typeof (Teacher))]
public class Person
...
```

Here's what a serialized Student now looks like:

```
<Person xmlns="..."
        xmlns:i="http://www.w3.org/2001/XMLSchema-instance"
        i:type="Student" >
  ...
<Person>
```

Because we specified Person as the root type, the root element still has that name. The actual subclass is described separately—in the type attribute.

The NetDataContractSerializer suffers a performance hit when serializing subtypes—with either formatter. It seems that when it encounters a subtype, it has to stop and think for a while!

Serialization performance matters on an application server that's handling many concurrent requests.

Object References

References to other objects are serialized, too. Consider the following classes:

```
[DataContract] public class Person
{
  [DataMember] public string Name;
  [DataMember] public int Age;
  [DataMember] public Address HomeAddress;
}

[DataContract] public class Address
{
  [DataMember] public string Street, Postcode;
}
```

Here's the result of serializing this to XML using the DataContractSerializer:

```
<Person...>
  <Age>...</Age>
  <HomeAddress>
    <Street>...</Street>
    <Postcode>...</Postcode>
  </HomeAddress>
  <Name>...</Name>
</Person>
```

The `DeepClone` method we wrote in the preceding section would clone `HomeAddress`, too—distinguishing it from a simple `MemberwiseClone`.

If you're using a `DataContractSerializer`, the same rules apply when subclassing `Address` as when subclassing the root type. So, if we define a `USAddress` class, for instance:

```
[DataContract]
public class USAddress : Address { }
```

and assign an instance of it to a `Person`:

```
Person p = new Person { Name = "John", Age = 30 };
p.HomeAddress = new USAddress { Street="Fawcett St", Postcode="02138" };
```

p could not be serialized. The solution is either to apply the `KnownType` attribute to `Address`, as shown next:

```
[DataContract, KnownType (typeof (USAddress))]
public class Address
{
    [DataMember] public string Street, Postcode;
}
```

or to tell `DataContractSerializer` about `USAddress` in construction:

```
var ds = new DataContractSerializer (typeof (Person),
    new Type[] { typeof (USAddress) } );
```

(We don't need to tell it about `Address` because it's the declared type of the `HomeAddress` data member.)

Preserving object references

The `NetDataContractSerializer` always preserves referential equality. The `DataContractSerializer` does not, unless you specifically ask it to.

This means that if the same object is referenced in two different places, a `DataContractSerializer` ordinarily writes it twice. So, if we modify the preceding example so that `Person` also stores a work address:

```
[DataContract] public class Person
{
    ...
    [DataMember] public Address HomeAddress, WorkAddress;
}
```

and then serialize an instance as follows:

```
Person p = new Person { Name = "Stacey", Age = 30 };
p.HomeAddress = new Address { Street = "Odo St", Postcode = "6020" };
p.WorkAddress = p.HomeAddress;
```

we would see the same address details twice in the XML:

```
...
<HomeAddress>
  <Postcode>6020</Postcode>
  <Street>Odo St</Street>
</HomeAddress>
...
<WorkAddress>
  <Postcode>6020</Postcode>
  <Street>Odo St</Street>
</WorkAddress>
```

When this was later deserialized, WorkAddress and HomeAddress would be different objects. The advantage of this system is that it keeps the XML simple and standards-compliant. The disadvantages of this system include larger XML, loss of referential integrity, and the inability to cope with cyclical references.

You can request referential integrity by specifying true for preserveObjectReferences when constructing a DataContractSerializer:

```
var ds = new DataContractSerializer (typeof (Person),
                      null, 1000, false, true, null);
```

The third argument is mandatory when preserveObjectReferences is true: it indicates the maximum number of object references that the serializer should keep track of. The serializer throws an exception if this number is exceeded (this prevents a denial of service attack through a maliciously constructed stream).

Here's what the XML then looks like for a Person with the same home and work addresses:

```
<Person xmlns="http://schemas.datacontract.org/2004/07/SerialTest"
        xmlns:i="http://www.w3.org/2001/XMLSchema-instance"
        xmlns:z="http://schemas.microsoft.com/2003/10/Serialization/"
        z:Id="1">
  <Age>30</Age>
  <HomeAddress z:Id="2">
    <Postcode z:Id="3">6020</Postcode>
    <Street z:Id="4">Odo St</Street>
  </HomeAddress>
  <Name z:Id="5">Stacey</Name>
  <WorkAddress z:Ref="2" i:nil="true" />
</Person>
```

The cost of this is in reduced interoperability (notice the proprietary namespace of the Id and Ref attributes).

Version Tolerance

You can add and remove data members without breaking forward or backward compatibility. By default, the data contract deserializers do the following:

- Skip over data for which there is no [DataMember] in the type.
- Don't complain if any [DataMember] is missing in the serialization stream.

Rather than skipping over unrecognized data, you can instruct the deserializer to store unrecognized data members in a black box, and then replay them should the type later be reserialized. This allows you to correctly round-trip data that's been serialized by a later version of your type. To activate this feature, implement IExtensibleDataObject. This interface really means "IBlackBoxProvider." It requires that you implement a single property, to get/set the black box:

```
[DataContract] public class Person : IExtensibleDataObject{
  [DataMember] public string Name;
  [DataMember] public int Age;

  ExtensionDataObject IExtensibleDataObject.ExtensionData { get; set; }
}
```

Required members

If a member is essential for a type, you can demand that it be present with IsRequired:

```
[DataMember (IsRequired=true)] public int ID;
```

If that member is not present, an exception is then thrown upon deserialization.

Member Ordering

The data contract serializers are extremely fussy about the ordering of data members. The deserializers, in fact, *skip over any members considered out of sequence.*

Members are written in the following order when serializing:

1. Base class to subclass
2. Low Order to high Order (for data members whose Order is set)
3. Alphabetical order (using *ordinal* string comparison)

So, in the preceding examples, Age comes before Name. In the following example, Name comes before Age:

```
[DataContract] public class Person
{
  [DataMember (Order=0)] public string Name;
  [DataMember (Order=1)] public int Age;
}
```

If Person has a base class, the base class's data members would all serialize first.

The main reason to specify an order is to comply with a particular XML schema. XML element order equates to data member order.

If you don't need to interoperate with anything else, the easiest approach is *not* to specify a member Order and rely purely on alphabetical ordering. A discrepancy will then never arise between serialization and deserialization as members are added and removed. The only time you'll come unstuck is if you move a member between a base class and a subclass.

Null and Empty Values

There are two ways to deal with a data member whose value is null or empty:

1. Explicitly write the null or empty value (the default).
2. Omit the data member from the serialization output.

In XML, an explicit null value looks like this:

```
<Person xmlns="..."
           xmlns:i="http://www.w3.org/2001/XMLSchema-instance">
  <Name i:nil="true" />
</Person>
```

Writing null or empty members can waste space, particularly on a type with lots of fields or properties that are usually left empty. More importantly, you may need to follow an XML schema that expects the use of optional elements (e.g., `minOccurs="0"`) rather than `nil` values.

You can instruct the serializer not to emit data members for null/empty values as follows:

```
[DataContract] public class Person
{
  [DataMember (EmitDefaultValue=false)] public string Name;
  [DataMember (EmitDefaultValue=false)] public int Age;
}
```

`Name` is omitted if its value is `null`; `Age` is omitted if its value is `0` (the default value for the `int` type).

 The data contract deserializer, in rehydrating an object, by-passes the type's constructors and field initializers. This allows you to omit data members as described without breaking fields that are assigned nondefault values through an initializer or constructor. To illustrate, suppose we set the default `Age` for a `Person` to 30 as follows:

```
[DataMember (EmitDefaultValue=false)]
public int Age = 30;
```

Now suppose that we instantiate `Person`, explicitly set its `Age` from 30 to 0, and then serialize it. The output won't include `Age`, because 0 is the default value for the `int` type. This means that in deserialization, `Age` will be ignored and the field will remain at its default value—which fortunately is 0, given that field initializers and constructors were bypassed.

Data Contracts and Collections

The data contract serializers can save and repopulate any enumerable collection. For instance, suppose we define `Person` to have a `List<>` of addresses:

```
[DataContract] public class Person
{
  ...
  [DataMember] public List<Address> Addresses;
}

[DataContract] public class Address
{
  [DataMember] public string Street, Postcode;
}
```

Here's the result of serializing a Person with two addresses:

```
<Person ...>
  ...
  <Addresses>
    <Address>
      <Postcode>6020</Postcode>
      <Street>Odo St</Street>
    </Address>
    <Address>
      <Postcode>6152</Postcode>
      <Street>Comer St</Street>
    </Address>
  </Addresses>
  ...
</Person>
```

Notice that the serializer doesn't encode any information about the particular *type* of collection it serialized. If the Addresses field was instead of type Address[], the output would be identical. This allows the collection type to change between serialization and deserialization without causing an error.

Sometimes, though, you need your collection to be of a more specific type than you expose. An extreme example is with interfaces:

```
[DataMember] public IList<Address> Addresses;
```

This serializes correctly (as before), but a problem arises in deserialization. There's no way the deserializer can know which concrete type to instantiate, so it chooses the simplest option—an array. The deserializer sticks to this strategy even if you initialize the field with a different concrete type:

```
[DataMember] public IList<Address> Addresses = new List<Address>();
```

(Remember that the deserializer bypasses field initializers.) The workaround is to make the data member a private field and add a public property to access it:

```
[DataMember (Name="Addresses")] List<Address> _addresses;

public IList<Address> Addresses { get { return _addresses; } }
```

In a nontrivial application, you would probably use properties in this manner anyway. The only unusual thing here is that we've marked the private field as the data member, rather than the public property.

Subclassed Collection Elements

The serializer handles subclassed collection elements transparently. You must declare the valid subtypes just as you would if they were used anywhere else:

```
[DataContract, KnownType (typeof (USAddress))]
public class Address
{
  [DataMember] public string Street, Postcode;
}

public class USAddress : Address { }
```

Adding a USAddress to a Person's address list then generates XML like this:

```
...
  <Addresses>
    <Address i:type="USAddress">
      <Postcode>02138</Postcode>
      <Street>Fawcett St</Street>
    </Address>
  </Addresses>
```

Customizing Collection and Element Names

If you subclass a collection class itself, you can customize the XML name used to describe each element by attaching a CollectionDataContract attribute:

```
[CollectionDataContract (ItemName="Residence")]
public class AddressList : Collection<Address> { }

[DataContract] public class Person
{
  ...
  [DataMember] public AddressList Addresses;
}
```

Here's the result:

```
...
  <Addresses>
    <Residence>
      <Postcode>6020</Postcode
      <Street>Odo St</Street>
    </Residence>
    ...
```

CollectionDataContract also lets you specify a Namespace and Name. The latter is not used when the collection is serialized as a property of another object (such as in this example), but it is when the collection is serialized as the root object.

You can also use CollectionDataContract to control the serialization of dictionaries:

```
[CollectionDataContract (ItemName="Entry",
                         KeyName="Kind",
                         ValueName="Number")]
public class PhoneNumberList : Dictionary <string, string> { }
```

```
[DataContract] public class Person
{
  ...
  [DataMember] public PhoneNumberList PhoneNumbers;
}
```

Here's how this formats:

```
  ...
    <PhoneNumbers>
      <Entry>
        <Kind>Home</Kind>
        <Number>08 1234 5678</Number>
      </Entry>
      <Entry>
        <Kind>Mobile</Kind>
        <Number>040 8765 4321</Number>
      </Entry>
    </PhoneNumbers>
```

Extending Data Contracts

This section describes how you can extend the capabilities of the data contract serializer through serialization hooks, [Serializable] and IXmlSerializable.

Serialization and Deserialization Hooks

You can request that a custom method be executed before or after serialization, by flagging the method with one of the following attributes:

[OnSerializing]
:   Indicates a method to be called just *before* serialization

[OnSerialized]
:   Indicates a method to be called just *after* serialization

Similar attributes are supported for deserialization:

[OnDeserializing]
:   Indicates a method to be called just *before* deserialization

[OnDeserialized]
:   Indicates a method to be called just *after* deserialization

The custom method must have a single parameter of type StreamingContext. This parameter is required for consistency with the binary engine, and it is not used by the data contract serializer.

[OnSerializing] and [OnDeserialized] are useful in handling members that are outside the capabilities of the data contract engine, such as a collection that has an extra payload or that does not implement standard interfaces. Here's the basic approach:

```
[DataContract] public class Person
{
  public SerializationUnfriendlyType Addresses;
```

```
[DataMember (Name="Addresses")]
SerializationFriendlyType _serializationFriendlyAddresses;

[OnSerializing]
void PrepareForSerialization (StreamingContext sc)
{
  // Copy Addresses-> _serializationFriendlyAddresses
  // ...
}

[OnDeserialized]
void CompleteDeserialization (StreamingContext sc)
{
  // Copy _serializationFriendlyAddresses-> Addresses
  // ...
}
}
```

An [OnSerializing] method can also be used to conditionally serialize fields:

```
public DateTime DateOfBirth;

[DataMember] public bool Confidential;

[DataMember (Name="DateOfBirth", EmitDefaultValue=false)]
DateTime? _tempDateOfBirth;

[OnSerializing]
void PrepareForSerialization (StreamingContext sc)
{
  if (Confidential)
    _tempDateOfBirth = DateOfBirth;
  else
    _tempDateOfBirth = null;
}
```

Recall that the data contract deserializers bypass field initializers and constructors. An [OnDeserializing] method acts as a pseudoconstructor for deserialization, and it is useful for initializing fields excluded from serialization:

```
[DataContract] public class Test
{
  bool _editable = true;

  public Test() { _editable = true; }

  [OnDeserializing]
  void Init (StreamingContext sc)
  {
    _editable = true;
  }
}
```

If it wasn't for the Init method, _editable would be false in a deserialized instance of Test—despite the other two attempts at making it true.

Methods decorated with these four attributes can be private. If subtypes need to participate, they can define their own methods with the same attributes, and they will get executed, too.

Interoperating with [Serializable]

The data contract serializer can also serialize types marked with the binary serialization engine's attributes and interfaces. This ability is important, since support for the binary engine has been woven into much of what was written prior to Framework 3.0—including the .NET Framework itself!

The following things flag a type as being serializable for the binary engine:

- The [Serializable] attribute
- Implementing ISerializable

Binary interoperability is useful in serializing existing types as well as new types that need to support both engines. It also provides another means of extending the capability of the data contract serializer, because the binary engine's ISerializable is more flexible than the data contract attributes. Unfortunately, the data contract serializer is inefficient in how it formats data added via ISerializable.

A type wanting the best of both worlds cannot define attributes for both engines. This creates a problem for types such as string and DateTime, which for historical reasons cannot divorce the binary engine attributes. The data contract serializer works around this by filtering out these basic types and processing them specially. For all other types marked for binary serialization, the data contract serializer applies similar rules to what the binary engine would use. This means it honors attributes such as NonSerialized or calls ISerializable if implemented. It does not *thunk* to the binary engine itself—this ensures that output is formatted in the same style as if data contract attributes were used.

Types designed to be serialized with the binary engine expect object references to be preserved. You can enable this option through the DataContractSerializer (or by using the NetData ContractSerializer).

The rules for registering known types also apply to objects and subobjects serialized through the binary interfaces.

The following example illustrates a class with a [Serializable] data member:

```
[DataContract] public class Person
{
    ...
    [DataMember] public Address MailingAddress;
}
[Serializable] public class Address
{
    public string Postcode, Street;
}
```

Here's the result of serializing it:

```
<Person ...>
    ...
    <MailingAddress>
        <Postcode>6020</Postcode>
        <Street>Odo St</Street>
    </MailingAddress>
    ...
```

Had `Address` implemented `ISerializable`, the result would be less efficiently formatted:

```
<MailingAddress>
    <Street xmlns:d3p1="http://www.w3.org/2001/XMLSchema"
        i:type="d3p1:string" xmlns="">str</Street>
    <Postcode xmlns:d3p1="http://www.w3.org/2001/XMLSchema"
        i:type="d3p1:string" xmlns="">pcode</Postcode>
</MailingAddress>
```

Interoperating with IXmlSerializable

A limitation of the data contract serializer is that it gives you little control over the structure of the XML. In a WCF application, this can actually be beneficial, in that it makes it easier for the infrastructure to comply with standard messaging protocols.

If you do need precise control over the XML, you can implement `IXmlSerializable` and then use `XmlReader` and `XmlWriter` to manually read and write the XML. The data contract serializer allows you to do this just on the types for which this level of control is required. We describe the `IXmlSerializable` interface further in the final section of this chapter.

The Binary Serializer

The binary serialization engine is used implicitly by Remoting. It can also be used to perform such tasks as saving and restoring objects to disk. The binary serialization is highly automated and can handle complex object graphs with minimum intervention.

There are two ways to make a type support binary serialization. The first is attribute-based; the second involves implementing `ISerializable`. Adding attributes is simpler; implementing `ISerializable` is more flexible. You typically implement `ISerializable` to:

- Dynamically control what gets serialized.
- Make your serializable type friendly to being subclassed by other parties.

Getting Started

A type can be made serializable with a single attribute:

```
[Serializable] public sealed class Person
{
  public string Name;
  public int Age;
}
```

The `[Serializable]` attribute instructs the serializer to include all fields in the type. This includes both private and public fields (but not properties). Every field must itself be serializable; otherwise, an exception is thrown. Primitive .NET types such as `string` and `int` support serialization (as do many other .NET types).

The `Serializable` attribute is not inherited, so subclasses are not automatically serializable, unless also marked with this attribute.

With automatic properties, the binary serialization engine serializes the underlying compiler-generated field. The name of this field, unfortunately, can change when its type is recompiled with more properties, breaking compatibility with existing serialized data. The workaround is either to avoid automatic properties in `[Serializable]` types or to implement `ISerializable`.

To serialize an instance of `Person`, you instantiate a formatter and call `Serialize`. There are two formatters for use with the binary engine:

`BinaryFormatter`
This is the more efficient of the two, producing smaller output in less time. Its namespace is `System.Runtime.Serialization.Formatters.Binary`.

`SoapFormatter`
This supports basic SOAP-style messaging when used with Remoting. Its namespace is `System.Runtime.Serialization.Formatters.Soap`.

`BinaryFormatter` is contained in *mscorlib*; `SoapFormatter` is contained in *System.Runtime.Serialization.Formatters.Soap.dll*.

The `SoapFormatter` is less functional than the `BinaryFormatter`. The `SoapFormatter` doesn't support generic types or the filtering of extraneous data necessary for version tolerant serialization.

The two formatters are otherwise exactly the same to use. The following serializes a Person with a BinaryFormatter:

```
Person p = new Person() { Name = "George", Age = 25 };

IFormatter formatter = new BinaryFormatter();

using (FileStream s = File.Create ("serialized.bin"))
    formatter.Serialize (s, p);
```

All the data necessary to reconstruct the Person object is written to the file *serialized.bin*. The Deserialize method restores the object:

```
using (FileStream s = File.OpenRead ("serialized.bin"))
{
    Person p2 = (Person) formatter.Deserialize (s);
    Console.WriteLine (p2.Name + " " + p.Age);      // George 25
}
```

 The deserializer bypasses all constructors when re-creating objects. Behind the scenes, it calls FormatterServices.GetUninitia lizedObject to do this job. You can call this method yourself to implement some very grubby design patterns!

The serialized data includes full type and assembly information, so if we try to cast the result of deserialization to a matching Person type in a different assembly, an error would result. The deserializer fully restores object references to their original state upon deserialization. This includes collections, which are just treated as serializable objects like any other (all collection types in System.Collections.* are marked as serializable).

 The binary engine can handle large, complex object graphs without special assistance (other than ensuring that all participating members are serializable). One thing to be wary of is that the serializer's performance degrades in proportion to the number of references in your object graph. This can become an issue in a Remoting server that has to process many concurrent requests.

Binary Serialization Attributes

[NonSerialized]

Unlike data contracts, which have an *opt-in* policy in serializing fields, the binary engine has an *opt-out* policy. Fields that you don't want serialized, such as those used for temporary calculations, or for storing file or window handles, you must mark explicitly with the [NonSerialized] attribute:

```
[Serializable] public sealed class Person
{
  public string Name;
  public DateTime DateOfBirth;

  // Age can be calculated, so there's no need to serialize it.
  [NonSerialized] public int Age;
}
```

This instructs the serializer to ignore the Age member.

Nonserialized members are always empty or null when deserialized—even if field initializers or constructors set them
otherwise.

[OnDeserializing] and [OnDeserialized]

Deserialization bypasses all your normal constructors, as well as field initializers.
This is of little consequence if every field partakes in serialization, but it can be
problematic if some fields are excluded via [NonSerialized]. We can illustrate this
by adding a bool field called Valid:

```
public sealed class Person
{
  public string Name;
  public DateTime DateOfBirth;

  [NonSerialized] public int Age;
  [NonSerialized] public bool Valid = true;

  public Person() { Valid = true; }
}
```

A deserialized Person will not be Valid—despite the constructor and field initializer.

The solution is the same as with the data contract serializer: to define a special
deserialization "constructor" with the [OnDeserializing] attribute. A method that
you flag with this attribute gets called just prior to deserialization:

```
[OnDeserializing]
void OnDeserializing (StreamingContext context)
{
  Valid = true;
}
```

We could also write an [OnDeserialized] method to update the calculated Age field
(this fires just *after* deserialization):

```
[OnDeserialized]
void OnDeserialized (StreamingContext context)
{
  TimeSpan ts = DateTime.Now - DateOfBirth;
  Age = ts.Days / 365;                          // Rough age in years
}
```

```
```

[OnSerializing] and [OnSerialized]

The binary engine also supports the [OnSerializing] and [OnSerialized] attributes. These flag a method for execution before or after serialization. To see how they can be useful, we'll define a Team class that contains a generic List of players:

```
[Serializable] public sealed class Team
{
  public string Name;
  public List<Person> Players = new List<Person>();
}
```

This class serializes and deserializes correctly with the binary formatter but not the SOAP formatter. This is because of an obscure limitation: the SOAP formatter refuses to serialize generic types! An easy solution is to convert Players to an array just prior to serialization, then convert it back to a generic List upon deserialization. To make this work, we can add another field for storing the array, mark the original Players field as [NonSerialized], and then write the conversion code in as follows:

```
[Serializable] public sealed class Team
{
  public string Name;
  Person[] _playersToSerialize;

  [NonSerialized] public List<Person> Players = new List<Person>();

  [OnSerializing]
  void OnSerializing (StreamingContext context)
  {
    _playersToSerialize = Players.ToArray();
  }

  [OnSerialized]
  void OnSerialized (StreamingContext context)
  {
    _playersToSerialize = null;   // Allow it to be freed from memory
  }

  [OnDeserialized]
  void OnDeserialized (StreamingContext context)
  {
    Players = new List<Person> (_playersToSerialize);
  }
}
```

[OptionalField] and Versioning

By default, adding a field breaks compatibility with data that's already serialized, unless you attach the [OptionalField] attribute to the new field.

To illustrate, suppose we start with a Person class that has just one field. Let's call it Version 1:

```
[Serializable] public sealed class Person       // Version 1
{
  public string Name;
}
```

Later, we realize we need a second field, so we create Version 2 as follows:

```
[Serializable] public sealed class Person       // Version 2
{
  public string Name;
  public DateTime DateOfBirth;
}
```

If two computers were exchanging Person objects via Remoting, deserialization would go wrong unless they both updated to Version 2 at *exactly the same time*. The OptionalField attribute gets around this problem:

```
[Serializable] public sealed class Person       // Version 2 Robust
{
  public string Name;
  [OptionalField (VersionAdded = 2)] public DateTime DateOfBirth;
}
```

This tells the deserializer not to panic if it sees no DateOfBirth in the data stream, and instead to treat the missing field as nonserialized. This means you end up with an empty DateTime (you can assign a different value in an [OnDeserializing] method).

The VersionAdded argument is an integer that you increment each time you augment a type's fields. This serves as documentation, and it has no effect on serialization semantics.

 If versioning robustness is important, avoid renaming and deleting fields and avoid retrospectively adding the NonSerialized attribute. Never change a field's type.

So far we've focused on the backward-compatibility problem: the deserializer failing to find an expected field in the serialization stream. But with two-way communication, a forward-compatibility problem can also arise whereby the deserializer encounters an extraneous field with no knowledge of how to process it. The binary formatter is programmed to automatically cope with this by throwing away the extraneous data; the SOAP formatter instead throws an exception! Hence, you must use the binary formatter if two-way versioning robustness is required; otherwise, manually control the serialization by implementing ISerializable.

Serialization

Binary Serialization with ISerializable

Implementing ISerializable gives a type complete control over its binary serialization and deserialization.

Here's the ISerializable interface definition:

```
public interface ISerializable
{
    void GetObjectData (SerializationInfo info, StreamingContext context);
}
```

GetObjectData fires upon serialization; its job is to populate the SerializationInfo object (a name-value dictionary) with data from all fields that you want serialized. Here's how we would write a GetObjectData method that serializes two fields, called Name and DateOfBirth:

```
public virtual void GetObjectData (SerializationInfo info,
                                   StreamingContext context)
{
    info.AddValue ("Name", Name);
    info.AddValue ("DateOfBirth", DateOfBirth);
}
```

In this example, we've chosen to name each item according to its corresponding field. This is not required; any name can be used, as long as the same name is used upon deserialization. The values themselves can be of any serializable type; the Framework will recursively serialize as necessary. It's legal to store null values in the dictionary.

> It's a good idea to make the GetObjectData method virtual—unless your class is sealed. This allows subclasses to extend serialization without having to reimplement the interface.

SerializationInfo also contains properties that you can use to control the type and assembly that the instance should deserialize as. The StreamingContext parameter is a structure that contains, among other things, an enumeration value indicating to where the serialized instance is heading (disk, Remoting, etc., although this value is not always populated).

In addition to implementing ISerializable, a type controlling its own serialization needs to provide a deserialization constructor that takes the same two parameters as GetObjectData. The constructor can be declared with any accessibility and the runtime will still find it. Typically, though, you would declare it protected so that subclasses can call it.

In the following example, we implement ISerializable in the Team class. When it comes to handling the List of players, we serialize the data as an array rather than a generic list, so as to offer compatibility with the SOAP formatter:

```
[Serializable] public class Team : ISerializable
{
  public string Name;
  public List<Person> Players;

  public virtual void GetObjectData (SerializationInfo si,
                                     StreamingContext sc)
  {
    si.AddValue ("Name", Name);
    si.AddValue ("PlayerData", Players.ToArray());
  }

  public Team() {}

  protected Team (SerializationInfo si, StreamingContext sc)
  {
    Name = si.GetString ("Name");

    // Deserialize Players to an array to match our serialization:
    Person[] a = (Person[]) si.GetValue ("PlayerData", typeof (Person[]));

    // Construct a new List using this array:
    Players = new List<Person> (a);
  }
}
```

For commonly used types, the `SerializationInfo` class has typed "Get" methods such as `GetString`, in order to make writing deserialization constructors easier. If you specify a name for which no data exists, an exception is thrown. This happens most often when there's a version mismatch between the code doing the serialization and deserialization. You've added an extra field, for instance, and then forgotten about the implications of deserializing an old instance. To work around this problem, you can either:

- Add exception handling around code that retrieves a data member added in a later version.

- Implement your own version numbering system. For example:

```
public string MyNewField;

public virtual void GetObjectData (SerializationInfo si,
                                   StreamingContext sc)
{
  si.AddValue ("_version", 2);
  si.AddValue ("MyNewField", MyNewField);
  ...
}

protected Team (SerializationInfo si, StreamingContext sc)
{
  int version = si.GetInt32 ("_version");
  if (version >= 2) MyNewField = si.GetString ("MyNewField");
  ...
}
```

Subclassing Serializable Classes

In the preceding examples, we **sealed** the classes that relied on attributes for serialization. To see why, consider the following class hierarchy:

```
[Serializable] public class Person
{
  public string Name;
  public int Age;
}

[Serializable] public sealed class Student : Person
{
  public string Course;
}
```

In this example, both `Person` and `Student` are serializable, and both classes use the default runtime serialization behavior since neither class implements `ISerializable`.

Now imagine that the developer of `Person` decides for some reason to implement `ISerializable` and provide a deserialization constructor to control `Person` serialization. The new version of `Person` might look like this:

```
[Serializable] public class Person : ISerializable
{
  public string Name;
  public int Age;

  public virtual void GetObjectData (SerializationInfo si,
                                     StreamingContext sc)
  {
    si.AddValue ("Name", Name);
    si.AddValue ("Age", Age);
  }

  protected Person (SerializationInfo si, StreamingContext sc)
  {
    Name = si.GetString ("Name");
    Age = si.GetInt32 ("Age");
  }

  public Person() {}
}
```

Although this works for instances of `Person`, this change breaks serialization of `Student` instances. Serializing a `Student` instance would appear to succeed, but the `Course` field in the `Student` type isn't saved to the stream because the implementation of `ISerializable.GetObjectData` on `Person` has no knowledge of the members of the `Student`-derived type. Additionally, deserialization of `Student` instances throws an exception since the runtime is looking (unsuccessfully) for a deserialization constructor on `Student`.

The solution to this problem is to implement `ISerializable` from the outset for serializable classes that are public and nonsealed. (With `internal` classes, it's not so important because you can easily modify the subclasses later if required.)

If we started out by writing Person as in the preceding example, Student would then be written as follows:

```
[Serializable]
public class Student : Person
{
  public string Course;

  public override void GetObjectData (SerializationInfo si,
                                      StreamingContext sc)
  {
    base.GetObjectData (si, sc);
    si.AddValue ("Course", Course);
  }

  protected Student (SerializationInfo si, StreamingContext sc)
    : base (si, sc)
  {
    Course = si.GetString ("Course");
  }

  public Student() {}
}
```

XML Serialization

The Framework provides a dedicated XML serialization engine called XmlSerial izer in the System.Xml.Serialization namespace. It's suitable for serializing .NET types to XML files and is also used implicitly by ASMX Web Services.

As with the binary engine, there are two approaches you can take:

- Sprinkle attributes throughout your types (defined in System.Xml.Serialization).

- Implement IXmlSerializable.

Unlike with the binary engine, however, implementing the interface (i.e., IXmlSerializable) eschews the engine completely, leaving you to code the serialization yourself with XmlReader and XmlWriter.

Getting Started with Attribute-Based Serialization

To use XmlSerializer, you instantiate it and call Serialize or Deserialize with a Stream and object instance. To illustrate, suppose we define the following class:

```
public class Person
{
  public string Name;
  public int Age;
}
```

The following saves a Person to an XML file, and then restores it:

```
Person p = new Person();
p.Name = "Stacey"; p.Age = 30;
```

```
XmlSerializer xs = new XmlSerializer (typeof (Person));

using (Stream s = File.Create ("person.xml"))
  xs.Serialize (s, p);

Person p2;
using (Stream s = File.OpenRead ("person.xml"))
  p2 = (Person) xs.Deserialize (s);

Console.WriteLine (p2.Name + " " + p2.Age);   // Stacey 30
```

Serialize and Deserialize can work with a Stream, XmlWriter/XmlReader, or TextWriter/TextReader. Here's the resultant XML:

```
<?xml version="1.0"?>
<Person xmlns:xsi="http://www.w3.org/2001/XMLSchema-instance"
        xmlns:xsd="http://www.w3.org/2001/XMLSchema">
  <Name>Stacey</Name>
  <Age>30</Age>
</Person>
```

XmlSerializer can serialize types without any attributes—such as our Person type. By default, it serializes all *public fields and properties* on a type. You can exclude members you don't want serialized with the XmlIgnore attribute:

```
public class Person
{
  ...
  [XmlIgnore] public DateTime DateOfBirth;
}
```

Unlike the other two engines, XmlSerializer does not recognize the [OnDeserializ ing] attribute and relies instead on a parameterless constructor for deserialization, throwing an exception if one is not present. (In our example, Person has an *implicit* parameterless constructor.) This also means field initializers execute prior to deserialization:

```
public class Person
{
  public bool Valid = true;   // Executes before deserialization
}
```

Although XmlSerializer can serialize almost any type, it recognizes the following types and treats them specially:

- The primitive types, DateTime, TimeSpan, Guid, and nullable versions
- byte[] (which is converted to base 64)
- An XmlAttribute or XmlElement (whose contents are injected into the stream)
- Any type implementing IXmlSerializable
- Any collection type

The deserializer is version tolerant: it doesn't complain if elements or attributes are missing or if superfluous data is present.

Attributes, names, and namespaces

By default, fields and properties serialize to an XML element. You can request an XML attribute be used instead as follows:

```
[XmlAttribute] public int Age;
```

You can control an element or attribute's name as follows:

```
public class Person
{
  [XmlElement ("FirstName")] public string Name;
  [XmlAttribute ("RoughAge")] public int Age;
}
```

Here's the result:

```
<Person RoughAge="30" ...>
  <FirstName>Stacey</FirstName>
</Person>
```

The default XML namespace is blank (unlike the data contract serializer, which uses the type's namespace). To specify an XML namespace, [XmlElement] and [XmlAttribute] both accept a Namespace argument. You can also assign a name and namespace to the type itself with [XmlRoot]:

```
[XmlRoot ("Candidate", Namespace = "http://mynamespace/test/")]
public class Person { ... }
```

This names the person element "Candidate" as well as assigning a namespace to this element and its children.

XML element order

XmlSerializer writes elements in the order that they're defined in the class. You can change this by specifying an Order in the XmlElement attribute:

```
public class Person
{
  [XmlElement (Order = 2)] public string Name;
  [XmlElement (Order = 1)] public int Age;
}
```

If you use Order at all, you must use it throughout.

The deserializer is not fussy about the order of elements—they can appear in any sequence and the type will properly deserialize.

Subclasses and Child Objects

Subclassing the root type

Suppose your root type has two subclasses as follows:

```
public class Person { public string Name; }

public class Student : Person { }
public class Teacher : Person { }
```

and you write a reusable method to serialize the root type:

```
public void SerializePerson (Person p, string path)
{
  XmlSerializer xs = new XmlSerializer (typeof (Person));
  using (Stream s = File.Create (path))
    xs.Serialize (s, p);
}
```

To make this method work with a Student or Teacher, you must inform XmlSerializer about the subclasses. There are two ways to do this. The first is to register each subclass with the XmlInclude attribute:

```
[XmlInclude (typeof (Student))]
[XmlInclude (typeof (Teacher))]
public class Person { public string Name; }
```

The second is to specify each of the subtypes when constructing XmlSerializer:

```
XmlSerializer xs = new XmlSerializer (typeof (Person),
                     new Type[] { typeof (Student), typeof (Teacher) } );
```

In either case, the serializer responds by recording the subtype in the type attribute (just like with the data contract serializer):

```
<Person xmlns:xsi="http://www.w3.org/2001/XMLSchema-instance"
        xsi:type="Student">
  <Name>Stacey</Name>
</Person>
```

This deserializer then knows from this attribute to instantiate a Student and not a Person.

> You can control the name that appears in the XML type attribute by applying [XmlType] to the subclass:
>
> ```
> [XmlType ("Candidate")]
> public class Student : Person { }
> ```
>
> Here's the result:
>
> ```
> <Person xmlns:xsi="..."
>         xsi:type="Candidate">
> ```

Serializing child objects

XmlSerializer automatically recurses object references such as the HomeAddress field in Person:

```
public class Person
{
  public string Name;
  public Address HomeAddress = new Address();
}

public class Address { public string Street, PostCode; }
```

To demonstrate:

```
Person p = new Person(); p.Name = "Stacey";
p.HomeAddress.Street = "Odo St";
p.HomeAddress.PostCode = "6020";
```

Here's the XML to which this serializes:

```
<Person ... >
  <Name>Stacey</Name>
  <HomeAddress>
    <Street>Odo St</Street>
    <PostCode>6020</PostCode>
  </HomeAddress>
</Person>
```

 If you have two fields or properties that refer to the same object, that object is serialized twice. If you need to preserve referential equality, you must use another serialization engine.

Subclassing child objects

Suppose you need to serialize a Person that can reference *subclasses* of Address as follows:

```
public class Address { public string Street, PostCode; }
public class USAddress : Address {  }
public class AUAddress : Address {  }

public class Person
{
  public string Name;
  public Address HomeAddress = new USAddress();
}
```

There are two distinct ways to proceed, depending on how you want the XML structured. If you want the element name always to match the field or property name with the subtype recorded in a type attribute:

```
<Person ...>
  ...
  <HomeAddress xsi:type="USAddress">
    ...
  </HomeAddress>
</Person>
```

you use [XmlInclude] to register each of the subclasses with Address as follows:

```
[XmlInclude (typeof (AUAddress))]
[XmlInclude (typeof (USAddress))]
public class Address
{
  public string Street, PostCode;
}
```

If, on the other hand, you want the element name to reflect the name of the subtype, to the following effect:

```
<Person ...>
  ...
  <USAddress>
    ...
  </USAddress>
</Person>
```

you instead stack multiple [XmlElement] attributes onto the field or property in the parent type:

```
public class Person
{
  public string Name;

  [XmlElement ("Address", typeof (Address))]
  [XmlElement ("AUAddress", typeof (AUAddress))]
  [XmlElement ("USAddress", typeof (USAddress))]
  public Address HomeAddress = new USAddress();
}
```

Each XmlElement maps an element name to a type. If you take this approach, you don't require the [XmlInclude] attributes on the Address type (although their presence doesn't break serialization).

 If you omit the element name in [XmlElement] (and specify just a type), the type's default name is used (which is influenced by [XmlType] but not [XmlRoot]).

Serializing Collections

XmlSerializer recognizes and serializes concrete collection types without intervention:

```
public class Person
{
  public string Name;
  public List<Address> Addresses = new List<Address>();
}

public class Address { public string Street, PostCode; }
```

Here's the XML to which this serializes:

```
<Person ... >
  <Name>...</Name>
  <Addresses>
    <Address>
      <Street>...</Street>
      <Postcode>...</Postcode>
    </Address>
    <Address>
```

```
    <Street>...</Street>
    <Postcode>...</Postcode>
  </Address>
  ...
 </Addresses>
</Person>
```

The [XmlArray] attribute lets you rename the *outer* element (i.e., Addresses).

The [XmlArrayItem] attribute lets you rename the *inner* elements (i.e., the Address elements).

For instance, the following class:

```
public class Person
{
  public string Name;

  [XmlArray ("PreviousAddresses")]
  [XmlArrayItem ("Location")]
  public List<Address> Addresses = new List<Address>();
}
```

serializes to this:

```
<Person ... >
  <Name>...</Name>
  <PreviousAddresses>
    <Location>
      <Street>...</Street>
      <Postcode>...</Postcode>
    </Location>
    <Location>
      <Street>...</Street>
      <Postcode>...</Postcode>
    </Location>
    ...
  </PreviousAddresses>
</Person>
```

The XmlArray and XmlArrayItem attributes also allow you to specify XML namespaces.

To serialize collections *without* the outer element, for example:

```
<Person ... >
  <Name>...</Name>
  <Address>
    <Street>...</Street>
    <Postcode>...</Postcode>
  </Address>
  <Address>
    <Street>...</Street>
    <Postcode>...</Postcode>
  </Address>
</Person>
```

instead add [XmlElement] to the collection field or property:

```
public class Person
{
  ...
  [XmlElement ("Address")]
  public List<Address> Addresses = new List<Address>();
}
```

Working with subclassed collection elements

The rules for subclassing collection elements follow naturally from the other sub-classing rules. To encode subclassed elements with the **type** attribute, for example:

```
<Person ... >
  <Name>...</Name>
  <Addresses>
    <Address xsi:type="AUAddress">
    ...
```

add [XmlInclude] attributes to the base (**Address**) type as we did before. This works whether or not you suppress serialization of the outer element.

If you want subclassed elements to be named according to their type, for example:

```
<Person ... >
  <Name>...</Name>
  <!-start of optional outer element->
  <AUAddress>
    <Street>...</Street>
    <Postcode>...</Postcode>
  </AUAddress>
  <USAddress>
    <Street>...</Street>
    <Postcode>...</Postcode>
  </USAddress>
  <!-end of optional outer element->
</Person>
```

you must stack multiple [XmlArrayItem] or [XmlElement] attributes onto the collection field or property.

Stack multiple [XmlArrayItem] attributes if you want to *include* the outer collection element:

```
[XmlArrayItem ("Address",   typeof (Address))]
[XmlArrayItem ("AUAddress", typeof (AUAddress))]
[XmlArrayItem ("USAddress", typeof (USAddress))]
public List<Address> Addresses = new List<Address>();
```

Stack multiple [XmlElement] attributes if you want to *exclude* the outer collection element:

```
[XmlElement ("Address",   typeof (Address))]
[XmlElement ("AUAddress", typeof (AUAddress))]
[XmlElement ("USAddress", typeof (USAddress))]
public List<Address> Addresses = new List<Address>();
```

IXmlSerializable

Although attribute-based XML serialization is flexible, it has limitations. For instance, you cannot add serialization hooks—nor can you serialize nonpublic members. It's also awkward to use if the XML might present the same element or attribute in a number of different ways.

On that last issue, you can push the boundaries somewhat by passing an `XmlAttributeOverrides` object into `XmlSerializer`'s constructor. There comes a point, however, when it's easier to take an imperative approach. This is the job of `IXmlSerializable`:

```
public interface IXmlSerializable
{
  XmlSchema GetSchema();
  void ReadXml (XmlReader reader);
  void WriteXml (XmlWriter writer);
}
```

Implementing this interface gives you total control over the XML that's read or written.

 A collection class that implements `IXmlSerializable` bypasses `XmlSerializer`'s rules for serializing collections. This can be useful if you need to serialize a collection with a payload—in other words, additional fields or properties that would otherwise be ignored.

The rules for implementing `IXmlSerializable` are `ReadXml` should read the outer start element, then the content, and then the outer end element, and `WriteXml` should write just the content. For example:

```
using System;
using System.Xml;
using System.Xml.Schema;
using System.Xml.Serialization;

public class Address : IXmlSerializable
{
  public string Street, PostCode;

  public XmlSchema GetSchema() { return null; }

  public void ReadXml(XmlReader reader)
  {
    reader.ReadStartElement();
    Street   = reader.ReadElementContentAsString ("Street", "");
    PostCode = reader.ReadElementContentAsString ("PostCode", "");
    reader.ReadEndElement();
  }
```

```
public void WriteXml (XmlWriter writer)
{
  writer.WriteElementString ("Street", Street);
  writer.WriteElementString ("PostCode", PostCode);
}
}
```

Serializing and deserializing an instance of Address via XmlSerializer automatically calls the WriteXml and ReadXml methods. Further, if Person was defined as follows:

```
public class Person
{
  public string Name;
  public Address HomeAddress;
}
```

IXmlSerializable would be called upon selectively to serialize the HomeAddress field.

We describe XmlReader and XmlWriter at length in the first section of Chapter 11. Also in Chapter 11, in "Patterns for Using XmlReader/XmlWriter" on page 459, we provide examples of IXmlSerializable-ready classes.

17

Assemblies

An assembly is the basic unit of deployment in .NET and is also the container for all types. An assembly contains compiled types with their IL code, runtime resources, and information to assist with versioning, security, and referencing other assemblies. An assembly also defines a boundary for type resolution and security permissioning. In general, an assembly comprises a single Windows *Portable Executable* (PE) file—with an *.exe* extension in the case of an application, or a *.dll* extension in the case of a reusable library.

Most of the types in this chapter come from the following namespaces:

```
System.Reflection
System.Resources
System.Globalization
```

What's in an Assembly?

An assembly contains four kinds of things:

An assembly manifest
Provides information to the .NET runtime, such as the assembly's name, version, requested permissions, and other assemblies that it references

An application manifest
Provides information to the operating system, such as how the assembly should be deployed and whether administrative elevation is required

Compiled types
The compiled IL code and metadata of the types defined within the assembly

Resources
Other data embedded within the assembly, such as images and localizable text

Of these, only the *assembly manifest* is mandatory, although an assembly nearly always contains compiled types.

Assemblies are structured similarly whether they're executables or libraries. The main difference with an executable is that it defines an entry point.

The Assembly Manifest

The assembly manifest serves two purposes:

- It describes the assembly to the managed hosting environment.
- It acts as a directory to the modules, types, and resources in the assembly.

Assemblies are hence *self-describing*. A consumer can discover all of an assembly's data, types, and functions—without needing additional files.

An assembly manifest is not something you add explicitly to an assembly—it's automatically embedded into an assembly as part of compilation.

Here's a summary of the functionally significant data stored in the manifest:

- The simple name of the assembly
- A version number (AssemblyVersion)
- A public key and signed hash of the assembly, if strongly named
- A list of referenced assemblies, including their version and public key
- A list of modules that comprise the assembly
- A list of types defined in the assembly and the module containing each type
- An optional set of security permissions requested or refused by the assembly (SecurityPermission)
- The culture it targets, if a satellite assembly (AssemblyCulture)

The manifest can also store the following informational data:

- A full title and description (AssemblyTitle and AssemblyDescription)
- Company and copyright information (AssemblyCompany and AssemblyCopyright)
- A display version (AssemblyInformationalVersion)
- Additional attributes for custom data

Some of this data is derived from arguments given to the compiler, such as the list of referenced assemblies or the public key with which to sign the assembly. The rest comes from assembly attributes, indicated in parentheses.

You can view the contents of an assembly's manifest with the .NET tool *ildasm.exe*. In Chapter 18, we describe how to use reflection to do the same programmatically.

Specifying assembly attributes

You can control much of the manifest's content with assembly attributes. For example:

```
[assembly: AssemblyCopyright ("\x00a9 Corp Ltd. All rights reserved.")]
[assembly: AssemblyVersion ("2.3.2.1")]
```

These declarations are usually all defined in one file in your project. Visual Studio automatically creates a file called *AssemblyInfo.cs* in the *Properties* folder with every new C# project for this purpose, prepopulated with a default set of assembly attributes that provide a starting point for further customization.

The Application Manifest

An application manifest is an XML file that communicates information about the assembly to the operating system. An application manifest, if present, is read and processed before the .NET-managed hosting environment loads the assembly—and can influence how the operating system launches an application's process.

An application manifest has a root element called `assembly` in the XML namespace `urn:schemas-microsoft-com:asm.v1`:

```
<?xml version="1.0" encoding="utf-8"?>
<assembly manifestVersion="1.0" xmlns="urn:schemas-microsoft-com:asm.v1">
  <!-- contents of manifest -->
</assembly>
```

The following manifest instructs the OS to request administrative elevation when the assembly runs under Windows Vista:

```
<?xml version="1.0" encoding="utf-8"?>
<assembly manifestVersion="1.0" xmlns="urn:schemas-microsoft-com:asm.v1">
  <trustInfo xmlns="urn:schemas-microsoft-com:asm.v2">
    <security>
      <requestedPrivileges>
        <requestedExecutionLevel level="requireAdministrator" />
      </requestedPrivileges>
    </security>
  </trustInfo>
</assembly>
```

We describe the consequences of requesting administrative elevation in Chapter 20.

Deploying an application manifest

You can deploy an application manifest in two ways:

- As a specially named file located in the same folder as the assembly
- Embedded within the assembly itself

As a separate file, its name must match that of the assembly's, plus *.manifest*. If an assembly was named *MyApp.exe*, its manifest would be named *MyApp.exe.manifest*.

To embed an application manifest file into an assembly, first build the assembly and then call the .NET mt tool as follows:

```
mt -manifest MyApp.exe.manifest -outputresource:MyApp.exe;#1
```

 The .NET tool *ildasm.exe* is blind to the presence of an embedded application manifest. Visual Studio, however, indicates whether an embedded application manifest is present if you double-click the assembly in Solution Explorer.

Modules

The contents of an assembly are actually packaged within one or more intermediate containers, called *modules*. A module corresponds to a file containing the contents of an assembly. The reason for this extra layer of containership is to allow an assembly to span multiple files—a feature that's useful when building an assembly containing code compiled in a mixture of programming languages.

Figure 17-1 shows the normal case of an assembly with a single module. Figure 17-2 shows a multifile assembly. In a multifile assembly, the "main" module always contains the manifest; additional modules can contain IL and/or resources. The manifest describes the relative location of all the other modules that make up the assembly.

Figure 17-1. Single-file assembly

Multifile assemblies have to be compiled from the command line: there's no support in Visual Studio. To do this, you invoke the csc compiler with the /t switch to create each module, and then link them with the assembly linker tool, *al.exe*.

Although the need for multifile assemblies is rare, at times you need to be aware of the extra level of containership that modules impose—even when dealing just with single-module assemblies. The main scenario is with reflection (see "Reflecting Assemblies" on page 700 and "Emitting Assemblies and Types" on page 714 in Chapter 18).

Figure 17-2. Multifile assembly

The Assembly Class

The `Assembly` class in `System.Reflection` is a gateway to accessing assembly metadata at runtime. There are a number of ways to obtain an assembly object: the simplest is via a `Type`'s `Assembly` property:

```
Assembly a = typeof (Program).Assembly;
```

You can also obtain an `Assembly` object by calling one of `Assembly`'s static methods:

`GetExecutingAssembly`
> Returns the assembly of the type that defines the currently executing function

`GetCallingAssembly`
> Does the same as `GetExecutingAssembly`, but for the function that called the currently executing function

`GetEntryAssembly`
> Returns the assembly defining the application's original entry method

Once you have an `Assembly` object, you can use its properties and methods to query the assembly's metadata and reflect upon its types. Table 17-1 shows a summary of these functions.

Table 17-1. Assembly members

Functions	Purpose	See the section...
FullName, GetName	Returns the fully qualified name or an AssemblyName object	"Assembly Names" on page 655
CodeBase, Location	Location of the assembly file	"Resolving and Loading Assemblies" on page 671
Load, LoadFrom, LoadFile	Manually loads an assembly into the current application domain	"Resolving and Loading Assemblies" on page 671
GlobalAssemblyCache	Indicates whether the assembly is defined in the GAC	"The Global Assembly Cache" on page 661
GetSatelliteAssembly	Locates the satellite assembly of a given culture	"Resources and Satellite Assemblies" on page 663
GetType, GetTypes	Returns a type, or all types, defined in the assembly	"Reflecting and Activating Types" on page 682
EntryPoint	Returns the application's entry method, as a MethodInfo	"Reflecting and Invoking Members" on page 688
GetModules, ManifestModule	Returns all modules, or the main module, of an assembly	"Reflecting Assemblies" on page 700
GetCustomAttributes	Returns the assembly's attributes	"Working with Attributes" on page 701

Strong Names and Assembly Signing

A *strongly named* assembly has a unique and untamperable identity. It works by adding two bits of metadata to the manifest:

- A *unique number* that belongs to the authors of the assembly
- A *signed hash* of the assembly, proving that the unique number holder produced the assembly

This requires a public/private key pair. The *public key* provides the unique identifying number, and the *private key* facilitates signing.

Strong-name-signing is different from *Authenticode*-signing. We cover Authenticode later in this chapter.

The public key is valuable in guaranteeing the uniqueness of assembly references: a strongly named assembly incorporates the public key into its identity. The signature is valuable for security—it prevents a malicious party from tampering with your assembly. Without your private key, no one can release a modified version of the assembly without the signature breaking (causing an error when loaded). Of course, someone could re-sign the assembly with a different key pair—but this would give the assembly a different identity. Any application referencing the original assembly would shun the imposter because public key tokens are written into references.

 Adding a strong name to a previously "weak" named assembly changes its identity. For this reason, it pays to give production assemblies strong names from the outset.

A strongly named assembly can also be registered in the GAC.

How to Strongly Name an Assembly

To give an assembly a strong name, first generate a public/private key pair with the *sn.exe* utility:

```
sn.exe -k MyKeyPair.snk
```

This manufactures a new key pair and stores it to a file called *MyApp.snk*. If you subsequently lose this file, you will permanently lose the ability to recompile your assembly with the same identity.

You then compile with the /keyfile switch:

```
csc.exe /keyfile:MyKeyPair.snk Program.cs
```

Visual Studio assists you with both steps in the Project Properties window.

 A strongly named assembly cannot reference a weakly named assembly. This is another compelling reason to strongly name all your production assemblies.

The same key pair can sign multiple assemblies—they'll still have distinct identities if their simple names differ. The choice as to how many key pair files to use within an organization depends on a number of factors. Having a separate key pair for every assembly is advantageous should you later transfer ownership of a particular application (along with its referenced assemblies), in terms of minimum disclosure. But it makes it harder for you to create a security policy that recognizes all of your assemblies. It also makes it harder to validate dynamically loaded assemblies.

 Prior to C# 2.0, the compiler did not support the /keyfile switch and you would specify a key file with the AssemblyKey File attribute instead. This presented a security risk, because the path to the key file would remain embedded in the assembly's metadata. For instance, with *ildasm*, you can see quite easily that the path to the key file used to sign *mscorlib* in CLR 1.1 was as follows:

```
F:\qfe\Tools\devdiv\EcmaPublicKey.snk
```

Obviously, you need access to that folder on Microsoft's .NET Framework build machine to take advantage of that information!

Delay Signing

In an organization with hundreds of developers, you might want to restrict access to the key pairs used for signing assemblies, for a couple of reasons:

- If a key pair gets leaked, your assemblies are no longer untamperable.
- A test assembly, if signed and leaked, could be maliciously propagated as the real assembly.

Withholding key pairs from developers, though, means they cannot compile and test assemblies with their correct identity. *Delay signing* is a system for working around this problem.

A delay-signed assembly is flagged with the correct public key, but not *signed* with the private key. A delay-signed assembly is equivalent to a tampered assembly and would normally be rejected by the CLR. The developer, however, instructs the CLR to bypass validation for the delay-sign assemblies on *that computer*, allowing the unsigned assemblies to run. When it comes time for final deployment, the private key holder re-signs the assembly with the real key pair.

To delay-sign, you need a file containing *just* the public key. You can extract this from a key pair by calling sn with the -p switch:

```
sn -k KeyPair.snk
sn -p KeyPair.snk PublicKeyOnly.pk
```

KeyPair.snk is kept secure and *PublicKeyOnly.pk* is freely distributed.

 You can also obtain *PublicKeyOnly.pk* from an existing signed assembly with the -e switch:

```
sn -e YourLibrary.dll PublicKeyOnly.pk
```

You then delay-sign with *PublicKeyOnly.pk* by calling csc with the /delaysign+ switch:

```
csc /delaysign+ /keyfile: PublicKeyOnly.pk /target:library YourLibrary.cs
```

Visual Studio does the same if you tick the "Delay sign" checkbox.

The next step is to instruct the .NET runtime to skip assembly identity verification on the development computers running the delay-signed assemblies. This can be done on either a per-assembly or a per-public key basis, by calling the sn tool with the Vr switch:

```
sn -Vr YourLibrary.dll
```

 Visual Studio does not perform this step automatically. You must disable assembly verification manually from the command line. Otherwise, your assembly will not execute.

The final step is to fully sign the assembly prior to deployment. This is when you replace the null signature with a real signature that can be generated only with access to the private key. To do this, you call sn with the R switch:

```
sn -R YourLibrary.dll KeyPair.snk
```

You can then reinstate assembly verification on development machines as follows:

```
sn -Vu YourLibrary.dll
```

You won't need to recompile any applications that reference the delay-signed assembly, because you've changed only the assembly's signature, not its *identity*.

Assembly Names

An assembly's "identity" comprises four pieces of metadata from its manifest:

- Its simple name
- Its version ("0.0.0.0" if not present)
- Its culture ("neutral" if not a satellite)
- Its public key token ("null" if not strongly named)

The simple name comes not from any attribute, but from the name of the file to which it was originally compiled (less any extension). So, the simple name of the *System.Xml.dll* assembly is "System.Xml". Renaming a file doesn't change the assembly's simple name.

The version number comes from the AssemblyVersion attribute. It's a string divided into four parts as follows:

```
major.minor.build.revision
```

You can specify a version number as follows:

```
[assembly: AssemblyVersion ("2.5.6.7")]
```

The culture comes from the AssemblyCulture attribute and applies to satellite assemblies, described later in the section "Resources and Satellite Assemblies" on page 663.

The public key token comes from a key pair supplied at compile time via the /keyfile switch, as we saw earlier, in the section "Strong Names and Assembly Signing" on page 652.

Fully Qualified Names

A fully qualified assembly name is a string that includes all four identifying components, in this format:

```
simple-name, Version=version, Culture=culture, PublicKeyToken=public-key
```

For example, the fully qualified name of *System.Xml.dll* is:

```
"System.Xml, Version=2.0.0.0, Culture=neutral,
PublicKeyToken=b77a5c561934e089"
```

If the assembly has no `AssemblyVersion` attribute, the version appears as "0.0.0.0". If it is unsigned, its public key token appears as "null".

An `Assembly` object's `FullName` property returns its fully qualified name. The compiler always uses fully qualified names when recording assembly references in the manifest.

 A fully qualified assembly name does not include a directory path to assist in locating it on disk. Locating an assembly residing in another directory is an entirely separate matter that we pick up in "Resolving and Loading Assemblies" on page 671.

The AssemblyName Class

`AssemblyName` is a class with a typed property for each of the four components of a fully qualified assembly name. `AssemblyName` has two purposes:

- It parses or builds a fully qualified assembly name.
- It stores some extra data to assist in resolving (finding) the assembly.

You can obtain an `AssemblyName` object in any of the following ways:

- Instantiate an `AssemblyName`, providing a fully qualified name.
- Call `GetName` on an existing `Assembly`.
- Call `AssemblyName.GetAssemblyName`, providing the path to an assembly file on disk.

You can also instantiate an `AssemblyName` object without any arguments, and then set each of its properties to build a fully qualified name. An `AssemblyName` is mutable when constructed in this manner.

Here are its essential properties and methods:

```
string      FullName    { get; }          // Fully qualified name
string      Name        { get; set; }     // Simple name
Version     Version     { get; set; }     // Assembly version
CultureInfo CultureInfo { get; set; }     // For satellite assemblies
string      CodeBase    { get; set; }     // Location

byte[]      GetPublicKey();                // 160 bytes
void        SetPublicKey (byte[] key);
byte[]      GetPublicKeyToken();           // 8-byte version
void        SetPublicKeyToken (byte[] publicKeyToken);
```

`Version` is itself a strongly typed representation, with properties for `Major`, `Minor`, `Build`, and `Revision` numbers. `GetPublicKey` returns the full cryptographic public key; `GetPublicKeyToken` returns the last eight bytes used in establishing identity.

To use `AssemblyName` to obtain the simple name of an assembly:

```
Console.WriteLine (typeof (string).Assembly.GetName().Name);  // mscorlib
```

To get an assembly version:

```
string v = myAssembly.GetName().Version.ToString();
```

We'll examine the `CodeBase` property in the later section "Resolving and Loading Assemblies" on page 671.

Assembly Informational and File Versions

Because an integral part of an assembly name is its version, changing the `AssemblyVersion` attribute changes the assembly's identity. This affects compatibility with referencing assemblies, which can be undesirable when making nonbreaking updates. To address this, there are two other independent assembly-level attributes for expressing version-related information, both of which are ignored by the CLR:

`AssemblyInformationalVersion`
The version as displayed to the end-user. This is visible in the Windows File Properties dialog as "Product Version". Any string can go here, such as "5.1 Beta 2". Typically, all the assemblies in an application would be assigned the same informational version number.

`AssemblyFileVersion`
This is intended to refer to the build number for that assembly. This is visible in the Windows File Properties dialog as "File Version". As with `AssemblyVersion`, it must contain a string consisting of up to four numbers separated by periods.

Authenticode Signing

Authenticode is a code-signing system whose purpose is to prove the identity of the publisher. Authenticode and *strong-name* signing are independent: you can sign an assembly with either or both systems.

While strong-name signing can prove that assemblies A, B, and C came from the same party (assuming the private key hasn't been leaked), it can't tell you who that party was. In order to know that the party was Joe Albahari—or Microsoft Corporation—you need Authenticode.

Authenticode is useful when downloading programs from the Internet, because it can prove that a program came from whoever was named by the Certificate Authority and was not modified in transit. In fact, one of the main benefits of Authenticode is that it prevents the "Unknown Publisher" warning shown in Figure 17-3, when running a downloaded application for the first time. This makes Authenticode particularly applicable to setup programs or standalone executables. (A reason to apply Authenticode to assemblies more broadly is that it's a requirement for the Windows Logo program.)

Authenticode works with not only .NET assemblies, but also unmanaged executables and binaries such as ActiveX controls or *.msi* deployment files. Of course, Authenticode doesn't guarantee that a program is free from malware—although it does

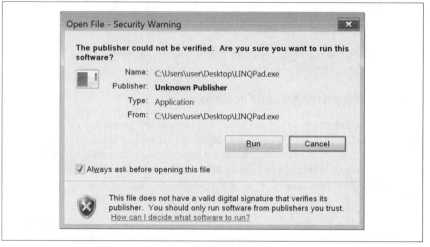

Figure 17-3. Unsigned file warning

make it less likely. A person or entity has been willing to put its name (backed by a passport or company document) behind the executable or library.

 The CLR does not treat an Authenticode signature as part of an assembly's identity. However, it can read and validate Authenticode signatures on demand, as we'll see soon.

Signing with Authenticode requires that you contact a *Certificate Authority* (CA) with evidence of your personal identity or company's identity (articles of incorporation, etc.). Once the CA has checked your documents, it will issue an X.509 code-signing certificate that is typically valid for one to five years. This enables you to sign assemblies with the *signtool* utility. You can also make a certificate yourself with the *makecert* utility; however, this is useful only for testing because the certificate won't be valid on other computers.

Authenticode relies on a public key infrastructure: essentially, it proves that a program was signed with a certificate whose credentials were verified by a CA. The CA itself is trusted because all CAs are loaded into the operating system (to see them, go to the Windows Control Panel and choose Internet Options→Content tab→Certificates button→Trusted Root Certification Authorities tab). A CA can revoke a publisher's certificate if leaked, so verifying an Authenticode signature requires periodically asking the CA for an up-to-date list of certification revocations.

Because Authenticode uses cryptographic signing, an Authenticode signature is invalid if someone subsequently tampers with the file. We discuss cryptography, hashing, and signing in Chapter 20.

How to Sign with Authenticode

Obtaining and installing a certificate

The first step is to obtain a code-signing certificate from a CA (see sidebar). You can then either work with the certificate as a password-protected file, or load the certificate into the computer's certificate store. The benefit of doing the latter is that you can sign without needing to specify a password. This is advantageous because it avoids having a password visible in automated build scripts or batch files.

Where to Get a Code-Signing Certificate

Just a handful of code-signing CAs are preloaded into Windows as root certification authorities. These include (with prices for one-year code-signing certificates at the time of publication) Comodo ($180), Go Daddy ($200), GlobalSign ($229), thawte ($299), and VeriSign ($499).

There is also a reseller called Ksoftware (*http://www.ksoftware.net*), which currently offers Comodo code-signing certificates for $99 per year.

The Authenticode certificates issued by Ksoftware, Comodo, Go Daddy, and GlobalSign are advertised as less restrictive in that they will also sign non-Microsoft programs such as Java applets. Aside from this, the products from all vendors are functionally equivalent.

Note that a certificate for SSL cannot generally be used for Authenticode signing (despite using the same X.509 infrastructure). This is, in part, because a certificate for SSL is about proving ownership of a domain; Authenticode is about proving who you are.

To load a certificate into the computer's certificate store, go to the Windows Control Panel and select Internet Options→Content tab→Certificates button→Import. Once the import is complete, click the View button on the certificate, go to the Details tab, and copy the certificate's *thumbprint*. This is the SHA-1 hash that you'll subsequently need to identity the certificate when signing.

 If you also want to strong-name-sign your assembly (which is highly recommended), you must do so *before* Authenticode signing. This is because the CLR knows about Authenticode signing, but not vice versa. So if you strong-name-sign an assembly *after* Authenticode-signing it, the latter will see the addition of the CLR's strong name as an unauthorized modification, and consider the assembly tampered.

Signing with signtool.exe

You can Authenticode-sign your programs with the *signtool* utility that comes with Visual Studio. It displays a UI if you call it with the `signwizard` flag; otherwise, you can use it in command-line style as follows:

```
signtool sign /sha1 (thumbprint) filename
```

The thumbprint is that of the certificate as shown in the computer's certificate store. (If the certificate is in a file instead, specify the filename with /f, and the password with /p.)

For example:

```
signtool sign /sha1 ff813c473dc93aaca4bac681df472b037fa220b3 LINQPad.exe
```

You can also specify a description and product URL with /d and /du:

```
... /d LINQPad /du http://www.linqpad.net
```

In most cases, you will also want to specify a *time-stamping server*.

Time stamping

After your certificate expires, you'll no longer be able to sign programs. However, programs that you signed *before* its expiry will still be valid—if you specified a *time-stamping server* with the /t switch when signing. The CA will provide you with a URI for this purpose: the following is for Comodo (or Ksoftware):

```
... /t http://timestamp.comodoca.com/authenticode
```

Verifying that a program has been signed

The easiest way to view an Authenticode signature on a file is to view the file's properties in Windows Explorer (look in the Digital Signatures tab). The *signtool* utility also provides an option for this.

Authenticode Validation

Both the operating system and the CLR may validate Authenticode signatures.

Windows validates Authenticode signatures before running programs marked as "blocked"—in practice, this means programs run for the first time after having been downloaded from the Internet. The status—or absence—of Authenticode information is then shown in the dialog we saw in Figure 17-3.

The CLR reads and validates Authenticode signatures when you ask for assembly evidence. Here's how to do that:

```
Publisher p = someAssembly.Evidence.GetHostEvidence<Publisher>();
```

The `Publisher` class (in `System.Security.Policy`) exposes a `Certificate` property. If this returns a non-null value, it has been Authenticode-signed. You can then query this object for the details of the certificate.

Prior to Framework 4.0, the CLR would read and validate Authenticode signatures when an assembly was loaded—rather than waiting until you called `GetHostEvidence`. This had potentially disastrous performance consequences, because Authenticode validation may round-trip to the CA to update the certificate revocation list—which can take up to 30 seconds (to fail) if there are Internet connectivity problems. For this reason, it's best to avoid Authenticode-signing .NET 3.5 or earlier assemblies if possible. (Signing *.msi* setup files, though, is fine.)

Regardless of the Framework version, if a program has a bad or unverifiable Authenticode signature, the CLR will merely make that information available via `GetHostEvidence`: it will never display a warning to the user or prevent the assembly from running.

As we said previously, an Authenticode signature has no effect on an assembly's identity or *name*.

The Global Assembly Cache

As part of the .NET Framework installation, a central repository is created on the computer for storing .NET assemblies, called the *Global Assembly Cache*, or GAC. The GAC contains a centralized copy of the .NET Framework itself, and it can also be used to centralize your own assemblies.

The main factor in choosing whether to load your assemblies into the GAC relates to versioning. For assemblies in the GAC, versioning is centralized at the machine level and controlled by the computer's administrator. For assemblies outside the GAC, versioning is handled on an application basis, so each application looks after its own dependency and update issues (typically by maintaining its own copy of each assembly that it references).

The GAC is useful in the minority of cases where machine-centralized versioning is genuinely advantageous. For example, consider a suite of interdependent plug-ins, each referencing some shared assemblies. We'll assume each plug-in is in its own directory, and for this reason, there's a possibility of there being multiple copies of a shared assembly (maybe some later than others). Further, we'll assume the hosting application will want to load each shared assembly just once for the sake of efficiency and type compatibility. The task of assembly resolution is now difficult for the hosting application, requiring careful planning and an understanding of the subtleties of assembly loading contexts. The simple solution here is to put the shared assemblies into the GAC. This ensures that the CLR always makes straightforward and consistent assembly resolution choices.

In more typical scenarios, however, the GAC is best avoided because it adds the following complications:

- XCOPY or ClickOnce deployment is no longer possible; an administrative setup is required to install your application.

- Updating assemblies in the GAC also requires administrative privileges.

- Use of the GAC can complicate development and testing, because *fusion*, the CLR's assembly resolution mechanism, always favors GAC assemblies over local copies.

- Versioning and *side-by-side* execution require some planning, and a mistake may break other applications.

On the positive side, the GAC can improve startup time for very large assemblies, because the CLR verifies the signatures of assemblies in the GAC only once upon installation, rather than every time the assembly loads. In percentage terms, this is relevant if you've generated native images for your assemblies with the *ngen.exe* tool, choosing nonoverlapping base addresses. A good article describing these issues is available online at the MSDN site, titled "The Performance Benefits of NGen."

 Assemblies in the GAC are always fully trusted—even when called from an assembly running in a limited-permissions sandbox. We discuss this further in Chapter 20.

How to Install Assemblies to the GAC

To install assemblies to the GAC, the first step is to give your assembly a strong name. Then you can install it using the .NET command-line tool, `gacutil`:

```
gacutil /i MyAssembly.dll
```

If the assembly already exists in the GAC with the *same public key and version*, it's updated. You don't have to uninstall the old one first.

To uninstall an assembly (note the lack of a file extension):

```
gacutil /u MyAssembly
```

You can also specify that assemblies be installed to the GAC as part of a setup project in Visual Studio.

Calling `gacutil` with the `/l` switch lists all assemblies in the GAC. You can do the same with the *mscorcfg* MMC snap-in (from Window→Administrative Tools→Framework Configuration).

Once an assembly is loaded into the GAC, applications can reference it without needing a local copy of that assembly.

 If a local copy *is* present, it's *ignored in favor of the GAC image*. This means there's no way to reference or test a recompiled version of your library—until you update the GAC. This holds true as long as you preserve the assembly's version and identity.

GAC and Versioning

Changing an assembly's `AssemblyVersion` gives it a brand-new identity. To illustrate, let's say you write a *utils* assembly, version it "1.0.0.0", strongly name it, and then install it in the GAC. Then suppose later you add some new features, change the version to "1.0.0.1", recompile it, and reinstall it into the GAC. Instead of overwriting the original assembly, the GAC now holds *both* versions. This means:

- You can choose which version to reference when compiling another application that uses *utils*.
- Any application previously compiled to reference *utils* 1.0.0.0 will *continue to do so*.

This is called *side-by-side* execution. Side-by-side execution prevents the "DLL hell" that can otherwise occur when a shared assembly is unilaterally updated: applications designed for the older version might unexpectedly break.

A complication arises, though, when you want to apply bug fixes or minor updates to existing assemblies. You have two options:

- Reinstall the fixed assembly to the GAC with the same version number.
- Compile the fixed assembly with a new version number and install that to the GAC.

The difficulty with the first option is that there's no way to apply the update *selectively* to certain applications. It's all or nothing. The difficulty with the second option is that applications will not normally use the newer assembly version without being recompiled. There is a workaround—you can create a *publisher policy* allowing assembly version redirection—at the cost of increasing deployment complexity.

Side-by-side execution is good for mitigating some of the problems of shared assemblies. If you avoid the GAC altogether—instead allowing each application to maintain its own private copy of *utils*—you eliminate *all* of the problems of shared assemblies!

Resources and Satellite Assemblies

An application typically contains not only executable code, but also content such as text, images, or XML files. Such content can be represented in an assembly through a *resource*. There are two overlapping use cases for resources:

- Incorporating data that cannot go into source code, such as images
- Storing data that might need translation in a multilingual application

An assembly resource is ultimately a byte stream with a name. You can think of an assembly as containing a dictionary of byte arrays keyed by string. This can be seen in *ildasm* if we disassemble an assembly that contains a resource called *banner.jpg* and a resource called *data.xml*:

```
.mresource public banner.jpg
{
  // Offset: 0x00000F58 Length: 0x000004F6
}
.mresource public data.xml
{
  // Offset: 0x00001458 Length: 0x0000027E
}
```

In this case, *banner.jpg* and *data.xml* were included directly in the assembly—each as its own embedded resource. This is the simplest way to work.

The Framework also lets you add content through intermediate *.resources* containers. There are designed for holding content that may require translation into different languages. Localized *.resources* can be packaged as individual satellite assemblies that are automatically picked up at runtime, based on the user's operating system language.

Figure 17-4 illustrates an assembly that contains two directly embedded resources, plus a *.resources* container called *welcome.resources*, for which we've created two localized satellites.

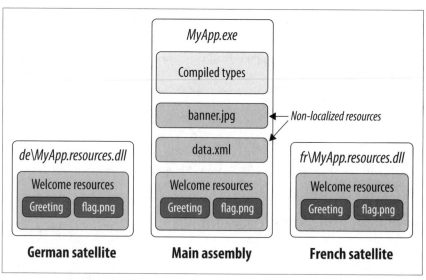

Figure 17-4. Resources

Directly Embedding Resources

To directly embed a resource at the command line, use the /resource switch when compiling:

```
csc /resource:banner.jpg /resource:data.xml MyApp.cs
```

You can optionally specify that the resource be given a different name in the assembly as follows:

```
csc /resource:<file-name>,<resource-name>
```

To directly embed a resource using Visual Studio:

- Add the file to your project.
- Set its build action to "Embedded Resource".

Visual Studio always prefixes resource names with the project's default namespace, plus the names of any subfolders in which the file is contained. So, if your project's default namespace was `Westwind.Reports` and your file was called *banner.jpg* in the folder *pictures*, the resource name would be *Westwind.Reports.pictures.banner.jpg*.

 Resource names are case-sensitive. This makes project subfolder names in Visual Studio that contain resources effectively case-sensitive.

To retrieve a resource, you call `GetManifestResourceStream` on the assembly containing the resource. This returns a stream, which you can then read as any other:

```
Assembly a = Assembly.GetEntryAssembly();

using (Stream s = a.GetManifestResourceStream ("TestProject.data.xml"))
using (XmlReader r = XmlReader.Create (s))
  ...

System.Drawing.Image image;
using (Stream s = a.GetManifestResourceStream ("TestProject.banner.jpg"))
  image = System.Drawing.Image.FromStream (s);
```

The stream returned is seekable, so you can also do this:

```
byte[] data;
using (Stream s = a.GetManifestResourceStream ("TestProject.banner.jpg"))
  data = new BinaryReader (s).ReadBytes ((int) s.Length);
```

If you've used Visual Studio to embed the resource, you must remember to include the namespace-based prefix. To help avoid error, you can specify the prefix in a separate argument, using a *type*. The type's namespace is used as the prefix:

```
using (Stream s = a.GetManifestResourceStream (typeof (X), "XmlData.xml"))
```

X can be any type with the desired namespace of your resource (typically, a type in the same project folder).

 Setting a project item's build action in Visual Studio to "Resource" within a WPF application is *not* the same as setting its build action to "Embedded Resource". The former actually adds the item to a *.resources* file called *<AssemblyName>.g.resources*, whose content you access through WPF's `Application` class, using a URI as a key.

To add to the confusion, WPF further overloads the term "resource." *Static resources* and *dynamic resources* are both unrelated to assembly resources!

`GetManifestResourceNames` returns the names of all resources in the assembly.

.resources Files

.resources files are containers for potentially localizable content. A *.resources* file ends up as an embedded resource within an assembly—just like any other kind of file. The difference is that you must:

- Package your content into the *.resources* file to begin with.
- Access its content through a `ResourceManager` or *pack URI*, rather than a `GetManifestResourceStream`.

.resources files are structured in binary and so are not human-editable; therefore, you must rely on tools provided by the Framework and Visual Studio to work with them. The standard approach with strings or simple data types is to use the *.resx* format, which can be converted to a *.resources* file either by Visual Studio or the `resgen` tool. The *.resx* format is also suitable for images intended for a Windows Forms or ASP.NET application.

In a WPF application, you must use Visual Studio's "Resource" build action for images or similar content needing to be referenced by URI. This applies whether localization is needed or not.

We describe how to do each of these in the following sections.

.resx Files

A *.resx* file is a design-time format for producing *.resources* files. A *.resx* file uses XML and is structured with name/value pairs as follows:

```
<root>
  <data name="Greeting">
    <value>hello</value>
  </data>
  <data name="DefaultFontSize" type="System.Int32, mscorlib">
    <value>10</value>
  </data>
</root>
```

To create a *.resx* file in Visual Studio, add a project item of type "Resources File". The rest of the work is done automatically:

- The correct header is created.
- A designer is provided for adding strings, images, files, and other kinds of data.
- The *.resx* file is automatically converted to the *.resources* format and embedded into the assembly upon compilation.
- A class is written to help you access the data later on.

The resource designer adds images as typed `Image` objects (*System.Drawing.dll*), rather than as byte arrays, making them unsuitable for WPF applications.

Creating a .resx file at the command line

If you're working at the command line, you must start with a *.resx* file that has a valid header. The easiest way to accomplish this is to create a simple *.resx* file programmatically. The `System.Resources.ResXResourceWriter` class (which, peculiarly, resides in the *System.Windows.Forms.dll* assembly) does exactly this job:

```
using (ResXResourceWriter w = new ResXResourceWriter ("welcome.resx")) { }
```

From here, you can either continue to use the `ResXResourceWriter` to add resources (by calling `AddResource`) or manually edit the *.resx* file that it wrote.

The easiest way to deal with images is to treat the files as binary data and convert them to an image upon retrieval. This is also more versatile than encoding them as a typed `Image` object. You can include binary data within a *.resx* file in base 64 format as follows:

```
<data name="flag.png" type="System.Byte[], mscorlib">
  <value>Qk32BAAAAAAAAHYAAAAoAAAAMAMDAwACAgIAAAAD/AA....</value>
</data>
```

or as a reference to another file that is then read by `resgen`:

```
<data name="flag.png"
  type="System.Resources.ResXFileRef, System.Windows.Forms">
  <value>flag.png;System.Byte[], mscorlib</value>
</data>
```

When you're done, you must convert the *.resx* file by calling `resgen`. The following converts *welcome.resx* into *welcome.resources*:

```
resgen welcome.resx
```

The final step is to include the *.resources* file when compiling, as follows:

```
csc /resources:welcome.resources MyApp.cs
```

Reading .resources files

If you create a *.resx* file in Visual Studio, a class of the same name is generated automatically with properties to retrieve each of its items.

The `ResourceManager` class reads *.resources* files embedded within an assembly:

```
ResourceManager r = new ResourceManager ("welcome",
                                  Assembly.GetExecutingAssembly());
```

(The first argument must be namespace-prefixed if the resource was compiled in Visual Studio.)

You can then access what's inside by calling `GetString` or `GetObject` with a cast:

```
string greeting = r.GetString ("Greeting");
int fontSize = (int) r.GetObject ("DefaultFontSize");
Image image = (Image) r.GetObject ("flag.png");      // (Visual Studio)
byte[] imgData = (byte[]) r.GetObject ("flag.png");   // (Command line)
```

To enumerate the contents of a *.resources* file:

```
ResourceManager r = new ResourceManager (...);
ResourceSet set = r.GetResourceSet (CultureInfo.CurrentUICulture,
                                     true, true);
foreach (System.Collections.DictionaryEntry entry in set)
  Console.WriteLine (entry.Key);
```

Creating a pack URI resource in Visual Studio

In a WPF application, XAML files need to be able to access resources by URI. For instance:

```
<Button>
  <Image Height="50" Source="flag.png"/>
</Button>
```

Or, if the resource is in another assembly:

```
<Button>
  <Image Height="50" Source="UtilsAssembly;Component/flag.png"/>
</Button>
```

(`Component` is a literal keyword.)

To create resources that can be loaded in this manner, you cannot use *.resx* files. Instead, you must add the files to your project and set their build action to "Resource" (not "Embedded Resource"). Visual Studio then compiles them into a *.resources* file called *<AssemblyName>.g.resources*—also the home of compiled XAML (*.baml*) files.

Call `Application.GetResource-Stream` to load a URI-keyed resource programmatically:

```
Uri u = new Uri ("flag.png", UriKind.Relative);
using (Stream s = Application.GetResourceStream (u).Stream)
```

Notice we used a relative URI. You can also use an absolute URI in exactly the following format (the three commas are not a typo):

```
Uri u = new Uri ("pack://application:,,,/flag.png");
```

If you'd rather specify an `Assembly` object, you can retrieve content instead with a `ResourceManager`:

```
Assembly a = Assembly.GetExecutingAssembly();
ResourceManager r = new ResourceManager (a.GetName().Name + ".g", a);
using (Stream s = r.GetStream ("flag.png"))
  ...
```

A `ResourceManager` also lets you enumerate the content of a *.g.resources* container within a given assembly.

Satellite Assemblies

Data embedded in *.resources* is localizable.

Resource localization is relevant when your application runs on a version of Windows built to display everything in a different language. For consistency, your application should use that same language too.

A typical setup is as follows:

- The main assembly contains *.resources* for the default or *fallback* language.
- Separate *satellite assemblies* contain localized *.resources* translated to different languages.

When your application runs, the Framework examines the language of the current operating system (from `CultureInfo.CurrentUICulture`). Whenever you request a resource using `ResourceManager`, the Framework looks for a localized satellite assembly. If one's available—and it contains the resource key you requested—it's used in place of the main assembly's version.

This means you can enhance language support simply by adding new satellites—without changing the main assembly.

 A satellite assembly cannot contain executable code, only resources.

Satellite assemblies are deployed in subdirectories of the assembly's folder as follows:

```
programBaseFolder\MyProgram.exe
                 \MyLibrary.exe
                 \XX\MyProgram.resources.dll
                 \XX\MyLibrary.resources.dll
```

XX refers to the two-letter language code (such as "de" for German) or a language and region code (such as "en-GB" for English in Great Britain). This naming system allows the CLR to find and load the correct satellite assembly automatically.

Building satellite assemblies

Recall our previous *.resx* example, which included the following:

```
<root>
  ...
  <data name="Greeting"
    <value>hello</value>
  </data>
</root>
```

We then retrieved the greeting at runtime as follows:

```
ResourceManager r = new ResourceManager ("welcome",
                                    Assembly.GetExecutingAssembly());
Console.Write (r.GetString ("Greeting"));
```

Suppose we want this to instead write "Hallo" if running on the German version of Windows. The first step is to add another *.resx* file named *welcome.de.resx* that substitutes *hello* for *hallo*:

```
<root>
  <data name="Greeting">
    <value>hallo<value>
  </data>
</root>
```

In Visual Studio, this is all you need to do—when you rebuild, a satellite assembly called *MyApp.resources.dll* is automatically created in a subdirectory called *de*.

If you're using the command line, you call **resgen** to turn the *.resx* file into a *.resources* file:

```
resgen MyApp.de.resx
```

and then call **al** to build the satellite assembly:

```
al /culture:de /out:MyApp.resources.dll /embed:MyApp.de.resources /t:lib
```

You can specify `/template:MyApp.exe` to import the main assembly's strong name.

Testing satellite assemblies

To simulate running on an operating system with a different language, you must change the `CurrentUICulture` using the `Thread` class:

```
System.Threading.Thread.CurrentThread.CurrentUICulture
   = new System.Globalization.CultureInfo ("de");
```

`CultureInfo.CurrentUICulture` is a read-only version of the same property.

Visual Studio designer support

The designers in Visual Studio provide extended support for localizing components and visual elements. The WPF designer has its own workflow for localization; other Component-based designers use a design-time-only property to make it appear that a component or Windows Forms control has a `Language` property. To customize for another language, simply change the `Language` property and then start modifying the component. All properties of controls that are attributed as `Localizable` will be persisted to a *.resx* file for that language. You can switch between languages at any time just by changing the `Language` property.

Cultures and Subcultures

Cultures are split into cultures and subcultures. A culture represents a particular language; a subculture represents a regional variation of that language. The

Framework follows the RFC1766 standard, which represents cultures and subcultures with two-letter codes. Here are the codes for English and German cultures:

```
en
de
```

Here are the codes for the Australian English and Austrian German subcultures:

```
en-AU
de-AT
```

A culture is represented in .NET with the `System.Globalization.CultureInfo` class. You can examine the current culture of your application as follows:

```
Console.WriteLine (System.Threading.Thread.CurrentThread.CurrentCulture);
Console.WriteLine (System.Threading.Thread.CurrentThread.CurrentUICulture);
```

Running this on a computer localized for Australia illustrates the difference between the two:

```
EN-AU
EN-US
```

`CurrentCulture` reflects the regional settings of the Windows control panel, whereas `CurrentUICulture` reflects the language of the operating system.

Regional settings include such things as time zone and the formatting of currency and dates. `CurrentCulture` determines the default behavior of such functions as `DateTime.Parse`. Regional settings can be customized to the point where they no longer resemble any particular culture.

`CurrentUICulture` determines the language in which the computer communicates with the user. Australia doesn't need a separate version of English for this purpose, so it just uses the U.S. one. If I spent a couple of months working in Austria, I would go to the control panel and change my `CurrentCulture` to Austrian-German. However, since I can't speak German, my `CurrentUICulture` would remain U.S. English.

`ResourceManager`, by default, uses the current thread's `CurrentUICulture` property to determine the correct satellite assembly to load. `ResourceManager` uses a fallback mechanism when loading resources. If a subculture assembly is defined, that one is used; otherwise, it falls back to the generic culture. If the generic culture is not present, it falls back to the default culture in the main assembly.

Resolving and Loading Assemblies

A typical application comprises a main executable assembly plus a set of referenced library assemblies. For example:

```
AdventureGame.exe
Terrain.dll
UIEngine.dll
```

Assembly resolution refers to the process of locating referenced assemblies. Assembly resolution happens both at compile time and at runtime. The compile-time system is simple: the compiler knows where to find referenced assemblies because it's told where to look. You (or Visual Studio) provide the full path to referenced assemblies that are not in the current directory.

Runtime resolution is more complicated. The compiler writes the strong names of referenced assemblies to the manifest—but not any hints as to where to find them. In the simple case where you put all referenced assemblies in the same folder as the main executable, there's no issue because that's (close to) the first place the CLR looks. The complexities arise:

- When you deploy referenced assemblies in other places
- When you dynamically load assemblies

Assembly and Type Resolution Rules

All types are scoped to an assembly. An assembly is like an address for a type. To give an analogy, we can refer to a person as "Joe" (type name without namespace), "Joe Bloggs" (full type name), or "Joe Bloggs of 100 Barker Ave, WA" (assembly-qualified type name).

During compilation, we don't need to go further than a full type name for uniqueness, because you can't reference two assemblies that define the same full type name (at least not without special tricks). At runtime, though, it's possible to have many identically named types in memory. This happens within the Visual Studio designer, for instance, whenever you *rebuild* the components you're designing. The only way to distinguish such types is by their assembly; therefore, an assembly forms an essential part of a type's runtime identity. An assembly is also a type's handle to its code and metadata.

The CLR loads assemblies at the point in execution when they're first needed. This happens when you refer to one of the assembly's types. For example, suppose that *AdventureGame.exe* instantiates a type called `TerrainModel.Map`. Assuming no additional configuration files, the CLR answers the following questions:

- What's the fully qualified name of the assembly that contained `TerrainModel.Map` when *AdventureGame.exe* was compiled?
- Have I already loaded an assembly with this fully qualified name into memory in the same (resolution) context?

If the answer to the second question is yes, it uses the existing copy in memory; otherwise, it goes looking for the assembly. The CLR first checks the GAC, then the *probing* paths (generally the application base directory), and as a final resort, fires the `AppDomain.AssemblyResolve` event. If none returns a match, the CLR throws an exception.

AssemblyResolve

The `AssemblyResolve` event allows you to intervene and manually load an assembly that the CLR can't find. If you handle this event, you can scatter referenced assemblies in a variety of locations and still have them load.

Within the `AssemblyResolve` event handler, you locate the assembly and load it by calling one of three static methods in the `Assembly` class: `Load`, `LoadFrom`, or `LoadFile`. These methods return a reference to the newly loaded assembly, which you then return to the caller:

```
static void Main()
{
  AppDomain.CurrentDomain.AssemblyResolve += FindAssembly;
  ...
}

static Assembly FindAssembly (object sender, ResolveEventArgs args)
{
  string fullyQualifiedName = args.Name;
  Assembly a = Assembly.LoadFrom (...);
  return a;
}
```

The `ResolveEventArgs` event is unusual in that it has a return type. If there are multiple handlers, the first one to return a non-null `Assembly` wins.

Loading Assemblies

The `Load` methods in `Assembly` are useful both inside and outside an `AssemblyResolve` handler. Outside the event handler, they can load and execute assemblies not referenced at compilation. An example of when you might do this is to execute a plug-in.

Think carefully before calling `Load`, `LoadFrom`, or `LoadFile`: these methods permanently load an assembly into the current application domain—even if you do nothing with the resultant `Assembly` object. Loading an assembly has side effects: it locks the assembly files as well as affecting subsequent type resolution.

The only way to unload an assembly is to unload the whole application domain.

If you just want to examine an assembly without executing any of its code, you can instead use the reflection-only context (see Chapter 18).

To load an assembly from a fully qualified name (without a location) call `Assembly.Load`. This instructs the CLR to find the assembly using its normal automatic resolution system. The CLR itself uses `Load` to find referenced assemblies.

To load an assembly from a filename, call `LoadFrom` or `LoadFile`.

To load an assembly from a URI, call `LoadFrom`.

To load an assembly from a byte array, call `Load`.

You can see what assemblies are currently loaded in memory by calling AppDomain's GetAssemblies method:

```
foreach (Assembly a in
AppDomain.CurrentDomain.GetAssemblies())
{
  Console.WriteLine (a.Location);         // file path
  Console.WriteLine (a.GetName().Name);   // simple name
}
```

Loading from a filename

LoadFrom and LoadFile can both load an assembly from a filename. They differ in two ways. First, if an assembly with the same identity has already been loaded into memory from another location, LoadFrom gives you the previous copy:

```
Assembly a1 = Assembly.LoadFrom (@"c:\temp1\lib.dll");
Assembly a2 = Assembly.LoadFrom (@"c:\temp2\lib.dll");
Console.WriteLine (a1 == a2);                          // true
```

LoadFile gives you a fresh copy:

```
Assembly a1 = Assembly.LoadFile (@"c:\temp1\lib.dll");
Assembly a2 = Assembly.LoadFile (@"c:\temp2\lib.dll");
Console.WriteLine (a1 == a2);                          // false
```

If you load twice from an *identical* location, however, both methods give you the previously cached copy. (In contrast, loading an assembly twice from an identical byte array gives you two distinct Assembly objects.)

Types from two identical assemblies in memory are incompatible. This is the primary reason to avoid loading duplicate assemblies, and hence a reason to favor LoadFrom over LoadFile.

Whether you use LoadFrom or LoadFile, the CLR always looks first for the requested assembly in the GAC, and then the *probing path* (normally the application base directory). If you *really* want to load an assembly from a particular path, the only way to do it is with ReflectionOnlyLoadFrom (which loads the assembly into a reflection-only context). Even loading from a byte array doesn't bypass the GAC, although it does bypass the probing path:

```
byte[] image = File.ReadAllBytes (assemblyPath);
Assembly a = Assembly.Load (image);
```

Loading from a byte array also gets around the problem of locking assembly files! The drawback is that you must handle the AppDomain's AssemblyResolve event in order to resolve any assemblies that the loaded assembly itself references.

The second difference between `LoadFrom` and `LoadFile` is that `LoadFrom` gives hints to the CLR as to the location of onward references, whereas `LoadFile` does not. To illustrate, suppose your application in *\folder1* loads an assembly in *\folder2* called *TestLib.dll*, which references *\folder2\Another.dll*:

```
\folder1\MyApplication.exe

\folder2\TestLib.dll
\folder2\Another.dll
```

If you load *TestLib* with `LoadFrom`, the CLR will find and load *Another.dll*.

If you load *TestLib* with `LoadFile`, the CLR will be unable to find *Another.dll* and will throw an exception—unless you also handle the `AssemblyResolve` event.

In the following sections, we demonstrate these methods in the context of some practical applications.

Deploying Assemblies Outside the Base Folder

Sometimes you might choose to deploy assemblies to locations other than the application base directory. For instance:

```
..\MyProgram\Main.exe
..\MyProgram\Libs\V1.23\GameLogic.dll
..\MyProgram\Libs\V1.23\3DEngine.dll
..\MyProgram\Terrain\Map.dll
..\Common\TimingController.dll
```

To make this work, you must assist the CLR in finding the assemblies outside the base folder. The easiest solution is to handle the `AssemblyResolve` event.

In the following example, we assume all additional assemblies are located in *c:\ExtraAssemblies*:

```
using System;
using System.IO;
using System.Reflection;

class Loader
{
  static void Main()
  {
    AppDomain.CurrentDomain.AssemblyResolve += FindAssembly;

    // We must switch to another class before attempting to use
    // any of the types in c:\ExtraAssemblies:
    Program.Go();
  }

  static Assembly FindAssembly (object sender, ResolveEventArgs args)
  {
    string simpleName = new AssemblyName (args.Name).Name;
    string path = @"c:\ExtraAssemblies\" + simpleName + ".dll";
```

```
      if (!File.Exists (path)) return null;    // Sanity check
      return Assembly.LoadFrom (path);          // Load it up!
    }
  }

  class Program
  {
    internal static void Go()
    {
      // Now we can reference types defined in c:\ExtraAssemblies
    }
  }
```

 It's vitally important in this example not to reference types in
c:\ExtraAssemblies directly from the Loader class (e.g., as fields),
because the CLR would then attempt to resolve the type before
hitting Main().

In this example, we could use either LoadFrom or LoadFile. In either case, the CLR
verifies that the assembly that we hand it has the exact identity it requested. This
maintains the integrity of strongly named references.

In Chapter 24, we describe another approach that can be used when creating new
application domains. This involves setting the application domain's PrivateBin
Path to include the directories containing the additional assemblies—extending the
standard assembly probing locations. A limitation of this is that the additional directories must all be *below* the application base directory.

Packing a Single-File Executable

Suppose you've written an application comprising 10 assemblies: 1 main executable
file, plus 9 DLLs. Although such granularity can be great for design and debugging,
it's also good to be able to pack the whole thing into a single "click and run"
executable—without demanding the user perform some setup or file extraction rit-
ual. You can accomplish this by including the compiled assembly DLLs in the main
executable project as embedded resources, and then writing an AssemblyResolve
event handler to load their binary images on demand. Here's how it's done:

```
using System;
using System.IO;
using System.Reflection;
using System.Collections.Generic;

public class Loader
{
  static Dictionary <string, Assembly> _libs
    = new Dictionary <string, Assembly>();

  static void Main()
  {
```

```
    AppDomain.CurrentDomain.AssemblyResolve += FindAssembly;
    Program.Go();
  }

  static Assembly FindAssembly (object sender, ResolveEventArgs args)
  {
    string shortName = new AssemblyName (args.Name).Name;
    if (_libs.ContainsKey (shortName)) return _libs [shortName];

    using (Stream s = Assembly.GetExecutingAssembly().
        GetManifestResourceStream ("Libs." + shortName + ".dll"))
    {
      byte[] data = new BinaryReader (s).ReadBytes ((int) s.Length);
      Assembly a = Assembly.Load (data);
      _libs [shortName] = a;
      return a;
    }
  }
}

public class Program
{
  public static void Go()
  {
    // Run main program...
  }
}
```

Because the Loader class is defined in the main executable, the call to Assembly.GetEx
ecutingAssembly will always return the main executable assembly, where we've included the compiled DLLs as embedded resources. In this example, we prefix the
name of each embedded resource assembly with "Libs.". If the Visual Studio IDE
was used, you would change "Libs." to the project's default namespace (go to
Project Properties→Application). You would also need to ensure that the "Build
Action" IDE property on each of the DLL files included in the main project was set
to "Embedded Resource".

The reason for caching requested assemblies in a dictionary is to ensure that if the
CLR requests the same assembly again, we return exactly the same object. Otherwise, an assembly's types will be incompatible with those loaded previously (despite
their binary images being identical).

A variation of this would be to compress the referenced assemblies at compilation,
then decompress them in FindAssembly using a DeflateStream.

Selective Patching

Suppose in this example that we want the executable to be able to autonomously
update itself—perhaps from a network server or website. Directly patching the executable not only would be awkward and dangerous, but also the required file I/O
permissions may not be forthcoming (if installed in *Program Files*, for instance). An
excellent workaround is to download any updated libraries to isolated storage (each
as a separate DLL) and then modify the FindAssembly method such that it first checks

for the presence of a library in its isolated storage area before loading it from a resource in the executable. This leaves the original executable untouched and avoids leaving any unpleasant residue on the user's computer. Security is not compromised if your assemblies are strongly named (assuming they were referenced in compilation), and if something goes wrong, the application can always revert to its original state—simply by deleting all files in its isolated storage.

Working with Unreferenced Assemblies

Sometimes it's useful to explicitly load assemblies that may not have been referenced in compilation.

If the assembly in question is an executable and you simply want to run it, calling `ExecuteAssembly` on the current application domain does the job. `ExecuteAssembly` loads the executable using `LoadFrom` semantics, and then calls its entry method with optional command-line arguments. For instance:

```
string dir = AppDomain.CurrentDomain.BaseDirectory;
AppDomain.CurrentDomain.ExecuteAssembly (Path.Combine (dir, "test.exe"));
```

`ExecuteAssembly` works synchronously, meaning the calling method is blocked until the called assembly exits. To work asynchronously, you must call `ExecuteAssembly` on another thread (see Chapter 21).

In most cases, though, the assembly you'll want to load is a library. The approach then is to call `LoadFrom`, and then use reflection to work with the assembly's types. For example:

```
string ourDir = AppDomain.CurrentDomain.BaseDirectory;
string plugInDir = Path.Combine (ourDir, "plugins");
Assembly a = Assembly.LoadFrom (Path.Combine (plugInDir, "widget.dll"));
Type t = a.GetType ("Namespace.TypeName");
object widget = Activator.CreateInstance (t);    // (See Chapter 18)
...
```

We used `LoadFrom` rather than `LoadFile` to ensure that any private assemblies *widget.dll* referenced in the same folder were also loaded. We then retrieved a type from the assembly by name and instantiated it.

The next step could be to use reflection to dynamically call methods and properties on `widget`; we describe how to do this in the following chapter. An easier—and faster—approach is to cast the object to a type that both assemblies understand. This is often an interface defined in a common assembly:

```
public interface IPluggable
{
  void ShowAboutBox();
  ...
}
```

This allows us to do this:

```
Type t = a.GetType ("Namespace.TypeName");
IPluggable widget = (IPluggable) Activator.CreateInstance (t);
widget.ShowAboutBox();
```

You can use a similar system for dynamically publishing services in a WCF or Remoting Server. The following assumes the libraries we want to expose end in "server":

```
using System.IO;
using System.Reflection;
...
string dir = AppDomain.CurrentDomain.BaseDirectory;
foreach (string assFile in Directory.GetFiles (dir, "*Server.dll"))
{
  Assembly a = Assembly.LoadFrom (assFile);
  foreach (Type t in a.GetTypes())
    if (typeof (MyBaseServerType).IsAssignableFrom (t))
    {
      // Expose type t
    }
}
```

This does make it very easy, though, for someone to add rogue assemblies, maybe even accidentally! Assuming no compile-time references, the CLR has nothing against which to check an assembly's identity. If everything that you load is signed with a known public key, the solution is to check that key explicitly. In the following example, we assume that all libraries are signed with the same key pair as the executing assembly:

```
byte[] ourPK = Assembly.GetExecutingAssembly().GetName().GetPublicKey();

foreach (string assFile in Directory.GetFiles (dir, "*Server.dll"))
{
  byte[] targetPK = AssemblyName.GetAssemblyName (assFile).GetPublicKey();
  if (Enumerable.SequenceEqual (ourPK, targetPK))
  {
    Assembly a = Assembly.LoadFrom (assFile);
    ...
```

Notice how `AssemblyName` allows you to check the public key *before* loading the assembly. To compare the byte arrays, we used LINQ's `SequenceEqual` method (`System.Linq`).

18

Reflection and Metadata

As we saw in the previous chapter, a C# program compiles into an assembly that includes metadata, compiled code, and resources. Inspecting the metadata and compiled code at runtime is called *reflection*.

The compiled code in an ssembly contains almost all of the content of the original source code. Some information is lost, such as local variable names, comments, and preprocessor statements. However, reflection can access pretty much everything else, even making it possible to write a decompiler.

Many of the services available in .NET and exposed via C# (such as dynamic binding, serialization, data binding, and Remoting) depend on the presence of metadata. Your own programs can also take advantage of this metadata, and even extend it with new information using custom attributes. The `System.Reflection` namespace houses the reflection API. It is also possible at runtime to dynamically create new metadata and executable instructions in IL (Intermediate Language) via the classes in the `System.Reflection.Emit` namespace.

The examples in this chapter assume that you import the `System` and `System.Reflec tion`, as well as `System.Reflection.Emit` namespaces.

When we use the term "dynamically" in this chapter, we mean using reflection to perform some task whose type safety is enforced only at runtime. This is similar in principle to *dynamic binding* via C#'s `dynamic` keyword, although the mechanism and functionality is different.

To compare the two, dynamic binding is much easier to use and leverages the DLR for dynamic language interoperability. Reflection is relatively clumsy to use, is concerned with the CLR only—but is more flexible in terms of what you can do with the CLR. For instance, reflection lets you obtain lists of types and members, instantiate an object whose name comes from a string, and build assemblies on the fly.

Reflecting and Activating Types

In this section, we examine how to obtain a `Type`, inspect its metadata, and use it to dynamically instantiate an object.

Obtaining a Type

An instance of `System.Type` represents the metadata for a type. Since `Type` is widely used, it lives in the `System` namespace rather than the `System.Reflection` namespace.

You can get an instance of a `System.Type` by calling `GetType` on any object or with C#'s `typeof` operator:

```
Type t1 = DateTime.Now.GetType();    // Type obtained at runtime
Type t2 = typeof (DateTime);         // Type obtained at compile time
```

You can use `typeof` to obtain array types and generic types as follows:

```
Type t3 = typeof (DateTime[]);          // 1-d Array type
Type t4 = typeof (DateTime[,]);         // 2-d Array type
Type t5 = typeof (Dictionary<int,int>); // Closed generic type
Type t6 = typeof (Dictionary<,>);       // Unbound generic type
```

You can also retrieve a `Type` by name. If you have a reference to its `Assembly`, call `Assembly.GetType` (we describe this further in the section "Reflecting Assemblies" on page 700 later in this chapter):

```
Type t = Assembly.GetExecutingAssembly().GetType ("Demos.TestProgram");
```

If you don't have an `Assembly` object, you can obtain a type through its *assembly qualified name* (the type's full name followed by the assembly's fully qualified name). The assembly implicitly loads as if you called `Assembly.Load(string)`:

```
Type t = Type.GetType ("System.Int32, mscorlib, Version=2.0.0.0, " +
                       "Culture=neutral, PublicKeyToken=b77a5c561934e089");
```

Once you have a `System.Type` object, you can use its properties to access the type's name, assembly, base type, visibility, and so on. For example:

```
Type stringType = typeof (String);
string name     = stringType.Name;      // String
Type baseType   = stringType.BaseType;  // typeof(Object)
Assembly assem  = stringType.Assembly;  // mscorlib.dll
bool isPublic   = stringType.IsPublic;  // true
```

A `System.Type` instance is a window into the entire metadata for the type—and the assembly in which it's defined.

> `System.Type` is abstract, so the `typeof` operator must actually give you a subclass of `Type`. The subclass that the CLR uses is internal to *mscorlib* and is called `RuntimeType`.

Obtaining array types

As we just saw, `typeof` and `GetType` work with array types. You can also obtain an array type by calling `MakeArrayType` on the *element* type:

```
Type tSimpleArray = typeof (int).MakeArrayType();
Console.WriteLine (tSimpleArray == typeof (int[]));      // True
```

`MakeArray` can be passed an integer argument to make multidimensional rectangular arrays:

```
Type tCube = typeof (int).MakeArrayType (3);      // cube shaped
Console.WriteLine (tCube == typeof (int[,,]));    // True
```

`GetElementType` does the reverse; it retrieves an array type's element type:

```
Type e = typeof (int[]).GetElementType();      // e == typeof (int)
```

`GetArrayRank` returns the number of dimensions of a rectangular array:

```
int rank = typeof (int[,,]).GetArrayRank();    // 3
```

Obtaining nested types

To retrieve nested types, call `GetNestedTypes` on the containing type. For example:

```
foreach (Type t in typeof (System.Environment).GetNestedTypes())
  Console.WriteLine (t.FullName);

OUTPUT: System.Environment+SpecialFolder
```

The one caveat with nested types is that the CLR treats a nested type as having special "nested" accessibility levels. For example:

```
Type t = typeof (System.Environment.SpecialFolder);
Console.WriteLine (t.IsPublic);            // False
Console.WriteLine (t.IsNestedPublic);      // True
```

Type Names

A type has `Namespace`, `Name`, and `FullName` properties. In most cases, `FullName` is a composition of the former two:

```
Type t = typeof (System.Text.StringBuilder);

Console.WriteLine (t.Namespace);    // System.Text
Console.WriteLine (t.Name);         // StringBuilder
Console.WriteLine (t.FullName);     // System.Text.StringBuilder
```

There are two exceptions to this rule: nested types and closed generic types.

> Type also has a property called `AssemblyQualifiedName`, which returns `FullName` followed by a comma and then the full name of its assembly. This is the same string that you can pass to `Type.GetType`, and it uniquely identifies a type within the default loading context.

Nested type names

With nested types, the containing type appears only in `FullName`:

```
Type t = typeof (System.Environment.SpecialFolder);

Console.WriteLine (t.Namespace);    // System
Console.WriteLine (t.Name);         // SpecialFolder
Console.WriteLine (t.FullName);     // System.Environment+SpecialFolder
```

The + symbol differentiates the containing type from a nested namespace.

Generic type names

Generic type names are suffixed with the ' symbol, followed by the number of type parameters. If the generic type is unbound, this rule applies to both `Name` and `FullName`:

```
Type t = typeof (Dictionary<,>); // Unbound
Console.WriteLine (t.Name);       // Dictionary'2
Console.WriteLine (t.FullName);   // System.Collections.Generic.Dictionary'2
```

If the generic type is closed, however, `FullName` (only) acquires a substantial extra appendage. Each type parameter's full *assembly qualified name* is enumerated:

```
Console.WriteLine (typeof (Dictionary<int,string>).FullName);

// OUTPUT:
System.Collections.Generic.Dictionary'2[[System.Int32, mscorlib,
Version=2.0.0.0, Culture=neutral, PublicKeyToken=b77a5c561934e089],
[System.String, mscorlib, Version=2.0.0.0, Culture=neutral,
PublicKeyToken=b77a5c561934e089]]
```

This ensures that `AssemblyQualifiedName` (a combination of the type's full name and assembly name) contains enough information to fully identify both the generic type and its type parameters.

Array and pointer type names

Arrays present with the same suffix that you use in a `typeof` expression:

```
Console.WriteLine (typeof ( int[]  ).Name);    // Int32[]
Console.WriteLine (typeof ( int[,] ).Name);    // Int32[,]
Console.WriteLine (typeof ( int[,] ).FullName); // System.Int32[,]
```

Pointer types are similar:

```
Console.WriteLine (typeof (byte*).Name);     // Byte*
```

ref and out parameter type names

A `Type` describing a `ref` or `out` parameter has an & suffix:

```
Type t = typeof (bool).GetMethod ("TryParse").GetParameters()[1]
                                  .ParameterType;
Console.WriteLine (t.Name);     // Boolean&
```

More on this in "Reflecting and Invoking Members" on page 688.

Base Types and Interfaces

Type exposes a `BaseType` property:

```
Type base1 = typeof (System.String).BaseType;
Type base2 = typeof (System.IO.FileStream).BaseType;

Console.WriteLine (base1.Name);    // Object
Console.WriteLine (base2.Name);    // Stream
```

The `GetInterfaces` method returns the interfaces that a type implements:

```
foreach (Type iType in typeof (Guid).GetInterfaces())
  Console.WriteLine (iType.Name);
```

```
IFormattable
IComparable
IComparable'1
IEquatable'1
```

Reflection provides two dynamic equivalents to C#'s static `is` operator:

`IsInstanceOfType`
> Accepts a type and instance

`IsAssignableFrom`
> Accepts two types

Here's an example of the first:

```
object obj  = Guid.NewGuid();
Type target = typeof (IFormattable);

bool isTrue   = obj is IFormattable;          // Static C# operator
bool alsoTrue = target.IsInstanceOfType (obj);   // Dynamic equivalent
```

`IsAssignableFrom` is more versatile:

```
Type target = typeof (IComparable), source = typeof (string);
Console.WriteLine (target.IsAssignableFrom (source));       // True
```

The `IsSubclassOf` method works on the same principle as `IsAssignableFrom`, but excludes interfaces.

Instantiating Types

There are two ways to dynamically instantiate an object from its type:

- Call the static `Activator.CreateInstance` method
- Call `Invoke` on a `ConstructorInfo` object obtained from calling `GetConstructor` on a `Type` (advanced scenarios)

`Activator.CreateInstance` accepts a `Type` and optional arguments that get passed to the constructor:

```
int i = (int) Activator.CreateInstance (typeof (int));

DateTime dt = (DateTime) Activator.CreateInstance (typeof (DateTime),
                                                   2000, 1, 1);
```

CreateInstance lets you specify many other options, such as the assembly from which to load the type, the target application domain, and whether to bind to a nonpublic constructor. A MissingMethodException is thrown if the runtime can't find a suitable constructor.

Calling Invoke on a ConstructorInfo is necessary when your argument values can't disambiguate between overloaded constructors. For example, suppose class X has two constructors: one accepting a parameter of type string, and another accepting a parameter of type StringBuilder. The target is ambiguous should you pass a null argument into Activator.CreateInstance. This is when you need to use a ConstructorInfo instead:

```
// Fetch the constructor that accepts a single parameter of type string:
ConstructorInfo ci = typeof (X).GetConstructor (new[] { typeof (string) };

// Construct the object using that overload, passing in null:
object foo = ci.Invoke (new object[] { null });
```

To obtain a nonpublic constructor, you need to specify BindingFlags—see "Accessing Nonpublic Members" on page 696 in the section "Reflecting and Invoking Members" on page 688.

 Dynamic instantiation adds a few microseconds onto the time taken to construct the object. This is quite a lot in relative terms because the CLR is ordinarily very fast in instantiating objects (a simple new on a small class takes in the region of tens of nanosecondsk).

To dynamically instantiate arrays based on just element type, call MakeArrayType first. You can also instantiate generic types: we describe this in the following section.

To dynamically instantiate a delegate, call Delegate.CreateDelegate. The following example demonstrates instantiating both an instance delegate and a static delegate:

```
class Program
{
  delegate int IntFunc (int x);

  static int Square (int x) { return x * x; }      // Static method
  int        Cube   (int x) { return x * x * x; }  // Instance method

  static void Main()
  {
    Delegate staticD = Delegate.CreateDelegate
      (typeof (IntFunc), typeof (Program), "Square");d

    Delegate instanceD = Delegate.CreateDelegate
      (typeof (IntFunc), new Program(), "Cube");
```

```
    Console.WriteLine (staticD.DynamicInvoke (3));      // 9
    Console.WriteLine (instanceD.DynamicInvoke (3));    // 27
  }
}
```

You can invoke the `Delegate` object that's returned by calling `DynamicInvoke`, as we did in this example, or by casting to the typed delegate:

```
IntFunc f = (IntFunc) staticD;
Console.WriteLine (f(3));          // 9 (but much faster!)
```

You can pass a `MethodInfo` into `CreateDelegate` instead of a method name. We describe `MethodInfo` shortly, in the section "Reflecting and Invoking Members" on page 688, along with the rationale for casting a dynamically created delegate back to the static delegate type.

Generic Types

A `Type` can represent a closed or unbound generic type. Just as at compile time, a closed generic type can be instantiated whereas an unbound type cannot:

```
Type closed = typeof (List<int>);
List<int> list = (List<int>) Activator.CreateInstance (closed);  // OK

Type unbound   = typeof (List<>);
object anError = Activator.CreateInstance (unbound);    // Runtime error
```

The `MakeGenericType` method converts an unbound into a closed generic type. Simply pass in the desired type arguments:

```
Type unbound = typeof (List<>);
Type closed = unbound.MakeGenericType (typeof (int));
```

The `GetGenericTypeDefinition` method does the opposite:

```
Type unbound2 = closed.GetGenericTypeDefinition();  // unbound == unbound2
```

The `IsGenericType` property returns `true` if a `Type` is generic, and the `IsGenericType Definition` property returns `true` if the generic type is unbound. The following tests whether a type is a nullable value type:

```
Type nullable = typeof (bool?);
Console.WriteLine (
  nullable.IsGenericType &&
  nullable.GetGenericTypeDefinition() == typeof (Nullable<>));    // True
```

`GetGenericArguments` returns the type arguments for closed generic types:

```
Console.WriteLine (closed.GetGenericArguments()[0]);     // System.Int32
Console.WriteLine (nullable.GetGenericArguments()[0]);   // System.Boolean
```

For unbound generic types, `GetGenericArguments` returns pseudotypes that represent the placeholder types specified in the generic type definition:

```
Console.WriteLine (unbound.GetGenericArguments()[0]);    // T
```

At runtime, all generic types are either *unbound* or *closed*. They're unbound in the (relatively unusual) case of an expression such as typeof(Foo<>); otherwise, they're closed. There's no such things as an *open* generic type at runtime: all open types are closed by the compiler. The method in the following class always prints False:

```
class Foo<T>
{
  public void Test()
  {
    Console.Write (GetType().IsGenericTypeDefinition);
  }
}
```

Reflecting and Invoking Members

The GetMembers method returns the members of a type. Consider the following class:

```
class Walnut
{
  private bool cracked;
  public void Crack() { cracked = true; }
}
```

We can reflect on its public members as follows:

```
MemberInfo[] members = typeof (Walnut).GetMembers();
foreach (MemberInfo m in members)
  Console.WriteLine (m);
```

This is the result:

```
Void Crack()
System.Type GetType()
System.String ToString()
Boolean Equals(System.Object)
Int32 GetHashCode()
Void .ctor()
```

When called with no arguments, GetMembers returns all the public members for a type (and its base types). GetMember retrieves a specific member by name—though it still returns an array because members can be overloaded:

```
MemberInfo[] m = typeof (Walnut).GetMember ("Crack");
Console.WriteLine (m[0]);                              // Void Crack()
```

MemberInfo also has a property called MemberType of type MemberTypes. This is a flags enum with these values:

| All | Custom | Field | NestedType | TypeInfo |
| Constructor | Event | Method | Property | |

When calling GetMembers, you can pass in a MemberTypes instance to restrict the kinds of members that it returns. Alternatively, you can restrict the result set by calling GetMethods, GetFields, GetProperties, GetEvents, GetConstructors, or GetNested Types. There are also singular versions of each of these to hone in on a specific member.

 It pays to be as specific as possible when retrieving a type member, so your code doesn't break if additional members are added later. If you're retrieving a method by name, specifying all parameter types ensures your code will still work if the method is later overloaded (we provide examples shortly, in the section "Method Parameters" on page 693).

A MemberInfo object has a Name property and two Type properties:

DeclaringType
> Returns the Type that defines the member

ReflectedType
> Returns the Type upon which GetMembers was called

The two differ when called on a member that's defined in a base type: Declaring Type returns the base type, whereas ReflectedType returns the subtype. The following example highlights this:

```
class Program
{
  static void Main()
  {
    // MethodInfo is a subclass of MemberInfo; see Figure 18-1.

    MethodInfo test = typeof (Program).GetMethod ("ToString");
    MethodInfo obj  = typeof (object) .GetMethod ("ToString");

    Console.WriteLine (test.DeclaringType);     // System.Object
    Console.WriteLine (obj.DeclaringType);      // System.Object

    Console.WriteLine (test.ReflectedType);     // Program
    Console.WriteLine (obj.ReflectedType);      // System.Object

    Console.WriteLine (test == obj);            // False
  }
}
```

Because they have different ReflectedTypes, the test and obj objects are not equal. Their difference, however, is purely a fabrication of the reflection API; our Program type has no distinct ToString method in the underlying type system. We can verify that the two MethodInfo objects refer to the same method in either of two ways:

```
Console.WriteLine (test.MethodHandle == obj.MethodHandle);   // True

Console.WriteLine (test.MetadataToken == obj.MetadataToken   // True
                   && test.Module == obj.Module);
```

A `MethodHandle` is unique to each (genuinely distinct) method within an application domain; a `MetadataToken` is unique across all types and members within an assembly module.

`MemberInfo` also defines methods to return custom attributes (see the section "Retrieving Attributes at Runtime" on page 705 later in this chapter).

 You can obtain the `MethodBase` of the currently executing method by calling `MethodBase.GetCurrentMethod`.

Member Types

`MemberInfo` itself is light on members because it's an abstract base for the types shown in Figure 18-1.

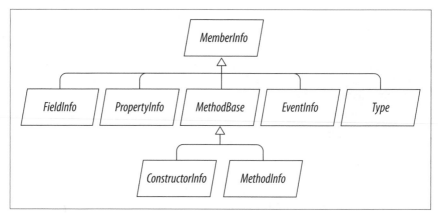

Figure 18-1. Member types

You can cast a `MemberInfo` to its subtype—based on its `MemberType` property. If you obtained a member via `GetMethod`, `GetField`, `GetProperty`, `GetEvent`, `GetConstructor`, or `GetNestedType` (or their plural versions), a cast isn't necessary. Table 18-1 summarizes what methods to use for each kind of C# construct.

Table 18-1. Retrieving member metadata

C# construct	Method to use	Name to use	Result
Method	GetMethod	Method name	MethodInfo
Property	GetProperty	Property name	PropertyInfo
Indexer	GetDefaultMembers		MemberInfo[] (containing PropertyInfo objects if compiled in C#)
Field	GetField	Field name	FieldInfo
Enum member	GetField	Member name	FieldInfo

C# construct	Method to use	Name to use	Result
Event	GetEvent	Event name	EventInfo
Constructor	GetConstructor		ConstructorInfo
Finalizer	GetMethod	"Finalize"	MethodInfo
Operator	GetMethod	"op_" + operator name	MethodInfo
Nested type	GetNestedType	Type name	Type

Each `MemberInfo` subclass has a wealth of properties and methods, exposing all aspects of the member's metadata. This includes such things as visibility, modifiers, generic type arguments, parameters, return type, and custom attributes.

Here is an example of using `GetMethod`:

```
MethodInfo m = typeof (Walnut).GetMethod ("Crack");
Console.WriteLine (m);                    // Void Crack()
Console.WriteLine (m.ReturnType);         // System.Void
```

All `*Info` instances are cached by the reflection API on first use:

```
MethodInfo method = typeof (Walnut).GetMethod ("Crack");
MemberInfo member = typeof (Walnut).GetMember ("Crack") [0];

Console.Write (method == member);         // True
```

As well as preserving object identity, caching improves the performance of what is otherwise a fairly slow API.

C# Members Versus CLR Members

The preceding table illustrates that some of C#'s functional constructs don't have a 1:1 mapping with CLR constructs. This makes sense because the CLR and reflection API were designed with all .NET languages in mind—you can use reflection even from Visual Basic.

Some C# constructs—namely indexers, enums, operators, and finalizers—are contrivances as far as the CLR is concerned. Specifically:

- A C# indexer translates to a property accepting one or more arguments, marked as the type's [DefaultMember].
- A C# enum translates to a subtype of `System.Enum` with a static field for each member.
- A C# operator translates to a specially named static method, starting in "op_"; for example, "op_Addition".
- A C# finalizer translates to a method that overrides `Finalize`.

Another complication is that properties and events actually comprise two things:

- Metadata describing the property or event (encapsulated by `PropertyInfo` or `EventInfo`)
- One or two backing methods

In a C# program, the backing methods are encapsulated within the property or event definition. But when compiled to IL, the backing methods present as ordinary methods that you can call like any other. This means GetMethods returns property and event backing methods alongside ordinary methods. To illustrate:

```
class Test { public int X { get { return 0; } set {} } }

void Demo()
{
  foreach (MethodInfo mi in typeof (Test).GetMethods())
    Console.Write (mi.Name + "  ");
}

// OUTPUT:
get_X  set_X  GetType  ToString  Equals  GetHashCode
```

You can identify these methods through the IsSpecialName property in MethodInfo. IsSpecialName returns true for property, indexer, and event accessors—as well as operators. It returns false only for conventional C# methods—and the Finalize method if a finalizer is defined.

Here are the backing methods that C# generates:

C# construct	Member type	Methods in IL
Property	Property	get_*XXX* and set_*XXX*
Indexer	Property	get_Item and set_Item
Event	Event	add_*XXX* and remove_*XXX*

Each backing method has its own associated MethodInfo object. You can access these as follows:

```
PropertyInfo pi = typeof (Console).GetProperty ("Title");
MethodInfo getter = pi.GetGetMethod();           // get_Title
MethodInfo setter = pi.GetSetMethod();           // set_Title
MethodInfo[] both = pi.GetAccessors();           // Length==2
```

GetAddMethod and GetRemoveMethod perform a similar job for EventInfo.

To go in the reverse direction—from a MethodInfo to its associated PropertyInfo or EventInfo—you need to perform a query. LINQ is ideal for this job:

```
PropertyInfo p = mi.DeclaringType.GetProperties()
                   .First (x => x.GetAccessors (true).Contains (mi));
```

Generic Type Members

You can obtain member metadata for both unbound and closed generic types:

```
PropertyInfo unbound = typeof (IEnumerator<>)   .GetProperty ("Current");
PropertyInfo closed = typeof (IEnumerator<int>).GetProperty ("Current");

Console.WriteLine (unbound);   // T Current
Console.WriteLine (closed);    // Int32 Current
```

```
Console.WriteLine (unbound.PropertyType.IsGenericParameter);   // True
Console.WriteLine (closed.PropertyType.IsGenericParameter);    // False
```

The MemberInfo objects returned from unbound and closed generic types are always distinct—even for members whose signatures don't feature generic type parameters:

```
PropertyInfo unbound = typeof (List<>) .GetProperty ("Count");
PropertyInfo closed = typeof (List<int>).GetProperty ("Count");

Console.WriteLine (unbound);    // Int32 Count
Console.WriteLine (closed);     // Int32 Count

Console.WriteLine (unbound == closed);   // False

Console.WriteLine (unbound.DeclaringType.IsGenericTypeDefinition); // True
Console.WriteLine (closed.DeclaringType.IsGenericTypeDefinition); // False
```

Members of unbound generic types cannot be *dynamically invoked*.

Dynamically Invoking a Member

Once you have a MemberInfo object, you can dynamically call it or get/set its value. This is called *dynamic binding* or *late binding*, because you choose which member to invoke at runtime rather than compile time.

To illustrate, the following uses ordinary *static binding*:

```
string s = "Hello";
int length = s.Length;
```

Here's the same thing performed dynamically with reflection:

```
object s = "Hello";
PropertyInfo prop = s.GetType().GetProperty ("Length");
int length = (int) prop.GetValue (s, null);        // 5
```

GetValue and SetValue get and set the value of a PropertyInfo or FieldInfo. The first argument is the instance, which can be null for a static member. Accessing an indexer is just like accessing a property called "Item," except that you provide indexer values as the second argument when calling GetValue or SetValue.

To dynamically call a method, call Invoke on a MethodInfo, providing an array of arguments to pass to that method. If you get any of the argument types wrong, an exception is thrown at runtime. With dynamic invocation, you lose compile-time type safety, but still have runtime type safety (just as with the **dynamic** keyword).

Method Parameters

Suppose we want to dynamically call string's Substring method. Statically, this would be done as follows:

```
Console.WriteLine ("stamp".Substring(2));          // "amp"
```

Here's the dynamic equivalent with reflection:

```
Type type = typeof (string);
Type[] parameterTypes = { typeof (int) };
MethodInfo method = type.GetMethod ("Substring", parameterTypes);

object[] arguments = { 2 };
object returnValue = method.Invoke ("stamp", arguments);
Console.WriteLine (returnValue);                          // "amp"
```

Because the Substring method is overloaded, we had to pass an array of parameter types to GetMethod to indicate which version we wanted. Without the parameter types, GetMethod would throw an AmbiguousMatchException.

The GetParameters method, defined on MethodBase (the base class for MethodInfo and ConstructorInfo), returns parameter metadata. We can continue our previous example as follows:

```
ParameterInfo[] paramList = method.GetParameters();
foreach (ParameterInfo x in paramList)
{
  Console.WriteLine (x.Name);              // startIndex
  Console.WriteLine (x.ParameterType);     // System.Int32
}
```

Dealing with ref and out parameters

To pass ref or out parameters, call MakeByRefType on the type before obtaining the method. For instance, this code:

```
int x;
bool successfulParse = int.TryParse ("23", out x);
```

can be dynamically executed as follows:

```
object[] args = { "23", 0 };
Type[] argTypes = { typeof (string), typeof (int).MakeByRefType() };
MethodInfo tryParse = typeof (int).GetMethod ("TryParse", argTypes);
bool successfulParse = (bool) tryParse.Invoke (null, args);

Console.WriteLine (successfulParse + " " + args[1]);      // True 23
```

This same approach works for both ref and out parameter types.

Retrieving and invoking generic methods

Explicitly specifying parameter types when calling GetMethod can be essential in disambiguating overloaded methods. However, it's impossible to specify generic parameter types. For instance, consider the System.Linq.Enumerable class, which overloads the Where method as follows:

```
public static IEnumerable<TSource> Where<TSource>
  (this IEnumerable<TSource> source, Func<TSource, bool> predicate);

public static IEnumerable<TSource> Where<TSource>
  (this IEnumerable<TSource> source, Func<TSource, int, bool> predicate);
```

To retrieve a specific overload, we must retrieve all methods and then manually find the desired overload. The following query retrieves the former overload of Where:

```
from m in typeof (Enumerable).GetMethods()
where m.Name == "Where" && m.IsGenericMethod
let parameters = m.GetParameters()
where parameters.Length == 2
let genArg = m.GetGenericArguments().First()
let enumerableOfT = typeof (IEnumerable<>).MakeGenericType (genArg)
let funcOfTBool = typeof (Func<,>).MakeGenericType (genArg, typeof (bool))
where parameters[0].ParameterType == enumerableOfT
    && parameters[1].ParameterType == funcOfTBool
select m
```

Calling .Single() on this query gives the correct MethodInfo object with unbound type parameters. The next step is to close the type parameters by calling MakeGenericMethod:

```
var closedMethod = unboundMethod.MakeGenericMethod (typeof (int));
```

In this case, we've closed TSource with int, allowing us to call Enumerable.Where with a source of type IEnumerable<int>, and a predicate of type Func<int,bool>:

```
int[] source = { 3, 4, 5, 6, 7, 8 };
Func<int, bool> predicate = n => n % 2 == 1;    // Odd numbers only
```

We can now invoke the closed generic method as follows:

```
var query = (IEnumerable<int>) closedMethod.Invoke
  (null, new object[] { source, predicate });

foreach (int element in query) Console.Write (element + "|");  // 3|5|7|
```

 If you're using the System.Linq.Expressions API to dynamically build expressions (Chapter 8), you don't need to go to this trouble to specify a generic method. The Expression.Call method is overloaded to let you specify the closed type arguments of the method you wish to call:

```
int[] source = { 3, 4, 5, 6, 7, 8 };
Func<int, bool> predicate = n => n % 2 == 1;

var sourceExpr = Expression.Constant (source);
var predicateExpr = Expression.Constant (predicate);

var callExpression = Expression.Call (
  typeof (Enumerable), "Where",
  new[] { typeof (int) },  // Closed generic arg type.
  sourceExpr, predicateExpr);
```

Using Delegates for Performance

Dynamic invocations are relatively inefficient, with an overhead typically in the few-microseconds region. If you're calling a method repeatedly in a loop, you can shift the per-call overhead into the nanoseconds region by instead calling a dynamically instantiated delegate that targets your dynamic method. In the following example, we dynamically call string's Trim method a million times without significant overhead:

```
delegate string StringToString (string s);

static void Main()
{
  MethodInfo trimMethod = typeof (string).GetMethod ("Trim", new Type[0]);
  var trim = (StringToString) Delegate.CreateDelegate
                               (typeof (StringToString), trimMethod);
  for (int i = 0; i < 1000000; i++)
    trim ("test");
}
```

This is faster because the costly dynamic binding (shown in bold) happens just once.

Accessing Nonpublic Members

All of the methods on types used to probe metadata (e.g., GetProperty, GetField, etc.) have overloads that take a BindingFlags enum. This enum serves as a metadata filter and allows you to change the default selection criteria. The most common use for this is to retrieve nonpublic members.

For instance, consider the following class:

```
class Walnut
{
  private bool cracked;
  public void Crack() { cracked = true; }

  public override string ToString() { return cracked.ToString(); }
}
```

We can *uncrack* the walnut as follows:

```
Type t = typeof (Walnut);
Walnut w = new Walnut();
w.Crack();
FieldInfo f = t.GetField ("cracked", BindingFlags.NonPublic |
                                      BindingFlags.Instance);
f.SetValue (w, false);
Console.WriteLine (w);         // False
```

Using reflection to access nonpublic members is powerful, but it is also dangerous, since you can bypass encapsulation, creating an unmanageable dependency on the internal implementation of a type.

The BindingFlags enum

BindingFlags is intended to be bitwise-combined. In order to get any matches at all, you need to start with one of the following four combinations:

```
BindingFlags.Public    | BindingFlags.Instance
BindingFlags.Public    | BindingFlags.Static
BindingFlags.NonPublic | BindingFlags.Instance
BindingFlags.NonPublic | BindingFlags.Static
```

NonPublic includes internal, protected, protected internal, and private.

The following example retrieves all the public static members of type `object`:

```
BindingFlags publicStatic = BindingFlags.Public | BindingFlags.Static;
MemberInfo[] members = typeof (object).GetMembers (publicStatic);
```

The following example retrieves all the nonpublic members of type `object`, both static and instance:

```
BindingFlags nonPublicBinding =
    BindingFlags.NonPublic | BindingFlags.Static | BindingFlags.Instance;

MemberInfo[] members = typeof (object).GetMembers (nonPublicBinding);
```

The `DeclaredOnly` flag excludes functions inherited from base types, unless they are overridden.

The `DeclaredOnly` flag is somewhat confusing in that it *restricts* the result set (whereas all the other binding flags *expand* the result set).

Generic Methods

Generic methods cannot be invoked directly; the following throws an exception:

```
class Program
{
  public static T Echo<T> (T x) { return x; }

  static void Main()
  {
    MethodInfo echo = typeof (Program).GetMethod ("Echo");
    Console.WriteLine (echo.IsGenericMethodDefinition);    // True
    echo.Invoke (null, new object[] { 123 } );             // Exception
  }
}
```

An extra step is required, which is to call `MakeGenericMethod` on the `MethodInfo`, specifying concrete generic type arguments. This returns another `MethodInfo`, which you can then invoke as follows:

```
MethodInfo echo = typeof (Program).GetMethod ("Echo");
MethodInfo intEcho = echo.MakeGenericMethod (typeof (int));
Console.WriteLine (intEcho.IsGenericMethodDefinition);      // False
Console.WriteLine (intEcho.Invoke (null, new object[] { 3 } ));   // 3
```

Anonymously Calling Members of a Generic Interface

Reflection is useful when you need to invoke a member of a generic interface and you don't know the type parameters until runtime. In theory, the need for this arises rarely if types are perfectly designed; of course, types are not always perfectly designed.

Reflection

For instance, suppose we want to write a more powerful version of ToString that could expand the result of LINQ queries. We could start out as follows:

```
public static string ToStringEx <T> (IEnumerable<T> sequence)
{
  ...
}
```

This is already quite limiting. What if sequence contained *nested* collections that we also want to enumerate? We'd have to overload the method to cope:

```
public static string ToStringEx <T> (IEnumerable<IEnumerable<T>> sequence)
```

And then what if sequence contained groupings, or *projections* of nested sequences? The static solution of method overloading becomes impractical—we need an approach that can scale to handle an arbitrary object graph, such as the following:

```
public static string ToStringEx (object value)
{
  if (value == null) return "<null>";
  StringBuilder sb = new StringBuilder();

  if (value is List<>)                                          // Error
    sb.Append ("List of " + ((List<>) value).Count + " items"); // Error

  if (value is IGrouping<,>)                                    // Error
    sb.Append ("Group with key=" + ((IGrouping<,>) value).Key); // Error

  // Enumerate collection elements if this is a collection,
  // recursively calling ToStringEx()
  // ...

  return sb.ToString();
}
```

Unfortunately, this won't compile: you cannot invoke members of an *unbound* generic type such as List<> or IGrouping<>. In the case of List<>, we can solve the problem by using the nongeneric IList interface instead:

```
  if (value is IList)
    sb.AppendLine ("A list with " + ((IList) value).Count + " items");
```

 We can do this because the designers of List<> had the foresight to implement IList classic (as well as IList *generic*). The same principle is worthy of consideration when writing your own generic types: having a nongeneric interface or base class upon which consumers can fall back can be extremely valuable.

The solution is not as simple for IGrouping<,>. Here's how the interface is defined:

```
public interface IGrouping <TKey,TElement> : IEnumerable <TElement>,
                                             IEnumerable
{
  TKey Key { get; }
}
```

There's no nongeneric type we can use to access the Key property, so here we must use reflection. The solution is not to invoke members of an unbound generic type (which is impossible), but to invoke members of a *closed* generic type, whose type arguments we establish at runtime.

 In the following chapter, we solve this more simply with C#'s dynamic keyword. A good indication for dynamic binding is when you would otherwise have to perform *type gymnastics*— as we are doing right now.

The first step is to determine whether value implements IGrouping<,>, and if so, obtain its closed generic interface. We can do this most easily with a LINQ query. Then we retrieve and invoke the Key property:

```
public static string ToStringEx (object value)
{
  if (value == null) return "<null>";
  if (value.GetType().IsPrimitive) return value.ToString();

  StringBuilder sb = new StringBuilder();

  if (value is IList)
    sb.Append ("List of " + ((IList)value).Count + " items: ");

  Type closedIGrouping = value.GetType().GetInterfaces()
    .Where (t => t.IsGenericType &&
                 t.GetGenericTypeDefinition() == typeof (IGrouping<,>))
    .FirstOrDefault();

  if (closedIGrouping != null)    // Call the Key property on IGrouping<,>
  {
    PropertyInfo pi = closedIGrouping.GetProperty ("Key");
    object key = pi.GetValue (value, null);
    sb.Append ("Group with key=" + key + ": ");
  }

  if (value is IEnumerable)
    foreach (object element in ((IEnumerable)value))
      sb.Append (ToStringEx (element) + " ");

  if (sb.Length == 0) sb.Append (value.ToString());

  return "\r\n" + sb.ToString();
}
```

This approach is robust: it works whether IGrouping<,> is implemented implicitly or explicitly. The following demonstrates this method:

```
Console.WriteLine (ToStringEx (new List<int> { 5, 6, 7 } ));
Console.WriteLine (ToStringEx ("xyyzzz".GroupBy (c => c) ));

List of 3 items: 5 6 7
```

Reflection

```
Group with key=x: x
Group with key=y: y y
Group with key=z: z z z
```

Reflecting Assemblies

You can dynamically reflect an assembly by calling `GetType` or `GetTypes` on an `Assembly` object. The following retrieves from the current assembly, the type called `TestProgram` in the `Demos` namespace:

```
Type t = Assembly.GetExecutingAssembly().GetType ("Demos.TestProgram");
```

The next example lists all the types in the assembly *mylib.dll* in *e:\demo*:

```
Assembly a = Assembly.LoadFrom (@"e:\demo\mylib.dll");

foreach (Type t in a.GetTypes())
  Console.WriteLine (t);
```

`GetTypes` returns only top-level and not nested types.

Loading an Assembly into a Reflection-Only Context

In the preceding example, we loaded an assembly into the current application domain in order to list its types. This can have undesirable side effects, such as executing static constructors or upsetting subsequent type resolution. The solution, if you just need to inspect type information (and not instantiate or invoke types), is to load the assembly into a *reflection-only* context:

```
Assembly a = Assembly.ReflectionOnlyLoadFrom (@"e:\demo\mylib.dll");
Console.WriteLine (a.ReflectionOnly);   // True

foreach (Type t in a.GetTypes())
  Console.WriteLine (t);
```

This is the starting point for writing a class browser.

There are three methods for loading an assembly into the reflection-only context:

* `ReflectionOnlyLoad (byte[])`
* `ReflectionOnlyLoad (string)`
* `ReflectionOnlyLoadFrom (string)`

 Even in a reflection-only context, it is not possible to load multiple versions of *mscorlib.dll*. For this reason, class browsers such as Lutz Roeder's .NET Reflector are written with custom classes and structs that map to the unmanaged metadata interfaces.

Modules

Calling GetTypes on a multimodule assembly returns all types in all modules. As a result, you can ignore the existence of modules and treat an assembly as a type's container. There is one case, though, where modules are relevant—and that's when dealing with metadata tokens.

A metadata token is an integer that uniquely refers to a type, member, string, or resource within the scope of a module. IL uses metadata tokens, so if you're parsing IL, you'll need to be able to resolve them. The methods for doing this are defined in the Module type and are called ResolveType, ResolveMember, ResolveString, and ResolveSignature. We revisit this in the final section of this chapter, on writing a disassembler.

You can obtain a list of all the modules in an assembly by calling GetModules. You can also access an assembly's main module directly—via its ManifestModule property.

Working with Attributes

The CLR allows additional metadata to be attached to types, members, and assemblies through attributes. This is the mechanism by which many CLR functions such as serialization and security are directed, making attributes an indivisible part of an application.

A key characteristic of attributes is that you can write your own, and then use them just as you would any other attribute to "decorate" a code element with additional information. This additional information is compiled into the underlying assembly and can be retrieved at runtime using reflection to build services that work declaratively, such as automated unit testing.

Attribute Basics

There are three kinds of attributes:

- Bit-mapped attributes
- Custom attributes
- Pseudocustom attributes

Of these, only *custom attributes* are extensible.

 The term "attribute" by itself can refer to any of the three, although in the C# world, it most often refers to custom attributes or pseudocustom attributes.

Bit-mapped attributes (our terminology) map to dedicated bits in a type's metadata. Most of C#'s modifier keywords, such as public, abstract, and sealed, compile to bit-mapped attributes. These attributes are very efficient because they consume

Reflection

minimal space in the metadata (usually just one bit), and the CLR can locate them with little or no indirection. The reflection API exposes them via dedicated properties on `Type` (and other `MemberInfo` subclasses), such as `IsPublic`, `IsAbstract`, and `IsSealed`. The `Attributes` property returns a flags enum that describes most of them in one hit:

```
static void Main()
{
  TypeAttributes ta = typeof (Console).Attributes;
  MethodAttributes ma = MethodInfo.GetCurrentMethod().Attributes;
  Console.WriteLine (ta + "\r\n" + ma);
}
```

Here's the result:

```
AutoLayout, AnsiClass, Class, Public, Abstract, Sealed, BeforeFieldInit
PrivateScope, Private, Static, HideBySig
```

In contrast, *custom attributes* compile to a blob that hangs off the type's main metadata table. All custom attributes are represented by a subclass of `System.Attribute` and, unlike bit-mapped attributes, are extensible. The blob in the metadata identifies the attribute class, and also stores the values of any positional or named argument that was specified when the attribute was applied. Custom attributes that you define yourself are architecturally identical to those defined in the .NET Framework.

Chapter 4 describes how to attach custom attributes to a type or member in C#. Here, we attach the predefined `Obsolete` attribute to the `Foo` class:

```
[Obsolete] public class Foo {...}
```

This instructs the compiler to incorporate an instance of `ObsoleteAttribute` into the metadata for `Foo`, which can then be reflected at runtime by calling `GetCustomAttributes` on a `Type` or `MemberInfo` object.

Pseudocustom attributes look and feel just like standard custom attributes. They are represented by a subclass of `System.Attribute` and are attached in the standard manner:

```
[Serializable] public class Foo {...}
```

The difference is that the compiler or CLR internally optimizes pseudocustom attributes by converting them to bit-mapped attributes. Examples include [Serializable] (Chapter 16), `StructLayout`, `In`, and `Out` (Chapter 25). Reflection exposes psuedocustom attributes through dedicated properties such as `IsSerializable`, and in many cases they are also returned as `System.Attribute` objects when you call `GetCustomAttributes` (`SerializableAttribute` included). This means you can (almost) ignore the difference between pseudo- and non-pseudo-custom attributes (a notable exception is when using `Reflection.Emit` to generate types dynamically at runtime; see "Emitting Assemblies and Types" on page 714 later in this chapter).

The AttributeUsage Attribute

AttributeUsage is an attribute applied to attribute classes. It tells the compiler how the target attribute should be used:

```
public sealed class AttributeUsageAttribute : Attribute
{
    public AttributeUsageAttribute (AttributeTargets validOn);

    public bool AllowMultiple          { get; set; }
    public bool Inherited              { get; set; }
    public AttributeTargets ValidOn    { get; }
}
```

AllowMultiple controls whether the attribute being defined can be applied more than once to the same target; Inherited controls whether the attribute can be subtyped. ValidOn determines the set of targets (classes, interfaces, properties, methods, parameters, etc.) to which the attribute can be attached. It accepts any combination of values from the AttributeTargets enum, which has the following members:

All	Delegate	GenericParameter	Parameter
Assembly	Enum	Interface	Property
Class	Event	Method	ReturnValue
Constructor	Field	Module	Struct

To illustrate, here's how the authors of the .NET Framework have applied AttributeUsage to the Serializable attribute:

```
[AttributeUsage (AttributeTargets.Delegate |
                 AttributeTargets.Enum     |
                 AttributeTargets.Struct   |
                 AttributeTargets.Class,     Inherited = false)
]
public sealed class SerializableAttribute : Attribute
{
}
```

This is, in fact, almost the complete definition of the Serializable attribute. Writing an attribute class that has no properties or special constructors is this simple.

Defining Your Own Attribute

Here's how you write your own attribute:

1. Derive a class from System.Attribute or a descendent of System.Attribute. By convention, the class name should end with the word "Attribute," although this isn't required.

2. Apply the AttributeUsage attribute, described in the preceding section.

   If the attribute requires no properties or arguments in its constructor, the job is done.

3. Write one or more public constructors. The parameters to the constructor define the positional parameters of the attribute and will become mandatory when using the attribute.

4. Declare a public field or property for each named parameter you wish to support. Named parameters are optional when using the attribute.

 Attribute properties and constructor parameters must be of the following types:

- A sealed primitive type: in other words, bool, byte, char, double, float, int, long, short, or string
- The Type type
- An enum type
- A one-dimensional array of any of these

When an attribute is applied, it must also be possible for the compiler to statically evaluate each of the properties or constructor arguments.

The following class defines an attribute for assisting an automated unit-testing system. It indicates that a method should be tested, the number of test repetitions, and a message in case of failure:

```
[AttributeUsage (AttributeTargets.Method)]
public sealed class TestAttribute : Attribute
{
  public int      Repetitions;
  public string   FailureMessage;

  public TestAttribute () : this (1)      { }
  public TestAttribute (int repetitions) { Repetitions = repetitions; }
}
```

Here's a Foo class with methods decorated in various ways with the Test attribute:

```
class Foo
{
  [Test]
  public void Method1() { ... }

  [Test(20)]
  public void Method2() { ... }

  [Test(20, FailureMessage="Debugging Time!")]
  public void Method3() { ... }
}
```

Retrieving Attributes at Runtime

There are two standard ways to retrieve attributes at runtime:

- Call `GetCustomAttributes` on any `Type` or `MemberInfo` object.
- Call `Attribute.GetCustomAttribute` or `Attribute.GetCustomAttributes`.

These latter two methods are overloaded to accept any reflection object that corresponds to a valid attribute target (`Type`, `Assembly`, `Module`, `MemberInfo`, or `ParameterInfo`).

 From Framework 4.0, you can also call `GetCustomAttri butesData()` on a type or member to obtain attribute information. The difference between this and `GetCustomAttributes()` is that the former tells you *how* the attribute was instantiated: it reports the constructor overload that was used, and the value of each constructor argument and named parameter. This is useful when you want to emit code or IL to reconstruct the attribute to the same state (see the section "Emitting Type Members" on page 717 later in this chapter).

Here's how we can enumerate each method in the preceding `Foo` class that has a `TestAttribute`:

```
foreach (MethodInfo mi in typeof (Foo).GetMethods())
{
  TestAttribute att = (TestAttribute) Attribute.GetCustomAttribute
    (mi, typeof (TestAttribute));

  if (att != null)
    Console.WriteLine ("Method {0} will be tested; reps={1}; msg={2}",
                        mi.Name, att.Repetitions, att.FailureMessage);
}
```

Here's the output:

```
Method Method1 will be tested; reps=1; msg=
Method Method2 will be tested; reps=20; msg=
Method Method3 will be tested; reps=20; msg=Debugging Time!
```

To complete the illustration on how we could use this to write a unit-testing system, here's the same example expanded so that it actually calls the methods decorated with the `Test` attribute:

```
foreach (MethodInfo mi in typeof (Foo).GetMethods())
{
  TestAttribute att = (TestAttribute) Attribute.GetCustomAttribute
    (mi, typeof (TestAttribute));

  if (att != null)
    for (int i = 0; i < att.Repetitions; i++)
      try
```

Reflection

```
    {
      mi.Invoke (new Foo(), null);    // Call method with no arguments
    }
    catch (Exception ex)        // Wrap exception in att.FailureMessage
    {
      throw new Exception ("Error: " + att.FailureMessage, ex);
    }
  }
```

Returning to attribute reflection, here's an example that lists the attributes present on a specific type:

```
[Serializable, Obsolete]
class Test
{
  static void Main()
  {
    object[] atts = Attribute.GetCustomAttributes (typeof (Test));
    foreach (object att in atts) Console.WriteLine (att);
  }
}
```

Output:

```
System.ObsoleteAttribute
System.SerializableAttribute
```

Retrieving Attributes in the Reflection-Only Context

Calling GetCustomAttributes on a member loaded in the reflection-only context is prohibited because it would require instantiating arbitrarily typed attributes (remember that object instantiation isn't allowed in the reflection-only context). To work around this, there's a special type called CustomAttributeData for reflecting over such attributes. Here's an example of how it's used:

```
IList<CustomAttributeData> atts = CustomAttributeData.GetCustomAttributes
                                  (myReflectionOnlyType);
foreach (CustomAttributeData att in atts)
{
  Console.Write (att.GetType());                   // Attribute type

  Console.WriteLine (" " + att.Constructor);   // ConstructorInfo object

  foreach (CustomAttributeTypedArgument arg in att.ConstructorArguments)
    Console.WriteLine ("   " +arg.ArgumentType + "=" + arg.Value);

  foreach (CustomAttributeNamedArgument arg in att.NamedArguments)
    Console.WriteLine ("   " + arg.MemberInfo.Name + "=" + arg.TypedValue);
}
```

In many cases, the attribute types will be in a different assembly from the one you're reflecting. One way to cope with this is to handle the ReflectionOnlyAssemblyRe solve event on the current application domain:

```
ResolveEventHandler handler = (object sender, ResolveEventArgs args)
                  => Assembly.ReflectionOnlyLoad (args.Name);
```

```
AppDomain.CurrentDomain.ReflectionOnlyAssemblyResolve += handler;

// Reflect over attributes...

AppDomain.CurrentDomain.ReflectionOnlyAssemblyResolve -= handler;
```

Dynamic Code Generation

The System.Reflection.Emit namespace contains classes for creating metadata and
IL at runtime. Generating code dynamically is useful for certain kinds of programming tasks. An example is the regular expressions API, which emits performant types
tuned to specific regular expressions. Other uses of Reflection.Emit in the Framework include dynamically generating transparent proxies for Remoting and generating types that perform specific XSLT transforms with minimum runtime overhead.
LINQPad uses Reflection.Emit to dynamically generate typed DataContext classes.

Generating IL with DynamicMethod

The DynamicMethod class is a lightweight tool in the System.Reflection.Emit namespace for generating methods on the fly. Unlike TypeBuilder, it doesn't require that
you first set up a dynamic assembly, module, and type in which to contain the
method. This makes it suitable for simple tasks—as well as serving as a good introduction to Reflection.Emit.

 A DynamicMethod and the associated IL are garbage-collected
when no longer referenced. This means you can repeatedly generate dynamic methods without filling up memory. In contrast,
dynamic *assemblies* cannot be unloaded from memory unless
the containing application domain is torn down.

Here is a simple use of DynamicMethod to create a method that writes Hello world to
the console:

```
public class Test
{
  static void Main()
  {
    var dynMeth = new DynamicMethod ("Foo", null, null, typeof (Test));
    ILGenerator gen = dynMeth.GetILGenerator();
    gen.EmitWriteLine ("Hello world");
    gen.Emit (OpCodes.Ret);
    dynMeth.Invoke (null, null);                    // Hello world
  }
}
```

OpCodes has a static read-only field for every IL opcode. Most of the functionality is
exposed through various opcodes, although ILGenerator also has specialized methods for generating labels and local variables and for exception handling. A method
always ends in Opcodes.Ret, which means "return." The EmitWriteLine method on
ILGenerator is a shortcut for Emitting a number of lower-level opcodes. We could

have replaced the call to EmitWriteLine with this, and we would have gotten the same result:

```
MethodInfo writeLineStr = typeof (Console).GetMethod ("WriteLine",
                              new Type[] { typeof (string) });
gen.Emit (OpCodes.Ldstr, "Hello world");    // Load a string
gen.Emit (OpCodes.Call, writeLineStr);      // Call a method
```

Note that we passed typeof(Test) into DynamicMethod's constructor. This gives the dynamic method access to the nonpublic methods of that type, allowing us to do this:

```
public class Test
{
  static void Main()
  {
    var dynMeth = new DynamicMethod ("Foo", null, null, typeof (Test));
    ILGenerator gen = dynMeth.GetILGenerator();

    MethodInfo privateMethod = typeof(Test).GetMethod ("HelloWorld",
      BindingFlags.Static | BindingFlags.NonPublic);

    gen.Emit (OpCodes.Call, privateMethod);    // Call HelloWorld
    gen.Emit (OpCodes.Ret);

    dynMeth.Invoke (null, null);               // Hello world
  }

  static void HelloWorld()        // private method, yet we can call it
  {
    Console.WriteLine ("Hello world");
  }
}
```

Understanding IL requires a considerable investment of time. Rather than understand all the opcodes, it's much easier to compile a C# program then to examine, copy, and tweak the IL. An assembly viewing tool such as *ildasm* or Lutz Roeder's Reflector is perfect for the job.

The Evaluation Stack

Central to IL is the concept of the *evaluation stack*. The evaluation stack is distinct from the stack used to store local variables and method parameters.

To call a method with arguments, you first push ("load") the arguments onto the evaluation stack, and then call the method. The method then pops the arguments it needs from the evaluation stack. We demonstrated this previously, in calling Console.WriteLine. Here's a similar example with an integer:

```
var dynMeth = new DynamicMethod ("Foo", null, null, typeof(void));
ILGenerator gen = dynMeth.GetILGenerator();
MethodInfo writeLineInt = typeof (Console).GetMethod ("WriteLine",
                              new Type[] { typeof (int) });

// The Ldc* op-codes load numeric literals of various types and sizes.
```

```
gen.Emit (OpCodes.Ldc_I4, 123);        // Push a 4-byte integer onto stack
gen.Emit (OpCodes.Call, writeLineInt);

gen.Emit (OpCodes.Ret);
dynMeth.Invoke (null, null);           // 123
```

To add two numbers together, you first load each number onto the evaluation stack, and then call Add. The Add opcode pops two values from the evaluation stack and pushes the result back on. The following adds 2 and 2, and then writes the result using the writeLine method obtained previously:

```
gen.Emit (OpCodes.Ldc_I4, 2);          // Push a 4-byte integer, value=2
gen.Emit (OpCodes.Ldc_I4, 2);          // Push a 4-byte integer, value=2
gen.Emit (OpCodes.Add);                // Add the result together
gen.Emit (OpCodes.Call, writeLineInt);
```

To calculate 10 / 2 + 1, you can do either this:

```
gen.Emit (OpCodes.Ldc_I4, 10);
gen.Emit (OpCodes.Ldc_I4, 2);
gen.Emit (OpCodes.Div);
gen.Emit (OpCodes.Ldc_I4, 1);
gen.Emit (OpCodes.Add);
gen.Emit (OpCodes.Call, writeLineInt);
```

or this:

```
gen.Emit (OpCodes.Ldc_I4, 1);
gen.Emit (OpCodes.Ldc_I4, 10);
gen.Emit (OpCodes.Ldc_I4, 2);
gen.Emit (OpCodes.Div);
gen.Emit (OpCodes.Add);
gen.Emit (OpCodes.Call, writeLineInt);
```

Passing Arguments to a Dynamic Method

You can load an argument passed into a dynamic method onto the stack with the Ldarg and Ldarg_XXX opcodes. To return a value, leave exactly one value on the stack upon finishing. For this to work, you must specify the return type and argument types when calling DynamicMethod's constructor. The following creates a dynamic method that returns the sum of two integers:

```
DynamicMethod dynMeth = new DynamicMethod ("Foo",
  typeof (int),                          // Return type = int
  new[] { typeof (int), typeof (int) },  // Parameter types = int, int
  typeof (void));

ILGenerator gen = dynMeth.GetILGenerator();

gen.Emit (OpCodes.Ldarg_0);     // Push first arg onto eval stack
gen.Emit (OpCodes.Ldarg_1);     // Push second arg onto eval stack
gen.Emit (OpCodes.Add);         // Add them together (result on stack)
gen.Emit (OpCodes.Ret);         // Return with stack having 1 value

int result = (int) dynMeth.Invoke (null, new object[] { 3, 4 } );   // 7
```

When you exit, the evaluation stack must have exactly 0 or 1 items (depending on whether your method returns a value). If you violate this, the CLR will refuse to execute your method. You can remove an item from the stack without processing it with `OpCodes.Pop`.

Rather than calling `Invoke`, it can be more convenient to work with a dynamic method as a typed delegate. The `CreateDelegate` method achieves just this. To illustrate, suppose we define a delegate called `BinaryFunction`:

```
delegate int BinaryFunction (int n1, int n2);
```

We could then replace the last line of our preceding example with this:

```
BinaryFunction f = (BinaryFunction) dynMeth.CreateDelegate
                                    (typeof (BinaryFunction));
int result = f (3, 4);      // 7
```

 A delegate also eliminates the overhead of dynamic method invocation—saving a few microseconds per call.

We demonstrate how to pass by reference later in the section "Emitting Type Members" on page 717.

Generating Local Variables

You can declare a local variable by calling `DeclareLocal` on an `ILGenerator`. This returns a `LocalBuilder` object, which can be used in conjunction with opcodes such as `Ldloc` (load a local variable) or `Stloc` (store a local variable). `Ldloc` pushes the evaluation stack; `Stloc` pops it. For example, consider the following C# code:

```
int x = 6;
int y = 7;
x *= y;
Console.WriteLine (x);
```

The following generates the preceding code dynamically:

```
var dynMeth = new DynamicMethod ("Test", null, null, typeof (void));
ILGenerator gen = dynMeth.GetILGenerator();

LocalBuilder localX = gen.DeclareLocal (typeof (int));   // Declare x
LocalBuilder localY = gen.DeclareLocal (typeof (int));   // Declare y

gen.Emit (OpCodes.Ldc_I4, 6);        // Push literal 6 onto eval stack
gen.Emit (OpCodes.Stloc, localX);    // Store in localX
gen.Emit (OpCodes.Ldc_I4, 7);        // Push literal 7 onto eval stack
gen.Emit (OpCodes.Stloc, localY);    // Store in localY

gen.Emit (OpCodes.Ldloc, localX);    // Push localX onto eval stack
gen.Emit (OpCodes.Ldloc, localY);    // Push localY onto eval stack
```

```
gen.Emit (OpCodes.Mul);              // Multiply values together
gen.Emit (OpCodes.Stloc, localX);    // Store the result to localX

gen.EmitWriteLine (localX);          // Write the value of localX
gen.Emit (OpCodes.Ret);

dynMeth.Invoke (null, null);         // 42
```

 Lutz Roeder's Reflector is also great for examining dynamic methods for errors. If you decompile to C#, it's usually obvious where you've gone wrong! We explain how to save dynamic emissions to disk in the section "Emitting Assemblies and Types" on page 714.

Branching

In IL, there are no while, do, and for loops; it's all done with labels and the equivalent of goto and conditional goto statements. These are the branching opcodes, such as Br (branch unconditionally), Brtrue (branch if the value on the evaluation stack is true), and Blt (branch if the first value is less than the second value).

To set a branch target, first call DefineLabel (this returns a Label object), and then call MarkLabel at the place you want to anchor the label. e.g., consider this C# code:

```
int x = 5;
while (x <= 10) Console.WriteLine (x++);
```

We can emit this as follows:

```
ILGenerator gen = ...

Label startLoop = gen.DefineLabel();              // Declare labels
Label endLoop = gen.DefineLabel();

LocalBuilder x = gen.DeclareLocal (typeof (int)); // int x
gen.Emit (OpCodes.Ldc_I4, 5);                     //
gen.Emit (OpCodes.Stloc, x);                      // x = 5
gen.MarkLabel (startLoop);
  gen.Emit (OpCodes.Ldc_I4, 10);                  // Load 10 onto eval stack
  gen.Emit (OpCodes.Ldloc, x);                    // Load x onto eval stack

  gen.Emit (OpCodes.Blt, endLoop);                // if (x > 10) goto endLoop

  gen.EmitWriteLine (x);                          // Console.WriteLine (x)

  gen.Emit (OpCodes.Ldloc, x);                    // Load x onto eval stack
  gen.Emit (OpCodes.Ldc_I4, 1);                   // Load 1 onto the stack
  gen.Emit (OpCodes.Add);                         // Add them together
  gen.Emit (OpCodes.Stloc, x);                    // Save result back to x

  gen.Emit (OpCodes.Br, startLoop);               // return to start of loop
gen.MarkLabel (endLoop);

gen.Emit (OpCodes.Ret);
```

Instantiating Objects and Calling Instance Methods

The IL equivalent of new is the `Newobj` opcode. This takes a constructor and loads the constructed object onto the evaluation stack. For instance, the code shown next constructs a `StringBuilder`:

```
var dynMeth = new DynamicMethod ("Test", null, null, typeof (void));
ILGenerator gen = dynMeth.GetILGenerator();

ConstructorInfo ci = typeof (StringBuilder).GetConstructor (new Type[0]);
gen.Emit (OpCodes.Newobj, ci);
```

Once an object is on the evaluation stack, you can call its instance methods using the `Call` or `Callvirt` opcode. Extending this example, we'll query the `StringBuilder`'s `MaxCapacity` property by calling the property's get accessor, and then write out the result:

```
gen.Emit (OpCodes.Callvirt, typeof (StringBuilder)
                    .GetProperty ("MaxCapacity").GetGetMethod());

gen.Emit (OpCodes.Call, typeof (Console).GetMethod ("WriteLine",
                                    new[] { typeof (int) } ));
gen.Emit (OpCodes.Ret);
dynMeth.Invoke (null, null);        // 2147483647
```

To emulate C# calling semantics:

- Use `Call` to invoke static methods and value type instance methods.
- Use `Callvirt` to invoke reference type instance methods (whether or not they're declared virtual).

In our example, we used `Callvirt` on the `StringBuilder` instance—even though `MaxProperty` is not virtual. This doesn't cause an error: it simply performs a nonvirtual call instead. Always invoking reference type instance methods with `Callvirt` avoids risking the opposite condition: invoking a virtual method with `Call`. (The risk is real. The author of the target method may later *change* its declaration.)

 Invoking a virtual method with `Call` bypasses virtual calling semantics, and calls that method directly. This is rarely desirable and, in effect, violates type safety.

In the following example, we construct a `StringBuilder` passing in two arguments, append ", world!" to the `StringBuilder`, and then call `ToString` on it:

```
// We will call:   new StringBuilder ("Hello", 1000)

ConstructorInfo ci = typeof (StringBuilder).GetConstructor (
                    new[] { typeof (string), typeof (int) } );

gen.Emit (OpCodes.Ldstr, "Hello");    // Load a string onto the eval stack
gen.Emit (OpCodes.Ldc_I4, 1000);      // Load an int onto the eval stack
gen.Emit (OpCodes.Newobj, ci);        // Construct the StringBuilder
```

```
Type[] strT = { typeof (string) };
gen.Emit (OpCodes.Ldstr, ", world!");
gen.Emit (OpCodes.Call, typeof (StringBuilder).GetMethod ("Append", strT));
gen.Emit (OpCodes.Callvirt, typeof (object).GetMethod ("ToString"));
gen.Emit (OpCodes.Call, typeof (Console).GetMethod ("WriteLine", strT));
gen.Emit (OpCodes.Ret);
dynMeth.Invoke (null, null);        // Hello, world!
```

For fun we called GetMethod on typeof(object), and then used Callvirt to perform
a virtual method call on ToString. We could have gotten the same result by calling
ToString on the StringBuilder type itself:

```
gen.Emit (OpCodes.Callvirt, typeof (StringBuilder).GetMethod ("ToString",
                                                          new Type[0] ));
```

(The empty type array is required in calling GetMethod because StringBuilder overloads ToString with another signature.)

> Had we called object's ToString method nonvirtually:
>
> ```
> gen.Emit (OpCodes.Call,
>           typeof (object).GetMethod ("ToString"));
> ```
>
> the result would have been "System.Text.StringBuilder". In
> other words, we would have circumvented StringBuilder's
> ToString override and called object's version directly.

Exception Handling

ILGenerator provides dedicated methods for exception handling. The translation for
the following C# code:

```
try                                   { throw new NotSupportedException(); }
catch (NotSupportedException ex)      { Console.WriteLine (ex.Message);     }
finally                               { Console.WriteLine ("Finally");      }
```

is this:

```
MethodInfo getMessageProp = typeof (NotSupportedException)
                            .GetProperty ("Message").GetGetMethod();

MethodInfo writeLineString = typeof (Console).GetMethod ("WriteLine",
                                          new[] { typeof (object) } );
gen.BeginExceptionBlock();
  ConstructorInfo ci = typeof (NotSupportedException).GetConstructor (
                                          new Type[0] );
  gen.Emit (OpCodes.Newobj, ci);
  gen.Emit (OpCodes.Throw);
gen.BeginCatchBlock (typeof (NotSupportedException));
  gen.Emit (OpCodes.Callvirt, getMessageProp);
  gen.Emit (OpCodes.Call, writeLineString);
gen.BeginFinallyBlock();
  gen.EmitWriteLine ("Finally");
gen.EndExceptionBlock();
```

Just as in C#, you can include multiple catch blocks. To rethrow the same exception, emit the Rethrow opcode.

 ILGenerator provides a helper method called ThrowException. This contains a bug, however, preventing it from being used with a DynamicMethod. It works only with a MethodBuilder (see the next section).

Emitting Assemblies and Types

Although is convenient, it can generate only methods. If you need to emit any other construct—or a complete type—you need to use the full "heavyweight" API. This means dynamically building an assembly and module. The assembly need not have a disk presence, however; it can live entirely in memory.

Let's assume we want to dynamically build a type. Since a type must live in a module within an assembly, we must first create the assembly and module before we can create the type. This is the job of the AssemblyBuilder and ModuleBuilder types:

```
AppDomain appDomain = AppDomain.CurrentDomain;

AssemblyName aname = new AssemblyName ("MyDynamicAssembly");

AssemblyBuilder assemBuilder =
  appDomain.DefineDynamicAssembly (aname, AssemblyBuilderAccess.Run);

ModuleBuilder modBuilder = assemBuilder.DefineDynamicModule ("DynModule");
```

 You can't add a type to an existing assembly, because an assembly is immutable once created.

Once we have a module where the type can live, we can use TypeBuilder to create the type. The following defines a class called Widget:

```
TypeBuilder tb = modBuilder.DefineType ("Widget", TypeAttributes.Public);
```

The TypeAttributes flags enum supports the CLR type modifiers you see when disassembling a type with *ildasm*. As well as member visibility flags, this includes type modifiers such as Abstract and Sealed—and Interface for defining a .NET interface. It also includes Serializable, which is equivalent to applying the [Serializable] attribute in C#, and Explicit, which is equivalent to applying [StructLayout(LayoutKind.Explicit)]. We describe how to apply other kinds of attributes later in this chapter, in the section "Attaching Attributes" on page 722.

The `DefineType` method also accepts an optional base type:

- To define a struct, specify a base type of `System.ValueType`.
- To define a delegate, specify a base type of `System.Multi castDelegate`.
- To implement an interface, use the constructor that accepts an array of interface types.
- To define an interface, specify `TypeAttributes.Interface | TypeAttributes.Abstract`.

Defining a delegate type requires a number of extra steps. In his weblog at *http://blogs.msdn.com/joelpob/*, Joel Pobar demonstrates how this is done in his article titled "Creating delegate types via Reflection.Emit."

We can now create members within the type:

```
MethodBuilder methBuilder = tb.DefineMethod ("SayHello",
                                             MethodAttributes.Public,
                                             null, null);
ILGenerator gen = methBuilder.GetILGenerator();
gen.EmitWriteLine ("Hello world");
gen.Emit (OpCodes.Ret);
```

We're now ready to create the type, which finalizes its definition:

```
Type t = tb.CreateType();
```

Once the type is created, we use ordinary reflection to inspect and perform dynamic binding:

```
object o = Activator.CreateInstance (t);
t.GetMethod ("SayHello").Invoke (o, null);       // Hello world
```

Saving Emitted Assemblies

The `Save` method on writes a dynamically generated assembly to a specified filename. For this to work, though, you must do two things:

- Specify an `AssemblyBuilderAccess` of `Save` or `RunAndSave` when constructing the `AssemblyBuilder`.
- Specify a filename when constructing the `ModuleBuilder` (this should match the assembly filename unless you want to create a multimodule assembly).

You can also optionally set properties of the `AssemblyName` object, such as `Version` or `KeyPair` (for signing).

For example:

```
AppDomain domain = AppDomain.CurrentDomain;

AssemblyName aname = new AssemblyName ("MyEmissions");
aname.Version = new Version (2, 13, 0, 1);
```

```
AssemblyBuilder assemBuilder = domain.DefineDynamicAssembly (
  aname, AssemblyBuilderAccess.RunAndSave);

ModuleBuilder modBuilder = assemBuilder.DefineDynamicModule (
  "MainModule", "MyEmissions.dll");

// Create types as we did previously...
// ...

assemBuilder.Save ("MyEmissions.dll");
```

This writes the assembly to the application's base directory. To save to a different location, you must provide the alternative directory when constructing AssemblyBuilder:

```
AssemblyBuilder assemBuilder = domain.DefineDynamicAssembly (
  aname, AssemblyBuilderAccess.RunAndSave, @"d:\assemblies" );
```

A dynamic assembly, once written to a file, becomes an ordinary assembly just like any other. A program could statically reference the assembly we just built and do this:

```
Widget w = new Widget();
w.SayHello();
```

The Reflection.Emit Object Model

Figure 18-2 illustrates the essential types in . Each type describes a CLR construct and is based on a counterpart in the System.Reflection namespace. This allows you to use emitted constructs in place of normal constructs when building a type. For example, we previously called Console.WriteLine as follows:

```
MethodInfo writeLine = typeof(Console).GetMethod ("WriteLine",
                            new Type[] { typeof (string) });
gen.Emit (OpCodes.Call, writeLine);
```

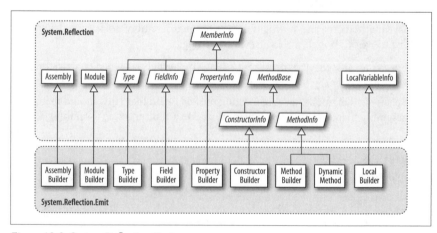

Figure 18-2. System.Reflection.Emit

We could just as easily call a dynamically generated method by calling gen.Emit with a MethodBuilder instead of a MethodInfo. This is essential—otherwise, you couldn't write one dynamic method that called another in the same type.

Recall that you must call CreateType on a TypeBuilder when you've finished populating it. Calling CreateType seals the TypeBuilder and all its members—so nothing more can be added or changed—and gives you back a real Type that you can instantiate.

Before you call CreateType, the TypeBuilder and its members are in an "uncreated" state. There are significant restrictions on what you can do with uncreated constructs. In particular, you cannot call any of the members that return MemberInfo objects, such as GetMembers, GetMethod, or GetProperty—these all throw an exception. If you want to refer to members of an uncreated type, you must use the original emissions:

```
TypeBuilder tb = ...

MethodBuilder method1 = tb.DefineMethod ("Method1", ...);
MethodBuilder method2 = tb.DefineMethod ("Method2", ...);

ILGenerator gen1 = method1.GetILGenerator();

// Suppose we want method1 to call method2:

gen1.Emit (OpCodes.Call, method2);                      // Right
gen1.Emit (OpCodes.Call, tb.GetMethod ("Method2"));     // Wrong
```

After calling CreateType, you can reflect on and activate not only the Type returned, but also the original TypeBuilder object. The TypeBuilder, in fact, morphs into a proxy for the real Type. We'll see why this feature is important later in this chapter in the section "Awkward Emission Targets" on page 725.

Emitting Type Members

All the examples in this section assume a TypeBuilder, tb, has been instantiated as follows:

```
AppDomain domain = AppDomain.CurrentDomain;
AssemblyName aname = new AssemblyName ("MyEmissions");

AssemblyBuilder assemBuilder = domain.DefineDynamicAssembly (
  aname, AssemblyBuilderAccess.RunAndSave);

ModuleBuilder modBuilder = assemBuilder.DefineDynamicModule (
  "MainModule", "MyEmissions.dll");

TypeBuilder tb = modBuilder.DefineType ("Widget", TypeAttributes.Public);
```

Emitting Methods

You can specify a return type and parameter types when calling `DefineMethod`, in the same manner as when instantiating a `DynamicMethod`; e.g., the following method:

```
public static double SquareRoot (double value)
{
  return Math.Sqrt (value);
}
```

can be generated like this:

```
MethodBuilder mb = tb.DefineMethod ("SquareRoot",
  MethodAttributes.Static | MethodAttributes.Public,
  CallingConventions.Standard,
  typeof (double),                   // Return type
  new[] { typeof (double) } );       // Parameter types

mb.DefineParameter (1, ParameterAttributes.None, "value");  // Assign name

ILGenerator gen = mb.GetILGenerator();
gen.Emit (OpCodes.Ldarg_0);                                 // Load 1st arg
gen.Emit (OpCodes.Call, typeof(Math).GetMethod ("Sqrt"));
gen.Emit (OpCodes.Ret);

Type realType = tb.CreateType();
double x = (double) tb.GetMethod ("SquareRoot").Invoke (null,
                                      new object[] { 10.0 });
Console.WriteLine (x);   // 3.16227766016838
```

Calling `DefineParameter` is optional and is typically done to assign the parameter a name. The number 1 refers to the first parameter (0 refers to the return value). If you call `DefineParameter`, the parameter is implicitly named __p1, __p2, and so on. Assigning names makes sense if you will write the assembly to disk; it makes your methods friendly to consumers.

> `DefineParameter` returns a `ParameterBuilder` object upon which you can call `SetCustomAttribute` to attach attributes (see "Attaching Attributes" on page 722, later in this chapter).

To emit pass-by-reference parameters, such as in the following C# method:

```
public static void SquareRoot (ref double value)
{
  value = Math.Sqrt (value);
}
```

call `MakeByRefType` on the parameter type(s):

```
MethodBuilder mb = tb.DefineMethod ("SquareRoot",
  MethodAttributes.Static | MethodAttributes.Public,
  CallingConventions.Standard,
  null,
  new Type[] { typeof (double).MakeByRefType() } );
```

```
mb.DefineParameter (1, ParameterAttributes.None, "value");

ILGenerator gen = mb.GetILGenerator();
gen.Emit (OpCodes.Ldarg_0);
gen.Emit (OpCodes.Ldarg_0);
gen.Emit (OpCodes.Ldind_R8);
gen.Emit (OpCodes.Call, typeof (Math).GetMethod ("Sqrt"));
gen.Emit (OpCodes.Stind_R8);
gen.Emit (OpCodes.Ret);

Type realType = tb.CreateType();
object[] args = { 10.0 };
tb.GetMethod ("SquareRoot").Invoke (null, args);
Console.WriteLine (args[0]);                    // 3.16227766016838
```

The opcodes here were copied from a disassembled C# method. Notice the difference in semantics for accessing parameters passed by reference: Ldind and Stind mean "load indirectly" and "store indirectly," respectively. The R8 suffix means an 8-byte floating-point number.

The process for emitting out parameters is identical, except that you call DefinePara meter as follows:

```
mb.DefineParameter (1, ParameterAttributes.Out, "value");
```

Generating instance methods

To generate an instance method, specify MethodAttributes.Instance when calling DefineMethod:

```
MethodBuilder mb = tb.DefineMethod ("SquareRoot",
  MethodAttributes.Instance | MethodAttributes.Public
  ...
```

With instance methods, argument zero is implicitly this; the remaining arguments start at 1. So, Ldarg_0 loads this onto the evaluation stack; Ldarg_1 loads the first real method argument.

HideBySig

If you're subclassing another type, it's nearly always worth specifying MethodAttri butes.HideBySig when defining methods. HideBySig ensures that C#-style method hiding semantics are applied, which is that a base method is hidden only if a subtype defines a method with an identical *signature*. Without HideBySig, method hiding considers only the *name*, so Foo(string) in the subtype will hide Foo() in the base type, which is generally undesirable.

Emitting Fields and Properties

To create a field, you call DefineField on a TypeBuilder, telling it the desired field name, type, and visibility. The following creates a private integer field called "length":

```
FieldBuilder field = tb.DefineField ("length", typeof (int),
                                      FieldAttributes.Private);
```

Creating a property or indexer requires a few more steps. First, call `DefineProp` `erty` on a `TypeBuilder`, telling it the name and type of the property:

```
PropertyBuilder prop = tb.DefineProperty (
                    "Text",                     // Name of property
                    PropertyAttributes.None,
                    typeof (string),            // Property type
                    new Type[0]                 // Indexer types
                );
```

(If you're writing an indexer, the final argument is an array of indexer types.) Note that we haven't specified the property visibility: this is done individually on the accessor methods.

The next step is to write the get and set methods. By convention, their names are csn3ed with "get_" or "set_". You then attach them to the property by calling `SetGetMethod` and `SetSetMethod` on the `PropertyBuilder`.

To give a complete example, we'll take the following field and property declaration:

```
string _text;
public string Text
{
  get          { return _text; }
  internal set { _text = value; }
}
```

and generate it dynamically:

```
FieldBuilder field = tb.DefineField ("_text", typeof (string),
                                     FieldAttributes.Private);
PropertyBuilder prop = tb.DefineProperty (
                    "Text",                     // Name of property
                    PropertyAttributes.None,
                    typeof (string),            // Property type
                    new Type[0]);               // Indexer types

MethodBuilder getter = tb.DefineMethod (
    "get_Text",                                 // Method name
    MethodAttributes.Public | MethodAttributes.SpecialName,
    typeof (string),                            // Return type
    new Type[0]);                               // Parameter types

ILGenerator getGen = getter.GetILGenerator();
getGen.Emit (OpCodes.Ldarg_0);      // Load "this" onto eval stack
getGen.Emit (OpCodes.Ldfld, field); // Load field value onto eval stack
getGen.Emit (OpCodes.Ret);          // Return

MethodBuilder setter = tb.DefineMethod (
    "set_Text",
    MethodAttributes.Assembly | MethodAttributes.SpecialName,
    null,                                       // Return type
    new Type[] { typeof (string) } );           // Parameter types
```

```
ILGenerator setGen = setter.GetILGenerator();
setGen.Emit (OpCodes.Ldarg_0);          // Load "this" onto eval stack
setGen.Emit (OpCodes.Ldarg_1);          // Load 2nd arg, i.e., value
setGen.Emit (OpCodes.Stfld, field);     // Store value into field
setGen.Emit (OpCodes.Ret);              // return

prop.SetGetMethod (getter);             // Link the get method and property
prop.SetSetMethod (setter);             // Link the set method and property
```

We can test the property as follows:

```
Type t = tb.CreateType();
object o = Activator.CreateInstance (t);
t.GetProperty ("Text").SetValue (o, "Good emissions!", new object[0]);
string text = (string) t.GetProperty ("Text").GetValue (o, null);

Console.WriteLine (text);               // Good emissions!
```

Notice that in defining the accessor `MethodAttributes`, we included `SpecialName`. This instructs compilers to disallow direct binding to these methods when statically referencing the assembly. It also ensures that the accessors are handled appropriately by reflection tools and Visual Studio's IntelliSense.

 You can emit events in a similar manner, by calling `DefineEvent` on a `TypeBuilder`. You then write explicit event accessor methods, and attach them to the `EventBuilder` by calling `SetAddOnMethod` and `SetRemoveOnMethod`.

Emitting Constructors

You can define your own constructors by calling `DefineConstructor` on a type builder. You're not obliged to do so—a default parameterless constructor is provided automatically if you don't. The default constructor calls the base class constructor if subtyping, just like in C#. Defining one or more constructors displaces this default constructor.

If you need to initialize fields, the constructor's a good spot. In fact, it's the only spot: C#'s field initializers don't have special CLR support—they are simply a syntactic shortcut for assigning values to fields in the constructor. So, to reproduce this:

```
class Widget
{
  int _capacity = 4000;
}
```

you would define a constructor as follows:

```
FieldBuilder field = tb.DefineField ("_capacity", typeof (int),
                                     FieldAttributes.Private);
ConstructorBuilder c = tb.DefineConstructor (
  MethodAttributes.Public,
  CallingConventions.Standard,
  new Type[0]);                         // Constructor parameters
```

```
ILGenerator gen = c.GetILGenerator();
```

```
gen.Emit (OpCodes.Ldarg_0);          // Load "this" onto eval stack
gen.Emit (OpCodes.Ldc_I4, 4000);     // Load 4000 onto eval stack
gen.Emit (OpCodes.Stfld, field);     // Store it to our field
gen.Emit (OpCodes.Ret);
```

Calling base constructors

If subclassing another type, the constructor we just wrote would *circumvent the base class constructor*. This is unlike C#, where the base class constructor is always called, whether directly or indirectly. For instance, given the following code:

```
class A     { public A() { Console.Write ("A"); } }
class B : A { public B() {} }
```

the compiler, in effect, will translate the second line into this:

```
class B : A { public B() : base() {} }
```

This is not the case when generating IL: you must explicitly call the base constructor if you want it to execute (which nearly always, you do). Assuming the base class is called B, here's how to do it:

```
gen.Emit (OpCodes.Ldarg_0);
ConstructorInfo baseConstr = typeof (B).GetConstructor (new Type[0]);
gen.Emit (OpCodes.Call, baseConstr);
```

Calling constructors with arguments is just the same as with methods.

Attaching Attributes

You can attach custom attributes to a dynamic construct by calling SetCustomAttri
bute with a CustomAttributeBuilder. For example, suppose we want to attach the
following attribute declaration to a field or property:

```
[XmlElement ("FirstName", Namespace="http://test/", Order=3)]
```

This relies on the XmlElementAttribute constructor that accepts a single string. To
use CustomAttributeBuilder, we must retrieve this constructor, as well as the two
additional properties we wish to set (Namespace and Order):

```
Type attType = typeof (XmlElementAttribute);

ConstructorInfo attConstructor = attType.GetConstructor (
  new Type[] { typeof (string) } );

var att = new CustomAttributeBuilder (
  attConstructor,                       // Constructor
  new object[] { "FirstName" },         // Constructor arguments
  new PropertyInfo[]
  {
    attType.GetProperty ("Namespace"),  // Properties
    attType.GetProperty ("Order")
  },
  new object[] { "http://test/", 3 }    // Property values
);
```

```
myFieldBuilder.SetCustomAttribute (att);
// or propBuilder.SetCustomAttribute (att);
// or typeBuilder.SetCustomAttribute (att);   etc
```

Emitting Generic Methods and Types

All the examples in this section assume that modBuilder has been instantiated as follows:

```
AppDomain domain = AppDomain.CurrentDomain;
AssemblyName aname = new AssemblyName ("MyEmissions");

AssemblyBuilder assemBuilder = domain.DefineDynamicAssembly (
  aname, AssemblyBuilderAccess.RunAndSave);

ModuleBuilder modBuilder = assemBuilder.DefineDynamicModule (
  "MainModule", "MyEmissions.dll");
```

Defining Generic Methods

To emit a generic method:

1. Call DefineGenericParameters on a MethodBuilder to obtain an array of GenericTypeParameterBuilder objects.

2. Call SetSignature on a MethodBuilder using these generic type parameters.

3. Optionally, name the parameters as you would otherwise.

For example, the following generic method:

```
public static T Echo<T> (T value)
{
  return value;
}
```

can be emitted like this:

```
TypeBuilder tb = modBuilder.DefineType ("Widget", TypeAttributes.Public);

MethodBuilder mb = tb.DefineMethod ("Echo", MethodAttributes.Public |
                                            MethodAttributes.Static);
GenericTypeParameterBuilder[] genericParams
  = mb.DefineGenericParameters ("T");

mb.SetSignature (genericParams[0],    // Return type
                 null, null,
                 genericParams,       // Parameter types
                 null, null);

mb.DefineParameter (1, ParameterAttributes.None, "value");   // Optional

ILGenerator gen = mb.GetILGenerator();
gen.Emit (OpCodes.Ldarg_0);
gen.Emit (OpCodes.Ret);
```

The DefineGenericParameters method accepts any number of string arguments—these correspond to the desired generic type names. In this example, we needed just one generic type called T. GenericTypeParameterBuilder is based on System.Type, so it can be used in place of a TypeBuilder when emitting opcodes.

GenericTypeParameterBuilder also lets you specify a base type constraint:

```
genericParams[0].SetBaseTypeConstraint (typeof (Foo));
```

and interface constraints:

```
genericParams[0].SetInterfaceConstraints (typeof (IComparable));
```

To replicate this:

```
public static T Echo<T> (T value) where T : IComparable<T>
```

you would write:

```
genericParams[0].SetInterfaceConstraints (
  typeof (IComparable<>).MakeGenericType (genericParams[0]) );
```

For other kinds of constraints, call SetGenericParameterAttributes. This accepts a member of the GenericParameterAttributes enum, which includes these values:

```
DefaultConstructorConstraint
NotNullableValueTypeConstraint
ReferenceTypeConstraint
Covariant
Contravariant
```

The last two are equivalent to applying the out and in modifiers to the type parameters.

Defining Generic Types

You can define generic types in a similar fashion. The difference is that you call DefineGenericParameters on the TypeBuilder rather than the MethodBuilder. So, to reproduce this:

```
public class Widget<T>
{
  public T Value;
}
```

you would do the following:

```
TypeBuilder tb = modBuilder.DefineType ("Widget", TypeAttributes.Public);

GenericTypeParameterBuilder[] genericParams
  = tb.DefineGenericParameters ("T");

tb.DefineField ("Value", genericParams[0], FieldAttributes.Public);
```

Generic constraints can be added just as with a method.

Awkward Emission Targets

All the examples in this section assume that a `modBuilder` has been instantiated as in previous sections.

Uncreated Closed Generics

Suppose you want to emit a method that uses a closed generic type:

```
public class Widget
{
  public static void Test() { var list = new List<int>(); }
}
```

The process is fairly straightforward:

```
TypeBuilder tb = modBuilder.DefineType ("Widget", TypeAttributes.Public);

MethodBuilder mb = tb.DefineMethod ("Test", MethodAttributes.Public |
                                            MethodAttributes.Static);
ILGenerator gen = mb.GetILGenerator();

Type variableType = typeof (List<int>);

ConstructorInfo ci = variableType.GetConstructor (new Type[0]);

LocalBuilder listVar = gen.DeclareLocal (variableType);
gen.Emit (OpCodes.Newobj, ci);
gen.Emit (OpCodes.Stloc, listVar);
gen.Emit (OpCodes.Ret);
```

Now suppose that instead of a list of integers, we want a list of widgets:

```
public class Widget
{
  public static void Test() { var list = new List<Widget>(); }
}
```

In theory, this is a simple modification; all we do is replace this line:

```
Type variableType = typeof (List<int>);
```

with this:

```
Type variableType = typeof (List<>).MakeGenericType (tb);
```

Unfortunately, this causes a `NotSupportedException` to be thrown when we then call `GetConstructor`. The problem is that you cannot call `GetConstructor` on a generic type closed with an uncreated type builder. The same goes for `GetField` and `GetMethod`.

The solution is unintuitive. `TypeBuilder` provides three static methods as follows:

```
public static ConstructorInfo GetConstructor (Type, ConstructorInfo);
public static FieldInfo       GetField       (Type, FieldInfo);
public static MethodInfo      GetMethod      (Type, MethodInfo);
```

Reflection

Although it doesn't appear so, these methods exist specifically to obtain members of generic types closed with uncreated type builders! The first parameter is the closed generic type; the second parameter is the member you want on the *unbound* generic type. Here's the corrected version of our example:

```
MethodBuilder mb = tb.DefineMethod ("Test", MethodAttributes.Public |
                                            MethodAttributes.Static);
ILGenerator gen = mb.GetILGenerator();

Type variableType = typeof (List<>).MakeGenericType (tb);

ConstructorInfo unbound = typeof (List<>).GetConstructor (new Type[0]);
ConstructorInfo ci = TypeBuilder.GetConstructor (variableType, unbound);

LocalBuilder listVar = gen.DeclareLocal (variableType);
gen.Emit (OpCodes.Newobj, ci);
gen.Emit (OpCodes.Stloc, listVar);
gen.Emit (OpCodes.Ret);
```

Circular Dependencies

Suppose you want to build two types that reference each other. For instance:

```
class A { public B Bee; }
class B { public A Aye; }
```

You can generate this dynamically as follows:

```
var publicAtt = FieldAttributes.Public;

TypeBuilder aBuilder = modBuilder.DefineType ("A");
TypeBuilder bBuilder = modBuilder.DefineType ("B");

FieldBuilder bee = aBuilder.DefineField ("Bee", bBuilder, publicAtt);
FieldBuilder aye = bBuilder.DefineField ("Aye", aBuilder, publicAtt);

Type realA = aBuilder.CreateType();
Type realB = bBuilder.CreateType();
```

Notice that we didn't call `CreateType` on `aBuilder` or `bBuilder` until we populated both objects. The principle is: first hook everything up, and then call `CreateType` on each type builder.

Interestingly, the `realA` type is valid but *dysfunctional* until you call `CreateType` on `bBuilder`. (If you started using `aBuilder` prior to this, an exception would be thrown when you tried to access field `Bee`.)

You might wonder how `bBuilder` knows to "fix up" `realA` after creating `realB`. The answer is that it doesn't: `realA` can fix *itself* the next time it's used. This is possible because after calling `CreateType`, a `TypeBuilder` morphs into a proxy for the real runtime type. So, `realA`, with its references to `bBuilder`, can easily obtain the metadata it needs for the upgrade.

This system works when the type builder demands simple information of the unconstructed type—information that can be *predetermined*—such as type, member, and object references. In creating `realA`, the type builder doesn't need to know, for instance, how many bytes `realB` will eventually occupy in memory. This is just as well, because `realB` has not yet been created! But now imagine that `realB` was a struct. The final size of `realB` is now critical information in creating `realA`.

If the relationship is noncyclical—for instance:

```
struct A { public B Bee; }
struct B {                }
```

you can solve this by first creating struct `B`, and then struct `A`. But consider this:

```
struct A { public B Bee; }
struct B { public A Aye; }
```

We won't try to emit this because it's nonsensical to have two structs contain each other (C# generates a compile-time error if you try). But the following variation is both legal and useful:

```
public struct S<T> { ... }    // S can be empty and this demo will work.

class A { S<B> Bee; }
class B { S<A> Aye; }
```

In creating `A`, a `TypeBuilder` now needs to know the memory footprint of `B`, and vice versa. To illustrate, we'll assume that struct `S` is defined statically. Here's the code to emit classes `A` and `B`:

```
var pub = FieldAttributes.Public;

TypeBuilder aBuilder = modBuilder.DefineType ("A");
TypeBuilder bBuilder = modBuilder.DefineType ("B");

aBuilder.DefineField ("Bee", typeof(S<>).MakeGenericType (bBuilder), pub);
bBuilder.DefineField ("Aye", typeof(S<>).MakeGenericType (aBuilder), pub);

Type realA = aBuilder.CreateType();    // Error: cannot load type B
Type realB = bBuilder.CreateType();
```

`CreateType` now throws a `TypeLoadException` no matter in which order you go:

- Call `aBuilder.CreateType` first and it says "cannot load type B".
- Call `bBuilder.CreateType` first and it says "cannot load type A"!

 You'll run into this problem if you emit typed LINQ to SQL `DataContext`s dynamically. The generic `EntityRef` type is a struct, equivalent to `S` in our examples. The circular reference happens when two tables in the database link to each other through reciprocal parent/child relationships.

To solve this, you must allow the type builder to create `realB` partway through creating `realA`. This is done by handling the `TypeResolve` event on the current application domain just before calling `CreateType`. So, in our example, we replace the last two lines with this:

```
TypeBuilder[] uncreatedTypes = { aBuilder, bBuilder };

ResolveEventHandler handler = delegate (object o, ResolveEventArgs args)
{
  var type = uncreatedTypes.FirstOrDefault (t => t.FullName == args.Name);
  return type == null ? null : type.CreateType().Assembly;
};

AppDomain.CurrentDomain.TypeResolve += handler;

Type realA = aBuilder.CreateType();
Type realB = bBuilder.CreateType();

AppDomain.CurrentDomain.TypeResolve -= handler;
```

The `TypeResolve` event fires during the call to `aBuilder.CreateType`, at the point when it needs you to call `CreateType` on `bBuilder`.

> Handling the `TypeResolve` event as in this example is also necessary when defining a nested type, when the nested and parent types refer to each other.

Parsing IL

You can obtain information about the content of an existing method by calling `GetMethodBody` on a `MethodBase` object. This returns a `MethodBody` object that has properties for inspecting a method's local variables, exception handling clauses, stack size—as well as the raw IL. Rather like the reverse of `Reflection.Emit`!

Inspecting a method's raw IL can be useful in profiling code. A simple use would be to determine which methods in an assembly have changed, when an assembly is updated.

To illustrate parsing IL, we'll write an application that disassembles IL in the style of *ildasm*. This could be used as the starting point for a code analysis tool or a higher-level language disassembler.

> Remember that in the reflection API, all of C#'s functional constructs are either represented by a `MethodBase` subtype, or (in the case of properties, events, and indexers) have `MethodBase` objects attached to them.

Writing a Disassembler

> You can download the source code for this at *http://www.alba hari.com/nutshell/*.

Here is a sample of the output our disassembler will produce:

```
IL_00EB:  ldfld        Disassembler._pos
IL_00F0:  ldloc.2
IL_00F1:  add
IL_00F2:  ldelema      System.Byte
IL_00F7:  ldstr        "Hello world"
IL_00FC:  call         System.Byte.ToString
IL_0101:  ldstr        " "
IL_0106:  call         System.String.Concat
```

To obtain this output, we must parse the binary tokens that make up the IL. The first step is to call the GetILAsByteArray method on MethodBody to obtain the IL as a byte array. In order to make the rest of the job easier, we will write this into a class as follows:

```
public class Disassembler
{
  public static string Disassemble (MethodBase method)
  {
    return new Disassembler (method).Dis();
  }

  StringBuilder _output;    // The result to which we'll keep appending
  Module _module;           // This will come in handy later
  byte[] _il;               // The raw byte code
  int _pos;                 // The position we're up to in the byte code

  Disassembler (MethodBase method)
  {
    _module = method.DeclaringType.Module;
    _il = method.GetMethodBody().GetILAsByteArray();
  }

  string Dis()
  {
    _output = new StringBuilder();
    while (_pos < _il.Length) DisassembleNextInstruction();
    return _output.ToString();
  }
}
```

The static Disassemble method will be the only public member of this class. All other members will be private to the disassembly process. The Dis method contains the "main" loop where we process each instruction.

With this skeleton in place, all that remains is to write DisassembleNextInstruction. But before doing so, it will help to load all the opcodes into a static dictionary, so we can access them by their 8- or 16-bit value. The easiest way to accomplish this is to use reflection to retrieve all the static fields whose type is OpCode in the OpCodes class:

```
static Dictionary<short,OpCode> _opcodes = new Dictionary<short,OpCode>();

static Disassembler()
{
  Dictionary<short, OpCode> opcodes = new Dictionary<short, OpCode>();
    foreach (FieldInfo fi in typeof (OpCodes).GetFields
                            (BindingFlags.Public | BindingFlags.Static))
      if (typeof (OpCode).IsAssignableFrom (fi.FieldType))
      {
        OpCode code = (OpCode) fi.GetValue (null);    // Get field's value
        if (code.OpCodeType != OpCodeType.Nternal)
          _opcodes.Add (code.Value, code);
      }
}
```

We've written it in a static constructor so that it executes just once.

Now we can write `DisassembleNextInstruction`. Each IL instruction consists of a 1- or 2-byte opcode, followed by an operand of zero, one, two, four, or eight bytes. (An exception is inline switch opcodes, which are followed by a variable number of operands). So, we read the opcode, then the operand, and then write out the result:

```
void DisassembleNextInstruction()
{
  int opStart = _pos;

  OpCode code = ReadOpCode();
  string operand = ReadOperand (code);

  _output.AppendFormat ("IL_{0:X4}:  {1,-12} {2}",
                        opStart, code.Name, operand);
  _output.AppendLine();
}
```

To read an opcode, we advance one byte and see whether we have a valid instruction. If not, we advance another byte and look for a 2-byte instruction:

```
OpCode ReadOpCode()
{
  byte byteCode = _il [_pos++];
  if (_opcodes.ContainsKey (byteCode)) return _opcodes [byteCode];

  if (_pos == _il.Length)  throw new Exception ("Unexpected end of IL");

  short shortCode = (short) (byteCode * 256 + _il [_pos++]);

  if (!_opcodes.ContainsKey (shortCode))
    throw new Exception ("Cannot find opcode " + shortCode);

  return _opcodes [shortCode];
}
```

To read an operand, we first must establish its length. We can do this based on the operand type. Because most are four bytes long, we can filter out the exceptions fairly easily in a conditional clause.

The next step is to call `FormatOperand`, which will attempt to format the operand:

```
string ReadOperand (OpCode c)
{
  int operandLength =
    c.OperandType == OperandType.InlineNone
      ? 0 :
    c.OperandType == OperandType.ShortInlineBrTarget ||
    c.OperandType == OperandType.ShortInlineI ||
    c.OperandType == OperandType.ShortInlineVar
      ? 1 :
    c.OperandType == OperandType.InlineVar
      ? 2 :
    c.OperandType == OperandType.InlineI8 ||
    c.OperandType == OperandType.InlineR
      ? 8 :
    c.OperandType == OperandType.InlineSwitch
      ? 4 * (BitConverter.ToInt32 (_il, _pos) + 1) :
      4;   // All others are 4 bytes

  if (_pos + operandLength > _il.Length)
    throw new Exception ("Unexpected end of IL");

  string result = FormatOperand (c, operandLength);
  if (result == null)
  {                              // Write out operand bytes in hex
    result = "";
    for (int i = 0; i < operandLength; i++)
      result += _il [_pos + i].ToString ("X2") + " ";
  }
  _pos += operandLength;
  return result;
}
```

If the `result` of calling `FormatOperand` is `null`, it means the operand needs no special formatting, so we simply write it out in hexadecimal. We could test the disassembler at this point by writing a `FormatOperand` method that always returns `null`. Here's what the output would look like:

```
IL_00A8:  ldfld       98 00 00 04
IL_00AD:  ldloc.2
IL_00AE:  add
IL_00AF:  ldelema     64 00 00 01
IL_00B4:  ldstr       26 04 00 70
IL_00B9:  call        B6 00 00 0A
IL_00BE:  ldstr       11 01 00 70
IL_00C3:  call        91 00 00 0A
...
```

Although the opcodes are correct, the operands are not much use. Instead of hexadecimal numbers, we want member names and strings. The `FormatOperand` method, once written, will address this—identifying the special cases that benefit from such formatting. These comprise most 4-byte operands and the short branch instructions:

```
string FormatOperand (OpCode c, int operandLength)
{
  if (operandLength == 0) return "";

  if (operandLength == 4)
    return Get4ByteOperand (c);
  else if (c.OperandType == OperandType.ShortInlineBrTarget)
    return GetShortRelativeTarget();
  else if (c.OperandType == OperandType.InlineSwitch)
    return GetSwitchTarget (operandLength);
  else
    return null;
}
```

There are three kinds of 4-byte operands that we treat specially. The first is references to members or types—with these, we extract the member or type name by calling the defining module's ResolveMember method. The second case is strings—these are stored in the assembly module's metadata and can be retrieved by calling ResolveString. The final case is branch targets, where the operand refers to a byte offset in the IL. We format these by working out the absolute address *after* the current instruction (+ 4 bytes):

```
string Get4ByteOperand (OpCode c)
{
  int intOp = BitConverter.ToInt32 (_il, _pos);

  switch (c.OperandType)
  {
    case OperandType.InlineTok:
    case OperandType.InlineMethod:
    case OperandType.InlineField:
    case OperandType.InlineType:
      MemberInfo mi;
      try   { mi = _module.ResolveMember (intOp); }
      catch { return null; }
      if (mi == null) return null;

      if (mi.ReflectedType != null)
        return mi.ReflectedType.FullName + "." + mi.Name;
      else if (mi is Type)
        return ((Type)mi).FullName;
      else
        return mi.Name;

    case OperandType.InlineString:
      string s = _module.ResolveString (intOp);
      if (s != null) s = "'" + s + "'";
      return s;

    case OperandType.InlineBrTarget:
      return "IL_" + (_pos + intOp + 4).ToString ("X4");

    default:
      return null;
  }
}
```

The point where we call ResolveMember is a good window for a code analysis tool that reports on method dependencies.

For any other 4-byte opcode, we return null (this will cause ReadOperand to format the operand as hex digits).

The final kinds of operand that need special attention are short branch targets and inline switches. A short branch target describes the destination offset as a single signed byte, as at the end of the current instruction (i.e., + 1 byte). A switch target is followed by a variable number of 4-byte branch destinations:

```
string GetShortRelativeTarget()
{
  int absoluteTarget = _pos + (sbyte) _il [_pos] + 1;
  return "IL_" + absoluteTarget.ToString ("X4");
}

string GetSwitchTarget (int operandLength)
{
  int targetCount = BitConverter.ToInt32 (_il, _pos);
  string [] targets = new string [targetCount];
  for (int i = 0; i < targetCount; i++)
  {
    int ilTarget = BitConverter.ToInt32 (_il, _pos + (i + 1) * 4);
    targets [i] = "IL_" + (_pos + ilTarget + operandLength).ToString ("X4");
  }
  return "(" + string.Join (", ", targets) + ")";
}
```

This completes the disassembler. We can test it by disassembling one of its own methods:

```
MethodInfo mi = typeof (Disassembler).GetMethod (
  "ReadOperand", BindingFlags.Instance | BindingFlags.NonPublic);

Console.WriteLine (Disassembler.Disassemble (mi));
```

Reflection

19

Dynamic Programming

In Chapter 4, we explained how dynamic binding works in the C# language. In this chapter, we look briefly at the DLR, and then explore the following dynamic programming patterns:

- Numeric type unification
- Dynamic member overload resolution
- Implementing dynamic objects
- Interoperating with dynamic languages

In Chapter 25, we'll describe how `dynamic` can improve COM interoperability.

The types in this chapter live in the `System.Dynamic` namespace, except for `CallSite<>`, which lives in `System.Runtime.CompilerServices`.

The Dynamic Language Runtime

C# relies on the *Dynamic Language Runtime* (DLR) to perform dynamic binding.

Contrary to its name, the DLR is not a dynamic version of the CLR. Rather, it's a library that sits atop the CLR—just like any other library such as *System.Xml.dll*. Its primary role is to provide runtime services to *unify* dynamic programming—in both statically and dynamically typed languages. This means that languages such as C#, VB, IronPython, and IronRuby all use a common protocol for calling functions dynamically, allowing them to share libraries and call code written in other languages.

The DLR also makes it relatively easy to write new dynamic languages in .NET. Instead of having to emit IL, dynamic language authors work at the level of *expression trees* (the same expression trees in `System.Linq.Expressions` that we talked about in Chapter 8).

The DLR further ensures that all consumers get the benefit of *call-site caching*, an optimization whereby the DLR avoids unnecessarily repeating the potentially expensive member resolution decisions made during dynamic binding.

 Framework 4.0 is the first Framework version to ship with the DLR. Prior to that, the DLR existed as a separate download on Codeplex. That site still contains some additional useful resources for language developers.

What Are Call Sites?

When the compiler encounters a dynamic expression, it has no idea who will evaluate that expression at runtime. For instance, consider the following method:

```
public dynamic Foo (dynamic x, dynamic y)
{
    return x / y;    // Dynamic expression
}
```

The x and y variables could be any CLR object, a COM object, or even an object hosted in a dynamic language. The compiler cannot, therefore, take its usual static approach of emitting a call to a known method of a known type. Instead, the compiler emits code that eventually results in an expression tree that describes the operation, managed by a *call site* that the DLR will bind at runtime. The call site essentially acts as an intermediary between caller and callee.

A call site is represented by the `CallSite<>` class in *System.Core.dll*. We can see this by disassembling the preceding method—the result is something like this:

```
static CallSite<Func<CallSite,object,object,object>> divideSite;

[return: Dynamic]
public object Foo ([Dynamic] object x, [Dynamic] object y)
{
    if (divideSite == null)
        divideSite =
            CallSite<Func<CallSite,object,object,object>>.Create (
                Microsoft.CSharp.RuntimeBinder.Binder.BinaryOperation (
                CSharpBinderFlags.None,
                ExpressionType.Divide,
                /* Remaining arguments omitted for brevity */ ));

    return divideSite.Target (divideSite, x, y);
}
```

As you can see, the call site is cached in a static field to avoid the cost of re-creating it on each call. The DLR further caches the result of the binding phase and the actual method targets. (There may be multiple targets depending on the types of x and y.)

The actual dynamic call then happens by calling the site's `Target` (a delegate), passing in the x and y operands.

Notice that the `Binder` class is specific to C#. Every language with support for dynamic binding provides a language-specific binder to help the DLR interpret expressions in a manner specific to that language, so as not to surprise the programmer. For instance, if we called `Foo` with integer values of 5 and 2, the C# binder would ensure that we got back 2. In contrast, a VB.NET binder would give us 2.5.

Numeric Type Unification

We saw in Chapter 4 how `dynamic` lets us write a single method that works across all numeric types:

```
static dynamic Mean (dynamic x, dynamic y)
{
  return (x + y) / 2;
}

static void Main()
{
  int x = 3, y = 5;
  Console.WriteLine (Mean (x, y));
}
```

 It's a humorous reflection on C# that the keywords `static` and `dynamic` can appear adjacently! The same applies to the keywords `internal` and `extern`.

However, this (unnecessarily) sacrifices static type safety. The following compiles without error, but then fails at runtime:

```
string s = Mean (3, 5);   // Runtime error!
```

We can fix this by introducing a generic type parameter, and then casting to `dynamic` within the calculation itself:

```
static T Mean<T> (T x, T y)
{
  dynamic result = ((dynamic) x + y) / 2;
  return (T) result;
}
```

Notice that we *explicitly* cast the result back to T. If we omitted this cast, we'd be relying on an implicit cast, which might at first appear to work correctly. The implicit cast would fail at runtime, though, upon calling the method with an 8- or 16-bit integral type. To understand why, consider what happens with ordinary static typing when you sum two 8-bit numbers together:

```
byte b = 3;
Console.WriteLine ((b + b).GetType().Name);  // Int32
```

We get an `Int32`—because the compiler "promotes" 8- or 16-bit numbers to `Int32` prior to performing arithmetic operations. For consistency, the C# binder tells the DLR to do exactly the same thing, and we end up with an `Int32` that requires an explicit cast to the smaller numeric type. Of course, this could create the possibility of overflow if we were, say, summing rather than averaging the values.

Dynamic binding incurs a small performance hit—even with call-site caching. You can mitigate this by adding statically typed overloads that cover just the most commonly used types. For example, if subsequent performance profiling showed that calling `Mean` with `doubles` was a bottleneck, you could add the following overload:

```
static double Mean (double x, double y)
{
  return (x + y) / 2;
}
```

The compiler will favor that overload when `Mean` is called with arguments that are known at compile time to be of type `double`.

Dynamic Member Overload Resolution

Calling a statically known method with dynamically typed arguments defers member overload resolution from compile time to runtime. This is useful in simplifying certain programming tasks—such as simplifying the *Visitor* design pattern. It's also useful in working around limitations imposed by C#'s static typing.

Simplifying the Visitor Pattern

In essence, the Visitor pattern allows you to "add" a method to a class hierarchy without altering existing classes. Although useful, this pattern in its static incarnation is subtle and unintuitive compared to most other design patterns. It also requires that visited classes be made "Visitor-friendly" by exposing an `Accept` method, which can be impossible if the classes are not under your control.

With dynamic binding, you can achieve the same goal more easily—and without needing to modify existing classes. To illustrate, consider the following class hierarchy:

```
class Person
{
  public string FirstName { get; set; }
  public string LastName  { get; set; }

  // The Friends collection may contain Customers & Employees:
  public readonly IList<Person> Friends = new Collection<Person> ();
}

class Customer : Person { public decimal CreditLimit { get; set; } }
class Employee : Person { public decimal Salary      { get; set; } }
```

Suppose we want to write a method that programmatically exports a `Person`'s details to an XML `XElement`. The most obvious solution is to write a virtual method called `ToXElement()` in the `Person` class that returns an `XElement` populated with a `Person`'s properties. We would then override it in `Customer` and `Employee` classes such that the `XElement` was also populated with `CreditLimit` and `Salary`. This pattern can be problematic, however, for two reasons:

- You might not own the `Person`, `Customer`, and `Employee` classes, making it impossible to add methods to them. (And extension methods wouldn't give polymorphic behavior.)

- The `Person`, `Customer`, and `Employee` classes might already be quite big. A frequent antipattern is the "God Object," where a class such as `Person` attracts so much functionality that it becomes a nightmare to maintain. A good antidote is to avoid adding functions to `Person` that don't need to access `Person`'s private state. A `ToXElement` method might be an excellent candidate.

With dynamic member overload resolution, we can write the `ToXElement` functionality in a separate class, without resorting to ugly switches based on type:

```
class ToXElementPersonVisitor
{
  public XElement DynamicVisit (Person p)
  {
    return Visit ((dynamic)p);
  }

  XElement Visit (Person p)
  {
    return new XElement ("Person",
      new XAttribute ("Type", p.GetType().Name),
      new XElement ("FirstName", p.FirstName),
      new XElement ("LastName", p.LastName),
      p.Friends.Select (f => DynamicVisit (f))
    );
  }

  XElement Visit (Customer c)   // Specialized logic for customers
  {
    XElement xe = Visit ((Person)c);   // Call "base" method
    xe.Add (new XElement ("CreditLimit", c.CreditLimit));
    return xe;
  }

  XElement Visit (Employee e)   // Specialized logic for employees
  {
    XElement xe = Visit ((Person)e);   // Call "base" method
    xe.Add (new XElement ("Salary", e.Salary));
    return xe;
  }
}
```

The `DynamicVisit` method performs a dynamic dispatch—calling the most specific version of `Visit` as determined at runtime. Notice the line in boldface, where we call

`DynamicVisit` on each person in the `Friends` collection. This ensures that if a friend is a `Customer` or `Employee`, the correct overload is called.

We can demonstrate this class as follows:

```
var cust = new Customer
{
  FirstName = "Joe", LastName = "Bloggs", CreditLimit = 123
};
cust.Friends.Add (
  new Employee { FirstName = "Sue", LastName = "Brown", Salary = 50000 }
);

Console.WriteLine (new ToXElementPersonVisitor().DynamicVisit (cust));
```

Here's the result:

```
<Person Type="Customer">
  <FirstName>Joe</FirstName>
  <LastName>Bloggs</LastName>
  <Person Type="Employee">
    <FirstName>Sue</FirstName>
    <LastName>Brown</LastName>
    <Salary>50000</Salary>
  </Person>
  <CreditLimit>123</CreditLimit>
</Person>
```

Variations

If you plan more than one visitor class, a useful variation is to define an abstract base class for visitors:

```
abstract class PersonVisitor<T>
{
  public T DynamicVisit (Person p) { return Visit ((dynamic)p); }

  protected abstract T Visit (Person p);
  protected virtual T Visit (Customer c) { return Visit ((Person) c); }
  protected virtual T Visit (Employee e) { return Visit ((Person) e); }
}
```

Subclasses then don't need to define their own `DynamicVisit` method: all they do is override the versions of `Visit` whose behavior they want to specialize. This also has the advantages of centralizing the methods that encompass the `Person` hierarchy, and allowing implementers to call base methods more naturally:

```
class ToXElementPersonVisitor : PersonVisitor<XElement>
{
  protected override XElement Visit (Person p)
  {
    return new XElement ("Person",
      new XAttribute ("Type", p.GetType().Name),
      new XElement ("FirstName", p.FirstName),
      new XElement ("LastName", p.LastName),
      p.Friends.Select (f => DynamicVisit (f))
    );
```

```
        }
        protected override XElement Visit (Customer c)
        {
          XElement xe = base.Visit (c);
          xe.Add (new XElement ("CreditLimit", c.CreditLimit));
          return xe;
        }

        protected override XElement Visit (Employee e)
        {
          XElement xe = base.Visit (e);
          xe.Add (new XElement ("Salary", e.Salary));
          return xe;
        }
      }
```

You can even then subclass `ToXElementPersonVisitor` itself.

Multiple Dispatch

C# and the CLR have always supported a limited form of dynamism in the form of virtual method calls. This differs from true dynamic programming in that for virtual method calls, the compiler must commit to a particular virtual member at compile time—based on the name and signature of a member in the base class. This means that:

- The calling expression must be fully understood by the compiler (e.g., it must decide at compile time whether a target member is a field or property).
- Overload resolution must be completed entirely by the compiler, based on the compile-time argument types.

A consequence of that last point is that the ability to perform virtual method calls is known as *single dispatch*. To see why, consider the following method call (where `Walk` is a virtual method):

```
        animal.Walk (owner);
```

The runtime decision of whether to invoke a dog's `Walk` method or a cat's `Walk` method depends only on the type of the *receiver*, `animal` (hence "single"). If many overloads of `Walk` accept different kinds of owner, an overload will be selected at compile time without regard to the actual runtime type of the `owner` object. In other words, only the runtime type of the receiver can vary which method gets called.

In contrast, a dynamic call defers overload resolution until runtime:

```
        animal.Walk ((dynamic) owner);
```

The final choice of which `Walk` method to call now depends on the types of both `animal` and `owner`—this is called *multiple dispatch* since the runtime types of arguments, in addition to the receiver type, contribute to the determination of which `Walk` method to call.

Anonymously Calling Members of a Generic Type

The strictness of C#'s static typing is a two-edged sword. On one hand, it provides guarantees of program correctness at compile time. On the other hand, it occasionally makes certain kinds of code difficult or impossible to express, at which point you have to resort to reflection. In these situations, dynamic binding is a cleaner and faster alternative to reflection.

An example is when you need to work with an object of type G<T> where T is unknown. We can illustrate this by defining the following class:

```
public class Foo<T> { public T Value; }
```

Suppose we then write a method as follows:

```
static void Write (object obj)
{
  if (obj is Foo<>)                          // Illegal
    Console.WriteLine ((Foo<>) obj).Value);  // Illegal
}
```

This method won't compile: you can't invoke members of *unbound* generic types.

Dynamic binding offers two means by which we can work around this. The first is to access the Value member dynamically as follows:

```
static void Write (dynamic obj)
{
  try { Console.WriteLine (obj.Value); }
  catch (Microsoft.CSharp.RuntimeBinder.RuntimeBinderException) {...}
}
```

This has the (potential) advantage of working with any object that defines a Value field or property. However, there are a couple of problems. First, catching an exception in this manner is somewhat messy and inefficient (and there's no way to ask the DLR in advance, "Will this operation succeed?"). Second, this approach wouldn't work if Foo was an interface (say, IFoo<T>), and either of the following conditions was true:

• Value was implemented explicitly.

• The type that implemented IFoo<T> was inaccessible (more on this soon).

A better solution is to write an overloaded helper method called GetFooValue and to call it using *dynamic member overload resolution*:

```
static void Write (dynamic obj)
{
  object result = GetFooValue (obj);
  if (result != null) Console.WriteLine (result);
}

static T GetFooValue<T> (Foo<T> foo) { return foo.Value; }
static object GetFooValue (object foo) { return null; }
```

Notice that we overloaded GetFooValue to accept an object parameter, which acts as a fallback for any type. At runtime, the C# dynamic binder will pick the best overload when calling `GetFooValue` with a dynamic argument. If the object in question is not based on `Foo<T>`, it will choose the object-parameter overload instead of throwing an exception.

> An alternative is to write just the first `GetFooValue` overload, and then catch the `RuntimeBinderException`. The advantage is that it distinguishes the case of `foo.Value` being null. The disadvantage is that it incurs the performance overhead of throwing and catching an exception.

In Chapter 18, we solved the same problem with an interface using reflection—with a lot more effort (see "Anonymously Calling Members of a Generic Interface" on page 697). The example we used was to design a more powerful version of `ToString()` that could understand objects such as `IEnumerable` and `IGrouping<,>`. Here's the same example solved more elegantly with dynamic binding:

```
static string GetGroupKey<TKey,TElement> (IGrouping<TKey,TElement> group)
{
  return "Group with key=" + group.Key + ": ";
}

static string GetGroupKey (object source) { return null; }

public static string ToStringEx (object value)
{
  if (value == null) return "<null>";
  if (value is string) return (string) value;
  if (value.GetType().IsPrimitive) return value.ToString();

  StringBuilder sb = new StringBuilder();

  string groupKey = GetGroupKey ((dynamic)value);    // Dynamic dispatch
  if (groupKey != null) sb.Append (groupKey);

  if (value is IEnumerable)
    foreach (object element in ((IEnumerable)value))
      sb.Append (ToStringEx (element) + " ");

  if (sb.Length == 0) sb.Append (value.ToString());

  return "\r\n" + sb.ToString();
}
```

In action:

```
Console.WriteLine (ToStringEx ("xyyzzz".GroupBy (c => c) ));

Group with key=x: x
Group with key=y: y y
Group with key=z: z z z
```

Notice that we used dynamic *member overload resolution* to solve this problem. If we did the following instead:

```
dynamic d = value;
try { groupKey = d.Value); }
catch (Microsoft.CSharp.RuntimeBinder.RuntimeBinderException) {...}
```

it would fail, because LINQ's `GroupBy` operator returns a type implementing `IGroup ing<,>` which itself is internal, and therefore inaccessible:

```
internal class Grouping : IGrouping<TKey,TElement>, ...
{
  public TKey Key;
  ...
}
```

Even though the `Key` property is declared `public`, its containing class caps it at `internal`, making it accessible only via the `IGrouping<,>` interface. And as we explained in Chapter 4, there's no way to tell the DLR to bind to that interface when invoking the `Value` member dynamically.

Implementing Dynamic Objects

An object can provide its binding semantics by implementing `IDynamicMetaObject Provider`—or more easily by subclassing `DynamicObject`, which provides a default implementation of this interface. We demonstrated this briefly in Chapter 4, with the following example:

```
static void Main()
{
  dynamic d = new Duck();
  d.Quack();                // Quack method was called
  d.Waddle();               // Waddle method was called
}

public class Duck : DynamicObject
{
  public override bool TryInvokeMember (
    InvokeMemberBinder binder, object[] args, out object result)
  {
    Console.WriteLine (binder.Name + " method was called");
    result = null;
    return true;
  }
}
```

DynamicObject

In the preceding example, we overrode `TryInvokeMember`, which allows the consumer to invoke a method on the dynamic object—such as a `Quack` or `Waddle`. `DynamicOb ject` exposes other virtual methods that enable consumers to use other programming constructs as well. The following correspond to constructs that have representations in C#:

Method	Programming construct
TryInvokeMember	Method
TryGetMember, TrySetMember	Property or field
TryGetIndex, TrySetIndex	Indexer
TryUnaryOperation	Unary operator such as !
TryBinaryOperation	Binary operator such as ==
TryConvert	Conversion (cast) to another type
TryInvoke	Invocation on the object itself—e.g., d("foo")

These methods should return `true` if successful. If they return `false`, then the DLR will fall back to the language binder, looking for a matching member on the `DynamicObject` (subclass) itself. If this fails, then a `RuntimeBinderException` is thrown.

We can illustrate `TryGetMember` and `TrySetMember` with a class that lets us dynamically access an attribute in an `XElement` (`System.Xml.Linq`):

```
static class XExtensions
{
  public static dynamic DynamicAttributes (this XElement e)
  {
    return new XWrapper (e);
  }

  class XWrapper : DynamicObject
  {
    XElement _element;
    public XWrapper (XElement e) { _element = e; }

    public override bool TryGetMember (GetMemberBinder binder,
                                       out object result)
    {
      result = _element.Attribute (binder.Name).Value;
      return true;
    }

    public override bool TrySetMember (SetMemberBinder binder,
                                       object value)
    {
      _element.SetAttributeValue (binder.Name, value);
      return true;
    }
  }
}
```

Here's how to use it:

```
XElement x = XElement.Parse (@"<Label Text=""Hello"" Id=""5""/>");
dynamic da = x.DynamicAttributes();
Console.WriteLine (da.Id);            // 5
da.Text = "Foo";
Console.WriteLine (x.ToString());     // <Label Text="Foo" Id="5" />
```

The following does a similar thing for System.Data.IDataRecord, making it easier to use data readers:

```
public class DynamicReader : DynamicObject
{
  readonly IDataRecord _dataRecord;
  public DynamicReader (IDataRecord dr) { _dataRecord = dr; }

  public override bool TryGetMember (GetMemberBinder binder,
                                     out object result)
  {
    result = _dataRecord [binder.Name];
    return true;
  }
}
...
using (IDataReader reader = someDbCommand.ExecuteReader())
{
  dynamic dr = new DynamicReader (reader);
  while (reader.Read())
  {
    int id = dr.ID;
    string firstName = dr.FirstName;
    DateTime dob = dr.DateOfBirth;
    ...
  }
}
```

The following demonstrates TryBinaryOperation and TryInvoke:

```
static void Main()
{
  dynamic d = new Duck();
  Console.WriteLine (d + d);          // foo
  Console.WriteLine (d (78, 'x'));    // 123
}

public class Duck : DynamicObject
{
  public override bool TryBinaryOperation (BinaryOperationBinder binder,
                                           object arg, out object result)
  {
    Console.WriteLine (binder.Operation);   // Add
    result = "foo";
    return true;
  }

  public override bool TryInvoke (InvokeBinder binder,
                                  object[] args, out object result)
  {
    Console.WriteLine (args[0]);     // 78
    result = 123;
    return true;
  }
}
```

`DynamicObject` also exposes some virtual methods for the benefit of dynamic languages. In particular, overriding `GetDynamicMemberNames` allows you to return a list of all member names that your dynamic object provides.

> Another reason to implement `GetDynamicMemberNames` is that Visual Studio's debugger makes use of this method to display a view of a dynamic object.

ExpandoObject

Another simple application of `DynamicObject` would be to write a dynamic class that stored and retrieved objects in a dictionary, keyed by string. However, this functionality is already provided via the `ExpandoObject` class:

```
dynamic x = new ExpandoObject();
x.FavoriteColor = ConsoleColor.Green;
x.FavoriteNumber = 7;
Console.WriteLine (x.FavoriteColor);    // Green
Console.WriteLine (x.FavoriteNumber);   // 7
```

`ExpandoObject` implements `IDictionary<string,object>`—so we can continue our example and do this:

```
var dict = (IDictionary<string,object>) x;
Console.WriteLine (dict ["FavoriteColor"]);    // Green
Console.WriteLine (dict ["FavoriteNumber"]);   // 7
Console.WriteLine (dict.Count);                // 2
```

Interoperating with Dynamic Languages

Although C# 4.0 supports dynamic binding via the `dynamic` keyword, it doesn't go as far as allowing you to execute an expression described in a string at runtime:

```
string expr = "2 * 3";
// We can't "execute" expr
```

> This is because the code to translate a string into an expression tree requires a lexical and semantic parser. These features are built into the C# compiler and are not available as a runtime service. At runtime, C# merely provides a *binder*—which tells the DLR how to interpret an already-built expression tree.

True dynamic languages such as IronPython and IronRuby do allow you to execute an arbitrary string, and this is useful in tasks such as scripting, dynamic configuration, and implementing dynamic rules engines. So although you may write most of your application in C#, it can be useful to call out to a dynamic language for such tasks. In addition, you might want to leverage an API that is written in a dynamic language where no equivalent functionality is available in a .NET library.

In the following example, we use IronPython to evaluate an expression created at runtime from within C#. This script could be used to write a calculator.

To run this code, download IronPython (search the Internet for *IronPython*), and then reference the *IronPython*, *Microsoft.Scripting*, and *Microsoft.Scripting.Core* assemblies from your C# application.

```
using System;
using IronPython.Hosting;
using Microsoft.Scripting;
using Microsoft.Scripting.Hosting;

class Calculator
{
  static void Main()
  {
    int result = (int) Calculate ("2 * 3");
    Console.WriteLine (result);            // 6
  }

  static object Calculate (string expression)
  {
    ScriptEngine engine = Python.CreateEngine();
    return engine.Execute (expression);
  }
}
```

Because we're passing a string into Python, the expression will be evaluated according to Python's rules and not C#'s. It also means we can use Python's language features, such as lists:

```
var list = (IEnumerable) Calculate ("[1, 2, 3] + [4, 5]");
foreach (int n in list) Console.Write (n);  // 12345
```

Passing State Between C# and a Script

To pass variables from C# to Python, a few more steps are required. The following example illustrates those steps, and could be the basis of a rules engine:

```
// The following string could come from a file or database:
string auditRule = "taxPaidLastYear / taxPaidThisYear > 2";

ScriptEngine engine = Python.CreateEngine ();

ScriptScope scope = engine.CreateScope ();
scope.SetVariable ("taxPaidLastYear", 20000m);
scope.SetVariable ("taxPaidThisYear", 8000m);

ScriptSource source = engine.CreateScriptSourceFromString (
                        auditRule, SourceCodeKind.Expression);

bool auditRequired = (bool) source.Execute (scope);
Console.WriteLine (auditRequired);   // True
```

You can also get variables back by calling `GetVariable`:

```
string code = "result = input * 3";

ScriptEngine engine = Python.CreateEngine();

ScriptScope scope = engine.CreateScope();
scope.SetVariable ("input", 2);

ScriptSource source = engine.CreateScriptSourceFromString (code,
                                SourceCodeKind.SingleStatement);
source.Execute (scope);
Console.WriteLine (engine.GetVariable (scope, "result"));   // 6
```

Notice that we specified `SourceCodeKind.SingleStatement` in the second example (rather than `Expression`) to tell the engine that we want to execute a statement.

Types are automatically marshaled between the .NET and Python worlds. You can even access members of .NET objects from the scripting side:

```
string code = @"sb.Append ("""World""")";

ScriptEngine engine = Python.CreateEngine ();

ScriptScope scope = engine.CreateScope ();
var sb = new StringBuilder ("Hello");
scope.SetVariable ("sb", sb);

ScriptSource source = engine.CreateScriptSourceFromString (
                          code, SourceCodeKind.SingleStatement);
source.Execute (scope);
Console.WriteLine (sb.ToString());   // HelloWorld
```

20

Security

In this chapter, we discuss the two main components of .NET security:

- Permissions
- Cryptography

Permissions, in .NET, provide a layer of security independent of that imposed by the operating system. Their job is twofold:

Sandboxing
Limiting the kinds of operations that partially trusted .NET assemblies can perform

Authorization
Limiting *who* can do what

The cryptography support in .NET allows you to store or exchange high-value secrets, prevent eavesdropping, detect message tampering, generate one-way hashes for storing passwords, and create digital signatures.

The types covered in this chapter are defined in the following namespaces:

```
System.Security;
System.Security.Permissions;
System.Security.Principal;
System.Security.Cryptography;
```

In Chapter 14, we covered *isolated storage*, which serves another useful role in a secure environment.

Permissions

The Framework uses permissions for both sandboxing and authorization. A *permission* acts as a gate that conditionally prevents code from executing. Sandboxing uses *code access* permissions; authorization uses *identity* and *role* permissions.

Although both follow a similar model, they feel quite different to use. Part of the reason for this is that they typically put you on a different side of the fence: with code access security, you're usually the *untrusted* party; with identity and role security, you're usually the *untrusting* party. Code access security is most often forced upon you by the CLR or a hosting environment such as ASP.NET or Internet Explorer, whereas authorization is usually something you implement to prevent unprivileged callers from accessing your program.

As an application developer, you'll need to understand code access security (CAS) in order to write assemblies that will run in a limited permissions environment. If you're writing and selling a component library, it's easy to overlook the possibility that your customers will call your library from a *sandboxed* environment such as a SQL Server CLR host.

Another reason to understand CAS is if you want to create your own hosting environment that sandboxes other assemblies. For example, you might write an application that allows third parties to write plug-in components. Running those plugins in an application domain with limited permissions reduces the chance of a plug-in destabilizing your application or compromising its security.

The main scenario for identity and role security is when writing middle tier or web application servers. You typically decide on a set of roles, and then for each method that you expose, you demand that callers are members of a particular role.

CodeAccessPermission and PrincipalPermission

There are essentially two kinds of permissions:

CodeAccessPermission
: The abstract base class for all code access security (CAS) permissions, such as FileIOPermission, ReflectionPermission, or PrintingPermission

PrincipalPermission
: Describes an identity and/or role (e.g., "Mary" or "Human Resources")

The term *permission* is somewhat misleading in the case of CodeAccessPermission, because it suggests something has been granted. This is not necessarily the case. A CodeAccessPermission object describes a *privileged operation*.

For instance, a FileIOPermission object describes the privilege of being able to Read, Write, or Append to a particular set of files or directories. Such an object can be used in a variety of ways:

- To verify that you and all your callers have the rights to perform these actions (Demand)
- To verify that your immediate caller has the rights to perform these actions (LinkDemand)
- To temporarily escape a sandbox and Assert your assembly-given rights to perform these actions, regardless of callers' privileges

Framework 4.0 deprecates support for Deny, RequestMinimum, RequestOptional, and RequestRefuse, and strongly discourages the use of PermitOnly. Its new transparency model also makes link demands effectively redundant.

PrincipalPermission is much simpler. Its only security method is Demand, which checks that the specified user or role is valid given the current execution thread.

IPermission

Both CodeAccessPermission and PrincipalPermission implement the IPermission interface:

```
public interface IPermission
{
  void Demand();
  IPermission Intersect (IPermission target);
  IPermission Union (IPermission target);
  bool IsSubsetOf (IPermission target);
  IPermission Copy();
}
```

The crucial method here is Demand. It performs a spot-check to see whether the permission or privileged operation is currently permitted, and it throws a SecurityException if not. If you're the *untrusting* party, *you* will be Demanding. If you're the *untrusted* party, code that you *call* will be Demanding.

For example, to ensure that only Mary can run management reports, you could write this:

```
new PrincipalPermission ("Mary", null).Demand();
// ... run management reports
```

In contrast, suppose your assembly was sandboxed such that file I/O was prohibited, so the following line threw a SecurityException:

```
using (FileStream fs = new FileStream ("test.txt", FileMode.Create))
  ...
```

The Demand, in this case, is made by code that you call—in other words, File Stream's constructor:

```
...
new FileIOPermission (...).Demand();
```

A code access security Demand checks right up the call stack, in order to ensure that the requested operation is allowed for every party in the calling chain (within the current application domain). Effectively, it's asking, "Is this application domain entitled to this permission?"

With code access security, an interesting case arises with assemblies that run in the GAC, which are considered *fully trusted*. If a such an assembly runs in a sandbox, any Demands that it makes are still subject to the sandbox's permission set. Fully trusted assemblies can, however, temporarily *escape* the sandbox by calling Assert on a CodeAccessPermission object. After doing so, Demands for the permissions that were asserted always succeed. An Assert ends either when the current method finishes or when you call CodeAccessPermission.RevertAssert.

The Intersect and Union methods combine two same-typed permission objects into one. The result of Intersect is *less* restrictive when Demanded, requiring *intersected* permissions to be met. The result of Union is *more* restrictive when Demanded, requiring both permission sets to be met.

IsSubsetOf returns true if the given target contains at least its permissions:

```
PrincipalPermission jay = new PrincipalPermission ("Jay", null);
PrincipalPermission sue = new PrincipalPermission ("Sue", null);

PrincipalPermission jayOrSue = (PrincipalPermission) jay.Union (sue);
Console.WriteLine (jay.IsSubsetOf (jayOrSue));  // True
```

In this example, calling Intersect on jay and sue would generate an empty permission, because they don't overlap.

PermissionSet

A PermissionSet represents a collection of differently typed IPermission objects. The following creates a permission set with three code access permissions, and then Demands all of them in one hit:

```
PermissionSet ps = new PermissionSet (PermissionState.None);

ps.AddPermission (new UIPermission (PermissionState.Unrestricted));
ps.AddPermission (new SecurityPermission (
                      SecurityPermissionFlag.UnmanagedCode));
ps.AddPermission (new FileIOPermission (
                      FileIOPermissionAccess.Read, @"c:\docs"));
ps.Demand();
```

PermissionSet's constructor accepts a PermissionState enum, which indicates whether the set should be considered "unrestricted." An unrestricted permission set is treated as though it contained every possible permission (even though its collection is empty). Assemblies that execute with unrestricted code access security are said to be *fully trusted*.

When you call AddPermission, the permission set looks to see whether a same-typed permission is already present. If so, it Unions the new and existing permissions; otherwise, it adds the new permission to its collection. Calling AddPermission on an unrestricted permission set has no effect (as it already has, logically, all possible permissions).

You can Union and Intersect permission sets just as you can with IPermission objects.

Declarative Versus Imperative Security

So far, we manually instantiated permission objects and called Demand on them. This is *imperative security*. You can achieve the same result by adding attributes to a method, constructor, class, struct, or assembly—this is *declarative security*. Although imperative security is more flexible, declarative security has three advantages:

- It can mean less coding.
- It allows the CLR to determine in advance what permissions your assembly requires.
- It can improve performance.

For example:

```
[PrincipalPermission (SecurityAction.Demand, Name="Mary")]
public ReportData GetReports()
{
    ...
}

[UIPermission(SecurityAction.Demand, Window=UIPermissionWindow.AllWindows)]
public Form FindForm()
{
    ...
}
```

This works because every permission type has a sister attribute type in the .NET Framework. PrincipalPermission has a PrincipalPermissionAttribute sister. The first argument of the attribute's constructor is always a SecurityAction, which indicates what security method to call once the permission object is constructed (usually Demand). The remaining named parameters mirror the properties on the corresponding permission object.

Code Access Security (CAS)

The CodeAccessPermission types that are enforced throughout the .NET Framework are listed by category in Tables 20-1 through 20-6. Collectively, these are intended to cover all the means by which a program can do mischief!

Table 20-1. Core permissions

Type	Enables
SecurityPermission	Advanced operations, such as calling unmanaged code
ReflectionPermission	Use of reflection
EnvironmentPermission	Reading/writing command-line environment settings
RegistryPermission	Reading or writing to the Windows Registry

SecurityPermission accepts a SecurityPermissionFlag argument. This is an enum that allows any combination of the following:

AllFlags	ControlThread
Assertion	Execution
BindingRedirects	Infrastructure
ControlAppDomain	NoFlags
ControlDomainPolicy	RemotingConfiguration
ControlEvidence	SerializationFormatter
ControlPolicy	SkipVerification
ControlPrincipal	UnmanagedCode

The most significant member of this enum is Execution, without which code will not run. The other members should be granted only in full-trust scenarios, because they enable a grantee to compromise or escape a sandbox. ControlAppDomain allows the creation of new application domains (see Chapter 24); UnmanagedCode allows you to call native methods (see Chapter 25).

ReflectionPermission accepts a ReflectionPermissionFlag enum, which includes the members MemberAccess and RestrictedMemberAccess. If you're sandboxing assemblies, the latter is safer to grant while permitting reflection scenarios required by APIs such as LINQ to SQL.

Table 20-2. I/O and data permissions

Type	Enables
FileIOPermission	Reading/writing files and directories
FileDialogPermission	Reading/writing to a file chosen through an Open or Save dialog
IsolatedStorageFilePermission	Reading/writing to own isolated storage
ConfigurationPermission	Reading of application configuration files
SqlClientPermission, OleDbPermission, OdbcPermission	Communicating with a database server using the SqlClient, OleDb, or Odbc class
DistributedTransactionPermission	Participation in distributed transactions

FileDialogPermission controls access to the OpenFileDialog and SaveFileDialog classes. These classes are defined in Microsoft.Win32 (for use in WPF applications) and in System.Windows.Forms (for use in Windows Forms applications). For this to work, UIPermission is also required. FileIOPermission is not also required, however, if you access the chosen file by calling `OpenFile` on the `OpenFileDialog` or `SaveFileDialog` objects.

Table 20-3. Networking permissions

Type	Enables
DnsPermission	DNS lookup
WebPermission	WebRequest-based network access
SocketPermission	Socket-based network access
SmtpPermission	Sending mail through the SMTP libraries
NetworkInformationPermission	Use of classes such as `Ping` and `NetworkInterface`

Table 20-4. Encryption permissions

Type	Enables
DataProtectionPermission	Use of the Windows data protection methods
KeyContainerPermission	Public key encryption and signing
StorePermission	Access to X.509 certificate stores

Table 20-5. UI permissions

Type	Enables
UIPermission	Creating windows and interacting with the clipboard
WebBrowserPermission	Use of the `WebBrowser` control
MediaPermission	Image, audio, and video support in WPF
PrintingPermission	Accessing a printer

Table 20-6. Diagnostics permissions

Type	Enables
EventLogPermission	Reading or writing to the Windows event log
PerformanceCounterPermission	Use of Windows performance counters

Demands for these permission types are enforced within the .NET Framework. There are also some permission classes for which the intention is that Demands are enforced in your own code. The most important of these are concerned with establishing identity of the calling assembly, and are listed in Table 20-7. The caveat is that (as with all CAS permissions) a Demand always succeeds if the application domain is running in full trust (see the following section).

Table 20-7. Identity permissions

Type	Enforces
GacIdentityPermission	The assembly is loaded into the GAC
StrongNameIdentityPermission	The calling assembly has a particular strong name

Type	Enforces
PublisherIdentityPermission	The calling assembly is Authenticode-signed with a particular certificate

How Code Access Security Is Applied

When you run a .NET executable from the Windows shell or command prompt, it runs with unrestricted permissions. This is called *full trust*.

If you execute an assembly via another hosting environment—such as a SQL Server CLR integration host, ASP.NET, ClickOnce, or a custom host—the host decides what permissions to give your assembly. If it restricts permissions in any way, this is called *partial trust* or *sandboxing*.

More accurately, a host does not restrict permissions to your *assembly*. Rather, it creates an application domain with restricted permissions, and then loads your assembly into that sandboxed domain. This means that any other assemblies that load into that domain (such as assemblies that you reference) run in that same sandbox with the same permission set. There are two exceptions, however:

- Assemblies registered in the GAC (including the .NET Framework)
- Assemblies that a host has nominated to fully trust

Assemblies in those two categories are considered *fully trusted* and can escape the sandbox by Asserting any permission they want. They can also call methods marked as [SecurityCritical] in other fully trusted assemblies, run unverifiable (unsafe) code, and call methods that enforce link demands, and those link demands will always succeed.

So when we say that a *partially trusted* assembly calls a *fully trusted* assembly, we mean that an assembly running in a sandboxed application domain calls a GAC assembly—or an assembly nominated by the host for full trust.

Testing for Full Trust

You can test whether you have unrestricted permissions as follows:

```
new PermissionSet (PermissionState.Unrestricted).Demand();
```

This throws an exception if your application domain is sandboxed. However, it might be that your assembly is, in fact, fully trusted and so can Assert its way out of the sandbox. You can test for this by querying the IsFullyTrusted property on the Assembly in question.

Allowing Partially Trusted Callers

Allowing an assembly to accept partially trusted callers creates the possibility of an elevation of privilege attack, and is therefore disallowed by the CLR unless you request otherwise. To see why this is so, let's look first at an elevation of privilege attack.

Elevation of Privilege

Let's suppose the CLR didn't enforce the rule just described, and you wrote a library intended to be used in full-trust scenarios. One of your properties was as follows:

```
public string ConnectionString
{
  get { return File.ReadAllText (_basePath + "cxString.txt"); }
}
```

Now, assume that the user who deploys your library decides (rightly or wrongly) to load your assembly into the GAC. That user then runs a totally unrelated application hosted in ClickOnce or ASP.NET, inside a restrictive sandbox. The sandboxed application now loads your fully trusted assembly—and tries to call the Connection String property. Fortunately, it throws a SecurityException because File.ReadAll Text will demand a FileIOPermission, which the caller won't have (remember that a Demand checks right up the calling stack). But now consider the following method:

```
public unsafe void Poke (int offset, int data)
{
  int* target = (int*) _origin + offset;
  *target = data;
  ...
}
```

Without an implicit Demand, the sandboxed assembly can call this method—and use it to inflict damage. This is an *elevation of privilege* attack.

The problem in this case is that you never intended for your library to be called by partially trusted assemblies. Fortunately, the CLR helps you by preventing this situation by default.

APTCA and [SecurityTransparent]

To help avoid elevation of privilege attacks, the CLR does not allow partially trusted assemblies to call fully trusted assemblies by default.*

To allow such calls, you must do one of two things to X:

- Apply the [AllowPartiallyTrustedCallers] attribute (called APTCA for short).
- Apply the [SecurityTransparent] attribute.

Applying these attributes means that you must think about the possibility of being the *untrusting* party (rather than the *untrusted* party).

Prior to CLR 4.0, only the APTCA attribute was supported. And all that it did was to enable partially trusted callers. From CLR 4.0, the APTCA also has the effect of implicitly marking all the methods (and functions) in your assembly as *security transparent*. We'll explain this in detail in the next section; for now, we can

---

* Before CLR 4.0, partially trusted assemblies could not even call other partially trusted assemblies if the target was strongly named (unless you applied the APTCA). This restriction didn't really aid security, and so was dropped in CLR 4.0.

summarize it by saying that security transparent methods can't do any of the following (whether running in full or partial trust):

- Run unverifiable (`unsafe`) code.
- Run native code via P/Invoke or COM.
- Assert permissions to elevate their security level.
- Satisfy a link demand.
- Call methods in the .NET Framework marked as [`SecurityCritical`]. Essentially, these comprise methods that do one of the preceding four things without appropriate safeguards or security checks.

> The rationale is that an assembly that doesn't do any of these things cannot, in general, be susceptible to an elevation of privilege attack.

The [`SecurityTransparent`] attribute applies a stronger version of the same rules. The difference is that with APTCA, you can nominate selected methods in your assembly as nontransparent, whereas with [`SecurityTransparent`], all methods must be transparent.

> If your assembly can work with [`SecurityTransparent`], your job is done as a library author. You can ignore the nuances of the transparency model and skip ahead to "Operating System Security" on page 772!

Before we look at how to nominate selected methods as nontransparent, let's first look at when you'd apply these attributes.

The first (and more obvious) scenario is if you plan to write a fully trusted assembly that will run in a partially trusted domain. We walk through an example in "Sandboxing Another Assembly" on page 769.

The second (and less obvious) scenario is writing a library without knowledge of how it will be deployed. For instance, suppose you write an object relational mapper and sell it over the Internet. Customers have three options in how they call your library:

1. From a fully trusted environment
2. From a sandboxed domain
3. From a sandboxed domain, but with your assembly fully trusted (e.g., by loading it into the GAC)

It's easy to overlook the third option—and this is where the transparency model helps.

The Transparency Model in CLR 4.0

To follow this, you'll need to have read the previous section and understand the scenarios for applying APTCA and [Security Transparent].

The security transparency model makes it easier to secure assemblies that might be fully trusted and then called from partially trusted code.

By way of analogy, let's imagine that being a partially trusted assembly is like being convicted of a crime and being sent to prison. In prison, you discover that there are a set of privileges (permissions) that you can earn for good behavior. These permissions entitle you to perform activities such as watching TV or playing basketball. There are some activities, however, that you can never perform—such as getting the keys to the TV room (or the prison gates)—because such activities (methods) would undermine the whole security system. These methods are called *security-critical*.

If writing a fully trusted library, you would want to protect those security-critical methods. One way to do so is to Demand that callers be fully trusted. This was the approach prior to CLR 4.0:

```
[PermissionSet (SecurityAction.Demand, Unrestricted = true)]
public Key GetTVRoomKey() { ... }
```

This creates two problems. First, Demands are slow because they must check right up the call stack; this matters because *security-critical* methods are sometimes *performance-critical*. A Demand can become particularly wasteful if a security-critical method is called in a loop—perhaps from another trusted assembly in the Framework. The CLR 2.0 workaround with such methods was to instead enforce *link demands*, which check only the immediate caller. But this also comes at a price. To maintain security, methods that call link-demanded methods must themselves perform demands or link demands—or be audited to ensure that they don't allow anything potentially harmful if called from a less-trusted party. Such an audit becomes burdensome when call graphs are complicated.

The second problem is that it's easy to forget to perform a demand or link demand on security-critical methods (again, complex call graphs exacerbate this). It would be nice if the CLR could somehow help out and enforce that security-critical functions are not unintentionally exposed to inmates.

The transparency model does exactly that.

The introduction of the transparency model is totally unrelated to the removal of CAS *policy* (see "Security Policy in CLR 2.0" on page 768).

How the Transparency Model Works

In the transparency model, security-critical methods are marked with the [SecurityCritical] attribute:

```
[SecurityCritical]
public Key GetTVRoomKey() { ... }
```

All "dangerous" methods (containing code that the CLR considers could breach security and allow an inmate to escape) must be marked with [SecurityCritical] or [SecuritySafeCritical]. This comprises:

- Unverifiable (unsafe) methods
- Methods that call unmanaged code via P/Invoke or COM interop
- Methods that Assert permissions or call link-demanding methods
- Methods that *call* [SecurityCritical] methods
- Methods that *override* virtual [SecurityCritical] methods

[SecurityCritical] means "this method could allow a partially trusted caller to escape a sandbox."

[SecuritySafeCritical] means "this method does security-critical things—but with appropriate safeguards and so is safe for partially trusted callers."

Partially trusted assemblies can never call security critical methods in fully trusted assemblies. [SecurityCritical] methods can be called only by:

- Other [SecurityCritical] methods
- Methods marked as [SecuritySafeCritical]

Security-safe critical methods act as gatekeepers for security-critical methods (see Figure 20-1), and can be called by any method in any assembly (fully or partially trusted, subject to permission-based CAS demands). To illustrate, suppose that as an inmate you want to watch television. The WatchTV method that you'll call will need to call GetTVRoomKey, which means that WatchTV must be *security-safe-critical*:

```
[SecuritySafeCritical]
public void WatchTV()
{
  new TVPermission().Demand();
  using (Key key = GetTVRoomKey())
    PrisonGuard.OpenDoor (key);
}
```

Notice that we Demand a TVPermission to ensure that the caller actually has TV-watching rights, and carefully dispose of the key we create. We are wrapping a *security-critical* method, making it *safe* to be called by anyone.

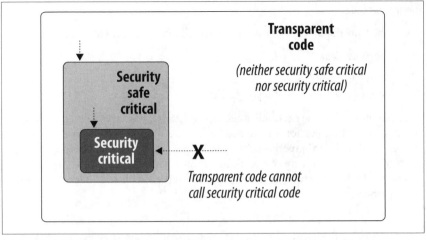

Figure 20-1. Transparency model; only the area in gray needs security auditing

Some methods partake in the activities considered "dangerous" by the CLR, but are not actually dangerous. You can mark these methods directly with [SecuritySafeCritical] instead of [SecurityCritical]. An example is the Array.Copy method: it has an unmanaged implementation for efficiency, and yet cannot be abused by partially trusted callers.

The UnsafeXXX Pattern

There's a potential inefficiency in our TV-watching example in that if a prison guard wants to watch TV via the WatchTV method, he must (unnecessarily) satisfy a TVPermission demand. As a remedy, the CLR team recommends a pattern whereby you define two versions of the method. The first is security-critical and is prefixed by the word *Unsafe*:

```
[SecurityCritical]
public void UnsafeWatchTV()
{
  using (Key key = GetTVRoomKey())
    PrisonGuard.OpenDoor(key);
}
```

The second is security-safe-critical, and calls the first after satisfying a full stack-walking demand:

```
[SecuritySafeCritical]
public void WatchTV()
{
  new TVPermission().Demand();
  UnsafeWatchTV();
}
```

Transparent code

Under the transparency model, all methods fall into one of three categories:

- *Security-critical*
- *Security-safe-critical*
- Neither (in which case, they're called *transparent*)

Transparent methods are so called because you can ignore them when it comes to auditing code for elevation of privilege attacks. All you need to focus on are the [SecuritySafeCritical] methods (the gatekeepers), which typically comprise just a small fraction of an assembly's methods. If an assembly comprises entirely transparent methods, the entire assembly can be marked with the [SecurityTransparent] attribute:

```
[assembly: SecurityTransparent]
```

We then say that the *assembly itself* is transparent. Transparent assemblies don't need auditing for elevation of privilege attacks and implicitly allow partially trusted callers—you don't need to apply APTCA.

Settings the transparency default for an assembly

To summarize what we said previously, there are two ways to specify transparency at the assembly level:

- Apply the APTCA. All methods are then implicitly transparent except those you mark otherwise.
- Apply the [SecurityTransparent] assembly attribute. All methods are then implicitly transparent, without exception.

The third option is to do nothing. This still opts you *into* the transparency rules, but with every method implicitly [SecurityCritical] (apart from any virtual [SecuritySafeCritical] methods that you override, which will remain safe-critical). The effect is that you can call any method you like (assuming you're fully trusted), but transparent methods in other assemblies won't be able to call you.

How to Write APTCA Libraries with Transparency

To follow the transparency model, first identify the potentially "dangerous" methods in your assembly (as described in the previous section). Unit tests will pick these up, because the CLR will refuse to run such methods—even in a fully trusted environment. (Framework 4.0 also ships with a tool called *SecAnnotate.exe* to help with this.) Then mark each such method with:

- [SecurityCritical], if the method might be harmful if called from a less trusted assembly
- [SecuritySafeCritical], if the method performs appropriate checks/safeguards and can be safely called from a less trusted assembly

To illustrate, consider the following method, which calls a security-critical method in the .NET Framework:

```
public static void LoadLibraries()
{
  GC.AddMemoryPressure (1000000);    // Security critical
  ...
}
```

This method could be abused by being called repeatedly from less trusted callers. We could apply the [SecurityCritical] attribute, but then the method would be callable only from other trusted parties via critical or safe-critical methods. A better solution is to fix the method so that it's secure and then apply the [SecuritySafe Critical] attribute:

```
static bool _loaded;

[SecuritySafeCritical]
public static void LoadLibraries()
{
  if (_loaded) return;
  _loaded = true;
  GC.AddMemoryPressure (1000000);
  ...
}
```

(This has the benefit of making it safer for trusted callers, too.)

Securing unsafe methods

Next, suppose we have an unsafe method that is potentially harmful if called by a less trusted assembly. We simply decorate it with [SecurityCritical]:

```
[SecurityCritical]
public unsafe void Poke (int offset, int data)
{
  int* target = (int*) _origin + offset;
  *target = data;
  ...
}
```

 If you write unsafe code in a transparent method, the CLR will throw a VerificationException ("Operation could destabilize the runtime") before executing the method.

We then secure the upstream methods, marking them with [SecurityCritical] or [SecuritySafeCritical] as appropriate.

Next, consider the following unsafe method, which filters a bitmap. This is intrinsically harmless, so we can mark it SecuritySafeCritical:

```
[SecuritySafeCritical]
unsafe void BlueFilter (int[,] bitmap)
{
```

```
int length = bitmap.Length;
fixed (int* b = bitmap)
{
  int* p = b;
  for (int i = 0; i < length; i++)
    *p++ &= 0xFF;
}
}
```

Conversely, you might write a function that doesn't perform anything "dangerous" as far as the CLR is concerned, but poses a security risk nonetheless. You can decorate these, too, with [SecurityCritical]:

```
public string Password
{
  [SecurityCritical] get { return _password; }
}
```

P/Invokes and [SuppressUnmanagedSecurity]

Finally, consider the following unmanaged method, which returns a window handle from a Point (System.Drawing):

```
[DllImport ("user32.dll")]
public static extern IntPtr WindowFromPoint (Point point);
```

Remember that you can call unmanaged code only from [SecurityCritical] and [SecuritySafeCritical] methods.

 You could say that all **extern** methods are implicitly [SecurityCritical], although there is a subtle difference: applying [SecurityCritical] explicitly to an **extern** method has the subtle effect of advancing the security check from runtime to JIT time. To illustrate, consider the following method:

```
static void Foo (bool exec)
{
  if (exec) WindowFromPoint (...)
}
```

If called with **false**, this will be subject to a security check only if WindowFromPoint is marked explicitly with [SecurityCriti cal].

Because we've made the method public, other fully trusted assemblies can call WindowFromPoint directly from [SecurityCritical] methods. For partially trusted callers, we expose the following secure version, which eliminates the danger, by Demanding UI permission and returning a managed class instead of an IntPtr:

```
[UIPermission (SecurityAction.Demand, Unrestricted = true)]
[SecuritySafeCritical]
public static System.Windows.Forms.Control ControlFromPoint (Point point)
{
  IntPtr winPtr = WindowFromPoint (point);
  if (winPtr == IntPtr.Zero) return null;
```

```
        return System.Windows.Forms.Form.FromChildHandle (winPtr);
    }
```

Just one problem remains: the CLR performs an implicit Demand for unmanaged permission whenever you P/Invoke. And because a Demand checks right up the call stack, the WindowFromPoint method will fail if the caller's caller is partially trusted. There are two ways around this. The first is to *assert* permission for unmanaged code in the first line of the ControlFromPoint method:

```
    new SecurityPermission (SecurityPermissionFlag.UnmanagedCode).Assert();
```

Asserting our assembly-given unmanaged right here will ensure that the subsequent implicit Demand in WindowFromPoint will succeed. Of course, this assertion would fail if the assembly itself wasn't fully trusted (by virtue of being loaded into the GAC or being nominated as fully trusted by the host). We'll cover assertions in more detail in "Sandboxing Another Assembly" on page 769.

The second (and more performant) solution is to apply the [SuppressUnmanagedCodeSecurity] attribute to the unmanaged method:

```
    [DllImport ("user32.dll"), SuppressUnmanagedCodeSecurity]
    public static extern IntPtr WindowFromPoint (Point point);
```

This tells the CLR to skip the expensive stack-walking unmanaged Demand (an optimization that could be particularly valuable if WindowFromPoint was called from other trusted classes or assemblies). We can then dump the unmanaged permission assertion in ControlFromPoint.

 Because you're following the transparency model, applying this attribute to an extern method doesn't create the same security risk as in CLR 2.0. This is because you're still protected by the fact that P/Invokes are implicitly security-critical, and so can be called only by other critical or safe-critical methods.

Transparency in Full-Trust Scenarios

In a fully trusted environment, you might want to write critical code and yet avoid the burden of security attributes and method auditing. The easiest way to achieve this is not to attach any assembly security attributes—in which case all your methods are implicitly [SecurityCritical].

This works well as long as *all* partaking assemblies do the same thing—or if the transparency-enabled assemblies are at the *bottom* of the call graph. In other words, you can still call transparent methods in third-party libraries (and in the .NET Framework).

To go in the reverse direction is troublesome; however, this trouble typically guides you to a better solution. Suppose you're writing assembly T, which is partly or wholly transparent, and you want to call assembly X, which is unattributed (and therefore fully critical). You have three options:

- Go fully critical yourself. If your domain will always be fully trusted, you don't need to support partially trusted callers. Making that lack of support *explicit* makes sense.

- Write [SecuritySafeCritical] wrappers around calls to X. This then highlights the security vulnerability points (although this can be burdensome).

- Ask the author of X to consider transparency. If X does nothing critical, this will be as simple as applying [SecurityTransparent] to X. If X does perform critical functions, the process of following the transparency model will force the author of X to at least identify (if not address) X's vulnerability points.

Security Policy in CLR 2.0

Prior to CLR 4.0, the CLR granted a default set of permissions to .NET assemblies based on a complex set of rules and mappings. This was called CAS *policy* and was defined in the computer's .NET Framework configuration. Three standard grant sets resulted from policy evaluation, customizable at the enterprise, machine, user, and application domain levels:

- "Full trust," which was granted to assemblies that ran on the local hard drive
- "LocalIntranet," granted to assemblies that ran over a network share
- "Internet," granted to assemblies that ran within Internet Explorer

Only "Full trust" was fully trusted by default. This meant that if you ran a .NET executable over a network share, it would run with a limited permission set and usually fail. This was supposed to offer some protection, but in reality it offered none—because a malicious party could simply replace the .NET executable with an unmanaged executable and be subject to no permission restrictions. All that this restriction achieved was to frustrate people who wanted to run .NET assemblies in full trust over a network share.

Therefore, the designers of CLR 4.0 decided to abolish these security policies. All assemblies now run in a permission set defined entirely by the hosting environment. Executables that you double-click or run from the command prompt will always run in full trust—whether on a network share or on a local hard drive.

In other words, it's now *entirely up to the host* as to how permissions should be restricted—a machine's CAS policy is irrelevant.

If you still need to work with CLR 2.0's security policy (which will be the case if your entry executable targets Framework Version 3.5 or earlier) you can view and adjust security policy with either the *mscorcfg.msc* MMC plug-in (Control Panel→Administrative Tools→Microsoft .NET Framework Configuration) or the *caspol.exe* command-line tool. The MMC plug-in no longer ships as standard with the .NET Framework: you must install the .NET Framework 3.5 SDK.

The security configuration is ultimately stored in an XML file called *security.config*, in the Framework's configuration folder. You can obtain this as follows:

```
string dir = Path.Combine
  (System.Runtime.InteropServices.RuntimeEnvironment
                  .GetRuntimeDirectory(), "config");
string configFile = Path.Combine (dir, "security.config");
```

Sandboxing Another Assembly

Suppose you write an application that allows consumers to install third-party plug-ins. Most likely you'd want to prevent plug-ins from leveraging your privileges as a trusted application, so as not to destabilize your application—or the end user's computer. The best way to achieve this is to run each plug-in in its own sandboxed application domain.

For this example, we'll assume a plug-in is packaged as a .NET assembly called *plugin.exe* and that activating it is simply a matter of starting the executable. (In Chapter 24, we describe how to load a library into an application domain and interact with it in a more sophisticated way.)

Here's the complete code, for the *host* program:

```
using System;
using System.IO;
using System.Net;
using System.Reflection;
using System.Security;
using System.Security.Policy;
using System.Security.Permissions;

class Program
{
  static void Main()
  {
    string pluginFolder = Path.Combine (
      AppDomain.CurrentDomain.BaseDirectory, "plugins");

    string plugInPath = Path.Combine (pluginFolder, "plugin.exe");

    PermissionSet ps = new PermissionSet (PermissionState.None);

    ps.AddPermission
      (new SecurityPermission (SecurityPermissionFlag.Execution));

    ps.AddPermission
      (new FileIOPermission (FileIOPermissionAccess.PathDiscovery |
                             FileIOPermissionAccess.Read, plugInPath));

    ps.AddPermission (new UIPermission (PermissionState.Unrestricted));

    AppDomainSetup setup = AppDomain.CurrentDomain.SetupInformation;
    AppDomain sandbox = AppDomain.CreateDomain ("sbox", null, setup, ps);
    sandbox.ExecuteAssembly (plugInPath);
    AppDomain.Unload (sandbox);
```

```
        }
    }
```

 You can also pass a list of assemblies to fully trust into the CreateDomain method. We'll give an example in the following section.

First, we create a limited permission set to describe the privileges we want to give to the sandbox. This must include at least execution rights and permission for the plug-in to read its own assembly; otherwise, it won't start. In this case, we also give unrestricted UI permissions. Then we construct a new application domain, specifying our custom permission set, which will be awarded to all assemblies loaded into that domain. We then execute the plug-in assembly in the new domain, and unload the domain when the plug-in finishes executing.

 In this example, we load the plug-in assemblies from a subdirectory called *plugins*. Putting plug-ins in the same directory as the fully trusted host creates the potential for an elevation of privilege attack, whereby the fully trusted domain implicitly loads and runs code in a plug-in assembly in order to resolve a type. An example of how this could happen is if the plug-in throws a custom exception whose type is defined in its own assembly. When the exception bubbles up to the host, the host will implicitly load the plug-in assembly if it can find it—in an attempt to deserialize the exception. Putting the plug-ins in a separate folder prevents such a load from succeeding.

Asserting Permissions

Permission assertions are useful when writing methods that can be called from a partially trusted assembly. They allow fully trusted assemblies to temporarily escape the sandbox in order to perform actions that would otherwise be prohibited by downstream Demands.

 Assertions in the world of CAS have nothing to do with diagnostic or contract-based assertions. Calling Debug.Assert, in fact, is more akin to Demanding a permission than Asserting a permission. In particular, asserting a permission has *side effects* if the assertion succeeds, whereas Debug.Assert does not.

Recall that we previously wrote an application that ran third-party plug-ins in a restricted permission set. Suppose we want to extend this by providing a library of safe methods for plug-ins to call. For instance, we might prohibit plug-ins from accessing a database directly, and yet still allow them to perform certain queries through methods in a library that we provide. Or we might want to expose a method for writing to a log file—without giving them any file-based permission.

The first step in doing this is to create a separate assembly for this (e.g., *utilities*) and add the `AllowPartiallyTrustedCallers` attribute. Then we can expose a method as follows:

```
public static void WriteLog (string msg)
{
  // Write to log
  ...
}
```

The difficulty here is that writing to a file requires `FileIOPermission`. Even though our *utilities* assembly will be fully trusted, the caller won't be, and so any file-based Demands will fail. The solution is to first `Assert` the permission:

```
public class Utils
{
  string _logsFolder = ...;

  [SecuritySafeCritical]
  public static void WriteLog (string msg)
  {
    FileIOPermission f = new FileIOPermission (PermissionState.None);
    f.AddPathList (FileIOPermissionAccess.AllAccess, _logsFolder);
    f.Assert();

    // Write to log
    ...
  }
}
```

> Because we're asserting a permission, we must mark the method as `[SecurityCritical]` or `[SecuritySafeCritical]` (unless we're targeting an earlier version of the Framework). In this case, the method is safe for partially trusted callers, so we choose SecuritySafeCritical. This, of course, means that we can't mark the assembly as a whole with `[SecurityTransparent]`; we must use APTCA instead.

Remember that `Demand` performs a spot-check and throws an exception if the permission is not satisfied. It then walks the stack, checking that all callers also have that permission (within the current `AppDomain`). An assertion checks only that the *current assembly* has the necessary permissions, and if successful, makes a mark on the stack, indicating that from now on, the caller's rights should be ignored and only the current assembly's rights should be considered with respect to those permissions. An `Assert` ends when the method finishes or when you call `CodeAccessPermission.RevertAssert`.

To complete our example, the remaining step is to create a sandboxed application domain that fully trusts the *utilities* assembly. Then we can instantiate a `StrongName` object that describes the assembly, and pass it into `AppDomain`'s `CreateDomain` method:

```
static void Main()
{
  string pluginFolder = Path.Combine (
    AppDomain.CurrentDomain.BaseDirectory, "plugins");

  string plugInPath = Path.Combine (pluginFolder, "plugin.exe");

  PermissionSet ps = new PermissionSet (PermissionState.None);

  // Add desired permissions to ps as we did before
  // ...

  Assembly utilAssembly = typeof (Utils).Assembly;
  StrongName utils = utilAssembly.Evidence.GetHostEvidence<StrongName>();

  AppDomainSetup setup = AppDomain.CurrentDomain.SetupInformation;
  AppDomain sandbox = AppDomain.CreateDomain ("sbox", null, setup, ps,
                                              utils);
  sandbox.ExecuteAssembly (plugInPath);
  AppDomain.Unload (sandbox);
}
```

For this to work, the *utilities* assembly must be strong-name signed.

> Prior to Framework 4.0, you couldn't obtain a StrongName by
> calling GetHostEvidence as we did. The solution was to instead
> do this:
>
> ```
> AssemblyName name = utilAssembly.GetName();
> StrongName utils = new StrongName (
>   new StrongNamePublicKeyBlob (name.GetPublicKey()),
>   name.Name,
>   name.Version);
> ```
>
> The old-fashioned approach is still useful when you don't want
> to load the assembly into the host's domain. This is because you
> can obtain an AssemblyName without needing an Assembly or Type
> object:
>
> ```
> AssemblyName name = AssemblyName.GetAssemblyName
>                     (@"d:\utils.dll");
> ```

Operating System Security

The operating system can further restrict what an application can do, based on the
user's login privileges. In Windows, there are two types of accounts:

- An administrative account that imposes no restrictions in accessing the local
  computer
- A limited permissions account that restricts administrative functions and visibility of other users' data

A feature called User Access Control (UAC) introduced in Windows Vista means that administrators receive two tokens or "hats" when logging in: an administrative hat and an ordinary user hat. By default, programs run wearing the ordinary user hat—with restricted permissions—unless the program requests *administrative elevation*. The user must then approve the request via a dialog that's presented.

For application developers, UAC means that *by default*, your application will run with restricted user privileges. This means you must either:

- Write your application such that it can run without administrative privileges.
- Demand administrative elevation in the application manifest.

The first option is safer and more convenient to the user. Designing your program to run without administrative privileges is easy in most cases: the restrictions are much less draconian than those of a typical *code access security* sandbox.

 You can find out whether you're running under an administrative account with the following method:

```
[DllImport ("shell32.dll", EntryPoint = "#680")]
static extern bool IsUserAnAdmin();
```

With UAC enabled, this returns true only if the current process has administrative elevation.

Running in a Standard User Account

Here are the key things that you *cannot* do in a standard Windows user account:

- Write to the following directories:
  — The operating system folder (typically *Windows*) and subdirectories
  — The program files folder (*Program Files*) and subdirectories
  — The root of the operating system drive (e.g., *C:*\\)
- Write to the HKEY_LOCAL_MACHINE branch of the Registry
- Read performance monitoring (WMI) data

Additionally, as an ordinary user (or even as an administrator), you may be refused access to files or resources that belong to other users. Windows uses a system of Access Control Lists (ACLs) to protect such resources—you can query and assert your own rights in the ACLs via types in System.Security.AccessControl. ACLs can also be applied to cross-process wait handles, described in Chapter 21.

If you're refused access to anything as a result of operating system security, an UnauthorizedAccessException is thrown. This is different from the SecurityException thrown when a .NET permission demand fails.

The .NET code access permission classes are mostly independent of ACLs. This means you can successfully `Demand` a `FileIO Permission`—but still get an `UnauthorizedAccessException` due to ACL restrictions when trying to access the file.

In most cases, you can deal with standard user restrictions as follows:

- Write files to their recommended locations.
- Avoid using the Registry for information that can be stored in files (aside of the HKEY_CURRENT_USER hive, which you will have read/write access to).
- Register ActiveX or COM components during setup.

The recommended location for user documents is `SpecialFolder.MyDocuments`:

```
string docsFolder = Environment.GetFolderPath
                    (Environment.SpecialFolder.MyDocuments);

string path = Path.Combine (docsFolder, "test.txt");
```

The recommended location for configuration files that a user might need to modify outside of your application is `SpecialFolder.ApplicationData` (current user only) or `SpecialFolder.CommonApplicationData` (all users). You typically create subdirectories within these folders, based on your organization and product name.

A good place to put data that need only be accessed within your application is isolated storage.

Perhaps the most inconvenient aspect of running in a standard user account is that a program doesn't have write access to its files, making it difficult to implement an automatic update system. One option is to deploy with ClickOnce: this allows updates to be applied without administrative elevation, but places significant restrictions on the setup procedure (e.g., you cannot register ActiveX controls). Applications deployed with ClickOnce may also be sandboxed with code access security, depending on their mode of delivery. We described another, more sophisticated solution in "Packing a Single-File Executable" on page 676.

Administrative Elevation and Virtualization

In Chapter 17, we described how to deploy an application manifest. With an application manifest, you can request that Windows prompt the user for administrative elevation whenever running your program:

```xml
<?xml version="1.0" encoding="utf-8"?>
<assembly manifestVersion="1.0" xmlns="urn:schemas-microsoft-com:asm.v1">
  <trustInfo xmlns="urn:schemas-microsoft-com:asm.v2">
    <security>
      <requestedPrivileges>
        <requestedExecutionLevel level="requireAdministrator" />
      </requestedPrivileges>
    </security>
  </trustInfo>
</assembly>
```

If you replace `requireAdministrator` with `asInvoker`, it instructs Windows that administrative elevation is *not* required. The effect is almost the same as not having an application manifest at all—except that *virtualization* is disabled. Virtualization is a temporary measure introduced with Windows Vista to help old applications run correctly without administrative privileges. The absence of an application manifest with a `requestedExecutionLevel` element activates this backward-compatibility feature.

Virtualization comes into play when an application writes to the *Program Files* or *Windows* directory, or the HKEY_LOCAL_MACHINE area of the Registry. Instead of throwing an exception, changes are redirected to a separate location on the hard disk where they can't impact the original data. This prevents the application from interfering with the operating system—or other well-behaved applications.

Identity and Role Security

Identity and role-based security is useful when writing a middle tier server or an ASP.NET application, where you're potentially dealing with many users. It allows you to restrict functionality according to the authenticated user's name or role. An *identity* describes a username; a *role* describes a group. A *principal* is an object that describes an identity and/or a role. Hence, a `PrincipalPermission` class enforces identity and/or role security.

In a typical application server, you demand a `PrincipalPermission` on all methods exposed to the client for which you want to enforce security. For example, the following requires that the caller be a member of the "finance" role:

```
[PrincipalPermission (SecurityAction.Demand, Role = "finance")]
public decimal GetGrossTurnover (int year)
{
  ...
}
```

To enforce that only a particular user can call a method, you can specify a Name instead:

```
[PrincipalPermission (SecurityAction.Demand, Name = "sally")]
```

(Of course, the necessity to hardcode names makes this hard to manage.) To allow a combination of identities or roles, you have to use imperative security instead. This means instantiating `PrincipalPermission` objects, calling `Union` to combine them, and then calling `Demand` on the end result.

Assigning Users and Roles

Before a `PrincipalPermission` demand can succeed, you must attach an `IPrincipal` object to the current thread.

You can instruct that the current Windows user be used as an identity in either of two ways, depending on whether you want to impact the whole application domain or just the current thread:

```
AppDomain.CurrentDomain.SetPrincipalPolicy (PrincipalPolicy.
                                            WindowsPrincipal);
// or:
Thread.CurrentPrincipal = new WindowsPrincipal (WindowsIdentity.
                                                GetCurrent());
```

If you're using WCF or ASP.NET, their infrastructures can help with impersonating the client's identity. You can also do this yourself with the GenericPrincipal and GenericIdentity classes. The following creates a user called "Jack" and assigns him three roles:

```
GenericIdentity id = new GenericIdentity ("Jack");
GenericPrincipal p = new GenericPrincipal
  (id, new string[] { "accounts", "finance", "management" } );
```

For this to take effect, you'd assign it to the current thread as follows:

```
Thread.CurrentPrincipal = p;
```

A principal is thread-based because an application server typically processes many client requests concurrently—each on its own thread. As each request may come from a different client, it needs a different principal.

You can subclass GenericIdentity and GenericPrincipal—or implement the IIdentity and IPrincipal interfaces directly in your own types. Here's how the interfaces are defined:

```
public interface IIdentity
{
  string Name { get; }
  string AuthenticationType { get; }
  bool IsAuthenticated { get; }
}

public interface IPrincipal
{
  IIdentity Identity { get; }
  bool IsInRole (string role);
}
```

The key method is IsInRole. Notice that there's no method returning a list of roles, so you're obliged only to rule on whether a particular role is valid for that principal. This can be the basis for more elaborate authorization systems.

Cryptography Overview

Table 20-8 summarizes the cryptography options in .NET. In the remaining sections, we explore each of these.

Table 20-8. Encryption and hashing options in .NET

Option	Keys to manage	Speed	Strength	Notes
File.Encrypt	0	Fast	Depends on user's password	Protects files transparently with file-system support. A key is derived implicitly from the logged-in user's credentials.
Windows Data Protection	0	Fast	Depends on user's password	Encrypts and decrypts byte arrays using an implicitly derived key.
Hashing	0	Fast	High	One-way (irreversible) transformation. Used for storing passwords, comparing files, and checking for data corruption.
Symmetric Encryption	1	Fast	High	For general-purpose encryption/decryption. The same key encrypts and decrypts. Can be used to secure messages in transit.
Public Key Encryption	2	Slow	High	Encryption and decryption use different keys. Used for exchanging a symmetric key in message transmission and for digitally signing files.

The Framework also provides more specialized support for creating and validating XML-based signatures in `System.Security.Cryptography.Xml` and types for working with digital certificates in `System.Security.Cryptography.X509Certificates`.

Windows Data Protection

In the section "File and Directory Operations" on page 559 in Chapter 14, we described how you could use `File.Encrypt` to request that the operating system transparently encrypt a file:

```
File.WriteAllText ("myfile.txt", "");
File.Encrypt ("myfile.txt");
File.AppendAllText ("myfile.txt", "sensitive data");
```

The encryption in this case uses a key derived from the logged-in user's password. You can use this same implicitly derived key to encrypt a byte array with the Windows Data Protection API. The Data Protection API is exposed through the `ProtectedData` class—a simple type with two static methods:

```
public static byte[] Protect (byte[] userData, byte[] optionalEntropy,
                              DataProtectionScope scope);

public static byte[] Unprotect (byte[] encryptedData, byte[] optionalEntropy,
                                DataProtectionScope scope);
```

Most types in `System.Security.Cryptography` live in *mscorlib.dll* and *System.dll*. `ProtectedData` is an exception: it lives in *System.Security.dll*.

Whatever you include in `optionalEntropy` is added to the key, thereby increasing its security. The `DataProtectionScope` enum argument allows two options: `CurrentUser` or `LocalMachine`. With `CurrentUser`, a key is derived from the logged-in user's credentials; with `LocalMachine`, a machine-wide key is used, common to all users. A `LocalMachine` key provides less protection, but works under a Windows Service or a program needing to operate under a variety of accounts.

Here's a simple encryption and decryption demo:

```
byte[] original = {1, 2, 3, 4, 5};
DataProtectionScope scope = DataProtectionScope.CurrentUser;

byte[] encrypted = ProtectedData.Protect (original, null, scope);
byte[] decrypted = ProtectedData.Unprotect (encrypted, null, scope);
// decrypted is now {1, 2, 3, 4, 5}
```

Windows Data Protection provides moderate security against an attacker with full access to the computer, depending on the strength of the user's password. With `LocalMachine` scope, it's effective only against those with restricted physical and electronic access.

Hashing

Hashing provides one-way encryption. This is ideal for storing passwords in a database, as you might never need (or want) to see a decrypted version. To authenticate, simply hash what the user types in and compare it to what's stored in the database.

A hash code is always a small fixed size regardless of the source data length. This makes it good for comparing files or detecting errors in a data stream (rather like a checksum). A single-bit change anywhere in the source data results in a significantly different hash code.

To hash, you call `ComputeHash` on one of the `HashAlgorithm` subclasses such as `SHA256` or `MD5`:

```
byte[] hash;
using (Stream fs = File.OpenRead ("checkme.doc"))
  hash = MD5.Create().ComputeHash (fs);        // hash is 16 bytes long
```

The `ComputeHash` method also accepts a byte array, which is convenient for hashing passwords:

```
byte[] data = System.Text.Encoding.UTF8.GetBytes ("stRhong%pword");
byte[] hash = SHA256.Create().ComputeHash (data);
```

The `GetBytes` method on an `Encoding` object converts a string to a byte array; the `GetString` method converts it back. An `Encoding` object cannot, however, convert an encrypted or hashed byte array to a string, because scrambled data usually violates text encoding rules. Instead, use the following:

- `Convert.ToBase64String`
- `Convert.FromBase64String`

These convert between any byte array and a legal (and XML-friendly) string.

`MD5` and `SHA256` are two of the `HashAlgorithm` subtypes provided by the .NET Framework. Here are all the major algorithms, in ascending order of security (and hash length, in bytes):

$$MD5(16) \rightarrow SHA1(20) \rightarrow SHA256(32) \rightarrow SHA384(48) \rightarrow SHA512(64)$$

The shorter the algorithm, the faster it executes. `MD5` is more than 20 times faster than `SHA512` and is well suited to calculating file checksums. You can hash hundreds of megabytes per second with `MD5`, and then store its result in a `Guid`. (A `Guid` happens to be exactly 16 bytes long, and as a value type it is more tractable than a byte array; you can meaningfully compare `Guid`s with the simple equality operator, for instance.) However, shorter hashes increase the possibility of *collision* (two distinct files yielding the same hash).

Use *at least* `SHA256` when hashing passwords or other security-sensitive data. `MD5` and `SHA1` are considered insecure for this purpose, and are suitable to protect only against accidental corruption, not deliberate tampering.

`SHA384` is no faster than `SHA512`, so if you want more security than `SHA256`, you may as well use `SHA512`.

The longer SHA algorithms are suitable for password hashing, but they require that you enforce a strong password policy to mitigate a *dictionary attack*—a strategy whereby an attacker builds a password lookup table by hashing every word in a dictionary. You can provide additional protection against this by "stretching" your password hashes—repeatedly rehashing to obtain more computationally intensive byte sequences. If you rehash 100 times, a dictionary attack that might otherwise take 1 month would take 8 years. The `Rfc2898DeriveBytes` and `PasswordDerive Bytes` classes perform exactly this kind of stretching.

Another technique to avoid dictionary attacks is to incorporate "salt"—a long series of bytes that you initially obtain via a random number generator, and then combine with each password before hashing. This frustrates hackers in two ways: hashes take longer to compute, and they made not have access to the salt bytes.

The Framework also provides a 160-bit RIPEMD hashing algorithm, slightly above SHA1 in security. It suffers an inefficient .NET implementation, though, making it slower to execute than even SHA512.

Symmetric Encryption

Symmetric encryption uses the same key for encryption as for decryption. The Framework provides four symmetric algorithms, of which Rijndael is the premium (pronounced "Rhine Dahl" or "Rain Doll"). Rijndael is both fast and secure and has two implementations:

- The Rijndael class, which was available since Framework 1.0
- The Aes class, which was introduced in Framework 3.5

The two are almost identical, except that Aes does not let you weaken the cipher by changing the block size. Aes is recommended by the CLR's security team.

Rijndael and Aes allow symmetric keys of length 16, 24, or 32 bytes: all are currently considered secure. Here's how to encrypt a series of bytes as they're written to a file, using a 16-byte key:

```
byte[] key = {145,12,32,245,98,132,98,214,6,77,131,44,221,3,9,50};
byte[] iv  = {15,122,132,5,93,198,44,31,9,39,241,49,250,188,80,7};

byte[] data = { 1, 2, 3, 4, 5 };   // This is what we're encrypting.

using (SymmetricAlgorithm algorithm = Aes.Create())
using (ICryptoTransform encryptor = algorithm.CreateEncryptor (key, iv))
using (Stream f = File.Create ("encrypted.bin"))
using (Stream c = new CryptoStream (f, encryptor, CryptoStreamMode.Write))
  c.Write (data, 0, data.Length);
```

The following code decrypts the file:

```
byte[] key = {145,12,32,245,98,132,98,214,6,77,131,44,221,3,9,50};
byte[] iv  = {15,122,132,5,93,198,44,31,9,39,241,49,250,188,80,7};

byte[] decrypted = new byte[5];

using (SymmetricAlgorithm algorithm = Aes.Create())
using (ICryptoTransform decryptor = algorithm.CreateDecryptor (key, iv))
using (Stream f = File.OpenRead ("encrypted.bin"))
using (Stream c = new CryptoStream (f, decryptor, CryptoStreamMode.Read))
  for (int b; (b = c.ReadByte()) > -1;)
    Console.Write (b + " ");                          // 1 2 3 4 5
```

In this example, we made up a key of 16 randomly chosen bytes. If the wrong key was used in decryption, CryptoStream would throw a CryptographicException. Catching this exception is the only way to test whether a key is correct.

As well as a key, we made up an IV, or *Initialization Vector*. This 16-byte sequence forms part of the cipher—much like the key—but is not considered *secret*. If transmitting an encrypted message, you would send the IV in plain text (perhaps in a message header) and then *change it with every message*. This would render each encrypted message unrecognizable from any previous one—even if their unencrypted versions were similar or identical.

If you don't need—or want—the protection of an IV, you can defeat it by using the same 16-byte value for both the key and the IV. Sending multiple messages with the same IV, though, weakens the cipher and might even make it possible to crack.

The cryptography work is divided among the classes. Aes is the mathematician; it applies the cipher algorithm, along with its encryptor and decryptor transforms. CryptoStream is the plumber; it takes care of stream plumbing. You can replace Aes with a different symmetric algorithm, yet still use CryptoStream.

CryptoStream is *bidirectional*, meaning you can read or write to the stream depending on whether you choose CryptoStreamMode.Read or CryptoStreamMode.Write. Both encryptors and decryptors are read- *and* write-savvy, yielding four combinations— the choice can have you staring at a blank screen for a while! It can be helpful to model reading as "pulling" and writing as "pushing." If in doubt, start with Write for encryption and Read for decryption; this is often the most natural.

Use RandomNumberGenerator in System.Cryptography to generate a random key or IV. The numbers it produces are genuinely unpredictable, or *cryptographically strong* (the System.Random class does not offer the same guarantee). Here's an example:

```
byte[] key = new byte [16];
byte[] iv  = new byte [16];
RandomNumberGenerator rand = RandomNumberGenerator.Create();
rand.GetBytes (key);
rand.GetBytes (iv);
```

If you don't specify a key and IV, cryptographically strong random values are generated automatically. You can query these through the Aes object's Key and IV properties.

Encrypting in Memory

With a MemoryStream, you can encrypt and decrypt entirely in memory. Here are helper methods that do just this, with byte arrays:

```
public static byte[] Encrypt (byte[] data, byte[] key, byte[] iv)
{
  using (Aes algorithm = Aes.Create())
  using (ICryptoTransform encryptor = algorithm.CreateEncryptor (key, iv))
    return Crypt (data, key, iv, encryptor);
}

public static byte[] Decrypt (byte[] data, byte[] key, byte[] iv)
```

```
    {
      using (Aes algorithm = Aes.Create())
      using (ICryptoTransform decryptor = algorithm.CreateDecryptor (key, iv))
        return Crypt (data, key, iv, decryptor);
    }

    static byte[] Crypt (byte[] data, byte[] key, byte[] iv,
                         ICryptoTransform cryptor)
    {
      MemoryStream m = new MemoryStream();
      using (Stream c = new CryptoStream (m, cryptor, CryptoStreamMode.Write))
        c.Write (data, 0, data.Length);
      return m.ToArray();
    }
```

Here, `CryptoStreamMode.Write` works best for both encryption and decryption, since in both cases we're "pushing" into a fresh memory stream.

Here are overloads that accept and return strings:

```
    public static string Encrypt (string data, byte[] key, byte[] iv)
    {
      return Convert.ToBase64String (
        Encrypt (Encoding.UTF8.GetBytes (data), key, iv));
    }

    public static string Decrypt (string data, byte[] key, byte[] iv)
    {
      return Encoding.UTF8.GetString (
        Decrypt (Convert.FromBase64String (data), key, iv));
    }
```

The following demonstrates their use:

```
    byte[] kiv = new byte[16];
    RandomNumberGenerator.Create().GetBytes (kiv);

    string encrypted = Encrypt ("Yeah!", kiv, kiv);
    Console.WriteLine (encrypted);              // R1/5gYvcxyR2vzPjnT7yaQ==

    string decrypted = Decrypt (encrypted, kiv, kiv);
    Console.WriteLine (decrypted);              // Yeah!
```

Chaining Encryption Streams

`CryptoStream` is a decorator, meaning it can be chained with other streams. In the following example, we write compressed encrypted text to a file, and then read it back:

```
    // Use default key/iv for demo.
    using (Aes algorithm = Aes.Create())
    {
      using (ICryptoTransform encryptor = algorithm.CreateEncryptor())
      using (Stream f = File.Create ("serious.bin"))
      using (Stream c = new CryptoStream (f,encryptor,CryptoStreamMode.Write))
      using (Stream d = new DeflateStream (c, CompressionMode.Compress))
      using (StreamWriter w = new StreamWriter (d))
```

```
      w.WriteLine ("Small and secure!");

  using (ICryptoTransform decryptor = algorithm.CreateDecryptor())
  using (Stream f = File.OpenRead ("serious.bin"))
  using (Stream c = new CryptoStream (f, decryptor, CryptoStreamMode.Read))
  using (Stream d = new DeflateStream (c, CompressionMode.Decompress))
  using (StreamReader r = new StreamReader (d))
    Console.WriteLine (r.ReadLine());              // Small and secure!
}
```

In this example, all one-letter variables form part of a chain. The mathematicians—algorithm, encryptor, and decryptor—are there to assist CryptoStream in the cipher work. Figure 20-2 shows this diagrammatically.

Figure 20-2. *Chaining encryption and compression streams*

Chaining streams in this manner demands little memory, regardless of the ultimate stream sizes.

> As an alternative to nesting multiple using statements, you can construct a chain as follows:
>
> ```
> using (ICryptoTransform encryptor = algorithm.CreateEncryptor())
> using
>   (StreamWriter w = new StreamWriter (
>     new DeflateStream (
>       new CryptoStream (
>         File.Create ("serious.bin"),
>         encryptor,
> ```

```
                    CryptoStreamMode.Write
                ),
                CompressionMode.Compress)
            )
        )
```

This is less robust than the previous approach, however, because should an exception be thrown in an object's constructor (e.g., `DeflateStream`), any objects already instantiated (e.g., `FileStream`) would not be disposed.

Disposing Encryption Objects

Disposing a `CryptoStream` ensures that its internal cache of data is flushed to the underlying stream. Internal caching is necessary for encryption algorithms because they process data in blocks, rather than one byte at a time.

`CryptoStream` is unusual in that its `Flush` method does nothing. To flush a stream (without disposing it), you must call `FlushFinalBlock`. In contrast to `Flush`, `FlushFinalBlock` can be called only once, and then no further data can be written.

In our examples, we also disposed the mathematicians—the `Aes` algorithm and `ICryptoTransform` objects (`encryptor` and `decryptor`). Disposal is actually optional with the Rijndael transforms, because their implementations are purely managed. Disposal still serves a useful role, however: it wipes the symmetric key and related data from memory, preventing subsequent discovery by other software running on the computer (we're talking malware). You can't rely on the garbage collector for this job because it merely flags sections of memory as available; it doesn't write zeros over every byte.

The easiest way to dispose an `Aes` object outside of a `using` statement is to call `Clear`. Its `Dispose` method is hidden via explicit implementation (to signal its unusual disposal semantics).

Key Management

It is inadvisable to hardcode encryption keys because popular tools exist to decompile assemblies with little expertise. A better option is to manufacture a random key for each installation, storing it securely with Windows Data Protection (or encrypt the entire message with Windows Data Protection). If you're encrypting a message stream, public key encryption provides the best option still.

Public Key Encryption and Signing

Public key cryptography is *asymmetric*, meaning that encryption and decryption use different keys.

Unlike symmetric encryption, where any arbitrary series of bytes of appropriate length can serve as a key, asymmetric cryptography requires specially crafted key pairs. A key pair contains a *public key* and *private key* component that work together as follows:

- The public key encrypts messages.
- The private key decrypts messages.

The party "crafting" a key pair keeps the private key secret while distributing the public key freely. A special feature of this type of cryptography is that you cannot calculate a private key from a public key. So, if the private key is lost, encrypted data cannot be recovered; conversely, if a private key is leaked, the encryption system becomes useless.

A public key handshake allows two computers to communicate securely over a public network, with no prior contact and no existing shared secret. To see how this works, suppose computer *Origin* wants to send a confidential message to computer *Target*:

1. *Target* generates a public/private key pair, and then sends its public key to *Origin*.

2. *Origin* encrypts the confidential message using *Target*'s public key, then sends it to *Target*.

3. *Target* decrypts the confidential message using its private key.

An eavesdropper will see the following:

- *Target*'s public key
- The secret message, encrypted with *Target*'s public key

But without *Target*'s private key, the message cannot be decrypted.

> This doesn't prevent against a man-in-the-middle attack: in other words, *Origin* cannot know that *Target* isn't some malicious party. In order to authenticate the recipient, the originator needs to already know the recipient's public key, or be able to validate its key through a *digital site certificate*.

The secret message sent from *Origin* to *Target* typically contains a fresh key for subsequent *symmetric* encryption. This allows public key encryption to be abandoned for the remainder of the session, in favor of a symmetric algorithm capable of handling larger messages. This protocol is particularly secure if a fresh public/private key pair is generated for each session, as no keys then need to be stored on either computer.

> The public key encryption algorithms rely on the message being smaller than the key. This makes them suitable for encrypting only small amounts of data, such as a key for subsequent symmetric encryption. If you try to encrypt a message much larger than half the key size, the provider will throw an exception.

The RSA Class

The .NET Framework provides a number of asymmetric algorithms, of which RSA is the most popular. Here's how to encrypt and decrypt with RSA:

```
byte[] data = { 1, 2, 3, 4, 5 };   // This is what we're encrypting.

using (var rsa = new RSACryptoServiceProvider())
{
  byte[] encrypted = rsa.Encrypt (data, true);
  byte[] decrypted = rsa.Decrypt (encrypted, true);
}
```

Because we didn't specify a public or private key, the cryptographic provider automatically generated a key pair, using the default length of 1,024 bits; you can request longer keys in increments of eight bytes, through the constructor. For security-critical applications, it's prudent to request 2,048 bits:

```
var rsa = new RSACryptoServiceProvider (2048);
```

Generating a key pair is computationally intensive—taking perhaps 100 ms. For this reason, the RSA implementation delays this until a key is actually needed, such as when calling Encrypt. This gives you the chance to load in an existing key—or key pair, should it exist.

The methods ImportCspBlob and ExportCspBlob load and save keys in byte array format. FromXmlString and ToXmlString do the same job in a string format, the string containing an XML fragment. A boolean flag lets you indicate whether to include the private key when saving. Here's how to manufacture a key pair and save it to disk:

```
using (var rsa = new RSACryptoServiceProvider())
{
  File.WriteAllText ("PublicKeyOnly.xml", rsa.ToXmlString (false));
  File.WriteAllText ("PublicPrivate.xml", rsa.ToXmlString (true));
}
```

Since we didn't provide existing keys, ToXmlString forced the manufacture of a fresh key pair (on the first call). In the next example, we read back these keys and use them to encrypt and decrypt a message:

```
byte[] data = Encoding.UTF8.GetBytes ("Message to encrypt");

string publicKeyOnly = File.ReadAllText ("PublicKeyOnly.xml");
string publicPrivate = File.ReadAllText ("PublicPrivate.xml");

byte[] encrypted, decrypted;

using (var rsaPublicOnly = new RSACryptoServiceProvider())
{
  rsaPublicOnly.FromXmlString (publicKeyOnly);
  encrypted = rsaPublicOnly.Encrypt (data, true);

  // The next line would throw an exception because you need the private
  // key in order to decrypt:
  // decrypted = rsaPublicOnly.Decrypt (encrypted, true);
}
```

```
using (var rsaPublicPrivate = new RSACryptoServiceProvider())
{
  // With the private key we can successfully decrypt:
  rsaPublicPrivate.FromXmlString (publicPrivate);
  decrypted = rsaPublicPrivate.Decrypt (encrypted, true);
}
```

Digital Signing

Public key algorithms can also be used to digitally sign messages or documents. A
signature is like a hash, except that its production requires a private key and so
cannot be forged. The public key is used to verify the signature. Here's an example:

```
byte[] data = Encoding.UTF8.GetBytes ("Message to sign");
byte[] publicKey;
byte[] signature;
object hasher = SHA1.Create();             // Our chosen hashing algorithm.

// Generate a new key pair, then sign the data with it:
using (var publicPrivate = new RSACryptoServiceProvider())
{
  signature = publicPrivate.SignData (data, hasher);
  publicKey = publicPrivate.ExportCspBlob (false);     // get public key
}

// Create a fresh RSA using just the public key, then test the signature.
using (var publicOnly = new RSACryptoServiceProvider())
{
  publicOnly.ImportCspBlob (publicKey);
  Console.Write (publicOnly.VerifyData (data, hasher, signature)); // True

  // Let's now tamper with the data, and recheck the signature:
  data[0] = 0;
  Console.Write (publicOnly.VerifyData (data, hasher, signature)); // False

  // The following throws an exception as we're lacking a private key:
  signature = publicOnly.SignData (data, hasher);
}
```

Signing works by first hashing the data, and then applying the asymmetric algorithm
to the resultant hash. Because hashes are of a small fixed size, large documents can
be signed relatively quickly (public key encryption is much more CPU-intensive than
hashing). If you want, you can do the hashing yourself, and then call SignHash instead
of SignData:

```
using (var rsa = new RSACryptoServiceProvider())
{
  byte[] hash = SHA1.Create().ComputeHash (data);
  signature = rsa.SignHash (hash, CryptoConfig.MapNameToOID ("SHA1"));
  ...
}
```

`SignHash` still needs to know what hash algorithm you used; `CryptoConfig.MapName ToOID` provides this information in the correct format from a friendly name such as "SHA1".

`RSACryptoServiceProvider` produces signatures whose size matches that of the key. Currently, no mainstream algorithm produces secure signatures significantly smaller than 128 bytes (suitable for product activation codes, for instance).

 For signing to be effective, the recipient must know, and trust, the sender's public key. This can happen via prior communication, preconfiguration, or a site certificate. A site certificate is an electronic record of the originator's public key and name—itself signed by an independent trusted authority. The namespace `System.Security.Cryptography.X509Certificates` defines the types for working with certificates.

21

Threading

C# allows you to execute code in parallel through multithreading.

A thread is analogous to the operating system process in which your application runs. Just as processes run in parallel on a computer, threads run in parallel *within a single process*. Processes are fully isolated from each other; threads have just a limited degree of isolation. In particular, threads share (heap) memory with other threads running in the same application. This, in part, is why threading is useful: one thread can fetch data in the background, for instance, while another thread can display the data as it arrives.

This chapter describes the language and Framework features for creating, configuring, and communicating with threads, and how to coordinate their actions through locking and signaling. It also covers the basic predefined types that assist threading, such as `BackgroundWorker` and the `Timer` classes.

Threading's Uses and Misuses

Multithreading has many uses; here are the most common:

Maintaining a responsive user interface
 By running time-consuming tasks on a parallel "worker" thread, the main UI thread is free to continue processing keyboard and mouse events.

Making efficient use of an otherwise blocked CPU
 Multithreading is useful when a thread is awaiting a response from another computer or piece of hardware. While one thread is blocked while performing the task, other threads can take advantage of the otherwise unburdened computer.

Parallel programming
 Code that performs intensive calculations can execute faster on multicore or multiprocessor computers if the workload is shared among multiple threads in a "divide-and-conquer" strategy (the following chapter is dedicated to this).

Speculative execution

On multicore machines, you can sometimes improve performance by predicting something that might need to be done, and then doing it ahead of time. LINQ-Pad uses this technique to speed up the creation of new queries. A variation is to run a number of different algorithms in parallel that all solve the same task. Whichever one finishes first "wins"—this is effective when you can't know ahead of time which algorithm will execute fastest.

Allowing requests to be processed simultaneously

On a server, client requests can arrive concurrently and so need to be handled in parallel (the .NET Framework creates threads for this automatically if you use ASP.NET, WCF, Web Services, or Remoting). This can also be useful on a client (e.g., handling peer-to-peer networking—or even multiple requests from the user).

With technologies such as ASP.NET and WCF, you may be unaware that multi-threading is even taking place—unless you access shared data (perhaps via static fields) without appropriate locking, running afoul of thread safety.

Threads also come with strings attached. The biggest is that multithreading can increase complexity. Having lots of threads does not in and of itself create much complexity; it's the interaction between threads (typically via shared data) that does. This applies whether or not the interaction is intentional, and can cause long development cycles and an ongoing susceptibility to intermittent and nonreproducible bugs. For this reason, it pays to keep interaction to a minimum, and to stick to simple and proven designs wherever possible. This chapter focuses largely on dealing with just these complexities; remove the interaction and there's much less to say!

 A good strategy is to encapsulate multithreading logic into reusable classes that can be independently examined and tested. The Framework itself offers many higher-level threading constructs, which we cover in this and the following chapter.

Threading also incurs a resource and CPU cost in scheduling and switching threads (when there are more active threads than CPU cores)—and there's also a creation/tear-down cost. Multithreading will not always speed up your application—it can even slow it down if used excessively or inappropriately. For example, when heavy disk I/O is involved, it can be faster to have a couple of worker threads run tasks in sequence than to have 10 threads executing at once. (In "Signaling with Wait and Pulse" on page 840, we describe how to implement a producer/consumer queue, which provides just this functionality.)

Getting Started

A *client* program (Console, WPF, or Windows Forms) starts in a single thread that's created automatically by the CLR and operating system (the "main" thread). Here it lives out its life as a single-threaded application, unless you do otherwise, by creating more threads (directly or indirectly).*

You can create and start a new thread by instantiating a `Thread` object and calling its `Start` method. The simplest constructor for `Thread` takes a `ThreadStart` delegate: a parameterless method indicating where execution should begin. For example, see the code listing following the note.

> All examples assume the following namespaces are imported:
>
> ```
> using System;
> using System.Threading;
> ```

```
class ThreadTest
{
  static void Main()
  {
    Thread t = new Thread (WriteY);     // Kick off a new thread
    t.Start();                          // running WriteY()

    // Simultaneously, do something on the main thread.
    for (int i = 0; i < 1000; i++) Console.Write ("x");
  }

  static void WriteY()
  {
    for (int i = 0; i < 1000; i++) Console.Write ("y");
  }
}

// Output:
xxxxxxxxxxxxxxxxxxxxyyyyyyyyyyyyyyyyyyyyyyyyyyyyyyyyyyyyyyyyyyy
xxxxxxxxxxxxxxxxxxxxxxxxxxxxxxxxxxxxxxxxxxyyyyyyyyyyyyyyyyy
yyyyyyyyyyyyyyyyyyyyyyyyyyyyyyyyyyyxxxxxxxxxxxxxxxxxxxxxxxxx
xxxxxxxxxxxxxxxxxxxxxxxxxxxxyyyyyyyyyyyyyyyyyyyyyyyyyyyyyyyy
yyyyyyyyyyyyyxxxxxxxxxxxxxxxxxxxxxxxxxxxxxxxxxxxxxxxxxxxxxxx
...
```

The main thread creates a new thread t on which it runs a method that repeatedly prints the character "y". Simultaneously, the main thread repeatedly prints the character "x", as shown in Figure 21-1. On a single-core computer, the operating system must allocate "slices" of time to each thread (typically 20 ms in Windows) to simulate concurrency, resulting in repeated blocks of "x" and "y". On a multicore or multiprocessor machine, the two threads can genuinely execute in parallel (subject to competition by other active processes on the computer), although you still get

---

* The CLR creates other threads behind the scenes for garbage collection and finalization.

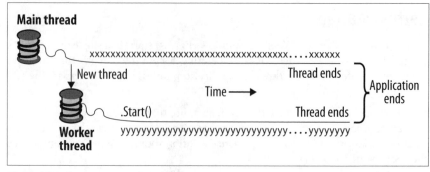

Figure 21-1. Starting a new thread

repeated blocks of "x" and "y" because of subtleties in the mechanism by which Console handles concurrent requests.

> A thread is said to be *preempted* at the points where its execution is interspersed with the execution of code on another thread. The term often crops up in explaining why something has gone wrong!

Once started, a thread's IsAlive property returns true, until the point where the thread ends. A thread ends when the delegate passed to the Thread's constructor finishes executing. Once ended, a thread cannot restart.

You can wait for another thread to end by calling its Join method. Here's an example:

```
static void Main()
{
  Thread t = new Thread (Go);
  t.Start();
  t.Join();
  Console.WriteLine ("Thread t has ended!");
}

static void Go() { for (int i = 0; i < 1000; i++) Console.Write ("y"); }
```

This prints "y" 1,000 times, followed by "Thread t has ended!" immediately afterward. You can include a timeout when calling Join, either in milliseconds or as a TimeSpan. It then returns true if the thread ended or false if it timed out.

Thread.Sleep pauses the current thread for a specified period:

```
Thread.Sleep (TimeSpan.FromHours (1));  // sleep for 1 hour
Thread.Sleep (500);                     // sleep for 500 milliseconds
```

> While a thread waits during a Sleep or Join, it's said to be *blocked*. We describe blocking in more detail in "Synchronization" on page 805.

`Thread.Sleep(0)` relinquishes the thread's current time slice immediately, voluntarily handing over the CPU to other threads. Framework 4.0's new `Thread.Yield()` method does the same thing—except that it relinquishes only to threads running on the *same* processor.

 `Sleep(0)` or `Yield` is occasionally useful in production code for advanced performance tweaks. It's also an excellent diagnostic tool for helping to uncover thread safety issues: if inserting `Thread.Yield()` anywhere in your code makes or breaks the program, you almost certainly have a bug.

Each thread has a `Name` property that you can set for the benefit of debugging. This is particularly useful in Visual Studio, since the thread's name is displayed in the Threads Window and Debug Location toolbar. You can set a thread's name just once; attempts to change it later will throw an exception.

The static `Thread.CurrentThread` property gives you the currently executing thread:

```
Console.WriteLine (Thread.CurrentThread.Name);
```

Passing Data to a Thread

The easiest way to pass arguments to a thread's target method is to execute a lambda expression that calls the method with the desired arguments:

```
static void Main()
{
  Thread t = new Thread ( () => Print ("Hello from t!") );
  t.Start();
}

static void Print (string message) { Console.WriteLine (message); }
```

With this approach, you can pass in any number of arguments to the method. You can even wrap the entire implementation in a multistatement lambda:

```
new Thread (() =>
{
  Console.WriteLine ("I'm running on another thread!");
  Console.WriteLine ("This is so easy!");
}).Start();
```

You can do the same thing almost as easily in C# 2.0 with anonymous methods:

```
new Thread (delegate()
{
  ...
}).Start();
```

Another technique is to pass an argument into `Thread`'s `Start` method:

```
static void Main()
{
  Thread t = new Thread (Print);
  t.Start ("Hello from t!");
}

static void Print (object messageObj)
{
  string message = (string) messageObj;    // We need to cast here
  Console.WriteLine (message);
}
```

This works because Thread's constructor is overloaded to accept either of two delegates:

```
public delegate void ThreadStart();
public delegate void ParameterizedThreadStart (object obj);
```

The limitation of ParameterizedThreadStart is that it accepts only one argument. And because it's of type object, it usually needs to be cast.

Lambda expressions and captured variables

As we saw, a lambda expression is the most powerful way to pass data to a thread. However, you must be careful about accidentally modifying *captured variables* after starting the thread. For instance, consider the following:

```
for (int i = 0; i < 10; i++)
  new Thread (() => Console.Write (i)).Start();
```

The output is nondeterministic! Here's a typical result:

```
0223557799
```

The problem is that the i variable refers to the *same* memory location throughout the loop's lifetime. Therefore, each thread calls Console.Write on a variable whose value may change as it is running! The solution is to use a temporary variable as follows:

```
for (int i = 0; i < 10; i++)
{
  int temp = i;
  new Thread (() => Console.Write (temp)).Start();
}
```

> This is analogous to the problem we described in "Captured Variables" on page 325 in Chapter 8. The problem is less about multithreading and more about C#'s rules for capturing variables (which are somewhat undesirable in the case of for and foreach loops).

Variable temp is now local to each loop iteration. Therefore, each thread captures a different memory location and there's no problem. We can illustrate the problem in the earlier code more simply with the following example:

```
string text = "t1";
Thread t1 = new Thread ( () => Console.WriteLine (text) );

text = "t2";
Thread t2 = new Thread ( () => Console.WriteLine (text) );

t1.Start();
t2.Start();
```

Here's the output:

```
t2
t2
```

Sharing Data Between Threads

The preceding example demonstrated that captured variables are shared between threads. Let's take a step back and examine what happens with local variables in the simpler case where no lambda expressions or anonymous methods are involved. Consider this program:

```
static void Main()
{
  new Thread (Go).Start();     // Call Go() on a new thread
  Go();                        // Call Go() on the main thread
}

static void Go()
{
  // Declare and use a local variable - 'cycles'
  for (int cycles = 0; cycles < 5; cycles++) Console.Write (cycles);
}

// OUTPUT:  0123401234
```

Each thread gets a separate copy of the cycles variable as it enters the Go method and so is unable to interfere with another concurrent thread. The CLR and operating system achieve this by assigning each thread its own private memory stack for local variables.

If threads do want to share data, they do so via a common reference. This can be a captured variable as we saw previously—but much more often it's a *field*. Here's an example:

```
static void Main()
{
  Introducer intro = new Introducer();
  intro.Message = "Hello";

  var t = new Thread (intro.Run);
  t.Start(); t.Join();

  Console.WriteLine (intro.Reply);
}
```

```
class Introducer
{
  public string Message;
  public string Reply;

  public void Run()
  {
    Console.WriteLine (Message);
    Reply = "Hi right back!";
  }
}

// Output:
Hello
Hi right back!
```

Shared fields allow both for passing data to a new thread and for receiving data back from it later on. Moreover, they allow threads to communicate with each other as they're running. Shared fields can be either instance or static.

> Shared data is the primary cause of complexity and obscure errors in multithreading. Although often essential, it pays to keep it as simple as possible. Sometimes it's possible to avoid shared state altogether—in which case, you entirely avoid the complexities and overhead of synchronization (which we'll describe later).

Foreground and Background Threads

By default, threads you create explicitly are *foreground threads*. Foreground threads keep the application alive for as long as any one of them is running, whereas *background threads* do not. Once all foreground threads finish, the application ends, and any background threads still running abruptly terminate.

> A thread's foreground/background status has no relation to its priority or allocation of execution time.

You can query or change a thread's background status using its `IsBackground` property. Here's an example:

```
class PriorityTest
{
  static void Main (string[] args)
  {
    Thread worker = new Thread ( () => Console.ReadLine() );
    if (args.Length > 0) worker.IsBackground = true;
    worker.Start();
  }
}
```

If this program is called with no arguments, the worker thread assumes foreground status and will wait on the `ReadLine` statement for the user to press Enter. Meanwhile, the main thread exits, but the application keeps running because a foreground thread is still alive.

On the other hand, if an argument is passed to `Main()`, the worker is assigned background status, and the program exits almost immediately as the main thread ends (terminating the `ReadLine`).

When a process terminates in this manner, any `finally` blocks in the execution stack of background threads are circumvented. This is a problem if your program employs `finally` (or `using`) blocks to perform cleanup work such as releasing resources or deleting temporary files. To avoid this, you can explicitly wait out such background threads upon exiting an application. There are two ways to accomplish this:

- If you've created the thread yourself, call `Join` on the thread.
- If you're on a pooled thread (see "Thread Pooling" on page 800) use an event wait handle (see "Signaling with Event Wait Handles" on page 832).

In either case, you should specify a timeout, so you can abandon a renegade thread should it refuse to finish for some reason. This is your backup exit strategy: in the end, you want your application to close—without the user having to enlist help from the Task Manager!

> If a user uses the Task Manager to forcibly end a .NET process, all threads "drop dead" as though they were background threads. This is observed rather than documented behavior, and it could vary depending on the CLR and operating system version.

Foreground threads don't require this treatment, but you must take care to avoid bugs that could cause the thread not to end. A common cause for applications failing to exit properly is the presence of active foreground threads.

Thread Priority

A thread's `Priority` property determines how much execution time it gets relative to other active threads in the operating system, on the following scale:

```
enum ThreadPriority { Lowest, BelowNormal, Normal, AboveNormal, Highest }
```

This becomes relevant only when multiple threads are simultaneously active.

> Think carefully before elevating a thread's priority—it can lead to problems such as resource starvation for other threads.

Elevating a thread's priority doesn't make it capable of performing real-time work, because it's still throttled by the application's process priority. To perform

real-time work, you must also elevate the process priority using the `Process` class in
`System.Diagnostics` (we didn't tell you how to do this):

```
using (Process p = Process.GetCurrentProcess())
  p.PriorityClass = ProcessPriorityClass.High;
```

`ProcessPriorityClass.High` is actually one notch short of the highest priority:
`Realtime`. Setting a process priority to `Realtime` instructs the OS that you never want
the process to yield CPU time to another process. If your program enters an accidental infinite loop, you might find even the operating system locked out, with
nothing short of the power button left to rescue you! For this reason, `High` is usually
the best choice for real-time applications.

> If your real-time application has a user interface, elevating the
> process priority gives screen updates excessive CPU time, slow-
> ing down the entire computer (particularly if the UI is complex).
> Lowering the main thread's priority in conjunction with raising
> the process's priority ensures that the real-time thread doesn't
> get preempted by screen redraws, but doesn't solve the problem
> of starving other applications of CPU time, because the operat-
> ing system will still allocate disproportionate resources to the
> process as a whole. An ideal solution is to have the real-time
> worker and user interface run as separate applications with dif-
> ferent process priorities, communicating via Remoting or
> memory-mapped files. Memory-mapped files are ideally suited
> to this task; we explain how they work in Chapters 14 and 25.

Even with an elevated process priority, there's a limit to the suitability of the managed environment in handling hard real-time requirements. In Chapter 12, we described the issues of garbage collection and the workarounds. Further, the operating
system may present additional challenges—even for unmanaged applications—that
are best solved with dedicated hardware or a specialized real-time platform.

Exception Handling

Any `try`/`catch`/`finally` blocks in scope when a thread is created are of no relevance
to the thread when it starts executing. Consider the following program:

```
public static void Main()
{
  try
  {
    new Thread (Go).Start();
  }
  catch (Exception ex)
  {
    // We'll never get here!
    Console.WriteLine ("Exception!");
  }
}

static void Go() { throw null; }    // Throws a NullReferenceException
```

The try/catch statement in this example is ineffective, and the newly created thread will be encumbered with an unhandled NullReferenceException. This behavior makes sense when you consider that each thread has an independent execution path.

The remedy is to move the exception handler into the Go method:

```
public static void Main()
{
    new Thread (Go).Start();
}

static void Go()
{
    try
    {
        ...
        throw null;    // The NullReferenceException will get caught below
        ...
    }
    catch (Exception ex)
    {
        Typically log the exception, and/or signal another thread
        that we've come unstuck
        ...
    }
}
```

You need an exception handler on all thread entry methods in production applications—just as you do (usually at a higher level, in the execution stack) on your main thread. An unhandled exception causes the whole application to shut down. With an ugly dialog!

In writing such exception handling blocks, rarely would you *ignore* the error: typically, you'd log the details of the exception, and then perhaps display a dialog allowing the user to automatically submit those details to your web server. You then might shut down the application—because it's possible that the error corrupted the program's state. However, the cost of doing so is that the user will lose his recent work—open documents, for instance.

The "global" exception handling events for WPF and Windows Forms applications (Application.DispatcherUnhandledException and Application.ThreadException) fire only for exceptions thrown on the main UI thread. You still must handle exceptions on worker threads manually.

AppDomain.CurrentDomain.UnhandledException fires on any unhandled exception, but provides no means of preventing the application from shutting down afterward.

There are, however, some cases where you don't need to handle exceptions on a worker thread, because the .NET Framework does it for you. These are covered in upcoming sections, and are:

- Asynchronous delegates
- `BackgroundWorker`
- The Task Parallel Library (conditions apply)

Thread Pooling

Whenever you start a thread, a few hundred microseconds are spent organizing such things as a fresh private local variable stack. Each thread also consumes (by default) around 1 MB of memory. The *thread pool* cuts these overheads by sharing and re-cycling threads, allowing multithreading to be applied at a very granular level without a performance penalty. This is useful when leveraging multicore processors to execute computationally intensive code in parallel in "divide-and-conquer" style.

The thread pool also keeps a lid on the total number of worker threads it will run simultaneously. Too many active threads throttle the operating system with administrative burden and render CPU caches ineffective. Once a limit is reached, jobs queue up and start only when another finishes. This makes arbitrarily concurrent applications possible, such as a web server. (The *asynchronous method* pattern takes this further by making highly efficient use of the pooled threads; see Chapter 23.)

There are a number of ways to enter the thread pool:

- Via the Task Parallel Library or PLINQ (from Framework 4.0)
- By calling `ThreadPool.QueueUserWorkItem`
- Via asynchronous delegates
- Via `BackgroundWorker`

> The following constructs use the thread pool *indirectly*:
>
> - WCF, Remoting, ASP.NET, and ASMX Web Services application servers
> - `System.Timers.Timer` and `System.Threading.Timer`
> - Framework methods that end in *Async*, such as those on `WebClient` (the *event-based asynchronous pattern*), and most `BeginXXX` methods (the *asynchronous programming model* pattern)

The *Task Parallel Library* (TPL) and PLINQ are sufficiently powerful and high-level that you'll want to use them to assist in multithreading even when thread pooling is unimportant. We discuss this fully in the following chapter. Right now, we'll look briefly at how you can use the `Task` class as a simple means of running a delegate on a pooled thread.

There are a few things to be wary of when using pooled threads:

- You cannot set the Name of a pooled thread, making debugging more difficult (although you can attach a description when debugging in Visual Studio's Threads window).

- Pooled threads are always *background threads* (this is usually not a problem).

- Blocking a pooled thread may trigger additional latency in the early life of an application unless you call Thread Pool.SetMinThreads (see the section "Optimizing the Thread Pool" on page 805).

You are free to change the priority of a pooled thread—it will be restored to normal when released back to the pool.

You can query if you're currently executing on a pooled thread via the property Thread.CurrentThread.IsThreadPoolThread.

Entering the Thread Pool via TPL

You can enter the thread pool easily using the Task classes in the Task Parallel Library. These were introduced in Framework 4.0: if you're familiar with the older constructs, consider the nongeneric Task class a replacement for ThreadPool.QueueU serWorkItem, and the generic Task<TResult> a replacement for asynchronous delegates. The newer constructs are faster, more convenient, and more flexible than the old.

To use the nongeneric Task class, call Task.Factory.StartNew, passing in a delegate of the target method:

```
static void Main()     // The Task class is in System.Threading.Tasks
{
  Task.Factory.StartNew (Go);
}

static void Go()
{
  Console.WriteLine ("Hello from the thread pool!");
}
```

Task.Factory.StartNew returns a Task object, which you can then use to monitor the task—for instance, you can wait for it to complete by calling its Wait method.

Any unhandled exceptions are conveniently rethrown onto the host thread when you call a task's Wait method. (If you don't call Wait and abandon the task, an unhandled exception will shut down the process, as with an ordinary thread.)

The generic Task<TResult> class is a subclass of the nongeneric Task. It lets you get a return value back from the task after it finishes executing. In the following example, we download a web page using Task<TResult>:

```
static void Main()
{
  // Start the task executing:
  Task<string> task = Task.Factory.StartNew<string>
    ( () => DownloadString ("http://www.linqpad.net") );

  // We can do other work here and it will execute in parallel:
  RunSomeOtherMethod();

  // When we need the task's return value, we query its Result property:
  // If it's still executing, the current thread will now block (wait)
  // until the task finishes:
  string result = task.Result;
}

static string DownloadString (string uri)
{
  using (var wc = new System.Net.WebClient())
    return wc.DownloadString (uri);
}
```

(The <string> type argument in boldface is for clarity: it would be *inferred* if we omitted it.)

Any unhandled exceptions are automatically rethrown when you query the task's Result property, wrapped in an AggregateException. However, if you fail to query its Result property (and don't call Wait), any unhandled exception will take the process down.

The Task Parallel Library has many more features, and is particularly well suited to leveraging multicore processors. We'll resume our discussion of TPL in the following chapter.

Entering the Thread Pool Without TPL

You can't use the Task Parallel Library if you're targeting an earlier version of the .NET Framework (prior to 4.0). Instead, you must use one of the older constructs for entering the thread pool: ThreadPool.QueueUserWorkItem and asynchronous delegates. The difference between the two is that asynchronous delegates let you return data from the thread. Asynchronous delegates also marshal any exception back to the caller.

QueueUserWorkItem

To use QueueUserWorkItem, simply call this method with a delegate that you want to run on a pooled thread:

```
static void Main()
{
  ThreadPool.QueueUserWorkItem (Go);
  ThreadPool.QueueUserWorkItem (Go, 123);
  Console.ReadLine();
}

static void Go (object data)    // data will be null with the first call.
{
  Console.WriteLine ("Hello from the thread pool! " + data);
}

// Output:
Hello from the thread pool!
Hello from the thread pool! 123
```

Our target method, Go, must accept a single object argument (to satisfy the WaitCallback delegate). This provides a convenient way of passing data to the method, just like with ParameterizedThreadStart. Unlike with Task, QueueUserWorkItem doesn't return an object to help you subsequently manage execution. Also, you must explicitly deal with exceptions in the target code—unhandled exceptions will take down the program.

Asynchronous delegates

ThreadPool.QueueUserWorkItem doesn't provide an easy mechanism for getting return values back from a thread after it has finished executing. Asynchronous delegate invocations (asynchronous delegates for short) solve this, allowing any number of typed arguments to be passed in both directions. Furthermore, unhandled exceptions on asynchronous delegates are conveniently rethrown on the original thread (or more accurately, the thread that calls EndInvoke), and so they don't need explicit handling.

 Don't confuse asynchronous delegates with asynchronous methods (methods starting with *Begin* or *End*, such as File.BeginRead/File.EndRead). Asynchronous methods follow a similar protocol outwardly, but they exist to solve a much more difficult problem, which we describe in Chapter 23.

Here's how you start a worker task via an asynchronous delegate:

1. Instantiate a delegate targeting the method you want to run in parallel (typically one of the predefined Func delegates).

2. Call BeginInvoke on the delegate, saving its IAsyncResult return value.

   BeginInvoke returns immediately to the caller. You can then perform other activities while the pooled thread is working.

3. When you need the results, call EndInvoke on the delegate, passing in the saved IAsyncResult object.

In the following example, we use an asynchronous delegate invocation to execute concurrently with the main thread, a simple method that returns a string's length:

```
static void Main()
{
  Func<string, int> method = Work;
  IAsyncResult cookie = method.BeginInvoke ("test", null, null);
  //
  // ... here's where we can do other work in parallel...
  //
  int result = method.EndInvoke (cookie);
  Console.WriteLine ("String length is: " + result);
}

static int Work (string s) { return s.Length; }
```

EndInvoke does three things. First, it waits for the asynchronous delegate to finish executing, if it hasn't already. Second, it receives the return value (as well as any ref or out parameters). Third, it throws any unhandled worker exception back to the calling thread.

 If the method you're calling with an asynchronous delegate has no return value, you are still (technically) obliged to call EndIn voke. In practice, this is open to debate; there are no EndInvoke police to administer punishment to noncompliers! If you choose not to call EndInvoke, however, you'll need to consider exception handling on the worker method to avoid silent failures.

You can also specify a callback delegate when calling BeginInvoke—a method accepting an IAsyncResult object that's automatically called upon completion. This allows the instigating thread to "forget" about the asynchronous delegate, but it requires a bit of extra work at the callback end:

```
static void Main()
{
  Func<string, int> method = Work;
  method.BeginInvoke ("test", Done, method);
  // ...
  //
}

static int Work (string s) { return s.Length; }

static void Done (IAsyncResult cookie)
{
  var target = (Func<string, int>) cookie.AsyncState;
  int result = target.EndInvoke (cookie);
  Console.WriteLine ("String length is: " + result);
}
```

The final argument to BeginInvoke is a user state object that populates the AsyncState property of IAsyncResult. It can contain anything you like; in this case, we're using it to pass the `method` delegate to the completion callback, so we can call `EndInvoke` on it.

Optimizing the Thread Pool

The thread pool starts out with one thread in its pool. As tasks are assigned, the pool manager "injects" new threads to cope with the extra concurrent workload, up to a maximum limit. After a sufficient period of inactivity, the pool manager may "retire" threads if it suspects that doing so will lead to better throughput.

You can set the upper limit of threads that the pool will create by calling `Thread Pool.SetMaxThreads`; the defaults are:

- 1023 in Framework 4.0 in a 32-bit environment
- 32768 in Framework 4.0 in a 64-bit environment
- 250 per core in Framework 3.5
- 25 per core in Framework 2.0

(These figures may vary according to the hardware and operating system.) The reason for there being that many is to ensure progress should some threads be blocked (idling while awaiting some condition, such as a response from a remote computer).

You can also set a lower limit by calling `ThreadPool.SetMinThreads`. The role of the lower limit is subtler: it's an advanced optimization technique that instructs the pool manager not to *delay* in the allocation of threads until reaching the lower limit. Raising the minimum thread count improves concurrency when there are blocked threads (see sidebar).

 The default lower limit is one thread per processor core—the minimum that allows full CPU utilization. On server environments, though (such ASP.NET under IIS), the lower limit is typically much higher—as much as 50 or more.

Synchronization

So far, we've described how to start a task on a thread, configure a thread, and pass data in both directions. We've also described how local variables are private to a thread and how references can be shared among threads, allowing them to communicate via common fields.

The next step is *synchronization*: coordinating the actions of threads for a predictable outcome. Synchronization is particularly important when threads access the same data; it's surprisingly easy to run aground in this area.

Synchronization constructs can be divided into four categories:

Simple blocking methods
These wait for another thread to finish or for a period of time to elapse. `Sleep`, `Join`, and `Task.Wait` are simple blocking methods.

Locking constructs

These limit the number of threads that can perform some activity or execute a section of code at a time. *Exclusive* locking constructs are most common—these allow just one thread in at a time, and allow competing threads to access common data without interfering with each other. The standard exclusive locking constructs are `lock` (`Monitor.Enter`/`Monitor.Exit`), `Mutex`, and `SpinLock`. The nonexclusive locking constructs are `Semaphore`, `SemaphoreSlim`, and `ReaderWriterLockSlim` (we cover reader/writer locks later in this chapter).

Signaling constructs

These allow a thread to pause until receiving a notification from another, avoiding the need for inefficient polling. There are two commonly used signaling devices: event wait handles and `Monitor`'s `Wait`/`Pulse` methods. Framework 4.0 introduces the `CountdownEvent` and `Barrier` classes.

Nonblocking synchronization constructs

These protect access to a common field by calling upon processor primitives. The CLR and C# provide the following nonblocking constructs: `Thread.MemoryBarrier`, `Thread.VolatileRead`, `Thread.VolatileWrite`, the `volatile` keyword, and the `Interlocked` class.

Blocking is essential to all but the last category. Let's briefly examine this concept.

How Does the Minimum Thread Count Work?

Increasing the thread pool's minimum thread count to x doesn't actually force x threads to be created right away—threads are created only on demand. Rather, it instructs the pool manager to create up to x threads the *instant* they are required. The question, then, is why would the thread pool otherwise delay in creating a thread when it's needed?

The answer is to prevent a brief burst of short-lived activity from causing a full allocation of threads, suddenly swelling an application's memory footprint. To illustrate, consider a quad-core computer running a client application that enqueues 40 tasks at once. If each task performs a 10 ms calculation, the whole thing will be over in 100 ms, assuming the work is divided among the four cores. Ideally, we'd want the 40 tasks to run on *exactly four threads*:

- Any less and we'd not be making maximum use of all four cores.
- Any more and we'd be wasting memory and CPU time creating unnecessary threads.

And this is exactly how the thread pool works. Matching the thread count to the core count allows a program to retain a small memory footprint without hurting performance—as long as the threads are efficiently used (which in this case they are).

But now suppose that instead of working for 10 ms, each task queries the Internet, waiting half a second for a response while the local CPU is idle. The pool manager's thread-economy strategy breaks down; it would now do better to create more threads, so all the Internet queries could happen simultaneously.

Fortunately, the pool manager has a backup plan. If its queue remains stationary for more than half a second, it responds by creating more threads—one every half-second—up to the capacity of the thread pool.

The half-second delay is a two-edged sword. On the one hand, it means that a one-off burst of brief activity doesn't make a program suddenly consume an extra unnecessary 40 MB (or more) of memory. On the other hand, it can needlessly delay things when a pooled thread blocks, such as when querying a database or calling WebClient.DownloadFile. For this reason, you can tell the pool manager not to delay in the allocation of the first *x* threads, by calling SetMinThreads, for instance:

```
ThreadPool.SetMinThreads (50, 50);
```

(The second value indicates how many threads to assign to I/O completion ports, which are used by the APM, described in Chapter 23.)

The default value is one thread per core.

Blocking

A thread is deemed *blocked* when its execution is paused for some reason, such as when Sleeping or waiting for another to end via Join or EndInvoke. A blocked thread immediately *yields* its processor time slice, and from then on consumes no processor time until its blocking condition is satisfied. You can test for a thread being blocked via its ThreadState property:

```
bool blocked = (someThread.ThreadState & ThreadState.WaitSleepJoin) != 0;
```

 ThreadState is a flags enum, combining three "layers" of data in a bitwise fashion. Most values, however, are redundant, unused, or deprecated. The following code strips a ThreadState to one of four useful values: Unstarted, Running, WaitSleepJoin, and Stopped:

```
public static ThreadState SimpleThreadState (ThreadState ts)
{
  return ts & (ThreadState.Unstarted |
               ThreadState.WaitSleepJoin |
               ThreadState.Stopped);
}
```

The ThreadState property is useful for diagnostic purposes, but unsuitable for synchronization, because a thread's state may change in between testing ThreadState and acting on that information.

When a thread blocks or unblocks, the operating system performs a *context switch*. This incurs an overhead of a few microseconds.

Blocking Versus Spinning

Sometimes a thread must pause until a certain condition is met. Signaling and locking constructs achieve this efficiently by *blocking* until a condition is satisfied. However, there is a simpler alternative: a thread can await a condition by *spinning* in a polling loop. For example:

```
while (!proceed);
```

or:

```
while (DateTime.Now < nextStartTime);
```

In general, this is very wasteful on processor time: as far as the CLR and operating system are concerned, the thread is performing an important calculation, and so gets allocated resources accordingly!

Sometimes a hybrid between blocking and spinning is used:

```
while (!proceed) Thread.Sleep (10);
```

Although inelegant, this is (in general) far more efficient than outright spinning. Problems can arise, though, due to concurrency issues on the proceed flag. Proper use of locking and signaling avoids this.

> Spinning *very briefly* can be effective when you expect a condition to be satisfied soon (perhaps within a few microseconds) because it avoids the overhead and latency of a context switch. The .NET Framework provides special methods and classes to assist—these are covered in the following chapter (see "Spin-Lock and SpinWait" on page 920).

Locking

Exclusive locking is used to ensure that only one thread can enter particular sections of code at a time. The two main exclusive locking constructs are lock and Mutex. Of the two, the lock construct is faster and more convenient. Mutex, though, has a niche in that its lock can span applications in different processes on the computer.

In this section, we'll start with the lock construct and then move on to Mutex and semaphores (for nonexclusive locking). Later in the chapter we'll cover reader/writer locks.

> From Framework 4.0, there is also the SpinLock struct for high-concurrency scenarios, which we cover in the following chapter.

Let's start with the following class:

```
class ThreadUnsafe
{
  static int _val1 = 1, _val2 = 1;

  static void Go()
  {
    if (_val2 != 0) Console.WriteLine (_val1 / _val2);
    _val2 = 0;
  }
}
```

This class is not thread-safe: if Go was called by two threads simultaneously, it would be possible to get a division-by-zero error, because _val2 could be set to zero in one thread right as the other thread was in between executing the if statement and Console.WriteLine.

Here's how lock can fix the problem:

```
class ThreadSafe
{
  static readonly object _locker = new object();
  static int _val1, _val2;

  static void Go()
  {
    lock (_locker)
    {
      if (_val2 != 0) Console.WriteLine (_val1 / _val2);
      _val2 = 0;
    }
  }
}
```

Only one thread can lock the synchronizing object (in this case, _locker) at a time, and any contending threads are blocked until the lock is released. If more than one thread contends the lock, they are queued on a "ready queue" and granted the lock on a first-come, first-served basis.[†] Exclusive locks are sometimes said to enforce *serialized* access to whatever's protected by the lock, because one thread's access cannot overlap with that of another. In this case, we're protecting the logic inside the Go method, as well as the fields _val1 and _val2.

A thread blocked while awaiting a contended lock has a ThreadState of WaitSleep Join. In "Interrupt and Abort" on page 855, we describe how a blocked thread can be forcibly released via another thread. This is a fairly heavy-duty technique that might be used in ending a thread.

[†] Nuances in the behavior of Windows and the CLR mean that the fairness of the queue can sometimes be violated.

Monitor.Enter and Monitor.Exit

C#'s lock statement is in fact a syntactic shortcut for a call to the methods Monitor.Enter and Monitor.Exit, with a try/finally block. Here's (a simplified version of) what's actually happening within the Go method of the preceding example:

```
Monitor.Enter (_locker);
try
{
  if (_val2 != 0) Console.WriteLine (_val1 / _val2);
  _val2 = 0;
}
finally { Monitor.Exit (_locker); }
```

Calling Monitor.Exit without first calling Monitor.Enter on the same object throws an exception.

The lockTaken overloads

The code that we just demonstrated is exactly what the C# 1.0, 2.0, and 3.0 compilers produce in translating a lock statement.

There's a subtle vulnerability in this code, however. Consider the (unlikely) event of an exception being thrown within the implementation of Monitor.Enter, or between the call to Monitor.Enter and the try block (due, perhaps, to Abort being called on that thread—or an OutOfMemoryException being thrown). In such a scenario, the lock may or may not be taken. If the lock *is* taken, it won't be released—because we'll never enter the try/finally block. This will result in a leaked lock.

To avoid this danger, CLR 4.0's designers added the following overload to Monitor.Enter:

```
public static void Enter (object obj, ref bool lockTaken);
```

lockTaken is false after this method if (and only if) the Enter method throws an exception and the lock was not taken.

Here's the correct pattern of use (which is exactly how C# 4.0 translates a lock statement):

```
bool lockTaken = false;
try
{
  Monitor.Enter (_locker, ref lockTaken);
  // Do your stuff...
}
finally { if (lockTaken) Monitor.Exit (_locker); }
```

TryEnter

Monitor also provides a TryEnter method that allows a timeout to be specified, either in milliseconds or as a TimeSpan. The method then returns true if a lock was obtained, or false if no lock was obtained because the method timed out. TryEnter can also be called with no argument, which "tests" the lock, timing out immediately if the lock can't be obtained right away.

As with the `Enter` method, it's overloaded in CLR 4.0 to accept a `lockTaken` argument.

Choosing the Synchronization Object

Any object visible to each of the partaking threads can be used as a synchronizing object, subject to one hard rule: it must be a reference type. The synchronizing object is typically private (because this helps to encapsulate the locking logic) and is typically an instance or static field. The synchronizing object can double as the object it's protecting, as the `_list` field does in the following example:

```
class ThreadSafe
{
  List <string> _list = new List <string>();

  void Test()
  {
    lock (_list)
    {
      _list.Add ("Item 1");
      ...
```

A field dedicated for the purpose of locking (such as `_locker`, in the example prior) allows precise control over the scope and granularity of the lock. The containing object (`this`)—or even its type—can also be used as a synchronization object:

```
lock (this) { ... }
```

or:

```
lock (typeof (Widget)) { ... }    // For protecting access to statics
```

The disadvantage of locking in this way is that you're not encapsulating the locking logic, so it becomes harder to prevent deadlocking and excessive blocking. A lock on a type may also seep through application domain boundaries (within the same process—see Chapter 24).

You can also lock on local variables captured by lambda expressions or anonymous methods.

 Locking doesn't restrict access to the synchronizing object itself in any way. In other words, `x.ToString()` will not block because another thread has called `lock(x)`; both threads must call `lock(x)` in order for blocking to occur.

When to Lock

As a basic rule, you need to lock around accessing *any writable shared field*. Even in the simplest case—an assignment operation on a single field—you must consider synchronization. In the following class, neither the `Increment` nor the `Assign` method is thread-safe:

```
class ThreadUnsafe
{
  static int _x;
  static void Increment() { _x++; }
  static void Assign()    { _x = 123; }
}
```

Here are thread-safe versions of Increment and Assign:

```
class ThreadSafe
{
  static readonly object _locker = new object();
  static int _x;

  static void Increment() { lock (_locker) _x++; }
  static void Assign()    { lock (_locker) _x = 123; }
}
```

In "Nonblocking Synchronization" on page 825, we explain how this need arises, and how the memory barriers and the Interlocked class can provide alternatives to locking in these situations.

Locking and Atomicity

If a group of variables are always read and written within the same lock, you can say the variables are read and written *atomically*. Let's suppose fields x and y are always read and assigned within a lock on object locker:

```
lock (locker) { if (x != 0) y /= x; }
```

One can say x and y are accessed atomically, because the code block cannot be divided or preempted by the actions of another thread in such a way that it will change x or y and *invalidate its outcome*. You'll never get a division-by-zero error, providing x and y are always accessed within this same exclusive lock.

> The atomicity provided by a lock is violated if an exception is thrown within a lock block. For example, consider the following:
>
> ```
> decimal _savingsBalance, _checkBalance;
>
> void Transfer (decimal amount)
> {
>   lock (_locker)
>   {
>     _savingsBalance += amount;
>     _checkBalance -= amount + GetBankFee();
>   }
> }
> ```
>
> If an exception was thrown by GetBankFee(), the bank would lose money. In this case, we could avoid the problem by calling GetBankFee earlier. A solution for more complex cases is to implement "rollback" logic within a catch or finally block.

Instruction atomicity is a different, although analogous concept: an instruction is atomic if it executes indivisibly on the underlying processor (see "Nonblocking Synchronization" on page 825).

Nested Locking

A thread can repeatedly lock the same object in a nested (*reentrant*) fashion:

```
lock (locker)
  lock (locker)
    lock (locker)
    {
        // Do something...
    }
```

or:

```
Monitor.Enter (locker); Monitor.Enter (locker);  Monitor.Enter (locker);
// Do something...
Monitor.Exit (locker);  Monitor.Exit (locker);   Monitor.Exit (locker);
```

In these scenarios, the object is unlocked only when the outermost `lock` statement has exited—or a matching number of `Monitor.Exit` statements have executed.

Nested locking is useful when one method calls another within a lock:

```
static readonly object _locker = new object();

static void Main()
{
  lock (_locker)
  {
    AnotherMethod();
    // We still have the lock - because locks are reentrant.
  }
}

static void AnotherMethod()
{
  lock (_locker) { Console.WriteLine ("Another method"); }
}
```

A thread can block on only the first (outermost) lock.

Deadlocks

A deadlock happens when two threads each wait for a resource held by the other, so neither can proceed. The easiest way to illustrate this is with two locks:

```
object locker1 = new object();
object locker2 = new object();


new Thread (() => {
                    lock (locker1)
                    {
                      Thread.Sleep (1000);
```

```
                    lock (locker2);        // Deadlock
                }
            }).Start();
    lock (locker2)
    {
        Thread.Sleep (1000);
        lock (locker1);                    // Deadlock
    }
```

More elaborate deadlocking chains can be created with three or more threads.

> The CLR, in a standard hosting environment, is not like SQL Server and does not automatically detect and resolve deadlocks by terminating one of the offenders. A threading deadlock causes participating threads to block indefinitely, unless you've specified a locking timeout. (Under the SQL CLR integration host, however, deadlocks *are* automatically detected and a [catchable] exception is thrown on one of the threads.)

Deadlocking is one of the hardest problems in multithreading—especially when there are many interrelated objects. Fundamentally, the difficulty is that you can't be sure what locks your *caller* has taken out.

So, you might innocently lock private field a within your class x, unaware that your caller (or caller's caller) has already locked field b within class y. Meanwhile, another thread is doing the reverse—creating a deadlock. Ironically, the problem is exacerbated by (good) object-oriented design patterns, because such patterns create call chains that are not determined until runtime.

The popular advice, "lock objects in a consistent order to avoid deadlocks," although helpful in our initial example, is hard to apply to the scenario just described. A better strategy is to be wary of locking around calling methods in objects that may have references back to your own object. Also, consider whether you really need to lock around calling methods in other classes (often you do—as we'll see in "Thread Safety" on page 543—but sometimes there are other options). Relying more on declarative and data parallelism (Chapter 22), immutable types, and nonblocking synchronization constructs (later in this chapter) can lessen the need for locking.

> Here is an alternative way to perceive the problem: when you call out to other code while holding a lock, the encapsulation of that lock subtly *leaks*. This is not a fault in the CLR or .NET Framework, but a fundamental limitation of locking in general. The problems of locking are being addressed in various research projects, including *Software Transactional Memory*.

Another deadlocking scenario arises when calling Dispatcher.Invoke (in a WPF application) or Control.Invoke (in a Windows Forms application) while in possession of a lock. If the UI happens to be running another method that's waiting on the same lock, a deadlock will happen right there. This can often be fixed simply by calling

BeginInvoke instead of Invoke. Alternatively, you can release your lock before calling Invoke, although this won't work if your *caller* took out the lock. We explain Invoke and BeginInvoke in the section "Rich Client Applications and Thread Affinity" on page 822.

Performance

Locking is fast: you can expect to acquire and release a lock in less than 100 nanoseconds on a 2010-era computer if the lock is uncontended. If it is contended, the consequential context switch moves the overhead closer to the microsecond region, although it may be longer before the thread is actually rescheduled. You can avoid the cost of a context switch with the SpinLock class described in the following chapter—if you're locking very briefly.

If used excessively, locking can degrade concurrency by causing other threads to wait unnecessarily. This can also increase the chance of deadlock.

Mutex

A Mutex is like a C# lock, but it can work across multiple processes. In other words, Mutex can be *computer-wide* as well as *application-wide*.

> Acquiring and releasing an uncontended Mutex takes a few microseconds—about 50 times slower than a lock.

With a Mutex class, you call the WaitOne method to lock and ReleaseMutex to unlock. Closing or disposing a Mutex automatically releases it. Just as with the lock statement, a Mutex can be released only from the same thread that obtained it.

A common use for a cross-process Mutex is to ensure that only one instance of a program can run at a time. Here's how it's done:

```
class OneAtATimePlease
{
  static void Main()
  {
    // Naming a Mutex makes it available computer-wide. Use a name that's
    // unique to your company and application (e.g., include your URL).

    using (var mutex = new Mutex (false, "oreilly.com OneAtATimeDemo"))
    {
      // Wait a few seconds if contended, in case another instance
      // of the program is still in the process of shutting down.

      if (!mutex.WaitOne (TimeSpan.FromSeconds (3), false))
      {
        Console.WriteLine ("Another instance of the app is running. Bye!");
        return;
      }
      RunProgram();
```

```
        }
    }

    static void RunProgram()
    {
        Console.WriteLine ("Running. Press Enter to exit");
        Console.ReadLine();
    }
}
```

If running under Terminal Services, a computer-wide Mutex is ordinarily visible only to applications in the same terminal server session. To make it visible to all terminal server sessions, prefix its name with *Global*.

Semaphore

A semaphore is like a nightclub: it has a certain capacity, enforced by a bouncer. Once it's full, no more people can enter, and a queue builds up outside. Then, for each person that leaves, one person enters from the head of the queue. The constructor requires a minimum of two arguments: the number of places currently available in the nightclub and the club's total capacity.

A semaphore with a capacity of one is similar to a Mutex or lock, except that the semaphore has no "owner"—it's *thread-agnostic*. Any thread can call Release on a Semaphore, whereas with Mutex and lock, only the thread that obtained the lock can release it.

There are two functionally similar versions of this class: Semaphore and SemaphoreSlim. The latter was introduced in Framework 4.0 and has been optimized to meet the low-latency demands of parallel programming. It's also useful in traditional multithreading because it lets you specify a cancellation token when waiting (see "Safe Cancellation" on page 857). It cannot, however, be used for interprocess signaling.

Semaphore incurs about 1 microsecond in calling WaitOne or Release; SemaphoreSlim incurs about a quarter of that.

Semaphores can be useful in limiting concurrency—preventing too many threads from executing a particular piece of code at once. In the following example, five threads try to enter a nightclub that allows only three threads in at once:

```
class TheClub      // No door lists!
{
    static SemaphoreSlim _sem = new SemaphoreSlim (3);    // Capacity of 3
```

```
static void Main()
{
  for (int i = 1; i <= 5; i++) new Thread (Enter).Start (i);
}

static void Enter (object id)
{
  Console.WriteLine (id + " wants to enter");
  _sem.Wait();
  Console.WriteLine (id + " is in!");          // Only three threads
  Thread.Sleep (1000 * (int) id);              // can be here at
  Console.WriteLine (id + " is leaving");      // a time.
  _sem.Release();
}
}

1 wants to enter
1 is in!
2 wants to enter
2 is in!
3 wants to enter
3 is in!
4 wants to enter
5 wants to enter
1 is leaving
4 is in!
2 is leaving
5 is in!
```

If the Sleep statement was instead performing intensive disk I/O, the Semaphore would improve overall performance by limiting excessive concurrent hard-drive activity.

A Semaphore, if named, can span processes in the same way as a Mutex.

Thread Safety

A program or method is thread-safe if it has no indeterminacy in the face of any multithreading scenario. Thread safety is achieved primarily with locking and by reducing the possibilities for thread interaction.

General-purpose types are rarely thread-safe in their entirety, for the following reasons:

- The development burden in full thread safety can be significant, particularly if a type has many fields (each field is a potential for interaction in an arbitrarily multithreaded context).

- Thread safety can entail a performance cost (payable, in part, whether or not the type is actually used by multiple threads).

- A thread-safe type does not necessarily make the program using it thread-safe, and often the work involved in the latter makes the former redundant.

Thread safety is hence usually implemented just where it needs to be, in order to handle a specific multithreading scenario.

There are, however, a few ways to "cheat" and have large and complex classes run safely in a multithreaded environment. One is to sacrifice granularity by wrapping large sections of code—even access to an entire object—within a single exclusive lock, enforcing serialized access at a high level. This tactic is, in fact, essential if you want to use thread-unsafe third-party code (or most Framework types, for that matter) in a multithreaded context. The trick is simply to use the same exclusive lock to protect access to all properties, methods, and fields on the thread-unsafe object. The solution works well if the object's methods all execute quickly (otherwise, there will be a lot of blocking).

 Primitive types aside, few .NET Framework types, when instantiated, are thread-safe for anything more than concurrent read-only access. The onus is on the developer to superimpose thread safety, typically with exclusive locks. (The collections in System.Collections.Concurrent are an exception; we'll cover them in the next chapter.)

Another way to cheat is to minimize thread interaction by minimizing shared data. This is an excellent approach and is used implicitly in "stateless" middle-tier application and web page servers. Since multiple client requests can arrive simultaneously, the server methods they call must be thread-safe. A stateless design (popular for reasons of scalability) intrinsically limits the possibility of interaction, since classes do not persist data between requests. Thread interaction is then limited just to the static fields one may choose to create, for such purposes as caching commonly used data in memory and in providing infrastructure services such as authentication and auditing.

The final approach in implementing thread safety is to use an automatic locking regime. The .NET Framework does exactly this, if you subclass ContextBoundObject and apply the Synchronization attribute to the class. Whenever a method or property on such an object is then called, an object-wide lock is automatically taken for the whole execution of the method or property. Although this reduces the thread-safety burden, it creates problems of its own: deadlocks that would not otherwise occur, impoverished concurrency, and unintended reentrancy. For these reasons, manual locking is generally a better option—at least until a less simplistic automatic locking regime becomes available.

Thread Safety and .NET Framework Types

Locking can be used to convert thread-unsafe code into thread-safe code. A good application of this is the .NET Framework: nearly all of its nonprimitive types are not thread-safe (for anything more than read-only access) when instantiated, and yet they can be used in multithreaded code if all access to any given object is protected via a lock. Here's an example, where two threads simultaneously add an item to the same List collection, then enumerate the list:

```
class ThreadSafe
{
  static List <string> _list = new List <string>();

  static void Main()
  {
    new Thread (AddItem).Start();
    new Thread (AddItem).Start();
  }

  static void AddItem()
  {
    lock (_list) _list.Add ("Item " + _list.Count);

    string[] items;
    lock (_list) items = _list.ToArray();
    foreach (string s in items) Console.WriteLine (s);
  }
}
```

In this case, we're locking on the _list object itself. If we had two interrelated lists, we would have to choose a common object upon which to lock (we could nominate one of the lists, or better: use an independent field).

Enumerating .NET collections is also thread-unsafe in the sense that an exception is thrown if the list is modified during enumeration. Rather than locking for the duration of enumeration, in this example we first copy the items to an array. This avoids holding the lock excessively if what we're doing during enumeration is potentially time-consuming. (Another solution is to use a reader/writer lock; see "Reader/Writer Locks" on page 865.)

Locking around thread-safe objects

Sometimes you also need to lock around accessing thread-safe objects. To illustrate, imagine that the Framework's List class was, indeed, thread-safe, and we want to add an item to a list:

```
if (!_list.Contains (newItem)) _list.Add (newItem);
```

Whether or not the list was thread-safe, this statement is certainly not! The whole if statement would have to be wrapped in a lock in order to prevent preemption in between testing for containership and adding the new item. This same lock would then need to be used everywhere we modified that list. For instance, the following statement would also need to be wrapped in the identical lock:

```
_list.Clear();
```

to ensure that it did not preempt the former statement. In other words, we would have to lock exactly as with our thread-unsafe collection classes (making the List class's hypothetical thread safety redundant).

Locking around accessing a collection can cause excessive blocking in highly concurrent environments. To this end, Framework 4.0 provides a thread-safe queue, stack, and dictionary, which we describe in the following chapter.

Static methods

Wrapping access to an object around a custom lock works only if all concurrent threads are aware of—and use—the lock. This may not be the case if the object is widely scoped. The worst case is with static members in a public type. For instance, imagine if the static property on the `DateTime` struct, `DateTime.Now`, was not thread-safe, and that two concurrent calls could result in garbled output or an exception. The only way to remedy this with external locking might be to lock the type itself—`lock(typeof(DateTime))`—before calling `DateTime.Now`. This would work only if all programmers agreed to do this (which is unlikely). Furthermore, locking a type creates problems of its own.

For this reason, static members on the `DateTime` struct have been carefully programmed to be thread-safe. This is a common pattern throughout the .NET Framework: *static members are thread-safe; instance members are not.* Following this pattern also makes sense when writing types for public consumption, so as not to create impossible thread-safety conundrums. In other words, by making static methods thread-safe, you're programming so as not to *preclude* thread safety for consumers of that type.

Thread safety in static methods is something that you must explicitly code: it doesn't happen automatically by virtue of the method being static!

Read-only thread safety

Making types thread-safe for concurrent read-only access (where possible) is advantageous because it means that consumers can avoid excessive locking. Many of the .NET Framework types follow this principle: collections, for instance, are thread-safe for concurrent readers.

Following this principle yourself is simple: if you document a type as being thread-safe for concurrent read-only access, don't write to fields within methods that a consumer would expect to be read-only (or lock around doing so). For instance, in implementing a `ToArray()` method in a collection, you might start by compacting the collection's internal structure. However, this would make it thread-unsafe for consumers that expected this to be read-only.

Read-only thread safety is one of the reasons that enumerators are separate from "enumerables": two threads can simultaneously enumerate over a collection because each gets a separate enumerator object.

In the absence of documentation, it pays to be cautious in assuming whether a method is read-only in nature. A good example is the Random class: when you call Random.Next(), its internal implementation requires that it update private seed values. Therefore, you must either lock around using the Random class, or maintain a separate instance per thread.

Thread Safety in Application Servers

Application servers need to be multithreaded to handle simultaneous client requests. WCF, ASP.NET, and Web Services applications are implicitly multithreaded; the same holds true for Remoting server applications that use a network channel such as TCP or HTTP. This means that when writing code on the server side, you must consider thread safety if there's any possibility of interaction among the threads processing client requests. Fortunately, such a possibility is rare; a typical server class either is stateless (no fields) or has an activation model that creates a separate object instance for each client or each request. Interaction usually arises only through static fields, sometimes used for caching in memory parts of a database to improve performance.

For example, suppose you have a RetrieveUser method that queries a database:

```
// User is a custom class with fields for user data
internal User RetrieveUser (int id) { ... }
```

If this method was called frequently, you could improve performance by caching the results in a static Dictionary. Here's a solution that takes thread safety into account:

```
static class UserCache
{
  static Dictionary <int, User> _users = new Dictionary <int, User>();

  internal static User GetUser (int id)
  {
    User u = null;

    lock (_users)
      if (_users.TryGetValue (id, out u))
        return u;

    u = RetrieveUser (id);          // Method to retrieve from database;
    lock (_users) _users [id] = u;
    return u;
  }
}
```

We must, at a minimum, lock around reading and updating the dictionary to ensure thread safety. In this example, we choose a practical compromise between simplicity and performance in locking. Our design actually creates a very small potential for inefficiency: if two threads simultaneously called this method with the same previously unretrieved id, the RetrieveUser method would be called twice—and the dictionary would be updated unnecessarily. Locking once across the whole method would prevent this, but would create a worse inefficiency: the entire cache would be locked up for the duration of calling `RetrieveUser`, during which time other threads would be blocked in retrieving *any* user.

Rich Client Applications and Thread Affinity

Both the Windows Presentation Foundation (WPF) and Windows Forms libraries follow models based on thread affinity. Although each has a separate implementation, they are both very similar in how they function.

The objects that make up a rich client are based primarily on `DependencyObject` in the case of WPF, or `Control` in the case of Windows Forms. These objects have *thread affinity*, which means that only the thread that instantiates them can subsequently access their members. Violating this causes either unpredictable behavior, or an exception to be thrown.

On the positive side, this means you don't need to lock around accessing a UI object. On the negative side, if you want to call a member on object X created on another thread Y, you must marshal the request to thread Y. You can do this explicitly as follows:

- In WPF, call `Invoke` or `BeginInvoke` on the element's `Dispatcher` object.

- In Windows Forms, call `Invoke` or `BeginInvoke` on the control.

`Invoke` and `BeginInvoke` both accept a delegate, which references the method on the target control that you want to run. `Invoke` works *synchronously*: the caller blocks until the marshal is complete. `BeginInvoke` works *asynchronously*: the caller returns immediately and the marshaled request is queued up (using the same message queue that handles keyboard, mouse, and timer events).

Assuming we have a window that contains a text box called `txtMessage`, whose content we wish a worker thread to update, here's an example for WPF:

```
public partial class MyWindow : Window
{
  public MyWindow()
  {
    InitializeComponent();
    new Thread (Work).Start();
  }

  void Work()
  {
    Thread.Sleep (5000);              // Simulate time-consuming task
    UpdateMessage ("The answer");
  }

  void UpdateMessage (string message)
  {
    Action action = () => txtMessage.Text = message;
    Dispatcher.Invoke (action);
  }
}
```

The code is similar for Windows Forms, except that we call the (Form's) Invoke method instead:

```
void UpdateMessage (string message)
{
  Action action = () => txtMessage.Text = message;
  this.Invoke (action);
}
```

The Framework provides two constructs to simplify this process:

- BackgroundWorker (see the section "Background-Worker" on page 852)
- Task continuations (see "Continuations" on page 904)

Worker threads versus UI threads

It's helpful to think of a rich client application as having two distinct categories of threads: UI threads and worker threads. UI threads instantiate (and subsequently "own") UI elements; worker threads do not. Worker threads typically execute long-running tasks such as fetching data.

Most rich client applications have a single UI thread (which is also the main application thread) and periodically spawn worker threads—either directly or using BackgroundWorker. These workers then marshal back to the main UI thread in order to update controls or report on progress.

So, when would an application have multiple UI threads? The main scenario is when you have an application with multiple top-level windows, often called a *Single Document Interface* (SDI) application, such as Microsoft Word. Each SDI window typically shows itself as a separate "application" on the taskbar and is mostly isolated, functionally, from other SDI windows. By giving each such window its own UI thread, the application can be made more responsive.

Immutable Objects

An immutable object is one whose state cannot be altered—externally or internally. The fields in an immutable object are typically declared read-only and are fully initialized during construction.

Immutability is a hallmark of functional programming—where instead of *mutating* an object, you create a new object with different properties. LINQ follows this paradigm. Immutability is also valuable in multithreading in that it avoids the problem of shared writable state—by eliminating (or minimizing) the writable.

One pattern is to use immutable objects to encapsulate a group of related fields, to minimize lock durations. To take a very simple example, suppose we had two fields as follows:

```
int _percentComplete;
string _statusMessage;
```

and we wanted to read/write them atomically. Rather than locking around these fields, we could define the following immutable class:

```
class ProgressStatus      // Represents progress of some activity
{
  public readonly int PercentComplete;
  public readonly string StatusMessage;

  // This class might have many more fields...

  public ProgressStatus (int percentComplete, string statusMessage)
  {
    PercentComplete = percentComplete;
    StatusMessage = statusMessage;
  }
}
```

Then we could define a single field of that type, along with a locking object:

```
readonly object _statusLocker = new object();
ProgressStatus _status;
```

We can now read/write values of that type without holding a lock for more than a single assignment:

```
var status = new ProgressStatus (50, "Working on it");
// Imagine we were assigning many more fields...
// ...
lock (_statusLocker) _status = status;      // Very brief lock
```

To read the object, we first obtain a copy of the object (within a lock). Then we can read its values without needing to hold on to the lock:

```
ProgressStatus status;
lock (_locker ProgressStatus) status = _status;   // Again, a brief lock
int pc = statusCopy.PercentComplete;
string msg = statusCopy.StatusMessage;
...
```

> Technically, the last two lines of code are thread-safe by virtue of the preceding lock performing an implicit *memory barrier*. We'll discuss this in the next section.

Note that this lock-free approach prevents inconsistency within a group of related fields. But it doesn't prevent data from changing while you subsequently act on it—for this, you usually need a lock. In Chapter 22, we'll see more examples of using immutability to simplify multithreading—including PLINQ.

It's also possible to safely assign a new `ProgressStatus` object based on its preceding value (e.g., it's possible to "increment" the `PercentComplete` value)—without locking over more than one line of code. In fact, we can do this without using a single lock, through the use of explicit memory barriers, `Interlocked.CompareExchange`, and spin-waits. This is an advanced technique, which we demonstrate in the final section of Chapter 22.

Nonblocking Synchronization

Earlier, we said that the need for synchronization arises even in the simple case of assigning or incrementing a field. Although locking can always satisfy this need, a contended lock means that a thread must block, suffering the overhead of a context switch and the latency of being descheduled, which can be undesirable in highly concurrent and performance-critical scenarios. The .NET Framework's *nonblocking* synchronization constructs can perform simple operations without ever blocking, pausing, or waiting.

Writing nonblocking or lock-free multithreaded code properly is tricky! Memory barriers, in particular, are easy to get wrong (the `volatile` keyword is even easier to get wrong). Think carefully whether you really need the performance benefits before dismissing ordinary locks.

The nonblocking approaches also work across multiple processes. An example of where this might be useful is in reading and writing process-shared memory.

Memory Barriers and Volatility

Consider the following example:

```
class Foo
{
  int _answer;
  bool _complete;

  void A()
  {
    _answer = 123;
    _complete = true;
  }

  void B()
  {
    if (_complete) Console.WriteLine (_answer);
  }
}
```

If methods A and B ran concurrently on different threads, might it be possible for B to write "0"? The answer is yes—for the following reasons:

- The compiler, CLR, or CPU may *reorder* your program's instructions to improve efficiency.
- The compiler, CLR, or CPU may introduce caching optimizations such that assignments to variables won't be visible to other threads right away.

C# and the runtime are very careful to ensure that such optimizations don't break ordinary single-threaded code—or multithreaded code that makes proper use of locks. Outside of these scenarios, you must explicitly defeat these optimizations by creating *memory barriers* (also called *memory fences*) to limit the effects of instruction reordering and read/write caching.

Full fences

The simplest kind of memory barrier is a *full memory barrier* (*full fence*), which prevents any kind of instruction reordering or caching around that fence. Calling Thread.MemoryBarrier generates a full fence; we can fix our example by applying four full fences as follows:

```
class Foo
{
  int _answer;
  bool _complete;

  void A()
  {
    _answer = 123;
    Thread.MemoryBarrier();    // Barrier 1
    _complete = true;
    Thread.MemoryBarrier();    // Barrier 2
  }

  void B()
  {
    Thread.MemoryBarrier();    // Barrier 3
    if (_complete)
    {
      Thread.MemoryBarrier();        // Barrier 4
      Console.WriteLine (_answer);
    }
  }
}
```

Barriers 1 and 4 prevent this example from writing "0". Barriers 2 and 3 provide a *freshness* guarantee: they ensure that if B ran after A, reading _complete would evaluate to true.

A full fence takes a few tens of nanoseconds.

The following implicitly generate full fences:

- C#'s lock statement (`Monitor.Enter`/`Monitor.Exit`)
- All methods on the `Interlocked` class (we'll cover these soon)
- Asynchronous callbacks that use the thread pool—these include asynchronous delegates, APM callbacks (Chapter 23), and `Task` continuations (Chapter 22)
- Setting and waiting on a signaling construct
- Anything that relies on signaling, such as starting or waiting on a `Task`

By virtue of that last point, the following is thread-safe:

```
int x = 0;
Task t = Task.Factory.StartNew (() => x++);
t.Wait();
Console.WriteLine (x);    // 1
```

You don't necessarily need a full fence with every individual read or write. If we had three *answer* fields, our example would still need only four fences:

```
class Foo
{
  int _answer1, _answer2, _answer3;
  bool _complete;

  void A()
  {
    _answer1 = 1; _answer2 = 2; _answer3 = 3;
    Thread.MemoryBarrier();
    _complete = true;
    Thread.MemoryBarrier();
  }

  void B()
  {
    Thread.MemoryBarrier();
    if (_complete)
    {
      Thread.MemoryBarrier();
      Console.WriteLine (_answer1 + _answer2 + _answer3);
    }
  }
}
```

A good approach is to start by putting memory barriers before and after every instruction that reads or writes a shared field, and then strip away the ones that you don't need. If you're uncertain of any, leave them in. Or better: switch back to using locks!

Do We Really Need Locks and Barriers?

Working with *shared writable fields* without locks or fences is asking for trouble. There's a lot of misleading information on this topic—including the MSDN documentation, which states that `MemoryBarrier` is required only on multiprocessor systems with weak memory ordering, such as a system employing multiple Itanium processors. We can demonstrate that memory barriers are important on ordinary Intel Core-2 and Pentium processors with the following short program. You'll need to run it with optimizations enabled and without a debugger (in Visual Studio, select Release Mode in the solution's configuration manager, and then start without debugging):

```
static void Main()
{
  bool complete = false;
  var t = new Thread (() =>
  {
    bool toggle = false;
    while (!complete) toggle = !toggle;
  });
  t.Start();
  Thread.Sleep (1000);
  complete = true;
  t.Join();         // Blocks indefinitely
}
```

This program *never terminates* because the `complete` variable is cached in a CPU register. Inserting a call to `Thread.MemoryBarrier` inside the `while` loop (or locking around reading `complete`) fixes the error.

The volatile keyword

Another (more advanced) way to solve this problem is to apply the `volatile` keyword to the `_complete` field:

```
volatile bool _complete;
```

The `volatile` keyword instructs the compiler to generate an *acquire-fence* on every read from that field, and a *release-fence* on every write to that field. An acquire-fence prevents other reads/writes from being moved *before* the fence; a release-fence prevents other reads/writes from being moved *after* the fence. These "half-fences" are faster than full fences because they give the runtime and hardware more scope for optimization.

As it happens, Intel's X86 and X64 processors always apply acquire-fences to reads and release-fences to writes—whether or not you use the volatile keyword—so this keyword has no effect on the *hardware* if you're using these processors. However, volatile *does* have an effect on optimizations performed by the compiler and the CLR—as well as on 64-bit AMD and (to a greater extent) Itanium processors. This means that you cannot be more relaxed by virtue of your clients running a particular type of CPU.

(And even if you *do* use volatile, you should still maintain a healthy sense of anxiety, as we'll see shortly!)

The effect of applying volatile to fields can be summarized as follows:

First instruction	Second instruction	Can they be swapped?
Read	Read	No
Read	Write	No
Write	Write	No[a]
Write	Read	**Yes!**

a The CLR ensures that write-write operations are never swapped, even without the volatile keyword.

Notice that applying volatile doesn't prevent a write followed by a read from being swapped, and this can create brainteasers. Joe Duffy illustrates the problem well with the following example: if Test1 and Test2 run simultaneously on different threads, it's possible for a and b to both end up with a value of 0 (despite the use of volatile on both x and y):

```
class IfYouThinkYouUnderstandVolatile
{
  volatile int x, y;

  void Test1()        // Executed on one thread
  {
    x = 1;            // Volatile write (release-fence)
    int a = y;        // Volatile read (acquire-fence)
    ...
  }

  void Test2()        // Executed on another thread
  {
    y = 1;            // Volatile write (release-fence)
    int b = x;        // Volatile read (acquire-fence)
    ...
  }
}
```

The MSDN documentation states that use of the volatile keyword ensures that the most up-to-date value is present in the field at all times. This is incorrect, since as we've seen, a write followed by a read *can* be reordered.

This presents a strong case for avoiding volatile: even if you understand the subtlety in this example, will other developers working on your code also understand it? A full fence between each of the two assignments in Test1 and Test2 (or a lock) solves the problem.

The volatile keyword is not supported with pass-by-reference arguments or captured local variables: in these cases, you must use the VolatileRead and VolatileWrite methods.

VolatileRead and VolatileWrite

The static VolatileRead and VolatileWrite methods in the Thread class read/write a variable while enforcing (technically, a superset of) the guarantees made by the volatile keyword. Their implementations are relatively inefficient, though, in that they actually generate full fences. Here are their complete implementations for the integer type:

```
public static void VolatileWrite (ref int address, int value)
{
  MemoryBarrier(); address = value;
}

public static int VolatileRead (ref int address)
{
  int num = address; MemoryBarrier(); return num;
}
```

You can see from this that if you call VolatileWrite followed by VolatileRead, no barrier is generated in the middle: this enables the same brainteaser scenario that we saw earlier.

Memory barriers and locking

As we said earlier, Monitor.Enter and Monitor.Exit both generate full fences. So if we ignore a lock's mutual exclusion guarantee, we could say that this:

```
lock (someField) { ... }
```

is equivalent to this:

```
Thread.MemoryBarrier(); { ... } Thread.MemoryBarrier();
```

Interlocked

Use of memory barriers is not always enough when reading or writing fields in lock-free code. Operations on 64-bit fields, increments, and decrements require the heavier approach of using the Interlocked helper class. Interlocked also provides the

Exchange and CompareExchange methods, the latter enabling lock-free read-modify-write operations, with a little additional coding.

A statement is intrinsically *atomic* if it executes as a single indivisible instruction on the underlying processor. Strict atomicity precludes any possibility of preemption. A simple read or write on a field of 32 bits or less is always atomic. Operations on 64-bit fields are guaranteed to be atomic only in a 64-bit runtime environment, and statements that combine more than one read/write operation are never atomic:

```
class Atomicity
{
  static int _x, _y;
  static long _z;

  static void Test()
  {
    long myLocal;
    _x = 3;              // Atomic
    _z = 3;              // Nonatomic on 32-bit environs (_z is 64 bits)
    myLocal = _z;        // Nonatomic on 32-bit environs (_z is 64 bits)
    _y += _x;            // Nonatomic (read AND write operation)
    _x++;                // Nonatomic (read AND write operation)
  }
}
```

Reading and writing 64-bit fields is nonatomic on 32-bit environments because it requires two separate instructions: one for each 32-bit memory location. So, if thread X reads a 64-bit value while thread Y is updating it, thread X may end up with a bitwise combination of the old and new values (a *torn read*).

The compiler implements unary operators of the kind x++ by reading a variable, processing it, and then writing it back. Consider the following class:

```
class ThreadUnsafe
{
  static int _x = 1000;
  static void Go() { for (int i = 0; i < 100; i++) _x--; }
}
```

Putting aside the issue of memory barriers, you might expect that if 10 threads concurrently run Go, _x would end up as 0. However, this is not guaranteed, because a *race condition* is possible whereby one thread preempts another in between retrieving _x's current value, decrementing it, and writing it back (resulting in an out-of-date value being written).

Of course, you can address these issues by wrapping the nonatomic operations in a lock statement. Locking simulates atomicity if consistently applied, but the Interlocked class provides an easier and faster solution for such simple operations:

```
class Program
{
  static long _sum;
```

```
static void Main()
{                                                                // _sum
    // Simple increment/decrement operations:
    Interlocked.Increment (ref _sum);                            // 1
    Interlocked.Decrement (ref _sum);                            // 0

    // Add/subtract a value:
    Interlocked.Add (ref _sum, 3);                               // 3

    // Read a 64-bit field:
    Console.WriteLine (Interlocked.Read (ref _sum));             // 3

    // Write a 64-bit field while reading previous value:
    // (This prints "3" while updating _sum to 10)
    Console.WriteLine (Interlocked.Exchange (ref _sum, 10));     // 10

    // Update a field only if it matches a certain value (10):
    Console.WriteLine (Interlocked.CompareExchange (ref _sum,
                                          123, 10));             // 123
}
}
```

> All of Interlocked's methods generate a full fence. Therefore, fields that you access via Interlocked don't need additional fences—unless they're accessed in other places in your program without Interlocked or a lock.

Interlocked's mathematical operations are restricted to Increment, Decrement, and Add. If you want to multiply—or perform any other calculation—you can do so in lock-free style by using the CompareExchange method (typically in conjunction with spin-waiting). We give an example in the final section in the following chapter.

Interlocked works by making its need for atomicity known to the operating system and virtual machine.

> Interlocked's methods have a typical overhead of 50 ns—half that of an uncontended lock. Further, they can never suffer the additional cost of context switching due to blocking. The flip side is that using Interlocked within a loop with many iterations can be less efficient than obtaining a single lock *around* the loop (although Interlocked enables greater *concurrency*).

Signaling with Event Wait Handles

Event wait handles are used for *signaling*. Signaling is when one thread waits until it receives notification from another. Event wait handles are the simplest of the signaling constructs, and they are unrelated to C# events. They come in three flavors: AutoResetEvent, ManualResetEvent, and (from Framework 4.0) CountdownEvent. The former two are based on the common `EventWaitHandle` class, where they derive all their functionality.

AutoResetEvent

An `AutoResetEvent` is like a ticket turnstile: inserting a ticket lets exactly one person through. The "auto" in the class's name refers to the fact that an open turnstile automatically closes or "resets" after someone steps through. A thread waits, or blocks, at the turnstile by calling `WaitOne` (wait at this "one" turnstile until it opens), and a ticket is inserted by calling the `Set` method. If a number of threads call `WaitOne`, a queue‡ builds up behind the turnstile. A ticket can come from any thread; in other words, any (unblocked) thread with access to the `AutoResetEvent` object can call `Set` on it to release one blocked thread.

You can create an `AutoResetEvent` in two ways. The first is via its constructor:

```
var auto = new AutoResetEvent (false);
```

(Passing `true` into the constructor is equivalent to immediately calling `Set` upon it.) The second way to create an `AutoResetEvent` is as follows:

```
var auto = new EventWaitHandle (false, EventResetMode.AutoReset);
```

In the following example, a thread is started whose job is simply to wait until signaled by another thread (see Figure 21-2):

```
class BasicWaitHandle
{
  static EventWaitHandle _waitHandle = new AutoResetEvent (false);

  static void Main()
  {
    new Thread (Waiter).Start();
    Thread.Sleep (1000);                // Pause for a second...
    _waitHandle.Set();                  // Wake up the Waiter.
  }

  static void Waiter()
  {
    Console.WriteLine ("Waiting...");
    _waitHandle.WaitOne();             // Wait for notification
    Console.WriteLine ("Notified");
  }
}

// Output:
Waiting... (pause) Notified.
```

‡ As with locks, the fairness of the queue can sometimes be violated due to nuances in the operating system.

Figure 21-2. Signaling with an EventWaitHandle

If Set is called when no thread is waiting, the handle stays open for as long as it takes until some thread calls WaitOne. This behavior helps avoid a race between a thread heading for the turnstile, and a thread inserting a ticket ("Oops, inserted the ticket a microsecond too soon, bad luck, now you'll have to wait indefinitely!"). However, calling Set repeatedly on a turnstile at which no one is waiting doesn't allow a whole party through when they arrive: only the next single person is let through and the extra tickets are "wasted."

Calling Reset on an AutoResetEvent closes the turnstile (should it be open) without waiting or blocking.

WaitOne accepts an optional timeout parameter, returning false if the wait ended because of a timeout rather than obtaining the signal.

 Calling WaitOne with a timeout of 0 tests whether a wait handle is "open," without blocking the caller. Bear in mind, though, that doing this resets the AutoResetEvent if it's open.

Disposing Wait Handles

Once you've finished with a wait handle, you can call its Close method to release the operating system resource. Alternatively, you can simply drop all references to the wait handle and allow the garbage collector to do the job for you sometime later (wait handles implement the disposal pattern whereby the finalizer calls Close). This is one of the few scenarios where relying on this backup is (arguably) acceptable, because wait handles have a light OS burden (asynchronous delegates rely on exactly this mechanism to release their IAsyncResult's wait handle).

Wait handles are released automatically when an application domain unloads.

Two-way signaling

Let's say we want the main thread to signal a worker thread three times in a row. If the main thread simply calls Set on a wait handle several times in rapid succession, the second or third signal may get lost, since the worker may take time to process each signal.

The solution is for the main thread to wait until the worker's ready before signaling it. This can be done with another AutoResetEvent, as follows:

```
class TwoWaySignaling
{
  static EventWaitHandle _ready = new AutoResetEvent (false);
  static EventWaitHandle _go = new AutoResetEvent (false);
  static readonly object _locker = new object();
  static string _message;

  static void Main()
  {
    new Thread (Work).Start();

    _ready.WaitOne();                  // First wait until worker is ready
    lock (_locker) _message = "ooo";
    _go.Set();                         // Tell worker to go

    _ready.WaitOne();
    lock (_locker) _message = "ahhh";  // Give the worker another message
    _go.Set();

    _ready.WaitOne();
    lock (_locker) _message = null;    // Signal the worker to exit
    _go.Set();
  }

  static void Work()
  {
    while (true)
    {
      _ready.Set();                          // Indicate that we're ready
      _go.WaitOne();                         // Wait to be kicked off...
      lock (_locker)
      {
        if (_message == null) return;        // Gracefully exit
        Console.WriteLine (_message);
      }
    }
  }
}

// Output:
ooo
ahhh
```

Figure 21-3 shows this process visually.

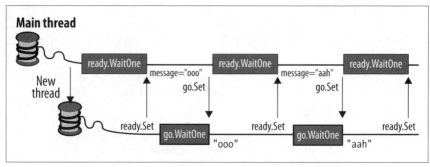

Figure 21-3. Two-way signaling

Here, we're using a null message to indicate that the worker should end. With threads that run indefinitely, it's important to have an exit strategy!

ManualResetEvent

A `ManualResetEvent` functions like an ordinary gate. Calling `Set` opens the gate, allowing *any* number of threads calling `WaitOne` to be let through. Calling `Reset` closes the gate. Threads that call `WaitOne` on a closed gate will block; when the gate is next opened, they will be released all at once. Apart from these differences, a `ManualRese tEvent` functions like an `AutoResetEvent`.

As with `AutoResetEvent`, you can construct a `ManualResetEvent` in two ways:

```
var manual1 = new ManualResetEvent (false);
var manual2 = new EventWaitHandle (false, EventResetMode.ManualReset);
```

> From Framework 4.0, there's another version of `ManualResetE vent` called `ManualResetEventSlim`. The latter is optimized for short waiting times—with the ability to opt into spinning for a set number of iterations. It also has a more efficient managed implementation and allows a `Wait` to be canceled via a `Cancel lationToken` (see "Cancellation" on page 886). It cannot, however, be used for interprocess signaling. `ManualResetEventSlim` doesn't subclass `WaitHandle`; however, it exposes a `WaitHandle` property that returns a `WaitHandle`-based object when called (with the performance profile of a traditional wait handle).

A `ManualResetEvent` is useful in allowing one thread to unblock many other threads. The reverse scenario is covered by `CountdownEvent`.

CountdownEvent

`CountdownEvent` lets you wait on more than one thread. The class is new to Framework 4.0 and has an efficient, fully managed implementation. To use the class, instantiate it with the number of threads or "counts" that you want to wait on:

```
var countdown = new CountdownEvent (3);  // Initialize with "count" of 3.
```

Calling `Signal` decrements the "count"; calling `Wait` blocks until the count goes down to zero. For example:

```
static CountdownEvent _countdown = new CountdownEvent (3);

static void Main()
{
  new Thread (SaySomething).Start ("I am thread 1");
  new Thread (SaySomething).Start ("I am thread 2");
  new Thread (SaySomething).Start ("I am thread 3");
  _countdown.Wait();   // Blocks until Signal has been called 3 times
  Console.WriteLine ("All threads have finished speaking!");
}

static void SaySomething (object thing)
{
  Thread.Sleep (1000);
  Console.WriteLine (thing);
  _countdown.Signal();
}
```

> Problems for which `CountdownEvent` is effective can sometimes be solved more easily using the *structured parallelism* constructs that we'll cover in the following chapter (PLINQ and the `Parallel` class).

You can reincrement a `CountdownEvent`'s count by calling `AddCount`. However, if it has already reached zero, this throws an exception: you can't "unsignal" a `Countdow nEvent` by calling `AddCount`. To avoid the possibility of an exception being thrown, you can instead call `TryAddCount`, which returns `false` if the countdown is zero.

To unsignal a countdown event, call `Reset`: this both unsignals the construct and resets its count to the original value.

Like `ManualResetEventSlim`, `CountdownEvent` exposes a `WaitHandle` property for scenarios where some other class or method expects an object based on `WaitHandle`.

Creating a Cross-Process EventWaitHandle

`EventWaitHandle`'s constructor allows a "named" `EventWaitHandle` to be created, capable of operating across multiple processes. The name is simply a string, and it can be any value that doesn't unintentionally conflict with someone else's! If the name is already in use on the computer, you get a reference to the same underlying `EventWaitHandle`; otherwise, the operating system creates a new one. Here's an example:

```
EventWaitHandle wh = new EventWaitHandle (false, EventResetMode.AutoReset,
                                          "MyCompany.MyApp.SomeName");
```

If two applications each ran this code, they would be able to signal each other: the wait handle would work across all threads in both processes.

Wait Handles and the Thread Pool

If your application has lots of threads that spend most of their time blocked on a wait handle, you can reduce the resource burden by calling `ThreadPool.Register WaitForSingleObject`. This method accepts a delegate that is executed when a wait handle is signaled. While it's waiting, it doesn't tie up a thread:

```
static ManualResetEvent _starter = new ManualResetEvent (false);

public static void Main()
{
  RegisteredWaitHandle reg = ThreadPool.RegisterWaitForSingleObject
   (_starter, Go, "Some Data", -1, true);
  Thread.Sleep (5000);
  Console.WriteLine ("Signaling worker...");
  _starter.Set();
  Console.ReadLine();
  reg.Unregister (_starter);    // Clean up when we're done.
}

public static void Go (object data, bool timedOut)
{
  Console.WriteLine ("Started - " + data);
  // Perform task...
}

// Output:
(5 second delay)
```

```
Signaling worker...
Started - Some Data
```

When the wait handle is signaled (or a timeout elapses), the delegate runs on a pooled thread.

In addition to the wait handle and delegate, `RegisterWaitForSingleObject` accepts a "black box" object that it passes to your delegate method (rather like `Parameteri zedThreadStart`), as well as a timeout in milliseconds (–1 meaning no timeout), and a boolean flag indicating whether the request is one-off rather than recurring.

`RegisterWaitForSingleObject` is particularly valuable in an application server that must handle many concurrent requests. Suppose you need to block on a `ManualResetEvent` and simply call `WaitOne`:

```
void AppServerMethod()
{
  _wh.WaitOne();
  // ... continue execution
}
```

If 100 clients called this method, 100 server threads would be tied up for the duration of the blockage. Replacing `_wh.WaitOne` with `RegisterWaitForSingleObject` allows the method to return immediately, wasting no threads:

```
void AppServerMethod
{
  RegisteredWaitHandle reg = ThreadPool.RegisterWaitForSingleObject
  (_wh, Resume, null, -1, true);
  ...
}

static void Resume (object data, bool timedOut)
{
  // ... continue execution
}
```

The data object passed to `Resume` allows continuance of any transient data.

WaitAny, WaitAll, and SignalAndWait

In addition to the `Set`, `WaitOne`, and `Reset` methods, there are static methods on the `WaitHandle` class to crack more complex synchronization nuts. The `WaitAny`, `WaitAll`, and `SignalAndWait` methods perform atomic signaling and waiting operations on multiple handles. The wait handles can be of differing types (including `Mutex` and `Semaphore`, since these also derive from the abstract `WaitHandle` class). `ManualResetEventSlim` and `CountdownEvent` can also partake in these methods via their `WaitHandle` properties.

WaitAll and SignalAndWait have a weird connection to the legacy COM architecture: these methods require that the caller be in a multithreaded apartment, the model least suitable for interoperability. The main thread of a WPF or Windows application, for example, is unable to interact with the clipboard in this mode. We'll discuss alternatives shortly.

WaitHandle.WaitAny waits for any one of an array of wait handles; WaitHandle.WaitAll waits on all of the given handles, atomically. This means that if you wait on two AutoResetEvents:

- WaitAny will never end up "latching" both events.
- WaitAll will never end up "latching" only one event.

SignalAndWait calls Set on one WaitHandle, and then calls WaitOne on another WaitHandle. The atomicity guarantee is that after signaling the first handle, it will jump to the head of the queue in waiting on the second handle: you can think of it as "swapping" one signal for another. You can use this method on a pair of EventWaitHandles to set up two threads to rendezvous or "meet" at the same point in time. Either AutoResetEvent or ManualResetEvent will do the trick. The first thread executes the following:

```
WaitHandle.SignalAndWait (wh1, wh2);
```

whereas the second thread does the opposite:

```
WaitHandle.SignalAndWait (wh2, wh1);
```

Alternatives to WaitAll and SignalAndWait

WaitAll and SignalAndWait won't run in a single-threaded apartment. Fortunately, there are alternatives. In the case of SignalAndWait, it's rare that you need its atomicity guarantee: in our rendezvous example, for instance, you could simply call Set on the first wait handle, and then WaitOne on the other. In "The Barrier Class" on page 849, we'll explore yet another option for implementing a thread rendezvous.

In the case of WaitAll, an alternative in some situations is to use the Parallel class's Invoke method, which we'll cover in the following chapter. (In that chapter we'll also cover Tasks and continuations, and see how Task.ContinueWithAny provides an alternative to WaitAny.)

In all other scenarios, the answer is to take the low-level approach that solves all signaling problems: Wait and Pulse.

Signaling with Wait and Pulse

The Monitor class provides a low-level signaling construct via the static methods Wait and Pulse (and PulseAll). The principle is that you write the signaling logic yourself using custom flags and fields (enclosed in lock statements), and then introduce Wait and Pulse commands to prevent spinning. With just these methods and the `lock` statement, you can achieve the functionality of `AutoResetEvent`, `Manual ResetEvent`, and `Semaphore`, as well as (with some caveats) `WaitHandle`'s static methods `WaitAll` and `WaitAny`. Furthermore, `Wait` and `Pulse` can be amenable in situations where all of the wait handles are parsimoniously challenged.

`Wait` and `Pulse` signaling, however, has a number of disadvantages over event wait handles:

- `Wait`/`Pulse` cannot span application domains or processes on a computer.
- `Wait`/`Pulse` cannot be used in the asynchronous method pattern (see Chapter 23) because the thread pool offers `Monitor.Wait` no equivalent of `RegisterWaitForSingleObject`, so a blocked `Wait` cannot avoid monopolizing a thread.
- You must remember to protect all variables related to the signaling logic with locks.
- `Wait`/`Pulse` programs may confuse developers relying on Microsoft's documentation.

The documentation problem arises because it's not obvious how `Wait` and `Pulse` are supposed to be used, even when you've read up on how they work. `Wait` and `Pulse` also have a peculiar aversion to dabblers: they will seek out any holes in your understanding and then delight in tormenting you! Fortunately, there is a simple pattern of use that tames `Wait` and `Pulse`.

In terms of performance, calling `Pulse` takes a few hundred nanoseconds—about half the time it takes to call `Set` on a wait handle. Calling `Wait` will always block and incur the overhead of a context switch—but you don't necessarily need to `Wait` if you follow our suggested pattern of use.

How to Use Wait and Pulse

Here's how to use `Wait` and `Pulse`:

1. Define a single field for use as the synchronization object, such as:

   ```
   readonly object _locker = new object();
   ```

2. Define field(s) for use in your custom blocking condition(s). For example:

   ```
   bool _go;   or:  int _semaphoreCount;
   ```

3. Whenever you want to block, include the following code:

   ```
   lock (_locker)
     while ( <blocking-condition> )
       Monitor.Wait (_locker);
   ```

4. Whenever you change (or potentially change) a blocking condition, include this code:

   ```
   lock (_locker)
   {
     < alter the field(s) or data that might
       impact the blocking condition(s) >
   ```

Threading

```
      Monitor.Pulse (_locker);    // or: Monitor.PulseAll (_locker)
    }
```

(If you change a blocking condition *and* want to block, you can incorporate steps 3 and 4 in a single lock statement.)

This pattern allows any thread to wait at any time for any condition. Here's a simple example, where a worker thread waits until the _go field is set to true:

```
class SimpleWaitPulse
{
  static readonly object _locker = new object();
  static bool _go;

  static void Main()
  {                                 // The new thread will block
    new Thread (Work).Start();      // because _go==false.

    Console.ReadLine();             // Wait for user to hit Enter

    lock (_locker)                  // Let's now wake up the thread by
    {                               // setting _go=true and pulsing.
      _go = true;
      Monitor.Pulse (_locker);
    }
  }

  static void Work()
  {
    lock (_locker)
      while (!_go)
        Monitor.Wait (_locker);     // Lock is released while we're waiting

    Console.WriteLine ("Woken!!!");
  }
}

// Output
Woken!!!   (after pressing Enter)
```

For thread safety, we ensure that all shared fields are accessed within a lock. Hence, we add lock statements around both reading and updating the _go flag. This is essential (unless you're willing to follow the nonblocking synchronization principles).

The Work method is where we block, waiting for the _go flag to become true. The Monitor.Wait method does the following, in order:

1. Releases the lock on _locker.
2. Blocks until _locker is "pulsed."
3. Reacquires the lock on _locker. If the lock is contended, then it blocks until the lock is available.

This means that despite appearances, *no* lock is held on the synchronization object while `Monitor.Wait` awaits a pulse:

```
lock (_locker)
{
  while (!_go)
    Monitor.Wait (_locker);   // _lock is released
  // lock is regained
  ...
}
```

Execution then continues at the next statement. `Monitor.Wait` is designed for use within a `lock` statement; it throws an exception if called otherwise. The same goes for `Monitor.Pulse`.

In the `Main` method, we signal the worker by setting the _go flag (within a lock) and calling `Pulse`. As soon as we *release the lock*, the worker resumes execution, reiterating its `while` loop.

The `Pulse` and `PulseAll` methods release threads blocked on a `Wait` statement. `Pulse` releases a maximum of one thread; `PulseAll` releases them all. In our example, just one thread is blocked, so their effects are identical. If more than one thread is waiting, calling `PulseAll` is *usually* safest with our suggested pattern of use.

In order for `Wait` to communicate with `Pulse` or `PulseAll`, the synchronizing object (`_locker`, in our case) must be the same.

In our pattern, pulsing indicates that *something might have changed*, and that waiting threads should recheck their blocking conditions. In the `Work` method, this check is accomplished via the `while` loop. The *waiter* then decides whether to continue, *not the notifier*. If pulsing by itself is taken as instruction to continue, the `Wait` construct is stripped of any real value; you end up with an inferior version of an `AutoResetEvent`.

If we abandon our pattern, removing the `while` loop, the _go flag, and the `ReadLine`, we get a bare-bones `Wait`/`Pulse` example:

```
static void Main()
{
  new Thread (Work).Start();
  lock (_locker) Monitor.Pulse (_locker);
}

static void Work()
{
  lock (_locker) Monitor.Wait (_locker);
  Console.WriteLine ("Woken!!!");
}
```

It's not possible to display the output, because it's nondeterministic! A race ensues between the main thread and the worker. If `Wait` executes first, the signal works. If

Pulse executes first, the *pulse is lost* and the worker remains forever stuck. This differs from the behavior of an `AutoResetEvent`, where its `Set` method has a memory or "latching" effect, so it is still effective if called before `WaitOne`.

`Pulse` has no latching effect because you're expected to write the latch yourself, using a "go" flag as we did before. This is what makes `Wait` and `Pulse` versatile: with a boolean flag, we can make it function as an `AutoResetEvent`; with an integer field, we can imitate a `Semaphore`. With more complex data structures, we can go further and write such constructs as a producer/consumer queue.

Producer/Consumer Queue

A producer/consumer queue is a common requirement in threading. Here's how it works:

- A queue is set up to describe work items—or data upon which work is performed.
- When a task needs executing, it's enqueued, allowing the caller to get on with other things.
- One or more worker threads plug away in the background, picking off and executing queued items.

The advantage of this model is that you have precise control over how many worker threads execute at once. This can allow you to limit consumption of not only CPU time, but other resources as well. If the tasks perform intensive disk I/O, for instance, you might have just one worker thread to avoid starving the operating system and other applications. Another type of application may have 20. You can also dynamically add and remove workers throughout the queue's life. The CLR's thread pool itself is a kind of producer/consumer queue.

A producer/consumer queue typically holds items of data upon which (the same) task is performed. For example, the items of data may be filenames, and the task might be to encrypt those files. By making the item a delegate, however, we can write a very general-purpose producer/consumer queue where each item can do anything. Here's an example that does exactly that:

> Framework 4.0 provides a new class called `BlockingCollection<T>` that implements the functionality of a producer/consumer queue. We'll cover this in "Concurrent Collections" on page 914 in the following chapter.
>
> Our manually written producer/consumer queue is still valuable—not only to illustrate `Wait`/`Pulse` and thread safety, but also as a basis for more sophisticated structures. For instance, if you wanted a *bounded blocking queue* (limiting the number of enqueued elements) that allowed cancellation (and removal) of enqueued work items, the following code would provide an excellent starting point.

```csharp
using System;
using System.Threading;
using System.Collections.Generic;

public class PCQueue : IDisposable
{
  readonly object _locker = new object();
  Thread[] _workers;
  Queue<Action> _itemQ = new Queue<Action>();

  public PCQueue (int workerCount)
  {
    _workers = new Thread [workerCount];

    // Create and start a separate thread for each worker
    for (int i = 0; i < workerCount; i++)
      (_workers [i] = new Thread (Consume)).Start();
  }

  public void Dispose()
  {
    // Enqueue one null item per worker to make each exit.
    foreach (Thread worker in _workers) EnqueueItem (null);
  }

  public void EnqueueItem (Action item)
  {
    lock (_locker)
    {
      _itemQ.Enqueue (item);          // We must pulse because we're
      Monitor.Pulse (_locker);        // changing a blocking condition.
    }
  }

  void Consume()
  {
    while (true)                      // Keep consuming until
    {                                 // told otherwise.
      Action item;
      lock (_locker)
      {
        while (_itemQ.Count == 0) Monitor.Wait (_locker);
        item = _itemQ.Dequeue();
      }
      if (item == null) return;       // This signals our exit.
      item();                         // Execute item.
    }
  }
}
```

Again we have an exit strategy: enqueuing a null item signals a consumer to finish after completing any outstanding items (if we want it to quit sooner, we could use an independent "cancel" flag). Because we're supporting multiple consumers, we must enqueue one null item per consumer to completely shut down the queue.

Here's a `Main` method that starts a producer/consumer queue, specifying two concurrent consumer threads, and then enqueues 10 delegates to be shared among the two consumers:

```
static void Main()
{
  using (PCQueue q = new PCQueue (2))
  {
    for (int i = 0; i < 10; i++)
    {
      int itemNumber = i;        // To avoid the captured variable trap
      q.EnqueueItem (() =>
      {
        Thread.Sleep (1000);          // Simulate time-consuming work
        Console.Write (" Task" + itemNumber);
      });
    }

    Console.WriteLine ("Enqueued 10 items");
    Console.WriteLine ("Waiting for items to complete...");
  }

  // Exiting the using statement runs PCQueue's Dispose method, which
  // tells the consumers to end when outstanding items are complete.
}

// Output:
Enqueued 10 items
Waiting for items to complete...
 Task1 Task0 (pause...) Task2 Task3 (pause...) Task4 Task5 (pause...)
 Task6 Task7 (pause...) Task8 Task9 (pause...)
```

Let's revisit `PCQueue` and examine the `Consume` method, where a worker picks off and executes an item from the queue. We want the worker to block while there's nothing to do; in other words, when there are no items on the queue. Hence, our blocking condition is `_itemQ.Count == 0`:

```
              Action item;
              lock (_locker)
              {
                while (_itemQ.Count == 0) Monitor.Wait (_locker);
                item = _itemQ.Dequeue();
              }
              if (item == null) return;      // This signals our exit
              item();                        // Perform task.
```

The `while` loop exits when `_itemQ.Count` is nonzero, meaning that (at least) one item is outstanding. We must dequeue the item *before* releasing the lock—otherwise, the item may not be there for us to dequeue; the presence of other threads means things can change while you blink. In particular, another consumer just finishing a previous job could sneak in and dequeue our item if we weren't meticulous with locking.

After the item is dequeued, we release the lock immediately. If we held on to it while performing the task, we would unnecessarily block other consumers and producers.

We don't pulse after dequeuing, as no other consumer can ever unblock by there being fewer items on the queue.

Locking briefly is advantageous when using `Wait` and `Pulse` (and in general), as it avoids unnecessarily blocking other threads. Locking across many lines of code is fine—providing they all execute quickly. Remember that you're helped by `Monitor.Wait`'s releasing the underlying lock while awaiting a pulse!

For the sake of efficiency, we call `Pulse` instead of `PulseAll` when enqueuing an item. This is because (at most) one consumer needs to be woken per item. If you had just one ice cream, you wouldn't wake a class of 30 sleeping children to queue for it; similarly, with 30 consumers, there's no benefit in waking them all—only to have 29 spin a useless iteration on their `while` loop before going back to sleep. We wouldn't break anything functionally, however, by replacing `Pulse` with `PulseAll`.

Wait Timeouts

You can specify a timeout when calling `Wait`, either in milliseconds or as a `TimeSpan`. The `Wait` method then returns `false` if it gave up because of a timeout. The timeout applies only to the *waiting phase*. Hence, a `Wait` with a timeout does the following:

1. Releases the underlying lock
2. Blocks until pulsed, *or the timeout elapses*
3. Reacquires the underlying lock

Specifying a timeout is like asking the CLR to give you a "virtual pulse" after the timeout interval. A timed-out `Wait` will still perform step 3 and reacquire the lock—just as if pulsed.

Should `Wait` block in step 3 (while reacquiring the lock), any timeout is ignored. This is rarely an issue, though, because other threads will lock only briefly in a well-designed `Wait`/`Pulse` application. So, reacquiring the lock should be a near-instant operation.

`Wait` timeouts have a useful application. Sometimes it may be unreasonable or impossible to `Pulse` whenever an unblocking condition arises. An example might be if a blocking condition involves calling a method that derives information from periodically querying a database. If latency is not an issue, the solution is simple—you can specify a timeout when calling `Wait`, as follows:

```
lock (_locker)
  while ( <blocking-condition> )
    Monitor.Wait (_locker, <timeout> );
```

This forces the blocking condition to be rechecked at the interval specified by the timeout, as well as when pulsed. The simpler the blocking condition, the smaller the timeout can be without creating inefficiency. In this case, we don't care whether the Wait was pulsed or timed out, so we ignore its return value.

The same system works equally well if the pulse is absent due to a bug in the program. It can be worth adding a timeout to all Wait commands in programs where synchronization is particularly complex, as an ultimate backup for obscure pulsing errors. It also provides a degree of bug immunity if the program is modified later by someone not on the Pulse!

 Monitor.Wait returns a bool value indicating whether it got a "real" pulse. If this returns false, it means that it timed out: sometimes it can be useful to log this or throw an exception if the timeout was unexpected.

Simulating Wait Handles

We can use Wait and Pulse to simulate a ManualResetEvent as follows:

```
readonly object _locker = new object();
bool _signal;

void WaitOne()
{
  lock (_locker)
  {
    while (!_signal) Monitor.Wait (_locker);
  }
}

void Set()
{
  lock (_locker) { _signal = true; Monitor.PulseAll (_locker); }
}

void Reset() { lock (_locker) _signal = false; }
```

We used PulseAll because there could be any number of blocked waiters. Simulating an AutoResetEvent is simply a matter of replacing the code in WaitOne with this:

```
lock (_locker)
{
  while (!_signal) Monitor.Wait (_locker);
  _signal = false;
}
```

and replacing PulseAll with Pulse in the Set method:

```
lock (_locker) { _signal = true; Monitor.Pulse (_locker); }
```

Use of PulseAll would forgo fairness in the queuing of back-logged waiters, because each call to PulseAll would result in the queue breaking and then re-forming.

Replacing _signal with an integer field would form the basis of a Semaphore.

Simulating the static methods that work across a set of wait handles is easy in simple scenarios. The equivalent of calling WaitAll is nothing more than a blocking condition that incorporates all the flags used in place of the wait handles:

```
lock (_locker)
  while (!_flag1 && !_flag2 && !_flag3...)
    Monitor.Wait (_locker);
```

This can be particularly useful given that WaitAll is often unusable due to COM legacy issues. Simulating WaitAny is simply a matter of replacing the && operator with the || operator.

 If you have dozens of flags, this approach becomes less efficient because they must all share a single synchronizing object in order for the signaling to work atomically. This is where wait handles have an advantage.

The Barrier Class

The Barrier class is a signaling construct new to Framework 4.0. It implements a *thread execution barrier*, which allows many threads to rendezvous at a point in time. The class is very fast and efficient, and is built upon Wait, Pulse, and spinlocks.

To use this class:

1. Instantiate it, specifying how many threads should partake in the rendezvous (you can change this later by calling AddParticipants/RemoveParticipants).
2. Have each thread call SignalAndWait when it wants to rendezvous.

Instantiating Barrier with a value of 3 causes SignalAndWait to block until that method has been called three times. It then starts over: calling SignalAndWait again blocks until called another three times. This keeps each thread "in step" with every other thread.

In the following example, each of three threads writes the numbers 0 through 4, while keeping in step with the other threads:

```
static Barrier _barrier = new Barrier (3);

static void Main()
{
  new Thread (Speak).Start();
  new Thread (Speak).Start();
  new Thread (Speak).Start();
```

```
  }

  static void Speak()
  {
    for (int i = 0; i < 5; i++)
    {
      Console.Write (i + " ");
      _barrier.SignalAndWait();
    }
  }
}
```

OUTPUT: 0 0 0 1 1 1 2 2 2 3 3 3 4 4 4

A really useful feature of Barrier is that you can also specify a *post-phase action* when constructing it. This is a delegate that runs after SignalAndWait has been called *n* times, but *before* the threads are unblocked (as shown in the shaded area in Figure 21-4). In our example, if we instantiate our barrier as follows:

```
static Barrier _barrier = new Barrier (3, barrier => Console.WriteLine());
```

then the output is:

```
0 0 0
1 1 1
2 2 2
3 3 3
4 4 4
```

Figure 21-4. Barrier

A post-phase action can be useful for coalescing data from each of the worker threads. It doesn't have to worry about preemption, because all workers are blocked while it does its thing.

The Event-Based Asynchronous Pattern

The event-based asynchronous pattern (EAP) provides a simple means by which classes can offer multithreading capability without consumers needing to explicitly start or manage threads. It also provides the following features:

- A cooperative cancellation model
- The ability to safely update WPF or Windows Forms controls when the worker completes
- Forwarding of exceptions to the completion event

The EAP is just a pattern, so these features must be written by the implementer. Just a few classes in the Framework follow this pattern, most notably `Background Worker` (which we'll cover next), and `WebClient` in `System.Net`. Essentially the pattern is this: a class offers a family of members that internally manage multithreading, similar to the following.

```
// These members are from the WebClient class:

public byte[] DownloadData (Uri address);      // Synchronous version
public void DownloadDataAsync (Uri address);
public void DownloadDataAsync (Uri address, object userToken);
public event DownloadDataCompletedEventHandler DownloadDataCompleted;

public void CancelAsync (object userState);    // Cancels an operation
public bool IsBusy { get; }                    // Indicates if still running
```

The *Async methods execute asynchronously: in other words, they start an operation on another thread and then return immediately to the caller. When the operation completes, the *Completed event fires—automatically calling `Invoke` if required by a WPF application. This event passes back an event arguments object that contains:

- A flag indicating whether the operation was canceled (by the consumer calling `CancelAsync`)
- An `Error` object indicating an exception that was thrown (if any)
- The `userToken` object if supplied when calling the `Async` method

Here's how we can use `WebClient`'s EAP members to download a web page:

```
var wc = new WebClient();
wc.DownloadStringCompleted += (sender, args) =>
{
  if (args.Cancelled)
    Console.WriteLine ("Canceled");
  else if (args.Error != null)
    Console.WriteLine ("Exception: " + args.Error.Message);
  else
  {
    Console.WriteLine (args.Result.Length + " chars were downloaded");
    // We could update the UI from here...
  }
};
wc.DownloadStringAsync (new Uri ("http://www.linqpad.net")); // Start it
```

A class following the EAP may offer additional groups of asynchronous methods. For instance:

```
public string DownloadString (Uri address);
public void DownloadStringAsync (Uri address);
public void DownloadStringAsync (Uri address, object userToken);
public event DownloadStringCompletedEventHandler DownloadStringCompleted;
```

However, these will share the same CancelAsync and IsBusy members. Therefore, only one asynchronous operation can happen at once.

> The EAP offers the *possibility* of economizing on threads, if its internal implementation follows the APM (see Chapter 23).

We'll see in the next chapter how Tasks offer similar capabilities—including exception forwarding, continuations, cancellation tokens, and support for synchronization contexts. This makes *implementing* the EAP less attractive—except in simple cases where BackgroundWorker will do.

BackgroundWorker

BackgroundWorker is a helper class in the System.ComponentModel namespace for managing a worker thread. It can be considered a general-purpose implementation of the EAP, and provides the following features:

- A cooperative cancellation model
- The ability to safely update WPF or Windows Forms controls when the worker completes
- Forwarding of exceptions to the completion event
- A protocol for reporting progress
- An implementation of IComponent allowing it to be sited in Visual Studio's designer

BackgroundWorker uses the thread pool, which means you should never call Abort on a BackgroundWorker thread.

Using BackgroundWorker

Here are the minimum steps in using BackgroundWorker:

1. Instantiate BackgroundWorker and handle the DoWork event.
2. Call RunWorkerAsync, optionally with an object argument.

This then sets it in motion. Any argument passed to RunWorkerAsync will be forwarded to DoWork's event handler, via the event argument's Argument property. Here's an example:

```
class Program
{
  static BackgroundWorker _bw = new BackgroundWorker();

  static void Main()
  {
    _bw.DoWork += bw_DoWork;
    _bw.RunWorkerAsync ("Message to worker");
    Console.ReadLine();
  }

  static void bw_DoWork (object sender, DoWorkEventArgs e)
  {
    // This is called on the worker thread
    Console.WriteLine (e.Argument);        // writes "Message to worker"
    // Perform time-consuming task...
  }
}
```

BackgroundWorker has a RunWorkerCompleted event that fires after the DoWork event handler has done its job. Handling RunWorkerCompleted is not mandatory, but you usually do so in order to query any exception that was thrown in DoWork. Further, code within a RunWorkerCompleted event handler is able to update user interface controls without explicit marshaling; code within the DoWork event handler cannot.

To add support for progress reporting:

1. Set the WorkerReportsProgress property to true.

2. Periodically call ReportProgress from within the DoWork event handler with a "percentage complete" value, and optionally, a user-state object.

3. Handle the ProgressChanged event, querying its event argument's ProgressPercentage property.

4. Code in the ProgressChanged event handler is free to interact with UI controls just as with RunWorkerCompleted. This is typically where you will update a progress bar.

To add support for cancellation:

1. Set the WorkerSupportsCancellation property to true.

2. Periodically check the CancellationPending property from within the DoWork event handler. If it's true, set the event argument's Cancel property to true, and return. (The worker can also set Cancel and exit without CancellationPending being true if it decides that the job is too difficult and it can't go on.)

3. Call CancelAsync to request cancellation.

Here's an example that implements all the preceding features:

```
using System;
using System.Threading;
using System.ComponentModel;
```

```csharp
class Program
{
  static BackgroundWorker _bw;

  static void Main()
  {
    _bw = new BackgroundWorker
    {
      WorkerReportsProgress = true,
      WorkerSupportsCancellation = true
    };
    _bw.DoWork += bw_DoWork;
    _bw.ProgressChanged += bw_ProgressChanged;
    _bw.RunWorkerCompleted += bw_RunWorkerCompleted;

    _bw.RunWorkerAsync ("Hello to worker");

    Console.WriteLine ("Press Enter in the next 5 seconds to cancel");
    Console.ReadLine();
    if (_bw.IsBusy) _bw.CancelAsync();
    Console.ReadLine();
  }

  static void bw_DoWork (object sender, DoWorkEventArgs e)
  {
    for (int i = 0; i <= 100; i += 20)
    {
      if (_bw.CancellationPending) { e.Cancel = true; return; }
      _bw.ReportProgress (i);
      Thread.Sleep (1000);        // Just for the demo... don't go sleeping
    }                             // for real in pooled threads!

    e.Result = 123;     // This gets passed to RunWorkerCompleted
  }

  static void bw_RunWorkerCompleted (object sender,
                                     RunWorkerCompletedEventArgs e)
  {
    if (e.Cancelled)
      Console.WriteLine ("You canceled!");
    else if (e.Error != null)
      Console.WriteLine ("Worker exception: " + e.Error.ToString());
    else
      Console.WriteLine ("Complete: " + e.Result);        // from DoWork
  }

  static void bw_ProgressChanged (object sender,
                                  ProgressChangedEventArgs e)
  {
    Console.WriteLine ("Reached " + e.ProgressPercentage + "%");
  }
}

// Output:
Press Enter in the next 5 seconds to cancel
Reached 0%
```

```
Reached 20%
Reached 40%
Reached 60%
Reached 80%
Reached 100%
Complete: 123

Press Enter in the next 5 seconds to cancel
Reached 0%
Reached 20%
Reached 40%

You canceled!
```

Interrupt and Abort

All blocking methods (such as Sleep, Join, EndInvoke, and Wait) block forever if the unblocking condition is never met and no timeout is specified. Occasionally, it can be useful to release a blocked thread prematurely; for instance, when ending an application. Two methods accomplish this:

- Thread.Interrupt
- Thread.Abort

The Abort method is also capable of ending a nonblocked thread—stuck, perhaps, in an infinite loop. Abort is occasionally useful in *niche* scenarios; Interrupt is almost never needed.

> Interrupt and Abort can cause considerable trouble: it's precisely because they *seem* like obvious choices in solving a range of problems that it's worth examining their pitfalls.

Interrupt

Calling Interrupt on a blocked thread forcibly releases it, throwing a ThreadInterruptedException, as follows:

```
static void Main()
{
  Thread t = new Thread (delegate()
  {
    try { Thread.Sleep (Timeout.Infinite); }
    catch (ThreadInterruptedException) { Console.Write ("Forcibly "); }
    Console.WriteLine ("Woken!");
  });
  t.Start();
  t.Interrupt();
}

// Output:
Forcibly Woken!
```

Interrupting a thread does not cause the thread to end, unless the `ThreadInterrup tedException` is unhandled.

If `Interrupt` is called on a thread that's not blocked, the thread continues executing until it next blocks, at which point a `ThreadInterruptedException` is thrown. This avoids the need for the following test:

```
if ((worker.ThreadState & ThreadState.WaitSleepJoin) > 0)
    worker.Interrupt();
```

which is not thread-safe because of the possibility of preemption between the `if` statement and `worker.Interrupt`.

Interrupting a thread arbitrarily is dangerous, however, because any framework or third-party methods in the calling stack could unexpectedly receive the interrupt rather than your intended code. All it would take is for the thread to block briefly on a simple lock or synchronization resource, and any pending interruption would kick in. If the method isn't designed to be interrupted (with appropriate cleanup code in `finally` blocks), objects could be left in an unusable state or resources incompletely released.

Moreover, `Interrupt` is unnecessary: if you are writing the code that blocks, you can achieve the same result more safely with a signaling construct—or Framework 4.0's cancellation tokens (see "Safe Cancellation" on page 857). And if you want to "unblock" someone else's code, `Abort` is nearly always more useful.

Abort

A blocked thread can also be forcibly released via its `Abort` method. This has an effect similar to calling `Interrupt`, except that a `ThreadAbortException` is thrown instead of a `ThreadInterruptedException`. Furthermore, the exception will be rethrown at the end of the `catch` block (in an attempt to terminate the thread for good) unless `Thread.ResetAbort` is called within the `catch` block. In the interim, the thread has a `ThreadState` of `AbortRequested`.

> An unhandled `ThreadAbortException` is one of only two types of exception that does not cause application shutdown (the other is `AppDomainUnloadException`).

The big difference between `Interrupt` and `Abort` is what happens when it's called on a thread that is not blocked. Whereas `Interrupt` waits until the thread next blocks before doing anything, `Abort` throws an exception on the thread right where it's executing (unmanaged code excepted). This is a problem because .NET Framework code might be aborted; code that is not abort-safe. For example, if an abort occurs while a `FileStream` is being constructed, it's possible that an unmanaged file handle will remain open until the application domain ends. This rules out using `Abort` in almost any nontrivial context.

For a discussion as to why aborting .NET Framework code is not safe, see the topic "Aborting Threads" at *http://www.alba hari.com/threading/*.

There are two cases, though, where you can safely use `Abort`. One is if you are willing to tear down a thread's application domain after it is aborted. A good example of when you might do this is in writing a unit-testing framework. (We discuss application domains fully in Chapter 24.) Another case where you can call `Abort` safely is on your own thread (because you know exactly where you are). Aborting your own thread throws an "unswallowable" exception: one that gets rethrown after each catch block. ASP.NET does exactly this when you call `Redirect`.

LINQPad aborts threads when you cancel a runaway query. After aborting, it dismantles and re-creates the query's application domain to avoid the potentially polluted state that could otherwise occur.

Safe Cancellation

As we saw in the preceding section, calling `Abort` on a thread is dangerous in most scenarios. The alternative, then, is to implement a *cooperative* pattern whereby the worker periodically checks a flag that indicates whether it should abort (like in `BackgroundWorker`). To cancel, the instigator simply sets the flag, and then waits for the worker to comply. This `BackgroundWorker` helper class implements such a flag-based cancellation pattern, and you easily implement one yourself.

The obvious disadvantage is that the worker method must be written explicitly to support cancellation. Nonetheless, this is one of the few safe cancellation patterns. To illustrate this pattern, we'll first write a class to encapsulate the cancellation flag:

```
class RulyCanceler
{
  object _cancelLocker = new object();
  bool _cancelRequest;
  public bool IsCancellationRequested
  {
    get { lock (_cancelLocker) return _cancelRequest; }
  }

  public void Cancel() { lock (_cancelLocker) _cancelRequest = true; }

  public void ThrowIfCancellationRequested()
  {
    if (IsCancellationRequested) throw new OperationCanceledException();
  }
}
```

`OperationCanceledException` is a Framework type intended for just this purpose. Any exception class will work just as well, though.

We can use this as follows:

```
class Test
{
  static void Main()
  {
    var canceler = new RulyCanceler();
    new Thread ((() => {
                  try { Work (canceler); }
                  catch (OperationCanceledException)
                  {
                    Console.WriteLine ("Canceled!");
                  }
                }).Start();
    Thread.Sleep (1000);
    canceler.Cancel();              // Safely cancel worker.
  }

  static void Work (RulyCanceler c)
  {
    while (true)
    {
      c.ThrowIfCancellationRequested();
      // ...
      try      { OtherMethod (c); }
      finally  { /* any required cleanup */ }
    }
  }

  static void OtherMethod (RulyCanceler c)
  {
    // Do stuff...
    c.ThrowIfCancellationRequested();
  }
}
```

We could simplify our example by eliminating the `RulyCanceler` class and adding the static boolean field `_cancelRequest` to the `Test` class. However, doing so would mean that if several threads called `Work` at once, setting `_cancelRequest` to `true` would cancel all workers. Our `RulyCanceler` class is therefore a useful abstraction. Its only inelegance is that when we look at the `Work` method's signature, the intention is unclear:

```
static void Work (RulyCanceler c)
```

Might the `Work` method itself intend to call `Cancel` on the `RulyCanceler` object? In this instance, the answer is no, so it would be nice if this could be enforced in the type system. Framework 4.0 provides *cancellation tokens* for this exact purpose.

Cancellation Tokens

Framework 4.0 provides two types that formalize the cooperative cancellation pattern that we just demonstrated: `CancellationTokenSource` and `CancellationToken`. The two types work in tandem:

- A `CancellationTokenSource` defines a `Cancel` method.
- A `CancellationToken` defines an `IsCancellationRequested` property and `ThrowIfCancellationRequested` method.

Together, these amount to a more sophisticated version of the `RulyCanceler` class in our previous example. But because the types are separate, you can isolate the ability to cancel from the ability to check the cancellation flag.

To use these types, first instantiate a `CancellationTokenSource` object:

```
var cancelSource = new CancellationTokenSource();
```

Then, pass its `Token` property into a method for which you'd like to support cancellation:

```
new Thread (() => Work (cancelSource.Token)).Start();
```

Here's how `Work` would be defined:

```
void Work (CancellationToken cancelToken)
{
  cancelToken.ThrowIfCancellationRequested();
  ...
}
```

When you want to cancel, simply call `Cancel` on `cancelSource`.

> `CancellationToken` is actually a struct, although you can treat it like a class. When implicitly copied, the copies behave identically and reference the original `CancellationTokenSource`.

The `CancellationToken` struct provides two additional useful members. The first is `WaitHandle`, which returns a wait handle that's signaled when the token is canceled. The second is `Register`, which lets you register a callback delegate that will be fired upon cancellation.

Cancellation tokens are used within the .NET Framework itself, most notably in the following classes:

- `ManualResetEventSlim` and `SemaphoreSlim`
- `CountdownEvent`
- `Barrier`
- `BlockingCollection` (see Chapter 22)
- PLINQ and the Task Parallel Library (see Chapter 22)

Most of these classes' use of cancellation tokens is in their `Wait` methods. For example, if you `Wait` on a `ManualResetEventSlim` and specify a cancellation token, another thread can `Cancel` its wait. This is much tidier and safer than calling `Interrupt` on the blocked thread.

Lazy Initialization

A common problem in threading is how to lazily initialize a shared field in a thread-safe fashion. The need arises when you have a field of a type that's expensive to construct:

```
class Foo
{
  public readonly Expensive Expensive = new Expensive();
  ...
}
class Expensive {  /* Suppose this is expensive to construct */  }
```

The problem with this code is that instantiating `Foo` incurs the performance cost of instantiating `Expensive`—whether or not the `Expensive` field is ever accessed. The obvious answer is to construct the instance *on demand*:

```
class Foo
{
  Expensive _expensive;
  public Expensive                    // Lazily instantiate Expensive
  {
    get
    {
      if (_expensive == null) _expensive = new Expensive();
      return _expensive;
    }
  }
  ...
}
```

The question then arises, is this thread-safe? Aside from the fact that we're accessing `_expensive` outside a lock without a memory barrier, consider what would happen if two threads accessed this property at once. They could both satisfy the `if` statement's predicate and each thread might end up with a *different* instance of `Expensive`. As this may lead to subtle errors, we would say, in general, that this code is not thread-safe.

The solution to the problem is to lock around checking and initializing the object:

```
Expensive _expensive;
readonly object _expenseLock = new object();

public Expensive
{
  get
  {
    lock (_expenseLock)
    {
```

```
            if (_expensive == null) _expensive = new Foo();
            return _expensive;
        }
    }
}
```

Lazy<T>

Framework 4.0 provides a new class called Lazy<T> to help with lazy initialization.
If instantiated with an argument of true, it implements the thread-safe initialization
pattern just described.

> Lazy<T> actually implements a slightly more efficient version of
> this pattern, called *double-checked locking*. Double-checked
> locking performs an additional volatile read to avoid the cost of
> obtaining a lock if the object is already initialized.

To use Lazy<T>, instantiate the class with a value factory delegate that tells it how to
initialize a new value, and the argument true. Then access its value via the Value
property:

```
Lazy<Expensive> _expensive = new Lazy<Expensive>
    (() => new Expensive(), true);

public static Expensive Expensive { get { return _expensive.Value; } }
```

If you pass false into Lazy<T>'s constructor, it implements the thread-unsafe lazy
initialization pattern that we described at the start of this section—this makes sense
when you want to use Lazy<T> in a single-threaded context.

LazyInitializer

LazyInitializer is a static class that works exactly like Lazy<T> except:

- Its functionality is exposed through a static method that operates directly on a
  field in your own type. This avoids a level of indirection, improving performance
  in cases where you need extreme optimization.

- It offers another mode of initialization that has multiple threads race to
  initialize.

To use LazyInitializer, call EnsureInitialized before accessing the field, passing
a reference to the field and the factory delegate:

```
Expensive _expensive;
public Expensive Expensive
{
    get            // Implement double-checked locking
    {
        LazyInitializer.EnsureInitialized (ref _expensive,
                                    () => new Expensive());
        return _expensive;
```

```
    }
  }
```

You can also pass in another argument to request that competing threads *race* to initialize. This sounds similar to our original thread-unsafe example, except that the first thread to finish always wins—and so you end up with only one instance. The advantage of this technique is that it's even faster (on multicores) than double-checked locking—because it can be implemented entirely without locks. This is an extreme optimization that you rarely need, and one that comes at a cost:

- It's slower when more threads race to initialize than you have cores.
- It potentially wastes CPU resources performing redundant initialization.
- The initialization logic must be thread-safe (in this case, it would be thread-unsafe if `Expensive`'s constructor wrote to static fields, for instance).
- If the initializer instantiates an object requiring disposal, the "wasted" object won't get disposed without additional logic.

For reference, here's how double-checked locking is implemented:

```
volatile Expensive _expensive;
public Expensive Expensive
{
  get
  {
    if (_expensive == null)
    {
      var expensive = new Expensive();
      lock (_expenseLock) if (_expensive == null) _expensive = expensive;
    }
    return _expensive;
  }
}
```

And here's how the race-to-initialize pattern is implemented:

```
volatile Expensive _expensive;
public Expensive Expensive
{
  get
  {
    if (_expensive == null)
    {
      var instance = new Expensive();
      Interlocked.CompareExchange (ref _expensive, instance, null);
    }
    return _expensive;
  }
}
```

Thread-Local Storage

Much of this chapter has focused on synchronization constructs and the issues arising from having threads concurrently access the same data. Sometimes, however, you want to keep data isolated, ensuring that each thread has a separate copy. Local variables achieve exactly this, but they are useful only with transient data.

The solution is *thread-local storage*. You might be hard-pressed to think of a requirement: data you'd want to keep isolated to a thread tends to be transient by nature. Its main application is for storing "out-of-band" data—that which supports the execution path's infrastructure, such as messaging, transaction, and security tokens. Passing such data around in method parameters is extremely clumsy and alienates all but your own methods; storing such information in ordinary static fields means sharing it among all threads.

 Thread-local storage can also be useful in optimizing parallel code. It allows each thread to exclusively access its own version of a thread-unsafe object without needing locks—and without needing to reconstruct that object between method calls.

There are three ways to implement thread-local storage.

[ThreadStatic]

The easiest approach to thread-local storage is to mark a static field with the ThreadStatic attribute:

```
[ThreadStatic] static int _x;
```

Each thread then sees a separate copy of _x.

Unfortunately, [ThreadStatic] doesn't work with instance fields (it simply does nothing), nor does it play well with field initializers—they execute only *once* on the thread that's running when the static constructor executes. If you need to work with instance fields—or start with a nondefault value—ThreadLocal<T> provides a better option.

ThreadLocal<T>

ThreadLocal<T> is new to Framework 4.0. It provides thread-local storage for both static and instance fields—and allows you to specify default values.

Here's how to create a ThreadLocal<int> with a default value of 3 for each thread:

```
static ThreadLocal<int> _x = new ThreadLocal<int> (() => 3);
```

You then use _x's Value property to get or set its thread-local value. A bonus of using ThreadLocal is that values are lazily evaluated: the factory function evaluates on the first call (for each thread).

ThreadLocal<T> and instance fields

ThreadLocal<T> is also useful with instance fields and captured local variables. For example, consider the problem of generating random numbers in a multithreaded environment. The Random class is not thread-safe, so we have to either lock around using Random (limiting concurrency) or generate a separate Random object for each thread. ThreadLocal<T> makes the latter easy:

```
var localRandom = new ThreadLocal<Random>(() => new Random());
Console.WriteLine (localRandom.Value.Next());
```

Our factory function for creating the Random object is a bit simplistic, though, in that Random's parameterless constructor relies on the system clock for a random number seed. This may be the same for two Random objects created within ~10 ms of each other. Here's one way to fix it:

```
var localRandom = new ThreadLocal<Random>
  ( () => new Random (Guid.NewGuid().GetHashCode()) );
```

We use this in the following chapter (see the parallel spellchecking example in "PLINQ" on page 877).

GetData and SetData

The third approach is to use two methods in the Thread class: GetData and SetData. These store data in thread-specific "slots." Thread.GetData reads from a thread's isolated data store; Thread.SetData writes to it. Both methods require a LocalDataS toreSlot object to identify the slot. The same slot can be used across all threads and they'll still get separate values. Here's an example:

```
class Test
{
  // The same LocalDataStoreSlot object can be used across all threads.
  LocalDataStoreSlot _secSlot = Thread.GetNamedDataSlot ("securityLevel");

  // This property has a separate value on each thread.
  int SecurityLevel
  {
    get
    {
      object data = Thread.GetData (_secSlot);
      return data == null ? 0 : (int) data;   // null == uninitialized
    }
    set { Thread.SetData (_secSlot, value); }
  }
  ...
```

In this instance, we called Thread.GetNamedDataSlot, which creates a named slot—this allows sharing of that slot across the application. Alternatively, you can control a slot's scope yourself by instantiating a LocalDataStoreSlot explicitly—without providing any name:

```
class Test
{
  LocalDataStoreSlot _secSlot = new LocalDataStoreSlot();
  ...
```

Thread.FreeNamedDataSlot will release a named data slot across all threads, but only once all references to that LocalDataStoreSlot have dropped out of scope and have been garbage-collected. This ensures that threads don't get data slots pulled out from under their feet, as long as they keep a reference to the appropriate LocalDataStoreSlot object while the slot is needed.

Reader/Writer Locks

Quite often, instances of a type are thread-safe for concurrent read operations, but not for concurrent updates (nor for a concurrent read and update). This can also be true with resources such as a file. Although protecting instances of such types with a simple exclusive lock for all modes of access usually does the trick, it can unreasonably restrict concurrency if there are many readers and just occasional updates. An example of where this could occur is in a business application server, where commonly used data is cached for fast retrieval in static fields. The ReaderWriter LockSlim class is designed to provide maximum-availability locking in just this scenario.

> ReaderWriterLockSlim was introduced in Framework 3.5 and is a replacement for the older "fat" ReaderWriterLock class. The latter is similar in functionality, but it is several times slower and has an inherent design fault in its mechanism for handling lock upgrades.
>
> When compared to an ordinary lock (Monitor.Enter/Exit), ReaderWriterLockSlim is still twice as slow, though.

With both classes, there are two basic kinds of lock—a read lock and a write lock:

- A write lock is universally exclusive.
- A read lock is compatible with other read locks.

So, a thread holding a write lock blocks all other threads trying to obtain a read *or* write lock (and vice versa). But if no thread holds a write lock, any number of threads may concurrently obtain a read lock.

ReaderWriterLockSlim defines the following methods for obtaining and releasing read/write locks:

```
public void EnterReadLock();
public void ExitReadLock();
public void EnterWriteLock();
public void ExitWriteLock();
```

Additionally, there are "Try" versions of all EnterXXX methods that accept timeout arguments in the style of Monitor.TryEnter (timeouts can occur quite easily if the resource is heavily contended). ReaderWriterLock provides similar methods, named AcquireXXX and ReleaseXXX. These throw an ApplicationException if a timeout occurs, rather than returning false.

Reader/Writer Locks | 865

The following program demonstrates ReaderWriterLockSlim. Three threads continually enumerate a list, while two further threads append a random number to the list every second. A read lock protects the list readers, and a write lock protects the list writers:

```
class SlimDemo
{
  static ReaderWriterLockSlim _rw = new ReaderWriterLockSlim();
  static List<int> _items = new List<int>();
  static Random _rand = new Random();

  static void Main()
  {
    new Thread (Read).Start();
    new Thread (Read).Start();
    new Thread (Read).Start();

    new Thread (Write).Start ("A");
    new Thread (Write).Start ("B");
  }

  static void Read()
  {
    while (true)
    {
      _rw.EnterReadLock();
      foreach (int i in _items) Thread.Sleep (10);
      _rw.ExitReadLock();
    }
  }

  static void Write (object threadID)
  {
    while (true)
    {
      int newNumber = GetRandNum (100);
      _rw.EnterWriteLock();
      _items.Add (newNumber);
      _rw.ExitWriteLock();
      Console.WriteLine ("Thread " + threadID + " added " + newNumber);
      Thread.Sleep (100);
    }
  }

  static int GetRandNum (int max) { lock (_rand) return _rand.Next(max); }
}
```

In production code, you'd typically add try/finally blocks to ensure that locks were released if an exception was thrown.

Here's the result:

```
Thread B added 61
Thread A added 83
Thread B added 55
Thread A added 33
...
```

ReaderWriterLockSlim allows more concurrent Read activity than a simple lock would. We can illustrate this by inserting the following line in the Write method, at the start of the while loop:

```
Console.WriteLine (_rw.CurrentReadCount + " concurrent readers");
```

This nearly always prints "3 concurrent readers" (the Read methods spend most of their time inside the foreach loops). As well as CurrentReadCount, ReaderWriterLock Slim provides the following properties for monitoring locks:

```
public bool IsReadLockHeld             { get; }
public bool IsUpgradeableReadLockHeld { get; }
public bool IsWriteLockHeld            { get; }

public int  WaitingReadCount           { get; }
public int  WaitingUpgradeCount        { get; }
public int  WaitingWriteCount          { get; }

public int  RecursiveReadCount         { get; }
public int  RecursiveUpgradeCount      { get; }
public int  RecursiveWriteCount        { get; }
```

Upgradeable Locks and Recursion

Sometimes it's useful to swap a read lock for a write lock in a single atomic operation. For instance, suppose you want to add an item to a list only if the item wasn't already present. Ideally, you'd want to minimize the time spent holding the (exclusive) write lock, so you might proceed as follows:

1. Obtain a read lock.

2. Test if the item is already present in the list, and if so, release the lock and return.

3. Release the read lock.

4. Obtain a write lock.

5. Add the item.

The problem is that another thread could sneak in and modify the list (e.g., adding the same item) between steps 3 and 4. ReaderWriterLockSlim addresses this through a third kind of lock called an *upgradeable lock*. An upgradeable lock is like a read lock except that it can later be promoted to a write lock in an atomic operation. Here's how you use it:

1. Call EnterUpgradeableReadLock.

2. Perform read-based activities (e.g., test whether the item is already present in the list).

3. Call `EnterWriteLock` (this converts the upgradeable lock to a write lock).

4. Perform write-based activities (e.g., add the item to the list).

5. Call `ExitWriteLock` (this converts the write lock back to an upgradeable lock).

6. Perform any other read-based activities.

7. Call `ExitUpgradeableReadLock`.

From the caller's perspective, it's rather like nested or recursive locking. Functionally, though, in step 3, `ReaderWriterLockSlim` releases your read lock and obtains a fresh write lock, atomically.

There's another important difference between upgradeable locks and read locks. While an upgradeable lock can coexist with any number of *read* locks, only one upgradeable lock can itself be taken out at a time. This prevents conversion deadlocks by *serializing* competing conversions—just as update locks do in SQL Server:

SQL Server	ReaderWriterLockSlim
Share lock	Read lock
Exclusive lock	Write lock
Update lock	Upgradeable lock

We can demonstrate an upgradeable lock by changing the `Write` method in the preceding example such that it adds a number to list only if not already present:

```
while (true)
{
  int newNumber = GetRandNum (100);
  _rw.EnterUpgradeableReadLock();
  if (!_items.Contains (newNumber))
  {
    _rw.EnterWriteLock();
    _items.Add (newNumber);
    _rw.ExitWriteLock();
    Console.WriteLine ("Thread " + threadID + " added " + newNumber);
  }
  _rw.ExitUpgradeableReadLock();
  Thread.Sleep (100);
}
```

 `ReaderWriterLock` can also do lock conversions—but unreliably because it doesn't support the concept of upgradeable locks. This is why the designers of `ReaderWriterLockSlim` had to start afresh with a new class.

Lock recursion

Ordinarily, nested or recursive locking is prohibited with `ReaderWriterLockSlim`. Hence, the following throws an exception:

```
var rw = new ReaderWriterLockSlim();
rw.EnterReadLock();
rw.EnterReadLock();
rw.ExitReadLock();
rw.ExitReadLock();
```

It runs without error, however, if you construct `ReaderWriterLockSlim` as follows:

```
var rw = new ReaderWriterLockSlim (LockRecursionPolicy.SupportsRecursion);
```

This ensures that recursive locking can happen only if you plan for it. Recursive locking can create undesired complexity because it's possible to acquire more than one kind of lock:

```
rw.EnterWriteLock();
rw.EnterReadLock();
Console.WriteLine (rw.IsReadLockHeld);     // True
Console.WriteLine (rw.IsWriteLockHeld);    // True
rw.ExitReadLock();
rw.ExitWriteLock();
```

The basic rule is that once you've acquired a lock, subsequent recursive locks can be less, but not greater, on the following scale:

Read Lock→Upgradeable Lock→Write Lock

A request to promote an upgradeable lock to a write lock, however, is always legal.

Timers

If you need to execute some method repeatedly at regular intervals, the easiest way is with a *timer*. Timers are convenient and efficient in their use of memory and resources—compared with techniques such as the following:

```
new Thread (delegate() {
                        while (enabled)
                        {
                          DoSomeAction();
                          Thread.Sleep (TimeSpan.FromHours (24));
                        }
                      }).Start();
```

Not only does this permanently tie up a thread resource, but without additional coding, `DoSomeAction` will happen at a later time each day. Timers solve these problems.

The .NET Framework provides four timers. Two of these are general-purpose multithreaded timers:

- `System.Threading.Timer`
- `System.Timers.Timer`

The other two are special-purpose single-threaded timers:

- `System.Windows.Forms.Timer` (Windows Forms timer)
- `System.Windows.Threading.DispatcherTimer` (WPF timer)

The multithreaded timers are more powerful, accurate, and flexible; the single-threaded timers are safer and more convenient for running simple tasks that update Windows Forms controls or WPF elements.

Multithreaded Timers

`System.Threading.Timer` is the simplest multithreaded timer: it has just a constructor and two methods (a delight for minimalists, as well as book authors!). In the following example, a timer calls the `Tick` method, which writes "tick..." after five seconds have elapsed, and then every second after that, until the user presses Enter:

```
using System;
using System.Threading;

class Program
{
  static void Main()
  {
    // First interval = 5000ms; subsequent intervals = 1000ms
    Timer tmr = new Timer (Tick, "tick...", 5000, 1000);
    Console.ReadLine();
    tmr.Dispose();          // This both stops the timer and cleans up.
  }

  static void Tick (object data)
  {
    // This runs on a pooled thread
    Console.WriteLine (data);        // Writes "tick..."
  }
}
```

You can change a timer's interval later by calling its `Change` method. If you want a timer to fire just once, specify `Timeout.Infinite` in the constructor's last argument.

The .NET Framework provides another timer class of the same name in the `System.Timers` namespace. This simply wraps the `System.Threading.Timer`, providing additional convenience while using the identical underlying engine. Here's a summary of its added features:

- A `Component` implementation, allowing it to be sited in Visual Studio's designer
- An `Interval` property instead of a `Change` method
- An `Elapsed` *event* instead of a callback delegate
- An `Enabled` property to start and stop the timer (its default value being `false`)
- `Start` and `Stop` methods in case you're confused by `Enabled`
- An `AutoReset` flag for indicating a recurring event (default value is `true`)
- A `SynchronizingObject` property with `Invoke` and `BeginInvoke` methods for safely calling methods on WPF elements and Windows Forms controls

Here's an example:

```
using System;
using System.Timers;   // Timers namespace rather than Threading
```

```
class SystemTimer
{
  static void Main()
  {
    Timer tmr = new Timer();        // Doesn't require any args
    tmr.Interval = 500;
    tmr.Elapsed += tmr_Elapsed;     // Uses an event instead of a delegate
    tmr.Start();                    // Start the timer
    Console.ReadLine();
    tmr.Stop();                     // Stop the timer
    Console.ReadLine();
    tmr.Start();                    // Restart the timer
    Console.ReadLine();
    tmr.Dispose();                  // Permanently stop the timer
  }

  static void tmr_Elapsed (object sender, EventArgs e)
  {
    Console.WriteLine ("Tick");
  }
}
```

Multithreaded timers use the thread pool to allow a few threads to serve many timers. This means that the callback method or Tick event may fire on a different thread each time it is called. Furthermore, a Tick always fires (approximately) on time— regardless of whether the previous Tick has finished executing. Hence, callbacks or event handlers must be thread-safe.

The precision of multithreaded timers depends on the operating system, and is typically in the 10–20 ms region. If you need greater precision, you can use native interop and call the Windows multimedia timer. This has precision down to 1 ms and it is defined in *winmm.dll*. First call timeBeginPeriod to inform the operating system that you need high timing precision, and then call timeSetEvent to start a multimedia timer. When you're done, call timeKillEvent to stop the timer and timeEndPeriod to inform the OS that you no longer need high timing precision. Chapter 25 demonstrates calling external methods with P/Invoke. You can find complete examples on the Internet that use the multimedia timer by searching for the keywords *dllimport winmm.dll timesetevent*.

Single-Threaded Timers

The .NET Framework provides timers designed to eliminate thread-safety issues for WPF and Windows Forms applications:

- System.Windows.Threading.DispatcherTimer (WPF)
- System.Windows.Forms.Timer (Windows Forms)

> The single-threaded timers are not designed to work outside their respective environments. If you use a Windows Forms timer in a Windows Service application, for instance, the Timer event won't fire!

Both are like `System.Timers.Timer` in the members that they expose (`Interval`, `Tick`, `Start`, and `Stop`) and are used in a similar manner. However, they differ in how they work internally. Instead of using the thread pool to generate timer events, the WPF and Windows Forms timers rely on the message pumping mechanism of their underlying user interface model. This means that the `Tick` event always fires on the same thread that originally created the timer—which, in a normal application, is the same thread used to manage all user interface elements and controls. This has a number of benefits:

- You can forget about thread safety.
- A fresh `Tick` will never fire until the previous `Tick` has finished processing.
- You can update user interface elements and controls directly from `Tick` event handling code, without calling `Control.Invoke` or `Dispatcher.Invoke`.

It sounds too good to be true, until you realize that a program employing these timers is not really multithreaded—*there is no parallel execution*. One thread serves all timers—as well as the processing UI events. This brings us to the disadvantage of single-threaded timers:

- Unless the `Tick` event handler executes quickly, the user interface becomes unresponsive.

This makes the WPF and Windows Forms timers suitable for only small jobs, typically those that involve updating some aspect of the user interface (e.g., a clock or countdown display). Otherwise, you need a multithreaded timer.

In terms of precision, the single-threaded timers are similar to the multithreaded timers (tens of milliseconds), although they are typically less *accurate*, because they can be delayed while other user interface requests (or other timer events) are processed.

22

Parallel Programming

In this chapter, we cover the multithreading APIs and constructs aimed at leveraging multicore processors:

- Parallel LINQ or *PLINQ*
- The `Parallel` class
- The *task parallelism* constructs
- The *concurrent collections*
- `SpinLock` and `SpinWait`

These are new to Framework 4.0 and are collectively known (loosely) as PFX (Parallel Framework). The `Parallel` class together with the task parallelism constructs is called the *Task Parallel Library* or TPL.

Framework 4.0 also adds a number of lower-level threading constructs that are aimed equally at traditional multithreading. We covered these in the previous chapter:

- The low-latency signaling constructs:
  — `SemaphoreSlim` (see the section "Locking" on page 808)
  — `ManualResetEventSlim` (see the section "Signaling with Event Wait Handles" on page 832)
  — `CountdownEvent` (see the section "Signaling with Event Wait Handles" on page 832)
  — `Barrier` (see the section "The Barrier Class" on page 849)
- Cancellation tokens for cooperative cancellation (see the section "Safe Cancellation" on page 857)
- The lazy initialization classes (see the section "Lazy Initialization" on page 860)
- `ThreadLocal<T>` (see the section "Thread-Local Storage" on page 862)

You'll need to be comfortable with the fundamentals in Chapter 21 before reading this chapter—particularly locking and thread safety.

Why PFX?

In recent times, CPU clock speeds have stagnated and manufacturers have shifted their focus to increasing core counts. This is problematic for us as programmers because our standard single-threaded code will not automatically run faster as a result of those extra cores.

Leveraging multiple cores is easy for most server applications, where each thread can independently handle a separate client request, but is harder on the desktop—because it typically requires that you take your computationally intensive code and do the following:

1. *Partition* it into small chunks.
2. Execute those chunks in parallel via multithreading.
3. *Collate* the results as they become available, in a thread-safe and performant manner.

Although you can do all of this with the classic multithreading constructs, it's awkward—particularly the steps of partitioning and collating. A further problem is that the usual strategy of locking for thread safety causes a lot of contention when many threads work on the same data at once.

The PFX libraries have been designed specifically to help in these scenarios.

> Programming to leverage multicores or multiple processors is called *parallel programming*. This is a subset of the broader concept of multithreading.

PFX Concepts

There are two strategies for partitioning work among threads: *data parallelism* and *task parallelism*.

When a set of tasks must be performed on many data values, we can parallelize by having each thread perform the (same) set of tasks on a subset of values. This is called *data parallelism* because we are partitioning the *data* between threads. In contrast, with *task parallelism* we partition the *tasks*; in other words, we have each thread perform a different task.

In general, data parallelism is easier and scales better to highly parallel hardware, because it reduces or eliminates shared data (thereby reducing contention and thread-safety issues). Also, data parallelism leverages the fact that there are often more data values than discrete tasks, increasing the parallelism potential.

Data parallelism is also conducive to *structured parallelism*, which means that parallel work units start and finish in the same place in your program. In contrast, task parallelism tends to be unstructured, meaning that parallel work units may start and finish in places scattered across your program. Structured parallelism is simpler and less error-prone and allows you to farm the difficult job of partitioning and thread coordination (and even result collation) out to libraries.

PFX Components

PFX comprises two layers of functionality, as shown in Figure 22-1. The higher layer consists of two *structured data parallelism* APIs: PLINQ and the `Parallel` class. The lower layer contains the task parallelism classes—plus a set of additional constructs to help with parallel programming activities.

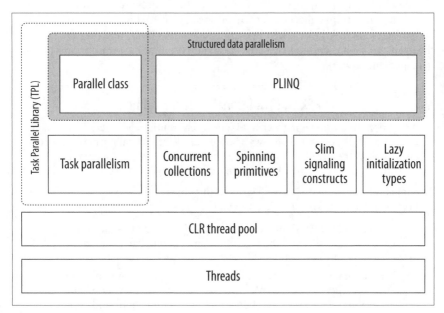

Figure 22-1. PFX components

PLINQ offers the richest functionality: it automates all the steps of parallelization—including partitioning the work into tasks, executing those tasks on threads, and collating the results into a single output sequence. It's called *declarative*—because you simply declare that you want to parallelize your work (which you structure as a LINQ query), and let the Framework take care of the implementation details. In contrast, the other approaches are *imperative*, in that you need to explicitly write code to partition or collate. In the case of the `Parallel` class, you must collate results yourself; with the task parallelism constructs, you must partition the work yourself, too:

	Partitions work	Collates results
PLINQ	Yes	Yes
The Parallel class	Yes	No
PFX's task parallelism	No	No

The concurrent collections and spinning primitives help you with lower-level parallel programming activities. These are important because PFX has been designed to work not only with today's hardware, but also with future generations of processors with far more cores. If you want to move a pile of chopped wood and you have 32 workers to do the job, the biggest challenge is moving the wood without the workers getting in each other's way. It's the same with dividing an algorithm among 32 cores: if ordinary locks are used to protect common resources, the resultant blocking may mean that only a fraction of those cores are ever actually busy at once. The concurrent collections are tuned specifically for highly concurrent access, with the focus on minimizing or eliminating blocking. PLINQ and the `Parallel` class themselves rely on the concurrent collections and on spinning primitives for efficient management of work.

PFX and Traditional Multithreading

A traditional multithreading scenario is one where multithreading can be of benefit even on a single-core machine—with no true *parallelization* taking place. We covered these in the previous chapter: they include such tasks as maintaining a responsive user interface and downloading two web pages at once.

Some of the constructs that we'll cover in this chapter are also sometimes useful in traditional multithreading. In particular:

- PLINQ and the `Parallel` class are useful whenever you want to execute operations in parallel and then wait for them to complete (*structured* parallelism). This includes non-CPU-intensive tasks such as calling a web service.

- The task parallelism constructs are useful when you want to run some operation on a pooled thread (we introduced this in the previous chapter), and also to manage a task's workflow through continuations and parent/child tasks.

- The concurrent collections are sometimes appropriate when you want a thread-safe queue, stack, or dictionary.

- `BlockingCollection` provides an easy means to implement producer/consumer structures.

When to Use PFX

The primary use case for PFX is *parallel programming*: leveraging multicore processors to speed up computationally intensive code.

A challenge in leveraging multicores is Amdahl's law, which states that the maximum performance improvement from parallelization is governed by the portion of

---

the code that must execute sequentially. For instance, if only two-thirds of an algorithm's execution time is parallelizable, you can never exceed a threefold performance gain—even with an infinite number of cores.

So, before proceeding, it's worth verifying that the bottleneck is in parallelizable code. It's also worth considering whether your code *needs* to be computationally intensive—optimization is often the easiest and most effective approach. There's a trade-off, though, in that some optimization techniques can make it harder to parallelize code.

The easiest gains come with what's called *embarrassingly parallel* problems—where a job can be divided easily into tasks that execute efficiently on their own (structured parallelism is very well suited to such problems). Examples include many image processing tasks, ray tracing, and brute force approaches in mathematics or cryptography. An example of a nonembarrassingly parallel problem is implementing an optimized version of the quicksort algorithm—a good result takes some thought and may require unstructured parallelism.

PLINQ

PLINQ automatically parallelizes local LINQ queries. PLINQ has the advantage of being easy to use in that it offloads the burden of both work partitioning and result collation to the Framework.

To use PLINQ, simply call `AsParallel()` on the input sequence and then continue the LINQ query as usual. The following query calculates the prime numbers between 3 and 100,000—making full use of all cores on the target machine:

```
// Calculate prime numbers using a simple (unoptimized) algorithm.

IEnumerable<int> numbers = Enumerable.Range (3, 100000-3);

var parallelQuery =
  from n in numbers.AsParallel()
  where Enumerable.Range (2, (int) Math.Sqrt (n)).All (i => n % i > 0)
  select n;

int[] primes = parallelQuery.ToArray();
```

`AsParallel` is an extension method in `System.Linq.ParallelEnumerable`. It wraps the input in a sequence based on `ParallelQuery<TSource>`, which causes the LINQ query operators that you subsequently call to bind to an alternate set of extension methods defined in `ParallelEnumerable`. These provide parallel implementations of each of the standard query operators. Essentially, they work by partitioning the input sequence into chunks that execute on different threads, collating the results back into a single output sequence for consumption (see Figure 22-2).

Calling `AsSequential()` unwraps a `ParallelQuery` sequence so that subsequent query operators bind to the standard query operators and execute sequentially. This is necessary before calling methods that have side effects or are not thread-safe.

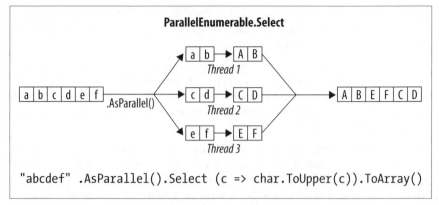

```
"abcdef" .AsParallel().Select (c => char.ToUpper(c)).ToArray()
```

Figure 22-2. PLINQ execution model

For query operators that accept two input sequences (Join, GroupJoin, Concat, Union, Intersect, Except, and Zip), you must apply AsParallel() to both input sequences (otherwise, an exception is thrown). You don't, however, need to keep applying AsParallel to a query as it progresses, because PLINQ's query operators output another ParallelQuery sequence. In fact, calling AsParallel again introduces inefficiency in that it forces merging and repartitioning of the query:

```
mySequence.AsParallel()               // Wraps sequence in ParallelQuery<int>
          .Where (n => n > 100)       // Outputs another ParallelQuery<int>
          .AsParallel()               // Unnecessary - and inefficient!
          .Select (n => n * n)
```

Not all query operators can be effectively parallelized. For those that cannot (see "PLINQ Limitations" on page 880), PLINQ implements the operator sequentially instead. PLINQ may also operate sequentially if it suspects that the overhead of parallelization will actually slow a particular query.

PLINQ is only for local collections: it doesn't work with LINQ to SQL or Entity Framework because in those cases the LINQ translates into SQL, which then executes on a database server. However, you *can* use PLINQ to perform additional local querying on the result sets obtained from database queries.

 If a PLINQ query throws an exception, it's rethrown as an AggregateException whose InnerExceptions property contains the real exception (or exceptions). See "Working with AggregateException" on page 912 for more details.

Parallel Execution Ballistics

Like ordinary LINQ queries, PLINQ queries are lazily evaluated. This means that execution is triggered only when you begin consuming the results—typically via a `foreach` loop (although it may also be via a conversion operator such as `ToArray` or an operator that returns a single element or value).

As you enumerate the results, though, execution proceeds somewhat differently from that of an ordinary sequential query. A sequential query is powered entirely by the consumer in a "pull" fashion: each element from the input sequence is fetched exactly when required by the consumer. A parallel query ordinarily uses independent threads to fetch elements from the input sequence slightly *ahead* of when they're needed by the consumer (rather like a teleprompter for newsreaders, or an antiskip buffer in CD players). It then processes the elements in parallel through the query chain, holding the results in a small buffer so that they're ready for the consumer on demand. If the consumer pauses or breaks out of the enumeration early, the query processor also pauses or stops so as not to waste CPU time or memory.

You can tweak PLINQ's buffering behavior by calling `WithMergeOptions` after `AsParallel`. The default value of `AutoBuffered` generally gives the best overall results. `NotBuffered` disables the buffer and is useful if you want to see results as soon as possible; `FullyBuffered` caches the entire result set before presenting it to the consumer (the `OrderBy` and `Reverse` operators naturally work this way, as do the element, aggregation, and conversion operators).

PLINQ and Ordering

A side effect of parallelizing the query operators is that when the results are collated, it's not necessarily in the same order that they were submitted (see Figure 22-2). In other words, LINQ's normal order-preservation guarantee for sequences no longer holds.

If you need order preservation, force it by calling `AsOrdered()` after `AsParallel()`:

```
myCollection.AsParallel().AsOrdered()...
```

Calling `AsOrdered` incurs a performance hit with large numbers of elements because PLINQ must keep track of each element's original position.

You can negate the effect of `AsOrdered` later in a query by calling `AsUnordered`: this introduces a "random shuffle point," which allows the query to execute more efficiently from that point on. So if you wanted to preserve input-sequence ordering for just the first two query operators, you'd do this:

```
inputSequence.AsParallel().AsOrdered()
  .QueryOperator1()
  .QueryOperator2()
  .AsUnordered()          // From here on, ordering doesn't matter
  .QueryOperator3()
  ...
```

`AsOrdered` is not the default because for most queries, the original input ordering doesn't matter. In other words, if `AsOrdered` was the default, you'd have to apply `AsUnordered` to the majority of your parallel queries to get the best performance, which would be burdensome.

PLINQ Limitations

There are currently some practical limitations on what PLINQ can parallelize. These limitations may loosen with subsequent service packs and Framework versions.

The following query operators prevent a query from being parallelized, unless the source elements are in their original indexing position:

- `Take`, `TakeWhile`, `Skip`, and `SkipWhile`
- The indexed versions of `Select`, `SelectMany`, and `ElementAt`

Most query operators change the indexing position of elements (including those that remove elements, such as `Where`). This means that if you want to use the preceding operators, they'll usually need to be at the start of the query.

The following query operators are parallelizable, but use an expensive partitioning strategy that can sometimes be slower than sequential processing:

- `Join`, `GroupBy`, `GroupJoin`, `Distinct`, `Union`, `Intersect`, and `Except`

The `Aggregate` operator's *seeded* overloads in their standard incarnations are not parallelizable—PLINQ provides special overloads to deal with this (see "Optimizing PLINQ" on page 886).

All other operators are parallelizable, although use of these operators doesn't guarantee that your query will be parallelized. PLINQ may run your query sequentially if it suspects that the overhead of parallelization will slow down that particular query. You can override this behavior and force parallelism by calling the following after `AsParallel()`:

```
.WithExecutionMode (ParallelExecutionMode.ForceParallelism)
```

Example: Parallel Spellchecker

Suppose we want to write a spellchecker that runs quickly with very large documents by leveraging all available cores. By formulating our algorithm into a LINQ query, we can very easily parallelize it.

The first step is to download a dictionary of English words into a `HashSet` for efficient lookup:

```
if (!File.Exists ("WordLookup.txt"))    // Contains about 150,000 words
  new WebClient().DownloadFile (
    "http://www.albahari.com/ispell/allwords.txt", "WordLookup.txt");

var wordLookup = new HashSet<string> (
  File.ReadAllLines ("WordLookup.txt"),
  StringComparer.InvariantCultureIgnoreCase);
```

We'll then use our word lookup to create a test "document" comprising an array of 1 million random words. After building the array, we'll introduce a couple of spelling mistakes:

```
var random = new Random();
string[] wordList = wordLookup.ToArray();

string[] wordsToTest = Enumerable.Range (0, 1000000)
  .Select (i => wordList [random.Next (0, wordList.Length)])
  .ToArray();

wordsToTest [12345] = "woozsh";    // Introduce a couple
wordsToTest [23456] = "wubsie";    // of spelling mistakes.
```

Now we can perform our parallel spellcheck by testing `wordsToTest` against `wordLookup`. PLINQ makes this very easy:

```
var query = wordsToTest
  .AsParallel()
  .Select ((word, index) => new IndexedWord { Word=word, Index=index })
  .Where   (iword => !wordLookup.Contains (iword.Word))
  .OrderBy (iword => iword.Index);

foreach (var mistake in query)
  Console.WriteLine (mistake.Word + " - index = " + mistake.Index);

// OUTPUT:
// woozsh - index = 12345
// wubsie - index = 23456
```

IndexedWord is a custom struct that we define as follows:

```
struct IndexedWord { public string Word; public int Index; }
```

The wordLookup.Contains method in the predicate gives the query some "meat" and makes it worth parallelizing.

> We could simplify the query slightly by using an anonymous type instead of the IndexedWord struct. However, this would degrade performance because anonymous types (being classes and therefore reference types) incur the cost of heap-based allocation and subsequent garbage collection.
>
> The difference might not be enough to matter with sequential queries, but with parallel queries, favoring stack-based allocation can be quite advantageous. This is because stack-based allocation is highly parallelizable (as each thread has its own stack), whereas all threads must compete for the same heap—managed by a single memory manager and garbage collector.

Using ThreadLocal<T>

Let's extend our example by parallelizing the creation of the random test-word list itself. We structured this as a LINQ query, so it should be easy. Here's the sequential version:

```
string[] wordsToTest = Enumerable.Range (0, 1000000)
  .Select (i => wordList [random.Next (0, wordList.Length)])
  .ToArray();
```

Unfortunately, the call to random.Next is not thread-safe, so it's not as simple as inserting AsParallel() into the query. A potential solution is to write a function that locks around random.Next; however, this would limit concurrency. The better option is to use ThreadLocal<Random> (see "Thread-Local Storage" on page 862 in the preceding chapter) to create a separate Random object for each thread. We can then parallelize the query as follows:

```
var localRandom = new ThreadLocal<Random>
  ( () => new Random (Guid.NewGuid().GetHashCode()) );

string[] wordsToTest = Enumerable.Range (0, 1000000).AsParallel()
```

```
.Select (i => wordList [localRandom.Value.Next (0, wordList.Length)])
.ToArray();
```

In our factory function for instantiating a Random object, we pass in a Guid's hash code to ensure that if two Random objects are created within a short period of time, they'll yield different random number sequences.

When to Use PLINQ

It's tempting to search your existing applications for LINQ queries and experiment with parallelizing them. This is usually unproductive, because most problems for which LINQ is obviously the best solution tend to execute very quickly and so don't benefit from parallelization. A better approach is to find a CPU-intensive bottleneck and then consider, "Can this be expressed as a LINQ query?" (A welcome side effect of such restructuring is that LINQ typically makes code smaller and more readable.)

PLINQ is well suited to embarrassingly parallel problems. It also works well for structured blocking tasks, such as calling several web services at once (see "Calling Blocking or I/O-Intensive Functions" on page 884).

PLINQ can be a poor choice for imaging, because collating millions of pixels into an output sequence creates a bottleneck. Instead, it's better to write pixels directly to an array or unmanaged memory block and use the Parallel class or task parallelism to manage the multithreading. (It is possible, however, to defeat result collation using ForAll—we discuss this in "Optimizing PLINQ" on page 886. Doing so makes sense if the image processing algorithm naturally lends itself to LINQ.)

Parallel
Programming

Functional Purity

Because PLINQ runs your query on parallel threads, you must be careful not to perform thread-unsafe operations. In particular, writing to variables is *side-effecting* and therefore thread-unsafe:

```
// The following query multiplies each element by its position.
// Given an input of Enumerable.Range(0,999), it should output squares.
int i = 0;
var query = from n in Enumerable.Range(0,999).AsParallel() select n * i++;
```

We could make incrementing i thread-safe by using locks or Interlocked (see "Nonblocking Synchronization" on page 825 in the preceding chapter), but the problem would still remain that i won't necessarily correspond to the position of the input element. And adding AsOrdered to the query wouldn't fix the latter problem, because AsOrdered ensures only that the elements are output in an order consistent with them having been processed sequentially—it doesn't actually *process* them sequentially.

Instead, this query should be rewritten to use the indexed version of Select:

```
var query = Enumerable.Range(0,999).AsParallel().Select ((n, i) => n * i);
```

For best performance, any methods called from query operators should be thread-safe by virtue of not writing to fields or properties (non-side-effecting, or *functionally pure*). If they're thread-safe by virtue of *locking*, the query's parallelism potential will be limited—by the duration of the lock divided by the total time spent in that function.

Calling Blocking or I/O-Intensive Functions

Sometimes a query is long-running not because it's CPU-intensive, but because it *waits* on something—such as a web page to download or some hardware to respond. PLINQ can effectively parallelize such queries, providing that you hint it by calling `WithDegreeOfParallelism` after `AsParallel`. For instance, suppose we want to ping six websites simultaneously. Rather than using clumsy asynchronous delegates or manually spinning up six threads, we can accomplish this effortlessly with a PLINQ query:

```
from site in new[]
{
    "www.albahari.com",
    "www.linqpad.net",
    "www.oreilly.com",
    "www.google.com",
    "www.takeonit.com",
    "stackoverflow.com"
}
.AsParallel().WithDegreeOfParallelism(6)
let p = new Ping().Send (site)
select new
{
    site,
    Result = p.Status,
    Time = p.RoundtripTime
}
```

`WithDegreeOfParallelism` forces PLINQ to run the specified number of tasks simultaneously. This is necessary when calling *blocking* functions such as `Ping.Send` because PLINQ otherwise assumes that the query is CPU-intensive and allocates tasks accordingly. On a two-core machine, for instance, PLINQ may default to running only two tasks at once, which is clearly undesirable in this situation.

> PLINQ typically serves each task with a thread, subject to allocation by the thread pool. You can accelerate the initial ramping up of threads by calling `ThreadPool.SetMinThreads` (see "Thread Pooling" on page 800 in the preceding chapter).

To give another example, suppose we were writing a surveillance system and wanted to repeatedly combine images from four security cameras into a single composite image for display on a CCTV. We'll represent a camera with the following class:

```
class Camera
{
  public readonly int CameraID;
  public Camera (int cameraID) { CameraID = cameraID; }

  // Get image from camera: return a simple string rather than an image
  public string GetNextFrame()
  {
    Thread.Sleep (123);        // Simulate time taken to get snapshot
    return "Frame from camera " + CameraID;
  }
}
```

To obtain a composite image, we must call `GetNextFrame` on each of four camera objects. Assuming the operation is I/O-bound, we can quadruple our frame rate with parallelization—even on a single-core machine. PLINQ makes this possible with minimal programming effort:

```
Camera[] cameras = Enumerable.Range (0, 4)      // Create 4 camera objects.
  .Select (i => new Camera (i))
  .ToArray();

while (true)
{
  string[] data = cameras
    .AsParallel().AsOrdered().WithDegreeOfParallelism (4)
    .Select (c => c.GetNextFrame()).ToArray();

  Console.WriteLine (string.Join (", ", data));   // Display data...
}
```

`GetNextFrame` is a blocking method, so we used `WithDegreeOfParallelism` to get the desired concurrency. In our example, the blocking happens when we call `Sleep`; in real life it would block because fetching an image from a camera is I/O-intensive rather than CPU-intensive.

Calling `AsOrdered` ensures the images are displayed in a consistent order. Because there are only four elements in the sequence, this would have a negligible effect on performance.

Changing the degree of parallelism

You can call `WithDegreeOfParallelism` only once within a PLINQ query. If you need to call it again, you must force merging and repartitioning of the query by calling `IsParallel()` again within the query:

```
"The Quick Brown Fox"
  .AsParallel().WithDegreeOfParallelism (2)
  .Where (c => !char.IsWhiteSpace (c))
  .AsParallel().WithDegreeOfParallelism (3)   // Forces Merge + Partition
  .Select (c => char.ToUpper (c))
```

Cancellation

Canceling a PLINQ query whose results you're consuming in a foreach loop is easy: simply break out of the foreach and the query will be automatically canceled as the enumerator is implicitly disposed.

For a query that terminates with a conversion, element, or aggregation operator, you can cancel it from another thread via a *cancellation token* (see "Safe Cancellation" on page 857 in the preceding chapter for a discussion of cancellation tokens). To insert a token, call WithCancellation after calling AsParallel, passing in the Token property of a CancellationTokenSource object. Another thread can then call Cancel on the token source, which throws an OperationCanceledException on the query's consumer:

```
IEnumerable<int> million = Enumerable.Range (3, 1000000);

var cancelSource = new CancellationTokenSource();

var primeNumberQuery =
  from n in million.AsParallel().WithCancellation (cancelSource.Token)
  where Enumerable.Range (2, (int) Math.Sqrt (n)).All (i => n % i > 0)
  select n;

new Thread ((() => {
                Thread.Sleep (100);      // Cancel query after
                cancelSource.Cancel();   // 100 milliseconds.
              }
            ).Start();
try
{
  // Start query running:
  int[] primes = primeNumberQuery.ToArray();
  // We'll never get here because the other thread will cancel us.
}
catch (OperationCanceledException)
{
  Console.WriteLine ("Query canceled");
}
```

PLINQ doesn't preemptively abort threads, because of the danger of doing so (see "Interrupt and Abort" on page 855 in the preceding chapter). Instead, upon cancellation, it waits for each worker thread to finish with its current element before ending the query. This means that any external methods that the query calls will run to completion.

Optimizing PLINQ

Output-side optimization

One of PLINQ's advantages is that it conveniently collates the results from parallelized work into a single output sequence. Sometimes, though, all that you end up doing with that sequence is running some function once over each element:

```
foreach (int n in parallelQuery)
    DoSomething (n);
```

If this is the case—and you don't care about the order in which the elements are processed—you can improve efficiency with PLINQ's `ForAll` method.

The `ForAll` method runs a delegate over every output element of a `ParallelQuery`. It hooks right into PLINQ's internals, bypassing the steps of collating and enumerating the results. To give a trivial example:

```
"abcdef".AsParallel().Select (c => char.ToUpper(c)).ForAll (Console.Write);
```

Figure 22-3 shows the process.

 Collating and enumerating results is not a massively expensive operation, so the `ForAll` optimization yields the greatest gains when there are large numbers of quickly executing input elements.

Figure 22-3. PLINQ ForAll

Input-side optimization

PLINQ has three partitioning strategies for assigning input elements to threads:

Strategy	Element allocation	Relative performance
Chunk partitioning	Dynamic	Average
Range partitioning	Static	Poor to excellent
Hash partitioning	Static	Poor

For query operators that require comparing elements (`GroupBy`, `Join`, `GroupJoin`, `Intersect`, `Except`, `Union`, and `Distinct`), you have no choice: PLINQ always uses *hash partitioning*. Hash partitioning is relatively inefficient in that it must precalculate the hash code of every element (so that elements with identical hash codes can be processed on the same thread). If you find this too slow, your only option is to call `AsSequential` to disable parallelization.

For all other query operators, you have a choice as to whether to use range or chunk partitioning. By default:

- If the input sequence is *indexable* (if it's an array or implements `IList<T>`), PLINQ chooses *range partitioning*.
- Otherwise, PLINQ chooses *chunk partitioning*.

In a nutshell, range partitioning is faster with long sequences for which every element takes a similar amount of CPU time to process. Otherwise, chunk partitioning is usually faster.

To force *range partitioning*:

- If the query starts with `Enumerable.Range`, replace the latter with `ParallelEnumerable.Range`.
- Otherwise, simply call `ToList` or `ToArray` on the input sequence (obviously, this incurs a performance cost in itself which you should take into account).

> `ParallelEnumerable.Range` is not simply a shortcut for calling `Enumerable.Range(...).AsParallel()`. It changes the performance of the query by activating range partitioning.

To force *chunk partitioning*, wrap the input sequence in a call to `Partitioner.Create` (in `System.Collection.Concurrent`) as follows:

```
int[] numbers = { 3, 4, 5, 6, 7, 8, 9 };
var parallelQuery =
    Partitioner.Create (numbers, true).AsParallel()
    .Where (...)
```

The second argument to `Partitioner.Create` indicates that you want to *load-balance* the query, which is another way of saying that you want chunk partitioning.

Chunk partitioning works by having each worker thread periodically grab small "chunks" of elements from the input sequence to process (see Figure 22-4). PLINQ starts by allocating very small chunks (one or two elements at a time), then increases the chunk size as the query progresses: this ensures that small sequences are effectively parallelized and large sequences don't cause excessive round-tripping. If a worker happens to get "easy" elements (that process quickly) it will end up getting more chunks. This system keeps every thread equally busy (and the cores "balanced"); the only downside is that fetching elements from the shared input sequence requires synchronization (typically an exclusive lock)—and this can result in some overhead and contention.

Range partitioning bypasses the normal input-side enumeration and preallocates an equal number of elements to each worker, avoiding contention on the input sequence. But if some threads happen to get easy elements and finish early, they sit idle while the remaining threads continue working. Our earlier prime number

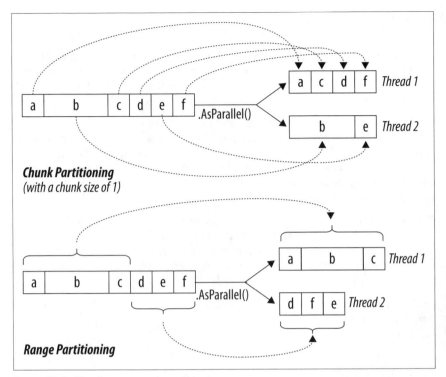

Chunk Partitioning
(with a chunk size of 1)

Range Partitioning

Figure 22-4. Chunk versus range partitioning

calculator might perform poorly with range partitioning. An example of when range partitioning would do well is in calculating the sum of the square roots of the first 10 million integers:

```
ParallelEnumerable.Range (1, 10000000).Sum (i => Math.Sqrt (i))
```

`ParallelEnumerable.Range` returns a `ParallelQuery<T>`, so you don't need to subsequently call `AsParallel`.

> Range partitioning doesn't necessarily allocate element ranges in *contiguous* blocks—it might instead choose a "striping" strategy. For instance, if there are two workers, one worker might process odd-numbered elements while the other processes even-numbered elements. The `TakeWhile` operator is almost certain to trigger a striping strategy to avoid unnecessarily processing elements later in the sequence.

Optimizing custom aggregations

PLINQ parallelizes the `Sum`, `Average`, `Min`, and `Max` operators efficiently without additional intervention. The `Aggregate` operator, though, presents special challenges for PLINQ. As described in Chapter 9, `Aggregate` performs custom aggregations. For example, the following sums a sequence of numbers, mimicking the `Sum` operator:

```
int[] numbers = { 1, 2, 3 };
int sum = numbers.Aggregate (0, (total, n) => total + n);   // 6
```

We also saw in Chapter 9 that for *unseeded* aggregations, the supplied delegate must be associative and commutative. PLINQ will give incorrect results if this rule is violated, because it draws *multiple seeds* from the input sequence in order to aggregate several partitions of the sequence simultaneously.

Explicitly seeded aggregations might seem like a safe option with PLINQ, but unfortunately these ordinarily execute sequentially because of the reliance on a single seed. To mitigate this, PLINQ provides another overload of `Aggregate` that lets you specify multiple seeds—or rather, a *seed factory function*. For each thread, it executes this function to generate a separate seed, which becomes a *thread-local* accumulator into which it locally aggregates elements.

You must also supply a function to indicate how to combine the local and main accumulators. Finally, this `Aggregate` overload (somewhat gratuitously) expects a delegate to perform any final transformation on the result (you can achieve this as easily by running some function on the result yourself afterward). So, here are the four delegates, in the order they are passed:

seedFactory
> Returns a new local accumulator

updateAccumulatorFunc
> Aggregates an element into a local accumulator

combineAccumulatorFunc
> Combines a local accumulator with the main accumulator

resultSelector
> Applies any final transformation on the end result

> In simple scenarios, you can specify a *seed value* instead of a seed factory. This tactic fails when the seed is a reference type that you wish to mutate, because the same instance will then be shared by each thread.

To give a very simple example, the following sums the values in a `numbers` array:

```
numbers.AsParallel().Aggregate (
  () => 0,                                  // seedFactory
  (localTotal, n) => localTotal + n,        // updateAccumulatorFunc
  (mainTot, localTot) => mainTot + localTot, // combineAccumulatorFunc
  finalResult => finalResult)               // resultSelector
```

This example is contrived in that we could get the same answer just as efficiently using simpler approaches (such as an unseeded aggregate, or better, the `Sum` operator). To give a more realistic example, suppose we wanted to calculate the frequency of each letter in the English alphabet in a given string. A simple sequential solution might look like this:

```
string text = "Let's suppose this is a really long string";
var letterFrequencies = new int[26];
foreach (char c in text)
{
  int index = char.ToUpper (c) - 'A';
  if (index >= 0 && index <= 26) letterFrequencies [index]++;
};
```

 An example of when the input text might be very long is in gene sequencing. The "alphabet" would then consist of the letters *a*, *c*, *g*, and *t*.

To parallelize this, we could replace the `foreach` statement with a call to `Parallel.ForEach` (as we'll cover in the following section), but this will leave us to deal with concurrency issues on the shared array. And locking around accessing that array would all but kill the potential for parallelization.

`Aggregate` offers a tidy solution. The accumulator, in this case, is an array just like the `letterFrequencies` array in our preceding example. Here's a sequential version using `Aggregate`:

```
int[] result =
  text.Aggregate (
    new int[26],                  // Create the "accumulator"
    (letterFrequencies, c) =>     // Aggregate a letter into the accumulator
    {
      int index = char.ToUpper (c) - 'A';
      if (index >= 0 && index <= 26) letterFrequencies [index]++;
      return letterFrequencies;
    });
```

And now the parallel version, using PLINQ's special overload:

```
int[] result =
  text.AsParallel().Aggregate (
    () => new int[26],            // Create a new local accumulator

    (localFrequencies, c) =>      // Aggregate into the local accumulator
    {
      int index = char.ToUpper (c) - 'A';
      if (index >= 0 && index <= 26) localFrequencies [index]++;
      return localFrequencies;
    },
                                  // Aggregate local->main accumulator
    (mainFreq, localFreq) =>
      mainFreq.Zip (localFreq, (f1, f2) => f1 + f2).ToArray(),

    finalResult => finalResult    // Perform any final transformation
  );                              // on the end result.
```

Notice that the local accumulation function *mutates* the `localFrequencies` array. This ability to perform this optimization is important—and is legitimate because `localFrequencies` is local to each thread.

The Parallel Class

PFX provides a basic form of structured parallelism via three static methods in the Parallel class:

Parallel.Invoke
:   Executes an array of delegates in parallel

Parallel.For
:   Performs the parallel equivalent of a C# `for` loop

Parallel.ForEach
:   Performs the parallel equivalent of a C# `foreach` loop

All three methods block until all work is complete. As with PLINQ, after an unhandled exception, remaining workers are stopped after their current iteration and the exception (or exceptions) are thrown back to the caller—wrapped in an AggregateException (see "Working with AggregateException" on page 912).

Parallel.Invoke

Parallel.Invoke executes an array of Action delegates in parallel, and then waits for them to complete. The simplest version of the method is defined as follows:

```
public static void Invoke (params Action[] actions);
```

Here's how we can use Parallel.Invoke to download two web pages at once:

```
Parallel.Invoke (
  () => new WebClient().DownloadFile ("http://www.linqpad.net", "lp.html"),
  () => new WebClient().DownloadFile ("http://www.jaoo.dk", "jaoo.html"));
```

On the surface, this seems like a convenient shortcut for creating and waiting on two Task objects (or asynchronous delegates). But there's an important difference: Parallel.Invoke still works efficiently if you pass in an array of 1 million delegates. This is because it *partitions* large numbers of elements into batches which it assigns to a handful of underlying Tasks—rather than creating a separate Task for each delegate.

As with all of Parallel's methods, you're on your own when it comes to collating the results. This means you need to keep thread safety in mind. The following, for instance, is thread-unsafe:

```
var data = new List<string>();
Parallel.Invoke (
  () => data.Add (new WebClient().DownloadString ("http://www.foo.com")),
  () => data.Add (new WebClient().DownloadString ("http://www.far.com")));
```

Locking around adding to the list would resolve this, although locking would create a bottleneck if you had a much larger array of quickly executing delegates. A better solution is to use the thread-safe collections that we'll cover in later sections—ConcurrentBag would be ideal in this case.

Parallel.Invoke is also overloaded to accept a ParallelOptions object:

```
public static void Invoke (ParallelOptions options,
                           params Action[] actions);
```

With `ParallelOptions`, you can insert a cancellation token, limit the maximum concurrency, and specify a custom task scheduler. A cancellation token is relevant when you're executing (roughly) more tasks than you have cores: upon cancellation, any unstarted delegates will be abandoned. Any already-executing delegates will, however, continue to completion. See "Cancellation" on page 886 for an example of how to use cancellation tokens.

Parallel.For and Parallel.ForEach

`Parallel.For` and `Parallel.ForEach` perform the equivalent of a C# `for` and `foreach` loop, but with each iteration executing in parallel instead of sequentially. Here are their (simplest) signatures:

```
public static ParallelLoopResult For (
  int fromInclusive, int toExclusive, Action<int> body)

public static ParallelLoopResult ForEach<TSource> (
  IEnumerable<TSource> source, Action<TSource> body)
```

The following sequential `for` loop:

```
for (int i = 0; i < 100; i++)
  Foo (i);
```

is parallelized like this:

```
Parallel.For (0, 100, i => Foo (i));
```

or more simply:

```
Parallel.For (0, 100, Foo);
```

And the following sequential `foreach`:

```
foreach (char c in "Hello, world")
  Foo (c);
```

is parallelized like this:

```
Parallel.ForEach ("Hello, world", Foo);
```

To give a practical example, if we import the `System.Security.Cryptography` namespace, we can generate six public/private key-pair strings in parallel as follows:

```
var keyPairs = new string[6];

Parallel.For (0, keyPairs.Length,
              i => keyPairs[i] = RSA.Create().ToXmlString (true));
```

As with `Parallel.Invoke`, we can feed `Parallel.For` and `Parallel.ForEach` a large number of work items and they'll be efficiently partitioned onto a few tasks.

The latter query could also be done with PLINQ:

```
string[] keyPairs =
  ParallelEnumerable.Range (0, 6)
  .Select (i => RSA.Create().ToXmlString (true))
  .ToArray();
```

Outer versus inner loops

`Parallel.For` and `Parallel.ForEach` usually work best on outer rather than inner loops. This is because with the former, you're offering larger chunks of work to parallelize, diluting the management overhead. Parallelizing both inner and outer loops is usually unnecessary. In the following example, we'd typically need more than 100 cores to benefit from the inner parallelization:

```
Parallel.For (0, 100, i =>
{
  Parallel.For (0, 50, j => Foo (i, j));    // Sequential would be better
});                                          // for the inner loop.
```

Indexed Parallel.ForEach

Sometimes it's useful to know the loop iteration index. With a sequential `foreach`, it's easy:

```
int i = 0;
foreach (char c in "Hello, world")
  Console.WriteLine (c.ToString() + i++);
```

Incrementing a shared variable, however, is not thread-safe in a parallel context. You must instead use the following version of `ForEach`:

```
public static ParallelLoopResult ForEach<TSource> (
  IEnumerable<TSource> source, Action<TSource,ParallelLoopState,long> body)
```

We'll ignore `ParallelLoopState` (which we'll cover in the following section). For now, we're interested in `Action`'s third type parameter of type `long`, which indicates the loop index:

```
Parallel.ForEach ("Hello, world", (c, state, i) =>
{
  Console.WriteLine (c.ToString() + i);
});
```

To put this into a practical context, we'll revisit the spellchecker that we wrote with PLINQ. The following code loads up a dictionary along with an array of 1 million words to test:

```
if (!File.Exists ("WordLookup.txt"))    // Contains about 150,000 words
  new WebClient().DownloadFile (
    "http://www.albahari.com/ispell/allwords.txt", "WordLookup.txt");

var wordLookup = new HashSet<string> (
  File.ReadAllLines ("WordLookup.txt"),
  StringComparer.InvariantCultureIgnoreCase);
```

```
var random = new Random();
string[] wordList = wordLookup.ToArray();

string[] wordsToTest = Enumerable.Range (0, 1000000)
  .Select (i => wordList [random.Next (0, wordList.Length)])
  .ToArray();

wordsToTest [12345] = "woozsh";      // Introduce a couple
wordsToTest [23456] = "wubsie";      // of spelling mistakes.
```

We can perform the spellcheck on our wordsToTest array using the indexed version of Parallel.ForEach as follows:

```
var misspellings = new ConcurrentBag<Tuple<int,string>>();

Parallel.ForEach (wordsToTest, (word, state, i) =>
{
  if (!wordLookup.Contains (word))
    misspellings.Add (Tuple.Create ((int) i, word));
});
```

Notice that we had to collate the results into a thread-safe collection: having to do this is the disadvantage when compared to using PLINQ. The advantage over PLINQ is that we avoid the cost of applying an indexed Select query operator—which is less efficient than an indexed ForEach.

ParallelLoopState: Breaking early out of loops

Because the loop body in a parallel For or ForEach is a delegate, you can't exit the loop early with a break statement. Instead, you must call Break or Stop on a ParallelLoopState object:

```
public class ParallelLoopState
{
  public void Break();
  public void Stop();

  public bool IsExceptional { get; }
  public bool IsStopped { get; }
  public long? LowestBreakIteration { get; }
  public bool ShouldExitCurrentIteration { get; }
}
```

Obtaining a ParallelLoopState is easy: all versions of For and ForEach are overloaded to accept loop bodies of type Action<TSource,ParallelLoopState>. So, to parallelize this:

```
foreach (char c in "Hello, world")
  if (c == ',')
    break;
  else
    Console.Write (c);
```

do this:

```
Parallel.ForEach ("Hello, world", (c, loopState) =>
{
  if (c == ',')
    loopState.Break();
  else
    Console.Write (c);
});

// OUTPUT: Hlloe
```

You can see from the output that loop bodies may complete in a random order. Aside from this difference, calling Break yields *at least* the same elements as executing the loop sequentially: this example will always output *at least* the letters H, e, l, l, and o in some order. In contrast, calling Stop instead of Break forces all threads to finish right after their current iteration. In our example, calling Stop could give us a subset of the letters H, e, l, l, and o if another thread was lagging behind. Calling Stop is useful when you've found something that you're looking for—or when something has gone wrong and you won't be looking at the results.

> The Parallel.For and Parallel.ForEach methods return a ParallelLoopResult object that exposes properties called IsCompleted and LowestBreakIteration. These tell you whether the loop ran to completion, and if not, at what cycle the loop was broken.
>
> If LowestBreakIteration returns null, it means that you called Stop (rather than Break) on the loop.

If your loop body is long, you might want other threads to break partway through the method body in case of an early Break or Stop. You can do this by polling the ShouldExitCurrentIteration property at various places in your code; this property becomes true immediately after a Stop—or soon after a Break.

> ShouldExitCurrentIteration also becomes true after a cancellation request—or if an exception is thrown in the loop.

IsExceptional lets you know whether an exception has occurred on another thread. Any unhandled exception will cause the loop to stop after each thread's current iteration: to avoid this, you must explicitly handle exceptions in your code.

Optimization with local values

Parallel.For and Parallel.ForEach each offer a set of overloads that feature a generic type argument called TLocal. These overloads are designed to help you optimize the collation of data with iteration-intensive loops. The simplest is this:

```
public static ParallelLoopResult For <TLocal> (
    int fromInclusive,
    int toExclusive,
    Func <TLocal> localInit,
    Func <int, ParallelLoopState, TLocal, TLocal> body,
    Action <TLocal> localFinally);
```

These methods are rarely needed in practice because their target scenarios are covered mostly by PLINQ (which is fortunate because these overloads are somewhat intimidating!).

Essentially, the problem is this: suppose we want to sum the square roots of the numbers 1 through 10,000,000. Calculating 10 million square roots is easily parallelizable, but summing their values is troublesome because we must lock around updating the total:

```
object locker = new object();
double total = 0;
Parallel.For (1, 10000000,
              i => { lock (locker) total += Math.Sqrt (i); });
```

The gain from parallelization is more than offset by the cost of obtaining 10 million locks—plus the resultant blocking.

The reality, though, is that we don't actually *need* 10 million locks. Imagine a team of volunteers picking up a large volume of litter. If all workers shared a single trash can, the travel and contention would make the process extremely inefficient. The obvious solution is for each worker to have a private or "local" trash can, which is occasionally emptied into the main bin.

The TLocal versions of For and ForEach work in exactly this way. The volunteers are internal worker threads, and the *local value* represents a local trash can. In order for Parallel to do this job, you must feed it two additional delegates that indicate:

1. How to initialize a new local value

2. How to combine a local aggregation with the master value

Additionally, instead of the body delegate returning void, it should return the new aggregate for the local value. Here's our example refactored:

```
object locker = new object();
double grandTotal = 0;

Parallel.For (1, 10000000,

  () => 0.0,                     // Initialize the local value.

  (i, state, localTotal) =>      // Body delegate. Notice that it
     localTotal + Math.Sqrt (i), // returns the new local total.

  localTotal =>                         // Add the local value
     { lock (locker) grandTotal += localTotal; }  // to the master value.
);
```

We must still lock, but only around aggregating the local value to the grand total. This makes the process dramatically more efficient.

 As stated earlier, PLINQ is often a good fit in these scenarios. Our example could be parallelized with PLINQ simply like this:

```
ParallelEnumerable.Range (1, 10000000)
    .Sum (i => Math.Sqrt (i))
```

(Notice that we used `ParallelEnumerable` to force *range partitioning*: this improves performance in this case because all numbers will take equally long to process.)

In more complex scenarios, you might use LINQ's `Aggregate` operator instead of `Sum`. If you supplied a local seed factory, the situation would be somewhat analogous to providing a local value function with `Parallel.For`.

Task Parallelism

Task parallelism is the lowest-level approach to parallelization with PFX. The classes for working at this level are defined in the `System.Threading.Tasks` namespace and comprise the following:

Class	Purpose
Task	For managing a unit for work
Task<TResult>	For managing a unit for work with a return value
TaskFactory	For creating tasks
TaskFactory<TResult>	For creating tasks and continuations with the same return type
TaskScheduler	For managing the scheduling of tasks
TaskCompletionSource	For manually controlling a task's workflow

Essentially, a task is a lightweight object for managing a parallelizable unit of work. A task avoids the overhead of starting a dedicated thread by using the CLR's thread pool: this is the same thread pool used by `ThreadPool.QueueUserWorkItem`, tweaked in CLR 4.0 to work more efficiently with `Task`s (and more efficiently in general).

Tasks can be used whenever you want to execute something in parallel. However, they're *tuned* for leveraging multicores: in fact, the `Parallel` class and PLINQ are internally built on the task parallelism constructs.

Tasks do more than just provide an easy and efficient way into the thread pool. They also provide powerful features for managing units of work, including the ability to:

* Tune a task's scheduling
* Establish a parent/child relationship when one task is started from another
* Implement cooperative cancellation

- Wait on a set of tasks—without a signaling construct
- Attach "continuation" task(s)
- Schedule a continuation based on multiple antecedent tasks
- Propagate exceptions to parents, continuations, and task consumers

Tasks also implement *local work queues*, an optimization that allows you to efficiently create many quickly executing child tasks without incurring the contention overhead that would otherwise arise with a single work queue.

The Task Parallel Library lets you create hundreds (or even thousands) of tasks with minimal overhead. But if you want to create millions of tasks, you'll need to partition those tasks into larger work units to maintain efficiency. The `Parallel` class and PLINQ do this automatically.

Visual Studio 2010 provides a new window for monitoring tasks (Debug→Window→Parallel Tasks). This is equivalent to the Threads window, but for tasks. The Parallel Stacks window also has a special mode for tasks.

Creating and Starting Tasks

As we described in Chapter 21 (in our discussion of thread pooling), you can create and start a `Task` by calling `Task.Factory.StartNew`, passing in an `Action` delegate:

```
Task.Factory.StartNew (() => Console.WriteLine ("Hello from a task!"));
```

The generic version, `Task<TResult>` (a subclass of `Task`), lets you get data back from a task upon completion:

```
Task<string> task = Task.Factory.StartNew<string> (() =>      // Begin task
{
  using (var wc = new System.Net.WebClient())
    return wc.DownloadString ("http://www.linqpad.net");
});

RunSomeOtherMethod();           // We can do other work in parallel...

string result = task.Result;  // Wait for task to finish and fetch result.
```

`Task.Factory.StartNew` creates and starts a task in one step. You can decouple these operations by first instantiating a `Task` object, and then calling `Start`:

```
var task = new Task (() => Console.Write ("Hello"));
...
task.Start();
```

A task that you create in this manner can also be run synchronously (on the same thread) by calling `RunSynchronously` instead of `Start`.

You can track a task's execution status via its Status property.

Specifying a state object

When instantiating a task or calling Task.Factory.StartNew, you can specify a *state* object, which is passed to the target method. This is useful should you want to call a method directly rather than using a lambda expression:

```
static void Main()
{
  var task = Task.Factory.StartNew (Greet, "Hello");
  task.Wait();  // Wait for task to complete.
}

static void Greet (object state) { Console.Write (state); }   // Hello
```

Given that we have lambda expressions in C#, we can put the *state* object to better use, which is to assign a meaningful name to the task. We can then use the AsyncState property to query its name:

```
static void Main()
{
  var task = Task.Factory.StartNew (state => Greet ("Hello"), "Greeting");
  Console.WriteLine (task.AsyncState);   // Greeting
  task.Wait();
}

static void Greet (string message) { Console.Write (message); }
```

 Visual Studio displays each task's AsyncState in the Parallel Tasks window, so having a meaningful name here can ease debugging considerably.

TaskCreationOptions

You can tune a task's execution by specifying a TaskCreationOptions enum when calling StartNew (or instantiating a Task). TaskCreationOptions is a flags enum with the following (combinable) values:

```
LongRunning
PreferFairness
AttachedToParent
```

LongRunning suggests to the scheduler to dedicate a thread to the task. This is beneficial for long-running tasks because they might otherwise "hog" the queue, and force short-running tasks to wait an unreasonable amount of time before being scheduled. LongRunning is also good for blocking tasks.

The task queuing problem arises because the task scheduler ordinarily tries to keep just enough tasks active on threads at once to keep each CPU core busy. Not *oversubscribing* the CPU with too many active threads avoids the degradation in performance that would occur if the operating system was forced to perform a lot of expensive time slicing and context switching.

`PreferFairness` tells the scheduler to try to ensure that tasks are scheduled in the order they were started. It may ordinarily do otherwise, because it internally optimizes the scheduling of tasks using local work-stealing queues. This optimization is of practical benefit with very small (fine-grained) tasks.

`AttachedToParent` is for creating *child tasks*.

Child tasks

When one task starts another, you can optionally establish a parent-child relationship by specifying `TaskCreationOptions.AttachedToParent`:

```
Task parent = Task.Factory.StartNew (() =>
{
  Console.WriteLine ("I am a parent");

  Task.Factory.StartNew (() =>        // Detached task
  {
    Console.WriteLine ("I am detached");
  });

  Task.Factory.StartNew (() =>        // Child task
  {
    Console.WriteLine ("I am a child");
  }, TaskCreationOptions.AttachedToParent);
});
```

A child task is special in that when you wait for the *parent* task to complete, it waits for any children as well. This can be particularly useful when a child task is a continuation, as we'll see shortly.

Waiting on Tasks

You can explicitly wait for a task to complete in two ways:

- Calling its `Wait` method (optionally with a timeout)
- Accessing its `Result` property (in the case of `Task<TResult>`)

You can also wait on multiple tasks at once—via the static methods `Task.WaitAll` (waits for all the specified tasks to finish) and `Task.WaitAny` (waits for just one task to finish).

`WaitAll` is similar to waiting out each task in turn, but is more efficient in that it requires (at most) just one context switch. Also, if one or more of the tasks throw an unhandled exception, `WaitAll` still waits out every task—and then rethrows a single `AggregateException` that accumulates the exceptions from each faulted task. It's equivalent to doing this:

```
// Assume t1, t2, and t3 are tasks:
var exceptions = new List<Exception>();
try { t1.Wait(); } catch (AggregateException ex) { exceptions.Add (ex); }
try { t2.Wait(); } catch (AggregateException ex) { exceptions.Add (ex); }
try { t3.Wait(); } catch (AggregateException ex) { exceptions.Add (ex); }
if (exceptions.Count > 0) throw new AggregateException (exceptions);
```

Calling `WaitAny` is equivalent to waiting on a `ManualResetEventSlim` that's signaled by each task as it finishes.

As well as a timeout, you can also pass in a *cancellation token* to the `Wait` methods: this lets you cancel the wait—*not the task itself*. For a discussion on cancellation tokens, see "Safe Cancellation" on page 857.

Exception-Handling Tasks

When you wait for a task to complete (by calling its `Wait` method or accessing its `Result` property), any unhandled exceptions are conveniently rethrown to the caller, wrapped in an `AggregateException` object (see "Working with AggregateException" on page 912). This usually avoids the need to write code within task blocks to handle unexpected exceptions:

```
int x = 0;
Task<int> calc = Task.Factory.StartNew (() => 7 / x);
try
{
  Console.WriteLine (calc.Result);
}
catch (AggregateException aex)
{
  Console.Write (aex.InnerException.Message);  // Attempted to divide by 0
}
```

You still need to exception-handle detached autonomous tasks (unparented tasks that are not waited upon) in order to prevent an unhandled exception taking down the application when the task drops out of scope and is garbage-collected (subject to the following note). The same applies for tasks waited upon with a timeout, because any exception thrown *after* the timeout interval will otherwise be "unhandled."

The static `TaskScheduler.UnobservedTaskException` event provides a final last resort for dealing with unhandled task exceptions. By handling this event, you can intercept task exceptions that would otherwise end the application—and provide your own logic for dealing with them.

For parented tasks, waiting on the parent implicitly waits on the children—and any child exceptions then bubble up:

```
TaskCreationOptions atp = TaskCreationOptions.AttachedToParent;
var parent = Task.Factory.StartNew (() =>
{
  Task.Factory.StartNew (() =>    // Child
  {
    Task.Factory.StartNew (() => { throw null; }, atp);    // Grandchild
  }, atp);
});

// The following call throws a NullReferenceException (wrapped
// in nested AggregateExceptions):
parent.Wait();
```

 Interestingly, if you check a task's Exception property after it
has thrown an exception, the act of reading that property will
prevent the exception from subsequently taking down your application. The rationale is that PFX's designers don't want you
ignoring exceptions—as long as you acknowledge them in some
way, they won't punish you by terminating your program.

 An unhandled exception on a task doesn't cause *immediate* application termination: instead, it's delayed until the garbage
collector catches up with the task and calls its finalizer. Termination is delayed because it can't be known for certain that you
don't plan to call Wait or check its Result or Exception property
until the task is garbage-collected. This delay can sometimes
mislead you as to the original source of the error (although Visual Studio's debugger can assist if you enable breaking on first-
chance exceptions).

As we'll see soon, an alternative strategy for dealing with exceptions is with
continuations.

Canceling Tasks

You can optionally pass in a cancellation token when starting a task. This lets you
cancel tasks via the cooperative cancellation pattern described in "Safe Cancellation" on page 857 in Chapter 21:

```
var cancelSource = new CancellationTokenSource();
CancellationToken token = cancelSource.Token;

Task task = Task.Factory.StartNew (() =>
{
  // Do some stuff...
  token.ThrowIfCancellationRequested();  // Check for cancellation request
  // Do some stuff...
}, token);
...
cancelSource.Cancel();
```

To detect a canceled task, catch an `AggregateException` and check the inner exception as follows:

```
try
{
  task.Wait();
}
catch (AggregateException ex)
{
  if (ex.InnerException is OperationCanceledException)
    Console.Write ("Task canceled!");
}
```

> If you want to explicitly throw an `OperationCanceledException` (rather than calling `token.ThrowIfCancellationRequested`), you must pass the cancellation token into `OperationCanceledException`'s constructor. If you fail to do this, the task won't end up with a `TaskStatus.Canceled` status and won't trigger `OnlyOnCanceled` continuations.

If the task is canceled before it has started, it won't get scheduled—an `OperationCanceledException` will instead be thrown on the task immediately.

Because cancellation tokens are recognized by other APIs, you can pass them into other constructs and cancellations will propagate seamlessly:

```
var cancelSource = new CancellationTokenSource();
CancellationToken token = cancelSource.Token;

Task task = Task.Factory.StartNew (() =>
{
  // Pass our cancellation token into a PLINQ query:
  var query = someSequence.AsParallel().WithCancellation (token)...
  ... enumerate query ...
});
```

Calling `Cancel` on `cancelSource` in this example will cancel the PLINQ query, which will throw an `OperationCanceledException` on the task body, which will then cancel the task.

> The cancellation tokens that you can pass into methods such as `Wait` and `CancelAndWait` allow you to cancel the *wait* operation and not the task itself.

Continuations

Sometimes it's useful to start a task right after another one completes (or fails). The `ContinueWith` method on the `Task` class does exactly this:

```
Task task1 = Task.Factory.StartNew (() => Console.Write ("antecedant.."));
Task task2 = task1.ContinueWith (ant => Console.Write ("..continuation"));
```

As soon as task1 (the *antecedent*) finishes, fails, or is canceled, task2 (the *continuation*) automatically starts. (If task1 had completed before the second line of code ran, task2 would be scheduled to execute right away.) The ant argument passed to the continuation's lambda expression is a reference to the antecedent task.

Our example demonstrated the simplest kind of continuation, and is functionally similar to the following:

```
Task task = Task.Factory.StartNew (() =>
{
  Console.Write ("antecedent..");
  Console.Write ("..continuation");
});
```

The continuation-based approach, however, is more flexible in that you could first wait on task1, and then later wait on task2. This is particularly useful if task1 returns data.

> Another (subtler) difference is that by default, antecedent and continuation tasks may execute on different threads. You can force them to execute on the same thread by specifying TaskCon tinuationOptions.ExecuteSynchronously when calling Continue With: this can improve performance in very fine-grained continuations by lessening indirection.

Continuations and Task<TResult>

Just like ordinary tasks, continuations can be of type Task<TResult> and return data. In the following example, we calculate Math.Sqrt(8*2) using a series of chained tasks and then write out the result:

```
Task.Factory.StartNew<int> (() => 8)
  .ContinueWith (ant => ant.Result * 2)
  .ContinueWith (ant => Math.Sqrt (ant.Result))
  .ContinueWith (ant => Console.WriteLine (ant.Result));   // 4
```

Our example is somewhat contrived for simplicity; in real life, these lambda expressions would call computationally intensive functions.

Continuations and exceptions

A continuation can find out if an exception was thrown by the antecedent via the antecedent task's Exception property. The following writes the details of a NullReferenceException to the console:

```
Task task1 = Task.Factory.StartNew (() => { throw null; });
Task task2 = task1.ContinueWith (ant => Console.Write (ant.Exception));
```

> If an antecedent throws and the continuation fails to query the antecedent's Exception property (and the antecedent isn't otherwise waited upon), the exception is considered unhandled and the application dies (unless handled by TaskScheduler.Unob servedTaskException).

A safe pattern is to rethrow antecedent exceptions. As long as the continuation is Waited upon, the exception will be propagated and rethrown to the Waiter:

```
Task continuation = Task.Factory.StartNew      (() => { throw null; })
                                    .ContinueWith (ant =>
    {
      if (ant.Exception != null) throw ant.Exception;
      // Continue processing...
    });

continuation.Wait();     // Exception is now thrown back to caller.
```

Another way to deal with exceptions is to specify different continuations for exceptional versus nonexceptional outcomes. This is done with TaskContinuationOptions:

```
Task task1 = Task.Factory.StartNew (() => { throw null; });

Task error = task1.ContinueWith (ant => Console.Write (ant.Exception),
                          TaskContinuationOptions.OnlyOnFaulted);

Task ok = task1.ContinueWith (ant => Console.Write ("Success!"),
                          TaskContinuationOptions.NotOnFaulted);
```

This pattern is particularly useful in conjunction with child tasks, as we'll see very soon.

The following extension method "swallows" a task's unhandled exceptions:

```
public static void IgnoreExceptions (this Task task)
{
    task.ContinueWith (t => { var ignore = t.Exception; },
      TaskContinuationOptions.OnlyOnFaulted);
}
```

(This could be improved by adding code to log the exception.) Here's how it would be used:

```
Task.Factory.StartNew (() => { throw null; }).IgnoreExceptions();
```

Continuations and child tasks

A powerful feature of continuations is that they kick off only when all child tasks have completed (see Figure 22-5). At that point, any exceptions thrown by the children are marshaled to the continuation.

In the following example, we start three child tasks, each throwing a NullReferenceException. We then catch all of them in one fell swoop via a continuation on the parent:

```
TaskCreationOptions atp = TaskCreationOptions.AttachedToParent;
Task.Factory.StartNew (() =>
{
    Task.Factory.StartNew (() => { throw null; }, atp);
    Task.Factory.StartNew (() => { throw null; }, atp);
    Task.Factory.StartNew (() => { throw null; }, atp);
})
.ContinueWith (p => Console.WriteLine (p.Exception),
                TaskContinuationOptions.OnlyOnFaulted);
```

Conditional continuations

By default, a continuation is scheduled *unconditionally*—whether the antecedent completes, throws an exception, or is canceled. You can alter this behavior via a set of (combinable) flags included within the `TaskContinuationOptions` enum. The three core flags that control conditional continuation are:

```
NotOnRanToCompletion = 0x10000,
NotOnFaulted = 0x20000,
NotOnCanceled = 0x40000,
```

These flags are subtractive in the sense that the more you apply, the less likely the continuation is to execute. For convenience, there are also the following precombined values:

```
OnlyOnRanToCompletion = NotOnFaulted | NotOnCanceled,
OnlyOnFaulted = NotOnRanToCompletion | NotOnCanceled,
OnlyOnCanceled = NotOnRanToCompletion | NotOnFaulted
```

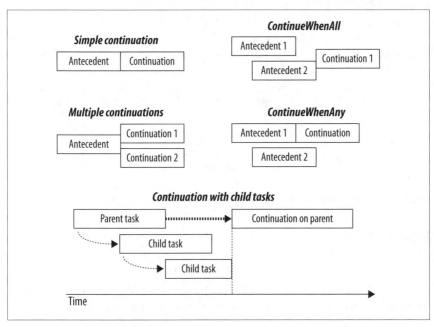

Figure 22-5. Continuations

(Combining all the `Not*` flags [`NotOnRanToCompletion`, `NotOnFaulted`, `NotOnCanceled`] is nonsensical, as it would result in the continuation always being canceled.)

"RanToCompletion" means the antecedent succeeded—without cancellation or unhandled exceptions.

"Faulted" means an unhandled exception was thrown on the antecedent.

"Canceled" means one of two things:

- The antecedent was canceled via its cancellation token. In other words, an `OperationCanceledException` was thrown on the antecedent—whose `CancellationToken` property matched that passed to the antecedent when it was started.

- The antecedent was implicitly canceled because *it* didn't satisfy a conditional continuation predicate.

It's essential to grasp that when a continuation doesn't execute by virtue of these flags, the continuation is not forgotten or abandoned—it's *canceled*. This means that any continuations on the continuation itself *will then run*—unless you predicate them with `NotOnCanceled`. For example, consider this:

```
Task t1 = Task.Factory.StartNew (...);

Task fault = t1.ContinueWith (ant => Console.WriteLine ("fault"),
                              TaskContinuationOptions.OnlyOnFaulted);

Task t3 = fault.ContinueWith (ant => Console.WriteLine ("t3"));
```

As it stands, `t3` will always get scheduled—even if `t1` doesn't throw an exception (see Figure 22-6). This is because if `t1` succeeds, the `fault` task will be *canceled*, and with no continuation restrictions placed on `t3`, `t3` will then execute unconditionally.

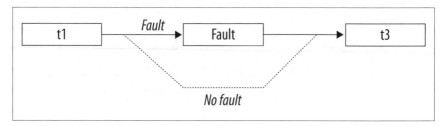

Figure 22-6. Conditional continuations

If we want `t3` to execute only if `fault` actually runs, we must instead do this:

```
Task t3 = fault.ContinueWith (ant => Console.WriteLine ("t3"),
                              TaskContinuationOptions.NotOnCanceled);
```

(Alternatively, we could specify `OnlyOnRanToCompletion`; the difference is that `t3` would not then execute if an exception was thrown within `fault`.)

Continuations with multiple antecedents

Another useful feature of continuations is that you can schedule them to execute based on the completion of multiple antecedents. `ContinueWhenAll` schedules execution when all antecedents have completed; `ContinueWhenAny` schedules execution when one antecedent completes. Both methods are defined in the `TaskFactory` class:

```
var task1 = Task.Factory.StartNew (() => Console.Write ("X"));
var task2 = Task.Factory.StartNew (() => Console.Write ("Y"));

var continuation = Task.Factory.ContinueWhenAll (
  new[] { task1, task2 }, tasks => Console.WriteLine ("Done"));
```

This writes "Done" after writing "XY" or "YX". The `tasks` argument in the lambda expression gives you access to the array of completed tasks, which is useful when the antecedents return data. The following example adds together numbers returned from two antecedent tasks:

```
// task1 and task2 would call complex functions in real life:
Task<int> task1 = Task.Factory.StartNew (() => 123);
Task<int> task2 = Task.Factory.StartNew (() => 456);

Task<int> task3 = Task<int>.Factory.ContinueWhenAll (
  new[] { task1, task2 }, tasks => tasks.Sum (t => t.Result));

Console.WriteLine (task3.Result);          // 579
```

 We've included the `<int>` type argument in our call to `Task.Factory` in this example to clarify that we're obtaining a generic task factory. The type argument is unnecessary, though, as it will be inferred by the compiler.

Multiple continuations on a single antecedent

Calling `ContinueWith` more than once on the same task creates multiple continuations on a single antecedent. When the antecedent finishes, all continuations will start together (unless you specify `TaskContinuationOptions.ExecuteSynchronously`, in which case the continuations will execute sequentially).

The following waits for one second, and then writes either "XY" or "YX":

```
var t = Task.Factory.StartNew (() => Thread.Sleep (1000));
t.ContinueWith (ant => Console.Write ("X"));
t.ContinueWith (ant => Console.Write ("Y"));
```

Task Schedulers and UIs

A *task scheduler* allocates tasks to threads. All tasks are associated with a task scheduler, which is represented by the abstract `TaskScheduler` class. The Framework provides two concrete implementations: the *default scheduler* that works in tandem with the CLR thread pool, and the *synchronization context scheduler*. The latter is designed (primarily) to help you with the threading model of WPF and Windows Forms, which requires that UI elements and controls are accessed only from the thread that created them (see "Rich Client Applications and Thread Affinity" on page 822 in the preceding chapter). For example, suppose we wanted to fetch some data from a web service in the background, and then update a WPF label called `lblResult` with its result. We can divide this into two tasks:

1. Call a method to get data from the web service (antecedent task).
2. Update `lblResult` with the results (continuation task).

If, for a continuation task, we specify the *synchronization context scheduler* obtained when the window was constructed, we can safely update `lblResult`:

```
public partial class MyWindow : Window
{
  TaskScheduler _uiScheduler;    // Declare this as a field so we can use
                                 // it throughout our class.
  public MyWindow()
  {
    InitializeComponent();

    // Get the UI scheduler for the thread that created the form:
    _uiScheduler = TaskScheduler.FromCurrentSynchronizationContext();

    Task.Factory.StartNew<string> (SomeComplexWebService)
      .ContinueWith (ant => lblResult.Content = ant.Result, _uiScheduler);
  }

  string SomeComplexWebService() { ... }
}
```

It's also possible to write our own task scheduler (by subclassing TaskScheduler), although this is something you'd do only in very specialized scenarios. For custom scheduling, you'd more commonly use TaskCompletionSource, which we'll cover soon.

TaskFactory

When you call Task.Factory, you're calling a static property on Task that returns a default TaskFactory object. The purpose of a task factory is to create tasks—specifically, three kinds of tasks:

- "Ordinary" tasks (via StartNew)
- Continuations with multiple antecedents (via ContinueWhenAll and Continue WhenAny)
- Tasks that wrap methods that follow the asynchronous programming model (via FromAsync)

> Interestingly, TaskFactory is the *only* way to achieve the latter two goals. In the case of StartNew, TaskFactory is purely a convenience and technically redundant in that you can simply instantiate Task objects and call Start on them.

We'll talk about FromAsync in the next chapter.

Creating your own task factories

TaskFactory is not an *abstract* factory: you can actually instantiate the class, and this is useful when you want to repeatedly create tasks using the same (nonstandard) values for TaskCreationOptions, TaskContinuationOptions, or TaskScheduler. For example, if we wanted to repeatedly create long-running *parented* tasks, we could create a custom factory as follows:

```
var factory = new TaskFactory (
  TaskCreationOptions.LongRunning | TaskCreationOptions.AttachedToParent,
  TaskContinuationOptions.None);
```

Creating tasks is then simply a matter of calling `StartNew` on the factory:

```
Task task1 = factory.StartNew (Method1);
Task task2 = factory.StartNew (Method2);
...
```

The custom continuation options are applied when calling `ContinueWhenAll` and `ContinueWhenAny`.

TaskCompletionSource

The `Task` class achieves two distinct things:

- It schedules a delegate to run on a pooled thread.
- It offers a rich set of features for managing work items (continuations, child tasks, exception marshaling, etc.).

Interestingly, these two things are not joined at the hip: you can leverage a task's features for managing work items without scheduling anything to run on the thread pool. The class that enables this pattern of use is called `TaskCompletionSource`.

To use `TaskCompletionSource` you simply instantiate the class. It exposes a `Task` property that returns a task upon which you can wait and attach continuations—just like any other task. The task, however, is entirely controlled by the `TaskCompletionSource` object via the following methods:

```
public class TaskCompletionSource<TResult>
{
  public void SetResult (TResult result);
  public void SetException (Exception exception);
  public void SetCanceled();

  public bool TrySetResult (TResult result);
  public bool TrySetException (Exception exception);
  public bool TrySetCanceled();
  ...
}
```

If called more than once, `SetResult`, `SetException`, or `SetCanceled` throws an exception; the `Try*` methods instead return `false`.

> `TResult` corresponds to the task's result type, so `TaskCompletion Source<int>` gives you a `Task<int>`. If you want a task with no result, create a `TaskCompletionSource` of `object` and pass in `null` when calling `SetResult`. You can then cast the `Task<object>` to `Task`.

The following example prints 123 after waiting for 5 seconds:

```
var source = new TaskCompletionSource<int>();

new Thread (() => { Thread.Sleep (5000); source.SetResult (123); })
  .Start();

Task<int> task = source.Task;        // Our "slave" task.
Console.WriteLine (task.Result);     // 123
```

In "Concurrent Collections" on page 914, we show how BlockingCollection
can be used to write a producer/consumer queue. We then demonstrate how
TaskCompletionSource improves the solution by allowing queued work items to be
waited upon and canceled.

Working with AggregateException

As we've seen, PLINQ, the Parallel class, and Tasks automatically marshal exceptions to the consumer. To see why this is essential, consider the following LINQ
query, which throws a DivideByZeroException on the first iteration:

```
try
{
  var query = from i in Enumerable.Range (0, 1000000)
              select 100 / i;
  ...
}
catch (DivideByZeroException)
{
  ...
}
```

If we asked PLINQ to parallelize this query and it ignored the handling of exceptions,
a DivideByZeroException would probably be thrown on a *separate thread*, bypassing
our catch block and causing the application to die.

Hence, exceptions are automatically caught and rethrown to the caller. But unfortunately, it's not quite as simple as catching a DivideByZeroException. Because
these libraries leverage many threads, it's actually possible for two or more exceptions to be thrown simultaneously. To ensure that all exceptions are reported, exceptions are therefore wrapped in an AggregateException container, which exposes
an InnerExceptions property containing each of the caught exception(s):

```
try
{
  var query = from i in Enumerable.Range (0, 1000000)
              select 100 / i;
  // Enumerate query
  ...
}
catch (AggregateException aex)
{
  foreach (Exception ex in aex.InnerExceptions)
    Console.WriteLine (ex.Message);
}
```

Both PLINQ and the `Parallel` class end the query or loop execution upon encountering the first exception—by not processing any further elements or loop bodies. More exceptions might be thrown, however, before the current cycle is complete. The first exception in `AggregateException` is visible in the `InnerException` property.

Flatten and Handle

The `AggregateException` class provides a couple of methods to simplify exception handling: `Flatten` and `Handle`.

Flatten

`AggregateException`s will quite often contain other `AggregateException`s. An example of when this might happen is if a child task throws an exception. You can eliminate any level of nesting to simplify handling by calling `Flatten`. This method returns a new `AggregateException` with a simple flat list of inner exceptions:

```
catch (AggregateException aex)
{
  foreach (Exception ex in aex.Flatten().InnerExceptions)
    myLogWriter.LogException (ex);
}
```

Handle

Sometimes it's useful to catch only specific exception types, and have other types rethrown. The `Handle` method on `AggregateException` provides a shortcut for doing this. It accepts an exception predicate, which it runs over every inner exception:

```
public void Handle (Func<Exception, bool> predicate)
```

If the predicate returns `true`, it considers that exception "handled." After the delegate has run over every exception, the following happens:

- If all exceptions were "handled" (the delegate returned `true`), the exception is not rethrown.
- If there were any exceptions for which the delegate returned `false` ("unhandled"), a new `AggregateException` is built up containing those exceptions, and is rethrown.

For instance, the following ends up rethrowing another `AggregateException` that contains a single `NullReferenceException`:

```
var parent = Task.Factory.StartNew (() =>
{
  // We'll throw 3 exceptions at once using 3 child tasks:

  int[] numbers = { 0 };

  var childFactory = new TaskFactory
    (TaskCreationOptions.AttachedToParent, TaskContinuationOptions.None);
```

```
    childFactory.StartNew (() => 5 / numbers[0]);    // Division by zero
    childFactory.StartNew (() => numbers [1]);       // Index out of range
    childFactory.StartNew (() => { throw null; });   // Null reference
  });

  try { parent.Wait(); }
  catch (AggregateException aex)
  {
    aex.Flatten().Handle (ex =>    // Note that we still need to call Flatten
    {
      if (ex is DivideByZeroException)
      {
        Console.WriteLine ("Divide by zero");
        return true;                          // This exception is "handled"
      }
      if (ex is IndexOutOfRangeException)
      {
        Console.WriteLine ("Index out of range");
        return true;                          // This exception is "handled"
      }
      return false;    // All other exceptions will get rethrown
    });
  }
```

Concurrent Collections

Framework 4.0 provides a set of new collections in the `System.Collections.Concur`
`rent` namespace. All of these are fully thread-safe:

Concurrent collection	Nonconcurrent equivalent
ConcurrentStack<T>	Stack<T>
ConcurrentQueue<T>	Queue<T>
ConcurrentBag<T>	(none)
BlockingCollection<T>	(none)
ConcurrentDictionary<TKey,TValue>	Dictionary<TKey,TValue>

The concurrent collections can sometimes be useful in general multithreading when
you need a thread-safe collection. However, there are some caveats:

- The concurrent collections are tuned for *parallel programming*. The conventional collections outperform them in all but highly concurrent scenarios.
- A thread-safe collection doesn't guarantee that the code using it will be thread-
  safe (see "Thread Safety" on page 543 in the preceding chapter).
- If you enumerate over a concurrent collection while another thread is modifying
  it, no exception is thrown—instead, you get a mixture of old and new content.
- There's no concurrent version of List<T>.

- The concurrent stack, queue, and bag classes are implemented internally with linked lists. This makes them less memory-efficient than the nonconcurrent Stack and Queue classes, but better for concurrent access because linked lists are conducive to lock-free or low-lock implementations. (This is because inserting a node into a linked list requires updating just a couple of references, while inserting an element into a List<T>-like structure may require moving thousands of existing elements.)

In other words, these collections don't merely provide shortcuts for using an ordinary collection with a lock. To demonstrate, if we execute the following code on a *single* thread:

```
var d = new ConcurrentDictionary<int,int>();
for (int i = 0; i < 1000000; i++) d[i] = 123;
```

it runs three times more slowly than this:

```
var d = new Dictionary<int,int>();
for (int i = 0; i < 1000000; i++) lock (d) d[i] = 123;
```

(*Reading* from a ConcurrentDictionary, however, is fast because reads are lock-free.)

The concurrent collections also differ from conventional collections in that they expose special methods to perform atomic test-and-act operations, such as TryPop. Most of these methods are unified via the IProducerConsumerCollection<T> interface.

IProducerConsumerCollection<T>

A producer/consumer collection is one for which the two primary use cases are:

- Adding an element ("producing")
- Retrieving an element while removing it ("consuming")

The classic examples are stacks and queues. Producer/consumer collections are significant in parallel programming because they're conducive to efficient lock-free implementations.

The IProducerConsumerCollection<T> interface represents a thread-safe producer/consumer collection. The following classes implement this interface:

```
ConcurrentStack<T>
ConcurrentQueue<T>
ConcurrentBag<T>
```

IProducerConsumerCollection<T> extends ICollection, adding the following methods:

```
void CopyTo (T[] array, int index);
T[] ToArray();
bool TryAdd (T item);
bool TryTake (out T item);
```

The TryAdd and TryTake methods test whether an add/remove operation can be performed, and if so, they perform the add/remove. The testing and acting are performed atomically, eliminating the need to lock as you would around a conventional collection:

```
int result;
lock (myStack) if (myStack.Count > 0) result = myStack.Pop();
```

TryTake returns false if the collection is empty. TryAdd always succeeds and returns true in the three implementations provided. If you wrote your own concurrent collection that prohibited duplicates, however, you'd make TryAdd return false if the element already existed (an example would be if you wrote a concurrent *set*).

The particular element that TryTake removes is defined by the subclass:

- With a stack, TryTake removes the most recently added element.
- With a queue, TryTake removes the least recently added element.
- With a bag, TryTake removes whatever element it can remove most efficiently.

The three concrete classes mostly implement the TryTake and TryAdd methods explicitly, exposing the same functionality through more specifically named public methods such as TryDequeue and TryPop.

ConcurrentBag<T>

ConcurrentBag<T> stores an *unordered* collection of objects (with duplicates permitted). ConcurrentBag<T> is suitable in situations when you *don't care* which element you get when calling Take or TryTake.

The benefit of ConcurrentBag<T> over a concurrent queue or stack is that a bag's Add method suffers almost *no* contention when called by many threads at once. In contrast, calling Add in parallel on a queue or stack incurs *some* contention (although a lot less than locking around a *nonconcurrent* collection). Calling Take on a concurrent bag is also very efficient—as long as each thread doesn't take more elements than it Added.

Inside a concurrent bag, each thread gets it own private linked list. Elements are added to the private list that belongs to the thread calling Add, eliminating contention. When you enumerate over the bag, the enumerator travels through each thread's private list, yielding each of its elements in turn.

When you call Take, the bag first looks at the current thread's private list. If there's at least one element,[*] it can complete the task easily and without contention. But if the list is empty, it must "steal" an element from another thread's private list and incur the potential for contention.

So, to be precise, calling Take gives you the element added most recently on that thread; if there are no elements on that thread, it gives you the element added most recently on another thread, chosen at random.

---

[*] Due to an implementation detail, there actually needs to be at least two elements to avoid contention entirely.

Concurrent bags are ideal when the parallel operation on your collection mostly comprises Adding elements—or when the Adds and Takes are balanced on a thread. We saw an example of the former previously, when using Parallel.ForEach to implement a parallel spellchecker:

```
var misspellings = new ConcurrentBag<Tuple<int,string>>();

Parallel.ForEach (wordsToTest, (word, state, i) =>
{
  if (!wordLookup.Contains (word))
    misspellings.Add (Tuple.Create ((int) i, word));
});
```

A concurrent bag would be a poor choice for a producer/consumer queue, because elements are added and removed by *different* threads.

BlockingCollection<T>

If you call TryTake on any of the producer/consumer collections we discussed previously:

```
ConcurrentStack<T>
ConcurrentQueue<T>
ConcurrentBag<T>
```

and the collection is empty, the method returns false. Sometimes it would be more useful in this scenario to *wait* until an element is available.

Rather than overloading the TryTake methods with this functionality (which would have caused a blowout of members after allowing for cancellation tokens and timeouts), PFX's designers encapsulated this functionality into a wrapper class called BlockingCollection<T>. A blocking collection wraps any collection that implements IProducerConsumerCollection<T> and lets you Take an element from the wrapped collection—blocking if no element is available.

A blocking collection also lets you limit the total size of the collection, blocking the *producer* if that size is exceeded. A collection limited in this manner is called a *bounded blocking collection*.

To use BlockingCollection<T>:

1. Instantiate the class, optionally specifying the IProducerConsumerCollection<T> to wrap and the maximum size (bound) of the collection.

2. Call Add or TryAdd to add elements to the underlying collection.

3. Call Take or TryTake to remove (consume) elements from the underlying collection.

If you call the constructor without passing in a collection, the class will automatically instantiate a ConcurrentQueue<T>. The producing and consuming methods let you specify cancellation tokens and timeouts. Add and TryAdd may block if the collection size is bounded; Take and TryTake block while the collection is empty.

Another way to consume elements is to call GetConsumingEnumerable. This returns a (potentially) infinite sequence that yields elements as they become available. You can force the sequence to end by calling `CompleteAdding`: this method also prevents further elements from being enqueued.

In the preceding chapter, we wrote a producer/consumer queue using `Wait` and `Pulse` (see "Signaling with Wait and Pulse" on page 840). Here's the same class refactored to use `BlockingCollection<T>` (exception handling aside):

```
public class PCQueue : IDisposable
{
  BlockingCollection<Action> _taskQ = new BlockingCollection<Action>();

  public PCQueue (int workerCount)
  {
    // Create and start a separate Task for each consumer:
    for (int i = 0; i < workerCount; i++)
      Task.Factory.StartNew (Consume);
  }

  public void Dispose() { _taskQ.CompleteAdding(); }

  public void EnqueueTask (Action action) { _taskQ.Add (action); }

  void Consume()
  {
    // This sequence that we're enumerating will block when no elements
    // are available and will end when CompleteAdding is called.

    foreach (Action action in _taskQ.GetConsumingEnumerable())
      action();      // Perform task.
  }
}
```

Because we didn't pass anything into `BlockingCollection`'s constructor, it instantiated a concurrent queue automatically. Had we passed in a `ConcurrentStack`, we'd have ended up with a producer/consumer stack.

`BlockingCollection` also provides static methods called `AddToAny` and `TakeFromAny`, which let you add or take an element while specifying several blocking collections. The action is then honored by the first collection able to service the request.

Leveraging TaskCompletionSource

The producer/consumer that we just wrote is inflexible in that we can't track work items after they've been enqueued. It would be nice if we could:

- Know when a work item has completed.
- Cancel an unstarted work item.
- Deal elegantly with any exceptions thrown by a work item.

An ideal solution would be to have the `EnqueueTask` method return some object giving us the functionality just described. The good news is that a class already exists to do exactly this—the `Task` class. All we need to do is to hijack control of the task via `TaskCompletionSource`:

```csharp
public class PCQueue : IDisposable
{
  class WorkItem
  {
    public readonly TaskCompletionSource<object> TaskSource;
    public readonly Action Action;
    public readonly CancellationToken? CancelToken;

    public WorkItem (
      TaskCompletionSource<object> taskSource,
      Action action,
      CancellationToken? cancelToken)
    {
      TaskSource = taskSource;
      Action = action;
      CancelToken = cancelToken;
    }
  }

  BlockingCollection<WorkItem> _taskQ = new BlockingCollection<WorkItem>();

  public PCQueue (int workerCount)
  {
    // Create and start a separate Task for each consumer:
    for (int i = 0; i < workerCount; i++)
      Task.Factory.StartNew (Consume);
  }

  public void Dispose() { _taskQ.CompleteAdding(); }

  public Task EnqueueTask (Action action)
  {
    return EnqueueTask (action, null);
  }

  public Task EnqueueTask (Action action, CancellationToken? cancelToken)
  {
    var tcs = new TaskCompletionSource<object>();
    _taskQ.Add (new WorkItem (tcs, action, cancelToken));
    return tcs.Task;
  }

  void Consume()
  {
    foreach (WorkItem workItem in _taskQ.GetConsumingEnumerable())
      if (workItem.CancelToken.HasValue &&
          workItem.CancelToken.Value.IsCancellationRequested)
      {
        workItem.TaskSource.SetCanceled();
      }
      else
        try
        {
          workItem.Action();
          workItem.TaskSource.SetResult (null);   // Indicate completion
        }
```

```
      catch (Exception ex)
      {
        workItem.TaskSource.SetException (ex);
      }
    }
  }
```

In `EnqueueTask`, we enqueue a work item which encapsulates the target delegate and a task completion source—which lets us later control the task that we return to the consumer.

In `Consume`, we first check whether a task has been canceled after dequeuing the work item. If not, we run the delegate and then call `SetResult` on the task completion source to indicate its completion.

Here's how we can use this class:

```
var pcQ = new PCQueue (1);
Task task = pcQ.EnqueueTask (() => Console.WriteLine ("Easy!"));
...
```

We can now wait on `task`, perform continuations on it, have exceptions propagate to continuations on parent tasks, and so on. In other words, we've got the richness of the task model while, in effect, implementing our own scheduler.

SpinLock and SpinWait

In parallel programming, a brief episode of spinning is often preferable to blocking, as it avoids the cost of context switching and kernel transitions. `SpinLock` and `Spin Wait` are designed to help in such cases. Their main use is in writing custom synchronization constructs.

 `SpinLock` and `SpinWait` are structs and not classes! This design decision was an extreme optimization technique to avoid the cost of indirection and garbage collection. It means that you must be careful not to unintentionally *copy* instances—by passing them to another method without the `ref` modifier, for instance, or declaring them as `readonly` fields. This is particularly important in the case of `SpinLock`.

SpinLock

The `SpinLock` struct lets you lock without incurring the cost of a context switch, at the expense of keeping a thread spinning (uselessly busy). This approach is valid in high-contention scenarios when locking will be very brief (e.g., in writing a thread-safe linked list from scratch).

If you leave a spinlock contended for too long (we're talking milliseconds at most), it will yield its time slice, causing a context switch just like an ordinary lock. When rescheduled, it will yield again—in a continual cycle of "spin yielding." This consumes far fewer CPU resources than outright spinning—but more than blocking.

On a single-core machine, a spinlock will start "spin-yielding" immediately if contended.

Using a `SpinLock` is like using an ordinary lock, except:

- Spinlocks are structs (as previously mentioned).
- Spinlocks are not reentrant, meaning that you cannot call `Enter` on the same `SpinLock` twice in a row on the same thread. If you violate this rule, it will either throw an exception (if *owner tracking* is enabled) or deadlock (if owner tracking is disabled). You can specify whether to enable owner tracking when constructing the spinlock. Owner tracking incurs a performance hit.
- `SpinLock` lets you query whether the lock is taken, via the properties `IsHeld` and, if owner tracking is enabled, `IsHeldByCurrentThread`.
- There's no equivalent to C#'s `lock` statement to provide `SpinLock` syntactic sugar.

Another difference is that when you call `Enter`, you *must* follow the robust pattern of providing a `lockTaken` argument (which is nearly always done within a `try/finally` block).

Here's an example:

```
var spinLock = new SpinLock (true);   // Enable owner tracking
bool lockTaken = false;
try
{
  spinLock.Enter (ref lockTaken);
  // Do stuff...
}
finally
{
  if (lockTaken) spinLock.Exit();
}
```

As with an ordinary lock, `lockTaken` will be `false` after calling `Enter` if (and only if) the `Enter` method throws an exception and the lock was not taken. This happens in very rare scenarios (such as `Abort` being called on the thread, or an `OutOfMemoryException` being thrown) and reliably lets you know whether to subsequently call `Exit`.

`SpinLock` also provides a `TryEnter` method, which accepts a timeout.

Given SpinLock's ungainly value-type semantics and lack of language support, it's almost as if they *want* you to suffer every time you use it! Think carefully before dismissing an ordinary lock.

A SpinLock makes the most sense when writing your own reusable synchronization constructs. Even then, a spinlock is not as useful as it sounds. It still limits concurrency. And it wastes CPU time doing *nothing useful*. Often, a better choice is to spend some of that time doing something *speculative*—with the help of SpinWait.

SpinWait

SpinWait helps you write lock-free code that spins rather than blocks. It works by implementing safeguards to avoid the dangers of resource starvation and priority inversion that might otherwise arise with spinning.

Lock-free programming with SpinWait is as *hardcore* as multi-threading gets and is intended for when none of the higher-level constructs will do. A prerequisite is to understand "Nonblocking Synchronization" on page 825 in the previous chapter.

Why we need SpinWait

Suppose we wrote a spin-based signaling system based purely on a simple flag:

```
bool _proceed;
void Test()
{
  // Spin until another thread sets _proceed to true:
  while (!_proceed) Thread.MemoryBarrier();
  ...
}
```

This would be highly efficient if Test ran when _proceed was already true—or if _proceed became true within a few cycles. But now suppose that _proceed remained false for several seconds—and that four threads called Test at once. The spinning would then fully consume a quad-core CPU! This would cause other threads to run slowly (resource starvation)—including the very thread that might eventually set _proceed to true (priority inversion). The situation is exacerbated on single-core machines, where spinning will nearly *always* cause priority inversion. (And although single-core machines are rare nowadays, single-core *virtual machines* are not.)

SpinWait addresses these problems in two ways. First, it limits CPU-intensive spinning to a set number of iterations, after which it yields its time slice on every spin (by calling Thread.Yield and Thread.Sleep), lowering its resource consumption. Second, it detects whether it's running on a single-core machine, and if so, it yields on every cycle.

How to use SpinWait

There are two ways to use SpinWait. The first is to call its static method, SpinUntil. This method accepts a predicate (and optionally, a timeout):

```
bool _proceed;
void Test()
{
  SpinWait.SpinUntil (() => { Thread.MemoryBarrier(); return _proceed; });
  ...
}
```

The other (more flexible) way to use SpinWait is to instantiate the struct and then to call SpinOnce in a loop:

```
bool _proceed;
void Test()
{
  var spinWait = new SpinWait();
  while (!_proceed) { Thread.MemoryBarrier(); spinWait.SpinOnce(); }
  ...
}
```

The former is a shortcut for the latter.

How SpinWait works

In its current implementation, SpinWait performs CPU-intensive spinning for 10 iterations before yielding. However, it doesn't return to the caller *immediately* after each of those cycles: instead, it calls Thread.SpinWait to spin via the CLR (and ultimately the operating system) for a set time period. This time period is initially a few tens of nanoseconds, but doubles with each iteration until the 10 iterations are up. This ensures some predictability in the total time spent in the CPU-intensive spinning phase, which the CLR and operating system can tune according to conditions. Typically, it's in the few-tens-of-microseconds region—small, but more than the cost of a context switch.

On a single-core machine, SpinWait yields on every iteration. You can test whether SpinWait will yield on the next spin via the property NextSpinWillYield.

If a SpinWait remains in "spin-yielding" mode for long enough (maybe 20 cycles) it will periodically *sleep* for a few milliseconds to further save resources and help other threads progress.

Lock-free updates with SpinWait and Interlocked.CompareExchange

SpinWait in conjunction with Interlocked.CompareExchange can atomically update fields with a value calculated from the original (read-modify-write). For example, suppose we want to multiply field x by 10. Simply doing the following is not thread-safe:

```
x = x * 10;
```

for the same reason that incrementing a field is not thread-safe, as we saw in "Nonblocking Synchronization" on page 825 in the preceding chapter.

The correct way to do this without locks is as follows:

1. Take a "snapshot" of *x* into a local variable.
2. Calculate the new value (in this case by multiplying the snapshot by 10).
3. Write the calculated value back *if* the snapshot is still up-to-date (this step must be done atomically by calling `Interlocked.CompareExchange`).
4. If the snapshot was stale, *spin* and return to step 1.

For example:

```
int x;

void MultiplyXBy (int factor)
{
  var spinWait = new SpinWait();
  while (true)
  {
    int snapshot1 = x;
    Thread.MemoryBarrier();
    int calc = snapshot1 * factor;
    int snapshot2 = Interlocked.CompareExchange (ref x, calc, snapshot1);
    if (snapshot1 == snapshot2) return;   // No one preempted us.
    spinWait.SpinOnce();
  }
}
```

We can improve performance (slightly) by doing away with the call to `Thread.MemoryBarrier`. We can get away with this because `CompareExchange` generates a memory barrier anyway—so the worst that can happen is an extra spin if `snapshot1` happens to read a stale value in its first iteration.

`Interlocked.CompareExchange` updates a field with a specified value *if* the field's current value matches the third argument. It then returns the field's old value, so you can test whether it succeeded by comparing that against the original snapshot. If the values differ, it means that another thread preempted you, in which case you spin and try again.

`CompareExchange` is overloaded to work with the `object` type, too. We can leverage this overload by writing a lock-free update method that works with all reference types:

```
static void LockFreeUpdate<T> (ref T field, Func <T, T> updateFunction)
  where T : class
{
  var spinWait = new SpinWait();
  while (true)
  {
    T snapshot1 = field;
    T calc = updateFunction (snapshot1);
    T snapshot2 = Interlocked.CompareExchange (ref field, calc, snapshot1);
    if (snapshot1 == snapshot2) return;
```

```
    spinWait.SpinOnce();
  }
}
```

Here's how we can use this method to write a thread-safe event without locks (this is, in fact, what the C# 4.0 compiler now does by default with events):

```
EventHandler _someDelegate;
public event EventHandler SomeEvent
{
  add    { LockFreeUpdate (ref _someDelegate, d => d + value); }
  remove { LockFreeUpdate (ref _someDelegate, d => d - value); }
}
```

SpinWait Versus SpinLock

We could solve these problems instead by wrapping access to the shared field around a SpinLock. The problem with spin locking, though, is that it allows only one thread to proceed at a time—even though the spinlock (usually) eliminates the context-switching overhead. With SpinWait, we can proceed speculatively and *assume* no contention. If we do get preempted, we simply try again. Spending CPU time doing something that *might* work is better than wasting CPU time in a spinlock!

Finally, consider the following class:

```
class Test
{
  ProgressStatus _status = new ProgressStatus (0, "Starting");

  class ProgressStatus     // Immutable class
  {
    public readonly int PercentComplete;
    public readonly string StatusMessage;

    public ProgressStatus (int percentComplete, string statusMessage)
    {
      PercentComplete = percentComplete;
      StatusMessage = statusMessage;
    }
  }
}
```

We can use our LockFreeUpdate method to "increment" the PercentComplete field in _status as follows:

```
LockFreeUpdate (ref _status,
  s => new ProgressStatus (s.PercentComplete + 1, s.StatusMessage));
```

Notice that we're creating a new ProgressStatus object based on existing values. Thanks to the LockFreeUpdate method, the act of reading the existing PercentComplete value, incrementing it, and writing it back can't get *unsafely* preempted: any preemption is reliably detected, triggering a spin and retry.

23

Asynchronous Methods

In Chapter 21, we saw how a thread provides a parallel execution path. We took for granted that whenever you needed to run something in parallel, you could assign a new or pooled thread to the job. Although this usually holds true, there are exceptions. Suppose you were writing a TCP sockets or web server application that needed to process 1,000 concurrent client requests. If you dedicated a thread to each incoming request, you would consume (by default) a gigabyte of memory purely on thread overhead.

Asynchronous methods address this problem through a pattern by which many concurrent activities are handled by a few pooled threads. This makes it possible to write highly concurrent applications—as well as highly *thread-efficient* applications.

To avoid getting lost, you'll need to be familiar with threading (Chapter 21) and streams (Chapter 14).

Why Asynchronous Methods Exist

The problem just described might be insoluble if every thread needed to be busy all of the time. But this is not the case: fetching a web page, for instance, might take up to several seconds from start to end (because of a potentially slow connection) and yet consume only a fraction of a millisecond of CPU time in total. Processing an HTTP request and response is not computationally intensive.

This means that a server thread dedicated to processing a single client request might spend 99% of its time blocked—representing huge economy potential. The *asynchronous method* pattern (also called the *asynchronous programming model* or APM) exploits just this potential, allowing a handful of fully utilized threads to take on thousands of concurrent jobs.

If you don't need such concurrency, avoid the APM; it will unnecessarily complicate your program. Further, asynchronous methods are not guaranteed to execute in parallel with the caller. If you need parallel execution, consider using a TPL `Task` or `BackgroundWorker`—or simply starting a new thread.

An asynchronous method aims never to block *any thread*, instead using a pattern of returning with a callback. (Blocking means entering a `WaitSleepJoin` state—or causing another thread to do the same—"wasting" a precious thread resource.) To achieve this, an asynchronous method must abstain from calling any blocking method.

The end goal of the APM is thread economy. This means that blocking *briefly* is OK—such as when locking around reading/writing fields.

A method that takes a while to execute because it performs computationally intensive work does not violate the APM. The purpose of asynchronous methods isn't to provide a convenient mechanism for executing a method in parallel with the caller; it's to *optimize thread resources*. Here's the golden rule of the APM:

> Make good use of the CPU, or exit with a callback!

This means an asynchronous method such as `BeginRead` may not return immediately to the caller. It can make the caller wait as long as it likes—while making good use of the processor or another constrained resource. It can even finish the entire task synchronously—providing it never blocked and never caused another thread to do the same.

 There is an exception to the don't-block rule. It's generally OK to block while calling a database server—if other threads are competing for the same server. This is because in a highly concurrent system, the database must be designed such that the majority of queries execute extremely quickly. If you end up with thousands of concurrent queries, it means that requests are hitting the database server *faster than it can process them*. Thread economy is then the least of your worries!

Similarly, reading or writing to a local hard drive *synchronously* is usually fine: concurrent I/O will choke the local filesystem *way* before exhausting the thread pool.

The primary use for asynchronous methods is handling many potentially long-running concurrent requests—typically over slow network connections.

Asynchronous Method Signatures

Asynchronous methods, by convention, all start with *Begin*, have a pairing method starting with *End*, and have signatures like those of asynchronous delegates:

```
IAsyncResult BeginXXX (in/ref-args, AsyncCallback callback, object state);

return-type EndXXX (out/ref-args, IAsyncResult asyncResult);
```

Here's an example from the Stream class:

```
public IAsyncResult BeginRead (byte[] buffer, int offset, int size,
                               AsyncCallback callback, object state);
public int EndRead (IAsyncResult asyncResult);
```

The Begin method returns an IAsyncResult object, which helps you to manage the asynchronous operation (as we'll see shortly). That same object is then passed to the completion callback. Here's its delegate:

```
public delegate void AsyncCallback (IAsyncResult ar);
```

As with asynchronous delegates, the EndXXX method allows the return value to be retrieved, as well as any out/ref arguments. This is also where exceptions are rethrown.

 If you fail to call the EndXXX method, exceptions won't get rethrown (meaning silent failure) and resources may circumvent cleanup.

To avoid blocking, you will nearly always call the EndXXX method from inside the callback method. Callbacks always run on pooled threads.

IAsyncResult

The IAsyncResult interface is defined as follows:

```
public interface IAsyncResult
{
  object AsyncState { get; }              // "state" object passed to Begin.
  WaitHandle AsyncWaitHandle { get; }     // Signaled when complete.
  bool CompletedSynchronously { get; }    // Did it complete on BeginX?
  bool IsCompleted { get; }               // Has it completed yet?
}
```

AsyncState lets you access the state argument passed to the BeginXXX method.

The wait handle is signaled when the operation is complete. To wait on this without blocking, call ThreadPool.RegisterWaitForSingleObject:

```
ThreadPool.RegisterWaitForSingleObject (
  result.AsyncWaitHandle,
  (data, timedOut) => { /* Callback */ },
  null, -1, true);
```

The CompletedSynchronously property indicates that the operation finished immediately after calling the BeginXXX method. This may be true for one of three reasons:

- The operation could be completed very quickly—and so was executed synchronously to avoid the overhead of managing an asynchronous operation.

- The underlying implementation—or operating system—doesn't support APM in that scenario.
- The operation was CPU-bound and could be completed without blocking.

When this property returns `true`, the callback will still be fired—but possibly on the *same thread* as that which called `BeginXXX`. Failing to consider this possibility can sometimes result in unintended recursion, leading to a stack overflow.

Asynchronous Methods Versus Asynchronous Delegates

Asynchronous delegate invocations implement the same pattern with their method signatures—but without the goal of thread economy:

Asynchronous methods	Asynchronous delegate invocations
Rarely or never blocks any thread	May block threads for any length of time (although not the calling thread)
Begin method may not return immediately to the caller	BeginInvoke returns immediately to the caller

The purpose of asynchronous methods is to allow many tasks to run on few threads; the purpose of asynchronous delegates is to execute a task in parallel with the caller.

You can use an asynchronous delegate to call an asynchronous method—so that execution is guaranteed to return immediately to the caller, while still following the APM. Or better: you can use Framework 4.0's new `Task` class to wrap an asynchronous method call to simplify management (we'll explain how to do this later in the chapter).

If you use an asynchronous delegate to call a blocking method, however, you're back to square one: the server will either suffer limited concurrency or need thousands of threads to do its job.

Using Asynchronous Methods

Let's rite a simple TCP sockets server that behaves as follows:

1. It waits for a client request.
2. It reads a 5,000-byte fixed-length message.
3. It reverses the bytes in the message, and then returns them to the client.

Let's first write this using a standard multithreaded *blocking* pattern. Here is the code, exception handling aside:

You can download a Visual Studio project containing all the code in this chapter—along with a client test harness—at *http: //www.albahari.com/nutshell/async40.zip*.

```
using System;
using System.Threading;
using System.Net;
using System.Net.Sockets;

public class Server
{
  public void Serve (IPAddress address, int port)
  {
    ThreadPool.SetMinThreads (50, 50);    // Refer to Chapter 21
    ThreadPool.SetMaxThreads (50, 50);    // Refer to Chapter 21
    TcpListener listener = new TcpListener (address, port);
    listener.Start();
    while (true)
    {
      TcpClient c = listener.AcceptTcpClient();
      ThreadPool.QueueUserWorkItem (Accept, c);
    }
  }

  void Accept (object clientObject)
  {
    using (TcpClient client = (TcpClient) clientObject)
    using (NetworkStream n = client.GetStream())
    {
      byte[] data = new byte [5000];

      int bytesRead = 0; int chunkSize = 1;
      while (bytesRead < data.Length && chunkSize > 0)
        bytesRead +=
          chunkSize = n.Read
            (data, bytesRead, data.Length - bytesRead);    // BLOCKS

      Array.Reverse (data);
      n.Write (data, 0, data.Length);                      // BLOCKS
    }
  }
}
```

 From Framework 4.0, you can replace ThreadPool.QueueUser
WorkItem with Task.Factory.StartNew. The end result is the
same.

Our use of the thread pool prevents an arbitrarily large number of threads from being created (possibly taking down the server) and eliminates the time wasted in creating a new thread per request. Our program is simple and fast, but it is limited to 50 concurrent requests.

In order to scale to 1,000 concurrent requests—without increasing the thread count—we must employ the asynchronous method pattern. This means avoiding the blocking I/O methods altogether and instead calling their asynchronous counterparts. Here's how to do it:

```
public class Server
{
  public void Serve (IPAddress address, int port)
  {
    ThreadPool.SetMinThreads (50, 50);
    TcpListener listener = new TcpListener (address, port);
    listener.Start();
    while (true)
    {
      TcpClient c = listener.AcceptTcpClient();
      ThreadPool.QueueUserWorkItem (ReverseEcho, c);
    }
  }

  void ReverseEcho (object client)
  {
    new ReverseEcho().Begin ((TcpClient)client);
  }
}

class ReverseEcho
{
  TcpClient _client;
  NetworkStream _stream;
  byte[] _data = new byte [5000];
  int _bytesRead = 0;

  internal void Begin (TcpClient c)
  {
    try
    {
      _client = c;
      _stream = c.GetStream();
      Read();
    }
    catch (Exception ex) { ProcessException (ex); }
  }

  void Read()               // Read in a nonblocking fashion.
  {
    while (true)
    {
      IAsyncResult r = _stream.BeginRead
        (_data, _bytesRead, _data.Length - _bytesRead, ReadCallback, null);

      // This will nearly always return in the next line:
      if (!r.CompletedSynchronously) return;   // Handled by callback
      if (!EndRead (r)) break;
    }
    Write();
  }

  void ReadCallback (IAsyncResult r)
  {
    try
    {
```

```
      if (r.CompletedSynchronously) return;
      if (EndRead (r))
      {
        Read();          // More data to read!
        return;
      }
      Write();
    }
    catch (Exception ex) { ProcessException (ex); }
  }

  bool EndRead (IAsyncResult r)    // Returns false if there's no more data
  {
    int chunkSize = _stream.EndRead (r);
    _bytesRead += chunkSize;
    return chunkSize > 0 && _bytesRead < _data.Length;    // More to read
  }

  void Write()
  {
    Array.Reverse (_data);
    _stream.BeginWrite (_data, 0, _data.Length, WriteCallback, null);
  }

  void WriteCallback (IAsyncResult r)
  {
    try { _stream.EndWrite (r); }
    catch (Exception ex) { ProcessException (ex); }
    Cleanup();
  }

  void ProcessException (Exception ex)
  {
    Cleanup();
    Console.WriteLine ("Error: " + ex.Message);
  }

  void Cleanup()
  {
    if (_stream != null) _stream.Close();
    if (_client != null) _client.Close();
  }
}
```

This program will handle 1,000 concurrent requests on fewer than 10 pooled threads.

Each client request is processed without calling any blocking methods (aside from the call to listener.AcceptTcpClient in the Serve method, which blocks just one thread).

In the Read method, we start by calling BeginRead on the stream, specifying a completion callback. We could simplify the entire method as follows and get the same result:

```
void Read()
{
  _stream.BeginRead
    (_data, _bytesRead, _data.Length - _bytesRead, ReadCallback, null);
}
```

However, there's a small chance that BeginRead could finish synchronously and then call ReadCallback on the same thread. Because ReadCallback calls Read again, this might lead to some fairly deep recursion and a stack overflow. To protect against this, we must check CompletedSynchronously after calling BeginRead, and if it returns true, use a *loop* to call Read until completion rather than relying on the potentially recursive call in ReadCallback.

This leads to why we called AcceptTcpClient in the Serve method—instead of its asynchronous version, BeginAcceptTcpClient. For the benefit of saving one thread, the latter would require the same pattern of use as with BeginRead to avoid a possible stack overflow.

The ReverseEcho class encapsulates a request's state for its lifetime. We can no longer use local variables for this job, because the execution stack disappears each time we exit (after each call to an asynchronous method). This also complicates cleanup and means that a simple using statement is no longer suitable for closing our TcpClient and stream.

Another complicating factor is that we can't use types such as BinaryReader and BinaryWriter, because they don't offer asynchronous versions of their methods. The asynchronous pattern often forces you to work at a lower level than you might otherwise.

Asynchronous Methods and Tasks

We saw in the preceding chapter how Framework 4.0's Task class can manage a unit of work that runs on a pooled thread. You can also use a Task to wrap asynchronous method calls—via the FromAsync method on TaskFactory.

The task that you get from calling FromAsync is merely a lightweight wrapper over calling a BeginXXX and EndXXX method—it does not get *scheduled* like an ordinary task. The reason to use FromAsync is to leverage features such as continuations and child tasks. FromAsync is internally implemented using TaskCompletionSource.

The FromAsync method requires the following parameters:

- A delegate specifying a BeginXXX method
- A delegate specifying an EndXXX method
- Additional arguments that will get passed to these methods

FromAsync is overloaded to accept delegate types and arguments that match nearly all the asynchronous method signatures found in the .NET Framework. For instance, assuming stream is a Stream, instead of doing this:

```
var buffer = new byte[1000];
stream.BeginRead (buffer, 0, 1000, MyCallback, null);
```

```
...
void MyCallback (IAsyncResult r)
{
  int bytesRead;
  try { bytesRead = stream.EndWrite (r); }
  catch (Exception ex) { Console.Write (ex.Message); }
  Console.Write (bytesRead + " bytes read");
}
```

we can do this:

```
var buffer = new byte[1000];

Task<int> readChunk = Task<int>.Factory.FromAsync (
  stream.BeginRead, stream.EndRead, buffer, 0, 1000, null);

readChunk.ContinueWith (ant => Console.Write (ant.Result + " bytes read"),
                        TaskContinuationOptions.NotOnFaulted);

readChunk.ContinueWith (ant => Console.Write (ant.Exception.Message),
                        TaskContinuationOptions.OnlyOnFaulted);
```

This doesn't deliver a huge saving in itself: the real benefit comes when you introduce
continuations with child antecedents. Revisiting our earlier example, suppose that
we refactor ReverseEcho's Begin method so that it calls Read on a new task. This
liberates Server.Serve from having to create a task itself, but more importantly, it
creates a parent for the FromAsync-created tasks upon which we can attach continuations. This avoids having to write separate exception-handling blocks or explicit
fault continuations for each child task. Cleanup can also be done easily as another
continuation on the parent:

```
public class Server
{
  public void Serve (IPAddress address, int port)
  {
    ThreadPool.SetMinThreads (50, 50);
    TcpListener listener = new TcpListener (address, port);
    listener.Start();
    while (true)
    {
      TcpClient c = listener.AcceptTcpClient();
      new ReverseEcho().BeginAsync (c);
    }
  }
}

class ReverseEcho
{
  TcpClient _client;
  NetworkStream _stream;
  byte[] _data = new byte [5000];
  int _bytesRead = 0;

  internal void BeginAsync (TcpClient c)
  {
    _client = c;
```

```
    _stream = c.GetStream();

    var task = Task.Factory.StartNew (Read);

    // Set up centralized error handling and cleanup:

    task.ContinueWith (ant =>
      Console.WriteLine ("Error: " + ant.Exception.Message),
      TaskContinuationOptions.OnlyOnFaulted);

    task.ContinueWith (ant =>
    {
      if (_stream != null) _stream.Close();
      if (_client != null) _client.Close();
    });
  }

  void Read()     // This will create a child task.
  {
    Task<int> readChunk = Task<int>.Factory.FromAsync (
      _stream.BeginRead, _stream.EndRead,
      _data, _bytesRead, _data.Length - _bytesRead, null,
      TaskCreationOptions.AttachedToParent);

    readChunk.ContinueWith (Write, TaskContinuationOptions.NotOnFaulted
                                 | TaskCreationOptions.AttachedToParent);
  }


  void Write (Task<int> readChunk)
  {
    _bytesRead += readChunk.Result;
    if (readChunk.Result > 0 && _bytesRead < _data.Length)
    {
      Read();       // More data to read!
      return;
    }
    Array.Reverse (_data);
    Task.Factory.FromAsync (_stream.BeginWrite, _stream.EndWrite,
                            _data, 0, _data.Length, null,
                            TaskCreationOptions.AttachedToParent);
  }
}
```

We also need not worry about Read going recursive and performing a stack dive: continuations don't happen synchronously unless you tell them to.

Asynchronous Methods and Iterators

In Visual Studio 2010's parallel programming samples for PFX, you'll find an extension method on TaskFactory called Iterate. With this, you can move the logic from the ReverseEcho class in our sample into a single iterator method. This is a terrific pattern in simple scenarios because it means you can replace ReverseEcho and its fields with a simple method with local variables. Here's our Server class refactored:

```
public class Server
{
  public void Serve (IPAddress address, int port)
  {
    ThreadPool.SetMinThreads (50, 50);
    TcpListener listener = new TcpListener (address, port);
    listener.Start();
    while (true)
    {
      TcpClient c = listener.AcceptTcpClient();
      Task.Factory.Iterate (ReverseEcho(c)).ContinueWith (t =>
        Console.WriteLine ("Error: " + t.Exception.Message),
        TaskContinuationOptions.OnlyOnFaulted);
    }
  }

  IEnumerable<Task> ReverseEcho (TcpClient client)
  {
    using (client)
    using (var stream = client.GetStream())
    {
      byte[] data = new byte[Program.MessageLength];
      int bytesRead = 0;
      while (true)
      {
        // ReadASync is an extension method in the samples.
        Task<int> readChunk = stream.ReadAsync
          (data, bytesRead, data.Length - bytesRead);
        yield return readChunk;
        bytesRead += readChunk.Result;
        if (readChunk.Result <= 0 || bytesRead >= data.Length)
          break;
      }
      Array.Reverse(data);
      yield return stream.WriteAsync (data, 0, bytesRead);
    }
  }
}
```

In more complex cases, however, having a class is helpful because you can abstract the code into as many methods (and classes) as you like. The problem with an iterator is that any methods that you call from the iterator can't themselves yield on behalf of the caller, and this cramps your ability to refactor large code blocks.

Writing Asynchronous Methods

Returning to our previous example, suppose that the 5,000-byte exchange was just a small part of a more sophisticated communication protocol. It would be nice to turn what we've already written into a method like this:

```
public byte[] ReverseEcho (TcpClient client);
```

The problem, of course, is that this method signature is synchronous; we need to offer an asynchronous version—in other words, BeginReverseEcho. Further, if an exception is encountered, it's no good writing it to the Console; we need to throw it back to the consumer at some point. So, to usefully partake in the pattern, we must also offer EndReverseEcho and write a class that implements IAsyncResult.

Our ReverseEcho class is an excellent candidate for IAsyncResult, since it already encapsulates the operation's state. All we really need to add is some plumbing code to rethrow any exception upon calling EndReverseEcho, and a wait handle to signal at completion.

Here's a real-world example, complete with exception handling and thread safety:

```
// This sample can be downloaded at http://www.albahari.com/nutshell/

public class MessagingServices
{
    public static IAsyncResult BeginReverseEcho (TcpClient client,
                                                 AsyncCallback callback,
                                                 object userState)
    {
        var re = new ReverseEcho();
        re.Begin (client, callback, userState);
        return re;
    }

    public static byte[] EndReverseEcho (IAsyncResult r)
    {
        return ((ReverseEcho)r).End();
    }
}

class ReverseEcho : IAsyncResult
{
    TcpClient _client;
    NetworkStream _stream;
    object _userState;
    ManualResetEvent _waitHandle = new ManualResetEvent (false);
    int _bytesRead = 0;
    byte[] _data = new byte [5000];
    Exception _exception;

    internal ReverseEcho() { }

    // IAsyncResult members:

    public object AsyncState { get { return _userState; } }
    public WaitHandle AsyncWaitHandle { get { return _waitHandle; } }
    public bool CompletedSynchronously { get { return false; } }
    public bool IsCompleted
    {
        get { return _waitHandle.WaitOne (0, false); }
    }

    internal void Begin (TcpClient c, AsyncCallback callback, object state)
    {
        _client = c;
        _userState = state;
```

```
_stream = _client.GetStream();

Task.Factory.StartNew (Read).ContinueWith (ant =>
{
  _exception = ant.Exception;    // In case an exception occurred.

  if (_stream != null)
    try { _stream.Close(); }
    catch (Exception ex) { _exception = ex; };

  _waitHandle.Set();

  if (callback != null) callback (this);
});
}

internal byte[] End()    // Wait for completion + rethrow any error.
{
  AsyncWaitHandle.WaitOne();
  if (_exception != null) throw _exception;
  return _data;
}

void Read()
{
  Task<int> readChunk = Task<int>.Factory.FromAsync (
    _stream.BeginRead, _stream.EndRead,
    _data, _bytesRead, _data.Length - _bytesRead, null);

  readChunk.ContinueWith (ContinueRead,
                          TaskContinuationOptions.NotOnFaulted
                        | TaskContinuationOptions.AttachedToParent);
}

void ContinueRead (Task<int> readChunk)
{
  _bytesRead += readChunk.Result;
  if (readChunk.Result > 0 && _bytesRead < _data.Length)
  {
    Read();        // More data to read!
    return;
  }
  Array.Reverse (_data);
  Task.Factory.FromAsync (_stream.BeginWrite, _stream.EndWrite,
                          _data, 0, _data.Length, null);
}
}
```

In Cleanup, we closed _stream but not _client, because the caller may want to continue using _client after performing the reverse echo.

When writing asynchronous methods, you must meticulously catch all exceptions, saving the exception object so that it can be rethrown when the consumer calls the End*XXX* method. The easiest way to achieve this is to attach a continuation to an overarching parent task (as in our example)—this catches all exceptions thrown by its child tasks.

Fake Asynchronous Methods

In general, any Framework method that starts with *Begin* and that returns an IASyncResult follows the APM. There are, however, some exceptions, based on the Stream class:

```
BufferedStream
CryptoStream
DeflateStream
MemoryStream
```

These types rely on fallback asynchronous implementations in the base Stream class, which offer no guarantees not to block. Instead, they use an asynchronous delegate to call a *blocking* method such as Read or Write. Although this approach is perfectly valid in the case of MemoryStream (it never blocks in the first place, so it is excused), it creates a problem with BufferedStream and CryptoStream—if wrapping anything other than a MemoryStream. In other words, if you call BeginRead or BeginWrite on a CryptoStream that wraps a NetworkStream, some thread is going to block at some point, violating the scalability of the asynchronous method pattern. This is a shame, because the CryptoStream's decorator architecture is otherwise efficient.

A workaround with CryptoStream is to first read the underlying stream asynchronously into a MemoryStream, and then have the CryptoStream wrap the MemoryStream. This means reading the whole stream into memory, though, which, on a highly concurrent server, is not great for scalability, either. If you really need an asynchronous encryption, a solution is to work at a lower level than CryptoStream—that is, ICryptoTransform. You can see exactly how CryptoStream uses ICryptoTransform to do its work with a disassembly tool such as Red Gate's Reflector.

DeflateStream does actually follow the asynchronous pattern—or at least tries to. The problem is that it doesn't properly handle exceptions. If the underlying stream is corrupt, for instance, BeginRead throws an exception on a pooled thread rather than marshaling it back to EndRead. This is an uncatchable exception that takes down your whole application.

The FileStream class is another violator—it touts *fake* asynchronous methods (i.e., it relies on Stream's default implementation). However, it does make an attempt at true asynchronous behavior if constructed as follows:

```
Stream s = new FileStream ("large.bin", FileMode.Create, FileAccess.Write,
                FileShare.None, 0x1000, true);
```

The boolean argument at the end instructs `FileStream` not to use asynchronous delegates—and instead (to attempt) a true APM approach. The problem is that asynchronous file I/O requires operating system support, which may not be forthcoming. If the OS fails to oblige, `BeginRead` blocks the calling thread in a `WaitSleep Join` state.

Lack of asynchronous file I/O is rarely a problem, though, assuming you're accessing a local filesystem (in fact, it can be a good idea not to use asynchronous file I/O at all). Small file requests are likely to be served from an operating system or hard-drive cache and so be brief and CPU-bound; large file I/O requests are going to seriously limit concurrency if not broken up or throttled in some way, no matter what the threading model. A more insidious blocking issue arises if you're using a `FileStream` on a UNC network path: the solution is instead to use lower-level networking classes (such as those described) for communicating between computers.

Alternatives to Asynchronous Methods

Chapter 21 described three analogous techniques—all of which coalesce many tasks onto a few threads:

- `ThreadPool.RegisterWaitForSingleObject`
- The producer/consumer queue
- The threading and system timers

`ThreadPool.RegisterWaitForSingleObject` can be helpful in implementing the asynchronous method pattern. A custom producer/consumer queue can provide a complete alternative—with your own pool of workers—but is of no help if you want to interoperate with the .NET Framework (e.g., to read from a `NetworkStream`). The threading and system timers are excellent if your work is executed in a periodic fashion, rather than in response to requests.

Asynchronous Methods

24

Application Domains

An *application domain* is the runtime unit of isolation in which a .NET program runs. It provides a managed memory boundary, a container for loaded assemblies and application configuration settings, as well as delineating a communication boundary for distributed applications.

Each .NET process usually hosts just one application domain: the default domain, created automatically by the CLR when the process starts. It's also possible—and sometimes useful—to create additional application domains within the same process. This provides isolation while avoiding the overhead and communication complications that arise with having separate processes. It's useful in scenarios such as load testing and application patching, and in implementing robust error recovery mechanisms.

Application Domain Architecture

Figure 24-1 illustrates the application domain architectures for single-domain, multidomain, and typical distributed client/server applications. In most cases, the processes housing the application domains are created implicitly by the operating system—when the user double-clicks your .NET executable file or starts a Windows service. However, an application domain can also be hosted in other processes such as IIS or in SQL Server through CLR integration.

In the case of a simple executable, the process ends when the default application domain finishes executing. With hosts such as IIS or SQL Server, however, the process controls the lifetime, creating and destroying .NET application domains as it sees fit.

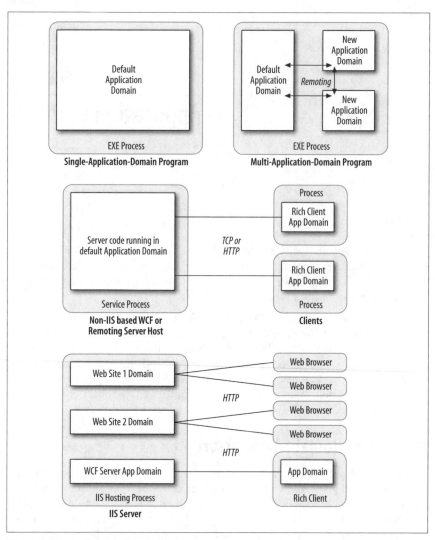

Figure 24-1. Application domain architecture

Creating and Destroying Application Domains

You can create and destroy additional application domains in a process by calling the static methods `AppDomain.CreateDomain` and `AppDomain.Unload`. In the following example, *test.exe* is executed in an isolated application domain, which is then unloaded:

```
static void Main()
{
  AppDomain newDomain = AppDomain.CreateDomain ("New Domain");
  newDomain.ExecuteAssembly ("test.exe");
  AppDomain.Unload (newDomain);
}
```

Note that when the default application domain (the one created by the CLR at startup) is unloaded, all other application domains automatically unload, and the application closes. A domain can "know" whether it's the default domain via the `AppDomain` property `IsDefaultDomain`.

The `AppDomainSetup` class allows options to be specified for a new domain. The following properties are the most useful:

```
public string ApplicationName { get; set; }        // "Friendly" name
public string ApplicationBase { get; set; }        // Base folder

public string ConfigurationFile { get; set; }
public string LicenseFile       { get; set; }

// To assist with automatic assembly resolution:
public string PrivateBinPath      { get; set; }
public string PrivateBinPathProbe { get; set; }
```

The `ApplicationBase` property controls the application domain base directory, used as the root for automatic assembly probing. In the default application domain, this is the main executable's folder. In a new domain that you create, it can be anywhere you like:

```
AppDomainSetup setup = new AppDomainSetup();
setup.ApplicationBase = @"c:\MyBaseFolder";
AppDomain newDomain = AppDomain.CreateDomain ("New Domain", null, setup);
```

It's also possible to subscribe a new domain to assembly resolution events defined in the instigator's domain:

```
static void Main()
{
  AppDomain newDomain = AppDomain.CreateDomain ("test");
  newDomain.AssemblyResolve += new ResolveEventHandler (FindAssem);
  ...
}

static Assembly FindAssem (object sender, ResolveEventArgs args)
{
  ...
}
```

App Domains

This is acceptable providing the event handler is a static method that is defined in a type available to both domains. The CLR is then able to execute the event handler in the correct domain. In this example, `FindAssem` would execute from within `newDomain`, even though it was subscribed from the default domain.

The `PrivateBinPath` property is a semicolon-separated list of subdirectories below the base directory that the CLR should automatically search for assemblies. (As with the application base folder, this can only be set prior to the application domain starting.) Take, for example, a directory structure where a program has a single executable (and perhaps a configuration file) in its base folder and all the referenced assemblies in subfolders as follows:

```
c:\MyBaseFolder\           -- Startup executable
              \bin
              \bin\v1.23    -- Latest assembly DLLs
              \bin\plugins  -- More DLLs
```

Here's how an application domain would be set up to use this folder structure:

```
AppDomainSetup setup = new AppDomainSetup();
setup.ApplicationBase = @"c:\MyBaseFolder";
setup.PrivateBinPath = @"bin\v1.23;bin\plugins";
AppDomain d = AppDomain.CreateDomain ("New Domain", null, setup);
d.ExecuteAssembly (@"c:\MyBaseFolder\Startup.exe");
```

Note that `PrivateBinPath` is always relative to, and below, the application base folder. Specifying absolute paths is illegal. `AppDomain` also provides a `PrivateBin PathProbe` property, which, if set to anything other than a blank string, excludes the base directory itself from being part of the assembly search path. (The reason `PrivateBinPathProbe` is a string rather than a `bool` type relates to COM compatibility.)

Just before any nondefault application domain unloads, the `DomainUnload` event fires. You can use this event for tear-down logic: the unloading of the domain (and the application as a whole, if necessary) is delayed until the execution of all `DomainUn load` event handlers completes.

Just before the application itself closes, the `ProcessExit` event fires on all loaded application domains (including the default domain). Unlike with the `DomainUnload` event, `ProcessExit` event handlers are timed: the default CLR host gives event handlers two seconds per domain, and three seconds in total, before terminating their threads.

Using Multiple Application Domains

Multiple application domains have the following key uses:

- Providing process-like isolation with minimum overhead
- Allowing assembly files to be unloaded without restarting the process

When additional application domains are created within the same process, the CLR provides each with a level of isolation akin to that of running in separate processes. This means that each domain has separate memory, and objects in one domain cannot interfere with those in another. Furthermore, static members of the same class have independent values in each domain. ASP.NET uses exactly this approach to allow many sites to run in a shared process without affecting each other.

With ASP.NET, the application domains are created by the infrastructure—without your intervention. There are times, however, when you can benefit from explicitly creating multiple domains inside a single process. Suppose you've written a custom authentication system, and as part of unit testing, you want to stress-test the server code by simulating 20 clients logging in at once. You have three options in simulating 20 concurrent logins:

- Start 20 separate processes by calling `Process.Start` 20 times.
- Start 20 threads in the same process and domain.
- Start 20 threads in the same process—each in its own application domain.

The first option is clumsy and resource-intensive. It's also hard to communicate with each of the separate processes, should you want to give them more specific instructions on what to do.

The second option relies on the client-side code being thread-safe, which is unlikely—especially if static variables are used to store the current authentication state. And adding a lock around the client-side code would prevent the parallel execution that we need to stress-test the server.

The third option is ideal. It keeps each thread isolated—with independent state—and yet within easy reach of the hosting program.

Another reason to create a separate application domain is to allow assemblies to be unloaded without ending the process. This stems from the fact that there's no way to unload an assembly other than closing the application domain that loaded it. This is a problem if it was loaded in the default domain, because closing this domain means closing the application. An assembly's file is locked while loaded and so cannot be patched or replaced. Loading assemblies in a separate application domain that can be torn down gets around this problem—as well as helping to reduce the memory footprint of an application that occasionally needs to load large assemblies.

App Domains

Using DoCallBack

Let's revisit the most basic multidomain scenario:

```
static void Main()
{
  AppDomain newDomain = AppDomain.CreateDomain ("New Domain");
  newDomain.ExecuteAssembly ("test.exe");
  AppDomain.Unload (newDomain);
}
```

Calling `ExecuteAssembly` on a separate domain is convenient but offers little opportunity to interact with the domain. It also requires that the target assembly is an executable, and it commits the caller to a single entry point. The only way to incorporate flexibility is to resort to an approach such as passing a string of arguments to the executable.

A more powerful approach is to use `AppDomain`'s `DoCallBack` method. This executes on another application domain, a method on a given type. The type's assembly is automatically loaded into the domain (the CLR will know where it lives if the current domain can reference it). In the following example, a method in the currently executing class is run in a new domain:

```
class Program
{
```

```
static void Main()
{
  AppDomain newDomain = AppDomain.CreateDomain ("New Domain");
  newDomain.DoCallBack (new CrossAppDomainDelegate (SayHello));
  AppDomain.Unload (newDomain);
}

static void SayHello()
{
  Console.WriteLine ("Hi from " + AppDomain.CurrentDomain.FriendlyName);
}
}
```

The example works because the delegate is referencing a static method, meaning it points to a type rather than an instance. This makes the delegate "domain-agnostic" or agile. It can run in any domain, and in the same way, as there's nothing tying it to the original domain. It's also possible to use DoCallBack with a delegate referencing an instance method. However, the CLR will attempt to apply Remoting semantics (described later), which in this case happens to be the opposite of what we want.

Monitoring Application Domains

From Framework 4.0, you can monitor the memory and CPU consumption of a specific application domain. For this to work, you must first enable application domain monitoring as follows:

```
AppDomain.MonitoringIsEnabled = true;
```

This enables monitoring for the current domain. Once enabled, you can't subsequently disable it—setting this property to false throws an exception.

> Another way to enable to enable domain monitoring is via the application configuration file. Add the following element:
>
> ```
> <configuration>
>   <runtime>
>     <appDomainResourceMonitoring enabled="true"/>
>   </runtime>
> </configuration>
> ```
>
> This enables monitoring for all application domains.

You can then query an AppDomain's CPU and memory usage via the following three instance properties:

```
MonitoringTotalProcessorTime
MonitoringTotalAllocatedMemorySize
MonitoringSurvivedMemorySize
```

The first two properties return the *total* CPU consumption and managed memory allocated by that domain since it was started. (These figures can only grow and never shrink.) The third property returns the actual managed memory consumption of the domain at the time of the last garbage collection.

You can access these properties from the same or another domain.

Domains and Threads

When you call a method in another application domain, execution blocks until the method finishes executing—just as though you called a method in your own domain. Although this behavior is usually desirable, there are times when you need to run a method concurrently. You can do that with multithreading.

We talked previously about using multiple application domains to simulate 20 concurrent client logins in order to test an authentication system. By having each client log in on a separate application domain, each would be isolated and unable to interfere with another client via static class members. To implement this example, we need to call a "Login" method on 20 concurrent threads, each in its own application domain:

```
class Program
{
  static void Main()
  {
    // Create 20 domains and 20 threads.
    AppDomain[] domains = new AppDomain [20];
    Thread[] threads = new Thread [20];

    for (int i = 0; i < 20; i++)
    {
      domains [i] = AppDomain.CreateDomain ("Client Login " + i);
      threads [i] = new Thread (LoginOtherDomain);
    }

    // Start all the threads, passing to each thread its app domain.
    for (int i = 0; i < 20; i++) threads [i].Start (domains [i]);

    // Wait for the threads to finish
    for (int i = 0; i < 20; i++) threads [i].Join();

    // Unload the app domains
    for (int i = 0; i < 20; i++) AppDomain.Unload (domains [i]);
    Console.ReadLine();
  }

  // Parameterized thread start - taking the domain on which to run.
  static void LoginOtherDomain (object domain)
  {
    ((AppDomain) domain).DoCallBack (Login);
  }

  static void Login()
  {
    Client.Login ("Joe", "");
    Console.WriteLine ("Logged in as: " + Client.CurrentUser + " on " +
      AppDomain.CurrentDomain.FriendlyName);
  }
}
```

```
class Client
{
  // Here's a static field that would interfere with other client logins
  // if running in the same app domain.
  public static string CurrentUser = "";

  public static void Login (string name, string password)
  {
   if (CurrentUser.Length == 0)    // If we're not already logged in...
   {
     // Sleep to simulate authentication...
     Thread.Sleep (500);
     CurrentUser = name;            // Record that we're authenticated.
   }
  }
}

// Output:
Logged in as: Joe on Client Login 0
Logged in as: Joe on Client Login 1
Logged in as: Joe on Client Login 4
Logged in as: Joe on Client Login 2
Logged in as: Joe on Client Login 3
Logged in as: Joe on Client Login 5
Logged in as: Joe on Client Login 6
...
```

See Chapter 21 for more information on multithreading.

Sharing Data Between Domains

Sharing Data via Slots

Application domains can use named slots to share data, as in the following example:

```
class Program
{
  static void Main()
  {
    AppDomain newDomain = AppDomain.CreateDomain ("New Domain");

    // Write to a named slot called "Message" - any string key will do.
    newDomain.SetData ("Message", "guess what...");

    newDomain.DoCallBack (SayMessage);
    AppDomain.Unload (newDomain);
  }

  static void SayMessage()
  {
    // Read from the "Message" data slot
    Console.WriteLine (AppDomain.CurrentDomain.GetData ("Message"));
  }
}
```

```
// Output:
guess what...
```

A slot is created automatically the first time it's used. The data being communicated (in this example, `"guess what ..."`) must either be *serializable* (see Chapter 16), or be based on `MarshalByRefObject`. If the data is serializable (such as the string in our example), it's copied to the other application domain. If it implements `MarshalByRefObject`, Remoting semantics are applied.

Intra-Process Remoting

The most flexible way to communicate with another application domain is to instantiate objects *in the other domain* via a proxy. This is called *Remoting*.

The class being "Remoted" must inherit from `MarshalByRefObject`. The client then calls a `CreateInstanceXXX` method on the remote domain's `AppDomain` class to remotely instantiate the object.

The following instantiates the type `Foo` in another application domain, and then calls its `SayHello` method:

```
class Program
{
  static void Main()
  {
    AppDomain newDomain = AppDomain.CreateDomain ("New Domain");

    Foo foo = (Foo) newDomain.CreateInstanceAndUnwrap (
                    typeof (Foo).Assembly.FullName,
                    typeof (Foo).FullName);

    Console.WriteLine (foo.SayHello());
    AppDomain.Unload (newDomain);
    Console.ReadLine();
  }
}

public class Foo : MarshalByRefObject
{
  public string SayHello()
  {
    return "Hello from " + AppDomain.CurrentDomain.FriendlyName;
  }

  public override object InitializeLifetimeService()
  {
    // This ensures the object lasts for as long as the client wants it
    return null;
  }
}
```

When the `foo` object is created on the other application domain (called the "remote" domain), we don't get back a direct reference to the object, because the application domains are isolated. Instead, we get back a transparent proxy; transparent because it *appears* as though it was a direct reference to the remote object. When we subsequently call the SayHello method on foo, a message is constructed behind the scenes, which is forwarded to the "remote" application domain, where it is then executed on the "real" foo. Any return value is turned into a message and sent back to the caller.

 Before Windows Communication Foundation was released in .NET Framework 3.0, Remoting was one of the two principal technologies for writing distributed applications (Web Services being the other). In a distributed Remoting application, you explicitly set up an HTTP or TCP/IP communication channel at each end, allowing communication to cross process and network boundaries.

Although WCF is superior to Remoting for distributed applications, Remoting still has a niche in interdomain communication within a process. Its advantage in this scenario is that it requires no configuration—the communication channel is automatically created (a fast in-memory channel), and no type registration is required. You simply start using it.

The methods on Foo can return more MarshalByRefObject instances, in which case more transparent proxies are generated when those methods are called. Methods on Foo can also accept MarshalByRefObject instances as arguments—in which Remoting happens in reverse. The caller will hold the "remote" object, while the callee will have a proxy.

As well as marshaling objects by reference, application domains can exchange scalar values, or any *serializable* object. A type is serializable if it either has the Serializable attribute or implements ISerializable. Then, when crossing the application domain boundary, a complete copy of the object is returned, rather than a proxy. In other words, the object is marshaled by *value* rather than reference.

Remoting within the same process is client-activated, meaning that the CLR doesn't attempt to share or reuse remotely created objects with the same or other clients. In other words, if the client creates two Foo objects, two objects will be created in the remote domain, and two proxies in the client domain. This provides the most natural object semantics; however, it means that the remote domain is dependent on the client's garbage collector: the foo object in the remote domain is released from memory only when the client's garbage collector decides that the foo (proxy) is no longer in use. If the client domain crashes, it may never get released. To protect against this scenario, the CLR provides a lease-based mechanism for managing the lifetime of remotely created objects. The default behavior is for remotely created objects to self-destruct after five minutes of nonuse.

App Domains

Because in this example the client runs in the default application domain, the client doesn't have the luxury of crashing. Once it ends, so does the whole process! Hence, it makes sense to disable the five-minute lifetime lease. This is the purpose of overriding InitializeLifetimeService—by returning a null lease, remotely created objects are destroyed only when garbage-collected by the client.

Isolating Types and Assemblies

In the preceding example, we remotely instantiated an object of type Foo as follows:

```
Foo foo = (Foo) newDomain.CreateInstanceAndUnwrap (
                typeof (Foo).Assembly.FullName,
                typeof (Foo).FullName);
```

Here's the method's signature:

```
public object CreateInstanceFromAndUnwrap (string assemblyName,
                                           string typeName)
```

Because this method accepts an assembly and type *name* rather than a Type object, you can remotely instantiate an object without loading its type locally. This is useful when you want to avoid loading the type's assembly into the caller's application domain.

> AppDomain also provides a method called CreateIn stanceFromAndUnwrap. The difference is:
>
> - CreateInstanceAndUnwrap accepts a *fully qualified assembly name* (see Chapter 17).
> - CreateInstanceFromAndUnwrap accepts a *path or filename*.

To illustrate, suppose we were writing a text editor that allows the user to load and unload third-party plug-ins. We demonstrated this in Chapter 20 in the section "Sandboxing Another Assembly" on page 769, from the perspective of security. When it came to actually executing the plug-in, however, all we did was call Execu teAssembly. With Remoting, we can interact with plug-ins in a richer fashion.

The first step is to write a common library that both the host and the plug-ins will reference. This library will define an interface describing what plug-ins can do. Here's a simple example:

```
namespace Plugin.Common
{
  public interface ITextPlugin
  {
    string TransformText (string input);
  }
}
```

Next, we need to write a simple plug-in. We'll assume the following is compiled to *AllCapitals.dll*:

```
namespace Plugin.Extensions
{
  public class AllCapitals : MarshalByRefObject, Plugin.Common.ITextPlugin
  {
    public string TransformText (string input) { return input.ToUpper(); }
  }
}
```

Here's how to write a host that loads *AllCapitals.dll* into a separate application domain, calls `TransformText` using Remoting, and then unloads the application domain:

```
using System;
using System.Reflection;
using Plugin.Common;

class Program
{
  static void Main()
  {
    AppDomain domain = AppDomain.CreateDomain ("Plugin Domain");

    ITextPlugin plugin = (ITextPlugin) domain.CreateInstanceFromAndUnwrap
      ("AllCapitals.dll", "Plugin.Extensions.AllCapitals");

    // Call the TransformText method using Remoting:
    Console.WriteLine (plugin.TransformText ("hello"));   // "HELLO"

    AppDomain.Unload (domain);

    // The AllCapitals.dll file is now completely unloaded and could
    // be moved or deleted.
  }
}
```

Because this program interacts with the plug-in solely through the common interface, `ITextPlugin`, the types in `AllCapitals` are never loaded into the caller's application domain. This maintains the integrity of the caller's domain and ensures that no locks are held on the plug-in assembly files after their domain is unloaded.

Type discovery

In our preceding example, a real application would need some means of discovering plug-in type names, such as `Plugin.Extensions.AllCapitals`.

You can achieve this by writing a discovery class in the *common* assembly that uses reflection as follows:

```
public class Discoverer : MarshalByRefObject
{
  public string[] GetPluginTypeNames (string assemblyPath)
  {
    List<string> typeNames = new List<string>();
    Assembly a = Assembly.LoadFrom (assemblyPath);
    foreach (Type t in a.GetTypes())
      if (t.IsPublic
          && t.IsMarshalByRef
          && typeof (ITextPlugin).IsAssignableFrom (t))
      {
        typeNames.Add (t.FullName);
      }
    return typeNames.ToArray();
  }
}
```

The catch is that `Assembly.LoadFrom` loads the assembly into the current application domain. Therefore, you must call this method *in the plug-in domain*:

```
class Program
{
  static void Main()
  {
    AppDomain domain = AppDomain.CreateDomain ("Plugin Domain");

    Discoverer d = (Discoverer) domain.CreateInstanceAndUnwrap (
      typeof (Discoverer).Assembly.FullName,
      typeof (Discoverer).FullName);

    string[] plugInTypeNames = d.GetPluginTypeNames ("AllCapitals.dll");

    foreach (string s in plugInTypeNames)
      Console.WriteLine (s);              // Plugin.Extensions.AllCapitals

    ...
```

In the *System.AddIn.Contract* assembly is an API that develops these concepts into a complete framework for program extensibility. It addresses such issues as isolation, versioning, discovery, activation, and so on. Visit *http://blogs.msdn.com* and search for "CLR Add-In Team Blog" for a good source of online information.

25

Native and COM Interoperability

This chapter describes how to integrate with native (unmanaged) DLLs and COM components. Unless otherwise stated, the types mentioned in this chapter exist in either the `System` or the `System.Runtime.InteropServices` namespace.

Calling into Native DLLs

P/Invoke, short for *Platform Invocation Services*, allows you to access functions, structs, and callbacks in unmanaged DLLs. For example, consider the `MessageBox` function, defined in the Windows DLL *user32.dll* as follows:

```
int MessageBox (HWND hWnd, LPCTSTR lpText, LPCTSTR lpCation, UINT uType);
```

You can call this function directly by declaring a static method of the same name, applying the `extern` keyword, and adding the `DllImport` attribute:

```
using System;
using System.Runtime.InteropServices;

class MsgBoxTest
{
  [DllImport("user32.dll")]
  static extern int MessageBox (IntPtr hWnd, string text, string caption,
                                int type);
  public static void Main()
  {
    MessageBox (IntPtr.Zero,
                "Please do not press this again.", "Attention", 0);
  }
}
```

The `MessageBox` classes in the `System.Windows` and `System.Windows.Forms` namespaces themselves call similar unmanaged methods.

The CLR includes a marshaler that knows how to convert parameters and return values between .NET types and unmanaged types. In this example, the `int` parameters translate directly to 4-byte integers that the function expects, and the string parameters are converted into null-terminated arrays of 2-byte Unicode characters. IntPtr is a struct designed to encapsulate an unmanaged handle, and is 32 bits wide on 32-bit platforms and 64 bits wide on 64-bit platforms.

Type Marshaling

Marshaling Common Types

On the unmanaged side, there can be more than one way to represent a given data type. A string, for instance, can contain single-byte ANSI characters or double-byte Unicode characters, and can be length-prefixed, null-terminated, or of fixed length. With the MarshalAs attribute, you can tell the CLR marshaler the variation in use, so it can provide the correct translation. Here's an example:

```
[DllImport("...")]
static extern int Foo ( [MarshalAs (UnmanagedType.LPStr)] string s );
```

The UnmanagedType enumeration includes all the Win32 and COM types that the marshaler understands. In this case, the marshaler was told to translate to LPStr, which is a null-terminated single-byte ANSI string. (All UnmanagedType members are listed at the end of this chapter.)

On the .NET side, you also have some choice as to what data type to use. Unmanaged handles, for instance, can map to IntPtr, int, uint, long, or ulong.

Most unmanaged handles encapsulate an address or pointer, and so must be mapped to IntPtr for compatibility with both 32- and 64-bit operating systems. A typical example is HWND.

Quite often with Win32 functions, you come across an integer parameter that accepts a set of constants, defined in a C++ header file such as *WinUser.h*. Rather than defining these as simple C# constants, you can define them within an enum instead. Using an enum can make for tidier code as well as increase static type safety. We provide an example in the later section "Shared Memory" on page 963.

When installing Microsoft Visual Studio, be sure to install the C++ header files—even if you choose nothing else in the C++ category. This is where all the native Win32 constants are defined. You can then locate all header files by searching for *.h* in the Visual Studio program directory.

Receiving strings from unmanaged code back to .NET requires that some memory management take place. The marshaler performs this work automatically if you declare the external method with a StringBuilder rather than a string, as follows:

```
using System;
using System.Text;
using System.Runtime.InteropServices;
```

```
class Test
{
  [DllImport("kernel32.dll")]
  static extern int GetWindowsDirectory (StringBuilder sb, int maxChars);

  static void Main()
  {
    StringBuilder s = new StringBuilder (256);
    GetWindowsDirectory (s, 256);
    Console.WriteLine (s);
  }
}
```

 If you are unsure how to call a particular Win32 method, you will usually find an example on the Internet if you search for the method name and *DllImport*. The site *http://www.pinvoke.net* is a wiki that aims to document all Win32 signatures.

Marshaling Classes and Structs

Sometimes you need to pass a struct to an unmanaged method. For example, GetSystemTime in the Win32 API is defined as follows:

```
void GetSystemTime (LPSYSTEMTIME lpSystemTime);
```

LPSYSTEMTIME conforms to this C struct:

```
typedef struct _SYSTEMTIME {
  WORD wYear;
  WORD wMonth;
  WORD wDayOfWeek;
  WORD wDay;
  WORD wHour;
  WORD wMinute;
  WORD wSecond;
  WORD wMilliseconds;
} SYSTEMTIME, *PSYSTEMTIME;
```

In order to call GetSystemTime, we must define a .NET class or struct that matches this C struct:

```
using System;
using System.Runtime.InteropServices;

[StructLayout(LayoutKind.Sequential)]
class SystemTime
{
  public ushort Year;
  public ushort Month;
  public ushort DayOfWeek;
  public ushort Day;
  public ushort Hour;
  public ushort Minute;
  public ushort Second;
```

```
    public ushort Milliseconds;
}
```

The `StructLayout` attribute instructs the marshaler how to map each field to its unmanaged counterpart. `LayoutKind.Sequential` means that we want the fields aligned sequentially on *pack-size* boundaries (we'll see what this means shortly), just as they would be in a C struct. The field names here are irrelevant; it's the ordering of fields that's important.

Now we can call `GetSystemTime`:

```
[DllImport("kernel32.dll")]
static extern void GetSystemTime (SystemTime t);

static void Main()
{
  SystemTime t = new SystemTime();
  GetSystemTime (t);
  Console.WriteLine (t.Year);
}
```

In both C and C#, fields in an object are located at n number of bytes from the address of that object. The difference is that in a C# program, the CLR finds this offset by looking it up using the field name; C field names are compiled directly into offsets. For instance, in C, `wDay` is just a token to represent whatever is at the address of a `SystemTime` instance plus 24 bytes.

For access speed, each field is placed at an offset that is a multiple of the field's size. That multiplier, however, is restricted to a maximum of x bytes, where x is the *pack size*. In the current implementation, the default pack size is 8 bytes, so a struct comprising a `sbyte` followed by an (8-byte) `long` occupies 16 bytes, and the 7 bytes following the `sbyte` are wasted. You can lessen or eliminate this wastage by specifying a *pack size* via the `Pack` property of the `StructLayout` attribute: this makes the fields align to offsets that are multiples of the specified pack size. So with a pack size of 1, the struct just described would occupy just 9 bytes. You can specify pack sizes of 1, 2, 4, 8, or 16 bytes.

The `StructLayout` attribute also lets you specify explicit field offsets (see "Simulating a C Union" on page 962).

In and Out Marshaling

In the previous example, we implemented `SystemTime` as a class. We could have instead chosen a struct—providing `GetSystemTime` was declared with a `ref` or `out` parameter:

```
[DllImport("kernel32.dll")]
static extern void GetSystemTime (out SystemTime t);
```

In most cases, C#'s directional parameter semantics work the same with external methods. Pass-by-value parameters are copied in, C# `ref` parameters are copied in/out, and C# `out` parameters are copied out. However, there are some exceptions for types that have special conversions. For instance, array classes and the

StringBuilder class require copying when coming out of a function, so they are in/out. It is occasionally useful to override this behavior, with the In and Out attributes. For example, if an array should be read-only, the in modifier indicates to only copy the array going into the function and not coming out of it:

```
static extern void Foo ( [In] int[] array);
```

Callbacks from Unmanaged Code

The P/Invoke layer does its best to present a natural programming model on both sides of the boundary, mapping between relevant constructs where possible. Since C# can not only call out to C functions but also can be called back from the C functions (via function pointers), the P/Invoke layer needs to map unmanaged function pointers onto something natural for the managed world. The managed equivalent of a function pointer is a delegate, so the P/Invoke layer automatically maps between delegates (in C#) and function pointers (in C).

As an example, you can enumerate all top-level window handles with this method in *User32.dll*:

```
BOOL EnumWindows (WNDENUMPROC lpEnumFunc, LPARAM lParam);
```

WNDENUMPROC is a callback that gets fired with the handle of each window in sequence (or until the callback returns false). Here is its definition:

```
BOOL CALLBACK EnumWindowsProc (HWND hwnd, LPARAM lParam);
```

To use this, we declare a delegate with a matching signature, and then pass a delegate instance to the external method:

```
using System;
using System.Runtime.InteropServices;

class CallbackFun
{
  delegate bool EnumWindowsCallback (IntPtr hWnd, IntPtr lParam);

  [DllImport("user32.dll")]
  static extern int EnumWindows (EnumWindowsCallback hWnd, IntPtr lParam);

  static bool PrintWindow (IntPtr hWnd, IntPtr lParam)
  {
    Console.WriteLine (hWnd.ToInt64());
    return true;
  }

  static void Main()
  {
    EnumWindows (PrintWindow, IntPtr.Zero);
  }
}
```

Simulating a C Union

Each field in a struct is given enough room to store its data. Consider a struct containing one int and one char. The int is likely to start at an offset of 0 and is guaranteed at least four bytes. So, the char would start at an offset of at least 4. If, for some reason, the char started at an offset of 2, you'd change the value of the int if you assigned a value to the char. Sounds like mayhem, doesn't it? Strangely enough, the C language supports a variation on a struct called a *union* that does exactly this. You can simulate this in C# using LayoutKind.Explicit and the FieldOffset attribute.

It might be hard to think of a case in which this would be useful. However, suppose you want to play a note on an external synthesizer. The Windows Multimedia API provides a function for doing just this via the MIDI protocol:

```
[DllImport ("winmm.dll")]
public static extern uint midiOutShortMsg (IntPtr handle, uint message);
```

The second argument, message, describes what note to play. The problem is in constructing this 32-bit unsigned integer: it's divided internally into bytes, representing a MIDI channel, note, and velocity at which to strike. One solution is to shift and mask via the bitwise <<, >>, &, and | operators to convert these bytes to and from the 32-bit "packed" message. Far simpler, though, is to define a struct with explicit layout:

```
[StructLayout (LayoutKind.Explicit)]
public struct NoteMessage
{
  [FieldOffset(0)] public uint PackedMsg;    // 4 bytes long

  [FieldOffset(0)] public byte Channel;      // FieldOffset also at 0
  [FieldOffset(1)] public byte Note;
  [FieldOffset(2)] public byte Velocity;
}
```

The Channel, Note, and Velocity fields deliberately overlap with the 32-bit packed message. This allows you to read and write using either. No calculations are required to keep other fields in sync:

```
NoteMessage n = new NoteMessage();
Console.WriteLine (n.PackedMsg);    // 0

n.Channel = 10;
n.Note = 100;
n.Velocity = 50;
Console.WriteLine (n.PackedMsg);    // 3302410

n.PackedMsg = 3328010;
Console.WriteLine (n.Note);         // 200
```

Shared Memory

Memory-mapped files, or *shared memory*, is a feature in Windows that allows multiple processes on the same computer to share data, without the overhead of Remoting or WCF. Shared memory is extremely fast and, unlike pipes, offers *random* access to the shared data. We saw in Chapter 14 how you can use Framework 4.0's new `MemoryMappedFile` class to access memory-mapped files; bypassing this and calling the Win32 methods directly is a good way to demonstrate P/Invoke.

The Win32 `CreateFileMapping` function allocates shared memory. You tell it how many bytes you need and the name with which to identify the share. Another application can then subscribe to this memory by calling `OpenFileMapping` with same name. Both methods return a *handle*, which you can convert to a pointer by calling `MapViewOfFile`.

Here's a class that encapsulates access to shared memory:

```
using System;
using System.Runtime.InteropServices;

public sealed class SharedMem : IDisposable
{
  // Here we're using enums because they're safer than constants

  enum FileProtection : uint      // constants from winnt.h
  {
    ReadOnly = 2,
    ReadWrite = 4
  }

  enum FileRights : uint          // constants from WinBASE.h
  {
    Read = 4,
    Write = 2,
    ReadWrite = Read + Write
  }

  static readonly IntPtr NoFileHandle = new IntPtr (-1);

  [DllImport ("kernel32.dll", SetLastError = true)]
  static extern IntPtr CreateFileMapping (IntPtr hFile,
                                          int lpAttributes,
                                          FileProtection flProtect,
                                          uint dwMaximumSizeHigh,
                                          uint dwMaximumSizeLow,
                                          string lpName);

  [DllImport ("kernel32.dll", SetLastError=true)]
  static extern IntPtr OpenFileMapping (FileRights dwDesiredAccess,
                                        bool bInheritHandle,
                                        string lpName);

  [DllImport ("kernel32.dll", SetLastError = true)]
  static extern IntPtr MapViewOfFile (IntPtr hFileMappingObject,
```

```
                              FileRights dwDesiredAccess,
                              uint dwFileOffsetHigh,
                              uint dwFileOffsetLow,
                              uint dwNumberOfBytesToMap);

  [DllImport ("Kernel32.dll", SetLastError = true)]
  static extern bool UnmapViewOfFile (IntPtr map);

  [DllImport ("kernel32.dll", SetLastError = true)]
  static extern int CloseHandle (IntPtr hObject);

  IntPtr fileHandle, fileMap;

  public IntPtr Root { get { return fileMap; } }

  public SharedMem (string name, bool existing, uint sizeInBytes)
  {
    if (existing)
      fileHandle = OpenFileMapping (FileRights.ReadWrite, false, name);
    else
      fileHandle = CreateFileMapping (NoFileHandle, 0,
                                      FileProtection.ReadWrite,
                                      0, sizeInBytes, name);
    if (fileHandle == IntPtr.Zero)
      throw new Win32Exception();

    // Obtain a read/write map for the entire file
    fileMap = MapViewOfFile (fileHandle, FileRights.ReadWrite, 0, 0, 0);

    if (fileMap == IntPtr.Zero)
      throw new Win32Exception();
  }

  public void Dispose()
  {
    if (fileMap != IntPtr.Zero) UnmapViewOfFile (fileMap);
    if (fileHandle != IntPtr.Zero) CloseHandle (fileHandle);
    fileMap = fileHandle = IntPtr.Zero;
  }
}
```

In this example, we set `SetLastError=true` on the `DllImport` methods that use the `SetLastError` protocol for emitting error codes. This ensures that the `Win32Excep`tion is populated with details of the error when that exception is thrown. (It also allows you to query the error explicitly by calling `Marshal.GetLastWin32Error`.)

In order to demonstrate this class, we need to run two applications. The first one creates the shared memory, as follows:

```
using (SharedMem sm = new SharedMem ("MyShare", false, 1000))
{
  IntPtr root = sm.Root;
  // I have shared memory!

  Console.ReadLine();        // Here's where we start a second app...
}
```

The second application subscribes to the shared memory by constructing a SharedMem object of the same name, with the existing argument true:

```
using (SharedMem sm = new SharedMem ("MyShare", true, 1000))
{
  IntPtr root = sm.Root;
  // I have the same shared memory!
  // ...
}
```

The net result is that each program has an IntPtr—a pointer to (the same) unmanaged memory. The two applications now need somehow to read and write to memory via this common pointer. One approach is to write a serializable class that encapsulates all the shared data, then serialize (and deserialize) the data to the unmanaged memory using an UnmanagedMemoryStream. This is inefficient, however, if there's a lot of data. Imagine if the shared memory class had a megabyte worth of data, and just one integer needed to be updated. A better approach is to define the shared data construct as a struct, and then map it directly into shared memory. We discuss this in the following section.

Mapping a Struct to Unmanaged Memory

A struct with a StructLayout of Sequential or Explicit can be mapped directly into unmanaged memory. Consider the following struct:

```
[StructLayout (LayoutKind.Sequential)]
unsafe struct MySharedData
{
  public int Value;
  public char Letter;
  public fixed float Numbers [50];
}
```

The fixed directive allows us to define fixed-length value-type arrays, and it is what takes us into the unsafe realm. Space in this struct is allocated inline for 50 floating-point numbers. Unlike with standard C# arrays, NumberArray is not a *reference* to an array—it *is* the array. If we run the following:

```
static unsafe void Main()
{
  Console.WriteLine (sizeof (MySharedData));
}
```

the result is 208: 50 4-byte floats, plus the 4 bytes for the Value integer, plus 2 bytes for the Letter character. The total, 206, is rounded to 208 due to the floats being aligned on 4-byte boundaries (4 bytes being the size of a float).

We can demonstrate MySharedData in an unsafe context, most simply, with stack-allocated memory:

```
MySharedData d;
MySharedData* data = &d;         // Get the address of d

data->Value = 123;
```

```
data->Letter = 'X';
data->Numbers[10] = 1.45f;
```

or:

```
// Allocate the array on the stack:
MySharedData* data = stackalloc MySharedData[1];

data->Value = 123;
data->Letter = 'X';
data->Numbers[10] = 1.45f;
```

Of course, we're not demonstrating anything that couldn't otherwise be achieved in a managed context. Suppose, however, that we want to store an instance of MySharedData on the *unmanaged heap*, outside the realm of the CLR's garbage collector. This is where pointers become really useful:

```
MySharedData* data = (MySharedData*)
    Marshal.AllocHGlobal (sizeof (MySharedData)).ToPointer();

data->Value = 123;
data->Letter = 'X';
data->Numbers[10] = 1.45f;
```

Marshal.AllocHGlobal allocates memory on the unmanaged heap. Here's how to later free the same memory:

```
Marshal.FreeHGlobal (new IntPtr (data));
```

(The result of forgetting to free the memory is a good old-fashioned memory leak.)

In keeping with its name, we'll now use MySharedData in conjunction with the SharedMem class we wrote in the preceding section. The following program allocates a block of shared memory, and then maps the MySharedData struct into that memory:

```
static unsafe void Main()
{
  using (SharedMem sm = new SharedMem ("MyShare", false, 1000))
  {
    void* root = sm.Root.ToPointer();
    MySharedData* data = (MySharedData*) root;

    data->Value = 123;
    data->Letter = 'X';
    data->Numbers[10] = 1.45f;
    Console.WriteLine ("Written to shared memory");

    Console.ReadLine();

    Console.WriteLine ("Value is " + data->Value);
    Console.WriteLine ("Letter is " + data->Letter);
    Console.WriteLine ("11th Number is " + data->Numbers[10]);
    Console.ReadLine();
  }
}
```

If you're targeting Framework 4.0, you can use its `MemoryMappedFile` class instead of `SharedMem` as follows:

```
using (MemoryMappedFile mmFile =
        MemoryMappedFile.CreateNew ("MyShare", 1000))
using (MemoryMappedViewAccessor accessor =
        mmFile.CreateViewAccessor())
{
  byte* pointer = null;
  accessor.SafeMemoryMappedViewHandle.AcquirePointer
   (ref pointer);
  void* root = pointer;
  ...
}
```

Here's a second program that attaches to the same shared memory, reading the values written by the first program. (It must be run while the first program is waiting on the `ReadLine` statement, since the shared memory object is disposed upon leaving its `using` statement.)

```
static unsafe void Main()
{
  using (SharedMem sm = new SharedMem ("MyShare", true, 1000))
  {
    void* root = sm.Root.ToPointer();
    MySharedData* data = (MySharedData*) root;

    Console.WriteLine ("Value is " + data->Value);
    Console.WriteLine ("Letter is " + data->Letter);
    Console.WriteLine ("11th Number is " + data->Numbers[10]);

    // Our turn to update values in shared memory!
    data->Value++;
    data->Letter = '!';
    data->Numbers[10] = 987.5f;
    Console.WriteLine ("Updated shared memory");
    Console.ReadLine();
  }
}
```

The output from each of these programs is as follows:

```
// First program:

Written to shared memory
Value is 124
Letter is !
11th Number is 987.5

// Second program:

Value is 123
Letter is X
11th Number is 1.45
Updated shared memory
```

Don't be put off by the pointers: C++ programmers use them throughout whole applications and are able to get everything working. At least most of the time! This sort of usage is fairly simple by comparison.

As it happens, our example is unsafe—quite literally—for another reason. We haven't considered the thread-safety (or more precisely, process-safety) issues that arise with two programs accessing the same memory at once. To use this in a production application, we'd need to add the volatile keyword to the Value and Letter fields in the MySharedData struct to prevent fields from being cached in CPU registers. Furthermore, as our interaction with the fields grew beyond the trivial, we would most likely need to protect their access via a cross-process Mutex, just as we would use lock statements to protect access to fields in a multithreaded program. We discussed thread safety in detail in Chapter 21.

fixed and fixed {...}

One limitation of mapping structs directly into memory is that the struct can contain only unmanaged types. If you need to share string data, for instance, you must use a fixed character array instead. This means manual conversion to and from the string type. Here's how to do it:

```
[StructLayout (LayoutKind.Sequential)]
unsafe struct MySharedData
{
    ...
    // Allocate space for 200 chars (i.e., 400 bytes).
    const int MessageSize = 200;
    fixed char message [MessageSize];

    // One would most likely put this code into a helper class:
    public string Message
    {
        get { fixed (char* cp = message) return new string (cp); }
        set
        {
            fixed (char* cp = message)
            {
                int i = 0;
                for (; i < value.Length && i < MessageSize - 1; i++)
                    cp [i] = value [i];

                // Add the null terminator
                cp [i] = '\0';
            }
        }
    }
}
```

 There's no such thing as a reference to a fixed array; instead, you get a pointer. When you index into a fixed array, you're actually performing pointer arithmetic!

With the first use of the `fixed` keyword, we allocate space, inline, for 200 characters in the struct. The same keyword has a different meaning when used later, in the property definition. It tells the CLR that should it decide to perform a garbage collection inside the `fixed` block, not to move the underlying struct about on the memory heap, since its contents are being iterated via direct memory pointers. Looking at our program, you might wonder how `MySharedData` could ever shift in memory, given that it lives not on the heap, but in the unmanaged world, where the garbage collector has no jurisdiction. The compiler doesn't know this, however, and is concerned that we *might* use `MySharedData` in a managed context, so it insists that we add the `fixed` keyword, to make our `unsafe` code safe in managed contexts. And the compiler does have a point—here's all it would take to put `MySharedData` on the heap:

```
object obj = new MySharedData();
```

This results in a boxed `MySharedData`—on the heap and eligible for transit during garbage collection.

This example illustrates how a string can be represented in a struct mapped to unmanaged memory. For more complex types, you also have the option of using existing serialization code. The one proviso is that the serialized data must never exceed, in length, its allocation of space in the struct; otherwise, the result is an unintended union with subsequent fields.

COM Interoperability

The .NET runtime has had special support for COM since its first version, enabling COM objects to be used from .NET and vice versa. C# 4.0 and CLR 4.0 significantly enhance the ability to use COM objects from .NET—in the aspects of both usability and deployment.

The Purpose of COM

COM is an acronym for Component Object Model, a binary standard for APIs released by Microsoft in 1993. The motivation for inventing COM was to enable components to communicate with each other in a language-independent and version-tolerant manner. Before COM, the approach in Windows was to publish Dynamic Link Libraries (DLLs) that declared structures and functions using the C programming language. Not only is this approach language-specific, but it's also brittle. The specification of a type in such a library is inseparable from its implementation: even updating a structure with a new field means breaking its specification.

The beauty of COM was to separate the specification of a type from its underlying implementation through a construct known as a *COM interface*. COM also allowed for the calling of methods on stateful *objects*—rather than being limited to simple procedure calls.

In a way, the .NET programming model is an evolution of the principles of COM programming: the .NET platform also facilitates cross-language development and allows binary components to evolve without breaking applications that depend on them.

The Basics of the COM Type System

The COM type system revolves around interfaces. A COM interface is rather like a .NET interface, but it's more prevalent because a COM type exposes its functionality *only* through an interface. In the .NET world, for instance, we could simply declare a type as follows:

```
public class Foo
{
  public string Test() { return "Hello, world"; }
}
```

Consumers of that type can use Foo directly. And if we later changed the *implementation* of Test(), calling assemblies would not require recompilation. In this respect, .NET separates interface from implementation—without requiring interfaces. We could even add an overload without breaking callers:

```
public string Test (string s) { return "Hello, world " + s; }
```

In the COM world, Foo exposes its functionality through an interface to achieve this same decoupling. So, in Foo's type library, an interface such as this would exist:

```
public interface IFoo { string Test(); }
```

(We've illustrated this by showing a C# interface—not a COM interface. The principle, however, is the same—although the plumbing is different.)

Callers would then interact with IFoo rather than Foo.

When it comes to adding the overloaded version of Test, life is more complicated with COM than with .NET. First, we would avoid modifying the IFoo interface—because this would break binary compatibility with the previous version (one of the principles of COM is that interfaces, once published, are *immutable*). Second, COM doesn't allow method overloading. The solution is to instead have Foo implement a *second interface*:

```
public interface IFoo2 { string Test (string s); }
```

(Again, we've transliterated this into a .NET interface for familiarity.)

Supporting multiple interfaces is of key importance in making COM libraries versionable.

IUnknown and IDispatch

All COM interfaces are identified with a GUID.

The root interface in COM is `IUnknown`—all COM objects must implement it. This interface has three methods:

- `AddRef`
- `Release`
- `QueryInterface`

`AddRef` and `Release` are for lifetime management, since COM uses reference counting rather than automatic garbage collection (COM was designed to work with unmanaged code, where automatic garbage collection isn't feasible). The `QueryInterface` method is for type discovery, and returns all the COM interfaces that the object supports.

To enable dynamic programming (e.g., scripting and Automation), a COM object may also implement `IDispatch`. This enables dynamic languages such as VBScript to call COM objects in a late-bound manner—just as with `dynamic` in C#.

Calling a COM Component from C#

The CLR's built-in support for COM means that you don't work directly with `IUnknown` and `IDispatch`. Instead, you work with CLR objects and the runtime marshals your calls to the COM world via Runtime-Callable Wrappers (RCWs). The runtime also handles lifetime management by calling `AddRef` and `Release` (when the .NET object is finalized) and takes care of the primitive type conversions between the two worlds. Type conversion ensures that each side sees, for example, the integer and string types in their familiar forms.

Additionally, there needs to be some way to access RCWs in a statically typed fashion. This is the job of *COM interop types*. COM interop types are automatically generated proxy types that expose a .NET member for each COM member. The type library importer tool (*tlimp.exe*) generates COM interop types from the command line, based on a COM library that you choose, and compiles them into a *COM interop assembly*.

> If a COM component implements multiple interfaces, the *tlimp.exe* tool generates a single type that contains a union of members from all interfaces.

You can create a COM interop assembly in Visual Studio by going to the Add Reference dialog and choosing a library from the COM tab. For example, if you have Microsoft Excel 2007 installed, adding a reference to the Microsoft Excel 12.0 Office Library allows you to interoperate with Excel's COM classes. Here's the C# 4.0 code to create and show a workbook, and then populate a cell in that workbook:

```
using System;
using Excel = Microsoft.Office.Interop.Excel;

class Program
```

```
{
  static void Main()
  {
    var excel = new Excel.Application();
    excel.Visible = true;
    Workbook workBook = excel.Workbooks.Add();
    excel.Cells [1, 1].Font.FontStyle = "Bold";
    excel.Cells [1, 1].Value2 = "Hello World";
    workBook.SaveAs (@"d:\temp.xlsx");
  }
}
```

The Excel.Application class is a COM interop type whose runtime type is an RCW. When we access the Workbooks and Cells properties, we get back more interop types.

This code is fairly simple, thanks to a number of enhancements in the C# 4.0 language. In C# 3.0, we would have to write the Main method like this instead:

```
var missing = System.Reflection.Missing.Value;

var excel = new Excel.Application();
excel.Visible = true;
Workbook workBook = excel.Workbooks.Add (missing);
var range = (Excel.Range) excel.Cells [1, 1];
range.Font.FontStyle = "Bold";
range.Value2 = "Hello world";

workBook.SaveAs (@"d:\temp.xlsx", missing, missing, missing, missing,
    missing, Excel.XlSaveAsAccessMode.xlNoChange, missing, missing,
    missing, missing, missing);
```

We'll look now at what those language enhancements are, and how they help with COM programming.

Optional Parameters and Named Arguments

Because COM APIs don't support function overloading, it's very common to have functions with numerous parameters, many of which are optional. Prior to C# 4.0, all optional parameters had to be explicitly passed default argument values. C# 4.0's new support for optional parameters puts an end to this verbosity and allows us to replace the following:

```
var missing = System.Reflection.Missing.Value;

workBook.SaveAs (@"d:\temp.xlsx", missing, missing, missing, missing,
    missing, Excel.XlSaveAsAccessMode.xlNoChange, missing, missing,
    missing, missing, missing);
```

with this:

```
workBook.SaveAs (@"d:\temp.xlsx");
```

(As we stated in Chapter 3, the compiler translates the latter into the former.)

With named arguments, you can easily specify additional arguments, regardless of their position:

```
workBook.SaveAs (@"c:\test.xlsx", Password:"foo");
```

Implicit ref Parameters

Some COM APIs (Microsoft Word, in particular) expose functions that declare *every* parameter as pass-by-reference—whether or not the function modifies the parameter value. This is because of the perceived performance gain from not copying argument values.

Calling such methods from C# is clumsy because you must specify the ref keyword with every argument. For instance, to open a Word document in C# 3.0, you must do the following:

```
object filename = "foo.doc";
object notUsed1 = Missing.Value;
object notUsed2 = Missing.Value;
object notUsed3 = Missing.Value;
...
Open (ref filename, ref notUsed1, ref notUsed2, ref notUsed3, ...);
```

C# 4.0 relaxes the rules by allowing you to omit the ref modifier on COM function calls. Leveraging this feature in conjunction with optional parameters can drastically simplify method calls:

```
word.Open ("foo.doc");
```

The only caveat is that you will get neither a compile-time nor a runtime error if the COM method you're calling actually does mutate an argument value.

Indexers

The ability to omit the ref modifier has another benefit: COM indexers with ref parameters are now accessible via ordinary C# indexer syntax. Previously, this was forbidden because ref/out parameters are not supported with C# indexers (the somewhat clumsy workaround was to call the backing methods such as get_*XXX* and set_*XXX*; this workaround is still legal for backward compatibility).

Interop with indexers has been further enhanced in C# 4.0 such that you can now call COM properties that accept arguments. In the following example, Foo is a property that accepts an integer argument:

```
myComObject.Foo [123] = "Hello";
```

Writing such properties yourself in C# is still prohibited: a type can expose an indexer only on itself (the "default" indexer). Therefore, if you wanted to write code in C# that would make the preceding statement legal, Foo would need to return another type that exposed a (default) indexer.

Dynamic Binding

There are two ways that dynamic binding can help when calling COM components. The first is if you want to access a COM component without a COM interop type. To do this, call Type.GetTypeFromProgID with the COM component name to obtain a COM instance, and then use dynamic binding to call members from then on. Of course, there's no IntelliSense, and compile-time checks are impossible:

```
Type excelAppType = Type.GetTypeFromProgID ("Excel.Application", true);
dynamic excel = Activator.CreateInstance (excelAppType);
excel.Visible = true;
dynamic wb = excel.Workbooks.Add();
excel.Cells [1, 1].Value2 = "foo";
```

(The same thing can be achieved, much more clumsily, with reflection instead of dynamic binding.)

 A variation of this theme is calling a COM component that supports *only* IDispatch. Such components are quite rare, however.

Dynamic binding can also be useful (to a lesser extent) in dealing with the COM variant type. COM API functions are often peppered with this type, which is roughly equivalent to object in .NET. The runtime maps variant to object prior to C# 4.0, with the effect that you must explicitly cast return values—as in the following example:

```
var excel = new Excel.Application();
excel.Visible = true;
Workbook workBook = excel.Workbooks.Add (System.Reflection.Missing.Value);
var range = (Excel.Range) excel.Cells [1, 1];
range.Font.FontStyle = "Bold";
```

 The fact that some COM methods return variants is often due to poor design more than to necessity.

From C# 4.0, variant types are instead mapped to dynamic (if Embed Interop Types is enabled; more on this soon), allowing you to replace the last two lines with this:

```
excel.Cells [1, 1].Font.FontStyle = "Bold";
```

The disadvantage of working in this way is that you lose auto-completion, so you must know that a property called Font happens to exist. For this reason, it's usually easier to *dynamically* assign the result to its known interop type:

```
Excel.Range range = excel.Cells [1, 1];
range.Font.FontStyle = "Bold";
```

As you can see, this saves only five characters over the old-fashioned approach!

The mapping of variant to dynamic is the default from Visual Studio 2010, and is a function of enabling Embed Interop Types on a reference.

Embedding Interop Types

We said previously that C# ordinarily calls COM components via interop types that are generated by calling the *tlimp.exe* tool (directly, or via Visual Studio).

Prior to C# 4.0, you would *reference* interop assemblies just like any other assembly. This could be troublesome, however, because interop assemblies can get quite large with complex COM components. A tiny add-in for Microsoft Word, for instance, requires an interop assembly that is orders of magnitude larger than itself.

In C# 4.0, rather than *referencing* an interop assembly, you have the option of *linking* to it. When you do this, the compiler analyzes the assembly to work out precisely the types and members that your application actually uses. It then embeds definitions for those types and members directly in your application. This means that you don't have to worry about bloat, because only the COM interfaces that you actually use are included in your application.

Interop linking is the default in Visual Studio 2010 for COM references. If you want to *disable* it, select the reference in the Solution Explorer, and then go to its properties and set Embed Interop Types to False.

To enable interop linking from the command-line compiler, call `csc` with `/link` instead of `/reference` (or `/L` instead of `/R`).

Type Equivalence

CLR 4.0 supports *type equivalence* for linked interop types. That means that if two assemblies each link to an interop type, those types will be considered equivalent if they wrap the same COM type. This holds true even if the interop assemblies to which they linked were generated independently.

> Type equivalence relies on the `TypeIdentifierAttribute` attribute in the `System.Runtime.InteropServices` namespace. The compiler automatically applies this attribute when you link to interop assemblies. COM types are then considered equivalent if they have the same GUID.

Type equivalence does away with the need for *Primary Interop Assemblies*.

Primary Interop Assemblies

Before C# 4.0, there was no interop linking and no option of type equivalence. This created a problem in that if two developers each ran the *tlimp.exe* tool on the same COM component, they'd end up with incompatible interop assemblies, hindering interoperability. The workaround was for the author of each COM library to release an official version of the interop assembly, called the *Primary Interop Assembly* (PIA).

PIAs, however, were a poor solution for the following reasons:

PIAs were not actually used
Since everyone could run the type library importer tool, they often did so, rather than using the official version. In some cases, there was no choice as the authors of the COM library didn't actually publish a PIA.

PIAs require registration
PIAs require registration in the GAC. This burden falls on developers writing simple add-ins for a COM component.

PIAs bloat deployment
PIAs exemplify the problem of interop assembly bloat that we described earlier. In particular, the Microsoft Office team chose not to deploy their PIAs with their product.

Exposing C# Objects to COM

It's also possible to write classes in C# that can be consumed in the COM world. The CLR makes this possible through a proxy called a COM-Callable Wrapper (CCW). A CCW marshals types between the two worlds (as with an RCW) and implements IUnknown (and optionally IDispatch) as required by the COM protocol. A CCW is lifetime-controlled from the COM side via reference counting (rather than through the CLR's garbage collector).

You can expose any public class to COM. The one requirement is to define an assembly attribute that assigns a GUID to identify the COM type library:

```
[assembly: Guid ("...")]    // A unique GUID for the COM type library
```

By default, all public types will be visible to COM consumers. You can make specific types invisible, however, by applying the [ComVisible(false)] attribute. If you want all types invisible by default, apply [ComVisible(false)] to the assembly, and then [ComVisible(true)] to the types you wish to expose.

The final step is to call the *tlbexp.exe* tool:

```
tlbexp.exe myLibrary.dll
```

This generates a COM type library (*.tlb*) file which you can then register and consume in COM applications. COM interfaces to match the COM-visible classes are generated automatically.

26

Regular Expressions

The regular expressions language identifies character patterns. The .NET types supporting regular expressions are based on Perl 5 regular expressions and support both search and search/replace functionality.

Regular expressions are used for tasks such as:

- Validating text input such as passwords and phone numbers (ASP.NET provides the `RegularExpressionValidator` control just for this purpose)
- Parsing textual data into more structured forms (e.g., extracting data from an HTML page for storage in a database)
- Replacing patterns of text in a document (e.g., whole words only)

This chapter is split into both conceptual sections teaching the basics of regular expressions in .NET and reference sections describing the regular expressions language.

All regular expression types are defined in `System.Text.RegularExpressions`.

> For more on regular expressions, *http://regular-expressions* *.info* is a good online reference with lots of examples, and *Mastering Regular Expressions* by Jeffrey E. F. Friedl, is invaluable for the serious.
>
> The samples in this chapter are all preloaded into LINQPad. There is also an interactive utility available called Expresso (*http://www.ultrapico.com*), which assists in building and visualizing regular expressions, and comes with its own expression library.

Regular Expression Basics

One of the most common regular expression operators is a *quantifier*. ? is a quantifier that matches the preceding item 0 or 1 time. In other words, ? means *optional*. An item is either a single character or a complex structure of characters in square brackets. For example, the regular expression "colou?r" matches color and colour, but not colouur:

```
Console.WriteLine (Regex.Match ("color",   @"colou?r").Success);  // True
Console.WriteLine (Regex.Match ("colour",  @"colou?r").Success);  // True
Console.WriteLine (Regex.Match ("colouur", @"colou?r").Success);  // False
```

Regex.Match searches within a larger string. The object that it returns has properties for the Index and Length of the match, as well as the actual Value matched:

```
Match m = Regex.Match ("any colour you like", @"colou?r");

Console.WriteLine (m.Success);     // True
Console.WriteLine (m.Index);       // 4
Console.WriteLine (m.Length);      // 6
Console.WriteLine (m.Value);       // colour
Console.WriteLine (m.ToString());  // colour
```

You can think of Regex.Match as a more powerful version of the string's IndexOf method. The difference is that it searches for a *pattern* rather than a literal string.

The IsMatch method is a shortcut for calling Match and then testing the Success property.

The regular expressions engine works from left to right by default, so only the leftmost match is returned. You can use the NextMatch method to return more matches:

```
Match m1 = Regex.Match ("One color? There are two colours in my head!",
                        @"colou?rs?");
Match m2 = m1.NextMatch();
Console.WriteLine (m1);        // color
Console.WriteLine (m2);        // colours
```

The Matches method returns all matches in an array. We can rewrite the preceding example as follows:

```
foreach (Match m in Regex.Matches
        ("One color? There are two colours in my head!", @"colou?rs?"))
    Console.WriteLine (m);
```

Another common regular expressions operator is the *alternator*, expressed with a vertical bar, |. An alternator expresses alternatives. The following matches "Jen", "Jenny", and "Jennifer":

```
Console.WriteLine (Regex.IsMatch ("Jenny", "Jen(ny|nifer)?"));  // True
```

The parentheses around an alternator separate the alternatives from the rest of the expression.

Compiled Regular Expressions

In some of the preceding examples, we called a static `RegEx` method repeatedly with the same pattern. An alternative approach in these cases is to instantiate a `Regex` object with the pattern and then call instance methods:

```
Regex r = new Regex (@"sausages?");
Console.WriteLine (r.Match ("sausage"));    // sausage
Console.WriteLine (r.Match ("sausages"));   // sausages
```

This is not just a syntactic convenience: under the covers, a `RegEx` instance uses lightweight code generation (`DynamicMethod` in `Reflection.Emit`) to dynamically build and compile code tailored to that particular regular expression. This results in (up to 10 times) faster matching, at the expense of a small initial compilation cost (a few tens of microseconds).

A `Regex` instance is immutable.

 The regular expressions engine is fast. Even without compilation, a simple match typically takes less than a microsecond.

RegexOptions

The `RegexOptions` flags enum lets you tweak matching behavior. A common use for `RegexOptions` is to perform a case-insensitive search:

```
Console.WriteLine (Regex.Match ("a", "A", RegexOptions.IgnoreCase)); // a
```

Most of the `RegexOptions` flags can also be activated within a regular expression itself, using a single-letter code as follows:

```
Console.WriteLine (Regex.Match ("a", @"(?i)A"));                     // a
```

You can turn options on and off throughout an expression as follows:

```
Console.WriteLine (Regex.Match ("AAAa", @"(?i)a(?-i)a"));            // Aa
```

Another useful option is `IgnorePatternWhitespace` or (?x). This allows you to insert whitespace to make a regular expression more readable—without the whitespace being taken literally.

Table 26-1 lists all `RegExOptions` values along with their single-letter codes.

Table 26-1. Regular expression options

Enum value	Regular expressions code	Description
None		
IgnoreCase	i	Ignores case (by default, regular expressions are case-sensitive)
Multiline	m	Changes ^ and $ so that they match the start/end of a line instead of start/end of the string
ExplicitCapture	n	Captures only explicitly named or explicitly numbered groups

Enum value	Regular expressions code	Description
Compiled	c	Forces compilation of regular expression to IL
Singleline	s	Makes . match every character (instead of matching every character except \n)
IgnorePattern Whitespace	x	Eliminates unescaped whitespace from the pattern
RightToLeft	r	Searches from right to left; can't be specified midstream
ECMAScript		Forces ECMA compliance (by default, the implementation is not ECMA-compliant)
CultureInvariant		Turns off culture-specific behavior (by default, CultureInfo.CurrentCulture influences string comparison rules)

Character Escapes

Regular expressions have the following metacharacters, which have a special rather than literal meaning:

\ * + ? | { [( ) ^ $. #

To refer to a metacharacter literally, you must prefix the character with a backslash. In the following example, we escape the ? character to match the string "what?":

```
Console.WriteLine (Regex.Match ("what?", @"what\?")); // what? (correct)
Console.WriteLine (Regex.Match ("what?", @"what?"));   // what  (incorrect)
```

 If the character is inside a *set* (square brackets), this rule does not apply, and the metacharacters are interpreted literally. We discuss sets in the following section.

The Regex's Escape and Unescape methods convert a string containing regular expression metacharacters by replacing them with escaped equivalents, and vice versa. For example:

```
Console.WriteLine (Regex.Escape   (@"?"));   // \?
Console.WriteLine (Regex.Unescape (@"\?"));  // ?>
```

All the regular expression strings in this chapter we express with the C# @ literal. This is to bypass C#'s escape mechanism, which also uses the backslash. Without the @, a literal backslash would require four backslashes:

```
Console.WriteLine (Regex.Match ("\\", "\\\\"));   // \
```

Unless you include the (?x) option, spaces are treated literally in regular expressions:

```
Console.Write (Regex.IsMatch ("hello world", @"hello world")); // True
```

Character Sets

Character sets act as wildcards for a particular set of characters.

Expression	Meaning	Inverse ("not")
[abcdef]	Matches a single character in the list	[^abcdef]
[a-f]	Matches a single character in a *range*	[^a-f]
\d	Matches a decimal digit	\D
	Same as [0-9]	
\w	Matches a *word* character (by default, varies according to CultureInfo.CurrentCulture; for example, in English, same as [a-zA-Z_0-9])	\W
\s	Matches a whitespace character	\S
	Same as [\n\r\t\f]	
\p{*category*}	Matches a character in a specified *category*	\P
.	(Default mode) Matches any character except \n	\n
.	(SingleLine mode) Matches any character	\n

To match exactly one of a set of characters, put the character set in square brackets:

```
Console.Write (Regex.Matches ("That is that.", "[Tt]hat").Count);   // 2
```

To match any character *except* those in a set, put the set in square brackets with a ^ symbol before the first character:

```
Console.Write (Regex.Match ("quiz qwerty", "q[^aeiou]").Index);   // 5
```

You can specify a range of characters with a hyphen. The following regular expression captures a chess move:

```
Console.Write (Regex.Match ("b1-c4", @"[a-h]\d-[a-h]\d").Success);   // True
```

\d indicates a digit character, so \d will match any digit. \D matches any nondigit character.

\w indicates a word character, which includes letters, numbers, and the underscore. \W matches any nonword character. These work as expected for non-English letters too, such as Cyrillic.

. matches any character except \n (but allows \r).

\p matches a character in a specified category, such as {Lu} for uppercase letter or {P} for punctuation (we list the categories in the reference section later in the chapter):

```
Console.Write (Regex.IsMatch ("Yes, please", @"\p{P}"));   // True
```

We will find more uses for \d, \w, and . when we combine them with *quantifiers*.

Quantifiers

Quantifiers match an item a specified number of times.

Quantifier	Meaning
*	Zero or more matches
+	One or more matches
?	Zero or one match
{*n*}	Exactly *n* matches
{*n*,}	At least *n* matches
{*n*,*m*}	Between *n* and *m* matches

The * quantifier matches the preceding character or group zero or more times. The following matches *cv.doc*, along with any numbered versions of the same file (e.g., *cv2.doc*, *cv15.doc*):

```
Console.Write (Regex.Match ("cv15.doc", @"cv\d*\.doc").Success);  // True
```

Notice that we have to escape out the period in the file extension with a backslash.

The following allows anything between *cv* and *.doc* and is equivalent to `dir cv*.doc`:

```
Console.Write (Regex.Match ("cvjoint.doc", @"cv.*\.doc").Success);  // True
```

The + quantifier matches the preceding character or group one or more times. For example:

```
Console.Write (Regex.Matches ("slow! yeah slooow!", "slo+w").Count);  // 2
```

The {} quantifier matches a specified number (or range) of repetitions. The following matches a blood pressure reading:

```
Regex bp = new Regex (@"\d{2,3}/\d{2,3}");
Console.WriteLine (bp.Match ("It used to be 160/110"));  // 160/110
Console.WriteLine (bp.Match ("Now it's only 115/75"));   // 115/75
```

Greedy Versus Lazy Quantifiers

By default, quantifiers are *greedy*, as opposed to *lazy*. A greedy quantifier repeats as *many* times as it can before proceeding. A lazy quantifier repeats as *few* times as it can before proceeding. You can make any quantifier lazy by suffixing it with the ? symbol. To illustrate the difference, consider the following HTML fragment:

```
string html = "<i>By default</i> quantifiers are <i>greedy</i> creatures";
```

Suppose we want to extract the two phrases in italics. If we execute the following:

```
foreach (Match m in Regex.Matches (html, @"<i>.*</i>"))
    Console.WriteLine (m);
```

the result is not two matches, but a *single* match, as follows:

```
<i>By default</i> quantifiers are <i>greedy</i>
```

The problem is that our * quantifier greedily repeats as many times as it can before matching </i>. So, it chomps right through the first </i>, stopping only at the final </i> (the *last point* at which the rest of the expression can still match).

If we make the quantifier lazy:

```
foreach (Match m in Regex.Matches (html, @"<i>.*?</i>"))
    Console.WriteLine (m);
```

the * bails out at the *first* point at which the rest of the expression can match. Here's the result:

```
<i>By default</i>
<i>greedy</i>
```

Zero-Width Assertions

The regular expressions language lets you place conditions on what should occur *before* or *after* a match, through lookbehind, lookahead, anchors, and word boundaries. These are called *zero-width* assertions, because they don't increase the width (or length) of the match itself.

Lookahead and Lookbehind

The (*?=expr*) construct checks whether the text that follows matches *expr*, without including *expr* in the result. This is called *positive lookahead*. In the following example, we look for a number followed by the word "miles":

```
Console.WriteLine (Regex.Match ("say 25 miles more", @"\d+\s(?=miles)"));
```

OUTPUT: 25

Notice the word "miles" was not returned in the result, even though it was required to *satisfy* the match.

After a successful lookahead, matching continues as though the sneak preview never took place. So, if we append .* to our expression as follows:

```
Console.WriteLine (Regex.Match ("say 25 miles more", @"\d+\s(?=miles).*"));
```

the result is 25 miles more.

Lookahead can be useful in validating a strong password. Suppose a password has to be at least six characters and contain at least one digit. With a lookup, we could achieve this as follows:

```
string password = "...";
bool ok = Regex.IsMatch (password, @"(?=.*\d).{6,}");
```

This first performs a lookahead to ensure that a digit occurs somewhere in the string. If satisfied, it returns to its position before the sneak preview began and matches six or more characters. (In "Cookbook Regular Expressions" on page 988, we include a more substantial password validation example.)

The opposite is the *negative lookahead* construct, `(?!expr)`. This requires that the match *not* be followed by *expr*. The following expression matches "good"—unless "however" or "but" appears later in the string:

```
string regex = "(?i)good(?!.*(however|but))";
Console.WriteLine (Regex.IsMatch ("Good work! But...",  regex));  // False
Console.WriteLine (Regex.IsMatch ("Good work! Thanks!", regex));  // True
```

The `(?<=expr)` construct denotes *positive lookbehind* and requires that a match be *preceded* by a specified expression. The opposite construct, `(?<!expr)`, denotes *negative lookbehind* and requires that a match *not be preceded* by a specified expression. For example, the following matches "good"—unless "however" appears *earlier* in the string:

```
string regex = "(?i)(?<!however.*)good";
Console.WriteLine (Regex.IsMatch ("However good, we...", regex)); // False
Console.WriteLine (Regex.IsMatch ("Very good, thanks!", regex));  // True
```

We could improve these examples by adding *word boundary assertions*, which we will introduce shortly.

Anchors

The anchors `^` and `$` match a particular *position*. By default:

`^`

Matches the *start* of the string

`$`

Matches the *end* of the string

> `^` has two context-dependent meanings: an *anchor* and a *character class negator*.
>
> `$` has two context-dependent meanings: an *anchor* and a *replacement group denoter*.

For example:

```
Console.WriteLine (Regex.Match ("Not now", "^[Nn]o"));  // No
Console.WriteLine (Regex.Match ("f = 0.2F", "[Ff]$"));  // F
```

If you specify `RegexOptions.Multiline` or include `(?m)` in the expression:

- `^` matches the start of the string or *line* (directly after a \n).
- `$` matches the end of the string or *line* (directly before a \n).

There's a catch to using `$` in multiline mode: a new line in Windows is nearly always denoted with \r\n rather than just \n. This means that for `$` to be useful, you must usually match the \r as well, with a *positive lookahead*:

```
(?=\r?$)
```

The positive lookahead ensures that \r doesn't become part of the result. The following matches lines that end in ".txt":

```
string fileNames = "a.txt" + "\r\n" + "b.doc" + "\r\n" + "c.txt";
string r = @".+\.txt(?=\r?$)";
foreach (Match m in Regex.Matches (fileNames, r, RegexOptions.Multiline))
  Console.Write (m + " ");

OUTPUT: a.txt c.txt
```

The following matches all empty lines in string s:

```
MatchCollection emptyLines = Regex.Matches (s, "^(?=\r?$)",
                                            RegexOptions.Multiline);
```

The following matches all lines that are either empty or contain only whitespace:

```
MatchCollection blankLines = Regex.Matches (s, "^[ \t]*(?=\r?$)",
                                            RegexOptions.Multiline);
```

 Since an anchor matches a position rather than a character, specifying an anchor on its own matches an empty string:

```
Console.WriteLine (Regex.Match ("x", "$").Length);   // 0
```

Word Boundaries

The word boundary assertion \b matches where word characters (\w) adjoin either:

- Nonword characters (\W)
- The beginning/end of the string (^ and $)

\b is often used to match whole words. For example:

```
foreach (Match m in Regex.Matches ("Wedding in Sarajevo", @"\b\w+\b"))
  Console.WriteLine (m);

Wedding
In
Sarajevo
```

The following statements highlight the effect of a word boundary:

```
int one = Regex.Matches ("Wedding in Sarajevo", @"\bin\b").Count; // 1
int two = Regex.Matches ("Wedding in Sarajevo", @"in").Count;     // 2
```

The next query uses positive lookahead to return words followed by "(sic)":

```
string text = "Don't loose (sic) your cool";
Console.Write (Regex.Match (text, @"\b\w+\b\s(?=\(sic\))"));   // loose
```

Groups

Sometimes it's useful to separate a regular expression into a series of subexpressions, or *groups*. For instance, consider the following regular expression that represents a U.S. phone number such as 206-465-1918:

```
\d{3}-\d{3}-\d{4}
```

Suppose we wish to separate this into two groups: area code and local number. We can achieve this by using parentheses to *capture* each group:

```
(\d{3})-(\d{3}-\d{4})
```

We then retrieve the groups programmatically as follows:

```
Match m = Regex.Match ("206-465-1918", @"(\d{3})-(\d{3}-\d{4})");

Console.WriteLine (m.Groups[1]);    // 206
Console.WriteLine (m.Groups[2]);    // 465-1918
```

The zeroth group represents the entire match. In other words, it has the same value as the match's `Value`:

```
Console.WriteLine (m.Groups[0]);    // 206-465-1918
Console.WriteLine (m);              // 206-465-1918
```

Groups are part of the regular expressions language itself. This means you can refer to a group within a regular expression. The \n syntax lets you index the group by group number n within the expression. For example, the expression (\w)ee\1 matches **deed** and **peep**. In the following example, we find all words in a string starting and ending in the same letter:

```
foreach (Match m in Regex.Matches ("pop pope peep", @"\b(\w)\w+\1\b"))
    Console.Write (m + " ");  // pop peep
```

The brackets around the \w instruct the regular expressions engine to store the submatch in a group (in this case, a single letter), so it can be used later. We refer to that group later using \1, meaning the first group in the expression.

Named Groups

In a long or complex expression, it can be easier to work with groups by *name* rather than index. Here's a rewrite of the previous example, using a group that we name 'letter':

```
string regEx =
    @"\b"             + // word boundary
    @"(?'letter'\w)"  + // match first letter, and name it 'letter'
    @"\w+"            + // match middle letters
    @"\k'letter'"     + // match last letter, denoted by 'letter'
    @"\b";              // word boundary

foreach (Match m in Regex.Matches ("bob pope peep", regEx))
    Console.Write (m + " ");  // bob peep
```

To name a captured group:

```
(?'group-name'group-expr)  or  (?<group-name>group-expr)
```

To refer to a group:

```
\k'group-name'  or  \k<group-name>
```

The following example matches a simple (nonnested) XML/HTML element, by looking for start and end nodes with a matching name:

```
string regFind =
  @"<(?'tag'\w+?).*>" +   // match first tag, and name it 'tag'
  @"(?'text'.*?)"    +   // match text content, name it 'text'
  @"</\k'tag'>";         // match last tag, denoted by 'tag'

Match m = Regex.Match ("<h1>hello</h1>", regFind);
Console.WriteLine (m.Groups ["tag"]);    // h1
Console.WriteLine (m.Groups ["text"]);   // hello
```

Allowing for all possible variations in XML structure, such as nested elements, is more complex. The .NET regular expressions engine has a sophisticated extension called "matched balanced constructs" that can assist with nested tags—information on this is available on the Internet and in *Mastering Regular Expressions* by Jeffrey E. F. Friedl.

Replacing and Splitting Text

The `RegEx.Replace` method works like `string.Replace`, except that it uses a regular expression.

The following replaces "cat" with "dog". Unlike with `string.Replace`, "catapult" won't change into "dogapult", because we match on word boundaries:

```
string find = @"\bcat\b";
string replace = "dog";
Console.WriteLine (Regex.Replace ("catapult the cat", find, replace));
```

OUTPUT: catapult the dog

The replacement string can reference the original match with the $0 substitution construct. The following example wraps numbers within a string in angle brackets:

```
string text = "10 plus 20 makes 30";
Console.WriteLine (Regex.Replace (text, @"\d+", @"<$0>"));
```

OUTPUT: <10> plus <20> makes <30>

You can access any captured groups with $1, $2, $3, and so on, or ${*name*} for a named group. To illustrate how this can be useful, consider the regular expression in the previous section that matched a simple XML element. By rearranging the groups, we can form a replacement expression that moves the element's content into an XML attribute:

```
string regFind =
  @"<(?'tag'\w+?).*>" +   // match first tag, and name it 'tag'
  @"(?'text'.*?)"    +   // match text content, name it 'text'
  @"</\k'tag'>";         // match last tag, denoted by 'tag'

string regReplace =
  @"<${tag}"   +   // <tag
  @"value=""" +   // value="
  @"${text}";  +   // text
```

```
@"""/>";              // "/>
```

```
Console.Write (Regex.Replace ("<msg>hello</msg>", regFind, regReplace));
```

Here's the result:

```
<msg value="hello"/>
```

MatchEvaluator Delegate

`Replace` has an overload that takes a `MatchEvaluator` delegate, which is invoked per match. This allows you to delegate the content of the replacement string to C# code when the regular expressions language isn't expressive enough. For example:

```
Console.WriteLine (Regex.Replace ("5 is less than 10", @"\d+",
                   m => (int.Parse (m.Value) * 10).ToString()) );
```

```
OUTPUT: 50 is less than 100
```

In the cookbook, we show how to use a `MatchEvaluator` to escape Unicode characters appropriately for HTML.

Splitting Text

The static `Regex.Split` method is a more powerful version of the `string.Split` method, with a regular expression denoting the separator pattern. In this example, we split a string, where any digit counts as a separator:

```
foreach (string s in Regex.Split ("a5b7c", @"\d"))
  Console.Write (s + " ");     // a b c
```

The result, here, doesn't include the separators themselves. You can include the separators, however, by wrapping the expression in a positive lookahead. The following splits a camel-case string into separate words:

```
foreach (string s in Regex.Split ("oneTwoThree", @"(?=[A-Z])"))
  Console.Write (s + " ");     // one Two Three
```

Cookbook Regular Expressions

Recipes

Matching U.S. Social Security number/phone number

```
string ssNum = @"\d{3}-\d{2}-\d{4}";
```

```
Console.WriteLine (Regex.IsMatch ("123-45-6789", ssNum));     // True
```

```
string phone = @"(?x)
  ( \d{3}[-\s] | \(\d{3}\)\s? )
  \d{3}[-\s]?
  \d{4}";
```

```
Console.WriteLine (Regex.IsMatch ("123-456-7890",   phone));  // True
Console.WriteLine (Regex.IsMatch ("(123) 456-7890", phone));  // True
```

Extracting "name = value" pairs (one per line)

Note that this starts with the *multiline* directive (?m):

```
string r = @"(?m)^\s*(?'name'\w+)\s*=\s*(?'value'.*)\s*(?=\r?$)";

string text =
  @"id = 3
    secure = true
    timeout = 30";

foreach (Match m in Regex.Matches (text, r))
  Console.WriteLine (m.Groups["name"] + " is " + m.Groups["value"]);
id is 3 secure is true timeout is 30
```

Strong password validation

The following checks whether a password has at least six characters, and whether it contains a digit, symbol, or punctuation mark:

```
string r = @"(?x)^(?=.* ( \d | \p{P} | \p{S} )).{6,}";

Console.WriteLine (Regex.IsMatch ("abc12", r));    // False
Console.WriteLine (Regex.IsMatch ("abcdef", r));   // False
Console.WriteLine (Regex.IsMatch ("ab88yz", r));   // True
```

Lines of at least 80 characters

```
string r = @"(?m)^.{80,}(?=\r?$)";

string fifty = new string ('x', 50);
string eighty = new string ('x', 80);

string text = eighty + "\r\n" + fifty + "\r\n" + eighty;

Console.WriteLine (Regex.Matches (text, r).Count);   // 2
```

Parsing dates/times (N/N/N H:M:S AM/PM)

This expression handles a variety of numeric date formats—and works whether the year comes first or last. The (?x) directive improves readability by allowing white-space; the (?i) switches off case-sensitivity (for the optional AM/PM designator). You can then access each component of the match through the Groups collection:

```
string r = @"(?x)(?i)
(\d{1,4}) [./-]
(\d{1,2}) [./-]
(\d{1,4}) [\sT]
(\d+):(\d+):(\d+) \s? (A\.?M\.?|P\.?M\.?)?";

string text = "01/02/2008 5:20:50 PM";

foreach (Group g in Regex.Match (text, r).Groups)
  Console.WriteLine (g.Value + " ");
01/02/2008 5:20:50 PM 01 02 2008 5 20 50 PM
```

Matching Roman numerals

```
string r =
    @"(?i)\bm*"        +
    @"(d?c{0,3}|c[dm])" +
    @"(l?x{0,3}|x[lc])" +
    @"(v?i{0,3}|i[vx])" +
    @"\b";

Console.WriteLine (Regex.IsMatch ("MCMLXXXIV", r));   // True
```

Removing repeated words

Here, we capture a named grouped called dupe:

```
string r = @"(?'dupe'\w+)\W\k'dupe'";

string text = "In the the beginning...";
Console.WriteLine (Regex.Replace (text, r, "${dupe}"));
```

In the beginning

Word count

```
string r = @"\b(\w|[-'])+\b";

string text = "It's all mumbo-jumbo to me";
Console.WriteLine (Regex.Matches (text, r).Count);   // 5
```

Matching a Guid

```
string r =
    @"(?i)\b"            +
    @"[0-9a-fA-F]{8}\-"  +
    @"[0-9a-fA-F]{4}\-"  +
    @"[0-9a-fA-F]{4}\-"  +
    @"[0-9a-fA-F]{4}\-"  +
    @"[0-9a-fA-F]{12}"   +
    @"\b";

string text = "Its key is {3F2504E0-4F89-11D3-9A0C-0305E82C3301}.";
Console.WriteLine (Regex.Match (text, r).Index);            // 12
```

Parsing an XML/HTML tag

Regex is useful for parsing HTML fragments—particularly when the document may
be imperfectly formed:

```
string r =
    @"<(?'tag'\w+?).*>"  + // match first tag, and name it 'tag'
    @"(?'text'.*?)"      + // match text content, name it 'textd'
    @"</\k'tag'>";         // match last tag, denoted by 'tag'

string text = "<h1>hello</h1>";

Match m = Regex.Match (text, r);
```

```
Console.WriteLine (m.Groups ["tag"]);      // h1
Console.WriteLine (m.Groups ["text"]);     // hello
```

Splitting a camel-cased word

This requires a positive lookahead to include the uppercase separators:

```
string r = @"(?=[A-Z])";

foreach (string s in Regex.Split ("oneTwoThree", r))
  Console.Write (s + " ");      // one Two Three
```

Obtaining a legal filename

```
string input = "My \"good\" <recipes>.txt";

char[] invalidChars = System.IO.Path.GetInvalidPathChars();
string invalidString = Regex.Escape (new string (invalidChars));

string valid = Regex.Replace (input, "[" + invalidString + "]", "");
Console.WriteLine (valid);

My good recipes.txt
```

Escaping Unicode characters for HTML

```
string htmlFragment = "© 2007";

string result = Regex.Replace (htmlFragment, @"[\u0080-\uFFFF]",
                m => @"&#" + ((int)m.Value[0]).ToString() + ";");

Console.WriteLine (result);      // &#169; 2007
```

Unescaping characters in an HTTP query string

```
string sample = "C%23 rocks";

string result = Regex.Replace (
    sample,
    @"%[0-9a-f][0-9a-f]",
    m => ((char) Convert.ToByte (m.Value.Substring (1), 16)).ToString(),
    RegexOptions.IgnoreCase
);

Console.WriteLine (result);   // C# rocks
```

Parsing Google search terms from a web stats log

This should be used in conjunction with the previous example to unescape characters in the query string:

```
string sample =
  "http://google.com/search?hl=en&q=greedy+quantifiers+regex&btnG=Search";

Match m = Regex.Match (sample, @"(?<=google\..+search\?.*q=).+?(?=(&|$))");

string[] keywords = m.Value.Split (
```

RegEx

```
    new[] { '+' }, StringSplitOptions.RemoveEmptyEntries);

    foreach (string keyword in keywords)
        Console.Write (keyword + " ");        // greedy quantifiers regex
```

Regular Expressions Language Reference

Table 26-2 through Table 26-12 summarize the regular expressions grammar and syntax supported in the .NET implementation.

Table 26-2. Character escapes

Escape code sequence	Meaning	Hexadecimal equivalent
\a	Bell	\u0007
\b	Backspace	\u0008
\t	Tab	\u0009
\r	Carriage return	\u000A
\v	Vertical tab	\u000B
\f	Form feed	\u000C
\n	Newline	\u000D
\e	Escape	\u001B
nnn	ASCII character *nnn* as octal (e.g., \n052)	
\x*nn*	ASCII character *nn* as hex (e.g., \x3F)	
\c*l*	ASCII control character *l* (e.g., \cG for Ctrl-G)	
\u*nnnn*	Unicode character *nnnn* as hex (e.g., \u07DE)	
symbol	A nonescaped symbol	

Special case: within a regular expression, \b means word boundary, except in a [ ] set, in which \b means the backspace character.

Table 26-3. Character sets

Expression	Meaning	Inverse ("not")
[abcdef]	Matches a single character in the list	[^abcdef]
[a-f]	Matches a single character in a *range*	[^a-f]
\d	Matches a decimal digit	\D
	Same as [0-9]	
\w	Matches a *word* character (by default, varies according to CultureInfo.CurrentCulture; for example, in English, same as [a-zA-Z_0-9])	\W
\s	Matches a whitespace character	\S
	Same as [\n\r\t\f]	

Expression	Meaning	Inverse ("not")
\p{category}	Matches a character in a specified *category* (see Table 26-6)	\P
.	(Default mode) Matches any character except \n	\n
.	(SingleLine mode) Matches any character	\n

Table 26-4. *Character categories*

Quantifier	Meaning
\p{L}	Letters
\p{Lu}	Uppercase letters
\p{Ll}	Lowercase letters
\p{N}	Numbers
\p{P}	Punctuation
\p{M}	Diacritic marks
\p{S}	Symbols
\p{Z}	Separators
\p{C}	Control characters

Table 26-5. *Quantifiers*

Quantifier	Meaning
*	Zero or more matches
+	One or more matches
?	Zero or one match
{n}	Exactly *n* matches
{n,}	At least *n* matches
{n,m}	Between *n* and *m* matches

The ? suffix can be applied to any of the quantifiers to make them *lazy* rather than *greedy*.

Table 26-6. *Substitutions*

Expression	Meaning
$0	Substitutes the matched text
$group-number	Substitutes an indexed *group-number* within the matched text
${group-name}	Substitutes a text *group-name* within the matched text

Substitutions are specified only within a replacement pattern.

Table 26-7. Zero-width assertions

Expression	Meaning
^	Start of string (or line in *multiline* mode)
$	End of string (or line in *multiline* mode)
\A	Start of string (ignores *multiline* mode)
\z	End of string (ignores *multiline* mode)
\Z	End of line or string
\G	Where search started
\b	On a word boundary
\B	Not on a word boundary
(?=*expr*)	Continue matching only if expression *expr* matches on right (positive lookahead)
(?!*expr*)	Continue matching only if expression *expr* doesn't match on right (negative lookahead)
(?<=*expr*)	Continue matching only if expression *expr* matches on left (positive lookbehind)
(?<!*expr*)	Continue matching only if expression *expr* doesn't match on left (negative lookbehind)
(?>*expr*)	Subexpression *expr* is matched once and not backtracked

Table 26-8. Grouping constructs

Syntax	Meaning
(*expr*)	Capture matched expression *expr* into indexed group
(?*number*)	Capture matched substring into a specified group *number*
(?'*name*')	Capture matched substring into group *name*
(?'*name1-name2*')	Undefine *name2*, and store interval and current group into *name1*; if *name2* is undefined, matching backtracks; *name1* is optional
(?:*expr*)	Noncapturing group

Table 26-9. Back references

Parameter syntax	Meaning
index	Reference a previously captured group by *index*
\k<*name*>	Reference a previously captured group by *name*

Table 26-10. Alternation

Expression syntax	Meaning
|	Logical OR
(?(*expr*)*yes*|*no*)	Matches *yes* if expression matches; otherwise, matches *no* (*no* is optional)
(?(*name*)*yes*|*no*)	Matches *yes* if named group has a match; otherwise, matches *no* (*no* is optional)

Table 26-11. Miscellaneous constructs

Expression syntax	Meaning
(?#*comment*)	Inline comment
#*comment*	Comment to end of line (works only in `IgnorePatternWhitespace` mode)

Table 26-12. Regular expression options

Option	Meaning
(?i)	Case-insensitive match ("ignore" case)
(?m)	Multiline mode; changes ^ and $ so that they match beginning and end of any line
(?n)	Captures only explicitly named or numbered groups
(?c)	Compiles to IL
(?s)	Single-line mode; changes meaning of "." so that it matches every character
(?x)	Eliminates unescaped whitespace from the pattern
(?r)	Searches from right to left; can't be specified midstream

RegEx

Index

Symbols

#define directive, 175
#else directive, 175
#end directive, 175
#endif directive, 175
#error directive, 175
#if directive, 175
#line directive, 175
#region directive, 175
#undef directive, 175
#warning directive, 175
( ) (parentheses)
    regex named groups, 987
8- and 16-bit integral types, 25
< (less-than) operator
    order comparison, 28, 255, 257
    overloading, 155
    use with nullable types, 151
<< (shift left) operator, 25
> (greater-than) operator
    order comparison, 28, 255, 257
    overloading, 155
    use with nullable types, 151
>> (shift right) operator, 25
& (address of) operator, 171
&& (and) operator, 29
* (dereference operator), 171
@ (at symbol), 11
\ (backslash), 31
    escaping in regex, 980
` (backtick) and generic type names, 684
{} (braces), 12, 51
^ (caret)
    regex character set negator, 981
    regex start of string anchor, 984
? (conditional) operator, 29
/// (documentation comment), 176

$ (dollar sign) regex end of string anchor, 984
// (double forward slash), 7, 12
== (equality operator), 28, 150, 245, 247
    Equals method compared to, 250
    overriding, 253
    string comparisons with, 199
    string equality comparisons, 200
= (equals sign), 12
!= (inequality operator), 28, 245, 247
- (minus) operator, 117
/*...*/ (multiline comment), 12
* (multiplication) operator, 9
! (not operator), 500
?? (null coalescing) operator, 152
|| (or operator), 29, 500
( ) (parentheses), 12
    regex alternator, 978
    regex lookahead and lookbehind, 983
. (period), 12
    regex character matching, 981
+ (plus) operator, 31, 117
-> (pointer-to-member) operator, 172
(preprocessor directives), 499
? (question mark)
    in nullable type, 149
    regex quantifier, 978
; (semicolon, 7, 12
' (single quotes), 30
[ ] (square brackets)
    arrays, 32
    attributes, 172
    in regular expressions, 978, 981
    indexers, 71
-= (subtract from self) operator, 117
~ (tilde)
    finalizers, 74
| (vertical bar)
    regex alternator, 978

We'd like to hear your suggestions for improving our indexes. Send email to *index@oreilly.com*.

GetUnicodeCategory method, 195
GetUtcOffset method, 214, 215
GetValue method, 276
Global Assembly Cache (see GAC)
globalization, 235
    checklist, 236
    testing, 236
goto statement, 55
greater-than (>) operator
    order comparison, 28, 255, 257
greedy quantifiers (regex)
    greedy versus lazy quantifiers, 982
groups (regex), 985
Guid struct, 245
GZipStream class, 571

H

hash partitioning (PLINQ), 887
HashAlgorithm class, 778
hashing (cryptography), 776, 778
HashSet<T>, 289
Hashtable class, 292
hashtables, 252
heap, 36
hexadecimal (converting), 233
Hexadecimal, specifying literals, 21
HideBySig, 719
hiding inherited members, 81
hiding interface members, 93
HTTP, 580, 592
    cookies, 594
    form data, uploading, 593
    forms, authentication, 595
    headers, 592
    HttpListener class, writing servers
        with, 597–600
    query strings, 593
    SSL, 596
HybridDictionary, 296

I

I/O (input/output) types, 537
IAsyncResult interface, 929
ICollection interface, 271
ICollection<T> and ICollection
        interfaces, 272
IComparable interface, 256

versus Equals method, 256
IComparable interfaces, 255
    implementation, 257
IComparer interface, 307
identifiers, 10
IDictionary interface, 293
IDictionary<TKey,TValue>, 293
IDispatch interface, 971
IDisposable interface, 266, 475–480
IDMOP (IDynamicMetaObjectProvider),
        162
IDynamicMetaObjectProvider, 162 (see
        IDMOP)
IEnumerable interface, 143, 264
IEnumerable<T>, 265
    IDisposable and, 266
    LINQ, querying with (see LINQ)
IEnumerator interface, 143, 264
IEnumerator<T>, 266
IEqualityComparer, 255
IEqualityComparer interface, 304
IEqualityComparer<T>, 304
IEquatable<T>, 254
IEquatable<T> interface, 250
if statement, 50
IFormatProvider and ICustomFormatter,
        223
IFormatProvider interface, 221
IFormattable, 220
IIdentity, 776
IL (Intermediate Language), 3
    DynamicMethod class, generating
        with, 707
    evaluation stack, 708
    parsing, 728–733
        disassemblers, writing, 729–733
ILGenerator class, 713
IList and IList<T> interfaces, 283
IList<T> and IList interfaces, 273
immutable objects, 823
imperative security, 755
implicit conversions, 23
implicit conversions, overloading, 155
implicit parameterless constructors, 66
<include> documentation tag, 178
increment operator, 24
indexed filtering, 373
indexers, 71

increment and decrement operators, 24

precedence and associativity, 46

table of operators, 46

optional parameters, 5, 42

or (||) operator, 29

order comparison, 199, 255–257

< and > operators, 257

IComparable interfaces, 256

implementation, 257

OrderBy operator, 314

OrderedDictionary class, 292, 295

ordinal comparisons, 199

out modifier, 40, 111

outer variables, 132

overflow checking, 25

overloading

inheritance, impact on method overloading, 84

operator overloading, 153

override keyword, 80

P

P/Invoke (Platform Invocation Services), 957

PadRight and PadLeft, 197

<para>documentation tag, 178

Parallel class, 892–898

Parallel.For and Parallel.ForEach, 893

breaking out of loops, 895

indexed Parallel.ForEach, 894

optimization with local values, 896

outer versus inner loops, 894

Parallel.Invoke, 892

Parallel Framework (see PFX)

Parallel LINQ (see PLINQ)

parallel programming, 874, 876

PFX (see PFX)

parallel queries, 879

<param> documentation tag, 177

parameterless constructors, 66

parameters, 8, 38–44

named arguments, 43

object initializers versus optional parameters, 68

optional parameters, 42

out modifier, 40

params modifier, 41

passing arguments by value, 39

passing by reference, implications, 41

ref parameter modifier, 39

<paramref> documentation tag, 178

parentheses ( ), 12

regex alternator, 978

regex lookahead and lookbehind, 983

regex named groups, 987

Parse method, 210

ParseExact method, 210

parsing, 219

DateTime and DateTimeOffset, 212, 230

DateTimeStyles and, 231

enum format strings, 231

with format providers, 223

Parse method, 220

parsing and misparsing of DateTimes, 230

TryParse method, 220

type converters, 234

partial classes, 75

partial methods, 76

partially trusted callers, 758

passing by reference

ref modifier, 39

password hashing, 778

Path class, 559, 564

PE (Portable Executable) file, 647

Peek method, 288

performance counters, 530–535

creating counters, 533

enumeration of available counters, 531

reading counter data, 532

writing performance data, 533

period (.), 12

regex character matching, 981

<permission> documentation tag, 177

permissions, 751–755

CodeAccessPermission and PrincipalPermission, 752

IPermission interface, 753

declarative versus imperative security, 755

PermissionSet, 754

PFX (Parallel Framework), 874–877

PIA (Primary Interop Assembly), 975

About the Authors

Joe Albahari is the author of LINQPad (*http://www.linqpad.net*) and other C# tools, and he writes about C# at *http://www.albahari.com/nutshell/*. He is a C# MVP and has been developing large-scale applications on .NET and other platforms for more than 15 years. Joe is currently a freelance consultant.

Ben Albahari is a former program manager at Microsoft and has been a coauthor of *C# in a Nutshell* since the first edition. He is the founder of TakeOnIt, a website for comparing opinions of experts, leaders, and organizations on important topics.

Colophon

The animal on the cover of *C# 4.0 in a Nutshell* is a numidian crane. The Numidian crane (*Antropoides virgo*) is also called the demoiselle crane because of its grace and symmetry. This species of crane is native to Europe and Asia and migrates to India, Pakistan, and northeast Africa in the winter.

Though numidian cranes are the smallest cranes, they defend their territories as aggressively as other crane species, using their loud voices to warn others of trespassing. If necessary, they will fight. Numidian cranes nest in uplands rather than wetlands and will even live in the desert if there is water within 200 to 500 meters. They sometimes make nests out of pebbles in which to lay their eggs, though more often they will lay eggs directly on the ground, protected only by spotty vegetation.

Numidian cranes are considered a symbol of good luck in some countries and are sometimes even protected by law.

The cover image is an original engraving from the 19th century. The cover font is Adobe ITC Garamond. The text font is Linotype Birka; the heading font is Adobe Myriad Condensed; and the code font is LucasFont's TheSansMonoCondensed.